Integrating Simulation Tools Into Entrepreneurship Education

Andreas N. Masouras
Neapolis University Pafos, Cyprus

Georgios A. Deirmentzoglou
Neapolis University Pafos, Cyprus

Sofia Anastasiadou
University of Western Macedonia, Greece

Harry Ph. Sophocleous
Neapolis University Pafos, Cyprus

Eleni E. Anastasopoulou
Neapolis University Pafos, Cyprus

IGI Global
Scientific Publishing
Publishing Tomorrow's Research Today

Vice President of Editorial Melissa Wagner
Managing Editor of Acquisitions Mikaela Felty
Managing Editor of Book Development Jocelynn Hessler
Production Manager Mike Brehm
Cover Design Phillip Shickler

Published in the United States of America by
IGI Global Scientific Publishing
701 East Chocolate Avenue
Hershey, PA, 17033, USA
Tel: 717-533-8845
Fax: 717-533-8661
Website: https://www.igi-global.com E-mail: cust@igi-global.com

Library of Congress Cataloging-in-Publication Data

Names: Masouras, Andreas, 1980- editor. | Anastasiadou, Sofia D., 1968- editor. | Deirmentzoglou, Georgios A., 1988- editor. | Sophocleous, Harry Ph., editor. | Anastasopoulou, Eleni, 1993- editor.
Title: Cases on integrating simulation tools into entrepreneurship education / edited by: Andreas Masouras, Sofia Anastasiadou, Georgios Deirmentzoglou, Harry Sophocleous, Eleni Anastasopoulou.
Description: Hershey, PA : IGI Global Scientific Publishing, [2025] | Includes bibliographical references and index. | Summary: "The objective of the book is to provide educators, researchers, and practitioners with a comprehensive understanding of how simulation tools can be effectively integrated into entrepreneurship education"-- Provided by publisher.
Identifiers: LCCN 2024054430 (print) | LCCN 2024054431 (ebook) | ISBN 9798369390405 (hardcover) | ISBN 9798369390412 (paperback) | ISBN 9798369390429 (ebook)
Subjects: LCSH: Simulation games in education. | Business education.
Classification: LCC LB1029.S53 C38 2025 (print) | LCC LB1029.S53 (ebook) | DDC 371.39/7--dc23/eng/20250213
LC record available at https://lccn.loc.gov/2024054430
LC ebook record available at https://lccn.loc.gov/2024054431

British Cataloguing in Publication Data
A Cataloguing in Publication record for this book is available from the British Library.

Table of Contents

Detailed Table of Contents

This chapter explores the integration of simulation-based learning in entrepreneurship and business education through a case study of the 'Business Simulation-Games' course offered at the University of Piraeus. Developed to address the growing need for practical, experiential learning, the course leverages business simulations to provide students with hands-on experience in managing real-world scenarios. The chapter highlights how the course fosters critical skills such as strategic decision-making, risk management, adaptability, and teamwork, all while following Kolb's Experiential Learning Cycle. Key components, including course design, the use of simulation tools, and reflective learning practices, are examined in detail. The chapter also addresses challenges related to technology, pedagogy, and student adaptation, as well as the strategies implemented to overcome them. Finally, the chapter offers practical recommendations for educators interested in adopting simulation-based approaches to enhance entrepreneurial skill development and improve learning outcomes in higher education.

This chapter examines simulation tools in business education, showcasing their ability to bridge theory and practice while developing skills like problem-solving, decision-making, and teamwork. Rooted in experiential and collaborative learning, simulations enable students to engage in real-world scenarios. Tools such as the Business Strategy Game, SimVenture, and Markstrat demonstrate value in teaching strategic management, SME operations, and marketing strategies. Key benefits include active participation, real-time feedback, and adaptability, though challenges like costs, technical issues, and training requirements persist. The chapter highlights the need for curriculum integration, teacher training, and advanced technologies like AI and AR to fully utilize simulations. While not a universal solution, they effectively prepare students for the complexities of modern business education.

This chapter explores the potential contributing role of simulation tools to finance school students' performance within Greek higher education. By applying a qualitative research method, this study examines the perspectives and experiences of 12 professors on the introduction of simulation tools into the respective learning processes. Findings indicated that simulations increase student engagement

The rapidly evolving landscape of entrepreneurship necessitates innovative educational approaches that effectively prepare students for real-world challenges. This study explores the synergistic potential of industry-academia partnerships in enhancing research and development (R&D) success within entrepreneurship education, particularly through the integration of simulation tools. By collaborating with industry experts, academic institutions can create dynamic learning environments that bridge theoretical knowledge with practical applications. Simulation tools serve as critical resources, enabling students to engage in experiential learning, risk assessment, and decision-making in a controlled setting. This chapter examines case studies of successful partnerships, illustrating how these collaborations enhance curriculum design, foster entrepreneurial skills, and drive innovation.

The current study has confirmed the strategic role and impact simulation tools play within higher education. Specifically, it does so from the students' perspective. The aim of this work was to primarily obtain valuable insight into students' experiences through the active use of simulation tools during their studies, and how this use has enabled university graduates to apply their acquired knowledge at the workplace. Considering the impact of technology and simulation tools on businesses' sustainable development, this empirical study strives to further contribute to the existing knowledge in this area. In total, 12 university graduates from economic schools in Greece participated in in-depth interviews on the basis of a qualitative research method. The research has highlighted, among others, the need for adjusting the university curricula in order to match the current and future trends related to university education in economic schools, and the technological advancements, in which simulation tools play an increasingly important role.

Entrepreneurship pedagogy is crucial in modern economies, particularly in Tunisia, where it helps tackle youth unemployment and promote economic transformation. Higher education institutions must prioritize practical entrepreneurial skills, yet many criticize their curricula for being overly theoretical and misaligned with labor market needs. In Tunisia, entrepreneurship education requires a shift from traditional teaching to more hands-on, practical training to build competitive skills. This study examines the effectiveness of current methods and challenges through interviews with educators and students.

In today's dynamic digital economy, mobile applications have become essential drivers of entrepreneurial success, enabling ventures to reach global markets and meet evolving consumer needs. This chapter explores the integration of mobile application prototyping as a core simulation activity within digital entrepreneurship education. The purpose of this chapter is to present a methodology for digital entrepreneurship programs regarding the prototyping of mobile applications for international markets. The proposed simulation activity consists of seven steps: 1) introduction to prototyping, 2) overview of the design tool Figma, 3) demonstration of Figma and its user interface, 4) gathering references and inspiration, 5) sketching ideas, 6) designing prototypes in Figma, and 7) peer testing and feedback. By integrating this simulation activity into digital entrepreneurship curricula, educators can better prepare students to meet the demands of a fast-paced digital landscape while cultivating entrepreneurial mindsets and technical expertise.

The chapter focuses on the examination of the strategic role of artificial intelligence (AI) and simulation tools in the context of higher education, and most importantly, how these two elements can substantially contribute towards enhancing effective learning and engagement. The chapter has identified the increasing role of AI in contemporary societies, with its impact in education (AIEd) to have gained an increasing role as a result of rapid growth of technological tools, and the need for higher institutions to incorporate such technological developments into their educational practices. This requires universities to identify the emerging opportunities and focus on the development of their technological infrastructure both tangible (equipment) and intangible (human). AI contributes towards the development of smart personalised education, therefore enabling both educators and students to fully develop their unique skills, leading towards improved educational and learning results for all parties involved in the process.

Today, entrepreneurship education has attracted attention as a suitable contribution to innovative and economic development. Individualized and more frequent methods, including lectures and case studies, are ineffective because they do not provide the best form of skill preparation to take on the baton of an entrepreneur. Hence, the gap in coverage through simulation-based training has been widened. This chapter aims to examine the prospects of simulation-based training for future entrepreneurs, particularly the development of technology in this area. In particular, developments in educational technologies—serious games, artificial intelligence (AI), augmented reality (AR), and virtual reality (VR)—make it possible to arrange risk-free simulation environments for participants where they can test business strategies. Respective steps and see how their decisions evolve in real time.

This chapter explores the potential and challenges of "Meta-Preneurship"an entrepreneurial learning capability emerging within the Metaverse. It reviews immersive technologies such as virtual reality (VR), augmented reality (AR), and mixed reality (MR) and explores their contribution to simulating entrepreneurial tasks, fostering creativity, adaptability, and collaboration. Ethical considerations and barriers to digital inclusion for persons with disabilities are examined in relation to the implementation of Metaverse technologies, which are carving the path towards inclusive and innovative pedagogy. The Metaverse could bridge gaps between traditional, online, and immersive learning and equip learners with skills to navigate interconnected societies and global economies.

Given the emphasis on innovation, adaptability, and an entrepreneurial attitude brought about by global economic transformations, entrepreneurship education has become an essential part of modern educational systems. The significance of developing entrepreneurial competencies that go beyond theoretical knowledge has been increasingly recognized by training organizations and higher education institutions in recent decades. This change emphasizes the value of hands-on training and experience learning. The need for effective pedagogical techniques in entrepreneurship education has grown as economies shift toward knowledge-based and innovation-focused models. Because they offer dynamic, interactive, and immersive learning environments that go against traditional pedagogical approaches, simulation games are becoming more and more acknowledged as a potentially successful educational strategy.

Entrepreneurial leadership is critical in navigating crises, requiring adaptability, resilience, and strategic decision-making. This chapter explores how simulation-based learning enhances leadership and organizational behavior skills, bridging the gap between theory and real-world crisis management. Using a case study, it examines transformational, situational, and adaptive leadership within high-pressure entrepreneurial environments. The simulation immerses participants in dynamic crisis scenarios, fostering decision-making under uncertainty, conflict resolution, and stakeholder communication.

The investigation has imperative managerial consequences and supports the inclusion of experiential learning and simulation-based learning in curriculum.

Preface

INTRODUCTION

Entrepreneurship education has undergone a significant transformation in recent years, with the integration of simulation tools playing a pivotal role in shaping how students engage with and understand the entrepreneurial process. Traditional pedagogical approaches, while foundational, often fail to provide students with the experiential learning necessary to navigate the real-world challenges of starting and managing a business. Simulation tools address this gap by offering immersive, interactive environments where learners can experiment, make strategic decisions, and witness the consequences of their choices in real time.

This book, *Integrating Simulation Tools Into Entrepreneurship Education,* explores the profound impact of these tools on the teaching and learning of entrepreneurship. Through a collection of carefully curated case studies, we examine innovative applications, emerging challenges, and key outcomes associated with the use of simulation technologies in educational settings. By presenting diverse real-world examples, this volume provides valuable insights for educators, researchers, and practitioners seeking to enhance entrepreneurship curricula through technology-driven experiential learning.

The objective of this book is to offer a comprehensive understanding of how simulation tools can be effectively integrated into entrepreneurship education. By showcasing practical implementations and best practices, we aim to inspire innovation in teaching methods and support the development of entrepreneurial skills critical for success in today's fast-paced business landscape. This compilation highlights the benefits and challenges of simulation-based learning while also addressing key pedagogical strategies that can optimize its effectiveness in different educational contexts.

The target audience for this book includes educators, curriculum developers, and academic administrators within the field of entrepreneurship and business education. Researchers interested in entrepreneurship pedagogy will find valuable insights into the role of simulation tools in fostering creativity and decision-making skills. Additionally, practitioners involved in training and developing entrepreneurial competencies in both academic and corporate environments will benefit from the practical applications discussed in this volume. Furthermore, policymakers and educational consultants seeking to implement or support innovative teaching methodologies that incorporate technology and experiential learning will find this book to be a crucial resource in advancing entrepreneurship education.

We hope that this book serves as both a guide and an inspiration for those dedicated to enriching entrepreneurship education through cutting-edge technology and pedagogy. By bridging theory and practice, we aim to contribute to the ongoing evolution of entrepreneurial learning and the cultivation of an entrepreneurial mindset among students and future business leaders.

ORGANIZATION OF THE BOOK

Chapter 1: Integrating Educationally Coherent Online Tools into Entrepreneurship Education

Incorporating online tools into entrepreneurship education has become increasingly relevant, particularly in the wake of the Covid-19 pandemic, which accelerated the transition to digital learning. This chapter explores how these tools are integrated based on established learning theories, ensuring that their use aligns with the unique pedagogical needs of entrepreneurship education. By examining four distinct case studies, the chapter demonstrates the diverse approaches—ranging from constructivist to pragmatic—used to enhance learning experiences. The discussion provides key insights into the future trajectory of digital entrepreneurship education and its broader implications for educators and learners.

Chapter 2: A Literature Review on The Emergence of Entrepreneurship Education: Development, Trends, and Challenges

Tracing the evolution of entrepreneurship education from a niche subject to a globally recognized discipline, this chapter presents a comprehensive literature review that highlights key developments, trends, and persistent challenges. The discussion emphasizes modern pedagogical strategies such as experiential learning and simulation technologies, which are pivotal in fostering student engagement. Additionally, the chapter examines the internationalization of entrepreneurship education, the growing role of social entrepreneurship, and the impact of digital technologies. Through this analysis, it provides a forward-looking perspective on the future of entrepreneurship education.

Chapter 3: Integrating Innovative Simulation Tools into Sustainable Continuous Vocational Educational Training (CVET) in Tourism SMEs

The demand for innovative educational methods has led to the exploration of simulation tools in Continuous Vocational Education and Training (CVET), particularly within tourism SMEs. This chapter introduces a visual model that serves as a roadmap for integrating simulation tools, demonstrating their potential benefits for educators, learners, and business stakeholders. By emphasizing the role of technology in fostering vocational training, the chapter contributes to ongoing discussions on educational innovation and its long-term impact on workforce development in the tourism industry.

Chapter 4: Incorporating Simulation Tools in Distant Educational Entrepreneurship: Enhancing Entrepreneurial Skills through Virtual Simulation in Online Learning

As entrepreneurship education increasingly shifts towards online and hybrid learning models, simulation tools have gained prominence as effective pedagogical instruments. This chapter delves into the advantages of using virtual simulations in entrepreneurship education, highlighting their ability to create interactive, realistic business scenarios. By discussing the challenges and best practices in implementing these tools, the chapter provides a valuable framework for educators seeking to enhance student learning outcomes through immersive experiences.

Chapter 5: Integrating Sustainable Corporate Performance into Entrepreneurship Education

The integration of sustainability principles into entrepreneurship education is crucial for fostering responsible business leadership. This chapter explores the role of simulation tools in embedding sustainability concepts within curricula, equipping students with competencies in ethical decision-making, innovation, and corporate responsibility. Through case studies and analysis, the discussion underscores the challenges and strategies associated with sustainability-focused learning. The chapter also highlights the importance of emerging technologies and interdisciplinary collaboration in preparing future entrepreneurs for sustainable business practices.

Chapter 6: Fostering Entrepreneurial Skills through Business Simulations: The Pedagogical Approach of the 'Business Simulation-Games' Course

Drawing on the case study of the 'Business Simulation-Games' course at the University of Piraeus, this chapter examines the effectiveness of simulation-based learning in entrepreneurship education. The course provides students with hands-on experience in strategic decision-making, risk management, and teamwork, following Kolb's Experiential Learning Cycle. The discussion covers course design, technological integration, and pedagogical challenges while offering recommendations for educators interested in adopting simulation-based methodologies.

Chapter 7: Pedagogical Approaches Using Simulations to Enhance Learning Outcomes in Business Education

This chapter presents a critical analysis of simulation tools as a bridge between theoretical concepts and real-world business practice. Highlighting well-known simulation programs such as the Business Strategy Game, SimVenture, and Markstrat, the discussion emphasizes their role in teaching strategic management, SME operations, and marketing strategies. The chapter also identifies key challenges such as costs, technical issues, and training requirements while advocating for curriculum integration and the adoption of emerging technologies like AI and AR.

Chapter 8: The Impact of Simulation Tools in Finance Schools as a Learning Strategy from Educators' Perspective

Exploring the role of simulation tools in finance education, this chapter presents insights from Greek higher education professors on their effectiveness in enhancing student engagement and problem-solving skills. The study highlights both the benefits—such as increased realism and interactivity—and the obstacles, including resource constraints and curriculum misalignment. The discussion contributes to the broader discourse on the integration of simulation technologies in finance education and their implications for policy development.

Chapter 9: Business Simulation Games Supporting School Entrepreneurship Education with the Application of Project-Based Methodology

Business simulation games offer an innovative approach to teaching entrepreneurship in schools by transforming theoretical concepts into practical, experiential learning experiences. This chapter evaluates how these games support project-based learning methodologies, enabling students to visualize complex business concepts such as costs, profit, and loss. The discussion outlines the design and implementation of educational scenarios, emphasizing the role of structured problem-solving tasks in enhancing entrepreneurial competence.

Chapter 10: Enhancing Entrepreneurship Education: The Role of Simulation Tools in Teaching and Learning

Focusing on the integration of simulation technologies in entrepreneurship education, this chapter examines their impact on student learning outcomes and entrepreneurial skill development. Using a mixed-methods approach, the study analyzes pre- and post-assessment data alongside qualitative student feedback to assess the effectiveness of virtual business environments. The findings indicate significant improvements in decision-making, strategic planning, and critical thinking, reinforcing the value of simulation-based learning in entrepreneurship curricula.

Chapter 11: Enhancing R&D Success in Entrepreneurship Education With Industry-Academia Collaboration and Simulation Tools

Effective entrepreneurship education requires strong collaborations between academia and industry to bridge the gap between theoretical knowledge and real-world application. This chapter explores the role of industry-academia partnerships in enhancing research and development (R&D) success through the use of simulation tools. By examining case studies of successful collaborations, the chapter demonstrates how these partnerships foster innovation, improve curriculum relevance, and equip students with practical entrepreneurial skills. The discussion provides insights into best practices for integrating experiential learning into entrepreneurship education through industry engagement.

Chapter 12: Opinions and Experiences of Economics Graduates on the Integration of Simulation Tools in Greek Higher Education towards Sustainable Entrepreneurship

The integration of simulation tools in higher education has proven to be a critical factor in equipping students with practical, real-world skills. This chapter examines the experiences of economics graduates from Greek universities, focusing on their use of simulation tools during their studies and their subsequent application in professional settings. Through qualitative research involving in-depth interviews with twelve graduates, the study highlights the transformative role of technology in fostering sustainable entrepreneurship. Findings suggest that universities must adapt their curricula to align with emerging technological advancements and industry trends, ensuring that future graduates possess the competencies needed to drive business sustainability.

Chapter 13: Pedagogical Methodologies and the Cultivation of Innovative Competencies Among Learners: An Examination of the Pedagogical Practices in Entrepreneurship

Entrepreneurship education plays a pivotal role in fostering innovation and economic development, particularly in Tunisia, where it serves as a tool to combat youth unemployment. This chapter critiques traditional pedagogical approaches, arguing for a shift toward hands-on, experiential learning methodologies that better align with labor market demands. Through interviews with educators and students, the study reveals that while project-based learning is favored, institutional and cultural barriers often hinder creativity and innovation. The findings advocate for cross-disciplinary collaboration and educational reforms to cultivate a more dynamic and innovation-driven learning environment, offering valuable insights for educators and policymakers aiming to enhance entrepreneurship education.

Chapter 14: Entrepreneurial Ecosystems in a Virtual World: Simulation Tools and Economic Education

As entrepreneurship education evolves, the role of simulation tools in bridging the gap between theory and practice has become increasingly significant. This chapter explores the intersection of entrepreneurial ecosystems, economic theory, and experiential learning, emphasizing the value of business and economic simulators in replicating real-world market scenarios. The discussion highlights how these tools enhance decision-making and economic literacy among students, fostering a deeper understanding of entrepreneurial challenges. The chapter concludes by addressing the challenges and opportunities associated with integrating simulation tools into educational frameworks, offering strategic recommendations for educators and policymakers.

Chapter 15: International Agritourism Ventures and Digital Tools: Enhancing Entrepreneurship Education Through Simulation

Digital tools are revolutionizing agritourism by expanding market reach and improving operational efficiency. This chapter examines how simulation-based learning can prepare students for success in agritourism entrepreneurship by immersing them in real-world digital business scenarios. Two key simulation activities are presented—one focusing on e-commerce and the other on social media—both designed to enhance students' understanding of digital marketing and consumer engagement. The implications of these activities extend beyond agritourism education, equipping students with practical digital skills applicable across various industries and entrepreneurial ventures.

Chapter 16: Prototyping Mobile Applications for International Markets: A Simulation Activity for Digital Entrepreneurship Education

With mobile applications playing an increasingly vital role in global entrepreneurship, this chapter introduces a structured simulation activity designed to teach students the fundamentals of mobile app prototyping. The step-by-step methodology, which incorporates tools such as Figma, guides students through ideation, design, and peer review processes. By engaging in this simulation, students develop both technical and entrepreneurial competencies, preparing them to navigate the fast-paced digital economy.

The chapter underscores the importance of integrating such experiential learning activities into digital entrepreneurship curricula to enhance innovation and market readiness.

Chapter 17: Transforming Higher Education: The Role of AI and Simulation Tools in Enhancing Learning and Engagement

Artificial intelligence (AI) and simulation tools are reshaping the educational landscape, offering personalized and immersive learning experiences. This chapter explores how universities can leverage AI to develop smart, adaptive learning environments that cater to individual student needs. The discussion highlights the necessity of investing in both technological infrastructure and human capital to maximize the benefits of AI-driven education. By fostering personalized learning and skill development, AI and simulation tools have the potential to revolutionize higher education, ensuring more effective engagement and improved learning outcomes.

Chapter 18: The Future of Simulation-Based Entrepreneurship Education and the Evolving Role of Technology in This Field

Entrepreneurship education is undergoing a transformation as simulation-based learning gains prominence. This chapter examines the future prospects of technology-driven training methods, including the integration of serious games, artificial intelligence, augmented reality (AR), and virtual reality (VR). These tools create risk-free environments where students can experiment with business strategies and observe real-time consequences. The chapter provides insights into how educational institutions can implement these technologies to enhance entrepreneurial preparedness, ultimately shaping the next generation of business leaders.

Chapter 19: Meta-Preneurship Education: Pathways to Entrepreneurial Skillsets Through Metaverse for Inclusive Learning

The Metaverse presents new opportunities for entrepreneurship education, fostering immersive and interactive learning experiences. This chapter investigates the role of virtual reality (VR), augmented reality (AR), and mixed reality (MR) in developing entrepreneurial competencies such as creativity, adaptability, and collaboration. Additionally, it examines ethical considerations and challenges related to digital inclusion, particularly for individuals with disabilities. By bridging the gap between traditional and digital education, the Metaverse has the potential to create more inclusive and innovative pedagogical frameworks for future entrepreneurs.

Chapter 20: The Effect of Simulation Games in Entrepreneurship Education

Simulation games have emerged as a powerful pedagogical tool for entrepreneurship education, offering dynamic, interactive, and immersive learning environments. This chapter explores the increasing recognition of simulation games as a method for developing entrepreneurial competencies beyond theoretical instruction. By providing hands-on experience in risk assessment, decision-making, and business strategy, simulation games equip students with the skills necessary to navigate complex entrepreneurial landscapes. The chapter emphasizes the need for educational institutions to integrate these tools into curricula to foster experiential learning.

Chapter 21: Developing Entrepreneurial Leadership and Organizational Behavior Skills: A Case Study on Leading Through Crisis Times With Simulation-Based Learning

Leadership in entrepreneurship requires resilience, adaptability, and strategic decision-making, particularly in times of crisis. This chapter examines how simulation-based learning can cultivate these skills by immersing students in high-pressure scenarios that mirror real-world challenges. Using a case study approach, the chapter explores transformational, situational, and adaptive leadership models, demonstrating how experiential learning enhances crisis management capabilities. The findings underscore the effectiveness of simulation tools in preparing future entrepreneurs to lead with confidence in volatile business environments.

Chapter 22: Navigating Ethical Challenges in Entrepreneurship: A Case Study on Simulation-Based Learning for Ethical Decision-Making

Ethical decision-making is a critical competency for entrepreneurs navigating complex business landscapes. This chapter explores how simulation-based learning fosters ethical awareness by exposing students to real-time, high-stakes dilemmas. Through structured exercises, participants develop moral reasoning, stakeholder communication, and corporate social responsibility skills. The findings highlight the effectiveness of experiential ethics training in bridging the gap between theoretical knowledge and practical application, offering insights into how entrepreneurship education can cultivate principled business leaders.

Chapter 23: Integrating Simulation Tools Effect on Entrepreneurship Education by Mediation of Real-World Entrepreneurial Practices

The role of simulation tools in entrepreneurship education extends beyond theoretical instruction, providing students with tangible, hands-on experiences that mirror real-world business environments. This chapter examines the impact of simulation-based learning on entrepreneurial skill development, emphasizing its role in bridging the gap between academia and industry. The discussion explores how simulation tools mediate real-world entrepreneurial practices, offering evidence-based recommendations for their integration into educational curricula to enhance student readiness for the business world.

CONCLUSION

As the landscape of entrepreneurship education continues to evolve, the integration of simulation tools and digital innovations has emerged as a transformative force in fostering practical, experiential learning. The chapters in this volume collectively highlight the critical role of technology-driven pedagogy in bridging the gap between theoretical instruction and real-world application. From economic education to agritourism ventures, from mobile application prototyping to the Metaverse, each contribution underscores the necessity of immersive learning environments that enhance problem-solving skills, adaptability, and entrepreneurial competencies.

The findings presented in this book reinforce the importance of interdisciplinary collaboration in designing entrepreneurship curricula that reflect the dynamic and competitive nature of modern economies. By leveraging artificial intelligence, augmented and virtual reality, serious gaming, and real-time simulation exercises, educators can cultivate a new generation of innovative thinkers and ethical leaders equipped to navigate the complexities of global markets. Moreover, the emphasis on ethical decision-making, crisis leadership, and inclusive digital education demonstrates a growing awareness of entrepreneurship's broader social responsibilities.

As we look toward the future, it is imperative that academic institutions, policymakers, and industry leaders continue to invest in digital learning infrastructures that empower students with hands-on, technology-enhanced experiences. By embracing simulation-based education, we not only enhance entrepreneurial readiness but also contribute to sustainable economic growth, innovation, and societal advancement. We hope this volume serves as a valuable resource for educators, researchers, and practitioners striving to redefine entrepreneurship education in an increasingly digital world.

Andreas N. Masouras
Neapolis University Pafos, Cyprus

Sofia Anastasiadou
University of Western Macedonia, Greece

Georgios A. Deirmentzoglou
Neapolis University Pafos, Cyprus

Harry Ph. Sophocleous
Neapolis University Pafos, Cyprus

Eleni E. Anastasopoulou
Neapolis University Pafos, Cyprus

Chapter 1
Integrating Educationally Coherent Online Tools Into Entrepreneurship Education

Alexandros Kakouris
https://orcid.org/0000-0002-1484-9019
University of the Peloponnese, Greece

Ioannis Sitaridis
https://orcid.org/0000-0002-1260-670X
University of Macedonia, Greece

ABSTRACT

Online tools have become widespread in many forms of education, gaining popularity after the restrictions of the Covid-19 pandemic which mandated online education overnight. The chapter disçusses how entrepreneurship education incorporates online tools based on various learning theories to reach contemporary audiences either purely online or hybrid. The goal is not merely to introduce tools and technologies, which are evolving and abundant, but to address how such tools align with learning theories and the idiosyncrasy of entrepreneurship education. After discussing educational underpinnings of online tools, four representative and complementary cases of educationally coherent online tools are presented and compared. These tools range from constructivist to pragmatic approaches to learning, fundamental to the teaching of entrepreneurship and its constructive alignment. Since online education paves the way for the future of entrepreneurship education, the insights from the present study introduce certain implications for educational practice, discussed in the last part of the chapter.

1. INTRODUCTION

The rise of online tools and gamification in contemporary education has gained outstanding influence on how educators and educational institutions plan and implement courses and programs to maximize learning outcomes (Maraza-Quispe et al., 2024). The "digitization" of education was recently accelerated by the sudden Covid-19 pandemic that forced educational institutions worldwide to implement online courses overnight (Kratochvil et al., 2023). Thus, online education gained popularity despite the various

DOI: 10.4018/979-8-3693-9040-5.ch001

hesitations of both teachers and students and the various shortcomings that this type of learning can cause (Macayan et al., 2022). Concurrently, the rapid development of artificial intelligence (AI) tools supports digitization through the introduction of AI-assisted learning (Chen & Chang, 2024; Vargas-Murillo et al., 2023). With these evolutions taken for granted, entrepreneurship education scholars are reflecting on their implications for entrepreneurship education (e.g., Liguori & Winkler, 2020) due to its inherently experiential learning nature. Therefore, amidst the rapid expansion of online educational tools and the observed "digitization" of education, it is timely to focus and reflect on online entrepreneurship education as an inevitable trend that challenges its own experiential nature. Authenticity for experience has long been considered a cornerstone for this type of education and scholars are concerned with how these "authentic" events can be transferred online. Human creativity, affection and agency are also key aspects of modern entrepreneurship that are challenged by generative AI and the online teaching.

All of the forms of entrepreneurship education (e.g., Kakouris & Liargovas, 2021) require, to varying degrees, the acquisition of skills through experience. Although most scholars would agree on this, there are different learning theories addressing experiential learning and there are different kinds of experience. So, a pertinent research question is "how could digital tools offer meaningful learning experiences for entrepreneurship students?" Regarding the practice of entrepreneurship education, it is a common credit that it employs a variety of methods and pedagogies. These include lectures, business plans and models, bricolage, design thinking, challenge-based learning, business games, hackathons, pitches, and others mostly unrelated to technical aspects (Mansoori & Lackéus, 2020). It has also been suggested that entrepreneurship needs to develop its own signature pedagogy, suitable for delivering entrepreneurship education in different contexts (Jones, 2019; Ramsgaard & Blenker, 2022), as it is distinct from other, more common pedagogies encountered in other curricula. On the other hand, there are suggestions that entrepreneurship pedagogies have to align more precisely with underlying learning theories (e.g., Kakouris & Morselli, 2020, Kakouris, Morselli & Pittaway, 2023) in order to be effective and constructively aligned (Biggs, 1996). In line with these requirements, the chapter suggests that entrepreneurship pedagogies should also be aligned with learning theories for their online tools and learning environments.

The remainder of the chapter first introduces the concept of an online learning environment and then illustrates some examples of online tools for entrepreneurship education, discussed from the perspective of related learning theories that are scarcely addressed in the literature. Specifically, the "Academic Business Planner" (Xinaris et al., 2011) presents an online learning environment for entrepreneurship that is compatible with the experiential learning environments proposed by Kolb and Fry (1974). The TeleCC online platform (Kakouris, 2017) introduces a learning environment based on social constructivism (David, 2014). The "Bikorama" case is an online simulation game (Drieschner et al., 2024) that offers possibilities for learning-by-doing. Finally, "SimVenture" incorporates the principles of experiential learning and game-based learning (Williams, 2015a,b). After discussing the previous online tools for entrepreneurship education, a comparison between them is provided focusing on their coherence with learning theories along with some recommendations for constructive alignment (Biggs, 1996). The selection of the cases was made to illustrate online tools with different learning perspectives. The main focus pertains to the examination of the theoretical consistency of tools with the practice of education and the instructional design, including learning objectives, methods, processes and assessment.

2. ONLINE TOOLS, LEARNING ENVIRONMENTS AND DIGITIZATION OF EDUCATION

2.1. A Variety of Digital Tools

Online educational tools span to a variety of products embedded in different learning environments, including Learning Management Systems (Moodle, Google Classroom, Blackboard), Collaborative Learning Platforms (Miro, Trello, Slack), Gamified Online Learning Tools (Kahoot, Quizizz, Formative, etc.), and Simulations. Online educational tools specific for entrepreneurship education include a plethora of software products such as business simulations (SimVenture, GoVenture, Startup Wars, BizSim, etc.), startup launch and business development tools (Bizplan, Canvanizer), pitch and presentation tools (Pitcherific, Prezi), collaboration and networking tools (Linkedin, CofounderLab), idea generation tools (IdeaFlip, MindMeister), skill building tools (MindTools, Skillshare) and many more. A large portion of these tools incorporate gamification principles to maintain user engagement. Gamification in education is rooted in Csíkszentmihályi's theory of flow, which emphasizes creating an optimal learning environment where students are fully immersed and focused. Flow refers to an individual's complete sensory immersion in an activity, serving as a powerful source of self-motivation that positively impacts performance and productivity (Csikszentmihalyi, 2014). All these digital tools and platforms employ a wide range of technologies, either open source or proprietary, to develop learning management systems, MOOC (massive open online course) platforms, virtual simulators, and case-based tools.

2.2. Building Online Learning Environments

Although tools can be used alone or in combination with other instructional methods, they should be considered as elements of a learning environment. The *learning environment* refers to the physical settings (places), contexts and cultures in which students learn. It goes beyond the concept of the "classroom" since learning can take place outside the classroom. A learning environment includes its *physical* dimension as well as its *psychological* and *emotional* dimensions. The former refers to the physical assets offered to students for learning (also called learning space) while the psychological dimension focuses on the encouragement along with trust and safety needed by students in their learning process. The emotional dimension offers attention to students' sentiments during their learning to ensure that they enjoy a positive experience from the teaching they receive.

Illeris (2007) has developed a synthetic theory of learning by comparing a large variety of learning theories (p. 257). He concludes that human learning encompasses the internal process of *acquisition* (the balance between cognition and emotion) and the process of *interaction* of the individual with the environment. Based on Illeris' theory we are able to decode what constitutes a learning environment. The *content*, including teachers and teaching methods, refers to the cognitive dimension, the *incentives*, including the feelings, refer to the affective dimension, while the *interaction* refers to both the immediate social environment in which education takes place (the classroom, the school, the people involved, etc. - i.e., the learning situation) and the broader societal context (the society, the culture, etc.) in which education is embedded. Thus, the interaction process of Illeris makes connections with both situated learning (Lave & Wenger, 1991) and social learning (Bandura, 1977). The Illerian framework is inclusive to the majority of teaching and learning approaches and signifies the dimensions of the learning environment that need to be examined in educational assessment (e.g., Apostolopoulos et al., 2018).

Apparently, online learning environments follow the logic of typical learning environments. They may substitute or complement the latter depending on the form of education delivered (purely online, hybrid, etc.). Online platforms for entrepreneurship education aim to act as integrated learning environments themselves (e.g., Kakouris, 2009). MOOC platforms, such as the well-known Coursera and Udemy, are another example of online learning environments but with a main focus on the content (cognition). Learning Management Systems (LMS) are also virtual learning environments (e.g., Moodle) that are essential for many types of online learning. Other cases like business simulators and case-specific tools (e.g., games, virtual collaboration tools) may not stand alone as learning "environments" but they can be integrated into them.

Ergo, digitization of education requires not only the occasional use of digital tools, but also their integration into online, or hybrid, learning environments capable of accommodating specific pedagogies. In this way, digital tools exhibit benefits, such as accessibility, scalability, interactive and collaborative learning, engagement and flow, but they also face challenges. For instance, engagement appears low in MOOCs (the drop-out rate is high), personal communication can be low, while technological barriers can be high increasing the costs of education. But the main challenge, discussed in the next section, is whether these technological developments are coherent with the pedagogy and the instructional design of online courses. Specifically for online entrepreneurship education, the main issue concerns its inherently experiential nature and the variance between the pursued pedagogies (Kakouris, 2009; Liguori & Winkler, 2020).

2.3. Connections With Learning Theories

Different online tools can facilitate different forms of pedagogy based on different learning theories (Conole et al., 2004). For example, synergistic learning environments follow the social constructivist paradigm (Kakouris, 2017; Land & Jonassen, 2012; Morselli & Kakouris, 2022), virtual reality immersive learning environments and simulation games facilitate the situated learning theory (Lave & Wenger, 1991; Spanellis et al., 2022), specific online tools can conform with Dewey's learning-by-doing (Dewey, 1933; Lau, 2023), while others can assist cognition in the individual level (e.g., Kolb's experiential learning, Kolb, 1984), or Piaget's equilibration process (Kakouris, 2017). While the synergistic learning environments approach is based on Vygotsky's social constructivism theory (or activity theory), which views learning as a social interaction process in which knowledge is assimilated especially through the social contact with knowledgeable others (Morselli & Kakouris, 2022), experiential learning focuses on the individual, seeking student's engagement by aligning practical experience with the actual knowledge development process. According to scholars, personalization of learning is closely connected to Vygotsky's *zone of proximal development* (Morselli & Kakouris, 2022). Vygotsky posits that each learner operates within a zone of proximal development, where external assistance is necessary to progress beyond their current capabilities. Learning in such an active manner is highly valued by students. On the other hand, Kolb's theory is rooted to individualistic experiential learning. Kolb describes learning as a continuous process - conceptualized as a cycle or spiral - of hands-on experience, reflection, abstract conceptualization, and active experimentation in new, authentic situations (Kolb, 1984). A significant step in this process involves *reflective observation*, where individuals mentally connect actions and experiences, not only based on memorized knowledge, but also on information, guidance, and advice from experts.

Emerging from Vygotsky's activity theory, *situated learning* (Lave & Wenger, 1991) suggests that learning occurs through active participation in real-life situations and communities (the communities of practice). The novices (the newcomers) can enter such a community through *legitimate peripheral participation* (a concept introduced by Lave) and gradually acquire practical knowledge and skills by performing rudimentary activities, thus moving from the periphery to the center sustained by the community experts. This learning approach argues that knowledge is best acquired when learners engage in practice-oriented activities within a meaningful, authentic context, rather than through abstract instruction detached from its practical application. Since knowledge is intertwined with practice, it is also essential that situated learning is contextual, meaning that knowledge gained in one context cannot be transferred to other contexts. Therefore, when applying situated learning to entrepreneurship, it is fundamental that the practice we refer to is entrepreneuring and the associated community of practice is an entrepreneurial one where the center is populated by expert entrepreneurs.

Although entrepreneurship courses still largely follow cognitive teaching (e.g., recorded lectures, case studies and MOOCs, for example, exhibit a cognitive orientation), entrepreneurship is best approached through experiential learning techniques as they archive a higher impact on students (Piperopoulos & Dimov, 2015). For this reason, entrepreneurship education has been observed to move from cognitive to constructivist pedagogies over time (Hägg & Gabrielsson, 2020). As a result, experiential approaches dominate the landscape of contemporary entrepreneurship education (Williams, 2015b). The experiential approach in teaching entrepreneurship has given way to the notion of *hands-on* experience, which generally means "doing" rather than "discussing" or "lecturing". Unlike in-person teaching where experience can be obtained in a variety of ways, in online environments hands-on experience can be provided by simulations. Simulations are known to be an essential tool for situated learning and they contribute significantly to experiential learning by enabling a safe and controlled environment for learners to acquire knowledge from practice. Besides, active coaching, mentoring, and expert feedback in an online learning environment can greatly assist learners by providing personalized guidance, fostering deeper understanding, and enhancing skill development. Such active learning is highly valued by students and raises their confidence and motivation to persevere through challenges, thereby increasing engagement. Online simulations allow learners to actively engage in real-world scenarios, which helps them retain knowledge more effectively than passive learning methods like lectures. Secondly, they provide a safe environment for experimentation, where students can learn from their mistakes and avoid unwanted consequences. This experimentation fosters critical thinking and helps them develop problem-solving skills. Simulations often provide instant feedback, allowing learners to reflect on their decisions and adjust their approach, aligning with Kolb's experiential learning cycle. Simulations often involve team-based tasks that promote interpersonal skills, collaboration and communication, key components of experiential learning. However, the major advantage of simulation-based learning environments is that they bridge theory and practice, linking abstract concepts to practical applications and helping learners understand how theoretical knowledge applies in real-world situations.

The previous are some examples, from a range of online teaching approaches, on how online tools can tie with underlying learning theories (Conole et al., 2004). Following the recent trend in entrepreneurship education, we primarily discuss constructivist approaches, leaving aside the cognitive ones, as the latter dominate the traditional pedagogies and there are plenty of online tools to assist them (e.g., lectures, cases, quizzes, assignments, online evaluation sheets, and so on). But entrepreneurship needs development of soft skills, communication, collaboration, experience, mentoring and others that are usually met in constructivist theories. The next section presents specific examples of online environments and tools that align with the context of entrepreneurship and constructivist instructional approaches.

3. EXAMPLES OF ONLINE TOOLS FOR ENTREPRENEURSHIP EDUCATION

This section presents and discusses four examples of online tools for entrepreneurship education. The selected cases address online teaching from different perspectives - they are grounded in different learning approaches. The "Academic Business Planner" is an online, distance learning platform that accommodates the usual team-based business planning process, "TeleCC" is an online platform that utilizes asynchronous, group-oriented discussions and enables reflection, "Bikorama" is an online simulation game that enables learning-by-doing to acquire economic knowledge and entrepreneurial skills, and "SimVenture" is a business simulation game that replicates a real-world business environment to enable game-based learning. While the first two examples can be considered as integrated learning environments, the rest two games are presented as online tools that can be introduced in other, purely online or hybrid, learning environments.

3.1. The "Academic Business Planner" (Xinaris et al., 2011)

The "Academic Business Planner" (Xinaris et al., 2011) presents an online learning environment for entrepreneurship that conforms to the experiential learning environments proposed by Kolb and Fry (1974). Drawing upon the four learning modes of Kolb's (1984) model, i.e., concrete experience, reflective observation, abstract conceptualization and active experimentation, the corresponding learning environments are: the *affective*, the *symbolic*, the *perceptual* and the *behavioral* (Kakouris, 2009). Each of them facilitates a specific learning mode: the affective points to concrete experience, the perceptual to reflective observation, the symbolic to abstract conceptualization, and the behavioral to active experimentation. These environments can be developed online (e.g., Richmond & Cummings, 2005). For example, if reflection on entrepreneurship is a main learning objective, the perceptual leaning environment seems more appropriate. In this kind of instruction, the project results are not considered "unique" and are discussed and evaluated comparatively. The instructor acts as a facilitator focusing on the process rather than the outcome. Any discussions are aimed at reflecting on experience and can take different perspectives according to the needs of the learners. For other environments, the symbolic one matches the traditional teacher-centered pedagogy, the affective one promotes gaining experience through activities in an informal and non-competitive base, and the behavioral one aims at gaining practical knowledge though practical problem-solving under the coaching of the educator.

The development of a business plan for a virtual venture is an open-ended, problem-solving procedure. The "Academic Business Planner" is an innovative online collaborative business planning platform (developed through Microsoft's .NET software architecture) that supports remote organic group-based virtual business plan development projects, enabling interdisciplinary learning, collaboration and competition among students. The platform accommodates three independent roles: those of administrators, professors and users. Administrators create projects and grant users access to the various stages of the project. Each user creates a personal profile and undertakes different responsibilities and permissions depending on their role in the project. In fact, an online learning community of different groups is formed and provided with the necessary tools (e.g., asynchronous communication, wikis, announcements, forums, financial calculation tools, profit inference, sensitivity analysis, risk analysis, etc.) to develop and present their own business plans. These tools are especially helpful for non-business students who lack financial literacy. The users propagate on a canvas of 16 unique business activities (tasks such as: investment costs, finance, loans, profits, balance sheets and ratios), developing required entrepreneurial skills through collaboration. Educators act as external observers, facilitators and mentors. Each project is evaluated by peers based on a scoreboard of project milestones. This game-based learning approach enhances students' sense of internal flow (Csikszentmihalyi, 2014) and offers them an engaging, gamified business planning learning experience.

The underlying learning approach of Academic Business Planner is based on experiential learning, mostly referring to Kolb's (1984) theory. The whole educational experience is scheduled to achieve specific learning objectives. The virtual environment follows the theoretically predefined steps of a typical business plan, and it can hardly be considered an "authentic" experience as Dewey's learning-by-doing demands. It develops a learning community, rather than a community of practice where situated learning can occur. Certainly, there is a possibility to transform the educational "Academic Business Planner" platform into a community of practice tool for newcomers if it is adopted by a community of expert entrepreneurs (forming the core of the community) and experienced mentors (active members) who step-by-step supervise the newcomers' projects. This could be possible, for example, in a business incubator environment. As it stands and operated so far, the platform is educational and accommodates a perceptual learning environment (Kolb & Fry, 1974) in which educators aim to provide feedback in order to enable reflection on student experience and innovation. The online community and gamification techniques (e.g., competition, collaboration, peer assessment, grading and awarding - also used in non-formal settings and hackathons) support communication and engagement of distance learners.

3.2. The "TeleCC" Platform (Kakouris, 2017)

The second online platform is "TeleCC" (Kakouris, 2017) - an acronym for tele-career counseling. It was generally developed to provide informal online career counseling through reflective, asynchronous discussions. Its design (based on open-source code - Drupal) introduces a form of social learning, that is, learning from peers administrated by "more knowledgeable others" (the facilitators). This approach refers to Vygotsky's theory of *social constructivism* (or the *activity theory*, Jonassen & Rohrer-Murphy, 1999; Morselli & Kakouris, 2022) where participation is structured through activities and asynchronous online discussions. In this way, knowledge is co-constructed rather than "transmitted" by educators. One of the TeleCC themes was "entrepreneurship" aiming at providing reflective activities for informal, graduate-level adult learners in Greece. The topics of the activities (15 in total) were not pre-defined and were developed on the spot in accordance with the learners' needs. The duration of the course was five months. The educator introduced the activity and initiated the discussion. Subsequently, the educator facilitated the group discussion and summarized the conclusions. As a means of socialization and engagement (independent of the course activities), a synchronous discussion forum was continuously available to the participants and career counseling could take place on a personal basis. As a learning setting it points to an affective environment (Kolb & Fry, 1974) for experiential learning in which experience is gained through activities and reflective discussions in a non-competitive basis. At the time of its introduction, TeleCC was one of the first innovative online approaches to provide a flexible, engaging and supportive learning environment aimed at assisting learners to develop meta-knowledge, critical thinking and skills needed to deal with entrepreneurship.

The learning approach underlying TeleCC is the *mediated act*, a tenet of Vygotsky's theory, where tools and signs (tangible or psychological) mediate the response to a stimulus. Each TeleCC activity is considered a mediated act since its content (the problem and the associated materials - videos, documents, narratives, etc.) are auxiliary stimuli (related to language and culture) available to the participants to develop their own responses and learning. In this way, the set of 15 activities aimed to develop the participants' zone of proximal development where new and novel concepts can emerge. Participants in Greece appeared to enjoy this kind of online interaction and declared that they reflected on several entrepreneurial notions (Kakouris, 2017). Asynchronicity was preferred for online discussions to support personal reflections, which are known to take time and occur at different moments for each participant. Asynchronicity also maximizes the autonomy of participation in distance learning (Conole et al., 2004). Besides, participation was allowed through *avatars*, i.e., profiles that users created themselves, revealing as much personal information as they wished. Users' real identities were known only to administrators. This option aimed to provide safety in learning where opinions could be seamlessly expressed, thus relating to the psychological dimension of the learning environment. To develop a highly communicative framework, the users could upvote or downvote messages, thus providing instant feedback, and use emojis, pictures and videos in their posts. These tools facilitated the emotional dimension of the learning environment and provided the educator and participants with information about the ongoing classroom climate. At the end of the course, users could return to their own posts and comments to track their own learning trajectories. In sum, the TeleCC platform is an online learning environment designed to facilitate reflection on entrepreneurial notions based on Vygotsky's activity theory.

3.3. The "Bikorama" Online Game (Drieschner et al., 2024)

The "Bikorama" case (Drieschner et al., 2024) is an online simulation game that offers possibilities for learning-by-doing. "Bikorama" is a serious game designed to help students aged 14-20 learn about the concepts of environmental entrepreneurship and sustainable development. The game simulates the challenges and opportunities of running and growing a bike rental business, with a focus on sustainable practices and environmental impact. "Bikorama" offers an interactive and immersive gaming experience that keeps students motivated and engaged. The game simulates real-world business scenarios, including financial management, marketing, operations, and human resources. It also emphasizes the importance of sustainable practices and encourages students to make environmentally conscious decisions throughout the three levels of increasing complexity, allowing students to gradually develop their entrepreneurial knowledge and skills. The game adapts to individual player choices and strategies, providing a personalized, active learning experience. "Bikorama" helps students develop a range of essential skills, including: decision-making, problem-solving, financial management, strategic thinking, teamwork and communication. The game also introduces students to key concepts in business, economics, and environmental science, encouraging them to analyze complex situations, evaluate options, and make informed decisions. A key innovation of the game, stemming from its sustainable focus, is that profit is measured not solely in terms of financial results, but also in terms of the player's achievements in carbon dioxide emissions reduction. The game's interactive nature and competitive elements increase student motivation and engagement. By simulating real-world business challenges, “Bikorama” prepares students for future careers and entrepreneurial endeavors.

“Bikorama” focuses on developing students' knowledge and skills in sustainable entrepreneurship. The learning approach behind “Bikorama” is based on the principles of Dewey’s (1933) learning-by-doing, a pragmatic self-regulated active learning approach that can take advantage of gamification techniques that emulate real-world (authentic) experiences. The five different phases of the game are highly didactic, following Bloom’s taxonomy of learning outcomes to enable a variety of entrepreneurial knowledge (Drieschner et al., 2024). Faced with a real-life scenario (a problem), students can develop an effective strategy to deal with the requirements of the game, which in the long run leads to improved academic achievement. During the game, the students perceive and elaborate the problem along with its conditions, self-reflect, collaborate, receive feedback and apply a strategy to solve it. These are the basic stages of learning-by-doing that builds upon reflective practice through interconnected “cycles” of experience.

Although “Bikorama” is a standalone application, designed primarily for classroom implementation rather than as an online collaborative environment, certain classroom settings have shown that the game can be used as a tool for competition between student teams. The software's accommodation of instant feedback and competition contributes to a collaborative learning experience. The game effectively captures players' engagement by involving them in business processes like decision-making related to cycling equipment procurement, human resource management, and cost calculations, while the playful game environment increases the sense of Csíkszentmihályi’s flow. During the game the students experience a range of emotions, from uncertainty and frustration to joy, as they interact within a synergistic communication scheme.

3.4. The “SimVenture” Simulation Game (Williams, 2015a,b)

SimVenture is a business simulation game designed to replicate a real-world business environment, incorporating the principles of game-based methodologies (Williams, 2015b, 2015a). The user engages with real-world business operations and is asked to make decisions based on available information, in order to create value and sustain business growth. Through realistic scenarios, the user can develop skills such as risk tolerance, coping with failure and decision-making under pressure or with incomplete data, while receiving immediate feedback on financial and other outcomes. The main benefit of using such simulations is that the variety of scenarios encountered by the player surpasses what could be experienced in comparable real-world situations. Another advantage over simulated real-world experiences is the ability to highly customize each scenario using a wide range of parameters, such as available finance, enquiries, orders, product stock and more. The latest versions of the software enable instructors to create customized scenarios on demand, serving specific thematic areas. Finally, tutors can design an enhanced user experience by providing their own financial documents or other types of information as feedback (Yasin & Hafeez, 2018). “SimVenture Evolution” uses AI integration to create realistic market conditions and competitors that react dynamically to user decisions. The platform simulates the lifecycle of a business startup, from creation to growth, with AI helping to adjust market demands and competitive pressures. Key features of this version include real-time feedback, business model development, and adaptive learning paths, which increase the features of personalized learning (Bhardwaj, 2020).

The underlying learning approach of “SimVenture” follows situated learning (Lave & Wenger, 1991). “SimVenture” facilitates a wide range of “authentic” scenarios and applies principles of legitimate peripheral participation to enrich the practical experience and the contextual knowledge of inexperienced students, allowing participants to reflect and experiment under the tutors' guidance. The platform accommodates a behavioral experiential learning environment (Kolb & Fry, 1974), through which learners receive practical knowledge via experimentation (practical problem-solving) and automated feedback on successful performance as well as failures (Yasin & Hafeez, 2018). The online game community and the use of gamification techniques, especially those offered within the "SimVenture Evolution" module (e.g., virtual business operation, within the team messaging system), facilitate active business idea development, strengthen students' communication skills and promote learner engagement by immersing them in AI-assisted scenarios with unique, time-sensitive challenges and uncertainty in decision outcomes (in line with Csíkszentmihályi's concept of flow). The learning environment also offers instructors the means to easily implement formative, summative or diagnostic assessments on a variety of entrepreneurship related educational topics, as well as ample opportunities for mentoring during game sessions and group discussions (Yasin & Hafeez, 2018). Finally, "SimVenture"'s design facilitates the implementation of exercises and promotes greater opportunities for active and self-directed learning.

The description of each one of the digital entrepreneurship learning environments under study, are summarized in Table 1.

Table 1. Description of online entrepreneurship learning environments

	"Academic Business Planner"	"TeleCC"	"Bikorama"	"SimVenture"
Learning environment	• Online Learning • Collaborative Learning • Online community features	• Informal Online Learning • Constructivist learning • Group discussions • Anonymous participation	• Game-Based Learning • Blended Learning	• Authentic Simulation • Collaborative approach • Flexible - Adaptable mission complexity
Pedagogical Methodology	• Experiential Learning • Gamification • Comparative evaluation	• Constructivist Learning • Social and Collaborative Learning • Asynchronous, reflective online discussions	• Learning by doing • Gamification • Collaborative Learning • Personalized Learning • Reflective practice	• Situated learning • Constructivist approach • Formative and summative assessment
Workflow	• Organic group formation • Collaborative business plan development • Comparative evaluation & competition	• 15 sequential group activities & follow-up discussions • Facilitator guidance • Empowerment evaluation	• Storyline introduction • Structured Inception, Survival, Growth, Expansion, and Maturity stages • Decision making • Feedback-Reflection and Evaluation	• Work in teams • Active decision making • Real world, temporal project structure • Rewards based on market and customer research
Software characteristics & capabilities	• Web 2.0 features • Administrative features • Microsoft .NET software architecture	• Asynchronous communication tools • Multimedia enabled • Open-source code - Drupal	• Python using the Pygame library	• Business functions simulation • Interconnected processes • Realistic feedback tools on actions and consequences • Web or Windows-based content and tools • AI integration

4. AN EDUCATIONAL COMPARISON BETWEEN THE FOUR EXAMPLES

In order to compare the four cases educationally, the learning environment they imply or conform to, the learning theory they are based on, the role of educators, the tools and innovations they introduce, and the overall constructive alignment need to be addressed. These characteristics are summarized in Table 2. All cases introduce entrepreneurial constructive approaches to teaching in different ways.

Table 2. Description of online entrepreneurship learning environments

	"Academic Business Planner"	**"TeleCC"**	**"Bikorama"**	**"SimVenture"**	
				"Classic"	**"Evolution"**
Learning environment	An online platform with community features	An online platform with communication tools	Standalone, offline cross-platform application	Standalone Windows application	Online platform with virtual community features
• Physical	Platform with digital community (network) features, communication and calculation tools embedded	Platform with asynchronous communication tools embedded	Standalone application based on Python (Pygame library)	Standalone application with embedded tools (notes, calculator, glossary and player log)	Server based, virtual simulation (similar to the classic version), rollback feature
• Psychological	A safe environment for synergistic learning, deliberate participation	Safety (use of avatars), transparency and volitional and seamless participation	Individual player or team-based class competition, Immersive experience	Individual player or team-based class competition, Immersive experience	Individual player or (remote) collaborative sessions, Immersive experience, Anonymous login option, Encrypted credentials
• Emotional	Group communication and transparent interaction with educators and peers	Embedded tools for instant expression of sentiments (voting, emojis, pictures, etc.)	Fictional and playful world game interface, transmits joyful emotions	Emoticons represent estimated stress level	Messaging facility, User monitoring through Control Tower functionality
Learning theory	Experiential learning (Kolb)	Activity theory (Vygotsky)	Learning-by-doing (Dewey)	Situated, game-based learning (Lave & Wenger)	
Role of educators	Coaching, facilitation and evaluation	Facilitators, more knowledgeable others	Supportive entity, lecturing only on basic concepts, technical assistance	Facilitators, coaching and tutoring	Tutoring, guidance and evaluation
Digital tools	Web 2.0 tools, Microsoft .NET software architecture, embedded calculation tools	Drupal open software, online forums, profiles, embedded multimedia	Developed in Python, using Pygame library, No Internet connection required	Web or Windows based content embedder tool, Built in activity log	History log, playback of weekly performance
Integrity and scalability	Standalone and scalable	Standalone and scalable	Standalone application	Standalone game	Web browser based

continued on following page

Table 2. Continued

	"Academic Business Planner"	"TeleCC"	"Bikorama"	"SimVenture"	
				"Classic"	"Evolution"
Innovation	Full digitization of the collaborative business plan process	Critical reflection and self-reflection on entrepreneurial notions through online social learning	Environment, social and sustainable development related learning objectives and outcomes	Built in AI-assisted scenarios and flexible starting options, Predefined student feedback feature	
Constructive alignment	Experiential learning toward skill acquisition	Reflective practice toward meaning-making on entrepreneurial notions	Acquisition of knowledge and skills articulated in Bloom's terms	Situated learning toward acquisition of practical knowledge. Practical problem-solving	
• Learning outcomes	Entrepreneurial skills	Critical thinking and critical reflection	Business skills, Economic knowledge, Soft skills, Sustainability skills	Core business skills, Entrepreneurial attitudes & skills	Business skills, Soft skills
• Teaching method	Collaborative experimentation with tools to develop the business plan	Asynchronous group discussions on given activities	A. Lecturing, B. Explanatory Questions and answers, C. Play Phase, D. Open round debriefing discussion *Targeted debriefing after sessions promotes knowledge sharing and self-reflection	Self-directed business processes experimentation scenarios, performance monitoring	Active learning business processes experimentation, performance monitoring, Online team collaboration
• Assessment	Comparative, summative evaluation of each group's business plan through which skills are demonstrated	Formative evaluation and empowerment during the online dialogues. Finally, students' reflections and reconsiderations are noted	Quantitative and qualitative self-evaluation based on pre/post test statements, bootstrapping and student self-assessment based on predefined learning objectives	Formative, summative or diagnostic assessment, individual or team reflection on decisions made and consequent outcomes	

The "Academic Business Planner" and "TeleCC" are integrated, standalone online platforms for entrepreneurship education with all the necessary tools embedded. Both of them build learning communities and seek collaborative learning. "Bikorama" is a cross-platform and standalone game playing environment developed in Python using the Pygame library. It is intended to be used as a training software in entrepreneurship courses for students, both in secondary and tertiary education, in order to develop their economic, social and sustainable development knowledge and skills. "SimVenture" is offered in two versions, "SimVenture Classic", a standalone MS Windows application, and "SimVenture Evolution", a collaborative server-based online platform. The physical dimension of the learning environment consists of the platforms and their tools or standalone software packages. By including educators and their teaching, the content dimension of Illeris' learning (2007) is defined. The psychological and emotional dimensions pertain to engagement, safety and instant expression of feelings during the course that are accommodated by users' profiles, communication, voting and interactive participation through appropriate Web 2.0 or Windows-based tools (emojis, pictures, videos, etc.). These elements refer to Illeris' (2007) incentives and emotions dimension. Illeris' social interaction includes the participating organic groups in the "Academic Business Planner" platform and by the learning community that is formed in "TeleCC", "Bikorama" and "SimVenture Evolution". In the case of "SimVenture Classic", these dimensions are accomplished through physical communication taking place mostly in classroom active learning designs incorporating exercises or competitions (Bhardwaj, 2020).

As already mentioned, the "Academic Business Planner" follows the perceptual learning environment (Kakouris, 2009) of Kolb and Fry (1974). The resulting business plans are not considered "unique" (right or wrong) and are evaluated on a comparative base. Thus, gamification techniques for business planning are provided to some extent. Communication between educators and coaches with the students is reflective, aiming at Kolb's mode of reflective observation, which is a reflection on the concrete experience that students have at different stages of their business plan development. Through reflective observation, abstract conceptualization is possible. Reflection is also the aim of "TeleCC" but in a more critical way. The activities (problems) presented to the students are initial stimuli for individual or collective reflection mediated by the associated tools and signs (included in each activity) and by the communicative interaction between them (peers) and with the educator (more knowledgeable other). This approach follows the methods of social constructivism introduced by Vygotsky and also refers to an affective experiential learning environment (Kolb & Fry, 1974) where experience is obtained informally and through activities. "Bikorama" follows an elaborate didactic model that includes four different phases. Phase A consists of a lecture in which basic concepts related to entrepreneurship, sustainability and information about the game itself are presented by teachers. In phase B, the consolidation of the required knowledge by the learners is checked through a series of predefined questions and answers, followed by a game playing session in phase C. Finally, in phase D, an open round discussion among the players is required, in order for the learners to make a reflective analysis of the different strategies and decisions made by each individual (Drieschner et al., 2024). Bikorama's learning objectives are fully aligned with Bloom's taxonomy and follow the Dewey's pragmatic learning-by-doing method. Therefore, it allows educators to teach more complex knowledge, corresponding to higher levels in Bloom's hierarchy, using these four phases in repetitive cycles of teaching, paying and reflection. "SimVenture" offers an active learning pedagogical approach based on situated learning (Lave & Wenger) which can be used either for classroom ("Classic" version) or fully online ("Evolution" version) situated, game-based learning implementations, where novices get practical and contextual knowledge through experimentation in an authentic business context. This is consistent with Kolb and Fry's (1974) behavioral experiential learning environment where practical problem-solving occurs.

The first two platforms utilize online tools either for group formation and communication or for the financial calculations and analyses that are needed in business plans and help the financially inexperienced participants. These tools and technologies are accessible, scalable and well-known. In the first case, the entire collaborative business plan development is digitized and offered online, while in the second case, the whole experience and discussion takes place and is stored online giving participants the opportunity to trace and reflect on their own learning trajectories. The third case offers the tools for sustainable education in a playful way, while the fourth case builds in AI-assisted scenarios and predefined student feedback in an "authentic" business context. In this way, all examples introduce complementary learning innovations to online entrepreneurship education. These innovations are not only technically new to the field but also new in the way that online tools accommodate the underlying experiential learning approaches.

Finally, the constructive alignment (Biggs, 1996) within the examples presented is educationally important in constructivist methods. Constructive alignment builds on the constructivist theory of learning and instructional design that aims to achieve specific and intended learning outcomes (Macht & Ball, 2016). It demands full alignment between the expected learning outcomes with the teaching method, the content and the assessment of the course. The "Academic Business Planner" aims at cultivating specific skills to students and its components (tools and methods) are specialized to them. The assessment of the resulting collaborative business plans is summative and examines the extent to which these skills have been achieved by each group. So there is an alignment between methods, tools and assessment. "TeleCC" aims at critical reflection. It adopts online asynchronous group dialogues on given activities as a teaching method. Evaluation is formative and empowers students to critically think on entrepreneurial concepts and tools. Critical thinking can be identified during the discussions and at the end of the course through personal reflections and possible reconsiderations expressed by the participants. The outcome depends on the nature of the activities and the educator's capacity to instill critical thinking during the dialogues. Similarly, "Bikorama" aims to cultivate learning objectives and outcomes related to environmental, social and sustainable development, alongside entrepreneurial knowledge and skills, in a gamified learning environment designed to provide a joyful experience for learners. Its expected learning outcomes are articulated in Blooms' terms that can be verified in the assessment (pre/post test statements, bootstrapping and student's self-assessment). Notably, "Bikorama" requires a successful firm operation not to be measured only upon financial profit but also by environmental benefits. The four didactic phases of "Bikorama" are fully aligned with the learning objectives and combine a lecturing/playing/reflecting methodology. "SimVenture", in its both versions, aims to cultivate core business skills, as well as entrepreneurial attitudes in a gamified approach. Both versions offer student messaging facilitation and log, with weekly performance reports. "SimVenture Evolution" additionally, offers the feature of customary initial firm conditions and activity rollback capability allowing learners' teams to get involved and test various authentic situations, increasing engagement and allowing for purposeful discussions and reflective analysis. The instructional method is consistent with the expected learning outcomes while assessment is both formative and summative based on decisions made during the game and consequent performance. In summary, the four constructivist cases presented in this chapter offer constructive alignment between learning outcomes, instructional methods and assessment.

5. DISCUSSION AND IMPLICATIONS

The adoption of online educational environments provides educators with the opportunity to shift from traditional teaching models to constructivism and pragmatism. And also to enhance entrepreneurship education through innovative student-centered methodologies where students actively construct knowledge through reflection, critical thinking, collective and personal exploration (e.g., "TeleCC" and "Bikorama" focus on reflection and meta-learning). Experiential learning approaches provide opportunities for hands-on activities such as simulations (e.g., "SimVenture Classic" and "SimVenture

Evolution"), interactive case studies (e.g., "TeleCC"), and group-based business planning (e.g., "The Academic Business Planner"), while the use of real-world scenarios similar to authentic entrepreneurial challenges ensure students' learning-by-doing. Nevertheless, experiential leaning appears mixed in entrepreneurship education literature (Kakouris & Morselli, 2020). The present examples clarify the meaning of "experience" in different learning theories.

Moreover, collaborative and flexible learning environments promote peer-to-peer (social) learning, through group activities and discussions enabling co-construction of knowledge and problem-solving. Platforms like "TeleCC" demonstrate the importance of asynchronous, collaborative dialogues where learners critically engage with one another. The use of asynchronous platforms and online tools, as seen in the "TeleCC", "Bikorama" and "SimVenture" examples, support diverse learning needs, especially for adult learners with professional or geographical constraints, and allow students to progress at their own pace. The use of platforms like "SimVenture Classic" simulate entrepreneurial decision-making, financial planning and team dynamics in a safe environment, and are also essential for focused skills development, such as customer discovery and customer needs analysis. The facilitation of "trial-and-error" in simulations to mimic real-world entrepreneurship, along with the use of gamification, motivate learners. This is accomplished through the incorporation of gaming elements such as leaderboards, challenges, and real-time feedback (e.g., "Bikorama" and "SimVenture Evolution"), which increase engagement and motivation. Additionally, reflective practice is encouraged during activities that prompt students to think deeply before making decisions, based on personal assumptions (e.g., "TeleCC"). Reflective or debriefing sessions after simulations or activities also help students internalize knowledge, while frequent group discussions and debates challenge students to examine entrepreneurial concepts from different perspectives, promoting critical thinking and deepening understanding. Educators act as facilitators, coaches and mentors. This transition from traditional lecturing to a coaching role guides learners through challenges while giving them autonomy (e.g., "SimVenture" and "TeleCC" approaches), and personalized support through career counseling and private mentoring. The utilization of external role models, such as entrepreneurs or industry professionals as guest mentors or observers, exposes students to real-world experiences and perspectives. "Bikorama", for instance, supports personalized learning by adapting to individual choices, providing chances for reflective discussion, and encouraging self-paced growth. It also enables mentoring opportunities for educators to guide, evaluate, and inspire students throughout the learning process. Therefore, the digital environments for entrepreneurship education presented here and the alternative roles for educators they imply introduce learning innovations to the field that are coherent with different learning theories.

Finally, all of the digital entrepreneurship environments in the sample connect theoretical concepts (e.g., practical entrepreneurial frameworks, such as effectuation theory, innovation, and business model design) with practice. There is an extensive use of case studies, role-playing, and simulation exercises to illustrate the application of concepts like customer discovery or resource management, in all four applications. Additionally, educators are offered the possibility to design scalable programs that cater to adult learners with diverse backgrounds and learning styles, address learners' tacit needs and support their personal development by building self-awareness and adaptability. Finally, new forms of evaluation are opened, taking into account not only business knowledge but also on personal growth, decision-making abilities, and critical thinking skills of learners. Additionally, diagnostic tools, analytics, or formative feedback can be used to identify strengths and areas for improvement of educational programs, alongside the use of reflective capacity, team collaboration, and creative problem-solving as assessment metrics, instead of traditional ones such as grades in exams or profits in simulations.

Summarizing the main benefits for learners across all four digital entrepreneurship learning environments, we can highlight skill development, team collaboration, practice and hands-on experience, decision making, self-paced learning, immediate feedback, motivation and engagement through gamification elements and a sense of flow, reflection on outcomes, metacognitive analysis of decisions, and flexibility in participation. On the other hand, educators and educational agencies can benefit from these digital tools to schedule courses and programs that incorporate gamification, real-world projects, and interdisciplinary approaches that are coherent with underlying leaning theories and are constructively aligned. Future research may focus on recent developments of digital technologies, such as artificial intelligence (AI), and their potential for teaching in online entrepreneurship education. Generative AI tools can be very helpful in the modern conception of entrepreneurship as a method and as a science of the artificial (Venkataraman et al., 2012).

6. CONCLUSION

This chapter focused on online educational tools and environments that are coherent with learning theories and provide alternatives for delivering entrepreneurship education online. Four constructivist examples of complementary approaches to online entrepreneurship education were presented and discussed. These align with different learning approaches, such as Kolb's experiential learning, social constructivist learning, Dewey's learning-by-doing, Lave and Wenger's situated learning and game-based learning. The specific learning environments include physical, psychological and emotional dimensions as well as the Illeris' (2007) three basic learning dimensions corresponding to content, incentives and environment. So, they are integrated and can be evaluated accordingly. The implementations of the four examples to date indicate that students enjoy this type of instruction and acquire knowledge and skills through hands-on experiences. Thus, online tools are fully consistent with the nature of learning in entrepreneurship education that is inherently experiential. The chapter also addressed the importance of integrating online tools into learning environments under teaching approaches that are coherent with learning theories. Only in this way can specific learning outcomes be expected from instructional design models and constructive alignment is possible. Given that recent technological developments are meteoric, with artificial intelligence paving the way and challenging existing forms of education, it is timely to delve back to educational theory to examine how these developments add value for students. Technological advances are not educational *per se,* but they can become so under pedagogically informed frameworks. The four examples of online environments and tools presented here retain their educational coherence, can be extended to other audiences and settings and can be further enhanced by recent developments in artificial intelligence. Entrepreneurial experiences, which are the main concern of online entrepreneurship education (Liguori & Winkler, 2020), are offered online in different ways, with "authenticity" being their more challenging aspect for situated or pragmatist learning. As entrepreneurship education expands to reach large populations around the world, its online delivery is inevitable yet possible through educationally coherent digital environments and tools.

REFERENCES

Apostolopoulos, N., Kakouris, A., Liargovas, P., Dermatis, Z., & Komninos, D. (2018). Evaluating the learning environment of a cross-institutional postgraduate programme in entrepreneurship. *Entrepreneurship Education*, *1*(1), 105–123.

Ballard, J., & Butler, P. (2011). Personalised learning: Developing a Vygotskian framework for e-learning. *International Journal of Technology, Knowledge and Society*, *7*(2), 21–36. Advance online publication. DOI: 10.18848/1832-3669/CGP/v07i02/56198

Bhardwaj, J. (2020). Working with others and enjoying it: CS1 students' experience of small-group collaboration on a business simulation. *Proceedings - Frontiers in Education Conference, FIE, 2020-Octob*. DOI: 10.1109/FIE44824.2020.9274161

Biggs, J. (1996). Enhancing teaching through constructive alignment. *Higher Education*, *32*(3), 347–364.

Chen, C. H., & Chang, C. L. (2024). Effectiveness of AI-assisted game-based learning on science learning outcomes, intrinsic motivation, cognitive load, and learning behavior. *Education and Information Technologies*, *29*(14), 18621–18642. Advance online publication. DOI: 10.1007/s10639-024-12553-x

Csikszentmihalyi, M. (2014). Flow and the foundations of positive psychology: The collected works of Mihaly Csikszentmihalyi. In *Flow and the Foundations of Positive Psychology*. The Collected Works of Mihaly Csikszentmihalyi., DOI: 10.1007/978-94-017-9088-8

David, L. (2014). *Social Development Theory (Vygotsky) - Learning Theories*. Learning Theories.

Dewey, J. (1933). *How we think: a restatement of the relation of reflective thinking to the educative process*. D.C. Heath & Co Publishers.

Drieschner, C., Xiong, F., Bajraktari, F., Utesch, M., Weking, J., & Krcmar, H. (2024). Measuring the Effectiveness of Learning Economic Principles in a Sustainable Entrepreneurship Game-Based Setting: A Bootstrapping Approach. *IEEE Transactions on Learning Technologies*, 1–12. DOI: 10.1109/TLT.2024.3492073

Hägg, G., & Gabrielsson, J. (2020). A systematic literature review of the evolution of pedagogy in entrepreneurial education research. *International Journal of Entrepreneurial Behaviour & Research*, *26*(5), 829–861. DOI: 10.1108/IJEBR-04-2018-0272

Jones, C. (2019). A signature pedagogy for entrepreneurship education. *Journal of Small Business and Enterprise Development*, *26*(2), 243–254. Advance online publication. DOI: 10.1108/JSBED-03-2018-0080

Kakouris, A. (2017). *Constructivist entrepreneurial teaching: The telecc online approach in Greece*. Contemporary Issues in Entrepreneurship Research. DOI: 10.1108/S2040-724620170000007015

Kakouris, A., & Liargovas, P. (2021). On the about/for/through framework of entrepreneurship education: A critical analysis. *Entrepreneurship Education and Pedagogy*, *4*(3), 396–421.

Kakouris, A., & Morselli, D. (2020). Addressing the pre/post-university pedagogy of entrepreneurship coherent with learning theories. Entrepreneurship education: A lifelong learning approach, 35-58.

Kakouris, A., Morselli, D., & Pittaway, L. (2023). Educational theory driven teaching in entrepreneurship. *International Journal of Management Education, 21*(2), 100814.

Kolb, D. A. (1984). Experiential learning: Experience as the source of learning and development, David A. Kolb, Prentice-Hall International, Hemel Hempstead, Herts., 1984. No. of pages: xiii + 256. *Journal of Organizational Behavior*.

Kolb, D. A., & Fry, R. E. (1974). Toward an Applied Theory of Experiential Learning. *Theories of Group Process*.

Kratochvil, T., Vaculik, M., & Macak, M. (2023). Gamification tailored for novelty effect in distance learning during COVID-19. *Frontiers in Education, 8*, 1051227. Advance online publication. DOI: 10.3389/feduc.2023.1051227

Land, S., & Jonassen, D. (2012). *Theoretical foundations of learning environments*. Routledge. DOI: 10.4324/9780203813799

Lave, J., & Wenger, E. (1991). *Situated learning: Legitimate peripheral participation*. Cambridge University Press. DOI: 10.1017/CBO9780511815355

Liguori, E., & Winkler, C. (2020). From offline to online: Challenges and opportunities for entrepreneurship education following the COVID-19 pandemic. *Entrepreneurship Education and Pedagogy, 3*(4), 346–351. DOI: 10.1177/2515127420916738

Macayan, V. D., Baguistan, D. C., & Golias, J. B. (2022). *Game-based activities and gamification in the mastery of science process skills: a systematic literature review. EPRA International Journal of Multidisciplinary Research*. IJMR. DOI: 10.36713/epra10950

Macht, S. A., & Ball, S. (2016). "Authentic Alignment"–a new framework of entrepreneurship education. *Education + Training, 58*(9), 926–944. DOI: 10.1108/ET-07-2015-0063

Mansoori, Y., & Lackéus, M. (2020). Comparing effectuation to discovery-driven planning, prescriptive entrepreneurship, business planning, lean startup, and design thinking. *Small Business Economics, 54*(3), 791–818. Advance online publication. DOI: 10.1007/s11187-019-00153-w

Maraza-Quispe, B., Traverso-Condori, L. C., Torres-Gonzales, S. B., Reyes-Arco, R. E., Tinco-Túpac, S. T., Reyes-Villalba, E., & Carpio-Ventura, J. D. R. (2024). Impact of the Use of Gamified Online Tools: A Study with Kahoot and Quizizz in the Educational Context. *International Journal of Information and Education Technology (IJIET), 14*(1), 132–140. Advance online publication. DOI: 10.18178/ijiet.2024.14.1.2033

Ramsgaard, M. B., & Blenker, P. (2022). Reinterpreting a signature pedagogy for entrepreneurship education. *Journal of Small Business and Enterprise Development, 29*(2), 182–202. Advance online publication. DOI: 10.1108/JSBED-03-2021-0115

Richmond, A. S., & Cummings, R. (2005). Implementing Kolb's learning styles into online distance education. *International Journal of Technology in Teaching and Learning, 1*(1), 45–54.

Scott, J. M., Pavlovich, K., Thompson, J. L., & Penaluna, A. (2020). Constructive (mis)alignment in team-based experiential entrepreneurship education. *Education + Training*. Advance online publication. DOI: 10.1108/ET-06-2019-0113

Vargas-Murillo, A. R., de la Asuncion Pari-Bedoya, I. N. M., & de Jesús Guevara-Soto, F. (2023). Challenges and Opportunities of AI-Assisted Learning: A Systematic Literature Review on the Impact of ChatGPT Usage in Higher Education. *International Journal of Learning, Teaching and Educational Research*. DOI: 10.26803/ijlter.22.7.7

Venkataraman, S., Sarasvathy, S. D., Dew, N., & Forster, W. R. (2012). Reflections on the 2010 AMR decade award: Whither the promise? Moving forward with entrepreneurship as a science of the artificial. *Academy of Management Review*, *37*(1), 21–33. DOI: 10.5465/armr.2011.0079

Williams, D. (2015a). Impact of Business Simulation Games in Enterprise Education University of Huddersfield Repository. *2010 University of Huddersfield Annual Learning and Teaching Conference, February 2011*.

Williams, D. (2015b). The Impact of SimVenture on the Development of Entrepreneurial Skills in Management Students. *Industry and Higher Education*, *29*(5), 379–395. DOI: 10.5367/ihe.2015.0270

Xinaris, C., Kourtellis, A., Kakouris, A., & Georgiadis, P. (2011). Game based learning in entrepreneurship: The academic business planner. *Proceedings of the European Conference on Games-Based Learning*.

Yasin, N., & Hafeez, K. (2018). Enterprise Simulation Gaming: Effective Practices for Assessing Student Learning with SimVenture Classic and VentureBlocks. In *Experiential Learning for Entrepreneurship* (pp. 51–69). Springer International Publishing. DOI: 10.1007/978-3-319-90005-6_3

Chapter 2
A Literature Review on the Emergence of Entrepreneurship Education:
Development, Trends, and Challenges

Marcos Komodromos
https://orcid.org/0000-0002-2910-6541
University of Nicosia, Cyprus

ABSTRACT

The chapter provides a comprehensive literature review on entrepreneurship education's evolution, trends, and challenges. It outlines the historical progression of this field from a specialized area of study to its current status as a globally recognized discipline. The chapter delves into modern pedagogical strategies, emphasising experiential learning and using simulation technologies to enhance student engagement. It also explores the growing adoption of interdisciplinary and cross-disciplinary methods to foster innovation and adaptability in learners. Additionally, the chapter examines key emerging trends, including the internationalization of entrepreneurship education, the growing significance of social entrepreneurship, and the impact of digital technologies. Through a thorough analysis, the chapter offers valuable insights into the current landscape of entrepreneurship education while providing a forward-looking perspective on its potential future developments.

INTRODUCTION

Entrepreneurship education has become increasingly important in business and management studies over the last few decades (Hanandeh et al., 2024; Zeithaml & Rice 1987). Its importance lies in its ability to equip individuals with the skills, knowledge, and mindset necessary to identify opportunities, create value, and address complex global challenges. In an era characterized by rapid technological advancements and globalization, entrepreneurship education is no longer confined to teaching business fundamentals but fosters creativity, leadership, adaptability, and resilience. These qualities are essential for navigating the dynamic global economic landscape and addressing pressing issues such as unem-

DOI: 10.4018/979-8-3693-9040-5.ch002

ployment, inequality, and sustainability. As a result, entrepreneurship education has become a strategic priority for policymakers, educators, and institutions worldwide.

Several authors argue that online learner engagement in blended synchronous learning can be increased by initiating frequent interactions, letting learners play active roles, continuous assessment, optimizing technological conditions, and professional development (Wang & Huang, 2024). Introducing entrepreneurial character education at a young age can nurture essential qualities like independence, creativity, leadership, discipline, and risk-taking in students, laying a solid groundwork for future entrepreneurial success (Badawi, 2024).

Entrepreneurship education has undergone notable transformation since it began in the mid-20th century. Originally confined to a select number of prestigious business schools emphasizing small business management, it gained traction during the 1980s and 1990s as the global economy increasingly acknowledged entrepreneurship's role in driving innovation and economic growth competitiveness. By the early 2000s, the field expanded to include fostering entrepreneurial mindsets and integrating technology into learning processes. The rise of blended and online learning environments further transformed entrepreneurship education by making it more accessible and interactive. Technologies such as simulation tools, social media platforms, and massive open online courses (MOOCs) have enabled experiential learning that mirrors real-world business challenges. These advancements have broadened the scope of entrepreneurship education and introduced new complexities.

Entrepreneurship drives economic growth, creates jobs, and fosters societal development in today's dynamic and innovation-driven global economies. As a result, entrepreneurship education has evolved from being a niche subject at a few business schools to an international phenomenon embraced by universities, colleges, and even secondary schools worldwide (Zhao, Yang & Sheng, 2024). This literature review aims to explore the emergence, trends, and obstacles related to the growth of entrepreneurship education, offering an in-depth analysis of the existing knowledge base and the future direction of entrepreneurship education.

Entrepreneurship education originated in the mid-20th century, but it gained significant momentum in the 1980s and 1990s. Initially, entrepreneurship was seen as a specialized study offered by only a few elite business schools, often focusing on the practical aspects of starting and managing small businesses (Badri & Badri, 2020). As the global economy evolved, so did the understanding of entrepreneurship. By the early 2000s, entrepreneurship education began to be recognized as a crucial component of business and management studies, with a broader focus on fostering entrepreneurial mindsets, creativity, and innovation (Petek et al, 2015). The expansion of entrepreneurship education during this period was driven by the recognition of entrepreneurship as a critical driver of economic development, particularly in globalization and technological advancement.

Moreover, despite its expansion, entrepreneurship education continues to encounter several practical challenges. A prominent issue is the assurance of learner engagement within blended synchronous learning environments. Research indicates that frequent interactions, active learner participation, continuous assessment, optimized technological conditions, and professional development are essential for enhancing engagement. However, the consistent implementation of these strategies across diverse educational contexts poses a significant challenge. Furthermore, there exists a disconnect between theoretical knowledge and practical application. Although simulation technologies provide hands-on experience, their effectiveness in accurately representing real-world complexities remains a subject of debate. Additionally, access to high-quality entrepreneurship education remains unequal globally due to disparities in resources and infrastructure.

Integrating technology and education has led to a significant transformation, particularly in entrepreneurship education (Mirr et al., 2022; Zainal & Yong, 2020). As the global economy becomes more interconnected and technology-driven, there is an increasing demand for entrepreneurial skills such as adaptability, innovation, and real-world experience (Kraus et al., 2019). In response to this demand, educational institutions and educators are incorporating innovative tools and methods to enhance learning. Among these, simulation technologies have emerged as a noteworthy pedagogical tool, providing practical learning opportunities that closely simulate real-world business challenges. (Komodromos, 2021; Watson, McGowan, & Cunningham, 2018).

Simulation technologies create a dynamic and interactive environment where students can experiment with business strategies, make decisions, and observe the outcomes of those decisions within a controlled setting (Khoshtaria et al., 2024; Williams, 2015). These tools improve the quality of entrepreneurship education and provide greater accessibility to experiential learning, enabling students from diverse backgrounds and geographical locations to acquire practical experience in business management and decision-making (Simpson, Tuck, & Bellamy, 2004).

Entrepreneurship is increasingly considered a key part of economic strategy. This has led to the development of entrepreneurship education as a distinct field of study. Entrepreneurship education aims to equip people with the knowledge, skills, and attitudes necessary to recognize opportunities, be innovative, and create new businesses (Apostu, 2022; Carpenter & Wilson, 2021). In recent years, there has been substantial growth in this field, with the introduction of various courses, programs, and research initiatives focused on nurturing entrepreneurial mindsets.

Several research gaps persist within this domain. For example, although a substantial body of literature has been produced regarding the pedagogical advantages of blended learning in entrepreneurship education, there exists a scarcity of empirical evidence concerning its long-term effects on entrepreneurial success. Likewise, the significance of character education in entrepreneurship at a younger age—while acknowledged as crucial—has not been sufficiently investigated across diverse cultural contexts. Furthermore, research focused on the optimization of digital tools to ensure inclusive and equitable access to entrepreneurship education remains limited.

This chapter aims to fill these gaps by thoroughly analyzing emerging trends in entrepreneurship education, particularly within blended and online learning environments. It will investigate methods to boost learner engagement and evaluate the efficacy of simulation technologies in connecting theoretical knowledge with practical application. By highlighting best practices and suggesting innovative solutions, this chapter seeks to inform future researchers and policymakers in developing more effective entrepreneurship education frameworks.

This literature review chapter centers on the question: ***How can blended and online entrepreneurship education be improved to boost learner engagement and connect theory with practice?*** This inquiry highlights the necessity to investigate innovative methods that enhance the effectiveness and accessibility of entrepreneurship education. By tackling this question, the chapter seeks to support the formation of an inclusive and dynamic educational landscape that equips individuals to succeed in a complex global economy. Furthermore, the literature review offers a thorough examination of the growth of entrepreneurship education, detailing its trends and challenges (Kurotimi, 2017; Lei et al., 2021).

1. HISTORICAL DEVELOPMENT OF ENTREPRENEURSHIP EDUCATION IN THE LATE 20TH AND 21ST CENTURY

Entrepreneurship education first became part of broader business education in the early 1900s. The earliest recorded instance of entrepreneurship education was a course on small business management offered at Harvard University in 1947. This "Management of New Enterprises" course marked the formal beginning of academic interest in entrepreneurship (Katz, 2003). Despite this, at that time, entrepreneurship was still considered a peripheral topic within business schools, with little emphasis on creating new ventures (Mikić, Sopta, & Horvatinović, 2019).

During the 1970s and 1980s, there was a growing recognition of the importance of entrepreneurship (Birley, 1985). Economic shifts, such as the decline of traditional industries, the rise of technology startups, and the increased focus on innovation, drove this. This period also saw the establishment of dedicated university entrepreneurship courses and programs. Notable developments included founding the first academic entrepreneurship centres, such as the Center for Entrepreneurial Studies at Stanford University in 1978 and the Babson College Entrepreneurship Program in 1970 (Ronstadt, Shuman & Vesper, 2020). Vesper & Gartner, 1997).

During this period, entrepreneurship education became more institutionalized. This involved developing specialized curricula, creating academic journals, and establishing professional organizations like the United States Association for Small Business and Entrepreneurship (USASBE) (Kuratko, 2005). These advancements formed the foundation for recognizing entrepreneurship education as an academic discipline. The 21st century has seen a significant increase in entrepreneurship education. The spread of entrepreneurship programs worldwide reflects the global understanding of entrepreneurship as a crucial factor in economic development. Universities and business schools worldwide have included entrepreneurship in their curricula, providing various courses, degrees, and certificates (Passaro et al, 2018; Schmitz). In addition, authors note that higher levels of education and specific entrepreneurial characteristics play a crucial role in developing entrepreneurial intention and human capital (Maas & Jones, 2015).

The rise of online education and Massive Open Online Courses (MOOCs) has made entrepreneurship education more accessible. Platforms such as Coursera, edX, and Udemy offer courses from top universities, allowing entrepreneurship education to reach a global audience (Vorbach, Poandl, & Korajman, 2019). The growing availability of online resources has contributed to the widespread sharing of entrepreneurial knowledge and skills.

2. CONTEMPORARY TRENDS AND PEDAGOGICAL APPROACHES IN ENTREPRENEURSHIP EDUCATION

In recent years, several key trends have emerged in entrepreneurship education. Many authors argue that entrepreneurship is now wider than business schools and has **become integrated into various disciplines** such as engineering, health sciences, and the arts (Kuratko, 2005). This interdisciplinary approach encourages students from diverse backgrounds to engage with entrepreneurial concepts and practices, thus broadening the scope of entrepreneurship education (Ratten & Usmanij, 2020). Authors agree that the teaching methods utilized in entrepreneurship education have evolved to align with the diverse objectives of entrepreneurship programs and the varying needs of students (Antonelli et al., 2023).

As the field has evolved, there has been a shift towards experiential and active learning methods, emphasizing the importance of engaging students in hands-on activities that simulate real-world **entrepreneurial experiences** (Thomsen, Muurlink & Best, 2019). In the early stages of entrepreneurship education, traditional lecture-based approaches were the primary mode of instruction, involving disseminating theoretical knowledge through lectures, readings, and examinations. While lecture-based teaching remains a component of many entrepreneurship courses, it is often criticized for needing to be more active and provide students with the practical skills necessary for entrepreneurship (Curtis, Moon & Penaluna, 2020).

Furthermore, **experiential and active learning** is increasingly important in entrepreneurship education (Hockerts, 2018). Programs now incorporate practical experiences such as business simulations, internships, and startup incubators to supplement theoretical knowledge. This hands-on approach enables students to apply entrepreneurial theories in real-world situations, thus fostering critical thinking and problem-solving skills (Pittaway & Cope, 2007). According to the literature review (Boldureanu et al., 2020; Fang & Luo, 2018; Febrianti et al., 2023; Kim et al., 2018; Pardo-Garcia & Barac, 2020; Pittaway & Cope, 2007; Russell, Atchison & Brooks, 2008), essential methods include:

- **Business Plan Competitions:** Students create and present business plans, gaining practical venture creation experience and receiving feedback from industry experts.
- **Case Studies:** Analyzing real-world cases of successful and failed entrepreneurship helps students develop problem-solving skills and understand their complexities.
- **Simulations and Games:** Computer-based simulations and role-playing games enable students to experience the intricacies of operating a business in a risk-free environment.
- **Internships and Field Projects**: Students acquire hands-on experience and establish connections within the entrepreneurial ecosystem by working with startups or participating in community-based projects.

The **globalization of entrepreneurship education** means that institutions worldwide offer entrepreneurship programs for local and international students (Gibb, 2002; Torres-Coronas & Vidal-Blasco, 2021). This reflects the recognition that entrepreneurship is crucial for driving global economic growth and innovation and necessitates education that goes beyond national borders.

The emergence of digital technologies has transformed **entrepreneurship education.** Integrating multimedia and digital tools in education can significantly enhance students' interest and engagement in developing entrepreneurial skills (Hsieh & Maritz, 2023). Online courses, Massive Open Online Courses (MOOCs), and virtual incubators have increased access to entrepreneurship education on a global scale, allowing individuals to pursue entrepreneurial education regardless of their location or time constraints (Guerrero, Heaton, & Urbano, 2021). This change has democratized access to entrepreneurial knowledge and resources, allowing aspiring entrepreneurs from various backgrounds to learn and innovate.

2.1 Design Thinking and Lean Startup Methodology

The combination of design thinking and lean startup methodologies in entrepreneurship education marks a notable transition towards more hands-on, customer-centric approaches. These methodologies are increasingly acknowledged for their ability to prepare students with the necessary skills to adapt and innovate in fast-paced markets (Iandoli, 2023). In recent years, there has been a shift in entrepreneurship education towards integrating design thinking and lean startup methodologies (Sarooghi, 2019).

These approaches focus on customer-centric innovation and iterative development. Design thinking encourages students to empathize with users, define problems, generate ideas, create prototypes, and conduct testing (Ghezzi & Cavallo, 2020). In addition, design thinking enables students to engage deeply with user needs and challenges. It fosters creativity and innovation by allowing students to explore multiple solutions and iterate based on feedback (Lynch, 2019).

On the other hand, the lean startup methodology, popularized by Eric Ries in 2011, promotes the creation of minimal viable products (MVPs) and emphasizes continuously using customer feedback to refine business models (Ghezzi & Cavallo, 2020). Incorporating lean startup principles into entrepreneurship education involves teaching students to develop minimum viable products (MVPs), conduct experiments, and pivot based on customer insights. This approach aligns with experiential learning, where students learn by doing (Shepherd & Gruber, 2020).

As a result, these educational shifts align with modern entrepreneurial practices and provide students with the tools to innovate effectively in dynamic markets. Several authors suggest that the lean startup methodology helps students cultivate a mindset of experimentation and resilience, promoting the embrace of failure as a learning opportunity and the continuous quest for validation from the market (Felin et al., 2020).

2.2 Integration of Design Thinking and Lean Startup

Integrating user-focused design methods, such as design thinking and lean startup, into the innovation process can significantly impact the development of new organizational opportunities. Several authors agree that design thinking, lean startup, and high-technology marketing can improve systems engineering processes, design, and adoption of new technology (Sarooghi, 2019; Shepherd & Gruber, 2020). They can also address culture change challenges and engage potential users and sponsors more effectively. Additionally, integrating design thinking and lean startup processes can be effectively used in agile methodology to facilitate the development of a minimum viable product (MVP) in collaborative teaching practices.

As previously mentioned, design thinking and lean startup methodologies complement each other by combining user-centered design with agile business development (Allen, 2020). Design thinking provides a creative framework, while lean startup offers a structured approach to testing and iteration. Additionally, several researchers have noted that integrating these methodologies into entrepreneurship education provides a comprehensive approach to innovation. Students learn to empathize with users, rapidly prototype solutions, and iteratively refine their ideas based on real-world feedback (Činčera, et al., 2018; Leal et al., 2021).

Integrating design thinking and lean startup methodologies in entrepreneurship education has many benefits. However, educators need to address challenges such as balancing theory with practice and ensuring that students have access to diverse perspectives and resources (Sarooghi et al., 2019). This approach equips students with the skills and mindsets required to innovate effectively in dynamic markets. As entrepreneurship education evolves, adopting design thinking and lean startup methodologies will likely play a crucial role in preparing students for the challenges and opportunities of the modern business landscape (Hockerts, 2018; Komodromos 2021).

3. INTERDISCIPLINARY AND CROSS-DISCIPLINARY APPROACHES IN ENTREPRENEURSHIP EDUCATION

Entrepreneurship is a multidisciplinary field encompassing technology, design, economics, and social sciences. Many authors have observed that entrepreneurship education is now essential to higher education programs worldwide (Antonelli et al., 2023; Komodromos, 2021; Ratten, & Usmanij, 2020). This shift has resulted in integrating entrepreneurship with different disciplines, promoting a multidisciplinary approach to provide students with a wide range of skills and encourage innovative thinking (Ireland & Webb, 2007). In addition, experts argue that it draws from various disciplines. In response, educational institutions increasingly adopt interdisciplinary and cross-disciplinary approaches to entrepreneurship education (Reinhardt, 2023).

3.1 Interdisciplinary Approaches

Interdisciplinary approaches involve integrating knowledge and methods from different disciplines to address complex problems. This means combining insights from business, technology, and social sciences to foster innovation in entrepreneurship (Torres-Coronas & Vidal-Blasco, 2021). Experts also emphasize that interdisciplinary programs in entrepreneurship education often include courses that blend business principles with technical skills and social awareness (Febrianti et al., 2023; Khoshtaria et al, 2024). These programs encourage students to think holistically and develop solutions considering multiple perspectives. Research suggests that interdisciplinary education enhances students' ability to think critically and creatively, fostering adaptability and problem-solving skills crucial for entrepreneurial success (Apostu et al., 2022).

3.2 Cross-Disciplinary Approaches

Cross-disciplinary approaches involve collaboration between different academic disciplines, allowing students to apply entrepreneurial thinking in various contexts (Antoncic & Hisrich, (2001). This approach is particularly relevant in fields like social entrepreneurship and intrapreneurship. Cross-disciplinary programs often involve partnerships between different departments or faculties. For example, a program might combine business, engineering, and design courses to provide a comprehensive entrepreneurial education. Cross-disciplinary education encourages students to apply entrepreneurial skills in diverse settings and promotes innovation by exposing students to different ways of thinking and problem-solving (Gibb, 2002).

3.3 Integration of Interdisciplinary and Cross-Disciplinary Approaches

Interdisciplinary and cross-disciplinary approaches complement each other by providing a broad and flexible framework for entrepreneurship education (Goch, 2023). Interdisciplinary approaches focus on integrating knowledge, while cross-disciplinary approaches emphasize collaboration across fields.

Researchers suggest that these methods assist students in developing the skills and perspectives needed to tackle complex challenges (Lei et al., 2021). They also encourage exploring entrepreneurial opportunities in technology, social impact, and corporate innovation. Implementing these methods requires close coordination between academic departments and a commitment to creating a collaborative learning environment. Educators must also ensure that students receive a comprehensive education covering both theoretical and practical aspects of entrepreneurship (Adedeji et al., 2020).

4. TRENDS IN ENTREPRENEURSHIP EDUCATION

Entrepreneurship education constantly changes in response to shifts in the global economy, technological advancements, and educational paradigms. Current trends in entrepreneurship education indicate a shift towards an anthropocentric view of education, linking it to emerging employment trends such as the gig economy and the digital transformation of the workplace (Khoshtaria et al., 2024; Ratten & Usmanij, 2020). Several authors have recently observed vital trends (Zhao et al., 2024).

4.1 Globalization of Entrepreneurship Education

The globalization of entrepreneurship education has been fueled by the growing acknowledgement of entrepreneurship as a crucial element in global economic development. Universities in both developed and developing countries have set up entrepreneurship programs, frequently in partnership with international collaborators. Efforts such as global entrepreneurship competitions, study-abroad initiatives, and cross-border incubators facilitate global entrepreneurial learning (Gibb, 2002). The exchange of knowledge and best practices across borders has enriched entrepreneurship education, making it more inclusive and diverse.

4.2 Focus on Social Entrepreneurship

The growing interest in social entrepreneurship reflects a broader shift towards socially responsible and sustainable business practices. Social entrepreneurship education is designed to equip students with the skills to establish ventures that address social and environmental issues (Badawi, 2024; Kurotimi et al., 2017). These programs often emphasize the triple bottom line—people, planet, and profit—and encourage students to pursue entrepreneurial ventures that generate social and financial returns. This trend has led to developing specialized curricula and research focused on social innovation, impact investing, and sustainable business models (Pardo-Garcia & Barac, 2020).

4.3 Integration of Technology and Digital Entrepreneurship

The rapid advancement of digital technologies has transformed the entrepreneurship landscape, resulting in the emergence of digital entrepreneurship. Education in digital entrepreneurship centers on the opportunities and challenges related to initiating and expanding ventures in the digital domain (Duong et al., 2022). Subjects such as e-commerce, digital marketing, platform-based business models, and the utilization of artificial intelligence and blockchain in entrepreneurship are progressively being integrated into entrepreneurship curricula. The emphasis on digital entrepreneurship underscores the growing importance of technology in fostering innovation and economic expansion (Wang & Huang, 2024).

4.4 Entrepreneurial Ecosystem Development

Entrepreneurial ecosystems, which consist of networks of institutions, resources, and support mechanisms, play a crucial role in promoting entrepreneurship (Kuratko, 2005). As a result, entrepreneurship education has increasingly focused on ecosystem development. Universities and educational institutions often anchor these ecosystems by providing educational resources such as incubators, accelerators, and funding opportunities (Febrianti et al., 2023). The emphasis on ecosystem development highlights the importance of creating supportive environments where entrepreneurship can thrive.

4.5 Emphasis on Lifelong Learning and Continuous Education

Entrepreneurship is a constantly evolving field that requires continuous learning and adaptation. As a result, there is a growing emphasis on lifelong learning in entrepreneurship education. Aside from traditional degree programs, educational institutions and organizations offer short courses, workshops, and executive education programs to cater to the ongoing learning needs of entrepreneurs at different stages of their careers (Antoncic & Hisrich, 2001). Lifelong learning is considered a vital skill that requires changes in teaching approaches and learner responsibilities, with individuals taking on more accountability for their learning process (Collins, 2009). The concept of lifelong learning reflects the idea that entrepreneurial skills must be regularly updated in response to changing markets and technologies.

5. SIMULATION TECHNOLOGIES IN EDUCATION

Simulation-based learning is a practical educational approach that allows learners to engage in interactive, risk-free environments. Research has shown that simulation-based learning in higher education effectively facilitates the learning of complex skills (Chernikova et al., 2020). Different types of scaffolding and technology support different phases of learning. This method will enable students to apply theoretical knowledge to practical scenarios, enhancing their learning experience. This enables them to apply theoretical knowledge to practical scenarios. Simulations can range from simple role-playing exercises to complex computer-based models replicating intricate business processes (Faisal et al., 2022). Recent advancements in simulation technology have been driven by developments in artificial intelligence (AI), machine learning (ML), virtual reality (VR), and augmented reality (AR) (Muthukannan., Gozman, & Johnson, 2020). These technologies make simulations more immersive and realistic, enabling personalized and adaptive learning experiences.

5.1 Artificial Intelligence and Machine Learning in Simulation

Artificial Intelligence (AI) and Machine Learning (ML) are essential to modern simulation technologies. They enhance these systems' adaptability, intelligence, and effectiveness (Janiesch et al., 2021). By analyzing learner behavior, predicting outcomes, and providing customized feedback, AI and ML have transformed simulations from static, pre-programmed experiences into dynamic, responsive, and personalized learning environments (Lynch et al., 2019). AI methods such as machine learning, pattern recognition, and deep learning offer compelling alternatives to classical modeling techniques in structural engineering. They address uncertainties, save time, and increase computational efficiency (Salehi & Burgueño, 2018). This literature review delves into the incorporation of AI and ML into simulation technologies, emphasizing their benefits, challenges, and future potential.

Integrating AI and ML into simulations has been shown to improve learner engagement. Adaptive simulations that respond to the learner's actions and provide personalized feedback are more engaging and interactive, helping to maintain the learner's interest and motivation (Crampon et al., 2021). Research has demonstrated that these tailored experiences lead to better information retention and greater satisfaction with the learning process.

Research shows that AI and ML enhanced simulations can enhance learning outcomes (Janiesch et al., 2021). These technologies personalize the learning experience to meet individual needs so that learners are engaged by manageable challenges and supported through easier tasks. This personalized approach maximizes the effectiveness of simulations, leading to improved skill acquisition and knowledge retention.

AI and ML make it possible to create scalable simulation systems that can accommodate many learners without significantly increasing resources. Automated feedback, personalized content delivery, and predictive analytics reduce the need for instructor involvement, making it feasible to deploy high-quality simulations in large educational settings or remote learning environments (Lynch et al., 2019).

As a result, AI and ML are now essential parts of modern simulation technologies. These technologies improve the adaptability and intelligence of simulations by allowing systems to analyze learner behavior, predict outcomes, and provide customized feedback (Ho et al., 2018). Simulations driven by AI can adjust the difficulty level based on the learner's performance, ensuring that the educational experience is both challenging and supportive. In entrepreneurship education, AI-powered simulations can model complex market environments, predict customer behaviour, and simulate real-time business decision-making processes (Komodromos et al., 2024). This gives students a deeper understanding of business dynamics and the implications of their decisions in a controlled environment (Duong et al., 2022).

5.2 Virtual Reality and Augmented Reality

Integrating virtual reality (VR) and augmented reality (AR) into simulation-based learning has created exciting new possibilities for developing highly immersive educational experiences. Integrating Virtual Reality (VR) and Augmented Reality (AR) into SBL has significantly enhanced the potential of these educational experiences, providing immersive, interactive, and highly realistic environments (Shankar et al., 2023). VR technology enables the creation of fully immersive 3D environments, allowing learners to interact with virtual objects and scenarios that closely resemble real-world business situations.

On the other hand, AR overlays digital information onto the physical world, offering contextual learning opportunities directly relevant to the learner's surroundings (Bhatti et al., 2021). In entrepreneurship education, VR and AR simulations can replicate various business environments, from startup incubators to international markets, allowing students to hone skills such as negotiation, product development, and crisis management in realistic settings.

Recent technological advancements have made virtual reality (VR) and augmented reality (AR) more accessible and practical for educational purposes. VR provides a fully immersive environment, while AR overlays digital information onto the real world, enhancing the learner's perception of reality. Both technologies have benefited from improvements in hardware (e.g., headsets and sensors) and software (e.g., realistic 3D models and intuitive user interfaces). In addition, virtual reality (VR) and augmented reality (AR) enable high levels of interactivity, which is essential for effective simulation-based learning (Birtill et al., 2021). In VR, learners can engage with objects and environments in a manner that replicates real-life scenarios, improving skill acquisition and retention (Pellas, Dengel & Christopoulos, 2020). On the other hand, AR allows learners to interact with their physical surroundings while receiving additional contextual information, as this aspect can be particularly beneficial in medical training, where real-world context is crucial (Hair et al., 2017).

5.3 Complex Computer-Based Models

The effectiveness of computer-based models in improving educational outcomes has been extensively researched. Several studies have examined the impact of these models on various aspects of learning, including cognitive skills, academic performance, and student engagement (Kleij, Feskens & Eggen, 2013). Recent advancements have led to the creation of advanced computer-based models replicating complex processes, such as business operations and medical procedures. These models provide learners with a deeper understanding of intricate systems. Many experts believe computer-based models are increasingly common in educational and industrial settings (Musso, Hernández & Cascallar, 2020). These models simulate complex processes and offer users valuable insights into intricate systems. They improve learning and decision-making by providing a virtual environment for experimentation and analysis.

The authors argue that complex computer-based models are valuable tools for understanding intricate processes (Kleij, Feskens & Eggen, 2013). These models provide significant educational benefits by offering learners insights into complex systems and enhancing their problem-solving skills. Future developments in AI and ML will likely lead to more adaptive and intelligent models that can provide personalized learning experiences and offer real-time feedback to users. Experts support the potential for developing collaborative and interdisciplinary models that integrate knowledge from multiple fields. Such models could provide a more comprehensive understanding of complex systems and foster interdisciplinary learning (Kim et al., 2018).

Integrating complex models into education and industry can revolutionize learning and decision-making. They provide realistic simulations that prepare learners for real-world challenges. As technology advances, these models are expected to play an increasingly important role in education and industry, offering immersive and interactive learning experiences that can revolutionize our understanding of complex systems (Watson et al., 2018).

6. IMPACT ON ENTREPRENEURSHIP EDUCATION

Entrepreneurship education aims to provide students with the skills, knowledge, and mindset needed to navigate the complex and often unpredictable world of business creation and management. Advanced simulation technologies in entrepreneurship education have recently become a powerful tool for improving learning outcomes (Duong et al., 2022).

Incorporating advanced simulation technologies into entrepreneurship education offers several advantages (Adedeji et al., 2020). Advanced simulation technologies facilitate experiential learning, a vital element of entrepreneurship education. Through simulations, students can test various business strategies and decisions without the risks associated with real-world business ventures. Entrepreneurship requires making informed decisions under uncertainty (Kurotimi et al., 2017).

According to several authors, using simulation technologies helps students develop essential skills by immersing them in dynamic and complex environments. In these environments, students must analyze data, anticipate outcomes, and make strategic decisions (Muthukannan, et al., 2020). Through repeated practice with simulations, students learn to think critically, evaluate risks, and gain a more nuanced understanding of business management.

Authors support the idea that tailored advanced simulations can meet students' individualized learning needs, providing personalized experiences catering to different levels of expertise and interest (Shepherd & Gruber, 2020). For example, students can participate in simulations focusing on specific entrepreneurship aspects, such as marketing, finance, or operations. This personalized approach enhances the relevance of the learning experience, making it more engaging and effective.

On the contrary, numerous simulation technologies promote collaborative learning by enabling students to work in teams to solve problems and make business decisions. This collaborative approach mirrors the demands of entrepreneurship, where teamwork and communication are indispensable (Leal et al., 2021). Through simulations, students develop interpersonal skills, learn to negotiate, collaborate, and experience the dynamics of working within a team to accomplish common goals. This risk-free environment fosters innovation and creativity, allowing learners to test hypotheses, learn from failures, and refine their approaches before applying them in real-world scenarios (Adedeji et al., 2020).

Students are provided with hands-on experience in a safe environment, allowing them to test different business strategies without the risk of real-world failure. This learning approach bridges the gap between theoretical knowledge and practical application, crucial for developing entrepreneurial skills (Birtill et al., 2021). The use of AI and ML in simulations allows for personalized learning paths, enabling students to progress at their own pace and receive tailored feedback to meet their individual learning needs (Crampon et al., 2021). This is particularly beneficial in entrepreneurship education, where students' learning curves vary significantly. Moreover, VR and AR technologies offer opportunities for collaborative learning. Students can join forces in virtual environments to tackle business challenges, enhancing their teamwork and communication skills, which are crucial for entrepreneurial success (Hair et al., 2017).

Furthermore, these technologies empower educators to develop diverse and inclusive learning experiences by simulating various cultural, economic, and social contexts. This exposure to different business environments equips students with the globalized nature of modern entrepreneurship (Komodromos, 2021).

7. CHALLENGES AND CRITICISMS IN ENTREPRENEURSHIP EDUCATION

Entrepreneurship education is rapidly growing and evolving, but it faces several challenges that must be addressed to ensure its ongoing relevance and effectiveness. One of the main challenges is the need for a standardized curriculum or pedagogical framework (Badawi, 2024; Činčera, et al., 2018). Entrepreneurship is a highly diverse field, and what defines effective entrepreneurship education can vary greatly depending on the context. This lack of standardization can lead to inconsistencies in the quality and content of entrepreneurship education programs (Hair, 2017).

Finding the right balance between theoretical knowledge and practical application is challenging in education. Critics argue that focusing too much on hands-on activities may result in a superficial understanding of entrepreneurial concepts. However, relying solely on theory may not prepare students with the skills needed for real-world entrepreneurship (Kim et al., 2018; Pittaway & Cope, 2007). Students must grasp the theoretical foundations of entrepreneurship and gain practical experience through experiential learning. Balancing these two aspects can be difficult, especially in programs with limited resources or faculty primarily focused on practical experience.

According to experts, there are several critical challenges in entrepreneurship education. One of these challenges is defining and measuring success. Unlike traditional fields of study, where success can be measured through exams and grades, the outcomes of entrepreneurship education are more complex and multidimensional (Vorbach et al., 2019). Success in entrepreneurship education can be measured by various metrics, including the number of startups created, the survival rate of ventures, the acquisition of entrepreneurial skills, and the impact on students' career trajectories. However, these metrics are often difficult to quantify, and there needs to be a consensus on the most appropriate measures for success (Felin et al., 2020).

Challenges exist in entrepreneurship education. One of these challenges is finding the right balance between theoretical and practical aspects. While theoretical knowledge helps comprehend the principles of entrepreneurship, practical experience is necessary for developing the skills required to handle the unpredictability of entrepreneurial endeavors (Apostu et al., 2022). Educators need to find a middle ground between these two aspects, ensuring that students have both the theoretical knowledge and the practical tools essential for entrepreneurship. This balance can be achieved through innovative teaching methods that combine theory with real-world application.

According to other authors, evaluating the effects of entrepreneurship education on students and society presents a unique challenge (Kraus et al., 2019). Unlike traditional fields of study, where outcomes can be assessed through exams and standardized tests, the success of entrepreneurship education is often judged by more intangible metrics such as the capacity to innovate, generate employment, and stimulate economic advancement. Creating reliable assessment tools to measure these outcomes remains an ongoing challenge for educators and researchers (Sarooghi et al., 2019).

Additionally, ensuring inclusivity and accessibility in entrepreneurship education poses a significant challenge. Various studies suggest that entrepreneurship education can be accessible and effective for diverse populations, including students from different socioeconomic backgrounds, cultures, and regions, especially when culturally responsive curricula, diverse learning environments, and exposure to successful entrepreneurial models are utilized (Boldureanu et al., 2020; Cadenas et al., 2020; Pittaway & Cope, 2007). However, factors like geographic location, financial constraints, and language barriers often limit access to entrepreneurship education. To tackle these challenges, institutions must develop strategies to promote inclusivity in entrepreneurship education, such as offering scholarships, creating online programs, and supporting underrepresented groups.

On the other hand, the rapid pace of technological change presents opportunities and challenges for entrepreneurship education. Technological advancements offer new tools and platforms for delivering education and fostering innovation (Febrianti et al., 2023). However, the fast-evolving nature of technology requires continuous updates to curricula and teaching methods. Educators must stay updated on technological trends to ensure that entrepreneurship education remains relevant in digital transformation (Ghezzi & Cavallo, 2020). This demands flexibility and adaptability in program design and delivery.

Experts stress the importance of customizing entrepreneurship education to meet the needs of the industry and the broader economy (Kraus et al., 2019; Shankar et al., 2023). This ensures that graduates have the skills and knowledge that are in demand by the market. However, this can be challenging due to the rapidly changing business environment and the diverse nature of entrepreneurship. Collaboration between educational institutions and industry stakeholders is essential to bridge this gap. By partnering with businesses, entrepreneurs, and investors, valuable insights into industry trends can be gained, helping to shape curricula relevant and responsive to market needs (Zainal & Yong, 2020).

Following this, it is essential to ensure that entrepreneurship education is accessible to a diverse range of students. Various studies suggest that entrepreneurship education is accessible to a diverse range of students, but its effectiveness and long-term outcomes are influenced by factors such as cultural responsiveness, diversity in learning environments, and subjective norms (Cadenas et al., 2020; Maresch et al., 2016; Pittaway & Cope, 2007; Simpson et al., 2004). In addition, other studies confirmed that a diverse learning environment positively influences students' entrepreneurial intentions and competencies. This environment, combined with knowledge transfer and self-efficacy, helps develop entrepreneurial skills among higher education students (Haddad, Haddad, & Nagpal, 2021). While digital learning has improved access, disparities in technology, resources, and support systems can hinder participation, especially in underrepresented and underserved communities.

8. THE FUTURE OF ENTREPRENEURSHIP EDUCATION

Entrepreneurship education is rapidly evolving to meet the demands of a dynamic global economy, influenced by international economic trends, technological advancements, and shifts in educational paradigms. Many studies suggest that the future of entrepreneurship education will be shaped by integrating emerging employment trends, digital transformation, and new educational paradigms while addressing labour market needs and leveraging educational technology (Khoshtaria et al., 2024; Rashid, 2019; Vanevenhoven, 2013). Several key directions are likely to influence the evolution of the field. Technological advancements and shifting market needs are disrupting traditional business models, and academic institutions are rethinking how they prepare students for entrepreneurial success.

One of the most significant trends in entrepreneurship education is ***technology integration***. Digital tools such as online platforms and simulation software are increasingly utilized to create interactive and immersive learning experiences (Zainal & Yong, 2020). Numerous emerging trends will influence the future of simulation technologies in entrepreneurship education.

Researchers have observed that the increasing focus on ***personalization and customization in education*** is expected to influence entrepreneurship education substantially. Research studies proved that the growing emphasis on personalization and customization in education is expected to dramatically influence entrepreneurship education by enhancing entrepreneurial intentions, competencies, and perceptions of feasibility, especially for those with less prior exposure (Lacatus & Stăiculescu, 2016; Nabi et al., 2017; Peterman & Kennedy, 2003). Progress in technology, especially in artificial intelligence and data analytics, allows for the creation of personalized learning experiences designed to meet individual students' specific needs, preferences, and career aspirations. Tailored learning paths can offer students more pertinent and focused educational experiences, thereby improving their potential for achieving entrepreneurial success.

Artificial intelligence (AI) and data analytics are expected to play a growing role in entrepreneurship education. Artificial intelligence (AI) and data analytics have been increasingly recognized in recent years for their transformative potential across various fields, including entrepreneurship education (Obschonka & Audretsch, 2019; Lévesque, Obschonka & Nambisan, 2020). This synthesis explores the growing role of AI and data analytics in entrepreneurship education, drawing insights from multiple research papers.

The future of simulation technologies in entrepreneurship education will likely involve integration with other emerging technologies, such as artificial intelligence (AI) and augmented reality (AR). AI can enhance simulations by providing personalized feedback and adaptive learning experiences. At the same time, AR can overlay digital information onto the physical world, creating hybrid learning environments that combine virtual and real-world elements (Chae & Goh, 2020). AI can be used to analyze market trends, predict entrepreneurial success, and provide personalized feedback to students (Lévesque, Obschonka & Nambisan, 2020). Data analytics can help educators track student progress, identify areas for improvement, and tailor educational content to meet learners' evolving needs. Integrating AI and data analytics into entrepreneurship education can enhance the effectiveness of teaching and learning, providing students with valuable insights and tools for entrepreneurial decision-making (Chae & Goh, 2020; Guerrero, Heaton & Urbano, 2021).

Numerous studies have shown that global challenges such as climate change, inequality, and social injustice are becoming increasingly urgent. As a result, there will be a greater emphasis on ***sustainability and ethical entrepreneurship in education***. Many studies suggest that sustainability and moral entrepreneurship in education contribute to society and the environment by integrating sustainability principles, promoting responsible consumption, and addressing complex community problems through interdisciplinary programs (Hermann & Bossle, 2020; Lans, Blok & Wesselink, 2014; Rashid, 2019; Žalėnienė & Pereira, 2021).

Entrepreneurship programs must highlight the significance of establishing ventures that positively contribute to society and the environment. This change will necessitate new curricula incorporating sustainability principles, corporate social responsibility, and ethical decision-making into entrepreneurship education.

In addition, these studies have led to a greater emphasis on sustainability and social entrepreneurship in educational programs aiming to equip students with the skills to create ventures that generate economic and social benefits (Bruksle et al., 2023; Kickul, et al., 2018). Developing an entrepreneurial mindset—marked by creativity, resilience, adaptability, and a willingness to take risks—will continue to be a central focus of entrepreneurship education. As the nature of work evolves, with a growing emphasis on innovation, problem-solving, and self-employment, the entrepreneurial mindset will become increasingly valuable across various careers and industries (Činčera, et al., 2018). Entrepreneurship education will need to highlight mindset development alongside technical skills to prepare students for the uncertainties and opportunities of the future.

As entrepreneurship education continues to evolve, there will be a greater focus on innovative teaching methods, including artificial intelligence, virtual reality, and other emerging technologies to enhance learning experiences. The COVID-19 pandemic accelerated the adoption of ***online and hybrid learning models***, and this trend is likely to continue in the future. Many studies suggest that the adoption of online and hybrid learning models is essential in entrepreneurship education for enhancing cooperation, engagement, creativity, international collaboration, entrepreneurial spirit, self-efficacy, professional qualities, employability, and user behavior (Elenurm, 2022; Mittal & Raghuvaran, 2021; Woraphiphat & Roopsuwankun, 2021).

Online and hybrid models offer flexibility and accessibility, allowing students to learn at their own pace and from any location. These models also enable institutions to reach a global audience, expanding the impact of entrepreneurship education (Guerrero, Heaton & Urbano, 2021; Lacatus & Stăiculescu, 2016). The challenge will be to ensure that online and hybrid learning experiences are as engaging and effective as traditional in-person education.

Expanding entrepreneurship education into emerging economies presents opportunities and challenges. As these regions seek to foster economic development through entrepreneurship, there will be a growing demand for educational programs tailored to their unique needs and contexts (Badri & Badri 2020). Expanding entrepreneurship education into emerging economies offers opportunities and challenges that are critical to consider for fostering economic development. With their rapid growth and industrialization, emerging economies provide fertile ground for entrepreneurial activities that can drive innovation and job creation (Iandoli, 2023). However, implementing entrepreneurship education in these regions requires careful adaptation to local contexts and needs.

Several studies suggest that expanding entrepreneurship education into emerging economies presents opportunities such as job creation, economic growth, and enhanced student motivation while facing challenges like academic legitimacy, resource mobilization, and contextual limitations (Foo, Vissa & Wu, 2020). Lim, Oh & Clercq, 2016). In addition, research indicates that educational programs must be tailored to address specific cultural, economic, and institutional factors unique to each region. For example, curricula should incorporate local business practices, regulatory environments, and market conditions to be effective (Lei, Hock & Karim, 2021). Additionally, educators must build the capacity to deliver these programs effectively, which may involve training and resources often limited in emerging economies.

Furthermore, partnerships between educational institutions, government bodies, and the private sector can enhance the relevance and impact of entrepreneurship education. Despite these challenges, the potential benefits of such educational initiatives are significant, as they can empower individuals with the skills and knowledge necessary to start and sustain successful businesses, ultimately contributing to broader economic growth and development (Nabi et al., 2017).

As technology becomes more affordable and digital tools become more accessible, advanced simulation technologies are expected to become more widely available in entrepreneurship education. This development will allow more institutions, including those in underserved areas, to integrate these tools into their curricula, making high-quality entrepreneurship training accessible to more people (Schmitz et al., 2017).

Strengthening the connections between ***academic institutions and industry*** is essential to ensuring entrepreneurship education's ongoing relevance and impact. Collaborative initiatives, including industry partnerships, mentorship programs, and joint research projects, will be pivotal in ensuring that entrepreneurship education stays aligned with the needs of the business world (Kraus, et al., 2019). Several authors note that we must continue researching the most effective ways to incorporate simulation technologies into entrepreneurship education (Činčera, et al., 2018; Haddad et al., 2021). This involves studying the effects of these tools on learning outcomes, identifying best practices for implementation, and creating new simulation models to meet the changing needs of entrepreneurship education.

CONCLUSION

Entrepreneurship education has become recognized as a distinct field of study due to the increasing importance of entrepreneurship in today's global economy. It has evolved into a dynamic, interdisciplinary field that fosters innovation and economic growth. This evolution has involved a shift from traditional business education to more experiential and interdisciplinary approaches, reflecting the changing nature of entrepreneurship itself. However, as the field expands, it must address several challenges, including standardization, balancing theory and practice, and ensuring inclusivity in entrepreneurship education. By addressing these challenges, entrepreneurship education can continue to progress and play a crucial role in preparing the next generation of entrepreneurs to tackle the complex challenges of the 21st century.

Developing entrepreneurship education involves integrating various teaching methods, including theoretical frameworks, and adapting to global and technological trends. However, the field also faces significant challenges, such as balancing theory and practice, ensuring inclusivity, and aligning with industry needs.

Entrepreneurship education has transformed from a specialized area of study to a global educational movement, highlighting the growing importance of entrepreneurship in driving economic growth, innovation, and societal progress. While there has been significant progress in expanding and diversifying entrepreneurship education, challenges remain in curriculum design, accessibility, and outcome assessment. As the field continues to evolve, ongoing research and innovation will be crucial in addressing these challenges and ensuring that entrepreneurship education continues to empower the next generation of entrepreneurs.

Integrating advanced simulation technologies into entrepreneurship education provides numerous benefits. These benefits include enhanced hands-on learning, the development of critical thinking and decision-making skills, personalized learning experiences, and opportunities for collaboration. However, there are also challenges such as cost, technical complexity, and the need to balance realism with educational goals. Nevertheless, the potential advantages of these technologies are considerable.

Academic programs that emphasize sustainability and social entrepreneurship are essential for developing students' abilities to create ventures that generate economic and social benefits. These programs enhance sustainability awareness, foster entrepreneurial competencies through extracurricular activities, and positively influence students' intentions to engage in sustainable entrepreneurship. Despite challenges, innovative pedagogical approaches and community interventions significantly promote a culture of social responsibility and sustainable development.

In the future, entrepreneurship education will be influenced by technological advancements, the global economy, and educational approaches. Trends such as AI integration, a focus on sustainability, and the growth of online learning will shape the field. As entrepreneurship education continues to evolve, it will play a vital role in preparing individuals to navigate the complexities of the modern world and contribute to creating a more innovative, inclusive, and sustainable global economy. With the advancement of technology and increased use of simulation tools, entrepreneurship education is expected to offer new opportunities for learners to gain the necessary skills and knowledge.

REFERENCES

Adedeji, S. B., Rahman, M. M., Abdul, M. B., Ghani, M. F. B. A., Uddin, M. J., & Rahaman, M. S. (2020). Innovative teaching methods and entrepreneurship education: A synthesised literature review [Educational Administration Research and Review]. *EARR*, *2*(1), 1–8. DOI: 10.17509/earr.v2i1.21713

Allen, G. (2020). Concepturealize™: A new contribution to generate real-needs-focussed, user-centred, lean business models. *Journal of Innovation and Entrepreneurship*, *11*(1), 6. Advance online publication. DOI: 10.1186/s13731-022-00198-4 PMID: 35096505

Antoncic, B., & Hisrich, R. (2001). Intrapreneurship: Construct refinement and cross-cultural validation. *Journal of Business Venturing*, *16*(5), 495–527. DOI: 10.1016/S0883-9026(99)00054-3

Antonelli, G., Venesaar, U., Riviezzo, A., Kallaste, M., Dorożyński, T., & Kłysik-Uryszek, A. (2023). Find your limits and break them! Nurturing students' entrepreneurship competence through innovative teaching methods and self-assessment. Journal of Enterprising Communities: People and Places in the Global Economy. .DOI: 10.1108/JEC-10-2022-0148

Apostu, S., Mukli, L., Panait, M., Gigauri, I., & Hysa, E. (2022). Economic Growth through the Lenses of Education, Entrepreneurship, and Innovation. *Administrative Sciences*, *12*(3), 74. Advance online publication. DOI: 10.3390/admsci12030074

Badawi, B. (2024). Entrepreneurial Character Education from an Early Age. Al-Hayat: Journal of Islamic Education. .DOI: 10.35723/ajie.v8i1.481

Badri, A., & Badri, P. (2020). Investigating The Impact Of Entrepreneurship And Education On Economic Growth. Open Journal of Management Science (ISSN: 2734-2107). DOI: 10.52417/ojms.v1i1.77

Bhatti, M. A., Al Doghan, M. A., Saat, S. A. M., Juhari, A. S., & Alshagawi, M. (2021). Entrepreneurial intentions among women: Does entrepreneurial training and education matters? (Pre-and post-evaluation of psychological attributes and its effects on entrepreneurial intention). *Journal of Small Business and Enterprise Development*, *28*(2), 167–184. DOI: 10.1108/JSBED-09-2019-0305

Birley, S. (1985). Encouraging Entrepreneurship: Britain's New Enterprise Program. *Journal of Small Business Management*, *23*, 6.

Birtill, M., King, J., Jones, D., Thyer, L., Pap, R., & Simpson, P. (2021). The use of immersive simulation in paramedicine education: A scoping review. *Interactive Learning Environments*, *31*(4), 2428–2443. DOI: 10.1080/10494820.2021.1889607

Boldureanu, G., Ionescu, A., Bercu, A., Bedrule-Grigoru ă, M., & Boldureanu, D. (2020). Entrepreneurship Education through Successful Entrepreneurial Models in Higher Education Institutions. *Sustainability (Basel)*, *12*(3), 1267. Advance online publication. DOI: 10.3390/su12031267

Bruksle, I., Chwallek, C., & Krastina, A. (2023). Strengthening Sustainability in Entrepreneurship Education -Implications for Shifting Entrepreneurial Thinking Towards Sustainability at Universities. *ACTA PROSPERITATIS*, *14*(1), 37–48. DOI: 10.37804/1691-6077-2023-14-37-48

Cadenas, G., Cantú, E., Lynn, N., Spence, T., & Ruth, A. (2020). A programmatic intervention to promote entrepreneurial self-efficacy, critical behavior, and technology readiness among underrepresented college students. *Journal of Vocational Behavior, 116*, 103350. DOI: 10.1016/j.jvb.2019.103350

Carpenter, A., & Wilson, R. (2021). A systematic review looking at the effect of entrepreneurship education on higher education student. *International Journal of Management Education*. Advance online publication. DOI: 10.1016/j.ijme.2021.100541

Chae, B., & Goh, G. (2020). Digital Entrepreneurs in Artificial Intelligence and Data Analytics: Who Are They? *Journal of Open Innovation, 6*(3), 56. Advance online publication. DOI: 10.3390/joitmc6030056

Chernikova, O., Heitzmann, N., Stadler, M., Holzberger, D., Seidel, T., & Fischer, F. (2020). Simulation-Based Learning in Higher Education: A Meta-Analysis. *Review of Educational Research, 90*(4), 499–541. DOI: 10.3102/0034654320933544

Činčera, J., Biberhofer, P., Binka, B., Boman, J., Mindt, L., & Rieckmann, M. (2018). Designing a sustainability-driven entrepreneurship curriculum as a social learning process: A case study from an international knowledge alliance project. *Journal of Cleaner Production, 172*, 4357–4366. DOI: 10.1016/j.jclepro.2017.05.051

Collins, J. (2009). Lifelong learning in the 21st century and beyond. *Radiographics, 29*(2), 613–622. DOI: 10.1148/rg.292085179 PMID: 19325069

Crampon, K., Giorkallos, A., Deldossi, M., Baud, S., & Steffenel, L. (2021). Machine-learning methods for ligand-protein molecular docking. *Drug Discovery Today*. Advance online publication. DOI: 10.1016/j.drudis.2021.09.007 PMID: 34560276

Curtis, V., Moon, R., & Penaluna, A. (2020). Active entrepreneurship education and the impact on approaches to learning: Mixed methods evidence from a six-year study into one entrepreneurship educator's classroom. *Industry and Higher Education, 35*(4), 443–453. DOI: 10.1177/0950422220975319

Duong, C. D., Wach, K., Vu, N. X., Ha, S. T., & Nguyen, B. N. (2022). Entrepreneurial education, government policies and programmes, and entrepreneurial behaviour: A serial moderated mediation model. *Entrepreneurial Business and Economics Review, 10*(4), 37–54.

Elenurm, T. (2022). Choosing Collaborative Learning Options for Preparing Innovative Entrepreneurs. *European Conference on Innovation and Entrepreneurship*. DOI: 10.34190/ecie.17.1.379

Faisal, N., Chadhar, M., Goriss-Hunter, A., & Stranieri, A. (2022). Business Simulation Games in Higher Education: A Systematic Review of Empirical Research. *Human Behavior and Emerging Technologies, 2022*, 1–28. Advance online publication. DOI: 10.1155/2022/1578791

Fang, F., & Luo, X. (2018). Entrepreneurship Teaching Design Based On Case Study. .DOI: 10.2991/icesem-18.2018.299

Febrianti, B., Kussudyarsana, K., Setyawan, A., Sholahuddin, M., & Maimun, M. (2023). *The Role of Internship Program and Entrepreneurship Training to Hole Entrepreneur Capability and Startup Performance*. Jurnal Manajemen Bisnis. DOI: 10.18196/mb.v14i2.19251

Felin, T., Gambardella, A., Stern, S., & Zenger, T. (2020). Lean startup and the business model: Experimentation revisited. *Long Range Planning, 53*(4), 101889. Advance online publication. DOI: 10.1016/j.lrp.2019.06.002

Foo, M., Vissa, B., & Wu, B. (2020). Entrepreneurship in Emerging Economies. PSN: Other Comparative Capitalism (Topic). DOI: 10.2139/ssrn.3666851

Ghezzi, A., & Cavallo, A. (2020). Agile Business Model Innovation in Digital Entrepreneurship: Lean Startup Approaches. *Journal of Business Research, 110*, 519–537. Advance online publication. DOI: 10.1016/j.jbusres.2018.06.013

Gibb, A. (2002). In Pursuit of a New 'Enterprise' and 'Entrepreneurship' Paradigm for Learning: Creative Destruction, New Values, New Ways of Doing Things and New Combinations of Knowledge. *International Journal of Management Reviews, 4*(3), 233–269. DOI: 10.1111/1468-2370.00086

Goch, M. (2023). Interdisciplinary students' reflections on the development of their epistemic fluency. *Frontiers in Education, 8*, 1145227. Advance online publication. DOI: 10.3389/feduc.2023.1145227

Guerrero, M., Heaton, S., & Urbano, D. (2021). Building universities' intrapreneurial capabilities in the digital era: The role and impacts of Massive Open Online Courses (MOOCs). *Technovation, 99*, 102139. Advance online publication. DOI: 10.1016/j.technovation.2020.102139

Haddad, G., Haddad, G., & Nagpal, G. (2021). Can students' perception of the diverse learning environment affect their intentions toward entrepreneurship? *Journal of Innovation & Knowledge, 6*(3), 167–176. DOI: 10.1016/j.jik.2021.04.002

Hair, J. F., Sarstedt, M., Ringle, C.M. and Gudergan, S.P. (2017), Advanced Issues in Partial Least Squares Structural Equation Modeling, Sage Publications, Thousand Oaks, CA.

Hanandeh, R., Alharafsheh, M., Albloush, A., Lehyeh, S., & Kilani, Q. (2024). The impact of entrepreneurship self-concept, work motivation, and risk-taking on human resource department performance and business overall performance at Jordan private universities. *Uncertain Supply Chain Management, 12*(1), 143–150. Advance online publication. DOI: 10.5267/j.uscm.2023.10.010

Hermann, R., & Bossle, M. (2020). Bringing an entrepreneurial focus to sustainability education: A teaching framework based on content analysis. *Journal of Cleaner Production, 246*, 119038. DOI: 10.1016/j.jclepro.2019.119038

Ho, M. H. R., Uy, M. A., Kang, B. N., & Chan, K. Y. (2018). Impact of entrepreneurship training on entrepreneurial efficacy and alertness among adolescent youth. *Frontiers in Education, 3*(13), 1–10. DOI: 10.3389/feduc.2018.00013

Hockerts, K. (2018). The Effect of Experiential Social Entrepreneurship Education on Intention Formation in Students. *Journal of Social Entrepreneurship, 9*(3), 234–256. DOI: 10.1080/19420676.2018.1498377

Hsieh, H., & Maritz, A. (2023). A Study of the Impact of the Application of Digital Technology-Integrated Entrepreneurship Education on Entrepreneurship and Entrepreneurial Performance. *International Journal of Emerging Technologies in Learning, 18*(20), 126–136. Advance online publication. DOI: 10.3991/ijet.v18i20.43907

Iandoli, L. (2023). Annual review article: The dual mindset of design-driven entrepreneurship: The case for a pedagogy of making and artefact-centred entrepreneurship education. *International Small Business Journal, 41*(4), 349–370. DOI: 10.1177/02662426231160525

Ireland, R., & Webb, J. (2007). A Cross-Disciplinary Exploration of Entrepreneurship Research. *Journal of Management, 33*(6), 891–927. DOI: 10.1177/0149206307307643

Janiesch, C., Zschech, P., & Heinrich, K. (2021). Machine learning and deep learning. *Electronic Markets, 31*(3), 685–695. DOI: 10.1007/s12525-021-00475-2

Khoshtaria, T., Matin, A., Komodromos, M., & Kikutadze, V. (2024). The Impact of Word- of-Mouth Communication on Consumer Choices and Satisfaction: An Empirical Study of Students' Perspective. International Journal of Marketing. *Communication and New Media, 12*(22), 6–33. DOI: 10.54663/2182-9306.2024

Kickul, J., Gundry, L., Mitra, P., & Berçot, L. (2018). Designing With Purpose: Advocating Innovation, Impact, Sustainability, and Scale in Social Entrepreneurship Education. *Entrepreneurship Education and Pedagogy, 1*(2), 205–221. DOI: 10.1177/2515127418772177

Kim, N., Belland, B., & Walker, A. (2018). Effectiveness of Computer-Based Scaffolding in the Context of Problem-Based Learning for Stem Education: Bayesian Meta-analysis. *Educational Psychology Review, 30*(2), 397–429. DOI: 10.1007/s10648-017-9419-1

Kleij, F., Feskens, R., & Eggen, T. (2013). Effects of Feedback in a Computer-Based Learning Environment on Students' Learning Outcomes. *Review of Educational Research, 85*(4), 475–511. DOI: 10.3102/0034654314564881

Komodromos, M. (2021). *Innovative Learning and Education Practices in European Universities: A Pathway to Modern Pedagogy*. Ktoridou (Ed.), *Cases on Engineering Management Education in Practice* (63-90). IGI Global.

Komodromos, M., Harkiolakis, T., Khoshtaria, T., & Vassiliou, M. (2024). Adoption of digital technology and investigation of the impact in the marketing industry for marketing communication professionals: The case study of Cyprus and Greece. *International Journal of Technology Enhanced Learning, 16*(2), 173–191. DOI: 10.1504/IJTEL.2024.137650

Kraus, S., Palmer, C., Kailer, N., Kallinger, F. L., & Spitzer, J. (2019). Digital entrepreneurship: A research agenda on new business models for the twenty-first century. *International Journal of Entrepreneurial Behaviour & Research, 25*(2), 353–375.

Kuratko, D. (2005). The Emergence of Entrepreneurship Education: Development, Trends, and Challenges. *Entrepreneurship Theory and Practice, 29*(5), 577–597. DOI: 10.1111/j.1540-6520.2005.00099.x

Kurotimi, M., Franklin, A., Aladei, G., & Helen, O. (2017). Entrepreneurship Education as a 21st Century Strategy for Economic Growth and Sustainable Development. World Academy of Science, Engineering and Technology, International Journal of Social, Behavioral, Educational, Economic. *Business and Industrial Engineering, 11*, 2242–2253.

Lacatus, M., & Stăiculescu, C. (2016). Entrepreneurship in Education. International conference Knowledge-Based Organization, 22, 438 - 443. DOI: 10.1515/kbo-2016-0075

Lans, T., Blok, V., & Wesselink, R. (2014). Learning apart and together: Towards an integrated competence framework for sustainable entrepreneurship in higher education. *Journal of Cleaner Production*, *62*, 37–47. DOI: 10.1016/j.jclepro.2013.03.036

Leal, L., Ribeiro, A., Romão, V., Amaral, G., Altmann, R., Kahn, R., Pacci, B., Avó, M., Salerno, M., Plonski, G., & Zancul, E. (2021). R&D approach based on multiple partners and Design Thinking, Lean Startup, and Agile concepts: case study in the electricity sector. .DOI: 10.14488/BJOPM.2021.003

Lei, J., Hock, O., & Karim, A. (2021). Exploration of Entrepreneurship Education and Innovative Talent Training Model: New Economic Perspective. *International Journal of Academic Research in Business & Social Sciences*, *11*(11). Advance online publication. DOI: 10.6007/IJARBSS/v11-i11/11319

Lévesque, M., Obschonka, M., & Nambisan, S. (2020). Pursuing Impactful Entrepreneurship Research Using Artificial Intelligence. *Entrepreneurship Theory and Practice*, *46*(4), 803–832. DOI: 10.1177/1042258720927369

Lim, D., Oh, C., & Clercq, D. (2016). Engagement in entrepreneurship in emerging economies: Interactive effects of individual-level factors and institutional conditions. *International Business Review*, *25*(4), 933–945. DOI: 10.1016/j.ibusrev.2015.12.001

Lynch, M., Kamovich, U., Longva, K., & Steinert, M. (2019). Combining technology and entrepreneurial education through design thinking: Students' reflections on the learning process. *Technological Forecasting and Social Change*, *119689*. Advance online publication. DOI: 10.1016/j.techfore.2019.06.015

Maas, G., & Jones, P. (2015). An Overview of Entrepreneurship Education., 22-95. .DOI: 10.1057/9781137509802_2

Maresch, D., Harms, R., Kailer, N., & Wimmer-Wurm, B. (2016). The impact of entrepreneurship education on the entrepreneurial intention of students in science and engineering versus business studies university programs. *Technological Forecasting and Social Change*, *104*, 172–179. DOI: 10.1016/j.techfore.2015.11.006

Mikić, M., Sopta, M., & Horvatinović, T. (2019). The Role Of Entrepreneurial Education In The Development Of Entrepreneurship. EMC Review - Časopis za ekonomiju - APEIRON. .DOI: 10.7251/EMC1802385M

Mir, A.A., Hassan, S. and Khan, S.J. (2022), "Understanding digital entrepreneurial intentions: a capital theory perspective", International Journal of Emerging Markets, Vol. ahead-of-print No. ahead-of-print, pp. 1-27.

Mittal, P., & Raghuvaran, S. (2021). Entrepreneurship education and employability skills: The mediating role of e-learning courses. *Entrepreneurship Education*, *4*(2), 153–167. DOI: 10.1007/s41959-021-00048-6

Musso, M., Hernández, C., & Cascallar, E. (2020). Predicting key educational outcomes in academic trajectories: A machine-learning approach. *Higher Education*, *80*(5), 1–20. DOI: 10.1007/s10734-020-00520-7

Muthukannan, P., Tan, B., Gozman, D., & Johnson, L. (2020). The emergence of a fintech ecosystem: A case study of the Vizag Fintech Valley in India. *Information & Management, 57*(8), 1–18. DOI: 10.1016/j.im.2020.103385

Nabi, G., Liñán, F., Fayolle, A., Krueger, N., & Walmsley, A. (2017). The Impact of Entrepreneurship Education in Higher Education: A Systematic Review and Research Agenda. *Academy of Management Learning & Education, 16*(2), 277–299. DOI: 10.5465/amle.2015.0026

Obschonka, M., & Audretsch, D. (2019). Artificial intelligence and big data in entrepreneurship: A new era has begun. *Small Business Economics, 55*(3), 529–539. DOI: 10.1007/s11187-019-00202-4

Pardo-Garcia, C., & Barac, M. (2020). Promoting Employability in Higher Education: A Case Study on Boosting Entrepreneurship Skills. *Sustainability (Basel), 12*(10), 4004. Advance online publication. DOI: 10.3390/su12104004

Passaro, R., Quinto, I., & Thomas, A. (2018). The impact of higher education on entrepreneurial intention and human capital. *Journal of Intellectual Capital, 19*(1), 135–156. DOI: 10.1108/JIC-04-2017-0056

Pellas, N., Dengel, A., & Christopoulos, A. (2020). A Scoping Review of Immersive Virtual Reality in STEM Education. *IEEE Transactions on Learning Technologies, 13*(4), 748–761. DOI: 10.1109/TLT.2020.3019405

Peterk, S., Koprivnjak, T., & Mezulić, P. (2015). Challenges Of Evaluation Of The Influence Of Entrepreneurship Education. *Econometric Reviews, 13*, 74–86.

Peterman, N., & Kennedy, J. (2003). Enterprise Education: Influencing Students' Perceptions of Entrepreneurship. *Entrepreneurship Theory and Practice, 28*(2), 129–144. DOI: 10.1046/j.1540-6520.2003.00035.x

Pittaway, L., & Cope, J. (2007). Simulating Entrepreneurial Learning. *Management Learning, 38*(2), 211–233. DOI: 10.1177/1350507607075776

Rashid, L. (2019). Entrepreneurship Education and Sustainable Development Goals: A literature Review and a Closer Look at Fragile States and Technology-Enabled Approaches. *Sustainability (Basel), 11*(19), 5343. Advance online publication. DOI: 10.3390/su11195343

Ratten, V., & Usmanij, P. (2020). Entrepreneurship education: Time for a change in research direction? *International Journal of Management Education*. Advance online publication. DOI: 10.1016/j.ijme.2020.100367

Reinhardt, K. (2023). Business Research Methods. SSRN Electronic Journal. DOI: 10.2139/ssrn.4488860

Ronstadt, R., Shuman, J., & Vesper, K. (2020). The early story: A brief history of the creation of entrepreneurship at Babson College and the discovery of innovation's missing imperative. *Industry and Higher Education, 35*(2), 75–82. DOI: 10.1177/0950422220978563

Russell, R., Atchison, M., & Brooks, R. (2008). Business plan competitions in tertiary institutions: Encouraging entrepreneurship education. *Journal of Higher Education Policy and Management, 30*(2), 123–138. DOI: 10.1080/13600800801938739

Salehi, H., & Burgueño, R. (2018). Emerging artificial intelligence methods in structural engineering. *Engineering Structures*, *171*, 170–189. Advance online publication. DOI: 10.1016/j.engstruct.2018.05.084

Sarooghi, H., Sunny, S., Hornsby, J., & Fernhaber, S. (2019). Design Thinking and Entrepreneurship Education: Where Are We, and What Are the Possibilities? *Journal of Small Business Management*, *57*, 78–93. DOI: 10.1111/jsbm.12541

Schmitz, A., Urbano, D., Dandolini, G., Souza, J., & Guerrero, M. (2017). Innovation and entrepreneurship in the academic setting: A systematic literature review. *The International Entrepreneurship and Management Journal*, *13*(2), 369–395. DOI: 10.1007/s11365-016-0401-z

Shankar, D., Tewari, D., Rahman, M., Mishra, D., & Bajaj, M. (2023). *Impact of Virtual Reality (Vr) and Augmented Reality (Ar) in Education*. Tuijin Jishu/Journal of Propulsion Technology., DOI: 10.52783/tjjpt.v44.i4.1014

Shepherd, D., & Gruber, M. (2020). The Lean Startup Framework: Closing the Academic–Practitioner Divide. *Entrepreneurship Theory and Practice*, *45*(5), 967–998. DOI: 10.1177/1042258719899415

Simpson, M., Tuck, N., & Bellamy, S. (2004). Small business success factors: The role of education and training. *Education + Training*, *46*(8/9), 481–491. DOI: 10.1108/00400910410569605

Thomsen, B., Muurlink, O., & Best, T. (2019). Backpack Bootstrapping: Social Entrepreneurship Education Through Experiential Learning. *Journal of Social Entrepreneurship*, *12*(2), 238–264. DOI: 10.1080/19420676.2019.1689155

Torres-Coronas, T., & Vidal-Blasco, M. (2021). *Predicting global entrepreneurship: An exploratory study*. Educar., DOI: 10.5565/rev/educar.1279

Vanevenhoven, J. (2013). Advances and Challenges in Entrepreneurship Education. *Journal of Small Business Management*, *51*(3), 466–470. DOI: 10.1111/jsbm.12043

Vorbach, S., Poandl, E., & Korajman, I. (2019). Digital Entrepreneurship Education - The Role of MOOCs. *Int. J. Eng. Pedagog.*, *9*(3), 99–111. DOI: 10.3991/ijep.v9i3.10149

Vorbach, S., Poandl, E. M., & Korajman, I. (2019). Digital entrepreneurship education: The role of MOOCs. *International Journal of Engineering Pedagogy*, *9*(3), 99–111. DOI: 10.3991/ijep.v9i3.10149

Wang, Q., & Huang, Q. (2024). Engaging Online Learners in Blended Synchronous Learning: A Systematic Literature Review. *IEEE Transactions on Learning Technologies*, *17*, 594–607. DOI: 10.1109/TLT.2023.3282278

Watson, K., McGowan, P., & Cunningham, J. A. (2018). An exploration of the Business Plan Competition as a methodology for effective nascent entrepreneurial learning. *International Journal of Entrepreneurial Behaviour & Research*, *24*(1), 121–146. DOI: 10.1108/IJEBR-05-2017-0158

Williams, D. (2015). The Impact of SimVenture on the Development of Entrepreneurial Skills in Management Students. *Industry and Higher Education*, *29*(5), 379–395. DOI: 10.5367/ihe.2015.0270

Woraphiphat, I., & Roopsuwankun, P. (2021). The impact of online design thinking-based learning on entrepreneurial intention: The case of vocational college. *Journal of Innovation and Entrepreneurship, 12*(1), 10. Advance online publication. DOI: 10.1186/s13731-023-00278-z PMID: 36911755

Zainal, N. T. A., & Yong, K. (2020). Examining the digital entrepreneurship education effectiveness on soft skills among undergraduates [PPIB]. *MANU Jurnal Pusat Penataran Ilmu Dan Bahasa, 31*, 139–151. DOI: 10.51200/manu.vi.2112

Žalėnienė, I., & Pereira, P. (2021). *Higher Education For Sustainability: A Global Perspective*. Geography and Sustainability., DOI: 10.1016/j.geosus.2021.05.001

Zeithaml, C., & Rice, G. (1987). Entrepreneurship-Small Business Education in American Universities. *Journal of Small Business Management, 25*, 44.

Zhao, M., Yang, X., & Sheng, S. (2024). Transferring Political Capabilities Into Formal Entrepreneurship: The Moderating Role of Market Development in Emerging Markets. *IEEE Transactions on Engineering Management, 71*, 1504–1518. DOI: 10.1109/TEM.2023.3335161

Chapter 3

Integrating Innovative Simulation Tools Into Sustainable Continuous Vocational Educational Training (CVET) in Tourism SMEs

Amvrosios Prodromou
https://orcid.org/0009-0008-4787-6292
Neapolis University, Pafos, Cyprus

Hary Sophocleous
Neapolis University, Pafos, Cyprus

ABSTRACT

This chapter is based on the fact that innovation in education has been the subject of extensive studies for at least two decades, thus bringing to the surface the need to diversify the ways and means by which education is provided by educators and acquired by learners, society in general, and business and economic activity in particular. Accordingly, the research leads to the estimated benefits for all stakeholders involved in the process, creating an accumulated perception of innovation in education. Hence, the chapter proposes a visual model that is likely to contribute as a roadmap for incorporating simulation tools in Continuous Vocational Education and Training (CVET) in tourism Small Medium Enterprises (SMEs).

1. INTRODUCTION AND RESEARCH CONTEXT

The recommended book chapter lies on the ground that innovation in education has been a subject of extensive studies for at least two decades, hence, bringing to the surface the need for diversifying the ways and means that education is delivered by educators as well as acquired by learners, society in general and in particular the business and economic activity. Therefore, the particular suggested research will lead to the estimated benefits for all stakeholders involved in the process, creating an accumulated perception of innovation in education (Blouin et al., 2009; Serdyukov, 2017; Rubia-Avi, 2022). Prenger

DOI: 10.4018/979-8-3693-9040-5.ch003

et al. (2022) enhance this argument by supporting that innovation in education not only is crucial for continuous development of all stakeholders, but most importantly, focusing on the issue requires strategies that will ensure innovation's sustainability, and ability to adapt the educational emerging needs. Furthermore, the implementation of innovative teaching methods requires the clarification of specific parameters such as the individuals' needs, curriculum characteristics, the organisational context, and collaboration between all parties in order to ensure a sustainable operational environment (Stirman et al., 2012). The role of innovation in education is gaining an increasing role, therefore, requiring from all stakeholders to ensure its uninterrupted development at all stages (Zhurakovskaya et al., 2020).

Based on this context, training should take into consideration the emerging impact of Green Human Resource Management (GHRM) which has reshaped the way that sustainability and climate protection should be addressed (Prodromou et al., 2024; Papademetriou et al., 2024). Moreover, the current book chapter aims to propose a new model of how VSBT should effectively be integrated into CVET in the tourism SMEs in order to enable SMEs to become more competitive through active, innovative, and diversified training of their labour force. Considering the effects of the post-pandemic on the tourism SMEs (Wang & Le, 2022), it is crucial for the sector's SMEs to establish a new business model that will focus on the human asset as a source of resilience (Rastegar et al., 2023). Such strategic choices should be developed within the context of nation branding, hence, enable a country to fully develop and effectively market its brand image within the current globalized environment (Masouras et al., 2024; Sophocleous, 2023). The need for such actions has intensified following the recent pandemic's negative consequences in which tourism SMEs have faced serious problems in several operational fields, hence, requiring a more extrovert approach (Prodromou et al., 2024). More specifically, the current chapter proposes a visual model that will contribute as a roadmap for incorporating simulation tools in CVET in tourism SMEs, as this constitutes an essential step forward for tourism SMEs and can substantially increase both workforce performance and customers' experience (UX) (Lobinger & Mele, 2021).

2. RESEARCH METHODOLOGY/ SUGGESTED APPROACH

The current book chapter has applied an effective research methodology based on scientific approaches and evidence in order to ensure its overall credibility and provide a more accurate understanding to the targeted audience which includes both academic and professionals. Providing the best possible scientific methodology can help the authors avoid possible pitfalls such as misinterpretation and bias, consequently, become more reliable in their overall analysis (Yarborough, 2021). Additionally, research has ensured obtaining data and information from credible resources from both academic and professional sources. This combination is expected to enhance the overall research confidence, and consequently, deliver the expected result related to a subject that has been gaining an increasing importance in global research.

2.1. Problem Formulation

The initial step of the current book chapter was to identify the research problem, as such identification not only is important for the structure of the chapter but can also be considered as a milestone which can become a roadmap for further steps, hence, avoid possible misleading in the overall process. The particular approach is essential for all academic research levels, hence, should be considered as a 'must take' step, as well as implementing all relevant methods to ensure proper analysis in the entire document (Rubenstein et al., 2020). Thus, the subsequent research problem has been identified:

> "Increasing challenges in tourism SMEs have led to the need for the industry's stakeholders to strategically focus on creating a sustainable framework for integrating simulation tools into Continuous Vocational Educational Training (CVET) in order to confront the challenges and create a more resilient operational framework which will take into consideration the market trends and employees' needs to upgrade their skills."

2.2. Literature Review: Conclusions, Recommendations, and Proposed Framework

An extensive and updated literature review has been incorporated with a total of 163 references. The authors focused on credible and relevant resources in order to structure the overall literature analysis and provide an adequate academic and professional background, all essential for such research (Kraus et al., 2024). This has led to the development of a set of Conclusions and practical recommendations, that are essential for the complete development of such an academic work (Bell et al., 2018). Finally, the current book chapter, has developed a specific operational model, namely "STTS - Simulation Training for Tourism SMEs" in order to provide a roadmap for delivering the most appropriate simulation tools practices. The current chapter pays exceptional attention to the role of Visual Modelling as this enables both authors and external readers to clearly understand the flow of proposed solutions within an easy-to-understand and logical flow (Bobek & Tversky, 2016). In the case of the proposed STTS Model, the authors take into serious consideration the interaction between all stakeholders related to the tourism industry, especially those linked to CVET and SMEs. This interaction cannot be underestimated, and therefore, the authors are attempting to connect these stakeholders in a logical flow.

3. LITERATURE REVIEW/ CONCEPTUAL FRAMEWORK

3.1. VET in Tourism / CVET

Vocational Educational Training (VET) has gradually gained ground in several sectors and disciplines and influences employees' knowledge, organizational commitment, and culture. (Hidalgo et al., 2020). Moreover, VET has been taking place as part of continuous development and aims to substantially increase the skills and competencies of people at their workplace and has been largely supported by the United Nations (UN) as a way of overcoming problems and enhancing their potentials (McGrath & Yamada, 2023). VET constitutes an integral part of Basic Professional Training (BTP) which strategically focuses on preparing students for the real workplace, with diversity in teaching to be a major part of the process, hence, helping students to become more competitive at work (Martínez-Carmona et al., 2022). In any case, effective VET should consider both sociological and psychological dimensions that should be enhanced by the appropriate support mechanism from both the public and private sectors in order to deliver the most appropriate and expected results (Milmeister et al., 2022).

In particular, VET has emerged as a major development tool for several business operations (Grobbelaar & Verma, 2020), such as marketing, supply chain management (SCM), and labor force, consequently, leading to exceptional results related to performance and productivity (Harris & Clayton, 2020).

Further, the authors support that strategic development of VET can lead to Continuing VET (CVET), an element with exceptional value for businesses that implement such approaches. The emergence of globalization has placed VET into a broader concept, that of the transferability of knowledge between countries, businesses, and chambers, thus creating new opportunities for all companies that wish to implement VET as part of their strategies (Li & Pilz, 2021). In this context, VET should be examined as part of the broader concept of political economy and political ecology which requires businesses to extensively analyze both internal and external environments, hence, ensuring a full coverage of the VET market potentials (Davoine & Deitmer, 2020).

VET constitutes an essential tool for Small and Medium Enterprises (SMEs) as the latter are usually suffering from lack of experience, acquiring the appropriate financial support, and limited managerial and strategic experience, leading to serious problems, such as poor competitiveness and cash flow management (Hlasny, 2023). Importantly, the authors support that such problems should be confronted with the contribution of the national authorities as SMEs are the backbone of the economy and should be supported in terms of VET. Gimmon et al. (2020) are highlighting the critical importance of VET in SMEs and suggest that not only SMEs' owners should strive towards this direction, but most importantly, employees should demand such training as it can substantially increase their earnings and strengthen their job position, especially in highly-competitive markets. CVET is exceedingly related to SMEs' sustainable development, requiring from businesses to diversify their business model and increase their attention in establishing improved relationships with all relevant stakeholders, such as the national authorities, industry, and labor unions as the latter represent their workforce (Lavía et al., 2021).

SMEs compose a substantial part of economy, and the capacity of their training is of vital importance (Nandi et al, 2020; Amoah et al., 2023). Moreover, SMEs are easily influenced by exogenous and operational factors (García, Ríos & Hernández, 2020). In particular, in the tourism industry are influenced by several factors such as labour shortage (Innerhofer et al., 2022) and seasonality which are causing serious problems related to their processes, productivity, and ability to ensure sustainable development (Rodríguez, et al., 2020), especially following difficult times requiring economic recovery and extrovert managerial thinking (Martínez et al., 2020).

In particular, VET in tourism SMEs have in recent years become an importance source of innovation in terms of processes, products and services, and employee performance, hence, leading to sustainable growth and higher competitiveness. This has been based on extensive Research & Development (R&D) which requires the relevant resources allocation (Demirkan et al., 2021). The application of simulation tools in SMEs VET requires from both educators and learners to collaborate effectively (Melo, et al., 2023), especially in cases in which learners are of an elder age and are not used in dealing with technology (Nyström & Ahn, 2024). Polikarpus et al. (2023) add to the previous argument by clarifying that the active involvement of trainers in the process of curriculum development, as this will ensure improved performance and collaboration.

Moreover, in recent years, the value of vocational education and training (VET) and VET research has become an increasingly important issue for researchers. Questions on this subject continue to be raised and debated frequently in most countries, and in almost all of them (with the exception of the German-speaking countries) the concerns revolve around the perceived low status and how it could be raised. In the European Union, two recent studies provide very interesting reading on the views of Europeans on initial VET and on adult learning and continuing VET. The first study involved 35,646 face-to-face interviews with citizens in the Member States. (Redondo et al, 2021) It provided data on citizens' opinions on the awareness, attractiveness, experience and effectiveness of VET in the EU. The results showed considerable differences between countries in terms of awareness of VET, ranging from 46% to 91% of respondents claiming to know what VET is. The research showed: EU citizens tend to have positive attitudes towards VET, its quality and its effectiveness. Respondents valued upper secondary VET as a way of finding jobs, strengthening the economy, reducing unemployment and promoting social inclusion. However, it still suffers from a lack of appreciation: VET is often perceived as a less attractive way of learning compared to general education and it continues to be seen as a second choice for the less able.

The second study concentrated on adult learning and continuing vocational education and training (CVET), defined as all learning activities undertaken by adults (employed or not) with the intention of improving their knowledge or skills. More than 40,000 interviews were conducted with a random sample of people aged 25 and over in the European Union, Norway and Iceland. (Heuer et al, 2024). At least two-thirds of adults in each Member State agreed that their government should prioritize investment in adult learning. Some 70% believed that adult education and training would become more important for career progression over the next decade, and 88% said that their job required them to keep their skills up to date. The benefits they saw were seen as supporting their personal development, necessary for career progression and job search, a route to higher earnings, and helping to reduce unemployment. They had positive perceptions of availability, access and information. In most countries, the family was seen as the main source of support for participation, although in the Netherlands, the United Kingdom and Norway it was the employer, in France professional or sectoral associations and in Luxembourg the government. Despite this positive image of learning and training, adults in 22 of the 30 countries said that their main reason for not participating was that they did not need to! The report concludes that this response is not due to negative attitudes towards adult learning and training, but to a lack of incentives. The positive image of CVET can thus provide policy makers with a strong basis for strengthening adult learning and CVET, while recognizing that challenges will include the need for complex institutional and governance arrangements, shifts in teaching and learning paradigms and modes beyond standard training provision, and ensuring synergies between the different policy areas supporting CVET systems. (Harris & Clayton, 2020)

Many of these concerns are resonating in Australia. One of the most recent reports (Billett et al, 2020) conducted a health check of Australia's vocational education and training sector to determine its readiness to meet the challenge of training more Australians now and in the future. The review identified that most participants were very enthusiastic about the VET model and believed that 'learning while you earn' was critical for a rapidly changing work environment (p.1). However, many were concerned about whether current VET systems and processes could deliver the kind of flexible, work-based learning models that would help Australians gain the skills they need for the jobs of the future. The report therefore argued for a significant upgrade in the architecture of the VET sector and proposed a new vision for VET in Australia. It recommended a six-point plan for change: stronger quality assurance, faster skills development, easier funding and skills matching, better careers information, clearer secondary pathways and greater access for disadvantaged Australians. Complemented by a roadmap showing how these points could be achieved, the report concludes that the plan would go a long way to boosting the confidence of employers, students and trainees in the VET sector, and to raising the status of VET so that it truly ranks alongside higher education in the aspirations of young Australians and their communities (p.2). Several other recent reports have also proclaimed the need to reimagine, revitalize, rethink, refresh and reform VET so that a true tertiary education sector, comprising both VET and higher education, can be established in Australia.

3.2. Simulation Tools

Virtual Simulation-Based Training (VSBT) which is essential for contemporary SMEs (Kijkasiwat et al., 2024), should be linked to university programs in order to ensure preparing students for the need of applying continuous development at their workplace, hence, being able to smoothly adapt to the ever-changing business environment. Hence, this demands for universities to work together with businesses in order to ensure this process (Navarro-Parra & Chiappe, 2024).

The application of simulators as a way to facilitate professional and vocational learning is gaining momentum, marking the emergence of a new VET teaching practice (Nyström & Ahn, 2024). There is extensive research on the outcomes of simulation training, concluding that it is an effective teaching method for students to train on specific tasks, apply knowledge and develop their ability to work independently (Chernikova et al., 2020; Cook et al., 2011; Issenberg et al., 2005, cf. Jossberger et al., 2015). Therefore, simulation training could facilitate and ease the work of teachers (Nyström & Ahn, 2024). There are also discussions and concerns about whether simulation training can replace learning with an authentic learning object (e.g. driving a real car or patient) and what role teachers have in such a teaching practice (Gustavsson, 2021; McKenna et al., 2011). However, research has overlooked what teachers' professional bodies do and mean in the context of simulation training (Persico & Lalor, 2019).

Pietsch et al. (2023) support the implementation of innovative methodologies and tools in all forms of education, however, the authors recommend that it is crucial for the relevant organizations to ensure the allocation of all appropriate and necessary resources. Lack to do so can potentially lead to negative results and become a massive barrier in the entire educational process. The essence for diversifying teaching methods and in particular online education, has changed substantially during the recent Covid-19 pandemic in which both educators and learners found themselves in front of a massive challenge, requiring from both parties, to adapt in order to ensure that they would not waste any valuable time and resources (Zheng et al., 2021). Essentially, the authors have identified that over 80 percent of both the educators and the learners would prefer to proceed by using online education to some extent. In any case, despite some benefits and positive lessons learned during the pandemic in terms of online education, this should not be taken for granted as several demographic parameters, such as gender, ethnicity, educational level, and income, should be considered. This is essential as various groups of people are facing different challenges, hence, calling for the relevant attention (Tosto et al., 2023).

Simulation-based education (SE) has been experiencing a massive growth in universities, occurring in both online and on-campus programs (Lefrid, et al., 2023), thus, providing the opportunity to educators to apply new methods and trigger the interest of their students (Campos et al., 2020). The implementation of such methods has been exceptionally beneficial for students in the STEM field (sciences, technology, engineering, mathematics). Therefore, organizations should evaluate their capacity and needs in order to allocate the appropriate scarce resources towards the right direction, avoiding possible waste (Kutz et al., 2016). The importance of SE in terms of Innovation should also be viewed as a major driver for overcoming barriers in crucial industries for the global economy, such as the automotive, in which companies effectively utilized their knowledge during the recent pandemic (Prodromou, 2021).

3.3. Artificial Intelligence as a Supportive Tool in the Tourism Industry

In recent years, AI has become a useful supportive tool in several industries as it has enabled businesses to diversify their business model and operations, helping employees at all levels to become both more efficient and effective, with the productivity to have increased substantially on several occasions (Davenport & Kalakota, 2019). However, the authors raise the importance of data quality, which on several occasions this can be highly influenced by the complexity and inability to analyse the data and provide the most appropriate real-time data for accurate decision-making. According to market experts Statista (2023), in 2022 the overall corporate global investment in AI reached $91.2 billion, which is a seven times fold increase in just seven years, as in 2015 the AI investments amounted to $12.75 billion.

AI's supportive role has been increasingly diversified in several other business and training areas, such as enabling organisations to increase their strategic focus on innovation and creativity, especially when high market competitive environments exist, requiring businesses to adjust accordingly (Ivcevic & Grandinetti, 2024). Within the specific context, academics have been benefited in order to increase their theoretical and empirical research, leading them to strategically incorporate AI in both research and professional training, hence, establishing a powerful environment for comprehensive development for all stakeholders involved in the process (Khalifa & Albadawy, 2024). Bhagat and Kanyal (2024) add to the impact of AI on innovation and creativity by suggesting that AI has enabled crucial sectors, such as the that of hospital and health care to proceed to the much-needed transformation actions, in which humans and machines had to become teams in order to increase their production efficiency and capacity.

AI and simulation tools can enable tourism industry organisations to become more focused and effective on issues related to marketing segmentation, and therefore, help the industry to move towards a more sustainable environment which is essential in the current tourism framework (García-Madurga & Grilló-Méndez, 2023). Bulchand-Gidumal et al. (2023) add to the need for incorporating AI and simulation tools in the concept of internal tourism operations, as training in divisions such as food and beverage, rooms division, reception, and reservations, require automation of action and development of know-how. Moreover, the authors raise the strategic role of managers in the tourism industry, calling for incorporating best practices that will lead to a more sustainable internal business environment. The role of AI and simulation tools in the tourism industry should not be restricted to the business operations, instead, the latter should strategically focus on training their clients in order to help them become more effective and independent in terms of booking and check-in, as this will save them valuable time and increase their experience (Sousa et al., 2024).

The broader tourism industry has been highly affected by the rapid development of AI, as this cutting-edge technology has been widely applied in several operations, creating opportunities for synergies, both internally and externally (Ku & Chen, 2024). Further, tourism scholars are taking advantage of this opportunity in order to enhance their research work by using AI as part of the 'Web of Science' data base which enables them to track and record both theoretical and practical trends, and consequently, establishing more sustainable business models based on the needs of each given organisation (Baiocco et al., 2022). In any case, despite AI's undisputed importance, tourism organisations should only view it as a supportive and training tool, and not as a replacement of human existence, as the tourism industry remains an anthropomorphic service which is directly linked to human emotions and experience, something that AI cannot replace and/or provide (Ku & Chen, 2024). As a result, this could seriously damage possible sustainability issues and drive organisations to introvert policies, in which the labour force would not be a priority, with obvious consequences on customers' experience (Andrade-Valbuena et al., 2022).

Climate change has long-been a subject of serious discussion and expression of different opinions, with its impact to be obvious in the economic activity across the world, especially in highly sensitive areas (Tol, 2018). Day et al. (2021, p.1) have strongly warned about the climate change on tourism operations in one of the most popular destinations of the United States of America (USA), that of Indiana, as "The direct impacts of climate change on Indiana include increases in the number of hot and extremely hot days each summer, fewer mild days, more rain, and less snow. Each direct impact will affect tourism and recreation." Importantly, the authors clarify that outdoor activities will be increasingly becoming more vulnerable to climate change, urging for a more sustainable business model, from both public and private sectors. Dangwal et al. (2023) and He (2022) suggest that tourism industry organisations, coupled with the strategic contribution of the public administration, should incorporate AI in their operations in order to predict weather forecast, and identify both opportunities and threats that exist in the business environment. In addition, the authors raise the importance of training their most valuable asset, their workforce, in order to ensure that they will become more aware of the climate change issue, and understand of how this can impact their personal, professional, family, and social development and cohesion. Tong et al. (2022) expand the previous approaches by raising the need to strategically incorporate AI as part of the overall vocational training within the tourism industry, in order to ensure that the understanding of climate change will influence the industry's businesses approach in areas. Amongst others, these should include environmental protection, social support and collaboration, sustainable corporate governance, and establishing synergies with other industry stakeholders.

3.4. Artificial Intelligence and Simulation Tools in SMEs

SMEs are facing increasing challenges as a result of high competition in the global market, therefore, requiring them to apply extrovert policies that will enable them to ensure healthy growth and sustainable development (Longenecker et al., 2019). Within this concept, elements such as transformational leadership and innovation are considered as fundamental in order for SMEs to establish a diversified operational environment that will confront the existing challenges and become more resilient (Nasir et al., 2022). Importantly, transformational leadership can enable increasing employees' voice as an essential part of communication and improving the potential for an improved working environment, with the role of contemporary technology to experience an increasing importance (Rasheed et al., 2021).

The adoption of AI and simulation tools is indeed evaluated as important within the SMEs' operations; however, this application can vary between small companies and medium-sized companies, with the latter to have managed to acquire significantly more benefits in several operations, including marketing, logistics, and human resource training that can establish sustainable development (Badghish & Soomro, 2024). Oldemeyer et al. (2024) clarify that the increasing role of AI and simulation tools in the current economic activities should not be underestimated, however, this should be done within a specific business model such as that of the Value Chain Analysis (Porter, 1985).

Despite the increasing importance of AI in contemporary economy, and therefore, in the SMEs' operations, the latter are facing serious problems in adapting to the new environment as well as adopting the new technological tools (Lemos et al., 2022). Limited financial resources, lack of national schemes, and poor human resource training are considered amongst the most important obstacles confronted by SMEs, with the problem to exist in several industries, such as construction, tourism, and retail (Nagy et al., 2023). Such problems lead to a serious negative impact on crucial sustainable elements, such as understanding contemporary consumer behavior and trends (Masouras & Papademetriou, 2018), as well as marketing strategy which can help SMEs become more focused on their market targets, save valuable time and resources, and most importantly, become more competitive (Sophocleous & Prodromou, 2024). Within this context, AI and simulation tools can become a powerful way of promoting sustainable development through the improvement of internal practices within an entrepreneurial ecosystem (Prodromou & Kountouridou, 2024), as well as improving the much-desired development of Green Human Resource Management (GHRM) which plays a key role in the operations of contemporary SMEs (Prodromou et al., 2024). Such issues related to AI and simulation tools are having an increasing importance in the training of SMEs in rural areas, as the latter are facing increasing obstacles of obtaining access and support, therefore, requiring the allocation of all appropriate resources (Apostolopoulos et al., 2020).

4. DISCUSSION AND CONCLUSIONS

Following the examination of all the above-mentioned elements, the current book chapter has come to some specific conclusions that need to be critically evaluated in order to enable deeper understanding of the current trends related to innovation considering simulation tools, and most importantly, of how such tools can effectively contribute towards a set of practical recommendations. The conclusions take into consideration the current trends in both the tourism industry and the technological development, as they both require extrovert thinking and understanding of the opportunities provided in the global marketplace. Further, such understanding will ensure the threats' mitigation should confront increased competition level.

Simulation tools have become a major element of effective training, therefore fulfilling the market's expectation and enabling contemporary organizations to establish a more resilient operational framework. Within this context, several industries have been highly benefited. The rapid technological development has led to a positive impact on both the quality and quantity of the simulation tools, therefore, enabling the distribution of knowledge to a greater percentage of businesses, across several industries. Within this framework, cutting edge technology should be viewed as the key elements which drives the need for incorporating simulation tools into their overall strategic approach in relation to technological infrastructure.

Labor shortage has intensified the existing problems of the tourism industry, with SMEs to face the majority of these problems. Considering the problems that SMEs are facing in relation to access to financial support and limited training. These lead to the need for a holistic strategic approach in order to enhance the industry's ability to fill the gaps in both quantity and quality. Labor shortage requires tourism organizations as well as related stakeholders to proceed to simulation training in order to increase the productivity of their existing labor force. Such a strategy can, to a certain degree, mitigate the short labor shortage with the role of technology to be a primary concern.

The current chapter has paid exceptional attention to the increasing role of AI in the entire global economy, with all industries facing serious challenges in regards of incorporating such tools in their operations. The challenge for tourism SMEs lies in the fact that such technology, which is directly related to the operations of simulation tools, may not be easily accessible to them. Therefore, this requires a strategic decision by the national authorities in order to enable tourism SMEs to gain access to such technology, as this can have a positive impact on both productivity and profitability, as these two elements are interrelated.

CVET has been experiencing rapid growth as a result of the need to ensure that businesses, especially those operating in highly demanding and vulnerable industries, such as that of tourism, shall increase their productivity and competitiveness. Within this context, the current chapter has clearly concluded that lack of implementing CVET as part of a broader strategic planning can lead tourism businesses towards negative consequences, especially since the industry has been facing consecutive problems, such as the financial crisis, the pandemic, and the ongoing political instability as a result of several military conflicts across the world. The combination of all the above raises the strategic role of CVET, therefore, requiring from tourism SMEs to view the issue as a turning point that will increase their potentials in the global market. Lack of understanding such crucial developments can become an internal instability factor, leading tourism SMEs towards negative operational paths, especially since the global competition in the tourism industry is rapidly increasing.

To all the above issues, tourism SMEs should consider the interconnection of training with the increasing role of the GHRM concept, as the latter constitutes an increasing trend which is directly related to the political decisions concerning environmental protection. Therefore, the incorporation of simulation tools as part of an overall GHRM training approach can be considered as a major challenge for tourism SMEs. The question for tourism SMEs is not whether GHRM training through the use of simulation tools should take place, but rather when and to what extent this training should occur in order to ensure that businesses will be aligned to the current political, ethical, and legal trends. As a result, this requires tourism SMEs to work closely together with the national authorities as well as other organizations, such as the local Chambers of Commerce, in order to enable all businesses to enjoy the same benefits. This should be viewed as a tool for holistic tourism development related to national branding, and not strictly considered as a tool for individual business development. Such an approach could be easily described as catastrophic as the contribution of the tourism industry, especially behalf the SMEs, is far too important.

The interdependence between CVET in tourism SMEs and technological infrastructure, including simulation tools, is in favour of the latter, as tourism SMEs are in urgent need of obtaining the best possible assistance from the rapid development of technology. This need is emerging as a result of the impact of AI which raises the strategic importance of simulation tools as an integral part of strategic planning as well as innovative and sustainable development. The fact that tourism and other service-related industries are highly affected by elements such as Intangibility, Inseparability, Variability, and Perishability (Kotler & Keller, 2007), makes the role of simulation tools as a major strategic requirement rather than a need. In this framework, tourism SMEs should also take into consideration the increasing competition within the industry, as this takes place at macro-level (national policies), meso-level (industry approach within the country, and micro-level (individual business strategy). All these can be considered as strategic requirements that should drive decision-makers towards a more extrovert approach that will enable them to (re)consider their overall approach to the industry. The services industry goes through a major transformation which requires an extensive and holistic training approach, with this need to be more obvious in SMEs as they lack experience and strategy development and implementation (Wirtz & Lovelock, 2021).

Therefore, these conclusions lead the authors to a set of proposal identified and justified in the Recommendations and Visual part, as this enables the practical identification of the current trends, realities, challenges, and opportunities within the tourism SMEs in relation to the need for establishing a more sustainable operational environment. Therefore, the following section can be considered as a pathway that enables tourism SMEs to become more resilient in an ever-changing environment which requires all parties involved to increase their market presence, in both quantity and quality, with the role of training through the use of cutting-edge simulation tools to be at the forefront of this process. Consequently, the current chapter, strongly concludes that lack of integrating technology and simulation tools within the CVET of tourism SMEs can become a negative factor that not only can hold businesses back from their operational performance, and therefore, have a negative impact on their productivity and profitability, but most importantly, at the long term, can become an instability factor which can lead to serious negative, and possibly, irreversible consequences.

5. RECOMMENDATION AND VISUAL

The current section of this chapter takes into consideration all the elements that have been extensively examined in order to proceed towards two major objectives, both equally important and interrelated. The first objective is related to the creation of a visual context which is essential for business decision-makers in order to understand the interconnection and interdependence of all variable factors included in the proposed visual context. The second one concerns the development of a set of practical recommendations that are important in both academic and professional level. The connection of academia with the industry should not be undermined, as academia, through its extensive knowledge, can shed light on the extensive problems confronted by the tourism industry, and especially by the industry's SMEs. In this context, somebody should also consider that a large proportion of the tourism industry's labor force, especially in managerial positions, are university graduates, therefore, the connection and interdependence can be easily considered as more than obvious. In any case, both objectives are focused on bringing the accumulated experience together, creating synergies, and therefore triggering the interest of all industry's stakeholders, both from public and private sectors, in order to collectively address the common challenges and take advantage of the opportunities provided within the domestic and global markets.

The recommendations and visual process shall enable a deeper understanding and analysis of the strategic role of technology, and most importantly, the training simulation tools, as an integral part of CVET within the fragile tourism industry. Recent experiences, including the financial crisis in 2008, the pandemic of 2020, as well as several regional military conflicts taking place around the world, have led to the serious exposure of the global tourism industry. This exposure creates uncertainty amongst national authorities and private sector's stakeholders, requiring them to work closely together in order to ensure the establishment of a sustainable, innovative, and resilient framework that will be mutually beneficial for the entire economy. The tourism industry is currently employing 348 million individuals across the world, and the number is expected to rise up to 449 million by 2034 (Statista, 2024). This will require from the industry not only to hire these people, but most importantly to train them to a level that they can contribute towards higher quality levels.

As a result, the following Visual "STTS - Simulation Training for Tourism SMEs" Model is proposed:

Figure 1. STTS: Simulation training for tourism SMEs

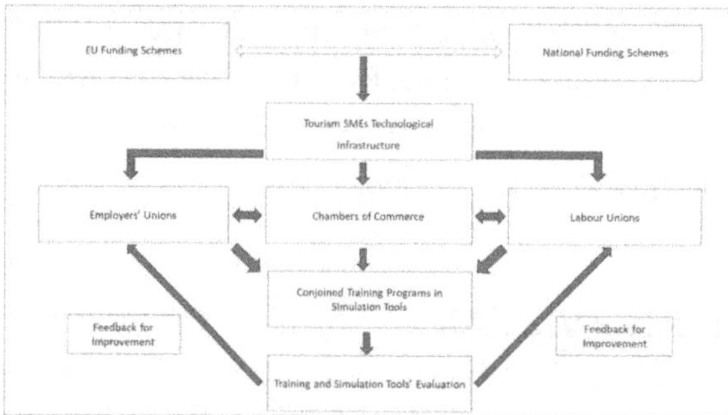

The main principles of the proposed STTS Model are based on the integration of stakeholders coming from various levels. The first level (macro level) refers to the role of political institutions, such as the EU and each country's national authorities. The second level (meso level) refers to the role of professional institutions such as the Chambers of Commerce, the Employers' Unions, and the Labour Unions. The third level (micro level) refers to the role of Conjoined Training Programs. The role of all these levels is of great importance, and therefore, this chapter aims to effectively propose their interdependence, as this is expected to establish the appropriate synergies that can lead towards a more sustainable and innovative model. In any case, all these synergies will require the establishment of the relevant strategies, policies, and actions. These are considered as fundamental in order to achieve this objective. Following there will be a discussion of the proposed STTS Model.

5.1. Macro Level: The Role of Political Institutions

The political institutions at both international (EU) and national levels are crucial as they enable the establishment of the appropriate Funding Schemes. This shall enable access to tourism SMEs to the much-needed financial resources, as the latter constitutes one of their most important problems. These policies shall enable the development of the appropriate and relevant technological infrastructure that will be clearly and directly linked to the needs of contemporary tourism SMEs. In the particular manner, the chapter strongly supports that lack of development of the proposed infrastructure will only lead to minor changes and improvements, and therefore, this will not lead to the desired innovation which is essential for transforming tourism SMEs through CVET.

5.2. Meso Level: The Role of Professional Institutions

Professional institutions such as Chambers, Employers' and Labor Unions are critical in order to ensure that simulation training in CVET shall take place. Their collaboration constitutes a major challenge as they will need to go beyond any possible differences related to professional and working matters, such as collective agreements. In this process, Chambers have a central role as they can act as mediators that will ensure effective and efficient collaboration. The accumulated experience of Chambers is identified as a major asset which needs to be utilized as part of a holistic strategic approach in order to develop Conjoined Training Programs in Simulation Tools.

5.3. Micro Level: The Role of Conjoined Training Programs

The role of Conjoined Training Programs as the final level which is linked to innovation and CVET through simulation tools, is considered as a real challenge for the tourism SMEs. Previous experience has indicated that training programs are suffering from lack of evaluation which will enable the appropriate measurement based on predetermined Key Performance Indices (KPIs). This evaluation is expected to provide the appropriate feedback to the professional institutions (meso level). This STTS Model proposes that feedback can contribute towards long-term positive results. Feedback can be crucial for introducing new methods and techniques in CVET, especially following difficult periods such as the recent pandemic and financial crisis. The establishment of KPIs creates opportunities for all stakeholders, at all three levels, to become more focused, improve performance, enhance innovation, and integrate simulation tools.

LIMITATIONS

As simulation tools in CVET are an emerging aspect in the development of CVET, there is insufficient information from both professional and academic sources in order to ensure that this chapter will effectively address the under-examination issues. Furthermore, SMEs in tourism industry are going through continuous changes as a result of consecutive crises; financial, health, and energy. This creates additional limitations as to the overall understanding and critical evaluation of the strategic role of technology and simulation tools as part of a comprehensive approach. The aforementioned limitations are expected to be lessened through the extensive literature review as well as the proposed STTS Model which focuses on dealing with the issue in a constructive and strategic manner.

REFERENCES

Amoah, J., Egala, S. B., Keelson, S., Bruce, E., Dziwornu, R., & Duah, F. A. (2023). Driving factors to competitive sustainability of SMEs in the tourism sector: An introspective analysis. *Cogent Business & Management*, *10*(1), 2163796. Advance online publication. DOI: 10.1080/23311975.2022.2163796

Andrade-Valbuena, N., Baier-Fuentes, H., & Gaviria-Marin, M. (2022). An Overview of Sustainable Entrepreneurship in Tourism, Destination, and Hospitality Research Based on the Web of Science. *Sustainability (Basel)*, *14*(22), 14944. DOI: 10.3390/su142214944

Apostolopoulos, N., Liargovas, P., Stavroyiannis, S., Makris, I., Apostolopoulos, S., Petropoulos, D., & Anastasopoulou, E. (2020). Sustaining Rural Areas, Rural Tourism Enterprises and EU Development Policies: A Multi-Layer Conceptualisation of the Obstacles in Greece. *Sustainability (Basel)*, *12*(18), 7687. DOI: 10.3390/su12187687

Badghish, S., & Soomro, Y. A. (2024). Artificial Intelligence Adoption by SMEs to Achieve Sustainable Business Performance: Application of Technology–Organization–Environment Framework. *Sustainability (Basel)*, *16*(5), 1864. DOI: 10.3390/su16051864

Baiocco, S., Leoni, L., & Paniccia, P. M. A. (2023). Entrepreneurship for sustainable development: Co-evolutionary evidence from the tourism sector. *Journal of Small Business and Enterprise Development*, *30*(7), 1521–1546. DOI: 10.1108/JSBED-01-2023-0003

Bell, E., Bryman, A., & Harley, B. (2018). *Business Research Methods* (5th ed.). Oxford University Press.

Bhagat, S. V., & Kanyal, D. (2024). Navigating the Future: The Transformative Impact of Artificial Intelligence on Hospital Management- A Comprehensive Review. *Cureus*, *16*(2), e54518. [REMOVED HYPERLINK FIELD]DOI: 10.7759/cureus.54518 PMID: 38516434

Billett, S., Choy, S., & Hodge, S. (2020). Enhancing the standing of vocational education and the occupations it serves: Australia. *Journal of Vocational Education and Training*, *72*(2), 270–296. DOI: 10.1080/13636820.2020.1751247

Blouin, R. A., Riffee, W. H., Robinson, E. T., Beck, D. E., Green, C., Joyner, P. U., Persky, A. M., & Pollack, G. M. (2009). Roles of innovation in education delivery. *American Journal of Pharmaceutical Education*, *73*(8), 154. DOI: 10.5688/aj7308154 PMID: 20221347

Bobek, E., & Tversky, B. (2016). Creating visual explanations improves learning. *Cognitive Research: Principles and Implications*, *1*(1), 27. [REMOVED HYPERLINK FIELD]DOI: 10.1186/s41235-016-0031-6 PMID: 28180178

Bulchand-Gidumal, J., Secin, E. W., O'Connor, P., & Buhalis, D. (2023). Artificial intelligence's impact on hospitality and tourism marketing: Exploring key themes and addressing challenges. *Current Issues in Tourism*, 1–18. DOI: 10.1080/13683500.2023.2229480

Campos, N., Nogal, M., Caliz, C., & Juan, A. A. (2020). Simulation-based education involving online and on-campus models in different European universities. *International Journal of Educational Technology in Higher Education*, *17*(1), 8. Advance online publication. DOI: 10.1186/s41239-020-0181-y

Chernikova, O., Heitzmann, N., Stadler, M., Holzberger, D., Seidel, T., & Fischer, F. (2020). Simulation-Based Learning in Higher Education: A Meta-Analysis. *Review of Educational Research, 90*(4), 499–541. DOI: 10.3102/0034654320933544

Cook, D. A., Hatala, R., Brydges, R., Zendejas, B., Szostek, J. H., Wang, A. T., Erwin, P. J., & Hamstra, S. J. (2011). Technology-Enhanced Simulation for Health Professions Education. *Journal of the American Medical Association, 306*(9). Advance online publication. DOI: 10.1001/jama.2011.1234 PMID: 21900138

Dangwal, A., Kukreti, M., Angurala, M., Sarangal, R., Mehta, M., & Chauhan, P. (2023). A Review on the Role of Artificial Intelligence in Tourism. 2023 10th International Conference on Computing for Sustainable Global Development (INDIACom), New Delhi, India, 2023, pp. 164-168. https://shorturl.at/G2NgW

Davenport, T., & Kalakota, R. (2019). The potential for artificial intelligence in healthcare. *Future Healthcare Journal, 6*(2), 94–98. [REMOVED HYPERLINK FIELD]DOI: 10.7861/futurehosp.6-2-94 PMID: 31363513

Davoine, R., & Deitmer, L. (2020). German Dual Training through Apprenticeships: An Exportable Model? 133–141. DOI: 10.1002/9781119694793.ch16

Day, J., Chin, N., Sydnor, S., Widhalm, M., Shah, K. U., & Dorworth, L. (2021). Implications of climate change for tourism and outdoor recreation: An Indiana, USA, case study. *Climatic Change, 169*(3-4), 29. DOI: 10.1007/s10584-021-03284-w PMID: 34924649

Demirkan, I., Srinivasan, R., & Nand, A. (2021). Innovation in SMEs: The role of employee training in German SMEs. *Journal of Small Business and Enterprise Development, 29*(3), 421–440. DOI: 10.1108/JSBED-07-2020-0246

García, J. Y. S., Ríos, J. E. N., & Hernández, C. L. (2020). Systemic complementarity, an integrative model of cooperation among small and medium-sized tourism enterprises in Mexico. *International Journal of Business Innovation and Research, 23*(3), 354. DOI: 10.1504/IJBIR.2020.110968

García-Madurga, M., & Grilló-Méndez, A. (2023). Artificial intelligence in the tourism industry: An overview of reviews. *Administrative Sciences, 13*(8), 172. DOI: 10.3390/admsci13080172

Gimmon, E., Farja, Y., & Greenberg, Z. (2020). Vocational education of owners and SME employment growth: Evidence from Israel. *International Journal of Training Research, 19*(1), 21–46. DOI: 10.1080/14480220.2020.1864440

Grobbelaar, W., & Verma, A. (2020). Vocational training and industry IR 4.0 in a smart city. SSRN Electronic Journal. DOI: 10.2139/ssrn.3713780

Gustavsson, S. (2021). Simulation in vocational education. Skandinavisk Tidsskrift for Yrker Og Profesjoner I Utvikling, 6(1). DOI: 10.7577/sjvd.4076

Harris, R., & Clayton, B. (2020). The value of vocational education and training. *International Journal of Training Research, 18*(3), 185–190. DOI: 10.1080/14480220.2020.1860309

He, F. (2022). Application Research on Intelligent Design System of Indoor Public Space Based on Computer AI Technology, 2022 IEEE 2nd International Conference on Data Science and Computer Application (ICDSCA), Dalian, China, 2022, pp. 864-868, DOI: 10.1109/ICDSCA56264.2022.9988571

Heuer, A., Serratos-Sotelo, L., & Motel-Klingebiel, A. (2024). How perception affects participation: The case of adult learning and continued vocational education and training in Europe. *International Journal of Lifelong Education*, 1–21. DOI: 10.1080/02601370.2024.2398516

Hidalgo-Peñate, A., Nieves, J., & Padrón-Robaina, V. (2020). The influence of employees' knowledge, organisational commitment, and culture on the innovativeness of vocational educational. *Knowledge Management Research and Practice*, *20*(5), 755–766. DOI: 10.1080/14778238.2020.1774431

Hlasny, V. (2023). Vocational training support and innovation at SMEs. *Asia Pacific Journal of Innovation and Entrepreneurship*, *17*(2), 99–120. DOI: 10.1108/APJIE-09-2022-0096

Innerhofer, J., Nasta, L., & Zehrer, A. (2022). Antecedents of labor shortage in the rural hospitality industry: A comparative study of employees and employers. *Journal of Hospitality and Tourism Insights*, *7*(1), 28–55. DOI: 10.1108/JHTI-04-2022-0125

Issenberg, S. B. (2005). Features and uses of high-fidelity medical simulations that lead to effective learning: A BEME systematic review. *Medical Teacher*, *27*(1), 1028. DOI: 10.1080/01421590500046924 PMID: 16147767

Ivcevic, Z., & Grandinetti, M. (2024). Artificial intelligence as a tool for creativity. *Journal of Creativity*, *34*(2), 100079. DOI: 10.1016/j.yjoc.2024.100079

Jossberger, H., Brand-Gruwel, S., van de Wiel, M. W. J., & Boshuizen, H. P. A. (2015). Teachers' Perceptions of Teaching in Workplace Simulations in Vocational Education. *Vocations and Learning*, *8*(3), 287–318. DOI: 10.1007/s12186-015-9137-0

Khalifa, M., & Albadawy, M. (2024). Using Artificial Intelligence in Academic Writing and Research: An Essential Productivity Tool. *Computer Methods and Programs in Biomedicine Update*, *5*, 100145. DOI: 10.1016/j.cmpbup.2024.100145

Kijkasiwat, P., Cave, J., Wellalage, N. H., & Locke, S. (2024). Forecasting symbiosis in tourism enterprise networks: Monte Carlo simulation of risk and return. *International Journal of Services Economics and Management*, *15*(1), 63–83. DOI: 10.1504/IJSEM.2024.136056

Kotler, P., & Keller, K. L. (2007). *A Framework for Marketing Management* (3rd ed.). Prentice Hall.

Kraus, S., Bouncken, R. B., & Aránega, A. Y. (2024). The burgeoning role of literature review articles in management research: An introduction and outlook. *Review of Managerial Science*, *18*(2), 299–314. DOI: 10.1007/s11846-024-00729-1

Ku, E. C., & Chen, C. (2024). Artificial intelligence innovation of tourism businesses: From satisfied tourists to continued service usage intention. *International Journal of Information Management*, *76*, 102757. DOI: 10.1016/j.ijinfomgt.2024.102757

Kutz, J. N., Brunton, S. L., Brunton, B. W., & Proctor, J. L. (2016). *Dynamic mode decomposition: data-driven modeling of complex systems*. Society for Industrial and Applied Mathematics., DOI: 10.1137/1.9781611974508

Lavía, C., Otero, B., Albizu, E., & Olazaran, M. (2021). Exploring the Intensity of Relationships with Vocational Education Centres: A Typology of Spanish SMEs. *Sustainability (Basel)*, *13*(16), 9287. DOI: 10.3390/su13169287

Lefrid, M., Cavusoglu, M., Richardson, S., & Donnelly, C. (2023). Simulation-Based Learning Acceptance Model (SBL-AM): Expanding the Technology Acceptance Model (TAM) into Hospitality Education. *Journal of Hospitality & Tourism Education*, 1–15. DOI: 10.1080/10963758.2023.2188217

Lemos, S. I. C., Ferreira, F. F., Zopounidis, C., Galariotis, E., & Ferreira, N. C. M. Q. F. (2022). Artificial intelligence and change management in small and medium-sized enterprises: An analysis of dynamics within adaptation initiatives. *Annals of Operations Research*. Advance online publication. DOI: 10.1007/s10479-022-05159-4 PMID: 36597501

Li, J., & Pilz, M. (2021). International transfer of vocational education and training: A literature review. *Journal of Vocational Education and Training*, *75*(2), 185–218. DOI: 10.1080/13636820.2020.1847566

Lobinger, K., & Mele, E. (2021). Visual Methods and Visual Analysis in Tourism Research. In Springer eBooks (pp. 1–28). DOI: 10.1007/978-3-030-05324-6 54-1

Longenecker, J. G., Petty, J. W., Palich, L. E., & Hoy, F. (2019). *Small Business Management: Launching and Growing Entrepreneurial Ventures* (19th ed.). Cengage.

Martínez, J. M. G., Martín, J. M. M., & Del Sol Ostos Rey, M. (2020). An analysis of the changes in the seasonal patterns of tourist behavior during a process of economic recovery. *Technological Forecasting and Social Change*, *161*, 120280. DOI: 10.1016/j.techfore.2020.120280

Martínez-Carmona, M. J., Gil Del Pino, C., & Álvarez-Castillo, J. L. (2022). The Basic Cycles of Vocational Training: Student Satisfaction and Perceived Benefit. *European Journal of Investigation in Health, Psychology and Education*, *12*(4), 417–430. DOI: 10.3390/ejihpe12040030 PMID: 35447748

Masouras, A., Daskou, S., Pistikou, V., Dimitriou, D., & Friesner, T. (2024). Global Developments in Nation Branding and Promotion. (2023). In Advances in marketing, customer relationship management, and e-services book series. DOI: 10.4018/978-1-6684-5902-7

Masouras, A., & Papademetriou, C. (2018). Digital Consumer Behaviour in Cyprus: From Uses and Gratifications Theory to 4C's Online Shopping Approach. *Journal of Advertising and Public Relations*, *1*(1), 1–11. DOI: 10.22259/2639-1953.0101006

McGrath, S., & Yamada, S. (2023). Skills for development and vocational education and training: Current and emergent trends. *International Journal of Educational Development*, *102*, 102853. DOI: 10.1016/j.ijedudev.2023.102853

McKenna, L., Innes, K., French, J., Streitberg, S., & Gilmour, C. (2010). Is history taking a dying skill? An exploration using a simulated learning environment. *Nurse Education in Practice*, *11*(4), 234–238. [REMOVED HYPERLINK FIELD]DOI: 10.1016/j.nepr.2010.11.009 PMID: 21195667

Melo, A., Melo, C., & Vasconcelos, S. (2023). 'Rota Dos Sabores' – Simulation-Based Learning in Tourism, Hospitality and Catering Education and Training. *INTED Proceedings*, 3384–3390. Advance online publication. DOI: 10.21125/inted.2023.0920

Milmeister, P., Rastoder, M., & Houssemand, C. (2022). Mechanisms of Participation in Vocational Education and Training in Europe. *Frontiers in Psychology*, *13*, 842307. Advance online publication. [REMOVED HYPERLINK FIELD]DOI: 10.3389/fpsyg.2022.842307 PMID: 35707674

Nagy, M., Lăzăroiu, G., & Valaskova, K. (2023). Machine Intelligence and Autonomous Robotic Technologies in the Corporate Context of SMEs: Deep Learning and Virtual Simulation Algorithms, Cyber-Physical Production Networks, and Industry 4.0-Based Manufacturing Systems. *Applied Sciences (Basel, Switzerland)*, *13*(3), 1681. DOI: 10.3390/app13031681

Nandi, V. T. N., Khan, S., Qureshi, M. A., & Ghias, S. (2020). Training & Development, Organizational Commitment and Turnover Intentions in SMEs. *Market Forces*, *15*(2), 24. DOI: 10.51153/mf.v15i2.457

Nasir, J., Ibrahim, R. M., Sarwar, M. A., Sarwar, B., Al-Rahmi, W. M., Alturise, F., Al-Adwan, A. S., & Uddin, M. (2022). The Effects of Transformational Leadership, Organizational Innovation, Work Stressors, and Creativity on Employee Performance in SMEs. *Frontiers in Psychology*, *13*, 772104. Advance online publication. [REMOVED HYPERLINK FIELD]DOI: 10.3389/fpsyg.2022.772104 PMID: 35529553

Navarro-Parra, S. L., & Chiappe, A. (2024). Simulated Learning Environments as an Interdisciplinary Option for Vocational Training: A Systematic Review. *Simulation & Gaming*, *55*(2), 135–158. DOI: 10.1177/10468781231221904

Nyström, S., & Ahn, S. E. (2024). Teaching with simulators in vocational education and training – From a storing place to a new colleague. *Teaching and Teacher Education*, *138*, 104409. DOI: 10.1016/j.tate.2023.104409

Oldemeyer, L., Jede, A., & Teuteberg, F. (2024). *Investigation of artificial intelligence in SMEs: a systematic review of the state of the art and the main implementation challenges*. Management Review Quarterly., DOI: 10.1007/s11301-024-00405-4

Papademetriou, C., Ragazou, K., Belias, D., Anastasiadou, S., Garefalakis, A., & Prodromou, A. (2024). The Importance of Green Human Resources: Green Ambidexterity and Environmental Performance. In *Sustainability Through Green HRM and Performance Integration*. IGI Global., DOI: 10.4018/979-8-3693-5981-5.ch004

Persico, L., & Lalor, J. D. (2019). A Review: Using Simulation-Based Education to Substitute Traditional Clinical Rotations. *Teaching and Learning in Nursing*, *14*(4), 274–278. DOI: 10.1016/j.teln.2019.03.006

Pietsch, M., Cramer, C., Brown, C., Aydin, B., & Witthöft, J. (2023). Open Innovation in Schools: A New Imperative for Organising Innovation in Education? *Technology Knowledge and Learning.*, *29*(2), 1051–1077. DOI: 10.1007/s10758-023-09705-2

Polikarpus, S., Luik, P., Poom-Valickis, K., & Ley, T. (2023). The Role of Trainers in Implementing Virtual Simulation-based Training: Effects on Attitude and TPACK Knowledge. *Vocations and Learning*, *16*(3), 459–486. DOI: 10.1007/s12186-023-09322-1

Porter, M. E. (1985). Competitive advantage: creating and sustaining superior performance: with a new introduction. Free Press, New York https://www.hbs.edu/faculty/Pages/item.aspx?num=193

Prenger, R., Tappel, A. P. M., Poortman, C. L., & Schildkamp, K. (2022). How can educational innovations become sustainable? A review of the empirical literature. *Frontiers in Education*, *7*, 970715. Advance online publication. DOI: 10.3389/feduc.2022.970715

Prodromou, A. (2021). The Impact of Covid-19 on the Global Automotive Industry - Future Challenges. *American International Journal of Social Science*, *10*(1), 1–11. DOI: 10.30845/aijss.v10n1p1

Prodromou, A., Efthimiou, I., & Apostolopoulos, S. (2024). Covid-19 and the Impact on Cyprus' SMEs Tourism - Enterprises: Lessons to be Learned. Conference Proceedings of the 19th European Conference on Innovation and Entrepreneurship ECIE 19(1), 2024 26-27 September 2024 CESI, Paris-Nanterre, France. DOI: 10.34190/ecie.19.1.2470

Prodromou, A., & Kountouridou, M. (2024). Local Entrepreneurial Ecosystems for Global Market Diversification. In *Security and Strategy Models for Key-Solving Institutional Frameworks*. IGI Global., DOI: 10.4018/979-8-3693-5583-1

Prodromou, A., Papademetriou, C., & Savvides, D. (2024). The Strategic Role of Green HRM in Hospitality Industry for Reaching Sustainable Development Goals. In *Sustainability Through Green HRM and Performance Integration*. IGI Global., DOI: 10.4018/979-8-3693-5981-5.ch001

Rastegar, R., Seyfi, S., & Shahi, T. (2023). Tourism SMEs' resilience strategies amidst the COVID-19 crisis: The story of survival. *Tourism Recreation Research*, 1–7. DOI: 10.1080/02508281.2023.2233073

Redondo, A., Castillo, S., Carro, L., & Martín, P. (2021). The Effects of European Recommendations on the Validation of Lifelong Learning: A Quality Assurance Model for VET in Spain. *Sustainability (Basel)*, *13*(13), 7283. DOI: 10.3390/su13137283

Research Anthology on Cross-Industry Challenges of Industry 4.0. (2021). In IGI Global eBooks. DOI: 10.4018/978-1-7998-8548-1

Rodríguez, A. J. G., Barón, N. J., & Martínez, J. M. G. (2020). Validity of dynamic capabilities in the operation based on new sustainability narratives on nature tourism SMEs and clusters. *Sustainability (Basel)*, *12*(3), 1004. DOI: 10.3390/su12031004

Rosário, A. T., & Raimundo, R. (2024). Enhancing Business Higher Education Through Simulation-Based Learning, Problem-Based Learning, and Challenge-Based Learning. DOI: 10.20944/preprints202407.0747.v1

Rubenstein, L. D., Callan, G. L., Neumeister, K. S., & Ridgley, L. M. (2020). Finding the problem: How students approach problem identification. *Thinking Skills and Creativity*, *35*, 100635. DOI: 10.1016/j.tsc.2020.100635

Rubia-Avi, B. (2022). The Research of Educational Innovation: Perspective and Strategies. *Education Sciences*, *13*(1), 26. DOI: 10.3390/educsci13010026

Serdyukov, P. (2017). Innovation in education: What works, what doesn't, and what to do about it? *Journal of Research in Innovative Teaching & Learning*, *10*(1), 4–33. DOI: 10.1108/JRIT-10-2016-0007

Sophocleous, H., & Prodromou, A. (2024). A Marketing - Business Plan and competition analysis for the Cyprus specialized /wellness tourism services / market. In *Real-World Tools and Scenarios for Entrepreneurship Exploration*. IGI Global. DOI: 10.4018/979-8-3693-3100-2.ch014

Sophocleous, H. P. H. (2023). Nation Branding as a Strategic Asset for Local SMEs. In Advances in marketing, customer relationship management, and e-services book series (pp. 124–155). DOI: 10.4018/978-1-6684-5902-7.ch006

Sousa, A. E., Cardoso, P., & Dias, F. (2024). The Use of Artificial Intelligence Systems in Tourism and Hospitality: The Tourists' Perspective. *Administrative Sciences*, *14*(8), 165. DOI: 10.3390/admsci14080165

Statista (2023). Global total corporate artificial intelligence (AI) investment from 2015 to 2022 (in billion U.S. dollars). https://shorturl.at/v35mo

Statista (2024). Number of travel and tourism jobs worldwide from 2019 to 2023, with a forecast for 2024 and 2034 (in millions). https://shorturl.at/KZIhr

Stirman, S. W., Kimberly, J., Cook, N., Calloway, A., Castro, F., & Charns, M. (2012). The sustainability of new programs and innovations: A review of the empirical literature and recommendations for future research. *Implementation Science : IS*, *7*(1), 17. Advance online publication. [REMOVED HYPERLINK FIELD]DOI: 10.1186/1748-5908-7-17 PMID: 22417162

Tol, R. S. J. (2018). The Economic Impacts of Climate Change. *Review of Environmental Economics and Policy*, *12*(1), 4–25. DOI: 10.1093/reep/rex027

Tong, L., Yan, W., & Manta, O. (2022). Artificial Intelligence Influences Intelligent Automation in Tourism: A Mediating Role of Internet of Things and Environmental, Social, and Governance Investment. *Frontiers in Environmental Science*, *10*, 853302. Advance online publication. DOI: 10.3389/fenvs.2022.853302

Tosto, S. A., Alyahya, J., Espinoza, V., McCarthy, K., & Tcherni-Buzzeo, M. (2023). Online learning in the wake of the COVID-19 pandemic: Mixed methods analysis of student views by demographic group. *Social Sciences & Humanities Open*, *8*(1), 100598. [REMOVED HYPERLINK FIELD]DOI: 10.1016/j.ssaho.2023.100598 PMID: 37366390

Wang, Z., & Le, T. T. (2022). The COVID-19 pandemic's effects on SMEs and travel agencies: The critical role of corporate social responsibility. *Economic Analysis and Policy*, *76*, 46–58. [REMOVED HYPERLINK FIELD]DOI: 10.1016/j.eap.2022.07.008 PMID: 35919271

Wirts, J., & Lovelock, C. (2021). *Services Marketing: People, Technology, Strategy* (9th ed.). World Scientific Publishing Company. DOI: 10.1142/y0024

Zheng, B., Zhang, Q., Geng, G., Chen, C., Shi, Q., Cui, M., Lei, Y., & He, K. (2021). Changes in China's anthropogenic emissions and air quality during the COVID-19 pandemic in 2020. *Earth System Science Data*, *13*(6), 2895–2907. DOI: 10.5194/essd-13-2895-2021

Zhurakovskaya, V., Sichinava, A., Simakova, T., Olicheva, O., Rykov, S., Valeeva, J., Kulachinskaya, A., & Ilyashenko, S. (2020). Innovations in Education—The Development of a New Pedagogical Technology of a Combinational Type, Focused on the Development of Personality of Students. *Journal of Open Innovation*, *6*(4), 123. DOI: 10.3390/joitmc6040123

Chapter 4
Incorporating Simulation Tools in Distant Educational Entrepreneurship:
Enhancing Entrepreneurial Skills Through Virtual Simulation in Online Learning

Stalo Georgiou
https://orcid.org/0009-0003-5004-0481
Neapolis University, Cyprus

ABSTRACT

Entrepreneurship education plays a vital role in equipping students with the skills and knowledge necessary to navigate the complex and dynamic world of business. Traditional instructional methods often focus on theoretical concepts, but they may not adequately prepare students for the real-world challenges of entrepreneurship. To address this gap, the integration of simulation tools in entrepreneurship education has gained significant attention in recent years. Simulation tools create immersive, interactive environments where students can experience realistic business scenarios and engage in decision-making processes that mirror actual entrepreneurial challenges. This paper explores the benefits, challenges, and best practices of integrating simulation tools into entrepreneurship education, offering insights into how they can enhance both teaching outcomes and student learning experiences.

1. INTRODUCTION

In the swiftly changing environment of education, simulation tools have become a significant transformative element, especially within the context of remote educational entrepreneurship. These innovative technologies serve not merely as supplementary resources; rather, they play a critical role in transforming the manner in which students interact with theoretical concepts and implement them in practical contexts. The incorporation of simulations within online learning environments allows educators to construct dynamic and immersive experiences that not only augment experiential learning

DOI: 10.4018/979-8-3693-9040-5.ch004

but also promote collaborative engagement and facilitate the connection between theoretical knowledge and practical application.

Entrepreneurship education generally encompasses the cultivation of competencies in areas such as decision-making, financial management, marketing strategy, and risk assessment. Nevertheless, imparting these skills through conventional lectures can prove challenging, especially within the context of distance learning environments. In this regard, simulation tools emerge as invaluable resources. The integration of digital platforms that replicate authentic business environments enables students to engage deeply in decision-making processes while experiencing the ramifications of their choices within a risk-free, virtual context. Simulation tools provide an interactive learning experience, affording learners the opportunity to experiment with concepts, encounter setbacks, and glean insights from their errors, thereby reflecting the inherent uncertainties associated with entrepreneurship.

A significant advantage of employing simulation tools in distance education lies in their capacity to offer experiential learning opportunities, which are frequently regarded as highly effective for imparting entrepreneurial skills. In contrast to traditional static learning resources, simulations provide students with the opportunity to engage in the management of virtual enterprises, compete with fellow learners, and adapt to fluctuations in the marketplace. This approach not only strengthens individuals' critical thinking and problem-solving skills but also facilitates the integration of theoretical knowledge with practical application. Additionally, simulation platforms can cater to a variety of learning styles, thereby rendering entrepreneurship education more inclusive and accessible to a wider audience (Liu, et al. 2019).

The integration of these tools promotes collaborative engagement among students within a remote learning context. Numerous simulations are structured to incorporate multiplayer or team-oriented elements, which facilitate collaborative engagement among learners, promote the exchange of ideas, and foster the development of strategic approaches. This aspect holds significant importance within the realm of entrepreneurship education, as collaborative efforts and networking are essential competencies for achieving success in business endeavors. Simulation tools serve to enhance these interactions within a virtual environment, thereby offering students the opportunity to participate in entrepreneurial ecosystems, even in a remote learning context (Nabi, et al. 2017).

As distance education progresses, the incorporation of simulation tools within entrepreneurship curricula provides a dynamic and interactive approach to learning. By facilitating students' engagement with authentic business challenges within a structured, virtual framework, these tools enrich both individual and collaborative learning experiences. Consequently, they more effectively equip students for the intricacies associated with entrepreneurial endeavors (Rahman, & Day, 2015).

The Goal of the Article

The objective of this article is to examine the effective integration of simulation tools within remote educational programs that emphasize entrepreneurship. With the expansion of online education, particularly in the realm of entrepreneurship, there is an increasing necessity to offer students experiential learning opportunities that effectively replicate real-world business challenges. This article seeks to illustrate the potential of simulation platforms to provide an immersive and interactive educational environment, thereby enabling students to cultivate essential competencies such as decision-making, financial management, and problem-solving.

By simulating intricate business scenarios within a virtual and risk-free environment, these tools facilitate the integration of theoretical knowledge with practical application, thereby providing essential experiential learning opportunities for emerging entrepreneurs. Furthermore, the article will underscore the role of simulation tools in enhancing collaboration among remote learners, thereby promoting teamwork, innovation, and networking—essential elements for successful entrepreneurship. The objective of this study is to elucidate the efficacy of these tools in providing students with the essential practical skills required to adeptly maneuver through the inherent uncertainties associated with entrepreneurship, even within a distance learning framework. This, in turn, aims to enhance educational outcomes as well as the preparedness of students for entrepreneurial endeavors.

Methodology

This study employs a descriptive analysis of the existing academic literature. The review of pertinent research and texts is intended to inform the formulation of the research question, grounded in the most reliable and relevant information available. Furthermore, it is essential to document and critically evaluate the methodologies and procedures employed by other researchers who have investigated the same or similar issues, in order to identify similarities and differences with the current hypothesis. This comparative analysis will facilitate the drawing of informed conclusions and the potential adoption of effective research methods and approaches.

2. DEFINITION OF TERMS

Experiential learning is a process of learning through experience, where students engage in hands-on activities and reflect on their actions to gain practical skills and knowledge. It emphasizes active participation and real-world application, fostering deeper understanding through practice and reflection (Wang, 2023).

Simulation tools are digital platforms that replicate real-world environments, allowing learners to engage in virtual scenarios for experiential learning. These tools enable students to apply theoretical concepts in controlled, risk-free settings, enhancing decision-making, problem-solving, and critical thinking (Williamson, et al, 2023).

Entrepreneurship education involves teaching individuals the skills and mindset needed to start, develop, and manage businesses. It focuses on fostering creativity, innovation, risk management, and strategic thinking, helping learners turn opportunities into viable business ventures (Petridou, & Sarri, 2011).

3. REVIEW OF LITERATURE

Enhancing Experiential Learning

Experiential learning is broadly acknowledged as one of the most effective pedagogical approaches, especially in disciplines such as entrepreneurship, where the development of practical skills and decision-making capabilities is essential. Conventional educational practices typically emphasize the acquisition of theoretical knowledge (Piperopoulos, 2012); however, experiential learning serves to connect theoretical frameworks with practical application, providing students with the opportunity to implement their learning in real-world situations. In the domain of distance education, the enhancement of experiential learning through the utilization of digital tools, including simulations, has emerged as an effective strategy for engaging students, advancing their comprehension, and equipping them to navigate the intricacies of the entrepreneurial environment (Stefanic, et al. 2020).

Simulation technologies afford learners the opportunity to immerse themselves in authentic scenarios while mitigating the inherent risks associated with practical applications. For example, healthcare education programs have effectively employed virtual patient simulations, enabling nursing and medical students to engage in diagnostic and therapeutic practice within a secure and regulated setting. Programs such as Labster provide virtual laboratory environments that enable students in the sciences to engage in experiments that would be difficult to implement or financially unfeasible in a conventional laboratory setting. This form of experiential learning not only reinforces theoretical knowledge but also enhances students' confidence, thereby equipping them to address real-world challenges (Wei, et al. 2019).

Entrepreneurship education is significantly enhanced by experiential learning, given the inherently practical nature of the discipline. Entrepreneurs are required to make rapid and informed decisions, adjust to fluctuating market dynamics, and formulate strategies for effective risk management. The acquisition of these skills poses significant challenges when approached through conventional pedagogical methods, underscoring the importance of experiential learning. This approach enables students to engage in active participation, thereby facilitating direct exposure to real-world business challenges. Through this process, learners are afforded the opportunity to make mistakes, reflect on these experiences, and refine their decision-making abilities within a structured context. In the context of distance learning, simulation tools serve to virtually replicate real-world experiences, thereby providing students with the opportunity to cultivate entrepreneurial skills despite being physically separated from their peers and instructors (Toledano, & Urbano, 2008).

Simulation Tools as a Catalyst for Experiential Learning

Simulation tools have emerged as one of the most effective ways to enhance experiential learning in distant education. These platforms create virtual environments where students can run businesses, manage resources, and respond to market changes. In entrepreneurship education, this type of hands-on learning is invaluable because it mimics the dynamic nature of real-world business operations. For instance, students might manage a startup, handle customer complaints, adjust their marketing strategies, and balance their finances within the simulation, all while receiving real-time feedback on their decisions.

These virtual environments offer a safe space for experimentation. Students can make risky decisions without the fear of real-world consequences, allowing them to test creative solutions, explore different business strategies, and learn from their mistakes. This type of interactive learning also enhances engagement, as students become active participants in their education rather than passive recipients of information. The process of "learning by doing" through simulations can accelerate understanding and retention of complex business concepts, better preparing students for the entrepreneurial challenges they will face after graduation (Wei, et al. 2019).

Simulation Platforms

Cesim presents a diverse array of business simulations that encompass scenarios ranging from managing startups to overseeing multinational corporations, and these simulations can be tailored to align with the specific objectives of the course.

Capsim engages students in simulated environments that require them to manage a virtual company, contend with market competition, and derive lessons from their decisions, thereby replicating authentic business contexts. Marketplace Simulations offers immersive environments that enable students to initiate and develop virtual enterprises while engaging in competition within fluctuating market conditions.

These tools support experiential learning by allowing students to engage with complex, real-world scenarios (Wei, et al. 2019).

4. LEARNING MANAGEMENT SYSTEMS (LMS) WITH COLLABORATION FEATURES

Learning management systems such as Moodle, Canvas, and Blackboard offer conducive environments for the integration of experiential learning through various tools, including discussion forums, collaborative wikis, and spaces designed for group projects. These platforms typically facilitate the use of multimedia resources, video conferencing, and mechanisms for peer-to-peer feedback, thereby rendering them particularly suitable for team-oriented experiential activities. Canvas provides educators with the capability to design assignments that replicate authentic real-world tasks, thereby fostering collaborative group work, critical reflection, and meaningful discussion among students. Moodle facilitates the integration of various plugins, such as H5P and Mahara, which significantly enhance interactivity within the platform. These tools enable students to create e-portfolios, effectively document their learning experiences, and obtain constructive feedback on their progress (Wei, et al. 2019).

5. VIRTUAL REALITY (VR) AND AUGMENTED REALITY (AR)

Technological platforms like ClassVR and ENGAGE play a crucial role in creating immersive three-dimensional experiences that closely mimic real-life environments. By leveraging these innovative tools, students are afforded the unique opportunity to immerse themselves in practical, real-world activities that enhance their learning experiences. For instance, they can practice their public speaking and presentation skills by delivering business proposals in virtual boardrooms, where they interact with realistic avatars representing colleagues and stakeholders. Furthermore, students can take part in virtual trade exhibitions, which allow them to showcase their projects and ideas to a broader audience, network with peers, and gain insights into industry practices—all from the comfort of their own classrooms. These engaging platforms not only enrich the educational process but also prepare students for the complexities of the professional world by providing them with hands-on experiences that are both relevant and impactful (Abdullah et al, 2017).

ClassVR plays a crucial role in fostering the development of interactive and immersive educational settings that empower students to participate in experiential skill-building activities. This innovative approach to learning enables students to actively engage with the material and apply their knowledge in practical scenarios. One of the standout features of this educational framework is ENGAGE, a cutting-edge virtual reality platform specifically designed to enhance student interaction within carefully crafted simulated environments. These environments are thoughtfully designed to mimic real-world business contexts, offering learners the opportunity to immerse themselves in situations that closely resemble authentic professional experiences (Abdullah et al, 2017).

By doing so, ENGAGE not only stimulates creativity but also significantly enhances students' problem-solving abilities, equipping them with the skills necessary to navigate complex challenges in their future careers. Through these immersive learning experiences, students are encouraged to think critically and work collaboratively, ultimately preparing them for success in the dynamic and ever-evolving landscape of the modern workforce.

6. CASE-BASED LEARNING PLATFORMS

Harvard Business Publishing offers a wide array of case-based learning materials designed to immerse students in the examination of real-world business dilemmas. These resources allow learners to explore and dissect genuine challenges faced by organizations, fostering critical thinking and practical problem-solving skills. By engaging with these case studies, students can gain valuable insights into the complexities of the business environment, encouraging them to apply theoretical concepts to actual situations they may encounter in their professional careers. This hands-on approach not only enhances their understanding of key business principles but also prepares them to navigate the multifaceted landscape of modern business effectively. These case studies can be thoroughly explored in various online discussion forums or through interactive video conferencing sessions, providing students with valuable opportunities to engage in practical experiences related to addressing complex business challenges (Amundam, 2019).

This innovative pedagogical approach not only enhances the development of critical thinking skills among students but also encourages them to effectively apply theoretical concepts to tangible real-world situations. By participating in these discussions and collaborative sessions, students can deepen their understanding of business dynamics, learn to analyze problems from multiple perspectives, and develop strategic solutions that are informed by both academic knowledge and practical insights. Ultimately, this method of learning prepares students for the realities of the business world, equipping them with the necessary tools to navigate and resolve issues they may encounter in their future careers (Amundam, 2019).

7. INTERACTIVE LEARNING PLATFORMS

Platforms such as Kahoot!, Quizlet, and Pear Deck provide interactive quizzes, games, and polling features that facilitate experiential learning for students. These resources are especially effective for reinforcing educational concepts through gamification and active participation, thereby enhancing the overall engagement and practicality of the learning experience.

Fostering Collaboration Among Distant Learners

A defining characteristic of simulation technologies is their capacity to facilitate collaboration among learners who may be situated in diverse geographical locations. Virtual environments, exemplified by platforms such as Gather or Mozilla Hubs, enable students to engage collaboratively on projects, partake in discussions, and address problems in real time. For instance, architecture students have the opportunity to engage in collaborative efforts to design a building within a three-dimensional virtual environment, effectively merging their theoretical understanding with practical application. This collaborative methodology not only improves educational outcomes but also cultivates a sense of community among students, a characteristic that is frequently absent in conventional online educational settings (Castaldi, et al, 2020).

In traditional classrooms, students naturally interact with one another, sharing ideas and building relationships through direct communication. However, in a distance learning scenario, the lack of physical presence can lead to feelings of isolation and disconnection. This absence of face-to-face interaction can hinder students' ability to form meaningful connections, which are vital for effective collaboration. Additionally, the reliance on technology for communication can create barriers; students may encounter technical difficulties, varying levels of digital literacy, or differing access to resources, all of which can impact their ability to work together effectively (Castaldi, et al, 2020).

To counter these challenges, educators must implement strategies that promote collaboration and ensure that students feel supported and connected despite the physical distance. This can include creating structured group activities, utilizing collaborative technology tools, and fostering an inclusive atmosphere where every student feels valued and empowered to contribute. By addressing these obstacles head-on, we can enhance the collaborative experience for students in remote learning environments, ultimately leading to richer educational experiences and improved academic outcomes. By utilizing a variety of digital tools, implementing organized group activities, and establishing clear communication protocols, learners who are participating from a distance can engage in effective collaboration. This approach allows them to share a wide range of perspectives and insights, fostering a rich learning environment. Furthermore, these interactions enable them to develop essential teamwork skills that are crucial in today's world, particularly in areas such as entrepreneurship and other practical fields where collaborative efforts are key to success. In an increasingly interconnected and digital landscape, the ability to work well with others, even when physically apart, has become an invaluable asset for learners as they prepare to enter the professional world (Castaldi, et al, 2020).

In summary, the importance of collaboration in learning cannot be overstated. It enriches the educational experience, promotes critical thinking, and equips students with the tools they need to thrive in both academic and professional environments. Collaborative tasks play a crucial role in the educational experience by encouraging students to engage in critical thinking, actively exchange ideas, and work together to solve problems. This collaborative approach not only enhances individual learning but also fosters a sense of community among students, even when they are physically separated by distance. In the realm of entrepreneurship education, where creativity and teamwork are essential components for success, nurturing a collaborative environment becomes increasingly important (Dal, et al, 2016).

By promoting collaboration, educators can help students develop the necessary skills to navigate complex challenges, think innovatively, and build strong relationships with their peers. This collaborative spirit not only prepares students for future professional endeavors but also enriches their overall learning experience, making it more dynamic and interactive. Entrepreneurs seldom operate in isolation; instead, they depend on a variety of skilled individuals who form diverse teams to successfully establish and grow their businesses.

Within this framework, the collaboration that takes place among learners who are geographically separated closely resembles the collaborative dynamics found in the real business world. This type of teamwork not only fosters a rich learning environment but also equips students with the essential skills and experiences they will need to navigate future entrepreneurial endeavors. By engaging in such collaborative efforts, students are better prepared to face the challenges of entrepreneurship, as they learn to communicate effectively, leverage different perspectives, and work harmoniously with others to achieve common goals. This prepares them for the complexities of real-world business interactions, where teamwork and collaboration are often critical to success (Haderer, & Ciolacu, 2022).

The swift advancement of digital tools has profoundly transformed the capacity of distant learners to collaborate in a more effective and cohesive manner. Platforms such as Google Workspace, Microsoft Teams, and Slack have revolutionized the way students interact by providing them with the ability to communicate in real-time, share files effortlessly, and work together on group projects with remarkable ease. These innovative platforms are designed to support both synchronous and asynchronous communication, which means that learners have the freedom to choose how and when they engage with their peers. This flexibility is particularly beneficial in accommodating different schedules, time zones, and learning styles, allowing for a more inclusive and comprehensive collaborative experience. As a result, students are not only able to stay connected with their classmates but also to contribute to discussions, share resources, and collaborate on assignments in a way that enhances their overall learning experience (Haderer, & Ciolacu, 2022).

The integration of these digital tools into the educational landscape has made it possible for distant learners to forge meaningful connections and work together effectively, despite the physical distance that may separate them. A prime example of this can be seen in Google Workspace, which offers a comprehensive suite of tools including Google Docs, Sheets, and Slides. These applications are designed to facilitate real-time collaboration among users, allowing multiple students to work on the same document at the same time. This collaborative feature not only enhances the spirit of teamwork among students but also instills a sense of accountability; each participant can easily observe and acknowledge the contributions made by their peers. In the context of entrepreneurship education, such tools become invaluable as they mimic authentic business environments. Students can engage in collaborative efforts to develop business plans, devise marketing strategies, or manage financial data, all while working remotely. This experience prepares them for the dynamics of the modern workplace, where teamwork and shared responsibility are essential for success. By utilizing these digital tools, students not only learn the technical skills necessary for the business world but also cultivate interpersonal skills that are crucial for effective collaboration in any entrepreneurial endeavor (Haderer, & Ciolacu, 2022).

Moreover, the integration of discussion forums can serve as an invaluable tool for fostering continuous dialogue and encouraging participation from all learners, regardless of their individual circumstances. These online platforms can facilitate asynchronous communication, enabling participants to contribute their thoughts and ideas at their convenience, thus accommodating varying schedules and time zones. By implementing these strategies, instructors can create an environment that not only promotes collaboration but also ensures that all learners feel connected and engaged, despite the physical distances that separate them (Iborra et al, 2016).

Promoting the adoption of video conferencing platforms such as Zoom or Microsoft Teams for group discussions can significantly alleviate the challenges posed by the absence of in-person interactions. These video calls provide students with the opportunity to observe non-verbal cues, such as facial expressions and body language, which are frequently absent in text-based communication. This visual component fosters a more intimate and personal connection among group members, enhancing collaboration and camaraderie. Furthermore, integrating collaborative project management tools like Trello or Asana into the workflow can be instrumental for remote learners in maintaining organization and ensuring that everyone remains focused on the project's objectives, even when they are engaging in their work asynchronously. By utilizing these tools, students can effectively coordinate tasks, set deadlines, and track progress, creating a structured environment that promotes productivity and accountability. This approach not only helps bridge the gap created by physical distance but also encourages a sense of community and teamwork, which is essential for successful group projects in a virtual learning landscape (Iborra et al, 2016).

Facilitating collaboration in distance education extends beyond the mere completion of group assignments; it encompasses the development of a robust learning community. Establishing avenues for informal interactions, such as online study groups or virtual social gatherings, can assist distance learners in cultivating relationships with their peers. The establishment of this sense of community is critical for maintaining motivation and engagement throughout the duration of the course. Educators can significantly influence collaborative learning by exemplifying collaborative behaviors and fostering an environment that encourages students to express their thoughts and perspectives without hesitation. Promoting peer feedback and reflective practices contributes to the establishment of a culture characterized by mutual respect and ongoing enhancement, both of which are critical for effective collaboration in diverse educational settings (Lloyd, et al, 2019).

Building Collaboration and Critical Thinking Skills

A significant advantage of experiential learning via simulations is that it promotes both collaboration and critical thinking among participants. Numerous simulation tools are specifically crafted to incorporate multiplayer or team-oriented components, which actively encourage students to engage in cooperative efforts as they tackle challenges, devise strategies, and strive to accomplish shared objectives. By working alongside their peers, students not only enhance their problem-solving skills but also learn to communicate effectively, negotiate differing viewpoints, and leverage the diverse strengths of their teammates. This collaborative environment not only deepens their understanding of the subject matter but also equips them with essential interpersonal skills that are invaluable in real-world contexts (Lloyd, et al, 2019).

Ultimately, the interactive nature of these simulations transforms the learning experience into a dynamic and enriching process, where students can explore complex ideas and concepts together, fostering a sense of community and shared purpose. In the realm of entrepreneurship, the ability to collaborate effectively stands out as an essential skill. Successful entrepreneurs frequently find themselves working alongside co-founders, investors, and diverse teams in order to transform their innovative ideas into tangible realities. The process of entrepreneurship is rarely a solitary endeavor; instead, it thrives on the synergy created by collaborative efforts.

To prepare aspiring entrepreneurs for this dynamic environment, simulation tools have emerged as invaluable resources. These tools replicate the collaborative nature of real-world entrepreneurial ventures, providing students with opportunities to engage actively with their peers. Through these interactive experiences, students can share their ideas, receive constructive feedback, and develop the interpersonal skills necessary to function efficiently within a team setting. Ultimately, this hands-on approach not only enhances their understanding of entrepreneurship but also equips them with the collaborative skills vital for success in their future endeavors (Lloyd, et al, 2019).

Furthermore, simulation tools play a crucial role in fostering critical thinking skills among students by immersing them in intricate, real-life scenarios that lack definitive right or wrong answers. In these situations, students are required to engage in thorough analysis of data, carefully evaluate various alternatives, and make well-informed decisions that are grounded in their comprehension of the business environment. This form of experiential learning not only encourages students to think quickly and effectively under pressure but also compels them to adjust to evolving circumstances and devise creative solutions to challenges they encounter. Such competencies are invaluable for aspiring entrepreneurs across all sectors, as they prepare students to navigate the complexities of the business world with confidence and ingenuity. By engaging with simulation tools, students not only enhance their problem-solving abilities but also cultivate a mindset that embraces adaptability and innovation—qualities that are essential for success in any entrepreneurial endeavor. In essence, these tools provide a dynamic learning experience that equips students with the necessary skills to thrive in an ever-changing marketplace (Middleton, & Donnellon, 2019).

Bridging Theory and Practice

The disparity between theoretical understanding and practical implementation has been a persistent challenge within the field of education. Simulation technologies serve as a crucial intermediary by offering a platform that enables students to implement their acquired knowledge within a controlled, simulated environment. Business schools have adopted the concept of experiential learning through the implementation of business simulation games, such as Capsim, which enable students to oversee virtual enterprises and make strategic decisions that yield immediate and measurable outcomes. These tools facilitate learners in comprehending the intricate nature of business operations while simultaneously fostering the development of critical thinking and decision-making abilities.

Challenges and Strategies for Implementation

Notwithstanding the multitude of advantages, entrepreneurs operating within the education sector may encounter obstacles in the implementation of simulation technologies. Substantial development expenses, the necessity for specialized technical knowledge, and the demand for a resilient infrastructure may present considerable obstacles. To address these challenges, educators ought to explore collaborations with technology providers in order to leverage shared resources and expertise (Embarak, 2022).

A significant challenge in the integration of simulation tools in educational settings is the technical barriers encountered by both students and institutions. The effective utilization of these tools typically necessitates substantial bandwidth, modern computing hardware, and consistent access to reliable internet connections. Consequently, many distance learners, particularly those residing in rural regions or from economically disadvantaged backgrounds, may experience difficulties in meeting these technological prerequisites. Enhancing Accessibility and Mobile Optimization: In order to address existing barriers, educational institutions should consider adopting simulation platforms specifically designed for mobile devices and low-bandwidth settings (Embarak, 2022).

By utilizing mobile-optimized simulation tools that demand fewer resources, institutions can significantly improve accessibility for a broader range of users. Institutional Support: Educational institutions, including schools and universities, ought to provide comprehensive technical assistance, which may encompass video tutorials, help desks, and discussion forums, to facilitate students' effective access to and utilization of simulation tools. Furthermore, the provision of computer lab facilities or loan programs for students who do not possess the requisite technological resources can serve to alleviate this challenge (Embarak, 2022).

A notable challenge is the financial burden associated with high-quality simulation tools. Numerous platforms require licensing fees that may be prohibitively expensive for both educational institutions and students. This issue is particularly pressing in the context of distance education, where institutions may be reluctant to allocate funds towards costly software in the absence of assured returns on investment. A viable strategy involves leveraging open-source and freemium simulation tools. Numerous high-quality platforms provide complimentary versions or discounted pricing for educational applications (Embarak, 2022).

Educational institutions have the opportunity to engage in negotiations for collective licensing agreements with vendors or to share resources with partner institutions, thereby mitigating individual expenditure. Furthermore, partnerships between universities and simulation developers can facilitate the creation of more cost-effective and customized solutions.

8. CONCLUSION

The integration of simulation tools into distance education programs focused on entrepreneurship entails several challenges, including technical obstacles, financial constraints, difficulties in student engagement, and complexities in assessment.

Facilitating collaboration among remote learners is fundamental to the development of a stimulating and effective online educational environment. By leveraging digital technologies, implementing structured group activities, and employing clear communication strategies, students are enabled to collaborate efficiently, cultivate essential teamwork skills, and foster a robust sense of community. These elements are vital for their success in both academic and professional contexts. In disciplines such as entrepreneurship, where collaborative efforts are integral to business achievement, gaining proficiency in virtual teamwork equips students to address the real-world challenges they will encounter in their future endeavors.

Nevertheless, the challenges can be addressed through the adoption of strategies such as the utilization of open-source software, the provision of adequate training, the implementation of competency-based assessment methods, and the incorporation of communication technologies. Simulation tools represent a potent mechanism for facilitating experiential learning in entrepreneurship education, and with careful implementation, they have the potential to substantially improve learning outcomes in distance education contexts.

In summary, the utilization of these tools—whether they be simulations, collaborative platforms, or immersive experiences—offers significant experiential learning opportunities that facilitate the integration of theoretical knowledge with practical application. When employed effectively, these tools can enhance student engagement, foster critical thinking, and promote the development of practical skills within the context of online entrepreneurship education.

REFERENCES

Abdullah, S. H., Rahim, M. S., & Zakaria, N. (2017). Riding the practice of technopreneur development: Innovative entrepreneurial teaching and learning in institutes of higher learning. *International Journal of Economic Research, 14*(15), 213–219.

Amundam, D. N. (2019). Enhancing potential social innovative thinking, responsibility, social entrepreneurship education: A curriculum content and teaching method model. *Journal of Entrepreneurship Education, 22*(5).

Castaldi, L., Sepe, E., Turi, C., & Iscaro, V. (2020). An experiential learning program for entrepreneurship education. *Global Business & Economics Review, 22*(1), 178–197. DOI: 10.1504/GBER.2020.105050

Dal, M., Elo, J., Leffler, E., Svedberg, G., & Westerberg, M. (2016). Research on pedagogical entrepreneurship-a literature review based on studies from Finland, Iceland and Sweden. *Education Inquiry, 7*(2), 159–182. DOI: 10.3402/edui.v7.30036

Embarak, O. H. (2022). Internet of Behaviour (IoB)-based AI models for personalized smart education systems. *Procedia Computer Science, 203*, 103–110. DOI: 10.1016/j.procs.2022.07.015

Haderer, B., & Ciolacu, M. (2022). Education 4.0: Artificial intelligence assisted task- and time planning System. *Procedia Computer Science, 200*, 1328–1337. DOI: 10.1016/j.procs.2022.01.334

Iborra, A., Álvarez, B., Sánchez, P., Pastor, J. A., & Suárez, T. (2016). ICT entrepreneurial ecosystem for engineering education. *International Journal of Engineering Education, 32*(5), 2033–2047.

Liu, F., Ma, J., & Li, R. (2019). Which role model is more effective in entrepreneurship education? An investigation of storytelling on Individual's entrepreneurial intention. *Frontiers in Psychology, 10*, 837. [REMOVED HYPERLINK FIELD]DOI: 10.3389/fpsyg.2019.00837 PMID: 31068853

Lloyd, R., Martin, M. J., Hyatt, J., & Tritt, A. (2019). A cold call on work-based learning: A "live" group project for the strategic selling classroom. *Higher Education. Skills & Work-Based Learning, 9*(3), 329–346. DOI: 10.1108/HESWBL-12-2017-0098

Middleton, K. W., & Donnellon, A. (2019). Personalizing entrepreneurial learning: A pedagogy for facilitating the know why. *Entrepreneurship Research Journal, 4*(2), 167–204. DOI: 10.1515/erj-2013-0040

Nabi, G., Liñán, F., Fayolle, A., Krueger, N., & Walmsley, A. (2017). The impact of entrepreneurship education in higher education: A systematic review and research agenda. *Academy of Management Learning & Education, 16*(2), 277–299. DOI: 10.5465/amle.2015.0026

Petridou, E., & Sarri, K. (2011). Developing "Potential Entrepreneurs" in Higher Education Institutes. *Journal of Enterprising Culture, 19*(1), 79–99. DOI: 10.1142/S0218495811000647

Piperopoulos, P. (2012). Could higher education programmes, culture and structure stifle the entrepreneurial intentions of students? Journal of Small Business and Enterprise Rahman, H., & Day, J. (2015). Involving the entrepreneurial role model: A possible development for entrepreneurship education. *Journal of Entrepreneurship Education, 18*(1), 86–95.

Stefanic, I., Campbell, R. K., Russ, J. S., & Stefanic, E. (2020). Evaluation of a blended learning approach for cross-cultural entrepreneurial education. *Innovations in Education and Teaching International*, *57*(2), 242–254. DOI: 10.1080/14703297.2019.1568901

Toledano, N., & Urbano, D. (2008). Promoting entrepreneurial mindsets at universities: A case study in the south of Spain. *European Journal of International Management*, *2*(4), 382–399. DOI: 10.1504/EJIM.2008.021244

Wang, Z. (2023). Online language education recommendation based on personalized learning and edge computing. *Internet Technology Letters*, *2*, e408.

Wei, X., Liu, X., & Sha, J. (2019). How does the entrepreneurship education influence the students' innovation? Testing on the multiple mediation model. *Frontiers in Psychology*, *10*, 1557. [REMOVED HYPERLINK FIELD]DOI: 10.3389/fpsyg.2019.01557 PMID: 31354574

Williamson, B., Macgilchrist, F., & Potter, J. (2023). Re-examining AI, automation and datafication in education. *Learning, Media and Technology*, *48*(1), 1–5. DOI: 10.1080/17439884.2023.2167830

Chapter 5
Integrating Sustainable Corporate Performance into Entrepreneurship Education

Aristi Karagkouni
https://orcid.org/0000-0003-4596-8069
Democritus University of Thrace, Greece

ABSTRACT

The landscape of entrepreneurship education is rapidly evolving to address pressing global challenges, emphasizing the need for sustainable corporate performance alongside profitability. This chapter explores the integration of sustainability into entrepreneurship education, focusing on the transformative role of simulation tools. By embedding sustainability principles into curricula, simulations bridge the gap between theory and practice, fostering competencies in ethical leadership, strategic decision-making, and innovation. Through case studies and analysis, the chapter highlights the benefits of sustainability-focused learning, identifies key challenges such as resource constraints and interdisciplinary collaboration, and proposes strategies for long-term integration. Future directions emphasize the adoption of emerging technologies, global partnerships, and inclusive approaches to prepare students as leaders who prioritize sustainable development while achieving business success.

INTRODUCTION

Entrepreneurship education is part of a rapidly changing world system, increasingly confronted with economic, social, and environmental challenges. Courses in entrepreneurship, in the past, targeted the more classical aspects of business creation: market analyses, financial planning, and management control. These are still relevant, but the rapidly changing needs of global markets need an approach that is both wider and more integrated. Contemporary entrepreneurs are increasingly judged not only by their ability to generate profit but also by their responsibility in managing environmental resources and contributing

DOI: 10.4018/979-8-3693-9040-5.ch005

to social welfare, which reflects the worldwide transition towards sustainability (Dimitriou et al., 2024; Kuckertz & Wagner, 2010).

Within this rapidly changing landscape, sustainability has emerged as a crucial element of contemporary business strategy, reshaping the criteria used to assess corporate performance. Stakeholders, including investors, consumers, and regulatory bodies, are placing greater importance on Environmental, Social, and Governance (ESG) metrics as essential factors influencing the enduring success of corporations (Clark, Feiner, & Viehs, 2015). On this point, research evidence has constantly shown that companies committed to sustainability ensure better financial performance, stakeholder trust, brand loyalty, and flexibility in times of market turbulence. Bansal & DesJardine (2014) suggest that all these changes in the nature of the business indicate a shift in what constitutes business success and thus calls for a different approach to entrepreneurship education.

Entrepreneurship curricula often fail to include sustainability as an integral part of business strategy, which is increasingly tied to corporate performance. Corporate performance today is not solely measured by financial success but by a firm's ability to align economic, social, and environmental objectives. Investors, consumers, and regulatory bodies now use Environmental, Social, and Governance (ESG) metrics to assess corporate performance, making sustainability a crucial component of long-term business viability (Clark, Feiner, & Viehs, 2015). However, many educational programs continue to treat sustainability as an isolated topic rather than embedding it within core entrepreneurship training (Russo, 2003). This fragmented approach prevents students from understanding the link between sustainability and corporate success, leaving them unprepared for a market where balancing financial, environmental, and social goals is a determinant of competitive advantage. Most of the freshly emerging entrepreneurs face problems due to a lack of preparedness to address a business environment that is increasingly being expected to balance economic returns with social and environmental responsibility (Porter & Kramer, 2011; Rosario and Raimundo, 2022). To be able to achieve such, a paradigmatic change in education is needed, focusing on sustainability as one of the areas of competence in entrepreneurship education, linking theory and practice.

Simulation tools represent a whole different direction in the resolution of this problem. These tools create an immersive, interactive learning environment to provide learning experiences to students that are very similar to real-life decision-making scenarios. Simulations afford learners the chance to explore the correlation between profitability and sustainability, enabling them to trial various strategies that encompass the reduction of carbon footprints, ethical sourcing practices, and endeavors associated with corporate social responsibility (Bocken et al., 2014). Additionally, these tools introduce students to crucial Environmental, Social, and Governance (ESG) metrics, thus fostering an understanding of the significance of sustainability in attaining long-term corporate success (Dimitriou & Karagkouni, 2022). Sustainability introduced via entrepreneurship education through simulation tools befits other wider international initiatives aimed at the adoption of responsible business behavior.

For example, the United Nations SDGs stress the role of innovation and entrepreneurship in addressing some of the most pressing global challenges, such as climate change, resource constraints, and social injustice (United Nations, 2015). Such philosophies, when included in the curriculum, would ultimately provide educators with an avenue to prepare students with the capacity to develop economically viable business models that were socially and environmentally sensitive.

This chapter explores the imperative role of inclusion of sustainable corporate performance that has a place in entrepreneurship education, enabled through the transformative power of simulation tools. This chapter will discuss the theoretical basis of sustainability in the business perspective, benefits derived from simulations in learning, and challenges of adopting such an approach in existing structures of education. Converse to this, this chapter points out, through cases and practical suggestions, that sustainability-focused simulations could actually foster an entrepreneurial mindset oriented toward ethical leadership, innovation, and the creation of long-term value.

It then goes on to outline how sustainability moved from a peripheral issue to one of the key concerns for companies today. The next section covers a number of pedagogic values of simulation tools in bringing both practice-based learning and strategic thinking together. Further sections develop the range of practical approaches from case and curriculum design to embedding sustainability into entrepreneurship courses. This chapter, therefore, tries to develop an integrative framework for sustainable entrepreneurship education that will help educators develop the required set of skills and mindset in students to lead effectively amidst increasingly interdependent economic, social, and ecological challenges.

Thus, the chapter contributes significantly to the fast-growing debate concerning the intersection between sustainability and entrepreneurship and underlines the need for educational innovation in preparing the next generation of business leaders. As global challenges evolve, it is, therefore, necessary that the approach to entrepreneurial capacity-building do so in a manner that future leaders, besides achieving marketplace success, really bring in considerable and sustainable changes to their communities and beyond.

BACKGROUND

In the present corporate world, the demands by stakeholders have increased, which have driven organizations to take social and environmental issues into consideration simultaneously with maintaining financial health. Stakeholders, including consumers, investors, and regulatory bodies, increasingly expect firms to make positive impacts on major global issues like climate change, social inequality, and resource depletion (Bansal & DesJardine, 2014). From a peripheral concern to a core business strategy, sustainability now permeates into the firms' decision-making processes at all levels. In view of the important contribution of entrepreneurship to economic development, understanding and integrating the concept of sustainability within entrepreneurial activities is increasingly indispensable for new entrepreneurs.

The business concept of sustainability is thus based on the rationale of the triple bottom line, which allows balancing economic, environmental, and social results (Elkington, 1997). Those entrepreneurs who will take on this model can place their companies as leaders in innovation while building stakeholder trust at the same time. Recent literature indeed suggests that companies with sound sustainability performance usually outperform their peers and are even more able to resist economic decline than their peers (Clark, Feiner, & Viehs, 2015). A growing body of evidence underlines a need to embed sustainability in entrepreneurship education in order to prepare students for the demands of the markets today. Research suggests that businesses with strong sustainability strategies demonstrate higher financial resilience, improved brand reputation, and greater stakeholder trust (Clark et al., 2015). Furthermore, scholars argue that entrepreneurship education must align with sustainability goals to address global challenges such as climate change, resource management, and ethical business practices (Bocken et al., 2014; Stubbs & Cocklin, 2008). As regulatory frameworks and consumer expectations continue to evolve, embedding sustainability into entrepreneurship curricula ensures that students are equipped to navigate these shifts and develop ventures that align with both economic and societal needs (Kuckertz & Wagner, 2010; United Nations, 2015). There are considerable risks for entrepreneurs who fail to include sustainability in their business strategy. Regulation pressures, changing consumer preferences, and increased investor scrutiny may threaten the going concern status of those businesses that have failed to consider environmental and social concerns (Kucketz & Wagner, 2010).

Industries based on activities seen as unsustainable-whether through overexploitation of natural resources or labor-face increasing prospects of litigation or reputational loss, thus affecting market value and stakeholder confidence. The competitive environment is shifting too: organizations perceived to be helping solve the global challenges-and, by implication, those leaving unsustainable operations-are competitively rewarded. Disregarding sustainability further constrains the potential for innovation. Those entrepreneurs who retain a narrow focus on short-term economic returns miss the opportunity to explore novel approaches that may meet the needs of the market but also societal challenges more effectively. Sustainability-driven innovation-renewable energy technologies, circular economy business models, and social impact ventures offer entrepreneurs different pathways to differentiation and long-term value creation (Bocken et al., 2014). It follows then that entrepreneurship education should equip students with the competencies to identify and leverage such opportunities.

Aligning Entrepreneurship Education with Global Sustainability Goals

The worldwide move to make the world sustainable is encapsulated in initiatives such as the SDGs, set by the United Nations, which stipulate guidelines for addressing issues ranging from poverty and hunger to climate action and sustainable consumption (United Nations, 2015). In addition, entrepreneurs play an important role in promoting such goals through the creation of novel approaches that balance economic development with the social and environmental demands of human civilization. To play this role, they need an education that embeds the principles of sustainability at the heart of entrepreneurial training.

Traditionally, education in entrepreneurship emphasizes competencies such as market research, financial modeling, and operational management. Nonetheless, these skills are inadequate in fully preparing students for the complexities of contemporary business, where decision-making must consider environmental limitations, ethical implications, and the expectations of various stakeholders (Russo, 2003; UNESCO, 2021). The integration of sustainability into the education framework ensures that students acquire the key tools necessary for such a challenging context and align their entrepreneurial activities with general social objectives.

A fundamental aspect of integrating sustainability education into entrepreneurship is the instruction of students regarding Environmental, Social, and Governance (ESG) metrics. These metrics offer a systematic framework for assessing and articulating a firm's sustainability performance, which includes aspects such as carbon emissions, diversity and inclusion, and governance transparency (Dimitriou et al., 2024). The rising utilization of these metrics by investors and various stakeholders to evaluate the long-term sustainability of enterprises underscores their importance as a crucial instrument for entrepreneurs.

Educators are in a place where they can use ESG metrics to teach students the ways in which sustainability impacts financial performance and stakeholder trust. For example, case studies and simulations can show how trade-offs and synergies between short-term profitability and long-term sustainability exist. Students, by cognizing such dynamics, develop the capability to make well-informed, balanced decisions that comply with both business objectives and societal expectations.

With global problems such as climate change and social inequalities manifesting themselves, the needs for sustainable entrepreneurs have gradually increased, thus putting pressure on entrepreneurship education to answer the call of the situation by the introduction of these concepts into the curriculum and emphasizing the significance of sustainability to business success. This will surely enable educators to help students become business leaders of enterprises that are economically viable and provide positive contributions to society.

Benefits of Integrating Sustainability into Entrepreneurship Education

The integration of sustainability into entrepreneurship education holds multifaceted benefits that enhance both the learning experience and the ensuing competence acquired. These benefits go beyond the classroom and will provide future entrepreneurs with ways of maneuvering through a quickly evolving business landscape, where social and environmental concerns are at the core.

In return, entrepreneurs embracing sustainability are well-positioned in light of rising consumer and investor demands, among others. Today, consumers are becoming increasingly selective, definitely favoring those showing environmental and social accountability. In a 2015 Nielsen survey, 73% of global consumers would consider changing their consumption patterns to reduce environmental harm, while 49% of those purchase products that have been labeled as sustainable (Nielsen 2015). This, therefore, is a great market opportunity that awaits entrepreneurs whose business model incorporates sustainability.

Companies that engage in environmental certification-for instance, Fair Trade or B Corporation recognition-can often see benefits. They expose their commitment to sustainability and build brand loyalty. Students who are taught to put such practices into their businesses position themselves to take advantage of such widely trending trends. This makes them more attractive to increasingly ethically-minded consumers. Entrepreneurship education with emphasis on sustainability entails that students understand how to align their ventures with market expectations and thus enhance their competitiveness and profitability.

Sustainability-driven business models are innate to reduce all kinds of risk from environmental and economic shocks. In this respect, entrepreneurs who focus on resource efficiency, renewable energy, and sustainable supply chains can adapt more quickly to various changes, such as sudden regulatory changes, resource depletion, and natural disasters. In fact, studies have proved that companies applying sustainability are less likely to experience supply chain disruption due to their diversified and localized raw materials (Bocken et al., 2014; Abbas and Bulut; 2024).

For instance, during the outbreak of COVID-19, organizations that featured resilience in supply chains and sustainability strategies responded better. Entrepreneurship training that integrates sustainability concepts shows students how to create systems that would survive such interruptions, building resilience that perpetuates long-term business success. Simulations and case studies help to illustrate, quite vividly, just how sustainability practices help an organization stabilize its processes, further helping students appreciate the importance of taking pre-emptive action on mitigating risks.

It nurtures a perspective of ethical leadership, which is characterized by openness, responsibility, and social justice, through sustainable entrepreneurship education. There is a growing expectation that entrepreneurs should efficiently manage companies for the prosperity of employees, customers, and society in general, as well as shareholders. Ethical leadership is of particular importance for handling issues that concern systems, such as labor exploitation, inequality, and ecological destruction (Freeman et al., 2007).

Ethical dilemma simulations will involve students through a series of simulations ranging in how to balance cost-cutting efforts and continuing to treat workers fairly. These opportunities will foster the development of critical thinking skills and develop knowledge about the impact business decisions have on society. The knowledge of sustainability measures also entails understanding gender diversity ratios and carbon footprint analysis so that students will be prepared to manage responsibly. By promoting these principles, entrepreneurship education shapes leaders who can navigate complex moral landscapes with integrity (Chandel, 2023).

The challenges created by sustainability create niche opportunities for entrepreneurial innovations. Finding ways to handle waste, renewable energy, and social inequality can be very innovative since these may require devising new ways of solving a problem. Companies such as Tesla and Beyond Meat have disrupted entire industries with their sustainable version of fossil fuel and animal-based commodities. These are just a few examples of how sustainability might spur innovative business ideas.

Identification and subsequent action towards the unmet needs in society are triggered in students through education in sustainable entrepreneurship. Areas such as pragmatic projects in biodegradable packaging, saving water technology, and low-income housing can be explored. These programs will eventually prepare the student for success as a leader in the sustainability-oriented industry by providing them with a venue for experimentation and creativity.

The benefits of integrating sustainability into entrepreneurship education are interconnected and provide a holistic framework for student development. Increased market relevance enhances resilience because business efforts will be in line with emerging consumer needs and changes in regulations. Ethical leadership builds trust and loyalty in different categories of stakeholders; hence, the strong market position. Innovation culture fosters the creation of value propositions at the same time, enhancing the resilience of an organization.

These synergies outline the high transformative potential of sustainability education within entrepreneurship curricula. Working through these dimensions, educators will be able to build entrepreneurial leaders capable of thriving in the cutthroat environment yet remaining committed to facilitating effective social transformation.

Challenges in Teaching Sustainability in Entrepreneurship

While there is an increasing awareness that sustainability is an integral part of entrepreneurship in the present context, translation of the same into education systems seems to present a lot of challenges. Such challenges are systemic in nature: deficits in curriculum, resource-related issues, and interdisciplinarity of the subject of sustainability. It is very important that educators understand such barriers while developing programs aimed at preparing successful, sustainability-conscious entrepreneurs.

One significant issue relating to the teaching of sustainability in entrepreneurship education refers to the fragmented inclusion of issues of sustainability in curricula. Many programs handle sustainability as a discrete topic that is unrelated to core business subjects like business strategy, financial planning, and innovation management, among others (Russo, 2003; Diepolder et al., 2021). This compartmental approach makes for less understanding of sustainability as an integral part of business operations and strategic decisions.

For instance, while the students may learn about environmental ethics, they hardly get to apply the same learning to some practical business scenarios. For learners to internalize how sustainability relates to entrepreneurship, a coherent framework that inculcates sustainability within the learning along with the progression of the curriculum is lacking. It's supposed to mean changes in the whole system, embedding sustainability issues right at the forefront of market analysis to product development in the entrepreneurial education process.

Another major barrier toward moving sustainability education in entrepreneurship forward is the pervasive lack of standardized metrics by which to measure both student learning and business outcomes. In companies, ESG metrics, which tap into issues such as carbon footprint, diversity and inclusion, and governance, have been widely used to measure sustainability performance (Clark, Feiner, & Viehs, 2015). However, adapting these metrics to academia is no small task. For example, student learning about matters of sustainability is commonly assessed through qualitative measures, like essay or presentation, and is thus liable to subjective and inconsistent judgments. In most entrepreneurship programs, students have little or no practical experience with metrics concerning sustainability; they would, therefore, be equally unprepared for the actual practical use of such tools. The development of consistent frameworks in teaching and assessment in the area of sustainability will be critical to close the gap.

Sustainability is also inherently inter-disciplinary, drawing significant lessons from disciplines such as environmental science, economics, sociology, and policy studies. This multiplicity of perspectives also presents another challenge for the entrepreneurship educator who may not have the skills or facilities to accommodate such diversity in the classroom environment. As Shrivastava (1995) noted, the conventional structures of academic institutions are generally hostile to inter-disciplinary approaches, and this puts further constraints on any attempts to give the students a well-rounded education in sustainability. For instance, courses to be taught in renewable energy technologies may equally be taught by faculty members coming from either engineering departments or those dealing with the circular economy framework. This does not often happen in real life due to conflicts in the schedule among faculties, financial resources, and the general silo approach adopted by the institutions. These barriers will only be overcome by a conscious effort toward interdisciplinary collaboration, which could be encouraged via course offerings, research projects, and combined teaching arrangements.

Sustainability is also a very dynamic field since practices, technologies, and regulations change continuously. There is an increasing number of things that an entrepreneur must keep pace with: new carbon accounting methods, changing renewable energies, and emerging consumer trends. Entrepreneurship education often cannot keep pace with these, and therefore it provides outdated or irrelevant curricula (Kuckertz & Wagner, 2010). For example, it's teaching students about sustainability initiatives that are no longer widely adopted. Linear recycling models are giving way to circular economy strategies; skills students may gain could already be out of step with today's industry. Given that this is a fact, educators should make it a point to have continuous communication with industry leaders so their course content is always current and relevant. Furthermore, the integration of adaptive learning technologies, especially AI-powered simulation tools, enables students to engage with state-of-the-art, advanced practices in sustainability in a timely manner.

Finally, a balance has to be struck between going down to a depth of sustainability without turning it into something too far out of reach for students who have no prior exposure to the subject. Sustainability is a large, interdisciplinary field ranging from global climate policies down to renewable energy science. Providing that knowledge within an entrepreneurship curriculum means summarizing those concepts without losing nuance or importance. For example, it is relevant to student learning to know basic carbon accounting; for students not from environmental studies, it can be too much to know about too many complicated technical aspects. The trick is designing the curriculum to support an obvious, general focus in the principles of sustainability while providing the option to delve more deeply into content via electives, projects, or individual study. Despite the clear necessity for sustainability in entrepreneurship education, several obstacles hinder its effective integration. These challenges include the gap between theoretical sustainability concepts and practical business application, resource constraints in implementing sustainability-focused curricula, resistance to change among faculty and institutions, and the complexity of interdisciplinary collaboration. Additionally, keeping curricula up to date with evolving sustainability standards, standardizing sustainability metrics for education, and incorporating global perspectives all present further difficulties. These challenges must be addressed to ensure that students gain the knowledge and competencies necessary to develop and manage sustainable business ventures. The next section presents strategies to overcome these barriers, providing solutions that enhance the effectiveness of sustainability education in entrepreneurship programs.

Strategies for Effective Sustainability Education

Addressing these challenges associated with integrating sustainability in entrepreneurship education requires an innovative, collaborative, and multilevel approach that combines innovation, collaboration, and institutional change. Targeted strategies are those enabling educators to fill existing curricular, metric, resource, and interdisciplinary collaboration gaps and provide the necessary skills and frames of mind for students to become sustainable entrepreneurs. The key strategies for overcoming the challenges mentioned above and enhancing effective sustainability education are presented in the figure below.

Figure 1. Key strategies for effective sustainability education (Authors' own work)

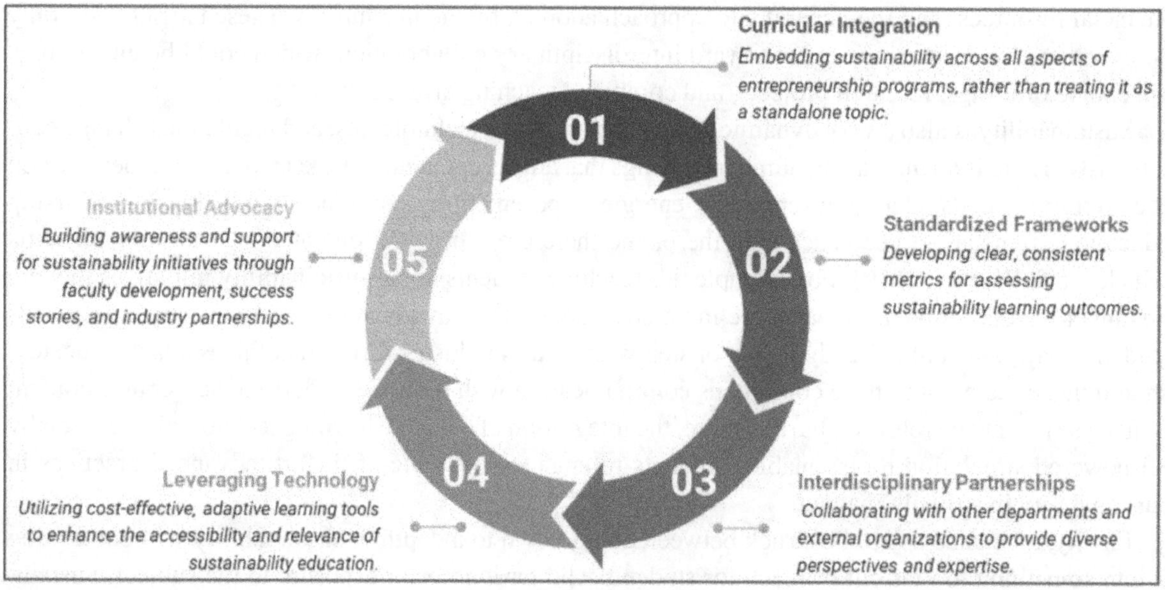

Curricular Integration

Therefore, integration across the curriculum would be another very effective method of integrating sustainability into entrepreneurship education. It does not stand on its own as a specific subject or an elective; it has to be integrated into core courses in business strategy, marketing, financial planning, and innovation management. This approach ensures that students recognize sustainability not merely as a standalone concern, but as a fundamental component of entrepreneurial success (Russo, 2003). For instance, sustainability principles can be integrated into case studies, simulations, and exercises related to business model development, demonstrating their importance in real-world decision-making scenarios. Also, project-oriented learning-developing sustainable business strategies or participation in sustainability-oriented community projects-would be allowed for students to transform theoretical knowledge into the solution of real problems. In this respect, entrepreneurship education shall develop deep understanding about the role of sustainability and eventually create a mindset focused on long-term value creation.

Standardized Frameworks

One other necessary method pertains to the development of uniform structures toward the assessment of sustainability learning outcomes. In the business world, ESG metrics are tools for measuring the performance of sustainability; these tools, however, are often too complicated or too specialized to be used in an academic setting directly (Clark, Feiner, & Viehs, 2015). It becomes necessary for instructors to adapt these structures in a manner that allows for the creation of metrics that are both rigorous yet reachable for students. Traditional assessment criteria may be how quantitatively students are able to analyze the sustainability impact of a business model, create innovative resolutions to environmental or social challenges, or apply ESG metrics in a decision-making context. Applying standard frameworks allows clarity and consistency; educators can grade objectively how well students understand and apply sustainability concepts in practice.

Interdisciplinary Partnerships

Sustainability possesses an inherently interdisciplinary nature, necessitating contributions from various domains, including environmental science, economics, sociology, and policy studies. In order to tackle this intricate issue, entrepreneurship curricula should deliberately promote interdisciplinary collaborations that unite a range of expert knowledge. Interdepartmental cooperation—specifically among business, engineering, and environmental science—can enhance the educational experience by equipping students with a well-rounded comprehension of the challenges and solutions associated with sustainability (Shrivastava, 1995). To this end, interdisciplinary curriculum development might allow education in renewable energy technologies to be combined with business-oriented discussion of market strategies relevant to a clean energy startup. Similarly, cooperative projects with external partners-which may involve nonprofit organizations as well as industry partners-place students in real-world situations where they tackle actual problems related to sustainability and learn from practitioners outside of academia.

Leveraging Technology

The embedding of technology, especially simulation tools, is one of the strong ways to overcome some of the challenges hitherto associated with sustainability education. Simulations provide a safe and interactive environment in which to test sustainability strategies as learners build experience-based learning that is connectedly linked to theory and practice (Bocken et al., 2014). Students can model, for example, the economic impact of reducing carbon emissions, improving supply chains, or implementing corporate social responsibility programs. Cost-effective and adaptive learning tools, open-source platforms, and AI-powered applications make technologies reach more and more institutions. Technology can help educators provide active learning experiences that deepen students' understanding of sustainability and its relevance to entrepreneurship.

Institutional Advocacy

This will, in the end, be enabled only through a supportive institutional culture. Faculty development programs, workshops, and collaborative forums build in further capacities for instructor integration of sustainability concepts within pedagogical approaches. Generally speaking, it remains important that such institutional leadership oversees the agenda on sustainability and provides resource support, among other features, in promoting faculty and student efforts toward the achievement of this common goal. These stories of alumni businesses solving challenges in sustainability, together with students' successes in various competitions on business model centrality around sustainability, will be incredibly useful in the appeal for more support and engagement. Such in-house advocacy is further enhanced in its message of value about sustainability education through collaborations with industrial and community partners.

By applying these methodologies, educators can confront some of the most significant challenges facing the inculcation of sustainability principles into entrepreneurship education and help develop curricula that will enable students in the future to lead innovative, profitable enterprises that are sensitive to both social and environmental concerns. Many such efforts are part of larger movements toward the reform of business education in light of a changing global context.

SIMULATION TOOLS AS TRANSFORMATIVE TEACHING METHODOLOGIES

Theoretical Benefits of Simulation Tools in Entrepreneurship Education

Simulation tools have emerged as transformative teaching methodologies in entrepreneurship education, offering an experiential learning approach that enhances students' ability to integrate sustainability into business decision-making. Traditional pedagogical methods, such as lectures and case studies, often struggle to convey the dynamic and multifaceted nature of sustainability in entrepreneurship. Simulations, however, provide students with hands-on experiences that replicate real-world business environments, allowing them to test sustainability strategies in a controlled setting. From a theoretical perspective, experiential learning theory (Kolb, 1984) underscores the importance of learning through active engagement rather than passive absorption of information. Simulation tools align with this theory by immersing students in complex decision-making scenarios, enabling them to navigate the trade-offs between financial performance, sustainability metrics, and corporate social responsibility. These tools facilitate systems thinking, an essential competency for sustainable entrepreneurship, as students learn to evaluate the long-term consequences of their decisions rather than focusing solely on short-term profitability (Bocken et al., 2014). Furthermore, simulations bridge the gap between theoretical knowledge and practical application, fostering essential entrepreneurial competencies such as risk assessment, adaptability, and ethical leadership. By incorporating sustainability as a key component of business strategy, these tools ensure that students perceive sustainability not as an external constraint but as a driver of innovation and corporate success (Porter & Kramer, 2011).

Practical Application of Simulation Tools in Entrepreneurship Education

Simulation tools are also a very good way to get to know frameworks like the triple bottom line, which includes economic, environmental, and social objectives, besides ESG metrics. By means of active learning, the student understands the influence of sustainability on the long-term outcome of a company. The empirical literature describes that the most adequate active learning methods ensure very good student learning and engagement, with high motivation and achievement of learning goals, above all for complex and multilevel themes such as sustainability (Kolb, 1984).

There is a wide variety of simulation tools to support entrepreneurship-related sustainability education, and they have been developed to meet different learning objectives. The main categories are: business strategy simulations, sustainability metrics tools, supply chain and operational simulations, and scenario-based learning environments.

Business strategy simulations place students in roles involving real decision-making within a stipulated organization, which needs to achieve a balance between profitability and sustainability. Such resources as The Triple Bottom Line Simulation challenge the course participants with making strategic choices aligned with financial, environmental, and social objectives. In such a direction, the simulation of sustainability metrics focuses on teaching students how to apply and interpret key performance indicators like carbon offsets, water consumption, and ESG scores. Platforms like En-ROADS enable users to model the impact of different sustainability policies that could affect climate outcomes, building a systems-thinking approach toward global problems.

The Supply Chain and Operations simulations model the challenges of managing sustainable supply chains, focusing on ethical sourcing, waste reduction, and logistics optimization. These tools show how decisions in one part of the supply chain can have cascading impacts on overall sustainability performance. References - Porter & Kramer, 2011; Bansal and Knox-Hayes; 2013. On the other hand, scenario-based simulations plunge students into a particular challenge, such as responding to a sustainability crisis or launching a green product. These situations favor creative problem-solving and practical implementation, allowing learners to acquire the necessary competencies for solving real-life sustainability challenges.

The benefits of the simulation tool in entrepreneurship education occur on various fronts: practical and pedagogical. First and foremost, simulations are non-threatening; students can experiment without the prospect of serious consequences. Students can apply certain measures for sustainability, like investments in renewable energies and improved resource use, sans the fear of losing money or damaging their brand. This liberating capacity for experimentation nurtures creativity and innovation, prompting students to explore unconventional approaches to sustainability issues (Bocken et al., 2014; Bruksle et al., 2023).

Simulations dramatically improve learner engagement and knowledge retention. Indeed, studies have found that active learning experiences far surpass traditional lectures in achieving deeper understanding. The more students invest through active engagement in making choices, the more they care about the outcomes, which supports a deeper learning of sustainability-related topics (Kolb, 1984). Moreover, learning through simulation gives feedback in real time; one can see what decisions lead to.

Transformative teaching methodologies in entrepreneurship education focus on reshaping students' perspectives on business success by integrating sustainability into decision-making processes. These methodologies leverage experiential learning techniques, such as simulation tools, case-based problem-solving, and interactive business modeling, to shift students' cognitive frameworks toward sustainability-driven entrepreneurship. Figure 2 illustrates how simulation tools facilitate transformative learning by moving students through a cycle of experiential engagement, reflective observation, conceptual analysis, and practical application (Kolb, 1984). This iterative process allows students to experience the direct consequences of sustainable and unsustainable business decisions, reinforcing the idea that corporate performance is a multidimensional construct that balances economic, social, and environmental objectives. The dynamic interaction between business profitability, regulatory compliance, and ethical decision-making within these simulations fosters a learning environment where sustainability is no longer seen as an external obligation but as a core strategic function of successful entrepreneurship.

Figure 2. Key features of simulation tools as transformative teaching methodologies (Authors' own work)

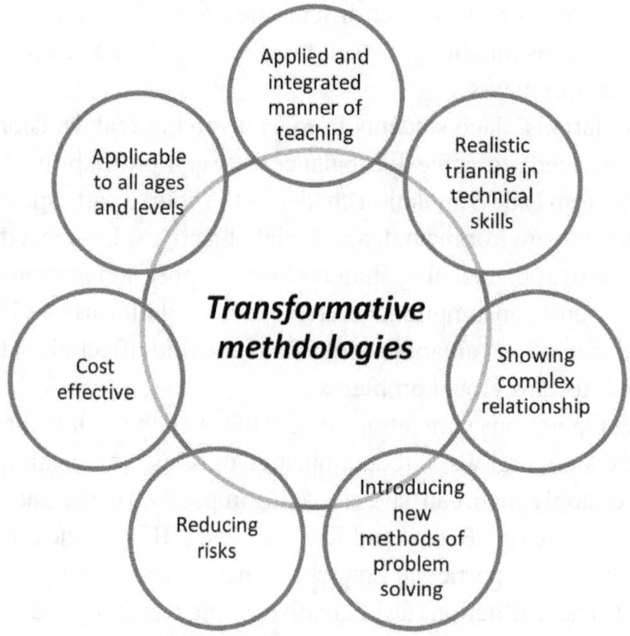

Integrating Simulation Tools into Entrepreneurship Curricula

The effective integration of simulation tools in entrepreneurship education requires planning and consistency with learning objectives. Educators first need to research and select tools which are accessible but relevant to the needs of their students. Easy-to-use platforms that also focus on current sustainability challenges are of particular use because they enable meaningful engagement by students with the subject matter at hand (Clark, Feiner & Viehs, 2015).

Once the relevant tools are identified, the simulations should be integrated into the core course modules. For example, a sustainability-themed simulation can be the capstone project in a business strategy course in which students apply their knowledge in a realistic integrative fashion. The facilitation of reflection and discussion after the simulations would be very helpful. Through an analysis of the decisions made and the outcome, students will further understand their learning processes and the areas that could be improved.

Industry partners can really extend simulation-based learning. The partnerships with businesses, non-profit organizations, and government agencies could make possible the usage of the most up-to-date resources and the most current data possible as students explore different learning situations. For example, partnerships with companies in renewable energy could enable students to model the economic and environmental impacts of making a switch to solar energy.

Although a number of benefits are associated with the use of simulation tools, there are also numerous drawbacks to their adoption. For example, many high-quality simulations require significant financial and technological investments that may be barriers for smaller institutions. Also, keeping simulations current with evolving sustainability knowledge and legislation requires ongoing investment and collaboration with industry experts (Kuckertz & Wagner 2010). Despite these challenges, the opportunity for educational innovation through the use of simulation-based pedagogies is significant. New opportunities for very interactive learning experiences arise with the development of AI and VR. As one simple example, VR simulations may enable students to visit sustainable production facilities virtually and thus have direct exposure to best practice in sustainability. Simulation tools hold great promise for an innovative approach to the teaching of entrepreneurship in sustainability and reducing the gap between theory and practice. These are tools that prepare students for the modern business environment challenges by putting a premium on long-term value creation within interactive and experience-based learning environments. As the demands from entrepreneurship continue to shift, simulation-based education also will increasingly play a crucial role in the shaping of the future generation of leaders.

Embedding Sustainability in Entrepreneurship Education Frameworks

The entrepreneurship curriculum on sustainability will have to be developed around integrative modeling of sustainability issues across learning, using simulation tools to help enhance learning in such a curriculum. Therefore, the gap between conceptual knowledge and practice will be bridged by instilling an entrepreneurial mindset that strives for continuous value creation hand in hand with environmental and social responsibility. With integration within curricula and infusion of activity-based learning methods, business educators would then be better positioned to create those critical competencies needed by students to thrive in today's highly interconnected business environment. The key steps for developing a sustainability embedded entrepreneurship education framework are presented in the figure below.

Figure 3. Key steps for embedding sustainability in entrepreneurship education frameworks (Authors' own work)

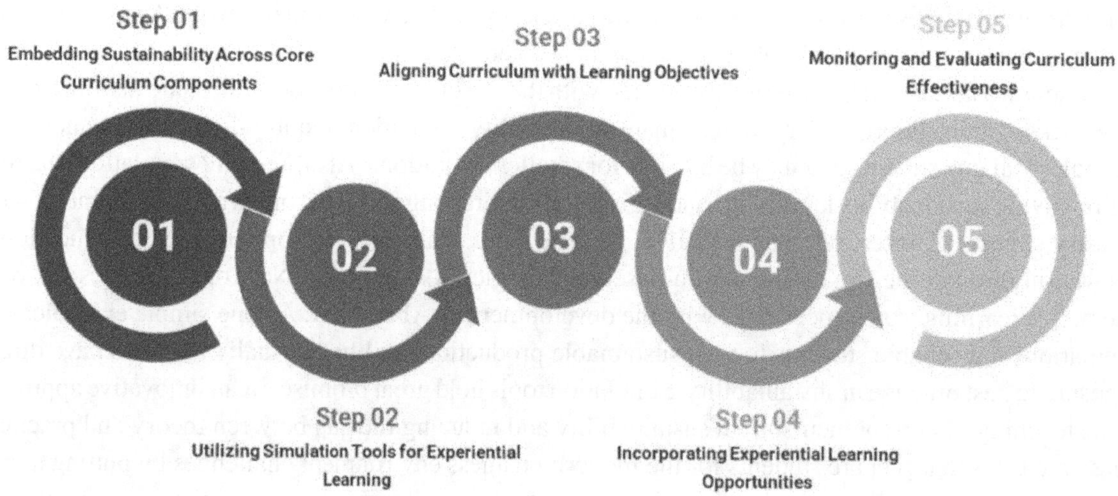

A key ingredient for elaboration of a sustainability-based curriculum lies within incorporating sustainability into core elements of entrepreneurship education, not as an add-on subject. Traditionally, sustainability is presented as a stand-alone course or as an elective; this may have the negative effect of marginalizing the subject and poorly illustrate how it can be related to core entrepreneurial endeavors (Russo, 2003). A really transformational curriculum would center sustainability within the disciplines of business strategy, marketing, operations, and finance. For instance, in business strategy, sustainability would be embedded by challenging students to think of businesses that truly reflect notions of the triple bottom line that balance economic, environmental, and social goals (Elkington, 1997). Students can learn in the marketing classes how green products could be marketed or how corporate social responsibility (CSR) could be communicated more effectively. Similarly, in the operations courses, students can be taught sustainable supply chains, resource efficiency, and waste reduction. By having sustainability embedded within these foundation areas, students take on a holistic perspective with regard to the relevance of sustainability to entrepreneurship and acquire the tools to apply it in diverse business contexts.

Simulation tools are highly relevant for training in sustainability, allowing students to use their imagination in an interactive investigation of realistic problems. Such simulation tools grant students the active learning opportunity in a virtual environment in which one can make decisions, test the consequences, and learn from decisions made in a no-consequence environment. Integration of simulation tools can be structured through the academic program in three distinct phases. The first level involves introductory simulations that aim at orienting the student toward basic ideas in sustainability. For instance, the student may be challenged to apply renewable energy initiatives in a virtual company within a simulation, balancing the goals of the maximization of profit with those of good environmental stewardship. At later stages, he introduces such scenarios as managing sustainable supply chains or solving ethical dilemmas. These simulations assist learners in enhancing their strategic decision-making abilities while concurrently enriching their comprehension of sustainability indicators, including ESG scores and carbon offsets (Clark, Feiner, & Viehs, 2015). It also covers capstone projects in which students will be able to integrate the insights gained from the simulations into viable real-life settings, such as the development of a sustainable startup or the solving of a specific sustainability-related challenge of a partner organization. It thus provides the students with conceptual and practical exposure.

This type of curriculum should refer, in other words, to fully acknowledged learning outcomes, which can be regarded as the shared objects in both entrepreneurial and sustainability education; the needed learning objectives are skills in modeling sustainable business, using relevant analytic tools for sustainability, enhancement of strategic decision making, and fostering responsible leadership behavior. Core competence includes understanding sustainable business models and thus requires a student to develop and evaluate businesses that can combine economic profitability with environmental and social goals. The understanding of the principles of the circular economy model and shared value creation is among such key building blocks and is well captured in the work of Porter and Kramer 2011. Apply sustainability measurements (ESG metrics, life cycle assessments, etc.) to evaluate the sustainability of business operations. Game-based tools are particularly effective in teaching these indicators, as they allow users to virtually experience assessment and improvement of sustainability performance in practice (Bocken et al., 2014). Other key objectives are strategic decision-making skills, since sustainability most often deals with trade-offs and tussles for primacy. Simulation-based learning in resource allocation, response to shifting market dynamics, and interaction with various stakeholders enhance these skills. Finally, the development of ethical leadership will help students to lead organizations with integrity and responsibility. Scenarios such as these, for instance, deciding between cost reductions or paying a fair cost of labor, help students reflect upon high levels of consequences for decision-making.

This is very important in enhancing experiential learning among students in the understanding of sustainability and its linkage with entrepreneurship. Whereas simulation tools are essentially part of an experiential pedagogy, they have to be complemented, where possible, with other opportunities for learning practically. Collaboration with industry is particularly important, since the students will later apply what they have learned in solving real-world problems about sustainability. For instance, students work out a plan with organizations on how to reduce carbon emissions or enhance energy efficiency. These classes complement academic knowledge with real-life learning obtained during the professional work experiences that are integrated within the curriculum. Besides that, sustainability-themed hackathons and business plan competitions are inclusive, allowing students to introduce their new ideas for solving the complex problems that the environment and society face. This encourages innovation and teamwork. Equally present are the internships and fieldwork with organizations that specialize in sustainability, so that students can apply theoretical knowledge in practice, trust in their strengths, and prepare themselves for the challenges of sustainability. Complemented by the use of simulation tools in these experiences, there is full development of a learning environment for the student leaders of sustainability.

Preparing a sustainability-based syllabus is not easy. Serious challenges are posed by the limitation on resources, resistance to change, and the essentially multidisciplinary nature of sustainability. In coping with the challenges, educators can use new approaches and make the best use of resources already available. The use of open-source simulation packages as inexpensive substitutes for commercial simulation packages is one such option. Simulation packages offer flexible simulations that can be used to meet many of the goals of sustainability education with limited high resource costs. Faculty development is also critical; it is necessary for faculty to learn how to incorporate sustainability into their curricula and use the simulation tool in their teaching methods. Professional development initiatives, workshops, and collaborative peer learning networks can assist in enhancing faculty proficiency (Shrivastava, 1995). Furthermore, interdisciplinary collaboration is crucial for addressing knowledge deficiencies and enhancing the curriculum. It allows students to get multiple perspectives through the collaboration of faculty from the environmental science, engineering, and public policy departments, among others. It has allowed more varied and deepened institutional focus on sustainability programs.

Essentially, such a curriculum addressing sustainability issues should be consistently followed through and evaluated for whether it effectively meets its educative objectives. There is a need to consider knowledge acquired about the concept of sustainability, competencies developed through the application of the concept into practice, and overall entrepreneurship competencies. Surveys, reflective essays, and performance measures during simulation activities may also yield valuable insights into student learning outcomes. Pre- and formative assessment could also be complemented with the continuous feedback of industrial partners and alumni in terms of relevance to evolving business and sustainability trends. A continuous improvement approach would allow educators to fine-tune the curriculum to the emerging challenges and opportunities inherent in sustainability education.

COMPETENCIES DEVELOPMENT FOR ETHICAL AND SUSTAINABLE ENTREPRENEURSHIP

Sustainability within entrepreneurship education surpasses being just a theoretically developed initiative; rather, it aims at consciously equipping students with an adequate set of competencies that will help them to function within a highly complex, increasingly oriented business environment towards sustainability. Consequences imply that learning outcomes change from single traditional entrepreneurial competencies to a more sophisticated capability in effectively managing inter-relationships between economic, environmental, and social objectives. This chapter will define the main competence expected to be developed among students, focusing on sustainable business models, integrated strategic decision-making approach, ethical leadership principles and adaptability with regard to innovation.

A key learning objective includes the development of an integrated understanding by the students of sustainable business models and their potential to create long-term value. Traditional business models are mostly designed to maximize short-term financial returns at the expense of the environmental and social impact of their operations. In contrast, sustainable business models adhere to the principles of the triple bottom line, balancing economic profitability with ecological sustainability and social responsibility (Elkington, 1997). Through these fields of study and simulation-focused activities, students will be prepared to propose ventures that address the above interrelated objectives. For example, they might design circular economy business models with goals of minimizing waste and increasing resource utilization or propose business strategies that align with the United Nations' SDGs. These activities prepare learners to develop innovative ventures that are grounded in the imperatives of the market while concurrently helping to solve global sustainability challenges.

Sustainability often involves trade-offs and requires decision-making from long-term perspectives. Among the competencies which a student should achieve is the art of making strategic decisions within complex and multi-dimensional scenarios. Indeed, simulation tools are very useful in developing this competency because students can test various strategies and see an outcome in a controlled environment. For example, a supply chain simulation would have to balance cost efficiency against the ethical consideration of sourcing and its environmental impact. Cases of this kind develop critical analytic skills and promote a system-thinking approach that will let students understand the greater impacts of their decisions regarding organizations and stakeholders. Development of strategic decision-making skills will also enable students to lead the organization toward a focus on profitability along with sustainability.

The most important other skill for sustainable entrepreneurship is the application of measures and metrics for sustainability. In the context of measuring and improving performance in sustainability, significant means are provided through various tools such as the ESG scores, carbon footprint assessment, and life cycle assessment (Clark, Feiner, & Viehs, 2015). However, most of the traditional programs in entrepreneurship have not put in place adequate emphasis on such metrics. These metrics are interpreted and integrated into the processes of business decision-making by the students, who learn through the use of simulation tools and case analyses. For example, in one simulation, students may be tasked with enhancing a company's ESG score by implementing renewable energy strategies or enhancing diversity and inclusion. By working directly with these metrics, the students learn to quantify and articulate the benefits of sustainability initiatives.

Cultivating Ethical Leadership and Innovation

Ethical leadership is a cornerstone of sustainable entrepreneurship that emphasizes accountability, transparency, and justice in decision-making. Entrepreneurship based on ethical considerations will develop better trust among stakeholders and reach further into the future. It is perceived by Freeman et al. (2007). The theoretical and empirical inputs toward a sustainability-based curriculum instill the values mentioned above. Very specifically, the scenario-based simulation is considered a suitable pedagogy for teaching ethical leadership. -Dimitriou (2022). These may include decisions on the trade-off between cost-cutting measures and fair play with employees, or the consideration of shareholder gains in light of community needs. Students will be able to reflect on the broader implications of the decisions they make and will be able to develop skills in moral reasoning which will serve them well in managing activities in an ethical manner.

The challenges associated with sustainability frequently necessitate inventive solutions, thereby rendering creativity and adaptability essential skills for emerging entrepreneurs. It is imperative for students to cultivate the ability to transcend traditional methods, investigating innovative strategies to tackle problems such as resource limitation, climate change, and social disparities (Dimitriou and Karagkouni, 2023). Simulation tools, hackathons, and project-based learning provide platforms for fostering this innovative mindset. For instance, students might be tasked with competing to produce a product that would help lower plastic waste or perhaps present a business model employing renewable energy technologies. This kind of activity gives the students the opportunity to explore new ideas while adjusting to changing market demands; this may help them when placed in any leading position in rapidly changing industries.

The integration of sustainability into entrepreneurship education was meant to develop an overall entrepreneurial mindset that focuses on long-term success rather than short-term gains. The trainees should be empowered to look at their business as part of the big picture and understand how their decisions impact their businesses and society at large, including the environment. Equipped with integrated technical competencies, strategic insight, and ethical principles, this course places students in leading roles that drive sustainable entrepreneurship and allows them to handle current business practice challenges while nurturing a just and sustainable future.

In order to ensure that these learning outcomes are indeed achieved, instructors should develop detailed systems of observation and feedback. Such systems may include reflective essays, group projects, and assessment of performances in simulation activities, among others. Moreover, valuable feedback from students and industry participants provides important information about the effectiveness of the curriculum. Continuous assessment not only helps in sustaining accountability but also highlights areas of improvement that could enable instructors to refine their programs and adapt to emerging trends. Because of paying attention to continuous improvement, educational institutions can provide courses that better prepare students to perform the tasks resulting from sustainable entrepreneurship. Finally, the integration of sustainability into entrepreneurship education gives students a wide range of competencies above traditional business skills. It covers everything from creating sustainable business models to developing ethical leadership. The learning outcomes listed above enable students to drive innovations that are not only innovative and socially relevant but also effective. By underpinning all these competencies, entrepreneurship programs help nurture a cadre of future leaders who would be better positioned to address complex challenges in the 21st century.

INNOVATIVE CASE STUDIES: SUSTAINABILITY IN ENTREPRENEURIAL EDUCATION

Incorporating sustainability simulations into entrepreneurship education represents a major turn towards new pedagogical directions; students have the opportunity to address real-world, complex challenges through activity-based and experiential learning (Nidumolu et al., 2009). This section examines a few examples of how sustainability simulations find effective use in varied educational contexts. Case studies provide important information on how to apply sustainability simulations within an entrepreneurship educational setting to better prepare students with practical knowledge of how complex issues apply to the real world. Such examples show how simulations can be used to develop students' capabilities for strategic decision-making, ethical leadership, innovation, and the use of sustainability metrics. This section further deconstructs how sustainability simulations can bring about considerable change in various industrial and educational settings through the presentation of more in-depth case studies.

Triple Bottom Line Business Strategy Simulation

The Triple Bottom Line Simulation has been used in many entrepreneurship classes to drive the nail home in ensuring the economic, environmental, and social objectives are in balance. One such session was conducted at a top business school where students were given charge of running a virtual company manufacturing and selling food and beverages. The goal was to allocate resources between and amongst power consumption reduction, community contribution, and supply chain streamlining. During the whole simulation, students appreciated the interdependencies of their decisions-for example, investments in renewable energy increased their costs in the short run but considerably improved brand reputation and customer loyalty. Conversely, those teams that focused on cost-cutting measures received regulatory fines and also lost market share as a result of their reputational losses. Student reflections after the simulation showed that they understood that embedding sustainability into business strategy actually creates value long term. This case study highlights the significance of simulations in demonstrating the trade-offs and synergies that are intrinsic to sustainable entrepreneurship (Elkington, 1997).

Climate Policy Simulation

Web-based En-ROADS Climate Policy Simulation: an unprecedented collaboration of Climate Interactive and MIT Sloan to explore how different climate policies can drive economic and environmental outcomes. In one European university, for instance, in one entrepreneurship course, students were formed into teams acting like different kinds of stakeholders-government, businesses, and NGOs-with mandates from each to propose policies that would reduce global warming without necessarily compromising economic stability. During the exercise, the representatives applied various tools: carbon tax, subsidies for renewable energy, afforestation, and so on. Yet another striking point of the integrated taxation policy of highly carbon-emitting sectors with the promotion of green innovation gave the maximum reduction in emission with maintained economic growth. Students also realized how important the role of cooperation and negotiations is: because for one goal, different stakeholder groups needed to reconcile their priorities. The present case study illustrated the importance of systemic thinking and collaboration across different sectors in tackling global sustainability issues (Bocken et al., 2014).

Supply Chain Sustainability in Business Operations

Supply chain management was thus considered a strategic area in which sustainability principles could be applied because of the pervasive impacts of environmental, social, and economic outcomes. In a simulation assignment focused on supply chain sustainability, the students could learn about sourcing, transportation, and production decisions, in addition to managing wastes that impact overall business performance. The exercise challenged the participants to balance the dual objectives of cost efficiency with environmental and social concerns during the management of a virtual company within a competitive market. In this game, students were responsible for choosing suppliers, optimizing logistic solutions, and designing packaging solutions according to Dimitriou et al. (2024) and Goyal et al. (2021).

A variety of suppliers offered different types of trade-offs: some provided lower costs, poor labor, and environmental standards, while others promised rigorous sustainability with a higher cost. In addition, participants were allowed to consider several environmental impacts of transport routes in relation to the carbon footprint of different methods of production. "The team focuses on responsible sourcing through the selection of suppliers who uphold ethics in employment practices, which again ensure that the raw materials used are friendly to the environment. While these decisions initially led to increased production costs, the group realized significant long-term benefits, such as reduced regulatory risks, increased brand equity, and improved customer loyalty. Their focus on sustainability also yielded a rise in the ESG score of their model company, thus attracting investing in social causes and opening up new avenues within the market.

In contrast, teams focusing on cost-reduction strategies based on the selection of suppliers with poor sustainability performance faced significant challenges. These also included public resistance, lower morale among employees, and decreased sales due to the damage their brands suffered. Additionally, the imposition of fines due to non-compliance with environmental legislation hurt their bottom line. The simulation showed financial and reputational risks associated with unsustainable supply chain practices and emphasized the need to include sustainability in supply chain decision-making.

What really drove home the message of innovation in pursuing sustainability within supply chains was this exercise. Teams that incorporated the latest technologies, such as automated logistical systems and biodegradable packaging solutions, really reduced waste while gaining great operational efficiency.

For example, one team rewired its supply chain to include local suppliers and modes of transportation that were energy-efficient, decreasing its carbon footprint significantly while still protecting its delivery schedule and quality of products.

Ethical Decision-Making in Tech Startups

A simulated, realistic intensive situation about ethics dilemmas in technology startups allowed students to experience active and intense learning. Students were in charge of a virtual company that was confronted with the prospect of venture capital investment by a firm notorious for seriously questionable labor practices. Students had to weigh the potential financial benefits of accepting this funding against the ethical and reputational risks involved. The teams that passed on the funding had strong morals, which in the context of the game changed into increased consumer trust and ultimately provided other investors who were far more coherently matched with the values of the company. Teams that took the funding had their brand destroyed and lost employees due to low morale, illustrating the long-term impact of an unethical decision. This case study therefore stressed how significant ethical leadership in entrepreneurship can be, proving that wise decision-making could enhance a firm's continued success due to Freeman et al. (2007) and Dimitriou (2022).

Renewable Energy Transition

The transition to sustainable energy is one of the most important focuses by which an organization can mitigate its harmful influence on the environment without necessarily compromising its economic viability. One of the simulations covered the aspect of sustainable energy transition, whereby students were allowed to handle its complexity and trade-off behind integrating renewable energy options into a business operation-Karagkouni and Dimitriou, 2022; Ordonez-Ponce, 2020. It was a challenge for the participating teams to manage the organization's energy portfolio in view of cost, environmental impact, and operational effectiveness. In this exercise, students looked into a number of different renewable energy options: photovoltaic systems, wind energy converters, and energy storage technologies. Each of these options had its positive and negative sides-the photoelectric systems needed high initial investment but provided savings in the long run, while the wind generation kinds were predictable in their generation but depended on site suitability. The simulation provided a lot of opportunities to adopt energy efficiency measures through retrofitting facilities with energy-efficient technologies, thus integrating it with smart energy management systems. Another team opted for this holistic approach by integrating the installation of solar energy with energy efficiency upgrades, such as LED lighting and automated heating systems. While the costs were significantly high in the beginning, this team had great reductions in their long-term operational expenses, alongside reductions of GHG emissions. Their improved ESG score lured in the socially responsible investors, thereby increasing their competitiveness in the market. Such exercises showcase how the adoption of renewable energy can bring with it real financial and reputational benefits along with helping contribute toward Global Sustainability Goals. Other teams argued for the adoption of a gradual energy transition approach using hybrid systems wherein conventional energy sources could work together with renewable ones.

This minimised disruption to business operations while the firm gradually reduced dependency on fossil fuel sources. Those teams that were slower to invest in renewable sources of energy were penalized during the game, with increased costs of operation due to higher carbon taxes and loss of customer confidence.

Among these key lessons learned through the game was making sure that the approach toward the energy transition aligns with the general business strategy. Companies that incorporated energy transition into the greater corporate system tended to outperform others because of the advantages of taking a unified approach to sustainability: for instance, one of the teams used renewable energy investment in product brand promotion to attract ecologically sensitive consumers and further achieved a strategic advantage.

Social Enterprise Development in Rural Communities

One simulation revolved around social entrepreneurship in the development of business models that would be sustainable for rural communities. Other areas of core prominence on which the participants tried to work included water shortage, unemployment, and food insecurity. One more simulation introduced an irrigation system with solar energy for small-scale farmers, preventing leakage of water and enhancing crop yields. Even this simulation requires the involvement of local stakeholders in identifying funding opportunities and framing a scalable business plan. Teams that emphasized the engagement of stakeholders and the empowerment of communities attained superior results, thereby illustrating the significance of harmonizing business goals with the requirements of the local populace. This case study underscored the function of social enterprises in confronting systemic sustainability issues and accentuated the importance of entrepreneurial innovation within marginalized areas (Shrivastava, 1995). These case studies further show the huge potential of sustainability simulations to contribute to entrepreneurship education in terms of both the necessary practical view and additional pedagogical benefits. The simulations put students into a real situation, developing their competencies in systems thinking, ethical decision-making, and strategic planning. Participants have hands-on practice with such tools as ESG metrics and carbon accounting, which provide them with insights and ways to cope with the complexity of sustainability challenges.

Simulations offer a route into how students can be brought together in stakeholder groups to reconcile conflicting priorities toward achieving shared objectives. Additionally, simulations detail the business case for sustainability by showing how ethical practices reinforce long-term profitability and maintain stakeholder confidence. These observations further emphasize that sustainability-themed simulations should be part of the learning curriculum and enable students to lead creative, ethical efforts toward global sustainability objectives. Analysis of these cases yields several implications concerning the transformational potential of sustainability simulations in entrepreneurship education, as described in the following figure.

Figure 4. Case studies' insights and implications for entrepreneurship education (Authors' own work)

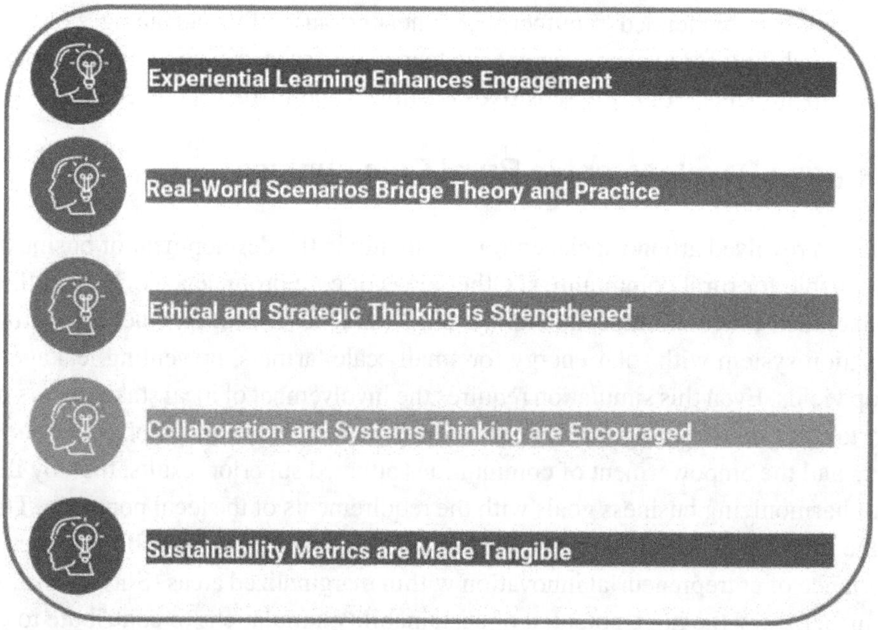

DISCUSSION AND CONCLUSION

The integration of sustainability into entrepreneurship education provides a critical foundation for equipping future business leaders with the competencies needed to navigate an increasingly complex economic and environmental landscape. Sustainability is no longer an optional consideration for businesses; rather, it has become a key driver of corporate performance, influencing profitability, stakeholder trust, and long-term strategic positioning (Clark, Feiner, & Viehs, 2015; Elkington, 1997). Simulation tools have emerged as valuable pedagogical methods, bridging the gap between theory and practice by enabling students to test sustainability-driven business strategies in controlled, experiential learning environments. Grounded in experiential learning theory (Kolb, 1984), simulations provide students with an interactive platform to analyze the impact of their decisions in real-time, fostering essential competencies such as strategic decision-making, risk assessment, and ethical leadership. The case studies presented illustrate the effectiveness of simulations in cultivating an entrepreneurial mindset that prioritizes sustainable business practices, reinforcing the notion that sustainability must be an embedded component of entrepreneurial education rather than an isolated concept (Bocken et al., 2014; Stubbs & Cocklin, 2008).

However, several challenges persist in fully embedding sustainability into entrepreneurship curricula. Resistance to change among faculty and institutions remains a significant obstacle, as many traditional business programs continue to emphasize short-term financial success over long-term corporate responsibility (Kuckertz & Wagner, 2010). The need for interdisciplinary collaboration further complicates this integration, as sustainability requires knowledge spanning business, environmental science, economics, and policy (Shrivastava, 1995). Additionally, resource constraints limit access to sophisticated simulation tools, particularly in institutions with fewer financial and technological resources (Bansal & Knox-Hayes, 2013). Addressing these challenges requires institutional commitment, innovative teaching strategies, and partnerships with industry to ensure that sustainability-focused education remains relevant and accessible. Open-source simulation platforms and cross-disciplinary course development can provide scalable solutions to these issues, ensuring that students receive a comprehensive sustainability education regardless of institutional limitations.

As the business environment continues to evolve, the role of sustainability in entrepreneurship education will only grow in importance. Institutions must take a long-term, strategic approach to embedding sustainability within entrepreneurship curricula, ensuring that students develop the necessary competencies to lead businesses that align profitability with social and environmental goals. The use of simulation tools presents a transformative opportunity to enhance experiential learning, allowing students to engage directly with sustainability-related challenges in a risk-free environment while also preparing them for the evolving expectations of investors, regulators, and consumers (Porter & Kramer, 2011). Sustainability is increasingly being measured using Environmental, Social, and Governance (ESG) metrics, requiring future entrepreneurs to integrate these frameworks into business decision-making (Dimitriou, Karagkouni, & Sartzetaki, 2024). By leveraging simulation tools, students can develop practical expertise in applying ESG principles to business models, ensuring they are prepared for emerging market trends that prioritize sustainability as a core component of corporate performance.

Future research should explore the role of emerging technologies, such as artificial intelligence (AI) and virtual reality (VR), in further enhancing sustainability-focused entrepreneurship education. Advances in these areas could create more immersive learning experiences, allowing students to engage with complex sustainability challenges in more dynamic and realistic settings (Sartzetaki & Dimitriou, 2023). Furthermore, future studies should examine the effectiveness of different simulation methodologies in developing specific entrepreneurial competencies, such as stakeholder management, sustainability reporting, and impact measurement. By continuing to refine sustainability education through technological advancements and pedagogical innovation, entrepreneurship programs can play a pivotal role in shaping the next generation of business leaders committed to creating long-term value for both society and the environment (United Nations, 2015).

REFERENCES

Abbas, M., & Bulut, M. (2024). Navigating the landscape of sustainable entrepreneurship research: A systematic literature review. *Discover Sustainability*, *5*(1), 171. Advance online publication. DOI: 10.1007/s43621-024-00293-4

Bansal, P., & DesJardine, M. R. (2014). Business sustainability: It is about time. *Strategic Organization*, *12*(1), 70–78. DOI: 10.1177/1476127013520265

Bansal, P., & Knox-Hayes, J. (2013). The time and space of materiality in organizations and the environment. *Organization & Environment*, *26*(1), 61–82. DOI: 10.1177/1086026612475069

Bocken, N. M., Short, S. W., Rana, P., & Evans, S. (2014). A literature and practice review to develop sustainable business model archetypes. *Journal of Cleaner Production*, *65*, 42–56. DOI: 10.1016/j.jclepro.2013.11.039

Bruksle, I., Chwallek, C., & Krastina, A. (2023). Strengthening Sustainability in Entrepreneurship Education -Implications for Shifting Entrepreneurial Thinking Towards Sustainability at Universities. *ACTA PROSPERITATIS.*, *14*(1), 37–48. DOI: 10.37804/1691-6077-2023-14-37-48

Chandel, Tarana. (2022). Green Entrepreneurship and Sustainable Development. .DOI: 10.4018/978-1-6684-4666-9.ch009

Clark, G. L., Feiner, A., & Viehs, M. (2015). *From the stockholder to the stakeholder: How sustainability can drive financial outperformance*. Oxford University Press.

Climate Interactive & MIT Sloan. (n.d.). En-ROADS Climate Policy Simulator. Retrieved from https://www.climateinteractive.org/tools/en-roads/

Diepolder, C. S., Weitzel, H., & Huwer, J. (2021). Competence Frameworks of Sustainable Entrepreneurship: A Systematic Review. *Sustainability (Basel)*, *13*(24), 13734. DOI: 10.3390/su132413734

Dimitriou, D. (2022). *Corporate Ethics: an arbitration of philosophical concepts and market practices*. CONATUS, International Journal of Philosophy, Scopus Indexed., DOI: 10.12681/cjp.29864

Dimitriou, D., & Karagkouni, A. (2022). Assortment of Airports' Sustainability Strategy: A Comprehensiveness Analysis Framework. *Sustainability (Basel)*, *14*(7), 4217. DOI: 10.3390/su14074217

Dimitriou D. and Karagkouni A., (2022). Du-diligence of transport infrastructure operators sustainability: a circular economy driven approach, Frondiers in Sustainability: Circular Economy, DOI: https://doi.org/DOI: 10.3389/frsus.2022.916038

Dimitriou, D., & Karagkouni, A. (2023). Appraisal of Critical Infrastructure Corporate Performance Upon Sustainability: An Analysis of Impact in National Branding and Welfare. In Masouras, A., Daskou, S., Pistikou, V., Dimitriou, D., & Friesner, T. (Eds.), *Global Developments in Nation Branding and Promotion: Theoretical and Practical Approaches* (pp. 1–24). IGI Global., DOI: 10.4018/978-1-6684-5902-7.ch001

Dimitriou, D., Sartzetaki, M., & Karagkouni, A. (2024). *Managing Airport Corporate Performance: Leveraging Business Intelligence and Sustainable Transition*. Elsevier., DOI: 10.1016/C2023-0-51427-2

Elkington, J. (1997). *Cannibals with Forks: The Triple Bottom Line of 21st Century Business*. Capstone.

Freeman, R. E., Harrison, J. S., & Wicks, A. C. (2007). *Managing for Stakeholders: Survival, Reputation, and Success*. Yale University Press.

Goyal, D P & Sharma, Sarika & Singh, Archana. (2021). Systematic review on sustainable entrepreneurship education (SME): A framework and analysis" World Journal of Entrepreneurship, Management and Sustainable Development. *World Review of Entrepreneurship, Management and Sustainable Development*, *17*, 372–395.

Karagkouni, A., & Dimitriou, D. (2022). 'Sustainability Performance Appraisal for Airports Serving Tourist Islands'. *Sustainability (Basel)*, *14*(20), 13363. DOI: 10.3390/su142013363

Kolb, D. A. (1984). *Experiential Learning: Experience as the Source of Learning and Development*. Prentice Hall.

Kuckertz, A., & Wagner, M. (2010). The influence of sustainability orientation on entrepreneurial intentions: Investigating the role of business experience. *Journal of Business Venturing*, *25*(5), 524–539. DOI: 10.1016/j.jbusvent.2009.09.001

Morales, B. (2020). Salvador & Martinez-Roig, Rosabel & Hernández-Amorós, María J. (2020). Sustainability and Educational Technology- A Description of the Teaching Self-Concept. *Sustainability (Basel)*, *12*(24), 10309. Advance online publication. DOI: 10.3390/su122410309

Nidumolu, R., Prahalad, C. K., & Rangaswami, M. R. (2009). Why sustainability is now the key driver of innovation. *Harvard Business Review*, *87*(9), 57–64.

Nielsen. (2015). The sustainability imperative: New insights on consumer expectations. Nielsen Global Consumer Survey.

Ordonez-Ponce, E., Clarke, A., & Colbert, B. (2020). Collaborative Sustainable Business Models: Understanding Organizations Partnering for Community Sustainability. *Business & Society*, 1–42. DOI: 10.1177/0007650320940241

Porter, M. E., & Kramer, M. R. (2011). Creating shared value. *Harvard Business Review*, *89*(1/2), 62–77.

Ribeiro, G., & Leitão, J. C. (2024). Sustainable leadership and sustainable entrepreneurship: A systematic literature review. *Discover Sustainability*, *5*(1), 188. Advance online publication. DOI: 10.1007/s43621-024-00383-3

Rosário, A. T., & Raimundo, R. (2024). Sustainable Entrepreneurship Education: A Systematic Bibliometric Literature Review. *Sustainability (Basel)*, *16*(2), 784. DOI: 10.3390/su16020784

Rosário, A. T., Raimundo, R. J., & Cruz, S. P. (2022). Sustainable Entrepreneurship: A Literature Review. *Sustainability (Basel)*, *14*(9), 5556. DOI: 10.3390/su14095556

Russo, M. V. (2003). The emergence of sustainable industries: Building on natural capital. *Strategic Management Journal*, *24*(4), 317–331. DOI: 10.1002/smj.298

Sartzetaki, M., Karagkouni, A., & Dimitriou, D. (2023). A Conceptual Framework for Developing Intelligent Services (a Platform) for Transport Enterprises: The Designation of Key Drivers for Action. *Electronics (Basel)*, *12*(22), 4690. DOI: 10.3390/electronics12224690

Shrivastava, P. (1995). The role of corporations in achieving ecological sustainability. *Academy of Management Review*, *20*(4), 936–960. DOI: 10.2307/258961

Shrivastava, P., & Hart, S. (1995). Creating sustainable value through environmental strategy. *The Academy of Management Perspectives*, *9*(4), 101–119.

Stubbs, W., & Cocklin, C. (2008). Conceptualizing a "sustainability business model". *Organization & Environment*, *21*(2), 103–127. DOI: 10.1177/1086026608318042

Tsironis, G., Karagkouni, A., Dimitriou, D., & Tsagarakis, K. P. (2023). Mapping sustainable practices and concepts in the transportation ecosystem for the EU-27 countries, based on LinkedIn company profiles. *Frontiers in Sustainability*, *4*, 1268575. Advance online publication. DOI: 10.3389/frsus.2023.1268575

United Nations. (2015). Transforming our world: The 2030 Agenda for Sustainable Development. United Nations General Assembly. https://www.un.org/sustainabledevelopment

United Nations Educational, Scientific, and Cultural Organization (UNESCO). (2021). Education for sustainable development: A roadmap. Retrieved from https://www.unesco.org

Xie, H., Qin, Z., & Li, J. (2024). Entrepreneurship and Corporate ESG Performance—A Case Study of China's A-Share Listed Companies. *Sustainability (Basel)*, *16*(18), 7964. DOI: 10.3390/su16187964

Chapter 6
Fostering Entrepreneurial Skills Through Business Simulations:
The Pedagogical Approach of the "Business Simulation-Games" Course

Ioannis Katsanakis
https://orcid.org/0000-0002-3603-5470
University of Piraeus, Greece

ABSTRACT

This chapter explores the integration of simulation-based learning in entrepreneurship and business education through a case study of the 'Business Simulation-Games' course offered at the University of Piraeus. Developed to address the growing need for practical, experiential learning, the course leverages business simulations to provide students with hands-on experience in managing real-world scenarios. The chapter highlights how the course fosters critical skills such as strategic decision-making, risk management, adaptability, and teamwork, all while following Kolb's Experiential Learning Cycle. Key components, including course design, the use of simulation tools, and reflective learning practices, are examined in detail. The chapter also addresses challenges related to technology, pedagogy, and student adaptation, as well as the strategies implemented to overcome them. Finally, the chapter offers practical recommendations for educators interested in adopting simulation-based approaches to enhance entrepreneurial skill development and improve learning outcomes in higher education.

1. INTRODUCTION

1.1. The Importance of Entrepreneurship Education in a Complex Business Landscape

Entrepreneurship education has emerged as a critical component in contemporary educational frameworks, particularly in light of the complexities and dynamism of today's business environment. As economies evolve and face challenges such as globalization, technological advancements, and shifting labor markets, the need for individuals equipped with entrepreneurial skills becomes increasingly

DOI: 10.4018/979-8-3693-9040-5.ch006

paramount. Integrating entrepreneurship education into curricula fosters individual competencies and contributes to broader economic growth and innovation (Aljohani, 2015; Sandirasegarane et al., 2016).

The significance of entrepreneurship education is underscored by its ability to cultivate transferable skills essential in a rapidly changing job landscape. Research indicates that programs combining vocational education and entrepreneurial training can enhance employability and instill enterprising behaviors among youth (Sandirasegarane et al., 2016). This dual approach not only prepares students for traditional employment but also empowers them to pursue entrepreneurial ventures, thereby contributing to local economies and job creation (Salavou et al., 2021; Sandirasegarane et al., 2016). Furthermore, the inclusion of entrepreneurship education in higher education institutions has been linked to increased entrepreneurial intentions among students, particularly in fields such as engineering and technology, where students often exhibit a higher propensity for entrepreneurial engagement when exposed to relevant educational experiences (Maresch et al., 2016; Nguy n et al., 2021).

Moreover, the role of human and cultural capital in fostering entrepreneurial potential cannot be overlooked. Positive role models and early exposure to business-related activities significantly influence students' entrepreneurial aspirations (Jayawarna et al., 2014). By integrating experiential learning opportunities, such as business simulations and real-world projects, educational institutions can enhance students' understanding of entrepreneurship and its practical applications (Pittaway et al., 2011). This experiential approach not only enriches the learning experience but also cultivates essential skills such as creativity, problem-solving, and critical thinking, which are vital for entrepreneurial success (Bell & Bell, 2020).

The effectiveness of entrepreneurship education is further enhanced by considering individual personality traits and psychological characteristics. Studies suggest that certain traits, such as openness to experience and creativity, can significantly impact the effectiveness of entrepreneurship programs in increasing entrepreneurial intentions (Fairlie & Holleran, 2012; Tsaknis et al., 2022). This highlights the importance of tailoring educational approaches to accommodate diverse learner profiles, thereby maximizing the potential benefits of entrepreneurship education (Tsaknis et al., 2022).

In addition, the pedagogical strategies employed in entrepreneurship education play a crucial role in shaping students' entrepreneurial competencies. A shift from traditional teacher-led instruction to more student-centered learning models has been advocated to foster greater engagement and ownership of the learning process (Robinson et al., 2016). This transition not only aligns with contemporary educational philosophies but also reflects the need for a more holistic approach to entrepreneurship education that encompasses cognitive, emotional, and social dimensions (Bell, 2021).

Furthermore, the impact of entrepreneurship education extends beyond individual competencies to encompass broader societal benefits. By nurturing an entrepreneurial mindset, educational programs can contribute to social justice and economic equality, providing individuals with the tools necessary to create their own opportunities and contribute to community development (Du Toit, 2023). This aligns with the growing recognition of entrepreneurship as a vital driver of economic growth and innovation, particularly in emerging economies where youth populations are rapidly expanding (Aljohani, 2015; Su et al., 2021).

Integrating sustainability into entrepreneurship education is another critical aspect that has gained traction in recent years. As businesses increasingly face pressures to operate sustainably, entrepreneurship education must equip students with the knowledge and skills to navigate these challenges effectively (Hagebakken et al., 2021; Lourenço et al., 2012). This includes understanding sustainable business practices and encouraging innovative solutions that align economic success with environmental and social responsibility (Egieya et al., 2023).

In conclusion, the importance of entrepreneurship education in today's complex business environment cannot be overstated. By fostering entrepreneurial skills through innovative pedagogical approaches, such as business simulations and experiential learning, educational institutions can prepare students to thrive in an ever-evolving landscape. The multifaceted benefits of entrepreneurship education, encompassing individual competencies, societal impact, and sustainability, underscore its critical role in shaping the future workforce and driving economic growth.

1.2 Overcoming the Limitations of Traditional Teaching Through Experiential Learning

Traditional teaching methods, often centered on lecture-based instruction and memorization, have long been criticized for promoting passive learning. In such approaches, students are positioned as recipients of information rather than active participants in their educational journey. This lack of engagement can diminish motivation and hinder the development of critical skills necessary for success in complex, real-world business environments (Dwiniasih & Khumaeroh, 2021). Research suggests that students exposed to predominantly traditional teaching methods often struggle to develop essential competencies such as critical thinking, problem-solving, and adaptability (Kiat et al., 2020).

A significant limitation of conventional pedagogy is its inability to accommodate diverse learning styles. When instruction is heavily lecture-driven, students with varying cognitive preferences may find it challenging to connect with the material (Mariappan, 2024). This approach can result in disengagement, particularly for students who benefit from interactive and hands-on learning experiences (Dwiniasih & Khumaeroh, 2021). Additionally, traditional methods often fail to provide opportunities for collaborative learning, a practice that enhances knowledge retention and deepens understanding through peer interaction and discussion (Rajeswarie et al., 2022). Without such opportunities, students may miss developing interpersonal skills vital for entrepreneurial and professional success (Colombelli et al., 2022; Feng, 2024).

There has been a growing shift toward experiential learning models in response to these shortcomings. Experiential learning emphasizes active participation and real-world application of knowledge, allowing students to engage with realistic scenarios that mirror the complexities of the business world (Colombelli et al., 2022). Through immersive activities like business simulations and case studies, students are encouraged to experiment, make decisions, and learn from the consequences of their actions. These experiences foster deeper learning by prompting students to take ownership of their education and remain engaged throughout the learning process (Colombelli et al., 2022).

Experiential learning also nurtures essential soft skills, including teamwork, communication, and leadership. Group projects and collaborative simulations allow students to navigate complex social dynamics, negotiate roles, and resolve conflicts (Colombelli et al., 2022; Rajeswarie et al., 2022). These collaborative experiences are particularly relevant in entrepreneurship, where success often depends on building networks and partnerships (Colombelli et al., 2022). Furthermore, experiential learning promotes a growth mindset by encouraging students to embrace challenges and learn from failure in a supportive environment (Colombelli et al., 2022).

Another critical advantage of experiential learning is its capacity to enhance adaptability and resilience. In contrast to traditional methods, which often focus on providing definitive answers, experiential approaches expose students to uncertainty and complexity - hallmarks of the entrepreneurial world

(Colombelli et al., 2022). By repeatedly facing and overcoming challenges, students develop confidence in their ability to navigate unpredictable circumstances (Colombelli et al., 2022). This iterative process builds both competence and resilience, preparing learners to thrive in dynamic business environments.

Technological advancements have further expanded the possibilities for experiential learning. Digital tools and platforms now facilitate interactive simulations, virtual collaboration, and access to extensive learning resources (Khanduri & Teotia, 2023). By integrating technology, educators can create engaging, scalable experiential learning experiences that prepare students for the digital economy (Colombelli et al., 2022). Virtual simulations, for example, provide opportunities for students to engage in global business scenarios, enabling them to apply their knowledge across diverse contexts (Mubaraz & Heikkilä, 2022).

In conclusion, traditional teaching methods often fail to equip students with the critical and adaptive skills necessary for entrepreneurial success. Experiential learning addresses these limitations by fostering active engagement, collaboration, and practical application of knowledge. By integrating hands-on activities, educators can prepare students to face the complexities and uncertainties of the business world with confidence and competence.

Having examined the importance of entrepreneurship education and the challenges posed by traditional methods, the following section delves into the theoretical underpinnings of experiential learning. This section explores key frameworks, including business simulations, and how they align with and enhance educational practices.

2. THEORETICAL BACKGROUND

2.1. Understanding Business Simulations

Business simulations are interactive learning environments designed to replicate real-world business scenarios, enabling participants to engage in decision-making processes and experience the consequences of their actions in a controlled, risk-free setting. These tools provide an immersive educational experience by bridging the gap between theoretical knowledge and practical application (Faria, 2001; Vojtko & Hesková, 2010; Wellington et al., 2016). Simulating business operations' complexities, simulations foster critical skills such as strategic thinking, problem-solving, and financial analysis (Blažič & Novak, 2015; Greco et al., 2013).

Business simulations can be classified based on complexity, format, educational objectives, and industry context. One classification distinguishes between simple and complex simulations. Simple simulations often focus on specific business functions, such as marketing or finance, and are designed to provide foundational knowledge in these areas (Faria, 2001). In contrast, complex simulations integrate multiple business functions, offering a comprehensive view of how different departments interact and affect overall business performance (Greco et al., 2013). These more advanced simulations are beneficial for developing a holistic understanding of business operations and strategic decision-making.

Another way to categorize business simulations is by their delivery format. Traditional, face-to-face simulations involve role-playing or team-based activities in a physical classroom setting (Faria, 2001). However, technological advancements have led to the rise of virtual simulations, which allow participants to engage in online, interactive environments (Hannig et al., 2012; Wellington et al., 2016). Virtual simulations facilitate collaboration among geographically dispersed teams, allowing students to engage with diverse perspectives and global business scenarios (Greco et al., 2013).

Simulations can also be classified by their educational objectives. Some are designed to develop specific competencies, such as negotiation, leadership, or financial management (Wellington et al., 2016). Others emphasize strategic decision-making, requiring participants to analyze data, forecast outcomes, and make informed choices to achieve business goals (Blažič & Novak, 2015; Greco et al., 2013). These strategic simulations are particularly valuable in entrepreneurship education, where navigating uncertainty and making sound decisions is essential for success.

Another key factor in differentiating business simulations is the target audience. Simulations for undergraduate students typically focus on foundational business concepts and skills (Faria, 2001). By contrast, simulations designed for graduate students or professionals often address advanced topics, such as strategic management and organizational leadership (Greco et al., 2013). This differentiation ensures that the learning experience aligns with participants' educational and professional development needs.

Additionally, business simulations can be tailored to specific industries, allowing learners to engage with challenges unique to sectors such as healthcare, manufacturing, or finance (Hannig et al., 2012; Wellington et al., 2016). Industry-specific simulations provide contextually relevant experiences that prepare students for careers in their chosen fields by simulating those industries' operational and strategic demands.

Pedagogically, business simulations are often grounded in constructivist learning theories, which emphasize active participation and hands-on learning. These simulations encourage learners to construct knowledge through direct engagement, reflection, and collaboration with peers (Greco et al., 2013; Vojtko & Hesková, 2010). By fostering experiential learning, simulations promote critical thinking, creativity, and adaptability, which are essential for entrepreneurial and business success.

In summary, business simulations are versatile educational tools that provide learners immersive experiences to develop entrepreneurial and business skills. Their classification by complexity, format, educational objectives, target audience, and industry context ensures that simulations can be tailored to meet diverse learning needs. As business education continues to evolve, the integration of simulations will remain crucial for preparing students to navigate the dynamic challenges of the global business environment.

2.2. Experiential Learning Theories: Kolb's Experiential Learning Cycle

Experiential learning theories have become pivotal in modern education, emphasizing the importance of active engagement and real-world application in fostering more profound learning. One of the most influential frameworks within this domain is David Kolb's Experiential Learning Cycle (ELC), introduced in 1984. Kolb's model posits that knowledge is created through the transformation of experience, with learning occurring across four interdependent stages: concrete experience, reflective observation, abstract conceptualization, and active experimentation (Davitadze et al., 2022; Kolb & Kolb, 2009; Stirling et al., 2017). While learners can enter the cycle at any point, optimal learning outcomes are achieved when all stages are engaged in sequence.

Figure 1. Kolb's experiential learning cycle (ELC) (Adapted from Kolb & Kolb, 2009)

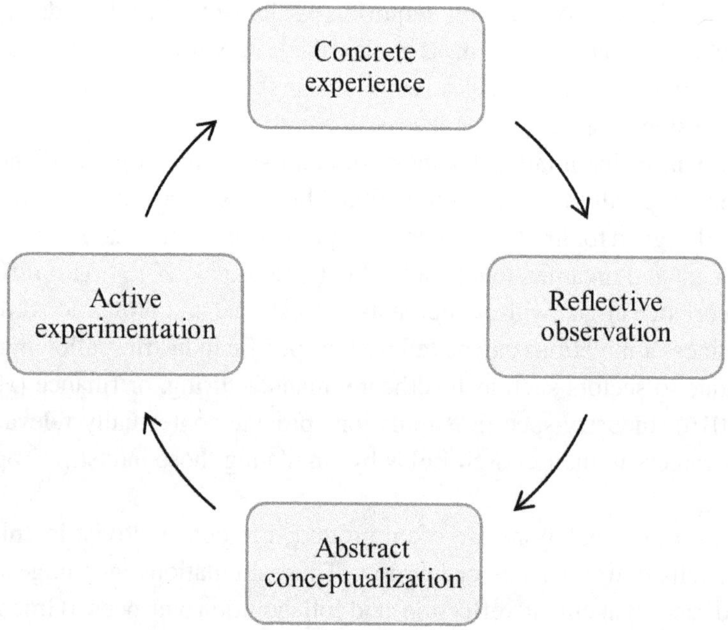

The first stage, concrete experience, involves direct, hands-on engagement with an activity or event. This stage serves as the foundation for learning by immersing individuals in real-world scenarios that provide rich experiential content (McCarthy, 2016). For example, in business education, students may participate in simulations where they manage virtual companies, encountering challenges that mirror the complexities of actual business operations. These experiences offer valuable opportunities for students to apply theoretical concepts and begin understanding business dynamics through practice.

Following concrete experience, learners enter the reflective observation stage, where they critically analyze their experiences. During this phase, learners evaluate what occurred, how they felt, and the outcomes of their actions, gaining insight into the effectiveness of their strategies (Lattacher & Wdowiak, 2020; Stirling et al., 2017). Reflective observation fosters critical thinking by prompting learners to identify patterns and connections between their actions and results. This reflective process enhances self-awareness and helps learners better understand their decision-making processes (Politis, 2005). For instance, students might reflect on their financial or marketing decisions after a business simulation, leading to greater insight into strategic planning.

The third stage, abstract conceptualization, involves synthesizing the insights gained from reflection into broader concepts and theories. Learners begin to form generalizations that can be applied to new situations, thus connecting experiential learning with academic knowledge (Maellaro, 2013). For example, students reflecting on market fluctuations in a simulation might develop a conceptual understanding of market dynamics or risk management. This stage is crucial for bridging the gap between theory and practice, as learners internalize their experiences and construct knowledge frameworks that inform future decision-making.

The final stage, active experimentation, encourages learners to apply their newly acquired knowledge in practical settings. In this phase, students test theories and strategies, refining their approaches based on feedback and real-world results (Stander et al., 2019). For example, students may implement new business strategies in subsequent rounds of a simulation or real-world projects, reinforcing their learning through iterative practice (Ellinger et al., 2007).

Kolb's Experiential Learning Cycle is not only a theoretical framework but also a practical guide for educators seeking to enhance learning outcomes. By guiding learners through experiences, reflection, conceptualization, and experimentation, the model supports the development of critical thinking, creativity, and problem-solving skills (Morris, 2019). These competencies are vital for success in today's rapidly changing business landscape (Ayad et al., 2019).

The applicability of Kolb's model extends beyond traditional classrooms to various educational contexts, including online and remote learning. Virtual simulations and collaborative projects provide meaningful opportunities for experiential learning, even in digital environments (Davitadze et al., 2022; Gürpınar et al., 2011). These approaches ensure that students continue to develop practical competencies, such as teamwork, communication, and strategic thinking, which are essential for their professional growth (Seaman, 2008).

Kolb's Experiential Learning Cycle is a robust theoretical and practical tool that enhances educational practices across diverse settings. It offers a structured framework for skill development through hands-on experience, reflection, and iterative learning. By systematically engaging students in concrete experiences, reflecting on those experiences, conceptualizing insights, and actively experimenting, educators can create transformative learning experiences that help students develop a deeper understanding of complex concepts, enhance their practical skills, and effectively meet the challenges of dynamic and complex business environments.

2.3. How Business Simulations Support Experiential Learning

Business simulations are increasingly recognized as practical tools for facilitating experiential learning, particularly in the context of entrepreneurship education. These simulations allow students to engage in realistic business scenarios and apply theoretical knowledge in practice while experiencing the complexities of decision-making in a controlled environment. The alignment of business simulations with experiential learning theories, particularly Kolb's Experiential Learning Cycle, underscores their pedagogical value in developing essential skills and competencies.

David Kolb's Experiential Learning Cycle (ELC) offers a robust framework for integrating business simulations into educational practices, particularly entrepreneurship education. The cycle consists of the four interconnected stages analyzed previously. Each stage is critical in enhancing the learning experience, helping students develop essential entrepreneurial skills through active engagement, reflection, and application (Ahn, 2008).

The first stage, concrete experience, involves active participation in a business simulation, where students engage in activities that replicate real-world business scenarios. This hands-on involvement immerses learners in a realistic context, allowing them to experience the complexities of business operations firsthand fostering a deeper understanding of business dynamics (Baden & Parkes, 2013; Buil et al., 2018; Wheadon & Duval-Couetil, 2014). For example, in a business simulation game, students may take on roles within a virtual company, making strategic decisions that influence the company's performance. Research shows that such experiences significantly improve student engagement and knowledge retention by fostering active involvement in the learning process (Yusof et al., 2020). By providing a practical foundation, concrete experiences help learners better understand complex business concepts and develop critical operational insights.

Following the concrete experience, learners move into the stage of reflective observation, where they critically analyze their actions and outcomes within the simulation. This phase involves questioning what strategies worked, what failed, and why specific results were achieved (Ahn, 2008). Reflective observation enhances critical thinking and self-awareness, as students assess the effectiveness of their decisions. This reflection often occurs in business simulations through structured debriefing sessions, where students share insights, discuss alternative approaches, and identify patterns in their decision-making processes (Stirling et al., 2017). Research confirms that this reflective practice deepens learning by promoting a more comprehensive understanding of business dynamics and encouraging students to apply lessons from their successes and failures to future scenarios (Piercy, 2013; Radford et al., 2015; Wheadon & Duval-Couetil, 2014). By reflecting on their experiences, students can identify patterns, draw insights, and develop a more nuanced understanding of business concepts, which is essential for effective decision-making in real-world scenarios (Morris, 2019).

The third stage, abstract conceptualization, involves synthesizing insights from reflection into broader theoretical concepts. During this phase, students generalize their experiences and connect them to established business theories or frameworks (Alstete, 2023; Brazhkin & Zimmerman, 2019). For example, after reflecting on a simulation, students might better understand market behavior, financial planning, or leadership dynamics (Dhliwayo, 2008). This conceptualization bridges the gap between theory and practice by helping learners internalize knowledge and apply it to diverse business contexts (Drury-Grogan & Russ, 2013).

The final stage, active experimentation, encourages learners to test and refine their newly acquired knowledge through practical application. In business simulations, this stage involves implementing strategies in subsequent rounds or applying insights to real-world projects (Raja & Najmonnisa, 2018). This iterative process reinforces learning by providing opportunities for continuous feedback and adjustment, as students must continuously refine their approaches based on feedback and changing circumstances (Memar et al., 2020; Yoehono & Liliani, 2018). Active experimentation fosters adaptability and resilience, critical traits for navigating uncertainty in the entrepreneurial landscape (Krakauer et al., 2017). Research demonstrates that students in this stage develop greater confidence in their ability to innovate and make strategic decisions in unpredictable environments (Monk & Lycett, 2014).

Moreover, technological advancements have expanded the potential for implementing Kolb's Experiential Learning Cycle through business simulations. Digital platforms offer interactive virtual simulations that enable students to collaborate across distances, engage with complex scenarios, and analyze outcomes in a risk-free setting (Baden & Parkes, 2013). These tools not only enhance accessibility but also prepare students for the digital economy by promoting technological proficiency, a crucial competency for modern entrepreneurs (Mubaraz & Heikkilä, 2022).

In addition to enhancing individual learning outcomes, business simulations also promote collaborative learning. Many simulations are designed to be team-based, requiring students to work together to achieve common goals. This collaborative aspect aligns with the principles of experiential learning, as it encourages communication, negotiation, and conflict resolution skills, essential competencies for future entrepreneurs (Chandwaskar & Jape, 2024; Loon et al., 2015). By engaging in teamwork within simulations, students learn to leverage diverse perspectives and expertise, which is vital for success in the increasingly interconnected business landscape (Zapalska, 2021).

Business simulations align seamlessly with experiential learning theories in entrepreneurship education. By guiding students through concrete experiences, reflective observation, abstract conceptualization, and active experimentation, educators can create transformative learning experiences that promote critical thinking, adaptability, and strategic problem-solving. As educational institutions continue to adapt to the evolving demands of the business landscape, integrating Kolb's framework into business simulations will remain essential for preparing students to succeed in dynamic business environments.

2.4. Business Simulations: A Key Tool for Developing Entrepreneurial Skills

Business simulations have emerged as a transformative tool in entrepreneurship education, offering students a dynamic and interactive platform for developing critical business competencies. These simulations create immersive, risk-free environments where learners can engage in realistic scenarios, apply theoretical knowledge, and experience the complexities of business operations firsthand (Peterková et al., 2022; Samašonok et al., 2020). By encouraging students to experiment with decision-making and assess the consequences of their actions, business simulations bridge the gap between academic concepts and practical application (Palmunen et al., 2013).

A key advantage of business simulations is their ability to replicate real-world business dynamics, providing experiential learning opportunities that align with Kolb's Experiential Learning Cycle. This model emphasizes the ELC's four stages. Simulations facilitate this process by immersing students in business operations (concrete experience), prompting them to analyze their decisions (reflective observation), encouraging the development of strategies (abstract conceptualization), and enabling them to test new approaches (active experimentation) (Dharmastuti et al., 2021; Xie, 2022). This iterative process fosters deep learning and skill acquisition, which are crucial for entrepreneurial success.

Research highlights that business simulations enhance both cognitive and interpersonal skills. In addition to improving critical thinking and strategic decision-making, simulations promote teamwork, communication, and leadership (van Krevelen et al., 2011; Rosenthal et al., 2021). Students often participate in team-based activities, where collaboration and negotiation are essential for achieving objectives. These experiences prepare learners to work effectively in entrepreneurial environments that require strong interpersonal and organizational capabilities.

The effectiveness of business simulations is further supported by empirical evidence demonstrating improved learning outcomes. Studies show that students who engage with simulations perform better in market analysis, financial management, and strategic planning than those who rely solely on traditional learning methods (Wheadon & Duval-Couetil, 2014; Williams, 2015). Additionally, simulations have been linked to higher student engagement and motivation levels. The interactive nature of these tools fosters a sense of involvement and relevance, making learning more meaningful and enjoyable (Avramenko, 2012; Fauzan et al., 2017).

Business simulations are also highly adaptable, allowing educators to tailor learning experiences to specific educational objectives and industry contexts. Simulations can focus on various business functions, such as marketing strategies, operational efficiency, or entrepreneurial finance, providing targeted and relevant skill development (Fajar & Sarno, 2019; Kurbjuhn et al., 2014). This flexibility enhances the overall educational experience and ensures that students acquire the competencies needed to navigate diverse business challenges (Wang et al., 2013). Moreover, simulations facilitate stronger connections between academia and industry by exposing students to scenarios that reflect real-world business practices. These experiences provide insights into industry standards and expectations, enhancing students' readiness for employment or entrepreneurial ventures (Angolia & Reed, 2019; Avramenko, 2012).

The integration of technology has further expanded the potential of business simulations. Virtual platforms enable students to participate in simulations remotely, collaborate across geographic boundaries, and utilize advanced analytical tools (Abdullah et al., 2013). This technological advancement enhances the realism and accessibility of simulations, equipping students with digital competencies essential for modern entrepreneurship (Mubaraz & Heikkilä, 2022).

Business simulations represent a powerful and versatile pedagogical tool for developing entrepreneurial skills. By fostering critical thinking, problem-solving, and collaboration, these simulations prepare students to tackle real-world business challenges confidently. Their alignment with experiential learning theories and capacity for technological integration make them an indispensable component of contemporary entrepreneurship education.

With a clear understanding of business simulations and their alignment with experiential learning theories, the following section examines current trends and challenges in entrepreneurship education. The discussion focuses on how experiential learning approaches, supported by these tools, shape and transform educational outcomes.

3. ENTREPRENEURSHIP EDUCATION AND EXPERIENTIAL LEARNING

3.1. Current Trends and Challenges in Entrepreneurship Education

Entrepreneurship education has evolved significantly over the past decade, adapting to rapid global economic changes and students' needs. Current trends emphasize experiential learning, technological integration, and the cultivation of entrepreneurial competencies while also addressing the challenges that accompany these developments.

One prominent trend in entrepreneurship education is the increasing focus on experiential learning. This approach prioritizes active engagement and real-world application of knowledge, allowing students to participate in hands-on activities such as business simulations, internships, and project-based learning (Bell & Bell, 2020). Studies show that experiential learning enhances both student engagement and knowledge retention by providing opportunities to apply theoretical concepts in practical contexts (Seikkula-Leino et al., 2019). For example, business simulation games have proven effective in fostering critical entrepreneurial skills, such as decision-making and risk management, in a controlled environment where students can learn through trial and error (Fox et al., 2018).

The integration of technology is another transformative trend in entrepreneurship education. Digital tools and platforms have expanded the accessibility and flexibility of learning opportunities. Virtual simulations, online entrepreneurship courses, and collaborative tools enable students to engage with content remotely, often in real-time, while interacting with peers across geographical boundaries (Abwamiah, 2023). Technological integration enhances learning by exposing students to digital business environments, which are increasingly relevant in today's economy (Tican, 2019). However, this trend also challenges educators, who must continuously update their curricula to stay aligned with emerging technological advancements (Yan, 2020).

A third key trend involves fostering an entrepreneurial mindset among students. This mindset emphasizes creativity, critical thinking, resilience, and the ability to identify and seize opportunities (Kaya et al., 2019). Educational programs now incorporate activities that encourage students to take initiative, solve complex problems, and innovate within diverse contexts. However, fostering such competencies requires educators to adopt innovative, student-centered teaching methods, which may differ from traditional approaches that focus heavily on theoretical instruction (Lackéus, 2020).

Despite these positive developments, entrepreneurship education continues to face several challenges. One major challenge is ensuring educators possess the necessary expertise to teach entrepreneurship effectively. Many instructors may lack practical entrepreneurial experience, hindering their ability to deliver impactful learning experiences (Pham et al., 2023). Professional development programs are needed to equip educators with relevant skills and knowledge to support experiential and technology-driven learning environments (Seikkula-Leino et al., 2019).

Another challenge is curriculum relevance. As industries evolve, entrepreneurship programs must stay aligned with the skills and competencies demanded by the labor market (Rippa et al., 2020). Maintaining this alignment requires close collaboration between educational institutions and industry stakeholders to identify emerging trends and adjust curricula accordingly (Suseno & Abbott, 2021). Without such collaboration, students may graduate without the practical skills necessary to succeed in entrepreneurial or business careers.

The integration of entrepreneurship education into broader academic programs also presents a challenge. In many institutions, entrepreneurship is treated as an elective or supplementary subject rather than a core component of business education (Kiyomi et al., 2022). This marginalization can limit students' exposure to essential entrepreneurial concepts and practices, reducing their preparedness for entrepreneurial ventures and traditional business roles (Li et al., 2020).

The COVID-19 pandemic has further complicated the delivery of entrepreneurship education. The sudden shift to remote learning disrupted traditional teaching methods and required educators to find innovative ways to maintain engagement in virtual settings (Sreenivasan & Suresh, 2023). Although online platforms have enabled continued access to education, the challenge of delivering experiential learning activities in digital environments remains significant. Educators have had to adapt by incorporating virtual simulations, online case studies, and collaborative digital projects to ensure students continue developing practical skills (Park & Kim, 2023).

Entrepreneurship education is shaped by evolving trends in experiential learning, technology integration, and the development of entrepreneurial mindsets. While these trends offer numerous opportunities for enhancing student learning and engagement, they also present challenges related to educator expertise, curriculum relevance, and adapting teaching methods to remote learning environments. Addressing these challenges through collaboration, innovation, and professional development will ensure that entrepreneurship education prepares students for success in an increasingly complex and dynamic business landscape.

3.2. How Experiential Learning Addresses Entrepreneurship Education Challenges

Experiential learning plays a crucial role in overcoming the challenges faced in entrepreneurship education, particularly in fostering active engagement, developing practical skills, and bridging the gap between theoretical knowledge and real-world application. By immersing students in hands-on, interactive experiences, this approach addresses key limitations associated with traditional pedagogical methods.

One of the main challenges in entrepreneurship education is the difficulty of developing practical, real-world skills through theoretical instruction alone. Traditional methods often fail to adequately prepare students for the complexities of entrepreneurship, where uncertainty and rapid change are constants (Monllor et al., 2023). Experiential learning mitigates this issue by allowing students to apply theoretical concepts in authentic business scenarios. Through activities such as business simulations, internships, and entrepreneurial projects, students gain valuable experience in decision-making, risk management, and strategic planning (Wang et al., 2022). For example, research shows that participation in entrepreneurship competitions enhances students' competencies by providing opportunities to tackle real-world challenges (Seikkula-Leino et al., 2019).

In addition to practical skills, experiential learning fosters critical soft skills like teamwork, communication, and leadership. Collaborative projects and simulations require students to interact with peers, negotiate roles, and resolve conflicts, experiences that mirror the interpersonal demands of entrepreneurial ventures (Kassean et al., 2015). By engaging in such activities, students learn how to build and leverage networks, an essential component of entrepreneurial success (Lackéus, 2020). Studies indicate that students who participate in experiential learning activities report increased confidence in their entrepreneurial abilities and are more likely to pursue ventures after graduation (Memar et al., 2020).

Another major challenge is ensuring that entrepreneurship curricula remain aligned with industry needs. As business environments evolve rapidly, educational institutions must continuously update their programs to reflect current market demands and technological advancements (Rippa et al., 2020). Experiential learning provides a mechanism for this alignment by exposing students to real-world problems and engaging them in projects that require industry collaboration. Partnerships between educational institutions and local businesses enable students to work on practical case studies and develop solutions directly applicable to current challenges (Macht & Ball, 2016). This collaboration helps students better understand industry practices and enhances their employability (Suseno & Abbott, 2021).

The adaptation of entrepreneurship education to online and remote settings, particularly during and after the COVID-19 pandemic, has posed additional challenges. Experiential learning methods traditionally rely on face-to-face interaction, which can be difficult to replicate in virtual environments (Sreenivasan & Suresh, 2023). However, educators have increasingly turned to digital tools, such as virtual business simulations and online collaborative platforms, to maintain student engagement and ensure practical skill development (Park & Kim, 2023). These tools enable students to participate in experiential learning from remote locations, expanding access to entrepreneurship education and fostering adaptability to the digital economy.

A key component of experiential learning is its emphasis on iterative learning. Unlike traditional methods that emphasize fixed outcomes, experiential learning encourages students to experiment, make mistakes, and refine their approaches based on feedback. This iterative process helps students develop resilience and adaptability, qualities vital for navigating the uncertainties inherent in entrepreneurship (Krakauer et al., 2017). Research highlights that students who engage in repeated cycles of experimentation and reflection are better equipped to handle complex business challenges and innovate effectively (Ellinger et al., 2007).

Experiential learning addresses many of the challenges in entrepreneurship education by fostering active engagement, developing practical and soft skills, and maintaining alignment with industry needs. Through hands-on activities, reflection, and iterative learning, this approach prepares students to succeed in dynamic business environments. As entrepreneurship education evolves, experiential learning will remain essential for equipping students with the competencies to thrive in entrepreneurial and professional contexts.

3.3. The Benefits of Hands-On, Risk-Free Experimentation

Hands-on, risk-free experimentation is a cornerstone of experiential learning, allowing students to develop entrepreneurial skills in a controlled environment. This approach provides practical exposure to real-world business scenarios without the financial or reputational risks associated with actual business ventures. By engaging in simulations, case studies, and other interactive learning experiences, students can experiment with decision-making, innovation, and problem-solving in a way that fosters confidence and adaptability (Apostu et al., 2022).

One significant advantage of hands-on experimentation is its promotion of active learning. Traditional education methods often rely on passive knowledge transfer, limiting student engagement and understanding (Longva & Foss, 2018). In contrast, hands-on activities encourage students to take ownership of their learning by applying theoretical concepts to practical challenges. For example, participation in entrepreneurship simulations allows students to explore business dynamics through direct involvement, such as market fluctuations and operational strategies (Kremel & Edman, 2019). Research confirms that students who engage in such activities demonstrate more knowledge retention and a deeper comprehension of complex concepts (Wheadon & Duval-Couetil, 2014).

Risk-free experimentation also nurtures a growth mindset, where students view mistakes and setbacks as opportunities for learning rather than failures. This mindset is particularly important in entrepreneurship, where uncertainty and risk are constant factors. By participating in controlled experiments, students can test their ideas and strategies without fear of severe consequences. This process builds resilience, as students learn to analyze failures, adapt their approaches, and persist in facing challenges (Hariyono, 2024). The iterative nature of experiential learning reinforces this adaptability, helping students develop problem-solving skills that are transferable to real-world contexts (Gopalan et al., 2020).

Another critical benefit of hands-on experimentation is the development of collaborative and interpersonal skills. Entrepreneurship often requires effective teamwork and communication, as entrepreneurs frequently work within networks of partners, investors, and employees (Klofsten et al., 2020). Experiential activities, such as team-based simulations and group projects, allow students to practice collaboration, negotiate roles, and resolve conflicts in realistic settings (D'Angelo et al., 2023). These experiences enhance students' ability to work in diverse teams and prepare them to lead and manage entrepreneurial ventures.

Experiential learning also fosters interdisciplinary knowledge integration, an essential skill in today's complex business landscape. Entrepreneurs must often synthesize insights from various domains, including finance, marketing, operations, and technology (Mariani & Nambisan, 2021). By engaging in experiential projects that require cross-functional thinking, students can develop a more holistic understanding of business operations. For example, creating a business plan in a simulation may involve financial forecasting, strategic marketing, and supply chain management, helping students build well-rounded competencies (Farooq et al., 2018).

The incorporation of technology further enhances the benefits of hands-on experimentation. Digital platforms and tools, such as virtual simulations and online collaborative environments, expand access to experiential learning by enabling remote participation. These technologies allow students to engage with complex business scenarios from anywhere, fostering digital literacy and preparing them for the demands of the digital economy (Englis & Frederiks, 2023). For instance, online entrepreneurship simulations allow students to analyze data, make strategic decisions, and collaborate with peers across geographical boundaries.

While the benefits of hands-on, risk-free experimentation are extensive, effective implementation requires educator expertise and well-defined assessment frameworks. Educators must be trained to design and facilitate experiential activities that align with learning objectives and provide meaningful feedback. Additionally, robust assessment criteria are needed to evaluate students' performance, including their decision-making processes, teamwork dynamics, and ability to apply theoretical knowledge in practical contexts. Clear assessment measures help ensure that experiential learning leads to measurable outcomes and continuous improvement (Olumekor, 2023; Sung & Park, 2018; Zhou et al., 2021).

Hands-on, risk-free experimentation is vital to entrepreneurship education. By promoting active learning, fostering a growth mindset, enhancing collaborative skills, and integrating interdisciplinary knowledge, experiential learning prepares students to navigate the complexities of entrepreneurial ventures. As technology continues to reshape education, incorporating digital tools in experiential activities will further expand opportunities for students to develop essential entrepreneurial competencies in a dynamic, risk-free environment.

The following case study illustrates how these concepts have been applied in practice through the "Business Simulation-Games" course at the University of Piraeus. This case provides a concrete example of how business simulations foster entrepreneurial skill development in an academic setting.

4. CASE STUDY: THE 'BUSINESS SIMULATION-GAMES' COURSE AT THE UNIVERSITY OF PIRAEUS

4.1. Course Development, Goals and Learning Outcomes

The 'Business Simulation-Games' course at the University of Piraeus was developed in 2003 as part of an EU co-financed initiative to enhance entrepreneurship education across Greek higher education institutions. This initiative responded to a growing recognition that traditional lecture-based education was insufficient for equipping students with the practical skills needed in dynamic and complex business environments. At the time, entrepreneurship was gaining prominence as a vital engine of economic growth, especially in the wake of globalization and technological advancements that were transforming business models. Greek higher education institutions, including the University of Piraeus, saw an opportunity to innovate curricula by adopting experiential learning methods emphasizing active participation and real-world application. As a result, business simulations were identified as a promising tool to address these needs.

The University of Piraeus, with its strong focus on economics and business studies, became a pioneer in integrating business simulations into its educational offerings. Since its introduction, the course has evolved in response to student needs and business education advancements. Initially part of the Department of Business Administration curricula as an elective course, it expanded to the newly established Department of Tourism Studies in 2020 to address the growing demand for experiential learning in this sector. The course was designed to bridge the gap between theoretical business concepts and practical skills, offering students a controlled, risk-free environment to experiment with business operations. This approach aligns with educational research that highlights the importance of experiential learning in fostering critical thinking, problem-solving, and decision-making capabilities (e.g. Bell & Bell, 2020; Kaya et al., 2019).

The primary goal of the 'Business Simulation-Games' course is to provide students with hands-on experience in management. Unlike traditional courses that rely heavily on lectures and textbook learning, this course also immerses students in interactive simulations where they assume the roles of business managers and entrepreneurs. Through these experiences, students develop a deeper understanding of how various business functions (e.g. finance, marketing, operations, and human resources) interact in a real-world context. Additionally, the course aims to cultivate key entrepreneurial competencies, including:

- Strategic decision-making, as students are challenged to make high-impact decisions under conditions of uncertainty and competition.
- Risk management, as simulations present scenarios where students must assess and mitigate risks, learning how to balance short-term and long-term goals.
- Adaptability, as the course encourages students to adapt their strategies in response to new challenges by exposing them to unpredictable market conditions.
- Team collaboration, as some simulations are team-based, requiring students to work together, negotiate roles, and leverage collective expertise to achieve objectives.
- Reflection and continuous learning, through debriefing sessions and reflective essays, where students analyze their decisions and outcomes, promoting self-awareness and learning from successes and failures.

The course is designed to align with the European Qualifications Framework (EQF) and the standards set by the Bologna Process, which emphasize learning outcomes and student-centered education. By focusing on both theoretical knowledge and practical application, the course supports the development of competencies that are highly valued by employers across Europe. According to the EQF descriptors for Level 6 (undergraduate / bachelor's degree), students are expected to:

- Demonstrate knowledge of advanced concepts within their field of study.
- Apply knowledge to solve complex problems in practical settings.
- Communicate effectively in diverse environments and collaborate with others on projects.
- Develop critical thinking and the ability to innovate.

The 'Business Simulation-Games' course addresses these outcomes through a curriculum that combines lectures, laboratory exercises with the use of simulation software, and self-directed study. Including simulation-based learning activities ensures that students acquire theoretical knowledge and develop the skills to apply this knowledge in professional contexts.

Upon completing the course, students are expected to achieve various learning outcomes that encompass technical and interpersonal skills. These outcomes include:

- *Understanding business simulations*: Students should be able to define and explain key concepts related to business simulations, including their applications, advantages, and limitations. They should also be familiar with the historical evolution of simulation techniques and their relevance to modern business practices.
- *Modeling and process simulation*: Students are trained to design and simulate business processes using specialized software. They learn to record historical data, calculate probabilities, generate random numbers, and model business operations. This technical knowledge forms the basis for more complex simulations that involve multiple variables and dynamic interactions
- *Application of business simulations*: The course emphasizes the practical application of simulation tools to solve business problems. Students engage with real-world data and case studies, enabling them to simulate scenarios such as inventory management, cash flow analysis, and performance improvement.
- *Critical thinking and problem-solving*: By participating in simulations, students develop the ability to analyze complex situations, identify key variables, and make data-driven decisions. This skill set is crucial for entrepreneurs and managers navigating uncertainty and risk in competitive environments.
- *Teamwork and communication*: Collaborative projects are a core component of the course, fostering teamwork, leadership, and negotiation skills. Students learn to communicate their ideas effectively, present their strategies, and justify their decisions during debriefing sessions and presentations.

4.2. Course Structure and Learning Activities

The 'Business Simulation-Games' course is carefully designed to balance theoretical instruction with practical, hands-on learning. It provides students with progressively challenging experiences aimed at cultivating entrepreneurial and management competencies. Throughout the semester, students engage in interactive simulations, collaborative projects, and reflective exercises that develop their technical and interpersonal skills. Integrating lectures, laboratory sessions, and real-world case studies ensures that students can handle the complexities of modern business environments.

The course follows a weekly schedule comprising three hours of lectures and one hour of laboratory work. In addition to this formal instruction, students dedicate time to self-directed study and team assignments. Over the semester, students participate in approximately 154 structured learning hours. Each week builds upon the previous one, with simulations becoming more complex. This gradual increase in difficulty allows students to develop core skills while gaining confidence in their ability to analyze and manage business scenarios.

The course begins with an introduction to business simulations and foundational concepts. During the initial weeks, students learn about the purpose and benefits of simulations in business education, including how simulations mimic real-world operations in a controlled, risk-free environment. Instructors provide an overview of the simulation tools used in the course, introducing key business functions such as financial planning, marketing, and operations. Early simulations focus on simple scenarios, such as launching a small business or entering a new market. These activities allow students to explore decision-making processes and become familiar with performance metrics without facing overwhelming complexity.

After gaining familiarity with basic concepts and tools, students advance to simulations that require strategic decision-making and cross-functional management. These scenarios often involve managing a business under competitive pressures, with decisions impacting multiple areas such as finance, marketing, and operations. For instance, students might need to develop marketing strategies while optimizing production schedules and managing cash flow. This phase emphasizes strategic planning and teamwork, as many simulations require students to collaborate in teams. Each team member assumes a specific role (e.g. marketing manager or financial officer), mirroring the division of responsibilities in real businesses. This collaborative approach fosters communication, leadership, and negotiation skills, essential for entrepreneurship and corporate management.

In later stages of the course, students face higher pressure simulations designed to develop their adaptability and crisis management abilities. These simulations introduce unexpected events, such as market disruptions, operational breakdowns, or competitive threats. Students are required to assess the situation quickly, prioritize responses, and implement strategic solutions. For example, a simulation might present a scenario where a hospitality business experiences a sudden drop in demand due to external factors. Students must devise strategies to mitigate revenue loss, such as adjusting pricing models or reallocating resources. This phase challenges students to think critically under time constraints, fostering resilience and problem-solving capabilities.

A culminating capstone simulation takes place near the end of the course, integrating all the knowledge and skills students have acquired. It builds on the feedback and insights students have gained throughout the semester, allowing them to apply refined strategies to complex, evolving business scenarios. This comprehensive exercise involves managing a business over multiple simulated time periods, during which market conditions evolve and new challenges emerge. Students are expected to demonstrate strategic consistency, balancing short-term actions with long-term business goals. They are also evaluated on their financial performance, including profitability and resource efficiency, as well as on team dynamics and communication effectiveness. Following the capstone simulation, students present their strategies and outcomes to their peers and instructors, articulating key insights and lessons learned. This capstone simulation is a pivotal component of the course, serving as a comprehensive test of students' ability to manage business complexities holistically.

Reflection is a cornerstone of the course structure. After each simulation, students participate in debriefing sessions led by the instructor. The instructor plays a crucial role in guiding students through the learning process by facilitating discussions and constructive feedback and promoting critical reflection. These sessions provide an opportunity to critically analyze decisions, discuss outcomes, and receive feedback. Students are encouraged to reflect on what worked, what did not, and how they can improve their strategies in future simulations. This reflective process enhances self-awareness and promotes continuous learning, helping students internalize the skills needed to navigate real-world business environments.

Assessment in the course is designed to capture both technical and interpersonal skill development. Simulation performance is a key component of the evaluation process, with students assessed on metrics such as financial results, operational efficiency, and strategic execution. Reflective essays further allow students to analyze their experiences, providing a narrative of their decision-making journey. Group presentations enable students to showcase their ability to communicate business insights, while peer evaluations provide additional feedback, emphasizing teamwork and collaboration. This holistic assessment approach ensures that students develop a balance of technical expertise, strategic thinking, and interpersonal skills essential for real-world business success.

Overall, the 'Business Simulation-Games' course at the University of Piraeus exemplifies how structured experiential learning can enhance educational outcomes. Through lectures, hands-on activities, and reflective practices, students gain practical experience and the confidence to effectively manage business operations in dynamic and competitive markets.

4.3. Pedagogical Approach

The pedagogical foundation of the 'Business Simulation-Games' course is centered on experiential learning, with Kolb's Experiential Learning Cycle providing the core framework. This model emphasizes that effective learning occurs through a dynamic, iterative process involving concrete experience, reflection, conceptualization, and experimentation. By following these stages, the course encourages students to develop critical thinking, adaptability, and problem-solving skills, skills essential for entrepreneurial success.

Simulations form the backbone of this approach, providing students with concrete experiences that mirror real-world business operations. Within these simulations, students assume roles that require them to make strategic decisions, such as managing resources, setting prices, and responding to operational challenges. These scenarios immerse students in the complexities of managing businesses, pushing them to engage directly with dynamic business dilemmas and opportunities.

Following each simulation, students transition to the reflective observation stage, where they analyze their decisions and outcomes. This reflection is not limited to structured debriefing sessions but is an ongoing process throughout the course. Students are encouraged to critically evaluate their actions, identify what worked and what did not, and consider how they can improve in future simulations. Guided by instructors, these reflective exercises foster greater self-awareness and continuous improvement. Instructors prompt students to articulate their reasoning, recognize successful strategies, and explore alternative approaches, helping them internalize lessons learned from both successes and failures.

As students progress, they engage in abstract conceptualization, connecting their reflections to theoretical frameworks introduced during lectures. Instructors help students link practical experiences with academic concepts such as competitive strategy, risk management, and organizational behavior. This stage deepens their theoretical understanding by demonstrating how business principles apply to real-world scenarios, reinforcing the relevance of both theory and practice.

The learning cycle ends with active experimentation, as students apply refined strategies in subsequent simulations. By integrating feedback and insights gained from earlier experiences, they improve their ability to navigate increasingly complex business environments. This iterative process resembles the entrepreneurial journey, where continuous learning, strategic adjustments, and experimentation are critical to success.

Active learning is a central pillar of the course. Rather than passively absorbing information through lectures, students actively engage with challenging tasks, make key decisions, and analyze the outcomes of their actions. This process fosters motivation and knowledge retention, as students are more likely to internalize concepts they have directly applied. Active learning is vital in entrepreneurship education, where uncertainty and complexity are defining characteristics. Simulations provide a controlled but dynamic environment where students can safely test and refine their ideas, simulating real-world risks and opportunities without immediate consequences.

Collaboration is another important element of the course's pedagogical design. Many simulations replicate team-based business operations, where success depends on effective communication, leadership, and coordination of roles. Students take on specific responsibilities within these teams, such as managing financial strategies or overseeing marketing initiatives. They must work together to develop cohesive strategies and achieve shared objectives. This team structure mirrors real-world business dynamics, fostering skills in negotiation, conflict resolution, and collaborative decision-making, competencies that are highly transferable across both entrepreneurial ventures and corporate settings.

The role of the instructor is equally essential, functioning not as a traditional lecturer but as a facilitator and mentor. Instructors guide students through each phase of the learning cycle, providing timely feedback and fostering critical reflection. Rather than offering ready-made solutions, they challenge students to think critically about their decisions and explore alternative strategies. This facilitative approach supports self-directed learning and encourages students to take ownership of their development. By fostering an environment where experimentation is encouraged, instructors help students build resilience and a growth mindset, key traits for success in both entrepreneurship and business leadership.

To ensure that students are fully prepared for the capstone simulation, the course offers multiple opportunities for iterative learning. Each simulation builds on the previous one, increasing in complexity and requiring students to apply their growing expertise to more challenging scenarios. This approach allows students to consolidate their knowledge while addressing areas for improvement. By the time students reach the capstone simulation, they have developed a strong foundation in both technical and strategic competencies, enabling them to manage complex business operations holistically.

One of the course's strengths is its ability to integrate theory and practice seamlessly. While simulations provide experiential learning opportunities, they are complemented by lectures and case studies that introduce key business concepts. For example, a lecture on strategic planning might precede a simulation in which students must develop and implement a market entry strategy. This combination of practical and theoretical learning equips students with a comprehensive skill set that prepares them for the challenges of modern business environments.

The course's assessment framework reflects its multidimensional learning objectives. Simulation performance is a critical component, with students assessed on their ability to meet business goals such as profitability, operational efficiency, and strategic execution. However, assessment is not limited to technical outcomes. Reflective essays allow students to analyze their decision-making processes, narrating the factors that influenced their choices and the lessons they derived from the experience. Group presentations further reinforce learning by requiring students to articulate their strategies and demonstrate an understanding of complex business concepts. Peer evaluations add another layer of feedback, promoting team accountability and collaboration by recognizing individual contributions to group success. Finally, a formal examination covering both theoretical and practical issues is conducted at the end of the semester, adding another layer of assessment.

Ultimately, this course's pedagogical approach exemplifies the transformative potential of experiential learning. By immersing students in cycles of experience, reflection, and experimentation, the course fosters a deep, active learning process that extends far beyond academic theory. Students gain the confidence, adaptability, and critical thinking skills needed to navigate complex business environments, positioning them to pursue entrepreneurial ventures or leadership roles successfully. Through its emphasis on experiential learning, active engagement, and reflective practice, the course aligns with modern pedagogical trends that prioritize skill development alongside theoretical knowledge. This approach enhances both educational outcomes and the development of resilient, innovative, and strategically minded professionals capable of meeting the demands of an ever-evolving business world.

4.4. Course Challenges and Successes

The development and implementation of the 'Business Simulation-Games' course have faced various challenges, particularly regarding technology, pedagogy, and student adaptation. These challenges, however, have been met with targeted improvements and continuous refinement, resulting in significant successes that have strengthened the course's ability to prepare students for complex business environments.

When the course was introduced in 2003, technological limitations posed one of the earliest obstacles. Business simulation platforms at the time were not as sophisticated or user-friendly as they are today. Many required extensive customization and technical support, leading to a steep learning curve for both students and instructors. Furthermore, the university needed to upgrade its infrastructure to support the installation and operation of simulation software, with financial resources often supplemented through European and national research projects. Over the years, these technological challenges were addressed through strategic partnerships with software providers and the adoption of cloud-based platforms, which facilitated smoother integration of simulations into both in-person and remote learning formats. These advancements enhanced accessibility, ensuring that students could participate in simulations regardless of location or external disruptions.

A second challenge was helping students adapt to the demands of simulation-based learning. Unlike traditional lecture-based courses, this course requires students to engage actively in decision-making under conditions of uncertainty. Many students initially struggled to grasp the complex interactions between business functions within the simulations, leading to confusion and anxiety. To ease this transition, the course was designed to introduce simulations in phases of increasing complexity. Early activities focus on individual business functions to build foundational knowledge, while later simulations incorporate cross-functional decision-making. Additionally, team-based learning fosters peer support, allowing students to share responsibilities and learn collaboratively.

Assessment posed another challenge, as traditional evaluation methods did not fully capture the experiential nature of the course. Measuring student performance solely based on a final examination or business outcomes of a simulation (e.g. profitability or market share) risks overlooking the learning process behind strategic decisions. To address this, the course implemented a multi-dimensional assessment framework that evaluates both technical performance and reflective analysis. Students submit reflective essays where they critically analyze their decision-making processes, discuss challenges encountered during simulations, and identify key lessons learned. Group presentations offer further opportunities for students to articulate their strategies and demonstrate their understanding of core business concepts, while peer evaluations promote accountability and highlight the importance of teamwork. Additionally, the course includes a final examination that combines theoretical and practical elements, ensuring that students are evaluated comprehensively on both conceptual knowledge and applied skills.

Despite these challenges, the course has achieved substantial successes. It has consistently enhanced student engagement, with many participants reporting that the hands-on simulations provide a deeper and more practical understanding of business operations than traditional methods. The course has also fostered entrepreneurial skills, particularly in strategic decision-making and risk management. The course has also strengthened students' collaborative and leadership skills. By working in teams to manage virtual businesses, students learn to negotiate roles, resolve conflicts, and coordinate strategies under time pressure. These experiences closely replicate real-world business environments, where effective teamwork is critical to organizational success.

5. CONCLUSIONS AND RECOMMENDATIONS

The case study of the 'Business Simulation-Games' course highlights the transformative potential of simulation-based learning in entrepreneurship and business education. By immersing students in dynamic, real-world scenarios, the course equips them with essential skills such as strategic decision-making, risk management, adaptability, and teamwork. Through iterative cycles of experience, reflection, conceptualization, and experimentation, guided by Kolb's Experiential Learning Cycle, the course bridges the gap between theoretical knowledge and practical application, preparing students for the complex realities of contemporary business environments (Kolb & Kolb, 2009).

One of the core insights from this case study is the importance of the course design in fostering meaningful learning outcomes. The structured, step-by-step approach used in the course, where simulations gradually increase in complexity, allows students to build confidence and competence incrementally (Greco et al., 2013). This approach is particularly effective in helping students transition from foundational knowledge to more advanced, cross-functional decision-making. It also ensures that students experience a balance of individual responsibility and team collaboration, which mirrors the realities of modern business operations (Colombelli et al., 2022).

The course also emphasizes the importance of selecting the right simulation tools that align with educational objectives. Early challenges related to technological limitations were overcome through strategic partnerships with software providers and the adoption of cloud-based platforms. These technological advancements have improved accessibility, flexibility, and user experience, enabling the course to offer consistent learning opportunities across both in-person and remote formats (Mubaraz & Heikkilä, 2022). For educators interested in adopting simulation-based learning, ensuring that tools are adaptable, user-friendly, and can reflect real-world business complexities is critical (Colombelli et al., 2022).

Another key insight is the role of reflection in fostering deep learning. Reflective exercises, including debriefing sessions, reflective essays, and peer evaluations, are integral to the course's pedagogical approach. These activities encourage students to critically analyze their decisions, identify lessons learned, and continuously refine their strategies (Stirling et al., 2017). By promoting self-awareness and critical thinking, the course helps students cultivate a growth mindset, a crucial attribute for entrepreneurs and leaders navigating rapidly evolving business landscapes (Bell & Bell, 2020). For educators, embedding structured reflection throughout the course can enhance both the retention of knowledge and the development of adaptable problem-solving skills (Fajar & Sarno, 2019).

In conclusion, the 'Business Simulation-Games' course demonstrates how experiential education can equip students with the critical skills needed to thrive in today's business world. By carefully balancing course design, technology integration, active engagement, and reflective practices, educators can create powerful learning environments that support deep learning and lifelong professional development. As higher education institutions strive to address the changing demands of the global economy, courses like this one provide a blueprint for equipping the next generation of business leaders and innovators.

REFERENCES

Abdullah, N. L., Hanafiah, M. H., & Hashim, N. A. (2013). Developing creative teaching module: Business simulation in teaching strategic management. *International Education Studies*, *6*(6). Advance online publication. DOI: 10.5539/ies.v6n6p95

Abwamiah, N., Maulani, G.A.F., Lindayani, & Hamdani, N.A. (2023). The effect of entrepreneurship education on student's entrepreneurship interest in entrepreneurship faculty of Universitas Garut. *Advances in Economics, Business and Management Research*, 1865-1876. .DOI: 10.2991/978-94-6463-234-7_197

Ahn, J. (2008). Application of the experiential learning cycle in learning from a business simulation game. *E-Learning and Digital Media*, *5*(2), 146–156. DOI: 10.2304/elea.2008.5.2.146

Aljohani, M. (2015). Innovation and entrepreneurship integration in education. Ohaio State Model. *International Journal of Teaching and Education*, *III*(3), 1–20. DOI: 10.20472/TE.2015.3.3.001

Alstete, J. W. (2023). Multiplying success: The power of multiple simulations with graduated weighting and coordinated sequencing for learner engagement. *Journal of International Education in Business*, *16*(3), 334–350. DOI: 10.1108/JIEB-04-2023-0018

Angolia, M., & Reed, A. H. (2019). A case for early semester utilization of business simulations. *Journal of Applied Research in Higher Education*, *11*(1), 90–101. DOI: 10.1108/JARHE-07-2017-0082

Apostu, S. A., Mukli, L., Panait, M., Gigauri, I., & Hysa, E. (2022). Economic growth through the lenses of education, entrepreneurship, and innovation. *Administrative Sciences*, *12*(3), 74. DOI: 10.3390/admsci12030074

Avramenko, A. (2012). Enhancing students' employability through business simulation. *Education + Training*, *54*(5), 355–367. DOI: 10.1108/00400911211244669

Ayad, A., Wilkinson, E., & Matthews, R. (2019). Systemic experiential learning model for the evaluation of technological learning: The case of small satellite capability-building in Algeria. *International Journal of Technology Management & Sustainable Development*, *18*(1), 75–100. DOI: 10.1386/tmsd.18.1.75_1

Baden, D., & Parkes, C. (2013). Experiential learning: Inspiring the business leaders of tomorrow. *Journal of Management Development*, *32*(3), 295–308. DOI: 10.1108/02621711311318283

Bell, R. (2021). Underpinning the entrepreneurship educator's toolkit: Conceptualising the influence of educational philosophies and theory. *Entrepreneurship Education*, *4*(1), 1–18. DOI: 10.1007/s41959-020-00042-4

Bell, R., & Bell, H. (2020). Applying educational theory to develop a framework to support the delivery of experiential entrepreneurship education. *Journal of Small Business and Enterprise Development*, *27*(6), 987–1004. DOI: 10.1108/JSBED-01-2020-0012

Blažič, A. J., & Novak, F. (2015). *Challenges of business simulation games - a new approach of teaching business*. E-Learning - Instructional Design, Organizational Strategy and Management. DOI: 10.5772/61242

Brazhkin, V., & Zimmerman, H. (2019). Students' perceptions of learning in an online multiround business simulation game: What can we learn from them? *Decision Sciences Journal of Innovative Education, 17*(4), 363–386. DOI: 10.1111/dsji.12189

Buil, I., Catalán, S., & Martínez, E. P. (2018). Exploring students' flow experiences in business simulation games. *Journal of Computer Assisted Learning, 34*(2), 183–192. DOI: 10.1111/jcal.12237

Chandwaskar, P., & Jape, S. (2024). Case of learnbiz simulations: Challenges and opportunities ahead. *Emerging Economies Cases Journal, 6*(2), 83–90. DOI: 10.1177/25166042241228367

Colombelli, A., Loccisano, S., Panelli, A., Pennisi, O. A. M., & Serraino, F. (2022). Entrepreneurship education: The effects of challenge-based learning on the entrepreneurial mindset of university students. *Administrative Sciences, 12*(1), 10. DOI: 10.3390/admsci12010010

D'Angelo, S., Ghezzi, A., Cavallo, A., Rangone, A., & Annunziata, S. (2023). Corporate experimentation: Antitode or oxymoron? *European Conference on Innovation and Entrepreneurship*, 18(1), 234-241. DOI: 10.34190/ecie.18.1.1771

Davitadze, M., Ooi, E., Ng, C. Y., Zhou, D., Thomas, L., Hanania, T., Blaggan, P., Evans, N., Chen, W., Melson, E., Arlt, W., & Kempegowda, P. (2021). Simba: Using Kolb's learning theory in simulation-based learning to improve participants' confidence. *BMC Medical Education, 22*(1), 116. [REMOVED HYPERLINK FIELD]DOI: 10.1186/s12909-022-03176-2 PMID: 35193557

Dharmastuti, C. F., Darmoyo, S., Gunawan, R. A., & Duka, M. N. (2021). Business simulation, student competency, and learning outcomes. *Jurnal Manajemen, 25*(1), 160. DOI: 10.24912/jm.v25i1.709

Dhliwayo, S. (2008). Experiential learning in entrepreneurship education. *Education + Training, 50*(4), 329–340. DOI: 10.1108/00400910810880560

Drury-Grogan, M. L., & Russ, T. L. (2013). A contemporary simulation infused in the business communication curriculum. *Business Communication Quarterly, 76*(3), 304–321. DOI: 10.1177/1080569913493923

Du Toit, A. (2023). Entrepreneurial Learning: Creating Value towards Social Justice. *Research in Educational Policy and Management, 5*(3), 1–19. DOI: 10.46303/repam.2023.18

Dwiniasih, D., & Khumaeroh, I. (2021). How do pre-service teachers deliver their instruction during teaching practicum?: Voice from EFL classrooms. *Research and Innovation in Language Learning, 4*(1), 1. DOI: 10.33603/rill.v4i1.3958

Egieya, Z. E., Ewuga, S. K., Omotosho, A., Adegbite, A. O., & Oriekhoe, O. I. (2023). A review of sustainable entrepreneurship practices and their impact on long-term business viability. *World Journal of Advanced Research and Reviews, 20*(3), 1283–1292. DOI: 10.30574/wjarr.2023.20.3.2588

Ellinger, A. D., Trent, R., Wang, Y., Wofford, G., Howard, Y., Cho, I., & Wooten, B. (2007). Experiencing scholarly writing through a collaborative course project. In Reynolds, M., & Vince, R. (Eds.), *The Handbook of Experiential Learning and Management Education* (pp. 309–326)., DOI: 10.1093/oso/9780199217632.003.0019

Englis, B. G., & Frederiks, A. (2023). Using experimental designs to study entrepreneurship education: A historical overview, critical evaluation of current practices in the field, and directions for future research. *Entrepreneurship Education and Pedagogy*, *7*(1), 93–149. DOI: 10.1177/25151274231161102

Fairlie, R. W., & Holleran, W. (2012). Entrepreneurship training, risk aversion and other personality traits: Evidence from a random experiment. *Journal of Economic Psychology*, *33*(2), 366–378. DOI: 10.1016/j.joep.2011.02.001

Fajar, A., & Sarno, R. (2019). Asynchronous agent-based simulation and optimization of parallel business. *Telkomnika*, *17*(4), 1731. DOI: 10.12928/telkomnika.v17i4.10846

Faria, A. J. (2001). The changing nature of business simulation/ gaming research: A brief history. *Simulation & Gaming*, *32*(1), 97–110. DOI: 10.1177/104687810103200108

Farooq, M. S., Salam, M., Rehman, S. U., Fayolle, A., Jaafar, N., & Ayupp, K. (2018). Impact of support from social network on entrepreneurial intention of fresh business graduates. *Education + Training*, *60*(4), 335–353. DOI: 10.1108/ET-06-2017-0092

Fauzan, A. C., Sarno, R., & Yaqin, M. A. (2017). Performance measurement based on coloured petri net simulation of scalable business processes. *Proceeding of the Electrical Engineering Computer Science and Informatics*, 4(1). DOI: 10.1109/EECSI.2017.8239121

Feng, Y., Lin, F., & Huang, M. (2024). Application of seminar teaching method combined with case-based learning and problem-based learning teaching models in oral clinical nursing teaching. *Journal of Contemporary Educational Research*, *8*(4), 176–181. DOI: 10.26689/jcer.v8i4.6521

Fox, J., Pittaway, L., & Uzuegbunam, I. (2018). Simulations in entrepreneurship education: Serious games and learning through play. *Entrepreneurship Education and Pedagogy*, *1*(1), 61–89. DOI: 10.1177/2515127417737285

Gopalan, M., Rosinger, K. O., & Ahn, J. B. (2020). Use of quasi-experimental research designs in education research: Growth, promise, and challenges. *Review of Research in Education*, *44*(1), 218–243. DOI: 10.3102/0091732X20903302

Greco, M., Baldissin, N., & Nonino, F. (2013). An exploratory taxonomy of business games. *Simulation & Gaming*, *44*(5), 645–682. DOI: 10.1177/1046878113501464

Gürpınar, E., Batı, H., & Tetik, C. (2011). Learning styles of medical students change in relation to time. *Advances in Physiology Education*, *35*(3), 307–311. [REMOVED HYPERLINK FIELD]DOI: 10.1152/advan.00047.2011 PMID: 21908841

Hagebakken, G., Reimers, C. S., & Solstad, E. (2021). Entrepreneurship education as a strategy to build regional sustainability. *Sustainability (Basel)*, *13*(5), 2529. DOI: 10.3390/su13052529

Hannig, A., Kuth, N., Özman, M., Jonas, S., & Spreckelsen, C. (2012). Emedoffice: A web-based collaborative serious game for teaching optimal design of a medical practice. *BMC Medical Education*, *12*(1), 104. Advance online publication. DOI: 10.1186/1472-6920-12-104 PMID: 23110606

Hariyono, H. (2024). Building a future generation of entrepreneurs: An experimental study of the integration of PBL and AI in entrepreneurial. *EDUTEC: Journal of Education and Technology*, *7*(4), 444–453. DOI: 10.29062/edu.v7i4.921

Jayawarna, D., Jones, O., & Macpherson, A. (2014). Entrepreneurial potential: The role of human and cultural capitals. *International Small Business Journal*, *32*(8), 918–943. DOI: 10.1177/0266242614525795

Kassean, H., Vanevenhoven, J., Liguori, E. W., & Winkel, D. (2015). Entrepreneurship education: A need for reflection, real-world experience and action. *International Journal of Entrepreneurial Behaviour & Research*, *21*(5), 690–708. DOI: 10.1108/IJEBR-07-2014-0123

Kaya, T., Erkut, B., & Thierbach, N. (2019). Entrepreneurial intentions of business and economics students in Germany and Cyprus: A cross-cultural comparison. *Sustainability (Basel)*, *11*(5), 1437. DOI: 10.3390/su11051437

Khanduri, V., & Teotia, D. A. (2023). Revolutionizing learning: An exploratory study on the impact of technology-enhanced learning using digital learning platforms and AI tools on the study habits of university students through focus group discussions. *International Journal of Research Publication and Reviews*, *4*(6), 663–672. DOI: 10.55248/gengpi.4.623.44407

Kiat, T. Y., Jumintono, J., Kriswanto, E. S., Sugiri, S., Handayani, E., Anggarini, Y., & Rofik, M. (2020). The effectiveness of multimedia learning on academic achievement in reproduction topic science subject. *Universal Journal of Educational Research*, *8*(8), 3625–3629. DOI: 10.13189/ujer.2020.080839

Kiyomi, A., Bayoumi, K. A., Din, N. S. E., Abuhassna, H., & Ali, E. A. (2022). Bibliometric analysis of entrepreneurship education research from 2012 to 2022. *International Journal of Academic Research in Business & Social Sciences*, *12*(11). Advance online publication. DOI: 10.6007/IJARBSS/v12-i11/15646

Klofsten, M., Jones-Evans, D., & Pereira, L. (2020). Teaching science and technology PhD students in entrepreneurship-Potential learning opportunities and outcomes. *The Journal of Technology Transfer*, *46*(2), 319–334. DOI: 10.1007/s10961-020-09784-8

Kolb, A., & Kolb, D. (2009). Experiential learning theory: a dynamic, holistic approach to management learning, education and development. In Armstrong, S. J., & Fukami, C. V. (Eds.), *The SAGE Handbook of Management Learning, Education and Development* (pp. 42–68). SAGE., DOI: 10.4135/9780857021038.n3

Krakauer, P. V. C., Serra, F. A. R., & de Almeida, M. I. R. (2017). Using experiential learning to teach entrepreneurship: A study with Brazilian undergraduate students. *International Journal of Educational Management*, *31*(7), 986–999. DOI: 10.1108/IJEM-09-2016-0189

Kremel, A., & Edman, K.W. (2019). Implementing design thinking as didactic method in entrepreneurship education. The importance of through. *The Design Journal*, 22(sup1), 163-175. .DOI: 10.1080/14606925.2019.1595855

Kurbjuhn, B., Kramer, F., & Turowski, K. (2014). Challenges for cloud-based simulation games. *Proceeding of the 47th Hawaii International Conference on System Sciences*. DOI: 10.1109/HICSS.2014.162

Lackéus, M. (2020). Comparing the impact of three different experiential approaches to entrepreneurship in education. *International Journal of Entrepreneurial Behaviour & Research, 26*(5), 937–971. DOI: 10.1108/IJEBR-04-2018-0236

Lattacher, W., & Wdowiak, M. A. (2020). Entrepreneurial learning from failure. A systematic review. *International Journal of Entrepreneurial Behaviour & Research, 26*(5), 1093–1131. DOI: 10.1108/IJEBR-02-2019-0085

Li, Y., Shen, W., & Lv, Y. (2020). Quality evaluation of entrepreneurship education in Chinese medical colleges–From the perspective of student cognition. *Frontiers in Psychology, 11*, 1093. Advance online publication. [REMOVED HYPERLINK FIELD]DOI: 10.3389/fpsyg.2020.01093 PMID: 32625132

Longva, K. K., & Foss, L. (2018). Measuring impact through experimental design in entrepreneurship education: A literature review and research agenda. *Industry and Higher Education, 32*(6), 358–374. DOI: 10.1177/0950422218804912

Loon, M., Evans, J., & Kerridge, C. (2015). Learning with a strategic management simulation game: A case study. *International Journal of Management Education, 13*(3), 227–236. DOI: 10.1016/j.ijme.2015.06.002

Lourenço, F., Jones, O., & Jayawarna, D. (2012). Promoting sustainable development: The role of entrepreneurship education. *International Small Business Journal, 31*(8), 841–865. DOI: 10.1177/0266242611435825

Macht, S., & Ball, S. (2016). "Authentic alignment" - A new framework of entrepreneurship education. *Education + Training, 58*(9), 926–944. DOI: 10.1108/ET-07-2015-0063

Macllaro, R. (2013). The learning journal bridge: From classroom concepts to leadership practices. *Journal of Leadership Education, 12*(1), 234–244. DOI: 10.12806/V12/I1/234

Maresch, D., Harms, R., Kailer, N., & Wimmer-Wurm, B. (2016). The impact of entrepreneurship education on the entrepreneurial intention of students in science and engineering versus business studies university programs. *Technological Forecasting and Social Change, 104*, 172–179. DOI: 10.1016/j.techfore.2015.11.006

Mariani, M. M., & Nambisan, S. (2021). Innovation analytics and digital innovation experimentation: The rise of research-driven online review platforms. *Technological Forecasting and Social Change, 172*, 121009. DOI: 10.1016/j.techfore.2021.121009

Mariappan, L. (2024). Mindful teaching, diverse learning: Harnessing multiple intelligences for students success. *Journal of Electrical Systems, 20*(7s), 1720–1725. DOI: 10.52783/jes.3768

McCarthy, M. C. (2016). Experiential learning theory: From theory to practice. *Journal of Business & Economics Research, 14*(3), 91–100. DOI: 10.19030/jber.v14i3.9749

Memar, N., Sundström, A., & Larsson, T. (2020). Teaching causation and effectuation in the large classroom: A production–trade game. *Journal of Management Education, 45*(3), 438–478. DOI: 10.1177/1052562920951971

Monk, E., & Lycett, M. (2014). Measuring business process learning with enterprise resource planning systems to improve the value of education. *Education and Information Technologies*, *21*(4), 747–768. DOI: 10.1007/s10639-014-9352-6

Monllor, J., Michels, N., & Adderley, S. (2023). Pivoting an entrepreneurship experiential learning module online: Applying a concrete experience framework. *Entrepreneurship Education and Pedagogy*, *7*(4), 416–438. DOI: 10.1177/25151274231217953

Morris, T. H. (2019). Experiential learning - A systematic review and revision of Kolb's model. *Interactive Learning Environments*, *28*(8), 1064–1077. DOI: 10.1080/10494820.2019.1570279

Mubaraz, S., & Heikkilä, J. (2022). Business simulations as effective virtual and experiential learning environment. INTED2022 Proceedings, 6743-6749. DOI: 10.21125/inted.2022.1705

Nguy n, T. T., Nguyen, L. T. P., Phan, H. T. T., & Vu, A. T. (2021). Impact of entrepreneurship extracurricular activities and inspiration on entrepreneurial intention: Mediator and moderator effect. *SAGE Open*, *11*(3), 21582440211032174. Advance online publication. DOI: 10.1177/21582440211032174

Olumekor, M., Mohiuddin, M., & Su, Z. (2023). Effective altruism and the dark side of entrepreneurship. *Frontiers in Psychology*, *14*, 1247331. Advance online publication. DOI: 10.3389/fpsyg.2023.1247331 PMID: 37908811

Park, S., & Kim, S. (2023). The Avaritia: Entrepreneurship practice to understand the problem of information control through gamification. *Sustainability (Basel)*, *15*(8), 6738. DOI: 10.3390/su15086738

Peterková, J., Repaská, Z., & Prachařová, L. (2022). Best practice of using digital business simulation games in business education. *Sustainability (Basel)*, *14*(15), 8987. DOI: 10.3390/su14158987

Pham, M., Nguyen, A. T. T., Tran, D. T., Mai, T. T., & Nguyen, V. T. (2023). The impact of entrepreneurship knowledge on students' e-entrepreneurial intention formation and the moderating role of technological innovativeness. *Journal of Innovation and Entrepreneurship*, *12*(1), 80. Advance online publication. DOI: 10.1186/s13731-023-00351-7

Piercy, N. (2013). Evaluating experiential learning in the business context: Contributions to group-based and cross-functional working. *Innovations in Education and Teaching International*, *50*(2), 202–213. DOI: 10.1080/14703297.2012.760870

Pittaway, L., Rodriguez-Falcon, E., Aiyegbayo, O., & King, A. S. (2011). The role of entrepreneurship clubs and societies in entrepreneurial learning. *International Small Business Journal*, *29*(1), 37–57. DOI: 10.1177/0266242610369876

Politis, D. (2005). The process of entrepreneurial learning: A conceptual framework. *Entrepreneurship Theory and Practice*, *29*(4), 399–424. DOI: 10.1111/j.1540-6520.2005.00091.x

Radford, S. K., Hunt, D. M., & Andrus, D. (2015). Experiential learning projects. *Journal of Macromarketing*, *35*(4), 466–472. DOI: 10.1177/0276146715573834

Raja, F. U., & Najmonnisa, K. (2018). Comparing Traditional Teaching Method and Experiential Teaching Method using Experimental Research. *Journal of Education and Educational Development*, *5*(2), 276. DOI: 10.22555/joeed.v5i2.1816

Rajeswarie, S., Praveen, K., Sangam, M. R., Vinay, G., Bokan, R. R., Deka, R., & Kaur, A. (2022). Comparison of team-based learning over conventional didactic lecture among second-year MBBS students. *Cureus*. Advance online publication. [REMOVED HYPERLINK FIELD]DOI: 10.7759/cureus.21792 PMID: 35251859

Rippa, P., Landi, G. C., Cosimato, S., Turriziani, L., & Gheith, M. H. (2020). Embedding entrepreneurship in doctoral students: The impact of a t-shaped educational approach. *European Journal of Innovation Management*, *25*(1), 249–270. DOI: 10.1108/EJIM-07-2020-0289

Robinson, S., Neergaard, H., Pedersen, L. T., & Krueger, N. (2016). New horizons in entrepreneurship education: From teacher-led to student-centered learning. *Education + Training*, *58*(7/8), 661–683. DOI: 10.1108/ET-03-2016-0048

Rosenthal, K., Ternes, B., & Strecker, S. (2021). Business process simulation on procedural graphical process models. *Business & Information Systems Engineering*, *63*(5), 569–602. DOI: 10.1007/s12599-021-00690-3

Salavou, H., Chalkos, G., & Lioukas, S. (2021). Linkages between entrepreneurial intentions and entrepreneurship education: New evidence on the gender imbalance. *Education + Training*, *63*(6), 906–919. DOI: 10.1108/ET-10-2020-0301

Samašonok, K., Išoraitė, M., & Žirnelė, L. (2020). Education of entrepreneurship by participation in a business simulation enterprise activities: Conditions of effectiveness and opportunities for improvement. *Entrepreneurship and Sustainability Issues*, *7*(4), 3122–3144. DOI: 10.9770/jesi.2020.7.4(36)

Sandirasegarane, S., Sutermaster, S., Gill, A., Volz, J., & Mehta, K. (2016). Context-driven entrepreneurial education in vocational schools. *International Journal for Research in Vocational Education and Training*, *3*(2), 106–126. DOI: 10.13152/IJRVET.3.2.3

Seaman, J. (2008). Experience, reflect, critique: The end of the "learning cycles" era. *Journal of Experiential Education*, *31*(1), 3–18. DOI: 10.1177/105382590803100103

Seikkula-Leino, J., Ruskovaara, E., Pihkala, T., Rodríguez, I. D., & Delfino, J. (2019). Developing entrepreneurship education in Europe: Teachers' commitment to entrepreneurship education in the UK, Finland and Spain. In Fayolle, A., Kariv, D., & Matlay, H. (Eds.), *The Role and Impact of Entrepreneurship Education* (pp. 130–145)., DOI: 10.4337/9781786438232.00014

Sreenivasan, A., & Suresh, M. (2023). Twenty years of entrepreneurship education: A bibliometric analysis. *Entrepreneurship Education*, *6*(1), 45–68. DOI: 10.1007/s41959-023-00089-z

Stander, J., Grimmer, K., & Brink, Y. (2019). Learning styles of physiotherapists: A systematic scoping review. *BMC Medical Education*, *19*(1), 2. Advance online publication. [REMOVED HYPERLINK FIELD]DOI: 10.1186/s12909-018-1434-5 PMID: 30606180

Stirling, A., Kerr, G., MacPherson, E., Banwell, J., Bandealy, A., & Battaglia, A. (2017). Do postsecondary internships address the four learning modes of experiential learning theory? An exploration through document analysis. *Canadian Journal of Higher Education*, *47*(1), 27–48. DOI: 10.47678/cjhe.v47i1.186196

Su, Y., Zhu, Z., Chen, J., Jin, Y., Wang, T., Lin, C., & Xu, D. (2021). Factors influencing entrepreneurial intention of university students in China: Integrating the perceived university support and theory of planned behavior. *Sustainability (Basel), 13*(8), 4519. DOI: 10.3390/su13084519

Sung, C. S., & Park, J. Y. (2018). Sustainability orientation and entrepreneurship orientation: Is there a tradeoff relationship between them? *Sustainability (Basel), 10*(2), 379. DOI: 10.3390/su10020379

Suseno, Y., & Abbott, L. (2021). Women entrepreneurs' digital social innovation: Linking gender, entrepreneurship, social innovation and information systems. *Information Systems Journal, 31*(5), 717–744. DOI: 10.1111/isj.12327

Tican, C. (2019). Pre-service primary school and pre-school teachers' perception of individual entrepreneurship and opinions about their creative thinking tendency. *International Journal of Educational Methodology, 5*(4), 591–606. DOI: 10.12973/ijem.5.4.591

Tsaknis, P. A., Sahinidis, A. G., & Vassiliou, E. E. (2022). Entrepreneurship education effectiveness: Does personality matter? *Development and Learning in Organizations, 36*(6), 8–11. DOI: 10.1108/DLO-12-2021-0230

van Krevelen, R., Warnier, M., Brazier, F. M. T., Verbraeck, A., & Corsi, T. M. (2011). Transparency, consistency and modularity of strategic reasoning: an agent architecture for interactive business simulations. *Proceedings of the 2011 Winter Simulation Conference (WSC)*, 1612-1623, DOI: 10.1109/WSC.2011.6147878

Vojtko, V., & Hesková, M. (2010). Constructivist use of business simulators in education. *Communications of the IBIMA*, 1–11. DOI: 10.5171/2010.366397

Wang, H. W., Liu, G., & Yang, Z. D. (2013). Business-task coupled process management for complex product simulation. *Applied Mechanics and Materials, 394*, 531–535. . DOI: 10.4028/www.scientific.net/AMM.394.531

Wang, J., Guo, Y., Zhang, M., Li, N., Li, K., Li, P., Huang, L., & Huang, Y. (2022). The impact of entrepreneurship competitions on entrepreneurial competence of Chinese college students. *Frontiers in Psychology, 13*, 784225. Advance online publication. [REMOVED HYPERLINK FIELD]DOI: 10.3389/fpsyg.2022.784225 PMID: 35295399

Wellington, W. J., Hutchinson, D., & Faria, A. J. (2016). Measuring the impact of a marketing simulation game. *Simulation & Gaming, 48*(1), 56–80. DOI: 10.1177/1046878116675103

Wheadon, J. D., & Duval-Couetil, N. (2014). Business plan development activities as a pedagogical tool in entrepreneurship education. *The Journal of Engineering Entrepreneurship, 5*(1), 31–48. DOI: 10.7814/jeen5v5p3wd

Williams, D. (2015). The impact of simventure on the development of entrepreneurial skills in management students. *Industry and Higher Education, 29*(5), 379–395. DOI: 10.5367/ihe.2015.0270

Xie, Q. (2022). Using task-based approach in business English courses for English-majors at a Chinese university. *International Journal of Chinese Education, 11*(2), 2212585X221099104. Advance online publication. DOI: 10.1177/2212585X221099104

Yan, Y. (2020). Exploration and practice of maker education mode in innovation and entrepreneurship education. *Frontiers in Psychology*, *11*, 1626. Advance online publication. DOI: 10.3389/fpsyg.2020.01626 PMID: 33013496

Yoehono, T., & Liliani, L. (2018). Innovativeness differences of studentpreneurs based on entrepreneurship experiential learning. *International Journal of Academic Research in Business & Social Sciences*, *8*(3). Advance online publication. DOI: 10.6007/IJARBSS/v8-i3/3932

Yusof, R., Yin, K. Y., Norwani, N. M., Ismail, Z., Ahmad, A. S., & Salleh, S. M. (2020). Teaching through experiential learning cycle to enhance student engagement in principles of accounting. *International Journal of Learning. Teaching and Educational Research*, *19*(10), 323–337. DOI: 10.26803/ijlter.19.10.18

Zapalska, A. M. (2021). Designing an experiential learning with simulations and games to improve education in an undergraduate engineering major. *Asean Journal of Engineering Education*, *5*(1), 32–43. DOI: 10.11113/ajee2021.5n1.59

Zhou, Y., Li, H., & Shahzad, F. (2021). Does college education promote entrepreneurship education in China? *SAGE Open*, *11*(3), 21582440211031616. Advance online publication. DOI: 10.1177/21582440211031616

Chapter 7
Pedagogical Approaches Using Simulations to Enhance Learning Outcomes in Business Education

Zacharias Dermatis
https://orcid.org/0000-0001-5605-3169
University of Peloponnese, Greece

Komninos Dimitrios
https://orcid.org/0009-0004-1461-7332
University of Peloponnese, Greece

Athanasios Anastasiou
University of Peloponnese, Greece

ABSTRACT

This chapter examines simulation tools in business education, showcasing their ability to bridge theory and practice while developing skills like problem-solving, decision-making, and teamwork. Rooted in experiential and collaborative learning, simulations enable students to engage in real-world scenarios. Tools such as the Business Strategy Game, SimVenture, and Markstrat demonstrate value in teaching strategic management, SME operations, and marketing strategies. Key benefits include active participation, real-time feedback, and adaptability, though challenges like costs, technical issues, and training requirements persist. The chapter highlights the need for curriculum integration, teacher training, and advanced technologies like AI and AR to fully utilize simulations. While not a universal solution, they effectively prepare students for the complexities of modern business education.

DOI: 10.4018/979-8-3693-9040-5.ch007

INTRODUCTION

The infusing of simulation tools in business education is appearing as an innovative and must needful teaching methodology relative to the scenario of the ever-changing work atmosphere. Considering the dynamics within the global market, fast technological advancements, and increasing business processes' complexities, there arises a compelling necessity for educational practices that extend beyond traditional instruction to incorporate students' active participation and internship.

Adapting simulation tools to the unique needs of the user is another reason for their acceptance. Today's platforms make it possible to design customized learning experiences corresponding to a given learner's level of knowledge, skills, and goals. This component enhances individualized instruction, enabling students to learn at their preferred rates (de Freitas & Oliver, 2006).

In recent years, the approach in entrepreneurial education has been changed to innovations that correspond to the requirements of a globalized and dynamically changing business environment. In such an environment, the application of simulation has developed as one of the best ways to improve experiential learning. This will facilitate such critical skills as problem solving, strategic thinking and decision making and enhance learner involvement (Lean et al., 2006).

Simulations invite the trainee into real business situations wherein the application of theoretical concepts to practical problems is demanded. Bridging the gap between theory and application, it enhances understanding and hones critical skills. According to Garris et al. (2002), this is because simulations create an environment for learning where a learner can apply various strategies, test them, evaluate the outcome and then make any necessary changes.

Perhaps one of the "basic" skills developed through simulation is problem solving, whereby participants are exposed to identifying and analyzing complex problems, developing alternatives and selecting the best course of action. Moreover, strategic thinking and capacity of making decisions are drawn out through managing limited resources, risk-taking, and operational conditions. (Faria & Dickinson, 1994).

1. The Importance of Simulation in Education

One of the most innovative and efficient teaching methods for business education in the current scenario is believed to be simulation. The major reason behind its widespread recognition has been its provision of a secure learning environment based on which learners can apply their theoretic knowledge, experiment, draw conclusions without really having to face failures in practice (Gredler, 2004). Specifically, in business training, it allows the provision of realistic scenarios in business crisis management, strategic product positioning, or financial analysis that make learners practice close to reality.

1.1. The Value of Simulation in Education

Simulation in education is a value that plays a bridging role between theory and actual practice. Concepts learned may be applied in a controlled environment to problems, and possible results observed for effective strategy management in real-life situations. As stressed by Gredler (2004), this helps in enhancing the understanding of issues and consolidating knowledge since the participants learn through experience and not theory.

These are the only risks involved to students—here adverse consequences do not occur: There is no loss of real money when using simulations, making it helpful in business education for brainstorming various scenarios and strategies without worrying about the financial or professional ripple they would have in a real working environment. (Kolb, 1984).

1.2. Applications in Business Education

Simulations have had numerous applications in business education, as they open up a window of exposure to lifelike business situations.

1. **Operational Crises Management**

Most high-stress job skills are ones that can be put to test in 'must-win' simulations. For example, imposition of managing a product recall or handling PR during post-negative advertising, to a given situation, like the defect case scenario, among other strategic 'games' for students keeps coming up in discussion relatively more often (Clarke, 2009).

2. **Strategic Product Placement**

Another use would be the possibility of strategic planning simulations, for example, the marketing of products. Here students would be required to assess market data, carry out competition analysis, devise pricing strategies or promotions for the success of a product. This helps familiarize students with actual strategic planning challenges (Faria & Dickinson, 1994).

3. **Financial Analysis**

Lean et al (2006) further claim that such activities facilitate knowledge and application of financial principles in real economic scenarios. Financial simulations or simulations are "playing" investments against real economic conditions and "playing" budgets in the management of the "just in time" environment.

These activities support the enhancement of economic principles and data-driven decision-making.

2. PEDAGOGICAL THEORIES SUPPORTING THE USE OF SIMULATIONS

Simulator learning philosophy comes from constructive and socio-cognitive epistemology, which formulates, as a theory, the theoretical underpinning that makes the use of simulators in educational theories so efficacious in learning and skills development.

2.1. Constructive Learning

Constructivism theory, according to Piaget (1971), attempts to explain that knowledge is not absorbed from the environment but learned actively through interaction with the environment. The simulation of the learning process further substantiates this, as it provides a controlled environment in which students can explore the concepts and find out things on their own.

The simulations are, therefore, an active means of involvement of the learner in the learning process. Learner involvement in real-life situations will ask them to relate to and apply the content of bookish knowledge. Such types of experiences lead to deep understanding, as the participants do not take information passively but create new knowledge through experience.

The simulations scaffold the construction of knowledge-referred to as feedback in chunks. This is because the students are given information directly regarding their decisions and actions regarding what specifically went wrong; thus, they can re-strategize as well as learn from their mistakes. This part of the simulation resonates Piaget's ideologies, emphasizing self-regulation and re-examination in learning.

2.2. Collaborative Learning and Simulations

Cooperative learning is how Vygotsky (1978) describes the social process of learning as being the most effective way to learn through other people. There's plenty of opportunity for collaboration in the simulations, too, since they can be designed to require interaction and a consensus from a group of people.

Participants frequently have to collaborate in simulation scenarios to solve problems, plan strategies, or make key decisions. All this enhances communication, conflict management, and understanding different perspectives. Students learn how to work in a team and bring their forces together for common goals.

Vygotsky's theory about the zone of proximal development is perhaps one of the best applications for simulations. Interaction with others may help learners attain much more understanding and skill above what they can do alone. For instance, in group simulations, advanced students can help the novices to learn in a social development situation.

2.3. Empirical Learning and Simulations

Kolb (1984) posited the experiential learning theory, which conceptualizes the experience as a core element of learning. In the opinion of Kolb learning does not proceed linearly but entails a cycle of four stages: experiencing, reflective observation, conceptualization and active experimentation.

Simulations present students with experience in real situations about real problems. From these experiences, participants develop critical thinking skills since they have to analyze data, assess different strategies, and take informed decisions. It also promotes self-knowledge since the student can identify his or her strengths and weaknesses through the reflective process.

Reflection is a key aspect of experiential learning and forms the core of simulations. Students are supposed to reflect on their actions and decisions, and what might have worked or not. Through this, the experience can be made into actionable knowledge thereby enhancing the potential for improvement in the future.

3. TEACHING METHODS USING SIMULATION TOOLS

The preregistration of simulation tools in the pedagogic set creates new opportunities to develop skills and knowledge on the basis of a combination of theoretical and practical methodologies. Case studies active teaching, real-time feedback, an approach to create a dynamic learning environment for participation. It enhances teaching through simulations methods case studies, active teaching, real-time feedback with an aim to create a dynamic learning environment which promotes participation, critical thinking and development of professional skills.

3.1. Case Studies Through Simulations

Case studies combined with simulation tools are among the most widely used pedagogical strategies. For instance, they can be applied in inviting the trainees to analyze and control actual operational state-based scenarios that would relate to aspects like crisis management, new product development, partner trading, or investment assessment.

Kim et al. (2006) argued that case studies by means of simulations enable learners to comprehend complex business problems and provide them with a chance to put theoretical concepts into practice.

For example, the simulation of strategic management incorporates an analysis of market data, and through this, students can be exposed to the actual practice of strategic decision-making based on certain sets of alternatives and live with the outcomes of their choices.

3.2. Energetic Teaching

Dynamic learning activities like projects also call for students to think of multiple alternatives, assess the advantages and disadvantages of each option and substantiate their choices. This becomes very handy in developing creativity for the learners since they can identify problems and think of innovative solutions.

Active teaching is all about getting learners to be actively involved in the learning process. Simulation tools further such practice by allowing students to step into roles like Director, Strategic Adviser, or Financial Analyst.

Assigning roles to students makes the learning experience more empiric and interesting. It allows them to apply their abilities through the given simulation operating in real work conditions. For example, in project management simulation, they can perform resource management, schedule tracking, and risk management.

A more active involvement and provision of the autonomy of information to students are associated with taking out a subscription. No longer do the trainees just absorb information – they become actors in the learning process and gain confidence and initiative (Prince, 2004). This would help students to relate better to course content and understand how theoretical concepts are actually applied in real situations.

3.3 Real-Time Feedback

Real-time feedback is perhaps the most important of the many benefits modern simulation tools offer. This enables students to view instant outcomes resulting from their decisions and serves to provoke reflection on decisions and modification of strategies.

Feedback often tends to concern data yielded by the simulation. For instance, in a finance simulation, students may track how investment choices impact a company's financial performance. Such data fosters reflection and continuous improvement because learners analyze their decisions and ways to improve (Hattie & Timperley, 2007).

Simulation tools enable students to try out different approaches and then check the outcomes in a safe environment, which enriches the entire process of learning since students do not just pay but learn from their mistakes without having to face the consequences that would exist in a real workplace..

4. SIMULATION TOOLS IN BUSINESS EDUCATION

Enabled to create learning for students that is as realistic as possible through realistic situations, the use of simulation tools in business education has gained great popularity. Three of the well-known simulation tools are the Business Strategy Game (BSG), SimVenture and Markstrat. Usually every one of these concentrates on different dimensions of business education-strategic management, entrepreneurship and small business management and marketing strategy respectively.

4.1. Business Strategy Game (BSG)

Today, one of the most famous simulations in business management is the Business Strategy Game (BSG). The BSG is intended for students of business administration. They are supposed to act as executives of a virtual company in the tough global market.

BSG is an integrated simulation environment in which participants make decisions pertaining to production, marketing, finance, operations, and strategic positioning of their company. Every decision taken affects the performance of the company, and the results are reflected through a number of financial and strategic indicators (Gove & Marquez, 2012).

BSG reinforces strategic thinking, data analysis, and decision-making within the context of a complex business environment. Students are confronted with "live" problems to solve, i.e., how to optimize productive resources, how to learn to market changes, and react to competitors' moves. This helps in understanding how markets work and grooms leadership skills.

Research shows that the use of BSG enhances student participation and understanding. For example, Faria et al. (2009) argue that BSG fosters collaborative learning since students go into group decision making and strategy development as far as the game is concerned. This also instills communication and teamwork within them.

4.2. SimVenture: Management of Small and Medium Enterprises

SimVenture is what can be claimed to be such a simulation tool for SME management learning. In a particular instance, it enables students to implement their start-up strategies in terms of growth, financial management, hiring, and marketing for a particular venture.

SimVenture covers many bases: writing a business plan, day-to-day operational management, and decision making in business growth. It allows students to try different strategies, assess the impact of their actions, and enhance their management through feedback (Scott et al., 2016).

SimVenture is a complete business management trainer that trains its users in handling limited resources, tackling the challenges imposed by the markets on attracting and retaining customers, etc. It also helps in improving business thinking and creativity.

It has been adopted at universities as a teaching tool for students in entrepreneurship programs. Bellotti et al. (2013) have reported that simulations increase engagement among students while providing a safe environment for risk-taking.

4.3. Markstrat: Marketing Strategy

Thus, Markstrat is a marketing strategy and market analysis-focused decision-making simulation instrument. Very exemplary are its applications in university instruction and corporate staff training in the marketing field.

It simulates a real-life market management scenario, where students make choices on product enhancements' pricing, distributions, and promotions based on analyzed market data and competitor tracking. (Larreche, 2001).

Learning simulation enables students to comprehend marketing strategy principles and develop market analysis skills. Through the process of decision-making, the participants refine their strategies aligned with the requirements of the markets and improve their judgment capabilities. (Cadotte, 2016).

Markstrat has been broadly applied in MBAs and executive training. One of its users, Larreche (2001), argues that -- through simulation--students grasp the fundamental role of marketing: the analysis of data and strategic decision-making.

4.4. Benchmarking of Tools

The three tools offer unique opportunities for learning, focusing on different aspects of entrepreneurship:

Table 1. Benchmarking of tools

Tool	Focus	Skills Developed	Educational Environment
Business strategy game	Strategic business management	Strategic thinking, data analysis, leadership	Collaborative learning
SimVenture	SME management	Business thinking, resource management	Individual or group involvement
Markstrat	Marketing strategy	Market analysis, decision making, adaptability	Market Simulation

5. ADVANTAGES AND CHALLENGES OF SIMULATION

5.1 Advantages

Simulation is one of the very innovative and effective teaching methodologies, which may provide various benefits to enhance the learning process at all levels. The possibilities provided by simulation tools are beyond that of the conventional mode of imparting education and create more interactivity, realism, and engagement in learning. The main benefits include:

- **Safe Learning Environments:** According to Alessi and Trollip (2001), students can experiment without real resources or fear of the consequences of wrong decisions.
- **Active Participation:** Thus, engagement is promoted: Simulations engage learners in the learning process more than do expository lectures. The former encourages independence and enterprise (Kolb, 1984).
- **Higher-Order Thinking:** Students are required to assess information, solve problems, or make decisions based on the evidence provided, fostering higher-order thinking (de Freitas & Oliver, 2006).
- **Flexible Adaptation:** The simulations can be tailored to the specific students or groups, thereby offering a customized learning experience for the students (Brockbank & McGill, 2007).
- **Real-Time Feedback:** Other simulation applications offer the means of returning instant feedback to students, who, in real-time, can see the implications of their choices. This furthers the learning process since they can go back over their error and fine-tune their strategy with the information they have (Hattie & Timperley, 2007).

5.2. Challenges

Regardless of their benefits, simulations pose certain challenges that need to be tackled so as to be efficiently applied in the educational process:

- **High Cost**: In general, purchasing and maintaining advanced simulation tools for education is expensive, especially in under-resourced institutions (Clarke, 2009).
- **Need for Specialization**: The further requirement is to train educators in the applied use of technical resources and deepen the need for training and support (Lean et al., 2006).
- **Technical Difficulties**: Technical glitches and errors faced with software or technology can pause the learning process and dishearten students (Alessi & Trollip, 2001).
- **Resistance to Change:** Perhaps, resistance to change may come from trainers or trainees who have grown accustomed to doing things the traditional way using traditional teaching resources – without simulations. Bringing in simulations requires a paradigm shift; it's that time-consuming.
- **Inequalities in access:** There is perhaps limited access to simulations for students or institutions that do not have the required technology to run the simulations. This indeed presents an issue on improving technology access.

6. IMPROVEMENT STRATEGIES

Though embedding simulations in the learning process provides many opportunities for enhancing learning, this can be maximized only after the required enhancement strategies have been implemented. This includes preservice teacher education, systemic incorporation of simulations into the curriculum, and continual review and refinement of simulation tools.

Teachers must have the requisite knowledge to understand how simulation tools operate. This includes understanding the user interface, feedback features, and simulations' data analysis tools . They should also know the available options for modifying simulations to the needs of their students (Lean et al., 2006).

Teachers need education on simulation-based instructional strategies besides the technical content to be conveyed; they must comprehend the conduct of these courses and the facilitation of students during simulations for maximum learning output (Bellotti et al., 2013).

6.1 Teacher Education

Implementation relies heavily on the teacher or trainers using these simulators effectively; however, not all teachers may know how to operate one or even the instructional functions. Thus, teacher training becomes very important in enhancing the performance of these technologies.

Teachers must know about the technical operation of simulation tools which involves how the simulations work, feedback indicators, and analytical tools embedded in simulations. They should also know about available options for customizing simulations to their students' needs (Lean et al., 2006).

Teacher training programs would have to include instruction on simulation over and above content knowledge. They must know how to manage these activities in the classroom and how to scaffold students during simulations for the best possible learning (Bellotti et al., 2013).

6.2. Integration Into Curricula

Simulations should not occur in isolation as a one-off extracurricular activity, but rather, they should be incorporated incrementally and systematically into curricula if they are to have any real impact on learning.

Simulation should be a part of particular teaching units and relate directly to the learning objectives determined. That is to say, in the teaching of strategic management, the business policy game, among other devices could emerge as a major vehicle for putting theory to practice and developing decision-making ability (Gove & Marquez, 2012).

Simulations integrated must consider the needs and capabilities of students. For instance, beginners may require basic simulations concentrating on fundamental concepts, while advanced learners may engage in more challenging activities that invoke very high levels of critical thinking.

6.3. Assessment and Adaptation

In order to ensure that simulations provide substantive value to the learning process, it is necessary to assess them on a regular basis and make any necessary adaptations based on the assessment.

The performance of students on the simulation should be assessed to determine if the set learning objectives are achieved. For instance, an analysis of the progress of students, particularly in decision-making, understanding of theoretical concepts, and collaboration would be appropriate (Hattie & Timperley, 2007).

Equally necessary is the obtaining of feedback from the students. The trainees will offer information on the effectiveness and usability of simulations and any problems they may have come across while using them. This feedback will help the instructors to fine-tune activities for students' use.

Increased application of cutting-edge technologies in simulation will further enhance the user experience by making it more lifelike by means of AI, AR, and analytics as the Cadotte (2016) argues.

7. THE ROLE OF EXPERIENTIAL LEARNING

Requiring the user to observe the situation and solve problems interactively, rather than just being a passive viewer, ensures a better learning experience; all these indeed imply that simulation is a space-friendly process. In another perspective, the teaching method transforms from the burden laid on the student to become the owner of the education. Lacking live lectures, learning became a self-propelled activity for the students. Trainees are involved in the learning process and have an active position that shapes outcomes (Kolb, 1984).

Immensely experiential simulations aid in anchoring knowledge and administering it in real professional environments. Referred to as 'players' during the simulation, the trainees can make and implement decisions in a very controlled environment and learn from their mistakes without losing actual resources. This makes simulations very useful while equipping students with skills to tackle labor market challenges (Clarke, 2009).

The author of the article argues that the advanced and enhanced learning experiences of students are attributed to the pedagogical shift from incorporating simulation assets as supplements to integrating them into immersive entrepreneurship education. This directs the use of such methodologies not only to promote engagement but to arm learners with work-relevant skills that will make them better placed and prepared for life as workers in the labor market.

While there are many benefits of the simulation tools, they are certainly not without problems. Financial implications in getting and keeping them and the necessity of teacher training and technical problems are just but a few of the hurdles that face educational institutions. However, the greater inclusion of artificial intelligence and augmented reality, and continued technological advancements open up new horizons for their usage in business education (Brockbank & McGill, 2007).

The concept of experiential learning, supported by Kolb's theory, has a long history in pedagogical science. From John Dewey to modern pedagogy and experience in learning technologies and digital simulation tools have existed to renew the consideration of the strategies formerly suggested for attaining truly accurate reproduction of complex business situations which would be beyond possibility without these innovations.

Integration of simulation tools into the learning process corresponds to experiential learning concepts of David Kolb. This technology insists that individuals are likely to grasp knowledge better if they actively participate in an experimental process of knowledge acquisition, reflect, and apply. Fittingly, this simulation process literally puts into the participation in situational exercises that approximate realistic business functions, be it strategic planning or response to a crisis.

8. THE IMPORTANCE OF SIMULATIONS

Strickland (2023) argues that the simulations provide authentic learning experiences be fully representative of strategic decision-making technical skills development and multi-dimensional problem solving in actual settings. For instance, learners practice strategic decisions, develop technical skills and solve multi-dimensional problems. For example, in business strategy simulations, learners might ended up trying out various scenarios like investment decisions or handling crises. It makes them assess the consequences of their actions, identify their mistakes and get better at what they do.

Delivering learners to complex environments: Its very last but not least is its capability of delivering learners to complex environments that otherwise may be very challenging or just impossible to reproduce. In the medical field, for example, simulations enable medical students to practice surgical techniques or deal with an emergency without risking a patient's health.

Simulation allows learners to explore and "experience" sophisticated business problems in a safe environment in which, let them make mistakes without fear. This element will help to create the atmosphere of the trial and error mode of learning and innovation as learners will be more likely to try out new methods and take risks.

Simulation tools have evolved into highly individualized and interactive ones with the rise of artificial intelligence and machine learning. They will form dynamic simulations in which conditions and challenges are determined by their decisions in a much more realistic deep learning style. It's not something subjective to the business sector only but rather spreads over various disciplines including medicine, engineering, public administration, among many others where complex and interconnected problems have to be handled by the trainees.

Learners through the simulations will have to realize how some interaction between varied business functions happens that is marketing, financial management, and human resource management. While participating in intergraded simulations, the trainees can develop a holistic outlook of the operation of businesses along with the enhancement of their negotiation skills, pressure decision-making, and efficacy in team working.

The knowledge that should be transferred by these simulations may not be only the technical knowledge but also other important 'soft' skills like working in a group, EI, adaptability, and time management. Moreover, it was also drawn that participation in simulations develops business acumen and strategic thinking, which are critical competencies in today's professional world, which is characterized by globalization and competition.

Simulation-based learning is an exciting way of learning that can be best understood by improving application and skill development through the application of knowledge under simulated virtual working conditions. This approach integrates technology into the learning process and develops an insulated environment in which trainees may later go out, work, and learn to ensure a production system's safety or its operation.

Advanced simulations have been made possible by technological evolution, which provides a much more personalized learning experience. Such simulations are easy to realize, depending on every student's requirement; hence, the learning process is more flexible and effective. For instance, AI-enhanced simulations may vary the complexity of scenarios according to student performance so that the latter is always presented with an appropriate learning challenge.

Also, by means of the simulations, it will be possible for the trainers to assess the performance of the trainees in a more objective and correct manner. By accumulating data on the performance of students under various conditions, teachers will be able to recognize the strong and weak points of each student's competences and fine-tune the educational process for them.

Overall, theoretical simulations in business education do not and have a tangible relationship to what is yet to be measured: the development of the professional within the educational sphere. The learners are, therefore, prone to finding their space within the labor markets because they do acquire practical skills like critical thinking, problem-solving, and communication, which today's businesses are desperately looking for in their employees. Today's business environment being much dynamic not only asks for flexible employees but adaptive ones who can solve real-time complex problems.

8.1. Research Findings on the Effectiveness of Simulation-Based Learning

Simulation based learning has been found effective in enhancing understanding of complex business concepts and overall learning experience for learners (Vivek, 2024). According to Entrepreneurship studies, simulation helps learners to deepen their market understanding enhances critical thinking and informed decision making. Similarly, in technology, trainees are more confident concerning capabilities and do better on challenging projects.

8.2 Advantages of Simulation-Based Learning

Increased Engagement: Less intrusiveness into everyday life and work, as simulation as a way of training can be performed at any place and time with results and without too much need for data from the learner outside the system, which also means reduced workload for learners who're already quite busy with other tasks. It can be used on its own and does not require additional hardware or physical models; knowledge is appropriate in a given file format, and skills are graded in an activity report or lab result. There are numerous benefits to this sort of learning approach – lower costs, increased availability, fewer demands on a human teacher, minimized risk, flexibility for updating when new data comes out, ease of conversion of the invisible to visible, simplicity of actualization of complex processes, etc.

Simulations are interactive. They draw the trainees into the educational process and involve them eagerly. Participants interact with the simulation environment, take decisions as to what they ought to do and observe what ensues from their actions. This results in higher attention, better retention, and deeper understanding of educational concepts. Further, engagement is related with inclusion of challenge or competition within the simulation, making it an interesting and effective learning atmosphere.

Flexibility: The primary benefit of simulation learning is the flexibility to cater to the educational experience as required to different students and groups. Simulations may be of varying difficulty or varied scenarios of real challenges for each trainee. For example, medical education may have scenario-based simulations designed at levels suitable to novices' understanding or experts in specific emergency scenarios.

Safety: The ability to practice in a controlled and safe environment is essential for acquiring skills without fear of actual repercussions. In fields such as aviation, medicine, and engineering it is possible that simulations might allow the trainee to err and still not jeopardize human life or infrastructure safety. Moreover, these simulations reduce the stress that any actor might feel during real conditions, providing room for the actual experiment and creativity.

Real-Time Feedback: Most simulations have it in them to show the learners what went wrong with their actions instantly. This is very important because it helps the participants immediately understand where they have erred, correct their steps, and enhance their performance. For example, in a flight simulation, a trainee can be provided with information on how an action of his is affecting the performance of the aircraft; in a project management simulation, one can look at how their choices change a schedule and budget.

Future Perspectives: The future of simulation-based learning is believed to involve further the incorporation of advanced technologies such as virtual reality (VR) and augmented reality (AR). These may lead to authentic, highly immersive reality-simulating environments. For instance, during emergency training, one can be placed in a virtual environment simulating a natural disaster for them to practice under complex conditions.

Challenges: While having their benefits, simulations have brought some challenges too. First, the cost of developing and sustaining the systems might be very high, more so for applications that would require specialized software or equipment. Second, the effectiveness of the simulation is directly proportional to a good design of the simulation and the training of trainers in its use. Finally, making sure that the simulations are really accessible and appropriate to the context is equally important.

While there are multiple advantages of simulation learning, there are certain challenges that need to be looked into. One of the major issues is pertaining to the development and maintenance costs associated with the simulation systems, which can turn out to be quite high, especially for the specialized applications designed. Another critical factor determining the effectiveness of the simulation is how intuitively designed and familiar the teachers are with it.

Simulations will be even more tightly integrated into the learning experience and will be also further by leveraging the potential of VR and AR technologies to make the learning experience even more realistic for the users.

9. PEDAGOGICAL FRAMEWORKS

A strong pedagogical framework must be used while requiring the design and implementation of activities guided under clearly defined learning objectives An effective pedagogical framework ensures the non-fragmentary operation of simulations and not merely as entertainment tools but an integral strategic part of the entire educational process.

9.1. Alignment With Learning Objectives

A development of simulations should be based on a well-defined set of learning objectives as described in the Bloom classification. The Bloom model comprises a framework that differentiates the levels of learning, starting from the simple recall of knowledge then up to the analysis, synthesis, and evaluation of it. Effective implementation for simulations needs a strong pedagogical framework in compliance with the set learning goals using the Bloom classification. (Vivek, 2024).

Simulations allow for increased engagement and active learning through real-world scenarios that 'trick' students into thinking critically and solving problems. Typically, this includes:

- The learners' capability is to review specific decisions in a given simulation and the effects and implications of their choices.
- They have an accumulated knowledge approach from different angles and can therefore propose remedies to complicated issues.
- They can compare alternative strategies and their application for different scenarios.

9.2. Pedagogical Approaches

Various Pedagogical Approaches Experiential Learning, and Problem-Based Learning are among the pedagogical approaches that have proved to be vital in inculcating the entrepreneurial attitudes and competences among learners (Hashim et al, 2024)

9.2.1 Experiential Learning

Kolb advocates experiential learning on the premise that people learn most when they experience it directly. Simulations are a space in which action research participants can ''live'' the reality of situations, interact with the environment, and learn from the experience. For instance, participants can take various roles within an imaginary organization in a business simulation, and execute certain strategic decisions for the good of the organization.

9.2.2 Problem Learning

Problem-based learning implies that learners must try to find solutions to real or hypothetical problems, requiring them to apply knowledge, cooperate and think critically. PBL simulations physically embed problem-based learning and make participants deal with challenges that approximate real complex problems. Such a medical simulation allows students to diagnose and manage patient cases based on real-time provided data.

9.2.3. Fostering Entrepreneurial Mindsets and Skills

Such simulation activities that are either experiential or problem-based are the most efficient in instilling entrepreneurial skills like innovation, resource management, and leadership amongst individuals. Provision of a controlled environment of entrepreneurship where exercises will help in designing and executing strategies as a business-related topic, and a crisis can be dealt with 'live' which might emanate from decisions of the same.

9.2.4. The Role of Trainers

The teacher should be actively involved in the simulation activities, acting as a facilitator for the learning process. He should be trained well in handling the simulation tools, give directions, and encourage discussion and reflection after the activity.

Effective training should be based on elaborate pedagogical models that fuse theory and practice, whereas, if appropriate learning objectives and methodologies are used, it may enhance involvement, and encourage analytical thinking and readiness towards real-life situations.

9.2.5. Skills Development

Since the inception of business simulations, they have been associated with the development of 21st-century skills, particularly entrepreneurship and employability; learners stated increased self-awareness of their skills (Sheik et al, 2023). Participation in simulations would give the trainees the chance to be practically involved in real scenarios, raising self-awareness and confidence in their abilities. More so, this experiential learning technique would offer a safe haven for initiative, decision-making and result analysis leading to a better understanding of business processes.

Online simulations can be accessed by a greater variety of learning environments and thus further support (Strickland, 2023). This more varied audience will not be subject to the limitations of location or program and will be quite beneficial to the user in either case. Moreover, the flexibility to design simulations will facilitate responding to various preferences and needs for learning, strengthen inclusivity, and maximize interaction. The varied learning opportunities offered through these platforms may correlate with the user's accessibility principles in that the simulations are appropriate for people with different backgrounds, skills and learning goals.

10. CHALLENGES AND PROSPECTS OF BUSINESS EDUCATION SIMULATION TOOLS

The educational process can be perceived in a creative perspective – something quite innovative in general, and especially for business education. Yet, as it is admitted to their considerable appeal, simulation tools still face various challenges and lay some potential prospects that could hamper their popular acceptance. From a Heavy financial burden to specialized training, it is no less a critical mountain that has to be climbed before simulating rather than learning can release its full potential.

10.1 Resource Constraints

The cost of simulation materials is hence a very bugging issue. As emphasized, for quality simulation, one must be ready to spend on acquisition as well as maintenance of the appropriate model. This goes beyond software to hardware and auxiliary support like very advanced computation and network infrastructure. Additionally, the development of customized simulations in response to unique educational needs heightens the costs, hence deeming it unviable for application in educational institutions that operate on a shoestring budget.

Partnerships with EdTech companies will have to be strategic and will provide for shared costs of development, as well as deployment. In addition to this, leveraging open educational resources (OER) and/or more cost-effective approaches like cloud-based simulations could prove to be a game-changer for better accessibility.

10.2 Need for Teacher Training

Teacher training is the other difficult obstacle to surmount. Special skills are needed for the use and incorporation of simulation tools in teaching. Many teachers have trouble fully understanding the potentials of the tools or changing their teaching methods to take advantage of the dynamics of simulations.

For solving this problem, instructional training has to be systemically developed for teachers. Comprehensive support and user guides should accompany the simulation tools on the training platforms that are available. Moreover, teacher communities of practice would share experience as well as good practices.

10.3. Technical Difficulties and Infrastructure

Another area where problems concerning simulation arise is in technological infrastructure. There should be very strong technical support for the simulation tools and very reliable networks, especially when it gets to online platforms. Technical problems, such as lags or system-based errors, can impede the efficiency of the educational process and dishearten their use by both teachers and students.

These problems can be addressed by enhancing the technological infrastructure of educational institutions. Moreover, careful selection of user-friendly tools that come with impeccable technical support can help reduce such related issues.

10.4 Cultural and Pedagogical Obstacles

Apart from the technical and economic issues already mentioned above, one major obstacle that stands in the way of the acceptance and use of simulation tools is the barrier created by culture. In many instances, it is taken that 'real' teaching is much more dependable and this thereby makes it tough for the acceptance of new technologies by teachers and students. Further, the cultural barriers to the learning tools may not fit with the cultural requirements of learners from different cultural backgrounds or educational levels.

The simulations' efficacy is contingent upon the customization of content to the requirements and preferences of various groups of students accessing the simulations. Instruments need to incorporate a variety of features and customization, empowering every individual to be in his or her mode and pace of learning.

10.5 Prospects for Enhancing the Use of Simulations

The future outlook of simulations in education may be said to be exciting if not for the challenges described above attributing to further development and adoption. Advancements in technology, particularly artificial intelligence and augmented reality, hint at enhancing simulation functionalities further and accessibility. Quite so, analysis-based intelligent simulations may offer personalized content and increased learning efficiency for each student.

Additionally, collaboration between universities and industry may result in the development of instruments that will correspond best to the demands of the labor market. The use of real scenario-based simulations that focus on highly demanded skills may contribute much to closing the gap between what the academic world feeds and what employers need.

These are powerful tools that have the capability to transform business education and more. Yet, it is necessary to address the economic, technical, cultural, and pedagogical challenges that limit their full impact. Strategic investment in technology infrastructure and teacher educational programs and the production of student-centric tools is a first imperative step in this direction. In the future of technology and deepening collaboration, simulations could have the driving role in an emergence of a more supple, participatory, and efficient education.

Among the best advantages of simulation tools is the ability to narrow the gap between theory and practice since it gives the trainee the chance to implement theoretical concepts in real applications and thus gain experiences that could barely be obtained through conventional teaching (Alessi & Trollip, 2001). For example, in strategic management simulations, students can really apply things like market analysis and decision-making models in real time to track the impact of their strategic choices.

CONCLUSION

A new and rather modern way of meeting the needs of the present times in education is through the incorporation of simulation tools, precisely what has been done in business education. Theory to practice is linked by these simulations in that they create safe 'controlled,' and realistic environments for the trainee, allowing them to acquire even the most critical skills and prepare for even the most complex professional challenges that lie ahead.

One of the main advantages claimed to be associated with the use of simulations is the development of critical skills – critical thinking, strategic decision-making, problem-solving – and effective cooperation. Meanwhile, learners get to experience truly professional scenarios, and gain self-confidence to take initiatives in mistake-learning rather than failure-causing environments.

Simulations make learning more experiential and help students participate actively and autonomously in situations so that they can appreciate and better grasp the realties of business. Furthermore, they provide differentiated instruction that is able to respond to the singular needs and knowledge levels of individual students.

However, embracing the technique has its hurdles. The cost of the systems is high; it will be necessary to educate the teachers, and there are technical challenges-all major hurdles that need to be overcome. Further, for simulations to bring maximum performance in the teaching function, strong pedagogical frameworks, very clear learning objectives and strategic planning have to be put in place.

Technological development will create new perspectives for the further development of simulation learning. In particular, the use of artificial intelligence, virtual reality, and augmented reality will allow for even more possibilities in terms of providing a life-like representation of professional scenarios and a highly-personalized experience to learners. Such technologies will make simulations more pertinent and broaden access to yet-to-be-imagined innovations in the application of simulations.

The use of simulation tools is a novelty but also a necessity in modern education. Properly applied, these tools may give students qualifications that do not relate to a particular area but specifically concern general adaptability and innovation and critical thinking amid an ever-changing professional environment. Sustainable incorporation of such methodologies may decisively contribute toward preparing a workforce able to face future challenges.

REFERENCES

Alessi, S. M., & Trollip, S. R. (2001). *Multimedia for Learning: Methods and Development.* Allyn & Bacon.

Bellotti, F., Berta, R., De Gloria, A., & Primavera, L. (2013). Enhancing the educational value of business simulations through gaming. *Computers in Human Behavior, 31*, 135–146.

Brockbank, A., & McGill, I. (2007). Facilitating Reflective Learning in Higher Education. McGraw-Hill Education.

Cadotte, E. R. (2016). Markstrat as a tool for teaching marketing strategy. *Marketing Education Review, 26*(1), 65–68.

Clarke, E. (2009). Learning outcomes from business simulation exercises: Challenges for the implementation of learning technologies. *Education + Training, 51*(5/6), 448–459.

de Freitas, S., & Oliver, M. (2006). How can exploratory learning with games and simulations within the curriculum be most effectively evaluated? *Computers & Education, 46*(3), 249–264.

Faria, A. J., & Dickinson, J. R. (1994). Simulation gaming for sales management training. *Journal of Management Development, 13*(1), 47–59.

Faria, A. J., Hutchinson, D., & Wellington, W. J. (2009). The role of business simulations in international business education. *Journal of Teaching in International Business, 20*(3), 207–223.

Garris, R., Ahlers, R., & Driskell, J. E. (2002). Games, motivation, and learning: A research and practice model. *Simulation & Gaming, 33*(4), 441–467.

Gove, S., & Marquez, J. (2012). The Business Strategy Game: Learning management principles. *Management Decision, 50*(8), 1356–1372.

Gredler, M. E. (2004). Games and simulations and their relationships to learning. Handbook of Research on Educational Communications and Technology, 571-581.

Hashim, Osman, & Elbadri. (2024). Pedagogical Approaches to Teaching Entrepreneurship to Higher Education Students: A Literature Review. DOI: 10.69481/PED06172024

Hattie, J., & Timperley, H. (2007). The power of feedback. *Review of Educational Research, 77*(1), 81–112. DOI: 10.3102/003465430298487

Kim, J., Park, M., & Shin, D. (2006). Case-based reasoning and simulation for decision support. *Expert Systems with Applications, 30*(3), 484–492.

Kolb, D. A. (1984). *Experiential learning: Experience as the source of learning and development.* Prentice Hall.

Larreche, J.-C. (2001). *Markstrat: A Marketing Strategy Simulation.* StratX International.

Lean, J., Moizer, J., Towler, M., & Abbey, C. (2006). Simulation and games: Use and barriers in higher education. *Active Learning in Higher Education, 7*(3), 227–242. DOI: 10.1177/1469787406069056

Piaget, J. (1971). The Theory of Stages in Cognitive Development. McGraw-Hill Education.

Prince, M. (2004). Does active learning work? A review of the research. *Journal of Engineering Education, 93*(3), 223–231. DOI: 10.1002/j.2168-9830.2004.tb00809.x

Scott, J. M., & Hall, M. (2016). SimVenture: Embedding business simulation games in entrepreneurship education. *Education + Training, 58*(1), 47–67.

Strickland, P. (2023). Business-Simulation Pedagogy, Assessments, and Barriers to Entry in an Australian Educational Environment. International Journal of Smart Business and Technology, 11(2), 1-14. DOI: 10.21742/IJSBT.2023.11.2.01

Vivek, A. (2024). Simulations in Business Education. Advances in educational technologies and instructional design book series, 1-21. DOI: 10.4018/979-8-3693-0716-8.ch001

Vygotsky, L. S. (1978). *Mind in Society: The Development of Higher Psychological Processes*. Harvard University Press.

Chapter 8

The Impact of Simulation Tools in Finance Schools as a Learning Strategy From Educators' Perspectives

Ilias A. Makris
https://orcid.org/0000-0002-4276-2375
University of the Peloponnese, Greece

Sotiris Apostolopoulos
Neapolis University, Pafos, Cyprus

Vasilios Babalos
University of the Peloponnese, Greece

Panagiotis Dimitrakopoulos
https://orcid.org/0009-0000-8188-4255
University of the Peloponnese, Greece

Panagiotis Charalampakis
https://orcid.org/0000-0003-0389-1075
University of Patras, Greece

ABSTRACT

This chapter explores the potential contributing role of simulation tools to finance school students' performance within Greek higher education. By applying a qualitative research method, this study examines the perspectives and experiences of 12 professors on the introduction of simulation tools into the respective learning processes. Findings indicated that simulations increase student engagement and enhance real-life scenarios and problem-based learning but also revealed the lack of resources and supporting mechanisms negatively affecting their seamless adoption. Additionally, it highlighted the emerging need for training of teaching personnel respectively while underscoring that oftentimes the content of certain curricula appears not being compatible with the notion of simulation games. This chapter adds evidence to the international literature towards simulation practices in financial education whilst its results could

DOI: 10.4018/979-8-3693-9040-5.ch008

be useful for responsible shaping educational policies.

1. INTRODUCTION

Simulation in finance and also within economic schools across the globe, as a learning strategy, has been continuously expanding over the past decades (Song et al., 2018; Marriott et al., 2015). Financial education, particularly because it relies on quantitative analyses and exercises, finds simulation tools much valuable as the latter increase student engagement while resulting in a positive impact on their performance (Bakoush, 2022; Aebersold et al., 2012). The research of Chulkov & Wang (2020) revealed that finance students who used simulation tools in the learning process performed better in their grades compared to those who did not use simulation. Similarly, the research by Bakoush (2022), which developed experiential learning in finance, based on simulation for graduate students of finance, highlighted the added value of simulation in providing practical experience in the real world. Simulation, as a method of facilitating learning in financial education, creates value for financial education itself (Jones et al., 2021; Wolmarans, 2005). It surpasses traditional teaching as it fosters collaboration and teamwork while it accurately enhances the integrated practical competence (Xie et al, 2018; Apostolopoulos et al., 2018a). Simulation has the advantage of being highly engaging and has the potential to improve the quality of learning for students in finance and economic sciences (Wang & Yang, 2024; Liu et al., 2018). However, issues have been identified, such as the lack of professional teaching staff in university infrastructures, outdated curriculum content, and the cost of purchasing simulation programs (Wang & Yang, 2024; Paunović et al, 2024; Apostolopoulos et al., 2024; Lean et al., 2006). Despite these weaknesses, the expansion of simulation tools in economic schools continues, with more schools adopting simulations as initiatives to improve the learning process (Moon, et al, 2018; Burdon & Munro, 2017). By using simulation tools, faculty lead their students to make decisions and tackle certain conflicts through safety and risk-free environments (Campos et al, 2021; Apostolopoulos et al, 2018b). In this light, students improve their critical thinking and upgrade their relevant knowledge and skills, while preparing themselves to deal with similar situations adequately in their future work settings (Jones et al, 2021; Makris & Apostolopoulos, 2021). However, the main barrier to the learning strategy with simulation tools certainly lies in potential of resources' availability (Wang & Yang, 2024; Agoraki et al, 2024; Lean et al, 2006). In recent decades, research interest has intensified regarding learning with simulation tools in economic schools, including finance and accounting departments (Bakoush, 2022; Peng & Abdullah, 2018; Burdon & Munro, 2017). However, a gap has been identified in understanding how the teaching staff themselves experience learning through simulation.

This research aims to fill the aforementioned gap by exploring the views, experiences, and expectations of teaching staff in finance and economic sciences regarding the outcomes of learning through simulation. The perspective of the teaching staff will highlight problems, obstacles, and prospects as they experience them in their daily work.

2. LITERATURE REVIEW

Computer-based business simulations hold significant promise as an educational tool in both academic courses and training programs (Gopinath & Sawyer, 1999). Especially in today's era, where the technologies range from broader fields such as computer science, application systems, and communication tools, to more specialized areas like renewable energy technologies, digital tools for green energy management, energy efficiency, and green energy capacity management, the need for alignment in addressing complex problems is becoming more and more essential (Apostolopoulos et al., 2024). Technology education is viewed not only as a way to build the technical skills needed in renewable energy sector, but also as a method for gaining transferable skills that can be applied across different industries (Apostolopoulos et al., 2024). Emerging technologies are revolutionizing the business simulation industry, introducing new features and enhancing its capabilities (Summers, 2004). The literature on this specific topic is quite recent and is continuously expanding.

Wang & Yang (2024), support that virtual simulation teaching is an innovative educational technology that provides a new path of teaching and reforms education with its unique advantages and strong vitality. It makes full use of advanced computer, network, multimedia, and simulation technologies to create a highly realistic environment, providing students with an immersive learning experience. Various studies endorse the use of simulation in education, highlighting its value in enhancing teaching and learning practices. It creates a highly realistic learning environment using modern information technology, allowing students to practice and learn in a virtual space, thereby facilitating the seamless integration of theoretical knowledge and practical skills.

Simulation-based learning methods are designed to mimic a system or process and aim to describe or predict the behavior of the subject being studied (Lean et al., 2006). As a result, the focus on the role of games in education has increasingly shifted toward their integration in schools. This approach helps address the limitations of traditional teaching methods (Ruben, 1999). Facer (2003) noted that the growing interest in educational gaming stems from the belief that individuals raised with modern technologies may develop different ways of thinking. However, she cautions against assuming the existence of a distinctly 'new' generation without careful consideration.

Kirriemuir & McFarlane (2004) suggest that playing computer games will continue to be a popular leisure activity, which will, in turn, shape how younger learners expect to engage with educational content. Lean et al., (2006), in their research within the UK higher education, observed that simulations, games and role play, are used for several teaching and learning methods, as long as barriers like limited time, resources and support are overcome. However they conclude that academics choose if they use these techniques, based upon their judgement of risk and benefit, rather than on the resources they have at their disposal.

Chulkov & Wang (2020), use a series of stock market simulation exercises in a finance investment course, in order to explore the impact of simulation in the finance classroom. Their goal was to illustrate the implementation of an investment simulation assignment within the finance curriculum at a business school. Their results were promising, indicating that simulation exercises can effectively replace certain traditional assignments and delivery methods. When properly integrated into the course, simulations enhance not only student knowledge and skills but also motivation and satisfaction. Additionally, they serve as a powerful tool for experiential learning.

Wolmarans, (2005), presents findings from three studies that explore the added value of this experiential learning method in a financial management course, as perceived by students. The research concluded that the impact on students' financial knowledge and their experience of team working, understanding financial statements and the interaction between critical variables was a significant positive learning experience. Wolmarans argues that total enterprise business simulations have a significant role in financial management education and finance instructors should consider this when planning future value-adding opportunities.

Wang & Yang (2024), report Immersion, Interactivity, Experimentation and Innovation as the main characteristics of virtual simulation teaching. According to them, the application of virtual simulation teaching especially in finance and economics colleges and universities is becoming increasingly popular. In finance and economics colleges, virtual simulation teaching can replicate real-world economic markets, financial transactions, and business operations. This allows students to engage and practice in a virtual setting, facilitating a seamless transition from theoretical knowledge to practical skills. Additionally, the virtual simulation teaching system can flexibly adjust simulation parameters and scenarios based on teaching requirements, allowing it to meet the learning objectives of various levels and disciplines. However, it is still in its early stages, facing challenges such as a shortage of qualified instructors, outdated teaching content, and slow development of teaching materials. Additionally, this method requires significant financial investment, making it a costly approach with limited effectiveness. It has become a key approach to enhancing teaching quality and developing well-rounded, innovative financial talents.

Gao (2020), conducted a rather detailed study on the construction of a virtual simulation experiment for teaching courses in Economics and Management Sciences and he quotes the advantages of virtual simulation experiment teaching. Scene reproduction, intuitiveness and vividness, safety and reliability are some of them. Furthermore, it is economic and controllable, accurate and precise, real and objective. China's Ministry of Education released the implementation guideline on the development of first-class undergraduate courses, aiming to establish 1,500 first-class national virtual simulation experiment teaching courses in universities nationwide focusing on student-centered virtual simulation experiment instruction. The virtual simulation business environment that Chinese Universities have built for their students, enables them to train their professional abilities such as problem solving, collaboration, communication and analytical way of thinking. However, author mentions that this kind of curriculum design is difficult to enhance talent training. Furthermore, the proportion of professional comprehensive experiments is relatively small and the system is not standardized enough, which means that teachers' arbitrariness in class affects the quality of teaching.

Hongyan (2018), states that Virtual Simulation Teaching enhances students' innovating ability, helps the overcoming of time and space constraints. Furthermore, it can replicate scenarios that are either challenging to implement or come with high costs, decreasing reliance on physical environments and lab equipment, thereby lowering the maintenance and management expenses of teaching experiments. Theoretical and practical teaching can occur simultaneously, leading to a significant improvement in teaching quality.

Achieving virtualization, digitization, and networking of lab resources, fosters open resource sharing, and addresses issues of redundant resource development and unequal distribution. Ming (2017), outlines the challenges and development directions for virtual simulation experimental teaching centers in application-oriented universities. These centers, often unclear in their goals and design, struggle with resource convergence and fail to meet the needs of economic transformation in personnel training. Unclear curriculum design, fragmented curriculum systems, lack of standardization, and ineffective quality monitoring, result in a lower quality of experimental teaching. The educational institution should harmonize the personal development motives expressed in the incentives dimension with the social factors, the immediate environment, and the content of the program (Apostolopoulos et al. 2018). Ming suggests that virtual simulation centers should enhance cooperation with enterprises, improve the utilization of experimental resources, and create shared platforms for high-quality teaching resources. This includes investing in cloud-based virtual teaching systems and expanding resource sharing among institutions, with the goal of improving the quality of training and fostering innovation and entrepreneurship among students. Furthermore, efforts should be made to integrate theory with practical and innovative practice and to develop interdisciplinary teaching systems, with a focus on building comprehensive and innovative teaching experiments.

3. METHODOLOGY

Material and Methods

A qualitative research method was employed in order to trace the multifaceted nature of topic (Neergaard & Ulhøi, 2007). The research team adopted a combination of convenience and purposive sampling to recruit relevant participants (Yin, 2007) which is very popular in qualitative studies (Apostolopoulos et al., 2022; Gregory and Austin, 2020). Particularly, the latter has the capacity to identify those persons who have deep knowledge towards the concrete subject thereby they could in-depth address potential issues and clarify the respective aspects (Patton, 2002) shedding light on the applications of simulation tools in Finance courses. Respondents were based throughout Greece, with a focus on university institutions featuring Finance Schools.

By following the respective phenomenological approach (Norlyk & Harder, 2010), certain semi-structured qualitative interviews (Creswell and Poth, 2016) were conducted in person, commonly used in primary investigation for tracing views of potential interviewees (Paunović et al., 2024; Makris et al., 2024). Moreover, the current research examined twelve Professors of higher education towards the presence of simulation games in educational process. Specifically, interview topic guide focused on their opinions and experiences with regard to the current status of simulation tools in Finance schools. Interviewing process reaching the thematic saturation, when no additional new information was being exported from participants (Saunders, 2018) whilst the sample size was such that it did not distort individual characteristics (Patton, 2002; Polit and Hungler, 1999; Morse and Field, 1996)

Individual interviews were carried out in Greek from October to December 2024. They lasted for 40 minutes on average. All interviews were conducted in person. Research guide had three sections. The first concerned simulation tools in finance and economic courses within Greek universities. Comparison with other countries. The second referred to the student focus and performance. Lastly, the third one focused on teaching personnel and learning through simulation tools. Furthermore, the participating educators were informed by the researchers about the purpose of the research and its goals. Additionally, they were also assured that their anonymity would be guaranteed.

Table 1. Description of study sample

Respondent	Participant's Status
R1	Professor of Higher Education / Finance School
R2	Professor of Higher Education / Finance School
R3	Professor of Higher Education / Finance School
R4	Professor of Higher Education / Finance School
R5	Professor of Higher Education / Finance School
R6	Professor of Higher Education / Finance School
R7	Professor of Higher Education / Finance School
R8	Professor of Higher Education / Finance School
R9	Professor of Higher Education / Finance School
R10	Professor of Higher Education / Finance School
R11	Professor of Higher Education / Finance School
R12	Professor of Higher Education / Finance School

Data Analysis

Data analysis has taken place by adopting a mixed-method featuring inductive & deductive reasoning (Gittins et al., 2025). The particular methodological approach is considered an accurate technique in analyzing qualitative data (Makris et al., 2025; Azungah, 2018). In this light, predefined subjects based on in-depth study of the existing literature were captured respectively through research guide and personal interviews examined as well before an inductively approach was applied (Bell & Waters, 2018) The latter led the research team to extract more relevant concepts. Coding and creating categories (Table 2) have been described in detail (Krippendorff, 2018).

Table 2. Thematic analysis

Theme	Sub-theme
Simulation tools in finance and economic courses within Greek universities. Comparison with other countries.	• Infrastructures/Simulation Laboratories • Teaching personnel • Curricula • Cost of purchasing simulation packages • State support for expansion of simulation laboratories
Student focus and performance	• Student focus and impact on their performance • Level of facilitation in learning process • Acquisition of decision-making capacity • Gaining the ability to solve problems • Level of entrepreneurial maturity • Knowledge and competencies
Teaching personnel and learning through simulation tools	• Engagement level of simulation methods • Extent of teaching personnel's familiarity with usage of simulation tools • Experience of comparing simulation methods with traditional lectures • Barriers and obstacles

4. FINDINGS

The findings were structured into three thematic sections. The first focused on simulation tools in financial and economic sciences within Greek universities, compared to other countries. The second explored the increase in student interest and its impact on their performance. The third examined the adequacy of academic staff in implementing simulation-based learning.

Simulation Tools in Financial and Economic Sciences at Greek Universities: Comparison With Other Countries

Participants in the study emphasized that the existence of simulation infrastructures and laboratories adds value to learning and better prepares students to handle complex problems in their future professional roles. They asserted that achieving strategic educational objectives is unattainable without the necessary infrastructure. However, they identified significant deficiencies in the support systems for simulation-based learning in Greek universities.

"The issue of infrastructure (e.g., simulation laboratories) is critical for achieving this educational strategy. Without the required infrastructure, achieving strategic objectives is impossible." (R2)

"The infrastructure needs to be upgraded to meet the demands of modern software and the increasing number of participants." (R5)

Moreover, the participants indicated that the lack of adequate academic staff in Greek financial university departments impedes the seamless implementation of simulation-based learning methods. This deficiency affects the development of optimal learning outcomes for students. Only two respondents reported that their institution has sufficient academic staff, though they acknowledged infrastructure-related issues.

"Unfortunately, there is insufficient academic staff. Adequate staffing is crucial, as is the need for continuous training." (R6)

"It depends on the institution. At the institution where I work, I would say there is sufficient professional teaching staff to develop simulation practices. The problem lies with the infrastructure, not staff adequacy." (R2)

On whether the existing academic staff possesses the professional competence to develop simulation practices in financial and economic schools, opinions were divided. Half of the participants believed that the current academic staff is sufficiently qualified, while an equally strong viewpoint highlighted shortcomings. Nonetheless, all participants agreed on the need for continuous training in simulation methods.

"In my view, these practices require ongoing training and development, as conditions are constantly changing. Overall, I would say the staff is adequately trained." (R3)

"I believe the staff is not adequately trained, but if there were more personnel and sufficient resources to acquire the necessary infrastructure, the instructors could acquire the required skills." (R10)

Participants' experiences revealed significant variation in the adoption of simulation tools across Greek universities. While some universities have incorporated simulation tools into their curricula, others are in the early stages of implementation due to resource constraints.

"Yes, in many departments, there are simulation laboratories for either business or financial models, and they form part of the students' courses. In departments where such programs are implemented, students engage with interest. Personally, I've adapted Excel-based simulations from foreign universities and adjusted them to the Greek context, but it required significant personal effort." (R1)

"The integration of simulation tools into curricula in Greece is unfortunately still at a very early stage." (R9)

The high cost of simulation software was identified as the main obstacle to its integration into the learning process.

"Cost is the primary barrier. A single-user license can cost €50–100 annually or up to €500 for a one-time installation. If you need to equip a lab with 30 or 35 computers, the cost becomes prohibitive. Adding to this the lack of staff to run and support the system, you can understand why its implementation is almost impossible in smaller regional departments." (R1)

"When the department's budget is lower than the cost of a simulation program for a reasonable number of students, it is easy to see why this becomes a major deterrent." (R7)

Participants emphasized the need for governmental support in creating or expanding simulation laboratories in financial and economic departments. However, they noted the lack of sufficient governmental intervention to date. Some also highlighted the importance of incentivizing private companies to collaborate with Greek universities to support the integration of simulation tools into the educational process.

"Government support is essential for developing infrastructure that will enhance the creation of simulation laboratories, but so far, the appropriate measures have not been taken." (R5)

"In my opinion, more flexibility and incentives should be provided to private companies to collaborate with Greek universities. This would facilitate the design and promotion of more simulations for inclusion in the educational process." (R3)

Student Interest and Performance

The respondents believed that simulations tools manage to increase student interest, by practically engaging theoretical context into interactional learning. The students though, that benefit the most are those that are already actively engaged and in those cases simulations tools substantially promote their performance and course achievement. Interest is mainly immersed by the closer to reality learning experience, their engagement in experiential learning as well as the opportunity to further research active problem solving in more complex situations.

"I believe that it rises their interest exponentially resulting into increased performance" (R4)

"It most definitely increases interest, in those that are already interested, not all because not all can be forced to show interest in learning..... In general, those that participate in such learning experiences increase their performance above average in a percentage as high as 80% ". (R1)

"Mostly yes, but it's not absolute. These is mostly observed in students that choose to participate in these types of exercises and laboratory tests, and are more conscientious students. Otherwise the result may not very be positive". (R11)

"Yes, combining theory with practical engagement increases student interests and also creates the opportunity to increase performance, through sources research and complex problem solving activity". (R7)

Simulation tools are thought to be very useful for economics and finance students, because they can see how economic and business sectors operate under real market conditions and can be further advanced with the use of games during class. They can offer the opportunity for practical understanding and application of theoretical knowledge, using scenarios like portfolio and risk management and market forecasting. Also, the interviewees believe that students can develop practical skills, as well as communication, collaboration and crisis management skills, that are known to be essential for their future employment. Some concerns though were risen about the students that these simulations will be applied, since there is the risk of wasting human and other resources in students that are not highly active and interested to start with.

"*It is important for the students that are interested in gaining practical skill, as they can observe how businesses operate under almost real-life circumstances*" (R2)

"Simulation methods offer students the opportunity to apply their learned theory on real data and scenarios. For example portfolio management, market forecasting and risk management etc……. Definitely the use of simulation is very important and useful". (R8)

"They are significantly important, if combined with other methods. For example, if the simulation is combined with a game in class, this will further advance the results of such a learning action". (R12)

"Also, they can develop through simulation very useful skills such as communication, collaboration and pressure management during the handling of difficult situations" (R3)

"Very useful since it will offer them skills that are necessary for their future employment". (R5)

"If they show interest, these processes can be really important. If not, they become a waste of resources, human and material". (R11)

As far as the students' ease of knowledge is concerned, the majority of participants believed that students that participate in simulation exercises acquire some practical understanding of real economy, which enhances their theoretical understanding of more complex contexts, their critical thinking and practical confidence, while motivating their learning. Those that are more hesitant about the benefits, agree that students certainly attain more stimuli, but if participation is compulsory, it might become more counteractive than it was first intended and depending on the students might be more beneficial or it might have no impact at all. The need for more long-term use and future simulation learning intervention may improve the understanding of how these processes enhance applied knowledge in a more structured manner.

"Yes, I believe that practical exercise facilitates theoretical understanding and enhances interest. Students that participate in such exercises, have a better understanding of real economy and stimulates their engagement in a more systematic manner" (R2)

"Students have a deeper understanding of concept after participating in simulation exercises". (R6)

"Maybe. They certainly have more knowledge stimuli and are more likely to attain better understanding on certain things. This is dependent on the commitment one has for these programmes and the interest one rises. If for example they are compulsory for all, it will have many participants that have to be there and are not truly engaged and interested". (R7)

«It depends on the students…..». R11

"I cannot know this for certain, since I have no means for comparison. Most programmes that have been done in my department are optional and completed in a day or two (short-term) and are not part of the whole semester" (R1)

"This can become a research intervention on how simulation-based learning can improve the understanding and application of knowledge". (R5)

Furthermore, interviewees believe that there is some decision making enhancement at the individual or team level in complex situations, as well as some practical evaluation of their decision making and critical thinking skills, through simulation learning. These advancements though can be seen if simulation learning is applied in a more systematic manner, with appropriate resources and organised processes that can offer real time evaluation of decision making. Although, it is also mentioned that other tools and exercises may be needed to advance students' decision making.

"I agree that my students when the participate in a simulation they learn how to reach to a decision on important real time business problems or demanding situations in investments, while receiving feedback on their action and what they could have done more efficiently". (R3)

"Simulation tools demand students action and therefore decision making. The ability to control decision making, leads students to more complex and broadly evaluated answers to certain questions". (R7)

"In order to have a significant impact, the simulation should be continuous and included in more courses. Otherwise, the improvement cannot be significant" (R1)

"Resources in terms of people and money are needed to create feedback on decision making. Then yes, there will be a significant impact on students in relation to the real world" (R11)

"Probably in a small extend. Although they have a better understanding on certain things, other pedagogical tools and teaching tools are needed to enhance develop and enhance students' Decision-making abilities". (R12)

On the other hand, students' problem-solving skills have the potential of being developed with simulation learning tools. It is believed that real-life working environment examples are often used by students when they are dealing with possible solutions that can be offered. Problem solving skills, like responsibility, patience, coordination, leadership, critical thinking, analytical approach and communication are usually experienced and employed during a simulation. These skills together with decision making skills, can prepare students for their working experience, within a safe environment that has no actual consequences. If performed in an organised manner it can be very beneficial. Certain personal, cognitive, social, cultural and background factors though, may play a pivotal role towards their learning experience and its actual applicability.

"In my opinion, experiential learning is very important in gaining real-life problem- solving abilities. Students familiarise with appropriate problem-solving skills such as responsibility, calmness, coordinated strategies, leadership and communication during virtual situations that are created during a simulation". (R3)

"It enhances the development of decision making in a safe environment, without the risk of failure. Students may develop certain skills that will reinforce their future working experience especially under pressure in a way that will develop their readiness for the real world". (R8)

"The potential is dependent on other learning, social, cultural factors. It is only a matter in the experiential exercise but of the personality and general cultural approach and the stimuli and background one carries". (R12)

The effect of simulations tools on the students' entrepreneurial maturity can be positively impacted and will enhance their professional skills in problem solving and decision making, it will bring them closer to their entrepreneurship maturity and will advance them later on in their career. These can be achieved if done in an appropriate manner by the professor and are addressed with somewhat professional maturity by the students. It can certainly enhance crisis management and situational analysis, but given the entrepreneurships multi-layered profile other factors are also involved and certain resources must be assigned in order to achieve a smaller or greater impact.

"Yes, the simulation of daily business decision making and dealing with the consequences brings decision making maturity". (R7)

"It certainly enhances crisis management, situational analysis, given that entrepreneurship is multi–layered (other factors are involved in the students' ability to create and manage business projects), but the simulation may provide them with necessary entrepreneurial skills". (R5)

"Entrepreneurial maturity requires time and experience. However, students that have the simulation experience are one step ahead to cope with real-life conditions". (R8)

"This is why resources are needed in order to implement such programmes and to stimulate students participation" (R11)

Academic Staff and Learning Through Simulation Tools

When interviewees were asked about the potential impact and acceptance of simulation tools amongst the teaching staff of business and finance schools, their responses were rather positive. Most believed that their colleagues perceive the use of simulation tools positively, given their learning benefits, only though under certain organisational, infrastructural and training conditions. Younger staff will adapt a more positive approach and simulation can enhance the curriculum quality when it is combined with excellent theory learning, but it will require time, effort and must be supported by most staff. One interviewee raised his concerns about the positive receptiveness, given his hesitance and his colleagues fear that workshops may replace theory. He did though agree that if implemented in moderation can create a more positive acceptance potential.

"In my opinion simulation methods will be very well received from the teaching staff because of the many advantages they incorporate, such as real life problem solving, familiarisation with decision making tools etch." (R3)

"I believe that younger faculty members of the Country's Universities would accept with ease the implementation of simulation methods in their modules if they had the appropriate support (infrastructures) and training.... " (R4)

"I do not believe they would be very receptive. On the one hand there are problems about support, funding and so on, and on the other hand many colleagues express their concerns about the workshops replacing theory. If you ask me, I think the truth is somewhere in the middle. They should be implemented in moderation and must be balanced with theoretical background. Given these circumstances I myself am positive. Not many of colleagues though.." (R1)

The degree of familiarity and training of such a teaching approach, may certainly play an inhibiting role in the implementation and broad application of the simulation tools, as well as for their successful use. Time constrains and familiarity may temporarily act as barriers that can be overcome with ongoing training, monitoring and support from appropriate human, financial and physical resources allocation, as well as close collaboration with simulation tools companies. One though interviewee believe their faculty's familiarly is already high, whereas another is confident that the faculty can familiarise rather quickly given its adaptability with other teaching tools in the past.

"I agree. In particular, I believe to a certain extend the familiarity of the faculty with simulation tools may temporarily act as a barrier for widely promoting simulations as a valuable teaching tool. It requires ongoing training and monitoring of the subject, which on the part of faculty certainly requires physical, monetary and time resources. Also, more information is needed from the private

companies that provide these tools and/or more interest from the universities themselves in order to disseminate these tools more widely and integrate them into the educational process" (R3)

"Yes, but I generally believe the degree of the faculty's familiarisation is rather high". (R10)

"No, as with other teaching tools faculty familiarisation is not a barrier, the teaching staff have largely responded in a short period of time previously". (R7)

As far as the advantages and disadvantages between traditional lectures and simulation teaching are concerned most responded that lectures promote the theoretical background that is required for practical testing during simulation learning. In particular, simulation requires a certain degree of engagement, activity and applicability of skills by the students, that is not always achieved by lectures and can reinforce theory assimilation in a more digestible and stimulating way. Its direct theory usage can promote real life experience, 'character' building and decision making, without though the appropriate theoretical mentality that this practises are stemming from. Therefore, simulation although important and with certain advantages, must only play a complementary role for applied knowledge, that is mostly acquired by theoretical lectures. One interviewee also mentioned that time management, classroom size and previously mentioned barriers are also listed as simulation learning disadvantages, whereas another preferred not to say due to lack of simulation teaching experience.

"Certainly, each method has advantages and disadvantages. Parts of the curriculum must be lectured, something that simulation cannot do. Simulation provides applied knowledge that the lecture is lacking. The coordinated use of methods can multiply the benefits". (R5)

"The two methods are complementary to each other. Traditional lectures give you the opportunity for a more comprehensive theoretical presentation of a subject, while simulation methods are more experiential learning". (R7)

"I think the disadvantages are the time management that a simulation requires. Sometimes the time of a lab course and the number of students per class create difficulties. Also as already noted a disadvantage is the adaptability of the teaching staff, which in some cases may require a lot of time". (R11)

The main barriers identified by the interviewees as far as simulation tools implementation is concerned were mostly lack of training, familiarity and experience by the faculty, as well as lack of funds, of qualified supporting staff and classroom infrastructures. In accordance, the number of students and the staffs' unwillingness to invest the time and effort required for the appropriate implementation of this teaching method were also raised. Only one responder raised his concerns on the risk that students might focus their interest only in simulation and distant themselves from lectures.

"The main problem is the lack of training and the lack of infrastructure, which limits its implementation". (R6)

"The lack of appropriate software, appropriate infrastructure and a large number of students". (R7)

"There is a risk that students will focus more on the simulation and less on theory, which may create a reaction towards lecturers of theoretical courses". (R8)

The culture of the faculty members is believed to affect the development of simulation teaching skills, since younger faculty members have more willingness to learn and implement new methods, which is closer to their mentality and digital familiarity. Although, without the appropriate support and incentives even those that have the skills and/or interest might lose purpose of engagement, the culture though is changing and positively contributes to such teaching changes. It was also mentioned that given the lack of academic community recognition for such approaches, faculty members will often avoid investing time and effort to implement them.

"Some faculty members are really interested and are already looking into it. Others are not particularly engaged and may not be positive because of the difficulties they need to face for the preparation and the lack of support, and also lack of familiarity with technical and technological issues". (R11)

"Yes, I believe the faculty members' culture can help their development. Thereare valuable members in staff who can make a significant contribution in this direction, provided they are given the "place", the time and the appropriate resources to do so". (R12)

"We must not forget that even if the culture is there, if the faculty has to work alone for long hours, without help, they will not be particularly engaged. Also, these actions are rarely recognized by the academic community as something special and would not help the faculty who implement them gain recognition among their older and more senior colleagues". (R1)

The potential constrains for the business and economics faculty to adopt simulation teaching, as previously mentioned, are unwillingness to invest time to something that lacks yearly resources, support, student interest, as well as recognition and appreciation from colleagues. Furthermore, the number of students, limited experience, training and monitoring approaches, lack of infrastructures, economic incentives for faculty members and fear of not being able to adequately meet the requirements of the methods which may consequently affect the results and acceptance by the students are also some of the constraints mentioned by the interviewees. It was interesting that one responder identified the complexity and uncertainty of economics and finance might limit the usefulness of simulation models.

"Lack of support, interest from all students, recognition and reward from colleagues and the department. The time mainly that one has to spend, due to these shortcomings, is perhaps the main problem". R1

"Lack of infrastructure, lack of training, lack of stable funding for relevant software which may not be continuously available on an annual basis". R5

"Limited financial resources. The lack of a financial incentive to compensate for the extra effort". R8

"The fear of not adequately meeting the requirements of the methods and possible non-acceptance/ support from students". R10

"The complexity and uncertainty that characterises economic and financial reality limits the usefulness of simulation models in the analysis and interpretation of real-world problems". R12

5. DISCUSSION

A series of intriguing conclusions emerged from the findings of the research. Regarding the first pillar of the research, simulation tools in finance and economic sciences in Greek universities and comparison with other countries, significant issues were identified, both in terms of existing infrastructure and the specialization of academic staff. The benefits of simulation methods, as also highlighted in the literature, are confirmed when those learning processes are properly integrated into courses (Chulkov & Wang, 2020). Traditional experimental courses have many limitations, regarding the need for proper equipment, the training of students' hands-on ability, etc., thus, failing to achieve the expected experimental teaching purpose. Thus, a reasonable experimental teaching method is needed, that can be used randomly, unlimited times, and is safe and convenient (Zhao, 2021). Experiments and exercises using simulations, however, have not been extensively developed, resulting in improper distribution of instructors and educational materials, which affects the quality of the education provided (Gao, 2020). Specifically for Greece, the resources are even more limited, as many respondents indicate, a phenomenon more pronounced in regional universities compared to central ones. Another crucial factor is the cost of acquiring simulation software and relevant equipment by educational institutions (Wang and Wang, 2024). The lack of resources and supporting mechanisms, both from the state and the institutions, is widely recognized as a significant barrier to such initiatives and actions (Ming, 2017, Lean et al., 2006).

Regarding student interest and performance from participating in such activities and exercises, the research confirmed the findings from other researchers, that simulations increase student engagement (Wolmarans, 2005, Chulkov & Wang, 2020, Kirriemuir & McFarlane, 2004), as they transform theoretical knowledge into practical experience, with practical examples (Wang and Yang, 2024). Simulation-based learning activity can provide students with a hands-on experience of the real-world practice, especially in financial and economic studies, helping them to engage in the learning process and become active learners (Bakoush, 2020). Thus, students become more satisfied with the educational process, they achieve better performance in their courses, but more importantly, they learn to manage and solve problems more effectively (Gao, 2020, Summers, 2004), and develop skills related to communication, decision-making, crisis management, and other constraints through different perspectives (Hongyan, 2018, Facer, 2003). As highlighted in literature, simulations provide positive learning reflections when compared to face-to-face simulation in a traditional course setting (Peng and Abdullah, 2018, Chulkov & Wang, 2020, Wang & Yang, 2024). The skills they acquire may be useful in their professional careers in the field of economics and finance. Simulations games have in general, a strong impact on students, because role-playing facilitates active learning, permits the acceptance of new concepts and generates increased student interest, enthusiasm and motivation (Zapalska et al., 2012). The findings of the present research confirm those results from other surveys, showing that participants in such teaching methods improve their understanding of more complex economic functions, markets, and businesses, while promoting teamwork and communication constitute essential skills now required for a modern executive. Instructors in the present survey, in line with the relevant literature, recognize the significant potential advantages of using simulation methods in the educational process (Gopinanth & Sawyer, 1999, Ruben, 1999) and the necessity to create conditions for applying these methods in Greek universities (Apostolopoulos et al., 2024). However, they acknowledge that they face significant challenges when integrating simulation methods into the educational process. In general, the integration mechanism of technology and education is not easy. Technical support needs to be further strengthened, and the evaluation criteria need to be clarified Lu et al., (2021). The instructors are not usually properly trained in new educational methods (particularly older instructors) and use outdated educational materials and teaching tools (Wang and Yang, 2024). The lack of supporting mechanisms and staff, as well as the general lack of resources such as non-properly designed classrooms, non-adequate time available, and others, are some of the issues identified in this research, and is also cited in the international literature as critical barriers (Lean et al., 2006). According to the responses from the research, many instructors believe that they either already have or could easily acquire the technological background to implement simulation methods in their courses, provided that the necessary support mechanisms are in place. That is easier, usually, for younger instructors, that are in general, more open and adaptable to new technological and educational tools. The findings of the research, also support the idea that simulation methods encourage the development of specific skills by students that are not covered by theoretical lectures, as they "translate" the latter into real-world conditions (Chulkov & Wang, 2020, Wang & Yang, 2024). Those methods, however, should be supplementary to theoretical lectures rather than replace them (Zhao, 2021), as they do not come with the necessary foundational knowledge. This view is reflected in our research too, as some of the respondents underline that the increased complexity of such systems and the distancing of students from traditional theory and teaching methods could disorient students and limit the usefulness of these methods.

6. CONCLUSION

In the present study, we adopted a qualitative approach using semi-structured interviews administered to personnel (educators) in higher educational institutions to examine the impact of simulation tools in finance schools. Simulation techniques in finance and economics studies have been continuously expanding over the past decades, resulting in a positive impact on students' performance. Our findings confirm that students who participate in such activities demonstrate increased engagement in the learning process, enjoy a hands-on experience of real-world scenarios, improve their decision-making and problem-solving abilities, and develop skills in communication and crisis management, among others. Instructors surveyed in the study recognize the significant potential advantages of using simulation methods in the educational process and emphasize the necessity of creating conditions for implementing these methods in Greek universities. However, several challenges have been identified, such as the lack of professionally trained teaching staff, inadequate university infrastructure, outdated curriculum content, and the high cost of acquiring simulation programs. Instructors are often not properly trained in new educational methods, and as they underlined, the absence of supporting mechanisms and adequate staff, coupled with the general lack of resources and funding in Greek Universities, are considered as critical barriers, to the broader use of simulation techniques.

REFERENCES

Aebersold, M., Tschannen, D., & Bathish, M. (2012). Innovative simulation strategies in education. *Nursing Research and Practice, 2012*(1), 765212. PMID: 22550573

Agoraki, K. K., Deirmentzoglou, G. A., Psychalis, M., & Apostolopoulos, S. (2024). Types of Innovation and Sustainable Development: Evidence from Medium-and Large-Sized Firms. *International Journal of Innovation and Technology Management, 21*(02), 1–18.

Apostolopoulos, N., Kakouris, A., Liargovas, P., Borisov, P., Radev, T., Apostolopoulos, S., & Anastasopoulou, E. E. (2023). Just transition policies, power plant workers and green entrepreneurs in Greece, Cyprus and Bulgaria: Can education and retraining meet the challenge? *Sustainability, 15*(23), 16307.

Apostolopoulos, N., Kakouris, A., Liargovas, P., Dermatis, Z., & Komninos, D. (2018). Evaluating the learning environment of a cross-institutional postgraduate programme in entrepreneurship. Entrepreneurship Education, 1, 105-123. https://doi.Org/10.1007/S41959-018-0007-6

Apostolopoulos, N., Kakouris, A., Liargovas, P., Dermatis, Z., & Komninos, D. (2018a). Evaluating the learning environment of a cross-institutional postgraduate programme in entrepreneurship. *Entrepreneurship Education, 1*, 105–123.

Apostolopoulos, N., Makris, I., Apostolopoulos, S., & Dimitrakopoulos, P. (n.d.). Resilience of rural micro-businesses in an adverse entrepreneurial environment: adapting to the energy crisis. Journal of Enterprising Communities: People and Places in the Global Economy. DOI: 10.1108/JEC-08-2023-0144

Apostolopoulos, N., Moon, C., & Walmsley, A. (2018b). The entrepreneurial university as an engine for sustainable development. *International Journal of Innovative Research and Development, 8*(4), 358–372.

Apostolopoulos, S., Makris, I., & Stavroyiannis, S. (2022, September). Health digitalisation and innovative entrepreneurship status. A qualitative exploration of private sector in Greece and synthesis of main issues. In *ECIE 2022 17th European Conference on Innovation and Entrepreneurship*. Academic Conferences and Publishing Limited.

Azungah, T. (2018). Qualitative research: Deductive and inductive approaches to data analysis. *Qualitative Research Journal, 18*(4), 383–400.

Bakoush, M. (2022). Evaluating the role of simulation-based experiential learning in improving satisfaction of finance students. *International Journal of Management Education, 20*(3), 100690.

Bell, J., & Waters, S. (2018). *Ebook: Doing Your Research Project: A Guide for First-Time Researchers*. McGraw-Hill Education.

Campos, N., Nogal, M., Caliz, C., & Juan, A. A. (2020). Simulation-based education involving online and on-campus models in different European universities. *International Journal of Educational Technology in Higher Education, 17*, 1–15.

Chulkov, D. & Wang, X. (2020). The Educational Value of Simulation as a Teaching Strategy in a Finance Course. e-Journal of Business Education & Scholarship of Teaching, 14(1), 40-56.

Creswell, J. W., & Poth, C. N. (2016). *Qualitative inquiry and research design: Choosing among five approaches*. Sage Publications.

Denzin, N., & Lincoln, Y. (Eds.). (1994). *Handbook of Qualitative Research*. SAGE Publications Ltd.

Facer, K. (2003). Computer games and learning. Futurelab discussion paper. Available at: www.futurelab .org.uk/resources/publications-reports-articles/discussion-papers/Discussion-Paper261

Gao, H. (2020). Research on the Construction of Virtual Simulation Experiment Teaching Courses of Economics and Management Majors. *Advances in Social Science, Education and Humanities Research, 416*.

Gao, H. (2020). Research on the construction of virtual simulation experiment teaching courses of economics and management majors. In *4th International Conference on Culture, Education and Economic Development of Modern Society (ICCESE 2020)* (pp. 973-978). Atlantis Press.

Gittins, P., Apostolopoulos, S., Anastasopoulou, E. E., & Apostolopoulos, N. (2025). Responding to Greece's constrained agricultural context: Farm diversification strategies used by family farmers. *Journal of Rural Studies*, *113*, 103522.

Gopinath, C., & Sawyer, J. E. (1999). Exploring the learning from an enterprise simulation. *Journal of Management Development*, *18*(5), 477–489.

Gregory, P. A., & Austin, Z. (2020). COVID-19: How did community pharmacies get through the first wave? *Canadian Pharmacists Journal/Revue des Pharmaciens du Canada, 153*(5), 243-251.

Hindle, K. (2004). Choosing Qualitative Methods for Entrepreneurial Cognition Research: A Canonical Development Approach. *Entrepreneurship Theory and Practice*, *28*(6), 575–607.

Hongyan, X. (2018). Construction and Practice of Virtual Simulation Experimental Teaching Platform for Economic Management. *Advances in Social Science, Education and Humanities Research, 264*.

Jones, P., Apostolopoulos, N., Kakouris, A., Moon, C., Ratten, V., & Walmsley, A. (Eds.). (2021). *Universities and entrepreneurship: meeting the educational and social challenges*. Emerald Publishing Limited.

Kallio, H., Pietilä, A. M., Johnson, M., & Kangasniemi, M. (2016). Systematic methodological review: Developing a framework for a qualitative semi-structured interview guide. *Journal of Advanced Nursing*, *72*(12), 2954–2965. PMID: 27221824

Karatas-Ozkan, M., Anderson, A., Fayolle, A., Howells, J., & Condor, R. (2014). Understanding entrepreneurship: Challenging dominant perspectives and theorising entrepreneurship through new post-positivist epistemologies. *Journal of Small Business Management*, *52*(4), 589–593.

Kirriemuir, J., & McFarlane, A. (2004). Games and learning. Futurelab Literature Review. Available at: www.futurelab.org.uk/resources/publications-reports-articles/literature reviews/Literature-Review378

Krippendorff, K. (2018). *Content Analysis: An Introduction to its Methodology*. Sage Publications.

Lean, J., Moizer, J., Towler, M., & Abbey, C. (2006). Simulations and games: Use and barriers in higher education. *Active Learning in Higher Education*, *7*(3), 227–242.

Liu, B., Zhu, W., Cao, Y., Liu, Y., & Sun, Y. (2018). Application of Virtual Reality Teaching Method in Combination with Practical Teaching Method in the Undergraduate Teaching of Colleges-Taking the Course of Rolling Technology as an Example. In *2018 International Conference on Social Science and Education Reform (ICSSER 2018)* (pp. 280-284). Atlantis Press.

Lu, H., Xu, J., Wang, L., & He, W. (2021, December). The Basic Problems of Virtual Simulation Experimental Teaching in Higher Education. In *2021 Tenth International Conference of Educational Innovation through Technology (EITT)* (pp. 69-74). IEEE.

Makris, I., & Apostolopoulos, S. (2021). Investing in healthcare enterprises in the non-metropolitan areas: Incentives, reflections, and innovative ideas. In *European Conference on Innovation and Entrepreneurship* (pp. 1160-R17). Academic Conferences International Limited.

Makris, I., Apostolopoulos, S., & Anastasopoulou, E. E. (2024). An Entrepreneurial Perspective on the Transition of Lignite Rural Areas to a New Regime within a Suffocating Timeframe. *Administrative Sciences, 14*(4), 64.

Makris, I. A., Apostolopoulos, S., & Masouras, A. (2025). EU policies and female entrepreneurship in Greek rural areas in relation to digital challenges. In *Real-World Tools and Scenarios for Entrepreneurship Exploration* (pp. 203–222). IGI Global.

Marriott, P., Tan, S. M., & Marriott, N. (2015). Experiential learning–A case study of the use of computerised stock market trading simulation in finance education. *Accounting Education, 24*(6), 480–497.

Ming, F. (2017). *Construction of experiment teaching center of virtual simulation of economic management in application-oriented Colleges Study on Shaan Xi Institute of International Trade & Commerce. In Advances in Engineering Research* (Vol. 123). Atlantis Press.

Moon, C., Walmsley, A., & Apostolopoulos, N. (2018). Sustainability and entrepreneurship education. A survey of 307 UN HESI signatories. Academic Press.

Morse, M. J., & Field, A. P. (1996). *Nursing Research: The Application of Qualitative Approach*. Chapman & Hall.

Moser, A., & Korstjens, I. (2018). Series: Practical guidance to qualitative research. Part 3: Sampling, data collection and analysis. *The European Journal of General Practice, 24*(1), 9–18. PMID: 29199486

Neergaard, H., & Ulhøi, J. P. (Eds.). (2007). Handbook of Qualitative Research Methods in Entrepreneurship. Edward Elgar Publishing.

Norlyk, A., & Harder, I. (2010). What makes a phenomenological study phenomenological? An analysis of peer-reviewed empirical nursing studies. *Qualitative Health Research, 20*(3), 420–431. PMID: 20068190

Patton, M. Q. (1990). *Qualitative evaluation and research methods*. SAGE Publications, inc.

Patton, M. Q. (2002). *Qualitative Research and Evaluation Methods* (3rd ed.). Sage.

Paunović, I., Apostolopoulos, S., Miljković, I. B., & Stojanović, M. (2024). Sustainable Rural Healthcare Entrepreneurship: A Case Study of Serbia. *Sustainability, 16*(3), 1143.

Peng, J., & Abdullah, I. (2018). Building a market simulation to teach business process analysis: Effects of realism on engaged learning. *Accounting Education, 27*(2), 208–222.

Polit, F. D., & Hungler, P. B. (1999). *Nursing Research: Principles and Methods.* Lippincott.

Ruben, B. D. (1999). Simulations, Games and Experience Based Learning: The Quest for a New Paradigm for Teaching and Learning. *Simulation & Gaming, 30*(4), 498–505.

Saunders, B., Sim, J., & Kingstone, T. (2018). Saturation in qualitative research: Exploring its conceptualization and operationalization. *Quality & Quantity, 52*, 1893–1907. PMID: 29937585

Song, R., Cao, Y., Xu, Z., Li, Y., & Liang, B. (2018). Exploring the Laboratory Construction in Finance and Economics Colleges and Universities by Adopting Virtual Simulation Technology. In *2018 2nd International Conference on Management, Education and Social Science (ICMESS 2018)* (pp. 491-494). Atlantis Press.

Summers, G. J. (2004). Today's business simulation industry. *Simulation & Gaming, 35*(2), 208–241.

Tuli, F. (2010). The basis of distinction between quantitative and qualitative in social science: Reflection on ontological, epistemological and methodological perspectives. *Ethiopian Journal of Education and Sciences, 6*(1), 97–108.

Wang, R., & Yang, R. (2024). Research and Exploration on Virtual Simulation Teaching in Universities of Finance and Economics. International Journal of New Developments in Education, 6(4), 182-187. DOI: 10.25236/IJNDE.2024.060431

Wolmarans, H. P. (2005). Business simulations in financial management courses: Are they valuable to learners? *Meditari. Research Journal of the School of Accounting, 13*(1), 121–133.

Xie, H. (2018). Construction and Practice of Virtual Simulation Experimental Teaching Platform for Economic Management. In *2018 5th International Conference on Education, Management, Arts, Economics and Social Science (ICEMAESS 2018)* (pp. 398-402). Atlantis Press.

Yin, R. (2007). *Qualitative research from start to finish* (2nd ed.). Guilford.

Zapalska, A., Brozik, D., & Rudd, D. (2012). *Development of active learning with simulations and games.* Online Submission.

Zhao, H. (2021, October). The Application of Virtual Simulation Technology in Experimental Practice Course Teaching. In *Proceedings of the 2021 5th International Conference on Electronic Information Technology and Computer Engineering* (pp. 1526-1530).

Chapter 9
Business Simulation Games Supporting School Entrepreneurship Education With the Application of Project-Based Methodology

Maria Anna Lykourentzou
https://orcid.org/0009-0009-3180-1701
University of Peloponnese, Greece

Achillefs Vratimos
https://orcid.org/0009-0004-5960-2505
National and Kapodistrian University of Athens, Greece

ABSTRACT

The aim of this chapter is to analyze how the category of Business simulation games – a non-educational category – can be efficiently utilized as a learning tool in a school environment. Since "Entrepreneurship" is a school subject that is difficult to be fully understood due to its extensive theoretical concepts and background, this chapter aims to evaluate in what extend the Business Simulation games could support its teaching through visual examples, activities, and experiments, as they could create a visualization of all these concepts, allowing the students to understand in real life terms such as "costs", "loss", "profit", etc. The educational scenario design will be based on the project-based learning (PBL) methodology, a systematic learning method that guides the learner to educate themselves wholistically via understanding and solving problems in designed real life scenarios. This methodology is developed to enrich learning through pre-defined tasks and goals, which when achieved lead the learner to the expected learning outcome.

DOI: 10.4018/979-8-3693-9040-5.ch009

INTRODUCTION

The swift evolution of information technology has significantly altered our lives. Students have been raised in media-rich settings, including videos, gaming consoles, and computer games. These games immerse players in fun and engaging experiences (Huang et al., 2022). The educational and professional approach leads the individual to create strategies that allow them to develop knowledge in an active way, to trigger solutions to a problem (López et al., 2020). Digital games have garnered the interest of scholars from a wide range of disciplines. Currently, experts from fields such as media design, literature, computer science, education, and theatre studies have collectively contributed to understanding this emerging medium and its role as a learning tool (Devlin-Scherer & Sardone, 2010). Business simulation games (BSGs) are linked to skills development, and the flipped classroom is acknowledged as a successful approach for encouraging student-centered learning through engagement. The BSG both improved learning achievement and situated students in learning with full involvement and enjoyment (Huang et al., 2022). Simulation games provide an experimental environment where participants share their tacit knowledge and obtain new experience via the simulator, which reproduces the real world of project management as accurately as possible and emulates all phases of the life cycle of a project. Using this tool, they can understand the different organizational approaches applied to project-oriented processes (Saenz & Cano, 2009). The purpose of this study is to examine how a business simulated game, with the application of project-based methodology, can enhance students' entrepreneurial skills and their capacity to engage in entrepreneurial activities in an education scenario.

LITERATURE REVIEW

Entrepreneurship and Education

Over the past two decades, entrepreneurship has arguably become one of the most powerful economic forces the world has ever seen. Entrepreneurship is new and it is about continual innovation and creativity (Kuratko, 2005). Entrepreneurship plays a key role in driving innovation, competitiveness, and economic growth, with a clear positive link between entrepreneurship and economic performance in areas such as growth, firm survival, innovation, job creation, technological advancements, productivity gains, and exports. Beyond its economic impact, entrepreneurship offers society another significant benefit: it serves as a pathway for personal development. It not only provides individuals the opportunity to start their own businesses but also acts as one of the most effective solutions to combat unemployment (Karanassios et al., 2006). In response, entrepreneurship education has become more widespread, equipping individuals with the skills and knowledge to navigate and succeed in this dynamic field (Kuratko, 2005).Universities are developing courses and programs that provide entrepreneurial knowledge and skills to students across a wide range of majors, not just business. They have also expanded experiential learning opportunities, including business plan and product development competitions, technology commercialization projects, and internships with start-up companies. These initiatives enable students to engage in entrepreneurial experiences, applying what they learn in practical, hands-on settings (Duval-Couetil, 2013).

Many universities have therefore established professorships in entrepreneurship, with the goal not only of encouraging business school students to take entrepreneurship courses, but also of promoting entrepreneurial thinking across other faculties, particularly in the natural sciences (Huebscher & Lendner,

2010). This cross-disciplinary approach can be further reinforced through classroom experiences, such as startup simulations, where students from various fields can apply entrepreneurial concepts in a practical, hands-on environment, mirroring real-world challenges and opportunities. (Huebscher & Lendner, 2010)

Digital Games

Digital games have emerged as an important means of recreational entertainment for consumers and have become a fairly important part in people's day-to-day lives (Lin et al., 2017). Digital games more than any other technology have the capability to bridge the constructivist learning goals with the constructivist conditions for instruction while controlling to some extent for the potential short comings that one-dimensional hands-on and discovery applications may have (Alexiou & Schippers, 2018).

Digital games span a wide range of genres, presenting players with diverse challenges and problems within a system of rules and mechanics that define the degrees of freedom available to players and govern the virtual environment (Lin et al., 2017). These experiences not only help players develop their logic and reflexes but also enhance their hand-eye coordination and cognitive abilities. As players build these skills, they gain a rewarding sense of accomplishment. Another key feature of digital games is graphic design, which plays a significant role in player engagement. With carefully crafted visuals, players are drawn deeply into the game world, experiencing it more vividly. The immersive 3-D effects and stimulating soundtracks elevate sensory pleasure, ultimately providing players with the ultimate enjoyment and enriching their sense of fun in life (Lin et al., 2017).

With the rapid advancement of technology and the digitalization of everyday life, digital games have surged in popularity worldwide, becoming a central part of our social and cultural landscape. As one of the most favored computer-based activities at home, digital games captivate players of all ages, from children to adults, who are spending increasing amounts of time engaged in gameplay. This widespread appeal has spurred substantial research into the implementation and impact of digital games across various fields, exploring how these games influence different aspects of life and learning (Oberle, & Leunig, 2016).

The sheer diversity of style, formats, and aesthetics of digital games is paralleled only by the range of experiences that they offer to their players. In fact, it could be argued that diversity in games is driven by the desire to offer new and compelling experiences to players (Cairns et al., 2014).There are numerous game genres, yet no single standard classification system exists. Research indicates that the industry, developers, and academics utilize various taxonomies, which can be categorized into seven main genres (Hamzeh et al., 2017):

Action Games (also known as platform games) – These are reaction-based games, and many early games belong to this genre.
Adventure Games – Players navigate a virtual world by solving a series of challenges.
Fighting Games – These involve combat against either computer-controlled characters or other players.
RPG (Role-Playing Games) – Players take on the roles of characters or creatures.
Simulations – Players must succeed within a simplified recreation of a location or scenario to achieve specific goals.
Sports Games – These games are centered around sports activities.

Strategy Games – These recreate historical or fictional situations, allowing players to develop strategies to reach objectives.

Applying this taxonomy can be challenging, as some games fit into multiple categories. For example, many modern sports games incorporate management elements, blending simulation and strategy aspects (Hong et al., 2009). Researchers studying computer games for learning are busy investigating the feasibility of using educational computer games to improve student learning of academic material and relevant cognitive skills (Mayer, 2019). A fundamental measure to take in this regard is to foster experiential learning which allows the students to learn through trial and error. To this end, the delivery of content and learning experience can be enhanced with the aid of simulation games where learners can engage in real-life problem-solving tasks (Yasin et al., 2022).

Digital Games in Education

Various researchers and scholars have studied the correlation between game behavior and learning. Effective content design is crucial to the success of digital game-based learning (Hong et al., 2009). Playing a game is an activity that involves improving skills in order to overcome these challenges. Play is therefore fundamentally a learning experience. Players actively construct ideas and relationships in their own minds based on experiments that they perform, rather than being told what to do, causing the learning to be more effective and efficient (Licorish et al., 2018).

Numerous studies on digital games have been conducted to explore various attributes that can advance the gaming industry and understand the effects of digital games on users. Many argue that the strong appeal of mainstream digital games could serve as a powerful tool for engaging students in serious games, potentially boosting their motivation to learn Computer Science concepts. However, it is crucial to compare user experiences between educational games and mainstream games to gain deeper insights into this dynamic (Egenfeldt-Nielsen, 2011). In education, there is a need for high-quality, learner-focused software that merges effective gaming techniques from game designers with proven educational strategies from teachers. This software should be developed for consoles that learners are already comfortable with, rigorously tested, independently evaluated, and widely promoted. The advantages of widely accessible gaming consoles—such as their stability, user-friendliness, and broadband connectivity—present valuable opportunities that should be fully leveraged (Cairns et al., 2014).

There has been a large increase, mainly in two areas: structural aspects of the games such as influence of digital games in digital literacy, learning styles, skills, etc, and the integration of videogames in schools to improve learning (Fox et al., 2018).Computer games may be particularly helpful in fostering generative processing but are susceptible to creating extraneous processing. The goal of the instructional design of educational computer games is to minimize extraneous processing, guide essential processing, and foster generative processing (Mayer, 2019).

To better understand game-based learning, it is essential to integrate two important elements: motivation and metacognition. An educational game is motivating when players choose to engage, persist in their efforts, and invest energy into mastering its challenges, fostering a sense of agency. Metacognition as an advantage for game-based learning is that it encourages players to become self-regulated learners who actively monitor and control their cognitive processes during gameplay. Furthermore, research on game-based learning can illuminate effective ways to incorporate metacognitive processes into existing cognitive theories of learning, enhancing our understanding of how these elements interact and contribute to a more comprehensive educational experience (Mayer, 2019). Therefore, the tool for assessing the effectiveness of game design is accordingly very important for parents and teachers, so that they may encourage or discourage students to play (Hong et al., 2009).

A properly applied, student-centered digital game-based learning approach and the use of serious games can serve as a powerful educational tool that not only enhances students' learning by promoting interaction, cooperation, and communication but also boosts their well-being, self-esteem, and soft skills. This approach supports critical thinking, decision-making, and problem-solving skills, helps maintain mental and psychological balance, and fosters a deeper interest in educational content, ultimately increasing motivation, engagement, and active participation in lessons(Anastasiadis et al., 2018).

METHODOLOGY

This section outlines the approach used to examine the role of business simulation games as digital tools for supporting entrepreneurship education within school settings, with a focus on project-based learning methodology. The online databases used were ScienceDirect & Scopus with no publication date time limit. The database was searched using not only the appropriate terms but also their combinations. The following search terms performed in the online database were: "Business simulation games", "Simulation games", "Simulation games education", "Project-based methodology".

Publications that include empirical studies will also be included. Publications will be excluded if they do not include information relevant to the purpose of the study. Papers and references will be excluded when only the abstract and not the full text are available. Posts will be excluded if they are not written in English or Greek. After the data was collected and categorized, a detailed summary of the findings will be written.

The methodology seeks to combine existing research to offer insights into how digital tools, such as simulation games, can enhance entrepreneurship education in schools. It also explores how project-based approaches can be effectively incorporated to help students develop entrepreneurial skills.

Project Based Learning Methodology

Project Based Methodology (PBL) is a dynamic educational approach that provides the students with an engaging environment where they could learn through the exploration of real – life problems, questions and challenges. Contrary to the traditional teaching methods where the student has the role of a passive recipient of knowledge, the PBL methodology offers a student – centric educational model, where the students take an active role in their learning developing not only their knowledge but also their soft skills. Fitriany. (2024) state that "Project-Based Learning is defined as a teaching method that supports, facilitates, and emphasizes active exploration and practical learning while promoting students' engagement and critical thinking.", followed by a more recent definition by Hogue et al, (2011) defining "Project-Based Learning is an active teaching method that emphasizes student engagement through real-world projects, fostering both cognitive and practical skills development." Both definitions clearly emphasize the active involvement of the students in the learning process, providing a wholistic development approach of all the key components of the students' personalities.

In PBL, learners are driven to go through an extensive research process in response to a complex question. In this way the learners feel that they have the freedom of choice to an extend when learning, while executing practical tasks and activities. These activities are very meticulously organized, designed and assessed by the educators, to help the learners not only learn core academic content but also develop and enhance their soft skills (collaboration, communication, critical thinking, decision making etc.) (López, 2020). For the successful application of PBL, academics suggest that educators should develop open – ended guiding questions or challenges, which will provide a framework for learnings and help depend on their knowledge by orienting them to research the relevant topics of interest. Additionally, through PBL students develop the needs to become familiar with the theoretical content and knowledge base that would support them in executing the real – life activities by applying this knowledge (Markham et al., 2003). To trigger the learners' interest, the methodology suggests for educators to always present the vision of the end -product or the learning outcome that is expected to be achieved as the course objective. This approach offers to the students a pragmatic understanding of how, when and where their knowledge and learning are applicable in real life. This will create a context for the students, motivating them to invest in their learning and understanding the theoretical frameworks. Also, the PBL methodology offers a sense of autonomy to the learners when they work on building up their knowledge on a specific subject (Petchamé et al., 2024). Common part of the PBL is the "learning through research" where students are prompted to initiate their own research on a topic, steadily developing real – life connections of theoretical concepts, based on their understanding of the research. The results would vary based on the ideas, understanding and interpretations of the students and their learning potential. The majority of researchers analyzing PBL as a learning methodology, have concluded that it embraces and ignites cognitive skills development such as critical thinking, problem solving, analytical thinking, as well as various forms of communication (Organ et al., 2022). With this methodology, students need to do much more than just remembering information and data, so they continuously use their higher order cognitive skills to proceed to conclusions and outcomes. They are also urged to learn to work as a team and contribute to a team effort with their personal input. Within the process of the team collaboration, the students get trained on how to listen to others, be articulate and make their ideas clear when discussing (Mutanga, 2024). At the same time, they develop their skill to be able to read a variety of materials, express themselves in multiple ways (written and verbal) and make eye – capturing presentations. These skills, abilities and habits are often labelled as "21st century skills" (Prensky, 2006).

As literature suggests, the PBL methodology prompts the students to work independently and take ownership of the choices and decisions they take during the activities. This educational setting Is designed to increase the students' engagement as they actively participate and interact with their peers and learning material. It is very frequently documented that learners build a stronger knowledge base through repetition of tasks and feedback (Sungur et al., 2006). The activities designed based on PBL, provide the same curriculum content in variations, allowing the students to explore different cases and situations and be let to the same outcome. When the students fail to grasp the required knowledge to move to the next stage, the educators are present to provide guidance and feedback without overshadowing or hijacking the learning process. Although, it might appear challenging for some students or demotivational after several failures Hanney & Savin-Baden (2013) indicate that the fact that these educational scenarios are based on real – life, boredom and exhaustion are very seldomly identified as students remain engaged for longer period due to interaction with peers. Finally, the PBL methodology includes the public presentation of the activity outcomes, among peers in an educational environment. In this way, students gain confidence and ownership not only for the knowledge they have obtained but also for the given opportunity to present their findings to their classmates and receive constructive feedback (Connolly & Stansfield, 2007).

Project Based Learning Methodology Characteristics

For fifty years, PBL methodology has been proven to be effective in building deep understanding, increasing academic achievement and motivating students to learn. Compared to the traditional teaching methodologies, the student engagement has been significantly increased as students get involved with real – life problems and try to apply their knowledge in solving questions and challenges that would potentially face in their lives out of the educational environment. According to Mallari (2024), PBL can be more effective that traditional teaching in applied sciences such as Math, Economics, Chemistry, Entrepreneurship etc., since it supports students in grasping abstract concepts and transforming them in real – life activities. In this way students learn more efficiently as their long – term knowledge retention increases, leading to the satisfaction of both teachers and students (Mutanga, 2024). The effectiveness of PBL has been proven even for students of lower cognitive level leading it to become an effective education model for the whole academic organization.

Pan (2017) states that PBL is easily applicable in the secondary educational environment as it can be incorporated with the main course curriculum, offering the educators a more engaging way of teaching. The educators have the option to design the project activities on their won and adjust them based on the classroom level, knowledge and cognitive understanding. The educators can also choose the duration of the activity, providing the students with the opportunity of an enriched learning session where they will be simultaneously developing their subject knowledge and their soft skills (Chee et al., 2015). Although PBL appears an "out-of-the-box" methodology, since it does not comply with the traditional academic system and curriculum teaching, this methodology supports wholistically the development of the students as personalities by fostering communication, collaboration, critical thinking, decision – making, feedback acceptance and public speaking (Mutanga, 2024).

Roles

Project Based Learning Methodology is student centric, based on group teaching and learning. Commonly, students are divided into groups and are dedicated to their assignments, continuously developing their personal understanding of the teaching subject. Following this process, will result in students obtaining ownership of the knowledge they have acquired. When students use technology as a means of communicating with others, they take on an active role as opposed to their passive role during the transmission of information by teachers, books or a TV/radio broadcast (Ke & Clark 2020).

The students' role is to ask questions, build knowledge, and determine a real solution to the problem/ question presented. Students must collaborate by developing active listening skills and are required to engage in intelligent and focused communication. Therefore, by allowing them to think logically about how to solve problems, students are encouraged to take responsibility for their own success through this method (Alper et al., 2021)). The students are now able to gradually choose how to receive, present and modify information. Technology makes it possible for students to actively think about the choices they make and execute, and every student could become a communicator of knowledge either as an individual or as a group. Project-based learning combines technology and questioning with students' daily learning-oriented curriculum. Students organize the research they will carry out with their team, and this enables them to develop valuable research skills as they engage in design, problem solving, decision making, and search activities (Chen et al., 2019).

On the other hand, teacher's role becomes that of the "facilitator". Teachers continue to control the class and the students' learning within an atmosphere of shared responsibility. The teachers should structure the guiding research question/problem to direct the students' search for knowledge towards the content – based material (Ergazakis & Metaxiotis 2011). Following this, the educators musth develop a robust activities' framework gradually leading the students to success with distinct transitional goals to ensure that students remain focused on the end goal and will gain deep understanding of research and curriculum concepts. Nonetheless, it is important for teachers not to provide students with any answers because this negates the learning and inquiry process (Liu et al., 2018). Once they students have completed their work, teachers should provide students with constructive feedback that will help them strengthen their skills for their next assignment. Despite the innovative structure that BPL offers to the classroom, research has shown that when the method is used effectively, it helps teachers organize a high – performing classroom, in which they and their students create a strong teaching and learning community.

Project Based Learning Methodology Limitations

As already mentioned, PBL requires significant time for all the phases of the learning process (preparation, execution, presentation and feedback), therefore educators are reluctant to use it as it can be challenging to fit under the standard academic schedule (Piu et al., 2016). Usually, in an academic environment the teaching plans for each course and class are meticulously designed by school or Ministry of Education committees, allowing a very limited flexibility for the educators to divert from the traditional methodologies or curriculum structure. In addition to this, to successfully apply PBL methodology and activities, teachers need to invest a significant amount of time in preparatory activities, to design engaging real – life scenarios with challenges and problems as well as find the resources (material, time) to effectively support the activity (Thavikulwat, 1995). Moreover, during the execution of the activity, teachers facilitate the whole collaborative process, providing guidance and feedback without interfering with the project progression. For teachers to successfully execute this role, they should be well – trained in modern teaching methods and processes, which is not always possible, due to lack of training, support or training funding. As a result, teachers, maintain teaching through the traditional teaching methods which might be outdated and out of touch for the younger generations of students (Ambrosio & Ford, 2016).

The most challenging aspect of implementing PBL methodologies is finding the right tools that will simulate the real – life scenarios. Technology has partially solved this problem with simulation tools, educational games and online guiding exercises and BPL activities. Unfortunately for all these tools to be accessed, specific technological equipment is required in large numbers for all the students to have access to the tools simultaneously and proceed with their activities (Fitriany, 2024). Although, in many regions, schools have computer labs available to all students, it has been identified that for many rural areas having technological equipment and sufficient training on how to use it, is a luxury (López, 2020). Another aspect that limits the usage of PBL methodology in classroom settings is the late development of ownership and accountability from students' side. A frequent phenomenon has been observed is that not all students collaborate equally in the group setting, whereas they are graded the same way based on their outcomes and results. This methodology requires the extensive involvement and observation by the evaluator to identify imbalances in workload within the groups and equalize it (Markham et al., 2003). Finally, the traditional assessment methods fail to comply with the collaborative setting of the PBL methodology as students will be evaluated as groups instead of individuals, with only minor components of the activity reviewed individually (e.g. the work sheet results, the individual presence during the group presentation and the personal feedback given to peers in classroom). Since these individual components are not significant for the complete evaluation of a student regarding a specific academic course, it is advised PBL to be used complementarily as a teaching tool instead of the main teaching methodology in an academic environment (Pan, 2017).

FINDINGS

Application of Business Simulation Games in Entrepreneurship

In recent decades, entrepreneurship has gained widespread recognition for its significant impact on a nation's economic activity and development. Encouraging entrepreneurship can be supported through education and training provided by higher education institutions (Shabbir & Pallares-Venegas, 2024). Various digital games have been specifically designed and implemented for educational purposes in the fields of entrepreneurship, innovation, and creativity. Online games and games supporting multiple scenarios seem to come closer to the issues and skills of real-world entrepreneurship. In multiplayer online games in particular, players perceive that action is indeed taking place in a real-world domain. The rest of the games approach parts of the reality, and could operate as instructional tools for more specific entrepreneurship topics (Tragazikis et al., 2012). The simulation tool encourages students to participate more actively in discussions and decisions. It not only empowered business knowledge but also changed their predisposition for undertaking entrepreneurial activities on their own (Huebscher & Lendner, 2010).

An important research community is working on the use of simulation games. With the increase in processing power and memory capabilities of new computers, there is an increasing demand for technically accurate simulations involving situations that would normally be impossible for the user to experience in real life. Adventure and simulation games provide complex learning environments that are appropriate for the acquisition of learning with meaningful materials that encourage the construction of relevant knowledge using the suitable models (Chen et al., 2019). Simulation-based games are an ideal fit for experiential learning environments, particularly for training manager trainees. They provide students with the chance to experience the outcomes of carrying out or neglecting key project management tasks. Trainees face complex challenges that arise during project development and can experiment with different approaches and solutions, learning from the results of their actions (Cadotte, 2022). The positive educational effect is achieved if briefings and debriefings become a part of a game-based learning process. Properly organized debriefing is the way to transfer knowledge and experience from a game to a real-life context. As games cannot simulate all possible real-life scenarios, a teacher, as a de-briefer, cannot be replaced by games (Tokarieva et al., 2019).

Business simulation games (BSGs) have been widely used in entrepreneurship education with positive effects. However, there are still some deficiencies in the BSGs, such as limited guidance, low uncertainty and limited simulation environment, which make it impossible to exert the maximum effect (Chen et al., 2022). Choosing the right simulation is critical to the success of the learning experience. It depends upon the level of education and maturity of the target audience plus the number of participants and available time for the exercise (Cadotte, 2022). Furthermore, the availability of e-learning materials, notably business simulation games, emerges as a critical catalyst in encouraging students' entrepreneurial aspirations (Shabbir & Pallares-Venegas, 2024).

As policymakers seek to support entrepreneurs, entrepreneurship simulation seminars serve as an effective method for teaching the complex interrelationships in business to both entrepreneurs and students across various disciplines. Data analysis indicates that these seminars result in significant learning outcomes, which participants, particularly entrepreneurs, find professionally valuable. Participants gain foundational entrepreneurial knowledge, develop new perspectives, and enhance their complex entrepreneurial thinking. Non-businessschool students can thereby be sensitized to the whole entrepreneurial field of action (Huebscher & Lendner, 2010). Both entrepreneurial abilities and institutional assistance play critical roles in developing and boosting students' entrepreneurship goals (Shabbir & Pallares-Venegas, 2024).

Concerns of Using Digital Games in Educational Environments

Teachers play a central role in both the creation and negotiation of context and their beliefs and understandings about games shape how, where, when and why they work with games with diverse learners (Beavis et al., 2014).Prior experience emerged as a key factor influencing science teachers' perceptions of educational computer games, with those who had previously used such games in teaching showing more positive attitudes toward their classroom use. Teachers lacking prior experience, however, expressed greater concerns about using games, suggesting that inexperience may be a major barrier to their adoption and integration. Additional obstacles to integrating educational games included limited computer availability, time constraints, the demands of preparing for high-stakes testing, and insufficient knowledge of science-related games. Teachers highlighted the need for computers and trial access to games to effectively incorporate them into their lessons (An et al., 2016). It's essential to recognize that for a game to be successfully introduced in formal education, the environment and activities supporting its integration play a crucial role in unlocking its full potential (Limone et al., 2023). The game's scope—meaning the time and effort a teacher needs to adapt gameplay to meet classroom requirements and the game's anticipated duration—also factors in when addressing the practical constraints of school settings. Ultimately, the suitability of any game, like other educational technologies, depends not only on its intrinsic educational value but also on the needs, characteristics, and limitations of the learning environment, as well as those of the teachers and students who will use it (Papadakis, 2018).

In learning through simulation games, the source of learning is what the participants do rather than what they are told by the trainer. The dynamics of learning through a simulation game provide a framework in which the dynamics between exploration and exploitation processes take place (Saenz & Cano, 2009). Entrepreneurship educators should recognize that simulations are not designed to replace traditional teaching methods (Barzilai, 2017). If this were to happen, it is possible that some barriers such as lack of access to resources and difficulties aligning games to curriculum will automatically diminish and others will be easier to address (Stieler-Hunt & Jones, 2017).Research shows that instructor-centered approaches often prove more effective for skill development than many alternative techniques, including simulations. However, simulations can enhance conventional methods by adding a valuable dimension: the practice of higher-order educational objectives in entrepreneurship education.

While these simulations still have room for improvement in accurately modeling entrepreneurial activities, they offer significant advantages (Justice & Ritzhaupt 2015). Instructors can effectively use simulations to teach key aspects of the entrepreneurial experience. Notably, they provide substantial practice and reinforcement of the general management competencies essential for entrepreneurs navigating the growth and consolidation phases of their firms. Thus, entrepreneurship instructors should consider total enterprise simulations as a valuable teaching technique (Bílek et al., 2018).

The key duties and responsibility of universities are to enhance the academic performance of the study. Business simulation games make it possible for students to think, communicate, and solve problems creatively and proactively, and these simulation games can be played at any location (Zulfiqar et al., 2021). These games incorporate strong problem-solving elements, with feedback loops that promote reflective learning. They also immerse students in narratives that offer insights into specific entrepreneurial contexts, particularly small business management, enabling them to explore virtual scenarios, make decisions, and navigate various choices dynamically (Fox et al., 2018). Additionally, simulation games provide different scenarios that provide the participants with an opportunity to interact, sharing their experiences and points of view about the situation they must tackle. This interaction in the core of the group is the driver of the team learning synergy(Saenz & Cano, 2009).

Simulation games are learning moving stations, which are available at the best cost for students. Therefore, educational institutes should enrich themselves with technology-oriented learning (Zulfiqar et al., 2021). With the evolution of project simulation models, many limitations of current simulation-based game will be addressed to provide a more realistic situation, increasing the number of training scenarios and enhancing knowledge transference (Faizan et al., 2019). The gaming landscape also continues to evolve with many more products on the market covering different entrepreneurial contexts and technological advancements, such as virtual reality and artificial intelligence offering many opportunities for improvements in technological and learning sophistication. While the current gaming landscape could improve, games provide a safe and risk-free pedagogy for learners to enhance their entrepreneurial preparedness before they launch or join a new venture (Fox et al., 2018).

Practical Implications

The application of the Project Based Learning methodology assists the educators in presenting how knowledge and academic courses apply in real life, with the support of technological tools. By creating real – life scenarios where students are called to resolve while applying their obtained knowledge, they encourage the exploration and learning growth through the execution of specific tasks and objectives (Adachi & Willoughby 2013). In this section we have developed a framework for an educational scenario that would be assisting in the teaching of the Entrepreneurship course fundamentals. For the effective implementation of PBL methodology the utilization of commercial digital games is required and specifically simulation games that offer the option for the users to create and develop their own business (e.g. Sims 2 expansion, Sims 4 expansion, RollerCoaster Tycoon, airport Tycoon, Two Point Hospital etc.) (Adams, 1998).

The proposed educational scenario aims to achieve the accomplishment of the targeted learning objectives, related to the entrepreneurship course following the guidelines of the Interdisciplinary Secondary Educational Curriculum Committee. More specifically, the goal of this scenario would be the teaching of the fundamental Entrepreneurship terminology “Costs”, “Profits”, “Loss” and their interdependency as well as the synergy of the “Supply and Demand” law / economic model, and how these terms affect the viability, sustainability and profitability of the Business (Cairns et al., 2014). The first teaching objective would be the understanding of the basic equations "Profit = Selling price – Cost price" and "Loss = Cost price – selling price", where the value of the selling price would be the determining factor of the business future and students should be able to understand that by using different variables the result would differ. The second teaching objective would be the application the application of several "Supply and Demand" variation – activities to help students understand how a business would remain profitable under alternate circumstances (Chen et al., 2022). Since the PBL activities are used in a complementary way by the educators, 6 teaching hours should be sufficient to cover all the teaching objectives in a meaningful manner.

Project Based Learning Educational Scenario Design

To provide a constructive teaching process, which will result to the learning for the fundamental entrepreneurship concepts, a detailed scenario should be designed and orchestrated by the educator with students actively participating in.

Phase 1: The educator would produce a collective design of all the activities / tasks that should be executed during the PBL session and prepare work sheets with all the research questions for the students to fill in during the gaming sessions (Lin et al., 2017). Following the PBL principles, the students are expected to experiment with the game and occasionally fail during the execution of their tasks, leading them to repeat them as a way of learning growth. Since there would be time constraints for the completion of the activity, the educator should include repetitive tasks, and variations of the same activity in the worksheet as well as a questionnaire with all the key objectives. In this way the students will be able to track their progress and analyze their results, in the next phases (Hogue et al., 2011).

Phase 2: Students would be instructed to work in groups, since according to the PBL literature references, collaboration and coordination among team members offers higher percentage for success and cognitive growth. As a result, students should be given the opportunity to work in teams, while assuming specific roles for the purposes of the gaming activity (Organ et al., 2022). These roles would represent the basic operational functions of a business giving the students a first – hand experience on how a business operates and which decisions impact its viability and stability. To achieve better results and develop their soft skills that students should be encouraged to switch roles among tasks.

The roles available would be:

Sales manager: They define the selling prices of the business' products, they document the cash flow during business opening hours, and its ranking, and draw conclusions regarding customer reactions towards the products' prices.

HR Manager: They are responsible for hiring and/or firing staff in the business. They evaluate potential candidates for the jobs available, they review their character and skillset, and they assign them on the most suitable open role. Additionally, they review the performance of the current employees during the gaming sessions, and they explore the growth of the employees' skillset considering giving them raises or demoting them.

Marketing Manager: They monitor and record the customers reaction and satisfaction levels towards the operational business model. In all business simulation games customer reactions are indicative of their satisfaction and they are influenced by product prices, service quality and sales persuasion by the virtual employees.

Phase 3: Prior to the initiation of the PBL scenario, students should be given a teaching hour to familiarize themselves with the game and execute all the preparatory tasks. As students could be easily destructed by the entertaining nature of the game, clear instructions should be given, including a strict time frame for their completion. During this teaching hour, the students should be prompted to design their avatars based on their taste and preferences and execute some basic quests / missions in the game, to familiarize themselves with the controls and gameplay (Huang et al., 2022). In cases where the games offer communication options during the gameplay, the educators should de-activate it, creating an isolated, safe and focused learning environment. Students should be ready for the PBL scenario post completing the below list of activities: a) selecting the business category by either creating one from scratch or purchase a pre-built one, a choice they will justify later in their worksheet. b) selecting the type of products they want to sell – if available through gameplay settings. Although their choice does not have an impact on the teaching objectives, if gives to the students a sense of ownership and develops their decision taking skills. c) design and furnish the business setting and having ready for opening day. d) decide on the selling prices of the products or fairy tickets and justify their choice on their worksheets, planning to track the customers' reaction to the prices in the coming phases (Aldrich, 2005).

Phase 4: During the six teaching hours of gameplay, the students will document their experiences and the results of their decisions on the worksheets, allowing them to evaluate the results at a later point and re-execute the same tasks with different variables if necessary for a better understanding of the learning scope (Tokarieva et al., 2019). The goal of the work sheets is to support the students in their exploration of the entrepreneurship fundamental terminology and the relationship between specific variables. For example, the relationship between wholesale and retail selling price of the products given the profit rate that each group of students has determined for their business. Also, the depreciation of the cost of opening the business. Students in each group experiment with the concepts of cost, breakeven, payback period and the profits the business must show to break even. What is the relationship that connects the assets or liabilities of the business to the profits of the business?

To better understand and experiment with the game the members of each group decide together, at the beginning of each activity session with the game, the changes they are going to implement in their business. These changes may concern a) the change in the selling prices of the products, b) the change in the number of employees of the company c) in decisions concerning the working conditions of the employees (e.g. days off, assigning tasks in accordance with their interests and skills, increasing or decreasing their salaries), c) expanding the business (Saenz & Cano, 2009). Whereas any changes will be jointly decided and implemented by the team member with the appropriate role (sales manager, HR manager, marketing manager). In any case, the implemented changes should be documented based on data related to the operation of the business and are also available from the game menus.

The information available to the group members at the end of each session feeds a discussion-debriefing between them, which will lead to decision-making and the formulation of the strategy to be followed in the next session. Indicative topics-questions to be discussed by the group members would be the following: "Has the cash flow to the business increased or decreased?", "Has the number of customers served increased or decreased?" or "How did the company's employees react to the changes made? Did they perform their duties more willingly or did they refuse to follow their supervisor's instructions?" As part of the operation and management of the business undertaken by each group of students, a total of three sessions with the game are foreseen. In this way, the recycling of roles within the team is ensured, since each role is assumed by each member of the team.

Phase 5: Following the completion of the gaming sessions, a session of evaluating and discussing the results should be initiated. Students should be the protagonists of this session, presenting their conclusions regarding the course of Entrepreneurship to their peers, showcasing examples of how they operated in different tasks during the game. The educator would coordinate the activity, allowing the feedback to be provided mainly by the students to their peers (Almaki et al., 2023). This session should be very thorough as it will produce the learning outcomes and presents whether the students developed a better understanding of the theoretical framework with the support of a real-life scenario (Tragazikis et al., 2012).

As a result, the student-members of each group should produce written reports, tables and charts to capture their course and progress of their business. The recorded results, as well as their evaluation should be discussed across the classroom. The groups should also present their results to the plenary session of the class and discuss these results with the members of the other groups who had been involved in similar activities or similar methods of handling specific tasks and quests (Hanney, & Savin-Baden, 2013). The educator should contribute to the discussion regarding issues related to the organization, management and operation of a business and how the students should perceive them after their active involvement in the educational activities with the digital game. The concepts that should be reviewed and discussed for further analysis are income, expenses, profit, loss, market needs, resources for the operation of the business, supply, demand, etc. Finally, the evaluation of the specific teaching objectives can be carried out by carrying out a final written examination (test). On the contrary, the achievement of the general teaching objectives (development of soft skills) can be assessed by direct observations made by the teacher, as well as by the work done by the students with the help of the worksheets and the game (Markham et al., 2003).

CONCLUSIONS

With the inclusion of Project Based Learning Methodology as our baseline, our research has provided a robust educational scenario design which includes all the main milestones and characteristics of the PBL. Through our analysis, we have presented a wholistic student centric teaching approach, which allows students to explore freely, engage with new technologies in an existing way and gain the curriculum knowledge through real – life challenges and activities (Fitriany, 2024). The concept of teaching the subject of "Entrepreneurship" with the assistance of Digital Simulation Games, would offer to the students' exposure to how a real business would operate and all the factors (internal and external) that would impact its viability, sustainability and profitability. Our research has attempted to provide a structured design of the utilization of digital games in a classroom setting as a complimentary teaching method with pre-defined and set teaching objectives and time.

As per the specific research evaluation, the Project Based Methodology learning, does not only focus on the curriculum teaching objectives but also enhances the soft skills of the students participating in the activities. Students are prompted to actively engage with the technological equipment and practice their motor skills, while expressing their personal taste through the design of their avatars and business. Moving on to the next activities, students are challenged to explore and make decisions regarding specific game tasks and quests. In this way students develop their critical thinking skills, their analytical thinking and while trying to justify their decisions they expand their conceptual thinking (Mutanga, 2024). In addition to this, while solving riddles or succeeding in challenges, students develop their problem-solving skills in combination with learning through "trial and error" allowing them to obtain ownership of their knowledge. Finally, as these activities are encouraged via PBL methodology to be executed in a group setting, the students expand their communication and collaboration skills as well as their reasoning and persuasion – through – arguments skills. As a result, the PBL educational scenario offers a wholistic development of the participants regarding both the teaching objectives and their personality.

Future Research

The specific chapter offers a detailed analysis of the Project Based Methodology and how it can be applied in an educational setting within the Secondary Education structure. It also gives an insight of how commercial digital games can be utilized in a structured and controlled manner, for the teaching of the subject of "Entrepreneurship", despite the limitations that have already been discussed and analyzed. Since this research offers a robust theoretical framework for the application of the BPL methodology and the simulation games in methodology, it can be used from future applicators as the baseline for their research and application of PBL methodology. The educational scenario design that has been produced as outcome of this research can contribute to better and more successful implementations and applications of PBL educational scenarios in the future for academic organizations, regarding subjects that are difficult to be grasped by students based on their educational level and cognitive understanding. It is important for future applicators to evaluate the described phases, apply them in all relevant stages of their teaching process and validate the results of specific set milestones.

REFERENCES

Adachi, P. J. C., & Willoughby, T. (2013). More than just fun and games: The longitudinal relationships between strategic video games, self-reported problem solving skills, and academic grades. *Journal of Youth and Adolescence*, *42*(7), 1041–1052. DOI: 10.1007/s10964-013-9913-9 PMID: 23344653

Adams, P. C. (1998). Teaching and learning with SimCity 2000. *The Journal of Geography*, *97*(2), 47–55. DOI: 10.1080/00221349808978827

Aldrich, C. (2005). *Learning by doing: A Comprehensive Guide to Simulations, Computer Games, and Pedagogy in e-Learning and Other Educational Experiences*. Academic Press.

Alexiou, A., & Schippers, M. C. (2018). Digital game elements, user experience and learning: A conceptual framework. *Education and Information Technologies*, *23*(6), 2545–2567. DOI: 10.1007/s10639-018-9730-6

Almaki, S. H., Gunda, M. A., Idris, K., Hashim, A. T. M., & Ali, S. R. (2023). A systematic review of the use of simulation games in K-12 education. *Interactive Learning Environments*, 1–25. DOI: 10.1080/10494820.2023.2205894

Alper, A., Şengün Öztaş, E., Atun, H., Çınar, D., & Moyenga, M. (2021). A systematic literature review towards the research of game-based learning with Augmented Reality. *International Journal of Technology in Education and Science*, *5*(2), 224–244. DOI: 10.46328/ijtes.176

Ambrosio Mawhirter, D., & Ford Garofalo, P. (2016). Expect the unexpected: Simulation games as a teaching strategy. *Clinical Simulation in Nursing*, *12*(4), 132–136. DOI: 10.1016/j.ecns.2015.12.009

An, Y.-J., Haynes, L., Alba, A., & Chumney, F. (2016). Using educational computer games in the classroom: Science teachers' experiences, attitudes, perceptions, concerns, and support needs. *Contemporary Issues in Technology & Teacher Education*, *16*(4), 415–433.

Anastasiadis, T., Lampropoulos, G., & Siakas, K. (2018). Digital game-based learning and serious games in education. *International Journal of Advances in Scientific Research and Engineering*, *4*(12), 139–144. DOI: 10.31695/IJASRE.2018.33016

Barzilai, S. (2017). "Half-reliable": A qualitative analysis of epistemic thinking in and about a digital game. *Contemporary Educational Psychology*, *51*, 51–66. DOI: 10.1016/j.cedpsych.2017.06.004

Beavis, C., Rowan, L., Dezuanni, M., McGillivray, C., O'Mara, J., Prestridge, S., Stieler-Hunt, C., Thompson, R., & Zagami, J. (2014). Teachers' beliefs about the possibilities and limitations of digital games in classrooms. *E-Learning and Digital Media*, *11*(6), 569–581. DOI: 10.2304/elea.2014.11.6.569

Bílek, M., Nodzyńska, M., Kopek-Putała, W., & Zimak-Piekarczyk, P. (2018). Balancing chemical equations using sandwich making computer simulation games as a supporting teaching method. *Problems of Education in the 21st Century*, *76*(6), 779–799. DOI: 10.33225/pec/18.76.779

Cadotte, E. R. (2022). How to use simulation games in the classroom? *The Journal of Entrepreneurship*, *31*(2, suppl), S90–S134. DOI: 10.1177/09713557221107442

Cairns, P., Cox, A., & Nordin, A. I. (2014). Immersion in digital games: Review of gaming experience research. In *Handbook of Digital Games* (pp. 337–361). John Wiley & Sons, Inc. DOI: 10.1002/9781118796443.ch12

Chee, Y. S., Mehrotra, S., & Ong, J. C. (2015). Professional development for scaling pedagogical innovation in the context of game-based learning: Teacher identity as cornerstone in "shifting" practice. *Asia-Pacific Journal of Teacher Education*, *43*(5), 423–437. DOI: 10.1080/1359866X.2014.962484

Chen, J., Chen, Y., Ou, R., Wang, J., & Chen, Q. (2022). How to use artificial intelligence to improve entrepreneurial attitude in business simulation games: Implications from a quasi-experiment. *Frontiers in Psychology*, *13*, 856085. DOI: 10.3389/fpsyg.2022.856085 PMID: 36467165

Chen, M.-H. M., Tsai, S.-T., & Chang, C.-C. (2019). Effects of game-based instruction on the results of primary school children taking a natural science course. *Education Sciences*, *9*(2), 79. DOI: 10.3390/educsci9020079

Connolly, T. M., & Stansfield, M. H. (2007). From eLearning to games-based eLearning: Using interactive technologies in teaching an IS course. *International Journal of Information Technology and Management*, *26*(2), 188–208.

Devlin-Scherer, R., & Sardone, N. B. (2010). Digital simulation games for social studies classrooms. The Clearing House: A. *The Clearing House: A Journal of Educational Strategies, Issues and Ideas*, *83*(4), 138–144.

Duval-Couetil, N. (2013). Assessing the impact of entrepreneurship education programs: Challenges and approaches. *Journal of Small Business Management*, *51*(3), 394–409. DOI: 10.1111/jsbm.12024

Egenfeldt-Nielsen, S. (2011). *Beyond edutainment: Exploring the educational potential of computer games*. Lulu. Com.

Ergazakis, K., & Metaxiotis, K. (2011). The knowledge-based development agenda:a perspective for 2010-2020. *Vine*, *41*(3), 358–377. DOI: 10.1108/03055721111171582

Fitriany, F. (2024). The implementation of Project Based Learning method in building creativity, encouraging learning motivation and improving language skills. *BRIGHT VISION Journal of Language and Education*, *4*(2), 108. DOI: 10.30821/brightvision.v4i2.3862

Fox, J., Pittaway, L., & Uzuegbunam, I. (2018). Simulations in entrepreneurship education: Serious games and learning through play. *Entrepreneurship Education and Pedagogy*, *1*(1), 61–89. DOI: 10.1177/2515127417737285

Hamzeh, F., Theokaris, C., Rouhana, C., & Abbas, Y. (2017). Application of hands-on simulation games to improve classroom experience. *European Journal of Engineering Education*, *42*(5), 471–481. DOI: 10.1080/03043797.2016.1190688

Hanney, R., & Savin-Baden, M. (2013). The problem of projects: Understanding the theoretical underpinnings of project-led PBL. *London Review of Education*, *11*(1), 7–19. DOI: 10.1080/14748460.2012.761816

Hogue, A., Kapralos, B., & Desjardins, F. (2011). The role of project-based learning in IT: A case study in a game development and entrepreneurship program. *Interactive Technology and Smart Education, 8*(2), 120–134. DOI: 10.1108/17415651111141830

Hong, J.-C., Cheng, C.-L., Hwang, M.-Y., Lee, C.-K., & Chang, H.-Y. (2009). Assessing the educational values of digital games: Assessing the educational values. *Journal of Computer Assisted Learning, 25*(5), 423–437. DOI: 10.1111/j.1365-2729.2009.00319.x

Huang, Y.-M., Silitonga, L. M., & Wu, T.-T. (2022). Applying a business simulation game in a flipped classroom to enhance engagement, learning achievement, and higher-order thinking skills. *Computers & Education, 183*(104494), 104494. DOI: 10.1016/j.compedu.2022.104494

Huebscher, J., & Lendner, C. (2010). Effects of entrepreneurship simulation game seminars on entrepreneurs' and students' learning. *Journal of Small Business and Entrepreneurship, 23*(4), 543–554. DOI: 10.1080/08276331.2010.10593500

Justice, J., & Ritzhaupt, L. (2015). Identifying the barriers to games and simulations in education. *Journal of Educational Technology Systems, 44*(1), 86–125.

Karanassios, N., Pazarskis, M., Mitsopoulos, K., & Christodoulou, P. (2006). EU strategies to encourage youth entrepreneurship: Evidence from higher education in Greece. *Industry and Higher Education, 20*(1), 43–50. DOI: 10.5367/000000006776150747

Ke, F. (2019). Mathematical problem solving and learning in an architecture-themed epistemic game. *Educational Technology Research and Development. Educational Technology Research and Development, 67*(5), 1085–1104. DOI: 10.1007/s11423-018-09643-2

Kuratko, D. F. (2005). The emergence of entrepreneurship education: Development,Trends and Challenges. *Entrepreneurship Theory and Practice, 29*(5), 577–597. DOI: 10.1111/j.1540-6520.2005.00099.x

Licorish, S. A., Owen, H. E., Daniel, B., & George, J. L. (2018). Students' perception of Kahoot!'s influence on teaching and learning. *Research and Practice in Technology Enhanced Learning, 13*(1), 9. Advance online publication. DOI: 10.1186/s41039-018-0078-8

Limone, P., Ragni, B., & Toto, G. A. (2023). The epidemiology and effects of video game addiction: A systematic review and meta-analysis. *Acta Psychologica, 241*(104047), 104047. DOI: 10.1016/j.actpsy.2023.104047 PMID: 37897856

Lin, Y.-L., Lin, H.-W., & Yang, Y.-T. (2017). Players' value structure in digital games. *Games and Culture, 12*(1), 72–99. DOI: 10.1177/1555412015581710

Liu, H., Ma, H., Meng, Q.-C., Fan, S.-S., & Dang, Z.-H. (2018). Reform and practice of electronic system design course based on CDIO educational philosophy. *DEStech Transactions on Social Science Education and Human Science, icss*. DOI: 10.12783/dtssehs/icss2017/19446

López, M. M. L. (2020). Project-based learning strategy: An innovative proposal for local education system. *International Journal of Psychosocial Rehabilitation, 24*(1), 1666–1681. DOI: 10.37200/IJPR/V24I1/PR200267

Mallari, A. (2024). Arcie Mallari. In *Advances in Educational Technologies and Instructional Design* (pp. 479–484). IGI Global.

Markham, T., Larmer, J., & Ravitz, J. (2003). *Project Based Learning Handbook: A Guide to Standards-Focused Project Based Learning for Middle and High School Students*. Academic Press.

Mayer, R. E. (2019). Computer games in education. *Annual Review of Psychology*, *70*(1), 531–549. DOI: 10.1146/annurev-psych-010418-102744 PMID: 30231003

Mutanga, M. B. (2024). Students' perspectives and experiences in project-based learning: A qualitative study. *Trends in Higher Education*, *3*(4), 903–911. DOI: 10.3390/higheredu3040052

Oberle, M., & Leunig, J. (2016). Simulation games on the European Union in civics: Effects on secondary school pupils' political competence. *Citizenship Social and Economics Education*, *15*(3), 227–243. DOI: 10.1177/2047173416689794

Organ, J., O'Neill, S., & Shanahan, B. W. (2022). Development of Social Technology Entrepreneurial Ventures: A challenge project-based learning approach. *IFAC-PapersOnLine*, *55*(39), 181–186. DOI: 10.1016/j.ifacol.2022.12.050

Pan, J. (2017). *An empirical study of the impact of project-based learning on English major students' critical thinking skills*. Academic Press.

Papadakis, S. (2018). The use of computer games in classroom environment. *International Journal of Teaching and Case Studies*, *9*(1), 1. DOI: 10.1504/IJTCS.2018.090191

Petchamé, J., Iriondo, I., Torné, O., & Solanellas, F. (2024). Student perceptions of project-Based Learning when studying 'Information Systems' in an ICT engineering program: Taking advantage of active learning. *Education Sciences*, *14*(11), 1148. DOI: 10.3390/educsci14111148

Piu, A., Fregola, C., & Santoro, A. (2016). Using a simulation game to make learning about angles meaningful. an exploratory study in primary school. *European Journal of Science and Mathematics Education*, *4*(4), 490–500. DOI: 10.30935/scimath/9488

Prensky, M. (2006). *Don't bother me mom — I'm learning!* Paragon House.

Saenz, M. J., & Cano, J. L. (2009). Experiential learning through simulation games: An empirical study. *International Journal of Engineering Education*, *25*(2), 296–307.

Shabbir, M. S., & Pallares-Venegas, E. (2024). Influences of entrepreneurship skills and universities on the promotion of entrepreneurial intentions of students; mediating role of business simulation games. *On the Horizon*, *32*(1), 1–14. DOI: 10.1108/OTH-10-2022-0062

Stieler-Hunt, C. J., & Jones, C. M. (2017). Feeling alienated – teachers using immersive digital games in classrooms. *Technology, Pedagogy and Education*, *26*(4), 457–470. DOI: 10.1080/1475939X.2017.1334227

Sungur, S., Tekkaya, C., & Geban, Ö. (2006). Improving achievement through problem-based learning. *Journal of Biological Education*, *40*(4), 155–160. DOI: 10.1080/00219266.2006.9656037

Thavikulwat, P. (1995). Computer-assisted gaming for entrepreneurship education. *Simulation & Gaming*, *26*(3), 328–345. DOI: 10.1177/1046878195263005

Tokarieva, A. V., Volkova, N. P., Harkusha, I. V., & Soloviev, V. N. (2019). Educational digital games: Models and implementation. *Educational Dimension*, *1*, 5–26. DOI: 10.31812/educdim.v53i1.3872

Tragazikis, P., Kirginas, S., & Gouscos, D. (2012). Digital games for entrepreneurial learning, innovation and creativity: Examples and evaluation criteria. *International Journal of Innovative Research and Development*, *4*(3/4), 314. DOI: 10.1504/IJIRD.2012.047564

Yasin, N., Gilani, S. A. M., Contu, D., & Fayaz, M. J. (2022). Simulation-based learning in business and entrepreneurship in higher education: A review of the games available. In *Technology and Entrepreneurship Education* (pp. 25–51). Springer International Publishing. DOI: 10.1007/978-3-030-84292-5_2

Zulfiqar, S., Al-reshidi, H. A., Al Moteri, M. A., Feroz, H. M. B., Yahya, N., & Al-Rahmi, W. M. (2021). Understanding and predicting students' entrepreneurial intention through business simulation games: A perspective of COVID-19. *Sustainability (Basel)*, *13*(4), 1838. DOI: 10.3390/su13041838

Chapter 10
Enhancing Entrepreneurship Education:
The Role of Simulation Tools in Teaching and Learning

Christos Papademetriou
https://orcid.org/0000-0002-7167-7786
Neapolis University, Pafos, Cyprus

Sofia Anastasiadou
Neapolis University, Pafos, Cyprus

ABSTRACT

This chapter examines the incorporation of simulation technologies into entrepreneurship education, evaluating their effect on student learning outcomes and the development of entrepreneurial skills. The study examines how these technologies might connect theoretical knowledge with practical application, equipping students for real-world issues. The research employs a mixed-methods approach, integrating quantitative analysis via pre- and post-assessment exams with qualitative insights via student surveys and interviews. Simulation tools were integrated into university entrepreneurship classes throughout a semester, allowing students to participate in experiential learning through virtual business settings. The results indicate that students show considerable enhancement in decision-making capabilities, strategic planning, and critical thinking skills.

1. INTRODUCTION

Over the past twenty years, entrepreneurship has emerged as a pivotal emphasis in institutions of higher learning. This transition addresses a fluid global economy and the urgent requirement for entrepreneurial mindset across sectors. Conventional teaching methods, centered on lectures and case studies, provide important basic knowledge but may inadequately prepare students with the crucial skills

DOI: 10.4018/979-8-3693-9040-5.ch010

necessary for successful entrepreneurship, including risk-taking, making smart choices, and flexibility to market fluctuations.

A primary shortcoming of conventional methods is their insufficient involvement with the practical, unexpected reality of corporate situations. Simulations address this gap by offering a controlled, immersive environment in which students can try, fail, and learn without the consequences of actual company failure. These instruments may encompass company simulations, market strategy games, and role-playing scenarios that enable students to "operate" virtual enterprises, make strategic choices, and analyze results depending on their actions.

This study examines the use of simulation tools in entrepreneurship education to assess their effect on students' development of vital entrepreneurial abilities, namely decision-making, critical thinking, and strategic planning. This study employs a mixed-methods approach to offer an extensive analysis of the impact of simulations on quantifiable results and student perceptions.

The study enquires:

- In what manner do simulation tools augment students' decision-making and critical thinking skills?
- What are students' views on the effectiveness of simulations in equipping them for real-world business challenges?

The findings seek to offer significant insights for educators and curriculum makers, emphasizing the efficacy of simulation technologies as a helpful complement to conventional teaching techniques.

2. LITERATURE REVIEW

2.1 The Shift Toward Experiential Learning in Entrepreneurship Education

Entrepreneurship education has progressively transitioned from solely theoretical frameworks to more practical methodologies, mirroring the dynamic and intricate character of entrepreneurial practice (Papademetriou and Charalampous, 2018; Papademetriou, 2012). Conventional lectures and textbooks provide essential core knowledge; nevertheless, they frequently inadequately develop the practical skills and critical thinking competencies required for success in entrepreneurial endeavors. Researchers underscore the significance of "learning by doing" in cultivating entrepreneurial capabilities, enabling students to acquire skills such as risk-taking, resilience, and adaptability, which are crucial for managing the uncertainties inherent in entrepreneurship (Neck & Greene, 2011).

Kolb's Experiential Learning Theory (1984) offers a fundamental framework for comprehending this transition, asserting that learning is a cyclical process comprising concrete experience, reflective observation, abstract conceptualization, and active experimentation. In entrepreneurship education, this manifests as a model wherein students actively participate in entrepreneurial activities, critically evaluate what they have learnt, and utilize newly gained knowledge to enhance their comprehension and performance. A new study by Hägg and Kurczewska (2019) corroborates Kolb's approach, illustrating that experiential learning techniques foster entrepreneurial attitudes and competencies through repeated cycles of action and reflection.

Furthermore, experiential learning cultivates competencies that are progressively esteemed in entrepreneurial contexts, including creativity, problem-solving, and opportunity identification. Nabi et al. (2018) assert that entrepreneurship programs emphasizing experiential learning yield graduates that exhibit greater confidence, innovation, and adaptability in fluctuating business contexts. Simulation technologies are especially efficacious in this setting, as they connect classroom theory with practical application, enabling students to engage in entrepreneurial processes without the significant dangers linked to actual companies.

2.2 The Efficacy of Simulation Tools Across Disciplines

Simulation technologies are extensively utilized in several educational domains—such as finance, medicine, and engineering—as efficient means for implementing theoretical knowledge in controlled, risk-free settings. These tools allow students the ability to participate in authentic scenarios, test strategies, and obtain feedback on their choices, so enhancing both engagement and retention.

In healthcare, Boyle et al. (2014) demonstrated that simulations markedly enhanced decision-making abilities and diminished error rates, highlighting the tool's efficacy in fostering rapid, adaptive cognition. Likewise, simulation-based learning in engineering education has demonstrated enhancement of students' problem-solving abilities by enabling them to analyze intricate systems and troubleshoot in real time (de Jong & Joolingen, 2018). These findings correspond with the principle of experiential learning, whereby students gain advantages from participating in "safe" practice sessions that replicate the obstacles they will encounter in their professions.

In business education, simulations are particularly beneficial for cultivating abilities like financial analysis, market strategy, and team management, enabling students to investigate business decisions without real-world consequences (Gredler, 1996). Shields (2002) discovered that business students utilizing simulations exhibited markedly superior performance on analytical tasks and shown enhanced confidence in their problem-solving skills. Vesci et al. (2021) has proved that simulations facilitate the development of adaptive tactics in competitive market situations, hence improving students' analytical skills and their responsiveness to changing conditions. These results underscore the significance of simulation technologies as adaptable educational resources that proficiently equip students for the practical requirements of diverse vocations.

2.3 Theoretical Underpinnings: Constructivist and Experiential Learning Theories

The application of simulation tools in education is based on numerous significant learning theories, particularly Constructivist Learning Theory and Experiential Learning Theory. Constructivist Learning Theory, articulated by Vygotsky (1978), asserts that knowledge is actively generated through experience and social interaction. This idea posits that students learn most effectively when they interact with materials in a relevant and contextualized manner, rather than passively receiving knowledge. Simulation tools correspond with this methodology by establishing interactive learning environments in which students may implement theoretical principles in real, contextually rich scenarios.

Kolb's Experiential Learning Theory (1984) enhances constructivism by conceptualizing learning as a dynamic interplay of experience, reflection, and experimentation. In entrepreneurship education, simulations encapsulate this cycle by enabling students to make decisions, evaluate outcomes, and modify their strategies in following iterations. This iterative approach enhances critical thinking and strategic planning skills, as students are persistently compelled to assess their activities and derive lessons from errors. Ngozwana (2022) asserts that simulations enhance profound learning by immersing students in authentic business scenarios, enabling them to "experience" entrepreneurship in ways that academic approaches cannot emulate.

Constructivist and experiential theories are particularly pertinent in entrepreneurship, where adaptation, innovation, and resilience are crucial. Ward (2021) posits that simulation-based learning establishes a connection between theory and practice, facilitating the development of cognitive and practical abilities essential for entrepreneurial success. These theoretical frameworks establish the foundation for comprehending the efficacy of simulation tools in education, especially in disciplines necessitating practical, adaptive skill sets.

2.4 Prior Research on Simulation Tools in Entrepreneurship

The utilization of simulation tools in entrepreneurship education is somewhat novel relative to other fields, although initial research suggests favorable results. Pittaway and Cope (2007) examined how simulations promote entrepreneurial cognition by prompting students to make strategic choices, evaluate potential risks, and adjust to fluctuating market conditions. Their research substantiates that simulation tools increase students' understanding of intricate business variables, including consumer requirements, competitive dynamics, and resource allocation.

Recent investigations corroborate similar conclusions. Fu et al. (2019) discovered that simulations in entrepreneurship courses improve students' capacity to formulate adaptable solutions, fostering both flexibility and inventiveness. Their research indicates that students utilizing simulation tools are more adept at managing the uncertainties intrinsic to entrepreneurship, as they acquire expertise in modifying plans in response to evolving circumstances. Vesci et al. (2021) assert that simulation-based learning cultivates vital competencies, like opportunity recognition and strategic planning, which are crucial for successful entrepreneurship. Ngozwana (2022) posits that simulation tools strengthen not only technical capabilities but also bolster students' confidence and resilience, attributes essential for entrepreneurial development.

These research correspond with the present study's aim of investigating how simulations cultivate essential entrepreneurial competencies. Simulations offer students an interactive, risk-free setting to test business concepts, enabling them to get practical experience and cultivate vital abilities in decision-making, critical thinking, and strategic planning. Prior research demonstrates that simulation tools possess considerable potential to enhance entrepreneurship education by allowing students to use theoretical knowledge in a manner that reflects the problems encountered in actual businesses.

3. METHODOLOGY

3.1 Research Design

A mixed-methods strategy was chosen because it allows collecting both quantitative data on skill learning and qualitative insights into students' experiences. The quantitative component included pre- and post-tests to assess progress in certain skills, while qualitative data were collected through surveys and interviews.

The quantitative component included pre- and post-assessments that examined skills including strategic planning, decision-making, and critical thinking. These tests offered objective information about the impact of simulations on skill development.

Qualitative Component: Open-ended surveys allowed students to express their learning experiences and attitudes towards simulations as a learning aid. In addition, ten in-depth interviews were performed to learn more about students' viewpoints on the importance of simulations in comprehending complicated business problems.

3.2 Participants

The sample included 100 undergraduate students participating in an introductory entrepreneurship course at a medium-sized university. Participation was voluntary, and students were told that their responses would be kept private. The demographic breakdown comprised students from various academic backgrounds, ensuring a varied range of opinions.

3.3 Data Collection Methods

Pre- and post-assessments evaluated students' decision-making, critical thinking, and strategic planning skills. The pre-test created a benchmark for students' abilities, while the post-test assessed any advances made following the simulation experience.

Surveys used Likert-scale and open-ended questions to get student feedback on the simulations' effectiveness.

Ten students participated in semi-structured interviews to explore engagement, skill growth, and simulation obstacles.

3.4 Data Analysis

Quantitative Analysis: Paired t-tests were employed to compare pre- and post-test scores, assessing if simulation tools significantly enhanced students' skills.

Qualitative Analysis: Survey and interview responses were systematically coded and thematically analysed. Data patterns were discerned to reveal prevalent themes, including enhanced confidence in decision-making and recognition of real-world applicability.

4. ANALYSIS AND DISCUSSION

4.1 Quantitative Findings: Measurable Improvement in Entrepreneurial Skills

Quantitative study indicated a significant enhancement in students' strategic planning, decision-making, and critical thinking abilities following their interaction with simulation tools. Post-test results were, on average, 25% higher than pre-test levels, highlighting the substantial impact of simulations on enhancing these competencies. The findings align with recent studies indicating that experiential and simulation-based learning methodologies enhance cognitive and practical competencies in business education contexts (Hägg & Kurczewska, 2019; Ngozwana, 2022).

Skills in Strategic Planning: Students exhibited significant advancement in strategic planning, enhancing their skills in recognizing market possibilities, resource allocation, and contingency planning. This improvement corresponds with the research of de la Fuente et al. (2021), who highlighted that simulations facilitate students' use of strategic frameworks in dynamic corporate environments. Frequent engagement in strategic decision-making simulations allowed students to see patterns, assess risks, and formulate action plans, cultivating proactive business acumen vital for entrepreneurship (Kuratko & Morris, 2018).

Decision-Making Competencies: A significant enhancement in decision-making capabilities was noted, as students became more proficient in assessing risks, predicting outcomes, and making informed decisions. Research indicates that simulation technologies substantially improve decision-making abilities by offering a practice setting devoid of real-world consequences (Ward, 2021). Kolb's (1984) experiential learning theory posits that decision-making necessitates experiencing contexts for optimal growth. Simulations facilitate a cycle of action, reflection, and refinement by enabling students to investigate intricate scenarios, thereby enhancing their decision-making skills (Bellotti et al., 2013).

Critical Thinking: Students demonstrated enhanced critical thinking abilities, since simulations compelled them to evaluate complex circumstances, discern essential difficulties, and investigate diverse solutions. Recent research by Hamilton et al. (2019) and Vesci et al. (2021) substantiates that simulation-based learning enhances critical thinking by engaging students in contexts that require problem-solving, adaptation, and ongoing learning. Participants in this study indicated that interacting with simulations offered a systematic framework for addressing business difficulties, resulting in a more analytical and critical approach to decision-making and analysis.

The quantitative results correspond with prior research on experiential learning techniques, reinforcing the conclusion that simulations significantly improve critical entrepreneurial skills. They not only emulate real-world difficulties but also offer a secure, engaging environment for skill enhancement in ways that conventional learning approaches may be deficient (Hägg & Kurczewska, 2019; Ngozwana, 2022).

4.2 Qualitative Findings: Student Perceptions of Simulation Tools

The qualitative examination of student input identified many critical themes concerning their experiences using simulation tools: improved engagement, practical application, and heightened confidence. These findings enhance the comprehension of the influence of simulation technologies on student attitudes and motivation within entrepreneurship education.

Increased Engagement: Students often indicated that simulations were more captivating than conventional lectures. They identified the interactive aspect and prompt feedback from simulations as elements that maintained their engagement in the learning process. A recent study by Ngozwana (2022) indicates that interactive technologies, such as simulations, enhance engagement by delivering real-time outcomes and promoting active participation. Hamilton et al. (2019) similarly discovered that students in virtual learning environments frequently exhibit increased motivation and enjoyment, resulting in enhanced retention and performance.

Practical Application: Students particularly valued the capacity to implement theoretical concepts in realistic contexts, reporting that simulations enhanced their comprehension of the intricacies of corporate situations. Vesci et al. (2021) indicated that students employing simulations acquired practical understanding of dynamic marketplaces and competitive business environments. This corresponds with Bellotti et al. (2013), who discovered that simulated learning environments enable students to engage with theoretical frameworks, therefore reinforcing their comprehension and execution of business strategies.

Enhanced Confidence: A prevalent theme was the assurance students acquired from engagement in simulations. A multitude of pupils credited their enhanced confidence to the secure setting, which permitted them to try without the apprehension of failure. Hägg and Kurczewska (2019) assert that simulations can alleviate entrepreneurial anxiety in students by offering a regulated environment for practice. Simulations foster resilience in pupils and cultivate a proactive mindset towards adversities, which are crucial attributes for successful entrepreneurs (Ward, 2021).

The qualitative findings support the idea that simulation tools provide value beyond skill development, positively impacting students' self-efficacy and engagement. By creating a learning environment where students feel supported and capable of experimenting, simulations contribute to a more holistic approach to entrepreneurship education.

4.3 Discussion: Implications for Educators and Curriculum Design

The study's results provide valuable information for educators and curriculum developers aiming to integrate simulation technologies into entrepreneurship education.

Curriculum Development Focused on Skills: The significant enhancement in students' post-assessment scores highlights the efficacy of simulation tools in fostering practical skills. Educators ought to develop entrepreneurial curricula that incorporate simulations as fundamental elements, in accordance with recent advocacy for experiential, skill-oriented learning methodologies in entrepreneurship education (Kuratko & Morris, 2018; Hägg & Kurczewska, 2019). A skills-focused curriculum equips students more effectively for practical business difficulties by providing experiential opportunities in strategic planning, decision-making, and critical thinking.

Enhanced Engagement and Knowledge Retention: The observed elevated levels of student involvement indicate that simulation tools can enhance learning outcomes and information retention. Hamilton et al. (2019) established that interactive, simulation-based learning environments significantly improve student motivation and understanding. Educators may employ simulation tools to enhance course engagement, thereby decreasing dropout rates and augmenting student happiness in entrepreneurship programs (Ngozwana, 2022).

Connecting Theory and Practice: Simulation tools facilitate the application of theoretical knowledge in authentic business contexts, thereby bridging the divide between theory and practice. Vesci et al. (2021) discovered that simulations facilitate the effective transfer of theoretical information into practical application, hence preparing students with essential skills for real-world entrepreneurial environments. The practical aspect is essential in entrepreneurship education, since it cultivates adaptable thinking and equips students for the unpredictable dynamics of the business environment (Ward, 2021).

Future Research on Simulation-Based Learning: This study underscores the opportunity for additional investigation into various simulation formats and their effects on particular entrepreneurial competencies. Competitive and collaborative simulations may provide distinct learning results, offering significant insights for customizing simulations to various educational aims. Longitudinal study may examine the sustained effects of simulation-based learning on students' career paths and entrepreneurial achievements, yielding insights into the lasting advantages of simulation technologies in education (de la Fuente et al., 2021).

This study's findings confirm that simulation tools are excellent for skill development and for increasing student engagement and confidence, thereby producing a holistic educational experience that equips students for entrepreneurial difficulties. Educators are urged to incorporate simulations into entrepreneurial curriculum, offering students a realistic, engaging, and supportive environment that connects academic principles with practical application.

5. CONCLUSION

This study emphasizes the significance of simulation tools in entrepreneurship education, illustrating their capacity to cultivate practical skills in a risk-free setting. Simulation technologies facilitate experiential learning, enabling students to cultivate and enhance their entrepreneurial skills through practical engagement.

Educators ought to incorporate simulation tools into entrepreneurial programs to promote active, experiential learning. Through simulations, educators can enable students to experiment with business ideas, cultivate adaptive abilities, and make data-driven decisions.

Future research may investigate the long-term impacts of simulation-based learning on students' entrepreneurial trajectories, along with the efficacy of various simulation modalities. The outcomes of this study indicate that simulation tools possess considerable potential for improving entrepreneurship education, providing students with an opportunity to acquire essential experience prior to entering the business realm.

5.1 Practical Implications

This study's findings provide several practical implications for educators, curriculum developers, and institutions dedicated to entrepreneurship education. This study emphasizes the efficacy of simulation technologies in developing essential entrepreneurial skills and proposes practical measures to improve entrepreneurship programs.

1. **Curriculum Integration:** Educators and curriculum designers should more extensively utilize simulation technologies inside entrepreneurship courses to offer students practical learning experiences. In contrast to conventional pedagogical approaches, simulations enable students to engage with authentic events, facilitating decision-making, outcome analysis, and strategic adjustments. This method facilitates the connection between theoretical comprehension and actual implementation, guaranteeing that students are adequately equipped for the intricacies of entrepreneurship.
2. **Skill Development Emphasis:** Simulations facilitate the cultivation of particular entrepreneurial competencies, including strategic planning, risk evaluation, and flexibility. These competencies are essential for maneuvering through the volatile landscape of the corporate realm. Institutions must contemplate the incorporation of simulations within a competency-based framework, emphasizing the cultivation of practical skills that students can apply in their professional endeavors.
3. **Improved Engagement and Retention:** The research indicated that students exhibited greater engagement and commitment to their learning while utilizing simulations. This indicates that simulation technologies can enhance student retention and course satisfaction by providing an engaging, immersive experience that encourages active participation in learning.
4. **Scalable Learning:** Simulation technologies can function as scalable resources that support extensive class sizes while maintaining educational quality. Universities and colleges experiencing budget limitations may consider simulations as a cost-efficient method to deliver high-quality, practical entrepreneurship instruction.
5. **Continuous Improvement via Feedback**: The prompt feedback from simulations enables students to make decisions, observe outcomes, and learn in real-time, fostering a continuous improvement cycle. Educators can utilize these characteristics to evaluate and enhance students' entrepreneurial thinking, thereby personalizing the learning experience and tailoring it to specific individual or group requirements.

By integrating these technologies into their curricula, universities can boost students' competencies and establish a reputation for providing creative, practical business education that aligns with the requirements of the contemporary corporate landscape.

5.2 Theoretical Implications

This study enhances the theoretical framework of entrepreneurship education by reinforcing and building upon several educational and learning theories pertinent to experiential learning and the development of entrepreneurial skills.

1. **Validation of Experiential Learning Theory:** The results of this study corroborate Kolb's Experiential Learning Theory (1984), which underscores the significance of learning by active engagement, reflection, and exploration. This study empirically supports the use of experiential learning in entrepreneurship education by demonstrating simulations that enhance entrepreneurial skills, including decision-making and strategic planning. This underscores the notion that business education must transcend mere passive knowledge acquisition to incorporate active, experiential learning.
2. **Expansion of Constructivist Theory in Business Education:** The research further develops Vygotsky's Constructivist Learning Theory (1978), which asserts that learners actively create knowledge via experience and interaction. Simulations provide a setting for students to participate

in entrepreneurial endeavors, develop new information through direct engagement, and implement their learning in intricate situations. The research validates that constructivist concepts can be successfully implemented in entrepreneurship education, indicating that interactive learning methods like as simulations are significant pedagogical assets.

3. **Contribution to the Theory of Simulation-Based Learning:** This research enhances the existing corpus of knowledge regarding simulation-based learning. Previous research on simulation tools in healthcare and engineering education (e.g., Boyle et al., 2014; Shields, 2002) has demonstrated beneficial effects on skill enhancement, and this study expands these conclusions to the field of entrepreneurship. This study demonstrates that simulations improve decision-making and critical thinking skills in entrepreneurial students, so affirming that simulation-based learning is a multifaceted educational instrument relevant to several fields.
4. **Addressing the Theory-Practice Discrepancy in Entrepreneurship Education:** A persistent difficulty in entrepreneurship education is reconciling theoretical concepts with practical application. The study indicates that simulations effectively facilitate this balance, enabling students to implement theoretical knowledge in a practical setting. This has theoretical significance for entrepreneurial curriculum design, as it endorses a blended learning paradigm that integrates both theoretical and experiential elements to promote holistic skill development.
5. **Framework for Future Research on Entrepreneurship Simulations:** This study paves the way for further enquiries in the domain of entrepreneurship education. The favorable results linked to simulations indicate that subsequent research could investigate diverse simulation types (e.g., competitive simulations, collaborative simulations) and their impact on various entrepreneurial competencies. Theoretical models can be constructed to evaluate the efficacy of these simulations across several tiers of entrepreneurship education, ranging from beginner courses to advanced programs.

This study indicates that educators and institutions may enhance entrepreneurial programs by including simulation technologies, emphasizing skill development, engagement, and scalability. Simultaneously, the theoretical implications underscore the significance of experiential and constructivist theories in entrepreneurship education, endorse simulation-based learning as an efficacious method, and emphasize avenues for future research in comprehending and enhancing simulations within entrepreneurial frameworks.

REFERENCES

Bellotti, F., Kapralos, B., Lee, K., Moreno-Ger, P., & Berta, R. (2013). Assessment in and of serious games: An overview. *Advances in Human-Computer Interaction, 2013*, 1–11. DOI: 10.1155/2013/120791

Boyle, E., MacArthur, E., Connolly, T. M., Hainey, T., Manea, M., Kärki, A., & van Rosmalen, P. (2014). A narrative literature review of games, animations and simulations to teach research methods and statistics. *Computers & Education, 74*, 1–14. DOI: 10.1016/j.compedu.2014.01.004

de Jong, T., & van Joolingen, W. R. (2018). Scientific discovery learning with computer simulations of conceptual domains. *Review of Educational Research, 68*(2), 179–201. DOI: 10.3102/00346543068002179

de la Fuente, J., Franco, C., Gabarda, V., & Zapata, L. (2021). The role of entrepreneurship education in the development of organizational resilience and value creation in new entrepreneurs. *Journal of Innovation & Knowledge, 6*(1), 27–34. DOI: 10.1016/j.jik.2020.06.001

Fu, H., Su, L., & Yu, X. (2019). Enhancing student engagement and learning outcomes through business simulations in entrepreneurship education. *Journal of Entrepreneurship Education, 22*(1), 1–10.

Gredler, M. E. (1996). Educational games and simulations: A technology in search of a (research) paradigm. In Jonassen, D. H. (Ed.), *Handbook of research on educational communications and technology* (pp. 521–539). Macmillan.

Hägg, G., & Kurczewska, A. (2019). Who is the student entrepreneur? Understanding the emergent adult through the pedagogy and andragogy of entrepreneurial learning. *Education + Training, 61*(9), 1071–1084.

Hamilton, L., Tee, S., & Considine, J. (2019). The impact of immersive simulation experiences on nurse educators' confidence, knowledge and skills. *Nurse Education Today, 78*, 37–42.

Kolb, D. A. (1984). *Experiential learning: Experience as the source of learning and development.* Prentice Hall.

Kuratko, D. F., & Morris, M. H. (2018). Examining the future trajectory of entrepreneurship education. *Journal of Small Business Management, 56*(1), 11–23. DOI: 10.1111/jsbm.12364

Nabi, G., Liñán, F., Fayolle, A., Krueger, N., & Walmsley, A. (2018). The impact of entrepreneurship education in higher education: A systematic review and research agenda. *Academy of Management Learning & Education, 16*(2), 277–299. DOI: 10.5465/amle.2015.0026

Neck, H. M., & Greene, P. G. (2011). Entrepreneurship education: Known worlds and new frontiers. *Journal of Small Business Management, 49*(1), 55–70. DOI: 10.1111/j.1540-627X.2010.00314.x

Ngozwana, N. (2022). Experiential learning through simulations in business management education. *Journal of Business Education & Learning, 18*(2), 147–161.

Papademetriou, C. (2012). Leadership Impact on Elementary School's Effectiveness and Improvement. Paper presented at the 8th European Conference on Management, Leadership and Governance, Pafos, Cyprus.

Papademetriou, C., & Charalampous, C. (2018). Entrepreneurship and Innovation in Education: The model of the Inclusive Leader. *1st International Conference on Marketing and Entrepreneurship (ICME 2018)*. Neapolis University.

Pittaway, L., & Cope, J. (2007). Simulating entrepreneurial learning: Integrating experiential and collaborative approaches to learning. *Management Learning*, *38*(2), 211–233. DOI: 10.1177/1350507607075776

Shields, M. (2002). Learning and teaching through simulation. *Simulation & Gaming*, *33*(1), 111–126. DOI: 10.1177/1046878102033001010

Vesci, M., Botti, A., & D'Auria, A. (2021). Simulation-based learning in higher education: Enhancing students' entrepreneurial skills through realistic virtual environments. *Computers & Education*, *170*, 104214. DOI: 10.1016/j.compedu.2021.104214

Vygotsky, L. S. (1978). *Mind in society: The development of higher psychological processes*. Harvard University Press.

Ward, T. B. (2021). Creative cognition in entrepreneurship: An overview and some new research directions. *Journal of Business Venturing*, *36*(3), 106102.

Chapter 11
Enhancing R&D Success in Entrepreneurship Education With Industry: Academia Collaboration and Simulation Tools

Vetrivel S. C.
https://orcid.org/0000-0003-3050-8211
Kongu Engineering College, India

Arun V. P.
JKKN College of Engineering and Technology, India

P. Vidhyapriya
https://orcid.org/0000-0002-1421-8743
Kongu Engineering College, India

ABSTRACT

The rapidly evolving landscape of entrepreneurship necessitates innovative educational approaches that effectively prepare students for real-world challenges. This study explores the synergistic potential of industry-academia partnerships in enhancing research and development (R&D) success within entrepreneurship education, particularly through the integration of simulation tools. By collaborating with industry experts, academic institutions can create dynamic learning environments that bridge theoretical knowledge with practical applications. Simulation tools serve as critical resources, enabling students to engage in experiential learning, risk assessment, and decision-making in a controlled setting. This chapter examines case studies of successful partnerships, illustrating how these collaborations enhance curriculum design, foster entrepreneurial skills, and drive innovation.

DOI: 10.4018/979-8-3693-9040-5.ch011

1. INTRODUCTION

1.1. The Importance of Collaboration in R&D

Research and Development (R&D) is the backbone of innovation, driving progress across industries and contributing to economic growth and societal advancement. Collaboration between industry and academia is crucial in R&D as it leverages the strengths of both sectors, fostering an environment conducive to groundbreaking discoveries and practical applications.

1.1.1 Leveraging Diverse Expertise

Industry-academia collaboration brings together diverse expertise, with academia offering deep theoretical knowledge and a focus on fundamental research, while industry provides practical insights and a market-oriented perspective, (Aasheim *et al.*, 2009). This synergy enhances the quality and applicability of research outcomes. Academic institutions, with their focus on curiosity-driven research, often explore novel concepts without immediate commercial constraints. In contrast, industry partners bring a pragmatic approach, emphasizing efficiency, scalability, and market relevance. By working together, these entities can bridge the gap between theory and practice, ensuring that innovations are not only scientifically sound but also commercially viable.

1.1.2 Access to Resources and Infrastructure

Collaborative efforts provide access to a broader range of resources and infrastructure. Academic institutions often have state-of-the-art laboratories, advanced research tools, and a pool of talented researchers and students, (Hanieh *et al.*, 2015). On the other hand, industries can offer funding, real-world data, and access to commercial-grade facilities and equipment. This pooling of resources accelerates the R&D process, enabling more ambitious projects that might be beyond the reach of individual entities, (Alshare & Sewailem, 2018). For instance, the development of new pharmaceuticals often requires extensive testing and regulatory compliance, processes that benefit from the combined efforts and resources of both academic researchers and industry professionals.

1.1.3 Innovation and Knowledge Transfer

One of the significant benefits of industry-academia collaboration is the facilitation of knowledge transfer and innovation. Academic research can sometimes be insulated within the confines of scholarly journals and conferences, limiting its impact on real-world problems. Industry partners can help translate academic findings into practical applications, leading to the development of new products, processes, and services. This not only benefits the industry but also enhances the societal impact of academic research, (Azmi *et al.*, 2018). Moreover, collaborative projects often result in intellectual property that can be commercialized, creating new revenue streams for both partners and fostering an innovation-driven economy.

1.1.4 Addressing Complex Challenges

Many of the world's most pressing challenges, such as climate change, healthcare, and sustainable development, are complex and multifaceted, requiring interdisciplinary approaches and substantial resources. Industry-academia partnerships are uniquely positioned to tackle these grand challenges. Academia's theoretical and exploratory research can uncover novel solutions, while industry expertise ensures these solutions are practical, scalable, and can be implemented effectively, (Bedwell, Salas, & Eduardo, 2014). For example, collaborations in renewable energy research have led to significant advancements in solar and wind technologies, driven by the combined efforts of academic innovation and industrial application.

1.1.5 Role of Simulation Tools in Entrepreneurship Education

Simulation tools play a crucial role in entrepreneurship education by providing a risk-free environment for students to experiment with business strategies, decision-making, and problem-solving. These tools replicate real-world market dynamics, allowing learners to develop practical skills in areas such as financial management, marketing, and operations without facing actual financial losses. By engaging in simulated business scenarios, students can test their ideas, analyze outcomes, and refine their approaches based on data-driven insights. Furthermore, simulation tools foster critical thinking, adaptability, and innovation, which are essential traits for aspiring entrepreneurs. The interactive and experiential nature of these tools enhances learning outcomes by bridging the gap between theoretical knowledge and practical application, preparing students to navigate the complexities of the entrepreneurial landscape effectively.

1.2 Historical Context of Industry-Academia Partnerships

Industry-academia partnerships have evolved significantly over the past century, reflecting broader changes in the economy, technology, and society. Understanding this historical context is crucial to appreciating the current landscape and the dynamics that shape these collaborations.

1.2.1 Early Beginnings and World War II

The roots of industry-academia partnerships can be traced back to the late 19th and early 20th centuries, a period marked by rapid industrialization and scientific discovery. Universities began to play a pivotal role in advancing scientific knowledge and producing skilled graduates, while industries sought to leverage this expertise to drive innovation and economic growth.

A major turning point occurred during World War II when the collaboration between academia and industry became critical to national security, (Boston Consulting Group Report, 2015). The U.S. government established partnerships with universities and industries to develop technologies that were essential for the war effort, such as radar, jet engines, and the atomic bomb. The establishment of the Office of Scientific Research and Development (OSRD) in 1941 exemplified this collaborative spirit, with universities providing the fundamental research and industries focusing on development and production.

1.2.2 Post-War Expansion and the Cold War Era

In the post-war period, the relationship between academia and industry continued to strengthen, driven by the Cold War and the space race. The launch of Sputnik by the Soviet Union in 1957 spurred significant investment in scientific research and education in the United States, leading to the creation of programs like the National Defense Education Act (NDEA) and the expansion of the National Science Foundation (NSF). Universities became key players in research and development, supported by substantial government funding, (Chan, 2011). During this era, industries increasingly turned to academic institutions for cutting-edge research and development. The symbiotic relationship was evident in the rapid advancements in fields such as aerospace, electronics, and computer science. The establishment of research parks, such as Stanford Research Park in the 1950s, provided a physical space where academia and industry could collaborate more closely.

1.2.3 The Rise of the Knowledge Economy

The latter part of the 20th century saw the emergence of the knowledge economy, characterized by the central role of information and technology in driving economic growth. This shift further deepened the connections between universities and industries. The Bayh-Dole Act of 1980 in the United States was a landmark piece of legislation that allowed universities to retain the intellectual property rights to inventions developed with federal funding, (Chea, Tan, & Huan, 2019). This act incentivized academic institutions to commercialize their research, leading to a surge in university patents and the formation of numerous university spin-offs and start-ups.Universities became incubators for innovation, fostering entrepreneurial ecosystems and collaborating with industries to bring new technologies to market. This period also saw the rise of interdisciplinary research centers and institutes within universities, designed to address complex problems and bridge the gap between academic research and industrial application.

1.2.4 Globalization and the Information Age

The advent of the internet and the globalization of economies in the late 20th and early 21st centuries further transformed industry-academia partnerships. The rapid pace of technological change and the global competition for talent and innovation necessitated closer collaboration between academia and industry on a global scale, (Crebert *et al.,* 2004). Universities began to forge international partnerships with multinational corporations, leading to a more interconnected and collaborative global research ecosystem.In this era, the focus expanded to include not only technological innovation but also social and environmental sustainability. Collaborative efforts increasingly addressed global challenges such as climate change, public health, and sustainable development. The integration of digital technologies and big data analytics became central to research and development efforts, fostering new forms of collaboration and innovation.

1.2.5 Recent Trends and Future Directions

Today, industry-academia partnerships are characterized by their diversity and complexity. They span multiple disciplines and sectors, involving a wide range of stakeholders, including government agencies, non-profit organizations, and international institutions. The rise of open innovation, where organizations seek external ideas and technologies, has further blurred the lines between academic and industrial research, (Dasgupta, 2015). Recent trends include the growing emphasis on translational research, which aims to move discoveries from the lab to the market more efficiently, and the increased focus on collaborative platforms and consortia that bring together multiple universities and companies to tackle large-scale challenges. The COVID-19 pandemic has underscored the importance of these partnerships, with unprecedented collaboration to develop vaccines and treatments at record speed.Looking ahead, the future of industry-academia partnerships will likely be shaped by emerging technologies such as artificial intelligence, biotechnology, and quantum computing, as well as by global imperatives for sustainable development and inclusive innovation, (Farkas & Nagy, 2008). As these partnerships continue to evolve, they will play a crucial role in driving scientific and technological progress, economic development, and societal well-being.

2. THEORETICAL FRAMEWORK AND LITERATURE REVIEW

2.1. Definitions and Key Concepts

2.1.1 Industry-Academia Partnerships

Industry-academia partnerships refer to collaborative arrangements between educational institutions, particularly universities, and private sector companies. These partnerships are designed to leverage the strengths and capabilities of both sectors to drive innovation, research, and development, (Gleason, 2018). Universities provide cutting-edge research, specialized knowledge, and a pool of talented students, while industries contribute practical experience, funding, and market insights. Such collaborations aim to bridge the gap between theoretical research and practical application, fostering an environment where theoretical knowledge can be transformed into real-world solutions.

2.1.2 Research and Development (R&D)

Research and Development (R&D) encompasses a wide range of activities undertaken by companies and academic institutions to innovate and introduce new products or services. R&D activities are crucial for technological advancement and economic growth. Within the context of industry-academia partnerships, R&D efforts are often focused on developing new technologies, improving existing products, and solving complex problems that require interdisciplinary approaches, (Groß, Siegert, & Bauernhansl, 2017). These activities can range from basic research, which seeks to expand fundamental knowledge, to applied research and experimental development, which aim to create practical applications and market-ready solutions.

2.1.3 Technology Transfer

Technology transfer is the process through which scientific findings and technological innovations developed within universities are moved to the commercial sector for further development and market introduction. This process involves licensing agreements, patents, and sometimes the creation of spin-off companies, (Hart & Smith-Glick, 1994). Effective technology transfer requires robust intellectual property management and clear agreements between academia and industry partners. The goal is to ensure that innovations reach the market where they can benefit society, while also providing financial returns to the academic institutions and researchers involved.

2.1.4 Innovation Ecosystems

Innovation ecosystems refer to the network of organizations, including academic institutions, businesses, government agencies, and other stakeholders, that collaborate and interact to drive innovation and economic development. These ecosystems provide the necessary infrastructure, resources, and supportive policies to foster collaboration and the exchange of ideas. Within these ecosystems, industry-academia partnerships play a pivotal role by combining the theoretical and practical aspects of innovation, thus accelerating the development and commercialization of new technologies.

2.1.5 Intellectual Property (IP)

Intellectual Property (IP) refers to creations of the mind, such as inventions, literary and artistic works, designs, and symbols, names, and images used in commerce. In the context of industry-academia partnerships, IP management is critical to ensure that both parties benefit from the collaboration, (Harvey & green, 1994). Universities and industries must navigate complex IP issues, including patent rights, copyright, and licensing agreements, to protect their innovations and ensure fair distribution of revenue generated from commercialized products. Effective IP management facilitates trust and cooperation between partners, enabling smoother technology transfer and commercialization processes.

2.1.6 Knowledge Exchange

Knowledge exchange in industry-academia partnerships involves the transfer of expertise, skills, and information between academic researchers and industry professionals. This exchange can occur through various mechanisms, including collaborative research projects, internships, workshops, and conferences. Knowledge exchange helps to align academic research with industry needs, ensuring that research outputs are relevant and can be practically applied. It also enhances the educational experience of students, providing them with real-world insights and preparing them for careers in industry, (Hecklau *et al.,* 2016). Understanding these key concepts provides a foundational framework for exploring the dynamics of industry-academia partnerships. These definitions highlight the multifaceted nature of collaboration, the importance of effective management of intellectual property, and the critical role of innovation ecosystems in supporting successful partnerships.

2.2. Models of Industry-Academia Collaboration

Industry-academia collaborations have evolved through various models that reflect the dynamic nature of research and development (R&D) and the diverse goals of the involved stakeholders. These models are designed to harness the complementary strengths of academic institutions and industry, fostering innovation and technological advancements. Below are some of the prominent models:

- **Contract Research:**In this model, companies outsource specific research projects to academic institutions. The industry provides funding and outlines the research goals, while academic researchers conduct the necessary investigations, (Henczi & Zöllei, 2007). This approach allows companies to access specialized expertise and advanced research facilities without maintaining them in-house. However, the focus is often on short-term, applied research, which may limit opportunities for fundamental, exploratory studies.
- **Collaborative Research:**Collaborative research involves joint efforts between industry and academia to pursue common research objectives. Both parties contribute resources, expertise, and infrastructure, and share the risks and rewards. This model encourages knowledge exchange and innovation by combining academic rigor with practical industry insights. Intellectual property (IP) agreements are crucial to define ownership and commercialization rights.
- **Research Consortia:**Research consortia are collaborative networks comprising multiple academic institutions, industries, and sometimes government agencies. These consortia address broad, complex research challenges that require multidisciplinary approaches and significant resources, (Hirschi, 2018). By pooling their efforts, participants can achieve outcomes that would be unattainable individually. Examples include the Semiconductor Research Corporation and the European Union's Horizon 2020 programs.
- **Licensing and Technology Transfer:**In this model, academic institutions license their patented technologies to industry partners. The industry then develops and commercializes these innovations. Technology transfer offices (TTOs) at universities play a crucial role in managing IP, negotiating licenses, and fostering relationships with industry, (Hobson *et al.,* 2014). This model helps bridge the gap between basic research and market-ready products, ensuring that academic discoveries have practical applications.
- **Spin-Off Companies:**Spin-offs are new companies formed to commercialize technologies developed within academic institutions. Researchers often become entrepreneurs, bringing their innovations to market. Universities may provide support through incubators, accelerators, and venture capital. Spin-offs can drive economic growth, create jobs, and bring academic research to the forefront of technological advancement.
- **Internships and Fellowships:** Internships and fellowships enable students and researchers to gain practical experience within industry settings, (Hurrell, 2016). These programs facilitate the transfer of knowledge and skills, preparing participants for careers in both academia and industry. They also help build personal networks that can lead to future collaborations.
- **Joint Labs and Research Centers:**Joint labs and research centers are established as permanent entities where academic and industry researchers work side by side. These centers focus on specific research areas and often involve long-term commitments, (Kinkel, Schemmann, & Lichtner, 2017). They provide a stable environment for sustained collaboration, enabling continuous innovation and development.

Figure 1. Models of industry-academia collaboration

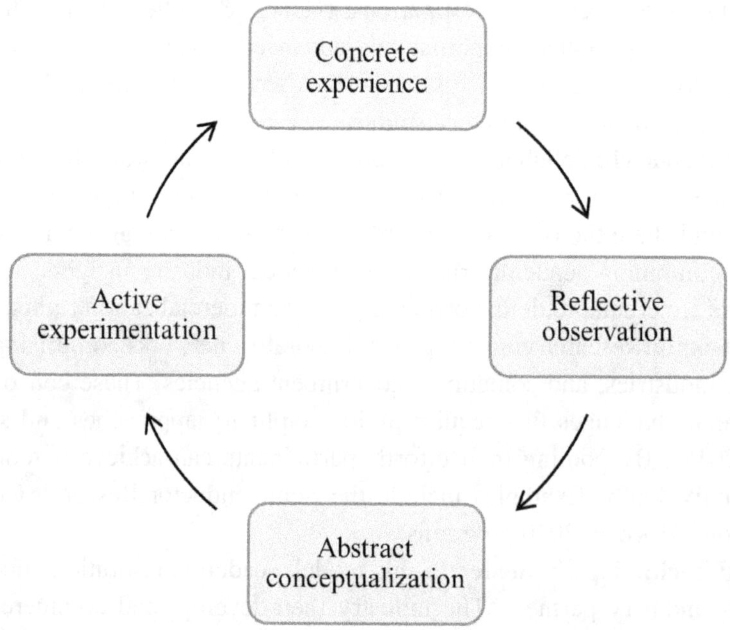

2.4. Theoretical Perspectives on Collaboration

Industry-academia collaborations are complex and multifaceted, often requiring a nuanced understanding of various theoretical frameworks to fully grasp their dynamics. Several theories provide insights into why and how these partnerships function, and they offer guidance on optimizing their effectiveness.

2.4.1. Resource-Based View (RBV)

The Resource-Based View (RBV) posits that organizations gain a competitive advantage by leveraging their unique resources and capabilities. In the context of industry-academia partnerships, RBV suggests that each partner brings distinct resources to the table. Academia typically provides cutting-edge research, theoretical knowledge, and a workforce of skilled graduates, while industry offers practical applications, funding, and market access, (Kleckner & Marshall, 2014). By combining these complementary resources, both parties can achieve outcomes that would be unattainable independently. For instance, a university might develop a novel technology that, with industry support, can be rapidly prototyped and commercialized, thus benefiting both entities.

2.4.2. Innovation Systems Theory

Innovation Systems Theory focuses on the systemic interactions between various actors within an innovation ecosystem. This perspective emphasizes the importance of networks and relationships in fostering innovation (Kuruczleki *et al.,* 2012). Industry-academia collaborations are seen as vital nodes within this system, where knowledge flows between universities, research institutions, firms, and government agencies. Effective partnerships can thus enhance the overall innovation capacity of a region or country. By fostering strong networks, sharing knowledge, and coordinating efforts, industry and academia can drive technological advancements and economic growth.

2.4.3. Transaction Cost Economics (TCE)

Transaction Cost Economics (TCE) examines the costs associated with economic exchanges, including the costs of negotiating, monitoring, and enforcing agreements. In industry-academia collaborations, transaction costs can be significant due to differences in organizational cultures, objectives, and expectations, (Larkin, 2014). TCE theory suggests that to minimize these costs, partners should establish clear, formal agreements that outline roles, responsibilities, intellectual property rights, and conflict resolution mechanisms. Additionally, building long-term relationships and trust can reduce the need for constant oversight and negotiation, thereby lowering transaction costs and increasing the efficiency of collaboration.

2.4.4. Social Capital Theory

Social Capital Theory highlights the value of social networks and relationships in facilitating cooperation and collective action. In industry-academia partnerships, social capital is built through trust, mutual respect, and shared norms. High levels of social capital can enhance communication, reduce misunderstandings, and foster a collaborative culture, (Lee, Kao, & Yang, 2014). This theory underscores the importance of informal interactions, joint problem-solving, and the establishment of a community of practice where both industry and academia can engage in continuous learning and knowledge exchange.

2.4.5. Open Innovation Theory

Open Innovation Theory advocates for the use of external ideas and innovations in conjunction with internal R&D efforts. This theory aligns closely with the concept of industry-academia partnerships, where firms open their innovation processes to include academic researchers and institutions, (Lowden *et al.,* 2011). By embracing open innovation, companies can access a broader pool of knowledge and technological advancements, while academia benefits from real-world applications and potential funding. This collaborative approach can accelerate innovation cycles, reduce costs, and enhance the scalability of new technologies.

2.4.6. Network Theory

Network Theory examines how the structure and dynamics of networks influence behavior and outcomes. In the context of industry-academia partnerships, network theory can help explain how the formation of strategic alliances, joint ventures, and research consortia impacts R&D success. Effective networks facilitate the flow of information, resources, and expertise, leading to increased innovation and problem-solving capabilities. By understanding the characteristics of successful networks, such as centrality, density, and diversity, stakeholders can design more effective collaborative structures, (Malik & Venkatraman, 2017). These theoretical perspectives provide a robust framework for analyzing and understanding the complexities of industry-academia partnerships. By applying these theories, stakeholders can identify best practices, anticipate potential challenges, and develop strategies to enhance the effectiveness and sustainability of their collaborations.

3. BENEFITS OF INDUSTRY-ACADEMIA PARTNERSHIPS

Industry-academia partnerships offer a range of benefits that extend beyond the immediate stakeholders, influencing broader societal, economic, and educational landscapes. These collaborations harness the strengths of both sectors, resulting in a synergy that can lead to groundbreaking advancements and innovations, (McGuinness & Ortiz, 2016). This section explores the key benefits, focusing on advancements in research and innovation, enhancements in educational outcomes, and the economic and societal impacts of such partnerships.

3.1. Advancements in Research and Innovation

One of the primary benefits of industry-academia partnerships is the significant boost they provide to research and innovation. By combining the practical expertise and resources of industry with the theoretical knowledge and investigative capabilities of academia, these collaborations can tackle complex problems more effectively. Industries often bring a wealth of real-world data, advanced technologies, and a focus on application-driven research, while academic institutions contribute with cutting-edge research methodologies, theoretical insights, and a culture of rigorous inquiry. These partnerships can lead to the development of new technologies, products, and processes that might not emerge from either sector working in isolation, (Patacsil & Tablatin, 2017). For instance, the pharmaceutical industry frequently collaborates with universities to conduct clinical trials and develop new drugs, resulting in innovative treatments for diseases. Similarly, the tech industry partners with academic researchers to advance fields such as artificial intelligence and quantum computing. Such collaborations often lead to joint patents and publications, driving both sectors forward and contributing to the global knowledge economy.

3.2. Enhancing Educational Outcomes

Industry-academia partnerships also play a crucial role in enhancing educational outcomes. By integrating industry insights into academic curricula, these collaborations ensure that educational programs remain relevant and aligned with current industry standards and practices, (Patil *et al.,* 2018). This alignment helps in producing graduates who are better prepared to meet the demands of the workforce, thus bridging the gap between academic knowledge and practical skills. Through internships, co-op programs, and industry-sponsored projects, students gain valuable hands-on experience and exposure to real-world challenges. These opportunities not only enhance their technical skills but also develop their problem-solving abilities, critical thinking, and teamwork. Furthermore, faculty members benefit from these partnerships by staying abreast of the latest industry trends and technologies, which they can then incorporate into their teaching and research, (Peters, 2017). Collaborations can also lead to the development of specialized training programs and certifications tailored to industry needs. These programs help in upskilling the existing workforce, ensuring that professionals remain competitive in a rapidly evolving job market. Overall, industry-academia partnerships contribute to a more dynamic and responsive educational ecosystem that supports lifelong learning and continuous professional development.

3.3. Economic and Societal Impact

The economic and societal impacts of industry-academia partnerships are profound and far-reaching. Economically, these collaborations drive innovation and competitiveness, leading to the creation of new industries, job opportunities, and economic growth. For example, research collaborations in fields like renewable energy, biotechnology, and information technology have spawned entire industries, generating significant economic value and contributing to sustainable development, (Rajnai & Kocsis, 2018). On a societal level, industry-academia partnerships can address pressing global challenges such as climate change, public health, and social inequality. By leveraging the combined expertise and resources of both sectors, these collaborations can develop innovative solutions that have a positive societal impact. For instance, partnerships in the healthcare sector can lead to the development of affordable medical technologies and treatments, improving healthcare access and outcomes for underserved populations. Moreover, these collaborations foster a culture of innovation and entrepreneurship within academic institutions, encouraging students and researchers to pursue entrepreneurial ventures, (Rao, 2014). This entrepreneurial spirit can lead to the creation of startups and spin-off companies, further stimulating economic activity and job creation.

4. CHALLENGES AND BARRIERS

4.1. Cultural Differences and Expectations

One of the most significant challenges in industry-academia partnerships is the cultural divide between the two entities. Academia is often driven by the pursuit of knowledge and long-term research goals, with a focus on publishing results and contributing to the academic community. In contrast, industry is typically motivated by market-driven outcomes, with an emphasis on short-term goals, product development, and profitability. These differing priorities can lead to conflicts in expectations and collaboration dynamics, (Roepen, 2017). Academics may prioritize open dissemination of findings, while industry partners might seek to protect proprietary information to maintain a competitive edge. Bridging this cultural gap requires fostering mutual respect and understanding, aligning goals, and creating a shared vision for the collaboration.

4.2. Intellectual Property and Confidentiality Issues

Intellectual property (IP) and confidentiality are critical concerns in industry-academia collaborations. Determining ownership of research outcomes and inventions can be contentious, as both parties may have invested significant resources. Universities often seek to retain rights to IP to support further research and academic dissemination, while industry partners aim to secure IP rights to capitalize on commercial opportunities. This can lead to protracted negotiations and legal disputes, (Rosenberg, Heimler, & Morote, 2012). Additionally, maintaining confidentiality of proprietary information is crucial for industry partners to safeguard competitive advantages, which may conflict with academia's emphasis on open research. Establishing clear agreements and frameworks at the outset, including IP ownership, licensing terms, and confidentiality clauses, is essential to mitigate these issues and ensure smooth collaboration.

4.3. Funding and Resource Allocation

Securing adequate funding and resources is a perennial challenge in R&D collaborations between industry and academia. Research projects often require substantial financial investment, advanced infrastructure, and skilled personnel. Disparities in funding availability and resource allocation priorities can hinder collaborative efforts, (Rubmann *et al.,* 2015). Academic institutions may face budget constraints and bureaucratic hurdles in accessing and managing funds, while industry partners may be hesitant to commit substantial resources without clear, tangible benefits. Effective partnerships necessitate transparent financial planning, equitable distribution of resources, and leveraging diverse funding sources, including government grants, private investments, and philanthropic contributions. Additionally, establishing joint management structures and shared accountability can help optimize resource utilization and enhance project outcomes.

4.4. Regulatory and Administrative Hurdles

Navigating regulatory and administrative landscapes poses another significant barrier to industry-academia partnerships. Compliance with various regulations, such as data protection laws, ethical standards, and industry-specific guidelines, can be complex and time-consuming. Differences in institutional policies and bureaucratic procedures can further complicate collaboration, leading to delays and inefficiencies, (Schofield, 2012). For instance, academia's emphasis on thorough ethical review processes may conflict with industry's need for rapid project progression. Streamlining administrative processes, harmonizing regulatory compliance efforts, and fostering open communication between legal and administrative teams are crucial to overcoming these hurdles. Establishing dedicated liaison offices or partnership coordinators can also facilitate smoother interactions and ensure adherence to regulatory and administrative requirements.

5. STRATEGIES FOR EFFECTIVE COLLABORATION

Effective collaboration between industry and academia is essential for the success of research and development (R&D) initiatives. The following sections delve into key strategies that can help build strong and productive partnerships.

5.1. Building Trust and Mutual Understanding

Building trust and mutual understanding is fundamental to any successful collaboration between industry and academia. Trust is the cornerstone that allows both parties to share knowledge, resources, and risks openly. This trust can be cultivated through consistent and transparent communication. Regular meetings, workshops, and informal gatherings can help bridge the cultural and operational differences between the two sectors. Mutual understanding involves recognizing and appreciating the distinct goals, strengths, and constraints of each partner. Academia often focuses on long-term, fundamental research aimed at generating new knowledge, while industry is typically driven by shorter-term goals focused on product development and market competitiveness. Acknowledging these differences can lead to more realistic expectations and a more collaborative approach to setting project objectives and timelines, (Schroder, 2016). Moreover, fostering an environment of mutual respect is crucial. Industry partners should value the academic freedom and intellectual contributions of researchers, while academics should appreciate the practical insights and financial investments made by industry. Jointly organized events, such as seminars and symposia, can serve as platforms for exchanging ideas and building rapport. An example of trust-building is the implementation of joint steering committees composed of representatives from both academia and industry. These committees can oversee the progress of collaborative projects, ensure alignment with shared goals, and address any issues that arise promptly. By involving members from both sides in decision-making processes, trust and mutual respect are reinforced.

5.2. Developing Clear Agreements and Frameworks

Clear agreements and frameworks are essential for managing expectations and protecting the interests of both academic and industry partners. These agreements typically cover aspects such as intellectual property (IP) rights, publication rights, confidentiality clauses, funding arrangements, and project timelines. Intellectual property is often a contentious issue in collaborations. Establishing clear guidelines on IP ownership, usage rights, and revenue sharing from the outset can prevent disputes later on. For instance, agreements should specify whether IP generated from the collaboration will be jointly owned or if one party will retain exclusive rights. Additionally, terms for licensing and commercialization should be outlined to ensure both parties benefit fairly from the outcomes, (Schwab, 2016). Publication rights are another critical element. Academic researchers may seek to publish their findings to contribute to the scientific community and advance their careers. Industry partners, however, may have concerns about protecting proprietary information. To address this, agreements can include provisions for delayed publication to allow time for patent filings or other protective measures. Confidentiality agreements are vital for safeguarding sensitive information shared during the collaboration. These should clearly define what constitutes confidential information, the obligations of both parties to protect this information, and the duration of the confidentiality obligations. Funding arrangements must also be explicitly detailed. This includes specifying the financial contributions of each party, the allocation of funds for different aspects of the project, and the mechanisms for financial reporting and accountability. Clear financial agreements help prevent misunderstandings and ensure that the project remains financially viable.

Project timelines and milestones should be clearly defined to provide a roadmap for the collaboration. These timelines should include regular review points where progress is assessed, and adjustments are made if necessary. Milestones help keep the project on track and ensure that both parties are aligned in their efforts.

5.3. Effective Communication and Conflict Resolution

Effective communication is the cornerstone of any successful partnership, especially in the context of industry-academia collaborations. These partnerships often involve diverse teams with varying objectives, working styles, and terminologies. To bridge these differences, establishing robust communication channels is essential. This includes regular meetings, clear documentation, and the use of collaborative tools. Regular meetings, whether face-to-face or virtual, ensure that all stakeholders are aligned on goals, progress, and challenges. These meetings should be structured with clear agendas, allowing for both information sharing and discussion. Additionally, documentation such as meeting minutes, project plans, and progress reports provides a tangible record that can be referenced, reducing the risk of misunderstandings.

Another critical aspect is the establishment of a common language. Academic and industry partners may use different terminologies and frameworks, leading to potential miscommunications. Joint training sessions or workshops can help bridge these gaps, fostering a shared understanding and vocabulary. Conflict resolution is an inevitable part of any collaboration. The key is to address conflicts promptly and constructively. This can be achieved through the following steps:

- **Identifying the Root Cause**: Understanding the underlying issues behind the conflict is crucial. This often involves active listening and empathetic communication.
- **Developing a Resolution Framework**: Establishing predefined conflict resolution protocols can streamline the process. This might include mediation by a neutral party, structured negotiation sessions, or escalation procedures.
- **Maintaining Objectivity**: It's essential to focus on the issue rather than the individuals involved. Objective discussions can lead to mutually beneficial solutions without personal biases clouding the judgment.
- **Continuous Improvement**: Post-resolution, it's beneficial to analyze what led to the conflict and how similar issues can be prevented in the future. This could involve updating communication protocols, revising agreements, or providing additional training.

5.4. Leveraging Technology and Infrastructure

In the digital age, technology and infrastructure play a pivotal role in enhancing the efficiency and effectiveness of industry-academia partnerships. Leveraging these resources can significantly streamline collaboration, foster innovation, and accelerate the achievement of research and development goals.

- **Digital Collaboration Tools**: Utilizing digital platforms such as project management software (e.g., Trello, Asana), communication tools (e.g., Slack, Microsoft Teams), and document sharing systems (e.g., Google Drive, Dropbox) can facilitate seamless collaboration. These tools enable real-time communication, centralized information sharing, and efficient task management, ensuring that all team members are on the same page and can contribute effectively, regardless of their physical location.
- **Data Management and Analytics**: Advanced data management systems and analytics platforms can handle large volumes of research data, allowing for sophisticated analysis and interpretation, (Srivastava, 2018). This is particularly beneficial in R&D projects that generate significant

amounts of data. Tools such as big data analytics, machine learning algorithms, and cloud computing can provide deeper insights, identify patterns, and support data-driven decision-making.

- **Research Infrastructure**: Access to state-of-the-art research facilities, such as laboratories, testing centers, and specialized equipment, is crucial for conducting high-quality research. Industry partners can provide funding and resources to enhance these facilities, while academic institutions can offer their expertise and innovative approaches. Jointly investing in research infrastructure ensures that both parties have the necessary tools to achieve their objectives.
- **Intellectual Property Management Systems**: Efficient management of intellectual property (IP) is essential in industry-academia partnerships. Technology platforms that facilitate the tracking, protection, and commercialization of IP can help prevent disputes and ensure that both parties benefit from the collaboration. This includes software for patent management, licensing agreements, and compliance tracking.
- **Virtual and Augmented Reality**: Emerging technologies such as virtual reality (VR) and augmented reality (AR) can enhance collaboration, particularly in fields requiring visualization of complex data or remote interaction with physical spaces. For instance, VR can be used for virtual lab simulations, while AR can assist in on-site troubleshooting and training.
- **Cybersecurity Measures**: Protecting sensitive data and intellectual property is paramount. Implementing robust cybersecurity protocols and technologies ensures that collaborative efforts are not compromised by data breaches or cyber-attacks. This includes encryption, secure access controls, and regular security audits.

6. CASE STUDIES

6.1. Global Examples of Successful Partnerships

6.1.1. MIT-IBM Watson AI Lab

The Massachusetts Institute of Technology (MIT) and IBM established the MIT-IBM Watson AI Lab in 2017, aiming to advance artificial intelligence (AI) research and innovation. This partnership leverages MIT's academic expertise and IBM's technological capabilities to address fundamental challenges in AI. One of the key elements of success in this collaboration is the focus on joint research projects. Researchers from both MIT and IBM work together on various projects, blending theoretical insights with practical applications in areas such as AI algorithms, deep learning, and AI's impact on different industries.Shared resources have been a cornerstone of this partnership. IBM provides access to its Watson AI technology, cloud computing resources, and extensive datasets, while MIT contributes cutting-edge academic research and a pool of talented students and faculty. This resource-sharing ensures that both parties can achieve more significant advancements than they could independently. Additionally, IBM's commitment of $240 million over ten years illustrates a substantial long-term investment in the collaboration, providing stable funding and support for ongoing research. The impact of the MIT-IBM Watson AI Lab has been profound, (Tabrizi *et al.*, 2019). The partnership has led to significant breakthroughs in AI, including advancements in natural language processing, machine learning, and AI ethics. It has also resulted in numerous publications, patents, and the development of new AI tools and applications.

This collaboration exemplifies how industry-academia partnerships can drive innovation and create substantial value in emerging technological fields.

6.1.2. University of Cambridge and AstraZeneca

The University of Cambridge and pharmaceutical giant AstraZeneca have formed a robust partnership, particularly in the field of biomedical science. This collaboration aims to accelerate drug discovery and development by combining Cambridge's academic prowess with AstraZeneca's industrial experience. A significant factor contributing to the success of this partnership is the physical proximity between the two entities. AstraZeneca relocated its global headquarters to Cambridge, facilitating closer interactions, quick decision-making, and seamless collaboration.Interdisciplinary research is another key element of this partnership. It spans multiple disciplines, including genomics, data science, and pharmacology, leveraging the strengths of both entities to tackle complex health challenges. This interdisciplinary approach enables comprehensive research that can lead to more innovative solutions in drug development and other areas of biomedical science.Talent development is also a critical component of the University of Cambridge and AstraZeneca partnership. Joint initiatives include PhD programs, internships, and fellowships, providing students with practical industry experience and fostering a new generation of scientists skilled in both academic and industrial research. These programs help bridge the gap between academic learning and real-world applications, preparing students for successful careers in both sectors, (Tran, 2016). The impact of this partnership has been substantial. Collaborative research has led to significant advancements in drug discovery and development, contributing to the creation of new therapies and medical treatments. Additionally, the partnership has resulted in numerous publications, patents, and the development of innovative research methodologies. This collaboration highlights the potential of industry-academia partnerships to drive progress in biomedical science and improve health outcomes globally.

6.2. Regional and Sectoral Variations

India's diverse regional and sectoral landscape significantly influences the dynamics of industry-academia partnerships. Each region in India has distinct strengths and challenges, which shape the nature and success of these collaborations.

North India

North India, encompassing states like Delhi, Punjab, Haryana, and Uttar Pradesh, has a strong presence in agriculture, manufacturing, and information technology. Prestigious institutions such as IIT Delhi, Punjab University, and the Indian Agricultural Research Institute (IARI) are at the forefront of research. Collaborations in this region often focus on agricultural innovations, manufacturing technologies, and software development. However, challenges like infrastructure limitations and funding gaps can hinder progress.

South India

South India, including states like Karnataka, Tamil Nadu, Andhra Pradesh, and Telangana, is renowned for its advancements in information technology, biotechnology, and manufacturing. Institutions like IISc Bangalore, Anna University, and IIIT Hyderabad are key players. Industry-academia partnerships here are driven by IT services, biotech innovations, and advanced manufacturing. The region benefits from a robust startup ecosystem and high-quality research output, although managing intellectual property and intense competition remain significant challenges.

East India

East India, with states such as West Bengal, Odisha, Bihar, and Jharkhand, has a rich history in mining, manufacturing, and agriculture. IIT Kharagpur, Jadavpur University, and NIT Rourkela are prominent institutions facilitating collaborations in mineral processing, industrial manufacturing, and crop improvement. The region faces issues like a lack of skilled workforce and inadequate infrastructure but offers substantial opportunities in mining technology and sustainable agriculture.

West India

West India, comprising Maharashtra, Gujarat, and Rajasthan, excels in finance, manufacturing, and information technology. Institutions like IIT Bombay, NMIMS, and Symbiosis International are leading academic partners. Collaborations often focus on financial technology, industrial automation, and software solutions. Regulatory hurdles and high operational costs can be challenging, but the region's strong industrial base and thriving fintech sector provide significant growth opportunities.

Central India

Central India, including states like Madhya Pradesh and Chhattisgarh, is known for its mining, agriculture, and manufacturing sectors. Key institutions such as IIT Kanpur, IIM Indore, and Banaras Hindu University (BHU) are involved in industry partnerships. Collaborations typically involve resource extraction, agricultural advancements, and industrial manufacturing. Challenges like resource depletion and environmental concerns must be addressed, but there are opportunities for enhancing mining techniques and promoting sustainable agricultural practices.

North-East India

North-East India, with states like Assam, Meghalaya, and Manipur, has a unique focus on agriculture, handicrafts, and tourism. Institutions like IIT Guwahati, NIT Silchar, and Tezpur University play vital roles in regional collaborations. The region's partnerships often involve agri-based technologies, local handicraft enhancement, and tourism management. Geographical isolation and limited funding are significant hurdles, yet the potential for agri-tourism, eco-friendly handicrafts, and tourism infrastructure development is immense.

6.3. Lessons Learned and Best Practices

6.3.1 Lessons Learned

- **Importance of Clear Objectives and Goals:** Industry-academia partnerships thrive when there are well-defined objectives and goals. Both parties must agree on the desired outcomes and have a shared vision. This clarity helps in aligning efforts and resources towards common goals, reducing conflicts and misunderstandings.
- **Mutual Trust and Respect:** Trust and respect are foundational for successful collaborations. Industry partners often face pressure to deliver commercial results quickly, while academic institutions prioritize knowledge generation and education. Understanding and valuing these different priorities fosters a collaborative environment where both sides can benefit.
- **Effective Communication:** Open and transparent communication is crucial. Regular meetings, progress updates, and clear documentation help keep all stakeholders informed and engaged. Miscommunications can lead to delays, frustration, and project failure.
- **Flexibility and Adaptability:** Projects may encounter unexpected challenges or opportunities. Flexibility in approach and the ability to adapt to changing circumstances can significantly enhance the partnership's success. This includes being open to modifying project plans, timelines, and roles as needed.
- **Leveraging Complementary Strengths:** Successful partnerships capitalize on the unique strengths of each partner. Academic institutions provide deep research expertise and innovative thinking, while industry partners offer practical insights, resources, and a focus on application and commercialization. Recognizing and leveraging these complementary strengths can lead to more impactful outcomes.
- **Managing Intellectual Property (IP):** Clear agreements on IP ownership and usage are essential to prevent disputes. Both parties should agree on how IP will be managed, shared, and protected from the outset. This ensures that both parties feel secure in sharing their knowledge and innovations.
- **Adequate Funding and Resource Allocation:** Securing sufficient funding and resources is critical. Both parties should contribute to the project's financial and resource needs. Additionally, seeking external funding sources, such as government grants or private investors, can provide additional support.

6.3.2 Best Practices

- **Establishing Clear Governance Structures:** Having a well-defined governance structure helps in managing the partnership effectively. This includes setting up steering committees, project management teams, and defining roles and responsibilities. Clear governance structures ensure accountability and streamline decision-making processes.
- **Regular Review and Feedback Mechanisms:** Implementing regular review and feedback mechanisms allows for continuous improvement. Periodic evaluations of the partnership's progress, achievements, and challenges help in identifying areas for improvement and making necessary adjustments.

- **Creating a Collaborative Culture:** Fostering a culture of collaboration, openness, and innovation is vital. Encouraging joint workshops, brainstorming sessions, and cross-functional teams can enhance creativity and problem-solving. A collaborative culture also helps in building strong relationships and trust between partners.
- **Investing in Capacity Building:** Training and development programs for both industry and academic partners can enhance collaboration. Providing opportunities for researchers to understand industry practices and for industry professionals to engage in academic research helps bridge the gap between the two sectors.
- **Utilizing Technology and Infrastructure:** Leveraging advanced technology and infrastructure can significantly enhance the partnership's effectiveness. Utilizing digital collaboration tools, data management systems, and state-of-the-art research facilities can streamline processes and foster innovation.
- **Focusing on Long-Term Relationships:** While short-term projects are important, building long-term relationships can yield more substantial benefits. Long-term partnerships allow for deeper collaboration, sustained innovation, and the development of trust and mutual understanding over time.
- **Engaging Stakeholders:** Involving all relevant stakeholders, including government bodies, funding agencies, and end-users, can enhance the partnership's impact. Engaging stakeholders ensures that the research is aligned with societal needs and increases the chances of successful implementation and adoption of outcomes.

7. POLICY IMPLICATIONS AND RECOMMENDATIONS

7.1. Role of Government and Policy Makers

The role of government and policymakers in fostering successful industry-academia partnerships is pivotal. Governments can facilitate these collaborations by designing and implementing policies that promote an environment conducive to mutual engagement. One key aspect is the creation of frameworks that encourage open dialogue between academic institutions and industry players, (Trauth, Farwsell, & Lee, 1993). This can be achieved through regular forums, workshops, and advisory councils that bring together representatives from both sectors to identify common goals and challenges. Incentivizing collaboration through financial support is another critical function of policymakers. Governments can provide grants, subsidies, and tax incentives to both academic institutions and businesses involved in R&D partnerships. Such financial incentives can reduce the risk for private companies and academic institutions, encouraging them to invest more in joint research initiatives. Additionally, establishing public-private partnership (PPP) programs can leverage both public resources and private expertise, enhancing the scale and impact of R&D efforts.

Policymakers also play a crucial role in setting up regulatory frameworks that protect intellectual property while facilitating the sharing of knowledge. Clear guidelines on intellectual property rights and commercialization processes help prevent disputes and ensure that both parties benefit from their contributions. Furthermore, governments should address any bureaucratic hurdles that may impede the progress of joint ventures. Streamlining approval processes and reducing administrative burdens can significantly enhance the efficiency of collaborations.

7.2. Creating a Supportive Ecosystem

Creating a supportive ecosystem for industry-academia partnerships involves fostering an environment that nurtures innovation, collaboration, and sustained engagement. One essential component is the establishment of innovation hubs or research clusters where academia and industry can interact more seamlessly. These hubs can offer shared facilities, resources, and networking opportunities, allowing partners to work closely and efficiently on research projects. By concentrating resources and expertise in designated areas, these hubs can drive advancements and encourage cross-disciplinary collaboration. Educational institutions should also be encouraged to integrate industry-relevant skills into their curricula. By aligning educational programs with the needs of the industry, academic institutions can better prepare students for future roles in research and development. This alignment can be achieved through industry partnerships that provide real-world projects, internships, and career development opportunities, ensuring that graduates possess the skills and knowledge required by employers. Moreover, establishing mentorship and training programs for both academic researchers and industry professionals can facilitate knowledge transfer and enhance collaboration. Such programs can provide insights into each sector's operational practices, expectations, and objectives, fostering a deeper understanding and smoother interactions between the two. Supportive ecosystems also involve creating platforms for sharing best practices and successful collaboration models. National and regional networks or databases that document case studies, lessons learned, and effective strategies can serve as valuable resources for organizations looking to engage in or improve their partnerships. These platforms can also facilitate the dissemination of research findings and innovations to a broader audience, amplifying the impact of collaborative efforts.

7.3. Funding and Incentive Structures

Effective funding and incentive structures are crucial to sustaining and enhancing industry-academia partnerships. These structures provide the financial support and motivation needed to initiate and maintain collaborative research and development efforts.

7.3.1 Funding Mechanisms

Governments and funding agencies can play a significant role by providing targeted grants and subsidies to support joint research projects between industry and academia. These funds can be allocated through competitive grant programs that require joint applications from both sectors. Such grants can help cover research costs, including personnel, equipment, and operational expenses. Funding agencies can also offer project-specific grants aimed at addressing particular scientific or technological challenges that require collaborative expertise. In addition to direct funding, creating innovation funds or venture capital initiatives specifically for industry-academia collaborations can help bridge the financial gap between research and commercialization. These funds can be designed to support early-stage projects, particularly those with high potential but high risk. Venture capitalists and angel investors could be incentivized to invest in these initiatives through co-investment schemes or matching fund arrangements, thereby amplifying the available resources.

7.3.2 Incentive Structures

To further encourage collaboration, policymakers can implement incentive structures that offer tax breaks or deductions for companies engaged in joint research projects with academic institutions. These tax incentives can reduce the financial burden on businesses and make it more appealing for them to invest in R&D activities. For example, offering tax credits for research expenditures or providing deductions for collaborative research activities can effectively stimulate private sector participation. Incentive structures should also encompass non-financial rewards, such as recognition programs that highlight successful collaborations and innovative outcomes. Awards and public recognition can serve as powerful motivators for both industry and academia, encouraging them to strive for excellence in their joint efforts. Recognizing achievements through industry awards, academic honors, or public accolades can enhance the reputation of the participating entities and attract further interest and investment in collaborative projects, (Tsitskaria *et al.*, 2016). Additionally, creating long-term incentive structures, such as research and development tax credits that accumulate over time based on the success and impact of the collaboration, can ensure sustained commitment from both parties. These structures can be linked to milestones and outcomes, rewarding progress and innovation over the duration of the partnership.

7.3.3 Private Sector Contributions

Encouraging private sector contributions through matching grants or co-funding arrangements can also be an effective way to leverage additional resources. Public-private partnership models that involve shared financial responsibilities and risk mitigation strategies can provide a balanced approach to funding. This collaboration can help ensure that both parties are equally invested in the success of the research and development activities.

7.4. Future Directions and Emerging Trends

As industry-academia partnerships continue to evolve, several future directions and emerging trends are likely to shape the landscape of research and development collaborations. These trends reflect the dynamic nature of technological advancement, societal needs, and the shifting priorities of both academia and industry.

7.4.1. Integration of Emerging Technologies

One of the most significant future directions is the integration of emerging technologies such as artificial intelligence (AI), machine learning, and blockchain into collaborative research efforts. AI and machine learning can enhance data analysis capabilities, leading to more sophisticated and efficient research methodologies. Blockchain technology has the potential to revolutionize intellectual property management and ensure transparency in the sharing of research data and results. Industry-academia partnerships that harness these technologies are likely to drive innovative solutions and breakthroughs across various fields.

7.4.2. Focus on Sustainability and Green Technologies

Sustainability is becoming a central focus of research and development activities. As environmental concerns and climate change become more pressing, there is an increasing emphasis on developing green technologies and sustainable practices. Industry-academia collaborations are expected to prioritize research that addresses environmental challenges, such as renewable energy sources, waste reduction, and resource efficiency. Partnerships aimed at creating sustainable solutions can lead to significant contributions toward achieving global sustainability goals and fostering a green economy.

7.4.3. Expanding Collaborative Models

Traditional models of industry-academia collaboration are evolving to include new and diverse approaches. For example, open innovation models encourage external collaboration and crowdsourcing, allowing for a broader range of ideas and solutions. Additionally, international partnerships are becoming more common, enabling cross-border collaboration and access to global expertise and resources. These expanded models offer new opportunities for joint research and development, fostering a more inclusive and innovative research environment.

7.4.4. Emphasis on Translational Research

There is a growing emphasis on translational research, which seeks to bridge the gap between basic scientific research and practical applications. Industry-academia partnerships are increasingly focused on translating scientific discoveries into commercial products and technologies that address real-world problems. This trend involves close collaboration between researchers and industry practitioners to ensure that research outcomes have tangible impacts and contribute to economic growth and societal benefits.

7.4.5. Strengthening Research Infrastructure

Future directions in industry-academia partnerships include the development and enhancement of research infrastructure, (Wikle & Fagin, 2014). This involves investing in state-of-the-art laboratories, facilities, and digital platforms that facilitate collaborative research. By providing access to advanced tools and resources, partnerships can accelerate the pace of innovation and improve the quality of research outcomes.

7.4.6. Increasing Focus on Diversity and Inclusion

Diversity and inclusion are becoming key priorities in research and development. Efforts to include diverse perspectives and voices in collaborative projects can lead to more innovative and equitable solutions. Industry-academia partnerships are likely to focus on promoting diversity in research teams and ensuring that collaborative efforts address the needs and interests of diverse populations.

7.4.7. Enhanced Data Sharing and Collaboration Platforms

The development of advanced data sharing and collaboration platforms is expected to play a crucial role in future partnerships. These platforms can facilitate real-time communication, data exchange, and joint analysis, improving the efficiency and effectiveness of collaborative research. Innovations in digital tools and platforms will enable more seamless interactions between academic and industry partners, fostering greater collaboration and information sharing.

7.4.8. Greater Emphasis on Policy and Ethical Considerations

As research and development activities become more complex, there will be a greater emphasis on policy and ethical considerations. Ensuring responsible research practices, addressing ethical dilemmas, and navigating regulatory requirements will be critical for successful collaborations. Industry-academia partnerships will need to address these considerations proactively to build trust and maintain the integrity of their research efforts.

8. CONCLUSION

Industry-academia partnerships are pivotal in bridging the gap between theoretical research and practical application, driving innovation, and addressing complex challenges in research and development. By combining the strengths of academic rigor with industry expertise, these collaborations create a dynamic environment that fosters groundbreaking discoveries and accelerates the translation of ideas into tangible solutions. As we look to the future, the evolving landscape of technology, sustainability, and collaborative models presents both opportunities and challenges. It is imperative for stakeholders to continuously refine funding mechanisms, incentivize engagement, and adapt to emerging trends to maximize the impact of these partnerships. By nurturing a supportive ecosystem and addressing policy and regulatory considerations, industry-academia collaborations can achieve greater success and contribute significantly to scientific advancement and societal progress. The continued commitment to bridging these sectors will be essential in navigating future research challenges and seizing opportunities for innovation, ensuring that the full potential of these partnerships is realized for the benefit of all.

REFERENCES

Abu Hanieh, A., Abdelall, S., Krajnik, P., & Hasan, A. (2015). Industry-academia partnership for sustainable development in Palestine. *Procedia CIRP*, *26*, 109–114. DOI: 10.1016/j.procir.2014.07.184

Alshare, K., & Sewailem, M. F. (2018). A gap analysis of business students' skills in the 21st century: A case study of Qatar. *Academy of Educational Leadership Journal*, *22*(1), 1–22.

Azmi, A. N., Kamin, Y., Noordin, M. K., &Nasir, A. N. M. (2018). Towards Industrial Revolution 4.0: Employers' expectations on fresh engineering graduates. International Journal of Engineering & Technology, 7(4.28), 267-272. https://doi.org/DOI: 10.14419/ijet.v7i4.28.23889

Bedwell, W. L., Salas, E. M., & Eduardo, J. (2014). Developing the future workforce: An approach for integrating interpersonal skills into the MBA classroom. *Academy of Management Learning & Education*, *13*(2), 171–186. DOI: 10.5465/amle.2011.0138

Bongomin, O., Ocen, G. G., Nganyi, E., Musinguzi, A., & Omara, T. (2020). Exponential disruptive technologies and the required skills of Industry 4.0. *Journal of Engineering*, *2020*, 1–17. DOI: 10.1155/2020/7074372

Boston Consulting Group Report. (2015). Man and machine in Industry 4.0: How will technology transform the industrial workforce through 2025. Boston Consulting Group.

Chan, V. (2011). Teaching oral communication in undergraduate science: Are we doing enough and doing it right? *Journal of Learning Design*, *4*(3), 71–79. DOI: 10.5204/jld.v4i3.123

Chea, C. C., Tan, J., & Huan, J. (2019). Higher education 4.0: The possibilities and challenges. *Journal of Social Sciences and Humanities*, *5*(2), 81–85.

Crebert, G., Bates, M., Bell, B., Patrick, C., & Cragnolini, V. (2004). Developing generic skills during work placement and in employment: Graduate perceptions. *Higher Education Research & Development*, *23*, 147–165. DOI: 10.1080/0729436042000206638

Dasgupta, A. (2015). Finding the right fit in academia and industry collaboration. Retrieved March 15, 2020, from https://www.geospatialworld.net/article/expectations-in-academia-and-industry-collaboration/amp/

Farkas, A., & Nagy, V. (2008). Student assessment of desirable technical skills: A correspondence analysis approach. *Acta Polytechnica Hungarica*, *5*(2), 43–57.

Gleason, N. W. (2018). Singapore's higher education systems in the era of the fourth industrial revolution: Preparing lifelong learners. In Higher education in the era of the fourth industrial revolution (pp. 145-169). Palgrave Macmillan, Singapore. DOI: 10.1007/978-981-13-0811-8_8

Groß, E., Siegert, J., & Bauernhansl, T. (2017). Changing requirements of competence building due to an increase of personalized products. *Procedia Manufacturing*, *9*, 291–298. DOI: 10.1016/j.promfg.2017.04.045

Hart, H., & Smith-Glick, J. (1994). Training in technical communication: Ideas for a partnership between the academy and the workplace. *Technical Communication (Washington)*, *41*(3), 399–405.

Harvey, L., & Green, D. (1994). *Employer satisfaction.* Quality in Higher Education Project.

Hecklau, F., Galeitzke, M., Flachs, S., & Kohl, H. (2016). Holistic approach for human resource management in Industry 4.0. *Procedia CIRP, 54*(1), 1–6. DOI: 10.1016/j.procir.2016.05.102

Henczi, L., & Zöllei, K. (2007). *Kompetenciamenedzsment (Competence management).* PerfektKiadó.

Hirschi, A. (2018). The fourth industrial revolution: Issues and implications for career research and practice. *The Career Development Quarterly, 66*(3), 192–204. DOI: 10.1002/cdq.12135

Hobson, C. J., Strupeck, D., Griffin, A., Szostek, J., & Rominger, A. S. (2014). Teaching MBA students teamwork and team leadership skills: An empirical evaluation of a classroom educational program. *American Journal of Business Education, 7*(3), 191–212. DOI: 10.19030/ajbe.v7i3.8801

Hurrell, S. A. (2016). Rethinking the soft skills deficit blame game: Employers, skills withdrawal and the reporting of soft skills gaps. *Human Relations, 69*(3), 605–628. DOI: 10.1177/0018726715608001

Kinkel, S., Schemmann, B., & Lichtner, R. (2017). Critical competencies for the innovativeness of value creation champions: Identifying challenges and work-integrated solutions. *Procedia Manufacturing, 9*, 323–330. DOI: 10.1016/j.promfg.2017.04.005

Kleckner, M. J., & Marshall, C. R. (2014). Critical communication skills: Developing course competencies to meet workforce needs. *Journal for Research in Business Education, 56*(2), 59–81.

Kuruczleki, E., Pelle, A., Laczi, R., & Fekete, B. (2012). The readiness of the European Union to embrace the fourth industrial revolution. *Journal Title, 11*, 327–347.

Larkin, M. (2014). Building successful partnerships between academia and industry. Elsevier Connect. Retrieved from https://www.elsevier.com/connect

Lee, J., Kao, H. A., & Yang, S. (2014). Service innovation and smart analytics for Industry 4.0 and big data environment. *Procedia CIRP, 16*(1), 3–8. DOI: 10.1016/j.procir.2014.02.001

Lowden, K., Hall, S., Elliot, D., &Lewin, J. (2011). A report on employers' perceptions of the employability skills of new graduates. SCRE Centre at the University of Glasgow. SCRE Centre Report.

Malik, G., & Venkatraman, A. (2017). The great divide: Skill gap between the employer's expectations and skills possessed by employees. *Industrial and Commercial Training, 49*(4), 175–182. DOI: 10.1108/ICT-11-2016-0071

McGuinness, S., & Ortiz, L. (2016). Skill gaps in the workplace: Measurement, determinants and impacts. *Industrial Relations Journal, 47*(3), 253–278. DOI: 10.1111/irj.12136

Patacsil, F., & Tablatin, L. (2017). Exploring the importance of soft and hard skills as perceived by IT internship students and industry: A gap analysis. *Journal of Technology and Science Education, 7*(3), 347–368. DOI: 10.3926/jotse.271

Patil, M., Meena, M., Maste, D., Deshpande, R., & Kallurkar, S. P. (2018). Building effective association amongst the academia world and industry world. *IOSR Journal of Engineering, 5*, 16–20. DOI: 10.9790/3021-0502061620

Peters, M. A. (2017). Technological unemployment: Educating for the fourth industrial revolution. *Educational Philosophy and Theory*, *49*(1), 1–6. DOI: 10.1080/00131857.2016.1177412

Rajnai, Z., & Kocsis, I. (2018). Assessing industry 4.0 readiness of enterprises. IEEE 16th World Symposium on Applied Machine Intelligence and Informatics (SAMI), 225-230.

Rao, M. (2014). Enhancing employability in engineering and management students through soft skills. *Industrial and Commercial Training*, *46*(1), 42–48. DOI: 10.1108/ICT-04-2013-0023

Roepen, D. (2017). Australian business graduates' perceptions of non-technical skills within the workplace. *Education + Training*, *59*(5), 571–582. DOI: 10.1108/ET-01-2017-0016

Rosenberg, S., Heimler, R., & Morote, E. S. (2012). Basic employability skills: A triangular design approach. *Education + Training*, *54*(1), 7–20. DOI: 10.1108/00400911211198869

Rubmann, M., Lorenz, M., Gerbert, P., Waldner, M., Justus, J., Engel, P., & Harnisch, M. (2015). Industry 4.0: The future of productivity and the growth in manufacturing industries. BCG Report. Retrieved from https://www.zvw.de/media/media.72e472fb-1698-4a15-8858-344351c8902f.original.pdf

Schofield, T. (2012). Critical success factors for knowledge transfer collaborations between university and industry. *The Journal of Research Administration*, *44*, 38–56.

Schroder, C. (2016). The challenges for Industry 4.0 for small and medium sized enterprises. Friedrich-Ebert-Stiftung. Retrieved from https://www.fes.de/aktuell/publikationen

Schwab, K. (2016). The Fourth Industrial Revolution: What it means, how to respond. World Economic Forum. Retrieved from https://www.weforum.org/agenda/2016/01/the-fourth-industrial-revolution-what-it-means-and-how-to-respond

Shrivastava, A. (2018). How to bridge the gap between academia and industry? Retrieved March 15, 2020, from https://www.peoplematters.in/article/campus-recruitment/how-to-bridge-the-gap-between-academia-and-industry-15203

Tabrizi, B., Lam, E., Girard, K., & Vernon, I. (2019). Change management: Digital transformation is not about technology. Harvard Business Review. Retrieved from https://hbr.org/2019/03/digital-transformation-is-not-about-technology

Tran, T. T. (2016). Enhancing graduate employability and the need for university-enterprise collaboration. *Journal of Teaching and Learning for Graduate Employability*, *7*(1), 58–71. DOI: 10.21153/jtlge2016vol7no1art598

Trauth, E. M., Farwsell, D. W., & Lee, D. (1993). The IS expectation gap: Industry expectations versus academic preparation. *Management Information Systems Quarterly*, *17*(3), 293–307. DOI: 10.2307/249773

Tsitskaria, E., Goudas, M., Tsalouchou, E., & Michalopoulou, M. (2016). Employers' expectations of the employability skills needed in the sport and recreation environment. *Journal of Hospitality, Leisure, Sport and Tourism Education*, *20*, 1–9. DOI: 10.1016/j.jhlste.2016.11.002

Wikle, T., & Fagin, T. (2014). Hard and soft skills in preparing GIS professionals: Comparing perceptions of employers and educators. *Transactions in GIS*, *19*(5), 641–799. DOI: 10.1111/tgis.12126

Chapter 12
Opinions and Experiences of Economics Graduates on the Integration of Simulation Tools in Greek Higher Education Towards Sustainable Entrepreneurship

Sotiris Apostolopoulos
Neapolis University, Pafos, Cyprus

Andreas Walmsley
https://orcid.org/0000-0002-2791-3315
Plymouth Marjon University, UK

Amvrosios Prodromou
https://orcid.org/0009-0008-4787-6292
Neapolis University, Pafos, Cyprus

ABSTRACT

The current study has confirmed the strategic role and impact simulation tools play within higher education. Specifically, it does so from the students' perspective. The aim of this work was to primarily obtain valuable insight into students' experiences through the active use of simulation tools during their studies, and how this use has enabled university graduates to apply their acquired knowledge at the workplace. Considering the impact of technology and simulation tools on businesses' sustainable development, this empirical study strives to further contribute to the existing knowledge in this area. In total, 12 university graduates from economic schools in Greece participated in in-depth interviews on the basis of a qualitative research method. The research has highlighted, among others, the need for adjusting the university curricula in order to match the current and future trends related to university education in economic schools, and the technological advancements, in which simulation tools play an increasingly important role.

DOI: 10.4018/979-8-3693-9040-5.ch012

1. INTRODUCTION

Simulation tools enable students to increase their learning abilities, and therefore, learn and undertake decisions within a safe and secure environment (Campos et al., 2021; Cook et al., 2012). As a result, simulation tools constitute an increasingly creative mechanism that enhances the overall students' interests, since it facilitates active problem solving (Silitonga et al., 2024) as well as establishing critical thinking skills that are essential in contemporary learning environments, preparing students for future challenges (Matute & Melero, 2016). Within this safe environment of simulation, students acquire crucial knowledge and skills, attitudes, and behaviors (Huang et al., 2022; Gough et al., 2012). This is considered as one of the major reasons why simulation tools have been gaining increasing popularity, thereby, leading to a substantial impact on students' performance (Ouahi et al., 2021; Aebersold et al., 2012). Learning through simulation is considered to be both more effective and efficient than traditional lectures due to the fact that it enables students to understand the consequences of their actions in virtual reality (McHaney et al., 2018) through understanding of the differences of real scenarios, and assessing both market opportunities and threats (Duchatelet & Donche, 2022).

This also applies to both undergraduate and graduate students involved in entrepreneurship who use simulation tools to enhance their learning experience (Amri et al., 2020). By using and applying simulation tools, students often take on the management of competing businesses, are asked to make business decisions within a simulated market, earn virtual money while being in charge of the business (Milosz & Milosz, 2012). Their decisions are translated into financial figures just as it happens in the real world of business (Dimitriou, 2016). This form of education contributes to the development of knowledge, skills and experience in managing and operating businesses in a competitive environment and in a demanding market (Jones et al., 2021; Neriz et al., 2020). After all, sustainable training of workforce utilising simulation tools constitutes an emerging practice within enterprises as well (Holuša et al., 2023).

Simulation tools are an important mechanism for teaching related to business sustainability since they enable students to operate a business in a sustainable way but without risk (Apostolopoulos et al, 2025; De la Torre et al., 2021; Moon et al., 2018). Certain economic universities that upgraded the simulation tools in the learning process ranked very well in the university evaluation (Kostenetskiy et al., 2021). In universities dealing with business administration and finance degrees, in both undergraduate and postgraduate degrees, such practical courses are highly considered as fundamental procedures if there are no laboratories with virtual simulation technology (Song et al., 2018; Marriott et al., 2015). Research has indicated that learning through the usage of simulation tools led students to perform better in their grades and have developed knowledge and skills in their working life in business (Bakoush, 2022; Chulkov & Wang, 2020). Despite the problems that research has highlighted about the lack of professional teaching staff and outdated curricula in many universities as well as the high cost of purchasing simulation programs (Wang & Yang, 2024; Lean et al., 2006), simulation tools in entrepreneurship courses are continuously expanding improving learning (Gao, 2020; Burdon & Munro, 2017).

Despite the spread of simulation tools in universities, the research findings on different contexts are limited, as are the studies on the opinions of the students themselves. This gap is filled by the present research. It seeks the views and experiences of graduates, both graduate and undergraduate, in the fields of economics and other closely related scientific fields, on the integration of simulation tools in Greek university education. It traces the views and experiences of business school graduates from the simulation tools used in Greek universities and how these tools contributed to their knowledge and skills in their work as business executives. The specific focus lies in the embedding of simulations in the context of sustainable entrepreneurship, and increasingly important and researched phenomenon (Klapper & Fayolle, 2023; Del Vecchio et al, 2021; Wagner et al, 2021). The study also seeks to understand to what extent this learning through simulation has helped them in their working life. This latter point is particularly important because many studies of educational interventions, especially in entrepreneurship, focus only on 'soft', i.e. attitudinal impact measures (Nabi et al. 2017) with limited assessment of actual impact beyond the university experience (Makris et al, 2024; Prodromou et al,2024).

2. LITERATURE REVIEW

Both the practice and the scholarship of entrepreneurship education (EE) continue to gather pace (e.g. Larios-Hernandez, Walmsley, & Lopez-Castro, 2022; Ligouri and Winkler, 2019; Neck and Corbett, 2018). This is on the back of a robust and equally expanding HE sector globally, from HE being regarded as elite to mass (Barakat and Shields, 2019), what is sometimes also referred to as the popularisation of higher education (e.g. Li, Xue, Wei, and He, 2024). This expansion has called forth a growing interest, and indeed expectation that courses in business and in entrepreneurship make reference to sustainability. The interest in sustainble entrepreneurship is now so developed that we are beginning to witness reviews of this concept (Fauske et al., 2024; Sharma et al. 2021). How best to teach sustainable entrepreneurship remains a moot point however, as Fauske et al. (2024) have identified, and others have confirmed (Lans et al., 2014). Perhaps, at least in part, this is due to the novelty of the concept of sustainable entrepreneurship (Shepherd & Patzelt, 2011).

More broadly, the discussion surrounding what the purpose of EE is, while evidently important, is no closer to finding a definitive answer than, say, ten years ago. If anything, the focus of EE has broadened from emphasis on business start-up (new venture creation) to developing a mindset and skillset in individuals that they can employ in a multitude of spheres of life (e.g. Walmsley and Wraae, 2022; Bacigalupo et al., 2016).

Papers that in their nature review the meaning, purpose but also methods of EE regularly refer to Fayolle and Gailly's (2008) work which offers a framework of EE around the key questions of: What? For whom? Why? How? For which results? (Fayolle & Gailly, 2008). As Fayolle and Gailly (2008) acknowledge, they are returning to these fundamental questions, which were in fact asked earlier by others. The history of how to deliver EE is as long as the question of what its purpose is (the two questions are not independent of each other). For example, Gibb (1996) compares conventional and enterprising teaching approaches. Among other things, the enterprising approach includes 'learning from mistakes' and 'emphasis on practice'. To illustrate further, and also to demonstrate the ongoing nature of these discussions surrounding the 'how' of EE, Sagar (2015) also distinguishes between conventional and entrepreneurial approaches. Here, Sagar (2015) writes of content and process orientated approaches (the latter being the entrepreneurial approach), which mirror in many respects what Gibb (1996) was writing almost twenty years earlier (indeed, she references Gibb's work).

The reason we have referenced Gibb's (1996) work here is because of its relevance to simulations as an educational tool to develop enterprising traits and, ultimately, behaviour. Simulation tools have numerous benefits, including limiting risk and thereby allowing for mistakes to occur that do not have disastrous results for the student. Simulations also deal with real-life practial problems. The EE literature is repleat with references to how EE is about practice, and that EE should be experiential (at least in part). To highlight just a few examples see Bell and Liu (2019), Curtis et al., (2021), Scheepers et al. (2019) and Warhuus et al., (2018).

Studies such as those by Pittaway and Cope (2007) and Usart and Romero (2014) have argued the case for simulation games in EE because they offer students a valuable means of experiencing the entrepreneurial process. So, what evidence is there of the use and efficacy of simulations in EE, and are there any findings that relate specifically to sustainable entrepreneurship? The answer to these questions is that some, albeit limited literature does exist (Fox, Pittaway and Uzuegbunam, 2018) and that early indications are that simulations are an important tool in supporting the development of sustainable entrepreneurship specifically, and developing work-ready graduates more generally. Starting with the generic, i.e. not specifically sustainability-focused literature, possibly the earliest documented study on the use of games in EE is that by Low et al. (1994). Their study introduced a game to see whether it was beneficial to both teaching and research and they confirmed that the game both stimulated enthusiasm among students, and supported knowledge development (Low et al. 1994).

A further early paper by Hindle (2002) draws on his experience in trying to introduce a simulation game to his entrepreneurship teaching. Using his own experience as a case study, Hindle (2002) developed guidelines for the use of simulations in EE. This study was not so much an evaluation of the value of simulations, which he clearly takes as a given, but more about how to develop important features of simulations as a teaching method in EE. Kriz and Auchter (2016) undertook an extensive study of the impact of using simulations in German EE. Their study covered more than 50 regular university courses with over 1000 students. Of the study's many findings one in particular stands out: students that engaged in a simulation game-based program were twice as likely to start their own businesses (around 16%) compared to the average rate in Germany. There could be an element of selection bias here, but the figures are so stark that it is hard to not put some of this increase down to the simulation game.

Newbery et al. (2018) draw on simulations as a means to test pedagogical approaches in EE within shortened timeframes. The authors used a simulation game to generate a dataset to enable a pre-post-test scenario relating to undergraduates' early entrepreneurship experiences. Findings did indicate cognitive dissonance between observed and experienced entrepreneurship on the development of students' entrepreneurial identities, with the authors acknowledging the important role the simulation had in providing data for their study (Newbery et al., 2018).

Fox, Pittaway and Uzuegbunam (2018) provided a systematic literature review of simulations and game-based learning in EE. Their analysis concluded that games (i.e. simulations) offer much value in EE. This occurs via an experiential and learning-by-doing apporach that simulations offer. As with many other studies that outline the beneifts of simulation, Fox et al. (2018) draw particular attention to the ability to experiment 'risk-free'. Despite the overall positive message the paper conveys about the use of simulations in EE, the authors do highlight a number of caveats: games must be realistic (fidelity), often students engage in short-term decision-making with a limit to critical thinking, and there is too much emphasis on a linear, de-contextual (limited situated contexts) scenarios.

A final study of great relevance to this paper because of its focus on responsible entrepreneurship as an outcome is the work by Gibbons et al., (2022). More specifically, this study was about developing students' responsible decision-making via the use of a simulation. The theoretical framework employed was the multiple identification theory (MIT) which suggests attitudinal change requires identificaiton with affective, cognitive and behavioural dimensions (Williams and Williams, 2011). Gibbons et al.'s (2022) findings confirmed the MIT approach, i.e. that simulations should target cognitive, affective and behavioural elements. They draw attention in particular to the important role emotions play in impacting responsible decision-making in an entrepreneurial context.

To summarise, the message from studies that have used simulations in EE is that they work in terms of learning broadly understood. Their design should not be left to chance however and in an ideal scenario will combine realism (fidelity), with cognitive, affective and behavioural aspects. Simulations are powerful learning tools, especially in EE, because they offer practice-relevant, risk free, experiential learning. With reference to research on the use of simulations in higher education and EE, the vast majority of studies have evaluated initiatives based on short-term measures (e.g. development of attitudes, knowledge, skills and students' enthusiasm). Long-term impacts of simulations are entirely lacking. Similarly, studies that have looked at the use of simulations in responsible/sustainable entrepreneurship are extremely scarce. This offers a gap that this study with its focus on the long-term, career-related impact on sustainable entrepreneurship is seeking to fill.

3. METHODOLOGICAL APPROACH

3.1 Material and Methods

Empirically, a qualitative strategy was adopted by the research team in order to identify the perceptions and opinions (Forman et al., 2008) of 12 graduates of economics and business schools about their experience with simulation tools during their studies within aforementioned relevant departments. It constitutes an accurate option when identigying human experiences in the field of management geneally as it is very often used by other studies as well (Apostolopoulos et al, 2024; Jones, 2024, Perkins et al., 2017). Thus, to capture the respective views of former students certain semi-structured interviews (Newbery, 2023; Jones,2017; Paunovic, 2024; Makris & Apostolopoulos, 2021; Steiner & Markantoni, 2014; Horton et., 2004) took place wherein the research guide covered predefined subjects reflecting to content analysis followed by inductive reasoning. A form of convenience sampling was applied to recruit participants (Robinson, 2014). Notably, half of them had completed postgraduate studies in entrepreneurship in Greece and as regards the other interviewees, they constituted individuals graduated from postgraduate programmes in entrepreneurship at universities abroad. Furthermore, it is widely known that sampling in qualitative research is based on the principle of appropriateness and adequacy (Morse, 1994) with a small sample so as not to lose the subjective and individual characteristics (Patton, 2002). Interviews were conducted from August 2024 to October 2024 and each one lasted approximately one hour. Interviews occurred by telephone or online, which are just as reliable as face-to-face collection of sample material (Apostolopoulos et al., 2022; Lo Iacono et al., 2016). The interviews were conducted in the native language of the respondents who participated in the survey (Greek). Lastly, the current study by utilising qualitative methodology examines how learning through simulation tools has contributed to the successful performance of former students' tasks in the real environment of competitive markets.

Table 1. Description of the study sample

Respondent	University Graduate	Postgraduate Studies
R1	Graduate of the Athens University of Economics and Business	Greece
R2	Graduate of the Economic University of Piraeus	Greece
R3	Graduate of the University of Ioannina in Economics	England
R4	Graduate in Economics from the University of Thessaloniki	England
R5	Graduate in Economics from the Aristotle University of Thessaloniki	Greece
R6	Graduate in Economics of the Athens University of Economics and Business	USA
R7	Graduate in Economics from the University of Patras	Greece
R8	Graduate in Economics of the National and Kapodistrian University of Athens	Greece
R9	Graduate in Economics of the University of Peloponnese	Germany
R10	Graduate in Economics of the University of Piraeus	England
R11	Graduate in Economics of the University of Crete	England
R12	Graduate in Economics of the University of Thessaloniki	Greece

3.2 Data Analysis

As mentioned before, a mixed-method technique was employed towards identifying and coding of the collected data, throughout the respective content analysis (Ndou et al, 2018). In this light, extracted concepts were captured by both inductive and deductive reasoning (Okoli, 2023; Rinehart, 2021). Specifically, by using an inductive approach (Creswell, 2005) the concrete personal interviews were reviewed and cross-checked with the themes (Yin, 1994). Additionally, the emergent themes identified in relation to the predefined concepts (Peterson, 2019; Clarke, 2015). Therefore, coding and creating categories have been described in detail (Krippendorff, 2018). There was a percentage weighting of agreement or non-agreement among the coding team (Hayes & Krippendorff, 2007). Table 2 reflects the respective themes and sub-themes ultimately used in this study.

Table 2. Content analysis

Themes	Sub-themes
Assessment of knowledge and skills using simulation tools compared to traditional lectures	• Critical thinking and cognitive engagement • Problem solving • Decision making
Experiences from economics university curricula	• Simulation workshops • Integration of simulation tools in curricula • Obstacles and barriers to learning through simulation
Application of knowledge gained from learning through simulation tools to entrepreneurship	• Entrepreneurial maturity issues • Knowledge and skills • Practical level of decision making and problem solving

4. FINDINGS

The findings were structured on the basis of three specific thematic sections. The section on "Assessment of knowledge and skills using simulation tools compared to traditional lectures". The section that dealt with "Experiences from the study programs of economic universities". Finally, the section on "Application of knowledge gained from learning through simulation tools in entrepreneurship."

4.1 Assessment of Knowledge and Skills Using Simulation Tools Compared to Traditional Lectures

The survey participants' assessment of the learning potential presented by the simulation tools appears to be positive. Participants believe that it creates added value in critical thinking and contributes to the upgrading of knowledge and skills in relation to their ability to solve problems and make decisions. Those with experience from universities outside Greece were more enthusiastic about learning methods through the use of simulation tools. Additionally, they believe that they are superior in terms of learning outcome compared to traditional lectures.

''I would say simulation methods are certainly essential for learning process, that's why most of the univesities across the globe utilise them respectively". (R1)

"Although in Greek universities learning through simulation is not among their priorities, I believe that cognitive engagement with simulation upgrades your critical thinking, your knowledge and your skills. Comparing the simulation to traditional lectures, simulation is superior." (R2)

"Having today a position of responsibility in the marketing department in the company I work for, I would say that my experience of the simulation as I experienced it at the university in England, has helped me to be able to make correct decisions, as well as solve difficult problems." (R10)

"Having experienced simulations in my student years at the university in Greece and a university in America where I completed my postgraduate studies, I can say that Greece needs to do a lot more. The experience I gained from the simulations gave a strong confidence in my workplace. I was prepared by virtual reality to deal positively with business problems in real life." (R6)

4.2 Experiences From Study Programs of Economics Universities

The research revealed differences in the use of learning tools in Greek universities. The regional universities use simulation methods less than the universities of Athens and Thessaloniki. Furthermore, overall Greece lags behind in these methods in relation to other universities abroad that have very good simulation laboratories. A deficit was identified in Greek universities in simulation laboratories and integration of simulation tools in the curricula. Additionally, non-compulsory attendance at university economics schools hinders the expansion of simulation methods. When there is no assessment and grading of students' participation in learning in simulation labs, students show little interest.

"I graduated from a regional university in which simulation labs are not developed there. As far as I am concerned, this is due to the cost of the software. However, my experience from my master's degree at a university abroad is positive in relation to simulation learning methods. Greece is lagging behind and this deficit should be covered." (R9)

"Greek universities reveal deficits in simulation laboratories and integration of these simulation methods in the curricula. However, my experience with the simulation is positive. It prepares you to deal effectively with the problems of the position of responsibility you will assume in your working life." (R5)

"I participated along with others in a simulated entrepreneurship course. A group of students had taken over from a competing business with the aim of conquering a green market. Unfortunately, in the middle of the process we abandoned the project because attendance was not compulsory and each time a large number of students were absent. This is exactly where the problem lies." (R1)

''There is a need for creating a decent context towards educational programs featuring simulation games, especially when it comes to the interdisciplinary concept of sustainable entepreneurship" (R4)

4.3 Applying Knowledge Gained From Learning Through Simulation Tools for Entrepreneurship

The participation of students in learning processes with simulation tools helped them in the positions of responsibility in companies they took following their graduation from the universities. Their learning experience was enhanced. They understood the consequences of their actions in order to avoid mistakes in their work. It helped them to solve problems as their knowledge and skills improved at a practical level. This has also shaped their attitude. They acquired business maturity that made it easier for them to make difficult decisions and solve complex problems.

"The theoretical knowledge you acquire at university is good and useful. However, learning through simulation tools is what strengthens your knowledge and skills on a practical level. Simulation expands your business maturity" (R3)

"Within the safe environment, you understand the consequences of your actions and shape your attitude and behaviour. You go to work with greater maturity in order to be able to effectively solve complex problems" (R7)

"The knowledge and skills I gained, especially during my studies in England, through simulation courses were my passport to my current position in the company I work for." (R11)

5. DISCUSSION

The current research has highlighted the importance of learning through the application of simulation tools and their dominance over traditional lectures. The learning process through simulation tools focuses on preparing students within a safe and non-threatening environment in order to acquire the appropriate knowledge and skills to make correct decisions in their working life, especially in solving complex business problems, such as presented by issues surrounding sustainability. However, the weaknesses of the universities' economic faculties in formulating learning strategies with simulation has also been highlighted. The research has revealed several inequalities and differences considering the simulation issues that exist between the universities' economic schools in two specific directions. Regional universities compared to universities in large urban centers lag behind in simulation-based learning methods. At the same time, the lag of the Greek economic faculties of the universities in learning methods with simulation was reflected in relation to the corresponding faculties of the universities in other countries. In many of the above findings there is compatibility and consistency with corresponding findings in the international literature. International research has revealed the superiority of simulation learning strategies over traditional lectures (Campos et al., 2021; Xie et al., 2018; McHaney et al., 2018), something confirmed in the entrepreneurship education-specific literature (e.g. Fox et al. 2018; Kris and Auchter, 2016; Newbery et al. 2018). They have highlighted the potential of simulation-based learning in providing students with the expected knowledge and skills in a safe and non-threatening environment, thus, following their graduation they can make business decisions and solve complex problems (Huang et al., 2022; Gibbons et al., 2022; Gough et al., 2012; Cook et al., 2012). Chulkov and Wang (2020) have highlighted the impact of performance on the scores of students who attended simulation compared to traditional lectures. Additionally, the research of Ke and Xu (2020) has proved that participatory simulation is effective in various academic fields. Economics schools whose simulation learning strategy had been upgraded, have managed to achieve higher rankings in the universities' evaluation (Kostenetskiy et al., 2021). Those universities' economic schools failed to emphasize on learning by using simulation, students' practical training was a formal process without substantial content (Song Song et al., 2018; Marriott et al., 2015). The international literature has revealed regional universities lagging in their ability to compete with central ones in simulation learning strategies. Further, an existing lag of the Greek economic schools in the development of learning processes with simulation in relation to universities abroad has been highlighted. Therefore, a deficit that in itself creates inequalities in education should be addressed based on specific policies.

Examining the experiences of students in economic universities in relation to the use of simulation tools showed that non-compulsory attendance limits learning with simulation tools since they require teamwork and collaborative processes. The daily presence and participation of students in the lectures in the economic faculties of Greek universities is limited compared to the registered students. Further, even those who attend the courses with simulation tools are not evaluated, nor does this participation have any impact on their grading. This situation does not increase the students' interest in participating in learning through the simulation tools. At the same time, simulation labs are developing at a slow pace and curricula remain adapted to traditional teaching. Based on the international literature, barriers to the development of simulation learning strategies have been identified. These barriers are mainly found in the simulation laboratories and various other necessary infrastructures, the professionalism of the teaching force, the curricula and the cost of the simulation programs (Wang & Yang, 2024; Burdon & Munro, 2017; Lean et al., 2006). However, in the international literature the current research did not identify any optional studies as a barrier to the development of simulation learning strategies by universities. Further, the research did not identify any obstacles to the development of the simulation with the non-evaluation and non-grading of the students who participated in the simulation-based learning process. These findings were highlighted by the present research. Wang and Yang (2024) examined teaching through virtual simulation, and found that in economics and finance schools, simulation has not been significantly expanded. The same research considers as an obstacle to the development of the simulation in the professionalism of the teachers, the outdated teaching content and the high cost of the teaching method. Bai and Yang (2023) add to the previous argument and highlighted as problems the insufficient investments, the poor connection of the simulations with the study system and the low enthusiasm of the students. It should be noted that the participants in this research expressed themselves positively about the results of learning by simulation. This finding is compatible with the findings of other studies (Silitonga et al., 2024; McHaney et al., 2018; Matute & Melero., 2016; Aebersold et al., 2012).

The present research highlighted the positive impact of simulation-based learning strategies on the positions of responsibility in companies taken by students after graduating from university. Simulation in learning was shown to improve the participants' learning experience and build entrepreneurial maturity.

Elements useful in working life that facilitate making difficult decisions and solving complex business problems. Understanding the consequences of the actions in the safe environment of the simulation not only improved knowledge and skills but also shaped the attitude of behaviour. Based on international literature, simulation improves knowledge and skills (Huang et al., 2022; Gough et al., 2012), creates entrepreneurial maturity (Faisal et al., 2022; Bell & Loon., 2015) and forms a behavioral attitude (Gillespie et al., 2021; Russo et al., 2007; Creed & Beale., 2005). Furthermore, it can support responsible decision-making (Gibbons et al., 2022) and incrase students' enthusiasm for learning (Low et al., 1994).

6. CONCLUSIONS AND RECOMMENDATIONS

The examiantion of all above elements, both from literature examination and participants' interviews, have enabled the researchers to gain deeper understanding of the role and impact of simulation tools in universities, and how these tools can potentially contribute towards graduates' professional development. As a result, the current reseachers have come to some intriguing conclusions and a set of practical recommendations. The latter aim to contribute to both the existing knowledge and practices applied in universities in relation to simulation tools, as well as to enable the development of best practices that will create a more positive educational environment and ability for sustainable professional development.

The primary conclusion lies on the fact that an increasing number Greek universities strategically strive towards incorporating simulation tools in their curricula, enabling students to become more familiar with the needs of real market arena. Such practices equip graduate students with the appropriate skills and confidence to fullfil their professional dreams and become more competitive within an increasingly demanding business battlefield. Therefore, the current research strongly suggests that relevant national authorities and universities should increase their efforts towards improving their technological infrastructure and create an increasingly positive environment for all stakeholders involved.The second conclusion focuses on the fact that graduate students that have managed to acquire experience during their studies, have managed to adapt a lot easier and with higher level of confidence at their new working environment. The fact that younger generations are a lot more familiar with contemporary technologies, such as artificial intelligence (AI) and machine learning (ML), should neither be neglected or underestimated. Consequently, this research supports that this should be viewed as a major requirement which universities should strive to meet, as an integral part of their overall strategy, in order to provide their students the best possible solutions and knowledge for their future professional career. The third major conclusion refers to the situation in Greek universities in relation to the existence and practical operation of simulation tools. Greek universities appear to seriously suffer, hence, creating concerns over both their ability and willingness to substantially improve their services provided to their students.

This study reveals a lack of consistency of how simulation tools are operating in the country. Lack of, and poor performance of simulation tools in Greek universities is highly considered as a major drawback which can potentially harm both graduates' professional development and the country's image as a quality higher education destination. Consequently, the country should strategically focus towards mitigating this serious gap through the allocation of all appropriate resources, such as human, financial, and technological. Simulation tools and cutting-edge technology are gaining an increasing importance in higher education, with the universities across the world facing serious challenges in order to ensure the smooth transition from the previous reality and the transition into the new era. Lastly, the current qualitative research concludes that universities are moving towards a new era in which contemporary technology, including simulation tools, will become a major requirement which derives from the need to remain competitive and address the increasing market needs.

REFERENCES

Aebersold, M., Tschannen, D., & Bathish, M. (2012). Innovative simulation strategies in education. *Nursing Research and Practice*, *2012*(1), 765212. PMID: 22550573

Amri, F., Djatmika, E. T., Wahyono, H., & Widjaja, S. U. M. (2020). The Effect of Using Simulation on Developing Students' Character Education in Learning Economics. *International Journal of Instruction*, *13*(4), 375–392.

Apostolopoulos, N., Liargovas, P., & Apostolopoulos, S. (2025). European Transnational Cooperation Programmes Involving the Academic Community and Their Contributions to Sustainable Entrepreneurship. In *Real-World Tools and Scenarios for Entrepreneurship Exploration* (pp. 1–24). IGI Global.

Apostolopoulos, N., Makris, I., Apostolopoulos, S., & Dimitrakopoulos, P. (2024). Resilience of rural micro-businesses in an adverse entrepreneurial environment: adapting to the energy crisis. Journal of Enterprising Communities: People and Places in the Global Economy.

Apostolopoulos, S., Makris, I., & Stavroyiannis, S. (2022). Healthcare innovation in Greece: The views of private health entrepreneurs on implementing innovative plans. *Journal of Open Innovation*, *8*(2), 78.

Bacigalupo, M., Kampylis, P., Punie, Y., & Van den Brande, G. (2016). *EntreComp: The Entrepreneurship Competence Framework*. European Commission.

Bai, C., & Yang, J. (2023). Exploration on the Application of Virtual Simulation Platforms in the Practice Teaching of Financial Management Majors in Private Colleges and Universities. In *3rd International Conference on Education Studies: Experience and Innovation (ICESEI 2022)* (pp. 71-76). Athena Publishing. DOI: 10.55060/s.atssh.230306.013

Bakoush, M. (2022). Evaluating the role of simulation-based experiential learning in improving satisfaction of finance students. *International Journal of Management Education*, *20*(3), 100690. DOI: 10.1016/j.ijme.2022.100690

Barakat, B., & Shields, R. (2019). Just Another Level? Comparing Quantitative Patterns of Global Expansion of School and Higher Education Attainment. *Demography*, *56*(3), 917–934. DOI: 10.1007/s13524-019-00775-5 PMID: 31001732

Bell, R., & Liu, P. (2019). Educator challenges in the development and delivery of constructivist active and experiential entrepreneurship classrooms in Chinese vocational higher education. *Journal of Small Business and Enterprise Development*, *26*(2), 209–227. DOI: 10.1108/JSBED-01-2018-0025

Bell, R., & Loon, M. (2015). The impact of critical thinking disposition on learning using business simulations. *International Journal of Management Education*, *13*(2), 119–127. DOI: 10.1016/j.ijme.2015.01.002

Burdon, W. M., & Munro, K. (2017). Simulation–is it all worth it? The impact of simulation from the perspective of accounting students. *International Journal of Management Education*, *15*(3), 429–448. DOI: 10.1016/j.ijme.2017.07.001

Campos, N., Nogal, M., Caliz, C., & Juan, A. A. (2020). Simulation-based education involving online and on-campus models in different European universities. *International Journal of Educational Technology in Higher Education, 17*(1), 1–15. DOI: 10.1186/s41239-020-0181-y

Chulkov, D., & Wang, X. (2020). The Educational Value of Simulation as a Teaching Strategy in a Finance Course. *E-Journal of Business Education & Scholarship of Teaching*, *14*(1), 40–56.

Clarke, V., Braun, V., Hayfield, N., & Smith, J. A. (2015). Qualitative psychology. A practical guide to research methods, 222, 248.

Cook, D. A., Brydges, R., Hamstra, S. J., Zendejas, B., Szostek, J. H., Wang, A. T., Erwin, P. J., & Hatala, R. (2012). Comparative effectiveness of technology-enhanced simulation versus other instructional methods: A systematic review and meta-analysis. *Simulation in Healthcare*, *7*(5), 308–320. DOI: 10.1097/SIH.0b013e3182614f95 PMID: 23032751

Creed, C., & Beale, R. (2005). Using emotion simulation to influence user attitudes and behavior. In *Proceedings of the 2005 Workshop on the role of emotion in HCI.*

Creswell, J. (2005). *Research Design: Qualitative, Quantitative, and Mixed Methods Approaches*. Sage Publications.

Curtis, V., Moon, R., & Penaluna, A. (2021). Active entrepreneurship education and the impact on approaches to learning: Mixed methods evidence from a six-year study into one entrepreneurship educator's classroom. *Industry and Higher Education*, *35*(4), 443–453. DOI: 10.1177/0950422220975319

De la Torre, R., Onggo, B. S., Corlu, C. G., Nogal, M., & Juan, A. A. (2021). The role of simulation and serious games in teaching concepts on circular economy and sustainable energy. *Energies*, *14*(4), 1138. DOI: 10.3390/en14041138

Del Vecchio, P., Secundo, G., Mele, G., & Passiante, G. (2021). Sustainable entrepreneurship education for circular economy: Emerging perspectives in Europe. *International Journal of Entrepreneurial Behaviour & Research*, *27*(8), 2096–2124. DOI: 10.1108/IJEBR-03-2021-0210

Dimitriou, D. J. (2016). Climate change implications in aviation and tourism market equilibrium. Climate Change Adaptation, Resilience and Hazards, 409-424.

Duchatelet, D., & Donche, V. (2022). Assessing student learning during simulations in education: Methodological opportunities and challenges when applying a longitudinal case study design. *Studies in Educational Evaluation*, *72*, 101129. DOI: 10.1016/j.stueduc.2022.101129

Earl Rinehart, K. (2021). Abductive analysis in qualitative inquiry. *Qualitative Inquiry*, *27*(2), 303–311. DOI: 10.1177/1077800420935912

Faisal, N., Chadhar, M., Goriss-Hunter, A., & Stranieri, A. (2022). Business simulation games in higher education: A systematic review of empirical research. *Human Behavior and Emerging Technologies*, *2022*(1), 1578791. DOI: 10.1155/2022/1578791

Fauske, I. M., Verhulst, E., Wigger, K. A., Solvoll, S., & Jakobsen, S. (2024). Teaching Entrepreneurship for Sustainability - a Review of Educational Tools. *Management Review*, *35*(1), 113–146.

Fayolle, A., & Gailly, B. (2008). From craft to science: Teaching models and learning processes in entrepreneurship education. *Journal of European Industrial Training*, *32*(7), 569–593. DOI: 10.1108/03090590810899838

Forman, J., Creswell, J. W., Damschroder, L., Kowalski, C. P., & Krein, S. L. (2008). Qualitative research methods: Key features and insights gained from use in infection prevention research. *American Journal of Infection Control*, *36*(10), 764–771. DOI: 10.1016/j.ajic.2008.03.010 PMID: 18834752

Fox, J., Pittaway, L., & Uzuegbunam, I. (2018). Simulations in Entrepreneurship Education: Serious Games and Learning Through Play. *Entrepreneurship Education and Pedagogy*, *1*(1), 61–69.

Gao, H. (2020). Research on the construction of virtual simulation experiment teaching courses of economics and management majors. In *4th International Conference on Culture, Education and Economic Development of Modern Society (ICCESE 2020)* (pp. 973-978). Atlantis Press. DOI: 10.2991/assehr.k.200316.214

Gibb, A. (1996). Entrepreneurship and Small Business Management: Can We Afford to Neglect Them in the Twenty-first Century Business School? *British Journal of Management*, *7*(4), 309–321. DOI: 10.1111/j.1467-8551.1996.tb00121.x

Gibbons, B., Fernando, M., & Spedding, T. (2022). Innovation Through Developing a Total Enterprise Computer Simulation: Teaching Responsible Decision Making. *Journal of Management Education*, *46*(1), 16–42. DOI: 10.1177/1052562920987591

Gillespie, G. L., Farra, S., Regan, S. L., & Brammer, S. V. (2021). Impact of immersive virtual reality simulations for changing knowledge, attitudes, and behaviors. *Nurse Education Today*, *105*, 105025. DOI: 10.1016/j.nedt.2021.105025 PMID: 34175566

Gough, S., Hellaby, M., Jones, N., & MacKinnon, R. (2012). A review of undergraduate interprofessional simulation-based education (IPSE). *Collegian (Royal College of Nursing, Australia)*, *19*(3), 153–170. DOI: 10.1016/j.colegn.2012.04.004 PMID: 23101350

Hayes, A. F., & Krippendorff, K. (2007). Answering the call for a standard reliability measure for coding data. *Communication Methods and Measures*, *1*(1), 77–89. DOI: 10.1080/19312450709336664

Hindle, K. (2002). A Grounded Theory for Teaching Entrepreneurship Using Simulation Games. *Simulation & Gaming*, *33*(2), 236–241. DOI: 10.1177/1046878102332012

Holuša, V., Vaněk, M., Beneš, F., Švub, J., & Staša, P. (2023). Virtual reality as a tool for sustainable training and education of employees in industrial enterprises. *Sustainability (Basel)*, *15*(17), 12886. DOI: 10.3390/su151712886

Horton, J., Macve, R., & Struyven, G. (2004). Qualitative research: experiences in using semi-structured interviews. In *The real life guide to accounting research* (pp. 339–357). Elsevier. DOI: 10.1016/B978-008043972-3/50022-0

Huang, Y. M., Silitonga, L. M., & Wu, T. T. (2022). Applying a business simulation game in a flipped classroom to enhance engagement, learning achievement, and higher-order thinking skills. *Computers & Education*, *183*, 104494. DOI: 10.1016/j.compedu.2022.104494

Jones, P. (2024). Engaging With Lived Experience: Towards a Sociological Biography of a Sociological Category. *Sociological Research Online*, *0*(0).

Jones, P., Apostolopoulos, N., Kakouris, A., Moon, C., Ratten, V., & Walmsley, A. (Eds.). (2021). *Universities and entrepreneurship: meeting the educational and social challenges*. Emerald Publishing Limited. DOI: 10.1108/S2040-7246202111

Jones, P., Jones, A., Williams-Burnett, N., & Ratten, V. (2017). Let's get physical: Stories of entrepreneurial activity from sports coaches/instructors. *International Journal of Entrepreneurship and Innovation*, *18*(4), 219–230. DOI: 10.1177/1465750317741878

Ke, F., & Xu, X. (2020). Virtual reality simulation-based learning of teaching with alternative perspectives taking. *British Journal of Educational Technology*, *51*(6), 2544–2557. DOI: 10.1111/bjet.12936

Klapper, R. G., & Fayolle, A. (2023). *A transformational learning framework for sustainable entrepreneurship education: The power of Paulo Freire's educational model. International Journal of Management Education (Elsevier Science), 21(1).*

Kostenetskiy, P. S., Chulkevich, R. A., & Kozyrev, V. I. (2021). HPC resources of the higher school of economics. *Journal of Physics: Conference Series*, *1740*(1), 012050. DOI: 10.1088/1742-6596/1740/1/012050

Krippendorff, K. (2018). *Content Analysis: An Introduction to Its Methodology*. Sage Publications.

Kriz, W. C., & Auchter, E. (2016). 10 Years of Evaluation Research Into Gaming Simulation for German Entrepreneurship and a New Study on Its Long-Term Effects. *Simulation & Gaming*, *47*(2), 179–205. DOI: 10.1177/1046878116633972

Lans, T., Blok, V., & Wesselink, R. (2014). Learning apart and together: Towards an integrated competence framework for sustainable entrepreneurship in higher education. *Journal of Cleaner Production*, *62*, 37–47. DOI: 10.1016/j.jclepro.2013.03.036

Larios-Hernandez, G., Walmsley, A., & Lopez-Castro, I. (Eds.). (2022). *Theorising Undergraduate Entrepreneurship Education. Reflections on the Development of the Entrepreneurial Mindset*. Palgrave MacMillan. DOI: 10.1007/978-3-030-87865-8

Lean, J., Moizer, J., Towler, M., & Abbey, C. (2006). Simulations and games: Use and barriers in higher education. *Active Learning in Higher Education*, *7*(3), 227–242. DOI: 10.1177/1469787406069056

Li, J., Xue, E., Wei, Y., & He, Y. (2024). How popularising higher education affects economic growth and poverty alleviation: Empirical evidence from 38 countries. *Humanities & Social Sciences Communications*, *11*(1), 520. DOI: 10.1057/s41599-024-03013-5

Liguori, E., Winkler, C., Neck, H., & Terjesen, S. (2019). Editorial: Special Issue on Entrepreneurship Education. *Journal of Small Business Management*, *57*(sup1, S1), 4–5. DOI: 10.1111/jsbm.12542

Lo Iacono, V., Symonds, P., & Brown, D. H. (2016). Skype as a tool for qualitative research interviews. *Sociological Research Online*, *21*(2), 103–117. DOI: 10.5153/sro.3952

Low, M., Venkataraman, S., & Srivatsan, V. (1994). Developing an Entrepreneurship Game for Teaching and Research. *Simulation & Gaming*, *25*(3), 383–401. DOI: 10.1177/1046878194253006

Makris, I., & Apostolopoulos, S. (2021, September). Investing in healthcare enterprises in the non-metropolitan areas: Incentives, reflections, and innovative ideas. In European Conference on Innovation and Entrepreneurship (pp. 1160-R17). Academic Conferences International Limited.

Makris, I., Apostolopoulos, S., & Dimitrakopoulos, P. (2024). Analysing supporting mechanisms, cultural shaping and incentives for circular economy: The case of local governments. *Interdisciplinary Environmental Review*, *23*(3), 218–235. DOI: 10.1504/IER.2024.139254

Marriott, P., Tan, S. M., & Marriott, N. (2015). Experiential learning–A case study of the use of computerised stock market trading simulation in finance education. *Accounting Education*, *24*(6), 480–497. DOI: 10.1080/09639284.2015.1072728

Matute, J., & Melero, I. (2016). *Game-based learning: using business simulators in the university classroom* [Aprender jugando: la utilización de simuladores empresariales en el aula universitaria]. No. ART.

McHaney, R., Reiter, L., & Reychav, I. (2018). Immersive simulation in constructivist-based classroom e-learning. *International Journal on E-Learning*, *17*(1), 39–64.

Milosz, E., & Milosz, M. (2012). Business simulation games during the summer schools–the case study. In *INTED2012 Proceedings* (pp. 1577-1583). IATED.

Moon, C., Walmsley, A., & Apostolopoulos, N. (2018). Sustainability and entrepreneurship education. A survey of 307 UN HESI signatories. Academic Press.

Morse, J. M. (1994). 'Emerging from the data': the cognitive processes of analysis in qualitative inquiry. In Morse, J. M. (Ed.), *Critical Issues in Qualitative Research Methods* (pp. 23–43). Sage.

Nabi, G., Liñan, F., Fayolle, A., Krueger, N., & Walmsley, A. (2017). The impact of entrepreneurship education in higher education: A systematic review and research agenda. *Academy of Management Learning & Education*, *16*(2), 277–299. DOI: 10.5465/amle.2015.0026

Ndou, V., Secundo, G., Schiuma, G., & Passiante, G. (2018). Insights for shaping entrepreneurship education: Evidence from the European entrepreneurship centers. *Sustainability (Basel)*, *10*(11), 4323. DOI: 10.3390/su10114323

Neck, H., & Corbett, A. (2018). The Scholarship of Teaching and Learning Entrepreneurship. *Entrepreneurship Education and Pedagogy*, *1*(1), 8–41. DOI: 10.1177/2515127417737286

Neriz, L., Núñez, A., Fuentes-Caceres, V., Ramis, F., & Jerez, O. (2020). Simulation-based training as a teaching and learning tool for management education. *Innovations in Education and Teaching International*, *57*(6), 701–713. DOI: 10.1080/14703297.2019.1631874

Newbery, R., Lean, J., Moizer, J., & Haddoud, M. (2018). Entrepreneurial identity formation during the initial entrepreneurial experience: The influence of simulation feedback and existing identity. *Journal of Business Research*, *85*, 51–59. DOI: 10.1016/j.jbusres.2017.12.013

Okoli, C. (2023). Inductive, abductive and deductive theorising. *International Journal of Management Concepts and Philosophy*, *16*(3), 302–316. DOI: 10.1504/IJMCP.2023.131769

Ouahi, M. B., Hou, M. A., & Hassoun, I. T. (2021). Opinions of Moroccan teachers towards the use of PhET simulations in teaching and learning physics–chemistry. In *2020 6th IEEE Congress on Information Science and Technology (CiSt)* (pp. 274-278). IEEE.

Patton, M. Q. (2002). *Qualitative Research and Evaluation Methods* (3rd ed.). Sage.

Paunović, I., Apostolopoulos, S., Miljković, I. B., & Stojanović, M. (2024). Sustainable Rural Healthcare Entrepreneurship: A Case Study of Serbia. *Sustainability (Basel)*, *16*(3), 1143. DOI: 10.3390/su16031143

Perkins, G., Lean, J., & Newbery, R. (2017). The role of organizational vision in guiding idea generation within SME contexts. *Creativity and Innovation Management*, *26*(1), 75–90. DOI: 10.1111/caim.12206

Peterson, J. S. (2019). Presenting a Qualitative Study: A Reviewer's Perspective. *Gifted Child Quarterly*, *63*(3), 147–158. DOI: 10.1177/0016986219844789

Pittaway, L., & Cope, J. (2007). Simulating Entrepreneurial Learning: Integrating Experiential and Collaborative Approaches to Learning. *Management Learning*, *38*(2), 211–233. DOI: 10.1177/1350507607075776

Prodromou, A., Efthimiou, I., & Apostolopoulos, S. (2024, September). Covid-19-The Impact on Cyprus' SMEs Tourism Enterprises–Lessons to be Learned. In *European Conference on Innovation and Entrepreneurship* (Vol. 19, No. 1, pp. 643-654). DOI: 10.34190/ecie.19.1.2470

Robinson, O. C. (2014). Sampling in interview-based qualitative research: A theoretical and practical guide. *Qualitative Research in Psychology*, *11*(1), 25–41. DOI: 10.1080/14780887.2013.801543

Russo, S. G., Eich, C., Barwing, J., Nickel, E. A., Braun, U., Graf, B. M., & Timmermann, A. (2007). Self-reported changes in attitude and behavior after attending a simulation-aided airway management course. *Journal of Clinical Anesthesia*, *19*(7), 517–522. DOI: 10.1016/j.jclinane.2007.04.007 PMID: 18063206

Sagar, H. (2015). *Entrepreneurial Schools. Part 2 - Entrepreneurial learning environments and a changed role for teachers., Entrepreneurship 360.* OECD and European Commission.

Scheepers, M. J. V., Barnes, R., Clements, M., & Stubbs, A. J. (2018). Preparing future-ready graduates through experiential entrepreneurship. *Education + Training*, *60*(4), 303–317. DOI: 10.1108/ET-11-2017-0167

Sharma, S., Goyal, D. P., & Singh, A. (2021). Systematic review on sustainable entrepreneurship education (SEE): A framework and analysis. *World Journal of Entrepreneurship, Management and Sustainable Development*, *17*(3), 372–395.

Shepherd, D. A., & Patzelt, H. (2011). The New Field of Sustainable Entrepreneurship: Studying Entrepreneurial Action Linking "What is to be Sustained" with "What is to be Developed". *Entrepreneurship Theory and Practice*, *35*(1), 137–163. DOI: 10.1111/j.1540-6520.2010.00426.x

Silitonga, L. M., Dharmawan, B., Murti, A. T., & Wu, T. T. (2024). Promoting Entrepreneurial Intentions and Competencies Through Business Simulation Games. *Journal of Educational Computing Research*, *62*(3), 725–755. DOI: 10.1177/07356331231209772

Song, R., Cao, Y., Xu, Z., Li, Y., & Liang, B. (2018, June). Exploring the Laboratory Construction in Finance and Economics Colleges and Universities by Adopting Virtual Simulation Technology. In *2018 2nd International Conference on Management, Education and Social Science (ICMESS 2018)* (pp. 491-494). Atlantis Press. DOI: 10.2991/icmess-18.2018.108

Steiner, A., & Markantoni, M. (2014). Unpacking community resilience through capacity for change. *Community Development Journal: An International Forum*, *49*(3), 407–425. DOI: 10.1093/cdj/bst042

Steiner, A., & Steinerowska-Streb, I. (2013). *Why Use Franchising?: The Perception of Scottish Entrepreneurs.* LAP LAMBERT Academic Publishing.

Talukder, S. C., Lakner, Z., & Temesi, Á. (2024). Development and State of the Art of Entrepreneurship Education: A Bibliometric Review. *Education Sciences*, *14*(3), 295. DOI: 10.3390/educsci14030295

Usart, M., & Romero, M. (2014). Entrepreneurship competence assessment through a game based learning MOOC. In De Gloria, A. (Ed.), Lecture Notes in Computer Science: Vol. 8605. *Games and Learning Alliance. GALA 2013* (pp. 252–264). DOI: 10.1007/978-3-319-12157-4_20

Wagner, M., Schaltegger, S., Hansen, E. G., & Fichter, K. (2021). University-linked programmes for sustainable entrepreneurship and regional development: How and with what impact? *Small Business Economics*, *56*(3), 1141–1158. DOI: 10.1007/s11187-019-00280-4

Walmsley, A., & Wraae, B. (2022). Entrepreneurship Education but not as we know it: Reflections on the relationship between Critical Pedagogy and Entrepreneurship Education. *International Journal of Management Education*, *20*(3), 1–11. DOI: 10.1016/j.ijme.2022.100726

Wang, R., & Yang, R. (2024). Research and Exploration on Virtual Simulation Teaching in Universities of Finance and Economics. *International Journal of New Developments in Education*, *6*(4).

Warhuus, J. P., Blenker, P., & Elmholdt, S. T. (2018). Feedback and assessment in higher-education, practice-based entrepreneurship courses: How can we build legitimacy? *Industry and Higher Education*, *32*(1), 1–10. DOI: 10.1177/0950422217750795

Williams, A. J., & Williams, R. H. (2011). Multiple Identification Theory: Attitude and Behavior Change in a Simulated International Conflict. *Simulation & Gaming*, *42*(6), 733–747. DOI: 10.1177/1046878111429228

Xie, H. (2018). Construction and Practice of Virtual Simulation Experimental Teaching Platform for Economic Management. In *2018 5th International Conference on Education, Management, Arts, Economics and Social Science (ICEMAESS 2018)* (pp. 398-402). Atlantis Press. DOI: 10.2991/icemaess-18.2018.83

Yin, R. K. (1994). Discovering the future of the case study. Method in evaluation research. *Evaluation Practice*, *15*(3), 283–290.

Chapter 13
Pedagogical Methodologies and the Cultivation of Innovative Competencies Among Learners:
An Examination of the Pedagogical Practices in Entrepreneurship

Nizar Mtibaa
https://orcid.org/0009-0005-4427-0680
Faculty of Economic Sciences and Management, Sfax, Tunisia

ABSTRACT

Entrepreneurship pedagogy is crucial in modern economies, particularly in Tunisia, where it helps tackle youth unemployment and promote economic transformation. Higher education institutions must prioritize practical entrepreneurial skills, yet many criticize their curricula for being overly theoretical and misaligned with labor market needs. In Tunisia, entrepreneurship education requires a shift from traditional teaching to more hands-on, practical training to build competitive skills. This study examines the effectiveness of current methods and challenges through interviews with educators and students. While project-based learning is favored, it often fails to foster sufficient creativity and innovation due to cultural, educational, and institutional barriers. Enhancing student innovation requires an integrated, cross-disciplinary approach and institutional reforms to promote a culture of innovation, with implications for policymakers and educators aiming to develop better educational strategies.

INTRODUCTION

In contemporary discourse, the pedagogy of entrepreneurship has emerged as an essential element within the economic frameworks of both advanced and emerging economies, particularly evident in countries such as Tunisia where the cultivation of entrepreneurial competencies is perceived as fundamental to mitigating issues such as youth unemployment and facilitating economic transformation (Iakovleva et al., 2020; Urbano et al., 2019). Entrepreneurs serve as pivotal agents in fostering innovation, generating employment opportunities, and catalyzing economic advancement, thereby rendering entrepreneurship

DOI: 10.4018/979-8-3693-9040-5.ch013

education a paramount national concern within the context of Tunisia's swiftly evolving economic environment (Klofsten et al., 2019; Edoho, 2015).

The worldwide transition towards innovation as a catalyst for economic competitiveness has positioned universities at the vanguard of the development of entrepreneurial competencies (Guerrero et al., 2016). Higher education institutions are increasingly expected not only to disseminate theoretical knowledge but also to function as incubators for practical, innovation-oriented entrepreneurship. Nevertheless, numerous Tunisian universities have faced criticism for their conventional, theory-laden curricula, which frequently fail to equip students with the practical competencies requisite for the labor market (Mwasalwiba, 2010; Smirnov et al., 2023). This incongruity between academic preparation and market requirements constitutes a significant impediment to the nation's economic advancement, underscoring the necessity for a comprehensive reform of educational methodologies that emphasize experiential learning (Mishra & Zachary, 2015).

Entrepreneurship education in Tunisia, akin to its counterparts in numerous developing nations, is increasingly regarded as an essential mechanism for mitigating unemployment and promoting novel economic prospects (Dana, 2020). It is anticipated that emerging entrepreneurs will assume a crucial role in addressing systemic employment issues, particularly in areas characterized by elevated youth unemployment rates (Chigunta, 2017). Nonetheless, to effectively nurture these entrepreneurs, educational institutions must transcend conventional pedagogical methods and provide more experiential, practical training that can robustly enhance the entrepreneurial and innovative competencies requisite in contemporary competitive markets (Walter et al., 2019; Kelley & Thomas, 2011).

While there exists an increasing agreement on the significance of experiential learning in entrepreneurship education, the inquiry into the optimal implementation of such pedagogical methodologies remains unresolved. Empirical evidence indicates that active learning strategies, including business simulations, case analyses, and project-based learning, are demonstrably more efficacious in cultivating entrepreneurial competencies compared to traditional educational approaches (Bae et al., 2014; Rideout & Gray, 2013). Nevertheless, in Tunisia, the uptake of these progressive instructional methods has been sluggish, primarily attributable to institutional limitations and insufficient resources (Bagheri et al., 2017).

This investigation aims to scrutinize two pivotal inquiries:

- Are the pedagogical strategies presently employed in entrepreneurship education in Tunisia effective in enhancing students' innovative capabilities?
- What elements facilitate or obstruct the implementation of these experiential teaching methodologies?

This article endeavors to respond to these inquiries through a systematic methodology. Initially, we will present a thorough review of the literature that investigates innovative capabilities and the pedagogical frameworks that foster their enhancement (Ndou et al., 2018). This segment will also evaluate the obstacles to the adoption of innovative teaching methodologies within higher education settings (Liguori & Winkler, 2020). The subsequent section of the article will analyze entrepreneurship education in Tunisia, emphasizing how universities are currently incorporating entrepreneurship into their curricular offerings. Ultimately, the findings of this analysis will be deliberated, particularly concerning the efficacy of these methodologies and the impediments to their successful deployment in developing nations such as Tunisia.

By examining these variables, this research contributes to the expansive discourse surrounding entrepreneurship education in developing economies, offering insights into how educational practices can be refined to more effectively equip students for entrepreneurial success in a globalized, innovation-centric economic landscape (Ratten, 2020).

1. LITERATURE REVIEW

1.1. Development of Innovation Capacities

Theoretically, the notion of innovation can be comprehended through various lenses: as an outcome, a procedural framework, or a competency. Crossan and Apaydin (2010) assert that innovation is predicated upon the generation of novelties and the creation of value, although this concept is profoundly contextual. Indeed, innovation is influenced by a multitude of cognitive, conative, emotional, and environmental variables, as elucidated by Burkhardt and Lubart (2010). In this discourse, we espouse a perspective of innovation as an interactive process characterized by the construction of knowledge and the cultivation of skills. This process seeks to effectively adopt or integrate novel ideas, methodologies, or products within a specific context (Rave-Habhab, 2011).

When examining innovation within the educational sphere, it can be perceived as a capacity, denoting a general and enduring trait that enhances an individual's efficacy in executing a diverse array of tasks (Van Zanten & Rayou, 2017). Consequently, innovation capabilities are constituted by a constellation of personal attributes, knowledge bases, skills, and attitudes that are intrinsically associated with the realization of new creations. These innovations frequently emerge from collaborative efforts embedded within intricate innovation processes. Similar to other competencies, innovation capabilities can be acquired and cultivated.

Concerning the academic milieu, the cultivation of innovation capabilities among students is paramount and can be characterized as a process designed to equip them with the requisite skills, resources, and motivation to access knowledge and perpetually enhance their abilities for the creation of novel entities (Fullan, 2010). Nonetheless, this process transcends the mere acquisition of technical skills. It necessitates, above all, a cultural transformation, as indicated by Cabrera and Cabrera (2023). This transformation pertains more to the beliefs and actions of individuals than to institutional programs or technological advancements. Thus, the metamorphosis hinges on the readiness of individuals to foster attitudes that are conducive to innovation.

Fostering innovation capabilities in higher education encompasses, among other elements, the acquisition of competencies in communication, collaborative work, problem-solving, leadership, critical analysis, information retrieval, and creative thinking (Hall et al., 2013). These competencies form the bedrock of innovation, as they facilitate self-directedness and learning across diverse contexts. Practically, this manifests in the cultivation of four principal types of capabilities among students: creative, entrepreneurial, soft skills, and technological (Maritz & Brown, 2013). Each of these dimensions is instrumental in enhancing students' capacity to innovate, both within academic settings and in professional environments.

Creative capabilities, which pertain to the generation of novel ideas and solutions, are predominantly bolstered by environments that promote experimentation. Urban and Silva (2019) contend that brainstorming techniques, co-creation workshops, and other interactive methodologies stimulate lateral thinking, a crucial component for addressing complex challenges. With regard to entrepreneurial competencies, these empower students to engage with innovation pragmatically, overseeing risks and resources to actualize new concepts. Ratten (2020) underscores the necessity for entrepreneurship programs to incorporate these pragmatic elements through simulations and case studies that immerse students in market realities.

Ultimately, non-technical competencies, commonly referred to as soft skills, including leadership and conflict resolution, are of paramount importance in collaborative settings, where the generation of innovative ideas is contingent upon the diversity of perspectives and the effective management of team dynamics (Panadero et al., 2019). Proficiency in technological instruments serves as another vital catalyst for innovation, as demonstrated by the findings of Garnett and O'Beirne (2019). In fact, within a landscape characterized by rapid technological advancement, it is imperative for students to cultivate digital competencies to maintain their competitiveness in the labor market.

In conclusion, fostering innovation capacities within higher education institutions necessitates a re-imagined pedagogical framework that emphasizes experiential learning and the cultivation of transversal skills. These methodologies enable students to effectively assimilate the requisite tools for innovation and to navigate more adeptly within perpetually evolving environments.

1.1.1. Creative Abilities

Non-technical competencies, commonly referred to as soft skills, including leadership and conflict resolution, are essential within collaborative settings, where innovation is fundamentally dependent on the heterogeneity of ideas and the effective management of team dynamics (Panadero et al., 2019). Proficiency in technological instruments represents another vital catalyst for innovation, as evidenced by the work of Garnett and O'Beirne (2019). Indeed, in an environment characterized by rapid technological advancement, creativity is recognized as a multidimensional and intricate construct that has engendered a multitude of definitions and theoretical frameworks over the decades. Sternberg and Lubart (2019) conceptualize creativity as an amalgamation of various individual, contextual, and environmental variables. Conversely, Parkhurst (1999) articulates creativity as "the capacity to produce new and appropriate work." This prevailing agreement concerning the principles of novelty and significance has endured in the academic discourse, while being further enriched by contemporary developments that incorporate cognitive, socio-cultural, and environmental perspectives.

Since the seminal work of Guilford (1950) and his groundbreaking investigations into divergent thinking, creativity has frequently been perceived as the capacity to consider a range of solutions to a specific problem, to challenge conventional paradigms, and to propose innovative alternatives (Kaufman et al., 2022). Divergent thinking serves as a fundamental attribute of creativity, enabling individuals to generate a plethora of original concepts and to conceive ideas beyond traditional boundaries (Lubart et al., 2015).

More recently, scholars have examined the interconnections between creativity and cognitive flexibility, defined as the capacity to shift between diverse cognitive modalities and to adapt to novel or fluctuating circumstances (Simonton, 2018). This cognitive flexibility is particularly salient in complex and dynamic contexts, such as those encountered by entrepreneurs, who frequently navigate uncertain and unpredictable environments (Panadero et al., 2019). At the tertiary education level, the creative capacities of students are instrumental in fostering their potential for innovation and problem-solving abilities. The cultivation of these creative competencies has emerged as a primary objective in higher education, particularly within disciplines pertinent to entrepreneurship (Ratten, 2020). Active pedagogical approaches, such as project-based learning, collaborative learning, and competency-based education, are increasingly being implemented to motivate students to enhance their creativity and acquire practical skills that will be advantageous in their professional pursuits (Beghetto & Kaufman, 2010).

One of the most critical dimensions of fostering creativity in educational settings is the establishment of an environment conducive to exploration and innovation. This necessitates the promotion of a culture characterized by curiosity and risk-taking, wherein students feel empowered to experiment and explore novel ideas without apprehension of failure (Hennessey & Amabile, 2010). This methodology further demands institutional support to incorporate technologies and resources that facilitate collaboration and innovation, such as creative laboratories and university incubators (Simonton, 2018).

Creativity is not confined to a specific discipline or domain; rather, it can be stimulated through a broad spectrum of activities and interactions. According to Fullan (2010), the advancement of creativity and innovation necessitates, above all, a cultural transformation within educational institutions, where the focus shifts to creative processes, critical thinking, and collaborative endeavors. This paradigm shift enables the training of individuals adept at navigating perpetually evolving environments and contributing to innovation within their respective domains.

Indeed, creativity constitutes a fundamental competency that can be cultivated and enhanced through intellectually stimulating educational contexts. Academic programs at the tertiary level, especially those focused on entrepreneurship, must implement instructional strategies that not only promote divergent thinking and cognitive adaptability but also furnish the requisite resources to actualize innovative concepts into tangible and feasible actions.

1.1.2. Entrepreneurial Skills

Entrepreneurship epitomizes a manifestation of human inventive prowess and, in this regard, it pervades diverse spheres of individual existence, commercial enterprises, societal constructs, and institutional frameworks. Central to this dynamic, entrepreneurship is conceptualized as the study of the sources of opportunities, the processes of discovering, evaluating and exploiting these opportunities, as well as the individuals who identify and exploit them (Kovid et al., 2022). To adeptly maneuver through the various stages of business opportunities, it is essential to cultivate a repertoire of entrepreneurial competencies.

To foster these competencies among students, educational initiatives can pursue three principal objectives. Primarily, the initial educational aim is to elucidate the entrepreneurial phenomenon. This entails the accumulation of foundational knowledge to comprehend the complexities, viewpoints, and challenges inherent to entrepreneurship. Enhancing awareness regarding the multifaceted nature of entrepreneurship is vital, as it establishes a robust groundwork upon which prospective entrepreneurs can construct their endeavors (Kuratko, 2020). For instance, contemporary investigations indicate that the incorporation of entrepreneurship modules into educational curricula enhances students' comprehension and acceptance of the entrepreneurial mindset (Goh et al., 2021).

Furthermore, the second objective concentrates on the cultivation of essential entrepreneurial behaviors within students. This encompasses the pursuit of opportunities, the initiation of actions, and the establishment of new ventures. By fostering these competencies, students are motivated to embrace a proactive approach and undertake calculated risks (Thompson, 2018). Moreover, pragmatic programs, such as university-based business incubators, have been recognized as conducive environments for nurturing these behaviors (Rae, 2018).

Building upon this analysis, the final objective pertains to the acquisition of generic and transversal entrepreneurial skills. This encompasses the capacity to identify and assess ideas, manage projects, and evaluate associated risks (Fayolle & Gailly, 2015). Recent scholarly work underscores that experiential learning, such as engagement in authentic entrepreneurial projects, not only fortifies technical competencies but also enhances critical interpersonal attributes, including teamwork and communication (Wang et al., 2020). Indeed, in an ever-evolving global landscape, the enhancement of entrepreneurial capacities in students has emerged as an imperative. By incorporating these three objectives into educational frameworks, institutions can equip students not only to emerge as proficient entrepreneurs but also to serve as catalysts for change within their communities. In doing so, they contribute to a dynamic entrepreneurial ecosystem that nurtures innovation and fosters economic advancement.

1.1.3. Soft Skills

As the exigency for knowledge dissemination and acquisition continues to escalate, interpersonal competencies, commonly denoted as soft skills, are emerging as indispensable. These competencies are progressively acknowledged as pivotal assets across diverse professional domains, as they augment collaboration and efficacy within teams. Nevertheless, it is imperative to underscore that technical competencies, frequently termed hard skills, will persist as a fundamental component in numerous occupational realms, particularly within technical and specialized industries.

Soft skills generally encompass a spectrum of abilities that are vital for professional accomplishment, such as leadership, communication, teamwork, negotiation, and emotional intelligence (MacDermott & Ortiz, 2017). According to a contemporary study, employers appraise interpersonal skills as equivalently or even more significant than technical skills in the context of recruitment and career advancement (Baker et al., 2020). This observation signifies a transformation in workplace priorities, wherein the capability to engage effectively with others is frequently essential for the attainment of organizational objectives.

In this regard, Dede's (2010) scholarly contribution delineates a compilation of interpersonal skills that are intricately interconnected, encompassing critical thinking, information retrieval, synthesis, dissemination, curiosity, and the application of existing knowledge to cultivate novel ideas, products, or processes. These skills are increasingly esteemed in an environment where innovation and adaptability are paramount. Indeed, recent investigations suggest that teams that foster the exchange of ideas and creativity tend to exhibit enhanced performance and are capable of adapting to swift market fluctuations (Nishikawa et al., 2021).

Moreover, collaboration, contextual learning, self-directedness, and communication skills are also recognized as fundamental competencies for contemporary professionals. The capacity to function effectively within a team is frequently cited as one of the most critical determinants of project success. Empirical studies demonstrate that teams characterized by a robust collaborative spirit are more inclined to surpass their competitors in terms of productivity and innovation (Salas et al., 2018).

It is also noteworthy that the cultivation of interpersonal skills necessitates a profound comprehension of oneself, typically acquired through introspection and feedback from others. Succi and Canovi (2020) emphasize the significance of self-reflection and feedback in identifying strengths and areas necessitating enhancement. Engaging in critical reflection enables individuals to assess their interactions and fortify their emotional intelligence, which is essential in the management of professional relationships.

As the professional environment rapidly transforms, the significance of interpersonal skills cannot be undervalued. Organizations that allocate resources towards the development of these skills in their personnel are more favorably positioned to innovate and adapt to forthcoming challenges. In this framework, the incorporation of interpersonal skills into training and professional development programs emerges as a crucial priority to guarantee a competent and responsive workforce.

1.1.3.1. Modern Technology Capabilities

In the contemporary landscape characterized by swift technological advancement and digital metamorphosis, it is crucial for students to cultivate competencies pertinent to the commercialization of emergent technologies and the administration of information systems. The commercialization of novel technology may be succinctly articulated as the transition of concepts from the research domain to the marketplace (Huang-Saad et al., 2017). This definition underscores the critical significance of knowledge transfer, which is vital for transforming scientific breakthroughs into tangible applications. Gbadegeshin (2017) elucidate that the commercialization of technology entails the process of generating ideas, augmenting complementary knowledge, formulating and producing marketable goods, and marketing the products in a commercial context.

The creation of educational resources associated with technology commercialization necessitates the incorporation of innovative content and pedagogical methodologies. This endeavor requires active collaboration among researchers, enterprises, academic institutions, and governmental entities to establish an ecosystem that fosters innovation (Nelson & Monsen, 2014). Such a collaborative framework guarantees that students receive training that equips them to navigate market challenges and fulfill industry-specific demands.

More specifically, the capabilities related to the commercialization of emerging technologies manifest in students' proficiency to engage effectively with inventors to comprehend the principal attributes of the new technology. They must also possess the ability to evaluate the novelty of this technology to determine the feasibility of securing a patent. This evaluation encompasses an analysis of the additional value that the new technology provides in addressing tangible real-world issues, alongside the preparation of a preliminary report regarding the status of the pertinent intellectual property (Phan, 2014). Moreover, it is imperative for students to acquire the skills necessary to appraise the feasibility of the technology to ascertain its market viability and potential impact.

In the domain of information systems management, these skills are reflected in a comprehensive understanding of the significance of information and information technologies in the facilitation and execution of innovations, both for individuals and organizations (Chege et al., 2020). In a milieu where data assumes a pivotal role in strategic decision-making, it is essential for students to learn how to assist organizations in employing information efficiently. This entails understanding the management of information flows and the utilization of information technologies, with a specific emphasis on contemporary social media and Web 2.0 technologies.

In this context, recent research underscores that proficiency with digital tools, encompassing online collaboration platforms and social networks, has emerged as a vital competency for contemporary professionals. Indeed, the capacity to navigate these digital environments can considerably affect an organization's ability to innovate and maintain competitiveness (Kumar & Gupta, 2021). Therefore, the cultivation of these skills within students signifies preparation for a professional future where digital agility and adaptability to new technologies will serve as crucial advantages.

In conclusion, in an environment marked by perpetual technological progression, the enhancement of competencies related to the commercialization of new technologies and the management of information systems is indispensable for students. By embedding these skills into educational frameworks, institutions can develop professionals who are equipped to confront the challenges of the contemporary market and contribute to the generation of meaningful innovations.

1.2. Teaching Methods Can Promote the Development of Students' Innovation Capacities

This point aims to identify teaching approaches capable of strengthening students' creative capacities, entrepreneurial skills, "soft skills" as well as modern technology skills.

1.2.1. Pedagogical Approaches to Cultivate Creative Competencies

The evolution of a creative disposition is predicated upon the principles of freedom regarding expression, cognition, and action. In order to nurture this creativity effectively, it is imperative to establish a learning environment that is devoid of threats and conducive to the initiation of independent thought and innovative ideation (Rajapathirana & Hui, 2018). Such an environment not only facilitates individualistic expression but also engenders a dynamic interplay among the cognitive, affective, conative, and sensory faculties of the learner.

Within the realm of management education, de Villiers Scheepers and Margarietha (2015) underscore the significance of the creative process as it pertains to problem-solving endeavors. Indeed, the capacity to discern, evaluate, and resolve intricate problems constitutes a foundational pillar of innovation. Mosyjowski and Seifert (2014) delineate that methodologies for problem-solving ought to be seamlessly integrated within project-based learning paradigms, thereby allowing students to engage with practical cases that mirror the complexities of real-world challenges.

The principles inherent in divergent thinking are equally vital for the enhancement of creativity. Kleibeuker, De Dreu, and Crone (2016) advocate for the inclusion of tasks such as "generating multiple solutions to an open-ended problem" and "reflecting on cognitive flexibility." These strategies empower students to traverse various pathways and cultivate the ability to contemplate diverse potential solutions, thereby fortifying their capacity for innovation.

Moreover, Chuang, Liu, and Shiu (2015) advocate for the incorporation of educational games as instrumental tools for fostering creativity among students. Such games afford interactive learning experiences, enabling students to immerse themselves in scenarios that evoke their imagination and enhance their capacity to engage in unconventional thinking.

Al-Samarraie and Hurmuzan (2018) contend that an environment conducive to creativity must incorporate brainstorming techniques. These methodologies facilitate the unimpeded exchange of ideas and the suspension of initial evaluative judgments, both of which are critical for the cultivation of creative potential. They further assert that in order to effectively embed creativity within the learning process, it is essential for it to be interwoven throughout the entirety of the program or curriculum, rather than being relegated to a series of isolated courses.

Formal education, which encompasses the accumulation of knowledge through structured educational systems and training, plays a pivotal role in the preparation of entrepreneurs. This educational framework must be meticulously designed to endow students with explicit knowledge while simultaneously furnishing them with experiential opportunities that enhance their creative competencies. Recent empirical investigations indicate that pedagogical methodologies that amalgamate theoretical and practical elements, such as project-based learning and problem-based learning, are particularly efficacious in the development of creative capabilities (Huang et al., 2021; Gül et al., 2023).

In conclusion, it is imperative to cultivate a culture of perpetual learning wherein students are encouraged to experiment, encounter failure, and derive lessons from their missteps. The establishment of such an environment can not only invigorate creativity but also foster the entrepreneurial spirit of students, thereby equipping them to innovate within an ever-evolving professional landscape.

1.2.2. Pedagogical Methods to Develop Entrepreneurial Capacities

Developing entrepreneurial capacities, such as identifying business opportunities, requires a collaborative approach. According to Rasmussen, Mosey, and Wright (2011), forming teams of students to work together on innovative projects is crucial. A "group pedagogy" not only helps generate innovative ideas, but also strengthens the interpersonal skills essential for entrepreneurship. However, it is imperative that this group work is accompanied by in-depth personal reflection. Students must explore various aspects of their personality, such as their social identity, their personal ambitions and goals, and their self-confidence. Qualities such as resilience, self-discipline, and the ability to tolerate uncertainty and ambiguity are also essential for navigating the entrepreneurial world, where failure and risk are often part of the process (Rasmussen et al., 2020).

Regarding educational tools, Mortara et al. (2014) argue that serious games are powerful resources to support the development of entrepreneurial capabilities. These games simulate real business environments, providing students with the opportunity to apply their theoretical knowledge in a practical setting, which increases their confidence and decision-making skills in complex situations.

San Tan and Frank (2006) also highlight the importance of creative problem-solving and critical thinking pedagogies in entrepreneurial education. By integrating these methods, students can learn to analyze situations, evaluate solutions, and adapt their approach based on the results obtained.

1.2.3. Educational Methods to Develop "Soft Skills"

"Soft skills" encompass a wide range of skills, among which leadership, teamwork, and communication are particularly emphasized in the development of innovation capabilities. Regarding leadership, several researchers, including Cacioppe (1998) and Hobson et al. (2014), highlight the essential role of teamwork and project-based learning to cultivate it. Boyatzis and Saatcioglu (2008) echo this idea by emphasizing the importance of emotional intelligence in team interactions.

Project-based learning, which promotes personal interactions, creates a learning environment conducive to collaboration. It places students in situations where they must make decisions, assume risks, and develop their interpersonal skills (Green & Blaszczynski, 2012). To do this, various assessment methods, such as the use of videos, role plays, group discussions, case analysis, and management simulations, are recommended to enrich the learning experience.

In the field of entrepreneurship education, Nielsen and Stovang (2015) highlight design thinking as an innovative approach to fostering creativity and problem solving. In addition, recent research shows that learning by doing is fundamental to acquiring entrepreneurial capabilities, as it allows students to actively engage in real-world experiences (Rasmussen, Mosey, & Wright, 2011). Instructional methods that support learning by doing typically involve group work, thus promoting knowledge sharing and collaborative learning.

Hyams-Ssekasi and Caldwell (2018) also recommend experiential learning to encourage students to develop a greater sense of self-efficacy, responsibility, cooperation, planning, and perseverance. By integrating hands-on and collaborative activities into the curriculum, higher education institutions can better prepare students to meet the challenges of the modern entrepreneurial world.

1.2.4. Teaching Methods to Develop Capacities in Modern Technologies

Developing capacities related to the commercialization of new technologies and the management of information systems requires a proactive opening of universities towards their socio-economic environment. This immersive approach allows students to better understand the crucial role of technology in the modern world, as well as the challenges associated with its implementation and commercialization (Mwasalwiba, 2020).

To strengthen skills in information systems management, it is essential that students have the opportunity to experience the internal dynamics of organizations. This can be done through internships, collaborative projects or mentoring initiatives within companies. These experiences allow students to grasp the importance of information management in strategic decision-making (Wang & Zhang, 2021). By observing how information technologies are integrated into organizational processes, students can identify good and bad practices. For example, they could analyse cases where poor information management led to failures, contrasting with situations where an effective approach generated positive results. This in-depth understanding is crucial for developing skills in innovation and information systems management, enabling students to become competent professionals in data and technology management.

Regarding the development of new technology commercialisation capabilities, universities can invite inventors and entrepreneurs to share their experiences with students. These interventions can address various themes such as intellectual property awareness, benchmarking the potential of a technology against its competitors, and analysing market trends (Levie, 2014). For example, students could be encouraged to interview real potential customers and industry experts to better understand market needs and commercialisation challenges.

Business model generation is also a key skill that can be developed through practical workshops and case studies. Students can work on projects where they have to design commercialization strategies based on innovative technologies, drawing on life stories of entrepreneurs who have successfully commercialized their innovations (Levie, 2014). This approach offers a concrete perspective on the real-world challenges encountered when commercializing new technologies and encourages students to think critically and creatively (Ziegler, 2022).

Other effective teaching methods include the use of market simulations and business scenarios, where students can apply their theoretical knowledge to practical situations, while developing analytical and decision-making skills. In addition, integrating digital platforms and project management tools into learning can help students become familiar with emerging technologies and gain practical expertise in information management and commercialization (Lichtenstein & Brush, 2019).

Indeed, collaboration between educational institutions and the private sector, as well as the inclusion of experience-based learning methods, are essential to prepare students to meet the technological challenges of the 21st century.

1.3. Factors That Promote or Inhibit the Adoption of Pedagogical Methods for Developing Innovation Capacities

On a global scale, one of the expected results of modern education systems is to promote an innovative and creative spirit among young people. However, the development of students' innovation capacities relies on a set of interdependent factors that interact in a systemic manner. To analyze these factors, we draw on the work of Gajda et al. (2017) and Filteau (2012), who identify five essential dimensions, called the "5Ps": people, process, product, time and place.

People refer to the different actors involved in the educational process, including teachers, university stakeholders, administrators and students themselves. The quality of the interaction between these actors plays a crucial role in the dynamics of innovation. For example, well-trained, motivated, and supported teachers can foster a learning environment that fosters creativity and experimentation (Eisenberg & Johnson, 2018).

Process refers primarily to pedagogical methods, whether strategic (such as educational strategy, curriculum engineering, and content) or operational (the different phases of implementing pedagogical and assessment methods). Active methods, such as project-based learning or problem-based learning, are recognized for stimulating student engagement and facilitating the development of their innovation capabilities (Mansour et al., 2021).

Products represent the results of the educational process in terms of innovation. Each new idea or product developed by students illustrates the different types of innovation, whether technological, process, product, organizational, or service innovations. Institutions that promote these products by communicating them widely or using them as case studies in their educational programs foster a climate conducive to innovation (Garcia et al., 2020).

In relation to the "5Ps", the literature highlights that teachers are a key resource for the development of innovation capacities in students. Their role requires a prior change in their acquired knowledge, values and pedagogical conceptions. They must be encouraged to unleash their creativity and imagination, engaging in pedagogical innovation processes that promote learning through exploration, experimentation and trial and error (Tardif, 2019). According to Vroom (1964), this change depends on both psychological and motivational factors in teachers, but also on favorable institutional, pedagogical and educational conditions (Mitchell, 2021).

At the student level, the development of innovation capacities is mainly based on motivation and personal commitment. The involvement of teachers in the evolution of their teaching practices, as well as the engagement of students in their own learning, largely depend on the culture and organizational structure of universities, as well as on learning conditions that are favorable to innovation (Sternberg & Lubart, 2019). If the different types of student innovations are valued and widely communicated, or even used as case studies, innovation-oriented learning can flourish.

At the same time, to foster an innovative spirit, it is essential that the organizational structure of universities is thought of in a transversal manner. This promotes collaboration between all departments and teachers in the framework of federating projects (Isaksen & Ekvall, 2010). The creation of communities of practice where teachers can exchange ideas and innovative teaching methods is also beneficial (Darling-Hammond et al., 2017).

In addition, universities must provide continuous and repetitive training to teachers so that they can acquire new skills and discover teaching methods oriented towards stimulating innovation in students. Such an objective requires the development of multidisciplinary content that integrates different perspectives and areas of expertise (Beckman & Barry, 2020). Universities must also devote more time to the assimilation and exploitation of content aimed at promoting innovation capacities in students. This involves establishing strong partnerships with external stakeholders, including companies and organizations in the regional economic fabric, in order to enrich the learning experience of students and ensure that their skills meet market needs.

2. TEACHING ENTREPRENEURSHIP IN TUNISIA

2.1. Research Methodology

To answer the questions of this research, we chose the field of entrepreneurship education as a field of study, because it offers a framework conducive to the development of innovation capacities that are both observable and assessable in students. This is particularly evident in their ability to identify business opportunities or design new products, technologies or processes (Selznick & Mayhew, 2018). This field thus makes it possible to explore the pedagogical mechanisms that promote innovation, while offering a rich ground for reflections on educational methodology and learning practices. An interpretivist stance was adopted for this research, favoring an inductive approach that aims to understand the lived experiences of the participants. This qualitative approach makes it possible to explore in depth the perceptions and motivations of teachers and students, giving them a voice in the research process (Creswell & Poth, 2018). To collect data, we conducted semi-structured interviews with 15 teachers (mean age 45, with an average of 10 years of experience in teaching entrepreneurship; among them, 10 were female) and 20 students who had followed an entrepreneurship module in different Master's programs (mean age 21, including 15 female). The average duration of the interviews was 50 minutes for teachers and 45 minutes for students, which allowed us to obtain rich and detailed data. Participants were recruited from 10 faculties of economic, legal and social sciences located in several cities, including Tunis, Nabeul, Sousse, Sfax, Gafsa and Gabès.

Regarding the choice of our qualitative sample, we respected the "principle of diversification", which emphasizes the variety of perspectives, including external or intergroup, rather than the principle of representativeness (Maxwell, 2020). This approach aims to leverage the wealth of information from different sources, allowing for a more nuanced understanding of the issues related to entrepreneurship education.

The semi-structured interview guide was developed based on our literature review on innovation capabilities, the teaching methods likely to foster them, and the factors determining the adoption of these methods. Pre-tests of the interview guides were conducted with a control group of two teachers and three students, allowing us to refine the questions and ensure their relevance (Rampersad et al., 2010). These pre-tests also allowed us to check the clarity and fluidity of the questions, which is essential for obtaining in-depth and meaningful responses during the interviews.

The data collected were transcribed in full, followed by a process of coding and in-depth analysis. Careful listening and repeated readings of the transcripts allowed us to identify themes of reflection from a thematic analysis, which will be used to structure the presentation of the results (Flick, 2018). To facilitate the analysis of qualitative data, we opted for a priori coding, by constituting a coding grid based on the relevant themes from the theoretical model developed. This rigorous methodology ensures the validity of the results and identifies emerging trends in the perceptions of teachers and students, while enriching the academic debate on the teaching of entrepreneurship and the development of innovation capacities. This research thus contributes to the literature by highlighting the importance of a reflexive and collaborative approach in the teaching of entrepreneurship, while identifying avenues for improvement for current teaching practices. By integrating varied perspectives and taking into account institutional dynamics, we hope to inform future initiatives aimed at enriching the learning experience of students in entrepreneurship.

2.2. Presentation of the Results

The presentation of the results of this research is divided into two main parts: the teaching methods used by entrepreneurship teachers and the factors that condition the adoption of these methods likely to develop innovation capacities in students. These factors will be analyzed according to the 5 "P" model: people, processes, products, period and place.

2.2.1. The Teaching Methods Used by Entrepreneurship Teachers

2.2.1.1. The Predominance of the Business Plan and Transmissive Pedagogies

The interviews conducted with entrepreneurship teachers and students reveal a diversity of teaching methods, but with a strong prevalence of traditional approaches. Indeed, 35% of teachers mention the use of project pedagogy, focused on the development of a business plan, which is then presented during classroom defenses or in front of professionals in the sector. This process is often seen as a realistic simulation of the entrepreneurial environment, allowing students to understand market requirements and investor expectations (Kuratko, 2020). For their part, students cite the business plan in 45% of cases, emphasizing that this method, although effective in structuring thinking, is often accompanied by more traditional approaches such as lectures and presentations. Indeed, they report that the presentation of the business plan is generally carried out in a theoretical framework followed by a practical application (25% of students), which demonstrates a hybridization of teaching methods.

2.2.1.2. The Use of Entrepreneur Testimonials and Discussions and Debates

To enrich learning around the business plan, 25% of teachers say they use entrepreneur testimonials as a first pedagogical approach. These testimonials, which can take the form of conferences or testimonials in class, offer students a direct perspective on the realities of the entrepreneurial world. At the same time, 10% of teachers integrate case studies on entrepreneurs, whether Tunisian or foreign, in order to contextualize learning. These case studies allow students to critically reflect on the strategies implemented by successful entrepreneurs and to explore real challenges that they face (Hägg & Gabrielsson, 2019). On the other hand, 20% of students mention that discussions and debates are essential to develop self-knowledge and explore broader themes related to entrepreneurship. However, they note that invitations to entrepreneurs and professionals remain rare, which limits learning opportunities outside of academic contexts. This insufficiency can potentially harm the motivation and engagement of students, who could benefit more from continued exposure to concrete examples of innovation and entrepreneurial success.

2.2.1.3. The Use of Case Studies

The case study is a pedagogical method commonly used in teaching entrepreneurship. Indeed, 18% of teachers and 15% of students mention the use of case studies, considered an effective way to inspire students and enable them to acquire knowledge and practical skills in entrepreneurship and innovation. Case studies provide a rich contextual framework that allows students to analyze real-life situations and apply entrepreneurial theories (Yin, 2018). This method also promotes critical thinking and the ability to solve complex problems, essential skills in the modern entrepreneurial world. By integrating contemporary case studies, teachers can also ensure that the content remains relevant and engaging for students.

2.2.1.4. The Low Use of the Most Active Teaching Methods

Despite the recognized benefits of active teaching methods in promoting the entrepreneurial spirit, the majority of teachers and students agree that these approaches are very little used. Entrepreneurship awareness workshops are mentioned by only 10% of teachers, while role-playing and action learning are mentioned by only 5%. In addition, only 2% of teachers integrate innovative methods such as the inverted classroom, error-based learning, simulation games, brainstorming, or the analysis of videos on real cases of entrepreneurs. This observation reveals a lack of commitment to the use of teaching methods that promote active student participation and experiential learning (Bessant & Tidd, 2019).

The use of these active methods, such as "learning by doing," is particularly crucial in the context of entrepreneurship education, where experimentation and innovation are at the heart of the skills to be acquired. Research has shown that students who participate in active learning methods are more likely to develop self-efficacy and self-confidence skills, essential elements for a successful entrepreneurial career (Morris et al., 2019).

2.2.2. Factors That Condition the Use of Teaching Methods Likely to Develop Innovation Capacities

Research on the factors that influence the adoption of teaching methods intended to develop innovation capacities among students has highlighted several key elements, organized according to the 5 "Ps": people, processes, products, period and place. These factors include the place of innovation in the national culture, the educational system, the context and role of the university, the act of teaching, as well as teachers and students.

2.2.2.1. Environmental Factors

Tunisian culture is often perceived as not very rewarding for the innovative entrepreneur. This perception directly influences students' commitment to innovation and their motivation to develop innovative capacities within the educational system. As one teacher pointed out: "in Tunisian culture, the entrepreneur, especially the innovative one, is not recognized as such compared to other classic types of entrepreneurs. Moreover, in Tunisia, the entrepreneur is only the one who has money". This narrow vision of entrepreneurship can discourage young people from embracing innovative ideas, instead favoring traditional business models that do not rely on innovation.

Previous research has shown that national culture plays a crucial role in how innovation is perceived and integrated into educational systems (Dinis & Lemos, 2021). In the case of Tunisia, a cultural environment that values traditional entrepreneurs more can hinder the development of an innovative spirit among students. For a culture of innovation to be implemented, it is essential to change social perceptions surrounding entrepreneurship and promote success models that integrate innovation as a key success factor.

Regarding the development of innovation capacities through appropriate teaching methods, 95% of interviewees highlighted that the university context represents a fundamental determinant in the adoption of these methods. Teachers highlight various aspects such as university management, departmental organization, university culture, and relations between the university and the productive sector. One teacher expressed that "it is difficult to get university administrative decision-makers to adhere to programs with long-term benefits. For some, innovation and entrepreneurship are not always their first concerns." The absence of an entrepreneurial culture within higher education institutions results in an inappropriate strategic positioning of entrepreneurship and innovation. This creates a disconnect between academic training and the needs of the labor market, making it difficult for students to integrate into the entrepreneurial environment after graduation. One student added that "for us, students, we do not perceive the existence of internal collaboration between university departments, nor external partnerships with the industrial world. Thus, we do not have real opportunities to develop our innovation capacities or implement them." This situation is corroborated by studies that show that universities that maintain close links with the private sector are more likely to create practical learning opportunities, which are essential for the development of entrepreneurial skills (Sánchez et al., 2020). Furthermore, the creation of a collaborative learning environment, which fosters interaction between students, teachers and industry professionals, is essential to catalyze innovation and entrepreneurship. The organization of the university into departments can also hinder the diffusion of innovative teaching methods, as academic silos limit the interdisciplinary exchanges necessary for innovation. To overcome these obstacles, it is crucial that higher education institutions adopt an integrated approach, promoting collaboration and the creation of interdepartmental programs that encourage creativity and innovation.

2.2.2.2. Process Factors

All study participants highlighted the crucial importance of the education system in developing innovation capabilities. In Tunisia, this system is often perceived as inadequate to instill in learners, from a young age, the values and skills that foster innovation. One teacher noted: "Teaching entrepreneurship and innovation is confronted with the fact that students view learning as quantitative. In these conditions, critical thinking and creativity are very rare. Thus, the education system hinders the innovative and entrepreneurial spirit, because it does not encourage students to take initiative and take risks" (Teacher 8).

This perception is corroborated by studies showing that the emphasis on memorization and rote learning, rather than critical thinking and experimentation, limits opportunities for innovation (Harrison et al., 2020). Educational programs need to evolve towards more active pedagogical approaches that encourage students to engage in practical projects and solve real-world problems. This requires a revision of curricula, incorporating elements such as project-based learning, where students can apply their knowledge in real-world contexts.

In addition, the development of innovation capacities requires teachers trained not only in their field of expertise, but also in innovative pedagogical methods that stimulate creativity. The continuous training of teachers and their ability to integrate digital tools into their teaching are also determining factors (Pérez et al., 2021).

2.2.2.3. *Factors Related to the Period*

Pedagogical methods are generally deployed during the act of teaching. However, for the teachers and students interviewed, this act faces several obstacles that hinder the development of innovation capacities. In particular, most teachers highlighted the insufficient volume of hours dedicated to Masters, as well as the problem of overcrowding of students. One teacher noted: "The training time is insufficient to equip students with entrepreneurial and creative skills. In addition, the overcrowding of students does not allow targeting those with an entrepreneurial predisposition or an inclination towards innovation."

This issue is widely documented in the literature, which indicates that the lack of time allocated to teaching entrepreneurial and creative skills can significantly reduce the effectiveness of educational programs (Meyer et al., 2019). In addition, the presence of a large number of students in a single class can make it difficult to achieve personalized interaction between teachers and students, which is essential to encourage engagement and motivation. Teaching methods must therefore be redesigned to integrate smaller classes or online learning devices that allow for greater flexibility and better monitoring of students (González et al., 2020).

Finally, the issue of the duration of training must also be addressed. Longer and more immersive training can foster a better assimilation of entrepreneurial and creative skills, allowing students to develop their innovative projects over an extended period. Therefore, it is crucial that educational institutions reconsider the temporal structure of their programs to integrate sufficient periods of practical learning and experimentation.

2.2.2.4. *People-Related Factors*

- **Students**

Certain factors associated with students significantly impede the advancement of their innovation capabilities. Initially, the educators interviewed underscore that students exhibit a pronounced inclination towards secure salaried positions as opposed to the establishment of innovative ventures. One educator articulated: "Due to the socio-economic backgrounds of the students (originating from predominantly average families), the attainment of a diploma is perceived as a pathway to upward mobility. The diploma constitutes the ultimate objective, while career selections tend to lean towards employment rather than entrepreneurial endeavors aimed at establishing one's own enterprise." This assertion is substantiated by research indicating that socio-economic determinants can shape students' career ambitions, compelling them to prioritize job stability over entrepreneurial pursuits (Blauth et al., 2019).

Moreover, all the students surveyed assert that financial resources are deemed more critical than innovative competencies when it comes to business creation. This restricted perspective is exacerbated by a negative assessment of the entrepreneurial landscape in Tunisia, where securing funding and resources is perceived as challenging. Consequently, despite the acknowledgment by some students regarding the significance of innovative abilities, they fail to cultivate a robust sense of confidence in their own innovation potential. One student remarked: "The student's recognition of his or her innovation capabilities ought to be facilitated through practical applications within the university curriculum, a practice that is notably rare in our educational framework."

Regarding personality characteristics, educators emphasize that Master's students often lack several fundamental attributes necessary for the cultivation of innovation capabilities. These educators identify factors such as diminished self-confidence, inadequate determination, apprehension towards failure, and aversion to risk. Such personality traits are imperative for entrepreneurship and innovation, as they influence students' responses to challenges and opportunities. Contemporary research indicates that self-confidence and resilience are critical determinants of entrepreneurial achievement (Krauss et al., 2020).

Furthermore, it is crucial to acknowledge that the educational milieu exerts a considerable influence on the development of these traits. An educational framework that fosters collaboration, experimentation, and risk-taking can significantly enhance students' self-confidence and innovative tendencies. The incorporation of experiential learning activities, such as social entrepreneurship initiatives or hackathons, could further augment students' perceptions of their innovativeness and capacity for entrepreneurship (Zhang et al., 2021).

Ultimately, educators and trainers must recognize the significance of nurturing an entrepreneurial mindset within their students. This encompasses not only motivating them to embrace proactive behaviors but also equipping them with emotional support and resources to surmount the perceived obstacles to innovation.

Teachers

From the students' perspective, the lack of experience and skills of teachers is a major obstacle to the development of innovation capacities. Students believe that many teachers do not have enough experience in innovative entrepreneurship, innovation management, or creativity techniques. One student expressed: "The lack of entrepreneurial or innovation experiences among teachers is a handicapping reality for the development of students' capacities." This perception is corroborated by recent studies that show that teachers' practical experience in the field of entrepreneurship is crucial to inspire and guide students (Nabi et al., 2019).

Moreover, even if a set of modern teaching methods is chosen and adopted, this does not necessarily guarantee the development of innovation capacities in students. The profile of teachers plays a determining role in this process. According to the students interviewed, "the teacher must be generalist, versatile, open-minded, available, attentive and patient, while constantly questioning himself. It is preferable that he has training in facilitation and support to instill a burst of freedom and creativity in students. In our Masters, this profile is very rare." This highlights the need for teachers to develop active pedagogy skills, which promote student-centered learning and creativity (Dewettinck et al., 2021).

Regardless of the teaching method used, the role of the teacher in the educational process is of crucial importance. For students, "the teacher does not play the role of sharing and transferring experience. He is also far from fulfilling the functions of accompanist, guide and facilitator. He often fails to engage students in networks of innovators and researchers, whether internally or externally." This highlights the importance of the connection between teaching and the professional world, which can offer students opportunities for collaboration and practical learning. Research has shown that teachers who act as facilitators and encourage exchanges with industry professionals can significantly improve student engagement and innovation (Gonzalez et al., 2020).

In sum, for students to develop their innovation capacities, it is essential that teachers have not only theoretical knowledge, but also practical skills and human qualities that foster a dynamic and engaging learning environment. Continuous training of teachers in facilitation, as well as the creation of strong links with the entrepreneurial sector, are therefore key elements to consider in order to improve entrepreneurship teaching in Tunisian universities.

3. DISCUSSION OF THE RESULTS

This discussion will focus on the reasons why some pedagogical methods adopted in entrepreneurship education fail to effectively develop students' innovation capacities. There is a significant gap between the recommendations of the literature and the pedagogical practices of Tunisian teachers, which we will explain by considering various cultural, educational and institutional factors.

In general, entrepreneurship teachers in Tunisia favor project-based pedagogies that focus mainly on the development of business plans, entrepreneurs' testimonies, theoretical discussions and case studies. This results in a limited use of pedagogical methods recognized in the literature to foster innovation, such as creative problem solving, divergent thinking, educational games, critical reflection, design thinking, brainstorming, as well as learning by design and experiential learning (Hennessey & Amabile, 2010; Beghetto & Kaufman, 2010).

The predominant use of the Business Plan, whose theoretical foundations are questionable (Mintzberg & Gosling, 2002; Castrogiovanni, 1996), raises questions about its ability to stimulate students' imagination and creativity. In theory, its use is anchored in an analytical and rational approach, not very conducive to the experimentation of new ideas (Honig & Karlsson, 2004). Despite these limitations, the Business Plan is widely used, partly because other teaching methods would require radical changes in class organization, such as managing heterogeneous groups, rigid schedules, and student overcrowding.

In addition, the profile of students also poses challenges. Many of them have an inadequate perception of innovation, limited interpersonal skills, and lack initiative, making group work difficult. The university context plays a crucial role: the absence of infrastructure dedicated to collaborative work and the lack of partnerships with the industrial world and research centers also limit the development of innovation capacities.

In addition, the lack of continuous training on these methods for teachers harms their motivation to engage in the development of their students' innovation capacities. Research shows that the perception of a lack of institutional recognition impacts teacher motivation (Lagziri et al., 2013). This observation is compounded by the fact that some teachers have not deliberately chosen to provide entrepreneurial education, leading them to focus more on awareness-raising than on the practical development of entrepreneurship and innovation skills (Fayolle & Gailly, 2015).

The use of case studies can be explained by the fact that many teachers come from management science backgrounds, where this method is valued. In addition, entrepreneur testimonies are not part of a deliberate university strategy but often result from personal relationships between teachers and the business world. For these testimonies to be inspiring, the speakers must have entrepreneurial qualities, a positive attitude towards the risks associated with innovation, and a high level of credibility (Garavan et al., 1994).

Finally, the literature highlights the importance of a range of teaching methods to develop innovation capacities (Klofsten et al., 2019; Ratten, 2020). However, achieving this goal requires cultural, educational and institutional changes. For Tunisia, it is essential to initiate changes within the educational system in order to foster critical thinking, creativity and risk acceptance. The university must transcend its traditional missions to adopt an entrepreneurial status, where teaching and promoting innovation would become strategic choices (Etzkowitz, 2004).

In conclusion, the development of innovation capacities among students must be seen as a transversal objective that goes beyond disciplinary boundaries, in order to guarantee a coherent and integrated approach to teaching entrepreneurship.

CONCLUSION

This research was designed to answer two fundamental questions: on the one hand, to what extent do the teaching methods implemented by entrepreneurship teachers contribute to the development of students' innovation capacities? On the other hand, what are the factors that promote or hinder the adoption of these teaching methods? The results of this study reveal that entrepreneurship teachers tend to favor teaching methods that, despite their intentionality, fail to effectively stimulate students' innovation capacities. These methods mainly include project-based pedagogies focused on the development of business plans, testimonies from entrepreneurs, as well as theoretical discussions and debates, not to mention case studies. The development of students' innovation capacities therefore seems to transcend solely pedagogical concerns, also affecting broader institutional and educational dimensions. Indeed, factors such as the place of innovation in the national culture, the intrinsic limits of the educational system, the context and role of the university and the quality of the teaching act are all key elements to consider. These dimensions encompass the roles of teachers, students themselves and the duration of entrepreneurship training.

In view of these results, this research offers theoretical and practical implications.

Regarding the theoretical implications, this study makes several contributions to the literature on entrepreneurial education, highlighting the link between pedagogical methodologies and the development of innovation capacities. On the one hand, it refines the conceptual framework of entrepreneurial education by emphasizing the importance of an integrative approach that combines pedagogies focused on creativity, entrepreneurship, general skills and modern technologies. On the other hand, it broadens the understanding of the role of pedagogical methods by demonstrating that innovation is not based solely on the acquisition of technical skills, but also on the adoption of active learning strategies, such as project-based learning, case studies and simulations.

Furthermore, the study highlights the need for an articulation between pedagogical practices and the socio-economic environment, emphasizing that entrepreneurial education must be adapted to local institutional and economic dynamics in order to optimize its impact on the entrepreneurial ecosystem. In addition, it enriches the scientific debate by identifying the obstacles to pedagogical innovation, including resistance to change, lack of resources and institutional rigidity, while opening up perspectives on ways to overcome them. Finally, by proposing a framework for assessing innovative skills, this research makes it possible to analyze the impact of different pedagogical approaches on students and to adapt training programs accordingly, thus contributing to the continuous improvement of entrepreneurship teaching systems.

For practical implications, they are useful for various actors, including decision-makers in education systems, university managers, teachers, and recruiters of university graduates. For example, education stakeholders could draw inspiration from them to design pedagogical strategies aimed at unleashing the creative and innovative potential of young students (Kuratko, 2020; Goh et al., 2021). For their part, teachers will be better able to adapt their strategies to foster pedagogical innovation in higher education (Morris et al., 2019; Garcia et al., 2020). Business leaders looking to recruit innovative graduates could also draw valuable lessons on the skills to look for in their future employees. It would thus be possible to understand, in the Tunisian context, the teaching methods likely to foster greater creativity and innovation among a certain population of students (Huang et al., 2021; Iakovleva et al., 2020).

However, while this research has interesting practical implications, it also suffers from some limitations that open the way for future research. Indeed, this study is exploratory in nature and is limited to a few universities and a single discipline, that of entrepreneurship education. Thus, the results obtained represent only a fragment of reality and their generalization requires more in-depth studies.

Furthermore, the use of semi-structured interviews presents potential biases, particularly in terms of social desirability and understanding of the questions and concepts used, which can influence the responses provided by participants (Flick, 2018; Creswell and Poth, 2018). These observations highlight the need for further research on the impact of pedagogical methods in entrepreneurship, taking into account different contextual and cultural variables, as well as diverse student profiles. Thus, future studies could further explore the interaction between pedagogical innovation and institutional dynamics, thus contributing to enriching the debate on entrepreneurship education in developing countries (Dana, 2020; Chigunta, 2017).

REFERENCES

Al-Samarraie, H., & Hurmuzan, S. (2018). A review of brainstorming techniques in higher education. *Thinking Skills and Creativity*, *27*, 78–91.

Bae, T. J., Qian, S., Miao, C., & Fiet, J. O. (2014). The relationship between entrepreneurship education and entrepreneurial intentions: A meta-analytic review. *Entrepreneurship Theory and Practice*, *38*(2), 217–254.

Bagheri, A., Lope Pihie, Z. A., & Krauss, S. E. (2017). Entrepreneurial leadership competencies among Malaysian university students: The pervasive effect of social support. *Asian Academy of Management Journal*, *22*(1), 79–101.

Baker, S. D. (2020). The role of soft skills in employability: A systematic review. *Journal of Education and Work*, *33*(6), 617–634.

Beckman, S. L., & Barry, M. (2020). Innovation and entrepreneurship education: A multidisciplinary approach. *Journal of Entrepreneurship Education*, *23*(4), 1–12.

Beghetto, R. A., & Kaufman, J. C. (2010). *Nurturing Creativity in the Classroom*. Cambridge University Press.

Bessant, J., & Tidd, J. (2019). *Managing Innovation: Integrating Technological, Market and Organizational Change*. John Wiley & Sons.

Blauth, M., Sinha, D., & Schmidt, C. (2019). Socio-economic background and entrepreneurial intentions: Evidence from a developing country. *Journal of Business Research*, *105*, 342–354.

Burkhardt, J. M., & Lubart, T. I. (2010). *Creativity and Innovation in Education: Theory, Research, and Practice*. Routledge.

Cabrera, D., & Cabrera, L. (2023). What is systems thinking? In *Learning, design, and technology: An international compendium of theory, research, practice, and policy* (pp. 1495–1522). Springer International Publishing.

Chege, S. M., Wang, D., & Suntu, S. L. (2020). Impact of information technology innovation on firm performance in Kenya. *Information Technology for Development*, *26*(2), 316–345.

Chigunta, F. (2017). Entrepreneurship as a possible solution to youth unemployment in Africa. Labour Market Institutions and Economic Outcomes in Africa, 433-451.

Creswell, J. W., & Poth, C. N. (2018). *Qualitative Inquiry and Research Design: Choosing Among Five Approaches*. Sage Publications.

Crossan, M. M., & Apaydin, M. (2010). A Multi-Dimensional Framework of Organizational Innovation: A Systematic Review of the Literature. *Journal of Management Studies*, *47*(6), 1154–1191.

Dana, L. P. (2020). *Entrepreneurship in developing countries*. Routledge.

Darling-Hammond, L., Hyler, M. E., & Gardner, M. (2017). *Effective teacher professional development*. Learning Policy Institute.

De Villiers Scheepers, M. (2015). Creative problem-solving in management education. *Management in Education, 15*(2), 101–115.

Dede, C. (2010). *Comparing frameworks for 21st century skills. In 21st Century Skills*. Rethinking How Students Learn.

Dewettinck, K., Van De Walle, J., & Galle, D. (2021). Active learning in higher education: Exploring the role of instructor and student engagement. *Teaching in Higher Education, 26*(3), 291–308.

Edoho, F. M. (2015). Entrepreneurship paradigm in the new millennium: A critique of public policy on entrepreneurship. *Journal of Educational Leadership, 15*(3), 27–39.

Fayolle, A., & Gailly, B. (2015). The impact of entrepreneurship education on entrepreneurial attitudes and intention: Hysteresis and persistence. *Journal of Small Business Management, 53*(1), 16–30.

Filteau, M. (2012). La créativité: Un processus complexe. *Review of Psychology, 42*(2), 73–85.

Flick, U. (2018). *An Introduction to Qualitative Research.* Sage Publications.

Fullan, M. (2010). *The Moral Imperative of School Leadership*. SAGE Publications.

Gajda, A., Karwowski, M., & Beghetto, R. A. (2017). Creativity and academic achievement: A meta-analysis. *Journal of Educational Psychology, 109*(2), 269.

Garcia, M. E., Guerrero, C. A., & Pérez, S. (2020). Enhancing innovative capacities in higher education: The importance of collaboration. *Innovation (Abingdon), 33*(3), 301–314.

Garnett, F., & O'Beirne, R. (2019). Digital Skills for Educators: Enhancing Technology Use in Teaching. *Educational Technology Research and Development, 67*(2), 207–221.

Gbadegeshin, S. A. (2017). Commercialization process of high technology: A study of Finnish University Spin-off. *Academy of Entrepreneurship Journal, 23*(2), 1–22.

Goh, Y. M., Lim, Y. T., & Ooi, K. B. (2021). Exploring the entrepreneurial intentions of university students: A comparative study between two Asian countries. *Asian Journal of Technology Innovation, 29*(1), 1–16.

Gonzalez, E., Rodriguez, M., & Martinez, A. (2020). The impact of entrepreneurial education on students' innovation skills: An analysis of the Spanish case. *Journal of Business Research, 118*, 63–71.

Guerrero, M., Urbano, D., Fayolle, A., Klofsten, M., & Mian, S. (2016). Entrepreneurial universities: Emerging models in the new social and economic landscape. *Small Business Economics, 47*(3), 551–563.

Guilford, J. P. (1950). Creativity. *The American Psychologist, 5*(9), 444–454. PMID: 14771441

Gül, H.. (2023). The impact of project-based learning on creative thinking skills: A meta-analysis. *Educational Research Review, 34*, 100405.

Hägg, G., & Gabrielsson, J. (2019). Entrepreneurial learning in practice: The role of narrative in the development of entrepreneurial competencies. *International Journal of Entrepreneurial Behaviour & Research, 25*(3), 478–498.

Hall, J. K., Matos, S., Sheehan, L., & Silvestre, B. S. (2013). Entrepreneurship and Innovation at the Base of the Pyramid: A Recipe for Inclusive Growth or Social Exclusion? *Journal of Management Studies*, *49*(4), 785–812.

Hennessey, B. A., & Amabile, T. M. (2010). Creativity. *Annual Review of Psychology*, *61*, 569–598. PMID: 19575609

Huang, C. (2021). The effects of experiential learning on creativity: A study of higher education. *Journal of Education and Training Studies*, *9*(1), 43–52.

Huang-Saad, A., Fay, J., & Sheridan, L. (2017). Closing the divide: Accelerating technology commercialization by catalyzing the university entrepreneurial ecosystem with I-Corps™. *The Journal of Technology Transfer*, *42*(6), 1466–1486.

Iakovleva, T., Kolvereid, L., & Stephan, U. (2020). Entrepreneurship and education in emerging economies. *Journal of Developmental Entrepreneurship*, *25*(4), 2050027.

Isaksen, S. G., & Ekvall, G. (2010). Managing for innovation: The importance of culture. *International Journal of Technology Management*, *51*(1/2), 112–130.

Kaufman, J. C., Beghetto, R. A., & Roberts, A. M. (2022). Creativity in the schools: Creativity models and new directions. In *Handbook of positive psychology in schools* (pp. 335–345). Routledge.

Kelley, D. J., & Thomas, B. (2011). *Entrepreneurship education: Learning by doing*. Edward Elgar Publishing.

Kleibeuker, S. W., De Dreu, C. K. W., & Crone, E. A. (2016). The role of cognitive flexibility in creative thinking: Evidence from a multi-method approach. *Psychological Science*, *27*(3), 366–373.

Klofsten, M., Urbano, D., & Heaton, S. (2019). Developing entrepreneurial competencies through education. *Journal of Small Business Management*, *57*(S2), 500–513.

Kovid, R. K., Rana, S., & Omrane, A. (2022). The promise of entrepreneurship and innovation as a strategic response to global turmoils. *FIIB Business Review*, *11*(1), 7–10.

Krauss, J., Reschke, C., & Hartmann, C. (2020). The role of self-efficacy in entrepreneurship education: Evidence from Germany. *Education + Training*, *62*(4), 455–473.

Kumar, S., & Gupta, S. (2021). The impact of digital skills on innovation: A study of small and medium-sized enterprises. *Journal of Small Business Management*, *59*(1), 142–165.

Kuratko, D. F. (2020). *Entrepreneurship: Theory, Process, and Practice*. Cengage Learning.

Levie, J. (2014). Entrepreneurial innovation: The importance of narratives in the commercialization of technology. *Journal of Business Research*, *67*(8), 1644–1650.

Lichtenstein, B. M., & Brush, C. (2019). How entrepreneurship education shapes students' attitudes towards risk and uncertainty. *Entrepreneurship Theory and Practice*, *43*(3), 511–534.

Liguori, E., & Winkler, C. (2020). From offline to online: Challenges and opportunities for entrepreneurship education following the COVID-19 pandemic. *Entrepreneurship Education and Pedagogy, 3*(4), 346–351.

Lubart, T. I., Zenasni, F., Barbot, B., & Botella, M. (2015). *The Creativity Maze: Implications for Teaching and Learning*. Creativity and Learning: A Theoretical Perspective, 17(4), 307-320.

MacDermott, C., & Ortiz, L. (2017). Beyond the business communication course: A historical perspective of the where, why, and how of soft skills development and job readiness for business graduates. *The IUP Journal of Soft Skills, 11*(2), 7–24.

Mansour, S., Mkhize, N., & Alam, S. (2021). Innovative pedagogies: The role of active learning in higher education. *International Journal of Educational Management, 35*(3), 569–586.

Maritz, A., & Brown, C. (2013). Enhancing Entrepreneurial Self-Efficacy and Learning Orientation: A Regional Australian Perspective. *Education + Training, 55*(6), 552–574.

Maxwell, J. A. (2021). Why qualitative methods are necessary for generalization. *Qualitative Psychology, 8*(1), 111.

Mishra, C., & Zachary, R. K. (2015). *The theory of entrepreneurship: Creating and sustaining entrepreneurial value*. Palgrave Macmillan.

Mitchell, T. R. (2021). Expectancy-value models in organizational psychology. In *Expectations and actions* (pp. 293–312). Routledge.

Morris, M. H., Kuratko, D. F., & Cornwall, J. R. (2019). Entrepreneurship Programs and the Development of Entrepreneurial Skills: An Exploration of the Student Experience. *The International Entrepreneurship and Management Journal, 15*(4), 1193–1216.

Mosyjowski, E. A., & Seifert, C. M. (2014). Integrating problem-solving methods in project-based learning. *International Journal of Educational Research, 64*, 53–61.

Mwasalwiba, E. S. (2010). Entrepreneurship education: A review of its objectives, teaching methods, and impact indicators. *Education + Training, 52*(1), 20–47.

Nabi, G., Holden, R., & Walmsley, A. (2019). The role of entrepreneurial education in fostering innovation. *International Journal of Entrepreneurial Behaviour & Research, 25*(2), 251–270.

Ndou, V., Mele, G., & Del Vecchio, P. (2018). Entrepreneurship education and entrepreneurial intention: The role of information exposure and knowledge acquisition. *Journal of Business Research, 94*, 209–221.

Nelson, R. R., & Monsen, E. (2014). The role of research in the commercialization of technology. *Research Policy, 43*(7), 1132–1143.

Nishikawa, K. (2021). The role of soft skills in enhancing team performance: A case study of Japanese companies. *Journal of Business Research, 124*, 233–243.

Panadero, E., Jonsson, A., & Botella, J. (2019). Effects of Self-Assessment on Self-Regulated Learning and Self-Efficacy: Four Meta-Analyses. *Educational Research Review, 28*, 100284.

Phan, P. H. (2014). The commercialization of technology: A review and future directions. *Research Policy, 43*(6), 1138–1149.

Rae, D. (2018). Entrepreneurial learning: A conceptual framework for the development of graduate entrepreneurship. *International Journal of Entrepreneurial Behaviour & Research, 24*(3), 724–744.

Rajapathirana, R. J., & Hui, Y. (2018). Relationship between innovation capability, innovation type, and firm performance. *Journal of Innovation & Knowledge, 3*(1), 44–55.

Rampersad, H., Ho, J., & Van der Meer, H. (2010). The role of pre-tests in qualitative research. *International Journal of Business Research, 10*(3), 130–138.

Ratten, V. (2020). Entrepreneurial Leadership and VUCA Management: Competencies for Creativity and Innovation. *Creativity and Innovation Management, 29*(2), 184–194.

Rideout, E. C., & Gray, D. O. (2013). Does entrepreneurship education really work? A review and methodological critique of the empirical literature on the effects of university-based entrepreneurship education. *Journal of Small Business Management, 51*(3), 329–351.

Salas, E. (2018). The power of teamwork: Building effective teams in organizations. *Organizational Psychology Review, 8*(2), 78–102.

Selznick, P., & Mayhew, L. (2018). Innovation in Higher Education: A Critical Perspective. *Journal of Higher Education Policy and Management, 40*(1), 1–15.

Simonton, D. K. (2018). Creative Genius: A Trait Theoretical and Multivariate Perspective. *Personality and Social Psychology Review, 22*(3), 218–240.

Smirnov, I., Tsvetkova, N., & Borisova, L. (2023). Innovation-driven entrepreneurship education: New strategies for success. *International Journal of Educational Research, 113*, 101965.

Sternberg, R. J., & Lubart, T. I. (2019). Developing a model for creativity. *The Cambridge Handbook of Creativity*, 2, 3-15.

Succi, C., & Canovi, M. (2020). Soft skills to enhance graduate employability: Comparing students and employers' perceptions. *Studies in Higher Education, 45*(9), 1834–1847.

Tardif, M. (2019). L'innovation pédagogique: Un levier pour la réussite des étudiants. *Revue internationale d'éducation*, 50(1), 55-73.

Thompson, P. (2018). Developing entrepreneurial attitudes in the classroom: The role of entrepreneurship education. *Journal of Education and Work, 31*(1), 27–40.

Urban, B., & Silva, M. (2019). The Influence of Creativity and Innovation on Entrepreneurial Intention. *International Journal of Entrepreneurial Behaviour & Research, 25*(4), 724–746.

Urbano, D., Aparicio, S., & Audretsch, D. B. (2019). Twenty-five years of research on institutions, entrepreneurship, and economic growth: What has been learned? *Small Business Economics, 53*(1), 21–49.

Van Zanten, A., & Rayou, P. (2017). *Dictionnaire de l'éducation.* Presses universitaires de France.

Vroom, V. H. (1964). *Work and motivation.* Wiley.

Walter, S. G., Parboteeah, K. P., & Walter, A. (2019). The role of culture and context in the relationship between entrepreneurship education and entrepreneurial intention. *Journal of Small Business Management, 57*(S1), 126–144.

Wang, C. L., Chugh, H., & Malik, M. (2020). Entrepreneurship education and intention: A systematic review of the literature. *Journal of Small Business Management, 58*(2), 343–367.

Wang, L., & Zhang, H. (2021). Leveraging experiential learning in higher education: The role of technology in shaping student outcomes. *International Journal of Educational Management, 35*(2), 285–299.

Yin, R. K. (2018). *Case Study Research and Applications: Design and Methods*. Sage Publications.

Zhang, J., Wang, C., & Zhao, H. (2021). Fostering entrepreneurial mindsets in higher education: A systematic review. *Journal of Entrepreneurship Education, 24*(1), 1–15.

Ziegler, R. (2022). Integrating technology and entrepreneurship: The role of higher education institutions. *Journal of Entrepreneurship Education, 25*(1), 1–20.

Chapter 14
Entrepreneurial Ecosystems in a Virtual World:
Simulation Tools and Economic Education

Christos N. Christodoulou-Volos
https://orcid.org/0000-0002-3188-844X
Neapolis University, Pafos, Cyprus

ABSTRACT

This chapter discusses the nexus between entrepreneurship education, economic theory, and the increasing application of simulation tools to improve learning outcomes. The evolving trends in entrepreneurship education, and the increasingly important role of an "experiential approach" to learning, are discussed at the outset. Next, the conceptual underpinning of entrepreneurial ecosystems and core economic concepts germane to entrepreneurship are revisited. Various types of simulation tools are discussed, including business and economic simulators, with a focus on those that are capable of simulating realistic, actual economic scenarios. This chapter describes how such a tool can help narrow the gap between theory and practice in enhancing economic literacy and decision-making among students. It finally concludes by focusing on some of the challenges and opportunities related to the integration of simulation tools within educational settings and then provides recommendations to educators and policymakers on how to enhance entrepreneurship education using innovative technologies.

1. INTRODUCTION

1.1. The Evolution of Entrepreneurship Education

Entrepreneurship education has undergone several changes over the last couple of decades. In traditional entrepreneurship teaching, theoretical lectures, case studies, and visitor guest speakers occasionally shared practical experiences about their businesses (Fiet, 2001). The traditional approach to teaching focused primarily on the foundational aspects of starting and managing a venture: business plans, interpreting financial statements, and strategies for marketing (Mankiw, 2024). While these remain imperative, the

DOI: 10.4018/979-8-3693-9040-5.ch014

dynamically changing economy of the world and the complex nature of business places have brought people to adopt more applied and experiential ways of learning (Kolb, 1984).

Rapid technological advancement and the continuous evolution of marketplace demands have drastically changed the face of entrepreneurship education in the 21st century (Blank, 2013). The modern educator increasingly perceives the limitation of traditional teaching techniques for the students to take up the challenges as entrepreneurs. There has, therefore, been a high onslaught towards experiential learning: an approach in pedagogy in which learners are engaged in direct experiences connected with the real world, to deepen the learning process regarding the entrepreneurial process (Gentry, 1990; Kolb, 1984).

The activities involved in the experiential learning process within entrepreneurship education encompass a wide array of exposures to internships, live projects, and simulations (Salas, Wildman, & Piccolo, 2009). Such methods are designed to immerse students in entrepreneurial experience so that students can experiment with ideas, learn from failures, and develop critical problem-solving skills (Dewey, 1938; Sarasvathy, 2001). Of these, the simulation tools have emerged as one of the most potent resources by providing students with a virtual environment in which to implement their business ideas and make strategic decisions while observing the result without real-world consequences of failure.

1.2. The Emergence and Growth of Simulation Tools in Education

Even though simulation tools have been discussed in the literature for several decades, their application to entrepreneurship education has been a consideration of substantial recent interest (Bloom, 2019; Salas, Wildman, & Piccolo, 2009) (Bloom, 2019; Salas, Wildman, & Piccolo, 2009). Simulation tools, which were developed originally for military and engineering training, evolved to serve other general educational purposes such as business and economics (Aldrich, 2004). Simulation tools include some of the most recent and up-to-date technological advancements, such as artificial intelligence, machine learning, and virtual reality, to visualize and create interactive, immersive learning environments (Bloom, 2019).

In entrepreneurship education, simulation tools can be viewed as virtual laboratories in which students can test themselves in complex enterprise situations or economic environments (Salas et al., 2009). Simulations allow students to experience real dynamic decision-making processes, not static case studies or abstract exercises that often occur in the classroom. Students may try various strategies, observe what happens due to their actions, and redo their ideas in the light of feedback that may be obtained from the simulation (Aldrich, 2004; Sarasvathy, 2001).

A number of reasons can be ascribed to the growth of simulation tools in entrepreneurship education. In the first instance, advances in technology make access to such facilities easier for educational institutions. Many of these simulation platforms are online; they have scalable solutions that can be tailored according to different course and program needs (Bloom, 2019). Second, there is an emerging awareness of the kind of preparation that each student needs in a world replete with unimagined perils and complexities. Simulation tools let students make mistakes in a zone of safety, practicing resilience and developing the set of skills needed to deal with the challenges entrepreneurship will bring (Gentry, 1990).

In addition, simulation tools today are even more sophisticated and realistic. Early business simulations were often narrow in scope and may have focused on simple management activities or making financial decisions. Today, on the other hand, it is possible to model an entire entrepreneurial ecosystem, taking into consideration market dynamics, competition, consumer behavior, and even macroeconomic trends (Bloom, 2019; Teece, 2010). This progress enables students to contemplate the whole process of entrepreneurship with a comprehensive gaze, together with the economic environment in which enterprises function.

1.3. The Intersection of Economics, Entrepreneurship, and Simulations

Economics thus becomes one of the critical determinants of entrepreneurship, since it undergirds the theoretical basis and framework within which market behavior, resource allocation, and growth are analyzed (Casson, 1982; Mankiw, 2024). However, over the years, the attempts at teaching economic principles to entrepreneurship students have not always been easy. Students often cannot appreciate how abstract economic concepts - supply and demand, market structures, or risk management - operate in the real world when these concepts are presented in a vacuum (Mankiw, 2024).

Simulation tools solve this problem in their own peculiar way because they actually bridge economic theory and the practical means of entrepreneurship. In simulations, the student gets to see how economic principles work in real-time in a controlled environment (Aldrich, 2004; Bloom, 2019). For example, students might participate in a simulation whereby they would have an opportunity to conduct their virtual business: set prices according to supply and demand, compete with others, or manage risks from market volatility (Salas, Wildman, & Piccolo, 2009). In fact, such reflection will provide students with a better understanding of how economic forces shape business outcomes and how they can make use of economic reasoning in making entrepreneurial decisions (Kolb, 1984).

The intersection of economics, entrepreneurship, and simulations holds special relevance to the entrepreneurial ecosystem. An entrepreneurial ecosystem refers to all interconnected entities that jointly influence the innovative and economic activities of entrepreneurs, investors, customers, and institutions (Davidsson, 2004; Shane, 2003). These are economies that deep-rooted call for knowledge of economic principles, coupled with the understanding of entrepreneurial dynamics. Such complex ecosystems will be modeled using simulation tools; students will be allowed to explore the interactions between the different actors, test their way forward in navigating the ecosystem, and understand the wider economic implications of their decisions (Teece, 2010; Wiklund, Patzelt, & Shepherd, 2009).

1.4. Objectives and Structure of the Chapter

The main purpose of this chapter is to discuss how simulation tools might be integrated into entrepreneurship education, focusing in particular on their connection with economics and the entrepreneurial ecosystem at large. This chapter, through an investigation of simulations for economic literacy and enhancement of entrepreneurial skills, aims to provide educators, students, and policymakers with a review of the many benefits and challenges brought about by this innovative approach to teaching.

This chapter aims to discuss how simulation tools could be integrated into entrepreneurship education, giving particular emphasis to their relationship with economics and the entrepreneurial ecosystem as a whole. The present chapter seeks to give educators, students, and policymakers an overview of the benefits and challenges this innovative teaching approach has brought forth by examining simulations for economic literacy and enhancement of entrepreneurial skills.

Structure of the chapter:

Section 2: Theoretical Underpinning - The section covers areas including entrepreneurial ecosystems and critical economic theories that underlie entrepreneurship. It thus provides a theoretical background relevant to conceptualizing the role of economics in entrepreneurship education.
Section 3: Simulation tools in entrepreneurship education - An overview of the various types developed and applied to teach entrepreneurship will be given, which includes business and economic simulations that would be useful to apply in real life for teaching enterprise skills.
Section 4: Embedding Economic Theories into Simulation-Based Learning Different methods and ways to embed theories in entrepreneurship simulations are included, together with a few case studies related to successful integration and best practices for educators.
Section 5: Impact on Students and Learning Outcomes: This section shall discuss how the use of simulation tools influenced students to have a better understanding of economic concepts, preparedness for actual business challenges, and enhance learning outcomes by using examples and samples from effective educators and testimony by the students themselves.
Section 6: Challenges and Opportunities -This section discusses various challenges with respect to the integration of simulation tools into entrepreneurship education and highlights opportunities for further development and innovation in this area.
Section 7: Conclusion - The last section summarizes the key messages of this chapter, discusses the implications for educators and policymakers, and provides directions for further research.

More importantly, after going through this chapter, the reader will know how simulation tools can revolutionize entrepreneurship education by bringing together different economic theories in ways that better prepare students for the challenges they face in real-world business.

2. Theoretical Foundations

2.1. Understanding Entrepreneurial Ecosystems

Entrepreneurial Ecosystems are interconnected, intricate networks of both actors and elements that facilitate innovation, new venture creation, and parallel economic growth (Davidsson, 2004; Shane, 2003; Wiklund, Patzelt, & Shepherd, 2009). Entities comprising the critical mass in such an ecosystem are entrepreneurs themselves, investors, mentors, academic institutions, government agencies, and support organizations like incubators and accelerators (Mitchell et al., 2002). Each is important in its own regard to foster entrepreneurship and create an enabling environment within which businesses thrive (Teece, 2010).

Recently, the entrepreneurial ecosystems idea has been popularized because scholars and policymakers have increasingly appreciated its holistic approach toward entrepreneurship (Shane, 2003). With this particular approach, the ecosystem view differs from the traditional views of entrepreneurship as an isolated activity driven solely by individual entrepreneurs. From the entrepreneurial ecosystem perspective, inter-relationships among multiple factors influencing entrepreneurial success are underlined (Davidsson, 2004). This perspective also converges with the broad economic view that no markets or industries exist in isolation; rather, they are part of a wide array of social, political, and economic forces (Casson, 1982).

Key Elements of Entrepreneurial Ecosystems:

i. Entrepreneurs: The main actors of this environment, composed of entrepreneurs, act as agents in the discovery of opportunities, risk-taking, and the start of new businesses. They introduce novelty into this environment; hence, driving innovation and economic growth in this system is always an affair of the entrepreneurs (Schumpeter, 1942; Kirzner, 1973.

ii. **Investors**: The stakeholders have included venture capitalists, angel investors, and other financial institutions that invest capital into company growth. Besides providing the financial element to catalyze the entrepreneurial process, investors provide strategic advice and valuable networks which their protégés benefit from greatly (Wilson, Kickul, & Marlino, 2007).

iii. Enabling Organizations: This includes incubators, accelerators, and coworking spaces that provide resources, mentorship, and physical infrastructures needed to build and scale a startup company. Support organizations are an important way to decrease barriers for new entrepreneurs (Gentry, 1990).

iv. Academic Institutions: These are those universities and research centers that help in the development of an ecosystem through knowledge creation, talent nurturing, and innovation through R&D, and provide required skills to would-be entrepreneurs through different educational and training programs (Fiet, 2001).

v. Government Agencies: Government agencies, through their policies, regulations, and incentives, either further or hinder the entrepreneurial ecosystems. Whereas favorable government policies may provide a propitious climate for startups, inhibitive regulations choke innovation (Porter, 1980).

vi. Markets: The extent of the local and global markets is quite a serious aspect when it comes to building up any kind of startup. Access to the market would determine the scope for earning revenues and expansion (Mankiw, 2024).

vii. Culture: The cultural environment, too, affects the ecosystem, with societal attitudes toward entrepreneurship, risk, and failure. Innovation is praised in an accepting culture of failure that encourages people to pursue entrepreneurial ventures (Schumpeter, 1942).

Dynamics of Entrepreneurial Ecosystems

Entrepreneurial ecosystems are never static; they are part of a constant motion and evolution (Wiklund et al., 2009). The ongoing interaction of the different components feeds into a self-reinforcing feedback loop, which acts on the health and vibrancy of the ecosystem as a whole. The successful entrepreneurs reinvest the profits into another venture, which may be a startup business, but it also involves investors and mentors for the next wave (Zimmerman & Zeitz, 2002). This is the "virtuous circle" when more cycles of reinvestment and knowledge transfer occur over time, the stronger the ecosystem gets.

Moreover, high-growth start-ups entail such strength in the ecosystem, as they are considered to provide strength to the driving forces of economic development (Teece, 2010). High-growth start-ups-sometimes referred to as "scale-ups" are actually those business entities that hold promises of providing greater economic impact through job creation, innovation, and enhanced factor productivity. These kinds of emerging business firms would get overall ecosystem support by availing resources, networks, and opportunities as required for their overall growth (Salas, Wildman, & Piccolo, 2009).

The complexity and interdependence in which entrepreneurial ecosystems exist are important to understand for educators and students alike (Gentry, 1990). It puts into perspective the relevance of not only the individual entrepreneurs themselves but the greater environment that bounds them. This perspective should go a long way in developing entrepreneurship education programs adequate for such ecosystems (Bloom, 2019).

2.2. Core Economic Theories Relevant to Entrepreneurship

Entrepreneurship and economics are interconnected; economic theory provides the instruments and models necessary to understand the market environment, make informed decisions, and assess risks and opportunities (Casson, 1982; Mankiw, 2024). Among various economic theories touching base with entrepreneurship, a number of key concepts are of real importance to budding entrepreneurs.

2.2.1. Supply and Demand

Supply and demand are basic concepts in economics that explain how prices and quantities of goods and services are determined in the market (Mankiw, 2024). The concept of supply and demand is important for an entrepreneur because of the following:

Pricing strategy: This means being able to rightly price products or services based on the relationship between supply and demand. A very high price decreases demand, and too low a price makes it impossible to cover the profits (Mankiw, 2024).
Market Entry: Market entry also helps an entrepreneur discover market opportunities and analyze the feasibility of market entry from the demand and supply perspective.
Resource Allocation: The entrepreneur has to plan his resources effectively against the anticipated demand. An overestimation leads to unused stock; an underestimation leads to the loss of a sale (Porter, 1980).

More educationally, the simulations of supply-and-demand equilibrium can be reproduced and thus provide opportunities for students to reflect on pricing policies, assess dynamics of responses in the marketplace, and, importantly, identify how exogenous factors such as competition and consumer preference can affect these dynamics (Bloom, 2019).

2.2.2. Market Structures

Market structure refers to the organization of a market, mainly based on the number of firms competing in a market and the nature of the competition. The following are the main types of market structures:

Perfect Competition: Numerous firms compete in producing homogeneous products, with no one firm having the power to influence the price of the market (Mankiw, 2024).
Monopoly: A market structure in which there is only one firm, and it controls total supply and has the right to fix prices (Porter, 1980).
Oligopoly: It is a form of market organization where there are a few firms whose individual actions must be strongly considered by the other competing firms (Teece, 2010).
Monopolistic Competition: A market structure containing a large number of firms selling differentiated products, but each individual firm has partial control over the price of its product (Mankiw, 2024).

Understanding market structures is important to the entrepreneur because it impacts his pricing power, the competitive strategies open to him, and his possible profitability (Teece, 2010). Simulations that model various market structures allow students to examine how their businesses would fare under different competitive conditions, thus preparing them for real-world market dynamics (Salas, Wildman, & Piccolo, 2009).

2.2.3. Innovation and Economic Growth

Perhaps no driving force has been as important to economic growth as innovation, and in practice, much of that innovation is pushed forward into the market through entrepreneurial activity with new products, services, and technologies (Schumpeter, 1942). Most economic theories, be it Schumpeter's "creative destruction" and others, express how innovation disbands existing markets and invents new industries. Innovating entrepreneurs can realize advantages over rivals in the competitive arena, capture market share, and hence contribute to general economic growth (Schumpeter, 1942).

Students in educational simulations can try out innovation-driven strategies, such as product differentiation or technological advancement, and learn how those affect market share, profitability, and the long-term success of the business (Kirzner, 1973; Shane, 2003). The results from such exercises help foster an understanding of the interrelationship between innovation and competition in relation to economic growth.

In fact, innovation can be considered one of the driving forces of economic growth whereby entrepreneurs create and bring new goods into the marketplace, as well as new services and technologies. A number of economic theories describe how innovation disrupts existing markets and opens up new industries. For example, Schumpeter's is called "creative destruction." Innovative entrepreneurs can develop competitive advantages capable of securing market share and having a positive effect on overall economic growth.

In educational simulations, students can try a number of innovation-driven strategies in a struggle for a higher share of a market, greater profitability, and long-term business success (Bloom, 2019). This kind of exercise helps students to contextualize the role of innovation and competition in economic growth.

2.2.4. Risk and Uncertainty in Economics

Any entrepreneurial activity is wrapped in risk and uncertainty. Various tools have been developed by economic theory to understand and manage those risks (Casson, 1982). For example,

- Expected Utility Theory: Helps an entrepreneur to decide uncertainty by considering the expected outcomes with their associated probabilities (McKeown, 2012).
- Portfolio Theory: Helps entrepreneurs to diversify their investments in order to reduce the risk of the sum of their investments (McKeown, 2012).
- Real Options Theory: Entitles the entrepreneur with the capability to value flexibility in making decisions at a later stage; for example, scaling up or abandoning a project depending upon prevailing market conditions (Teece, 2010).

Mastering these tools is of prime importance for the entrepreneur because he normally works in a scenario of high uncertainty. Simulation tools can easily mimic situations where students make decisions under uncertainty, evaluate risks, and come up with strategies to reduce those risks (Salas et al., 2009).

2.3. The Role of Economic Education in Shaping Entrepreneurs

Of course, the most significant elements to be included in entrepreneurship education would be those on economic literacy. If entrepreneurs understand how economics works, they will make far more pragmatic decisions and forecast the macro trends likely to harm or benefit their businesses (Casson, 1982; Mankiw, 2024). Traditional economics teaching in entrepreneurship courses typically involves lecturing, reading, and case analysis. While such methods help form the base level of understanding, they have limitations in conveying the dynamic and applied nature of entrepreneurship (Fiet, 2001).

Simulation-based learning creates an active and practical approach to learning economics in entrepreneurship. Such tools will take the student in a hands-on experience in the simulated business environment where real-time economic theories can be applied, strategies tried out, and results of decisions tested (Aldrich, 2004; Bloom, 2019). This process makes the concept of economics flow within the student-internalize to bring out the critical thinking skills, the most in-demand ingredient in entrepreneurs (Kolb, 1984).

Additionally, simulation-based economic education can make students aware of the spillover effect their entrepreneurial activities would cause in the economy at large. They might reason, for example, how business decisions involving themselves as entrepreneurs could affect supply chains, employment, and economic growth within a virtual economy (Davidsson, 2004; Shane, 2003). In other words, it is this holistic understanding - that of how economics interfaces with entrepreneurship - that is needed if responsible and effective entrepreneurship is to be brought forth (Teece, 2010).

In other words, the inclusion of economic theories in entrepreneurship studies via simulation tools offers a more holistic and applied learning experience. The student is thus better equipped to face the complex dynamic world of entrepreneurship, where a certain degree of economic literacy is no longer an advantage but a given (Salas, Wildman, & Piccolo, 2009).

3. SIMULATION TOOLS IN ENTREPRENEURSHIP EDUCATION

3.1. Overview of Simulation Tools

Simulation tools have become a huge part of modern education, where fields involve practical applications of complex theories that need a totally requisite skill in solving real-world problems (Aldrich, 2004; Salas, Wildman, & Piccolo, 2009). In entrepreneurship education, this tool makes for an interactive bridge between the theoretical knowledge in a classroom and the practical experience. This will be useful in the simulation of real-life business situations wherein the learners can perform decision-making processes, and strategies testing, and learn the outcomes of such moves within a controlled environment (Bloom, 2019).

The two major classes into which the entrepreneurship simulation tool may be divided include business simulation and economic simulation. Both kinds of simulation have a complementary role in the education of a future entrepreneur. Business simulations provide an operational and strategic perspective on how to conduct business (Salas et al., 2009), while economic simulations focus on the general economic environment in which businesses operate (Mankiw, 2024).

Characteristics of Simulation Tools:

- Interactivity: These simulation tools are interactive. Within that virtual environment, students can make decisions and immediately see the result of those decisions (Aldrich, 2004).
- Realism: The most sophisticated simulation tools will deploy real data and real scenarios to ensure realism as close as possible to actual business conditions (Bloom, 2019).
- Operating Feedback Mechanism: The simulation provides feedback in real-time, so the student learns from their mistakes and has the possibility to change their strategy quite fast (Kolb, 1984).
- Scalability: Most of the simulation tools are designed to be scalable; therefore, they can be tailored to a different level of complexity and will be suitable for both novice and advanced students (Salas et al., 2009).
- Collaborative Learning: Many simulation activities promote teamwork and collaboration, much like real-life entrepreneurship (Gentry, 1990).

These characteristics make the simulation tool a very valuable resource in entrepreneurship education since it assures the practical involvement of students alongside traditional ways of learning (Fiet, 2001).

3.2. Business Simulations

Business simulations are designed to simulate the problems and decision-making aspects that one encounters in running a business. They range from simple models, emphasizing basic functions of business, to very complex systems modeling entire industries or markets (Aldrich, 2004; Salas, Wildman, & Piccolo, 2009). They have been found very useful in making students understand business management, strategy, and operations in depth (Bloom, 2019).

3.2.1. Startup Simulators

The highest category of business simulations is the startup simulators, whereby the major factor concerns the early stages of business development. These kinds of tools allow students to develop experiences right from scratch: the generation of ideas, researching the market, planning a business, and its implementation (Sarasvathy, 2001). Some of the well-known startup simulators include:

- SimVenture: SimVenture was originally designed to teach the student how to start and then manage in fine detail a small business, including aspects like finance, marketing, operations, and human resource management (Salas et al., 2009).
- Lean LaunchPad: Lean LaunchPad is based on the lean startup methodology. The model focuses on rapid prototyping, customer feedback, and iterative development. It allows students to explore different business models and strategies without exposing actual businesses to risks (Blank, 2013).

In these simulators, students make critical decisions related to funding, marketing strategies, product development, and customer acquisition for their virtual businesses. This may vary in its potential business results because it is intended to simulate the business experience of being an entrepreneur to the fullest degree - so that students can learn from their successes as well as their failures (Kolb, 1984).

3.2.2. Market Simulators

Other categories of business simulation include market simulators, whereby this tool focuses on the dynamics that surround competition, markets, and consumer preference. This will give students an idea of how markets work and how businesses can put themselves forward for success in a competitive environment (Porter, 1980). An example of market simulators includes the following:

- Marketplace Simulations: This is a broad business simulation exercise encompassing virtually all business facets in a competitive environment. Students will be able to design products, set price levels, create and place advertisements, and distribute goods and services within the marketplace while competing against other teams (Teece, 2010).
- CAPSIM: CAPSIM does indeed allow a number of business simulations that teach market strategy, product development, and competitive analysis. Using this environment, the students get a feel for the pressures that competitors must face in their global market (Mankiw, 2024).

Market simulators enable students to gain a deeper understanding of how businesses interact with the market and of those external factors - economic trends, and consumer behavior - that weigh in on the decisions of a business (Shane, 2003). It is through these simulations that students will be able to put into practice the development of strategies that will give them a competitive advantage, optimize prices, and use resources effectively (Bloom, 2019).

3.3. Economic Simulations

While business simulations are about the operation of the individual business, economic simulations concern the larger economic environment (Mankiw, 2024). These models are called 'economic' because they represent a broader economic context; they help the student to understand the many interacting macroeconomic factors that impinge on businesses and indeed on the economy as a whole. With the economic simulations, students can better learn how government policy, foreign trade, and the economic cycles affect business (Casson, 1982; Mankiw, 2024).

3.3.1. Macroeconomic Models

The simulations of macroeconomics model the big forces that drive national and global economies (Mankiw, 2024). Students can enact a sequence of economic policy choices and observe the results through variables such as gross domestic product, inflation, unemployment, and trade balances (Schumpeter, 1942). The following are some examples of macroeconomic simulations:

- SimCity EDU: Traditionally a city-building video game, the contents of SimCity EDU can be wrung into teaching students urban economics, the management of resources, and the different impacts that economic policies have on city growth and development (Bloom, 2019).
- Econland: Econland is a macroeconomic simulation that students can use to manage a virtual economy. Students can make decisions on fiscal and monetary policies while observing the effects of such choices on economic indicators like GDP, unemployment, and inflation (Mankiw, 2024).

Simulation in macroeconomics allows students to view, for the first time, the big economic picture in which businesses operate: examine the relationships between government policies and the implications of those policies on business; and learn how overall economic trends and cycles influence entrepreneurial enterprises (Davidsson, 2004).

3.3.2. Microeconomic Simulations

Microeconomic simulations refer to those individual decisions made in the economy, including the price settings for commodities, consumer behavior, and allocation of means of production (Kirzner, 1973). The most interesting features of micro-economic simulations for teaching are those that generally involve market efficiency, competition, and scarce resource allocation (Mankiw, 2024). Examples of microeconomic simulations include:

- Lemonade Stand Game: This game is a classic microeconomic simulation that imparts knowledge in supply and demand, pricing, and inventory management through a simple scenario: running a lemonade stand (Schumpeter, 1942).
- Fishbanks: Fishbanks is a resource management simulation game through which students can learn ways to handle common-pool resources and also the concept of the tragedy of the commons. This activity will make the participants play the role of managing a fishing company by being concerned with profit without depleting the available resources and being as sustainable as possible (Ostrom, as cited in Teece, 2010).

Simulation in microeconomics allows students to explore how economic principles, put together with market forces, interact with individual business decisions (Porter, 1980). It is through this interaction that students develop a better understanding of how various microeconomic factors affect their businesses and how best to optimize strategies to realize maximum efficiency and profits (Teece, 2010).

3.4. Gamification in Economic and Entrepreneurial Education

Gamification is the incorporation of concepts and elements of game design into something that is essentially not a game but learning (Aldrich, 2004; Bloom, 2019). In the education of entrepreneurship and economics, gamification indeed proved to be handy for increasing the motivation of students to learn more. Competition, rewards, and other forms of interactive storytelling through gamified simulations facilitate fun learning and better engagement with learning (Gentry, 1990).

Benefits of Gamification:

- Increased Participation: In the gamified simulation, students are highly engaged and show quite active participation, making learning interactive and more entertaining (Salas, Wildman, & Piccolo, 2009).
- Motivation by Competition: Gamified simulations comprise various competitive streaks like leaderboards and challenges that actually make the students get motivated to perform better (Fiet, 2001).
- Immediate Feedback: Live-response gamification simulations allow students to receive instantaneous feedback on their decisions for the purpose of learning from mistakes to adapt new strategies in real time (Kolb, 1984).
- Collaborative Learning: Most gamification involves teams or collaboration - a highly social and collaborative process, not different from entrepreneurship itself (Shane, 2003).

Some examples of such game-like simulations in entrepreneurship education are:

[1] Startup Weekend: A fully immersed, gamified experience wherein participants, through teams, work out a business idea, create a prototype, and pitch their concept to judges within 54 hours. This is a high-intensity, competitive environment that emulates the pressures of real-world entrepreneurship (Sarasvathy, 2001).

[2] GoVenture Entrepreneur: This is a gamified business simulation in which students start and run a virtual business. These include customer interactions, marketing campaigns, and other activities-based entrepreneurship efforts that give experience to an individual in practice (Aldrich, 2004).

In this respect, gamification in entrepreneurship and economics education works to make the learning process much more participatory and active for students. Gamified simulations not only make learning fun but also develop critical thinking, problem-solving, and decision-making among students to succeed in entrepreneurship (Teece, 2010).

4. INTEGRATING ECONOMIC THEORIES INTO SIMULATION-BASED LEARNING

4.1. Pedagogical Approaches to Integration

Classic economic theory blended into simulation-based learning must be very thoughtful and well-entrenched to engage the student on one level while grasping richer underlying principles that drive business and economic decisions on another (Mankiw, 2024). There are several pedagogical ways of effectively bridging gaps between theoretical economics and practical entrepreneurship using simulations (Bloom, 2019; Aldrich, 2004).

4.1.1. Blending Theory With Practice

Simulation-based learning naturally has strong points in marrying theoretical knowledge with practical application. This could be done as elaborated below:

- Pre-simulation theoretical instructions: Before the students are put into any kind of simulation by the instructors, one could always provide a sound theoretical framework wherein central economic concepts are taught in reference to the simulation. For example, a lecture on market structure should precede the simulation where students would run businesses under various competitive conditions (Mankiw, 2024). This way, the students will finally understand the underlying economic principles they will be implementing within the simulated environment (Fiet, 2001).
- In-simulation scaffolding: step-by-step guidance and prompting by the instructors as students work their way through the simulation to encourage reflection about the underlying economic theories. For instance, in a simulation in which students are making a series of pricing decisions, instructors might ask, "What do you think would happen to your optimal price if demand increases?" (Kolb, 1984). This kind of scaffolding helps the students connect theory and practice in real-time (Salas, Wildman, & Piccolo, 2009).
- Post-simulation reflection and analysis: After a completed simulation, students can pursue some reflection activities that might reinforce the used economics concepts. This can be done through discussion groups, written reflection activities, and even debriefing activities whereby students analyze the outcome of their decisions and connect them back to the theoretical concepts of economics that they had learned. Reflection on the experience consolidates learning, allowing critical thinking to take hold (Gentry, 1990).

4.1.2. Active Learning Through Simulations

Active learning is a teaching methodology that involves students in the learning process, rather than simply receiving information (Kolb, 1984; Gentry, 1990). Simulations easily accommodate this approach to learning, since students must make decisions, solve problems, and respond to changing situations (Bloom, 2019).

Incorporating active learning principles into simulation-based education has the potential to facilitate deeper learning of economic theories in the following ways.

- Problem-Based Learning: Instructors can create a simulation with real-world economic problems and ask students to solve them using their understanding of theories. Using a company that is in an economic recession, a simulation could challenge students to manage the company and work out the theories of demand elasticity and cost-cutting measures necessary to keep the company profitable (Porter, 1980).
- Group learning: This would normally entail working in groups in simulations. Students are thus expected to work with other colleagues in order to realize common goals. Discussions or debates on how these theories of economics apply in such settings deepen their insight through interaction with their peers. Such a suggested example involves students being tasked to work in teams, in a market simulation, to devise a competitive strategy based on their analysis of market conditions and economic indicators (Salas et al., 2009).
- Scenario-based learning: the instructors can plan activities by placing students in various scenarios where they would have to use one or another economic theory. For example, students may be faced with sudden changes in consumer preference or changes in government regulation affecting their businesses; based on that, they would have to adjust their strategies according to the relevant economic principle (Teece, 2010).

Instructors will be able to allow learners a far more engaging experience and thus effective learning experience in economic theories and their application by embedding active learning techniques into simulation-based education (Mankiw, 2024; Sarasvathy, 2001).

4.2. Case Study: Effective Integration of Economics in Simulation Tools

The following section describes the case study of an entrepreneurship course in which simulations were put to successful use to teach core economic theories by means of simulation-based learning. Implementation, challenges, and outcomes reached by these courses are discussed.

4.2.1. Background of the Case

The said entrepreneurship course was from a leading business school and was designed to provide students with a panoramic view of how economic principles influence entrepreneurial decision-making. The course consisted of lectures and readings complemented with a capstone simulation project students would use throughout the semester to apply learned economic theories (Kolb, 1984; Fiet, 2001).

The capstone project therefore entailed a complex business simulator that contained a competitive market simulation. Students were requested to start a virtual company and make decisions about pricing, production, marketing, and financial management (Salas, Wildman, & Piccolo, 2009). The simulation included changes in macroeconomic variables, such as inflation rates and interest rates, that affected the business environment and had students change their set strategies to accommodate these changes in the business environment (Mankiw, 2024).

4.2.2. Implementation Process

The simulation-based capstone project was implemented in a structured process that allowed students to incorporate economic theories into their decision-making.

- Pre-simulation preparation: Well in advance of the simulation, students were exposed to lectures and discussions on related key economic concepts: supply and demand, market structures, pricing strategies, and macroeconomic indicators (Mankiw, 2024; Porter, 1980). The sessions aimed at giving students the theoretical input necessary for the simulation.
- Execution of Simulation: The simulation ran for a couple of weeks with students in teams operating their virtual companies. Instructors can provide real-time feedback and set prompts throughout the simulation that question students about the economic implications of each decision. For instance, when the demand falls, students are prompted to think about what they learned from the theory of elasticity of demand regarding the fall in price or the reduction of output (Bloom, 2019).
- Post-simulation analysis: The students were put through a post-simulation debriefing session, where the outcome of their decisions against the theories studied would be analyzed. This included discussion on what worked and what did not, and why. This would include a written report that links their experiences in the simulation to specific economic concepts (Gentry, 1990).

4.2.3. Results and Impact

This capstone project using simulations proved to be truly successful. There were reports from students on how much better they understand, theoretically, how economic theories relate to business in the real world. Most of them expressed the idea that the simulation made concepts that previously appeared quite abstract much more applicable (Aldrich, 2004; Bloom, 2019).

Key outcomes included:

1) Improved Economic Literacy: Students applied economic theories to practical situations. This is evidenced in the action of the simulation itself and in reporting the economic rationale for decisions made in the post-simulation analysis (Mankiw, 2024).
2) Better critical thinking skills: The simulation really put students in that place where they had to strongly think critically about how various determinants of economic factors-for instance, changes in consumer behavior or, perhaps, changes in market conditions - would affect their business. This helped foster in them the ability to analyze detailed economic environments (Shane, 2003).
3) Real-World Preparedness: Most of the students felt assured that through the simulation they learned certain skills and knowledge that would be useful in real settings while going ahead as entrepreneurs. The experience of simulation helped bridge the gap in using academic learning in real-life scenarios (Salas et al., 2009).

The case study, however, informs on the effectiveness of integrating economic theories into simulation-based learning. This course married theoretical instruction with practical application to give students insight into how economic principles influence entrepreneurial success (Teece, 2010).

4.3. Best Practices for Educators

Based on the case study but also based on other effective implementations, this section highlights best practices that educators may consider with regard to the integration of economic theories within simulation-based entrepreneurship education (Bloom, 2019; Aldrich, 2004).

1) Provide a good theoretical basis: Let them first get acquainted with the relevant underlying economic concepts they are going to practice using the simulations. This section, therefore, presented the best practices that educators could consider regarding the integration of economic theories within simulation-based entrepreneurship education, drawing from the case study and considering other effective implementations as well. This can be done through lectures, reading, and discussion about main theories (Mankiw, 2024; Fiet, 2001).
2) Choice of Right Simulation Tool: Ideally, one should choose simulations that relate to the learning outcomes of the course and use theories taught (Salas, Wildman, & Piccolo, 2009). The simulation needs to realistically model the level of complexity within the economic environment and be of an interacting nature (Teece, 2010).
3) Scaffold the Simulation: Use pointers and guidance throughout the simulation to assist students in making links between theory and practice (Kolb, 1984). At the end, ask students to reflect on whether the decisions taken are consistent with the economic principles learned and how other strategies might have produced another outcome (Gentry, 1990).

4) Allow for Reflection and Analysis: Once the simulation is finished, make sure to have activities that allow the students to reflect on their decisions, along with the repercussions of those decisions, in relation to the theories of economics that they learned (Shane, 2003; Sarasvathy, 2001). This can be done through group discussions, written reflections, or even formal presentations (Porter, 1980).
5) Encourage Collaboration: Many of the simulations are designed for group work, just like entrepreneurial collaboration in the real world (Wilson, Kickul, & Marlino, 2007). Allow for teamwork and peer learning; students can learn much from discussing and debating economic concepts with classmates (Salas et al., 2009).
6) Continuously Assess and Adapt: In the course of the simulation, students are to be regularly assessed on their understanding of the economic concepts. Be prepared to make a change if need be. This may come in the form of revisiting certain theories or even an addition of resources to help the students in overcoming some challenges (Fiet, 2001.
7) Leverage Technology: Avail of technology to enhance the learning experience of simulation. Most simulation tools today offer state-of-the-art features such as data analytics, real-time feedback, and immersive environments. These features help students understand deeply how the economic principle works (Aldrich, 2004; Bloom, 2019).

Hence, such best practices allow educators to provide a better and more engaging learning environment, where not only does one teach economic theories but also how to equip them for the impending challenges awaiting young entrepreneurs.

5. IMPACT ON STUDENTS AND LEARNING OUTCOMES

5.1 Enhancing Economic Literacy

Arguably, the most critical consequence of integrating simulation tools into entrepreneurship education relates to the increased economic literacy of the students (Mankiw, 2024; Bloom, 2019). In this regard, economic literacy refers to the extensive understanding and application of economic principles in decision-making processes, particularly within the business community (Casson, 1982). Simulations are an efficient and unique way of teaching such principles since they actually put the student in a situation that necessitates informed decisions as one works their way through a very complex economic landscape based on real data (Aldrich, 2004).

5.1.1 Gaining Economic Insights Through Simulation

Being able to apply theoretical and abstract concepts of economics in a practical, hands-on way is what simulation provides for a student. For instance, supply and demand become quite an abstract thing when dealt with solely on paper. However, this turns very concrete when students have to price their products given market fluctuations (Mankiw, 2024). Through simulation, students can realize how changes in supply or demand will directly affect business outcomes intuitively and may remember these basic economic principles longer (Salas, Wildman, & Piccolo, 2009).

Simulations also have the advantage of often putting students in a situation that calls for the application of several concepts in economic theory at once-mirroring real-world economic decision-making. The development of a pricing strategy could be when students are required to bring together knowledge of market structure and consumer behavior or balance short-run profit maximization with long-run growth through efficient resource management. This integrated approach enables the student to understand the practical links between economic theories and entrepreneurial choices while preparing them for real-world business complexities (Teece, 2010; Shane, 2003).

5.1.2 Retention of Economic Knowledge

There are numerous studies that have demonstrated better retention using active learning techniques, such as simulation, compared to traditional lectures (Kolb, 1984; Gentry, 1990). This is because the simulation method can engage several senses and cognitive processes, which would make the experience of learning much more memorable (Fiet, 2001). Furthermore, immediate feedback through simulations helps students learn from their mistakes while reinforcing correct economic principal applications (Bloom, 2019).

One business school that integrated economic simulations into the entrepreneurship curriculum demonstrated far superior retention of the economic concepts than their straight lecture counterparts, as evidenced through assessment performance as well as application of the very same economic theories in post-real projects. It also showed that students who participated in the simulations were confident in their mastery of economic principles and used the knowledge more in entrepreneurial ventures (Salas et al., 2009).

5.1.3 Application of Economic Literacy in Real-Life Situations

Perhaps the most telling evidence concerning the effectiveness of simulation-based learning about students' economic literacy is found in the application of knowledge in real-life situations. The graduates who have been exposed to the simulations in entrepreneurship education consequently report that this has helped them deal with the economic challenges of starting and running a business (Davidsson, 2004). For example, they could remind one how a simulation prepared them to respond to a sudden fall in demand with their pricing strategy or teach them how to manage cash flow during an economic downturn.

Basically, simulations allow for transitioning from theoretical practice to practical, which secures the very fact that students will be able to apply the concepts of economics acquired within the lecture in real-life business situations (Schumpeter, 1942). Such an approach to economic literacy will help entrepreneurs make weighted decisions in correspondence with their priorities, foresee market changes in advance, and adapt businesses in conformity with the changing economic situation (Teece, 2010).

5.2 Fostering Entrepreneurial Mindsets

Besides economic literacy, the simulations have an important role in developing an entrepreneurial mindset of the students. An entrepreneurial mindset means a creative, resilient, risk-taking, and active assumption toward a solution to a problem (Sarasvathy, 2001; Shane, 2003). The attributes regarded above are crucially important in entrepreneurship, where uncertainty and challenge happen to be routine (Schumpeter, 1942).

5.2.1 Problem-Solving Skills Development

After all, entrepreneurship is inherently about solving problems - whether it be an attempt to identify a market need, develop a product to meet that need, or find innovative ways to overcome obstacles (Teece, 2010). Simulations prove considerably effective in developing problem-solving skills since they place the student in situations where there is the need to analyze complex issues and make decisions under stress, as well as learn from the consequences of one's actions (Gentry, 1990).

For instance, during a simulation, a student acting as the head of a startup will be put into situations that are unexpected: sudden manufacturing cost escalation or even the entry of a new competitor. Their success depends on how fast they can analyze such situations, look for possible solutions, and then apply the best approach (Salas, Wildman, & Piccolo, 2009). The idea of trial and error allows practice through iteration to be built into developing critical thinking and problem-solving skills in students, important in entrepreneurship (Kolb, 1984).

5.2.2 Encouraging Creativity and Innovation

Simulations also nurture creativity and innovation by providing a risk-free environment in which experimentation can take place (Blank, 2013). In any real business, taking risks can also entail extremely high financial and reputational consequences. On the other hand, students can try various business models, marketing strategies, and product innovations with no apprehension of failure in a simulated environment. It is this kind of license to explore new ideas and take measured risks that engages the mindset that is open to innovation and is ready to question the status quo (Aldrich, 2004).

For instance, a simulation could provide students with the opportunity to test very unconventional marketing strategies, such as viral campaigns or influencer partnerships, in order to see how these methods affect brand awareness and sales. Placing students in an environment that necessitates lateral thinking to consider new possibilities and ideas-simulations stimulates the creativity and innovative thinking common among successful entrepreneurs (Teece, 2010).

5.2.3 Building Resilience and Adaptability

It is resilience and adaptability that enable entrepreneurs to successfully work out ups and downs in business (Sarasvathy, 2001). Simulations nurture these two characteristics because students are exposed to numerous difficult and unpredictable situations. In this regard, a student may witness the failure of a product launch, a big financial loss, or other surprising changes in market conditions. Such situations will then compel them to change strategies, learn from their mistakes, and never give up easily (Davidsson, 2004).

It is through such experiences in the simulated environment that students are able to develop their resiliency to setbacks that they will encounter in the real world. Students come to realize that failure is not the outcome but rather a lesson to learn and an opportunity to become better. This is a very important virtue in entrepreneurs; often they need to change business models or strategies in accordance with changes in circumstances (Wilson, Kickul, & Marlino, 2007).

5.2.4 Encouraging Pro-Activity

Finally, simulations reward proactive entrepreneurship. The student in a simulation generally does not have the luxury to sit back, wait for things to happen, and then react (Gentry, 1990). Instead, they have to anticipate problems, think ahead, and become proactive to achieve their objectives. For example, a simulation may reward those who plan a long-term growth strategy or take steps that might mitigate unfavorable circumstances before they have taken place (Teece, 2010).

This attitude is essential for entrepreneurs, who should always try to pursue opportunities with continuous pursuit in trying to outcompete or keep ahead of market developments. By instilling this attitude through the simulation exercises, the educator prepares the students to develop the forward-looking attitude that defines successful entrepreneurship (Bloom, 2019).

5.3 Preparing for Real-World Challenges

One of the focuses of entrepreneurship education is the preparation of students for what they are bound to find within the business environment as owners and innovators of businesses (Fiet, 2001; Shane, 2003). Simulations will fit into this perfectly, as they offer an experience that is realistic and hands-on, similar to the manner in which complexities in the business environment come across (Aldrich, 2004; Bloom, 2019).

5.3.1 Economic Decision-Making

Entrepreneurs have to make an incredible number of economic decisions, most of them under a great deal of time pressure and with sometimes very limited information. These decisions include but are not limited to how to price their products or control their costs, from making investment decisions to responding to economic downturns (Mankiw, 2024; Teece, 2010). Simulations put students into these situations as preparation for such decisions by requiring them to apply economic theories in a real application context (Salas, Wildman, & Piccolo, 2009).

In this regard, the simulation might ask the students to decide when to expand the business during times of economic growth and consolidate their market positions. For this, the simulation would show various economic indicators-interest rates, inflation, and consumer confidence, amongst others-which the student would have to weigh in to come to an informed decision (Davidsson, 2004). This experience is supposed to help students develop the analytical competencies that are necessary for the interpretation of economic data to support them in making good decisions in their real lives (Porter, 1980).

5.3.2 Adaptability and Problem-Solving

As identified above, adaptability and problem-solving are two of the important entrepreneurship skills. Simulations prepare students to handle the challenges in business by exposing them to numerous situations, which require prompt action and changes of strategies in an instant. How to respond to sudden drops in sales, supply chain disruptions, or regulatory changes-simulations allow students to train for how to adapt to the unexpected (Wilson, Kickul, & Marlino, 2007).

This adaptability is especially needed in today's rapidly changing business environment, wherein entrepreneurs must be able to make rapid pivots with sudden new information or each change in circumstance (Schumpeter, 1942). With the practice of these skills in a simulated environment, students build the confidence and competence needed to navigate the uncertainties of the real world (Bloom, 2019).

5.3.3 Long-Term Entrepreneurial Success

In the final analysis, the objectives of entrepreneurship education aim at long-term success for the students, equipping them with the necessary knowledge, competencies, and attitudes (Gentry, 1990; Teece, 2010). Simulations are an input toward such goals by providing a pedagogical experience that ties together theoretical economics, real decision-making, and entrepreneurial qualities: resilience, creativity, and adaptability (Kolb, 1984).

Graduates who have had the experience of simulation-based entrepreneurship education enter the market much better prepared for the creation and growth of a successful venture. They are decidedly better informed as to the economic drivers of business success and will have practiced in realistic, challenging situations how to apply that knowledge (Bloom, 2019; Salas et al., 2009. For this reason, they are more apt to make informed decisions, prepare and adapt to challenges, and pursue new innovative strategies leading to long-term growth and sustainability (Teece, 2010).

5.3.4 Testimonials and Feedback

Feedback from students who have undergone simulation-based entrepreneurship education testifies to how much these activities have added to their value. For many students, these simulations often remain at the forefront as among the most important impacts of education for providing real-world experience and knowledge useful to them as entrepreneurs right away (Aldrich, 2004).

One student shared how a simulation helped a student to take the course concepts of supply and demand in devising a pricing strategy in their startup. The other said, "The simulation experience taught me the importance of adapting to new situations, which became so invaluable when I found myself needing to change my business model entirely as market conditions changed."

These testimonies are enough to highlight how simulation-based learning can really alter the course of better preparation for students in real-life challenges and their ultimate success as an entrepreneurs in the long run (Sarasvathy, 2001; Teece, 2010).

6. CHALLENGES AND OPPORTUNITIES

6.1. Challenges in Implementing Simulation Tools

Whereas the benefits of integrating simulation tools in entrepreneurship education can easily be identified, challenges that need to be considered are manifold for efficient integration. They span from technical and logistical challenges to pedagogical and institutional (Aldrich, 2004; Bloom, 2019).

6.1.1. Technical Challenges

The major problem with applying simulation tools is technical complexity. The performance of qualitative simulations quite often requires advanced software and hardware, which are often expensive to buy or maintain (Salas, Wildman, & Piccolo, 2009). Educators and students also need to receive training in the effective use of these kinds of tools, which sometimes may be time-consuming (Kolb, 1984).

1) Access to Technology: Not everyone can afford to invest in state-of-the-art simulation technologies. This will make certain students studying in well-endowed schools have an advantage over others who come from less-well-endowed institutions (Mankiw, 2024). Now is the time for cheaper alternatives to be sought after, such as cloud-based simulations that require less local infrastructure, or even open-source simulation platforms that are free (Teece, 2010).
2) Technical Support: While having the enabling technology is one thing, the continuance of technical support arrangements is quite another thing for the seamless running of simulations. This involves problem solutions in software, the maintenance of hardware, and users' support both for teachers and learners (Aldrich, 2004). Without proper technical support, the effectiveness of simulation-based learning seriously deteriorates (Bloom, 2019).

6.1.2. Pedagogical Challenges

Besides these problems in technology, there are some serious pedagogical issues related to integrating simulations into entrepreneurship education.

Traditional methodologies in teaching are those with which most educators are comfortable, and educators are going to be very resistant to the integration of newer technologies (Gentry, 1990). This may be due to a lack of familiarity with the simulation tools, due to skepticism about the effectiveness of simulations for learning outcomes, or simply due to reluctance to change well-established teaching practices (Fiet, 2001). This resistance can be worn off by thorough training of educators, proof through pilot programs, and follow-up support in the way of helping instructors adjust to new methods (Salas et al., 2009).

One of the other challenges is how to balance theory and practice within teaching on one side and giving freedom to students by simulating on the other (Mankiw, 2024). As much as simulations are ideal for practical application, they work best when students have a good theoretical framework. Educators need to very carefully design their courses in a manner that integrates both aspects: the courses must be designed in such a way that students are aware of the underlying economic principles when participating in simulations (Kolb, 1984).

Other challenges with simulation-based learning environments have to do with the assessment of student performance. Traditional assessment methods, such as exams and written assignments, may not be fully applicable to capture learning outcomes realized through simulations (Shane, 2003). Educators need to devise new assessment strategies that gauge students' ability to apply theories of economics in practical situations, decision-making processes, and reflection on the simulation experience (Teece, 2010).

6.2. Opportunities for Enhancing Entrepreneurship Education

Besides these challenges, several opportunities arise for the enhancement of entrepreneurship education through the innovative use of simulation tools. These become possible with enabling factors in the form of technological advances, integration across disciplines, and the possibility of increased access (Aldrich, 2004; Bloom, 2019).

6.2.1. Technological Advancements

And with technology literally racing ahead at such a pace, the future of simulation-based learning holds promise. Newer technologies like AI, VR, and AR hold great promise in further enhancing the level of simulations that allow experience to be more immersive and realistic (Salas, Wildman, & Piccolo, 2009).

1) Artificial Intelligence: With the help of artificial intelligence, these simulations become rather dynamic, functional, and interactive (Bloom, 2019). For example, AI-based simulations may adapt to the progress students make in learning and include individualized challenges and responses based on how each performs. AI can also be applied in simulating complex market behavior or predicting the results of different business decisions in order to give students deeper insights into economic dynamics (Teece, 2010).
2) Virtual and Augmented Reality: VR and AR technologies have made it possible to create fully immersive simulation environments in which students interact with virtual markets, customers, and competitors (Aldrich, 2004). An example of such a thing is how VR simulations can place students into a virtual marketplace where they can observe consumer behavior, test product placements, and experiment with marketing strategies in a very realistic environment. AR offers the possibility for overlaying economic data onto real-world environments, thus creating a rich interactive learning experience for students while connecting theoretical knowledge with practice (Mankiw, 2024).

6.2.2. Cross-Disciplinary Integration

Another excellent opportunity exists in the integration of simulation tools across different disciplines. By nature, entrepreneurship is an interdisciplinary business: it involves several aspects, such as economics, finance, marketing, technology, and many others. It would be interesting if the integration of various simulations, each reflecting one or more fields, would make this teaching more complete for students (Shane, 2003; Sarasvathy, 2001).

1) Interdisciplinary Simulations: For example, a simulation that integrates the theory of economics with the tools of data science may enable the students to analyze market trends with big data analytics (Teece, 2010). Similarly, simulated interferences between finance and operations management may enable students to understand the jungle that is managing cash flows while optimizing production processes (Porter, 1980). Cross-disciplinary simulations enhance not only the grasp of entrepreneurship by students but also prepare them for real-world challenges-often multivariate in nature-which constitute the task of running a business (Davidsson, 2004).

2) Interdisciplinary Collaboration: Institutions can facilitate collaboration between departments in designing and implementing interdisciplinary simulations. For instance, the economics and business departments can collaborate in designing simulations that show students how economic policies affect business decisions (Mankiw, 2024). This will further enhance holistic and innovative simulation learning experiences.

6.2.3. Expanding Accessibility

As it has been discussed, access to simulation tools develops inequality for some institutions. However, the creation of more affordable and scalable solutions might improve this (Fiet, 2001).

The most promising solution to increase access to simulations is the leveraging of cloud-based platforms. These models allow institutions to access robust simulation tools without necessarily having to incur expensive hardware and software installations (Salas et al., 2009. Cloud-based simulations can be accessed with any device connected to the internet, which makes them ideal for remote and hybrid learning environments (Bloom, 2019).

Open-source tools themselves can be an opportunity to democratize access to high-value educational resources. The development of open-source simulation tools can be given away and modified freely to meet the needs of various curricula (Kolb, 1984). By the same virtue, campuses can leverage networks of educators and developers that enhance these open-source tools to gain a collective advantage without costs (Wilson, Kickul, & Marlino, 2007.

Partnerships among educational institutions, technology companies, and nonprofit organizations also have great potential for broadly scaling up access to simulation tools. Technology companies may provide educational institutions with free or significantly reduced-price access to their simulation platforms; on the other hand, non-profit organizations may fund such initiatives as those aimed at bringing simulation-based learning to under-resourced communities.

6.3. Future Directions for Research and Development

While entrepreneurship education continues to evolve, fully unlocking the potential of simulation-based learning requires ongoing research and development. There are quite a few areas that do call for further exploration and innovation.

[1] Research on Learning Outcomes: Although numerous studies have identified that simulations enhance learning outcomes for entrepreneurship education, much more research needs to be conducted in order to quantify the actual benefits and best practices. It may also be that future research investigates whether and how simulation-based learning impacts longer-term entrepreneurial success for students, and how specific types of simulations impact specific learning outcomes.

[2] New Models of Simulation Development: Besides the development of new economic theories and new business models, the need to develop new simulation models reflecting those changes is ever-growing. As a matter of fact, this trend started long ago and is continuing with the rise of the gig economy, digital platforms, and blockchain technology; each presents new challenges and opportunities for entrepreneurs, and inclusion in simulations makes the varying business landscapes understandable and negotiable (Teece, 2010).

It could also be that future research investigates whether and how simulation-based learning impacts longer-term entrepreneurial success for students, and the impact of specific kinds of simulations on specific learning outcomes (Aldrich, 2004; Bloom, 2019).

[3] New Models of Simulation Development: Besides the development of new economic theories, and the development of new business models, there is an ever-increasing need for the development of new simulation models reflecting those changes (Aldrich, 2004; Bloom, 2019). It would bring in the effectiveness of simulation-based education fully, meeting diverse ways of learning (Salas, Wildman, & Piccolo, 2009).

In this respect, there is a growing need within the community of educators, researchers, and developers in this field of learning for collaboration and sharing knowledge. Development platforms for best practices sharing, research findings, and newly developed simulation tools should be created to be of assistance to the education community so that it progresses with this aspect together and the simulation-based learning is continuously renewed and updated (Fiet, 2001; Shane, 2003).

7. CONCLUSION

7.1. Recap of Key Insights

In this direction, the employment of simulation tools in entrepreneurship education has been the most recent development that concerns methods of teaching economic theories and entrepreneurial skills (Aldrich, 2004; Bloom, 2019). This chapter has discussed various ways in which simulations may enrich the learning experience of students by providing them with practical, hands-on opportunities to apply economic principles in real world - like business situations (Salas, Wildman, & Piccolo, 2009).

Key Takeaways:

- Economics Literacy: It is realized that simulations highly develop economic literacy in students by enabling them to understand how to apply economics concepts in real life (Mankiw, 2024; Fiet, 2001).
- Entrepreneurship Mindsets: The development of the art of creativity, toughness, adaptability, and problem-solving will be important as students will be confronted with challenges dealing with simulations in entrepreneurship (Sarasvathy, 2001; Shane, 2003).
- Practical Preparedness: These simulations are quite realistic in outlook and interactive, partly like the challenges of running a business; this, in turn, prepares the student with the relevant skills and confidence for eventual success (Gentry, 1990).

7.2. Implications for Educators

From this perspective, educators will have to adopt a thoughtful and strategic way of embedding simulation tools into entrepreneurship education. The integration should be balanced with theoretical input, adequate technical support, and training, besides developing new methods of assessments that capture learning outcomes attained through simulations (Kolb, 1984; Bloom, 2019).

Recommendations:

- Invest in Training: Educators should invest in professional development and training to become proficient in using simulation tools and integrating them into their courses (Salas et al., 2009).
- Interdisciplinary Collaboration: An institution should make every effort to encourage interdisciplinary collaboration in developing simulations that give broad, interdisciplinary learning experiences (Teece, 2010).
- Embrace Technological Innovation: Educators should update themselves regarding the state of the art in simulation technology and find innovative ways to enhance learning with new tools further (Aldrich, 2004).

7.3. Policy Implications

It is also important that policymakers, too, do their part in the process of integration of simulation tools within entrepreneurship education. This would entail funding to support the development and implementation of simulation-based learning and sharing access to these facilities among a wide array of educational institutions, as well as the promotion of research into the impact of simulations on learning outcomes (Wilson, Kickul, & Marlino, 2007).

Recommendations for Policy Change:

- Increase Funding: It requires increased funding to avail the intervention of simulation tools, especially in under-resourced settings where access to technology may be scant. This should be invested in by Governments and Schools (Fiet, 2001).
- Access and Equity Promotion: Policymakers should work to ensure that all students - regardless of their socioeconomic status or geography - have access to a variety of quality simulation resources (Salas et al., 2009).
- Supporting Research and Innovation: Adapting the right amount of funds for effectiveness-oriented research on simulation-based learning is essential; best practices must be developed, and new technologies explored (Teece, 2010).

7.4. Future Outlook

The future of entrepreneurship education is great, and simulation tools will continue to play a more central role in shaping the next generation of entrepreneurs. With every advance in technology, there opens up fresh possibilities of making simulations not only more engaging but also closer to real life, which is, after all, the ultimate goal of the process of preparing students for all challenges awaiting them in the business world (Bloom, 2019).

Future Directions:

- New Developments: Developing new simulation models, integrating state-of-the-art technologies like AI and VR, and exploring new learning pathways will be the keys to future developments in simulation-based education (Aldrich, 2004).
- Global Collaboration: For the latest developments in simulation-based learning to take place, for all students in different schools and other educational institutions to benefit from these

new developments, it would require more collaboration on a global scale among educators, researchers, and developers (Salas et al., 2009).

- Sustainability and Impact: The more the increase in the use of simulation tools, the more the future consideration that will have to be given to their long-term sustainability and impact, not only on education outcomes but in the contribution they will make towards creating a resilient, innovative, and entrepreneurial global economy (Salas et al., 2009).

Call to Action:

This is an opportunity that educators, policymakers, and researchers must seize upon, and work together to develop ways of overcoming barriers that simulation-based learning has thus far put up (Gentry, 1990). It is only in this manner that we will allow the young entrepreneurs to garner knowledge, acquire the skill set needed, and get the mindset that would lead them successfully through an increasingly complex and dynamic world (Shane, 2003; Teece, 2010).

REFERENCES

Aldrich, C. (2004). *Simulations and the Future of Learning: An Innovative (and Perhaps Revolutionary) Approach to e-Learning*. Pfeiffer.

Blank, S. (2013). *The Four Steps to the Epiphany: Successful Strategies for Products that Win*. K&S Ranch.

Bloom, N. (2019). The Use of Simulations in Entrepreneurship Education. *Journal of Business Education, 87*(2), 34–48. DOI: 10.1080/08832323.2018.1536028

Casson, M. (1982). *The Entrepreneur: An Economic Theory*. Martin Robertson.

Davidsson, P. (2004). *Researching Entrepreneurship*. Springer.

Dewey, J. (1938). *Experience and Education*. Kappa Delta Pi.

Fiet, J. O. (2001). The Theoretical Side of Teaching Entrepreneurship. *Journal of Business Venturing, 16*(1), 1–24. DOI: 10.1016/S0883-9026(99)00041-5

Gartner, W. B. (1988). Who Is an Entrepreneur? Is the Wrong Question. *American Journal of Small Business, 12*(4), 11–32. DOI: 10.1177/104225878801200401

Gentry, J. W. (1990). *What is Experiential Learning? Guide to Business Gaming and Experiential Learning*. Nichols/GP Publishing.

Kirzner, I. M. (1973). *Competition and Entrepreneurship*. University of Chicago Press.

Kolb, D. A. (1984). *Experiential Learning: Experience as the Source of Learning and Development. Englewood Cliffs*. Prentice-Hall.

Mankiw, N. G. (2024). *Principles of Economics* (10th ed.). South-Western Cengage Learning.

McKeown, J. M. (2012). *Real Options in Practice*. Wiley.

Mitchell, R. K., Busenitz, L., Lant, T., McDougall, P. P., Morse, E. A., & Smith, J. B. (2002). Toward a Theory of Entrepreneurial Cognition: Rethinking the People Side of Entrepreneurship Research. *Entrepreneurship Theory and Practice, 27*(2), 93–104. DOI: 10.1111/1540-8520.00001

Porter, M. E. (1980). *Competitive Strategy: Techniques for Analyzing Industries and Competitors*. Free Press.

Salas, E., Wildman, J. L., & Piccolo, R. F. (2009). Using Simulation-Based Training to Enhance Management Education. *Academy of Management Learning & Education, 8*(4), 559–573. DOI: 10.5465/AMLE.2009.47785474

Sarasvathy, S. D. (2001). Causation and Effectuation: Toward a Theoretical Shift from Economic Inevitability to Entrepreneurial Contingency. *Academy of Management Review, 26*(2), 243–263. DOI: 10.2307/259121

Schumpeter, J. A. (1942). *Capitalism, Socialism, and Democracy*. Harper & Brothers.

Shane, S. (2003). *A General Theory of Entrepreneurship: The Individual-Opportunity Nexus*. Edward Elgar Publishing. DOI: 10.4337/9781781007990

Teece, D. J. (2010). Business Models, Business Strategy and Innovation. *Long Range Planning*, *43*(2-3), 172–194. DOI: 10.1016/j.lrp.2009.07.003

Von Mises, L. (1949). *Human Action: A Treatise on Economics*. Yale University Press.

Wiklund, J., Patzelt, H., & Shepherd, D. A. (2009). Building an Integrative Model of Small Business Growth. *Small Business Economics*, *32*(4), 351–374. DOI: 10.1007/s11187-007-9084-8

Wilson, F., Kickul, J., & Marlino, D. (2007). Gender, Entrepreneurial Self-Efficacy, and Entrepreneurial Career Intentions: Implications for Entrepreneurship Education. *Entrepreneurship Theory and Practice*, *31*(3), 387–406. DOI: 10.1111/j.1540-6520.2007.00179.x

Zimmerman, M. A., & Zeitz, G. J. (2002). Beyond Survival: Achieving New Venture Growth by Building Legitimacy. *Academy of Management Review*, *27*(3), 414–431. DOI: 10.2307/4134387

Chapter 15
International Agritourism Ventures and Digital Tools:
Enhancing Entrepreneurship Education Through Simulation

Georgios A. Deirmentzoglou
https://orcid.org/0000-0003-1687-0708
Neapolis University Pafos, Cyprus

Eleni E. Anastasopoulou
https://orcid.org/0000-0002-0918-8527
Neapolis University Pafos, Cyprus

Eirini Vlassi
University of the Aegean, Greece

Sotirios Varelas
University of Piraeus, Greece

Ioannis Anastasopoulos
University of Piraeus, Greece

ABSTRACT

Digital tools have become essential to the growth and sustainability of international agritourism ventures. E-commerce and social media enable agritourism businesses to expand their market reach, improve customer engagement, and streamline operations, ultimately increasing their competitiveness in the global tourism industry. As the agritourism sector continues to embrace digital transformation, it is critical to equip business students with the knowledge and skills necessary to effectively utilize these tools. This chapter aims to present two simulation activities tailored for agritourism education—one focused on e-commerce and the other on social media—and provide detailed insights into their design and implementation. The implications of these activities extend beyond agritourism education, fostering an entrepreneurial mindset and increasing students' readiness to implement digital tools and platforms in various business contexts.

DOI: 10.4018/979-8-3693-9040-5.ch015

1. INTRODUCTION

In the contemporary globalized and digitally interconnected world, the realm of agritourism finds itself at the nexus of conventional agricultural practices and contemporary tourism strategies (Mutipforo et al., 2024). The tourism and hospitality sectors have emerged as pivotal drivers of employment creation and economic growth at the local, regional, and national levels (Vlassi et al., 2023a). As rural destinations increasingly attract tourists seeking authentic and sustainable experiences, digital tools such as websites and social media have become indispensable for agritourism businesses to achieve visibility, communicate their value propositions, and expand their reach globally (Muwani et al., 2024; Król, 2019). Effective online presence allows agritourism enterprises to promote local culture, heritage, and eco-friendly practices while tapping into international markets (Fanelli, 2022).

Websites serve as the virtual storefronts of agritourism businesses, providing essential information, showcasing offerings, and facilitating bookings (Król, 2019; Platania, 2014). Social media platforms, on the other hand, create interactive spaces where businesses can engage directly with potential customers, share visual storytelling, and build online communities (Katsande et al., 2024; Tshuma et al., 2024; Hardesty, 2011). Leveraging these tools enhances brand recognition and fosters trust, enabling small agritourism businesses to compete in a highly competitive tourism sector. For entrepreneurs in this domain, the ability to manage websites and social media pages effectively can mean the difference between remaining a local attraction and becoming a global destination.

Given the critical role of digital tools in agritourism, it is imperative to equip future entrepreneurs with the knowledge and skills necessary to navigate and harness these technologies (Lalisan et al., 2024). Business and tourism education programs must evolve to integrate practical training methods that simulate real-world challenges. Simulation-based learning offers a dynamic and interactive approach, allowing students to design, develop, and manage digital tools within a controlled, risk-free environment (Sheikh et al., 2023). This pedagogical method fosters experiential learning, enabling students to experiment with strategies, analyze outcomes, and refine their approaches before applying them in professional contexts.

Simulation activities specifically tailored for agritourism entrepreneurship courses can prepare students to tackle the unique demands of the sector. These activities should mirror actual industry scenarios, providing learners with opportunities to create and manage websites, plan social media campaigns, and optimize online content for search engines. In doing so, students develop critical thinking, creativity, and problem-solving skills that are essential for entrepreneurial success.

This chapter explores the role of websites and social media pages as strategic tools for agritourism businesses and underscores the importance of integrating simulation-based learning in entrepreneurship education. It provides practical frameworks and methodologies for implementing such activities in agritourism courses, ensuring that students graduate with both theoretical knowledge and hands-on expertise. By bridging the gap between theory and practice, this approach empowers future agritourism entrepreneurs to leverage digital tools effectively and achieve sustainable growth in a competitive global market.

This chapter is organized into seven sections to provide a comprehensive analysis of the integration of e-commerce and social media in agritourism education through simulation-based activities. Section 2 begins with an overview of agritourism, offering a definition, discussing its significance, and examining its economic impact. Section 3 focuses on the role of e-commerce and social media in agritourism, highlighting how these digital tools influence marketing strategies, customer engagement, and business performance. In Section 4, we delve into the role of simulation-based learning in entrepreneurship education, emphasizing its experiential value and alignment with real-world business practices. Section

5 introduces two proposed simulation activities tailored for agritourism education—one focused on e-commerce and the other on social media—detailing their design and implementation. Section 6 evaluates the skills and competencies developed through these activities, demonstrating their relevance to the modern agritourism landscape. Finally, Section 7 concludes the chapter by offering recommendations for future activities, including the integration of emerging technologies such as artificial intelligence and the metaverse to further enhance digital competencies in agritourism education.

2. OVERVIEW OF AGRITOURISM

2.1. Defining Agritourism

Agritourism is a unique type of rural tourism that includes activities directly associated with agriculture and offers visitors some level of interaction with the day to day functions of a working farm (Barbieri, 2020). It brings together agriculture and tourism, offering a diversity of activities including guided tours on the farm, hands-on harvesting, educational courses and nights spent in the farms (Flanigan, Blackstock and Hunter 2014). Agritourism is different from many other forms of tourism as agritourism focuses on providing genuine rural experiences which connects urban with rural and deepens an insight into local agricultural experience and lifestyles (Hjalager, 2015).

Increasing demand for sustainable tourism and local food production has driven consumers to agritourism. Traditionally, tourism has been a rather passive activity, something that is now shifting towards in the direction of increased participation (Lane, 2018) as tourists are seeking more meaningful and immersive experiences; the ultimate place for such event to take place is through agritourism activities. Similarly, trend displays a large scale shift to experiential travel where visitors favour on hands-on activities and cultural immersions instead of regular observation (Tew and Barbieri, 2012).

2.2. Significance of Agritourism

Agritourism plays a significant role in rural economy as it allows farmers to diversify their incomes and helps contribute to regional economies (Barbieri, 2013; Sonnino, 2004). Farmers can obtain added income by diversifying their agricultural operation with a tourism component, which helps shield them from adverse economic impacts due to market and weather uncertainties (Santeramo and Barbieri, 2017). The opportunity to diversify income from traditional agriculture through tourism enterprises has established itself as a useful tool for the long-term viability of small farms (Fleischer et al., 2018).

In addition, agritourism is also a means of social and educational exchange. It provides urban visitors with an insight into sustainable farming methods and issues impacting rural communities (Hjalager, 2010). Encouraging public appreciation for local produce and sustainable agricultural practices through this interaction may, in turn, raise awareness of rural sustainability initiatives. The commercialization of rural tourism, through *alojamento* rural, as well as *agriturismo* there are several variants of these examples which preserves the manor in some way or to promote local culinary culture with preserved antique tools and methods (Flanigan et al., 2014).

2.3. Economic Impact of Agritourism

Economically, indirect and direct financial benefits of agritourism to rural areas are numerous (Tew and Barbieri, 2012). Farm tours, u-pick operations and farmers markets not only provide a direct income stream to farmers, but also provide indirect benefits by providing economic stimulus resulting from transportation costs of market-related services (e.g., hospitality, dining and retail) that will increase based on increased local spending power (Phillip et al., 2010). Agritourism expands the economic portfolio of rural communities and alleviates dependence on a monoculture (Lamie et al., 2021) by drawing clientele unlikely to travel to these areas otherwise.

Though in areas where agriculture is failing, agritourism can not only sustain the local communities but play a vital role in strengthening their economies. Ensuring the maturity and sustainability of farm diversification activities is a strategic objective that contributes to income stability for farmers, permitting them to develop new revenues streams and making their coping capacity higher towards external shocks (Nickerson et al., 2001). Farms that engage in agritourism receive much higher profit than farms producing traditional products (Schilling et al., 2014) This resilience to economic changes is a necessity, especially in areas with demographic issues like population out-migration and lower agricultural output.

In the last few years, digital technologies have gained more visibility in agritourism. The adoption of e-commerce and social media platforms has allowed agritourism businesses to expand their circle of customers, present their services more effectively, and even communicate directly with the consumers (Paliszkiewicz et al., 2024). Agritourism businesses could extend the circle of their customers, present their services more effectively, and communicate directly with the consumers through the adoption of social media and e-commerce. Such digital tools can help the small-scale farmer reach larger, even global markets; a better margin on sales to direct consumers is often realized with this model compared to more traditional models of distribution (Muwani et al., 2024).

Agritourism has emerged as one of the major drivers of rural development in a sustainable manner, while at the same time offering a realistic path toward economic diversification, cultural preservation, and enhancement of community participation. Backed by the strength of digital marketing strategies, its potential has been further enhanced by opening up new windows of opportunity for its expansion and innovation. The following section shall discuss the role of digital platforms like e-commerce and social media that agritourism may play with reference to entrepreneurship education.

3. THE ROLE OF E-COMMERCE AND SOCIAL MEDIA IN AGRITOURISM

Modern agritourism could be marked as being shaped most actively by digital technologies through effective promotion, customer interaction, and direct sales. E-commerce and social media will continue to bear prime importance due to their unique advantages they provide to the businesses by means of increasing visibility, connecting with audiences, and building strong brand identity.

3.1.E-Commerce: Facilitating Direct Sales and Market Expansion

E-commerce is the sale of products and services via the Internet (Deirmentzoglou and Deirmentzoglou, 2022). It is one of the most crucial strategies for agritourism businesses in their quest to diversify their operations from local markets (Apostolopoulos et al., 2024; Huang and Benyoucef, 2013). With e-commerce, agritourism businesses can sell direct products, such as fresh farm produce, handicrafts, and value-added foods. In this case, this stage of selling normally bypasses intermediaries, thereby increasing the rate of profit accruable to the business and at the same time providing a price level that is competitive enough to attract and retain customers (Lee et al., 2024).

Furthermore, guided tour bookings, workshops, and farm accommodation have become much easier with digital platforms. Provided with online booking tools, customers find it easy, while the administrative burden becomes lighter (Ananya, 2021). In this way, the automated processes enable the improvement of customer experiences and the gathering of data for effective promotions. E-commerce helps in diversifying the revenues of agritourism businesses, thus making them resilient to several economic fluctuations. In addition, outside the peak season, such establishments can still sell their products online to anyone in any part of the world, hence increasing profitability (Xu et al., 2023).

3.2.Social Media: Enhancing Customer Engagement and Brand Building

Social media platforms such as Instagram, Facebook, and YouTube provide powerful tools that allow the agritourism operations of farm businesses to communicate more effectively with their clients and market themselves to potential ones. Unlike traditional methods of marketing, social media methods involve businesses interacting on a personal basis with their target audience. This makes the tourism experience more personal, as Leung et al. (2013) points out. Social media has emerged as a pivotal component in the online pursuit of travel-related information, offering a comprehensive platform for exploring novel experiences and facilitating informed decision-making through user-generated content (Xiang and Gretzel, 2010). Specifically, visual media, such as photos and videos, has proven to be a particularly effective medium for capturing the allure of rural landscapes (Hays et al., 2013). The role of social media in this regard is twofold: it transforms tourists from passive spectators to active participants in shaping and creating value (Vlassi et al., 2023b).

One of the strong positive features of social media is user-generated content: satisfied visitors share their experiences on their personal social media profiles. In this way, organic promotion serves as a strong recommendation to bring in new customers who are influenced by the friends and family recommending it (Ashley and Tuten, 2015). Moreover, the analytics of social media can be employed by firms in compiling data about consumer tastes and behavior so that it allows more targeted and effective marketing strategies.

Besides, it helps develop one's brand identity through consistent and authentic storytelling. Agritourism operators could use new media to express sustainable commitments, show unique value propositions, and create a narrative regarding farm history and mission. This strategy of differentiation apart from distinguishing the business from its competitors, identifies itself with growing numbers of consumers looking for authenticity and naturalness. In this vein, Senyao and Ha (2022) and Adeyinka-Ojo and Abdullah (2021) have argued that such initiatives provide a clear distinction from competition while heightening appeal to consumers that increasingly look for genuine and natural experiences.

3.3. Building Synergies Between E-Commerce and Social Media

The eventual synergistic effect is that both e-commerce and social media, when combined, broaden the agritourism enterprise's marketing and sales potential. Social media campaigns, for example, will drive consumers to an agritourism business' e-commerce website, therefore increasing online sales and bookings of the establishment. Social media use is becoming more pervasive in the online search for information on travel; hence, these sites increase the visibility of businesses and shape consumer behavior, ultimately driving traffic onto their e-commerce websites (Xiang and Gretzel, 2010). More so, positive customers' reviews and testimonials on social media can help to build up the business's credibility by strengthening its brand reputation and trusting the potential visitors (Tanina et al., 2020; Navío-Marco et al., 2018; Yuan, Tseng and Li, 2022).

A holistic approach towards digital marketing will allow the integration of such business processes that will comprehensively offer online visibility to agritourism businesses, improving customer engagement, supporting direct sales, and enhancing generally their position in the marketplace. This is particularly important in the competitive environment of tourism, where a good line of sight and customer loyalty are the main drivers for success.

In this way, e-commerce and social media become very important tools for agritourism, offering infrastructure for direct sales, enhancing customer interaction, and providing powerful opportunities to strengthen the brand. When done correctly, e-commerce and social media create new marketing opportunities, help agritourism companies forge strong relationships with their guests, and create a model that supports long-term growth. The following sections discuss specific strategies for each of these platforms integrating agritourism education to train the future entrepreneur in navigating the demands of doing business in the digital age.

4. SIMULATION-BASED LEARNING IN ENTREPRENEURSHIP

Simulation-based learning represents an experiential teaching approach that immerses students in realistic, scenario-driven environments where they can apply theoretical knowledge to practical challenges (Chernikova et al., 2020; Costello, 2017). In entrepreneurship education, this method bridges the gap between academic concepts and real-world applications, enabling students to experience the complexities of starting and managing businesses without the risks associated with actual ventures. Through simulated activities, learners engage in decision-making, problem-solving, and strategic planning, helping them to develop critical skills and competencies required for entrepreneurial success (Yasin et al., 2022).

The significance of simulation-based learning in entrepreneurship education lies in its ability to provide hands-on experience while fostering creativity, adaptability, and resilience (Salamzadeh et al., 2022; Torres et al., 2020). By simulating real business operations, students are exposed to scenarios involving market analysis, financial planning, customer interactions, and crisis management. These activities not only enhance technical and managerial skills but also cultivate the entrepreneurial mindset needed to identify opportunities and address challenges effectively. Simulation tools such as business model canvases, digital prototyping software, and virtual marketplaces allow students to experiment with strategies and observe the outcomes, promoting deeper learning through reflection and iteration.

In the context of agritourism education, simulation-based learning holds particular relevance due to the sector's reliance on digital marketing, sustainable practices, and community engagement. Agritourism entrepreneurship requires a blend of business acumen and digital literacy to market products and services effectively while promoting eco-friendly values (Gadanakis, 2024; Siregar et al., 2024; Phelan and Sharpley, 2011). Simulation activities tailored to agritourism education provide learners with opportunities to design websites, manage social media campaigns, and create branding strategies that highlight sustainability and cultural heritage. Such activities mirror the dynamics of agritourism businesses, where entrepreneurs must integrate technology with traditional practices to reach broader audiences and generate economic benefits.

Moreover, these simulations emphasize the importance of environmental responsibility and ethical entrepreneurship, aligning with contemporary demands for sustainability (Moratis et al., 2006). Students gain exposure to scenarios that involve balancing profitability with eco-conscious practices, encouraging them to develop ventures that support both economic growth and environmental stewardship. By focusing on agritourism, simulation-based learning not only prepares students for entrepreneurship in rural and agricultural sectors but also promotes innovation and adaptability in leveraging digital tools for sustainable development.

The incorporation of simulation activities into entrepreneurship education, particularly in agritourism, fosters a dynamic learning environment where students can experiment, collaborate, and refine their ideas. It equips them with the skills and confidence to navigate uncertainties and capitalize on opportunities, ensuring they are well-prepared to launch and sustain successful ventures in an increasingly competitive and digitalized economy.

5. ACTIVITIES IN AGRITOURISM ENTREPRENEURSHIP EDUCATION

This section outlines two proposed activities designed to enhance students' competencies in agritourism entrepreneurship through hands-on digital tools and strategies. Activity 1 focuses on the design and development of websites for agritourism ventures, equipping students with technical and creative skills for building online platforms that showcase agritourism businesses. Activity 2 emphasizes the development and management of social media pages, enabling students to harness the power of digital marketing to promote agritourism services and engage with customers effectively. These activities aim to integrate technological proficiency with entrepreneurial acumen, ensuring that learners are prepared to establish and sustain successful agritourism ventures in the digital age.

5.1. Design and Development of Websites for Agritourism Ventures

This activity is designed to guide students through the process of creating functional and visually appealing websites or e-shops for agritourism business ventures. The goal is to equip students with practical skills in digital marketing and website development, fostering their entrepreneurial abilities.

5.1.1. Understanding E-commerce in Agritourism

The first step involves introducing students to the concept of e-commerce and its significance in modern business practices, particularly in the agritourism sector. The lecture begins with an overview of how e-commerce has transformed marketing and sales strategies for small and medium-sized enterprises (SMEs). E-commerce has enabled SMEs to reduce operational costs, streamline business processes, and enhance customer relationships through digital platforms (Choshin & Ghaffari, 2017). Special attention is given to agritourism ventures, emphasizing how online platforms can be used to promote products and services, reach wider audiences, and generate revenue. For instance, platforms such as online marketplaces and social media have provided agritourism businesses with tools to create virtual storefronts, facilitate online bookings, and manage customer interactions (Galloway et al., 2011).

Examples of successful agritourism websites are presented to demonstrate the impact of e-commerce on business growth and sustainability. Research highlights that digital marketing strategies, including search engine optimization (SEO) and social media advertising, have become critical for enhancing visibility and competitiveness in niche markets such as agritourism (Tew & Barbieri, 2012). By leveraging these strategies, agritourism enterprises not only expand their customer base but also build brand recognition and trust, ultimately leading to increased profitability and long-term sustainability (Lee, 2016).

5.1.2. Learning Key Elements of Website Development

Following this introduction, the next step outlines the fundamental elements required to create a professional website or e-shop, emphasizing the strategic planning and technical components involved in the process. Students first learn about selecting and registering a domain name, which serves as the online identity of a business and plays a critical role in branding and search engine optimization (SEO). The domain name is the "*name of the web server and it is usually selected to be the same as the name of the company*" (Chaffey et al., 2019). Choosing a domain name that reflects the business's purpose and is easy to remember can significantly enhance visibility and credibility (Murphy et al., 2003).

The course then examines the process of selecting a web hosting service, focusing on factors such as reliability, scalability, and security (Turban et al., 2018). Hosting services that provide 24/7 support and regular backups are emphasized to ensure continuous uptime and data protection, which are crucial for maintaining customer trust.

To address growing concerns about cybersecurity, students explore the integration of Secure Sockets Layer (SSL) certificates, which encrypt data and protect sensitive information during online transactions (Bisel, 2007). Maintaining secure transactions is further reinforced by analyzing the role of payment gateways and encryption technologies in safeguarding financial data and fostering consumer confidence (Bhatia et al., 2021).

Furthermore, students acquire knowledge regarding responsive web design principles, which guarantee that layouts are optimized for both desktop and mobile users. In light of the persistent growth of mobile commerce (M-commerce), responsive design enhances usability and accessibility, thereby exerting a direct impact on customer satisfaction and conversion rates (Li and Yeh, 2010; Lee and Benbasat, 2004). Given the pivotal role of customer satisfaction in the tourism industry, this subject matter is of particular relevance (Deirmentzoglou et al., 2022). The course also highlights the importance of user experience (UX) design, emphasizing intuitive navigation, fast loading speeds, and visually appealing aesthetics to attract and retain visitors.

5.1.3. Exploring Existing Websites for Inspiration

In the contemporary business world, innovation is of paramount importance (Agoraki et al., 2024a; Agoraki et al. 2024b; Pistikou et al. 2023). To this end, students are encouraged to explore and critically analyze existing agritourism websites, with the aim of inspiring creativity and innovation. This step involves examining effective design techniques, identifying user-friendly features, and recognizing e-commerce strategies that enhance customer experience. Special attention is given to intuitive navigation, which plays a pivotal role in guiding users seamlessly through the website and facilitating goal-oriented actions, such as making reservations or purchasing products. Students evaluate the use of clear menu structures, logical categorization, and visible search bars, which improve usability and minimize cognitive load (Yan and Guo, 2010; Matera et al., 2006).

Furthermore, they assess the integration of interactive features, such as chatbots, reviews, and multimedia content, which foster engagement and build trust (Aoki, 2020; Gefen et al., 2003). Research suggests that personalization, such as tailored product recommendations and dynamic content, enhances the browsing experience and increases customer satisfaction (Kumar and Benbasat, 2006).

Students also examine strategies for optimizing mobile responsiveness, as studies highlight that mobile-friendly designs directly impact user retention and conversion rates (Nawir and Hendrawan, 2024). Emphasis is placed on fast-loading pages, intuitive touch controls, and mobile payment options, ensuring accessibility across different devices.

Through this analysis, students brainstorm ideas and gather inspiration for their own projects by evaluating how existing websites attract and retain visitors. This process not only strengthens their understanding of usability principles but also encourages them to implement design elements that prioritize user experience, trust, and functionality.

5.1.4. Introduction to E-Commerce Platforms

The next phase introduces students to widely used content management systems (CMS), such as Wix[1], Shopify[2], and WordPress[3]. These platforms are highlighted for their user-friendly interfaces, scalability, and extensive customization options, making them suitable for small and medium-sized enterprises (SMEs) and agritourism ventures. The lecture begins with demonstrations of each platform's core functionalities, tools, and design flexibility. These platforms offer a drag-and-drop editor, built-in SEO tools, and AI-powered design capabilities, plugin integration, customizable themes, integrated payment gateways, inventory management systems, and advanced analytics tools, which streamline online sales processes and support scalability.

Students are advised to work on Wix, as it allows them to explore its features during the trial period without requiring a credit card, making it an accessible starting point for hands-on practice. Students are guided step-by-step through setting up demo accounts, customizing templates, and experimenting with plugins to create interactive features, such as chatbots, contact forms, and booking systems. Hands-on practice emphasizes usability testing, mobile responsiveness, and performance optimization, ensuring that students develop the technical skills needed to design professional, customer-centric websites.

Through this process, students gain insights into leveraging platform-specific tools to enhance user experience, improve search engine rankings, and integrate marketing strategies that drive traffic and conversions. By working directly with these platforms, they build confidence in employing digital tools for creating functional and visually appealing e-commerce websites.

5.1.5. Designing and Developing Websites

Building on this foundation, students proceed to design and develop their own websites or e-shops based on their agritourism business ideas. They draft wireframes, select themes and templates, and upload relevant content, including images, text, and product information. Interactive features such as booking systems, contact forms, and social media integration are added to enhance usability and engagement.

Throughout this process, instructors provide feedback and technical support to address challenges and refine designs.

5.1.6. Presentation and Peer Review

The activity concludes with a presentation session where students showcase their completed websites to the class. Each student delivers a short presentation highlighting the key features and functionalities of their website. Peer reviews are conducted to encourage constructive feedback and foster collaborative learning. Students are given the opportunity to revise and improve their websites based on the feedback received.

5.1.7. Activity's Learning Outcomes

By the end of this activity, students will have gained a comprehensive understanding of the importance of e-commerce in agritourism entrepreneurship. They will have acquired practical skills in website creation, from domain registration and design to integrating security features and user-friendly navigation. Additionally, they will develop creativity, teamwork, and problem-solving abilities through hands-on practice and peer collaboration. This structured approach ensures that students are prepared to leverage digital tools effectively, empowering them to establish a strong online presence for their agritourism ventures.

5.2. Developing and Managing Social Media Pages for Agritourism Ventures

This section outlines a series of interactive activities designed to enhance students' understanding and practical skills in developing and managing social media pages for agritourism ventures. These activities aim to provide hands-on experience and foster creativity, teamwork, and entrepreneurial thinking.

5.2.1. Introduction to the Importance of Social Media

Begin the activity with a lecture or discussion highlighting the transformative role of social media in modern business practices, particularly in promoting agritourism ventures. Social media has become a powerful marketing tool, enabling businesses to reach broader audiences, build relationships with customers, and promote their unique offerings through cost-effective strategies (Felix et al., 2017). Emphasize how platforms such as Facebook, Instagram, and TikTok facilitate content sharing, interactive communication, and community engagement, making them ideal channels for businesses to increase visibility and customer retention (Wang, 2024).

For agritourism ventures, social media offers the ability to showcase authentic experiences, highlight seasonal events, and leverage visual storytelling to attract tourists (Leung et al., 2013). Platforms like Instagram are particularly effective due to their focus on visual content, enabling businesses to share high-quality images and videos that evoke emotions and promote scenic rural landscapes (Dhanesh et al., 2022; Challa and Anute, 2021). Similarly, Facebook provides tools for creating business pages, running targeted advertisements, and receiving customer reviews, which help build trust and credibility (Jordan, 2020). Meanwhile, TikTok offers opportunities for viral marketing through short-form videos, allowing agritourism businesses to showcase activities like farm-to-table events, festivals, and interactive workshops in an engaging format (Du et al., 2022).

Discuss the consumer behavior shift toward relying on social media for discovery, evaluation, and decision-making regarding tourism experiences. Studies suggest that user-generated content (UGC) and online reviews significantly influence purchasing decisions, as they provide social proof and enhance perceived trustworthiness (Malthouse et al., 2016; Zeng & Gerritsen, 2014). Furthermore, hashtags, geotagging, and influencer partnerships amplify marketing efforts by expanding reach and encouraging peer-to-peer recommendations, which are crucial for attracting younger generations, such as Millennials and Gen Z.

To inspire students and demonstrate practical applications, provide real-life examples of successful agritourism ventures that leveraged social media to drive growth. Highlight cases where businesses used Instagram campaigns to showcase eco-friendly practices or Facebook ads to promote local food festivals and events, resulting in increased foot traffic and bookings. Incorporate student activities such as analyzing these examples, developing sample posts, and creating social media marketing plans to enhance learning outcomes.

5.2.2. Presentation of Basic Features of Social Media Platforms

Demonstrate how to use specific features of popular social media platforms relevant to business promotion. Begin with an overview of the fundamental elements of social media platforms, highlighting features that enable businesses to establish a strong digital presence, foster engagement, and track performance. Discuss the importance of profiles and pages, where businesses can share key information such as descriptions, contact details, and operating hours. Explain how multimedia content—including images, videos, and live streams—enhances user engagement by creating visually appealing and interactive experiences (Kaplan and Haenlein, 2010).

Illustrate the role of hashtags in expanding visibility and reaching target audiences through keyword-based searches (Aswani et al., 2018). Highlight analytics tools that measure engagement rates, impressions, and audience demographics, enabling businesses to evaluate their performance and refine strategies. Incorporate step-by-step tutorials and encourage students to explore each platform's features in real time to build their confidence and familiarity with the tools. Emphasize how businesses can adapt their strategies to each platform's unique strengths while maintaining consistent branding across channels.

5.2.3. Development of Social Media Pages for Agritourism Ventures

Ask students to develop social media pages based on their agritourism venture ideas. The process involves brainstorming business concepts and branding strategies before creating profiles or pages that reflect their ideas. Students should design logos, select cover photos, and write descriptions that effectively communicate their brand identity. They will also be responsible for developing and uploading initial content such as posts, images, and videos that align with their branding and messaging strategies. This phase encourages creativity and challenges students to think critically about their target audiences and content approaches.

5.2.4. Interaction Through Scenarios

Simulate real-life interactions by having students act as potential customers on their classmates' social media pages. Activities in this step include commenting on posts, asking questions, and providing feedback. Students will simulate inquiries about services, pricing, and bookings to practice professional communication. They will also share posts to simulate organic reach and engagement while providing constructive criticism and suggestions for improvement. This interactive component fosters collaborative learning and exposes students to diverse perspectives and strategies for engaging with customers online.

5.2.5. Presentation and Peer Feedback

Conclude the activity with student presentations where each team showcases their social media pages and strategies. During the presentations, teams will discuss key design choices, content strategies, and engagement tactics. They will share metrics such as likes, shares, and comments achieved during the interaction phase. Presentations will also include reflections on challenges faced and lessons learned. Peer and instructor feedback will provide students with constructive insights to refine their approach and identify areas for improvement, enhancing their ability to adapt and innovate in future entrepreneurial endeavors.

5.2.6. Activity's Learning Outcomes

By the end of this activity, students will understand the importance of social media in promoting agritourism ventures and develop technical skills in creating and managing social media pages. They will enhance creativity and problem-solving abilities through content creation and branding. Students will also gain experience in customer interaction and feedback management while improving teamwork and presentation skills through collaborative exercises and peer evaluations. These activities combine theory and practice, ensuring that students acquire the necessary skills to effectively leverage social media for entrepreneurial success in the agritourism sector.

6. SKILLS AND COMPETENCIES DEVELOPED THROUGH THE SIMULATION ACTIVITIES

The simulation activities outlined in this chapter are designed to provide students with hands-on experience and practical knowledge, equipping them with the essential skills and competencies required for successful agritourism entrepreneurship in the digital era. These activities not only focus on technical expertise but also emphasize soft skills and strategic thinking. The skills and competencies developed through these activities span several areas, ensuring a comprehensive learning experience.

Digital literacy and technical proficiency are central to the activities, enabling students to gain expertise in creating professional websites, including domain registration, web hosting, and e-commerce integration. Students develop proficiency in using website-building platforms such as Wix, Shopify, and WordPress, along with knowledge of cybersecurity practices, including SSL certificates and secure payment gateways. In addition, they acquire technical skills to set up and manage social media business pages, utilizing platform-specific features like Facebook ads, Instagram Stories, and TikTok trends.

Hands-on practice with analytics tools further enhances their ability to track performance metrics and optimize campaigns. Students also develop content creation and multimedia skills, learning to produce engaging visual and textual content, including videos, infographics, and blog posts, while gaining experience with editing tools and graphic design software to enhance their creative capabilities.

Marketing and branding competencies are another key area, where students learn to apply marketing principles to promote agritourism ventures online. They explore SEO techniques, keyword optimization, and email marketing strategies to boost visibility and sales. Emphasis is placed on crafting compelling brand identities, including logo design, taglines, and consistent visual themes, while practicing branding strategies that resonate with target audiences and build brand loyalty. Interactive scenarios help students develop skills in managing online inquiries, feedback, and complaints, as simulated customer interactions build professionalism and responsiveness.

Entrepreneurial and business skills are cultivated through activities that teach students to conceptualize and plan agritourism ventures, from identifying niche markets to defining unique value propositions. Skills in market analysis and competitive benchmarking are enhanced, alongside project management skills that involve organizing and executing tasks within deadlines. Activities such as developing wireframes, drafting content calendars, and scheduling posts promote time management and goal-setting.

Critical thinking and problem-solving abilities are developed as students evaluate and troubleshoot design flaws, usability issues, and technical errors during website and social media development. Activities promote brainstorming and ideation processes, encouraging students to devise creative solutions for real-world challenges in agritourism marketing. Communication and collaboration skills are also emphasized through group-based activities that foster teamwork, leadership, and conflict resolution. Students learn to divide responsibilities, collaborate on designs, and provide constructive feedback to peers. Formal presentations of their websites and social media pages enhance their ability to articulate ideas and present their work confidently.

Innovation and adaptability are promoted by encouraging students to adopt a growth mindset through experimentation with new tools and approaches. Activities emphasize adaptability to emerging trends, technologies, and customer preferences, preparing students for continuous learning in the dynamic digital landscape. Sustainability awareness is reinforced as students explore the intersection of sustainability and digital entrepreneurship, recognizing how agritourism ventures can contribute to eco-friendly practices and community development. Ethical considerations, including sustainable branding and eco-conscious messaging, are highlighted to promote responsible entrepreneurship.

Finally, networking and relationship-building skills are developed as students practice simulated collaborations and online engagement strategies. Emphasis is placed on fostering partnerships with influencers, suppliers, and local stakeholders to create mutually beneficial relationships that enhance business growth.

The simulation activities described in this chapter provide a comprehensive learning experience, equipping students with the technical, strategic, and interpersonal skills necessary for launching and managing successful agritourism ventures. By combining theoretical insights with practical exercises, the activities ensure that students develop confidence and competence in leveraging digital tools for global reach, business growth, and sustainability. These competencies not only prepare students for entrepreneurship but also empower them to innovate and adapt to the evolving digital landscape, making them well-positioned for long-term success in the agritourism sector.

7. CONCLUSION

In the intricate international economic and business landscape (Deirmentzoglou et al., 2024a), agritourism has established a notable niche within the broader domain of tourism, wherein agricultural production and tourism experiences intersect. These offer experiences that attract both domestic and international visitors in pursuit of geographic authenticity (Barbieri, 2013; Barbieri and Streifeneder, 2019; Barbieri, 2020). E-commerce and pervasiveness of social media indeed have been the very bases for new ways in which agritourism enterprises now function, market products, and interact with customers. For this reason, it is of critical relevance to provide agritourism ventures with digital skills that are crucial for their sustainable development and competitive advantage (Arroyo et al., 2013).

This chapter endeavored to address the critical absence of e-commerce and social media training in conventional agritourism education by underscoring the significance of these digital tools in the contemporary agritourism context. These platforms facilitate direct sales of goods and services, foster enhanced customer relationships, and contribute to the development of brand identity (Greenhow and Lewin, 2019). Such digital tools are to be maximized in a simulated learning approach whereby students can be given hands-on experiences to be prepared for the dynamic environment that characterizes digital marketing and online business management (Freberg, 2012). Simulation-based activities clearly fit into the theories of experiential learning; the student is prepared for hands-on experience similar to what actually happens in business environments (Kolb, 2014).

The objective of this chapter was to examine the integration of structured e-commerce and social media activities into entrepreneurship courses through simulation activities relevant to the contemporary industry. The use of digital tools has been shown to enhance students' learning experience and bridge the gap between academic knowledge and practical business skills (Mandalia, 2023). The chapter's culmination was the empowerment of tourism students to cultivate the competencies essential for the adept management of digital marketing strategies, the optimization of online sales channels, and the enhancement of customer engagement. This endowment of skills will undoubtedly facilitate the students' seamless integration into the agritourism industry.

While this chapter has laid the foundation for integrating e-commerce and social media activities into agritourism entrepreneurship education, future studies should expand the digital landscape by exploring emerging technologies such as the metaverse and artificial intelligence (AI).

The metaverse can hold immense potential for agritourism businesses by enabling immersive virtual experiences that showcase farms, vineyards, and rural landscapes to a global audience. Given the critical role of the metaverse in the tourism industry (Deirmentzoglou et al., 2024b; Buhalis et al., 2023), activities could use virtual reality (VR) and augmented reality (AR) technologies (Varelas, 2022) to simulate authentic agritourism experiences, allowing students to explore destinations, participate in virtual tastings, and even participate in agricultural activities from remote locations.

Similarly, with the rapid development of AI in the modern business world (Kourkoumelis et al., 2024; Stroumpoulis et al., 2022), AI-powered tools can revolutionize agritourism by enabling personalized marketing strategies, chatbots for customer engagement, and predictive analytics to optimize sales and inventory management. Activties could focus on how AI can support smart farming practices, such as precision agriculture and data-driven decision making, to improve the productivity and sustainability of agritourism businesses. In addition, AI applications in recommendation engines can be explored to tailor agritourism experiences to visitors' preferences, thereby improving customer satisfaction and loyalty.

Another promising direction involves examining the role of sustainable development in digital agritourism. As the concepts of corporate sustainable development and environmental, social and governance (ESG) practices are topics of utmost important in business management (e.g. Deirmentzoglou et al., 2024c; Patsoulis and Deirmentzoglou, 2024; Deirmentzoglou et al. 2020); future activities should focus on digital technologies their support to the United Nations Sustainable Development Goals (SDGs) and ESG regulations. Digital tools can be leveraged to promote eco-friendly practices, highlight organic farming, and reduce the carbon footprint of agritourism businesses by promoting virtual experiences as sustainable alternatives to traditional tourism.

Beyond their application to agritourism, the activities proposed in this chapter can be effectively adapted to other types of tourism, such as cruise tourism (Anastasopoulos et al., 2024) and tourism real estate (Anastasopoulos and Varelas, 2023), or to other types of businesses in the agricultural sector, such as agrifood. Agrifood businesses have similar needs for digital tools to improve marketing, streamline operations, and foster customer loyalty (Apostolopoulos et al., 2024; Apostolopoulos et al., 2024; Apostolopoulos et al., 2023; Apostolopoulos et al., 2021). E-commerce platforms and social media channels can facilitate direct-to-consumer sales, promote transparency in sourcing and production processes, and build strong brand identities focused on sustainability and quality.

As the agritourism industry continues to evolve in response to technological advancements and sustainability challenges, it is imperative to align entrepreneurship education with these emerging trends. By integrating metaverse applications, AI tools, and sustainable practices into agritourism curricula, educators can prepare students to navigate and thrive in a highly dynamic and competitive market. This chapter not only highlights the current gaps in digital training but also paves the way for innovative pedagogical approaches that leverage experiential learning to foster resilience, creativity, and adaptability among future agritourism entrepreneurs.

REFERENCES

Adeyinka-Ojo, S., & Abdullah, S. K. (2021). Social media marketing in rural hospitality and tourism destination research. *University of South Florida (USF) M3 Publishing, 5*, 11.

Agoraki, K. K., Deirmentzoglou, G. A., Psychalis, M., & Apostolopoulos, S. (2024a). Types of Innovation and Sustainable Development: Evidence from Medium-and Large-Sized Firms. *International Journal on Management of Innovation & Technology, 21*(02), 1–18. DOI: 10.1142/S0219877024500135

Agoraki, K. K., Deirmentzoglou, G. A., & Triantopoulos, C. (2024b). Cultural Values as Catalysts of Technological Innovation for a Sustainable Future. *Sustainability (Basel), 16*(5), 2064. DOI: 10.3390/su16052064

Ananya, S. A. (2021). Technology application in agri-tourism. In *Technology Application in the Tourism and Hospitality Industry of Bangladesh* (pp. 113-126). DOI: 10.1007/978-981-16-2434-6_7

Anastasopoulos, I., Georgopoulos, N., Katsanakis, I., Klada, N., Konstantopoulou, C., Kopanaki, E., Stroumpoulis, A., Tsoupros, G., & Varelas, S. (2024). Management of sustainable tourism in tourist destination ports: The use of sustainable indicators in the case study of Piraeus port, Greece. *WIT Transactions on Ecology and the Environment, 263*, 23–35. DOI: 10.2495/ST240031

Anastasopoulos, I., & Varelas, S. 2023, September. A Literature Review and Emerging Trends on key Topics of Risks and Challenges Facing Tourism real Estate Investments. In *European Conference on Innovation and Entrepreneurship* (Vol. 18, No. 1, pp. 39-47). DOI: 10.34190/ecie.18.1.1738

Aoki, N. (2020). An experimental study of public trust in AI chatbots in the public sector. *Government Information Quarterly, 37*(4), 101490. DOI: 10.1016/j.giq.2020.101490

Apostolopoulos, N., Kakouris, A., Liargovas, P., Petropoulos, D., & Anastasopoulou, E. (2024). Agri-food enterprises and relationship marketing during COVID-19: A primary data research through commitment-trust theory. *Journal of International Food & Agribusiness Marketing, 36*(1), 3–22. DOI: 10.1080/08974438.2023.2183300

Apostolopoulos, N., Kakouris, A., Liargovas, P., Petropoulos, D., & Anastasopoulou, E. E. (2024). Exploring the impact of crises on rural agri-food SMEs: The moderating role of support mechanisms, digitalisation, and networking. *International Journal of Entrepreneurship and Innovation*. DOI: 10.1177/14657503241270275

Apostolopoulos, N., Makris, I., Apostolopoulos, S., & Anastasopoulou, E. E. 2023, September. Aligning Agri-food Business with Sustainable Development and Quality of Life in Rural Areas: Stakeholders' Perspectives from Greece. In *ECIE 2023 18th European Conference on Innovation and Entrepreneurship Vol 1*. Academic Conferences and Publishing Limited.

Apostolopoulos, N., Petropoulos, D., Liargovas, P., & Anastasopoulou, E. 2024. Constraints to Green and Digital Transition in the Greek Agri-Food Sector. In *Proceedings of The 19th European Conference on Innovation and Entrepreneurship*. Academic Conferences International. DOI: 10.34190/ecie.19.1.2996

Apostolopoulos, N., Ratten, V., Petropoulos, D., Liargovas, P., & Anastasopoulou, E. (2021). Agri-food sector and entrepreneurship during the COVID-19 crisis: A systematic literature review and research agenda. *Strategic Change*, *30*(2), 159–167. DOI: 10.1002/jsc.2400

Arroyo, C. G., Barbieri, C., & Rich, S. R. (2013). Defining agritourism: A comparative study of stakeholders' perceptions in Missouri and North Carolina. *Tourism Management*, *37*, 39–47. DOI: 10.1016/j.tourman.2012.12.007

Ashley, C., & Tuten, T. (2015). Creative strategies in social media marketing: An exploratory study of branded social content and consumer engagement. *Psychology and Marketing*, *32*(1), 15–27. DOI: 10.1002/mar.20761

Aswani, R., Kar, A. K., Ilavarasan, P. V., & Dwivedi, Y. K. (2018). Search engine marketing is not all gold: Insights from Twitter and SEOClerks. *International Journal of Information Management*, *38*(1), 107–116. DOI: 10.1016/j.ijinfomgt.2017.07.005

Barbieri, C. (2013). Assessing the sustainability of agritourism in the US: A comparison between agritourism and other farm entrepreneurial ventures. *Journal of Sustainable Tourism*, *21*(2), 252–270.

Barbieri, C. (2020). Agritourism research: A perspective article. *Tourism Review*, *75*(1), 149–152. DOI: 10.1108/TR-05-2019-0152

Barbieri, C., & Mahoney, E. (2009). Why is diversification an attractive farm adjustment strategy? Insights from Texas farmers and ranchers. *Journal of Rural Studies*, *25*(1), 58–66. DOI: 10.1016/j.jrurstud.2008.06.001

Barbieri, C., & Streifeneder, T. (2019). Agritourism advances around the globe: A commentary from the editors. *Open Agriculture*, *4*(1), 712–714. DOI: 10.1515/opag-2019-0068

Bhatia, N. L., Shukla, V. K., Punhani, R., & Dubey, S. K. 2021, June. Growing aspects of cyber security in e-commerce. In *2021 International Conference on Communication information and Computing Technology (ICCICT)* (pp. 1-6). IEEE. DOI: 10.1109/ICCICT50803.2021.9510152

Bisel, L. D. (2007). The role of SSL in cybersecutiry. *IT Professional*, *9*(2), 22–25. DOI: 10.1109/MITP.2007.41

Buhalis, D., Leung, D., & Lin, M. (2023). Metaverse as a disruptive technology revolutionising tourism management and marketing. *Tourism Management*, *97*, 104724. DOI: 10.1016/j.tourman.2023.104724

Carpio, C. E., Wohlgenant, M. K., & Boonsaeng, T. (2008). The demand for agritourism in the United States. *Journal of Agricultural and Resource Economics*, 254–269.

Chaffey, D., Edmundson-Bird, D., & Hemphill, T. (2019). *Digital business and e-commerce management*. Pearson Uk.

Challa, A., & Anute, N. (2021). The effectiveness of Instagram content marketing on brand building of a company. *Journal of Sales. Service and Marketing Research*, *2*(2), 1–7. DOI: 10.46610/JSSMR.2021.v02i02.001

Chernikova, O., Heitzmann, N., Stadler, M., Holzberger, D., Seidel, T., & Fischer, F. (2020). Simulation-based learning in higher education: A meta-analysis. *Review of Educational Research, 90*(4), 499–541. DOI: 10.3102/0034654320933544

Choshin, M., & Ghaffari, A. (2017). An investigation of the impact of effective factors on the success of e-commerce in small- and medium-sized companies. *Computers in Human Behavior, 66*, 67–74. DOI: 10.1016/j.chb.2016.09.026

Costello, G. J. (2017). More than just a game: The role of simulation in the teaching of product design and entrepreneurship to mechanical engineering students. *European Journal of Engineering Education, 42*(6), 644–652. DOI: 10.1080/03043797.2016.1211992

Deirmentzoglou, G. A., Agoraki, K. K., & Fousteris, A. E. (2020). Organizational culture and corporate sustainable development: Evidence from Greece. *International Journal of Business and Social Science, 11*(5), 92–98. DOI: 10.30845/ijbss.v11n5a9

Deirmentzoglou, G. A., Agoraki, K. K., & Patsoulis, P. (2024c). The nexus between cultural values and perceptions of corporate sustainable development. *Social Responsibility Journal, 20*(2), 224–242. DOI: 10.1108/SRJ-09-2022-0373

Deirmentzoglou, G. A., Anastasopoulou, E. E., & Sklias, P. (2024a). International economic relations and energy security in the European Union: A systematic literature review. *International Journal of Sustainable Energy, 43*(1), 2385682. DOI: 10.1080/14786451.2024.2385682

Deirmentzoglou, G. A., & Deirmentzoglou, E. A. 2022, September. Pest analysis of the e-commerce industry: The case of Greece. In *Business Development and Economic Governance in Southeastern Europe: 13th International Conference on the Economies of the Balkan and Eastern European Countries (EBEEC),Pafos, Cyprus,2021* (pp. 315-323). Cham: Springer International Publishing.

Deirmentzoglou, G. A., Vlassi, E., & Agoraki, K. K. 2022, May. The Effect of the Hotel Attributes on Guest Satisfaction Due to the Covid-19 Pandemic Crisis: The Case of the Greek Tourism and Hospitality Sector. In *International Conference Economies of The Balkan And Eastern European Countries* (pp. 283-297). Cham: Springer Nature Switzerland.

Deirmentzoglou, G. A., Vlassi, E., & Anastasopoulou, E. E. (2024b). DDMMO Website Quality, Destination Image and Intention to Use Metaverse Platforms. *Platforms, 2*(4), 180–192. DOI: 10.3390/platforms2040012

Dhanesh, G., Duthler, G., & Li, K. (2022). Social media engagement with organization-generated content: Role of visuals in enhancing public engagement with organizations on Facebook and Instagram. *Public Relations Review, 48*(2), 102174. DOI: 10.1016/j.pubrev.2022.102174

Du, X., Liechty, T., Santos, C. A., & Park, J. (2022). 'I want to record and share my wonderful journey': Chinese Millennials' production and sharing of short-form travel videos on TikTok or Douyin. *Current Issues in Tourism, 25*(21), 3412–3424. DOI: 10.1080/13683500.2020.1810212

Fanelli, R. M. (2022). Agritourism farms: A great way to promote local products. *Tourism Analysis, 27*(3), 331–342. DOI: 10.3727/108354222X16449628077748

Felix, R., Rauschnabel, P. A., & Hinsch, C. (2017). Elements of strategic social media marketing: A holistic framework. *Journal of Business Research*, *70*, 118–126. DOI: 10.1016/j.jbusres.2016.05.001

Flanigan, S., Blackstock, K., & Hunter, C. (2014). Agritourism from the perspective of providers and visitors: A typology-based study. *Tourism Management*, *40*, 394–405. DOI: 10.1016/j.tourman.2013.07.004

Fleischer, A., Tchetchik, A., Bar-Nahum, Z., & Talev, E. (2018). Is agriculture important to agritourism? The agritourism attraction market in Israel. *European Review of Agriculture Economics*, *45*(2), 273–296. DOI: 10.1093/erae/jbx039

Freberg, K. (2012). Intention to comply with crisis messages communicated via social media. *Public Relations Review*, *38*(3), 416–421. DOI: 10.1016/j.pubrev.2012.01.008

Gadanakis, Y. (2024). Advancing farm entrepreneurship and agribusiness management for sustainable agriculture. *Agriculture*, *14*(8), 1288. DOI: 10.3390/agriculture14081288

Galloway, L., Sanders, J., & Deakins, D. (2011). Rural small firms' use of the internet: From global to local. *Journal of Rural Studies*, *27*(3), 254–262. DOI: 10.1016/j.jrurstud.2011.05.005

Gefen, D., Karahanna, E., & Straub, D. W. (2003). Trust and tam in online shopping: An integrated model1. *Management Information Systems Quarterly*, *27*(1), 51–90. DOI: 10.2307/30036519

Greenhow, C., & Lewin, C. (2019). Social media and education: Reconceptualizing the boundaries of formal and informal learning. In *Social Media and Education* (pp. 6–30). Routledge. DOI: 10.4324/9781315121697-2

Hardesty, S. (2011). Agritourism operators embrace social media for marketing. *California Agriculture*, *65*(02), 56–57. DOI: 10.3733/ca.v065n02p56a

Hays, S., Page, S. J., & Buhalis, D. (2013). Social media as a destination marketing tool: Its use by national tourism organisations. *Current Issues in Tourism*, *16*(3), 211–239. DOI: 10.1080/13683500.2012.662215

Hjalager, A. M. (2010). A review of innovation research in tourism. *Tourism Management*, *31*(1), 1–12. DOI: 10.1016/j.tourman.2009.08.012

Huang, Z., & Benyoucef, M. (2013). From e-commerce to social commerce: A close look at design features. *Electronic Commerce Research and Applications*, *12*(4), 246–259. DOI: 10.1016/j.elerap.2012.12.003

Jordan, T. (2020). *The Digital Economy*. Polity Press.

Kaplan, A. M., & Haenlein, M. (2010). Users of the world, unite! The challenges and opportunities of Social Media. *Business Horizons*, *53*(1), 59–68. DOI: 10.1016/j.bushor.2009.09.003

Katsande, C., Chigora, F., Mutipforo, G., & Marime, S. 2024. Redefining Social Media through Agritourism Business Marketing. In *Agritourism for Sustainable Development: Reflections from Emerging African Economies* (pp. 47-61). CABI. DOI: 10.1079/9781800623705.0004

Kolb, D. A. (2014). *Experiential learning: Experience as the source of learning and development*. FT Press.

Kourkoumelis, A., Anastasopoulou, E., Deirmentzoglou, G., Masouras, A., & Anastasiadou, S. (2024). Artificial Intelligence and Managerial Decision-Making in International Business. In *Proceedings of The 19th European Conference on Innovation and Entrepreneurship*. Academic Conferences International. DOI: 10.34190/ecie.19.1.2573

Król, K. (2019). Forgotten agritourism: Abandoned websites in the promotion of rural tourism in Poland. *Journal of Hospitality and Tourism Technology, 10*(3), 431–442. DOI: 10.1108/JHTT-09-2018-0092

Kumar, N., & Benbasat, I. (2006). Research note: The influence of recommendations and consumer reviews on evaluations of websites. *Information Systems Research, 17*(4), 425–439. DOI: 10.1287/isre.1060.0107

Lalisan, A. K., Fresnido, M. B. R., Ramli, H. R., Aung, A., Utama, A. A. G. S., & Ating, R. (2024, July). Empowering the ASEAN Community through Digitalization of Agriculture for Rural Tourism Development: An NVIVO Analysis. *IOP Conference Series. Earth and Environmental Science, 1366*(1), 012018. DOI: 10.1088/1755-1315/1366/1/012018

Lamie, R. D., Chase, L., Chiodo, E., Dickes, L., Flanigan, S., Schmidt, C., & Streifeneder, T. (2021). Agritourism around the globe: Definitions, authenticity, and potential controversy. *Journal of Agriculture, Food Systems, and Community Development, 10*(2), 573–577. DOI: 10.5304/jafscd.2021.102.002

Lane, B. (2009). Rural tourism: An overview. Academic Press.

Lee, I. (2016). *Encyclopedia of E-Commerce Development, Implementation, and Management.* IGI Global. DOI: 10.4018/978-1-4666-9787-4

Lee, K., Nguyen, A. T., Nguyen, N. P., Nguyen, T. H., Tran, N., Nguyen, T. L., & Vu, T. T. (2024). Determinants of agritourism development in green tea farms of the northern mountains of Vietnam. *Multidisciplinary Science Journal, 6*(4).

Lee, Y. E., & Benbasat, I. (2004). A framework for the study of customer interface design for mobile commerce. *International Journal of Electronic Commerce, 8*(3), 79–102. DOI: 10.1080/10864415.2004.11044299

Leung, D., Law, R., Van Hoof, H., & Buhalis, D. (2013). Social media in tourism and hospitality: A literature review. *Journal of Travel & Tourism Marketing, 30*(1-2), 3–22. DOI: 10.1080/10548408.2013.750919

Li, Y. M., & Yeh, Y. S. (2010). Increasing trust in mobile commerce through design aesthetics. *Computers in Human Behavior, 26*(4), 673–684. DOI: 10.1016/j.chb.2010.01.004

Malthouse, E. C., Calder, B. J., Kim, S. J., & Vandenbosch, M. (2016). Evidence that user-generated content that produces engagement increases purchase behaviours. *Journal of Marketing Management, 32*(5-6), 427–444. DOI: 10.1080/0267257X.2016.1148066

Mandalia, S. (2023, November). Tourism Education in the Digital Era: Navigating Innovation and Transformation. In *International Conference on Social Science and Education (ICoeSSE 2023)* (pp. 509-530). Atlantis Press. DOI: 10.2991/978-2-38476-142-5_48

Matera, M., Rizzo, F., & Carughi, G. T. (2006). Web usability: Principles and evaluation methods. *Web engineering*, 143-180.

Moratis, L., Hoff, J., & Reul, B. (2006). A dual challenge facing management education: Simulation-based learning and learning about CSR. *Journal of Management Development, 25*(3), 213–231. DOI: 10.1108/02621710610648150

Murphy, J., Raffa, L., & Mizerski, R. (2003). The Use of Domain Names in e-branding by the World's Top Brands. *Electronic Markets, 13*(3), 222–232. DOI: 10.1080/1019678032000108310

Mutipforo, G., Muwani, T. S., Katsande, C., Marime, S., & Ranganai, N. (2024). ICTs and Their Influence on Agritourism. In *Agritourism for Sustainable Development: Reflections from Emerging African Economies* (pp. 174-188). CABI. DOI: 10.1079/9781800623705.0013

Muwani, T. S., Marime, S., Ranganai, N., & Mutipforo, G. (2024). Digital technologies for sustainable agritourism and human development. In *Agritourism for Sustainable Development* (pp. 189-206). CABI. DOI: 10.1079/9781800623705.0014

Navío-Marco, J., Ruiz-Gómez, L. M., & Sevilla-Sevilla, C. (2018). Progress in information technology and tourism management: 30 years on and 20 years after the internet-Revisiting Buhalis & Law's landmark study about eTourism. *Tourism Management, 69*, 460–470. DOI: 10.1016/j.tourman.2018.06.002

Nawir, F., & Hendrawan, S. A. (2024). The Impact of Website Usability and Mobile Optimization on Customer Satisfaction and Sales Conversion Rates in E-commerce Businesses in Indonesia. *The Eastasouth Journal of Information System and Computer Science, 2*(01), 15–30. DOI: 10.58812/esiscs.v2i01.324

Nickerson, N. P., Black, R. J., & McCool, S. F. (2001). Agritourism: Motivations behind farm/ranch business diversification. *Journal of Travel Research, 40*(1), 19–26. DOI: 10.1177/004728750104000104

Paliszkiewicz, J., Chen, K., & Mendel, M. (2024). *Trust in Social and Business Relations*. Trust in Social and Business Relations., DOI: 10.4324/9781032633749

Patsoulis, P., & Deirmentzoglou, G. A. (2024). Entrepreneurship in the World of ESG Awareness: Tales from a Global Panel. *Available atSSRN* 4870078. DOI: 10.2139/ssrn.4870078

Phelan, C., & Sharpley, R. (2011). Exploring agritourism entrepreneurship in the UK. *Tourism Planning & Development, 8*(2), 121–136. DOI: 10.1080/21568316.2011.573912

Phillip, S., Hunter, C., & Blackstock, K. (2010). A typology for defining agritourism. *Tourism Management, 31*(6), 754–758. DOI: 10.1016/j.tourman.2009.08.001

Pistikou, V., Flouros, F., Deirmentzoglou, G. A., & Agoraki, K. K. (2023). Sustainability Reporting: Examining the Community Impact of the S&P500 Companies. *Sustainability (Basel), 15*(18), 13681. DOI: 10.3390/su151813681

Platania, M. (2014). Agritourism farms and the web. An exploratory evaluation of their websites. *AGRIS On-Line Papers in Economics and Informatics, 6*(3), 51–58.

Salamzadeh, A., Tajpour, M., & Hosseini, E. (2022). Measuring the impact of simulation-based teaching on entrepreneurial skills of the MBA/DBA students. In *Technology and entrepreneurship Education: Adopting creative digital approaches to learning and teaching* (pp. 77–104). Springer International Publishing. DOI: 10.1007/978-3-030-84292-5_4

Santeramo, F. G., & Barbieri, C. (2017). On the demand for agritourism: A cursory review of methodologies and practice. *Tourism Planning & Development, 14*(1), 139–148. DOI: 10.1080/21568316.2015.1137968

Schilling, B. J., Attavanich, W., & Jin, Y. (2014). Does agritourism enhance farm profitability? *Journal of Agricultural and Resource Economics*, 69–87.

Senyao, S., & Ha, S. (2022). How social media influences resident participation in rural tourism development: A case study of Tunda in Tibet. *Journal of Tourism and Cultural Change, 20*(3), 386–405. DOI: 10.1080/14766825.2020.1849244

Sheikh, R. A., Abdalkrim, G. M., & Shehawy, Y. M. (2023). Assessing the impact of business simulation as a teaching method for developing 21st century future skills. *Journal of International Education in Business, 16*(3), 351–370.

Siregar, O. M., Ginting, B., Jali, M. F. M., & Nasution, M. D. T. P. (2024). Challenges in Integrating Agritourism with Sustainable Farming Practices: How Do the Willingness, Attitudes, and Entrepreneurial Competencies of Rural Youth Influence This Integration? In Harnessing, A. I. (Ed.), *Machine Learning, and IoT for Intelligent Business* (Vol. 1, pp. 439–450). Springer Nature Switzerland.

Sonnino, R. (2004). For a 'piece of bread'? Interpreting sustainable development through agritourism in Southern Tuscany. *Sociologia Ruralis, 44*(3), 285–300. DOI: 10.1111/j.1467-9523.2004.00276.x

Stroumpoulis, A., Kopanaki, E., & Varelas, S. (2022). Role of artificial intelligence and big data analytics in smart tourism: A resource-based view approach. *WIT Transactions on Ecology and the Environment, 256*, 99–108. DOI: 10.2495/ST220091

Tanina, A., Konyshev, E., & Tsahaeva, K. (2020). Agritourism development model in digital economy. In *Innovations in Digital Economy* (pp. 1-6). DOI: 10.1145/3444465.3444518

Tew, C., & Barbieri, C. (2012). The perceived benefits of agritourism: The provider's perspective. *Tourism Management, 33*(1), 215–224. DOI: 10.1016/j.tourman.2011.02.005

Torres, A., Domańska-Glonek, E., Dzikowski, W., Korulczyk, J., & Torres, K. (2020). Transition to online is possible: Solution for simulation-based teaching during the COVID-19 pandemic. *Medical Education, 54*(9), 858–859. DOI: 10.1111/medu.14245 PMID: 32418247

Tshuma, S., Dube, M., & Dangaiso, P. (2024). Agritourism Digital and Social Media Marketing in Africa: The Case Study of Zimbabwe. In *Agritourism in Africa* (pp. 191-211). Routledge.

Turban, E., Pollard, C., & Wood, G. (2018). *Information technology for management: On-demand strategies for performance, growth and sustainability*. John Wiley & Sons.

Varelas, S. (2022). Virtual immersive platforms as a strategic innovative destination marketing tool in the COVID-19 era. *Sustainability (Basel), 14*(19), 12867. DOI: 10.3390/su141912867

Vlassi, E., Deirmentzoglou, G. A., Agoraki, K. K., & Papatheodorou, A. (2023a). When Tourism and Fashion Cocreate: Narratives From Greece. In *Fashion and Tourism: Parallel Stories* (pp. 93-106). Emerald Publishing Limited.

Vlassi, E., Deirmentzoglou, G. A., & Irakleidi, E. (2023b, September). Capturing Destination's Cognitive and Affective Image on Social Media. The Case of Pafos, Cyprus. In *The International Conference on Strategic Innovative Marketing and Tourism* (pp. 19-28). Cham: Springer Nature Switzerland.

Wang, K. (2024). Analysis of Image Interaction and Social Motivation in Virtual Communities:—Take the Example of Tiktok, Instagram Virtual Communities. *Transactions on Social Science. Education and Humanities Research*, *7*, 194–200.

Xiang, Z., & Gretzel, U. (2010). Role of social media in online travel information search. *Tourism Management*, *31*(2), 179–188. DOI: 10.1016/j.tourman.2009.02.016

Xu, R., Yu, H., Li, B., & Miao, D. (2023). Research on the development path of e-commerce for rural tourism. *Applied Mathematics and Nonlinear Sciences, 9*(1).

Yan, P., & Guo, J. (2010, February). The research of web usability design. In *2010 The 2nd International Conference on Computer and Automation Engineering (ICCAE)* (Vol. 4, pp. 480-483). IEEE.

Yasin, N., Gilani, S. A. M., Contu, D., & Fayaz, M. J. (2022). Simulation-based learning in business and entrepreneurship in higher education: A review of the games available. *Technology and Entrepreneurship Education: Adopting Creative Digital Approaches to Learning and Teaching*, 25-51.

Yuan, Y., Tseng, Y. H., & Li, C. (2022). e-Tourism research: A review. *Handbook of e-Tourism*, 75-93.

Zeng, B., & Gerritsen, R. (2014). What do we know about social media in tourism? A review. *Tourism Management Perspectives*, *10*, 27–36. DOI: 10.1016/j.tmp.2014.01.001

ENDNOTES

1 https://www.wix.com/

2 https://www.shopify.com/

3 https://wordpress.com/

Chapter 16
Prototyping Mobile Applications for International Markets:
A Simulation Activity for Digital Entrepreneurship Education

Georgios A. Deirmentzoglou
https://orcid.org/0000-0003-1687-0708
Neapolis University Pafos, Cyprus

Andreas N. Masouras
https://orcid.org/0000-0001-8989-3930
Neapolis University, Pafos, Cyprus

Konstantina K. Agoraki
https://orcid.org/0009-0007-5135-3091
University of Piraeus, Greece

Eleni E. Anastasopoulou
https://orcid.org/0000-0002-0918-8527
Neapolis University, Pafos, Cyprus

Andreas E. Fousteris
https://orcid.org/0009-0008-8381-8532
University of Piraeus, Greece

Evangelos A. Deirmentzoglou
https://orcid.org/0009-0002-9638-7520
University of Piraeus, Greece

ABSTRACT

In today's dynamic digital economy, mobile applications have become essential drivers of entrepreneurial success, enabling ventures to reach global markets and meet evolving consumer needs. This chapter explores the integration of mobile application prototyping as a core simulation activity within digital entrepreneurship education. The purpose of this chapter is to present a methodology for digital entrepreneurship programs regarding the prototyping of mobile applications for international markets. The proposed simulation activity consists of seven steps: 1) introduction to prototyping, 2) overview of the design tool Figma, 3) demonstration of Figma and its user interface, 4) gathering references and inspiration, 5) sketching ideas, 6) designing prototypes in Figma, and 7) peer testing and feedback. By integrating this simulation activity into digital entrepreneurship curricula, educators can better prepare students to meet the demands of a fast-paced digital landscape while cultivating entrepreneurial mindsets and technical expertise.

DOI: 10.4018/979-8-3693-9040-5.ch016

1. INTRODUCTION

In the rapidly evolving global economy, digital entrepreneurship has emerged as a transformative force, reshaping industries, markets, and business practices (Kraus et a., 2019). According to Kollman (2006) "*e-entrepreneurship refers to establishing a new company with an innovative business idea within the net economy, which, using an electronic platform in data networks, offers its products and/or services based upon a purely electronic creation of value. Essential is the fact that this value offer was only made possible through the development of information technology*". Sussan and Acs (2017) defined digital entrepreneurship as the combination of digital and entrepreneurial ecosystems and Davidson and Vaast (2010) included the concept of identifying opportunities through the use of digital technologies. Thus, digital entrepreneurship refers to the process of creating and managing businesses that leverage digital technologies, including e-commerce platforms, social media channels, and mobile applications, to deliver products and services. This mode of entrepreneurship not only reduces geographical barriers but also facilitates access to international markets, enabling businesses to scale globally with relative ease.

The proliferation of digital tools has democratized entrepreneurship, offering individuals and small enterprises the ability to compete with larger organizations (Elia et al., 2020). In today's interconnected world, technology is at the core of how businesses operate, innovate, and compete (Agoraki et al., 2024a). Digital entrepreneurship is no longer confined to traditional models but involves leveraging emerging technologies to address real-world challenges. This shift has placed immense pressure on educational institutions to adapt, equipping students with the tools and skills necessary to excel in a rapidly evolving market (Kondaveeti et al., 2021; Viswanathan et al., 2014; Fayolle & Gailly, 2008; Neck & Greene, 2011; Kraus et al., 2019). The entrepreneurial ecosystem demands graduates who can innovate, design, and adapt to the rapidly changing digital environment.

Mobile applications have become indispensable tools in the digital business landscape (Bharadwaj et al., 2013). With the widespread adoption of smartphones and mobile internet, apps provide seamless access to information, services, and transactions, making them central to modern entrepreneurship. Mobile applications enable businesses to engage directly with customers, personalize user experiences, and streamline operations (Faulds et al., 2018; Sun and May, 2014). From e-commerce and financial services to health and education, mobile apps facilitate diverse business models, fostering innovation and scalability. Their ability to harness data analytics and artificial intelligence further enhances customer insights, enabling targeted marketing strategies and improved decision-making (Kourkoumelis et al., 2024; Sarker et al., 2021). For entrepreneurs aiming to penetrate international markets, mobile applications offer a platform to adapt to local preferences while maintaining a consistent global presence. As such, mobile app development is a critical skill for aspiring entrepreneurs, equipping them to meet the demands of an increasingly mobile-driven economy.

Simulation-based learning has gained prominence as an effective pedagogical approach in entrepreneurship education (Hallinger and Wang, 2020). Simulations create realistic, risk-free environments where students can experiment with business concepts, test strategies, and develop problem-solving skills. However, traditional lecture-based teaching methods often fail to address the dynamic and practical needs of modern entrepreneurs. While theoretical knowledge provides the foundation, it does not suffice in developing the practical skills, creativity, and adaptability needed in entrepreneurship (Ahuja, 2024). According to Brown (2009), experiential learning methods, such as simulation-based activities, have proven effective in bridging the gap between academic theory and real-world application.

Mobile application prototyping has emerged as a particularly effective simulation activity. By allowing students to create tangible representations of their business ideas, prototyping provides an opportunity to explore design, functionality, and user experience (Ries, 2011). This process not only enhances technical and creative skills but also fosters an entrepreneurial mindset, preparing students to face the uncertainties of the digital economy (Norman, 2013). Moreover, students introduced to critical entrepreneurial processes, such as iterative development and user-centric design, which are essential in modern startups.

This chapter aims to provide a comprehensive framework for integrating mobile application design as a simulation activity within digital entrepreneurship programs. By focusing on international markets, the chapter highlights the importance of cultural adaptability (Deirmentzoglou et al., 2024a; Agoraki et al., 2024b), user-centered design, and scalable business models. It outlines step-by-step methodologies for creating prototype mobile applications, from conceptualization to deployment, emphasizing practical learning outcomes. The ultimate goal is to demonstrate how simulation activities can cultivate entrepreneurial competencies, enhance digital literacy, and prepare students for the complexities of global markets. This chapter serves as a valuable resource for educators, researchers, and practitioners seeking to enhance entrepreneurship education through experiential learning methodologies.

2. THEORETICAL FRAMEWORK FOR SIMULATION ACTIVITIES IN EDUCATION

The evolution of the digital economy over the last decade has led to the substantial development of mobile applications, which, in conjunction with technological advances, has given rise to a niche market for mobile applications. The emergence of this market has precipitated the necessity for the development of simulation-based learning methodologies, which demand the establishment and execution of real-world models. This paradigm shift has unveiled novel challenges in educational methodologies and activities, with the objective of equipping students with the necessary tools to apply their knowledge and cultivate soft skills within a novel and advanced conceptual framework that mirrors the evolving professional practices (Frasson & Blanchard, 2012).

Babin et al. (2019) argue that learning theories are the cornerstone for the development and the implementation of effective educational tools to gain the ultimate learning experience. Within this framework, simulation educators must be familiar with their contributions to education to improve teaching and learning. In reviewing the extant literature on the subject matter, Babin et al. (2019) discuss thoroughly the alternative learning theories which have been developed over the last two decades that are of importance in developing and implementing simulation-based education. The main finding of their analysis is that these alternative approaches are an integrated part of the designing simulation activities and to the designing of prototype mobile applications.

Recently, Lewandowski (2019) provides a thorough analysis on the development of simulation-learning tools which teachers and other educators could choose to implement and integrate into their clinical training. The combination of such tools is expected to form an evidence-based approach which amounts as a starting point the formal identification of the expected learning outcomes. This will be followed by the establishment of a set of metrics to determine under which conditions the expected learning outcomes are achieved and developing the methodologies for the evaluation of the specific metrics. Moreover, Lewandowski (2019) explains that it is of importance to select the appropriate interventions to accomplish the expected learning outcomes implementing a systems approach for both the simulators and the simulation approaches. Professional reports along with published academic research lying in the field of instructional and performance technology should be used to extract the tools under consideration. Finally, Lewandowski (2019) proposes the use of a holistic approach to determine the return on investment (ROI) along with the formation of specific guidelines and suggestions to develop the implementation plan of the simulation-learning methodologies.

Grierson et al. (2019) argue that an indirect hypothesis of simulation is that we can transfer to the actual clinical framework those learning skills obtained from the implementation of the simulation methodology. A by-product of this hypothesis is that the likelihood for a successful resemblance of "real life" is greater the better the simulation has been designed. Grierson et al. (2019) critically examine these assumptions. To this end, they use a large literature from the fields of psychology and motor learning which leads to the conclusion that the transfer from the laboratory to the real world is a difficult task in several cases. The authors also show that the transfer of those skills acquired is still far from done in a coherent way even in the case of a realistic resemblance. In addition, Grierson et al. (2019) analyze several features of simulation and the application of the corresponding developed curriculum which could lead to a higher likelihood to achieve a successful transfer.

Ingram and Jackson (2004) argue that there are several dimensions that theoretical underpinnings and their practical applications of simulation-based learning encompass. According to their research, teaching and learning approaches could be enhanced through simulations when genuine learning environments could be developed. Such simulations will provide the platform for students' problem-solving steps. This platform is required to create a safe and controlled environment through which the students will apply acquired knowledge, make mistakes, receive feedback, and adjust their understanding accordingly. Through this loop of knowledge, trial and error and feedback receipt there will be a higher likelihood for a successful transfer of learning to real-world settings and genuine learning. In his seminar work, Kolb (1984) explains the process of simulated learning with the development of a cycle of experiential learning which provides the theoretical framework of simulated learning. Kolb's (1984) theoretical framework considers a learning environment where students learn by doing, reflecting, and actively participating in the learning process (the cycle or the loop process of acquiring knowledge). Jonassen and Hung (2012) further explore this cycle of knowledge acquisition by considering that the development of instructional methods like the problem-based learning (PBL) which allow students to learn by solving problems which purposely have been constructed in a wrong way. Such simulation learning approach is expected to increase the level of thinking of students who will also discover self-directed methods.

Simulation learning experiences require the establishment of virtual laboratories which will allow students to conduct experiments tailored to a specific discipline. Moreover, in the case of science courses it is expected that such virtual laboratories allow students to conduct experiments without taking the risk of a hazardous and unexpected outcome. In addition, such virtual laboratories do not require substantial funding like the physical laboratories neither are time-consuming as in the case that physical presence is required. Johanssen and Hung (2012) explain that problem-based learning is an instructional method aimed at preparing students for real-world settings. Problem-based learning was originally developed and implemented seven decades ago to improve the clinical performances by medical students. The theoretical background is based upon the information processing process model of cognition, cognitive theories, and constructivist theories. This learning process has five characteristics, namely (a) problem-focused; (b) problem-structured content; (c) student-centered, self-directed learning; (d) self-reflective and (e) tutors/instructors as facilitators. In the field of social sciences, students can understand different perspectives and develop a range of feelings based on alternative scenarios.

The above-mentioned practical applications show how versatile and effective those simulations contribute to the promotion of active learning and engagement. According to Bell et al. (2008) there are four major features encompassed by simulation-based learning. Those instructional features are: (a) richness of the learning experience; (b) immersion; (c) interactivity; and finally, communication. The first instructional feature is related to the use of multimedia content which helps to create a realistic and relevant context. Hui et al. (2021) argue that immersion leads to the learners to be exposed to significant contextual characteristics. The third instructional feature refers to the interaction with different potential stakeholders like the simulation of competitors, co-workers, or clients. Finally, communication could provide instructional support, or develop environments for collaboration like face to face lectures and discussions and/or on-line instruction.

The creation of effective learning simulations is based on the following stages of development and implementation. The first stage involves the design of an activity which must be compatible with the learning objectives taken to be clearly defined. Such procedure must ensure that students are provided with the necessary challenges and tasks. Given the availability of necessary resources, you are asked to choose the resource that matches better the needs and context, and these resources may refer to multimedia, simulation software and virtual reality tools. The second stage is linked to simulated learning. Specifically, virtual reality and /or sophisticated media production may lead to an enhanced learning experience which of high-fidelity and 3D representation although as Kozlowski and Bell (2007) argue to enhance a learner's understanding and interpretation of the learning material may be necessarily linked to complex learning procedures. Therefore, it is argued by Kozlowski and Bell (2007) that there is no robust evidence that learning is necessarily enhanced if instead of using simple text we use alternative multimedia elements. In fact, such multimedia elements can be proved to create a substantial cost burden, being less user-friendly, while may lead to an extension of the duration of the learning process and learner's training. Kozlowski and Bell (2007) argue, though, that these multimedia elements which are generated by simulations could have significant contribution in training which require the acquaintance of more complex and adaptable skills.

Ross (2021) also confirms that simulation-based learning was first developed and employed in health-care professional education since the 1950s. However, Ross (2021) argues that while simulation-based learning at the same time it demands significant time to design and execute. Furthermore, Ross (2021) that one important element of health care education research appears to be an interchange of learning theory and pedagogy although there is an important difference between the two learning approaches. Finally, Ross (2021) presents and discusses four alternative learning theories which are commonly integrated into simulation-based learning, namely, Behaviorism; social cognitive theory; constructivism and experiential learning theory. Furthermore, each of these theories provides a solid theoretical framework for simulation-based learning.

Vlachopoulos and Makri (2017) argue that innovative teaching methods are utilized including games and simulations to provide additional means to the higher education institutions in preparing future professionals. These researchers focuse on the impact of games and simulations to achieve specific learning objectives. The empirical evidence indicates that games and/or simulations have a positive impact on learning goals. Vlachopoulos and Makri (2017) identify three learning outcomes when integrating games into the learning process: cognitive, behavioural, and affective. Simulations offer a new channel for genuine learning and training in higher education by providing students the opportunity to practice their skills in an environment that resembles their potential professional practice. Moreover, it is argued that students can engage actively in the learning process and eventually exhibit higher levels of thinking because of effective design and the implementation of appropriate learning technologies. Simulation-based learning provides a wide range of tools that will critically support the students to engage in high-quality learning experiences. Furthermore, such tools will give the opportunity to practice their skills in a safe environment which will also allow them to reflect on their learning and engage in knowledge discussion with their classmates and colleagues. Two other tools provided are the interactive document and the interactive video. The former, provides the flexibility of adding on-line questions by educators and the latter, provide the tools for asynchronous on-line education.

3. THE IMPORTANCE OF DIGITAL TOOLS IN ENTREPRENEURSHIP AND INTERNATIONAL MARKETS

Digital tools have become indispensable in modern entrepreneurship, transforming the ways businesses operate, innovate, and compete, especially in international markets (Apostolopoulos et al., 2024; Nambisan et al., 2019a). As globalization accelerates and digital technologies advance, entrepreneurs must leverage digital platforms, applications, and systems to remain competitive, access to international markets and seize new opportunities (Dana, 2022; Luo, 2021; Nambisan et al., 2019b).

Platforms such as e-commerce websites, social media, and online marketplaces enable businesses to reach global audiences without requiring physical infrastructure in multiple locations (Deirmentzoglou and Deirmentzoglou, 2022; Berthon et al., 2012; Wilson and Abel, 2002). Through digital marketing techniques, entrepreneurs can promote their products and services globally, targeting specific demographics with precision using data analytics and customer profiling tools (Jose, 2018).

Search Engine Optimization (SEO) and Pay-Per-Click (PPC) advertising are examples of strategies that allow businesses to enhance their visibility in competitive markets (Kritzinger and Weideman, 2013). Additionally, multilingual websites and translation tools lower language barriers, making it easier to attract and engage international customers. This democratization of access enables even small and medium-sized enterprises (SMEs) to compete on a global scale, fostering inclusivity and diversity in international commerce.

The integration of digital tools streamlines business operations, improving efficiency and productivity. Entrepreneurs can utilize Customer Relationship Management (CRM) systems to monitor customer interactions and manage relationships effectively (Chen and Popovich, 2003). Tools such as project management software and communication platforms facilitate collaboration among remote teams, supporting the growing trend of distributed workforces.

Accounting and financial management tools simplify budgeting, invoicing, and financial analysis, allowing entrepreneurs to make informed decisions. Cloud-based storage systems ensure data accessibility and security, enabling entrepreneurs to manage their businesses from anywhere in the world (Kloch et al., 2011).

Digital tools foster innovation by enabling entrepreneurs to prototype, test, and refine their products more efficiently (Elia et al., 2020). Prototyping platforms, such as Figma and Adobe XD, allow businesses to visualize and test ideas quickly, reducing time-to-market. Entrepreneurs can gather user feedback through surveys, usability testing, and analytics tools, ensuring products align with customer needs and expectations.

Moreover, advancements in artificial intelligence (AI) and machine learning support predictive modeling, automating decision-making processes and enhancing customer service through chatbots and virtual assistants (Bharadiya, 2023). Such innovations enable entrepreneurs to stay ahead of market trends and continuously improve their offerings.

Networking and collaboration are critical to entrepreneurial success, and digital tools have revolutionized these processes. Social media platforms and networking tools allow entrepreneurs to connect with investors, mentors, and partners worldwide (Mack et al., 2017). Online forums, webinars, and virtual conferences facilitate knowledge sharing and collaboration, providing access to expertise and resources previously limited to local markets.

Additionally, crowdfunding platforms like Kickstarter and Indiegogo enable entrepreneurs to raise capital from a global pool of investors, breaking down traditional funding barriers. These platforms not only provide financial support but also validate ideas through community engagement, reducing risk and increasing market confidence (Lehner, 2015).

While digital tools offer significant advantages, they also present challenges, particularly when operating in international markets. Entrepreneurs must address data privacy regulations, cybersecurity threats, and cultural differences to maintain trust and compliance (Mmango and Gundu, 2024). In addition, payment gateways, such as PayPal and Stripe, simplify cross-border transactions, but entrepreneurs must also consider currency fluctuations and local payment preferences. Addressing these complexities requires strategic use of digital tools to manage risks and optimize global operations.

The rapid pace of technological advancements means entrepreneurs must remain adaptable and forward-thinking. Emerging technologies, such as blockchain, augmented reality (AR), virtual reality (VR), metaverse and the Internet of Things (IoT), are poised to redefine international business landscapes. Blockchain, for example, enhances transparency and security in financial transactions (Deirmentzoglou, 2019), while metaverse enable immersive customer experiences that transcend geographical boundaries (Deirmentzoglou et al., 2024b).

Entrepreneurs who embrace these innovations and integrate them into their strategies will be better positioned to capitalize on future opportunities. Education and training programs must also evolve, equipping aspiring entrepreneurs with the skills and knowledge required to navigate this digital era effectively.

Digital tools play a transformative role in entrepreneurship, enabling businesses to access international markets, enhance efficiency, drive innovation, and build global networks. By leveraging these technologies, entrepreneurs can overcome traditional barriers, scale operations, and remain competitive in an increasingly digital economy. However, the successful adoption of digital tools requires ongoing learning, adaptability, and a strategic approach to managing challenges.

As the digital landscape continues to evolve, entrepreneurs must stay informed about emerging trends and technologies. Incorporating simulation-based activities, such as mobile app prototyping, into educational frameworks can further prepare future entrepreneurs for success in global markets. The integration of digital tools in entrepreneurship not only facilitates business growth but also fosters creativity, resilience, and inclusivity, laying the foundation for sustainable and scalable ventures.

4. PROTOTYPING MOBILE APPLICATIONS

Prototyping is a vital process in entrepreneurship, serving as a bridge between conceptual ideas and tangible products. It involves creating preliminary versions of products or systems that allow for testing and refinement before full-scale development. In the context of entrepreneurship, prototyping enables innovators to visualize their ideas, assess functionality, and gather feedback from stakeholders (Noyes, 2018). This iterative process reduces the risks associated with launching new products by highlighting potential flaws and areas for improvement early on (Petrakis et al., 2021). Entrepreneurs benefit from prototyping as it fosters creativity, encourages experimentation, and accelerates problem-solving. Furthermore, prototyping facilitates communication with investors, partners, and users, helping entrepreneurs secure buy-in and refine their offerings based on user needs (Paust et al., 2024).

Prototyping typically include conceptualization, design, testing, and refinement (Deininger et al., 2017). Initially, ideas are explored and defined based on identified market needs or problems. The design phase transforms concepts into tangible representations, whether through sketches, wireframes, or digital models. Testing follows, where prototypes are evaluated for usability and functionality, often involving direct feedback from potential users. Finally, refinements are made based on feedback to improve the design before launching the final product. This cyclical process ensures that products are developed with a user-centric approach, reducing the likelihood of failure and increasing market relevance.

In the realm of mobile applications, prototyping plays an increasingly important role due to the dynamic and competitive nature of the market. Mobile apps often serve as critical touchpoints between businesses and consumers, making it essential for entrepreneurs to create user-friendly and visually appealing designs (Flora et al., 2014). Prototyping mobile applications involves several key steps, starting with research and inspiration. Entrepreneurs analyze existing applications to identify best practices and gather ideas for their own designs. This phase also includes identifying user pain points and needs to ensure the application delivers meaningful value.

The design process begins with sketching ideas on paper, allowing entrepreneurs to quickly experiment with different layouts and structures. Sketching serves as a low-cost, flexible method for capturing concepts without being constrained by technical tools (Goldschmidt, 2014). Once initial sketches are reviewed and refined, entrepreneurs transition to digital tools like Figma to create wireframes and interactive prototypes. Figma enables collaborative design, making it easier for teams to build and refine interfaces in real time.

Creating a prototype in software like Figma involves defining the structure of the application, adding visual elements, and incorporating interactive features to simulate user navigation. This hands-on approach allows entrepreneurs to test functionality and identify usability issues early in the process. During this stage, careful attention must be paid to designing with a user-centric approach (Černezel Heričko, 2013). Entrepreneurs should prioritize intuitive navigation, consistent design patterns, and accessibility to enhance user experience. Elements such as color schemes, typography, and button placements should align with user expectations and cultural preferences, especially when targeting international markets.

Testing and feedback are integral components of mobile application prototyping (Samrgandi, 2021). Peer testing allows entrepreneurs to present their prototypes to others for evaluation, gathering insights into usability, clarity, and overall appeal. Feedback sessions often reveal overlooked issues and inspire further improvements. Iterative adjustments based on feedback ensure the final product meets user expectations and performs effectively in the market.

5. MOBILE APPLICATION PROTOTYPING AS A SIMULATION ACTIVITY

The role of simulation activities in education has been extensively studied, with consistent evidence pointing to their efficacy in enhancing student engagement and learning outcomes. According to Ahuja (2024), simulations offer a dynamic learning environment where students can experiment with business strategies, observe the outcomes, and refine their decision-making processes. These activities are particularly effective in entrepreneurship education, where practical experience is crucial.

Mobile application prototyping, as a specific form of simulation, stands out for its alignment with the needs of the digital economy. Ries (2011) highlights the importance of rapid prototyping in entrepreneurial contexts, particularly within the Lean Startup methodology, which advocates iterative development to test and validate business ideas quickly. This iterative approach minimizes risk while maximizing the potential for innovation.

Brown (2009) argues that design thinking, a methodology closely linked to prototyping, fosters a user-centric approach to problem-solving. This approach is critical in entrepreneurship, as it encourages students to empathize with end-users and design solutions that meet real needs. Lee (2021) emphasize the importance of scaffolding in supporting students as they navigate the complexities of prototyping, highlighting how structured guidance can enhance learning outcomes.

Despite its many benefits, implementing prototyping in educational settings is not without challenges. Laine (2010) & Hoidn (2014) point to resource limitations, technical skill gaps, and the need for continuous curriculum updates as significant barriers. Moreover, the rapidly evolving nature of technology requires educators to stay informed about the latest tools and trends to ensure relevance in their teaching practices.

5.1. Benefits of Mobile Application Prototyping

Using mobile application prototyping as a teaching tool offers numerous benefits that reach far beyond the classroom setting (Ocares-Cunyarachi and Andrade-Arenas, 2022). By engaging in the design and testing of apps, students step into a learning environment that reflects the complexities of real-world entrepreneurship. This hands-on approach not only teaches them technical skills but also fosters an entrepreneurial mindset necessary for thriving in today's fast-changing digital economy. Prototyping serves as a bridge between theory and application, immersing students in the creation of digital products. They gain hands-on experience with widely used tools like Figma and Adobe XD, mastering the skills needed to design intuitive interfaces and functional layouts (Norman, 2013). This direct exposure equips students to meet the technical demands of the industry.

Prototyping is an iterative process that pushes students to test, fail, and refine their ideas. This cycle not only improves their problem-solving abilities but also nurtures an entrepreneurial mindset that is flexible and open to uncertainty (Ries, 2011). Beckman and Barry (2007) emphasize how prototyping inspires creativity, especially when students explore multiple solutions to a given problem. Prototyping projects often rely on collaboration, mimicking real-life entrepreneurial environments. Working in teams teaches students how to effectively communicate, resolve disagreements, and leverage diverse perspectives—skills that are vital in any business setting (Seidel & Fixson, 2013).

By presenting their prototypes to classmates, teachers, or even industry experts, students receive valuable feedback to better align their designs with real-world needs. This not only refines their ideas but also gives them experience in pitching concepts and responding to constructive criticism (Fayolle & Liñán, 2014). Through this practice, students gain exposure to both technical expertise and entrepreneurial principles like adaptability and innovation. These skills prepare them for the demands of the modern workforce, making prototyping an essential addition to entrepreneurship programs in the digital era.

5.2. Challenges in Implementing Mobile Application Prototyping

Although mobile application prototyping provides substantial educational benefits, incorporating it into academic settings comes with several challenges related to resource constraints, skill disparities, time limitations, and subjective evaluation. High-quality software and hardware essential for prototyping can be expensive, making it difficult for many institutions to provide adequate access. While free prototyping tools are available, they often lack the advanced features required for more complex projects (Laine, 2010; Hoidn, 2014). Collaborating with technology providers to secure discounted or free licenses for educational use can help mitigate this issue. At the same time, students entering entrepreneurship programs often have different levels of technical expertise, which can hinder the effectiveness of prototyping exercises and leave some students struggling to keep pace (Ahuja, 2024; Lee, 2021). Offering thorough training sessions and ongoing support is vital to bridging these gaps and ensuring all students can participate effectively.

The iterative nature of prototyping also demands significant time for designing, testing, and refining. However, academic programs often operate within tight schedules, leaving limited time for in-depth exploration (Dreyfus, 1980). Balancing these activities with other coursework can be challenging (Ahuja, 2024). Flexible schedules or integrating prototyping into final-year capstone projects can provide the necessary time for meaningful engagement. Furthermore, assessing prototypes can be highly subjective, as it involves weighing creativity, technical functionality, and market relevance. To ensure fair assessments, educators must develop detailed rubrics that strike a balance between innovation, practicality, and user-centered design (Beckman, 2007; Brown, 2009).

Despite its practical value, academic prototyping often oversimplifies the complexities of app development, focusing primarily on front-end design while neglecting back-end processes like database management and system integration (Thomke, 1998). This limited exposure can leave students unprepared for the technical demands of full-scale app development (Ries, 2011). Similarly, students may prioritize creating visually appealing designs, sometimes at the expense of addressing practical or functional requirements (Kondaveeti, 2021; Lee, 2021). It is crucial to emphasize both functionality and aesthetics during prototyping activities to ensure students develop balanced designs.

While feedback from instructors and peers is valuable, it cannot replace the insights provided by real-world stakeholders. Engaging industry professionals or end-users in the evaluation process can enhance the authenticity and impact of the learning experience (Ries, 2011). Additionally, relying too much on specific prototyping tools can narrow students' focus, making them proficient in the tools themselves but less adept at broader entrepreneurial thinking (Laine, 2010; Hoidn, 2014). Educators must emphasize the importance of balancing technical and entrepreneurial skills to foster well-rounded development.

To overcome these obstacles, educators, institutions, and industry partners must work collaboratively. By investing in adequate resources, providing comprehensive training, and creating supportive learning environments, academic institutions can successfully integrate prototyping into their programs, enriching the student learning experience. Flexible scheduling, partnerships with industry stakeholders, and structured evaluation frameworks can further enhance learning outcomes. Recognizing these limitations and designing targeted interventions will ensure that mobile application prototyping serves as a powerful tool for preparing students to meet the entrepreneurial challenges of the digital age.

5.3. Recommendations for Effective Implementation

Mobile application prototyping should not be treated as an isolated activity. Instead, it needs to be integrated into a broader curriculum that covers business strategy, financial planning, marketing, and technology management (Brown, 2009). This approach ensures that students gain a holistic understanding of the entrepreneurial process, enhancing the value of prototyping activities by showing its role within the larger framework of business development.

To maximize its effectiveness, institutions should provide robust training sessions and workshops to familiarize students with prototyping tools. Ongoing technical support can bridge skill gaps and ensure equitable participation (Lee, 2021). Faculty development programs should also be implemented to help educators stay updated with the latest tools and methodologies (Beckman, 2007), enabling them to better guide students through the process. Additionally, engaging with industry professionals can enhance the realism and relevance of prototyping activities. Guest lectures, workshops, and mentorship programs provide insights into current industry practices, while partnerships with companies to simulate real-world challenges expose students to stakeholder feedback (Ries, 2011).

Academic schedules must allocate sufficient time for iterative prototyping processes. Breaking down activities into smaller milestones and providing structured timelines for ideation, prototyping, feedback, and revision can help manage time effectively (Laine, 2010; Hoidn, 2014). Incorporating summer projects or capstone activities can also provide additional opportunities for students to tackle more complex prototyping tasks. To further support these efforts, institutions should invest in technology infrastructure. Partnerships with software providers for free or discounted licenses can alleviate cost barriers (Ahuja, 2024). Creating makerspaces or innovation labs equipped with the necessary tools can also enhance hands-on learning experiences.

While peer and instructor feedback is valuable, integrating input from real stakeholders, such as potential users or investors, offers a more authentic evaluation of prototypes. Events like hackathons, demo days, or user-testing sessions can provide students with insights into real-world market dynamics and practical considerations (Ries, 2011). These opportunities allow students to present their prototypes to industry professionals, gaining valuable feedback that can inform further refinement (Seidel & Fixson, 2013).

By embedding mobile application prototyping within a comprehensive curriculum and complementing it with sufficient training, industry partnerships, and real-world engagement, educators can ensure students develop the technical, strategic, and entrepreneurial skills required to thrive in the digital economy.

6. METHODOLOGY FOR INTEGRATING MOBILE APPLICATION PROTOTYPING IN DIGITAL ENTREPRENEURSHIP EDUCATION

The methodology for integrating mobile application prototyping into digital entrepreneurship education revolves around providing students with a hands-on, simulation-based learning experience. This approach emphasizes experiential learning, enabling students to engage with real-world challenges while developing essential skills in creativity, problem-solving, and digital prototyping. The methodology is particularly important as it bridges the gap between theoretical knowledge and practical application, preparing students to navigate the fast-evolving landscape of digital entrepreneurship.

By working through this structured process, students learn to conceptualize, design, prototype, and test a mobile application, mirroring industry-standard practices. The step-by-step approach not only fosters technical skills in using tools like Figma but also highlights the importance of user-centered design, iterative development, and feedback integration. Each stage in the methodology builds upon the previous one, ensuring students gain confidence in transforming abstract ideas into tangible products.

The following sections outline the step-by-step process for conducting this lecture and guiding students through the assignment, emphasizing key stages that simulate real-world app development workflows and decision-making processes.

Figure 1. Methodology for integrating mobile application prototyping in digital entrepreneurship education

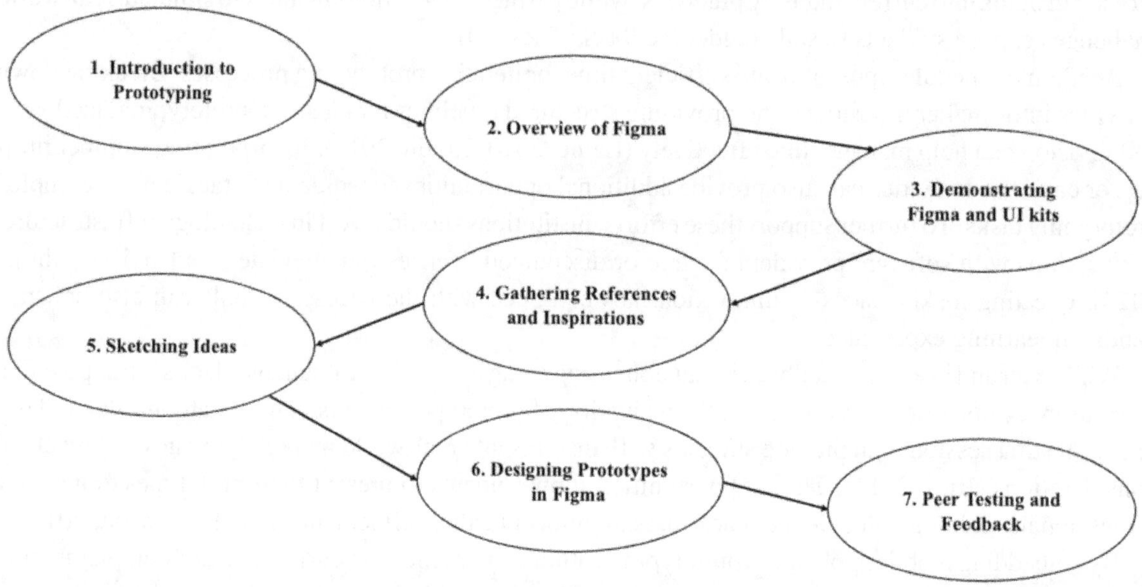

6.1 Introduction to Prototyping

The lecture begins with an introduction to the concept of prototyping. The lecturer explains that prototyping is an essential phase in the development of digital products. For entrepreneurs, prototyping is particularly valuable as it allows them to visualize their ideas, test functionality, and gather feedback before committing to full-scale development (Paust et al., 2024). The lecturer highlights the cost and time efficiency of prototyping, as well as its role in fostering innovation and communication with stakeholders.

6.2 Overview of Figma

The next step is introducing students to Figma[1], a tool for collaborative interface design. The lecturer provides an overview of Figma's key features, such as its cloud-based platform, which allows real-time collaboration, and its extensive library of design components and plugins. The benefits of using Figma for prototyping are emphasized, including its intuitive interface, accessibility, and the ability to create interactive prototypes that mimic the behavior of real applications (Staiano, 2022). The lecturer reassures students that the objective is not to become professional designers but to learn how to use design tools to effectively communicate entrepreneurial ideas.

6.3 Demonstrating Figma and UI Kits

During the lecture, the lecturer demonstrates the basic functions of Figma. This includes creating frames, adding elements, and utilizing user interface (UI) kits. UI kits are pre-designed components that simplify the design process ((Staiano, 2022), enabling students to quickly assemble a prototype without needing advanced design skills. The demonstration focuses on practical applications, showing students how to:

- Navigate the Figma interface
- Drag and drop UI components from kits
- Use layers and grids for organization
- Create interactive elements like buttons and navigation flows

The lecturer emphasizes that the goal is to create a functional prototype rather than a polished design. This approach ensures that students focus on the conceptualization and usability of their ideas rather than aesthetics.

6.4 Gathering References and Inspirations

Following the demonstration, students are tasked with gathering references and inspirations from mobile applications they admire. Inspiration in design can be defined as a process that integrates the use of any element in any form to elicit creative responses to extant problems (Gonçalves et al., 2014). This activity not only encourages students to identify apps they frequently use and enjoy but also helps them analyze what makes these apps appealing, whether in terms of user experience, features, or design. Documenting their observations and ideas for their own prototypes allows students to ground their designs in proven concepts while fostering creativity and originality. Understanding the strengths of existing applications provides a foundation for incorporating best practices and avoiding common pitfalls in mobile application design.

6.5 Sketching Ideas

Before diving into digital design, students are instructed to sketch their ideas on paper. Paper prototyping is "*a variation of usability testing where representative users perform realistic tasks by interacting with a paper version of the interface that is manipulated by a person 'playing computer', who does not explain how the interface in intented to work*" (Snyder, 2003). This step plays a crucial role in the creative process as it allows students to explore different layouts and functionalities freely. Sketching on paper encourages rapid ideation, reduces the pressure of dealing with technical constraints, and provides a visual medium for brainstorming and communicating initial concepts. By working through sketches first, students can refine their ideas and address usability concerns before translating them into digital prototypes. The lecturer provides feedback on these sketches, helping students improve their designs and prepare for the digital prototyping phase.

6.6 Designing Prototypes in Figma

With their sketches as a guide, students begin creating their prototypes in Figma. Designing prototypes is a critical step as it transforms abstract ideas into tangible, interactive models, bridging the gap between conceptualization and implementation (Petrakis et al., 2021). This process helps students practice translating user needs into functional layouts while developing essential digital design skills. While designing, students are encouraged to adopt a user-centric approach, prioritizing usability, simplicity, and intuitive navigation. They are also advised to pay attention to consistency in visual design, responsiveness across devices, and accessibility features to create inclusive experiences. This hands-on experience allows students to bring their concepts to life while practicing digital skills relevant to entrepreneurship.

6.7 Peer Testing and Feedback

The final step involves testing the prototypes with peers. Peer testing is an essential phase in the design process, as it provides an opportunity to evaluate usability, functionality, and overall appeal from an external perspective (Purchase, 2000). By presenting their designs and collecting feedback, students can identify areas for improvement and make necessary adjustments. This iterative process mirrors real-world product development, where feedback and revisions are fundamental to creating effective solutions. Peer testing not only improves design quality but also fosters collaboration and critical thinking, helping students develop valuable skills for refining and validating their ideas.

6.8 Proposed Alterations to the Methodology

While the outlined methodology provides a strong foundation, several enhancements can be proposed to improve its effectiveness. Incorporating market research analysis at the beginning of the process can help students identify market gaps and user needs, enabling data-driven design decisions. Integrating persona development as part of the planning phase could further align prototypes with target audience preferences by creating detailed user profiles that guide design choices. Additionally, the inclusion of usability testing tools, such as Maze[2], would allow students to collect structured feedback and analytics, improving their understanding of user interactions. Encouraging collaborative group projects can simulate startup environments, fostering teamwork and enabling students to take on specialized roles, such as project manager, designer, or marketer. Introducing iterative prototyping stages with structured feedback loops would emphasize the importance of refining designs through multiple phases, closely mirroring agile development processes. Finally, reflective journals and self-assessment exercises could be implemented to encourage students to document their design choices, challenges, and lessons learned, fostering critical thinking and continuous improvement. By following this methodology and incorporating the proposed alterations, students gain practical experience in mobile application design, enhance their entrepreneurial skills, and learn the value of prototyping as a tool for innovation and communication.

7. SKILLS AND COMPETENCIES DEVELOPED THROUGH MOBILE APP SIMULATION

The mobile app simulation activity provides students with a rich and multifaceted learning experience, enabling them to develop a diverse set of skills and competencies that are highly relevant in digital entrepreneurship. By engaging in hands-on prototyping and design tasks, students cultivate technical proficiency, creative problem-solving abilities, and entrepreneurial mindsets that prepare them to navigate the dynamic landscape of mobile application development.

One of the primary skills developed through this simulation is digital literacy (Wenngren and Rizk, 2024), as students are required to work with design tools such as Figma. They gain hands-on experience in creating wireframes, assembling interface elements, and building interactive prototypes. These activities equip students with practical knowledge of digital design processes and tools, enabling them to visualize and communicate complex concepts effectively. Such digital proficiency is increasingly essential in modern entrepreneurship (Scuotto and Morellato, 2013), where mobile and web technologies play a pivotal role in business operations.

The simulation also fosters critical thinking and problem-solving abilities (Sheikh et al., 2023). Students must assess user needs, brainstorm innovative solutions, and refine their designs through iterative feedback. This process challenges them to identify usability issues, anticipate potential obstacles, and develop functional prototypes that address market demands. The ability to think analytically and iteratively is invaluable for entrepreneurs who need to adapt quickly to changing circumstances and evolving customer preferences.

Creativity and innovative thinking is further strengthened as students tackle real-world challenges through the simulation (Jiwa et al., 2005). They are encouraged to identify issues, evaluate potential solutions, and experiment with new approaches during the design process. This iterative approach promotes resilience and adaptability, essential qualities for entrepreneurs facing uncertainty and competition in global markets. By emphasizing innovative thinking, the activity inspires students to create original solutions that address market gaps and leverage technology effectively. Moreover, students are encouraged to draw inspiration from existing applications while designing unique features that differentiate their prototypes. This balance between analysis and originality fosters an entrepreneurial mindset, pushing students to explore novel solutions and leverage technology to address unmet needs in international markets. As they develop their prototypes, students learn to merge technical feasibility with creative vision, resulting in products that are both functional and compelling.

Technical and digital literacy also play a central role in the simulation (Martínez et al., 2019). Students gain technical skills related to mobile app development, including user interface (UI) design, navigation structures, and functionality testing. These competencies enhance their ability to conceptualize and execute app designs that meet industry standards and user expectations. By learning the fundamentals of app development, students build confidence in working with digital tools and frameworks, making them well-prepared for future digital ventures.

Collaboration and teamwork are integral to the simulation, as students work together to test prototypes and provide constructive feedback (Hühn and Rausch, 2022; Riivari et al., 2021). This peer-driven process promotes effective communication and interpersonal skills, ensuring that participants can articulate ideas clearly, listen to feedback, and incorporate suggestions for improvement. Such collaborative experiences mirror real-world entrepreneurial environments, where cooperation with developers, designers, and stakeholders is crucial to project success.

Entrepreneurial competencies are also developed (Costin, et al., 2019; Auchter and Kriz, 2014), as students acquire business-related skills such as market analysis, product development, and value proposition design. They learn to evaluate competitive landscapes, define target audiences, and create strategies for successful app launches. These competencies prepare students to assess risks, seize opportunities, and develop scalable business models—key attributes of successful entrepreneurs operating in international markets.

Additionally, students develop project management skills by overseeing the design and development of their prototypes (Misfeldt, 2015). From conceptualization to completion, participants are required to manage timelines, allocate resources, and set milestones to ensure progress. These project management practices not only enhance organizational skills but also prepare students for the structured yet flexible approach required in entrepreneurship.

Market research principles are also reinforced during the simulation (Vos, 2015). Students analyze existing applications, identify design trends, and consider user preferences to inform their prototypes. This research-driven approach enhances their ability to evaluate market demands and develop customer-focused solutions. By prioritizing usability and accessibility, students learn the importance of creating products that resonate with diverse audiences in international markets.

Finally, the iterative testing and refinement process strengthens adaptability and resilience. Students learn to embrace constructive criticism, view setbacks as opportunities for growth, and make data-driven adjustments to their designs. This iterative mindset mirrors the agile methodologies widely used in software development and entrepreneurship, fostering a culture of continuous improvement.

Through this simulation, students not only acquire technical and creative skills but also develop entrepreneurial competencies that are transferable across industries. They emerge better equipped to conceptualize, design, and market digital products, positioning themselves as innovative thinkers and leaders in the global digital economy.

8. CONCLUSION: FUTURE TRENDS AND RECOMMENDATIONS

As the digital landscape continues to evolve, mobile technologies are becoming increasingly integrated with emerging advancements such as artificial intelligence (AI), augmented reality (AR), and virtual reality (VR). These technologies have the potential to transform digital entrepreneurship by enabling more personalized, immersive, and data-driven mobile applications. Future entrepreneurs will need to harness these innovations to create dynamic and engaging products that resonate with users. By incorporating AI for predictive analytics, AR for enhanced user experiences, and VR for virtual simulations, mobile app development is expected to expand into new realms of interaction and functionality. As such, integrating these technologies into simulation activities can prepare students to remain competitive and innovative in the ever-changing digital economy.

To further enhance the effectiveness of simulation activities, educators should continuously refine their design and delivery methods. Incorporating more sophisticated prototyping tools, expanding the scope of exercises to include AR/VR applications, and integrating usability testing with real user feedback can deepen the learning experience. Additionally, fostering interdisciplinary collaboration through team-based projects that combine technical, marketing, and business expertise can create more comprehensive learning environments. Simulations can also benefit from partnerships with industry stakeholders, providing students with exposure to real-world challenges and expectations.

International economic relations and sustainable development are emerging as crucial considerations for entrepreneurship (Deirmentzoglou et al. 2024c). As global markets become increasingly interconnected, entrepreneurs must address challenges related to cross-border trade, energy sustainability, and geopolitical stability. Mobile applications can support businesses in navigating these complexities by providing real-time data analytics, enhancing supply chain transparency, and facilitating international transactions. Preparing students to leverage these tools equips them to respond to economic and sustainability-related uncertainties effectively, ensuring resilience and sustainability in international markets.

Sustainability reporting is becoming a fundamental requirement for businesses operating in today's environmentally conscious markets (Pistikou et al., 2023). Mobile applications can be developed to track and report sustainability metrics, helping businesses demonstrate their commitment to sustainable practices. Simulation activities can incorporate sustainability-focused app designs, encouraging students to prioritize transparency and accountability. This approach not only aligns with global sustainability goals but also fosters a culture of responsible entrepreneurship.

Expanding the simulation model to other disciplines offers an exciting opportunity to broaden its impact. Fields such as tourism, education, and environmental sustainability could adopt similar activities to address sector-specific challenges. For instance, the tourism industry, driven by social media and customer satisfaction, presents another area for growth and innovation (Vlassi et al., 2023; Deirmentzoglou et al., 2022). Mobile applications play a central role in improving customer experiences through personalized recommendations, virtual tours, and streamlined booking systems. Simulations that focus on designing apps for tourism can teach students to integrate features that enhance user engagement and satisfaction. By analyzing customer feedback and social media trends, entrepreneurs can continuously refine their products to meet evolving consumer demands, promoting sustainable growth in the tourism sector.

In conclusion, this chapter has highlighted the importance of simulation-based learning for fostering digital entrepreneurship. Through hands-on experience in mobile app design, students develop essential skills such as problem-solving, technical literacy, and entrepreneurial competencies. The integration of emerging technologies and the expansion of simulation activities to other fields further underscore the potential of this approach to drive innovation and adaptability. As digital tools continue to shape global markets, equipping students with practical, forward-thinking skills will be vital for their success as future entrepreneurs.

REFERENCES

Agoraki, K. K., Deirmentzoglou, G. A., Psychalis, M., & Apostolopoulos, S. (2024a). Types of Innovation and Sustainable Development: Evidence from Medium-and Large-Sized Firms. *International Journal on Management of Innovation & Technology*, *21*(02), 1–18. DOI: 10.1142/S0219877024500135

Agoraki, K. K., Deirmentzoglou, G. A., & Triantopoulos, C. (2024b). Cultural Values as Catalysts of Technological Innovation for a Sustainable Future. *Sustainability (Basel)*, *16*(5), 2064. DOI: 10.3390/su16052064

Ahuja, V. (2024). Simulations in Business Education: Unlocking Experiential Learning. Practices and Implementation of Gamification in Higher Education, 1-21.

Apostolopoulos, N., Kakouris, A., Liargovas, P., Petropoulos, D., & Anastasopoulou, E. E. (2024). Exploring the impact of crises on rural agri-food SMEs: The moderating role of support mechanisms, digitalisation, and networking. *International Journal of Entrepreneurship and Innovation*. DOI: 10.1177/14657503241270275

Auchter, E., & Kriz, W. C. (2014). The impact of business simulations as a teaching method on entrepreneurial competencies and motivation—A review of 10 years of evaluation research in entrepreneurship education. *The shift from teaching to learning: Individual, collective and organizational learning through gaming & simulation*, 187-197.

Babin, M.-J., Rivière, E., & Chiniara, G. (2019). Theory for Practice: Learning Theories for Simulation. In *Clinical Simulation (Second Edition), Education, Operations, and Engineering* (pp. 97-114). Academic Press.

Beckman, G. D. (2007). "Adventuring" Arts Entrepreneurship Curricula in Higher Education: An Examination of Present Efforts, Obstacles, and Best Practices. *The Journal of Arts Management, Law, and Society*, *37*(2), 87–112. DOI: 10.3200/JAML.37.2.87-112

Beckman, S. L., & Barry, M. (2007). Innovation as a Learning Process: Embedding Design Thinking. *California Management Review*, *50*(1), 25–56. DOI: 10.2307/41166415

Bell, B. S., Kanar, A. M., & Kozlowski, S. W. J. (2008). Current issues and future directions in simulation-based training in North America. *International Journal of Human Resource Management*, *19*(8), 1416–1434. DOI: 10.1080/09585190802200173

Berthon, P. R., Pitt, L. F., Plangger, K., & Shapiro, D. (2012). Marketing meets Web 2.0, social media, and creative consumers: Implications for international marketing strategy. *Business Horizons*, *55*(3), 261–271. DOI: 10.1016/j.bushor.2012.01.007

Bharadiya, J. P. (2023). Machine learning and AI in business intelligence: Trends and opportunities. [IJC]. *International Journal of Computer*, *48*(1), 123–134.

Bharadwaj, A., El Sawy, O. A., Pavlou, P. A., & Venkatraman, N. V. (2013). Digital business strategy: Toward a next generation of insights. *Management Information Systems Quarterly*, *37*(2), 471–482. DOI: 10.25300/MISQ/2013/37:2.3

Brown, T. (2009). *Change by design: How design thinking creates new alternatives for business and society*. Collins Business.

Černezel, A., & Heričko, M. 2013. A user-centric approach for developing mobile applications. In *7th International Conference on Knowledge Management in Organizations: Service and Cloud Computing* (pp. 455-465). Springer Berlin Heidelberg. DOI: 10.1007/978-3-642-30867-3_41

Chen, I. J., & Popovich, K. (2003). Understanding customer relationship management (CRM): People, process and technology. *Business Process Management Journal*, *9*(5), 672–688. DOI: 10.1108/14637150310496758

Costin, Y., O'Brien, M. P., & Hynes, B. (2019). Developing cognitive and non-cognitive entrepreneurial competences through business simulation games. *Journal of Enterprising Culture*, *27*(04), 471–498. DOI: 10.1142/S0218495819500171

Dana, L. P., Salamzadeh, A., Mortazavi, S., & Hadizadeh, M. (2022). Investigating the impact of international markets and new digital technologies on business innovation in emerging markets. *Sustainability (Basel)*, *14*(2), 983. DOI: 10.3390/su14020983

Davidson, E., & Vaast, E. 2010, January. Digital entrepreneurship and its sociomaterial enactment. In *2010 43rd Hawaii International Conference on System Sciences* (pp. 1-10). IEEE. DOI: 10.1109/HICSS.2010.150

Deininger, M., Daly, S. R., Sienko, K. H., & Lee, J. C. (2017). Novice designers' use of prototypes in engineering design. *Design Studies*, *51*, 25–65. DOI: 10.1016/j.destud.2017.04.002 PMID: 29398740

Deirmentzoglou, E., Papakyriakopoulos, G., & Patsakis, C. (2019). A survey on long-range attacks for proof of stake protocols. *IEEE Access: Practical Innovations, Open Solutions*, *7*, 28712–28725. DOI: 10.1109/ACCESS.2019.2901858

Deirmentzoglou, G. A., Agoraki, K. K., & Patsoulis, P. (2024a). The nexus between cultural values and perceptions of corporate sustainable development. *Social Responsibility Journal*, *20*(2), 224–242. DOI: 10.1108/SRJ-09-2022-0373

Deirmentzoglou, G. A., Anastasopoulou, E. E., & Sklias, P. (2024c). International economic relations and energy security in the European Union: A systematic literature review. *International Journal of Sustainable Energy*, *43*(1), 2385682.

Deirmentzoglou, G. A., & Deirmentzoglou, E. A. 2022, September. Pest analysis of the e-commerce industry: The case of Greece. In *Business Development and Economic Governance in Southeastern Europe:13th International Conference on the Economies of the Balkan and Eastern European Countries (EBEEC),Pafos, Cyprus,2021* (pp. 315-323). Cham: Springer International Publishing.

Deirmentzoglou, G. A., Vlassi, E., & Agoraki, K. K. 2022, May. The Effect of the Hotel Attributes on Guest Satisfaction Due to the Covid-19 Pandemic Crisis: The Case of the Greek Tourism and Hospitality Sector. In *International Conference Economies of The Balkan And Eastern European Countries* (pp. 283-297). Cham: Springer Nature Switzerland.

Deirmentzoglou, G. A., Vlassi, E., & Anastasopoulou, E. E. (2024b). DDMMO Website Quality, Destination Image and Intention to Use Metaverse Platforms. *Platforms*, *2*(4), 180–192.

Dreyfus, S. E. (1980). *A Five-stage model of the mental activities involved in directed skill acquisition*. Storming Media. DOI: 10.21236/ADA084551

Elia, G., Margherita, A., & Passiante, G. (2020). Digital entrepreneurship ecosystem: How digital technologies and collective intelligence are reshaping the entrepreneurial process. *Technological Forecasting and Social Change*, *150*, 119791. DOI: 10.1016/j.techfore.2019.119791

Faulds, D. J., Mangold, W. G., Raju, P. S., & Valsalan, S. (2018). The mobile shopping revolution: Redefining the consumer decision process. *Business Horizons*, *61*(2), 323–338. DOI: 10.1016/j.bushor.2017.11.012

Fayolle, A., & Gailly, B. (2008). From Craft to Science: Teaching Models and Learning Processes in Entrepreneurship Education. *Journal of European Industrial Training*, *32*(7), 569–593. DOI: 10.1108/03090590810899838

Fayolle, A., & Liñán, F. (2014). The Future of Research on Entrepreneurial Intentions. *Journal of Business Research*, *67*(5), 663–666. DOI: 10.1016/j.jbusres.2013.11.024

Flora, H. K., Wang, X., & Chande, S. V. (2014). An investigation on the characteristics of mobile applications: A survey study. *IJ Information Technology and Computer Science*, *11*(11), 21–27. DOI: 10.5815/ijitcs.2014.11.03

Frasson, C., & Blanchard, E. G. (2012). Simulation-Based Learning. In Seel, N. M. (Ed.), *Encyclopedia of the Sciences of Learning*. Springer., DOI: 10.1007/978-1-4419-1428-6_129

Goldschmidt, G. (2014). Modeling the role of sketching in design idea generation. In *An anthology of theories and models of design: philosophy, approaches and empirical explorations* (pp. 433–450). Springer London. DOI: 10.1007/978-1-4471-6338-1_21

Gonçalves, M., Cardoso, C., & Badke-Schaub, P. (2014). What inspires designers? Preferences on inspirational approaches during idea generation. *Design Studies*, *35*(1), 29–53. DOI: 10.1016/j.destud.2013.09.001

Grierson, L., Norman, G., Monteiro, S., & Sibbald, M. (2019). Simulation-Based Education and the Challenge of Transfer. In *Clinical Simulation (Second Edition), Education, Operations, and Engineering* (pp. 115-127). Academic Press.

Hallinger, P., & Wang, R. (2020). Analyzing the intellectual structure of research on simulation-based learning in management education, 1960–2019: A bibliometric review. *International Journal of Management Education*, *18*(3), 100418. DOI: 10.1016/j.ijme.2020.100418

Hoidn, S., & Kärkkäinen, K. (2014). Promoting skills for innovation in higher education: A literature review on the effectiveness of problem-based learning and of teaching behaviours. Academic Press.

Hühn, C., & Rausch, A. (2022). Collaboration and emotions during simulation-based learning in general management courses. *Studies in Educational Evaluation*, *73*, 101130. DOI: 10.1016/j.stueduc.2022.101130

Hui, A. N. N., Eason, M. S., Cheung, R. C. C., Lai, L. C. H., Lau, D., & Lam, T. (2021) The Relationships Among Simulation-Based Learning Creativity and the Learning Approach in Higher Education. In A. Hui & C. Wagner (Eds.), *Creative and Collaborative Learning through Immersion*. Creativity in the Twenty First Century. Springer. DOI: 10.1007/978-3-030-72216-6_6

Ingram, K.W., & Jackson, M.K. (2004). Simulations as authentic learning strategies: Bridging the gap between theory and practice in performance technology. Academic Press.

Jiwa, S., Lavelle, D., & Rose, A. (2005). E-entrepreneurship: Learning in a simulated environment. *Journal of Electronic Commerce in Organizations*, *3*(3), 42–56. DOI: 10.4018/jeco.2005070103

Jonassen, D. H., & Hung, W. (2012). Problem-Based Learning. In Seel, N. M. (Ed.), *Encyclopedia of the Sciences of Learning*. Springer. DOI: 10.1007/978-1-4419-1428-6_210

Jose, S. (2018). Strategic use of digital promotion strategies among female emigrant entrepreneurs in UAE. *International Journal of Emerging Markets*, *13*(6), 1699–1718. DOI: 10.1108/IJoEM-10-2016-0268

Kloch, C., Petersen, E. B., & Madsen, O. B. (2011). Cloud based infrastructure, the new business possibilities and barriers. *Wireless Personal Communications*, *58*, 17–30.

Kolb, D. A. (1984). *Experiential learning: experience as the source of learning and development / David A. Kolb*. Prentice-Hall.

Kollmann, T. (2006). What is e-entrepreneurship? Fundamentals of company founding in the net economy. *International Journal of Technology Management*, *33*(4), 322–340. DOI: 10.1504/IJTM.2006.009247

Kondaveeti, H. K., Kumaravelu, N. K., Vanambathina, S. D., Mathe, S. E., & Vappangi, S. (2021). A systematic literature review on prototyping with Arduino: Applications, challenges, advantages, and limitations. *Computer Science Review*, *40*, 100364. DOI: 10.1016/j.cosrev.2021.100364

Kourkoumelis, A., Anastasopoulou, E., Deirmentzoglou, G., Masouras, A., & Anastasiadou, S. (2024). Artificial Intelligence and Managerial Decision-Making in International Business. In *Proceedings of The 19th European Conference on Innovation and Entrepreneurship*. Academic Conferences International. DOI: 10.34190/ecie.19.1.2573

Kozlowski, S. W. J., & Bell, B. S. (2007). A theory-based approach for designing distributed learning systems. In Fiore, S. M., & Salas, E. (Eds.), *Toward a science of distributed learning* (pp. 15–39). APA. DOI: 10.1037/11582-002

Kraus, S., Burtscher, J., Vallaster, C., & Angerer, M. (2019). Sustainable Entrepreneurship Orientation: A Reflection on Status-Quo Research and Future Research Directions. *Journal of Cleaner Production*, *235*, 1336–1350.

Kraus, S., Palmer, C., Kailer, N., Kallinger, F. L., & Spitzer, J. (2019). Digital entrepreneurship: A research agenda on new business models for the twenty-first century. *International Journal of Entrepreneurial Behaviour & Research*, *25*(2), 353–375.

Kritzinger, W. T., & Weideman, M. (2013). Search engine optimization and pay-per-click marketing strategies. *Journal of Organizational Computing and Electronic Commerce*, *23*(3), 273–286. DOI: 10.1080/10919392.2013.808124

Laine, K. (2010). Fostering Innovation in Collaboration between Higher Education and Industry. A Systemic Model Based on Case Study. Academic Press.

Lee, Y. L., & Tee, M. Y. (2021). Facilitator's Scaffolding Strategies in a Design-based Learning Context. *Journal of Social Sciences and Humanities*, *5*(2), 15–33.

Lehner, O. M., Grabmann, E., & Ennsgraber, C. (2015). Entrepreneurial implications of crowd-funding as alternative funding source for innovations. *Venture Capital*, *17*(1-2), 171–189. DOI: 10.1080/13691066.2015.1037132

Lewandowski, W. E. (2019). *Assessing and Planning for Simulation Implementation: An Approach to Instructional Design to Meet Organizational Needs*. Academic Press.

Luo, Y. (2021). New OLI advantages in digital globalization. *International Business Review*, *30*(2), 101797. DOI: 10.1016/j.ibusrev.2021.101797

Mack, E. A., Marie-Pierre, L., & Redican, K. (2017). Entrepreneurs' use of internet and social media applications. *Telecommunications Policy*, *41*(2), 120–139. DOI: 10.1016/j.telpol.2016.12.001

Martínez, J. G., Martí, M. C., & Cervera, M. G. (2019). Inside a 3D simulation: Realism, dramatism and challenge in the development of students' teacher digital competence. *Australasian Journal of Educational Technology*, *35*(5), 1–14.

Misfeldt, M. (2015). Scenario Based Education as a Framework for Understanding Students Engagement and Learning in a Project Management Simulation Game. *Electronic Journal of e-Learning*, *13*(3), 181–191.

Nambisan, S., Wright, M., & Feldman, M. (2019). The digital transformation of innovation and entrepreneurship: Progress, challenges and key themes. *Research Policy*, *48*(8), 103773. DOI: 10.1016/j.respol.2019.03.018

Nambisan, S., Zahra, S. A., & Luo, Y. (2019). Global platforms and ecosystems: Implications for international business theories. *Journal of International Business Studies*, *50*(9), 1464–1486. DOI: 10.1057/s41267-019-00262-4

Neck, H. M., & Greene, P. G. (2011). Entrepreneurship Education: Known Worlds and New Frontiers. *Journal of Small Business Management*, *49*(1), 55–70. DOI: 10.1111/j.1540-627X.2010.00314.x

Norman, D. A. (2013). *The Design of Everyday Things* (Revised and Expanded Edition). Basic Books.

Noyes, E. (2018). Teaching entrepreneurial action through prototyping: The prototype-it challenge. *Entrepreneurship Education and Pedagogy*, *1*(1), 118–134. DOI: 10.1177/2515127417737289

Ocares-Cunyarachi, L., & Andrade-Arenas, L. (2022). Mobile Application Prototype: Learning in the Programming Course in Computer Engineering Students. *International Journal of Advanced Computer Science and Applications*, *13*(7). Advance online publication. DOI: 10.14569/IJACSA.2022.0130791

Paust, S., Korsgaard, S., & Thrane, C. (2024). Entrepreneurial prototyping: The role of purpose, prototype recycling, and skills bricolage. *Small Business Economics*, 1–25.

Petrakis, K., Wodehouse, A., & Hird, A. (2021). Prototyping-driven entrepreneurship: Towards a prototyping support tool based on design thinking principles. *The Design Journal*, *24*(5), 761–781. DOI: 10.1080/14606925.2021.1957531

Pistikou, V., Flouros, F., Deirmentzoglou, G. A., & Agoraki, K. K. (2023). Sustainability Reporting: Examining the Community Impact of the S&P500 Companies. *Sustainability (Basel)*, *15*(18), 13681. DOI: 10.3390/su151813681

Purchase, H. C. (2000). Learning about interface design through peer assessment. *Assessment & Evaluation in Higher Education*, *25*(4), 341–352. DOI: 10.1080/026029300449245

Ries, E. (2011). *The Lean Startup: How Today's Entrepreneurs Use Continuous Innovation to Create Radically Successful Businesses.* Crown Business.

Riivari, E., Kivijärvi, M., & Lämsä, A. M. (2021). Learning teamwork through a computer game: For the sake of performance or collaborative learning? *Educational Technology Research and Development*, *69*(3), 1753–1771. DOI: 10.1007/s11423-021-10009-4

Ross, S. (2021). Simulation-based learning: From learning theory to pedagogical application. *The Internet Journal of Allied Health Sciences and Practice*, *19*(4), 15. DOI: 10.46743/1540-580X/2021.2056

Samrgandi, N. (2021). User interface design & evaluation of mobile applications. *International Journal of Computer Science & Network Security*, *21*(1), 55–63.

Sarker, I. H., Hoque, M. M., Uddin, M. K., & Alsanoosy, T. (2021). Mobile data science and intelligent apps: Concepts, AI-based modeling and research directions. *Mobile Networks and Applications*, *26*(1), 285–303. DOI: 10.1007/s11036-020-01650-z

Scuotto, V., & Morellato, M. (2013). Entrepreneurial knowledge and digital competence: Keys for a success of student entrepreneurship. *Journal of the Knowledge Economy*, *4*(3), 293–303. DOI: 10.1007/s13132-013-0155-6

Seidel, V., & Fixson, S. K. (2013). Adopting Design Thinking in Novice Multidisciplinary Teams: The Application and Limits of Design Methods and Reflexive Practices. *Journal of Product Innovation Management*, *30*(1), 19–33. DOI: 10.1111/jpim.12061

Sheikh, R. A., Abdalkrim, G. M., & Shehawy, Y. M. (2023). Assessing the impact of business simulation as a teaching method for developing 21st century future skills. *Journal of International Education in Business*, *16*(3), 351–370. DOI: 10.1108/JIEB-11-2022-0085

Snyder, C. (2003). *Paper prototyping: The fast and easy way to design and refine user interfaces.* Morgan Kaufmann.

Staiano, F. (2022). *Designing and Prototyping Interfaces with Figma: Learn essential UX/UI design principles by creating interactive prototypes for mobile, tablet, and desktop.* Packt Publishing Ltd.

Sussan, F., & Acs, Z. J. (2017). The digital entrepreneurial ecosystem. *Small Business Economics*, *49*(1), 55–73. DOI: 10.1007/s11187-017-9867-5

Thomke, S. (1998). Managing Experimentation in the Design of New Products. *Management Science, 44*(6), 743–762. DOI: 10.1287/mnsc.44.6.743

Viswanathan, V., Atilola, O., Goodman, J., & Linsey, J. (2014, October). Prototyping: a key skill for innovation and life-long learning. In 2014 IEEE Frontiers in Education Conference (FIE) Proceedings (pp. 1-8). IEEE. DOI: 10.1109/FIE.2014.7044423

Vlachopoulos, D., & Makri, A. (2017). The effect of games and simulations on higher education: A systematic literature review. *International Journal of Educational Technology in Higher Education, 14*(1), 2. DOI: 10.1186/s41239-017-0062-1

Vlassi, E., Deirmentzoglou, G. A., & Irakleidi, E. 2023, September. Capturing Destination's Cognitive and Affective Image on Social Media. The Case of Pafos, Cyprus. In *The International Conference on Strategic Innovative Marketing and Tourism* (pp. 19-28). Cham: Springer Nature Switzerland.

Vos, L. (2015). Simulation games in business and marketing education: How educators assess student learning from simulations. *International Journal of Management Education, 13*(1), 57–74. DOI: 10.1016/j.ijme.2015.01.001

Wenngren, J., & Rizk, A. (2024). Prototyping for Digital Innovation: Investigating the Impact of Digital Technology on Prototyping Elements. *Administrative Sciences, 14*(7), 142. DOI: 10.3390/admsci14070142

Wilson, S. G., & Abel, I. (2002). So you want to get involved in e-commerce. *Industrial Marketing Management, 31*(2), 85–94. DOI: 10.1016/S0019-8501(01)00188-2

ENDNOTES

1 https://www.figma.com/

2 https://maze.co/

Chapter 17
Transforming Higher Education: The Role of AI and Simulation Tools in Enhancing Learning and Engagement

Amvrosios Prodromou
https://orcid.org/0009-0008-4787-6292
Neapolis University, Pafos, Cyprus

Marilia Kountouridou
European University, Cyprus

ABSTRACT

The chapter focuses on the examination of the strategic role of artificial intelligence (AI) and simulation tools in the context of higher education, and most importantly, how these two elements can substantially contribute towards enhancing effective learning and engagement. The chapter has identified the increasing role of AI in contemporary societies, with its impact in education (AIEd) to have gained an increasing role as a result of rapid growth of technological tools, and the need for higher institutions to incorporate such technological developments into their educational practices. This requires universities to identify the emerging opportunities and focus on the development of their technological infrastructure both tangible (equipment) and intangible (human). AI contributes towards the development of smart personalised education, therefore enabling both educators and students to fully develop their unique skills, leading towards improved educational and learning results for all parties involved in the process.

INTRODUCTION

Artificial intelligence (AI) has managed to change many areas in modern life (Gardner et al., 2021). As a result of this widespread diffusion and adoption of artificial intelligence and other simulation tools, it inevitably has an impact on the education sector (Lee et al., 2024). Therefore, the education sector has seen tremendous changes due to the widespread use of such technologies (Wright et al., 2023; Fullan, 2023). As pointed out by Chu et al., (2022) and Scherer and Teo, (2019), the integration of artificial intelligence in the Higher Education (HE) sphere has grown dramatically in the last five years, garnering considerable scholarly interest. Indeed, AI and simulation tools are gaining significant popularity in HE (Alajmi et al., 2020), making them an integral part of the teaching and learning process (Dai &

DOI: 10.4018/979-8-3693-9040-5.ch017

Ke 2022). As suggested by Aldosari, (2020), AI-based learning strategies can be effectively applied by instructors to assess the performance of students, thus creating a more personalised program based on students' strengths and weaknesses. The integration of the previously mentioned tools in the learning process leads to various positive outcomes as students can acquire knowledge more effectively and improve their performance, especially when combined with practical experience (Campos et al., 2020).

It is of outmost importance for universities to optimize their entire learning environment by incorporating AI and stimulation tools as part their strategic planning in terms of both learning experience and strategy, as both are considered as essential in order to ensure a comprehensive experience (Bearman et al., 2022). Hence, universities will have to change drastically as this point of AI-dominated technological transformation becomes more commonplace for most universities (AwangHarun et al., 2022). Consequently, universities are confronted with the obligation of adapting their curricular and pedagogical strategies to reflect the continuous shift in AI technologies, thus ensuring its students will receive contemporary information that will enable them to navigate the rapidly changing environment (Thurzo et al., 2023). This will enable universities to compete effectively in this highly competitive environment, attract more students and improved their overall performance (Kountouridou and Domic, 2022a).

Given the importance of this topic, the present chapter focuses on providing a critical overview of the integration of AI and other simulation tools in Higher Education (AIEd). It will also examine the influence of these tools on the learning process and the advantages which emerge from these technologies. Because AIEd is fast growing and evolving, there is much room to develop an understanding of academic AIEd, therefore, this chapter aims to substantially contribute towards this emerging educational aspect, especially since this has been a major market requirement during the last decade as companies are asking for technological knowledge (Schwartz & Weber, 2015).

In this context, the role of Human Resource (HR) as a major asset in contemporary economy is gaining an increasing level of attention by the majority of organisations across most industries, with the latter to require from their workforce to be fully equipped with the relevant technological knowledge when they enter the market (Ali et al., 2023). Importantly, the authors support that the transfer of such knowledge is seriously taken into consideration by organisations when selecting, training, and developing their HR with the potential to become a long-term asset which can serve their strategic objectives.

Following the catastrophic consequence of the recent Covid-19 pandemic, the crucial sector of Health science has increased, diversifying its approach towards developing the technological skills of its existing HR as well as the students as potential workforce. These technological requirements consider advance technologies such as AI, Machine Leaning (ML) and simulation tools, all of critical importance in order for the sector to adapt to the new health and social realities that call for extrovert policies (Qin et al., 2023). This approach is further enhanced Alonso-Peña and Álvarez Álvarez (2023) who state that an increasing number of universities in most advanced countries are adopting AI and simulation tools as part of their training, with the incorporation of role playing to have become a popular method amongst both educators and students, and consequently, establishing more realistic scenarios that can be transferred to the workplace.

Considering such fact, the need for much more awareness of the power of AI in educational contexts is raised by scholars. It will, therefore, be the effort of the chapter to examine how AI and simulation tools can be integrated into practical levels and the academic curricula, so that they become a formal part of higher education. In this framework, AI and simulation tools can also tend to be a tool in the hands of educators with a view to influencing policymakers towards adapting their policies accordingly, by allocating all the relevant productive resources, such as human, financial and technological, to the higher institutions responsible for delivering students ready to confront real-life challenges. As a result of all the above-mentioned elements, a new model will be proposed in order to effectively reflect to the AI transformation in the higher education context, enabling educators to integrate such technologies in their learning process. The proposed model considers the market requirements and trends, as both are considered crucial in order to adequately prepare university students to enter the real market arena, and therefore, ensure that they will be competitive enough in order to enjoy a healthy career development within a highly demanding economic environment (Liu et al., 2022).

1. MAIN PART

1.1. Artificial Intelligence (AI) in Education (AIEd)

AI in education, often referred to as Artificial Intelligence in Education (AIEd), has been around for many decades, with a notable expansion in the past five years, leading to substantial changes, challenges, and improvements in the overall economic activity and business operations (Chu et al., 2022). Artificial intelligence made its appearance in the 1950s when John McCarthy in a workshop held in the US, referred to the word AI for the first time (Russel & Norvig, 2010). Importantly, the authors state that there are two fundamental schools related to the examination and implementation of AI in the economy; symbolic and connectionist. Critically assessing the work of Russel and Norvig, this constitutes a major contribution to the development of the current chapter as it refers to a series of other major research, such as that of Wilson and Keil (1999) who refer to the concept of Cognitive Science which enables development of machine learning (ML) and AI.

As AI has gained increasing popularity in recent years, studies conducted around this topic have diversified and deepened, as they aim to examine different aspects of AIEd, including the provision of a collaborative learning environment (Dillenbourg & Jermann, 2007), the engaging learning environment (Desmarais & Baker, 2012) and Student-centered strategies for revolutionizing e-learning (Woolf, 2010). Given this increased popularity, AIEd managed to attract significant scholarly attention as it can revolutionize traditional pedagogical approaches and provide a modern and engaging teaching environment (Chen et al., 2020; Luckin & Cukurova, 2019). Indeed, the application of AI in the realm of HE has grown impressively in recent years, significantly transforming the learning environment (Scherer & Teo, 2019). Further analysing the definitions provided to explain these emerging technologies, AI is defined as computer systems developed to implement cognitive tasks and more specifically problem-solving tasks, linked to the human mind. Another definition provided to explain what simulation-based learning environment is, refers to an interactive digital assisted learning environment that mimics a real process or situation. This enables students to examine their hypotheses and practice (Merchant et al., 2014). As noted by Baker and Smith (2019), AI is a generic term that includes a number of different technologies and methods such as machine learning, natural language processing, data mining, neural networks or an algorithm.

Chaudhry and Kazim (2021) support that the role of AIEd should be viewed well beyond its application within the academic institutions as its effective application in universities will lead to long-term effects, such as enhancing communication and exchange of information, providing incentives to businesses for implementing changes, and create opportunities for balanced employee growth. Importantly, the authors state that this has become a necessity following the recent pandemic in which companies had to rapidly adapt to the new business environment, with the expertise incorporated from AI and simulation tools to be considered as one of the most important elements. Polas et al. (2023) add to the discussion and suggest that the pandemic has accelerated the transition to cutting-edge technologies, such as AI, ML, and simulation tools in both academia and organisations.

Integrating AI tools including simulation-based learning, artificial neural networks (ANNs), machine learning, and deep learning, natural language processing (NLP), can provide an interactive environment for students (Dai and Ke, 2022). Similarly, Abbas et al. (2023), emphasise on the importance of incorporating AI technologies such as intelligent tutoring systems (ITS), adaptive learning, and automated assessments, educators can develop a personalised learning experience with leads to academic success. Such systems have been shown to enable effective personalised learning where the systems can provide optimal pathways to learning that matches students' needs, thereby improving engagement and performance (Chang et al., 2022; Bilad et al., 2023).

AIEd can improve students' engagement, improving their overall performance and retaining students to the university. As mentioned by Kim (2020), such tools help to design a personalised learning environment that enables students to receive individualised feedback about their overall performance, thus it improves the learning experience. In addition to this, by integrating AI technology, universities can reduce the attrition rate and increase students' retention by 30%. The results are numerous as it helps students stay more engaged during the learning process, improve their overall performance, as well as ease the grading process as it reduced the time required by 90%. Importantly, 37% of institutions have experienced higher levels of student satisfaction due to the integration of AI, and 12% increase in graduation rates (Shalwa, 2024). An extensive analysis of AIEd in the higher education sector conducted by Zawacki-Richter et al. (2019), identified four key areas that AI can be applied in HE. More specifically, they pointed out that AIEd can be used in HE for (1) profiling and prediction, (2) assessment and evaluation, (3) adaptive systems and personalisation, and (4) intelligent tutoring systems.

1.2. Artificial Intelligence and Smart Personalised Education

AI in the HE sectors plays a profound role that has managed to create a paradigm shift for HE and more specifically has modernized the traditional education approaches and improved the learning environment by providing personalised education for students, as well as increased teaching capacity to educators (Lee et al., 2022). The term personalisation in the educational context refers to the process of adjusting academic material as well as the education process based on students' needs and learning styles (Pane et al., 2017). As mentioned by Thimmanna et al. (2024) and Taylor et al. (2021) smart education reflects the utilisation of AI technologies in order to offer tailored education based on students' strengths and weaknesses. Importantly, the integration of AI in education provides endless opportunities as they offer individualised support and the ability to analyze student data on their overall performance. More precisely, AI algorithms can identify students' needs and areas that need improvement and thus provide personalised educational material in order to support them and facilitate the learning process (Imran, 2024). It is worth highlighting that different AI tools help instructors design an engaging learning environment where students will have the opportunity to interact and enjoy the learning process (Al-haimi, 2021).

As proposed by George (2023), there are different AI-aided systems including chatbots and virtual tutoring tools, that enable educators to create an interactive educational experience. Integrating such tools students are more engaged and motivated. In addition, they can monitor their performance by obtaining feedback and receiving recommendations for further study. Tapalova and Zhiyenbayeva (2022) expand this discussion by suggesting that personalised education as part of the broader context of AIEd should be viewed from a strategic point-of-view in order tom enable both national economies and industries to increase their production capacity, effectiveness, efficiency, and professionalisation, as this is essential to the smooth transition to e-science and data-driven decisions. The concept of e-science as an integral part of AIEd has long been attracting the attention of scholars across the world, such as Underwood et al. (2007, p. 535) who support that "E-Science has the potential to transform school science by enabling learners, teachers and research scientists to engage together in authentic scientific enquiry, collaboration and learning." Such statements are fully compatible with recent research such as Karakaş (2024) who clarifies that e-science within the higher education framework can help both educators and learners to expand their knowledge beyond typical economic issues and understand the gender inequality in science.

1.3. The Democratisation of AI in AIEd

According to Bondarenko and Kozulin (1991, p. 76) the Democratisation of Education has been evolving for centuries as a major social issue and has created controversy amongst social classes. The authors clarify that the "Democratisation of education involves the interaction of four major interrelated components (1) the democratization of the forms of educational activity… (2) the democratization of the content of education… (3) the humanization of the functioning of educational establishments…, and (4) the democratization of the interactions of education with other spheres of social life." The evolution of education and its overall impact on the economic and social activities of contemporary societies should bring to the surface the issue for rethinking the way that education is equally accessed and delivered at all levels, as this can help towards a more comprehensive approach, leading to sustainable and innovative results (Strand & Papastephanou, 2023).

Prinsloo and Khalil (2024) state that the current educational environment is directly linked to the concept of Democratisation of Education, with the impact of AI to be visible at all levels of education, therefore, requiring educational institutions to apply all the relevant measures. Bulathwela et al. (2024) add to the discussion by stating that the development of AI in education at all levels, especially in universities, is indeed important for all societies. Both national and universities' authorities should strategically focus on this direction, however, the authors support that AI will not lead to the democratisation of education due to pre-existing educational inequalities. Cupać et al. (2024) expand this discussion by supporting that the connection between AI in HE should be viewed from a different perspective, that of the democratisation of societies, as education and technology have a massive impact of how societies and economies are developed. Therefore, enabling access to students as well as the entire society towards AI constitutes a massive step forward, should the authorities be fully willing and committed in ensuring democratisation of education and AI. Such developments would require from national and university authorities to provide the appropriate resources, such as human, financial, and technological, in order to increase the potential of democratisation of education in the AI era (Costa et al., 2024). The democratisation of AI in education requires the establishment of appropriate strategies as this will ensure providing direction to all stakeholders (Ali et al., 2023). Such strategies should therefore be established at all educational levels in order to ensure the relevant continuation and transition to the new digital era which requires societies to become more adaptive and identify the opportunities provided (Berson et al., 2023).

1.4. Higher Educational Institutions Readiness for Adapting AI Culture

One of the main tasks of higher education institutions is to prepare students for a competitive workplace environment that requires knowledge and skills regarding the different AI technologies. Hence, instructors in HE should adopt a proactive approach and integrate such technologies in the learning process. Looking at the global level of how universities have adopted an AI culture Stanford and MIT have built specialized AI research centers and included AI into their curricula (Zawacki-Richter et al., 2019; Holmes et al., 2019). In contrast, universities that do not have the appropriate resources face significant challenges, including, among others, inexperienced instructors in AI technologies and inadequate facilities (OECD, 2021).

The following framework was proposed by Van Bure (2024) in order to help HE institutes to understand the level of AI readiness. As they mentioned, there are six key elements that are important for any sector that intends to participate in technologically advanced efforts namely technology, strategy, ethics, platform, people, and process. This framework illustrates the level of readiness of higher education institutions to engage with any AI tool in practice and their capabilities to adapt to AI. Strategy represents the first component of the framework that plays a decisive role since HEI should alight the strategic objectives in order to achieve AI integration. Focusing on the second component, technology and platforms can be assessed by the institution's architecture and tools, security and development models to assess the level or readiness. In the third component, namely process, HEI should evaluate HEI's delivery, governance, measurement, and funding. The fourth component represented by data security suggests that effective measures include an assessment regarding the privacy level, whether data is secure, data discipline and the organization's data strategy. Focusing on the fifth component of people is a key dimension for measuring the readiness of artificial intelligence and education, as their contribution is significant in the revolution in learning environments. Reuben, et al., (2024) highlight the importance of faculty development and training programmes in preparation for AI integration in the HE sectors. As they noted, a successful integration of AI into the learning process requires a high level of proficiency in AI technologies from instructors. The sixth dimension, ethics play a key role in confirming the willingness of any institute to adopt the culture of AI, because policies of transparency and explainability guide the creation of an unbiased and comprehensive approach to learning systems with the help of AI tools.

Figure 1. Framework for assessing higher educational institutions readiness (Van Bure, 2024)

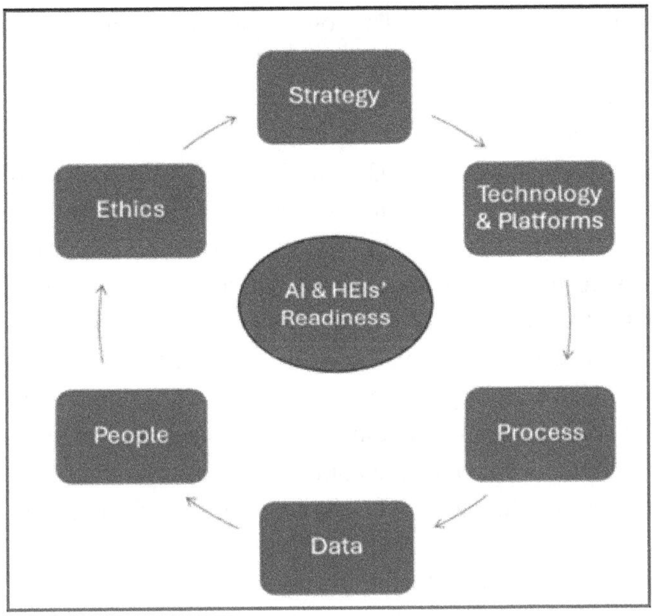

To all the above issues, especially to those linked to Strategy, Data, and Ethics, the concept of "Higher Educational Institutions Readiness for Adapting AI Culture" should take into consideration the current legal developments in European Union (EU) which has an impact on the global economy. "The EU Artificial Intelligence Act, the most comprehensive legal framework that sets out harmonized rules for the development, placing on the market, and use of artificial intelligence in the EU…" (EU AI Act, 2023). The specific Act is divided into thirteen chapters with attention on issues such as innovation, governance, information sharing, market surveillance, and penalties. The introduction of the EU AI Act is creating new and stricter challenges and implications for developers' software in order to ensure that AI will have a positive role in the economic and social development and ensure that it will become a risk for people's lives' (Van Kolfschooten & Van Oirschot, 2024). The EU AI Act will inevitably lead to substantial changes of how AI, and consequently, relevant digital tools such as simulation, in the HE (Colonna, 2023). The introduction of EU AI Act will have further impact on HE in areas such as Academic Performance Prediction (APP) which is crucial in ensuring quality and continuous performance improvement. This will require providing all the relevant information and data to students, hence, requiring from HE educators to become familiar with the specific Act (Lünich et al., 2024).

Universities should develop a strategic framework including certain policies that will enable them to integrate AI technologies effectively and efficiently. Countries that invest in education and take AI-related decisions can enjoy the important benefits resulting from AI. Chinese universities for example, have noted significant progress in the integration of AI in HE by implementing the China's "Next Generation Artificial Intelligence Development Plan" which constitutes a strategic priority for the entire country (Wang, 2024). Mehta (2023) adds to the strategic role and impact of the "Next Generation Artificial Intelligence Development Plan" by supporting that this is of a crucial importance for the country's overall development as China is at a decisive stage, therefore, the universities' readiness to incorporate the relevant AI infrastructure constitutes a fundamental pillar in this process.

Similarly, the European Union has initiated a program aiming to help AI research and integration in HE (European Commission, 2020). Such EU actions are largely based on the member states' ability to gradually incorporate the relevant AI in high schools' curriculum, as this will enable a smooth transition, and consequently, enable both educators and students to ensure a smooth transition into the universities' diversified environment (Bellas et al., 2022). In 2022, the European Commission has published the "Ethical Guidelines on the Use of Artificial Intelligence (AI) and data in teaching and learning for teachers", a move that intends to provide a comprehensive framework for all member states and all levels of education, as the rapid incorporation of AI in schools has not been monitored properly, and therefore, leading to serious regulatory and monitoring gaps (European Commission, 2022).

Highly profiled universities such as the Massachusetts Institute of Technology (MIT) in USA, University of Oxford in England, and Tsinghua University in China strategically focus on developing their readiness in order to adapt a holistic AI culture. Importantly, this readiness is based on two major pillars. The first one is the establishment of the appropriate culture and infrastructure at all levels and dimensions, and the second one refers to the development of the relevant academic research that will ensure that extrovert policies shall be produced in order to achieve dissemination of the accumulated knowledge which can create synergies for further success (Rios-Campos et al., 2024).

All these bring to the surface the need to incorporate AI in HE as this can help specific industries, such as the Automotive which has suffered massively during the recent pandemic (Prodromou, 2021) and provide the appropriate support to small and medium enterprises that faced challenges during the same period (Prodromou et al., 2024).

1.5. Intelligent Tutoring System

Intelligent tutoring systems (ITS) are an effective tool that instructors can used, which provides personalized feedback to students and hence to improve their skills. This process can enable substantial improvement of their performance, and therefore, create opportunities in terms of employment and competitiveness in the real marketplace which requires ability to adapt (Chang et al., 2022; Bilad et al., 2023). Therefore, ITS tools can improve students' engagement and their overall academic performance (Abbas et al., 2023). According to Mousavinasab et al. (2021), ITS tools and AI can be used together to offer a personalized learning environment based on students' skills and knowledge. Khalfallah and Slama (2018), developed an ITS application that enables engineering to perform various activities and experiments. The application of ITS in the HE sector can be extremely beneficial in scientific fields such as science, technology, engineering, and mathematics (STEM). This should co-exist with other tools such as AI and simulations tools as it can provide added value to all relevant stakeholders (Batsaikhan & Correia, 2024). The integration of ITS should be critically viewed as their efficiency and effectiveness is based on several variables such as their quality and the variability in terms of the ability of the professionals that oversee them. It is therefore important to ensure that any incorporation of ITS should take into consideration this parameter as it can lead to substantial fluctuations of the final educational results (Kulik & Fletcher, 2016).

Further, when incorporating ITS within the learning environment, several factors should be considered, such as academic material as they cannot all have the same influence on students and it requires significant attention by the educators (Chevalère et al., 2023). The result of this research suggests that the integration of ITS systems should also consider the psychological aspects and how students can be influenced by such technologies during their studies. Additionally, ITS can be perceived as a strategic tool that adds value on other technologies such as AI and other simulation tools. These are very important for developing a resilient and sustainable educational environment which will contribute towards providing excellent academic knowledge (Lin et al., 2023).

1.6. AIEd in Assessment and Evaluation

Chen et al. (2020) and Crompton et al. (2023) emphasize the benefits resulting from the integration of AI for instructors as well as students in HE. Hooda et al., (2022) characterized AIEd as a contemporary approach to providing individualized feedback on overall student performance and thereby evolving traditional practices and offering multiple benefits to students (Hooda et al., 2022). Indeed, integrating AI into HE revolutionizes the learning process and provides instant feedback to students with different educational backgrounds. Providing timely feedback is of outmost importance in the higher education sector, especially with the integration of AI system as it can design a dynamic environment where students will enjoy the learning process (González-Calatayud et al., 2021).

Similarly, Verdú et al., (2017) indicate that through the incorporation of AI tools students will have access to academic material based on their skills and knowledge and thus the education process is improved. In addition, it provides students with real-time feedback (Dever et al., 2020), it facilitates the assessment process and can predict their future performance (Çağataylı & Çelebi, 2022). Furthermore, AI enables automatic assessment and provides feedback to students about their overall performance. The benefits resulting for the instructors are significant since AI tools can reduce their workload (Rutner & Scott, 2022). In addition, these tools facilitate the preparation of instructors since it provides them with numerous exercises in order to give students hands-on experience and thus prepare them for employment (Yang et al., 2021). A relevant study conducted by Zhang and Xu (2022) sheds light on the topic. More precisely, they authors applied automatic assessment in real-world settings with the aim of improving the writing skills of Chinese students. The analysis of the results shows an increased overall engagement of students in the self-assessment system behaviorally, cognitively and emotionally. As a result, an improvement was observed in student writing skills and engagement.

AI-powered assessment tools can also provide detailed data about student activities. Such information is useful for students as they can track their academic progress, and this provides a rich learning environment (Hooda et al., 2022). The research conducted by Mousavi et al. (2020), makes an important contribution, since they developed an AI system that biology students can effectively utilize. Through this AI tool students can receive feedback based on their skills and backgrounds. The main conclusion resulting from the research suggests that AIEd tools can extensively analyses students' performance and thereby provide personalized feedback (Ouatik et al., 2021). As mentioned by Chu et al. (2022), the use of AI in HE has riced dramatically from 1996 to 2020 reaching an increase of 150% compared to 2019. As it presented in the following figure the integration of AI in, HE has noted a rapid grown from 2016 to 2022. However, a minor decrease was observed in 2019, which manage to increase dramatically thereafter.

Figure 2. Chronological trend in AIEd in HE (Crompton and Burke, 2023)

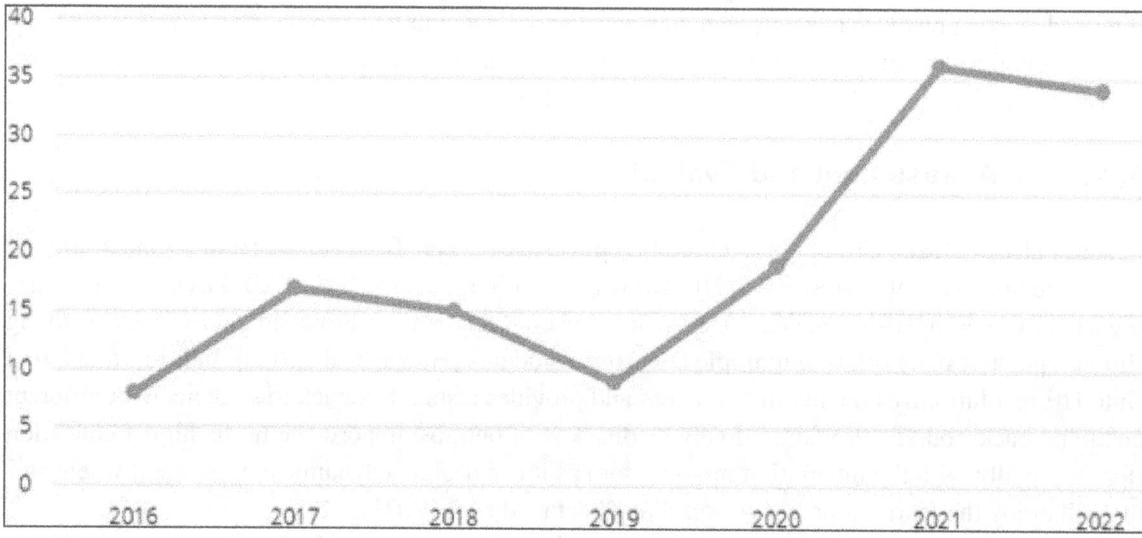

1.7. Development of Real-World Skills Through AI and Simulation Tools

Integrating tools such as AI, Virtual Reality (VR) and other simulation tools is an effective approach that helps students to improve their skill and knowledge. AI can be incorporated into different subjects and fields of studies to offer students with hands-on experience and real worlds exercises. These tools can revolutionize the old teaching approaches and develop an interactive learning environment for students. Taking an example of medical students, they can easily apply the different theories introduced in the classroom into real-life situations and thus to improve their understanding and skills. Virtual Operative Assistant (VOA) is another AI tool designed specifically for medical students, and it can be used for surgical training. Students can practice such tools in order to identify any areas that need further improvement, and they receive feedback regarding their overall performance (Mirchi et al., 2020). This innovative learning environment can improve their overall performance through the easier and more effective acquisition and development of surgical technical skills (Yilmaz et al., 2023).

Students should have the chance to develop their clinical skills in a simulation relatively risk-free environment. Therefore, the incorporation of Virtual Reality (VR) systems integrated with AI algorithms can be an ideal educational tool that provides multiple learning opportunities for the healthcare professionals and students (Esfahlani et al., 2019). Artificial intelligence is beginning to change this with real-world applications in the form of the Artificial Internet of Things (AIoT), which is integrating Computational Thinking (CT) capabilities and Augmented Reality (AR). Combining these technologies can potentially transform scientific methodologies by creating more interactive, and intelligent problem-solving environments. The benefits resulting from these approaches are numerous, since they can enhance problem solving and application planning skills in students making it easier for them to relate AIoT concepts in real life (Lin et al., 2021).

Another area that AI can be applied to improve students' skills and abilities is called Reinforcement Learning (RL). Through these technologies students can experience a simulation of the competitive landscape making the learning process more challenging and effective (Sharma et al., 2020). AI technologies can also be incorporated into the engineering field (Guillén-Yparrea, and Hernández-Rodríguez, 2024). Utilizing AI tools in the learning process offers a more interactive learning environment where students will enjoy the learning process. Furthermore, Bosman et al. (2022) point out that artificial intelligence tools can be effectively applied in order to explain the theoretical models. More precisely, from their research they found that these tools can also apply in different business management courses. For example, for students to understand the supply chain management process these tools can be utilised in order to show them in a role-play format how beer is distributed. This transition from theoretical analysis of different processes to practical application in the real-world examples enables students to acquire knowledge more effectively (Bosman et al., 2022).

2. CONCEPTUAL FRAMEWORK

By examining the existing literature, the following model (Figure 2), namely 'The influence of AI and simulation tools in HE on Student Success and University Brand Image Enhancement' (HESAIT: Higher Education Simulation with Artificial Intelligence Technologies) is developed and enables deeper understanding of all the issues related to the specific graph. As it is presented in the following figure, there are three main outcomes on students, because of the incorporation of AI and simulation tools. By integrating the previously mentioned tools in the learning process, students' motivation, engagement and skills can be increased. This optimized learning environment incorporating artificial intelligence and stimulation tools are vital elements that can prepare students for the competitive workforce. As a result, AI and other simulations tools enable students to gain a significant competitive advantage, as students who graduate from universities that incorporate these technologies in their learning processes are more skilled than that other students who graduate from other universities. This in turn can increase the university's appeal to prospective students and can lower the attrition rate. As a result, the overall profitability of the university is positively affected by both attracting new students and keeping the existing ones.

The HESAIT conceptual framework will be discussed and further developed in the Recommendations section, and therefore, further analysis and understanding will be gained. As is explained in the proposed conceptual framework, students remain at the heart of all these activities, as they are the ones that will receive, and therefore, benefit from the end results of this process. The development of AI and simulation skills has become a major issue in scientific fields such as medicine in which students use such simulations in order to increase their knowledge and "...enables personal evaluation and provides personalized feedback in surgical training simulations...however, barriers to wide-spread commercialization of such devices and software remain complex and multifactorial" (Park et al., p. 1). Harder (2023) adds to the impact of AI and simulation tools in the Medicine field and clarifies that such tools enable health professionals at all levels, including those in universities, to fully develop their skills and capacity, therefore, leading to higher levels of productivity as well as increased quality in the provided services. This will enable universities to increase their overall brand image which is essential in order to become more competitive in the already demanding HE sector (Kountouridou and Domic, 2022b).

Such scientific findings coming from renowned scientists and institutions provide a rather safe pathway which needs to be followed. Within this concept, the role of AI and its commercialization should be further examined of how it can be introduced into small and medium enterprises (Masouras et al., 2021), as well as co-create added value as an integral part of a broader strategic marketing plan (Daskou et al., 2021).

Figure 3. The influence of AI and other simulation tools in HE on student success and university brand image enhancement (HESAIT: Higher Education Simulation with Artificial Intelligence Technologies) (Authors' work)

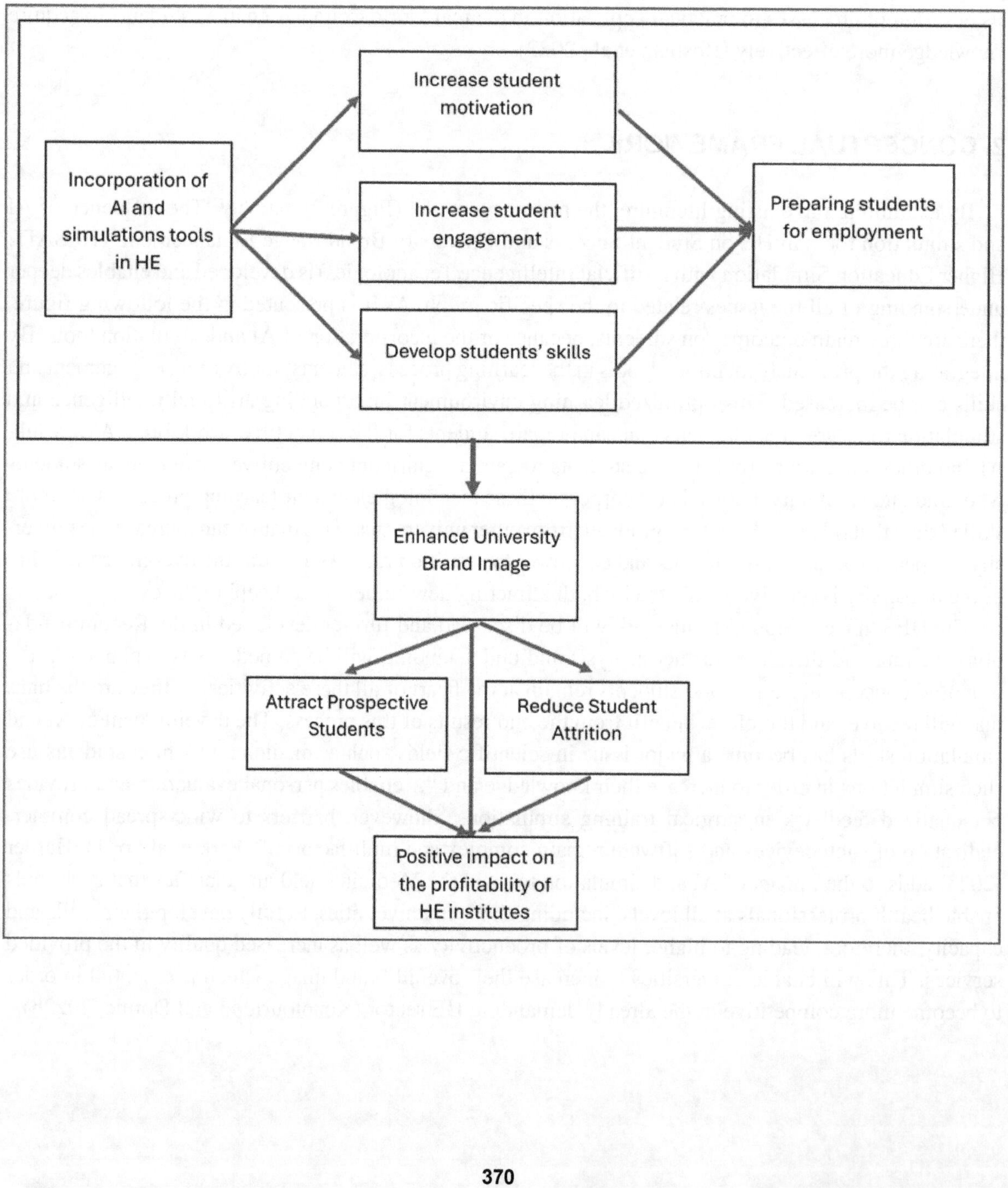

As it clearly stated through the proposed HESAIT visual conceptual framework, the final strategic objective is to ensure that HE will achieve the appropriate growth which can lead to the much-needed profitability. Considering the fact that funding has been a long-term challenge for universities (Hunter, 2013; Kudla, 2014 et al., 2014), especially following the recent Covid-19 pandemic which has caused anxiety and stress to a large percentage of students (Islam et al., 2020), this framework strongly supports that AI and simulation tools can provide innovative and sustainable solutions for all stakeholders involved.

3. CONCLUSION AND RECOMMENDATIONS

3.1. Conclusion

The current chapter has focused on the examination of the application and role of AI and simulation tools within the HE, as this issue has been emerging substantially during the last few decades, therefore, creating the need for deeper understanding of several elements. Such elements refer to the policies developed by national authorities, the ability of universities to incorporate such advanced technological tools as their introduction requires the relevant resources, including financial, building, and most importantly, human. Within this preliminary context, AI and simulation tools are considered as a necessity which will enable the sustainable development of several, HE institutions across the world. Therefore, the major question that should be addressed to these institutions is not whether they should incorporate AI and simulation tools in their infrastructure, but when this will occur.

AI in Education AIEd has led to massive changes in how contemporary HE institutions view the future in education, with simulation tools to have gained exceptional attention in both practical and theoretical levels. This chapter has deeply explored the specific issue, and therefore, concludes that AIEd can transform the entire educational system and experience for all its participants. AIEd will require institutions to adapt their curricula according to the students' needs, and consequently, educators will need to increase their digital skills. Such adaptation will require intensive training. Tools such as ML and simulation will no longer be a subject of choice, it will rather be an issue of necessity which educators will need to take into serious consideration whilst dealing with younger generation students.

Personalized education has become an issue of massive importance within HE, therefore, requiring HE institutions to apply all the relevant tools in order to enable such strategic approaches. The current market realities at which HE students will enter soon after their graduation, and even during their studies through placement programs, require them to be ready to adapt to their new working environment. Consequently, developing personalized education based on the specific needs, wants, and requirements of each student should be treated as of the outmost importance by HE and educators. Such an approach will substantially increase students' capacity and provide them with added confidence in their workplace, especially when this takes place in highly demanding markets. This chapter has identified the role of curricula in relation to personalized education which will require from the curricula developers to identify possible gaps in the educational process. This will enable a deeper understanding of each student's unique needs, with the impact of AI and simulation tools to be clearly visible during the entire process.

The Democratization of Education has been a subject of exceptional attention within the current chapter, as this is directly linked to several crucial issues that extend far beyond the typical academic concept. Issues such as equal access to education, allocation of the relevant resources, such as financial, technological, and human, have clearly been identified as major components that can add to the Democratization of Education. In any case, this issue cannot be left to the HE institutions, instead, it should be a subject of strategic choice by the relevant national authorities in order to ensure that all HE students will have equal access opportunities in technological tools, including AI and simulation tools. Considering the broader impact of education in developing sustainable and resilient societies, this chapter considers the current issue as a fundamental in delivering high-quality education.

The readiness for adapting to new AI and simulation tools changes, and consequently adopting all the relevant changes as an integral part of the entire process, has also been found to have an extremely important position in this chapter. The readiness of universities depends on several internal and external factors, therefore, the establishment of an extrovert strategy on behalf of all major stakeholders is considered as of the outmost importance. The examples of Stanford University and MIT, as well as the "Higher Educational Institutions Readiness for Adapting AI Culture" policy developed by the EU, constitute positive steps towards enhancing the overall readiness. The current chapter has paid exceptional attention to the concept of ethics, as this can help, HE institutions as well as policy makers to take the appropriate strategic decisions that will ensure the protection of all parties involved in the educational process. Additionally, focusing on ethics can contribute towards avoiding possible legal implications. It is therefore important for all HE that focus on implementing any kind of cutting-edge technology, such as AI, ML, ITS, and simulation tools, to increase their attention towards ethical issues as this can provide them with serious advantages, especially when this deals with the personal data of their students.

Intelligent Tutoring Systems (ITS) has also been another major part of discussion of the current chapter. ITS are indeed important parts of the overall technological infrastructure in contemporary HE institutions. Therefore, their introduction into this emerging framework should take into serious consideration all possible parameters, including psychological factors. The findings of Lin et al. (2023) related to the sustainability and resilience of the educational environment have been found to make a massive contribution to the current chapter. Such findings bring to the surface the need behalf of the HE institutions to establish the relevant infrastructure, especially in terms of internal culture, in order to provide both educators and students with the appropriate teaching and learning environment, respectively.

3.2. Recommendations

The following part will propose a set of practical recommendations that are considered as important in order to enable the introduction of AI and simulation tools in the HE context. These recommendations are believed to have practical value for all major stakeholders, especially educators and students, as these two groups are considered as the 'frontline' people that will interact with each other on a regular basis. Therefore, this interaction must be structured on realistic facts that will deliver all the appropriate results, and consequently, enable HE to increase their resilience and image within a highly demanding sector which requires continuous improvement and adaptation to the technological advancements, as well as educational and social demands.

Amongst others, the current chapter will focus on the proposed conceptual framework, namely "HESAIT: Higher Education Simulation with Artificial Intelligence Technologies." HESAIT constitutes the summary of the authors' findings that are considered to have the best possible practical application within the HE institutions. All elements included in the proposed HESAIT model are considered to have a major impact on HE sustainable development. However, other recommendations that will cover both public and private stakeholders shall be included in this section, as both are considered as of the outmost importance and can play a key role in the incorporation of AI and simulation tools in HE.

The first recommendation refers to the need for developing a holistic national strategy that will ensure that AI, simulation tools, as well as other advanced digital infrastructure, shall be incorporated into the educational process. Introducing a comprehensive national strategy will ensure the allocation of the relevant resources, including financial, human, land, buildings, equipment, and of course, technological. However, the biggest message is that the existence of a national strategy will provide direction to all statehooders, ensure commitment by everyone, and increase the attention related to the long-term benefits a strategy can provide. Therefore, this will hold accountable to all parties involved in the process, including HE students.

The second recommendation refers to the introduction of AI and simulation tools in the early stages of education, including primary schools. Considering that young people are born and raised within an environment which is highly affected by technological development, introducing such advanced technology in the classrooms will enable a smooth transition of both the children and teachers. Further, increasing young children's technological capacity will enable them to improve their understanding over the benefits and challenges related to technology, and consequently, making them more resilient when it comes to cybersecurity issues, and finally, prepare them for when they either enter the market or HE.

The third recommendation refers to the need for the public and private sectors to join forces together in order to ensure that AI, ML, ITS, and simulation tools to be incorporated within the entire educational system, and obviously, within the HE context. Increasing the public and private partnerships (PPP) will enable increasing private funding in universities, and therefore, enable them to identify several business opportunities. This recommendation is evaluated as a major component of the current chapter as the expectations from HE are increasing in terms of providing the market, especially highly-competitive industries, with the appropriate qualified human resources which can become an asset for the entire economy.

The fourth and final recommendation refers to the proposed conceptual framework "HESAIT: Higher Education Simulation with Artificial Intelligence Technologies." The incorporation of AI and simulation tools in HE is expected to lead to three major positive outcomes; (i) increasing students' motivation which is essential in order to create a future workforce based on skills and understanding the impact of technological tools that are increasingly introduced in the global market; (ii) increasing students' engagement in both educational and workplace environments. This issue is crucial in developing the workforce as several employers complain that younger employees are not motivated and do not take their job seriously, and therefore, they cannot develop. Despite that there is no yet adequate scientific evidence regarding the connection between AI and simulation tools to work engagement, the current chapter proposes that such development would be beneficial for all parties involved in the process; (iii) Develop students' skills which are essential in becoming more competitive in their educational and working environment. This can be extremely beneficial for those students that are working as part of placement year as part of their studies. All three elements are expected to contribute towards preparing students to enter the ever-challenging workplace which is characterized by rapid technological developments within a globalized environment. The proposed HESAIT Model proposes that all the above will lead to increased universities' overall brand image which is essential in order to become more competitive in the already demanding HE sector. The increase in brand image is expected to lead to two major benefits; (i) attract prospective students with solid high-school background and are willing to enter into this emerging educational environment; (ii) reduce students' attrition; and therefore, enable them to become more resilient in their educational and working environment, with obvious social and economic benefits. Finally, all the above issues are expected to lead to increased profitability of the HE institutions. Considering that several countries have a blend of both public and private universities, focusing on issues such as profitability is essential for their sustainable development and contribution to their societies.

REFERENCES

Abbas, M., Jam, F. A., & Khan, T. I. (2024). Is it harmful or helpful? Examining the causes and consequences of generative AI usage among university students. *International Journal of Educational Technology in Higher Education*, *21*(1), 10. Advance online publication. DOI: 10.1186/s41239-024-00444-7

Act, E. U. A. I. (n.d.). https://www.euaiact.com/#:~:text=The%20EU%20Artificial%20Intelligence%20Act,three%20years%20negotiations%20and%20entered

Al-Haimi, B., Hujainah, F., Nasir, D., & Alhroob, E. (2021). Higher Education Institutions with Artificial Intelligence: Roles, Promises, and Requirements. In *Studies in computational intelligence* (pp. 221–238). DOI: 10.1007/978-3-030-72080-3_13

Alajmi, Q., Al-Sharafi, M. A., & Abuali, A. (2020). Smart learning gateways for Omani HEIs towards educational technology: Benefits, challenges and solutions. *International Journal of Information Technology and Language Studies*, *4*(1), 12–17. https://www.scirp.org/reference/referencespapers?referenceid=2989533

Aldosari, S. A. M. (2020). The Future of Higher Education in the Light of Artificial Intelligence Transformations. *International Journal of Higher Education*, *9*(3), 145. DOI: 10.5430/ijhe.v9n3p145

Ali, O., Krsteska, K., Said, D., & Momin, M. (2023). Advanced technologies enabled human resources functions: Benefits, challenges, and functionalities: A systematic review. *Cogent Business & Management*, *10*(2), 2216430. Advance online publication. DOI: 10.1080/23311975.2023.2216430

Ali, O., Murray, P. A., Momin, M., Dwivedi, Y. K., & Malik, T. (2023). The effects of artificial intelligence applications in educational settings: Challenges and strategies. *Technological Forecasting and Social Change*, *199*, 123076. DOI: 10.1016/j.techfore.2023.123076

Alonso-Peña, M., & Álvarez Álvarez, C. (2023). Clinical simulation in health education: A systematic review. *Investigacion y Educacion en Enfermeria*, *41*(2), e08. DOI: 10.17533/udea.iee.v41n2e08 PMID: 38589326

AwangHarun, S., Md Hashim, N. H., & Kadiman, S. (2022). The Effectiveness of Simulation in Education 4.0: Application in a Transesophageal Echocardiography Training Program in Malaysia. *Frontiers in Surgery*, *9*, 749092. Advance online publication. DOI: 10.3389/fsurg.2022.749092 PMID: 35445072

Baker, T., & Smith, L. (2019). *Educ-AI-tion Rebooted? Exploring the future of artificial intelligence in schools and colleges*. https://media.nesta.org.uk/documents/Future_of_AI_and_education_v5_WEB.pdf

Batsaikhan, B., & Correia, A.-P. (2024). The effects of Generative Artificial Intelligence on Intelligent Tutoring Systems in higher education: A systematic review. *Studies in Technology Enhanced Learning*, *4*(1). Advance online publication. DOI: 10.21428/8c225f6e.33570bb1

Bearman, M., Ryan, J., & Ajjawi, R. (2022). Discourses of artificial intelligence in higher education: A critical literature review. *Higher Education*, *86*(2), 369–385. Advance online publication. DOI: 10.1007/s10734-022-00937-2

Bellas, F., Guerreiro-Santalla, S., Naya, M., & Duro, R. J. (2022). AI Curriculum for European High Schools: An Embedded Intelligence Approach. *International Journal of Artificial Intelligence in Education, 33*(2), 399–426. DOI: 10.1007/s40593-022-00315-0

Berson, I. R., & Berson, M. J. (2023). The Democratization of AI and its Transformative Potential in Social Studies Education. *Social Education, 87*(2). https://lists.aaai.org/ai4k12/cache/22236874/2.pdf

Bilad, M. R., Anwar, K., & Hayati, S. (2023). Nurturing Prospective STEM Teachers' Critical Thinking Skill through Virtual Simulation-Assisted Remote Inquiry in Fourier Transform Courses. *International Journal of Essential Competencies in Education, 1*(1), 1–10. Advance online publication. DOI: 10.36312/ijece.v1i1.728

Bondarenko, Y. G., & Kozulin, A. V. (1991). The Democratization of education: basic principles. *Higher education in Europe, 16*(1), 74-78. https://unesdoc.unesco.org/ark:/48223/pf0000093679

Bosman, L., Kotla, B., Madamanchi, A., Bartholomew, S., & Byrd, V. (2022). Preparing the future entrepreneurial engineering workforce using web-based AI-enabled tools. *European Journal of Engineering Education, 48*(5), 972–989. DOI: 10.1080/03043797.2022.2119122

Bulathwela, S., Pérez-Ortiz, M., Holloway, C., Cukurova, M., & Shawe-Taylor, J. (2024). Artificial Intelligence Alone Will Not Democratise Education: On Educational Inequality, Techno-Solutionism and Inclusive Tools. *Sustainability (Basel), 16*(2), 781. DOI: 10.3390/su16020781

Çağataylı, M., & Çelebi, E. (2022). Estimating academic success in higher education using big five personality traits, a machine learning approach. *Arabian Journal for Science and Engineering, 47*(2), 1289–1298. DOI: 10.1007/s13369-021-05873-4

Campos, N., Nogal, M., Caliz, C., & Juan, A. A. (2020). Simulation-based education involving online and on-campus models in different European universities. *International Journal of Educational Technology in Higher Education, 17*(1), 8. Advance online publication. DOI: 10.1186/s41239-020-0181-y

Chang, Y., Kao, J.-Y., & Wang, Y.-Y. (2022). Influences of virtual reality on design creativity and design thinking. *Thinking Skills and Creativity, 46*, 101127. DOI: 10.1016/j.tsc.2022.101127

Chaudhry, M. A., & Kazim, E. (2021). Artificial Intelligence in Education (AIEd): A high-level academic and industry note 2021. *AI and Ethics, 2*(1), 157–165. DOI: 10.1007/s43681-021-00074-z PMID: 34790953

Chen, L., Chen, P., & Lin, Z. (2020). Artificial Intelligence in Education: A Review. *IEEE Access : Practical Innovations, Open Solutions, 8*, 75264–75278. DOI: 10.1109/ACCESS.2020.2988510

Chevalère, J., Yun, H. S., Henke, A., Pinkwart, N., Hafner, V. V., & Lazarides, R. (2023). A sequence of learning processes in an intelligent tutoring system from topic-related appraisals to learning gains. *Learning and Instruction, 87*, 101799. DOI: 10.1016/j.learninstruc.2023.101799

Chu, H., Tu, Y., & Yang, K. (2022). Roles and research trends of artificial intelligence in higher education: A systematic review of the top 50 most-cited articles. *Australasian Journal of Educational Technology, 38*(3), 22–42. DOI: 10.14742/ajet.7526

Colonna, L. (2023). *The AI Regulation and Higher Education: Preliminary Observations and Critical Perspectives*. De Lege., DOI: 10.33063/dl.vi.428

Crompton, H., & Burke, D. (2023). Artificial Intelligence in Higher education: The State of the Field. *International Journal of Educational Technology in Higher Education*, *20*(1), 1–22. DOI: 10.1186/s41239-023-00392-8

Cupać, J., Schopmans, H., & Tuncer-Ebetürk, İ. (2024). Democratization in the age of artificial intelligence: Introduction to the special issue. *Democratization*, *31*(5), 899–921. DOI: 10.1080/13510347.2024.2338852

Dai, C., & Ke, F. (2022). Educational applications of artificial intelligence in simulation-based learning: A systematic mapping review. *Computers and Education Artificial Intelligence*, *3*, 100087. DOI: 10.1016/j.caeai.2022.100087

Daskou, S., Masouras, A., & Reppa, A. (2022). Service-Dominant Logic: The Road Map to Value Co-Creation in Place Marketing. In *Business Development and Economic Governance in Southeastern Europe: 13th International Conference on the Economies of the Balkan and Eastern European Countries (EBEEC), Pafos, Cyprus, 2021* (pp. 369-382). Cham: Springer International Publishing, 2022.

Desmarais, M. C., & Baker, R. S. D. (2012). A review of recent advances in learner and skill modeling in intelligent learning environments. *User Modeling and User-Adapted Interaction*, *22*(1-2), 9–38. DOI: 10.1007/s11257-011-9106-8

Dever, D. A., Azevedo, R., Cloude, E. B., & Wiedbusch, M. (2020). The impact of autonomy and types of informational text presentations in game-based environments on learning: Converging multi-channel processes data and learning outcomes. *International Journal of Artificial Intelligence in Education*, *30*(4), 581–615. DOI: 10.1007/s40593-020-00215-1

Dillenbourg, P., & Jermann, P. (2007). Designing Integrative Scripts. In *Springer eBooks* (pp. 275–301). DOI: 10.1007/978-0-387-36949-5_16

Esfahlani, S. S., Izsof, V., Minter, S., Kordzadeh, A., Shirvani, H., & Esfahlani, K. S. (2019). Development of an Interactive Virtual Reality for Medical Skills Training Supervised by Artificial Neural Network. In *Advances in intelligent systems and computing* (pp. 473–482). DOI: 10.1007/978-3-030-29513-4_34

European Commission. (2020). *Artificial intelligence: A European perspective*. European Union Publications.

European Commission. (2022). *The Commission publishes guidelines to help teachers address misconceptions about Artificial Intelligence and promote its ethical use*.https://ec.europa.eu/commission/presscorner/detail/en/ip_22_6338

Fullan, M. (2023). *The Principal 2.0: Three Keys to Maximizing Impact*. John Wiley & Sons.

Gardner, J., O'Leary, M., & Yuan, L. (2021). Artificial intelligence in educational assessment: 'Breakthrough? Or buncombe and ballyhoo? *Journal of Computer Assisted Learning*, *37*(5), 1207–1216. DOI: 10.1111/jcal.12577

George, B., & Wooden, O. (2023). Managing the Strategic Transformation of Higher Education through Artificial Intelligence. *Administrative Sciences*, *13*(9), 196. DOI: 10.3390/admsci13090196

González-Calatayud, V., Prendes-Espinosa, P., & Roig-Vila, R. (2021). Artificial Intelligence for Student Assessment: A Systematic Review. *Applied Sciences (Basel, Switzerland)*, *11*(12), 5467. DOI: 10.3390/app11125467

Guillén-Yparrea, N., & Hernández-Rodríguez, F. (2024). Unveiling Generative AI in Higher Education: Insights from Engineering Students and Professors. *2022 IEEE Global Engineering Education Conference (EDUCON)*, 1–5. https://doi.org/DOI: 10.1109/EDUCON60312.2024.10578876

Harder, N. (2023). Advancing healthcare simulation through artificial intelligence and Machine Learning: Exploring Innovations. *Clinical Simulation in Nursing*, *83*, 101456. DOI: 10.1016/j.ecns.2023.101456

Holmes, W., Bialik, M., & Fadel, C. (2019). *Artificial Intelligence in Education: Promises and Implications for Teaching and Learning*. Center for Curriculum Redesign.

Hooda, M., Rana, C., Dahiya, O., Rizwan, A., & Hossain, M. S. (2022). Artificial Intelligence for Assessment and Feedback to Enhance Student Success in Higher Education. *Mathematical Problems in Engineering*, *2022*, 1–19. DOI: 10.1155/2022/5215722

Hunter, P. (2013). Research funding is not enough. Universities need more support for teaching and facility maintenance to stay fit for the future. *EMBO Reports*, *14*(2), 140–142. DOI: 10.1038/embor.2012.226 PMID: 23318630

Imran, M., Almusharraf, N., Abdellatif, M. S., & Abbasova, M. Y. (2024). Artificial Intelligence in Higher Education: Enhancing Learning Systems and Transforming Educational Paradigms. *International Journal of Interactive Mobile Technologies*, *18*(18), 34–48. DOI: 10.3991/ijim.v18i18.49143

Islam, M. A., Barna, S. D., Raihan, H., Khan, M. N. A., & Hossain, M. T. (2020). Depression and anxiety among university students during the COVID-19 pandemic in Bangladesh: A web-based crosssectional survey. *PLoS One*, *15*(8), e0238162. DOI: 10.1371/journal.pone.0238162 PMID: 32845928

Karakaş, Ö. (2024). The Persistence of Gender Inequality in e-Science: The Case of eSec. *Minerva*, *62*(4), 611–634. Advance online publication. DOI: 10.1007/s11024-024-09530-6

Khalfallah, J., & Slama, J. B. H. (2018). The effect of emotional analysis on the improvement of experimental e-learning systems. *Computer Applications in Engineering Education*, *27*(2), 303–318. DOI: 10.1002/cae.22075

Kim, B., Suh, H., Heo, J., & Choi, Y. (2020). AI-Driven Interface Design for Intelligent Tutoring System Improves Student Engagement. *arXiv (Cornell University)*. /arxiv.2009.08976DOI: 10.48550

Kountouridou, M., & Dino Domic, . (2022a). Reconditioning the Freshman Gene: Can a 'Positive Visualisation Course' Successfully modify Freshmen Students' Perceptions of a University's Brand Image? *Transnational Marketing Journal*, *10*(2), 203–214. DOI: 10.33182/tmj.v10i2.1988

Kountouridou, M., & Domic, D. (2022b). 'The Impact of a Positive Visualisation Course in Brand Identity on Freshmen Students' Perceptions of University Brand Image'. *Interdisciplinary Journal of Management Studies*, *15*(4), 945–962. DOI: 10.22059/ijms.2022.326021.674612

Kudła, J., Stachowiak-Kudła, M., & Figurski, A. (2014). The impact of funding on the quality of public higher education in Poland. SSRN *Electronic Journal*. DOI: 10.2139/ssrn.2537075

Kulik, J. A., & Fletcher, J. D. (2016). Effectiveness of Intelligent Tutoring Systems: A Meta-Analytic Review. *Review of Educational Research, 86*(1), 42–78. DOI: 10.3102/0034654315581420

Lee, D., Arnold, M., Srivastava, A., Plastow, K., Strelan, P., Ploeckl, F., Lekkas, D., & Palmer, E. (2024). The impact of generative AI on higher education learning and teaching: A study of educators' perspectives. *Computers and Education Artificial Intelligence, 6*, 100221. DOI: 10.1016/j.caeai.2024.100221

Lee, M., Liang, P., & Yang, Q. (2022). CoAuthor: Designing a Human-AI Collaborative Writing Dataset for Exploring Language Model Capabilities. *CHI Conference on Human Factors in Computing Systems*. DOI: 10.1145/3491102.3502030

Lee, Y. J., Davis, R. O., & Ryu, J. (2024). Korean in-Service Teachers' Perceptions of Implementing Artificial Intelligence (AI) Education for Teaching in Schools and Their AI Teacher Training Programs. *International Journal of Information and Education Technology (IJIET), 14*(2), 214–219. DOI: 10.18178/ijiet.2024.14.2.2042

Lin, C., Huang, A. Y. Q., & Lu, O. H. T. (2023). Artificial intelligence in intelligent tutoring systems toward sustainable education: A systematic review. *Smart Learning Environments, 10*(1), 41. Advance online publication. DOI: 10.1186/s40561-023-00260-y

Lin, Y., Chen, S., Tsai, C., & Lai, Y. (2021). Exploring Computational Thinking Skills Training Through Augmented Reality and AIoT Learning. *Frontiers in Psychology, 12*, 640115. Advance online publication. DOI: 10.3389/fpsyg.2021.640115 PMID: 33708166

Liu, X., Sha, Y., & Yu, X. (2022). The Impact of Developmental HR Practices on Career Self-Management and Organizational Citizenship Behavior: A Moderated Mediation Model. *Psychology Research and Behavior Management, 15*, 1193–1208. DOI: 10.2147/PRBM.S355376 PMID: 35586698

Lu, O. H. T., Huang, A. Y. Q., Tsai, D. C. L., & Yang, S. J. H. (2021). Expert-authored and machine-generated short-answer questions for assessing students learning performance. *Journal of Educational Technology & Society, 24*(3), 159–173. https://www.jstor.org/stable/27032863

Luckin, R., & Cukurova, M. (2019). Designing educational technologies in the age of AI: A learning sciences-driven approach. *British Journal of Educational Technology, 50*(6), 2824–2838. DOI: 10.1111/bjet.12861

Lünich, M., Keller, B., & Marcinkowski, F. (2024). Diverging Perceptions of Artificial Intelligence in Higher Education: A Comparison of Student and Public Assessments on Risks and Damages of Academic Performance Prediction in Germany. *Computers and Education Artificial Intelligence, 100305*, 100305. Advance online publication. DOI: 10.1016/j.caeai.2024.100305

Masouras, A., Pistikou, V., & Komodromos, M. (2021). Innovation analysis in Cypriot small and medium-sized enterprises and the role of the European Union. In *Entrepreneurship, Institutional Framework and Support Mechanisms in the EU* (pp. 115-131). Emerald Publishing Limited. DOI: 10.1108/978-1-83909-982-320211011

Mehta, M. G. D. K. (2023, March 30). *China's Next-Gen Artificial Intelligence Development Plan (Part 1)*. IMR. https://imrmedia.in/chinas-next-gen-artificial-intelligence-development-plan-part-

Merchant, Z., Goetz, E. T., Cifuentes, L., Keeney-Kennicutt, W., & Davis, T. J. (2013). Effectiveness of virtual reality-based instruction on students' learning outcomes in K-12 and higher education: A meta-analysis. *Computers & Education, 70*, 29–40. DOI: 10.1016/j.compedu.2013.07.033

Mirchi, N., Bissonnette, V., Yilmaz, R., Ledwos, N., Winkler-Schwartz, A., & Maestro, R. (2020). The Virtual Operative Assistant: An explainable artificial intelligence tool for simulation-based training in surgery and medicine. *PLoS One, 15*(2), e0229596. Advance online publication. DOI: 10.1371/journal.pone.0229596 PMID: 32106247

Mousavi, S. M., & Beroza, G. C. (2020). A Machine-Learning Approach for Earthquake Magnitude Estimation. *Geophysical Research Letters, 47*(1). Advance online publication. DOI: 10.1029/2019GL085976

Mousavinasab, E., Zarifsanaiey, N., Kalhori, S. R. N., Rakhshan, M., Keikha, L., & Saeedi, M. G. (2018). Intelligent tutoring systems: A systematic review of characteristics, applications, and evaluation methods. *Interactive Learning Environments, 29*(1), 142–163. DOI: 10.1080/10494820.2018.1558257

OECD. (2021). *The state of AI adoption in higher education in developing countries.* OECD Publishing. https://www.oecd.org/en/topics/sub-issues/higher-education.html

Ouatik, F., Raoufi, M., Ouatik, F., & Skouri, M. (2021). E-Learning & decision making system for automate students assessment using remote laboratory and machine learning. *DOAJ (DOAJ: Directory of Open Access Journals).* DOI: 10.20368/1971-8829/1135285

Pane, J. F., Steiner, E. D., Baird, M. D., & Hamilton, L. S. (2017). *Informing Progress: Insights on Personalized Learning Implementation and Effects.* RAND Corporation. DOI: 10.7249/RR2042

Park, J. J., Tiefenbach, J., & Demetriades, A. K. (2022). The role of artificial intelligence in surgical simulation. *Frontiers in Medical Technology, 4*, 1076755. DOI: 10.3389/fmedt.2022.1076755 PMID: 36590155

Polas, M. R. H., Jahanshahi, A. A., Ahamed, B., & Molla, M. O. F. (2023). The Future of Artificial Intelligence in Education 4.0. In *Advances in educational technologies and instructional design book series* (pp. 1–20). DOI: 10.4018/978-1-6684-9103-4.ch001

Prinsloo, P., & Khalil, M. (2024). The Democratisation of AI in, for and through Education: A Position Paper. *Ubiquity Proceedings, 8*, 8. Advance online publication. DOI: 10.5334/uproc.130

Prodromou, A. (2021). The Impact of Covid-19 on the Global Automotive Industry - Future Challenges. *American International Journal of Social Science, 10*(1), 1–11. DOI: 10.30845/aijss.v10n1p1

Prodromou, A., Efthimiou, I., & Apostolopoulos, S. (2024). Covid-19 and the Impact on Cyprus' SMEs Tourism - Enterprises: Lessons to be Learned. *Conference Proceedings of the 19th European Conference on Innovation and Entrepreneurship ECIE 19(1), 2024 26-27 September 2024 CESI.* DOI: 10.34190/ecie.19.1.2470

Qin, X., Huang, Y.-N., Hu, Z., Chen, K., & Lin, L. (2023). Human resource management research in healthcare: a big data bibliometric study. *Human Resources for Health, 21*(1). https://www.ncbi.nlm.nih.gov/pmc/articles/PMC10696747/

Reuben, B., Samuel, O., & Lawal, A. (2024). *A Review of Artificial Intelligence (AI) Readiness in Higher Education Institutions: A Case Study of Northern States of Nigeria BY.*https://shorturl.at/XQ4zz

Rios-Campos, C., Zambrano, E. O. G., Cantos, M. F. M., Anchundia-Gómez, O., León, M. E. C., Moya, G. E. M., García, E. M., Batalla, E. P., De La Oliva, N. R., & Zelada, O. S. (2024). Universities and artificial intelligence. *South Florida Journal of Development*, *5*(6), e4016. DOI: 10.46932/sfjdv5n6-010

Russel, S., & Norvig, P. (2010). *Artificial intelligence - a modern approach.* Pearson Education.

Rutner, S., & Scott, R. (2022, September 1). *Use of Artificial Intelligence to Grade Student Discussion Boards: An Exploratory Study.* https://isedj.org/2022-20/n4/ISEDJv20n4p4.html

Scherer, R., & Teo, T. (2019). Unpacking teachers' intentions to integrate technology: A meta-analysis. *Educational Research Review*, *27*, 90–109. DOI: 10.1016/j.edurev.2019.03.001

Schwartz, R. A., & Weber, B. W. (2015). Simulation as a Research Tool for Market Architects. In Lee, C. F., & Lee, J. (Eds.), *Handbook of Financial Econometrics and Statistics*. Springer. DOI: 10.1007/978-1-4614-7750-1_4

Shalwa. (2024, November 16). AI in Education: 2025 Statistics & the Future of Learning. *ARTSMART AI*. https://artsmart.ai/blog/ai-in-education-statistics-2024/

Sharma, A., Ahn, M., Levine, S., Kumar, V., Hausman, K., & Gu, S. (2020). Emergent Real-World Robotic Skills via Unsupervised Off-Policy Reinforcement Learning. *ArXiv*, abs/2004.12974. DOI: 10.15607/RSS.2020.XVI.053

Staroverov, A., Muravyev, K., Yakovlev, K., & Panov, A. (2023). Skill Fusion in Hybrid Robotic Framework for Visual Object Goal Navigation. *Robotics (Basel, Switzerland)*, *12*(4), 104. Advance online publication. DOI: 10.3390/robotics12040104

Strand, T., & Papastephanou, M. (2023). Education and democratization. An introduction. *Ethics and Education*, *18*(3–4), 231–241. DOI: 10.1080/17449642.2023.2281856

Tapalova, O., & Zhiyenbayeva, N. (2022). Artificial Intelligence in Education: AIEd for Personalised Learning Pathways. *Electronic Journal of e-Learning*, *20*(5), 639–653. https://files.eric.ed.gov/fulltext/EJ1373006.pdf. DOI: 10.34190/ejel.20.5.2597

Taylor, D. L., Yeung, M., & Bashet, A. Z. (2021). Personalized and Adaptive Learning. In *SpringerBriefs in statistics* (pp. 17–34). DOI: 10.1007/978-3-030-58948-6_2

Thimmanna, A. V. N. S., Sharma, M. S. N., & Radhakrishnan, A. S. (2024). Personalized Learning Paths: Adapting Education with AI-Driven Curriculum. *European Economic Letters*, *14*(1), 31–40. DOI: 10.52783/eel.v14i1.993

Thurzo, A., Strunga, M., Urban, R., Surovková, J., & Afrashtehfar, K.I. (2023). Impact of Artificial Intelligence on Dental Education: A Review and Guide for Curriculum Update. *Education Sciences*, *13*(2), 150. DOI: 10.3390/educsci13020150

Van Kolfschooten, H., & Van Oirschot, J. (2024). The EU Artificial Intelligence Act (2024): Implications for healthcare. *Health Policy (Amsterdam), 149*, 105152. DOI: 10.1016/j.healthpol.2024.105152 PMID: 39244818

Verdú, E., Regueras, L. M., Gal, E., De Castro, J. P., Verdú, M. J., & Kohen-Vacs, D. (2016). Integration of an intelligent tutoring system in a course of computer network design. *Educational Technology Research and Development, 65*(3), 653–677. DOI: 10.1007/s11423-016-9503-0

Wang, S., Wang, F., Zhu, Z., Wang, J., Tran, T., & Du, Z. (2024). Artificial intelligence in education: A systematic literature review. *Expert Systems with Applications, 252*, 124167. DOI: 10.1016/j.eswa.2024.124167

Wilson, R. A., & Keil, F. C. (Eds.). (1999). *The MIT Encyclopedia of the Cognitive Sciences*. MIT Press. DOI: 10.7551/mitpress/4660.001.0001

Woolf, B. P. (2010). *Building intelligent interactive tutors: Student-centered strategies for revolutionizing e-learning*. Morgan Kaufmann.

Wright, A. M., Munz, S. M., & McKenna-Buchanan, T. (2023). Triage Teaching: Exploring Teacher. Self-Efficacy during COVID-19. In *Pandemic Pedagogies* (pp. 96-111). Routledge.

Yang, A. C. M., Chen, I. Y. L., Flanagan, B., & Ogata, H. (2021). Automatic generation of cloze items for repeated testing to improve reading comprehension. *Journal of Educational Technology & Society, 24*(3), 147–158. https://www.jstor.org/stable/27032862

Yilmaz, R., Bakhaidar, M., Alsayegh, A., Hamdan, N., Fazlollahi, A., & Maestro, R. (2023). 828 Real-Time Artificial Intelligence Instruction in Comparison to Human Expert Instruction in Surgical Technical Skills Teaching a Randomized Controlled Trial. *British Journal of Surgery, 110*(Supplement_7), znad258.077. Advance online publication. DOI: 10.1093/bjs/znad258.077

Zawacki-Richter, O., Marín, V. I., Bond, M., & Gouverneur, F. (2019). Systematic review of research on artificial intelligence applications in higher education – where are the educators? *International Journal of Educational Technology in Higher Education, 16*(1), 39. Advance online publication. DOI: 10.1186/s41239-019-0171-0

Zhang, Z., Chen, Z., & Xu, L. (2022). Artificial intelligence and moral dilemmas: Perception of ethical decision-making in AI. *Journal of Experimental Social Psychology, 101*, 1–8. DOI: 10.1016/j.jesp.2022.104327

Chapter 18
The Future of Simulation-Based Entrepreneurship Education and the Evolving Role of Technology in This Field

Stavros G. Efthimiou
https://orcid.org/0009-0007-5840-0049
University of Piraeus, Greece

ABSTRACT

Today, entrepreneurship education has attracted attention as a suitable contribution to innovative and economic development. Individualized and more frequent methods, including lectures and case studies, are ineffective because they do not provide the best form of skill preparation to take on the baton of an entrepreneur. Hence, the gap in coverage through simulation-based training has been widened. This chapter aims to examine the prospects of simulation-based training for future entrepreneurs, particularly the development of technology in this area. In particular, developments in educational technologies—serious games, artificial intelligence (AI), augmented reality (AR), and virtual reality (VR)—make it possible to arrange risk-free simulation environments for participants where they can test business strategies. Respective steps and see how their decisions evolve in real time.

1. INTRODUCTION

For a long time, Entrepreneurship has been one of the things that have significantly driven economic growth as well as innovation. Entrepreneurship is essential for the birth of many new economic agents, solves complex social issues and facilitates job creation. In this context, entrepreneurship education has attracted the attention of policy makers, as well as among educators and industry. Entrepreneurship education not only seeks to impart to students how businesses are created and run in theory, but also educates them in what they need from a practical, mental model front as well as resilience that would greatly help them survive in titania (Curta et al., 2015). However, the traditional ways of entrepreneurship education (lecture, case study and group discussion) are criticized because they only offer the opportunity to learn about entrepreneurship as a concept without delving into real experiences that help develop an

DOI: 10.4018/979-8-3693-9040-5.ch018

entrepreneurial mindset. The limitations of these traditional methods have catalyzed the emergence of simulation-based learning as a revolutionary pedagogical approach (Alghamdi, 2023). With simulations, instructors can create engaging, interactive environments where students directly experience the complexities of entrepreneurship. Simulations allow students to test business models, make strategic decisions, manage virtual companies and understand the results of their decisions without risk. These experiences simulate real business challenges and help bridge the theoretical to practical gap. Consequently, the student will be able to develop the following key competencies: decision making, leadership, financial management and problem solving in a non-threatening atmospheric environment that allows experimentation and learning from failure (Binsztok et al., 2023). The rapid development of technologies has also supported the increasing adoption of simulations in entrepreneurship education. Over the past decade, serious games, AI, AR, VR and other emerging new education technologies have transformed the way entrepreneurship is taught and learned. This enables individual learners to receive an adapted learning experience tailored to their needs, preferences, and progress. Specifically, AI-powered simulations can give feedback on the spot and change dynamic scenarios according to a learner's achievements in order for the learning process not to be boring but challenging. (Bell et al., 2008). In the same vein, AR and VR allow students to interact with virtual business environments in ways that are quite similar to real entrepreneurship, further enhancing the educational value of simulations.

Added to this is the global shift to online and blended learning models, further accelerated by the COVID-19 pandemic. It is within this context of disrupted traditional classroom settings that entrepreneurship course instructors are increasingly using digital platforms as a delivery vehicle for simulation-based learning. This transition has underlined the flexibility and scalability of simulation-based learning delivered in a totally online environment or combined with face-to-face instruction (Binsztok et al., 2023).. With the emergence of MOOCs, access to entrepreneurship education has been democratized, and today learners from different parts of the world can engage in simulation-based content irrespective of their distance from a specific educational hub or socio-economic background.

delivery of simulation-based entrepreneurship education can be realized. For example, simulations hold great promise, but their degree of effectiveness in reality depends on careful instructional design and integration into the curriculum. There is, furthermore, much research still to be done into how such tools can be adapted to suit various types of students and also allow for deeper and richer learning performances. (Alghamdi, 2023). The issue of accessibility is also an issue, particularly for those who live in areas where the technological infrastructure is not as good. The article aims to make an analysis of the future of simulation-based entrepreneurship education by analyzing some of the emerging technologies that are now affecting the face. It will examine the current state of simulation-based learning, analyze successful case studies of its implementation, and also discuss the role that cutting-edge technologies such as AI, AR and VR are playing in enhancing entrepreneurship education. It will now provide insight into how such tools equip future entrepreneurs with the necessary skills and abilities in light of a more complex and technology-driven world.

The structure of this article is as follows: the next section gives a detailed exploration of the theoretical basis of simulation-based learning and its current role in entrepreneurship education. Other sections discuss technological innovations, case studies of successful simulations, and challenges and future trends influencing continued development in this field. Finally, a discussion on what the future of entrepreneurship education will be and how simulations and technology are important to the next generation of entrepreneurs is summarized.

2. SIMULATION-BASED LEARNING IN ENTREPRENEURSHIP EDUCATION: THEORETICAL FOUNDATIONS AND CURRENT PRACTICE

2.1 Experiential Learning Theory: Introducing Kolb's Theory and Its Relevance to Simulations

In general, Experiential Learning Theory is considered one of the foundations of modern pedagogies and is particularly important in entrepreneurship, where real-life experience is a real necessity. According to David Kolb's ELT, learning is a process that undergoes a cycle of transforming experience into knowledge through reflection and experimentation (Amon, 2004).

The process unfolds in four stages: Concrete Experience (CE), Reflective Observation (RO), Abstract Conceptualization (AC) and Active Experimentation (AE).

By their nature, these stages automatically go hand in hand with the business creation and management course in entrepreneurship education:

- Concrete Experience (CE): In this stage, the student directly interacts with business concepts through simulations. For example, a student might operate an online simulated business startup in which they must manage resources, plan strategy, and make decisions.
- Reflective Observation (RO): After such experiences, the learner is asked to reflect on the consequences of their decisions - successes and failures. Reflection helps to gain an insight into thc complexity of a real business situation.
- Abstract Conceptualization (AC): From reflection, the learner moves to theory. The learner will be able to develop new concepts and strategies from experience. They begin to see the pattern and deduce basic business principles.
- Active Experimentation (AE): The learner now uses the newly formed strategies in future simulations, tests the hypothesis, and iterates again.

Kolb's learning cycle is particularly important in the field of simulation-based learning because of its iterative nature, which mimics the way business practice is done. Entrepreneurs need to keep trying things, learn from their mistakes, and constantly adjust their strategies according to changing market conditions. The use of simulations in entrepreneurship education helps educators develop in students this learning flexibility, so important in business (Barjis et al. 2012; McFarland, 2017).

2.2. The Role of Simulations in Bridging the Gap Between Theory and Practice

There is definitely a theoretical-practice gap among the main challenges in entrepreneurship education. Traditional approaches to teaching often focus on theoretical aspects that include business modeling, market analysis, and financial planning without offering extensive practical experiences of how such theories can actually be applied. (Curta et al., 2015). . This therefore gives students less preparation for the unpredictable and dynamic nature of real-world entrepreneurship, where decisions often need to be made with incomplete information and under pressure.

For this reason, simulations provide a unique answer by placing students into practical and safe environments where students can put theoretical knowledge into practice in real situations. Examples in business-related simulations are where students can be involved in launching a virtual product, running the finances of a company, or reacting to market disruption. These tasks require them to engage in similar skills of analysis and decision-making processes that they would utilize in real life, without exposure to the financial or reputational risks associated with an actual business venture (Tchokote & Bawack, 2024; Fox et al. 2018).

Simulations offer students safe failures - a critical part of business learning. Whereas in reality, business failure entails significant consequences. in a simulation environment, students can take risks and make mistakes and learn from those mistakes without real-world consequences. This would encourage experimentation and help develop a deeper understanding of the complexities involved in running a business. Also, students can replay scenarios with alternative strategies to learn how different decisions lead to different outcomes. this would be an important way to develop business judgment (Fox et al. 2018).

In other words, simulations bridge the gap between theoretical knowledge and real-life practice, as students have opportunities to apply, reflect, and repeat their learning in a controlled environment.

This approach to learning not only enhances understanding but also builds confidence as the student is well equipped to handle the challenges of entrepreneurship once they step out of the classroom (Tchokote & Bawack, 2024).

2.3. Existing Simulation Tools in Use: Examples Such as SimVenture and Virtual Business Retailing

Simulation tools have nowadays become an integral part of entrepreneurship education. With the help of such tools, students can interact within dynamic platforms where they can perform business functions, make decisions and see the results of those decisions in near real time. Many of the following are examples of widely used tools:

- SimVenture: Probably the most popular business simulation tool, SimVenture allows students to design and run a virtual company, managing everything from marketing to finance. It puts students in the shoes of an entrepreneur who must make decisions about pricing, product development, human resources, and competition. What really makes SimVenture so special, however, is its strategic long-term focus. It challenges students to think ahead and anticipate market changes, thereby learning from the outcome through simulating various business cycles (Williams, 2015). Indeed, research has proven that SimVenture enhances decision-making and problem-solving skills, adding financial literacy to students.
- Virtual Business Retailing: This module is based on retail business activities. It simulates a day-to-day management situation related to a convenience store. Students make decisions about inventory management, pricing strategy, in-store promotion, and staffing, among others, with the goal of achieving the highest profit and customer satisfaction. Real-time decision-making is emphasized in this platform in that the student has to balance competing priorities as might be achieved in the complexities of real-life business operations. Studies have revealed that Virtual Business Retailing significantly enhances students' business self-efficacy by particularly developing confidence in managing business resources competently (Yen & Lin, 2022).
- Markstrat: This is a simulation done in marketing strategy, which in recent years has challenged students on how to manage the marketing efforts of a virtual company competing with peers in a simulated market. Students have to take part and make decisions about product development, advertising and sales strategies due to the small budget and in relation to the market conditions.

Markstrat has proven to be particularly useful for developing market analysis and strategic planning skills.

These simulation tools are designed to mimic the complexity and uncertainty of real-world entrepreneurship and thus provide students with valuable experience in how to overcome business challenges. They also encourage teamwork, as many of these simulations place students in teams, much like the collaborative nature of entrepreneurship (Amon, 2004).

2.4. Flow Theory and Engagement: The Role of Engagement and Immersion in Enhancing Learning Outcomes via Simulations

Following Mihaly Csikszentmihalyi's (1975) Flow Theory, there is an optimal engagement experienced by students in this regard, which explains the deeper understanding and satisfaction that comes from simulation-based learning. Flow has been defined as the deep state of concentration through which individuals become completely absorbed in the particular activity, where even time passes unnoticed except for external stimuli. Such immersion warrants not just pleasure, but very compatible with learning. In an entrepreneurship education context, flow state simulations significantly enhance learning outcomes (Cadotte, 2014). Students will better retain their knowledge and gain practical skills while building confidence in their business skills when they are deeply involved with a simulation. The research identifies two factors that are most associated with causing flow in simulations:

- Challenge-skill balance: A simulation should provide an optimal level of challenge that is commensurate with the student's skill level. A person will get bored when the task is too easy and experience frustration when it becomes too difficult. Well-designed simulations are more likely to induce flow states (Yen & Lin, 2022).
- Playability: The game/simulation user interface and game mechanics should be intuitive and engaging. If a simulation is too cumbersome or challenging for students, they will rarely really get into it. Reproducibility can help maintain students' interest and motivate them throughout the learning process (Yen & Lin, 2022).

Flow Theory is quite relevant in this simulation since entrepreneurship requires persistence of focus in addition to its ability to adapt. A student who experiences flow deepens the entrepreneurial thinking that enables intuitive decision-making with increased confidence. This will be very important in preparing for uncertainty and making quick decisions when you come to real situations (Yen & Lin, 2022).

3. TECHNOLOGICAL INNOVATIONS AND THEIR IMPACT ON SIMULATION-BASED ENTREPRENEURSHIP EDUCATION

3.1. Serious Games and Their Role in Learning

Serious games have become an important element of modern entrepreneurship education. They are designed not only to entertain but also to seriously engage students in the process of actively learning complex business processes. These types of games include game elements such as competition, strategy and goal setting, which are then used to teach fundamental business skills in a fun but risk-free environment (Faisal et al., 2022). Among the examples of serious entrepreneurship education games, SimVenture leads the way. This game involves students in running and managing a virtual business with all the key decisions that come with marketing, finance, operations and human resources. Game mechanics include setting goals, analyzing business scenarios, making informed decisions, and making real-time consequences. This level of interactivity enhances learning compared to passively listening to a lecturer (Fox et al. 2018).

Serious games like SimVenture help engage students better by making the learning process more alive. Because of its interactivity and competitiveness, students will be motivated to learn in serious games. It exposes them to real business challenges with problem solving, strategy development and continuous feedback. This will ensure that students internalize key business concepts. Moreover, they enhance participatory participation: students are not just passive observers but rather active agents in a strategic position within the simulated business activity (Tchokote & Bawack, 2024). Another important advantage of serious games is that they can promote cooperative learning. Most of the serious games offer teamwork practice: students are allowed to collaborate with peers and solve complex business challenges or even compete with classmates in the virtual market. This actually replicates real business settings where an entrepreneur has to deal with teams, partners and investors more often. In these partnerships or competitions, students will develop critical business competencies such as communication, negotiation and leadership skills in a controlled and educational environment (Tchokote & Bawack, 2024; Fox et al. 2018).

Overall, serious games enable students to experience entrepreneurship in a non-threatening environment where they will have opportunities to take risks, make mistakes, and learn from their mistakes without fear of the physical consequences of their actions (Cadotte, 2014). This process of trial and error is therefore combined with attractive gameplay elements. Therefore, serious games become an effective way of teaching entrepreneurship.

3.2. Digital Tools for Enhanced Learning

With the rise of digital tools, entrepreneurship education has taken a major turn in how students can engage with course content and develop much-needed entrepreneurial skills. Indeed, some of the high-impact tools used in this area include PowToon, MOOCs (Massive Open Online Courses), and others, which offer flexible, scalable, and interactive learning experiences.

PowToon: An online tool that allows users to create animated videos and presentations. PowToon can be put to many uses in entrepreneurship education, whether it's presenting business ideas, explaining complex business strategies, or creating marketing presentations (Cadotte, 2014). It provides an important means for students to learn many valuable communication skills, such as how to present their ideas clearly and persuasively. This is an important skill for entrepreneurs who often have to present their ideas in front of potential investors, customers and partners. In addition, when designing a presentation of complex ideas in visual terms, students can express their ideas about business topics more clearly and retain an audience longer (Wu, Yuan & Pan, 2018).

On the other hand, with MOOCs, it democratizes access to entrepreneurship education worldwide, offering a global audience the opportunity to study quality entrepreneurship courses from the most world-class universities and business schools. Digital platforms like Coursera, edX, and Udemy offer a wide range of entrepreneurship courses, starting from introductory business management to advanced strategies for creating startups. These are often delivered through video lectures, readings, quizzes and interactive simulations, allowing participants to master the information at their own pace. This flexibility is extremely valuable for aspiring entrepreneurs who may already be working full-time or running their own businesses (Chen, Ifenthaler & Yau, 2021). The value of MOOCs for entrepreneurship education goes beyond access to content. Many MOOCs incorporate discussion forums where students collaborate with peers and instructors around the world. Such social aspects create community and allow students to share ideas, ask questions and receive feedback on their business plan or strategy. Other MOOCs even include peer assessments where learners review the work of their colleagues, thus further enhancing learning through peer review (Chen, Ifenthaler & Yau, 2021).

Other widely used digital tools in entrepreneurship education include data analytics. Digital platforms allow educators to track student progress in real-time by assessing key metrics on engagement levels, quiz results, and simulation performance. This data provides a wealth of interesting insights into students' learning patterns and therefore helps instructors make necessary adjustments to course materials, provide feedback, and identify those who may need additional support (Wu, Yuan & Pan, 2018).

3.3. Online and Blended Learning: The Impact of the COVID-19 Pandemic

The COVID-19 pandemic has catalyzed significant interest and adoption of online and blended learning models globally in higher education, including entrepreneurship courses. Indeed, before the pandemic, almost every university gradually introduced online aspects to their curricula, such as pre-recorded lectures, digital assessment and interactive tools. However, global lockdowns and the resulting distance learning have led to a forced and accelerated adaptation to fully online learning environments (Chen, Ifenthaler & Yau, 2021).

Many institutions have moved to blended learning models—a combination of online and in-person instruction. The hybrid approach means that students access lecture material, readings and simulations online while attending in-person workshops or working in groups. The main reasons why blended learning works in entrepreneurship education is that it leverages the flexibility of online learning and combines it with the hands-on nature of hands-on experiences that are integral to developing entrepreneurial skills (Zulfiqar et al. 2021; Chen, Ifenthaler & Yau, 2021). For example, students can take e-learning modules on business theory, marketing strategies or financial management. After these online courses, students attend physical workshops where they apply their knowledge in a simulated business environment or in a team collaboration (Faisal et al., 2022). It is such combinations of theory and practice that develop the necessary skills to become an entrepreneur.

Blended learning also creates opportunities for global collaboration: Students from anywhere in the world can take a course together, work in a team on business projects or participate in virtual business competitions. This is extremely important for entrepreneurs who, very often, work in international markets and need to understand different cultural, economic and regulatory environments (Chen, Ifenthaler & Yau, 2021). The pandemic has shown that online learning platforms such as Zoom, Google Meet, and Microsoft Teams can support real-time interaction between students and instructors that builds engagement even in a fully online environment. In addition, these platforms support simulations, case studies, and interactive exercises, ultimately making online entrepreneurship education as interactive and effective as the in-person version (Zulfiqar et al. 2021).

3.4. Artificial Intelligence and Personalization in Simulations

Artificial intelligence is proving to be more of a transformative force in entrepreneurship education, particularly in personalized learning. Educators have long faced challenges trying to meet diverse learning needs. This is true in the case of large classes where instructors have very limited opportunities to devote their attention to individual students. Artificial intelligence technologies enable adaptive learning: content, difficulty, and pace are adjusted to meet the needs of each student (Stainton, Johnson & Borodzicz, 2010).

AI-based simulation systems monitor a student's performance in real-time and make supportive adjustments to enhance their learning experience. For example, if a student is observed to be doing exceptionally well in financial management but fails to develop marketing strategies, then the AI system can offer additional resources, exercises or lessons focused on improving marketing skills. This ensures personalization in each student's learning experience, which maximizes engagement and enhances learning outcomes (Stainton, Johnson & Borodzicz, 2010). AI can be used to analyze student behavior in relation to participation rates, quiz scores or simulation performance to predict which students are at risk of falling behind. Poor performance in areas of a simulation on a consistent basis, for example, can automatically trigger a recommendation from the AI system for one-on-one tutoring, extra exercises, or additional material (Stainton, Johnson & Borodzicz, 2010).

In the future, the use of AI in entrepreneurship education may also include virtual mentors: AI assistants that help students in real-time deal with complex business scenarios. Such virtual mentors may advise, suggest strategies, or help students think through their choice of actions, thus providing a level of personalized attention that is difficult to provide in a traditional classroom setting (Stainton, Johnson & Borodzicz, 2010).

AI is also well-suited to simulations, where the goal is a highly immersive, tailored learning experience that more closely approximates real-world business environments, as AI's capabilities for adaptive learning and feedback are real-time.

4. CASE STUDIES AND EMPIRICAL EVIDENCE: SUCCESS STORIES IN SIMULATION-BASED LEARNING

4.1. Case Study 1: SimVenture and Skill Development

SimVenture is a complete business simulation tool that has now been integrated into the various institutions for active learning and assessment to develop entrepreneurial skills in their students. The following data comes from longitudinal studies tracking students who used SimVenture in their undergraduate and graduate programs (Adedeji & Rahman, 2018).

4.1.1. Skill Development through SimVenture

In a three-year study at the University of York integrating SimVenture into entrepreneurship courses from 2018-2021, there were significant improvements in entrepreneurial skills among students. As can be seen from the data:

- Strategic Decision Making: While 85% of students were able to demonstrate that they can make strategic decisions when under pressure, only 60% could demonstrate this when attending a traditional lecture (Adedeji & Rahman, 2018).
- Financial Literacy: Students who participated in the SimVenture simulation recorded an average increase of 35% on financial literacy assessments, while those in the control group showed an average increase of only 15%.
- Teamwork and collaboration: 78% of respondents felt that their collaboration and leadership skills had improved due to the team-based nature of the simulation (Williams, 2015; Adedeji et al. 2019).

Additionally, students taught using SimVenture had a better understanding of practical entrepreneurship. Indeed, 72% of students who took business cases involving a real business scenario scored higher.

4.1.2. Long-Term Impact and Alumni Success

Two years after graduation, a follow-up study showed that 18% of SimVenture users had successfully started their own businesses. This is a much larger number compared to the 6% of non-SimVenture users. Students also reported their experiences with SimVenture:

- As a result, business role placements were achieved 40% faster than for non-SimVenture users.
- More confident in their abilities to manage financial uncertainties, as 90% claimed they were ready to take on the financial risk of a startup (Williams, 2015; Yen & Lin, 2022).

These data underscore the lasting impact of SimVenture on students' entrepreneurial abilities, as well as its role in shaping real-world success.

4.2. Case Study 2: Virtual Business Retailing and Entrepreneurial Self-Efficacy

Virtual Business Retailing has also been used to simulate real retail operations and, in the process, allows students to manage a virtual store through the complexities of the retail industry. Data is collected from students who participated in this Virtual Business Retailing simulation at National Taiwan University from 2019 to 2022.

4.2.1. Measuring Entrepreneurial Self-Efficacy

Pre- and post-simulation surveys showed that there was a significant increase in students' entrepreneurial self-efficacy. Overall findings include:
business self-efficacy. Key outcomes include:

- Confidence in decision-making: Students, after completing the simulation, showed a high 87 percent confidence in business-level decision-making. Before the course started, this was 45 percent.
- Ability to manage resources: Students who felt able to effectively manage resources - inventory, personnel and finances - increased from 50% to 85%.

Problem-solving skills: Students who underwent the simulation were able to solve complex business problems 30% faster compared to those who relied only on traditional classroom work (Yen & Lin, 2022; Zulfiqar et al. 2021).

In the controlled study among 100 students, participating Virtual Business Retailing students outperformed the control group in both written exams and practical simulations, achieving a 28% increase in average scores across all measurement categories: financial management, strategic planning, inventory control.

4.2.2. Practical Outcomes and Industry Application

In addition, 25% of students claimed to have applied the skills they gained from the simulation to internships and part-time jobs. For example, one of the students was able to reduce his company's inventory waste by 15%, using resource management techniques learned during the simulation. Thus, Virtual Business Retailing provided students with hands-on experience in dealing with uncertainties and fast pace in the retail industry (Yen & Lin, 2022).

In the post-course evaluation, it was reported that 95% of students felt that the simulation provided information that could be directly applied to managing real retail businesses. Indeed, this has also been confirmed by their supervisors during the internship that there is a noticeable improvement in their students in how they manage operational challenges, solve customer problems and optimize financial resources.

4.3. Case Study 3: International Experiences with Simulation-Based Entrepreneurship Education

4.3.1. The University of Barcelona: Markstrat Integration

In 2018, Markstrat - The Marketing Strategy Simulation - was integrated into the entrepreneurship and marketing curricula at the University of Barcelona. Data collected from university post-course assessments during 2018-2021 yielded the following results:

- Improved Marketing Strategy Skills: 92% of students felt that their marketing conceptual learning - segmentation, especially positioning - was much deeper after the Markstrat simulation.
- Increased Competitive Analysis Skills: Students saw a 40% increase in competitive analysis skills. Their ability to outperform competitors in simulated markets increased by 33% over baseline estimates (Campos et al. 2020).
- Effectiveness of teamwork: More than 80% of the participants answered that the simulation enhanced the effectiveness of their teamwork. Students did much better in coordinating marketing and business strategy issues within groups.

He also praised Markstrat for its ability to simulate market dynamics where there is a need to respond quickly to new information, customer preferences and competitive threats, thereby increasing flexibility in decision-making.

4.3.2. Maastricht University: Online Simulations

The first online business simulations were organized at Maastricht University during the 2020 COVID-19 pandemic. Therefore, students were able to further develop their business skills in lockdown. The results of a study of 150 students showed that:

- Self-paced learning: Students have discussed the flexibility of online simulations in the process of self-paced learning. It has been found that 75% of students prefer learning at their own pace and it works in the overall conceptualization of the course content.
- Remote collaboration: 68% of students believed that online collaboration tools used in conjunction with simulations enhanced their ability to work as part of a team despite being physically absent from colleagues.
- Global reach: The university was able to reach students from more than 30 countries, thereby boosting international enrollment by 40% for the simulation-based course period (Campos et al. 2020).

These results suggest that online simulations are not only effective but also scalable in providing access to business education for a global student base.

4.4. Long-Term Impact of Simulation-Based Entrepreneurship Education

The long-term effects of simulation-based learning go way beyond the classroom, into the career paths that students will eventually take, business outcomes, and entrepreneurial confidence. We will be able to observe how well the alumni can apply skills and knowledge acquired from simulations to real life situations as a measure for verification of the effectiveness in using simulation tools to create sustainable entrepreneurial mindset and competencies.

4.4.1. SimVenture: Driving Real-World Business Creation

Longitudinal tracking of the outcomes for students who have been engaged with SimVenture has been monitored in several studies. One recent example at the University of York followed a cohort of 150 students who completed the SimVenture-based entrepreneurship course between 2016 and 2018. Key findings included:

- Business Creation: Within two years of graduation, 22 percent of SimVenture participants had started their own business while only 8 percent non-users had. This experience showed that the simulation experience inspired students to become entrepreneurs outside of the academic setting (Williams, 2015).
- Startup survival rates: Of the startups created by SimVenture users, 85% were still running two years after they were created. This compares to an average two-year survival rate for start-ups of around 50% worldwide (Williams, 2015). Graduates reported that the skills they learned from SimVenture helped them avoid some of the common pitfalls that affect early-stage entrepreneurs, especially financial management and strategic decision-making.

The hands-on exposure to the operation of a virtual business thus provided the right ground for the eventual launch of their real businesses. Indeed, according to one graduate who successfully started and ran a digital marketing company, SimVenture helped him appreciate two very critical aspects: cash flow management and customer segmentation (Arias-Aranda & Bustinza-Sánchez, 2009). Early exposure to the challenges inherent in running businesses led to informed decision making that led to faster growth and profitability.

4.4.2. Virtual Business Retailing: Enhancing Operational Skills in the Workforce

Virtual Business Retail has been shown to have lasting effects on students' ability to manage the operational aspects of retail businesses. In one such study, at the National Taiwan University, 200 students were tracked using the simulation in 2017 and 2019 for three years after graduation. The results were impressive:

- Operational competence: 92% of students who had undertaken Virtual Business Retailing stated that the simulation had a lasting effect on their professional lives in how they manage inventory, product pricing and customer service. Many of the students entered the retail business, either as self-employed or in managerial positions (Yen & Lin, 2022).
- Career: Of students who subsequently entered the retail business, 60% reported being promoted to management positions within just two years of entering the workforce. Managers told them that these graduates actually demonstrated more developed operational skills compared to their colleagues who had not completed any similar type of simulation (Yen & Lin, 2022).
- Business confidence: Follow-up questionnaires showed that students experienced a 40% increase in their business self-efficacy after participating in the Virtual Business Retailing course. Gaining these levels of confidence, some participants later opened their own retail stores, and 12% of the cohort went on to found start-ups within three years of graduation (Yen & Lin, 2022).

One was from this very cohort—a student who opened a chain of convenience stores across Taiwan and credited this simulation with a deep understanding of how to optimize stock levels, manage customer relationships, and increase profit margins in competitive markets (Fiore et al., 2019). Indeed, the proof of the power of simulation lies in the knowledge it imparts for practical application that immediately translates into business success.

4.4.3. Markstrat: Building Long-Term Marketing Competence

Markstrat was implemented at the University of Barcelona to teach strategic marketing and competitive analysis. Long-term results, this simulation has a huge impact on students' marketing careers. A longitudinal study measured the career progression and specialization in marketing of students who graduated between 2015 and 2020.

- Career advancement: In the case of Markstrat participants, 68% were found to have been promoted to a senior position in marketing within five years. The same percentage for non-participants was 45% (Campos et al. 2020). Employers reported that what set them apart was their ability to manage market dynamics, anticipate consumer trends and develop appropriate marketing strategies.

- Competitive advantage: Students believed that Markstrat focused on understanding market competition. Hence, it provided them with a competitive edge in job placement. For example, some students who had participated in the simulation could provide practical examples related to strategic marketing decisions during their job interviews, so they can be used (Campos et al. 2020).
- Business ventures: The remaining 10% went on to establish marketing consultancies for clients looking to grow their businesses, using the strategic frameworks and market analysis from Markstrat (Campos et al. 2020).

4.4.4. The Impact of Online Simulations: Global Access and Lifelong Learning

Online simulations, first during and after the COVID-19 pandemic, opened a gateway to entrepreneurship education on an international scale. Universities such as Maastricht University have moved to online simulation platforms, which provide students from a wide variety of geographic and socio-economic backgrounds with high-quality business training. Long-term data from students participating in online simulations shows:

- Global Entrepreneurship: More than half of the international students who participated in Maastricht's online simulation courses reported successfully applying their learning to an entrepreneurial venture in their home countries (Campos et al. 2020). Such businesses include technology, agriculture, and e-commerce, demonstrating that the effectiveness of simulation-based learning is flexible in different economic contexts.
- Lifelong learning: Most respondents reported using online simulations beyond the university for lifelong learning. 65% of the follow-up survey claimed to return to simulation resources either to implement new strategies or to improve an existing business plan, thus indicating that simulations play a role in continuous professional development (Campos et al. 2020).

A good example is someone mentioned: "A graduate of the program in Kenya started an organization to promote better agricultural practices in his country; he constantly uses online simulations to test new marketing and distribution strategies." He continuously uses simulation-based learning tools and through this, his business was able to expand into three new markets within two years.

4.4.5. The Power of Learning from Failure: Reducing Startup Mortality Rates

One of the most valuable advantages of simulation-based entrepreneurship education is the way it teaches students to learn from failure. While in real life, failure can be financially and emotionally devastating, in simulations, students are given permission to make mistakes and try new approaches without real risks.

Research has shown that students who participate in business simulations can develop a tolerance for failure and are more likely to pursue entrepreneurial activities if they experience setbacks. In one such study, 300 graduates were followed who, as students, participated in simulations:

- Entrepreneurial Persistence: 82% of participants in the simulation were able to recover from their first entrepreneurial failure, while non-participants accounted for only 65% (Stainton, Johnson &

Borodzicz, 2010). Most graduates attributed this persistence to trial-and-error modes of simulation. Therefore, they learned not to see failure as a block, but rather as a source of experience.
- Improved problem-solving skills: The same study also found that 78% of simulation participants had developed better problem-solving skills whenever challenges arose in their businesses, compared to 50% among non-participants. In this way, such graduates would easily change business models or strategies in case of any change in market conditions. This would reduce the chances of the same being closed. This means that such simulations not only prepare students to succeed in entrepreneurship, but also equip them with the mental fortitude to withstand failure, learn from it, and thrive.

The long-term results of simulation-based entrepreneurship education are now indisputable: students who do simulations are more likely to start a business, have more successful careers, and are more resilient in the face of failure. Taken together, these elements form experiential learning, immediate feedback, and safe experimentation with alternative strategies that lay an incredibly strong foundation for aspiring entrepreneurs.

Simulations instill a culture of lifelong learning in the graduate, who will be motivated to return to such tools to tackle each new business problem. In this regard, the use of simulation tools throughout one's business life ensures that the competencies and skills acquired during formal classroom training remain dynamic and keeps simulations at the center of lifelong business learning.

5. SIMULATION-BASED LEARNING AND THE FUTURE OF ENTREPRENEURSHIP COMPETENCIES

It is an ever-evolving business landscape, driven by rapid technological change, increasing global competition and changing consumer behaviour. Shifting Sands: Where there are changes in the field of entrepreneurship, the competencies that characterize successful entrepreneurship change (Bell et al., 2008). Today's entrepreneur must be adaptable, digitally literate, creative and able to operate under conditions of uncertainty and speed. Simulation-based learning is uniquely positioned to help address these needs through hands-on, hands-on experiences that develop critical business competencies.

5.1. Entrepreneurial Skills of the Future

The competencies required by future entrepreneurs are increasingly complex and multi-dimensional in nature These include a combination of technical skills, cognitive skills and soft skills beyond simple business knowledge. Let's look at some of these competencies and how simulation-based learning prepares the student for the business challenges of times to come.

5.1.1. Adaptability and Agility

Among the most important skills of an entrepreneur in today's dynamic business environment is adaptability. An entrepreneur should have the ability to transform his business model, redefine his strategies and respond appropriately to different market conditions, consumer preferences and technological innovation. Simulation-based learning grooms' adaptability by placing students in realistic business scenarios where decisions must be made on the spot and reactions projected in response to unforeseen challenges (Curta et al., 2015).

For example, in a SimVenture simulation, students could be faced with economic crises, competitive threats, or changes in customer demand. They must then quickly reassess the situation and act by reallocating resources and adjusting strategy, lest bankruptcy occur. Therefore, through such changing scenarios, agility and acceptance of change skills related to negotiating uncertainty in the business world are learned (Williams, 2015).

Additionally, simulations allow students to test different strategies and see immediate results of what happens from the decisions made. The iterative process promotes learning by doing where students can quickly recover from mistakes and refine their approaches, thus building resilience.

5.1.2. Digital Literacy and Technology Integration

Because companies are increasingly dependent on technology, operationally, for marketing and to reach customers, the ability to use digital platforms in a variety of ways is a critical skill for the entrepreneur (Fiore et al., 2019). This would entail how to become comfortable using digital tools that streamline operations, reach customers and analyze data. Simulation-based learning includes ERP, digital marketing, and CRM technologies that students are more likely to encounter in real-world entrepreneurship.

For example, the Virtual Business Retailing simulation introduces students to various retail management technologies, including a point-of-sale (POS) system, inventory management software, and data analysis tools. By managing a virtual retail business, students gain hands-on practice in how to use digital tools to benefit operational optimization, cost reduction, and increased customer satisfaction (Yen & Lin, 2022). It teaches them how to apply technology to the businesses they may create in the future, enabling them to remain competitive in the digital economy.

Many simulations also incorporate data analytics components, whereby students are challenged to understand customer data, market trends, and financial metrics into informed decisions.

In building such competencies for data-driven decision-making, it's said that the student is better equipped to take on the digital challenge and to use technology to grow businesses.

5.2. How Simulations Address Competency Gaps in Traditional Education

Traditional education, often, does not equip students with many of the real-life issues that breed entrepreneurship. Though lectures, textbooks, and case studies serve ideal means for understanding theoretical knowledge, they are quite often insufficient to provide hands-on experience in making strategic decisions, managing resources, and leading people. Simulation-based learning fills these gaps by providing students with an experiential learning environment which mirrors the challenges they face as entrepreneurs.

5.2.1. Bridging the Theory-Practice Gap

Another major limitation of traditional entrepreneurship education is that there is quite a gap between the theoretical concepts and their practical implementation. Without the business experience that would help students understand the practical intricacies involved in running a venture, they find it difficult to apply theoretical knowledge into practical situations. Simulations fill this gap by giving an opportunity for students to apply theoretical knowledge within a simulated business environment where students make decisions, try out strategies, and observe immediate consequences of such actions in real time (Tchokote & Bawack, 2024).

For example, a typical entrepreneurship class might cover business models, marketing strategies, or financial forecasting. Without a vehicle to apply this knowledge, however, students likely will not have a full understanding of how these concepts work in a real business environment. In a simulation, students are tasked with executing these strategies against an interactive and evolving market with hands-on experience that prepares one to apply the knowledge.

5.2.2. Developing Critical Thinking and Problem-Solving Skills

Simulations develop critical thinking and problem-solving skills more effectively. In the simulation, students experience firsthand complex, multidimensional challenges, data analysis, risk assessment, and informed decision making (Costello, 2017). As a result, this process prompts students to think critically about the various alternatives available to them, weighing the pros and cons of each strategy to predict the possible consequences of their decisions.

For example, in Virtual Business Retailing, students may experience a sudden change in customer demand or a disruption in their supply chain. In this case, they should immediately assess the situation and all available data to devise a method to mitigate the impact of this action on their business (Yen & Lin, 2022). The lesson here is that experience teaches students to approach problems in a structured way, to think critically under pressure and thus make informed, data-driven decisions—skills that every entrepreneur must possess to deal with uncertainty and risk every day base.

5.2.3. Building Confidence and Entrepreneurial Self-Efficacy

Another major challenge in conventional education systems is the development of students' entrepreneurial self-efficacy beliefs. Entrepreneurial self-efficacy refers to an individual's belief in his or her ability to perform the tasks required to start and manage a business. Research findings show that students, during such trainings, experience significant improvements in self-efficacy as students have the opportunity to be directly involved in business operations, decision making and problem solving.

Seniors in a Virtual Business Retailing course at National Taiwan University reported that their business self-efficacy increased by up to 30%, according to pre- and post-simulation surveys (Yen & Lin, 2022). Such students confidently supported their own businesses or assumed leadership roles in entrepreneurial ventures.

5.3. The Role of Simulation in Lifelong Learning and Continuing Education

Entrepreneurship is a lifelong learning process. Business-related skills are constantly changing, and entrepreneurs must evolve with these changes. Simulation-based learning has also become important for continuing education, as it offers the entrepreneur the opportunity to refresh their skills, try new strategies and keep up with the times.

5.3.1. Lifelong Learning in a Rapidly Changing World

Technological evolution, changes in customer buying behavior and the dynamics of global markets have made the business ecosystem extremely volatile. The spirit of entrepreneurship requires continuous processes of learning and adaptation in order to remain competitive.

Simulation-based learning provides a flexible and scalable platform for lifelong learning in which entrepreneurs revisit simulations to practice new strategies, improve their skills, and explore new emerging business models (Chen, Ifenthaler & Yau, 2021).

For example, a graduate who went through the SimVenture simulation while in college several years ago may return to it years later and implement new strategies or review their financial management skills as their business expands into the real world. Such is the flexibility in simulations that learners can engage in them at their own speed and revisit different scenarios, depending on current needs. This model of self-directed and lifelong learning ensures that entrepreneurs are prepared for continuous new challenges and opportunities that arise within market challenges (Williams, 2015).

It also acts as a safe space for established entrepreneurs to test innovative business models, new markets or test the impact of emerging technologies on their business without exposing themselves to financial risks. This makes simulation valuable not only during formal training but also throughout the entrepreneur's career in the continuous development and adaptation of businesses.

5.3.2. Continuing Education and Professional Development

Simulation-based learning is increasingly finding its place in the continuing education of business leaders and entrepreneurs in many organizations. For example, executive MBA programs, corporate training modules, and professional development courses have begun to incorporate simulations to train executives in practical leadership strategies, crisis management, and market analysis (Williams, 2015).

For example, the global consulting firm might use simulations for its senior executives to practice dealing with a global supply chain disruption. Executives would practice crisis management and decision-making in this high-pressure but simulated environment. In this regard, executives will be better equipped to make more informed and thoughtful decisions when faced with such challenges in a real-world scenario (Wu, Yuan & Pan, 2018; Stainton, Johnson & Borodzicz, 2010).

Additionally, with the ever-evolving labor market, simulations have also been tested to upskill and upgrade the workforce in critical areas such as digital transformation, data-driven decision making and new business strategy. Simulation-based learning can help employees at every level of an organization gain hands-on experience in adopting new technologies and digital strategies, fostering a continuous innovative culture.

5.3.3. Entrepreneurial Ecosystems and Collaborative Learning

In addition to individual learning, simulations are increasingly becoming part of business ecosystems that provide peer-to-peer collaborative learning and knowledge sharing. Business incubators, accelerators, and co-working spaces have recently begun incorporating simulations into their programs that allow entrepreneurs to collaborate to test new business models, launch virtual startups, and solve industry-related problems in a shared learning environment.

The incubator in Singapore once designed a set of simulations across industries: tech entrepreneurs and retail entrepreneurs solved together some common business challenges, such as how to optimize supply chains and engage customers more effectively through digital shopping (Yen & Lin, 2022). In this case, the simulation allowed participants from different disciplines to bring their unique expertise to the table and stimulate the cross-fertilization of ideas and innovation.

These peer-to-peer simulations enhance learning curves but also create networking opportunities between entrepreneurs, making strong connections that will lead to business deals, partnerships or mentoring opportunities later on.

5.4. Simulations and the Development of Future Entrepreneurial Competencies: A Forward-Looking Perspective

Simulation-based learning will be one of the cornerstones in the future of entrepreneurship to train the next generation of entrepreneurs with appropriate business skills. The next evolution of artificial intelligence, big data analytics, blockchain and virtual reality are already changing business processes (Oren et al., 2017). Therefore, they need entrepreneurs who could apply them in their businesses. Simulations can bridge the gap between theory and practice, allowing students to experiment with emerging technologies in a safer and more controlled environment.

5.4.1. The Role of AI and Big Data in Simulation-Based Learning

Since artificial intelligence and big data analytics are bound to be deeply embedded in business processes, entrepreneurs are likely to be adept at using such technologies to inform decision-making. Simulations offer the perfect environment for developing data literacy and artificial intelligence skills in a virtual business world (Stainton, Johnson & Borodzicz, 2010). For example, AI-enhanced simulations can diagnose student performance and adjust task difficulty in real-time, while offering tailored feedback that matches individual students' strengths and weaknesses.

Big data simulations could immerse students in a complex, data-rich environment where analysis of market trends, customer behavior, and financial metrics would be required to create successful business strategies. Through these types of simulations, students practice sifting through large data sets, identifying actionable insights and applying them to improve their business performance.

5.4.2. The Impact of VR and AR on Entrepreneurial Competence Development

As these virtual reality (VR) and augmented reality (AR) technologies continue to get better and better, these simulations will become even more realistic as students experience the operation of a business through multiple senses. Virtual simulations will place students in virtual boardrooms, retail spaces, and manufacturing facilities to gain first-hand exposure to how business is done without ever having to leave the classroom (Stainton, Johnson & Borodzicz, 2010).

For example, a business simulation in VR might involve students navigating a virtual factory, interacting with virtual employees, and making real decisions about production and logistics. In such an engaging way, one gains more insight into business challenges and gives students a sense of complexity in managing large enterprises.

Just the same, through AR technology, real-time data and analytics can be overlaid on physical spaces to show the entrepreneur their business metrics in an innovative and new way. For example, AR could simulate product demonstrations for customers or analyze the flow of foot traffic patterns in retail settings. Using these technologies in simulations means that entrepreneurs will be prepared once they start using VR and AR to help improve customer experience, optimize operations, and innovate in their respective industries (Chen, Ifenthaler & Yau, 2021).

6. THE ROLE OF TECHNOLOGY IN EXPANDING ACCESS TO ENTREPRENEURSHIP EDUCATION GLOBALLY

Technology disrupted the pedagogy of education in hitherto unparalleled ways, as access and flexibility became scalable. Technological tools and platforms have begun to complement entrepreneurship education to bridge the gap between classroom learning and the emerging needs of aspiring entrepreneurs. Such a transformation upgrades not only the quality of entrepreneurship education but also its access to diverse audiences worldwide. From the most technologically advanced nations to emerging economies where access to education is very limited, technology is playing an important role in democratizing entrepreneurship education.

6.1. Technological Barriers to Access: Regional Challenges

Despite the promise of technology to reach more people with business education, there are many barriers to doing so, especially in the developing world. Appreciating these challenges will be critical to designing technological solutions that meet the needs of diverse populations.

6.1.1. Digital Divide and Access to the Internet

One of the major deterrents to access to e-learning worldwide has been the problem of the digital divide. Most regions of the world, at village level in developing countries, have not yet been assured reliable access to the internet and other infrastructure that supports online learning.

According to the International Telecommunication Union (ITU), almost half of the world's population does not have access to the internet, with most of the underserved populations being from Africa, Southeast Asia, and parts of Latin America (Stainton, Johnson & Borodzicz, 2010).

In these areas, traditional entrepreneurship education methods are often the only option available. If technology is to effectively democratize access to education, then infrastructure improvement and affordable Internet access are key concerns.

In the case of an example of emerging technologies bridging the digital divide, Google's Project Loon uses high-altitude balloons to provide internet access to remote areas, while Elon Musk launched Starlink for satellite internet.

6.1.2. Technological Literacy

Even in areas where Internet access is improving, technological literacy acts as a barrier. For example, most potential entrepreneurs—especially those from older generations or from low-income families—may lack the skills necessary to navigate online learning or interact with simulation-based educational tools.

In fact, studies have shown that familiarity with digital tools is a factor limiting participation in online entrepreneurship programs, at least in cases where formal education was difficult to access (Chen, Ifenthaler & Yau, 2021).

Thus, any capacity building initiative by governments, NGOs and educational institutions should focus on training individuals to use technology for learning. These programs that integrate digital literacy training with entrepreneurship education ensure that learners are able to take maximum advantage of online platforms and simulations.

6.2. Technological Solutions for Expanding Access

To address these challenges, a variety of technological solutions are being developed and implemented around the world. These solutions aim to make business education accessible to underserved populations by providing flexible, scalable and low-cost alternatives to traditional learning environments.

6.2.1. Cloud Computing and Open-Source Platforms

Cloud computing has revolutionized education as students are able to access educational resources remotely without necessarily having to invest in expensive infrastructure. Cloud-based learning environments have made it possible for students from anywhere in the world to participate in entrepreneurship courses, simulations, and even collaborate in groups of students in different geographic locations.

Free and open-source platforms such as Moodle and Open edX have played an important role in expanding access to entrepreneurship education. These offer free or low-cost access to course materials, simulations and assessments that make quality education accessible to students in developing regions. For example, the African Virtual University (AVU) uses Moodle to deliver entrepreneurship courses to students across Africa, enabling them to engage in entrepreneurial theory, practice and simulation in an online environment (Stainton, Johnson & Borodzicz, 2010).

The flexibility of cloud computing allows students to access materials on low-cost devices such as smartphones and tablets, more commonly accessible in developing regions than laptops or desktop computers. This adaptability ensures access even for those with meager resources to participate in entrepreneurship programs using cloud-based options and reduces some of the barriers associated with hardware and infrastructure.

6.2.2. Mobile Learning (m-Learning)

Since in most developing countries, mobile phones are more accessible than the traditional computer, m-learning is therefore considered one of the main solutions that increase access to entrepreneurship education. There is increased interest in mobile-friendly platforms and applications that provide students with access via their mobile devices to learning materials, simulations and assessments. The GSM Association estimated that worldwide, 5 billion people use mobile phones and many of them depend on their phones as a means of accessing the Internet (Stainton, Johnson & Borodzicz, 2010).

Most online learning platforms, including Coursera and edX, optimize their courses for mobile devices. Students can now listen to lectures, participate in discussions and submit assignments while on the go. In areas where mobile phone penetration is high and internet connectivity poor, such as regions of sub-Saharan Africa, offline learning capabilities are being developed. For example, the Coursera mobile app supports downloading course material for offline access so that students can learn seamlessly even if their connectivity is poor (Chen, Ifenthaler & Yau, 2021).

In entrepreneurship education, mobile apps are used to deliver business simulations, which allow students to practice business skills in real time. For example, the Business Simulation App, developed by the African Management Institute (AMI), allows aspiring entrepreneurs to simulate the operation of a business from their mobile devices, focusing on key areas such as financial management, marketing and acquisition customers.

6.2.3. Online Learning Communities and Peer Collaboration

Online learning communities are powerful tools for expanding access to entrepreneurship education because of the ways in which students learn from each other through peer learning, mentoring, and collaboration. Such communities provide connections between students around the world, thereby enabling the sharing of knowledge, the exchange of ideas, and even collaboration on business projects.

Platforms such as FutureLearn, Udemy, and Khan Academy incorporate online forums, group projects, and student peer assessments into their courses to build a sense of community and promote collaborative learning. Global Entrepreneurship Network (GEN) provides online forums where budding entrepreneurs can connect and receive comments and suggestions from seasoned business leaders, as well as collaborate on global entrepreneurship challenges with other students elsewhere around the world (Campos et al. 2020).

That makes a very useful, peer-driven model of education in entrepreneurship because it closely mimics the collaborative nature of the entrepreneurial ecosystem. Throughout the process, entrepreneurs are frequently leveraging mentorship, networking, and partnerships to advance their businesses, many of which are replicated virtually in online learning communities.

6.3. The Future of Access: AI-Driven Personalization and Virtual Reality

While online platforms have greatly expanded access to entrepreneurship education, the future promises even more with the integration of AI-based personalization and virtual reality (VR).

6.3.1. AI-Driven Personalization

Artificial intelligence (AI) is innovating education by introducing a personalized learning experience that meets the specific needs, preferences and learning speed of each individual student. In entrepreneurship education, AI-driven personalization can dynamically adapt course content, simulations, and assessments based on student performance to better perform in providing targeted support and challenges to students at a level relevant to their skill levels.

Adaptive Learning Pathways

With AI-powered platforms, adaptive learning paths can be developed where course material will stabilize at an ideal level of difficulty in real-time, based on student progress. For example, a student may struggle with financial management in a business simulation. In this regard, an AI system can provide additional resources to help a student get better at it through things like tutorials, exercises, or case studies. Conversely, when a student performs well in a particular area, AI would increase the difficulty for tasks or add more challenging ones (Stainton, Johnson & Borodzicz, 2010).

This personalized approach ensures that each student is guaranteed a personalized learning experience, which is particularly important in entrepreneurship education because students come from different backgrounds and experience levels. Similarly, AI simulations can also be designed to provide real-time feedback to students to learn the outcomes of their decisions and enhance problem-solving skills more powerfully compared to traditional methods.

AI-Enhanced Simulations and Mentorship

Artificial intelligence can further expand business simulations to include virtual mentors, artificial entities that guide a student through the learning process. Such a virtual mentor would provide advice and suggestions as the student makes choices within the simulation. For example, in a virtual startup simulation, an AI mentor would provide advice on other ways to market one's product if a student's initial way isn't good enough to generate enough sales. This interactive coaching can be seen as an interaction with a real business advisor who provides feedback on activities and suggestions on what to do or change, taking into account the student's performance (Stainton, Johnson & Borodzicz, 2010).

AI mentors can also track a student's long-term progress and provide insight into areas a student needs to improve, making it easier for the student to focus on developing their weaknesses. This technology will be especially useful in areas that do not have access to human mentors. In this way, personalized business guidance can be provided at scale.

6.3.2. Virtual Reality (VR) and Augmented Reality (AR) in Entrepreneurship Education

Virtual reality (VR) and augmented reality (AR) are set to revolutionize entrepreneurship education by creating immersive learning environments that replicate real-world business scenarios.

Similarly, virtual reality will transport students into virtual meeting rooms, retail, and even manufacturing facilities, where they will engage a virtual workforce of employees, customers, and suppliers to solve critical business problems. Meanwhile, AR places digital information on top of the physical world.

Here, students can visualize real-world business data, such as customer metrics or inventory levels, in real-world settings.

Immersive Business Simulations

VR-based entrepreneurship simulations allow students to practice business management without the risks associated with running a company in the real world. For example, a student may be placed in a virtual retail store where they are required to monitor inventory, listen to and resolve customer complaints, and interpret sales data.

This multi-sense learning not only enhances student engagement but also provides a much more realistic view of day-to-day business operations (Stainton, Johnson & Borodzicz, 2010).

Other areas where VR and AR technologies can be very effective include simulating sophisticated business challenges, such as supply chain disruptions or market entry into new territories. Students will be able to walk through virtual factories to observe how products are made and make decisions while having a real-time impact on the business. In this regard, students can experiment with strategies that would not be practically possible in a real classroom.

Accessing Virtual Business Ecosystems

Of the recent developments in VR and AR for entrepreneurship education, perhaps the most exciting will be the development of virtual business ecosystems where students around the world can collaborate, compete and interact in a shared virtual space.

Using VR, for example, an aspiring entrepreneur in Nigeria can work with a UK-based student to develop a joint business venture, attend virtual meetings, pitch their business to virtual investors and launch virtual products.

These virtual ecosystems break down geographical barriers, allowing students from different countries to exchange knowledge, test global business strategies and build international networks. This is relevant for students in developing regions, as access to international markets may be limited at times. Using entrepreneurship ecosystems supported by virtual reality provides students with the global view they require to perform business in today's global business arena (Stainton, Johnson & Borodzicz, 2010).

6.4. Global Case Study: The Impact of Technology on Entrepreneurship Education in Emerging Markets

To further illustrate the transformative power of technology in expanding access to entrepreneurship education, consider the case of Emerging Markets Business Institute (EMBI), a non-profit organization based in Brazil. EMBI developed a cloud-based entrepreneurship platform that provides students in Latin America with access to simulations, online courses, and mentoring opportunities, all of which are tailored to the challenges faced by entrepreneurs in emerging markets.

6.4.1. Cloud-Based Learning for Rural Entrepreneurs

One of the key objectives of the EMBI platform is to extend its reach to rural entrepreneurs in areas where access to conventional business training is limited. By integrating mobile learning with cloud-based simulations, the platform enables rural farmers and smaller business owners to simulate financial management, market analysis, and supply chain optimization practices without physically attending classes.

Since its release, EMBI has trained upwards of 50,000 entrepreneurs across Brazil, Peru, and Colombia. Of all users, 80% confirmed how this platform had indeed enhanced their decision-making at the business level through data presentation (Campos et al. 2020). Additionally, 20% of participants were able to scale their businesses by completing the programs offered on this site. This goes further to give the platform its impact on the success level of entrepreneurs in areas considered underserved.

6.4.2. Virtual Mentorship for Social Entrepreneurs

Complementing cloud-based learning, EMBI offers a virtual mentoring program that matches aspiring social entrepreneurs with experienced business leaders from around the world. This kind of mentor could provide guidance on "how" to start or scale a social enterprise in impact measurement, fundraising and stakeholder management. By leveraging technology and connecting students with global mentors, EMBI is helping to develop a new cadre of social entrepreneurs who are solving some of the most intractable problems in their communities (Chen, Ifenthaler & Yau, 2021).

6.5. The Role of Technology in Bridging the Gender Gap in Entrepreneurship Education

The second major area where technology is opening up access to entrepreneurship education is closing the gender gap. Typically, women are underrepresented in both business education and leadership positions. However, technology is helping to close this gap by giving women more access to resources, guidance and support networks.

6.5.1. Online Platforms for Women Entrepreneurs

Such online platforms as SheEO and Women's Startup Lab created virtual communities for women entrepreneurs where they could be trained through mentoring and funding. Such online platforms provide entrepreneurship lessons on unique challenges women face in business: how to balance work-life responsibilities, overcome gender bias, and gain access to capital (Chen, Ifenthaler & Yau, 2021).

For example, SheEO's global community connects women entrepreneurs with a network of active investors and business leaders who invest in and support women to expand their businesses. Online courses include leadership, financial management and marketing skills - all of which go a long way in empowering women in these competitive industries.

6.5.2. Virtual Mentorship Programs for Female Entrepreneurs

In addition to virtual mentoring programs, there are online courses that aim to help women overcome entrepreneurial obstacles by connecting them with various experienced female business leaders.

Mentors guide them on a variety of issues, including how to handle gender bias, building an inclusive team, and getting investors to invest in their businesses, as those investors themselves could be biased against investing in companies run by women (Stainton, Johnson & Borodzicz, 2010).

According to a study on virtual mentoring by the Global Entrepreneurship Monitor (GEM), there is a 30% increase in the number of women starting their own businesses, and a 40% higher scale of businesses compared to those who did not have access to mentoring (Campos et al. 2020).

This will be an informative study on the transformative impact of technology on women's business education and how they can excel in business.

6.6 Advanced Technologies in Developed Economies

The same course of entrepreneurship education has gained immense inspiration from advanced technologies like AI and virtual reality in parts of North America and Asia. These emerging technologies have created truly immersive learning environments where students are presented with scenarios that may arise while running a business. Applications of artificial intelligence for personalized learning and virtual reality in immersive startup management create the foundation for students in fast-paced, technology-driven economies to innovate and adapt.

6.6.1. Bridging the Digital Divide

While there is a shift to the effective use of simulations in entrepreneurship education worldwide, challenges remain, such as the digital divide, especially in areas where access to technology and poor internet infrastructure will always be a problem. However, programs such as mobile learning platforms in Africa and satellite internet initiatives are trying to fill this gap, thereby making entrepreneurship education accessible to more students. Scaling up such efforts will be key to ensuring that everyone is provided with equal opportunities to access education around the world.

These regional case studies from Africa, Asia, Latin America, Europe and North America create a rich tapestry of the flexibility and transformative power that technology has brought to entrepreneurship education. From agriculture training in Africa through innovation-driven mobile simulations in Asia to personalized learning with artificial intelligence in North America, technology is playing an increasingly important role in spreading the network of access to business skills (Chen, Ifenthaler & Yau, 2021).

These technological innovations will overcome not only geographical but also economic barriers and enable the development of a global business ecosystem where students from different regions can collaborate, learn from each other and grow together.

From teaching farmers in rural Africa how to overcome agricultural challenges to preparing tech entrepreneurs for Asia's global markets, simulation-based learning and technology is empowering the next generation of entrepreneurs to tackle some of the world's problems while simultaneously encouraging economic growth and social impact.

7. THE FUTURE OF SIMULATION-BASED ENTREPRENEURSHIP EDUCATION: EMERGING TRENDS AND OPPORTUNITIES

Simulation-based learning will be at the forefront of the emerging global landscape for entrepreneurship education and an even more vital strategy to help future entrepreneurs develop skills and competencies for success in dynamic and uncertain environments. Technological advances are continuing to jump forward with each passing day, while innovation in the design, delivery, and integration of simulations into educational curricula is driven by the ever-changing needs of education across many dimensions. Below, we will discuss the most recent trends in shaping the future of simulation-based entrepreneurship education and the opportunities inherent in such a system.

7.1. The Integration of Artificial Intelligence (AI) and Machine Learning (ML)

The integration of artificial intelligence (AI) and machine learning (ML) technologies acts as one of the most promising points in the development of the future of simulation-based entrepreneurship education. Whereas these technologies already enhance simulations by allowing personalized learning experiences, immediate feedback, and adapted guidance based on students' performances, the integration of AI and ML in entrepreneurship education will continue to evolve and further develop.

7.1.1. Adaptive Learning Pathways Powered by AI

In the future, we are likely to experience AI-powered simulations that will adjust with each new move that the student makes. The individual weaknesses in students identified by the analysis of their decision-making patterns can be used by an AI system to present them with a unique learning path. For example, if a student is struggling with financial management, AI can provide them with additional practice scenarios or targeted tutorials or real-time coaching to improve their skills (Stainton, Johnson & Borodzicz, 2010).

It will allow simulations to predict learning outcomes based on the actions students have taken in the machine learning algorithms, thus helping educators find early signs of success or failure.

Therefore, this could provide educators with a predictive ability to intervene earlier to provide individualized support to those students who may be struggling with certain aspects of entrepreneurship.

7.1.2. AI-Powered Virtual Mentors and Coaches

The role of artificial intelligence will go beyond adaptive learning to simulate life-like coaching and mentoring. AI-powered virtual mentors will guide the student through simulations, giving expert advice, offering alternative approaches and leading students to reflect on the decisions they make.

Enhanced with natural language processing and ML, these virtual mentors will answer complex questions, have meaningful conversations, and give individual feedback based on student performance (Stainton, Johnson & Borodzicz, 2010).

For example, an AI mentor can play a venture capitalist who listens to the student's business proposal and guides them with tips on how to increase their chances of getting funding. A fully immersive coaching experience like this would be very instructive for the students, as would the real experience of interacting with industry experts.

7.2. Immersive Learning Environments: Virtual Reality (VR) and Augmented Reality (AR)

The rise of virtual reality (VR) and augmented reality (AR) technologies is set to revolutionize the way students engage with entrepreneurship education. VR and AR create immersive learning environments where students can experience the complexities of running a business in a more vivid and interactive way.

7.2.1. Full Immersion in Business Operations

In the future, virtual reality may place students in simulated virtual business environments based on real-world requirements. Therefore, the student will be able to enter a virtual production facility, interact with virtual employees and control the production process from start to finish.

They could also walk through a virtual retail store and study customer behavior while making pricing and inventory decisions and in-store marketing strategies in real time (Stainton, Johnson & Borodzicz, 2010).

These multi-sensory VR simulations will provide students with a much deeper understanding of the day-to-day running of a business, giving them a holistic view of entrepreneurship. Students, by interacting with simulated stakeholders - suppliers, customers and investors - will develop interpersonal and negotiation skills necessary to manage relationships in the real world of business.

7.2.2. Augmented Reality for Real-Time Decision Making

While VR provides a fully immersive environment, augmented reality (AR) that overlays digital information on the physical world provides real-world data and information to students in real-time as they interact with their environment. A good example could be found in entrepreneurship education, where a student is exposed to real-time business scenarios simulated through AR and based on live data streams, the student has to make decisions. For example, a student running a virtual restaurant will be able to visualize sales trends, customer feedback, and inventory levels by applying AR in a physical environment (Chen, Ifenthaler & Yau, 2021).

These experiences can be further extended to physical learning through AR, as students can collaborate with digital and physical tools integrated into one space. This technology will also allow educators to combine traditional methods with advanced simulation tools and thus provide a truly blended learning experience for students to prepare them for the future of business.

7.3. Blockchain and Decentralized Learning Platforms

Among the major benefits that blockchain could bring to education is the potential ability to provide secure, immutable records of student achievement. By implementing blockchain technology, everyone will receive blockchain-verified academic credentials upon completion of simulations, entrepreneurship courses, and mentoring programs, respectively. The electronic digital certificates obtained will be recognized globally and will be much easier to prove to future employers, venture capitalists or business partners once the need arises (Stainton, Johnson & Borodzicz, 2010).

7.3.1. Decentralized Education Platforms

Blockchain further enables the development of decentralized educational platforms where students will be able to access learning resources, simulations and coaching without necessarily transacting through traditional gatekeepers such as universities or certification entities. These platforms will facilitate a student-led process of ownership of their learning journeys to create a personalized curriculum that best meets their individual business goals.

In addition to providing open access to educational content, blockchain platforms can also allow students to crowdfund their business ventures by connecting to global networks of investors.

In this way, students will use their blockchain business idea for fundraising purposes through decentralized crowdfunding platforms. This new avenue offers aspiring entrepreneurs from resource-poor regions alternative access to sources of funds (Campos et al. 2020).

7.4. The Role of Industry Partnerships

Industry partnerships will be integral to the simulation-based learning ecosystem in support of continuous professional development. In this regard, a partnership with industry leaders will enable educational institutions to provide simulations that authentically represent modern business challenges across all industries. This will keep entrepreneurship education current, relevant and aligned with current developments in industry trends, technologies and best practices.

7.4.1. Real-World Simulations Powered by Industry Data

Industry partnerships will also enable educational institutions to simulate the development of real-world simulations supported by live industry data.

In this way, the simulations will reflect not only the current state of the market but also changes in regulations and technological advances to give the student a proper picture of both the challenges and opportunities inherent in the modern business environment (Walker et al., 1998).

For example, collaboration with financial institutions can lead to the development of simulations where students manage a company's finances from real market flows. Likewise, collaboration with technology companies can lead to simulations in which students are tasked with introducing new products into a competitive high-tech market (Stainton, Johnson & Borodzicz, 2010).

These reality-based scenarios will indeed ensure that learners are better placed to go out there and engage in the world of work and make informed decisions in their field of expertise in the face of rapid change.

7.4.2. Continuous Feedback Loops Between Academia and Industry

As academia continues to interact more deeply with industry, continuous feedback loops are created where industry professionals provide regular insights into evolving business needs.

This is where entrepreneurship simulations and curricula are updated with continuous feedback. This means students are better prepared with skills in greater demand from employers and investors.

With continued collaboration, educational institutions will be better able to create simulations that address some of the emerging challenges facing humanity, such as the development of artificial intelligence, climate change, and the disruption of supply chains around the world.

Educators will go a long way to adequately prepare entrepreneurs to build resilient and future-proof businesses once simulations capture inputs from industry (Campos et al. 2020).

7.5. The Future Role of Government and Policy in Simulation-Based Entrepreneurship Education

There is a growing realization by governments around the world that entrepreneurship serves as a primary driver for economic growth, job creation and innovation. Therefore, they take an active interest in promoting simulation-based learning as an important component in national and regional entrepreneurship strategies.

In the future, more emphasis will be placed on public-private partnerships and policy initiatives that promote access to entrepreneurship education using technology and simulations.

7.5.1. Government-Funded Simulation Platforms

Some governments in various regions have already started supporting simulation-based entrepreneurship education through financially supported open access learning platforms.

For example, the South Korean government supported and developed a national entrepreneurship simulation platform that would provide free simulation access to students, aspiring entrepreneurs, and small business owners in the country.

This platform covers issues of business planning, market analysis and financial management that help create a more entrepreneurial workforce across the country (Campos et al. 2020).

In this regard, more and more governments in the future may have similar initiatives realizing that simulation-based entrepreneurship training democratizes access to entrepreneurship training for underserved populations and equips them with the skills needed to create and grow businesses.

Public funding can go a long way in creating locally tailored simulations that address the challenges of entrepreneurship in different regions, from navigating regulatory environments, through accessing capital, to creating sustainable supply chains (Stainton, Johnson & Borodzicz, 2010).

7.5.2. Policy Support for Lifelong Entrepreneurial Learning

On the other hand, governments are supposed to take on more and more tasks to support lifelong business learning. By creating policies that promote the development of lifelong learning platforms, it should be ensured that at every stage of their career, entrepreneurs have opportunities for continuous professional development.

This may include tax breaks for businesses that offer entrepreneurship training or create grants and subsidies to educational institutions that develop simulations and state-of-the-art digital learning tools (Chen, Ifenthaler & Yau, 2021).

This can also be complemented by governments working with industry leaders through the development of certification programs that recognize skills and competencies gained through simulation-based learning.

Such nationally recognized credentials would help entrepreneurs demonstrate their capabilities to investors, employers and business partners, further validating the role of simulations in entrepreneurship education.

7.6. The Future of Entrepreneurship Education: A Global and Inclusive Approach

As entrepreneurship education continues to evolve, the future will be defined by global collaboration, inclusive learning environments, and the integration of emerging technologies that make entrepreneurship education accessible to all.

7.6.1. Global Collaboration for Inclusive Growth

The future of simulation-based entrepreneurship education will be a global collaborative effort by universities, industry leaders, governments and technology providers to build the entrepreneurship ecosystem to become integrated.

This is the right way to make sure that entrepreneurs from a different region, industry or socio-economic background receive resources, guidance and support on their journey to success (Hammoda, 2024).

Entrepreneurship education will be increasingly borderless in this increasingly interdependent world, where students from different countries collaborate on global simulations, cross-border business strategies and learn from international mentors.

Simulation-based learning will help break down these geographic barriers to creating global business networks. Therefore, innovation and opportunities will enable entrepreneurs to scale up in international markets (Campos et al. 2020; Stainton, Johnson & Borodzicz, 2010).

7.6.2. Inclusive Learning for Underserved Communities

Technology-based simulations will also continue to play a critical role in bridging educational gaps in underserved communities. By allowing access to entrepreneurship education for people in remote or economically disadvantaged areas, simulations offer the opportunity for communities to take part in and contribute to the global economy. Mobile learning platforms, cloud-based simulations, and decentralized education systems ensure that entrepreneurs of every walk of life can develop the skills necessary to build sustainable and effective businesses contingent (Chen, Ifenthaler & Yau, 2021).

Moreover, simulation-based entrepreneurship education will also serve women entrepreneurs, minority-owned businesses, and social enterprises in their quest for an inclusive and equitable entrepreneurial environment. These platforms provide personalized simulations and coaching opportunities to address challenges specific to these groups.

7.7. Seizing the Opportunities of Simulation-Based Entrepreneurship Education

The future for simulation-based entrepreneurship education is bright, opening up opportunities to harness the power of technology, global collaboration and inclusive learning to drive innovation and business growth worldwide.

In this new education landscape, simulations will become more immersive, personalized and accessible because AI, VR, AR and blockchain are going to change everything about learning (Hammoda, 2024).

Through this Simulation-based Learning, the next generation of entrepreneurs will be developed and able to solve some of the critical challenges facing humanity, to develop sustainable enterprises and drive inclusive economic growth for successive generations by providing broad access to lifelong learning. global collaboration and addressing unique challenges of regional entrepreneurship ecosystems.

8. CONCLUSION

Simulation-based entrepreneurship education can be a game-changer in how this skill is taught and learned. As we have explored throughout the paper, simulations represent the exception to an immersive approach to learning that brings theory into practice by involving students in real situations without putting them at risk. Business simulations are designed to mimic the intensive nature of business management, cornering a market, or developing innovative products that permit students to develop important decision-making, problem-solving, and leadership competencies necessary in today's fast-paced industry. This technological advancement in AI, VR, AR, and cloud computing has been a trendsetter toward changing the dimension in which entrepreneurship education stands today. AI-powered personalization will enable adaptive learning experiences that meet the needs of individual learners, while VR and AR are creating immersive learning environments that simulate real-world business scenarios with a realism previously unimaginable. These tools are not only improving educational quality but also expanding educational access to all learners, including remote and underserved areas.

The diverse case studies from around the world included in this article point out the flexibility of simulation-based learning across regions and industries.

Furthermore, the application of blockchain technology is poised to make entrepreneurship education even more accessible, as students can gain verified credentials and take part in decentralized learning platforms.

The future of entrepreneurship education will be one of global collaboration whereby universities, governments, industry leaders, and technology providers come together to develop a truly inclusive entrepreneurial ecosystem. Simulation-based entrepreneurship learning provides the necessary resources for skill development and mentoring from every walk of life, including women, minority-owned businesses, and businesses from economically disadvantaged parts of the world, to pursue successful businesses.

These partnerships will thus drive innovation and drive inclusive economic growth, solving some of the most pressing problems facing the world.

The role of lifelong learning and continuous professional development will be large in the future. Entrepreneurs should always adapt to emerging situations and new technologies, transforming market conditions. Simulation-based platforms are best positioned to address this need to enable on-demand learning for entrepreneurs and experience real-world simulations that reflect the latest trends and challenges in business.

In short, simulation-based entrepreneurship education has emerged as an important tool for creating the next generation of entrepreneurs. Basically, simulations are an exciting and effective means of acquiring skills and competencies through experiential learning combined with cutting-edge technology. This means that scaling access, personalizing learning and driving innovation through platforms has huge potential and, as technology continues to improve, is the impact that simulation-based learning will have on entrepreneurship education. The entrepreneurs of the future will not only be skilled and better prepared, but also resilient, innovative and globally connected, ready to lead businesses in every corner of the world that drive social impact, economic growth and sustainability.

REFERENCES

Adedeji, S., Rahman, M., Abdul, M., Faizal Bin A. Ghan, M., Uddin, M., & Rahaman, S. (2019). Innovative Teaching Methods and Entrepreneurship Education: A Review of Literature. *Journal of Educational Administration Research and Review*, *2*(1). Advance online publication. DOI: 10.17509/earr.v2i1.21713

Adedeji, S. B., & Rahman, M. M. (2018). Innovative Teaching Methods and Entrepreneurship Education: A Review of Literature. *Journal of Research in Business. Economics and Management*, *10*(1), 1807–1813.

Alghamdi, E. (2023). Digital Games use in Entrepreneurhip Education at the Undergraduate Level: A Systematic Review. *Journal of Management and Business Education*, *6*(2), 172–198. DOI: 10.35564/jmbe.2023.0009

Amon, T. (2004). Simulations and the Future of Learning: An Innovative (and Perhaps Revolutionary) Approach to e-Learning. *Journal of Educational Technology & Society*, *7*, 149–150.

Arias-Aranda, D., & Bustinza-Sánchez, O. (2009). Entrepreneurial attitude and conflict management through business simulations. *Industrial Management & Data Systems*, *109*(8), 1101–1117. DOI: 10.1108/02635570910991328

Barjis, J., Gupta, A., Sharda, R., Bouzdine-Chameeva, T., Lee, P. D., & Verbraeck, A. (2012). Innovative teaching using simulation and virtual environments. *Interdisciplinary Journal of Information, Knowledge, and Management*, *7*, 237–255.

Bell, B. S., Kanar, A. M., & Kozlowski, S. W. J. (2008). Current issues and future directions in simulation-based training in North America. *International Journal of Human Resource Management*, *19*(8), 1416–1434. DOI: 10.1080/09585190802200173

Binsztok, A., Butryn, B., Holowinska, K., Owoc, M. L., & Sobinska, M. (2023). Business Computer Simulations and its Role in Educational Processes from the Students' Perspective. *Procedia Computer Science*, *225*(7), 4006–4014. DOI: 10.1016/j.procs.2023.10.396

Cadotte, E. (2014). The use of simulations in entrepreneurship education: Opportunities, challenges and outcomes. *Business (Atlanta, Ga.)*, *2014*, 280–302. DOI: 10.4337/9781783471454.00021

Campos, N., Nogal, M., Caliz, C., & Juan, A. A. (2020). Simulation-based education involving online and oncampus models in different European universities. *International Journal of Educational Technology in Higher Education*, *17*(1), 1–15. DOI: 10.1186/s41239-020-0181-y

Chen, L., Ifenthaler, D. & Yau, J.YK. (2021). Online and blended entrepreneurship education: a systematic review of applied educational technologies. *Entrep Educ*, 4(2), 191–232. DOI: 10.1007/s41959-021-00047-7

Costello, G. J. (2017). More than just a game: The role of simulation in the teaching of product design and entrepreneurship to mechanical engineering students. *European Journal of Engineering Education*, *42*(6), 644–652. DOI: 10.1080/03043797.2016.1211992

Csikszentmihalyi, M. (1975). *Beyond Boredom and Anxiety*. Jossey-Bass Publishers.

Curta, N. C., Petrusel, R., & Iftinca, C. A. (2015). Business simulation of tourism companies using the level I exercise firm model. *Quaestus*, *7*, 65.

Faisal, N., Chadhar, M. A., Goriss-Hunter, A., & Stranieri, A. (2022). Business Simulation Games in Higher Education: A Systematic Review of Empirical Research. *Human Behavior and Emerging Technologies*, *2022*, 1–28. DOI: 10.1155/2022/1578791

Fiore, E., Sansone, G., & Paolucci, E. (2019). Entrepreneurship Education in a Multidisciplinary Environment: Evidence from an Entrepreneurship Programme Held in Turin. *Administrative Sciences*, *9*(1), 28. DOI: 10.3390/admsci9010028

Fox, J., Pittaway, L., & Uzuegbunam, I. (2018). Simulations in Entrepreneurship Education: Serious Games and Learning Through Play. *Entrepreneurship Education and Pedagogy*, *1*(1), 61–89. DOI: 10.1177/2515127417737285

Hammoda, B. (2024). The impact of educational technologies on entrepreneurial competencies: A systematic review of empirical evidence. *Knowledge Management & E-Learning*, *16*(2), 309–333. DOI: 10.34105/j.kmel.2024.16.015

McFarland, K. (2017). Entrepreneurship Education and Experiential E-Learning: A Literature Review. *Developments in Business Simulation and Experiential Learning*, 44.

Oren, T., Mittal, S., & Durak, U. (2017). *Guide to Simulation-Based Disciplines. Simulation Foundations, Methods and Applications*. Springer. DOI: 10.1007/978-3-319-61264-5

Stainton, A. J., Johnson, J. E., & Borodzicz, E. P. (2010). Educational Validity of Business Gaming Simulation: A Research Methodology Framework. *Simulation & Gaming*, *41*(5), 705–723. DOI: 10.1177/1046878109353467

Sunny Yang, S., & Chandra, Y. (2013). Growing artificial entrepreneurs: Advancing entrepreneurship research using agent-based simulation approach. *International Journal of Entrepreneurial Behaviour & Research*, *19*(2), 210–237. DOI: 10.1108/13552551311310383

Tchokote, I., & Bawack, R. (2024). Linking Business Games to Business and Entrepreneurship Education: Insights from a Bibliometric and Literature Review. *Theoretical Economics Letters*, *14*(2), 436–467. DOI: 10.4236/tel.2024.142024

Walker, P. A., Greiner, R., McDonald, D. A., & Lyne, V. (1998). The Tourism Futures Simulator: A systems thinking approach. *Environmental Modelling & Software*, *14*(1), 59–67. DOI: 10.1016/S1364-8152(98)00033-4

Williams, D. (2015). The Impact of SimVenture on the Development of Entrepreneurial Skills in Management Students. *Industry and Higher Education*, *29*(5), 379–395. DOI: 10.5367/ihe.2015.0270

Wu, Y. J., Yuan, C.-H., & Pan, C.-I. (2018). Entrepreneurship Education: An Experimental Study with Information and Communication Technology. *Sustainability (Basel)*, *10*(3), 691. DOI: 10.3390/su10030691

Yen, W. C., & Lin, H.-H. (2022). Investigating the effect of flow experience on learning performance and entrepreneurial self-efficacy in a business simulation systems context. *Interactive Learning Environments*, *30*(9), 1593–1608. DOI: 10.1080/10494820.2020.1734624

Zulfiqar, S., Al-reshidi, H. A., Al Moteri, M. A., Feroz, H. M. B., Yahya, N., & Al-Rahmi, W. M. (2021). Understanding and Predicting Students' Entrepreneurial Intention through Business Simulation Games: A Perspective of COVID-19. *Sustainability (Basel)*, *13*(4), 1838. DOI: 10.3390/su13041838

Chapter 19
Meta-Preneurship Education:
Pathways to Entrepreneurial Skillsets Through Metaverse for Inclusive Learning

Christina Morfaki
https://orcid.org/0000-0003-4505-6828
Neapolis University, Pafos, Cyprus

Alex Morfaki
Norland College, UK

ABSTRACT

This chapter explores the potential and challenges of "Meta-Preneurship"an entrepreneurial learning capability emerging within the Metaverse. It reviews immersive technologies such as virtual reality (VR), augmented reality (AR), and mixed reality (MR) and explores their contribution to simulating entrepreneurial tasks, fostering creativity, adaptability, and collaboration. Ethical considerations and barriers to digital inclusion for persons with disabilities are examined in relation to the implementation of Metaverse technologies, which are carving the path towards inclusive and innovative pedagogy. The Metaverse could bridge gaps between traditional, online, and immersive learning and equip learners with skills to navigate interconnected societies and global economies.

INTRODUCTION

Innovation in computer science and information technology has reshaped the global landscape, sparking revolutions that resonate across the environment, business, education, and society. Concurrently, rapid technological advancements and enhanced connectivity are transforming daily human life, altering communication, interaction, and behavior. From the perspective of end users, three major waves of technological innovation have been identified, marked by the advent of personal computers, the internet, and mobile devices, respectively (Mystakidis, 2022). Currently, the fourth wave of computational innovation revolves around spatial and immersive technologies like Virtual Reality (VR) and Augmented Reality (AR). This wave is poised to become the next ubiquitous computing paradigm, with the potential to reshape education, business, remote work, and entertainment (Mystakidis, 2022). Education has consistently evolved from chalkboards to Massive Open Online Courses (MOOCs), leveraging the potential of

DOI: 10.4018/979-8-3693-9040-5.ch019

emerging technologies. The Metaverse offers transformative opportunities to revolutionize entrepreneurial education through the enhancement of creativity, collaboration, and immersive learning experiences.

The term "Metaverse" originates from the Greek prefix "meta," meaning "beyond" or "transcending," combined with 'universe' (Qiu et al., 2023). First coined in Neal Stephenson's 1992 cyberpunk science fiction novel Snow Crash, the Metaverse represents a "meta-reality," or "meta-cosmos", a continuous and perpetual multi-user environment that fuses physical reality with the digital virtual world. Alternatively, the term "meta" can signify both initiation and completion, representing not only a new beginning but also a state of completeness that encompasses both the virtual past and the real, future world (Lin et al., 2022).

Digital technology, the internet, and electronic devices in interactive and social learning contexts have enhanced student-centered learning (Schwaiger et al., 2024). The sixth generation of communication networks, 6G, is anticipated to facilitate numerous novel applications and services that were unattainable with 4G or 5G infrastructures. Digital twins, holograms, robotic avatars, high-density Internet of Things (IoT), augmented reality (AR), and virtual reality (VR) are key applications for 6G communication networks. Notwithstanding their time past, these applications have been continuously improved, with advancements in technology expanding their scope and functionality (Al-Ansi et al., 2023).

The digital transformation has redefined traditional entrepreneurship, emphasizing the integration of innovative technologies with entrepreneurial education. In the context of the Metaverse, entrepreneurship education evolves by merging experiential learning with digital tools such as VR, AR, and blockchain technologies (Calandra et al., 2023). These tools facilitate immersive learning environments where learners can simulate entrepreneurial tasks, such as developing business models, creating digital prototypes, and engaging in global market simulations (Hsieh & Wu, 2019; Kraus et al., 2022).

Digital and entrepreneurial education intersect by focusing on the skills needed for adaptability, creativity, and collaboration in dynamic markets. Metaverse introduces a new dimension by offering a decentralized, boundary-free space for learning and collaboration. Students can interact with peers, educators, and mentors from around the world, fostering a global entrepreneurial mindset. Furthermore, the use of gamification, virtual communities, and co-design in educational settings encourages students to experiment and innovate without the constraints of real-world risks (Dwivedi et al., 2022).

Within the ever-changing landscape of digital technology and the Metaverse, the issues of inclusion and digital accessibility remain pertinent and should guide considerations governing the design and implementation of new technologies. The United Nations Convention on the Rights of People with Disabilities (2006) acknowledges the significant impact that Information and Communication Technologies could have in promoting independence and stipulates that persons with disabilities should be afforded equal opportunities to access information. Despite legal mandates reinforcing accessibility, the path to inclusion remains fraught with significant barriers. These need to be identified and explored in an effort to enhance awareness of the challenges that may be encountered and propose solutions to potential issues that may emerge.

This chapter examines how the Metaverse can transform entrepreneurship education by leveraging key frameworks to address challenges of accessibility, equity, and inclusion. It discusses how immersive and innovative practices foster entrepreneurial competencies such as creativity, collaboration, and adaptability. By analyzing the opportunities and limitations of Metaverse technologies, the chapter provides insights into bridging the digital divide and preparing learners to thrive in an interconnected and evolving entrepreneurial ecosystem.

IMMERSIVE TECHNOLOGIES IN EDUCATION: AR, VR, AND MR

Under the broad concept of "Extended Reality" or "Cross Reality," several different types of immersive technologies have been developed; these include digital and electronic settings that display and project data (Milgram et al., 1995). Virtual reality is a digitally created, artificial environment designed to immerse users in an alternative reality where they experience a sense of presence similar to being in a physical space. Users can interact with the virtual environment in ways that mimic real-world interactions, enhanced by specialized multimodal equipment such as VR headsets, immersive helmets, and omnidirectional treadmills (Mystakidis, 2022; Pellas et al., 2021). These tools engage multiple senses, such as sight, sound, touch, and movement, allowing users to interact with virtual objects in intuitive and natural ways. Virtual reality enables students to explore virtual environments that replicate real-world scenarios or represent abstract concepts (Garcia et al., 2019). This technology promotes active learning by fostering engagement and curiosity, encouraging students to take an active role in their educational experience (Akman & Çakır, 2023; Schwaiger et al., 2024).

Augmented Reality revolutionizes the educational landscape by blending the digital and physical worlds, creating an enriched learning environment that enhances engagement and understanding. By overlaying digital information into real-world settings, AR offers contextually relevant data about objects or environments, fostering a deeper connection between learners and their surroundings (Amani et al., 2024; Farshid et al., 2018). This spatial merging of the physical and virtual realms is achieved through devices like smartphones, tablets, AR glasses, or even VR headsets with pass-through camera capabilities, projecting layers of digital artifacts directly into the user's view (Bacca et al., 2014; Mystakidis, 2022)).

A distinctive feature of AR is its ability to gamify education, turning traditional lessons into interactive, immersive experiences. This gamification approach not only captivates students but also promotes collaboration and critical problem-solving skills (Amani et al., 2024; Martín-Gutiérrez et al., 2015; Sarkar et al., 2020). For instance, AR applications can simulate real-world challenges or scenarios, encouraging teamwork and active participation. The integration of virtual elements into physical spaces bridges the gap between theoretical knowledge and practical application, making learning more dynamic and personalized (Farshid et al., 2018).

Moreover, AR excels at addressing diverse learning preferences, offering dynamic and adaptable educational experiences. By enabling students to interact with their environment in novel ways, it addresses the limitations of traditional teaching methods and keeps learners engaged. The spatially projected layer of information enhances visualization but also adapts to individual preferences, ensuring a more inclusive educational experience (Bacca Acosta et al., 2014). As technology evolves, AR's integration with advanced devices like AR-enabled contact lenses or transparent surfaces holds the promise of even greater interactivity and accessibility, paving the way for a new era in education (Ibáñez & Delgado-Kloos, 2018; Mystakidis et al., 2021). Incorporating AR into educational frameworks, especially within entrepreneurial and meta-preneurial contexts, could amplify its impact by fostering creativity, innovation, and real-world problem-solving, underscoring its transformative potential in higher education.

Mixed Reality (MR) has evolved into a complex and pivotal technology, especially in the context of metaverse education, which leverages a combination of AR and VR. Mixed reality represents a spectrum where the physical and digital environments interact, characterized by real-time contextual adaptation. For example, in an MR-enabled educational game, digital elements such as a non-player character can engage dynamically with physical surroundings, hiding under a desk or interacting with real-world objects (Milgram et al., 1995b; Speicher et al., 2019). To conceptualize MR, Milgram & Kishino's,

(1994) reality-virtuality continuum provides a foundational framework. This continuum illustrates a progression from the physical environment (on the left) to fully virtual environments (on the right). AR resides near the physical end by overlaying digital elements onto real-world settings, whereas VR entirely immerses users in a simulated environment. Mixed reality encompasses both ends and intermediate states, including "augmented virtuality," offering extensive educational opportunities (Milgram et al., 1995b; Mystakidis, 2022). In meta-preneurship education, MR can provide immersive platforms for entrepreneurial simulation and collaborative problem-solving. By blending physical and digital realms, learners can experiment with complex scenarios and prototype innovative solutions in realistic, risk-free environments (Sin et al., 2023). Such educational experiences align closely with metaverse principles, enabling decentralized, interactive, and learner-centric paradigms.

Transforming Entrepreneurship Education: From Traditional Learning to Metaverse Environments

Education has undergone a profound transformation, evolving from its traditional roots to embrace technological advancements that redefine how learners engage with content, educators, and each other. Traditional education, grounded in physical classrooms and one-directional lectures, emphasized fixed curricula and limited global reach. While effective in creating structured learning environments, it struggled to address the diverse needs of learners (Jeong, 2019; Mishra, 2017). This model often lacked the flexibility to cultivate entrepreneurial competencies, such as creativity, problem-solving, and adaptability, which are essential for success in today's dynamic and competitive landscapes.

The advent of online education brought flexibility and accessibility, with asynchronous tools like Learning Management Systems (e.g., Moodle, Blackboard) and synchronous platforms (e.g., Zoom, Microsoft Teams) enabling "anytime, anywhere" learning (Anderson & Rivera Vargas, 2020; Stöhr et al., 2020). However, these two-dimensional (2D) platforms face inherent limitations, such as low self-perception, emotional isolation, and passive participation (Mystakidis, 2022). Challenges like "Zoom fatigue" (Han & Bailenson, 2024) and low completion rates in MOOCs highlight the pressing need for more engaging and immersive solutions (Anderson & Rivera Vargas, 2020; Jordan, 2014; Mystakidis, 2022). For entrepreneurship education, these limitations often result in missed opportunities for learners to engage in experiential activities such as business prototyping or collaborative decision-making.

Metaverse represents the next frontier in educational evolution. By integrating immersive 3D environments, blockchain-based systems, and advanced interactive technologies like VR and AR, it creates boundaryless environments where learners can actively explore, collaborate, and innovate (Lehikko, 2021; Parong & Mayer, 2021). For aspiring entrepreneurs, the Metaverse provides an innovative platform to experiment with real-world scenarios in a controlled, risk-free environment, enabling them to refine ideas and test strategies in ways that traditional or online platforms cannot. Unlike traditional 2D online platforms, the Metaverse spatially merges the physical and digital worlds, providing a heightened sense of presence through immersive interfaces (Chen et al., 2022; Lin et al., 2022; Sun et al., 2022). Tools such as VR headsets, AR glasses, and haptic devices offer realistic sensory feedback, bridging the gap between real-world and digital experiences (Chen et al., 2022; Lin et al., 2022). This advancement fosters the emotional and social dimensions of learning often absent in 2D platforms, enabling more dynamic and meaningful interactions (Kanematsu et al., 2010).

Furthermore, Metaverse addresses critical shortcomings of traditional and online education (Georgiou et al., 2021; Kanematsu et al., 2010; Lin et al., 2022):

- Low self-perception: customizable avatars allow learners to express their identity and creativity, essential for entrepreneurial confidence.
- Lack of presence: immersive collective meeting spaces encourage collaboration and idea-sharing, mirroring dynamic team environments often found in start-ups.
- Inactivity: interactive simulations and gamified activities engage learners in entrepreneurial tasks such as business model development or strategic planning. These activities not only mimic real-world entrepreneurial challenges but also encourage learners to develop resilience and adaptability—skills vital for navigating the complexities of today's markets.

The transformative potential of the Metaverse extends to its ability to foster creativity, collaboration, and adaptability—skills critical for entrepreneurial and lifelong learning (Mohan, 2019)Immersive environments support visualizing abstract concepts, conducting high-risk training in safe virtual settings, and promoting global collaboration. Blockchain technologies ensure academic integrity through tamper-proof records, while AI-driven analytics tailor learning pathways to individual preferences (Kanematsu et al., 2010; Lin et al., 2022). Entrepreneurship education particularly benefits from this integration, as learners can form virtual start-up teams, collaborate across cultures, and pitch ideas to global audiences within the Metaverse's immersive framework. Table 1 captures the evolution of educational modalities, illustrating how Metaverse builds on traditional and online learning to offer unprecedented opportunities for engagement and innovation.

Table 1. Comparison of educational characteristics: Traditional, online, and metaverse learning environments

Characteristic	Traditional Learning	Online Learning	Metaverse Learning Environment
Location	Fixed physical spaces (classrooms)	Flexible (home, office, remote access)	Decentralized, boundaryless (VR spaces, hybrid physical-virtual zones, IoT-enabled environments)
Equipment	Textbooks, chalkboards, projectors	Computers, tablets, smartphones	VR headsets, AR glasses, haptic devices, brain-computer interfaces
Learning Interaction	One-directional lectures	Video-based, interactive discussions	Immersive, real-time collaborations, peer-to-peer exchanges
Role of Educator	Teacher as knowledge provider	Knowledge facilitator, content curator	Experience designer, mentor, and entrepreneurial co-creator
Role of Learner	Passive recipient	Engaged learner	Active explorer, digital creator, entrepreneurial thinker
Customization	Standardized curricula	Flexible (MOOCs, adaptive LMS)	Fully personalized learning pathways, AI-guided content, dynamic content creation
Learning Tools	Blackboards, physical tools	LMS platforms, educational apps	Virtual labs, digital twins, blockchain certificates, interactive simulations
Global Reach	Limited to geographical proximity	Online access across time zones	Seamless global interaction with virtual collaborators
Experiential Learning	Case studies, on-site visits	Simulated models, online demonstrations	Immersive entrepreneurial simulations, virtual prototyping, experiential problem-solving
Assessment Methods	Exams, assignments	Quizzes, peer-reviewed projects	Blockchain-secured credentials, real-time AI-driven performance tracking

continued on following page

Table 1. Continued

Characteristic	Traditional Learning	Online Learning	Metaverse Learning Environment
Skill Development Focus	Academic knowledge	Practical and technical skills	Creativity, collaboration, adaptability, and entrepreneurial innovation
Social Interaction	Local peer networks	Online discussions	Virtual communities, networking hubs, immersive collaboration with avatars
Opportunities	Stable, consistent	Accessible, cost-effective	Immersive, innovative, boundary-breaking; integration of global entrepreneurial ecosystems
Challenges	Geographical and logistical limits	Digital divide, engagement hurdles	Technological complexity, inclusivity, ethical and governance challenges; infrastructure and digital literacy barriers

Innovating Futures: HEIs, the Metaverse, and Entrepreneurial Ecosystems

Entrepreneurship is a fundamental driver of societal progress and economic development, playing a pivotal role in fostering innovation to exploit emerging opportunities, enhance productivity, generate employment, and address critical global challenges such as the United Nations Sustainable Development Goals (SDGs) and other significant global crises (Global Entrepreneurship Monitor, 2024)

Small and medium-sized enterprises (SMEs) are particularly central to economic systems as significant contributors to job creation and employment. Globally, SMEs constitute 90% of all businesses and contribute over 50% of total employment (Morfaki, 2025). Within OECD economies, SMEs account for more than 99% of firms, over 60% of employment within the business sector, and a substantial proportion of value creation and new job opportunities. Furthermore, SMEs are indispensable to the social and economic fabric of local communities, underscoring their broader societal impact (OECD, 2023).

Higher education institutions (HEIs) are increasingly recognized as pivotal contributors to socio-economic development, serving as intellectual hubs capable of addressing complex societal challenges. Scholars emphasize the need for HEIs to shift from traditional roles centered on teaching, research, and service-related activities toward innovative practices that integrate entrepreneurship education to tackle real-world problems (Amani et al., 2024; Hoang et al., 2020; Maunze et al., 2020).

Research highlights the transformative role of HEIs in fostering entrepreneurial mindsets and intentions among students and communities, thereby combating unemployment and enhancing societal capacities. Studies argue that HEIs are uniquely positioned to nurture individual talents and abilities, transforming them into resources for social and economic growth (Amani et al., 2024; Miotto et al., 2020; Nzilano et al., 2022; Setiawan, 2014). Entrepreneurial programs, such as incubators, events, and experiential learning opportunities, effectively empower students to pursue entrepreneurial ventures (Neneh, 2022).

HEIs also play a critical role in promoting entrepreneurial attitudes, knowledge, and skills, creating a foundation for students to pursue entrepreneurial endeavors (Farhangmehr et al., 2016; Ismail, 2022). This capacity to stimulate entrepreneurial intentions is supported by the institutions' ability to integrate innovation into their curricula and extracurricular activities, thereby aligning with societal expectations of fostering entrepreneurship-driven economic and social progress.

HEIs are engines of socio-economic transformation, integrating entrepreneurial education and practices to address societal challenges. Their role extends beyond academic functions to building entrepreneurial ecosystems that prepare individuals and communities for dynamic participation in economic and social innovation. Thus, HEIs have a great importance as catalysts for cultivating entrepreneurial mindsets and bridging the gap between education and economic development.

The rapid advancements in digital technologies, coupled with evolving consumer demands and environmental uncertainties, have significantly transformed the global economic landscape (Patrício & Ferreira, 2024). These dynamics present multifaceted challenges for businesses, necessitating innovative approaches to navigate disruptive models (Stoiber et al., 2023).Addressing these challenges requires a robust entrepreneurial ecosystem—an interconnected network of actors including government entities, private sector stakeholders, society, universities, and entrepreneurs (Bouncken & Kraus, 2022; Patrício & Ferreira, 2024).

Entrepreneurial ecosystems, conceptualized as "sets of interdependent actors and factors coordinated to enable productive entrepreneurship within a particular territory," serve as platforms for innovation and economic growth (Stam 2015, p.5). In this context, the metaverse extends these ecosystems into virtual and hybrid spaces, dissolving geographical constraints and enabling the seamless interaction of actors across physical and digital realms. These virtual ecosystems amplify opportunities for collaboration, knowledge exchange, and resource access, aligning with Muldoon et al. (2023) exploration of ecosystems that span physical and cyber boundaries(Patrício & Ferreira, 2024). The metaverse not only enhances entrepreneurial ecosystems but also redefines their dynamics, enabling the creation of "extended ecosystems" that connect diverse actors in immersive virtual spaces. This evolution aligns with HEIs' transformative role in fostering entrepreneurial mindsets, promoting innovation, and addressing socio-economic challenges (Amani et al., 2024, Miotto et al., 2020).

THEORETICAL FOUNDATIONS FOR META-PRENEURSHIP EDUCATION

Theory of Planned Behavior

Entrepreneurship education in the Metaverse is underpinned by established theoretical models, such as the Theory of Planned Behavior, which suggests that an individual's subjective norm significantly influences their behavioral intentions, attitudes, and perceived behavioral control (Ajzen, 1991). This theory highlights how entrepreneurial education in immersive environments like the Metaverse can shape positive attitudes toward entrepreneurship by providing students with practical knowledge of the benefits and challenges of business creation (Amani et al., 2024; Maheshwari & Kha, 2022).

Moreover, entrepreneurship self-efficacy -the belief in one's capacity to start and manage a successful business—plays a critical role in influencing perceived behavioral control. Metaverse-based entrepreneurship education can bolster entrepreneurship self-efficacy by offering students immersive and risk-free environments to practice entrepreneurial tasks, such as virtual business modeling or market simulations. These experiences could increase confidence and resourcefulness, enhancing the likelihood of pursuing entrepreneurial ventures (Uddin et al., 2022; Wardana et al., 2020)

The entrepreneurial environment which includes supportive policies, community networks, and exposure to successful entrepreneurs, further strengthens perceived behavioral control. In the Metaverse, virtual role models and simulations of thriving entrepreneurial ecosystems can create a supportive environment for students. These digital interactions can amplify opportunities for networking, mentorship, and collaborative learning, helping students internalize the entrepreneurial process and fostering their intent to pursue business creation (Amani et al., 2024; Jena, 2020). By integrating immersive technologies, entrepreneurial ecosystems, and tailored experiential learning, Metaverse-based entrepreneurship education aligns theoretical constructs with innovative practices, offering a transformative pathway for aspiring entrepreneurs.

Experiential Learning Theory

The theory highlights the importance of experience in the learning process, defining learning as the process whereby knowledge is created through the transformation of experience (Kolb, 2014). This approach encourages learners to explore environments directly through interaction and discovery, fostering deep engagement and active knowledge construction (De Carvalho, 2013).

In entrepreneurial education, Metaverse offers a unique platform to implement Experiential Learning Theory by providing immersive and authentic experiences that are often too costly, risky, or logistically impossible in real-world settings. For example, virtual simulations can enable learners to practice high-stakes entrepreneurial skills such as negotiating investments or managing crises without real-world consequences (Carruth, 2017; Markowitz et al., 2018). Similarly, virtual prototyping and business modeling in VR environments can replicate market dynamics and customer interactions, allowing students to refine their entrepreneurial ideas.

Key design principles for experiential learning theory in the Metaverse include:

- Augmentation or Extension of Real-World Contexts: virtual reality environments should either enhance real-world phenomena or provide experiences unattainable in reality, such as diving into the micro-level workings of an economic system or simulating startup launches under varying market conditions (Bouchard et al., 2006; Kolb, 2014).
- Authenticity and Presence: to maximize learning, students must perceive virtual experiences as authentic and feel a strong sense of "being there" (Heater, 1992; Slater & Wilbur, 1997). The Metaverse's immersive nature, through high-resolution VR tools and interactive 3D models, enhances this presence, enabling active participation rather than passive observation (Johnston et al., 2018; Kwon, 2019).
- Cognitive Augmentation: virtual reality environments reduce cognitive load by integrating spatial information and realistic models, allowing students to focus on decision-making and entrepreneurial problem-solving (Duncan et al., 2012).

While VR replicates real-world scenarios effectively, its value lies in creating augmented or novel experiences that expand entrepreneurial thinking (Kalantari et al., 2021; Kim et al., 2023). For instance, the Metaverse can simulate dynamic, cross-cultural market interactions, empowering learners to develop adaptability, creativity, and strategic foresight.

Viewing the Metaverse for entrepreneurship education through the lens of Experiential Learning Theory promotes immersive, hands-on engagement, aligning virtual activities with the challenges and opportunities of real-world entrepreneurship. This approach equips learners with the confidence and skills necessary to navigate complex entrepreneurial landscapes effectively.

Distributed Cognition Theory

This theory expands on experiential learning by emphasizing that cognition occurs not only within the brain but also through interactions between individuals and their environment(Hutchins, 1995; Van Dijk et al., 2014). This perspective highlights the importance of tools, social interactions, and external knowledge representations (e.g., sketches or notes) in shaping learning outcomes (Deitrick et al., 2015; Hutchins, 2020; Kim et al., 2023).

In Metaverse-based entrepreneurship education, distributed cognition informs the design of immersive environments that reduce cognitive load and enhance engagement. Virtual reality platforms, for instance, can integrate features like interactive objects, dynamic content creation, and collaborative tools to support entrepreneurial tasks such as prototyping or strategic planning (Hollan et al., 2009; Kirsh, 2013). Social interaction spaces within VR enable nonverbal communication, feedback, and shared decision-making, fostering entrepreneurial teamwork and innovation (McVeigh-Schultz & Isbister, 2022).

Effective design must balance learner agency and structured progression, ensuring flexibility for users to explore and manipulate their environment without overwhelming them. Features like avatar-driven gestures, real-time annotations, and collaborative workspaces enhance visibility and interaction, simulating real-world entrepreneurial ecosystems. By leveraging Distributed Cognition Theory, the Metaverse transforms learning into an interconnected and dynamic process, ideal for developing entrepreneurial competencies.

Embodied Learning Theory

Embodied Learning Theory emphasizes the integration of bodily movements with cognitive processes, arguing that sensorimotor actions, such as gestures, play a critical role in developing mental models and strengthening memory (Goldin-Meadow, 2005; Kim et al., 2023; Nathan & Martinez, 2015; Piaget, 1952; Roth, 2001). This theory highlights how engaging the body in learning processes enhances understanding and retention, as evidenced by research showing that performing relevant gestures leads to better outcomes than merely observing them (Nathan & Martinez, 2015; Stieff et al., 2016).

In Metaverse, embodied learning becomes particularly impactful due to its immersive nature. Modern VR devices, such as Oculus Quest 2, allow users to interact with virtual environments using natural gestures and body movements, creating a deeper sense of presence and engagement (Bailey & Bailenson, 2017). For entrepreneurship education, this translates into opportunities to simulate real-world tasks, such as pitching ideas, collaborating in virtual teams, or managing operations, where learners' physical interactions with virtual objects mirror real-life scenarios.

For example, VR environments can guide learners to use their avatars to perform specific entrepreneurial activities, such as negotiating deals or visually mapping business strategies. These embodied interactions enhance understanding of complex concepts by connecting motor actions to cognitive learning outcomes, as demonstrated in studies where bodily engagement facilitated mastery of abstract systems (Price et al., 2020).

Design principles for embodied learning in entrepreneurship education within VR include:

- Facilitating Natural Movements: virtual reality environments should enable learners to use their body movements to interact meaningfully with virtual tools and scenarios, forging connections between physical actions and entrepreneurial problem-solving.

- Connecting Actions to Learning Goals: movements in VR should be carefully aligned with specific entrepreneurial tasks, such as using gestures to simulate market dynamics or team coordination.

From the perspective of embodied learning in the Metaverse, entrepreneurship education can offer hands-on, immersive experiences that deepen understanding, enhance memory retention, and cultivate critical skills like collaboration and innovation, essential for entrepreneurial success.

Inclusion in Higher Education and Entrepreneurship

Inclusion in education and higher education is embedded and underpinned by international and national policy and legislation initiatives which are not solely aimed at increasing participation for under-represented populations and minorities (Merry, 2024) but become preoccupied with the infrastructure, content and delivery of curricula that are geared at meeting the learning requirements of increasingly diverse populations of students (Dinmore & Stokes, 2015; Timu et al., 2024). Despite the emphasis placed upon inclusion, statistics indicate that access to education and meaningful academic engagement and attainment for persons with disability remains problematic. The United Nations Department of Economic and Social affairs reports that disability rates remain significantly higher among groups with lower educational attainment in the countries of the Organisation for Economic Co-operation and Development (OECD). On average, 19% of less educated people have disabilities, compared to 11% among the better educated. In OECD countries, despite governments' commitment to inclusivity, students with disabilities in higher education are under-represented. Underrepresentation in higher education remains unresolved and appears to go hand in hand with participation in paid labour (UN,n.d). The International Labour Organisation (ILO) reports that "on average across countries, having disabilities decreases the likelihood of labour market participation by 29 percentage points for men, and by 20 percentage points for women" (Ananian & Dellaferrera, 2024, p.14).

As means of countering participation in the labour market, the United States Department for Labour (2024) highlights the contribution of small businesses to the economy and advocates for the economic empowerment and personal and financial independence afforded to persons with disabilities by owning their own business. In the United Kingdom, the Federation of Small Business (FSB) reports that disabled-owned small businesses accounting for 8.6% of the turnover of all UK businesses (2024). Although self-employment is viewed as an effective means of establishing a balance between professional and personal life and, even a potential solution to tackling reduced employment opportunities and discrimination (Gouskova, 2020), the gap in income between persons with disabilities and non-disabled colleagues perseveres and points to entrenched inequalities in treatment, wage outcomes, and professional experiences. The ILO (2024) acknowledges the disparities and points countries and organisations to international legislation and national policy and guidance which aims to mandate, regulate and advocate the rights of persons with disabilities to equitable opportunities and remuneration (Ananian & Dellaferrera, 2024).

Based on the aforementioned, enhanced inclusion for people with disabilities at international and national level could be predicated in part on providing opportunities for entrepreneurship training which specifically focus on developing skills and competencies associated with enterprise, management, and leadership across a range of settings and organisations. Studies indicate a strong positive link between entrepreneurship education and subsequent action (Bell & Cui, 2023; Dakung et al., 2017) and call for the incorporation of entrepreneurship elements across all levels of education (Ahmad, 2013), which is not restricted to management and leadership courses, but encompasses a wide range of disciplines in an effort to instil individual and communal knowledge, capacity, and skills. In the United Kingdom, the Quality Assurance Agency for Higher Education (2018) has embraced the 'mainstreaming' of entrepreneurial elements across a range of tertiary courses and degree syllabi and called for the establishment of metrics that measure and evaluate the effectiveness of respective higher education institutions in promoting enterprise and entrepreneurial education.

The development of entrepreneurship among underrepresented populations is not only conducive to individual progression, through the provision of flexible labour alternatives. It could equally contribute to the development of shared communitarian values that enhance the employment conditions, standards of living and wellbeing of disadvantaged populations in local and wider communities (García & Capitán, 2021) thus promoting social, cultural and economic amelioration (QAA, 2018). Despite the potential benefits associated with fostering conditions that incentivise disabled minorities to engage and commence their own enterprise projects, there are reported challenges that hinder their materialisation. García and Capitán (2019) identify several exogenous and endogenous factors that erect barriers to the actualisation of entrepreneurship among individuals with disability including institutional and physical accessibility obstacles imposed upon them. Although institutional barriers and inequities have become deeply entrenched within the historical and societal nexus, there is potential for reorganisation through the formulation of policy initiatives that embed and contribute to widening participation at all levels of education including Further and Higher Education. In the absence of whole system reorganisation, the potential of digital technologies and the metaverse should be assessed to ascertain the opportunities and barriers erected for individuals with disabilities.

Digital Technology and Entrepreneurship: Inclusive Structures and Capacity Building

In Higher Education, emphasis on widening participation and improving inclusion has been an ongoing process which is oscillating between the quality standards and outcomes agenda. On one hand barriers, erected within Higher Education institutions are acknowledged and contextualised within the competitive climate imposed nationally and globally (Donnelly & Evans, 2019). On the other hand, the transformation of students into entrepreneurial individuals who are profitable and productive for the economy remains firmly embedded within a neoliberalist international agenda (Naidoo, 2016). The notion of entrepreneurship promoted in this article is not preoccupied solely with financial profitability and industrial readiness but advocates for creative and cultural enterprise (Naudin & Agusita, 2021) across a range of disciplines. This form of entrepreneurship could augment and enable alternative and various means of expression, promote representation, and should be based on the unique views and innovative capital of persons with disabilities.

While the traditional notion of entrepreneurship remains under review, the advent of digital technology and the metaverse appear to hail a new era in the technological and digital realms (Botelho, 2021). Current times are viewed as critical in fostering opportunities for heterogeneous populations to connect, formulate new experiences and forge new skills and capabilities through interactions within the context of virtual, augmented and extended reality. The evolution of technology has been ongoing, although the Covid and post-Covid era signalled new understandings as access to digital technology became a necessity, enhanced opportunities for social interaction and fostered alternative means of communication and learning among diverse communities of learners. Digital and virtual places replaced physical environments and approaches to teaching and learning had to be reconfigured and adapted to the new reality. However, this evolution came with both benefits and challenges (Bong & Chen, 2024; Botelho, 2021). Digital technology could simultaneously act as an enabler or barrier on the path to inclusion.

An increasing number of colleges and universities incorporate the principles of the Universal Design of Learning to promote equitable access to their curricula (LeGary Jr & LaRocco, 2022). The framework, which originally hails from architectural design centred on the removal of physical barriers, has been adopted and developed by the Centre for Applied Special Technology (CAST) to encompass a frame which is centred on meeting the learning needs and requirements of diverse student populations through multiple means of expression, representation and engagement (European Agency for Special Needs and Inclusive Education, 2024). Gilligan, (2020) notes the complementarity of digital technologies with the principles of UDL. Multiple means of engagement could be offered through the provision of flexible learning programmes that entail synchronous and asynchronous online delivery modes and personalised learning that could lead to diverse pathways and multiple specialisations within subjects. Expression could be enabled by allowing students to demonstrate knowledge and evidence their learning through practical assessments and the formulation of digital, physical and virtual artefacts. Representation is centred on the production and dissemination of a range of resources that comply with the Web Content Accessibility Guidelines (WCAG 2.2) issued by the World Wide Web Consortium (2024).

While the UDL provides an overview of inclusive practice, a complementary framework, the Universal Design for Instruction (UDI) is preoccupied specifically with the design of products and teaching resources and their practical application and seamless incorporation into teaching in Higher Education. The UDI adopts a proactive approach to inclusion which is aiming for the creation of artefacts and products that fulfil the needs of diverse populations of students (Burstahler et al., 2020; Wilkens et al.,2021). UDI is underpinned by seven principles which support its application: equitable use, flexibility in use, simple and intuitive use, perceptible information, tolerance for error, low physical effort and size and space for approach and use. The combination of both frameworks could be conducive to inclusive practice and dismantle some of the organisational barriers erected within Higher Education Institutions.

The WCAG guidelines further reinforce these principles. These have infiltrated government policies and regulations worldwide and are reinforced by the European Accessibility Act (2019). The former have placed a statutory duty on organisations, institutions and companies to make websites, apps and digital services accessible to all including persons with disabilities. The design principles are focussed on the products and services being perceivable, operable, understandable and robust. Although the technical stipulations of WCAG are beyond the scope of this chapter, the educational capacity of digital accessibility remains at the heart of considerations raised in relation to digital and technological inclusion. The rolling out of digital services and platforms, the organisation and dissemination of engaging materials and virtual resources, the delivery of online interactive sessions and the formulations of creative assessments predisposes the collaboration of professionals from different fields and departments within and outside academia (Boat and Cheng, 2023; Hope 2020). Concurrently, it places an onus on higher education teachers and lecturers to develop a comprehensive knowledge and working understanding of technology as means of improving the digital experiences of students, enhancing engagement and addressing learning requirements (Gilligan, 2020; Tondeur et al., 2023). The European Commission (2018) and UNESCO (2022) have developed respective frameworks providing overviews of digital competency areas or specific competencies addressed at educators of all levels with the aims of building capacity and enhancing technological accessibility.

Although these frameworks set out a roadmap that could be useful in capacity building, they have been critiqued due to their 'one-size fits all' approach which does not correspond to specific educational levels and does not take into account the digital needs and requirements of students at various levels (Gilligan, 2020). Moreover, the means by which frameworks are incorporated in undergraduate or ongoing professional development and materialise in teaching practice are devolved to individual institutions and organisations. This could result in significant variations observed between teachers and institutions. Tondeur et al. (2022) advocate for the formulation of context-specific frameworks in Higher Education that are sensitive to institutional and social specificities and respond to the needs and requirements of the student body.

Several studies note the proliferation of issues plaguing digital accessibility and exclusion. These range from insufficient technical knowledge on the part of teachers (Gilligan, 2020) and lack of professional development opportunities afforded by faculties (Bong & Chen, 2024) to ubiquitous, non-specific guidelines which might exacerbate confusion (Tondeur et al., 2023) and result in organisations or institutions evading accountability for application and implementation. Despite the challenges, there are elements of digital inclusion and immersive inclusion afforded by digital technologies and the metaverse which provide opportunities for users to develop new skills and craft knowledge which do not fall within the constraints imposed by physical environments and could afford new embodied social, educational, and professional experiences (Zallio & Clarkson, 2022).

Inclusive Futures: Challenges and Opportunities in Metaverse-Driven Education

Learning is considered to be a social and co-constructed process which is formulated and developed within and between communities of practice. Although the contribution of communities of practice to personal and professional development is not a new concept (Wenger et al., 2002) digital and online technologies have enabled individuals and groups of persons with disabilities to create communities of inquiry and practice (Sweet at al., 2022) which are not constrained by the barriers erected by actual physical environments. From an educational perspective, these online digital communities do not merely serve as virtual meeting places that enable students of various abilities and disabilities to meet and exchange ideas and perspectives on topics. They have the capacity to foster a sense of belonging, encourage participation and promote advocacy for groups which could result in the formulation of new personal, professional, and collective identities (Sweet et al., 2020).

Wilkens et al. (2021) conducted a survey that reported on the experiences of tertiary students with disabilities utilising digital technology. The results indicated that students found digital study more accessible than study requiring physical presence due to the flexibility and opportunities to work at one's own pace. Despite the benefits, a significant percentage of students reported challenges when using assistive technologies which were partly related to restrictions associated with the specific platform used by the university (Moodle) but were also ascribed to lecturers' quality of digital teaching and devices' compatibility and effectiveness at working together. This raises some relevant points related to accessibility, versatility and complementarity of different resources and devices that could be used to support digital learning. Botelho (2021) notes that despite the great strides made in technological evolution, there remain residual issues which are partly rooted in the development cycles observed during product design and calls for the production process of hardware and software to be harmonised and enable interoperability arrangements.

While issues associated with digital accessibility persevere and point to a digital divide (Gandasegui, 2013), the advent of the Metaverse seems to be promising new opportunities for users with disabilities to access immersive realities that could foster new ways of playing, socialising and learning (Zallio & Clarkson, 2022). In principle, the Metaverse appears to offer some solutions by removing some of the constraints imposed by physical environments, such as gravitational forces, which restrict participation for users with physical disabilities (Zallio & Clarkson, 2022). Recent studies (Altinay et al., 2024; Othman et al., 2024; Yenduri et al., 2023). highlight the potential of metaverse technologies to address or support the educational needs and requirements of students with disabilities. Equally, a number of ethical, design, and practical considerations are raised that call for collaboration among metaverse stakeholders to resolve potential challenges.

While it is acknowledged that learners with disabilities may face various challenges when accessing learning due to their specific needs, the services and provisions provided by the metaverse should not be restricted to a 'one size fits all' approach formulated solely on the basis of specific conditions or impairments. While a significant number of studies have emphasised the needs of specific sub-groups of persons with disability such as visually impaired learners. Altinay et al., (2024) the educational and personalised needs of other groups have not been afforded the same attention. Instead of assuming that learning needs correspond and are compatible with specific conditions, services offered by Metaverse should focus on the customisation of assistive technologies and educational aids (Yenduri et al., 2023). While mass customisation and multimodality could be perceived as a more inclusive approach, it could equally introduce additional complexity to the interface and experiences of users. Dudley et al. (2023) advocate for automatic personalisation which enables users to select and discard functions based on their requirements. The dilemmas associated with the commonality or additionality of provision have been documented extensively in inclusive studies (Norwich, 2014) and effect the digital and virtual reality realms.

While Metaverse design remains in its infancy, the creation of multimodality predisposes that developers of immersive applications are familiar with strategies that enhance accessibility (Altinay et al., 2024; Dudley et al., 2023). This requires comprehensive awareness of guidelines that transcend tokenistic compliance with W3C's Web Content Accessibility Guidelines. The participation and collaboration of users with disabilities should inform and assist with the formulation of carefully designed and well thought out guidelines that should govern the features supported (Dudley et al., 2023) and allow for the development of a new design language to be shared and critiqued by organisations and users (Zallio & Clarkson, 2022). Such guidelines and language should address interoperability standards within and among organisation and product designers to deliver verification and certification (Yenduri et al., 2023).

While issues surrounding the design and guidelines underpinning and governing the Metaverse form integral aspects of any new technology, the health, safety and well-being of users should be given equal consideration. The advent of social media, such as Instagram, has resulted in the promotion of the 'perfect bodies and false projections of 'ideal' physical aesthetics which could be seen as incompatible with physical impairment and disability. This has subsequently resulted in the compromise of some users' psychological and emotional well-being (Tiggemann et al., 2020). Although avatars may enable users to project selected virtual images of self, Zallio and Clarkson (2021) note that the physical, psychological and emotional implications of the social exchanges and interactions occurring within the context of virtual contexts should not be underestimated. This calls for the creation of ethical guidelines and protocols that will monitor interactions, filter or block avatars and scrutinise the ethicality of content generated in the virtual and augmented worlds (Zallio and Clarkson, 2022).

Securing users' physical, emotional and psychological well-being in the Metaverse goes hand in hand with data privacy and legal issues that might emerge because of its use. Data generated in the Metaverse will have to comply with legal mandates such as General Data Protection Regulations. However, these interactions will be subject to additional complexity particularly in the case of users with disability. Othman et al. (2024) note that privacy issues could emerge as users with disabilities are likely to be more reliant on assistive technologies and the utilisation of avatars in professional and social interactions which might result in discrimination and exclusion. The review and update of current legal and regulatory frameworks that govern the use of technology will have to be overhauled to take into account the intricacies and nuances presented by the Metaverse. This could become challenging within a decentralised and democratised context like the one proposed by the Foundation Web 3.0 where processes initiated and conducted within different Metaverses have to be dictated by uniform regulation focussed on equal opportunities, equity and diversity (Zallio & Clarkson, 2022).

Equity and the provision of equal opportunities in the context of Metaverse will have to be given particular consideration in relation to users with disability. These users could be adversely affected by financial and economic costs of acquiring resources or devices, which further hinders their engagement and participation in the digital technological world (Botelho, 2021). Moreover, training and frameworks should not be restricted to faculty members and web developers but empower higher education students with disabilities to develop lifelong learning skills which will not be restricted to academic requirements but incorporate problem-solving skills that will be applied to their future employment (Tondeur et al., 2023).

CONCLUSION

Meta-preneurship education has the potential to transform traditional educational approaches and equip learners with entrepreneurial skills in an era defined by immersive technologies and digital innovation. This chapter highlighted how established frameworks such as Universal Design for Learning (UDL) and Universal Design for Instruction (UDI) could be utilized within the new educational contexts emerging, to support diverse learners (Burstahler et al., 2020; Wilkens et al., 2021). These frameworks emphasize multimodal access, flexible resources, and personalized learning experiences, all of which could work in tandem with the opportunities afforded by the Metaverse.

The integration of Metaverse technologies fosters creativity, adaptability, and entrepreneurial competencies by providing immersive environments where students can experiment with real-world challenges in risk-free contexts (Altinay et al., 2024; Yenduri et al., 2023). Furthermore, these technologies promote cross-cultural collaboration, global networking, and the creation of entrepreneurial ecosystems, expanding the traditional boundaries of education. However, this evolution is accompanied by challenges, including issues of accessibility, interoperability, and digital equity (Zallio & Clarkson, 2022). The process of inclusion will be ongoing, as Metaverse evolves, and requires the adoption of sensitive and context-specific approaches to the design and implementation of services. These eschew 'one size-fit all' solutions and take into account the requirements and feedback of users.

Ethical considerations, such as data privacy, the fostering of psychological well-being, and the regulation of user interactions, require urgent attention. As avatars and virtual identities become central to these platforms, safeguarding the emotional and social experiences of users with disabilities should be prioritized and form the basis of ethical and legal protocols (Tiggemann et al., 2020; Othman et al., 2024).

Collaborative efforts among educators, technologists, and policymakers will be essential to develop and apply relevant and situated ethical regulations that govern Metaverse applications in education.

To fulfil its promise, Meta-preneurship education must embrace adaptability and innovation while ensuring equitable access to tools, platforms, and resources. Higher education institutions have a critical role in bridging the digital divide by equipping educators and learners with the knowledge and competencies needed to navigate the new digital field (Gilligan, 2020; Tondeur et al., 2023). By doing so, they will contribute to entrepreneurial ecosystems that promote communitarian values and foster sustainability, inclusivity, and creativity on a global scale.

REFERENCES

Ahmad, S. Z. (2013). The need for inclusion of entrepreneurship education in Malaysia lower and higher learning institutions. *Education + Training, 55*(2), 191–203. DOI: 10.1108/00400911311304823

Ajzen, I. (1991). The Theory of planned behavior. *Organizational Behavior and Human Decision Processes, 50*(2), 179–211. DOI: 10.1016/0749-5978(91)90020-T

Akman, E., & Çakır, R. (2023). The effect of educational virtual reality game on primary school students' achievement and engagement in mathematics. *Interactive Learning Environments, 31*(3), 1467–1484. DOI: 10.1080/10494820.2020.1841800

Al-Ansi, A. M., Jaboob, M., Garad, A., & Al-Ansi, A. (2023). Analyzing augmented reality (AR) and virtual reality (VR) recent development in education. *Social Sciences & Humanities Open, 8*(1), 100532. DOI: 10.1016/j.ssaho.2023.100532

Altinay, F., Tlili, A., Altinay, Z., Dagli, G., Adedoyin, O. B., Huang, R., Xu, L., Jemni, M., Mogavi, R. H., & Metwally, A. H. S. (2024). *Meta-In or Meta-Out of Students with Special Needs: A Systematic Review on the Use of Metaverse in Special Education*. DOI: 10.1007/978-981-97-1298-4_7

Amani, D., Ismail, I. J., Makona, A., Changalima, I. A., & Kazungu, I. (2024). Extending the mediation role of entrepreneurial self-efficacy on enhancing students' entrepreneurial intentions: A moderated mediation model. *International Journal of Management Education, 22*(1), 100915. Advance online publication. DOI: 10.1016/j.ijme.2023.100915

Ananian, S., & Dellaferrera, G. (2024). *A study on the employment and wage outcomes of people with disabilities*. ILO Working Paper.

Anderson, T., & Rivera Vargas, P. (2020). A critical look at educational technology from a distance education perspective. *Digital Education Review, 2020*(37), 208–229. DOI: 10.1344/der.2020.37.208-229

Bacca, J., Baldiris, S., Fabregat, R., & Graf, S. (2014). Augmented Reality Trends in Education: A Systematic Review of Research and Applications. *Journal of Educational Technology & Society, 17*(4).

Bacca Acosta, J. L., Baldiris Navarro, S. M., Fabregat Gesa, R., & Graf, S. (2014). Augmented reality trends in education: A systematic review of research and applications. *Journal of Educational Technology and Society, 17*(4), 133–149.

Bailey, J. O., & Bailenson, J. N. (2017). Considering virtual reality in children's lives. *Journal of Children and Media, 11*(1), 107–113. DOI: 10.1080/17482798.2016.1268779

Bell, R., & Cui, J. (2023). Addressing progressive educational reforms: Fusing acquisition approaches and participation in Chinese entrepreneurship education. *International Journal of Management Education, 21*(1), 100748. DOI: 10.1016/j.ijme.2022.100748

Bong, W. K., & Chen, W. (2024). Increasing faculty's competence in digital accessibility for inclusive education: A systematic literature review. *International Journal of Inclusive Education, 28*(2), 197–213. DOI: 10.1080/13603116.2021.1937344

Botelho, F. H. F. (2021). Accessibility to digital technology: Virtual barriers, real opportunities. *Assistive Technology, 33*(sup1), 27–34.

Bouchard, S., Côté, S., St-Jacques, J., Robillard, G., & Renaud, P. (2006). Effectiveness of virtual reality exposure in the treatment of arachnophobia using 3D games. *Technology and Health Care, 14*(1), 19–27. DOI: 10.3233/THC-2006-14103 PMID: 16556961

Bouncken, R. B., & Kraus, S. (2022). Entrepreneurial ecosystems in an interconnected world: Emergence, governance and digitalization. *Review of Managerial Science, 16*(1), 1–14. DOI: 10.1007/s11846-021-00444-1

Burgstahler, S., David, M. E., & Amey, M. J. (2020). Universal design for learning. In *The SAGE encyclopedia of higher education* (Vol. 4, pp. 1621–1622). SAGE Publications. DOI: 10.4135/9781529714395.n609

Calandra, D., Oppioli, M., Sadraei, R., Jafari-Sadeghi, V., & Biancone, P. Pietro. (2023). Metaverse meets digital entrepreneurship: a practitioner-based qualitative synthesis. *International Journal of Entrepreneurial Behavior & Research.*

Carruth, D. W. (2017). Virtual reality for education and workforce training. *2017 15th International Conference on Emerging ELearning Technologies and Applications (ICETA)*, 1–6.

Centre for Applied Special Technology (CAST). (2024). *About universal design for learning*. Retrieved from https://www.cast.org/impact/universal-design-for-learning-udl

Chen, Z., Wu, J., Gan, W., & Qi, Z. (2022). Metaverse security and privacy: An overview. *2022 IEEE International Conference on Big Data (Big Data)*, 2950–2959. DOI: 10.1109/BigData55660.2022.10021112

Dakung, R. J., Orobia, L., Munene, J. C., & Balunywa, W. (2017). The role of entrepreneurship education in shaping entrepreneurial action of disabled students in Nigeria. *Journal of Small Business and Entrepreneurship, 29*(4), 293–311. DOI: 10.1080/08276331.2017.1312217

De Carvalho, C. V. (2013). Improving experiential learning with haptic experimentation. *International Journal of Online Engineering, 9*(S8), 7–9. DOI: 10.3991/ijoe.v9iS8.3309

Deitrick, E., Shapiro, R. B., Ahrens, M. P., Fiebrink, R., Lehrman, P. D., & Farooq, S. (2015). Using distributed cognition theory to analyze collaborative computer science learning. *Proceedings of the Eleventh Annual International Conference on International Computing Education Research*, 51–60. DOI: 10.1145/2787622.2787715

Dinmore, S., & Stokes, J. (2015). Creating inclusive university curriculum: Implementing universal design for learning in an enabling program. *Widening Participation and Lifelong Learning : the Journal of the Institute for Access Studies and the European Access Network, 17*(4), 4–19. DOI: 10.5456/WPLL.17.4.4

Donnelly, M., & Evans, C. (2019). A 'home-international' comparative analysis of widening participation in UK higher education. *Higher Education, 77*(1), 97–114. DOI: 10.1007/s10734-018-0260-3

Dudley, J., Yin, L., Garaj, V., & Kristensson, P. O. (2023). Inclusive Immersion: A review of efforts to improve accessibility in virtual reality, augmented reality and the metaverse. *Virtual Reality (Waltham Cross), 27*(4), 2989–3020. DOI: 10.1007/s10055-023-00850-8

Duncan, I., Miller, A., & Jiang, S. (2012). A taxonomy of virtual worlds usage in education. *British Journal of Educational Technology*, *43*(6), 949–964. DOI: 10.1111/j.1467-8535.2011.01263.x

Dwivedi, Y. K., Hughes, L., Baabdullah, A. M., Ribeiro-Navarrete, S., Giannakis, M., Al-Debei, M. M., Dennehy, D., Metri, B., Buhalis, D., Cheung, C. M. K., Conboy, K., Doyle, R., Dubey, R., Dutot, V., Felix, R., Goyal, D. P., Gustafsson, A., Hinsch, C., Jebabli, I., & Wamba, S. F. (2022). Metaverse beyond the hype: Multidisciplinary perspectives on emerging challenges, opportunities, and agenda for research, practice and policy. *International Journal of Information Management*, *66*, 102542. DOI: 10.1016/j.ijinfomgt.2022.102542

European Commission. (2019). *European Accessibility Act.* Retrieved from https://eur-lex.europa.eu/legal-content/EN/TXT/?uri=CELEX%3A32019L0882

European eCompetence Framework. (n.d.). Retrieved from https://www.ecompetences.eu/

Farhangmehr, M., Gonçalves, P., & Sarmento, M. (2016). Predicting entrepreneurial motivation among university students: The role of entrepreneurship education. *Education + Training*, *58*(7/8), 861–881. DOI: 10.1108/ET-01-2016-0019

Farshid, M., Paschen, J., Eriksson, T., & Kietzmann, J. (2018). Go boldly!: Explore augmented reality (AR), virtual reality (VR), and mixed reality (MR) for business. *Business Horizons*, *61*(5), 657–663. DOI: 10.1016/j.bushor.2018.05.009

Gandasegui, V. D. (2013). Entornos virtuales para el desarrollo de la educación inclusiva: Una mirada hacia el futuro desde el pasado de Second Life. *RELATEC: Revista Latinoamericana de Tecnología Educativa*, *12*(2), 67–77.

García, P. O., & Capitán, Á. J. O. (2021). Entrepreneurship for people with disabilities: From skills to social value. *Frontiers in Psychology*, *12*, 699833. DOI: 10.3389/fpsyg.2021.699833 PMID: 34305761

García, P. O., & Capitán, Á. O. (2019). The uniqueness of entrepreneurship of persons with disabilities in Spain. *Suma de Negocios, 10*(SPE22), 1–8.

Garcia, S., Kauer, R., Laesker, D., Nguyen, J., & Andujar, M. (2019). A virtual reality experience for learning languages. *Extended Abstracts of the 2019 CHI Conference on Human Factors in Computing Systems*, 1–4.

Georgiou, Y., Tsivitanidou, O., & Ioannou, A. (2021). Learning experience design with immersive virtual reality in physics education. *Educational Technology Research and Development*, *69*(6), 3051–3080. DOI: 10.1007/s11423-021-10055-y

Gilligan, J. (2020). Competencies for educators in delivering digital accessibility in higher education. *Universal Access in Human-Computer Interaction. Applications and Practice: 14th International Conference, UAHCI 2020, Held as Part of the 22nd HCI International Conference, HCII 2020, Copenhagen, Denmark, July 19–24, 2020Proceedings*, *22*(Part II), 184–199.

Global Entrepreneurship Monitor. (2024). *GEM 2023/2024 Global Report 25 Years and Growing*. Author.

Goldin-Meadow, S. (2005). *Hearing gesture: How our hands help us think.* Harvard University Press. DOI: 10.2307/j.ctv1w9m9ds

Gouskova, E. (2020). Why self-employment rates are higher among people with work limitations. *Journal of Disability Policy Studies*, *31*(1), 15–25. DOI: 10.1177/1044207319851244

Han, E., & Bailenson, J. N. (2024). Lessons for/in virtual classrooms: designing a model for classrooms inside virtual reality. In *Communication Education* (Vol. 73, Issue 2, pp. 234–243). Routledge. DOI: 10.1080/03634523.2024.2312879

Heater, C. (1992). Being there: The subjective experience of presence. *Presence (Cambridge, Mass.)*, *1*(2), 262–271. DOI: 10.1162/pres.1992.1.2.262

Hoang, G., Le, T. T. T., Tran, A. K. T., & Du, T. (2020). Entrepreneurship education and entrepreneurial intentions of university students in Vietnam: The mediating roles of self-efficacy and learning orientation. *Education + Training*, *63*(1), 115–133. DOI: 10.1108/ET-05-2020-0142

Hollan, J., Hutchins, E., & Kirsh, D. (2009). Distributed Cognition: Toward a New Foundation for Human-Computer Interaction Research, 2000. *ACM Transactions on Computer-Human Interaction*, *7*(2), 175.

Hsieh, Y.-J., & Wu, Y. J. (2019). Entrepreneurship through the platform strategy in the digital era: Insights and research opportunities. *Computers in Human Behavior*, *95*, 315–323. DOI: 10.1016/j.chb.2018.03.033

Hutchins, E. (1995). How a cockpit remembers its speeds. *Cognitive Science*, *19*(3), 265–288. DOI: 10.1207/s15516709cog1903_1

Hutchins, E. (2020). The distributed cognition perspective on human interaction. In *Roots of human sociality* (pp. 375–398). Routledge. DOI: 10.4324/9781003135517-19

Ibáñez, M.-B., & Delgado-Kloos, C. (2018). Augmented reality for STEM learning: A systematic review. *Computers & Education*, *123*, 109–123. DOI: 10.1016/j.compedu.2018.05.002

Ismail, I. J. (2022). My intentions, my choice! How does lecturers' competency influence entrepreneurial intention among undergraduate university students in Tanzania? *Cogent Education*, *9*(1), 2151237. DOI: 10.1080/2331186X.2022.2151237

Jena, R. K. (2020). Measuring the impact of business management Student's attitude towards entrepreneurship education on entrepreneurial intention: A case study. *Computers in Human Behavior*, *107*, 106275. DOI: 10.1016/j.chb.2020.106275

Jeong, H. (2019). Rethinking Open Universities: What makes them unique? *International Review of Research in Open and Distance Learning*, *20*(4), 152–166. DOI: 10.19173/irrodl.v20i4.4163

Johnston, E., Olivas, G., Steele, P., Smith, C., & Bailey, L. (2018). Exploring pedagogical foundations of existing virtual reality educational applications: A content analysis study. *Journal of Educational Technology Systems*, *46*(4), 414–439. DOI: 10.1177/0047239517745560

Jordan, K. (2014). Initial trends in enrolment and completion of massive open online courses. *International Review of Research in Open and Distance Learning*, *15*(1), 133–160. DOI: 10.19173/irrodl.v15i1.1651

Kalantari, S., Rounds, J. D., Kan, J., Tripathi, V., & Cruz-Garza, J. G. (2021). Comparing physiological responses during cognitive tests in virtual environments vs. in identical real-world environments. *Scientific Reports*, *11*(1), 10227. DOI: 10.1038/s41598-021-89297-y PMID: 33986337

Kanematsu, H., Fukumura, Y., Barry, D. M., Sohn, S. Y., & Taguchi, R. (2010). Multilingual discussion in metaverse among students from the USA, Korea and Japan. *Knowledge-Based and Intelligent Information and Engineering Systems: 14th International Conference, KES 2010, Cardiff, UK, September 8-10, 2010Proceedings, 14*(Part IV), 200–209.

Kim, T., Planey, J., & Lindgren, R. (2023). Theory-Driven Design in Metaverse Virtual Reality Learning Environments: Two Illustrative Cases. *IEEE Transactions on Learning Technologies, 16*(6), 1141–1153. DOI: 10.1109/TLT.2023.3307211

Kirsh, D. (2013). Embodied cognition and the magical future of interaction design. *ACM Transactions on Computer-Human Interaction, 20*(1), 1–30. DOI: 10.1145/2442106.2442109

Kolb, D. A. (2014). *Experiential learning: Experience as the source of learning and development.* FT Press.

Kraus, S., Kanbach, D. K., Krysta, P. M., Steinhoff, M. M., & Tomini, N. (2022). Facebook and the creation of the metaverse: Radical business model innovation or incremental transformation? *International Journal of Entrepreneurial Behaviour & Research, 28*(9), 52–77. DOI: 10.1108/IJEBR-12-2021-0984

Kwon, C. (2019). Verification of the possibility and effectiveness of experiential learning using HMD-based immersive VR technologies. *Virtual Reality (Waltham Cross), 23*(1), 101–118. DOI: 10.1007/s10055-018-0364-1

LeGary, R. A.Jr, & LaRocco, D. J. (2022). Job-embedded professional learning: Facilitating faculty implementation of UDL. *New Directions for Teaching and Learning, 2022*(172), 93–103. DOI: 10.1002/tl.20521

Lehikko, A. (2021). Measuring self-efficacy in immersive virtual learning environments: A systematic literature review. *Journal of Interactive Learning Research, 32*(2), 125–146.

Lin, H., Wan, S., Gan, W., Chen, J., & Chao, H.-C. (2022). *Metaverse in Education: Vision, Opportunities, and Challenges.* DOI: 10.1109/BigData55660.2022.10021004

Maheshwari, G., & Kha, K. L. (2022). Investigating the relationship between educational support and entrepreneurial intention in Vietnam: The mediating role of entrepreneurial self-efficacy in the theory of planned behavior. *International Journal of Management Education, 20*(2), 100553. DOI: 10.1016/j.ijme.2021.100553

Markowitz, D. M., Laha, R., Perone, B. P., Pea, R. D., & Bailenson, J. N. (2018). Immersive virtual reality field trips facilitate learning about climate change. *Frontiers in Psychology, 9*, 2364. DOI: 10.3389/fpsyg.2018.02364 PMID: 30555387

Martín-Gutiérrez, J., Fabiani, P., Benesova, W., Meneses, M. D., & Mora, C. E. (2015). Augmented reality to promote collaborative and autonomous learning in higher education. *Computers in Human Behavior, 51*, 752–761. DOI: 10.1016/j.chb.2014.11.093

Maunze, O. R., Abratt, R., & Mingione, M. (2020). Impact of internal branding on student engagement: Insights from a South African University. *Services Marketing Quarterly, 41*(2), 124–144. DOI: 10.1080/15332969.2020.1742979

McVeigh-Schultz, J., & Isbister, K. (2022). A "beyond being there" for VR meetings: Envisioning the future of remote work. *Human-Computer Interaction, 37*(5), 433–453. DOI: 10.1080/07370024.2021.1994860

Merry, K. L. (2024). *Delivering inclusive and impactful instruction: Universal design for learning in higher education* (1st ed.). CAST Professional Publishing.

Milgram, P., & Kishino, F. (1994). A taxonomy of mixed reality visual displays. *IEICE Transactions on Information and Systems, 77*(12), 1321–1329.

Milgram, P., Takemura, H., Utsumi, A., & Kishino, F. (1995). Augmented reality: A class of displays on the reality-virtuality continuum. *Telemanipulator and Telepresence Technologies, 2351*, 282–292. DOI: 10.1117/12.197321

Miotto, G., Del-Castillo-Feito, C., & Blanco-González, A. (2020). Reputation and legitimacy: Key factors for Higher Education Institutions' sustained competitive advantage. *Journal of Business Research, 112*, 342–353. DOI: 10.1016/j.jbusres.2019.11.076

Mishra, S. (2017). Open educational resources: Removing barriers from within. *Distance Education, 38*(3), 369–380. DOI: 10.1080/01587919.2017.1369350

Mohan, V. (2019). On the use of blockchain-based mechanisms to tackle academic misconduct. *Research Policy, 48*(9), 103805. DOI: 10.1016/j.respol.2019.103805

Morfaki, C. (2025). From Passion to Success: A Journey Through the Emotional Landscape of Entrepreneurial (He) arts. In *Real-World Tools and Scenarios for Entrepreneurship Exploration* (pp. 169–202). IGI Global.

Muldoon, J., Liguori, E. W., Solomon, S., & Bendickson, J. (2023). Technological Innovation and the expansion of Entrepreneurship Ecosystems. *Review of Managerial Science, 17*(5), 1789–1808. DOI: 10.1007/s11846-022-00573-1

Mystakidis, S. (2022). Metaverse. *Encyclopedia, 2*(1), 486–497. DOI: 10.3390/encyclopedia2010031

Mystakidis, S., Papantzikos, G., & Stylios, C. (2021). Virtual reality escape rooms for STEM education in industry 4.0: Greek teachers perspectives. *2021 6th South-East Europe Design Automation, Computer Engineering,Computer Networks and Social Media Conference (SEEDA-CECNSM)*, 1–5.

Naidoo, R. (2016). The competition fetish in higher education: Varieties, animators and consequences. *British Journal of Sociology of Education, 37*(1), 1–10. DOI: 10.1080/01425692.2015.1116209

Nathan, M. J., & Martinez, C. V. J. (2015). Gesture as model enactment: The role of gesture in mental model construction and inference making when learning from text. *Learning: Research and Practice, 1*(1), 4–37. DOI: 10.1080/23735082.2015.1006758

Naudin, A., & Agusita, E. (2021). Rethinking Cultural and Creative Entrepreneurship Education. *European Conference on Innovation and Entrepreneurship.*

Neneh, B. N. (2022). Entrepreneurial passion and entrepreneurial intention: The role of social support and entrepreneurial self-efficacy. *Studies in Higher Education, 47*(3), 587–603. DOI: 10.1080/03075079.2020.1770716

Norwich, B. (2014). Recognising value tensions that underlie problems in inclusive education. *Cambridge Journal of Education*, *44*(4), 495–510. DOI: 10.1080/0305764X.2014.963027

Nzilano, K. L., Tundui, H. P., & Ndyetabula, D. W. (2022). Perceived university support and technical graduates' intentions to venture into business start-ups in Tanzania: Does institutional support matter? *Journal of Global Entrepreneurship Research*, *12*(1), 465–477. DOI: 10.1007/s40497-022-00334-0

OECD. (2023). *Managing Shocks and Transitions. Future-Proofing SME and Entrepreneurship Policies.* https://www.oecd.org/cfe/smes/key-issues-paper-oecd-sme-and-entrepreneurship-ministerial-meeting-2023.pdf

Othman, A., Chemnad, K., Hassanien, A. E., Tlili, A., Zhang, C. Y., Al-Thani, D., Altınay, F., Chalghoumi, H. S., Al-Khalifa, H., & Obeid, M. (2024). Accessible Metaverse: A Theoretical Framework for Accessibility and Inclusion in the Metaverse. *Multimodal Technologies and Interaction*, *8*(3), 21. DOI: 10.3390/mti8030021

Parong, J., & Mayer, R. E. (2021). Cognitive and affective processes for learning science in immersive virtual reality. *Journal of Computer Assisted Learning*, *37*(1), 226–241. DOI: 10.1111/jcal.12482

Patrício, L. D., & Ferreira, J. J. (2024). Unlocking the connection between education, entrepreneurial mindset, and social values in entrepreneurial activity development. *Review of Managerial Science*, *18*(4), 991–1013. DOI: 10.1007/s11846-023-00629-w

Pellas, N., Mystakidis, S., & Kazanidis, I. (2021). Immersive Virtual Reality in K-12 and Higher Education: A systematic review of the last decade scientific literature. *Virtual Reality (Waltham Cross)*, *25*(3), 835–861. DOI: 10.1007/s10055-020-00489-9

Piaget, J. (1952). *The origins of intelligence in children*. International University. DOI: 10.1037/11494-000

Price, S., Yiannoutsou, N., & Vezzoli, Y. (2020). Making the body tangible: Elementary geometry learning through VR. *Digital Experiences in Mathematics Education*, *6*(2), 213–232. DOI: 10.1007/s40751-020-00071-7

Qiu, Y., Isusi-Fagoaga, R., & García-Aracil, A. (2023). Perceptions and use of metaverse in higher education: A descriptive study in China and Spain. *Computers and Education: Artificial Intelligence*, *5*, 100185. Advance online publication. DOI: 10.1016/j.caeai.2023.100185

Quality Assurance Agency for Higher Education. (2018). *Enterprise and entrepreneurship education: Guidance for UK higher education providers.* Retrieved from https://www.qaa.ac.uk/the-quality-code/enterprise-and-entrepreneurship-education

Roth, W.-M. (2001). Gestures: Their role in teaching and learning. *Review of Educational Research*, *71*(3), 365–392. DOI: 10.3102/00346543071003365

Sarkar, P., Kadam, K., & Pillai, J. S. (2020). Learners' approaches, motivation and patterns of problem-solving on lines and angles in geometry using augmented reality. *Smart Learning Environments*, *7*(1), 1–23. DOI: 10.1186/s40561-020-00124-9

Schwaiger, M., Krajnčan, M., Vukovič, M., Jenko, M., & Doz, D. (2024). Educators' opinions about VR/AR/XR: An exploratory study. *Education and Information Technologies*, *29*(18), 24861–24880. Advance online publication. DOI: 10.1007/s10639-024-12808-7

Setiawan, J. L. (2014). Examining entrepreneurial self-efficacy among students. *Procedia: Social and Behavioral Sciences*, *115*, 235–242. DOI: 10.1016/j.sbspro.2014.02.431

Sin, Z. P. T., Zhao, I. D., Wu, A. C. H., Li, R. C., Ng, P. H. F., Huang, X., Baciu, G., Cao, J., & Li, Q. (2023). Towards a Metaverse of Knowledge: A Constructivist Proposition on Immersive Learning and Visual Literacy. *Lecture Notes in Computer Science (Including Subseries Lecture Notes in Artificial Intelligence and Lecture Notes in Bioinformatics), 13869 LNCS*, 214–225. DOI: 10.1007/978-3-031-33023-0_19

Slater, M., & Wilbur, S. (1997). A framework for immersive virtual environments (FIVE): Speculations on the role of presence in virtual environments. *Presence (Cambridge, Mass.)*, *6*(6), 603–616. DOI: 10.1162/pres.1997.6.6.603

Speicher, M., Hall, B. D., & Nebeling, M. (2019, May 2). What is mixed reality? *Conference on Human Factors in Computing Systems - Proceedings*. DOI: 10.1145/3290605.3300767

Stam, E. (2015). Entrepreneurial ecosystems and regional policy: A sympathetic critique. *European Planning Studies*, *23*(9), 1759–1769. DOI: 10.1080/09654313.2015.1061484

Stieff, M., Lira, M. E., & Scopelitis, S. A. (2016). Gesture supports spatial thinking in STEM. *Cognition and Instruction*, *34*(2), 80–99. DOI: 10.1080/07370008.2016.1145122

Stöhr, C., Demazière, C., & Adawi, T. (2020). The polarizing effect of the online flipped classroom. *Computers & Education*, *147*, 103789. DOI: 10.1016/j.compedu.2019.103789

Stoiber, K., Matzler, K., & Hautz, J. (2023). Ambidextrous structures paving the way for disruptive business models: A conceptual framework. *Review of Managerial Science*, *17*(4), 1439–1485. DOI: 10.1007/s11846-022-00589-7

Sun, J., Gan, W., Chen, Z., Li, J., & Yu, P. S. (2022). Big data meets metaverse: A survey. *ArXiv Preprint ArXiv:2210.16282*.

Sweet, K. S., LeBlanc, J. K., Stough, L. M., & Sweany, N. W. (2020). Community building and knowledge sharing by individuals with disabilities using social media. *Journal of Computer Assisted Learning*, *36*(1), 1–11. DOI: 10.1111/jcal.12377

Tiggemann, M., Anderberg, I., & Brown, Z. (2020). # Loveyourbody: The effect of body positive Instagram captions on women's body image. *Body Image*, *33*, 129–136. DOI: 10.1016/j.bodyim.2020.02.015 PMID: 32151992

Timu , N., Bartlett, M. E., Bartlett, J. E., Ehrlich, S., & Babutsidze, Z. (2024). Fostering inclusive higher education through universal design for learning and inclusive pedagogy–EU and US faculty perceptions. *Higher Education Research & Development*, *43*(2), 473–487. DOI: 10.1080/07294360.2023.2234314

Tondeur, J., Howard, S., Van Zanten, M., Gorissen, P., Van der Neut, I., Uerz, D., & Kral, M. (2023). The HeDiCom framework: Higher Education teachers' digital competencies for the future. *Educational Technology Research and Development, 71*(1), 33–53. DOI: 10.1007/s11423-023-10193-5 PMID: 37016717

Uddin, M., Chowdhury, R. A., Hoque, N., Ahmad, A., Mamun, A., & Uddin, M. N. (2022). Developing entrepreneurial intentions among business graduates of higher educational institutions through entrepreneurship education and entrepreneurial passion: A moderated mediation model. *International Journal of Management Education, 20*(2), 100647. DOI: 10.1016/j.ijme.2022.100647

UNESCO. (2018). *ICT competency framework for teachers (version 3).* Retrieved from https://unesdoc.unesco.org/ark:/48223/pf0000213475

United Nations. (2006). *Convention on the rights of persons with disabilities.* General Assembly of the United Nations. Retrieved from https://www.un.org/development/desa/disabilities/convention-on-the-rights-of-persons-with-disabilities.html#Fulltext

United Nations Department of Economic and Social Affairs. (n.d.). *Disability factsheet on persons with disabilities.* Retrieved from https://www.un.org/development/desa/disabilities/resources/factsheet-on-persons-with-disabilities.html#:~:text=Disability%20rates%20are%20significantly%20higher,cent%20among%20the%20better%20educated

Van Dijk, J., Van Der Lugt, R., & Hummels, C. (2014). Beyond distributed representation: embodied cognition design supporting socio-sensorimotor couplings. *Proceedings of the 8th International Conference on Tangible, Embedded and Embodied Interaction*, 181–188. DOI: 10.1145/2540930.2540934

Wardana, L. W., Narmaditya, B. S., Wibowo, A., Mahendra, A. M., Wibowo, N. A., Harwida, G., & Rohman, A. N. (2020). The impact of entrepreneurship education and students' entrepreneurial mindset: The mediating role of attitude and self-efficacy. *Heliyon, 6*(9), e04922. DOI: 10.1016/j.heliyon.2020.e04922 PMID: 32995616

Web Accessibility Initiative (WAI). (n.d.). *Curricula.* Retrieved from https://www.w3.org/WAI/curricula/

Wenger, E., McDermott, R., & Snyder, W. M. (2002). Seven principles for cultivating communities of practice. *Cultivating Communities of Practice: A Guide to Managing Knowledge, 4*, 1–19.

Wilkens, L., Haage, A., Lüttmann, F., & Bühler, C. R. (2021). Digital teaching, inclusion and students' needs: Student perspectives on participation and access in higher education. *Social Inclusion (Lisboa), 9*(3), 117–129. DOI: 10.17645/si.v9i3.4125

World Wide Web Consortium. (2024). *Web Content Accessibility Guidelines (WCAG) 2.1.* Retrieved from https://www.w3.org/TR/WCAG21/

Yenduri, G., Kaluri, R., Rajput, D. S., Lakshmanna, K., Gadekallu, T. R., Mahmud, M., & Brown, D. J. (2023). From Assistive Technologies to Metaverse - Technologies in Inclusive Higher Education for Students with Specific Learning Difficulties: A Review. *IEEE Access : Practical Innovations, Open Solutions, 11*, 64907–64927. DOI: 10.1109/ACCESS.2023.3289496

Zallio, M., & Clarkson, P. J. (2022). Designing the metaverse: A study on inclusion, diversity, equity, accessibility and safety for digital immersive environments. *Telematics and Informatics*, *75*, 101909. DOI: 10.1016/j.tele.2022.101909

Chapter 20
The Effect of Simulation Games in Entrepreneurship Education

Elena Polydorou
https://orcid.org/0009-0001-7490-5983
Neapolis University, Pafos, Cyprus

ABSTRACT

Given the emphasis on innovation, adaptability, and an entrepreneurial attitude brought about by global economic transformations, entrepreneurship education has become an essential part of modern educational systems. The significance of developing entrepreneurial competencies that go beyond theoretical knowledge has been increasingly recognized by training organizations and higher education institutions in recent decades. This change emphasizes the value of hands-on training and experience learning. The need for effective pedagogical techniques in entrepreneurship education has grown as economies shift toward knowledge-based and innovation-focused models. Because they offer dynamic, interactive, and immersive learning environments that go against traditional pedagogical approaches, simulation games are becoming more and more acknowledged as a potentially successful educational strategy.

1. INTRODUCTION: THE EFFECT OF SIMULATION GAMES IN ENTREPRENEURSHIP EDUCATION

Entrepreneurship education has emerged as a critical component of contemporary educational frameworks, especially in light of global economic transformations that emphasize innovation, adaptability, and entrepreneurial mindset. In recent decades, higher education institutions and training organizations have progressively acknowledged the importance of cultivating entrepreneurial competencies that extend beyond mere theoretical knowledge. This shift underscores the significance of experiential learning and practical application (Fayolle & Gailly, 2008). As economies transition towards knowledge-based and innovation-focused models, the necessity for effective pedagogical approaches in entrepreneurship education has become increasingly pronounced. Simulation games have increasingly been recognized as a potentially effective approach to education, providing dynamic, interactive, and immersive learning environments that challenge conventional pedagogical methods (Kraus et al, 2020). This chapter con-

DOI: 10.4018/979-8-3693-9040-5.ch020

ducts a critical analysis of the role of simulation games within the context of entrepreneurship education, investigating their efficacy, implications, and inherent limitations.

Entrepreneurship education holds a distinct role within the context of higher education and professional development, with the objective of reconciling theoretical understanding with practical implementation. In contrast to other academic disciplines, entrepreneurship is predominantly grounded in experiential and situational learning, as the achievement of entrepreneurial endeavors is significantly influenced by an individual's capacity to manage uncertainty, make swift decisions, and creatively address unforeseen challenges (Neck & Greene, 2011). Conventional pedagogical frameworks, which predominantly rely on lectures and case studies, frequently fall short in equipping students to navigate the dynamic and uncertain landscape of entrepreneurial ecosystems (Pittaway & Cope, 2007). This shortcoming has prompted educators to explore alternative instructional methodologies, resulting in the integration of tools such as simulation games that are congruent with experiential learning theories.

Simulation games are congruent with constructivist learning principles, which prioritize the active construction of knowledge through experiential learning and social interaction. Kolb's experiential learning cycle provides a robust theoretical framework for incorporating simulation games into the entrepreneurship curriculum, as it asserts that learning is a dynamic process encompassing concrete experiences, reflective observation, abstract conceptualization, and active experimentation (Kolb, 1984). In contrast to traditional passive learning approaches, simulation games facilitate an experiential learning process where participants engage in "learning by doing." This methodology permits individuals to explore entrepreneurial decision-making within a risk-free context, while also obtaining immediate feedback regarding their actions (Garris, Ahlers, & Driskell, 2002).

Simulation games fundamentally serve to emulate real-world situations, offering learners a range of challenges that necessitate the application of strategic thinking, problem-solving, and decision-making skills. These games can vary in complexity, from basic virtual marketplaces to intricate simulations that encompass entire entrepreneurial ecosystems, which include factors such as market dynamics, competition, resource management, and consumer relations. Participants frequently engage in activities such as establishing virtual enterprises, managing resources, adapting to fluctuations in the market, and competing against either their peers or AI-driven adversaries (Bellotti et al., 2013). The efficacy of simulation games can be attributed to their capacity to engage learners across various cognitive, emotional, and social dimensions. Firstly, these games serve as a platform for active experimentation, enabling students to formulate hypotheses and refine their strategies without incurring real-world repercussions. This process promotes critical thinking and iterative learning, both of which are vital for achieving success in entrepreneurship. Secondly, the competitive and interactive characteristics of simulation games enhance motivation and engagement, which are essential for maintaining learners' interest and facilitating knowledge retention (Garris et al., 2002). Finally, simulation games frequently necessitate teamwork and collaboration, thereby assisting participants in developing the interpersonal and communication skills that are indispensable in entrepreneurial endeavors (Hindle, 2007).

From an educational standpoint, simulation games provide educators with the capability to cater to the varied learning requirements of students. By integrating theoretical concepts with hands-on application, these tools effectively support both analytical and experiential learners. Additionally, simulations facilitate customized learning experiences, enabling educators to adjust game parameters to correspond with particular learning goals or to address specific challenges encountered by students (Bellotti et al., 2013).

An increasing volume of empirical research substantiates the effectiveness of simulation games within the realm of entrepreneurship education. Evidence indicates that students participating in simulation-based learning experiences frequently exhibit enhanced knowledge retention, elevated entrepreneurial intention, and improved self-efficacy in comparison to their peers who are instructed through conventional pedagogical approaches (Pittaway & Cope, 2007). For example, research conducted by Vogel et al. (2006) revealed that learners engaging with simulation games demonstrated a more profound comprehension of intricate concepts, including market dynamics and strategic planning. In a related study, Bellotti et al. (2013) found that students involved in entrepreneurship simulations exhibited enhanced confidence in their capacity to make informed business decisions.

The implementation of simulation games has been associated with the enhancement of non-cognitive skills, including resilience, adaptability, and risk tolerance. These qualities are especially pertinent in the field of entrepreneurship, where individuals frequently encounter failure and uncertainty. By offering a controlled environment for experimentation and learning from mistakes, simulation games promote learners' willingness to take calculated risks, assess the results of their decisions, and refine their strategies—actions that closely resemble actual entrepreneurial practices. (Neck & Greene, 2011).

Despite the myriad advantages associated with simulation games, they are not devoid of limitations. A central critique pertains to their dependence on simplified representations of reality, which may inadequately encompass the intricate dynamics of entrepreneurial ecosystems. Although simulations can effectively replicate certain elements of entrepreneurship, including financial decision-making and market competition, they frequently overlook essential social, cultural, and psychological dimensions that shape entrepreneurial behavior (Pittaway & Cope, 2007). This reductionist approach may result in an overly mechanistic interpretation of entrepreneurship, thereby misrepresenting its inherently multifaceted character. A further challenge pertains to the design and implementation of simulation games in educational contexts. The creation of high-quality simulations necessitates substantial investments of time, expertise, and financial resources, which may be unattainable for numerous educational institutions. Moreover, the efficacy of these tools is largely contingent upon their integration within the broader curriculum. In the absence of appropriate guidance and contextualization, simulation games may become isolated activities that do not align with overarching learning objectives (Bellotti et al., 2013).

Furthermore, students exhibit varying degrees of responsiveness to simulation-based learning experiences. While certain individuals may excel in competitive and interactive settings, others may find themselves feeling overwhelmed or disengaged, especially in the absence of prior experience or confidence in entrepreneurial competencies. This underscores the necessity for inclusive design and adaptive learning strategies that cater to a wide range of learner profiles. (Garris et al., 2002).

The increasing integration of simulation games into entrepreneurship education is indicative of wider trends within the realms of education and technology. Recent advancements in digital platforms and artificial intelligence have enhanced the capacity to develop sophisticated and immersive simulations, allowing educators to design increasingly intricate scenarios. This development is in harmony with the transition towards competency-based education, which prioritizes the cultivation of practical skills and attributes over the mere acquisition of theoretical knowledge (World Economic Forum, 2020). Moreover, the incorporation of simulation games within entrepreneurship education highlights the significance of interdisciplinary methodologies. Successful simulations frequently leverage knowledge from diverse fields such as economics, psychology, computer science, and game design, thereby promoting collaboration among various academic and professional sectors. This interdisciplinary approach not only enhances the educational experience but also equips students to navigate the complex challenges inherent in entrepreneurial endeavors (Fayolle & Gailly, 2008).

In the subsequent chapters, we will further investigate the theoretical underpinnings, practical applications, and empirical research pertaining to the use of simulation games in entrepreneurship education. Through a critical and analytical approach, this inquiry aims to enrich the ongoing dialogue regarding innovative pedagogical strategies within higher education. Simulation games serve as a potent instrument within the dynamic framework of entrepreneurship education. By merging experiential learning with advanced interactive technology, these tools confront essential challenges associated with adequately preparing students for the intricacies of entrepreneurial endeavors. Nevertheless, their effectiveness is contingent upon careful design, implementation, and seamless integration into the overarching curriculum. As this chapter examines, simulation games possess considerable potential to revolutionize entrepreneurship education, promoting not only the acquisition of technical competencies but also fostering the mindsets and behaviors essential for entrepreneurial achievement (Kraus et al, 2020).

2. ENTREPRENEURSHIP EDUCATION

Entrepreneurship education has historically depended on conventional instructional methods, including lectures, case studies, and project-based learning, to prepare students with the competencies and knowledge essential for achieving entrepreneurial success. Nevertheless, as the intricacies of contemporary business landscapes increase, there is a corresponding necessity for innovative pedagogical strategies. Simulation games have become an essential instrument within this domain, grounded in theoretical frameworks that prioritize active learning, experiential engagement, and the cultivation of higher-order cognitive skills. This section explores the theoretical underpinnings of simulation games in the context of entrepreneurship education, with particular emphasis on constructivist learning theories, experiential learning models, and the correspondence of these tools with entrepreneurial competencies (Kraus et al, 2020).

2.1 Constructivist Learning Theories

Constructivism asserts that individuals actively engage in the construction of knowledge through their experiences, reflective practices, and interactions with their surroundings (Piaget, 1950; Vygotsky, 1978). This theoretical framework emphasizes the significance of involving students in experiential and relevant activities that compel them to utilize their knowledge within practical settings. Simulation games are congruent with constructivist principles, as they offer immersive, problem-based learning environments that allow students to experiment with entrepreneurial concepts (Kakouris et al, 2021).

Key principles of constructivism in simulation games:

- Active Engagement: Learners are not merely passive recipients of information; rather, they actively participate in decision-making processes and problem-solving activities. Simulation games necessitate that students confront authentic entrepreneurial challenges, which may include resource management, negotiation, and strategic planning.

- Social Learning: Vygotsky's focus on the social aspects of learning is exemplified in multiplayer or team-based simulations, which facilitate collaboration and subsequently improve educational outcomes.
- Scaffolding and Feedback: Simulation games facilitate continuous feedback mechanisms, allowing learners to enhance their strategic approaches and cultivate a more profound comprehension of the subject matter (Kakouris et al, 2021).

For instance, research conducted by Bellotti et al. (2013) demonstrated that simulation games such as GoVenture Entrepreneur substantially improved students' comprehension of entrepreneurial concepts. This enhancement can be attributed mainly to the games' congruence with constructivist approaches that emphasize active, experiential learning.

2.2 Experiential Learning Models

Experiential Learning Theory (ELT), formulated by Kolb in 1984, represents a fundamental framework within the realm of simulation-based education. This theory posits that learning is a cyclical process that encompasses four distinct stages: concrete experience, reflective observation, abstract conceptualization, and active experimentation. Simulation games effectively embody this cyclical model, offering an interactive platform through which learners can both acquire and apply entrepreneurial knowledge.

- Concrete Experience: Simulations provide learners with immersive engagement in authentic business scenarios, such as initiating a startup or overseeing a virtual enterprise. These experiential learning opportunities enable students to acquire knowledge through active participation.
- Reflective Observation: Participants are prompted to critically assess the results of their decisions, engaging in a reflective process that considers both successes and failures in order to pinpoint opportunities for enhancement.
- Abstract Conceptualization: Reflections yield valuable insights that facilitate the development of novel strategies or conceptual frameworks, which are subsequently evaluated through further gameplay (Kakouris et al, 2021).

Kolb's experiential learning model holds particular significance in the realm of entrepreneurship education, as it closely reflects the iterative nature inherent in entrepreneurial endeavors: recognizing opportunities, testing concepts, and making adjustments informed by feedback. Empirical studies have indicated that engaging in experiential learning through simulations significantly bolsters students' entrepreneurial self-efficacy and their capacity for risk-taking (Neck et al., 2014).

2.3 Active and Experiential Learning in Entrepreneurship

Entrepreneurship education necessitates a comprehensive approach that extends beyond mere theoretical understanding; it involves the development of essential competencies, including critical thinking, opportunity identification, and decision-making in uncertain conditions. Simulation games are particularly effective in meeting these educational requirements, as they promote active learning, a concept articulated by Bonwell and Eison (1991) as instructional strategies that involve students in significant activities that surpass the limitations of passive listening.

Advantages of active learning in simulation:

- Decision-Making in High-Pressure Situations: Simulations frequently necessitate rapid cognitive processing and strategic prioritization, thereby reflecting the complexities and challenges encountered in real-world entrepreneurial contexts.
- Risk Management: Entrepreneurs must evaluate and address potential risks, an essential competency in their skill set.
- Iterative Problem-Solving: Engaging in repeated gameplay enables learners to explore various strategies and gain insights from their errors.

For instance, the CapsimCore Business Simulation offers students a simulated environment in which they can make informed decisions related to marketing, finance, and operations. Research indicates that students engaged in these types of simulations demonstrate enhanced confidence in their ability to apply entrepreneurial principles (Ratten & Jones, 2021).

2.4 Alignment With Entrepreneurial Competencies

Simulation games possess distinct characteristics that facilitate the development of competencies crucial for achieving entrepreneurial success, as delineated in frameworks such as the European Entrepreneurship Competence Framework (EntreComp). Among these key competencies are creativity, financial literacy, and strategic thinking, each of which can be effectively fostered through simulation-based learning methodologies (Zulfiqar et al, 2019).

- Creativity and Innovation: A multitude of simulation games necessitate that players engage in divergent thinking, thereby enhancing their creative problem-solving abilities. For example, games such as Startup Wars compel students to formulate distinctive business models within competitive market environments.
- Opportunity Recognition: Engaging in scenario-based gameplay facilitates the development of learners' competencies in identifying and assessing potential business opportunities. This process is congruent with the entrepreneurial framework, which frequently entails the identification of market inefficiencies.
- Leadership and Teamwork: Multiplayer simulations foster collaborative engagement, providing learners with opportunities to cultivate leadership competencies and refine their communication skills.
- Ethical Decision-Making: Certain simulations incorporate ethical dilemmas that assist students in grappling with the moral intricacies inherent in entrepreneurship. For instance, these scenarios may require individuals to reconcile profit-driven objectives with commitments to social responsibility (Zulfiqar et al, 2019).

2.5 Gamification and Motivation Theories

Simulation games effectively integrate various aspects of gamification, which includes game-based mechanics such as scoring systems, competitive elements, and reward structures. These components are designed to boost motivation and foster greater engagement among players. To better understand the efficacy of gamified learning environments, we can turn to theoretical frameworks like Deci and

Ryan's Self-Determination Theory (SDT), developed in 1985. This theory offers valuable insights into the psychological needs that drive human behavior and suggests that fulfilling these needs can enhance both motivation and learning outcomes. In gamified contexts, the incorporation of challenges, feedback, and clear goals aligns with these intrinsic motivators, making the learning experience not only more enjoyable but also more effective in achieving educational objectives (Jia et al, 2021). By leveraging the principles of SDT, designers of simulation games can create environments that not only capture players' interest but also promote a deeper understanding of the material being taught. Autonomy: Players are granted the ability to make their own choices, which cultivates a deep sense of ownership over their actions and experiences within the game. This freedom to decide not only empowers them but also enhances their intrinsic motivation, driving them to engage more fully and passionately with the gameplay. When individuals feel that they have the authority to steer their own course, they are more likely to invest themselves emotionally and intellectually, leading to a richer and more fulfilling gaming experience (Zulfiqar et al, 2019).

Ultimately, this sense of autonomy is crucial for fostering creativity and encouraging players to explore the various possibilities that the game has to offer. Competence: The inherent challenge of mastering a game, serves as a powerful motivator for learners, encouraging them to persist in their efforts and continually seek improvement in their skills and understanding. This drive to overcome obstacles and achieve a higher level of proficiency not only fosters resilience but also cultivates a sense of accomplishment and self-efficacy. As learners engage with the complexities of the game, they become more invested in the process, recognizing that each setback is an opportunity to learn and grow (Hyams-Ssekasi, et al,2018).

Hence, this journey towards mastery not only enhances their gaming abilities but also instills a lifelong passion for learning and self-improvement in various aspects of their lives. In a study conducted by Hamari et al. (2016), the researchers explored the impact of gamification on student engagement and found compelling evidence that it can boost motivation and academic performance, particularly in high-stakes educational settings such as entrepreneurship courses. The findings suggest that when gamification elements are integrated into educational frameworks, they can create an environment that is not only stimulating but also conducive to learning. This approach taps into the competitive spirit and intrinsic motivation of students, thereby making the learning process more dynamic and effective. As a result, educators are increasingly recognizing the potential of gamification to transform traditional teaching methods and enhance the overall educational experience for students (Hyams-Ssekasi, et al,2018).

2.6 Simulation Games and Bloom's Taxonomy

As we move up the hierarchy, we encounter higher-order skills that demand a greater level of cognitive engagement and complexity. These skills include analyzing, evaluating, and creating. Analyzing requires learners to break down information into its constituent parts, allowing them to identify relationships and patterns. Evaluating goes a step further by asking learners to make judgments based on criteria and standards, fostering critical thinking abilities. Finally, creating represents the pinnacle of cognitive engagement, as it involves synthesizing information and ideas to produce original work or solutions. This progression from lower-order to higher-order skills underscores the importance of a comprehensive approach to education that fosters deeper learning and critical thinking (Anderson et al., 2001).

Simulation games have emerged as an effective pedagogical tool that can adeptly address these various levels of Bloom's Taxonomy. By engaging students in immersive, interactive experiences, simulation games challenge them to apply their knowledge and skills in dynamic environments. This method not only reinforces lower-order skills like remembering and understanding through gameplay mechanics but also promotes higher-order skills such as analyzing complex scenarios, evaluating different strategies, and creating innovative solutions to problems encountered within the game. In this way, simulation games serve as a powerful medium through which educators can facilitate a more holistic approach to learning, encouraging students to develop a well-rounded skill set that prepares them for real-world challenges (Gao et al, 2022).

Bloom's Taxonomy is a well-established framework that educators use to categorize various educational objectives and goals. This framework is structured in a hierarchical manner, which distinguishes between lower-order cognitive skills and higher-order cognitive skills. At the foundational level, we find lower-order skills such as remembering and understanding. These skills are essential as they serve as the building blocks for more complex cognitive processes. Remembering involves the ability to recall information, facts, and concepts, while understanding entails comprehending the meaning of the information and being able to explain it in one's own words (Peterková et al, 2022).

For instance, research conducted by Gentry et al. (2010) underscores the effectiveness of simulations in enhancing critical thinking and problem-solving abilities among learners. These skills are crucial for reaching the upper tiers of Bloom's taxonomy, which emphasizes the importance of higher-order cognitive processes in education. By participating in such simulations, individuals are not only able to apply what they have learned but also to synthesize new ideas and evaluate the effectiveness of different approaches in a dynamic environment. This process significantly contributes to their overall cognitive development and prepares them for real-world challenges (Gao et al, 2022).

2.7 Critiques and Challenges

Although the theoretical foundations of simulation games are strong, challenges remain. Critics claim that: Moreover, the financial burden and technical intricacy associated with implementing advanced simulation technologies can pose significant barriers to their widespread adoption. This is particularly true for institutions that operate with limited funding, where the resources required to acquire, maintain, and effectively utilize these sophisticated simulation tools may be out of reach (Liang, et al, 2022).

As a result, students in underfunded educational settings may miss out on the potential benefits that such simulations could provide. In addition to financial and technical challenges, there is often a degree of reluctance among educators to embrace simulation-based teaching methods. This hesitation can stem from a lack of familiarity with these tools or a belief that they may not yield effective learning outcomes. Such concerns may prevent instructors from fully integrating simulations into their teaching practices, thereby limiting students' exposure to innovative and engaging learning experiences(Gao et al, 2022). To effectively address these concerns and critiques, it is essential to approach the integration of simulations into educational curricula with careful consideration. This involves not only selecting appropriate simulation tools that reflect real-world complexities but also implementing a system of continuous evaluation to assess their impact on student learning outcomes. By doing so, educators can ensure that simulations serve as a meaningful component of the learning process, rather than as a superficial representation of the entrepreneurial landscape (Faria et al., 2009).

3. SIMULATION GAMES IN ENTREPRENEURSHIP EDUCATION

Simulation games have emerged as significant pedagogical instruments in the realm of entrepreneurship education, providing students with the opportunity to participate in interactive and risk-free environments that closely mimic authentic business challenges. This section will analyze the various types of simulation games utilized in entrepreneurship education, review pertinent case studies, and delineate the skills cultivated through these methodologies. By incorporating simulation games into their curricula, educators can effectively connect theoretical knowledge with practical application, thereby enhancing students' comprehension of entrepreneurial principles (Liang, et al, 2022).

3.1 Types of Simulation Games Used in Entrepreneurship Education

Key features of simulation games include: Real-time Feedback: Learners receive prompt responses regarding their choices, facilitating a process of iterative learning. Gamification, defined as the integration of game mechanics including scoring systems, progression levels, and reward structures, has been shown to significantly enhance motivation and engagement among participants. Risk-free experimentation allows participants to evaluate various strategies without facing real-world repercussions, thereby fostering an environment conducive to innovation and exploration. Simulation games serve as a vital link between theoretical concepts and practical application by facilitating experiential learning. These games replicate authentic entrepreneurial challenges, including the navigation of uncertainties, the identification of opportunities, and the management of constrained resources. This congruence with real-world situations is essential for adequately equipping students for entrepreneurial endeavors (Liang, et al, 2022).

Examples of Entrepreneurship Simulation Games There are several simulation games that have been developed specifically for entrepreneurship education, each focusing on different aspects of running a business. Here are some widely used examples: Venture Strategy Simulation is an educational tool that emphasizes the intricacies of startup management and market entry strategies. Participants engage in the creation and administration of a virtual enterprise, where they are responsible for critical decision-making processes related to product development, marketing, pricing, and distribution. The simulation replicates the dynamics of a competitive marketplace, enabling learners to evaluate the actions of competitors and modify their strategies in response (source). The Startup Game is a pedagogical tool aimed at enhancing students' competencies in resource allocation and pitching. This interactive experience engages participants in the intricate process of obtaining funding for a business concept (Rogmans, & Abaza, 2019).

Players adopt various roles, including entrepreneurs, investors, and advisors, thereby acquiring insights into negotiation strategies and value creation dynamics. Marketplace Live is a comprehensive platform that provides a range of simulations tailored for business students, encompassing modules focused on the initiation of new ventures. The platform underscores the importance of customer-centric strategies and financial management, while also equipping students with the skills to analyze market trends and enhance operational efficiency. These simulations exhibit a diverse range of focal points and possess a high degree of flexibility in their implementation, rendering them appropriate for a variety of educational contexts, spanning from undergraduate studies to executive training programs (Rezghi et al, 2022).

Simulation games are based on well-defined rules and algorithms that mimic the complexities of real-world markets and businesses. Here is an overview of the mechanics:

Scenario Presentation: Learners are confronted with a problem or challenge, such as the establishment of a business within a particular industry or the revitalization of a struggling enterprise.
Decision-Making Framework: Participants engage in strategic decision-making processes that encompass various aspects, including product pricing, workforce recruitment, marketing expenditures, and innovation initiatives.
Evaluation of Outcomes: The simulation computes the consequences of these strategic choices utilizing established algorithms, providing analytical metrics such as profitability, market share, and levels of customer satisfaction. For instance, a simulation could immerse students in a context where they are tasked with launching a technology startup. In this scenario, they must allocate resources across product development, marketing, and staffing while adapting to market fluctuations and the actions of competitors. The simulation monitors their progress and offers insights regarding the efficacy of their strategic decisions (Newbery et al, 2016).

3.2 The Role of Technology

Recent technological advancements have markedly expanded the capabilities and efficacy of simulation games. Innovations such as artificial intelligence, machine learning, and virtual reality are contributing to the sophistication and realism of these educational tools. For example, virtual reality-based simulations can immerse learners in a three-dimensional business context, enabling them to engage with virtual customers, suppliers, and competitors. These developments render simulation games not only pedagogically valuable but also significantly engaging for participants. Cloud-based platforms facilitate scalability, enabling students worldwide to engage in a unified simulation experience. Additionally, the integration of data analytics within simulation games offers educators comprehensive reports on student performance, highlighting both strengths and areas requiring enhancement (Bell, & Federman, 2013).

3.3. Learning Objectives in Simulation Games

Simulation games in entrepreneurship education are structured to fulfill a number of essential learning objectives. Students are instructed in the art of situational analysis, enabling them to foresee potential challenges and develop comprehensive plans. For example, they may assess market conditions to identify the most advantageous timing for a product launch. Entrepreneurship is characterized by the necessity to operate within environments of ambiguity and unpredictability (Liu, & Bell, 2019).

Simulation games effectively replicate this phenomenon by presenting participants with variable market conditions and scenarios characterized by constrained information. The efficient allocation of financial, human, and physical resources is essential in the realm of entrepreneurship. Participants encounter the trade-offs and opportunity costs associated with these strategic decisions. Numerous simulations necessitate collaborative efforts, thereby educating students on the significance of effective communication, delegation, and leadership in the pursuit of organizational objectives. Experiencing failure is a frequent component of entrepreneurial endeavors. Simulation exercises provide students with the opportunity to confront setbacks within a structured environment, promoting resilience and the development of a growth mindset (Bell, & Federman, 2013).

4. ADVANTAGES OF SIMULATION GAMES

In summary, simulation games present a wealth of advantages that make them a powerful tool in modern education. By promoting active participation, real-world applicability, and the development of essential skills, these games can transform the learning experience and better prepare students for future challenges. Research has shown that students demonstrate a significantly higher likelihood of retaining knowledge and understanding concepts when they are actively engaged in the learning process (Liu, & Bell, 2019). This means that when learners participate in discussions, collaborate on projects, and apply what they have learned in practical situations, they are not just passively absorbing information but rather interacting with it in meaningful ways. Engaging students through hands-on activities, group work, and critical thinking exercises fosters a deeper connection to the material, allowing them to integrate new information with their existing knowledge base. Consequently, this active involvement not only enhances retention but also promotes critical thinking, creativity, and a greater overall enthusiasm for learning. In essence, when students take an active role in their education, they are more likely to internalize the content and develop a lasting understanding that extends beyond the classroom (Liu, & Bell, 2019).

The experiential aspect of simulations plays a crucial role in equipping students with the skills and knowledge necessary to tackle practical challenges they may encounter in their professional lives. By engaging in these immersive learning experiences, students are not only able to apply theoretical concepts to real-world scenarios but also develop critical problem-solving abilities that are essential in today's fast-paced and ever-evolving work environments. This active participation fosters a deeper understanding of the subject matter, allowing learners to navigate complex situations with greater confidence and competence. Ultimately, the hands-on experience gained through simulations bridges the gap between academic learning and real-world application, ensuring that students are well-prepared to face the demands of their future careers (Clark, et al, 2010).

Personalization and Adaptability: Educators have the ability to modify and customize simulations to accurately represent particular industries, geographical regions, or unique entrepreneurial challenges. This level of personalization allows instructors to create more relevant and engaging learning experiences that cater to the specific needs and contexts of their students (Clark, et al, 2010).

By aligning simulations with real-world scenarios, educators can enhance the educational value of the learning process, ensuring that the content is not only applicable but also resonates with the interests and aspirations of the learners. This adaptability empowers teachers to foster a deeper understanding of complex concepts, making it easier for students to grasp the intricacies of various fields and develop the skills necessary to navigate the challenges they may face in their professional journeys. The incorporation of real-time feedback provides students with immediate insights into the outcomes of their choices, enabling them to grasp the implications of their decisions. This timely information empowers them to refine and modify their strategies in response to the results they observe (Clark, et al, 2010).

By receiving instant feedback, students can engage in a more dynamic learning process, where they continuously assess their performance, identify areas for improvement, and implement adjustments that enhance their overall effectiveness. This iterative cycle of decision-making and feedback not only fosters a deeper understanding of the subject matter but also cultivates critical thinking skills, as students learn to analyze the impact of their actions and make informed choices moving forward. Ultimately, the ability to receive and act upon real-time feedback transforms the learning experience into a more interactive and responsive journey, encouraging students to take ownership of their educational development (Clark, et al, 2010)

4.1 Criticisms and Challenges

Despite the numerous advantages that simulation games offer, they are not exempt from criticism. One of the primary concerns is the high costs associated with advanced simulation tools. These sophisticated technologies often come with a hefty price tag, which can create significant financial barriers for educational institutions and organizations that operate on limited budgets. As a result, many schools, training centers, and other entities may find it challenging to invest in these valuable resources, potentially limiting their ability to provide high-quality training and learning experiences for their students or participants. This financial hurdle can hinder the widespread adoption of simulation games, preventing a broader audience from reaping their benefits and contributing to an uneven playing field in educational and professional training environments. Individuals who are new to gaming mechanics often face significant challenges when first encountering these systems (Michael,, & Chen, 2016).

Their lack of prior experience can lead to confusion and frustration, making it essential for instructors or experienced players to provide extra guidance and support. This additional assistance can take many forms, such as tutorials, one-on-one coaching, or even detailed instructional materials that break down the various components of gameplay. By offering these resources, we can help beginners navigate the complexities of gaming, allowing them to build confidence and gradually improve their understanding of the mechanics at play. Ultimately, fostering a supportive learning environment is crucial for helping novice players overcome initial hurdles and develop their skills in the gaming realm. One significant concern regarding the integration of gamification in educational settings is the potential for students to become overly fixated on the notion of "winning" the game itself (Michael,, & Chen, 2016).

This fixation can lead to a scenario where the primary objective shifts away from the essential goal of absorbing and internalizing valuable entrepreneurial lessons. Instead of engaging deeply with the material and developing critical thinking skills, students might prioritize achieving high scores, completing levels, or earning virtual rewards. This shift in focus can ultimately undermine the educational experience, as the rich and nuanced lessons inherent in entrepreneurship may be overshadowed by the competitive elements of the game. Consequently, educators must be mindful of striking a balance where gamification serves as a complementary tool rather than a distraction, ensuring that students remain engaged with the core principles and practices of entrepreneurship rather than merely chasing after points or accolades within a game framework (Morselli et al, 2022).

Evaluating learning outcomes through simulations presents a variety of challenges, particularly because the performance metrics employed may not completely or accurately reflect the full spectrum of skill acquisition. While simulations offer valuable opportunities to observe and measure participant behavior in controlled environments, the complexity of real-world scenarios often cannot be replicated (Morselli et al, 2022).As a result, the metrics used to assess performance may fall short in capturing not just the technical skills developed, but also the subtler nuances of critical thinking, adaptability, and decision-making that are essential in real-life situations. This limitation underscores the need for a more comprehensive approach to assessment that goes beyond surface-level performance indicators and takes into account the multifaceted nature of learning and skill mastery (Morselli et al, 2022).

5. CASE STUDIES AND EMPIRICAL EVIDENCE ON SIMULATION GAMES IN ENTREPRENEURSHIP EDUCATION

Simulation games are gaining widespread acknowledgment as powerful instruments for enhancing entrepreneurship education, offering students valuable chances to participate in immersive and interactive learning experiences. In the following sections, we will delve deeper into this topic by exploring a comprehensive analysis that includes recent case studies and empirical research findings from 2023. This expanded discussion will highlight how simulation games can foster critical thinking, decision-making skills, and practical knowledge in aspiring entrepreneurs, ultimately preparing them for real-world business challenges. By examining various examples and research outcomes, we aim to illustrate the significant impact that these innovative educational tools can have on the entrepreneurial landscape (Morselli et al, 2022).

5.1 Simulation Games in Promoting Higher-Order Thinking Skills

A recent study investigated the incorporation of business simulation games into flipped classroom settings, highlighting their capacity to promote higher-order thinking skills among students. This research was carried out in a university located in China and utilized a quasi-experimental design, focusing specifically on students enrolled in cross-border e-commerce courses. The results of the study indicated that the use of simulation games, when paired with project-based learning (PBL), led to significant improvements in various forms of engagement, including cognitive, emotional, and behavioral engagement (Morselli et al, 2022).

Additionally, students exhibited notable advancements in critical thinking, creativity, and problem-solving skills. This innovative approach facilitated an environment where students could actively engage in sustainability-oriented entrepreneurship, as they were able to simulate real-world decision-making processes within a dynamic and interactive framework. By experiencing these simulations, students gained practical insights into the complexities of entrepreneurship, allowing them to apply theoretical knowledge to practical situations in a meaningful way. Overall, the research underscores the potential of integrating simulation games in educational settings to cultivate essential skills that are increasingly valuable in today's rapidly evolving business landscape. (Hsu & Wu, 2023).

5.2 Inclusivity and Accessibility in Entrepreneurship Education

The findings indicated that while there were notable accessibility issues stemming from these socio-economic disparities, the availability of resources on campus played a significant role in alleviating some of these barriers. This support enabled a wider range of students to embrace and utilize simulation games effectively. Furthermore, the study emphasized the pivotal function that these games serve in democratizing entrepreneurial education. By bridging existing gaps in technological capabilities and financial resources, simulation games create opportunities for students from diverse backgrounds to access quality educational experiences that might otherwise be out of reach. In essence, this research underscores the potential of simulation tools not only to enhance learning but also to foster greater equity in educational access and outcomes within the entrepreneurial landscape of South Africa (Petersen, 2023).

5.3 Cross-Cultural Applications in Entrepreneurial Training

In these educational settings, the simulation games served as powerful learning instruments, offering participants tailored experiences that were not only culturally relevant but also economically pertinent to their unique circumstances. By immersing students in realistic scenarios, these simulations significantly enhanced their entrepreneurial competencies, equipping them with the necessary skills to thrive in various market conditions. Moreover, the ability to engage with these tools helped prepare students for the challenges they would encounter in the real world, fostering a more profound understanding of the interplay between local cultures and global business practices (Mueller et al, 2021).

This multifaceted approach underscores the potential of simulation games as effective pedagogical tools that bridge the gap between theoretical knowledge and practical application, ultimately empowering the next generation of entrepreneurs across different cultural landscapes. Simulation games have showcased a remarkable degree of versatility across a variety of cultural contexts, particularly in their implementation within educational institutions in both Africa and Europe. A notable example of this is a collaborative project involving multiple universities that conducted an in-depth analysis of how digital simulation tools were utilized to tackle specific entrepreneurial challenges faced by emerging businesses in these regions. The project focused on critical issues such as effectively navigating the complexities of informal economies, which are prevalent in many African nations, and developing scalable business models that can adapt to diverse market environments (Mueller et al, 2021).

5.4 Measuring Learning Outcomes and Engagement

A recent study has shed light on the significant effectiveness of simulation games in enhancing student engagement while also providing a robust mechanism for assessing learning outcomes through various gamification strategies. These innovative games uniquely blend theoretical knowledge with practical, real-world scenarios, making them invaluable tools for bridging the divide between academic concepts and their application in actual entrepreneurial contexts (Mueller et al, 2021).

By utilizing interactive platforms, students are afforded the opportunity to experiment with hypotheses, encounter failures in a safe environment, and refine their solutions through an iterative process. This hands-on learning approach cultivates essential skills that are vital for achieving success in the unpredictable and rapidly changing landscape of modern markets. The study emphasizes that by engaging with simulation games, students not only deepen their understanding of theoretical principles but also develop the practical competencies needed to navigate the complexities of entrepreneurship effectively. This interactive method of learning is increasingly recognized as a crucial component in preparing future entrepreneurs for the challenges they will face in their professional journeys (Emerald Insight, 2023).

5.5 Leveraging Gamification for Sustainable Entrepreneurship

Gamification techniques integrated into simulation games have proven to be effective tools in fostering sustainable entrepreneurship, aligning these educational efforts with the broader global sustainability objectives. Through the immersive experience of simulating the consequences of various business decisions on both environmental and social systems, students are provided with a unique opportunity to understand the complexities of balancing profitability with sustainability (Mueller et al, 2021).

This experiential learning environment encourages them to critically analyze the implications of their choices, allowing them to appreciate the importance of responsible decision-making in the business world. As a result, these innovative approaches not only enhance students' understanding of sustainable practices but also empower them to become forward-thinking entrepreneurs. They are equipped with the knowledge and skills necessary to launch ventures that not only aim for financial success but also contribute positively to society and the environment. Ultimately, this holistic educational strategy fosters a new generation of business leaders who are committed to driving meaningful change and creating enterprises that prioritize both economic viability and social responsibility. (Hsu & Wu, 2023).

The incorporation of simulation games into entrepreneurship education is experiencing a notable surge, providing significant advantages that go beyond traditional teaching methods. These benefits include heightened levels of student engagement, the cultivation of essential entrepreneurial skills, and a closer alignment with the intricate dynamics of real-world business environments. Recent empirical research has further substantiated the effectiveness of simulation games across a wide array of educational contexts, ranging from institutions with limited resources to sophisticated flipped classroom models. By utilizing these innovative tools, educators can not only enrich the learning experience but also equip students with the necessary competencies to navigate the complexities and challenges of entrepreneurship in a fast-paced, ever-changing global marketplace. As the landscape of business continues to evolve, the role of simulation games in preparing future entrepreneurs becomes increasingly vital, fostering a deeper understanding of practical applications and strategic thinking that are crucial for success in their entrepreneurial endeavors (Obschonka, et al, 2021).

6. BEST PRACTICES FOR IMPLEMENTATION OF SIMULATION GAMES IN ENTREPRENEURSHIP EDUCATION

Simulation games have emerged as a pivotal component in contemporary teaching methods for entrepreneurship education. By providing an experiential learning environment, these games closely replicate the complexities and dynamics of real-world business situations. To maximize the effectiveness of these educational tools, it is essential to follow a set of established best practices. In the following sections, we will delve into an in-depth exploration of these best practices, drawing upon recent research findings to support our discussion (Obschonka, et al, 2021).

6.1. Integration With Curricular Objectives

Simulation games are an essential component of entrepreneurship education, as they must be closely aligned with the educational objectives and desired learning outcomes of entrepreneurship courses. By incorporating business simulation games such as MonsoonSim into the curriculum, educators can significantly enhance students' abilities in critical thinking, decision-making, and problem-solving. These types of games, which are thoughtfully designed around specific themes and closely connected to the content of the course, provide a structured yet engaging way for students to interact with real-world business scenarios. This alignment not only helps students develop practical skills that are vital for their future careers but also ensures that they meet academic milestones effectively. By utilizing these interactive tools, educators can create a dynamic learning environment that encourages students to apply theoretical concepts in practical situations, thereby deepening their understanding and preparing them for the complexities of the entrepreneurial landscape (Okonkwo et al, 2022).

6.2. Incorporating Flipped Classroom Methodologies

To maximize the effectiveness of this approach, educators should thoughtfully design and curate pre-class materials—such as video lectures, readings, and other resources—that adequately prepare students for the immersive game scenarios they will encounter. By doing so, students can arrive in class equipped with the foundational knowledge necessary to fully engage with the simulation games, thereby enriching their learning experience. This preparation phase is crucial, as it sets the stage for deeper exploration and application of concepts during class time, transforming traditional learning dynamics into a more interactive and collaborative environment. Ultimately, the flipped classroom model, combined with simulation games, not only makes learning more engaging but also promotes critical thinking and innovation among students, equipping them with essential skills for their future endeavors (Obschonka, et al, 2021).

6.3. Balancing Challenge and Accessibility

To ensure successful implementation, it is essential that simulation games strike a delicate balance between being sufficiently challenging to encourage critical thinking and remaining accessible to students with diverse skill levels. Achieving this equilibrium is crucial, as it helps to keep learners engaged and motivated while preventing them from feeling overwhelmed or discouraged by the complexity of the tasks at hand (Okonkwo et al, 2022).

One effective way to manage this balance is through the incorporation of adjustable difficulty settings that allow students to tailor their experience according to their individual capabilities. Additionally, providing clear and concise instructions can significantly enhance the learning experience, making it easier for students to grasp the concepts being taught. A practical example of this approach can be observed in the entrepreneurial courses offered by UAEU, which effectively utilized customizable business simulation platforms. These platforms enabled students to navigate various scenarios and challenges at their own pace, fostering a productive learning environment that caters to a wide range of abilities and promotes active engagement in the learning process (Okonkwo et al, 2022).

6.4. Facilitating Collaboration and Group Dynamics

Engaging in group activities within simulation games fosters an environment of collaborative learning, effectively mirroring the dynamics of teamwork commonly observed in real-world business settings. To fully leverage the advantages offered by these group activities, it is essential for instructors to strategically form balanced groups. This process should take into account the varying skill sets and learning styles of individual participants, ensuring that each group is well-rounded and capable of tackling challenges from multiple perspectives (Raith & Lehmann, 2023).

Research has shown that the consistency of participation among group members plays a crucial role in determining the success of collaborative efforts. When all members actively engage and contribute, it not only enhances the quality of the group's output but also enriches the learning experience for each participant. Therefore, fostering an atmosphere that encourages active involvement from every member is vital for achieving positive outcomes in group activities within simulation games (Raith & Lehmann, 2023).

6.5. Training and Support for Instructors

To further enhance the teaching experience and ensure that educators are well-prepared to integrate simulation games into their curricula, it is essential to establish dedicated support systems tailored specifically for instructors. Such support systems can provide ongoing assistance, resources, and troubleshooting to address any technical or pedagogical challenges that may arise during the implementation of these tools. By fostering a supportive environment, educators are more likely to feel confident in their ability to effectively utilize simulation games, thereby maximizing the learning opportunities for their students and contributing to a successful educational experience overall. The effectiveness and overall success of simulation games are significantly influenced by the level of expertise and training that instructors possess (Raith & Lehmann, 2023).

It is crucial for educators to receive comprehensive training that not only covers the technical functionalities of these simulation tools but also delves into pedagogical strategies for utilizing them in the classroom. This training should encompass a thorough understanding of the platform's capabilities, enabling educators to navigate its features proficiently and utilize them to their full potential. Additionally, instructors should be equipped with methods for facilitating engaging discussions that stem from the outcomes of the games, allowing for deeper reflection and learning among students (Hussain and Li, 2022).

6.6. Assessment and Feedback Mechanisms

When developing assessment methods, it is essential to create approaches that evaluate more than merely the completion of simulation activities; they should also take into account the level of understanding that students have gained and the skills they have developed throughout the process. One effective strategy for achieving this is to implement structured debriefings following simulation exercises, which provide students with an opportunity to reflect critically on their decision-making processes and the outcomes of their actions(Alghamdi, 2023). Additionally, utilizing detailed rubrics that specifically assess various competencies such as problem-solving abilities, critical thinking skills, and the application of theoretical knowledge will contribute to a more holistic and comprehensive evaluation of student performance. This multifaceted assessment approach not only ensures that students are held accountable for their actions but also fosters a deeper learning experience by encouraging them to engage with the material on a more profound level. Ultimately, such methods can lead to a more meaningful understanding of the subject matter and prepare students more effectively for real-world challenges (Alghamdi, 2023).

7. LEVERAGING TECHNOLOGY AND ANALYTICS

Contemporary simulation platforms frequently come equipped with advanced analytics tools that meticulously monitor various aspects of student performance and engagement levels. These valuable insights can be leveraged to customize future simulation sessions, allowing educators to specifically target areas where students may be struggling or to place greater emphasis on certain competencies that require reinforcement. By examining the data collected, instructors can discern patterns in student behavior, which enables them to make informed adjustments to the game settings or to modify supplemental materials in a way that better meets the needs of their learners. This data-driven approach not only enhances the overall educational experience but also fosters a more personalized learning environment, ultimately contributing to improved student outcomes (Alghamdi, 2023).

7.1. Encouraging Reflection and Real-World Connections

Students derive the greatest advantages from simulations when they can effectively link their in-game experiences to tangible challenges faced in the realm of real-world entrepreneurship. To enhance this learning process, engaging in structured reflection activities is crucial. For instance, tasks like composing detailed post-simulation reports or taking part in in-depth discussions allow students to articulate and analyze their experiences, thereby reinforcing these important connections. Furthermore, the integration of case studies in conjunction with the simulations enriches the learning environment, offering a more comprehensive context that aids in the understanding of various business strategies and practices. This multifaceted approach not only deepens students' insights but also equips them with the skills necessary to navigate the complexities of the entrepreneurial landscape (Alghamdi, 2023).

7.2. Focusing on Sustainability and Long-Term Skills

These simulation games serve as a powerful tool to engage students in immersive learning experiences that challenge them to think critically about environmental and social impacts when making decisions. By placing students in realistic scenarios where they must balance economic objectives with ecological and societal considerations, these games foster a holistic perspective on entrepreneurship. This experiential learning approach encourages students to reflect on the broader implications of their choices and to develop a sense of responsibility towards sustainable practices (Sugahara, 2018). Moreover, by integrating sustainability into the educational framework, we are not only preparing students to contribute meaningfully to the achievement of sustainable development goals but also nurturing a mindset geared towards lifelong learning. This is crucial in an ever-evolving global landscape, where the ability to adapt and innovate in response to sustainability challenges is becoming increasingly important. Ultimately, this comprehensive educational strategy aims to empower future entrepreneurs to become catalysts for positive change, equipping them with the tools they need to make informed, ethical decisions that benefit both society and the planet (Sugahara, 2018).

8. CONCLUSION: THE ROLE OF SIMULATION GAMES IN ENTREPRENEURSHIP EDUCATION

8.1 Summary of Key Insights

Simulation games have increasingly established themselves as a highly effective pedagogical instrument within the realm of entrepreneurship education. They present a wide array of advantages, such as enhancing critical thinking, fostering creativity, and providing hands-on experience that traditional teaching methods may lack. However, alongside these benefits, there are also specific challenges that educators and students may encounter when integrating simulation games into the learning process. This section aims to deliver an in-depth summary of the most significant insights gleaned from the current body of research and practice regarding simulation games in entrepreneurship education (Sugahara, 2018). It will reflect on the vast potential these games hold for driving future innovations and advancements in teaching methodologies. Furthermore, the discussion will culminate in a thoughtful examination of the transformative impact that simulation games can have on equipping the next generation of entrepreneurs with the necessary skills, knowledge, and mindset to thrive in an ever-evolving business landscape. Through this exploration, we aim to better understand how simulation games can not only enhance learning outcomes but also contribute to the development of resilient and adaptable entrepreneurs capable of navigating the complexities of the modern economy (Sugahara, 2018).

Overall, simulation games serve as a powerful tool for enhanced experiential learning, equipping students with the necessary skills and confidence to thrive in their entrepreneurial pursuits. By bridging the gap between theory and practice, these immersive experiences prepare learners to tackle the complexities of the business world with greater competence and resilience. As they navigate through various challenges and opportunities presented in the simulations, students sharpen their abilities in several key areas (Sugahara, 2018). For instance, they learn to assess risks accurately, which involves not only identifying potential pitfalls but also evaluating the likelihood and impact of different outcomes. This skill is crucial for entrepreneurs who must make informed choices in uncertain environments. Moreover, the simulations require participants to manage resources effectively. This involves allocating limited assets, such as time, money, and human capital, in a way that maximizes their potential for success. By practicing this resource management in a simulated context, students gain insights into the strategic thinking and planning needed to operate a successful business. Additionally, the ever-changing nature of simulation games fosters adaptability among learners. As they encounter unexpected developments or shifts in the simulated market, students must adjust their strategies and responses accordingly (Sugahara, 2018).

This ability to pivot and respond to new information is a fundamental quality for any entrepreneur, who often faces unpredictable challenges in the real world. Moreover, these simulations often present business scenarios that necessitate active participation and collaboration among group members. By engaging in these interactive exercises, students have the chance to cultivate essential teamwork skills and enhance their interpersonal abilities. Such competencies are not merely advantageous; they are critical attributes that contribute significantly to achieving success in the entrepreneurial landscape. Through collaborative problem-solving and collective decision-making, participants not only develop a deeper understanding of business dynamics but also learn to value diverse perspectives and leverage the strengths of their peers, thereby laying a strong foundation for their future endeavors in the business world (Okonkwo et al, 2022).

Although simulation games offer significant opportunities for creativity and engagement, they also come with a range of challenges that need to be addressed. These challenges can impact both the development process and the overall player experience, making it essential for developers to navigate these obstacles effectively. From technical limitations to balancing realism with playability, the hurdles associated with simulation games can be complex and multifaceted. Moreover, players may encounter issues such as steep learning curves or the potential for repetitive gameplay, which can detract from the overall enjoyment of the game. As such, while the promise of simulation games is substantial, it is equally important to acknowledge and address the various difficulties that come with creating and enjoying these immersive experiences. To address these financial barriers and enhance access to simulation resources, several strategies can be employed (Sugahara, 2018).

One effective approach is fostering institutional collaborations, where multiple organizations pool their resources and expertise to share access to simulation technologies. This collaborative model not only maximizes the utilization of available resources but also promotes a community of practice that can lead to innovative teaching strategies and improved outcomes. Overall, by exploring various collaborative models and embracing open-source options, institutions can overcome the challenges posed by resource constraints and ensure that high-quality simulation platforms are accessible to a wider range of learners (Okonkwo et al, 2022).

This approach ultimately contributes to a more equitable educational landscape, enabling all students to benefit from cutting-edge simulation technology in their training. The successful implementation of simulation tools in educational settings hinges on the ability of educators to effectively utilize these technologies. To meet this critical requirement, it is essential to establish comprehensive training programs designed specifically for instructors. These programs should focus on equipping educators with the necessary skills and knowledge to effectively facilitate and guide students through the intricacies of the simulation experience. By providing thorough training, educators can not only enhance their own understanding of the tools but also improve the overall learning outcomes for their student (Okonkwo et al, 2022).

When it comes to the design of simulations, it is crucial to find a balance in complexity. Simulations that are overly intricate can easily overwhelm students, leading to confusion and frustration. On the other hand, simulations that are too simplistic may fail to adequately reflect the complexities and nuances inherent in the field of entrepreneurship. To create an effective learning environment, it is advisable to tailor the complexity of the simulations to align with the varying skill levels and experiences of the students involved. This approach ensures that students are both challenged and supported, promoting a more engaging and meaningful learning experience (Sugahara, 2018).

The process of measuring learning outcomes within simulation-based environments presents a notable challenge due to its inherently subjective nature. In order to address this issue effectively, it is essential to create comprehensive and robust rubrics that evaluate both the processes involved and the final outcomes achieved by students. By doing so, we can ensure a fair and equitable assessment of student performance. This dual focus not only facilitates a more accurate reflection of a student's abilities and understanding but also promotes a deeper engagement with the learning material. Ultimately, well-structured rubrics serve as invaluable tools for educators, enabling them to provide constructive feedback and support the continuous improvement of their students in these dynamic learning environments (Sugahara, 2018).

8.2 Future D. Technological Advancements: VR/AR Simulations

The incorporation of advanced technologies such as virtual reality (VR) and augmented reality (AR) has the potential to transform the landscape of entrepreneurship education. VR simulations can replicate intricate, realistic business scenarios, providing an exceptional level of immersion for learners. Evidence suggests that entrepreneurship programs utilizing VR have been effective in enhancing participants' decision-making and strategic planning capabilities. Furthermore, artificial intelligence (AI) facilitates personalized learning experiences by adapting simulations to accommodate individual learning speeds and preferences, thereby increasing their efficacy (Zulfiqar et al, 2019). AI algorithms are capable of analyzing performance metrics to deliver customized feedback, thereby fostering skill development. Sustainability and social entrepreneurship can be effectively integrated into future simulation games by addressing pressing global challenges such as climate change and social equity. These educational tools provide students with the opportunity to develop business models that are grounded in sustainable and ethical principles (Zulfiqar et al, 2019).

For instance, platforms like SimVenture Evolution are actively engaging with these themes in their simulations. Simulation games signify a transformative advancement in entrepreneurship education. They provide an interactive learning environment that equips students to navigate the intricacies of the entrepreneurial landscape. Through engaging in simulations, students can assess the repercussions of their decisions, gain insights from their errors, and cultivate the resilience and creativity essential for thriving as entrepreneurs (Zulfiqar et al, 2019). The body of research concerning the long-term effects of simulation games is extensive; however, additional investigation is necessary to elucidate their enduring influence on entrepreneurial success. Longitudinal studies that follow students from their educational experiences into their professional careers would yield significant insights. By confronting the implementation challenges and harnessing emerging technologies, educators can fully realize the potential of simulation games. As the educational landscape evolves, these tools are positioned to significantly influence the development of future business leaders, promote innovation, and support sustainable development initiatives (Zulfiqar et al, 2019).

REFERENCES

Abt, C. C. (1970). *Serious Games*. Viking Press.

Anderson, L. W., Krathwohl, D. R., & Bloom, B. S. (2001). *A taxonomy for learning, teaching, and assessing: A revision of Bloom's taxonomy of educational objectives*. Longman.

Bell, B. S., & Federman, J. E. (2013). E-Learning and Development: The Use of Simulation Games in Workforce Training. *Human Resource Management Review*, *23*(2), 239–251.

Bellotti, F., Kapralos, B., Lee, K., Moreno-Ger, P., & Berta, R. (2013). Assessment in and of serious games: An overview. *Advances in Human-Computer Interaction*, *2013*, 1–11. DOI: 10.1155/2013/120791

Bonwell, C., & Eison, J. A. (1991). Active Learning: Creating Excitement in the Classroom. *ASHE-ERIC Higher Education Report*.

Clark, R. E., Yates, K., Early, S., & Moulton, K. (2010). An Analysis of the Use of Simulation Games in Education. *Educational Technology Research and Development*, *58*(5), 575–595.

Deci, E. L., & Ryan, R. M. (1985). *Intrinsic motivation and self-determination in human behavior*. Springer. DOI: 10.1007/978-1-4899-2271-7

Faria, A. J., Hutchinson, D., Wellington, W. J., & Gold, S. (2009). Developments in business gaming: A review of the past 40 years. *Simulation & Gaming*, *40*(4), 464–487. DOI: 10.1177/1046878108327585

Gao, C. A., Howard, F. M., Markov, N. S., Dyer, E. C., Ramesh, S., Luo, Y., & Pearson, A. T. (2022). Comparing scientific abstracts generated by ChatGPT to original abstracts using an artificial intelligence output detector, plagiarism detector, and blinded human reviewers. *bioRxiv*. 2022.12.23.521610

Gentry, J. W. (1990). What is Experiential Learning? In *Guide to Business Gaming and Experiential Learning*. Nichols Publishing.

Gentry, J. W., Commuri, S., & Sulek, J. (2010). How experiential learning can be used in entrepreneurship education. *Simulation & Gaming*, *41*(1), 114–123.

Gentry, T., Wallace, J., Kvarfordt, C., & Lynch, K. (2010). Personal digital assistants as cognitive aids for high school students with autism: Results of a community-based trial. *Journal of Vocational Rehabilitation*, *32*(2), 101–107. DOI: 10.3233/JVR-2010-0499

Hamari, J., Koivisto, J., & Sarsa, H. (2014). Does Gamification Work? — A Literature Review of Empirical Studies on Gamification. *Proceedings of the ... Annual Hawaii International Conference on System Sciences. Annual Hawaii International Conference on System Sciences*, *10*, 1109. DOI: 10.1109/HICSS.2014.377

Hamari, J., Koivisto, J., & Sarsa, H. (2016). Does gamification work?—A literature review of empirical studies on gamification. *System Sciences*, *2016*, 3025–3034.

Hsu, C.-Y., & Wu, T.-T. (2023). Application of Business Simulation Games in Flipped Classrooms to Facilitate Student Engagement and Higher-Order Thinking Skills for Sustainable Learning Practices. *Sustainability (Basel)*, *15*(24), 16867. DOI: 10.3390/su152416867

Hyams-Ssekasi, D., & Caldwell, E. F. (2018). An exploration of experiential education as a catalyst for future entrepreneurs. In Hyams-Ssekasi, D., & Caldwell, E. F. (Eds.), *Experiential learning for entrepreneurship: theoretical and practical perspectives on enterprise education* (pp. 71–83). Springer International Publishing. DOI: 10.1007/978-3-319-90005-6_4

Insight, E. (2023). *Business Simulation Games and Entrepreneurial Education*. Retrieved from Emerald Insight.

. Jia, Q., Cui, J., Xiao, Y., Liu, C., Rashid, P., & Gehringer, E.F. (2021). ALL-IN-ONE: Multi-task learning BERT models for evaluating peer assessments. *arXiv*.

Kakouris, A., & Liargovas, P. (2021). On the about/for/through framework of entrepreneurship education: A critical analysis. *Entrepreneurship Education and Pedagogy*, *4*(3), 396–421. DOI: 10.1177/2515127420916740

Kolb, D. A. (1984). *Experiential learning: Experience as the source of learning and development.* Prentice Hall.

Kraus, M., Feuerriegel, S., & Oztekin, A. (2020). Deep learning in business analytics and operations research: Models, applications and managerial implications. *European Journal of Operational Research*, *281*(3), 628–641. DOI: 10.1016/j.ejor.2019.09.018

Lean, J., Moizer, J., Towler, M., & Abbey, C. (2006). Simulation and Games: Use and Barriers in Higher Education. *Active Learning in Higher Education*, *7*(3), 227–242. DOI: 10.1177/1469787406069056

Liang, P., Bommasani, R., Lee, T., Tsipras, D., Soylu, D., Yasunaga, M., Zhang, Y., & Narayanan, D.. (2022). *Holistic evaluation of language models*. Arxiv.

Liu, P., & Bell, R. (2019). Exploration of the initiation and process of business model innovation of successful Chinese ICT enterprises. *Journal of Entrepreneurship in Emerging Economies*, *11*(4), 515–536. DOI: 10.1108/JEEE-09-2018-0094

Michael, D. R., & Chen, S. L. (2016). *Serious Games: Games That Educate, Train, and Inform*. Thomson Course Technology.

Morselli, D., & Gorenc, J. (2022). Using the EntreComp framework to evaluate two entrepreneurship education courses based on the Korda Method. *International Journal of Management Education*, *20*(1), 100591. DOI: 10.1016/j.ijme.2021.100591

Mueller, S., & Anderson, A. R. (2014). Understanding the entrepreneurial learning process and its impact on students' personal development: A European perspective. *International Journal of Management Education*, *12*(3), 500–511. DOI: 10.1016/j.ijme.2014.05.003

Neck, H. M., Greene, P. G., & Brush, C. G. (2014). *Teaching entrepreneurship: A practice-based approach*. Edward Elgar Publishing. DOI: 10.4337/9781782540564

Newbery, R., Lean, J., & Moizer, J. (2016). Evaluating the impact of serious games: The effect of gaming on entrepreneurial intent. *Information Technology & People*, *29*(4), 733–749. DOI: 10.1108/ITP-05-2015-0111

Obschonka, M., & Audretsch, D. B. (2020). Artificial intelligence and big data in entrepreneurship: A new era has begun. *Small Business Economics*, *55*(3), 529–539. DOI: 10.1007/s11187-019-00202-4

Okonkwo, C. W., & Ade-Ibijola, A. (2021). Chatbots applications in education: A systematic review. *Computers and Education: Artificial Intelligence*, *2*, 100033. DOI: 10.1016/j.caeai.2021.100033

Peterková, J., Repaská, Z., & Prachařová, L. (2022). Best Practice of Using Digital Business Simulation Games in Business Education. *Sustainability (Basel)*, *14*(15), 8987. DOI: 10.3390/su14158987

Petersen, F. (2023). Business Simulation Games and Entrepreneurial Education. In Iwu, C. G., & Shambare, R. (Eds.), *Delivering Entrepreneurship Education in Africa*. Emerald Publishing Limited.

Ratten, V., & Jones, P. (2021). Transformational entrepreneurship education through gamification. *International Journal of Entrepreneurial Behaviour & Research*, *27*(5), 1241–1257.

Rezghi, S., Moghaddam, A., & Modarresi, M. (2022). The effect of digital games on entrepreneurial self-efficacy and occupational preferences of adolescents. Technology of Education Journal (TEJ), 339-350.

Rogmans, T., & Abaza, W. (2019). The impact of international business strategy simulation games on student engagement. *Simulation & Gaming*, *50*(3), 393–407. DOI: 10.1177/1046878119848138

Wolfe, J., & Crookall, D. (1998). Developing a Scientific Knowledge of Simulation/Gaming. *Simulation & Gaming*, *29*(1), 7–19. DOI: 10.1177/1046878198291002

Chapter 21
Developing Entrepreneurial Leadership and Organizational Behavior Skills:
A Case Study on Leading Through Crisis Times With Simulation-Based Learning

Maria Sartzetaki
https://orcid.org/0000-0002-9564-5332
Democritus University of Thrace, Greece

ABSTRACT

Entrepreneurial leadership is critical in navigating crises, requiring adaptability, resilience, and strategic decision-making. This chapter explores how simulation-based learning enhances leadership and organizational behavior skills, bridging the gap between theory and real-world crisis management. Using a case study, it examines transformational, situational, and adaptive leadership within high-pressure entrepreneurial environments. The simulation immerses participants in dynamic crisis scenarios, fostering decision-making under uncertainty, conflict resolution, and stakeholder communication. Findings highlight the effectiveness of experiential learning in equipping future leaders with the ability to pivot strategies, inspire teams, and maintain stability in volatile markets. By integrating simulation tools in entrepreneurship education, this study demonstrates how hands-on crisis management training strengthens leadership capabilities, preparing emerging entrepreneurs for the complexities of modern business challenges.

INTRODUCTION

Entrepreneurial leadership is one of the key determinants of success in the modern fast-changing and often turbulent business world. Entrepreneurs are not simply resource managers; they are visionary leaders who have to overcome intricate challenges, innovate in the face of adversity, and bring diverse groups of people together in pursuit of a common goal. This becomes an even more daunting task in moments of crisis, when uncertainty, swift change, and extreme pressure have the potential to undermine even the most carefully made plans. In these circumstances, being a strong leader is not only a wished-for

DOI: 10.4018/979-8-3693-9040-5.ch021

quality but an absolute survival imperative. The chapter examines the interactive nexus of entrepreneurial leadership and crisis management, with a precise interest in how simulation-based training can close the gap between theoretical foundations and practical implementation in live situations.

In entrepreneurship, leaders are often faced with crises that challenge not just their strategic thinking but also their emotional intelligence and flexibility. Crises can take many forms: economic crises, abrupt market changes, disruptive technological innovations, or internal organizational crises. All of these require swift decision-making and the capability to adjust strategies according to unexpected problems. The traditional wisdom of business school, which too frequently depends on classroom learning and theoretical frameworks, does not adequately prepare leaders for these high-stakes situations.

Entrepreneurial leadership in times of crisis entails more than risk management; it entails unleashing the potential of a team, building confidence in the face of uncertainty, and turning challenge into opportunity. Leadership theories—whether transformational and situational leadership or adaptive leadership—provide useful frameworks for explaining these dynamics. But although these theories give a basic understanding of effective leadership, they typically do not include the experiential element that leaders need in order to translate these principles into action in real-time, high-pressure circumstances.

This chapter contends that simulation-based education provides one such solution to this pedagogical deficit. By placing students into simulated crisis situations that reflect the problems encountered by actual entrepreneurial firms, simulation tools create a risk-free space for experimentation and discovery. These experiential settings enable future entrepreneurs to rehearse and hone their leadership abilities, converting esoteric theoretical abstractions into tangible, actionable plans.

Problem Statement: Bridging the Gap Between Practice and Theory

In spite of the large amount of literature on leadership theories and organizational behavior, there exists a substantial gap in the real-world application of these models in high-stress entrepreneurial environments. Conventional pedagogical methods in business education usually focus on conceptual knowledge and analytical frameworks but fail to provide the experiential insight necessary to deal with actual crises. This imbalance is especially pronounced in entrepreneurial environments where leaders are expected to dovetail short-term survival with long-term strategic vision.

Theoretical models such as transformational, situational, and adaptive leadership provide essential insights into effective leadership practices. However, these models are typically taught in isolation from the unpredictable and fluid realities of entrepreneurial crises. Students learn about inspiring teams, making ethical decisions, and managing conflict, yet they rarely have the opportunity to test these skills in a simulated environment that mimics the complexity and urgency of actual business emergencies. As a result, there is a pressing need for innovative teaching methods that combine theory with practice, enabling emerging leaders to develop the intuition and adaptability required to navigate crises effectively.

Simulation-based learning becomes an effective pedagogical aid in this situation. By mimicking the environments of an entrepreneurial crisis, simulations enable students to live out the pressures of fast-paced decision-making, resource paucity, and high-stakes team leadership. Not only does the experiential model anchor theoretical learning but also develops critical soft skills like resilience, conflict management, and ethical stakeholder communication skills—capabilities that are greatly needed during crises.

Purpose and Scope: Addressing the Educational Gap Through Simulation

The primary aim of this chapter is to demonstrate how simulation-based learning can serve as an effective bridge between theoretical leadership models and the practical demands of entrepreneurial crisis management. Through a detailed case study of a leadership simulation tool implemented in a business school entrepreneurship course, the chapter illustrates the process by which experiential learning transforms abstract leadership concepts into real-world skills.

The chapter's scope includes an in-depth exploration of the following areas:

1. Theoretical Foundations: An examination of key leadership theories—transformational, situational, and adaptive—and organizational behavior concepts that are pertinent to understanding the challenges of entrepreneurial leadership during crises.
2. Simulation-Based Learning: A review of current research on the application of simulation tools in entrepreneurship education and crisis management, highlighting both the benefits and limitations of this approach.
3. Case Study Analysis: A rich description of the simulation experience, including the organization and design of the simulation tool, the type of crises simulated, and the learning outcomes demonstrated among participants.
4. Skill Development: An analysis of how simulation-based learning facilitates the development of essential leadership skills, including decision-making under pressure, team management, and communication with stakeholders.

The chapter aims to provide educators, researchers, and practitioners with a comprehensive understanding of how experiential learning through simulation can enhance entrepreneurial leadership. The case study not only exemplifies the practical application of leadership theories but also serves as a blueprint for integrating similar simulation tools into entrepreneurship curricula.

BACKGROUND

Leadership Theories in Entrepreneurship

Entrepreneurial leadership is unique in its twin focus on innovation and the capacity to cope with uncertainty. Classical leadership theories, though enlightening, need to be translated to the fluid and frequently turbulent environment of entrepreneurial firms. Three leading leadership theories offer a valuable framework for making sense of the special challenges confronting entrepreneurs:

Transformational leadership, as explained by Bass and Riggio (2006) and elucidated in more recent research (Tang et al., 2020), focuses on a leader's ability to influence and inspire their followers to accomplish extraordinary results by transcending personal self-interests in the larger interest of the organization. In entrepreneurial settings, transformational leaders play a key role in establishing a strong vision that inspires team members to move forward with innovations in spite of limited resources or external ambiguities. Their capability to instill a sense of common purpose makes them particularly invaluable in times of crisis when unprecedented changes require strategic vision as well as moral encouragement (Lee et al., 2018).

Formulated by Hersey and Blanchard and reexamined in recent research (e.g., Martínez, 2017), situational leadership theory argues that there is no one "best" style of leadership. Rather, effective leadership depends on the leader's capacity to measure the readiness and competence of his followers and shift his style as appropriate. In the volatile context of entrepreneurship, the situational leadership model emerges as especially prominent. Entrepreneurs tend to encounter varied problems that call for a change in directive and supportive behavior. For example, in a crisis situation, the leader may have to become more authoritarian in order to make quick decisions, while in a period of relative calm, a participative style may work better (Dionne et al., 2014). Such flexibility is important in developing an adaptive organizational culture that is able to react to internal and external changes (Sharma et al., 2015).

Adaptive leadership, developed by Heifetz and Linsky and supplemented by more recent work (Oreg & Berson, 2019), builds on this conversation by highlighting the value of learning and adaptability in response to change. In contrast to conventional approaches that emphasize technical problem solving, adaptive leadership focuses on engaging people to address difficult challenges that demand new patterns of thinking and behaving. Adaptive leadership cannot be overemphasized in entrepreneurial practice. Entrepreneurs find themselves in ambiguous situations frequently, where past experience and current norms do not apply. Adaptive leaders shape a space by fostering the culture of incessant learning and experimentation where failures are regarded as prospects for learning, and resilience is constructed by constantly addressing predicaments (Hassan et al., 2013).

The volatile nature of entrepreneurial businesses calls for leaders who are not just visionary but also resilient and adaptable. Adaptability can be understood as the ability to change strategies midway in the face of unforeseen difficulties, and resilience is about bouncing back from adversity. Crisis management, which is a combination of these traits, demands that leaders take rapid, high-pressure decisions in critical situations. These competencies are symbiotic: adaptability enables leaders to modify their strategy in response to new information, resilience permits them to survive and learn from failure, and successful crisis management combines these traits to guide the organization through challenging circumstances.

Recent empirical research (e.g., Ensley, Hmieleski, & Pearce, 2006; replicated by McIntyre & Zhang, 2021) has validated the positive relationship between adaptive leadership styles and organizational effectiveness in entrepreneurial settings. Leaders with high emotional intelligence—a dimension of resilience Goleman (1995) highlighted and one that is echoed in current research by Rahim and Mansoor (2020)—are more able to maintain team morale under crisis, thus ensuring recovery and long-term success. Entrepreneurial leadership, in effect, involves not just strategic visioning but also the ability to adjust and maintain organizational momentum under pressure.

Organizational Behavior in Crisis

Organizational behavior (OB) literature offers valuable insights into the functioning of teams under pressure, a theme of specific interest in entrepreneurial crises. One of the most widely used models of group dynamics is Tuckman's model of group development, which describes the processes of forming, storming, norming, and performing. Under crisis, teams tend to revert back to previous stages—like the storming stage—marked by conflict, confusion, and dissolution of established norms. Such backsliding is particularly challenging for entrepreneurial leaders as they try to rebuild cohesion and direction in the face of escalated tensions.

Recent studies by Wood et al., (2020) point out that heterogeneous team configurations can both exacerbate and enrich group dynamics in the context of high-stakes situations. Fluidity in team dynamics is further aggravated during crises due to the occurrence of various personalities and expertise sets. During periods of high intensity, effective communication and conflict resolution become more essential. Research works by Jehn (1995) have since been developed further by current researchers (e.g., Liu et al., 2012), who identified that teams with open communication channels and proactive conflict management are in a better place to manage crises. Leaders who are able to create a climate of trust and teamwork can counteract the ill effects of stress and uncertainty and thereby save team performance even when pressure from the outside increases (Sung et al., 2014)

Decision making in the context of a crisis is quite distinct from decision making in more stable contexts. In normal times, decisions can frequently be made using deliberative processes that provide time for exhaustive analysis as well as consensus-building. Yet, crises call for swift, at times intuitive, decision-making to counter emerging threats. Organizational behavior studies have recognized that high-stakes situations can prompt cognitive biases like groupthink, in which the urge for agreement trumps critical analysis (Schmitt et al., 2016). Additionally, stress can compromise judgment and lower the potential for analytical reasoning, resulting in inferior outcomes.

Successful crisis management, then, demands leaders who excel at trading off speed and accuracy. Decision models, including the recognition-primed decision models

(Dimitriou et al., 2022), provide a valuable framework for explaining how experts can make rapid decisions through pattern recognition and experience instead of comprehensive analysis (Sartzetaki et al., 2024). This model has specific relevance in entrepreneurial settings, where leaders frequently make decisions under uncertainty and incomplete information. By drawing on their intuition and past experiences, successful leaders are able to balance the trade-offs between thoroughness and speed, making decisions that are not only timely but also contextually relevant. (Sklias et al., 2024)

Another key aspect of organizational behavior is the capacity for an organization to learn from crisis experiences. Cultures that place a high value on continuous improvement, innovation, and flexibility will be more resilient to come out even stronger following a crisis. Current research by Zorn et al., 2019) has reaffirmed that, in entrepreneurial enterprises—where formal structures can be less entrenched—establishing a culture of openness and learning can enable swift adaptation and recovery.

Learning and Simulation Tools

Experiential learning theory, as extended by more recent scholars such as Chollet eta l., 2017, posits that knowledge is constructed through the transformation of experience. Kolb's experiential learning cycle—comprising concrete experience, reflective observation, abstract conceptualization, and active experimentation—provides a robust framework for understanding how individuals learn in dynamic environments. In the context of entrepreneurship education, experiential learning enables students to integrate theoretical knowledge with practical skills by engaging in activities that mimic real-world challenges.

Simulation-based learning has emerged as a particularly effective application of experiential learning in business education. Simulations create immersive environments in which students can experiment with decision-making, strategic planning, and crisis management without the risks associated with real-world failures. In research studies such as Salas, et al., 2009) have documented the benefits of simulation tools in enhancing learning outcomes. These benefits include improved retention of theoretical concepts, heightened engagement, and the development of critical soft skills such as problem-solving, adaptability, and teamwork (Anastastasiadou et al., 2025)

In entrepreneurial education, simulations frequently mimic the problems of launching and growing a company, such as market competition, resource management, and operational emergencies. By inserting students into decision-making positions in these simulated contexts, instructors are able to create the space for real-time feedback and reflective learning. For example, a simulation might involve a sudden market downturn or a disruptive technological innovation, forcing participants to make rapid decisions and adapt their strategies on the fly. Such experiences not only reinforce theoretical models of leadership but also allow students to develop the intuition required for effective crisis management (Lee et., 2018).

Outside of entrepreneurship, simulation-based tools have been employed in domains like emergency management, military training, and healthcare for a long time to ready leaders for high-stakes situations (e.g., Gishu et al., 2015). Such simulations focus on quick decision-making, situational awareness, and stress management (Dimitriou et al., 2024). That these methods are crossing over into business education speaks to the interdisciplinary appeal of simulation-based learning. Empirical research indicates that crisis management simulation learning results in enhanced performance on future actual tasks. Trainees frequently indicate increased confidence, enhanced decision-making skill, and higher ability to handle team dynamics during stress. These results align with the objectives of entrepreneurial education, where crisis navigating skills are a determining factor towards long-term entrepreneurial success.

METHODOLOGY

This methodological framework that underpins the chapter, outlines the case study design, describing the simulation tool, detailing the implementation context, and explicating the data collection and analysis strategies. Together, these methodological components provide a structured approach to investigating how simulation-based learning bridges the gap between theoretical leadership models and practical application in entrepreneurial crisis management.

Case Study Design

The case study method was chosen to conduct this research because it is the most appropriate method for examining in-depth complex, context-dependent phenomena. Entrepreneurial leadership during crises entails a multitude of dynamic variables interacting in real time. As opposed to experimental designs that typically attempt to isolate variables under controlled environments, case study methodology permits an immersive investigation of a real setting—while enabling the observer to witness the intricacies of decision-making, team dynamics, and leadership behavior develop in the midst of simulated crises.

Using a case study methodology enables the research to:

- Embrace Complexity: Offer an in-depth investigation of the application of theoretical leadership concepts within a simulated, high-pressure entrepreneurial context.
- Contextual Understanding: Enable the analysis of interactions between participants, the simulation environment, and the inherent uncertainties of crisis scenarios.

- Generate Rich Qualitative Insights: Offer qualitative data that reveal insights into the cognitive and emotional processes of participants, which are essential for understanding the experiential learning process.

This approach is particularly valuable given that the study's objective is not only to measure performance outcomes but also to explore the transformative process through which simulation-based learning impacts leadership skills.

The case study approach is guided by the following research questions:

1. How does simulation-based learning facilitate the practical application of leadership theories in high-pressure entrepreneurial contexts?
2. What specific leadership competencies (e.g., adaptability, resilience, crisis management) are developed or enhanced through the simulation experience?
3. How do participants perceive the value of simulation as a bridge between theoretical concepts and real-world practice?

These questions drive the collection of both quantitative and qualitative data, aiming to provide a comprehensive understanding of the simulation's impact on leadership development. The simulation tool was created to model a crisis situation in an entrepreneurial context. The tool's design is modular, so participants can experience several crisis events sequentially and dynamically. The main elements of the simulation are depicted in Figure 1.

Each module represents a distinct crisis (e.g., market downturn, operational disruption, internal conflict) that unfolds over predetermined time intervals. These modules are interlinked to simulate the cascading effects of decisions made in earlier stages.

Figure 1. Scenario modules development

Decision Points	Embedded within each module are critical decision points where participants must choose between alternative strategies. These choices affect subsequent modules, thereby creating a feedback loop that mirrors real-world consequences
Role-Playing Components	Players receive designated roles (e.g., CEO, operations manager, marketing director) to promote an authentic team setting. The role allocation aims to replicate the multidisciplinary aspect of entrepreneurial leadership.
Resource Management Interface	A virtual dashboard offers real-time feedback on resource distribution, financial success, and staff morale. The interface is interactive, with players needing to adapt strategies according to changing circumstances.
Crisis Communication Simulator	An integrated module focuses on stakeholder communication, where participants craft messages to investors, customers, and employees. This element emphasizes the importance of transparency and ethical decision-making during crises.
Feedback Mechanism	Throughout the simulation, automated feedback is provided to participants, highlighting the immediate impacts of their decisions and offering insights for reflection.

The simulation tool is supported by core leadership theories of transformational, situational, and adaptive leadership, as depicted in Figure 2. The Transformational Leadership tasks learners with communicating a clear vision and motivating their team under resource constraints. The Situational Leadership Components demand that learners alternate between directive and supportive styles of leadership depending on the changing demands of the crisis situation. The Adaptive Leadership Emphasis asks participants to try new approaches and learn from setbacks, building a continuous improvement and resilience culture. This combination guarantees that the simulation not only examines technical decision-making ability but also builds soft skills that are necessary for successful leadership.

Figure 2. Core leadership theories components of simulation tool

Entrepreneurial Course Environment

The simulation was introduced in an advanced entrepreneurship course at a business school. The course is targeted at graduate students who are on the verge of starting their own businesses or joining startups as leaders. The classroom setting offered a controlled environment in which experimental learning techniques could be incorporated with standard coursework. The simulation was used as a capstone project, allowing students to integrate theoretical learning with real-world leadership dilemmas.

Participants in the study consisted of 35 graduate students enrolled in the entrepreneurship course. The cohort represented a diverse mix of backgrounds, including business, engineering, and social sciences, which enriched the team dynamics and broadened the range of perspectives during the simulation. Key characteristics of the participant group included:

- Educational Background: All participants had at least an undergraduate degree, with many holding professional experience in various industries.
- Experience Levels: While some students had prior exposure to entrepreneurship and leadership roles, others were encountering these concepts for the first time in a practical setting.
- Demographic Diversity: The group was diverse in terms of age, gender, and cultural backgrounds, which provided a fertile ground for exploring the interplay of different leadership styles and organizational behaviors.

The simulation was conducted over a two-day intensive workshop. The logistics were carefully planned to maximize the experiential learning outcomes:

1. Pre-Simulation Briefing: Prior to the simulation, participants attended a briefing session where the objectives, rules, and structure of the simulation were explained. This session also provided an overview of the leadership theories that would be applied during the exercise.
2. Simulation Environment: The simulation was hosted in a dedicated computer lab equipped with the necessary software and digital interfaces. The physical setup included round-table configurations to facilitate team discussions and real-time decision-making.
3. Facilitation: Two facilitators—experienced entrepreneurs and academic instructors—were present to guide the simulation, offer support, and ensure that the exercise adhered to the planned structure.
4. Time Management: A dedicated time box was assigned to each crisis module so that the simulation progressed at a fast pace but with adequate time for key decision points and feedback.

Data Collection and Analysis

A multi-method approach was adopted to capture both quantitative and qualitative data throughout the simulation. The following instruments and techniques were employed:

Observations

Facilitator Observations: During the simulation, facilitators recorded observations of participant behavior, team interactions, and decision-making processes. These field notes focused on key moments where leadership styles shifted or where significant challenges were encountered

Video Recording: The simulation sessions were video recorded to allow for the capture of non-verbal clues, team dynamics, and involuntary reactions. These recordings yielded rich contextual data for subsequent analysis.

Surveys and Questionnaires

Pre- and Post-Simulation Surveys: Participants took part in pre- and post-simulation surveys to measure changes in self-reported leadership competencies like adaptability, crisis management, and emotional intelligence.

Feedback Questionnaires: Directly after the simulation, formatted questionnaires solicited participant feedback on the simulation's effectiveness, the reality of the crisis scenarios, and the perceived value of the experiential learning experience.

Performance Metrics

Simulation Performance Data: Key performance indicators (KPIs), including the efficiency of resource management, decision turnaround time, and overall team performance, were automatically tracked in the digital dashboard of the simulation tool. The metrics provided quantitative measures of participants' performance in navigating the simulated crisis.

Scenario Outcome Analysis: Every crisis module was followed by a debriefing that quantified the outcome of decisions taken throughout the simulation. This provided a quantitative measure of decision quality in relation to pre-established benchmarks.

Interviews and Focus Groups

Semi-Structured Interviews: A subset of participants was invited to participate in semi-structured interviews after the simulation. These interviews probed deeper into individual experiences, challenges faced, and the evolution of leadership skills during the exercise.

Focus Group Discussions: Post-simulation focus groups were conducted to encourage collective reflection and discussion. These sessions provided insights into team dynamics, shared learning experiences, and the perceived impact of the simulation on future leadership practices.

Data Analysis Procedures

Qualitative Data Analysis

Thematic Analysis: Qualitative information from facilitator observations, video recordings, interviews, and focus groups were analyzed via thematic analysis. Themes were identified and coded concerning adaptability, resilience, management in crisis, and shifts in leadership style. This method facilitated the detection of patterns in participants' adaptations in leadership behaviors during the simulation.

Narrative Analysis: The development of team dynamics and personal decision-making processes was explored using narrative analysis, giving in-depth case narratives that demonstrate the interaction between theory and practice. These narratives assisted in the comprehension of the context-specific leadership effectiveness factors.

Quantitative Data Analysis

Descriptive Statistics: Pre- and post-simulation survey responses were subjected to descriptive statistics to quantify changes in self-perceived leadership competencies. Mean scores, standard deviations, and percentage enhancements were determined to measure the effect of the simulation.
Performance Metric Analysis: Statistics were applied to data collected from the dashboard of the simulation to establish correlations among decision-making pace, resource allocation, and overall team performance. Patterns and trends were plotted on graphs and charts, which allowed for easy comparison of performance on various crisis modules.
Comparative Analysis: Where possible, performance data were contrasted between various teams and positions to determine what factors led to successful outcomes. This comparative analysis revealed how different leadership styles affected the simulation outcomes.

The Simulation Case Study

This section presents an in-depth case study of a simulation designed to replicate the high-pressure environment of entrepreneurial crises. The simulation was integrated into an advanced entrepreneurship course to facilitate experiential learning in leadership and organizational behavior. The narrative below describes the simulation's timeline, outlines the key challenges and decision points, details how participants engaged with the scenario, and provides illustrative examples of critical moments and outcomes.

Scenario Description

The simulation was structured as a multi-stage crisis scenario that unfolded over the course of two days. The design intentionally mimicked the cascading nature of real-world crises, where early decisions would have ripple effects throughout the scenario. Participants were assigned roles within a startup environment, including positions such as CEO, operations manager, marketing director, and finance officer. Each role was crafted to reflect the interdisciplinary nature of entrepreneurial leadership, requiring a blend of strategic vision, tactical responsiveness, and interpersonal skills.

Timeline and Structure

The simulation was divided into three main phases:

1. Phase 1: Initialization and Early Warning (Day 1 Morning)

In this phase, participants were introduced to the startup scenario, including background information, organizational structure, and initial market conditions. A series of mild disturbances—such as a slight dip in sales figures and a low-level internal communication issue—served as early indicators that prompted participants to begin thinking about potential crises. The intention was to familiarize participants with the simulation environment and the interactive digital dashboard, which displayed real-time metrics on resource allocation, market performance, and team morale.

2. Phase 2: Crisis Escalation (Day 1 Afternoon to Day 2 Morning)

As the simulation progressed, the startup faced a major external crisis: an abrupt market downturn caused by a competitor launching a disruptive innovation. Simultaneously, internal challenges emerged, including a significant breakdown in team communication and a supply chain disruption. This phase was designed to test participants' abilities to prioritize, delegate, and make swift, informed decisions under increasing pressure. Critical decision points were inserted at regular intervals, where teams had to choose strategic responses from a pre-defined set of options (e.g., cost-cutting, innovation pivots, crisis communication strategies).

3. Phase 3: Resolution and Reflection (Day 2 Afternoon)

In the third phase, the immediate crisis started to resolve as the consequences of participants' decisions became evident. Teams were given time to stabilize operations, engage in a structured debriefing session, and reflect on their decision-making processes. During this phase, a post-crisis scenario was introduced to simulate the long-term impacts of crisis management on team morale and stakeholder trust. Participants were asked to develop recovery strategies and set plans for sustainable growth, which were later analyzed as part of the performance metrics.

Key Challenges

Throughout the simulation, several key challenges were strategically introduced to stimulate critical thinking and leadership adaptability. Among these were:

1. Market Shock: The sudden appearance of a disruptive competitor required rapid strategic realignment. Participants had to decide whether to invest in new technology, pivot the business model, or intensify marketing efforts to retain customer loyalty.
2. Internal Communication Breakdown: Conflicts and misunderstandings among team members jeopardized the organization's unity. This issue required leaders to step in promptly to rebuild trust and redefine roles.
3. Supply Chain Disruption: A key supplier abruptly defaulted on the delivery of vital components, compelling teams to redirect resources and seek new suppliers within stringent timeframes.
4. Stakeholder Pressure: External stakeholders, including investors and customers, demanded immediate explanations and assurances. Participants had to craft timely and ethical communication strategies to maintain credibility and manage expectations.

At each of these decision points, participants were provided with a limited window (ranging from 10 to 20 minutes) to deliberate and select from various response options. The outcomes of these decisions were immediately reflected in the simulation's digital dashboard, which updated key performance indicators (KPIs) in real time.

Participant Engagement

Students interacted with the simulation mainly through an interactive online platform that replicated the startup's operations dashboard. The dashboard provided real-time feedback on financial performance, market share, operational indicators, and team morale. Moreover, an integrated communications module allowed teams to send messages, prepare press releases, and hold virtual meetings—replicating the dynamics of a real startup under pressure. Each participant's role was tailored to challenge specific leadership competencies as depicted in Figure 3.

The CEO is tasked with setting the overall strategic direction and mediating between conflicting interests, so was central to navigating the external market shock and internal team conflicts. The Operations Manager is faced with supply chain issues, so needed to quickly identify alternative suppliers, reallocate resources, and manage operational disruptions. With the sudden market downturn, the marketing director had to innovate and reposition the brand, crafting a message that would reassure customers and differentiate the startup from competitors. Charged with monitoring cash flow and resource allocation, the finance officer's role was critical in ensuring that short-term decisions did not jeopardize the long-term financial stability of the venture.

Figure 3. Participants roles and leadership competencies

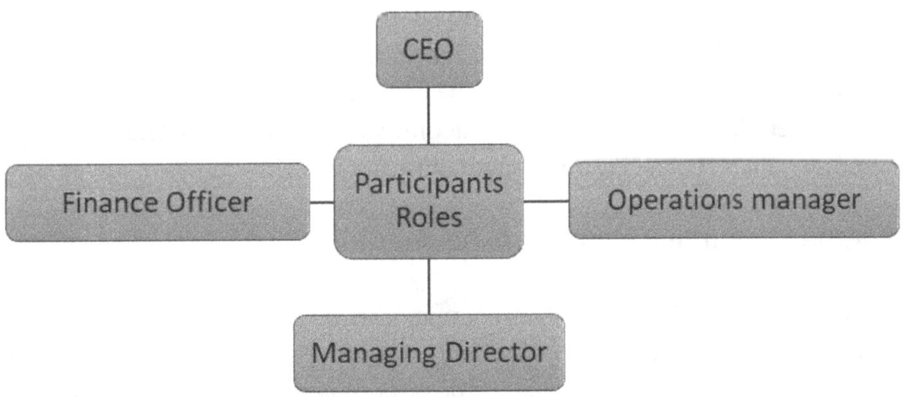

As the simulation unfolded, teams encountered scenarios that required real-time adaptive responses. For example, when the supply chain disruption occurred, the operations manager quickly convened a virtual team meeting via the dashboard's communication module. Participants engaged in rapid brainstorming sessions, weighing the pros and cons of various contingency plans. In one instance, a team opted to negotiate expedited shipping from a backup supplier—a decision that was immediately reflected in the simulation's performance metrics as a temporary dip in operational efficiency, followed by gradual recovery.

Throughout the simulation, automated feedback was provided at the conclusion of each decision point. The feedback incorporated graphical displays of the effect of decisions on important measures, such as cash holdings fluctuation and customer mood changes. Moreover, facilitators intervened at critical junctures to stimulate reflection and discussion and, as such, allow participants to gain insight into the rationale for decisions and encourage the use of different approaches. Peer-to-peer discussion in debriefing sessions enabled teams to go through their approaches, talk through different outcomes, and together derive best practices in the area of crisis management.

Illustrative Examples of Critical Moments

Managing the Market Shock

During the early stages of Phase 2, the simulation introduced a dramatic market shock. A disruptive competitor launched a similar product with advanced features, causing an immediate 15% decline in the startup's market share. At this critical juncture, the CEO and marketing director faced a pivotal decision: should they attempt to innovate on the fly, rebrand, or focus on customer retention through enhanced service offerings? In a team meeting facilitated via the dashboard, the CEO proposed an innovation pivot by reallocating funds towards research and development. However, the marketing director argued for a dual approach—simultaneously launching a targeted campaign to reinforce brand loyalty and initiating a small-scale pilot for product enhancement. The team adopted a combined strategy. The simulation's digital interface reflected this decision by showing a short-term increase in marketing expenditures but also a stabilization of customer retention rates. Over the next decision cycle, the market share loss was halted, and gradual recovery began. The immediate outcome was a learning moment for the team, as the decision underscored the value of balancing immediate tactical moves with long-term strategic innovation.

Overcoming Internal Communication Breakdowns

The second key instance arose when internal miscommunications gave rise to a running battle between the operations manager and the finance officer. The internal conflict led to slow reaction to supply chain problems, aggravating the situation. Recognizing the deteriorating team dynamics, the CEO convened an emergency virtual meeting. During the meeting, team members were encouraged to express their concerns, and the facilitator prompted discussion on conflict resolution strategies. Options included appointing a neutral mediator from within the team, reassigning conflicting roles, or implementing a temporary freeze on non-critical communications to focus on crisis resolution. The team elected to appoint a senior member as an impromptu mediator. This decision not only resolved the immediate conflict but also reinforced the importance of open communication channels. The simulation's feedback indicated that team morale improved by 20% following the intervention, and subsequent decisions were made more cohesively. The resolution of the communication breakdown was highlighted as a key learning point, demonstrating how effective interpersonal leadership can mitigate operational disruptions.

Managing Stakeholder Pressure

In one of the later phases, as the crisis began to subside, a simulated press release was required to address growing concerns among investors and customers. Stakeholder pressure had mounted due to the earlier market shock and internal turmoil. The marketing director and the finance officer collaborated to devise a response that reconciled transparency with an assurance. They had the difficult choice of either fully acknowledging the seriousness of the crisis or providing a moderated version that emphasized continued recovery efforts. During the drafting process, the simulation provided real-time sentiment analysis based on simulated social media dialogue and investor responses. The team decided to issue a measured press release that acknowledged the challenges while outlining concrete steps for recovery. This decision was immediately reflected in improved stakeholder sentiment metrics, with simulated investor confidence rising by 10% and customer trust beginning to rebuild. The exercise reinforced the critical importance of ethical communication and the need for timely, balanced stakeholder engagement during a crisis.

ANALYSIS AND DISCUSSION

This chapter analyzes the outcomes of the simulation in detail across four areas. First, it assesses how the simulation impacted the acquisition of key leadership competencies of adaptability, conflict resolution, and effective communication. Second, it outlines specific instances where theoretical frameworks—transformational, situational, and adaptive leadership—were utilized throughout the simulation. This is followed by a comparison of the learning outcomes of simulation-based learning and classroom-based methods, and lastly, an examination of the implications for entrepreneurship education and curriculum design in the future. One of the most significant leadership skills developed through the simulation was adaptability. Participants were continuously challenged by unforeseen events—such as sudden market shocks and internal disruptions—that required them to quickly adjust their strategies. The simulation's dynamic environment forced leaders to depart from rigid planning and adopt flexible, real-time responses.

The formalized decision points in every crisis module compelled teams to evaluate quickly changing data and pick suitable strategies. For instance, in responding to a disruptive competitor bringing out a new high-tech product, teams needed to decide between innovation pivots, intensified marketing, or a blend of both. The instant feedback through the simulation's dashboard enabled the participants to realize the effects of their decisions nearly immediately, underlining the value of agility. Adaptability was also developed through the simulation's iterative process. Every phase built on the results of earlier decisions, and leaders had to adjust their strategies as new issues cropped up. This process underscored the fact that adaptability is not a single event but a constantly changing ability, vital for working through the unpredictable environment of entrepreneurial initiatives. Conflict resolution emerged as another critical outcome of the simulation. The intentional introduction of internal communication breakdowns and role-specific tensions offered participants a realistic environment in which to practice resolving disputes.

In one instance, internal discord between the operations manager and the finance officer threatened to derail the entire team's progress. The CEO's decision to convene an emergency meeting and appoint an internal mediator was a direct application of conflict resolution strategies. The immediate improvement in team morale and subsequent smoother decision-making processes validated the efficacy of these strategies. The post-simulation debriefing sessions provided a platform for participants to reflect on conflict resolution strategies and share insights about what worked and what did not. This reflective practice not only solidified learning outcomes but also built an awareness that successful leadership often involves managing interpersonal dynamics as much as making strategic decisions.

Improvement in Effective Communication

Effective communication was another leadership competency that the simulation significantly enhanced. Throughout the exercise, participants were required to engage in various forms of communication—internal team discussions, crisis debriefings, and stakeholder messaging. Stakeholder Communication: For example, during the phase where stakeholder pressure was high, the finance officer and marketing director collaborated to craft a balanced press release. The simulation's real-time sentiment analysis provided immediate feedback on the tone and content of the communication, allowing them to adjust their messaging to better meet stakeholder expectations.

Internal Communication Dynamics: The simulation's integrated communication module, which mimicked both formal and informal communication channels, highlighted the importance of clear, consistent messaging. Teams that communicated effectively were better able to coordinate their responses to emerging crises, thereby reducing confusion and enhancing overall performance.

Leadership Competency Gains

Quantitative data from pre- and post-simulation surveys yielded clear evidence of measurable gains in self-perceived leadership competencies. Simulation participants registered significant gains on a number of dimensions, including adaptability, conflict resolution, and effective communication. These findings indicate that simulation-based learning is an effective vehicle for building the practical leadership skills that are critical to entrepreneurial success.

Adaptability Gains

One of the strongest improvements registered was in the adaptability of participants. The simulation was built to engage students in a dynamic context in which unforeseen difficulties and cascading situations demanded swift changes in strategy. Survey statistics indicated that the average self-rating scores on adaptability improved significantly following the simulation exercise. Students indicated that they had learned more about how to change strategies quickly to match evolving situations. For example, in the face of an unexpected market shock, most teams needed to reallocate resources and change their short-term strategy without losing focus on their long-term vision. The repeated decision points in the simulation, along with instant feedback through a digital dashboard, allowed students to go through the process of iterating on their strategy. This experiential involvement brought to the fore that adaptability is not an inherent quality but a developing competency, cultivated through continued exposure to uncertain and dynamic situations.

Conflict Resolution Gains

Besides adaptability, the simulation also significantly increased participants' conflict resolution competencies. During the simulation, intra-team conflicts and misunderstandings were purposely introduced to replicate real-world issues that entrepreneurial businesses often face. Participants indicated that these exercises had greatly enhanced their conflict management and resolution capacity. In the simulation, some groups had hot moments when conflicts almost derailed group efforts. In such cases, successful conflict resolution measures—such as the use of a neutral arbitrator or holding emergency sessions—were vital in restoring group unity. Both quantitative survey responses and qualitative feedback suggested that students were more confident in their ability to confront and resolve conflict quickly, a skill they recognized was too often underdeveloped in conventional learning contexts.

Effective Communication Gains

Effective communication was another area in which considerable growth was evident. The simulation highlighted the value of open, timely, and clear communication under conditions of high pressure. Participants had to undertake both internal communication with their teams as well as external communication with simulated stakeholders, including investors and customers. The immediate effect of lucid messaging through crisis stages was directly observable by improvements in stakeholder sentiment and team coordination in real time. Post-simulation feedback indicated that students not only appreciated the pivotal role that communication plays in crisis management, but also formulated pragmatic approaches to making their messages concise and compelling. In this manner, the simulation reaffirmed the fact that clear communication is one of the foundations of effective leadership, especially in entrepreneurial environments where quick decisions and ongoing adaptation are the order of the day.

Translating Theory Into Practice

Perhaps the strongest part of the simulation was the manner in which it connected leadership theoretical models with practice. There were several moments during the simulation where the application of conventional leadership theory was made visible in a very graphic way in terms of turning established leadership theory into practical, actionable strategies for everyday situations.

Transformational leadership theory focuses on vision, inspiration, and the capacity to inspire followers. In the simulation, the CEO's role was central to the demonstration of these principles. When normal operations were derailed by a sudden market shock, the CEO's capacity to communicate a clear and compelling vision was central to stabilizing the team. By suggesting a twin strategy that traded off innovation with customer retention, the CEO not only provided a clear direction but also gave team members a sense of common purpose. This vision articulation act is a classic illustration of transformational leadership. In addition, at times when the simulation challenged the team's emotional resilience—like in internal conflicts—the CEO's empathetic interventions and active attempts to mediate conflicts further illustrated the practice of transformational leadership. Such interventions served to restore trust and preserve morale, further entrenching the notion that crisis leadership demands strategic foresight as well as emotional intelligence.

Situational leadership theory argues that the most effective style of leadership is contingent on the situation and the maturity of the followers. This postulate was regularly seen in action during the simulation. In instances where quick decision-making was crucial—such as in the event of a critical supply chain breakdown—leaders tended to take on a more directive style automatically. For instance, when the operations manager had to respond to an urgent requirement to rebalance resources to counter a supply bottleneck, clear and firm directive approach was used. However, when the time demanded reflective problem-solving and brainstorming in a collaborative environment, team leaders moved to a participative style. Such seamless movement from directive to participative leadership style confirmed the underlying premises of situational leadership theory. It also showed that successful leadership is not fixed but is an ongoing interplay of different approaches that need to be modified in real time based on the unique requirements of the situation.

Adaptive leadership theory focuses on developing and learning from actions in the context of a rapidly changing context. This notion was perhaps the most immediately visible in the simulation. As teams suffered early setbacks or unexpected failures, they were forced to make repeated changes in strategy. The feedback loops built into the simulation allowed players to experiment with the short-term implications of their choices and then revise their strategies as needed. Leaders who fostered a culture that was receptive to experimentation—recognizing that not every decision would be an immediate success—were more effective at leading their teams through the crisis. This propensity for experimentation, risk-taking, and learning from results encapsulates the key attributes of adaptive leadership. Not only did this style reaffirm theory, but it also showed that learning from failures is a vital component of effective leadership in entrepreneurial settings.

Comparison With Classic Classroom Techniques

Classic classroom techniques, including lectures, case studies, and discussions of theory, have been the staple of business education for decades. These are especially useful for communicating foundational concepts, frameworks, and analytical models that are instrumental to comprehending entrepreneurial leadership. Yet, whereas they are excellent at imparting conceptual knowledge, they tend to be less effective at simulating the intricacies and uncertainties of real-world entrepreneurial problems. In traditional environments, students usually experience information passively. They hear lectures and study written cases, which, though instructional, seldom ask them to make decisions in the moment under pressure. Therefore, these customary approaches have a tendency to form an educational environment where immediacy of decision-making does not exist and feedback on actions is postponed or hypothetical.

One of the main shortcomings of traditional methods is the built-in lag in feedback. In case studies and classroom discussions, feedback typically comes only after the fact—often in the form of post-mortem analyses or theoretical critiques. This delayed feedback cycle means that students do not directly experience the immediate consequences of their decisions. For instance, though a case study can explain the aftermath of a strategic blunder, it cannot permit students to experience the pressure of an unfolding meltdown or witness directly how a timely remedial action can arrest a crisis. In the process, students are denied the ability to iterate and adapt their decision-making processes in the moment—a key element in acquiring effective crisis management abilities.

By comparison, simulation-based learning provides an interactive and immersive counterpart that explicitly overcomes these drawbacks. In a simulation, students must make key decisions within a controlled but dynamic setting that reproduces the pressures of actual entrepreneurial environments. The setting is built to be demanding but also responsive, with real-time performance data and automated feedback systems that immediately inform students of the results of their actions. The immediacy of this feedback serves to speed up the learning process. If a decision results in an undesirable outcome, the simulation instantly reflects the consequences, enabling participants to swiftly analyze what went wrong and adapt their strategy accordingly. This quick cycle of action, feedback, and modification not only enhances students' conceptual comprehension of theoretical principles but also serves to strengthen the practical application of those principles in a pressurized setting.

One of the most significant benefits of simulation-based learning is the increased level of engagement it provides. As opposed to the passive learning characteristic of lectures and case studies, simulations demand active involvement. Students are immersed in situations where they need to work through complicated issues, communicate clearly with teammates, and cope with unexpected crises. This active participation quite naturally results in the more effective retention of leadership principles since students aren't just learning theory—they're putting it into practice in a setting that reflects the volatility of the business environment. Consequently, the experiential learning within the simulation closes the gap between theory and practice, assuring that students gain a more subtle and practical appreciation of leadership under pressure.

Additionally, simulations' interactive elements enable detailed skills building. In conventional learning environments, attention is split between the development of technical skills (like analytical thinking and financial modelling) and interpersonal skills (like emotional intelligence and conflict management). Nevertheless, those environments seldom create venues to hone sets of those kinds of skills in a collective form. In a simulation, however, participants must apply both sets of skills together. For instance, a leader may have to make a rapid financial decision while also dealing with team morale and communicating with stakeholders—all simultaneously in real time. This integrated delivery not only strengthens the overall learning experience but also reflects the complex nature of real-world entrepreneurship, in which technical and interpersonal competencies are inextricably linked.

One other key advantage of simulation-based learning is that it allows for the creation of a safe space where experimentation is possible. Traditional approaches tend not to leave much space for trial and error; an error in a lecture or case discussion has no real-world impact, but it also does not have the concrete risk that leads to actual learning. In a simulation, errors have direct and observable consequences, but they take place in a risk-free sphere. This prepares students to be calculated risk takers, to experiment with creative solutions, and to learn through failure without experiencing real-world repercussions. Through repetition, this reinforces a mindset of ongoing improvement and flexibility— skills that are most necessary in navigating the rapid universe of entrepreneurship.

In addition, the interactivity of simulations, including dynamic dashboards, role-playing, and scenario-based exercises, enables a type of interactivity that is beyond the capabilities of conventional methods. Such features make it possible for instructors to capture a wide range of data—from the speed of decision-making to communication quality—that can be examined to gain additional insights into the learning experience. This empirical strategy not only assists in the improvement of the simulation itself, but also informs the creation of more successful teaching methods and curricular designs. Essentially, simulations are both a learning experience and a research tool, providing an integrated platform for assessing and improving leadership skills.

In summary, whereas conventional classroom techniques have been of great value in creating a sound theoretical base in entrepreneurship education, they tend to be less effective in equipping students with the practical demands of actual business situations. The passive nature of these techniques, along with postponed feedback and small space for active decision-making, limits the acquisition of essential crisis management and leadership abilities. Simulation-based learning, through its immersive, interactive, and iterative nature, offers an attractive alternative not only remedying these deficiencies but also delivering greater engagement, better retention, and comprehensive skill development. As it is, combining simulation-based techniques with conventional pedagogical methods holds the potential to create more effective and resilient entrepreneurial leaders who are more prepared to handle the complexity and uncertainty of the contemporary business environment.

Advantages of Stimulation Based learning

The unique strengths of simulation-based learning go far beyond the passive imparting of theoretical knowledge. By establishing a realistic and dynamic context, the simulation forced participants to actively immerse themselves in the complex problems of entrepreneurship. This active learning promoted an environment in which students were not passive absorbers of information, but active problem solvers who were able to directly test leadership theories in action. In this way, the simulation acted as an essential link between theoretical notions learned through lectures and their practical applications, successfully bridging the gap between theory and practice.

One of the greatest analytical benefits of learning through simulation is the capacity to receive instant and actionable feedback. The design of the simulation includes an electronic dashboard with real-time performance indicators, which enables the participants to witness the immediate effects of their choices as they progress. This feedback loop is critical for speeding up the iterative process of learning. When students observe the immediate impact of their choices, they are more easily able to discern what approaches are working and what approaches are not, allowing them to make quick modifications to their strategies. Such real-time reinforcement is invaluable because it transforms mistakes into learning opportunities and allows learners to refine their decision-making processes in a controlled yet dynamic environment.

Moreover, the immersive nature of the simulation encourages a holistic form of learning that integrates both technical and interpersonal competencies. Players must not only make strategic choices about managing resources and market position but also negotiate the intrigue of team dynamics and stakeholder communication. By having this two-pronged focus, we ensure that students learn a well-rounded set of skills. From a technical perspective, they get practice in data analysis, strategic planning, and operations management; from an interpersonal perspective, they practice clear communication, conflict management, and leadership under fire. This kind of integrated skill building is difficult to accomplish with traditional lectures or case studies alone, since they seldom replicate the concurrent demands of strategic decision-making and interpersonal dynamics in a high-stakes environment.

Analytically, the simulation serves as a microcosm of actual business reality. It mimics the unpredictability of entrepreneurial problems and compels players to deal with uncertainty directly. By doing this, it develops critical thinking and adaptive reasoning—skills that are vital for leadership in dynamic environments. As students work through the simulation, they are prompted to try out various strategies, learn from setbacks, and refine their approaches continuously. This experiential loop not only reinforces theoretical frameworks of leadership but also develops the practical skills necessary for successful crisis management. The simulation's immediate, data-driven feedback also enables students to evaluate the efficacy of their decisions in the moment, developing a profound appreciation for the cause-and-effect dynamics that drive successful entrepreneurship.

In addition, the analytical advantages of simulation-based education are evident in its ability to replicate the intrinsic complexity of actual entrepreneurial situations. Conventional pedagogical methods, including lectures and static case studies, frequently present sanitized versions of business problems that do not capture the complexity and urgency of real-world situations. Simulations, on the other hand, engage students in a dynamic process in which multiple variables interact at once, thus creating a truer reflection of the business environment. This complexity requires students to engage in multifaceted problem-solving, integrating quantitative data analysis with qualitative judgments about team morale and stakeholder sentiment. As a result, the simulation not only reinforces theoretical knowledge but also fosters the development of practical, analytical skills that are critical for navigating the unpredictable terrain of entrepreneurship.

In summary, simulation-based learning offers a range of advantages that are both profound and multifaceted. Its ability to deliver instant feedback, encourage integrated skill development, and simulate the complexity of real-world problems makes it an especially effective tool in the field of entrepreneurship education. By forcing students to actively engage with the content and constantly adjust their strategies according to real-time information, simulation-based learning develops a richer, more analytical understanding of leadership. This repetitive and experiential learning approach not only bridges the gap between theoretical understanding and practical implementation but also equips prospective entrepreneurs with flexible and analytical thinking skills necessary to thrive in a dynamic and uncertain business environment.

Implications for Entrepreneurship Education

The lessons learned from this simulation have far-reaching implications for entrepreneurship education going forward, as the business world continues to increase in complexity and uncertainty. Established methods of curriculum development, rooted frequently in lecturing, case studies, and theoretical discussion, need to be reconsidered based on the clear advantages of engaging, experiential learning demonstrated here. The simulation amply demonstrated that when students are immersed in dynamic, real-time settings that replicate the complex challenges of entrepreneurship, students are able to acquire pragmatic leadership capabilities—like adaptability, conflict management, and clear communication—that are essential to thrive in the turbulent market conditions of today.

Incorporating simulation-based learning modules into entrepreneurship curricula presents an encouraging solution to fill the age-old gap between theory and practice. When coupled with traditional lectures and case studies, these modules create a well-rounded learning experience that cements conceptual understanding while building practical skills concurrently. Students are able to try out alternative leadership approaches, see the immediate impact of their choices, and iteratively adjust their strategies in response to real-time feedback. This iterative process is essential to the cultivation of an agile mindset, which is highly capable of dealing with the fast pace of change and uncertainty inherent in entrepreneurial ventures.

Secondly, the simulation emphasizes the value of cross-disciplinary teamwork in entrepreneurship education. Business problems in the real world seldom fall neatly within the confines of a single discipline. As it is, it's imperative that curricula going forward prioritize cross-functional teamwork, getting students from different academic backgrounds to work together in solving multifaceted problems. Not only does this interdisciplinary modality enhance the learning experience through the exposure it provides to different ways of thinking, but it also reflects the reality of entrepreneurial activity today, where success tends to hinge on the combination of technical, managerial, and creative skills.

Along with curriculum revitalization, the simulation experience underlines the important requirement of continual faculty development. Faculty members have to be expert not just in entrepreneurship's theoretical foundations, but also in simulation tools' technical and pedagogical intricacies. Faculty who are expertly trained in simulation tools can conduct simulations more easily and guide reflective debriefings through which students internalize learning experiences. Investment in extensive training programs for faculty is thus imperative. These training programs must address both the technical nuances of using simulation software as well as the pedagogical methods required to shepherd students through the complicated, iterative process of learning. By doing this, instructors can foster a positive learning environment where continuous learning and adaptive learning are prevailing themes.

In addition, embracing a hybrid learning model that merges online simulation software and face-to-face interactions can create a more compelling and flexible learning experience. This blended model captures the best of both the digital and face-to-face learning modes. On one side, the simulation software delivers an interactive forum for real-time decisions and instantaneous feedback. On the other, face-to-face interaction allows for probing discussions, peer problem-solving, and customized mentoring. This kind of immersive learning setting not only raises the level of student engagement and knowledge retention but also supports the overall development of entrepreneurial leadership skills.

Finally, the effectiveness of the simulation-based learning method offers a strong argument for the re-evaluation of the future of entrepreneurship education. By incorporating experiential learning modules in the curriculum, stressing inter-disciplinary teamwork, and making significant investment in faculty development, business schools can more effectively prepare entrepreneurs of the future to excel in an increasingly dynamic business environment. Such a comprehensive approach guarantees that students are not just familiar with theoretical knowledge but are also endowed with practical, adaptive competencies required to lead successfully in intricate real-world settings.

DISCUSSION

The results in this chapter provide a strong argument for the incorporation of simulation-based learning in entrepreneurship education but also provide a number of discussion points and potential areas for further research. The evidence suggests that simulation-based learning effectively improves leadership competencies by giving instant feedback, allowing active learning, and providing the possibility of applying theoretical models in real time. This experiential methodology not only builds hard skills like strategic decision-making and resource allocation but also nurtures critical soft skills like adaptability, conflict resolution, and communication. By doing this, it closes a long-standing gap between theory and practice—a gap that is difficult for traditional classroom methodologies to fill.

One of the important discussion points arising from this research is how the learner's experience is revolutionized through active participation. The simulation context compels participants to deal with difficulties that reflect real-world uncertainties, making them think on their feet and make decisions in a pressured environment. This active learning experience underpins the theoretical underpinnings of transformational, situational, and adaptive leadership by locating them in situations where their practical application is instantly examined. On the other hand, conventional pedagogical methods tend to be passive in nature and only give feedback at a later time, which may hinder the development of critical crisis management skills. The strong and immediate feedback mechanisms that are part of simulation-based learning appear to be instrumental in accelerating the circular process of learning, thus leading to more adaptive and skilled entrepreneurial leaders.

Despite these promising results, several limitations should be noted. The focus of the present research was limited to a specific course with a relatively small, heterogeneous group of graduate students. This limitation generates concerns regarding the generalizability of the results to other educational contexts, disciplines, and larger groups. In addition, though the simulation was useful in terms of understanding leadership behavior and decision-making, some participants indicated that some scenarios would be more effective with added complexity and unpredictability to better reflect the subtleties of actual entrepreneurial crises in the real world. Also, while the assessment of soft skills, though promising, was based to a large extent on self-report measures, the use of more objective and multimethod assessment tools is indicated in future research.

In consideration of these factors, a number of directions for future research arise. Future research should seek to replicate and expand these findings in a broader variety of educational settings and with larger groups of students to determine the more generalizability of simulation-based learning in entrepreneurship. It would be especially worthwhile to investigate the long-term effect of simulation-based learning on entrepreneurial success using longitudinal research designs that follow participants' performance and career development over time. These studies might offer greater insight into how experiential learning affects not just near-term leadership skills but also long-term entrepreneurial efficacy in the distant future.

Finally, advances in technology offer exciting possibilities for enriching simulation-based learning. Future studies may explore the incorporation of more advanced digital platforms, including virtual reality and augmented reality, to develop even more immersive and interactive simulation experiences. These technologies have the potential to bridge the divide between theoretical learning and real-world practice even further, providing more vivid, detailed learning experiences. Researchers can also look into examining the impact of simulation-based learning in cross-cultural contexts to ascertain if cultural differences affect the efficacy of experiential learning approaches in building entrepreneurial leadership competencies.

One other area of promise for future research includes studying the ideal balance between autonomy and guidance in simulation environments. Although a certain level of structured feedback is necessary, excessive intervention may again suppress creativity and independent problem-solving. Researching the balance that optimizes both learning and innovation will be important to advancing simulation-based educational software.

Lastly, the incorporation of simulation-based learning within blended learning frameworks needs to be researched. The blending of web-based simulation tools with face-to-face learning may provide a balanced approach to entrepreneurship education, drawing on the strengths of both online and face-to-face learning methodologies. Future studies need to assess the impact of such blended frameworks on student engagement, retention, and acquisition of technical and social leadership skills.

In summary, though this chapter illustrates the immense value of simulation-based learning in developing entrepreneurial leadership and organizational behavior competencies, it also points to the necessity for ongoing research and development. Through examining the limitations outlined and investigating new technological and methodological avenues, future research can significantly enhance what is known regarding how experiential learning can be optimized in order to prepare future entrepreneurs to tackle the sophisticated and turbulent challenges in the business world today. Such endeavors will be critical for creating more efficacious, robust, and responsive entrepreneurial leaders who can thrive within perpetually shifting global contexts.

CONCLUDING REMARKS

In conclusion, this chapter has discussed the acquisition of entrepreneurial leadership and organizational behavior competencies using simulation-based learning, presenting an integrated review of both the theoretical and applied aspects of experiential education. The research initiated by establishing the imperative for strong leadership in entrepreneurial settings, especially during times of crisis, and emphasized the constraints of classroom methods for developing applied skills like adaptability, conflict management, and good communication. By comparison, the simulation approach offered a live, interactive setting that strongly resembles the sophistication and unpredictability of actual entrepreneurial problems.

The literature review highlighted the relevance of different leadership theories—transformational, situational, and adaptive—as underlying frameworks that guide successful crisis management. It also shed light on the wide gap between theory and practice, one that simulation-based learning is particularly well placed to fill. By combining experiential learning theory with advanced simulation technology, educators can establish a learning context in which students not only grasp leadership principles theoretically but also acquire the first-hand experience necessary to operate in volatile business environments.

The methodological framework outlined in this chapter illustrated the meticulous design and implementation of the simulation case study. The simulation was designed to reflect real-world entrepreneurial crises in several stages, enabling participants to experience decision-making processes with immediate and quantifiable results. With feedback in real time and iterative learning cycles, participants could adjust their strategies in real time, thus internalizing the theoretical as well as practical dimensions of leadership. The intensive data gathering and analysis—including quantitative surveys, qualitative observations, and performance data—yielded strong evidence of substantial improvement in leadership competencies, such as greater adaptability, better conflict resolution, and improved communication.

The case study itself dramatically demonstrated the use of leadership theories in action. Transformational leadership was on full display as the CEO managed to convey a clear vision in the midst of crisis, and situational and adaptive theories of leadership came alive in the dynamic changes in leadership styles according to changing challenges. These practical illustrations not only confirmed the theoretical frameworks explored in the literature review, but also served as real-life examples of how simulation-based learning can enhance a richer understanding of leadership in the crucible.

The trial and consideration also demonstrated that simulation-based learning is much more effective than traditional pedagogical approaches in building the extensive skill set necessary for entrepreneurial achievement. In contrast to standard lectures and case studies, which provide delayed feedback and primarily passive engagement, the simulation's real-time interactivity, instantaneous feedback, and contextual presence substantially increased both retention and applied application of leadership principles. The evidence is that simulation-based learning not only augments conventional pedagogical methods but also has the potential to radically change entrepreneurship education by preparing future leaders with the adaptive, strategic, and interpersonal abilities required to excel in a dynamic business environment.

The implications for entrepreneurship education are significant. The incorporation of simulation-based learning modules in curricula is a paradigm shift that can close the long-standing gap between theoretical instruction and practical application. By adopting a blended learning model that incorporates conventional methods with immersive simulations, educators can make the learning environment more engaging, flexible, and effective. Moreover, the effectiveness of this method highlights the necessity of interdisciplinary cooperation and continuous faculty development so that both the students and the instructors are equally well-prepared to take advantage of the strengths of simulation technology.

In the future, there is an evident need for more research to advance and extend the application of simulation-based learning for entrepreneurship. Future research would address methods that attempt to increase the realism and sophistication of simulations, include the use of cutting-edge technologies such as virtual reality, and investigate the long-term effect of experience-based learning on entrepreneurial success. Furthermore, it will be important to extend the use of these methods to other educational contexts and larger groups of students in order to permit generalizability of results and foster broad-scale curricular innovations.

In conclusion, this chapter illustrates that simulation-based learning provides a compelling, integrative methodology for entrepreneurial leadership competency development. Through bringing together theory and practice, it equips prospective entrepreneurs with the ability to tackle the complex problems of contemporary business contexts with confidence and resilience. As universities go on transforming to meet the needs of a more complicated world, the research and approaches outlined herein offer a strong basis for developing the future generation of adaptive, creative, and successful entrepreneurial leaders.

REFERENCES

Anastasiadou, S., Zirinoglou, P., Seremeti, L., Masouras, A., Komodromos, M., & Anastasiadis, L. (2025). Statistical implicative analysis: A distinguished statistical methodology in evaluating Greek students' attitudes toward the use of AI. In *Real-world tools and scenarios for entrepreneurship exploration* (pp. 133–168). IGI Global.

Banks, G. C., McCauley, K. D., Gardner, W. L., & Guler, C. E. (2016). A meta-analytic review of authentic and transformational leadership: A test for redundancy. *The Leadership Quarterly*, *27*(4), 634–652. DOI: 10.1016/j.leaqua.2016.02.006

Bass, B. M., & Riggio, R. E. (2006). *Transformational leadership* (2nd ed.). Lawrence Erlbaum Associates Publishers., DOI: 10.4324/9781410617095

Dimitriou, D., & Karagkouni, A. (2022). 'Airports' Sustainability Strategy: Evaluation framework upon environmental awareness'. *Frontiers in Sustainability.*, *3*, 880718. Advance online publication. DOI: 10.3389/frsus.2022.880718

Dimitriou, D., Sartzetaki, M., & Karagkouni, A. (2024). *Managing Airport Corporate Performance: Leveraging Business Intelligence and Sustainable Transition*. Elsevier. DOI: 10.1016/C2023-0-51427-2

Dionne, S. D., Gupta, A., Sotak, K. L., Shirreffs, K. A., Serban, A., Hao, C., & Yammarino, F. J. (2014). A 25-year perspective on levels of analysis in leadership research. *The Leadership Quarterly*, *25*(1), 6–35. DOI: 10.1016/j.leaqua.2013.11.002

Ghisu, T., Arca, B., Pellizzaro, G., & Duce, P. (2015). An improved cellular automata for wildfire spread. *Procedia Computer Science*, *51*, 2287–2296.

Hassan, S., Mahsud, R., Yukl, G., & Prussia, G. E. (2013). Ethical and empowering leadership and leader effectiveness. *Journal of Managerial Psychology*, *28*(2), 133–146. DOI: 10.1108/02683941311300252

Jehn, K. A. (1995). A multimethod examination of the benefits and detriments of intragroup conflict. *Administrative Science Quarterly*, *40*(2), 256–282. DOI: 10.2307/2393638

Lai, F.-Y., Tang, H.-C., Lu, S.-C., Lee, Y.-C., & Lin, C.-C. (2020). Transformational leadership and job performance: The mediating role of work engagement. *SAGE Open*, *10*(1), 1–12. DOI: 10.1177/2158244019899085

Lee, A., Willis, S., & Tian, A. W. (2018). Empowering leadership: A meta-analytic examination of incremental contribution, mediation, and moderation. *Journal of Organizational Behavior*, *39*(3), 306–325. DOI: 10.1002/job.2205

Liu, Y., Keller, R. T., & Shih, H.-A. (2011). The impact of team-member exchange, differentiation, team commitment, and knowledge sharing on R&D project team performance. *R & D Management*, *41*(3), 274–287.

Martínez-Martí, M. L., & Ruch, W. (2017). Character strengths predict resilience over and above positive affect, self-efficacy, optimism, social support, self-esteem, and life satisfaction. *The Journal of Positive Psychology*, *12*(2), 110–119. DOI: 10.1080/17439760.2016.1163403

Oreg, S., & Berson, Y. (2019). Leaders' impact on organizational change: Bridging theoretical and methodological chasms. *The Academy of Management Annals, 13*(1), 272–307. DOI: 10.5465/annals.2016.0138

Salas, E., Wildman, J. L., & Piccolo, R. F. (2009). Using simulation-based training to enhance management education. *Academy of Management Learning & Education, 8*(4), 559–573. DOI: 10.5465/AMLE.2009.47785474

Sartzetaki, M., Dimitriou, D., & Karagkouni, A. (2025). Assortment of the Regional Business Ecosystem Effects Driven by New Motorway Projects, Transportation Research. *Procedia, 82*, 515-529. DOI: 10.1016/j.trpro.2024.12.111

Schmitt, A., Den Hartog, D. N., & Belschak, F. D. (2016). Transformational leadership and proactive work behaviour: A moderated mediation model including work engagement and job strain. *Journal of Occupational and Organizational Psychology, 89*(3), 588–610. DOI: 10.1111/joop.12143

Sharma, P. N., & Kirkman, B. L. (2015). Leveraging leaders: A literature review and future lines of inquiry for empowering leadership research. *Group & Organization Management, 40*(2), 193–237. DOI: 10.1177/1059601115574906

Sklias, G., Gkelios, S., Dimitriou, D., Sartzetaki, M., & Chatzichristofis, S. A. (2024). Synergizing global and local strategies for dynamic project management: An advanced machine learning-enhanced framework. *IEEE Access : Practical Innovations, Open Solutions, 12*, 85955–85968. DOI: 10.1109/ACCESS.2024.3413890

Sung, S. Y., & Choi, J. N. (2014). Do organizations spend wisely on employees? Effects of training and development investments on learning and innovation in organizations. *Journal of Organizational Behavior, 35*(3), 393–412. DOI: 10.1002/job.1897 PMID: 25598576

Tena-Chollet, F., Tixier, J., Dandrieux, A., & Slangen, P. (2017). Training decision-makers: Existing strategies for natural and technological crisis management and specifications of an improved simulation-based tool. *Safety Science, 97*, 144–153. DOI: 10.1016/j.ssci.2016.03.025

Wood, J., Oh, J., Park, J., & Kim, W. (2020). The relationship between work engagement and work–life balance in organizations: A review of the empirical research. *Human Resource Development Review, 19*(3), 240–262. DOI: 10.1177/1534484320917560

Zorn, M. L., Sexton, J. C., Bhussar, M. S., & Lamont, B. T. (2019). Unfinished business: Nested acquisitions, managerial capacity, and firm performance. *Journal of Management, 45*(5), 1488–1516. DOI: 10.1177/0149206317737351

Chapter 22
Navigating Ethical Challenges in Entrepreneurship:
A Case Study on Simulation-Based Learning for Ethical Decision-Making

Maria Sartzetaki
https://orcid.org/0000-0002-9564-5332
Democritus University of Thrace, Greece

Dimitrios J. Dimitriou
https://orcid.org/0000-0002-5744-5110
Democritus University of Thrace, Greece

ABSTRACT

Ethical decision-making is a core challenge for entrepreneurs navigating complex business environments. This chapter explores how simulation-based learning enhances ethical competencies by immersing participants in real-time, high-stakes dilemmas that mirror actual business scenarios. Drawing on experiential learning theory, the study examines how entrepreneurs develop moral sensitivity, ethical reasoning, and leadership skills. Through structured decision-making exercises, participants refine their ability to balance financial imperatives with corporate social responsibility, stakeholder interests, and regulatory compliance. The findings demonstrate that simulations bridge the gap between ethical theory and practice, fostering resilience and adaptability in handling ethical crises. By integrating simulation-based ethics training into entrepreneurship education, this study highlights the potential to cultivate a new generation of ethical leaders capable of making principled, informed decisions in dynamic business landscapes.

INTRODUCTION

Entrepreneurship in contemporary times is not just characterized by competitive adaptability and innovation, but also by complex ethical challenges. Entrepreneurs are required to navigate decision landscapes in which financial, strategic, and operational issues intersect with ethical issues (Carroll & Buchholtz, 2003). Such challenges arise from the risky nature of entrepreneurship, resource constraints,

DOI: 10.4018/979-8-3693-9040-5.ch022

and the rapid emergence of digital technologies, which introduced new ethical challenges related to data protection, artificial intelligence, and business social accountability (Dimitriou, 2022). As a result, ethical decision-making has become a key capability for entrepreneurs to pursue sustainability over time without sacrificing public trust.

Cases of business scandals, such as ChoicePoint and TJX data breaches, shed lights on the serious consequences of ethical violations, such as consumer confidentiality and data protection (Culnan & Williams, 2009). Such cases indicate that breaches of ethics not only lead to loss of trust among various stakeholders, but also to financial loss, legal penalties, and loss of reputation. In entrepreneurship, in particular, where companies often operate with little supervision and in high-stake contexts, ethical aspects take on added seriousness. Entrepreneurs constantly face ethical dilemmas that range from financial honesty to transparency in dealing with investors, social accountability, to ecological sustainability. The dilemma between short-term financial survival versus long-term accountability is particularly intense in new start-ups, in which resource scarcity may lead decision makers to prefer profits over ethics (Ferrell et al., 2018; Elms et al., 2010). In view of the complexity of such ethical challenges, there is a heightened need for effective learning and training to equip potential entrepreneurs with capabilities to handle sophisticated ethical decisions. The use of artificial intelligence in entrepreneurship has introduced a new dimension of ethical challenges that require more sophisticated capabilities to handle (Dimitriou, 2022).

The traditional method of business ethics instruction has largely relied on lectures, theoretical case studies, and abstract discussions regarding ethical principles (Lawton & Gabriunas, 2014). Although such approaches provide a basic knowledge of ethical theory, they often fail to simulate the instant pressures and unexpected situations found in actual business scenarios. For instance, classroom case studies allow for retrospective analysis of ethical failures but fail to provide active student engagement in actual decision-making processes (Buckingham & Goodall, 2015). Consequently, many entrepreneurs struggle to apply their theory-based knowledge of ethics to actual challenges in business settings. Further, empirical studies support that decision making is more than a cognitive function; it is also a behavioral competency that requires experiential learning (Dimitriou, 2022; Briseño-García & Husted, 2015). The nature of ethical behavior in business settings is shaped by organizational culture, leadership style, and the effects of various stakeholders. Without active engagement and experiential application, entrepreneurship students can gain a theoretical knowledge of ethics without learning the competencies to apply it in actual business scenarios (Carroll & Buchholtz, 2003). The gap between theory and application highlights the need for new pedagogical approaches that enable experiential learning of ethical competencies.

Simulation-based learning has become a key method of closing the gap between theory of ethics and practical application of it. Underpinned by experiential learning theory (Kolb, 1984), this method of learning places participants in dynamic situations that simulate their involvement in decision-making in a controlled yet realistic setup. In contrast to traditional case studies, simulations capture real-time pressures, interactions with a wide range of stakeholders, and unexpected consequences, hence providing participants with a more realistic exposure to making decisions ethically (Salas et al., 2009). By going through simulation-based ethical learning, entrepreneurs can develop key competencies such as ethical sensitivity, decision-making in a condition of uncertainty, leadership, management of diverse stakeholders, and learning adaptability. Simulation-based learning is shown to not just improve ethical reasoning skills but also to better retain ethical principles compared to more traditional methods of learning (Alessi & Trollope-Kumar, 2018). By incorporating iterative learning processes coupled with instant feedback, simulations allow participants to sharpen their decision-making capabilities in ethical situations in ways that apply easily to entrepreneurship.

The current chapter presents a new conceptual framework of a module of simulation-based learning that seeks to enhance ethical decision-making in entrepreneurship. The key objectives consist of developing ethical competency by providing students and entrepreneurs with the competencies to detect, evaluate, and mitigate ethical challenges that arise in entrepreneurial settings; closing the gap between theory of ethics and application of it in practice by translating abstract principles to practical strategies using experiential learning; improving leadership competencies coupled with decision-making competencies by inculcating ethical decision-making habits in high-stake situations keeping in view diverse interests; and enabling cross-disciplinary learning by encouraging collective problem-solving among participants of diverse scholarly and professional backgrounds.

The chapter is structured as follows. The second section provides an overview of the theoretical foundations of ethical decision-making in entrepreneurship and the pedagogical rationale for simulation-based learning. The third section presents the design of the simulation-based learning environment, including its modular structure, scenario development, and key learning objectives. The fourth section outlines the implementation strategy for integrating simulation-based ethics training into entrepreneurship curricula. The fifth section explores the expected outcomes of the proposed simulation, including its impact on ethical competency, leadership skills, and stakeholder management. The sixth section discusses broader implications for research and curriculum development, emphasizing the transformative potential of simulation-based education. The final section offers concluding reflections on the role of simulation-based learning in shaping ethical entrepreneurs. Through this discussion, the chapter underscores the need for innovative, experiential approaches to ethics education in entrepreneurship. By leveraging simulation-based learning, educators and practitioners can cultivate a new generation of ethical entrepreneurs who are equipped to navigate the complex moral challenges of the business world.

LITERATURE BACKGROUND

The process of making ethical business decisions in entrepreneurship is complex and is guided by a range of moral, social, and economic variables. Entrepreneurs work in uncontrolled settings in which ethical situations often arise, making it a delicate balance between the need to produce a return on investment and the need to discharge higher-order duties to stakeholders, employees, and society (Dimitriou et al., 2024; Carroll & Buchholtz, 2003). Conceptual models of ethical decision-making provide a reference point for understanding how entrepreneurs manage moral decisions and face ethical issues. The rationale for using simulation-based learning is grounded in experiential learning theory, emphasizing active engagement and practical application of knowledge. This section examines ethical decision-making in entrepreneurship, examines underlying ethical theory and models of decision-making, and introduces the rationale for using simulation-based learning to enhance ethical competencies.

Ethical Decision-Making in Entrepreneurship

Entrepreneurial enterprises present unique ethical challenges owing to the dynamic nature of their working contexts. In the case of new start-up companies, resource constraints, competitive pressures, and pressures to scale up often create situations in which financial needs are weighed against ethical demands (Ferrell et al., 2018). Entrepreneurship's ethical challenges can include conflict of interest, issues of data protection, employment practices, transparency in dealing with investors, and efforts towards corporate social responsibility (Dimitriou, 2022). As companies scale up, the character of the ethical challenges evolves, pushing entrepreneurs to take decisions that impact increasingly diverse groups of stakeholders, such as customers, staff, investors, and regulatory institutions (Elms et al., 2010; Ardichvili et al., 2009).

Theoretical models shed light on ways in which entrepreneurs approach ethical decision-making. Kohlberg's Stages of Moral Development provide a cognitive approach to understanding how individuals move towards higher-order ethical reasoning (Rest, 1986). This approach argues that entrepreneurs, like other decision-makers, can operate at different levels of moral reasoning, such that some prioritize self-interest and others adhere to guided principles of ethics (Ferrell et al., 2018). In addition, Rest's (1986) Four-Component Model of ethical decision-making also throws more light on this, stating that ethical action is driven by moral sensitivity (sensitivity to recognizing ethical challenges), moral judgment (evaluation of potential action options), moral motivation (prioritizing ethical matters), and moral character (ability to act ethically in situations of adversity).

Entrepreneurs often use a combination of logical reasoning and intuitive judgment when dealing with ethical challenges. Dual-process models of ethics propose that ethical reasoning is a mixture of intentional, logical analysis and impulsive, emotional response (Elms et al., 2010). Under high-stress situations typical of entrepreneurship, contextual influences such as organizational culture, peer behavior, and regulative controls heavily impact the process of making ethical decisions (Carroll & Buchholtz, 2003). Such circumstances require strong training methods that allow entrepreneurs to use ethical reasoning in regulated, high-stress situations effectively.

Theoretical Foundations of Simulation-Based Learning

Simulation-based learning is grounded in experiential learning theory, which posits that learning is most effectively accomplished through active engagement over passive reception (Kolb, 1984). The theory traces a spiral process of concrete experience, reflection on that experience, abstract conceptualization, and active experimentation, hence reinforcing experiential engagement in learning (Kolb, 1984). In comparison, conventional ethics education often leans heavily on lectures and case studies, typically without immersion in this spiral process (Buckingham & Goodall, 2015; Chakrabarty & Bass, 2015). In contrast, simulation engages participants in realistic decision-making contexts that allow participants to work through ethical challenges and build up their moral reasoning iteratively.

The effectiveness of learning using simulations has been established in management education and organizational behavior studies (Salas et al., 2009; Kirkman et al., 2006). Simulation-based learning has been shown to facilitate the learning of theory in conjunction with practical competencies such as ethical reasoning, leadership, and crisis management (Werhane & Freeman, 1999; Alessi & Trollope-Kumar, 2018). In addition, simulation-based learning is uniquely beneficial in entrepreneurship learning, where ethical challenges arise in situ and require adaptability in decision-making strategies (Werhane & Freeman, 1999).

One strength of one such simulation model lies in its capability to simulate realistic situations in a controlled learning environment coupled with the provision of structured feedback. The provision of instant feedback mechanisms allows participants to assess their decisions in a controlled environment, hence reinforcing learning in ethics via trial and error (Dimitriou, 2022). The process is in line with constructivist learning theory, which argues that learning is a process in which learners build up knowledge via engagement in their learning environment in place of passive reception (Lawton & Gabriunas,

2014). By working through simulated ethical issues, entrepreneurs gain a better appreciation of decision implications and adapt their frameworks of ethics accordingly.

The Role of Simulation in Ethical Training

A recurring problem in business ethics education is the gap between theory-based frameworks and practical application (Carroll & Buchholtz, 2003; Christensen, 1997). Business schools and entrepreneurship programs teach students basic knowledge of ethical theory, principles of governance in companies, and legal frameworks, yet often fail to equip them with applicable decision-making capabilities in actual business settings. As a result, businesspeople may know a great deal about ethical principles but struggle to apply such knowledge proficiently in complex and dynamic business settings. Simulation learning addresses this problem by combining instruction based on ethical theory with experiential learning. Contrary to traditional case studies that review failed attempts in retrospect, simulations place learners in dynamic situations that require instant decision-making (Salas et al., 2009; Buxton et al., 2014). The approach not only increases sensitivity to ethical aspects but also enhances learners' capacity to navigate decision-making adaptively. By constantly working on ethical dilemmas, business practitioners hone their capabilities to anticipate potential disputes, assess trade-offs, and apply ethical reasoning in a time-sensitive manner.

Simulations also facilitate cross-disciplinary cooperation by demanding participants to work in groups to address ethical challenges (Ferrell et al., 2018). Decision-making in entrepreneurship is seldom a one-person job; it often requires bargaining, convincing, and compromising between different groups of actors. By going through role-playing simulations, learners gain leadership and communication skills that are fundamental aspects of ethical entrepreneurship. The interactive approach replicates realistic business situations in which ethical challenges are met collectively in problem-solving processes, not in individual contemplation (Dimitriou, 2022). The inherent cyclical nature of simulations allows for continued education and improvement of skills. In contrast to static tests that assess ethical knowledge at a given point in time, simulations allow for continued engagement, reflection, and improvement (Alessi & Trollope-Kumar, 2018). Learners are given a chance to trial different approaches to decision making, receive feedback on their decisions, and hone their frameworks of ethics across multiple simulated experiences. Such a dynamic learning process builds resilient ethical proficiency and prepares business owners to handle unexpected challenges that they would most likely face in their working lives.

DESIGN OF THE SIMULATION-BASED LEARNING ENVIRONMENT

The integration of simulation-based learning in entrepreneurship education is a productive approach to dealing with ethical decision making in that it places participants in dynamic and realistic situations. Compared to traditional pedagogical approaches that mainly focus on theory-oriented discussions, simulation-based learning encourages experiential engagement, allowing entrepreneurs to face ethical challenges in a controlled yet realistic manner (Kolb, 1984; Salas et al., 2009). The current section outlines the conceptual design of the proposed simulation, defining its purposes, structural elements, and instructional methods. In addition, it examines the role of scenario-based learning, systems of feedback, and collective decision-making processes, key aspects in strengthening entrepreneurs' ethical competencies.

Conceptual Framework and Objectives

The simulation learning environment is specifically designed to bridge theoretically grounded education in ethics to entrepreneurship decision-making in a real-world context. By placing participants in situations that are riddled with ethical challenges, the simulation fosters the cultivation of ethical sensitivity, reflection, and leadership competencies required in managing morally demanding business scenarios (Ferrell et al., 2018). Underpinned by experiential learning theory, the simulation marries action, reflection, and improvement in iterative settings that allow participants to view ethical decision-making as a learnable competency, not a passive theoretical notion (Kolb, 1984). The key objectives of the educational module linked to the simulation are to deepen ethical sensitivity by preparing participants to recognize, question, and challenge ethical issues in entrepreneurial contexts; sharpen practical decision-making competencies by offering participants a chance to try different approaches to ethics in a simulated, low-stakes learning environment; and to cultivate leadership competencies required in managing stakeholders through scenarios that force participants to negotiate, persuade, and navigate ethically demanding business scenarios. In addition, the simulation fosters learning flexibility via a self-renewal process in which participants sharpen their ethical judgment through continuing reflection and corrective action.

Figure 1. Conceptual flow of the simulation-based learning process design

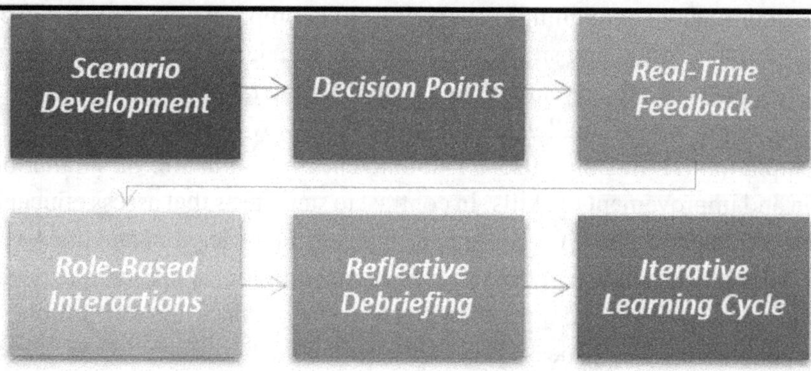

Structural Components of the Simulation

The efficacy of simulation-based learning in the field of entrepreneurship, specifically in the context of ethical education, is predicated on a carefully structured approach that facilitates immersive, interactive, and iterative decision-making (Daymond & Knight, 2023). The setup of the simulation should be in line with pedagogical objectives, learning objectives in ethics, and realistic entrepreneurial challenges to ensure that learners gain not just theoretical knowledge, but also practical competencies to inform ethically grounded decisions. An appropriately developed simulation includes key aspects of scenario design, decision points, instant feedback mechanisms, stakeholder engagement, transparently established roles, and debriefing processes, hence enabling a high-fidelity learning process. Essentially, a method of ethics training based on simulation needs to capture the dynamic nature of entrepreneurship, in which ethically demanding situations often present unexpectedly, pushing leaders to navigate high-stake decisions in situations of incomplete information and competing stakeholder interests. Compared to established case study approaches that present ethically demanding situations retrospectively, simulations place participants in dynamic, constantly evolving contexts that require reasoning, bargaining, and justifying decisions in situ in real time. The next subsections of this article will provide a close analysis of the structure of the simulation, with a focus on its function in inculcating ethically conscious awareness, leadership formation, and cross-disciplinary cooperation.

Scenario Development and Ethical Complexity

The efficacy of any ethics simulation is intrinsically linked to the approach taken in designing scenarios, in that realistic and contextually relevant ethical challenges are developed to actively involve students in decision-making processes. The ethical challenges of entrepreneurship arise from a wide range of sources, including financial constraints, investor pressures, regulatory requirements, technological advances, and social expectations. In order to accurately simulate these challenges, it is crucial that the scenarios in the simulation are carefully developed to capture multiple aspects of complexity, in that students face ethical challenges that echo those of actual entrepreneurs. Each scenario should be developed around a unique problem statement of ethics, applicable business contexts, and key decisions that require participants to weigh competing interests. For example, a challenge of protecting consumer data in artificial intelligence technology may force students to balance consumer transparency, regulation requirements, and competitive forces when making a decision regarding using consumer data to fuel product innovation. Similarly, a financial honesty scenario would pose a dilemma between maintaining short-term financial sustainability or reporting financial risks to investors.

In order to accurately simulate actual decision-making limitations, each scenario should also incorporate aspects of ambiguity, time pressures, and incomplete knowledge, in that students must navigate untested ethical terrains. The inclusion of unexpected events and ethically related uncertainties serves to further promote realism, in that students must also consider long-term consequences and ethic-trade-offs in business decisions. In addition, challenges of a particular nature should be developed to be applicable to a particular industry whenever possible, in that students get to interact with industry-specific challenges such as intellectual property disputes in tech start-ups, ecological challenges in green businesses, and fair labor practices in manufacturing processes.

Decision Points and Ethical Trade-offs

A crucial aspect of the simulation design is decision-making, in which students must choose between different ethical options. In contrast to educational settings that assess ethical decisions after the fact, simulations force students to make decisions in the moment, decisions that have both short-term and long-term consequences. Every decision point should pose conflicting ethical responsibilities that force students to assess the consequences of their decisions across various groups of stakeholders and in the business environment in total. The design of decision points should be in multiple rounds to allow students to witness the cumulative effects of their decisions over time. An example of a sustainability problem in the supply chain, for example, would initially face students with a decision between using low-cost material linked to dubious labor practices or a more ethically compliant but more expensive supply partner. As the simulation unfolds, such a preliminary decision would lead to consumer outrage, heightened scrutiny from investors, or regulation pressures that force students to revisit their strategies in response to altered behavioral expectations.

For a more in-depth analysis of ethical reasoning, decision points should be morally sophisticated situations that do not yield easy answers, compelling students to justify their ethical reasoning in terms of accepted theory such as utilitarianism, deontology, virtue theory, or stakeholder theory. Students should be asked to account for financial, legal, reputational, and ethical consequences before making a decision. By incorporating decision points that require a multidimensional analysis of ethics, the simulation ensures that students develop nimble decision capabilities relevant to actual business scenarios.

Real-Time Feedback and Ethical Impact Metrics

One of the most valuable aspects of simulation-based learning is the ability to provide real-time feedback on students' ethical decision-making processes. Immediate feedback allows participants to observe the impact of their choices, reinforcing the connection between ethical behavior and business outcomes. This feedback can take various forms, including quantitative performance metrics, qualitative narrative feedback, and stakeholder response indicators. A well-designed simulation should incorporate dynamic scoring systems that track key performance indicators such as:

- Stakeholder Trust Scores: Measuring how ethical decisions influence relationships with investors, employees, customers, and regulatory agencies.
- Financial Performance Metrics: Assessing the long-term profitability and sustainability of ethical vs. unethical business practices.
- Regulatory Compliance Indicators: Evaluating students' ability to adhere to legal and corporate governance requirements.

Beyond numerical feedback, simulations should also include narrative-based responses from virtual stakeholders, providing students with contextualized feedback on how their choices affect different interest groups. For example, a decision to prioritize shareholder returns at the expense of employee well-being may trigger virtual protests, employee resignations, or customer backlash, simulating real-world consequences of unethical decision-making.

Role-Based Interactions and Team Decision-Making

Entrepreneurial ethical dilemmas are rarely addressed by a single individual; rather, they involve collaborative decision-making among leadership teams, investors, regulators, and customers. To replicate this complexity, simulation-based ethics training should incorporate role-based decision-making structures, where students assume different leadership positions within a startup or corporate venture. Participants should be assigned to teams with clearly defined roles and responsibilities, such as:

- Chief Executive Officer (CEO): Responsible for strategic decision-making and balancing financial sustainability with ethical considerations.
- Chief Financial Officer (CFO): Managing financial transparency, investment risk, and corporate accountability.
- Operations Manager: Overseeing supply chain ethics, labor practices, and sustainability policies.
- Ethics and Compliance Officer: Ensuring legal compliance and promoting corporate social responsibility.

By engaging in role-playing exercises, students develop a deeper understanding of how ethical decision-making is influenced by different organizational perspectives. This approach also fosters collaborative problem-solving, negotiation skills, and interdisciplinary communication, preparing students for the complexities of ethical leadership in professional settings.

Reflective Debriefing and Ethical Learning Outcomes

The final structural aspect of the simulation is reflective debriefing, which is a key link between theory in ethics and resulting decision outcomes. Reflection is crucial in experiential learning, enabling in-depth scrutiny of decision processes, reasoning strategies, and contemplation of different methodologies that would lead to varying results. As compared to traditional examinations or standardized analysis, reflective debriefing engenders deep learning by encouraging self-assessment, spurring discussions among peers, and allowing instructors to review the ethical implications of decisions. There is a need to carry out debriefing sessions immediately after a simulation to allow participants to maintain a vivid memory of their experience and decisions. The sessions provide participants a chance to critically review their ethical decisions in the simulation, determine areas of strength and weakness in their decision strategies, and explore the wide-reaching implications of their decisions in business sustainability and trust among stakeholders. In addition, reflection allows for patterns in ethical reasoning to be established, hence improving business priorities, personal values, and their impact on decision processes.

An essential function of debriefing is to allow students to explore their reasoning processes in making ethical decisions and assess the extent to which their decisions conform to established ethical models, such as utilitarianism, deontology, virtue ethics, and stakeholder theory. By comparing different models of ethics, students can determine to what extent their decisions were largely driven by consequentialist reasoning (with a view to creating maximum benefits to the many), rule-based ethical principles (with a focus on duties or rules that guide one's behavior), or value-based leadership (with a focus on sustaining ethical character over short-term rewards). By engaging in such discussions, students can better describe their ethical decisions in logical, rule-based terms rather than relying on intuitive response or convenience. Another key aspect of debriefing is to review the long-term consequences of making decisions ethically for organizational success and credibility. Most of the ethical challenges that face entrepreneurship involve pressures to boost short-term profits, maintain investor confidence, or gain a competitive advantage in a hurry. However, impulsive decisions without careful reflection on their ethics can have serious long-term consequences such as fines, loss of credibility, loss of consumer trust, or organizational instability. In debriefing sessions, students assess to what extent their short-term business strategies conformed to responsible, long-term ethical principles. This underscores that more is required in ethical entrepreneurship than just mere compliance; it also requires developing a responsible business mindset that fosters credibility, trust, and resilience.

Discussions among peers form a basic aspect of debanking, given that ethical decision-making is never done in isolation in actual business settings. Interaction with a range of different perspectives of their peers and fellow students is beneficial, especially when dealing with ethical challenges that require compromises between financial objectives, social duties, and legal requirements. Organized discussions between peers force students to enunciate their ethical reasoning in a logical manner, support their arguments, and critically review potential ethical shortcomings that would be easily overlooked in simulated settings. Interactive discussions sharpen the capabilities of students in managing ethical decision-making in team-oriented settings throughout their professional careers, in which business practitioners often need to negotiate, accommodate, and synthesize competing demands without compromising their professional ethic. In order to facilitate in-depth engagement in reflective learning, processes related to debanking need to be taken beyond mere dialogue. The inclusion of written reflection and assignments for post-simulation analysis in the learning structure will force students to systematically document their processes of making ethical decisions. Such reflection mechanisms function as fundamental self-assessment tools, in that they allow students to build a reflective structure that can be applied in their professional careers in the future.

The provision of instructor feedback is a key aspect of debriefing, as it provides to students expert assessments of their ethical reasoning and application of best business ethics practices. Instructors should review students' written reflection assignments in conjunction with providing detailed feedback regarding how students handled ethical challenges, their capacity to take multiple stakeholders into account, and to what extent their ethical decisions were based on logical reasoning and established principles of ethics. The process of providing such a feedback system not just reinforces learning outcomes in students but also enhances their ethical capabilities across various rounds of simulation exercises. The process of reflection eventually allows for the consolidation of learned concepts of ethics in simulations to take place, moving beyond a one-time undertaking in a classroom to a higher-order perception of making decisions ethically. With guided reflection, peer discussions, and analysis guided by instructors, students build a more resilient ethical structure that equips them to anticipate and address challenges ethically in their business careers in the future. The focus on reflective practice not just enhances educational outcomes in ethics but also serves to catalyze long-term leadership in ethics, responsible business, and sustainable decision making in business.

Adaptive Learning and Iterative Decision-Making

A fundamental element of the simulation-based learning environment is role-playing coupled with team-based decision-making. The participants get to play their respective roles in a startup, such as Chief Executive Officer (CEO), Chief Financial Officer (CFO), Operations Manager, or Chief Ethics Officer. The roles used in the simulation are meant to simulate actual entrepreneurial interactions, hence enabling ethical decision-making in a cooperative multidisciplinary setup. By engaging in role-oriented decision-making, one is faced with the complexities that lie in applying ethical leadership, bargaining between stakeholders, and organizational accountability. The interactive nature of the simulation stimulates participants to articulate their ethical rationale, negotiate over alternative perspectives, and negotiate competing interest in a team setup. Literature shows that team-based decision-making enhances ethical perception by exposing one to diverse perspectives and frameworks of reasoning (Lawton & Gabriunas, 2014).

Moreover, in addition to team dynamics, there is also provision for stakeholder engagement in the simulation, in that participants interact with virtual stakeholders, such as investors, customers, regulators, or community members. Such interactions simulate pressures from outside forces and ethical-dilemma, hence replicating the multifaceted nature of making decisions ethically in entrepreneurship. The provision of stakeholder engagement ensures that participants gain a wide appreciation of ethically responsible behavior, not just accounting for organizational-intrinsic values, but also for extrinsic expectations of society (Dimitriou, 2022). The unique feature of the simulation-based learning setup is its adaptability to learning. In contrast to traditional approaches that assess ethical capability at a given point in time, the simulation allows participants to engage in multiple rounds of making decisions, hence developing their frameworks of reasoning ethically over time.

Each iteration of the simulation introduces participants to new cognitive models that enable their decision-making approaches to be refined based on their experiences and feedback given to them. The iterative improvement in educational settings is in line with contemporary pedagogical approaches that focus on incremental improvement, reflective learning, and responsiveness to ethical principles (Buckingham & Goodall, 2015). By using adaptive learning models, the simulated learning environment introduces ethical decision-making as a dynamic competency that evolves over time in place of a static set of skills. As a result, participants in the simulation become more attuned to ethical challenges, more self-assured in their decision-making capabilities, and more informed regarding the ethical complexities that surround entrepreneurship.

IMPLEMENTATION STRATEGY IN ENTREPRENEURSHIP CURRICULUM

The integration of simulation-based learning into entrepreneurship curricula requires a structured implementation strategy that ensures its effectiveness in fostering ethical decision-making skills. Traditional ethics education often falls short of equipping students with practical competencies, as it primarily relies on theoretical instruction and post-hoc case study analysis (Carroll & Buchholtz, 2003; Ferrell et al., 2018). By contrast, simulation-based learning immerses students in real-world ethical dilemmas, compelling them to engage in decision-making processes that mirror those encountered in entrepreneurial settings. This section outlines the key considerations for implementing the proposed simulation-based learning module, including curriculum integration, faculty and infrastructure requirements, logistical planning, and assessment methodologies.

Figure 2. Implementation framework for simulation-based learning

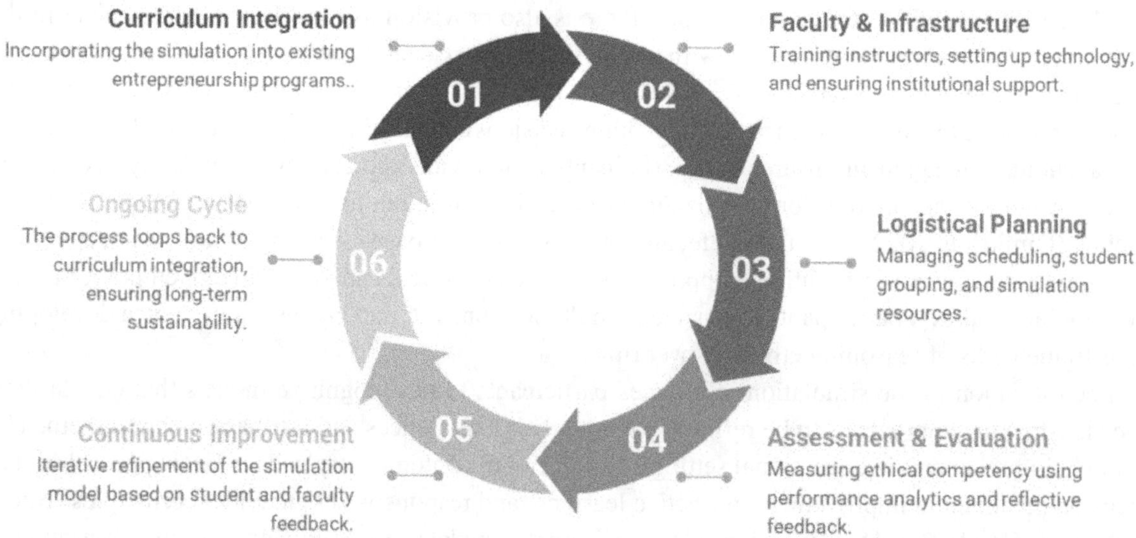

Curriculum Integration

The successful implementation of simulation-based learning in entrepreneurship education requires a well-structured integration strategy that aligns with existing curricula while ensuring students develop ethical decision-making competencies. Unlike traditional ethics education, which often relies on static case studies and theoretical discussions, simulation-based learning actively engages students in ethical dilemmas, providing a more interactive and experiential approach to ethical reasoning (Carroll & Buchholtz, 2003). To maximize its effectiveness, the simulation module must be thoughtfully embedded into entrepreneurship programs through a phased implementation process, incorporating preparatory instruction, guided simulation exercises, blended learning methodologies, and continuous assessment mechanisms.

Pre-Simulation Preparation: Establishing Ethical Foundations

Prior to their engagement in the simulation, it is crucial that students build a basic understanding of ethical theory, decision models, and the role of ethics in entrepreneurship. The preparation undertaken beforehand ensures that participants enter the experiential learning process armed with sufficient conceptual knowledge, hence enabling their undertaking of ethical decision-making challenges with confidence. The preparatory process begins with introductory lectures and readings on key ethical frameworks, including consequentialism, deontology, and virtue ethics, that provide students with multiple perspectives of moral reasoning (Ferrell et al., 2018). Such theoretical foundations help students determine how decisions that are ethically informed can be evaluated in terms of consequences, duties, or character-based standards. In addition to that, models such as Kohlberg's Stages of Moral Development and Rest's Four-Component Model provide frameworks that describe how people determine, evaluate, and react to moral dilemmas (Rest, 1986).

Parallel to theory discussions, students receive actual case studies that capture the ethical challenges often experienced in entrepreneurship. Such case studies can include ethical breaches in start-ups, social responsibility challenges in business, interest clashes, and transparency challenges in investors. By studying actual business decisions, students begin to build up the critical thinking skills required to determine ethical challenges and review potential reaction options. In order to properly prepare students for the simulation, educators use interactive discussions and exercises in reasoning ethically, in which students receive example scenarios of ethically challenging situations that require justification of their decision methods. Such activities support application of theory to practical scenarios, hence ensuring a correlation between theory and application. Self-assessment questionnaires can also be used to assess students' ethical awareness and personal principles of ethics before their exposure to the simulation.

Simulation Workshops: Structured Engagement with Ethical Dilemmas

Following the attainment of a basic understanding of ethics, students participate in structured simulation workshops that consist of role-based exercises in ethical decision making. The workshops are a key aspect of the process of curriculum integration, providing a progressively demanding learning process that is increasingly sophisticated over time. Prior to each workshop, students are divided into groups that take on key decision-maker roles in a startup company, such as Chief Executive Officer, Chief Financial Officer, Ethics Officer, or Operations Manager. Each group is given a business case involving ethical challenges, such as conflict of interest, financial honesty issues, data protection issues, or corporate social responsibilities.

The simulation is centered on key decision points that force teams to assess ethical challenges, propose practical alternatives, and choose a path to take. Each decision has immediate and long-term consequences, presented in real-time via digital systems that generate instant feedback, metrics of stakeholder response, and indicators of financial consequences. The experiential approach allows for a better appreciation of the impact of ethical decisions on business sustainability, stakeholder trust, and conformity to regulation requirements. After each decision point, students get instant feedback that is a combination of qualitative and quantitative metrics. Quantitative metrics may include stakeholder trust ratings, financial metrics of performance, or metrics of conformity to ethics, whereas qualitative analysis is provided in instructor reports and AI-based narrative analysis. The instant feedback process increases students' ability to reflect on their decisions and adjust their decision-making approaches accordingly.

Blended Learning Approach: Integrating Online and In-Person Components

To enhance learner engagement and accessibility, the simulation module adopts a blended learning approach that combines digital simulations with face-to-face debriefing sessions. The blended approach allows learners to interact with the simulation in active and interactive ways, yet also gain from structured face-to-face discussions that support ethically informed learning outcomes. In the digital module, learners use an online simulation platform to interact in real-time with scenarios, receive instant feedback, and track their improvement in making ethically informed decisions. In addition, the online learning module allows scalability, in that learners can undertake simulation exercises at their convenience, individually or in groups.

On the other hand, face-to-face debriefing sessions provide channels for collective reflection and sharing of knowledge. After each simulated exercise, learners undertake guided discussions in which they assess their approach to decision-making, reflect on ethically demanding scenarios, and review their rationale in response to varied scenarios. Instructors facilitate these discussions using reflection questions that invite learners to share their observations and devise ways of applying principles of ethics in practical business contexts. The blended learning approach also allows dynamic curriculum design, in that educators can adjust the complexity of the simulation in line with learner progression. Upon proficiency in basic ethically informed decision-making, educators can expose learners to more complex scenarios of multi-stakeholder bargaining, cross-national business ethics, and regulation challenges. The dynamic yet personalized nature of this approach means that learners are continually challenged, hence developing higher-order ethically informed competencies over time.

Continuous Assessment and Feedback Mechanisms

To enhance the effectiveness of the simulation-based learning module, a continuous assessment system is incorporated throughout the course of study. This method diverges from traditional ethics modules, which often rely on static examinations; simulation-based learning is centered around constant evaluation and reflection, allowing for sharpened ethical reasoning capabilities to be developed through iterative repetition and reflection on decisions. Pre-, in-, and post-simulation formative assessments provide regular checks on students' basic knowledge of ethics and their proclivity to make ethically sound decisions. In-simulation performance assessments track key indicators of financial sustainability, stakeholder impact ratings, and ethical decision-making accuracy.

Alongside quantitative measurement, systems of qualitative review help to support learning of ethics. The use of reflective journals permits students to describe their cognitive processes, encountered ethical challenges, and learned material during the simulation, hence enabling critical reflection. Such reflection is used as crucial tools of self-assessment, encouraging internalization of ethical principles in a manner that supports a sustainability approach to ethical entrepreneurship. Moreover, peer review and collective review introduce various outlooks on students' ethical reasoning capabilities. As ethical decision-making in a business environment is in essence a collective effort, mechanisms of peer review invite scrutiny of each participant's input, leadership capabilities, and ethical reasoning approaches. The system of multiple review ensures that learning of ethics is strengthened in multiple ways, ensuring a developed appreciation of responsible entrepreneurship in the ethic sphere.

Long-Term Integration and Curriculum Expansion

To enhance learning efficacy via simulation, it is crucial to place the module at the heart of entrepreneurship programs and not just a short-term educational endeavor. Such a venture requires institutional support, instructor training, and regular improvement of the system of simulation guided by learner feedback and business practices evolving over time. In addition, incorporating multiple disciplines of learning can greatly support the efficacy of the simulation by introducing knowledge of business ethics, business law, business psychology, and behavioral economics. By encouraging cross-disciplinary cooperation, entrepreneurship learners can gain a better appreciation of making decisions in line with ethical principles, hence enabling them to effectively handle business challenges that define the current marketplace. The key objective of incorporating such a course is to raise a generation of business leaders to view ethics as a key aspect of business success. By introducing learning via simulation in entrepreneurship studies, educational institutions can help produce ethically aware leadership, responsible entrepreneurship, and high standards of business morality, hence preparing graduates to face ethically demanding challenges throughout their careers.

Faculty and Infrastructure Requirements

The successful application of simulation-based learning in entrepreneurship education requires heavy investment in educators' professional development, as well as in technological infrastructure and administrative support. As compared to traditional ethics education, which relies mainly on conceptual frameworks and classroom discussions, simulation-based learning demands an experiential and interactive approach in which students interact dynamically with ethical issues in realistic contexts. Educators need to have competencies to facilitate learning processes, review student decisions, and give constructive feedback in a timely manner. In addition, educational institutions need to design a sophisticated technological infrastructure that ensures smooth functionality of the simulation platform, enabling students to immerse in their learning process. This section outlines key requirements in terms of faculty training, technological integration, information technology support, and enhancement strategies to ensure sustainability and scalability of simulation-based ethics education.

Faculty plays a key role in choreographing the simulation process by steering students through ethical issues, moderating discussions, and providing constructive feedback. As compared to one-way knowledge transfer in traditional lecture-oriented instruction, simulation-based learning forces instructors to take a more facilitatory and interactive role. This need is compounded by the need to provide specialist faculty training programs to equip educators to deliver simulation exercises effectively, hence enabling students to gain skills in making ethical decisions. Training of educators should include technical training in using simulation software, pedagogical strategies in experiential learning, and methods of evaluating student performance. Instructors need to become proficient in starting scenarios, observing student interactions, and interpreting patterns of decision making in the simulation process. Training to handle technical challenges that can arise during instructional time is also crucial to curbing interference in the process of instruction.

In conjunction with technical competencies, it is crucial to build a faculty that is in line with the principles of experiential learning theory, specifically as outlined in Kolb's (1984) theory, which underscores the active experimentation, concrete experiences, reflective observations, and abstract conceptualizations components. The faculty needs to be skilled in debriefing methods to allow for a structured reflection of learner decision making coupled with exposure to a wide range of ethical approaches. Training educators in experiential learning methods allows for the creation of a learning environment in which students can deeply interact with ethical challenges, hence ensuring constant improvement of their moral reasoning capabilities. Training in methods of assessment that include analysis of quantitative indicators of performance, impact studies from multiple stakeholders, and review of student reflection journals is equally crucial. Constructive feedback is a key aspect of learning using simulations to allow learners to become aware of their ethical blind spots and areas of improvement. Training in effective formative and summative methods of assessment equips learners with relevant guidance that maximizes their ethical capabilities.

The advancement of scholarly staff requires that facilitation of learning via simulations be founded on a solid technological infrastructure. In order to enable accessibility to learners that are in geographically remote locations using different devices, there is a need to implement a cloud-based platform for simulations. The platform needs to be skilled in providing instant analysis of data, hence enabling educators and learners to view decision processes and receive instant feedback. Institutions can opt to purchase commercially existing software or to design personalized simulations that cater to their particular entrepreneurship curriculum requirements. Considering that many of the ethical decision-making situations involve proprietary business details, it is crucial that the platform has mechanisms to ensure student confidentiality and maintain data integrity. The use of multi-factor authentication and encryption methods is crucial to participant information protection, hence ensuring institutional and legislative requirements for protection of data.

The integration of artificial intelligence-driven feedback mechanisms can further enhance the simulation experience by providing personalized insights into students' ethical decision-making patterns. AI-driven simulations can analyze historical decision-making trends and suggest tailored feedback, allowing students to refine their approaches to ethical challenges in real time. Adaptive learning algorithms can also modify the complexity of scenarios based on individual performance, ensuring that students encounter ethical dilemmas that challenge their existing skill levels while providing opportunities for continuous growth. To ensure that all students can fully participate in the simulation, institutions must also ensure high-speed internet access and device compatibility. The simulation platform should be designed to function across multiple devices, including laptops, tablets, and smartphones, to accommodate students with varying levels of access to technology. On-campus computer labs should be equipped with the necessary hardware and software, and institutions may consider implementing a laptop loan program for students who lack access to suitable devices.

Given the complexity of running simulation-based learning at scale, institutions must provide dedicated IT support and administrative coordination to ensure smooth implementation. A team of IT specialists should be available to troubleshoot technical issues, provide guidance to students, and maintain the stability of the simulation platform. IT support should be readily accessible during simulation sessions to prevent disruptions that could hinder the learning experience. In addition to technical support, institutions should appoint a program coordinator responsible for managing the logistics of the simulation, including scheduling, student onboarding, and faculty coordination. The coordinator should collaborate closely with faculty members to ensure that the ethical scenarios align with the learning objectives of the entrepreneurship curriculum.

Before participating in the simulation, students should undergo a structured orientation session that familiarizes them with the platform, the expected learning outcomes, and the rules governing ethical decision-making within the simulation environment. This orientation should include interactive tutorials that walk students through the decision-making process step by step, ensuring that they understand how to navigate the simulation and interpret feedback. Institutions may also provide self-paced learning modules that allow students to explore the simulation platform independently before engaging in live decision-making exercises.

To ensure the long-term sustainability of simulation-based learning, institutions must establish mechanisms for continuous evaluation and curriculum enhancement. Regular faculty feedback sessions should be conducted to refine simulation scenarios and improve facilitation techniques. Student surveys and performance analytics should be analyzed to assess the effectiveness of the simulation in achieving learning objectives and to identify areas for improvement. Annual updates to the simulation platform should be planned to incorporate new ethical dilemmas, emerging business trends, and technological advancements. Additionally, institutions should explore opportunities to expand the simulation beyond entrepreneurship programs, integrating it into business ethics courses, executive education programs, and interdisciplinary curricula.

Simulation-based learning is a fundamental shift in the field of ethics education that requires institutions of higher learning to continually invest in support services, new technologies, and professional development of their educators. By investing in key infrastructure and increasing educator competency, institutions of higher learning become better positioned to provide a transformative learning process that equips up-and-coming entrepreneurs to approach ethically challenging situations with confidence, honesty, and strategic vision. The combination of sophisticated technological systems, educator competency, and cooperative institutional action ensures that students become immersed in a demanding learning process that accurately balances theory and practical application. As ethical principles increasingly inform business practices, simulation-based learning is likely to become a key method of developing business leaders that support responsible decision making and accountability in their business models.

Furthermore, the effective application of simulation-based ethics instruction requires careful organization of logistics, such as scheduling, group dynamics, and resource allocation. The strategic inclusion of modules in entrepreneurship curricula should be aligned to key learning milestones. As such, introductory modules should be introduced at the beginning of a semester to raise awareness of ethics, while more complex scenarios can be used to build advanced decision-making capabilities (Ferrell et al., 2018). The formation of student groups should facilitate crossdisciplinary working to allow for varied input in the process of making ethical decisions. Proper group formation is required to allow for participants of different academic backgrounds, leadership approaches, and business knowledge. The literature shows that heterogeneous groups work better in making ethical decisions in that they can accommodate a wide range of input and analytical approaches (Elms et al., 2010). In addition to using digital platforms in simulations, institutions of learning need to provide areas for face-to-face discussions, debriefing, and interactive workshops. Purposely allocated meeting areas with multimedia capabilities enable face-to-face discussions, while online platforms accommodate distant learners in blended learning models. By incorporating digital and face-to-face learning modes, institutions can provide a wide range of simulation learning that maximizes accessibility and learner engagement.

Assessment and Evaluation Methodologies

Simulation-based learning in entrepreneurship ethics evaluates students' practical capabilities in making decisions and tackling ethical issues. In contrast to knowledge-based measurement, it employs a range of different measurements such as quantitative indicators, qualitative observations, feedback, and longitudinal monitoring. The system follows up on ethical capabilities over time, noting improvement during simulations to support professional decision-making. Measuring ethical decision-making is complex owing to its subjective nature; in contrast to technical subjects, ethical issues encompass interpretations, conflicting interests, and long-term effects. The measurements need to take account of decisions taken by the students, as well as their reasoning processes. This method appropriately assesses students' capabilities in identifying ethical issues, grasping contexts, applying ethical frameworks to justify decisions, and reacting to feedback and sustainability challenges.

The assessment process gauges performance in a simulated real-time environment for such key indicators as stakeholder trust, financial sustainability, and ethics. Measures indicate students' capacity to reconcile business objectives with ethics, making practical decisions. An example is a transparent team that is more likely to score high in trust compared to one that is concentrated on short-term profits at the expense of reputation. The metrics enable instructors to assess students' ethical reasoning in business. Reflective measurement during debriefings is crucial to assessment. Decision making in ethics increases over time, self-reflection, and peer review. Students keep reflection journals throughout a simulation, recording their rationale, challenges, and learning. The journals indicate students' perception of ethical issues and decision making. Faculty assess reflection using such metrics as analysis depth, reasoning clarity, and application of ethical theory to facilitate moral introspection.

Post-simulation debriefing reinforces learning in ethics and critiques decision making. Instructors need to facilitate discussions for students to revisit decisions, consider alternatives, and forecast ethical scenarios. Some questions to use are: What were the primary ethical challenges? How did you balance business objectives and ethics? Who guided your decisions? What would you do differently in a repeat simulation? Promoting rationale reinforces critical analysis and ethics. Instructors need to provide personalized feedback, pointing out strengths and areas to work on in ethical analysis. Incorporating team and peer review is crucial in assessment. Business is done in a team and requires negotiation. Institutions need to apply peer review for formal feedback on ethics and team working skills. The approach underscores that decisions in ethics take place in groups, mirroring actual business situations, and encourages student exposure to ethics and working in a team. In order to assess simulation-based ethics education, institutions need to carry out longitudinal studies of postgraduate behavior. Periodical examinations do not indicate graduates' application of ethical principles in business careers. Follow-up questionnaires can indicate if graduates continue to apply ethical practices in business. Such studies expose professional values, leadership style, and long-term effects of such education.

The assessment process needs to be integrated with feedback loops to facilitate learning in simulations. In contrast to standard examinations, simulations enable multiple rounds of refinements in ethical reasoning. Aspects such as instant feedback, live mentoring, and self-assessments facilitate learning from failure and incremental improvement. This is in line with experiential learning's action, reflection, and improvement principles. Institutions need to demonstrate that their methods of assessment meet accreditation and learning outcomes in business studies. As ethical decision-making is crucial to future business leadership, accreditation bodies might demand evidence of ethical competency testing. An appropriately planned simulation-based assessment enhances learning experiences and increases entrepreneurship programs' credibility, preparing graduates with crucial ethical reasoning capabilities. In conclusion, beyond grades, there is a need to assess ethical decision-making in simulation-based ethics training. With live metrics, reflection essays, and peer review, it is possible to effectively evaluate ethical competencies. Cross-disciplinary evaluations enable students to build stronger reasoning for entrepreneurship. With business success relying on ethical leadership, it is crucial to use simulation-based training to equip entrepreneurs to make responsible decisions.

EXPECTED OUTCOMES AND EDUCATIONAL IMPACT

The integration of simulation-based learning in entrepreneurship education is predicted to lead to considerable improvement in the ability to make ethically informed decisions, leadership competencies, and stakeholder engagement. Traditional learning approaches often heavily rely on abstract knowledge, sometimes without providing learners with the opportunity to apply ethical principles in dynamic, realistic contexts (Carroll & Buchholtz, 2003). Simulation-based learning, on the other hand, engages participants in interactive settings that force them to face ethical challenges in realistic business contexts, hence making it possible to gain key competencies in experiential learning, reflection, and constructive feedback (Salas, Wildman, & Piccolo, 2009). This section examines potential influences of simulations, such as heightened ethical awareness, improvement in practical decision-making competencies, cultivation of dynamic, team-oriented leadership competencies, and a profound impact on entrepreneurship education. In addition, it introduces a methodical approach to evaluating the efficacy of simulation-based instruction in ethics and its long-term impact on participants' professional ethical behavior.

Enhancing Ethical Competencies in Entrepreneurship

A fundamental objective of the simulation-based learning module is to enhance the ethical competencies of potential entrepreneurs. Decision-making is a crucial competency in business; yet it is often given inadequate treatment in conventional entrepreneurship curricula. Entrepreneurs constantly face situations that require a reconciliation between social responsibility and profitability, managing competing interests, and satisfying diverse groups of stakeholders. Such situations require a wide knowledge of ethical principles, in addition to their application in high-stake contexts (Ferrell et al., 2018). By repeatedly working through ethical challenges in a simulated environment, students become more cognizant of the ethical issues that can arise during entrepreneurial undertakings. One of the key challenges in making ethically informed decisions is the capability to anticipate ethical issues in a forward-looking manner, a capability that can avert their escalation to serious crises. Most business failures result not from a desire to behave unethically but a failure to anticipate potential ethical issues (Dimitriou, 2022). By engaging students in realistic business situations that intrinsically pose ethical challenges, the simulation inculcates sensitivity to ethical issues, enabling participants to detect potential challenges in a timely manner and to take preventive action.

In addition to inculcating ethical sensitivity, the simulation increases students' capabilities to estimate ethical trade-offs. Business decisions often involve competing interests, requiring a watchful consideration of ethical aspects in conjunction with financial, operational, or strategic goals. In a typical classroom setting, students generally review case studies after the fact, noting mistakes made by earlier companies. Such a method is not representative of time pressures and ambiguities associated with real-time decision-making (Carroll & Buchholtz, 2003). The simulation engages students in decision-maker status, forces them to review multiple alternatives, forecast probable results, and justify their decisions. Such experiential learning fosters students' competencies in careful analysis and ethical reasoning, preparing them to apply their analysis capabilities in dealing with complex ethical challenges. In addition, the simulation inculcates ethical resilience and fosters a strategic outlook over a protracted time horizon. Entrepreneurs often face pressures to sacrifice short-term profits in favor of compromising on ethical principles. Nevertheless, empirical evidence shows that unshakeable adherence to ethical business principles results in sustainable success, marked by increased trust, brand capital, and higher employee engagement (Elms et al., 2010). The simulation establishes a virtual learning platform in which students can determine the consequences of ethical or unethical decisions, reinforcing the long-term benefits of ethical leadership.

Developing Adaptive and Collaborative Leadership Skills

Beyond their ethical implications, simulations are designed to facilitate collective decision-making and adaptive leadership, competencies that are crucial for businesspeople to navigate unstable and complex business environments. The heart of entrepreneurial leadership is in making quick yet informed decisions, often in situations of incomplete information and high external pressures (Elms et al., 2010). The simulation accurately models such situations by exposing participants to dynamic, live situations that require quick decisions to be made. One of the leadership competencies developed using simulations is decision-making in situations of uncertainty. Business ethical challenges never present easy options; rather, they require leaders to assess risks, reconcile competing interests, and make decisions in situations of ambiguity (Ferrell et al., 2018). By going through time-sensitive decision-making situations, students gain confidence in their ability to act swiftly without compromising their adherence to ethical principles. This competency is highly relevant to entrepreneurs, who often face tough decisions in situations of market volatility, pressures from investors, and financial constraints.

Moreover, simulation facilitates cooperative problem-solving and engagement among stakeholders. The process of making ethical decisions is rarely in the hands of one person; it often requires bargaining and consensus among various groups of stakeholders such as co-founders, employees, investors, customers, and regulators (Culnan & Williams, 2009). The simulation includes role-playing aspects in which students take up different leadership positions in a startup team, such as CEO, CFO, or Ethics Officer. By working in groups to solve ethically related dilemmas, students enhance their communication, bargaining, and comprehension of various perspectives relevant to making ethically informed decisions. The simulation also highlights the importance of developing long-term relationships with stakeholders. Entrepreneurship done ethically is more than just avoiding legal consequences; it is developing sustainable companies that build trust between customers, employees, and investors (Lawton & Gabriunas, 2014). The measurement of trust metrics related to stakeholders in the simulation provides instant feedback regarding how ethically informed decisions can affect business reputation, financial results, and employee morale. The experiential learning approach highlights the key role of leadership in encouraging business sustainability.

Bridging the Gap Between Theory and Practice

A notable strength of simulation-based learning is its ability to link theory of ethics to practical application in professional settings. Traditional ethics education often exposes students to theoretical concepts of morality, expecting that they apply such concepts in their future careers. However, without experiential learning, such that students get to apply these principles in a realistic manner, it is challenging for students to internalize such principles and gain required competencies in actual application (Buckingham & Goodall, 2015). The simulation-based approach overcomes passive learning in that it requires active engagement of students in dealing with ethical issues in a controlled yet realistic setting. As compared to classic case studies that force students to review past failures in a detached manner, simulations immerse students in decision-making situations to a point of envisioning probable hazards, justifying their decisions, and dealing with the consequences of their decisions in real time (Salas et al.,

2009). The experiential nature of such learning reinforces ethical decision-making as a concrete competency rather than a mere concept. The simulation also fosters self-assessment and iterative learning. The students are challenged to reflect on their decisions, review feedback, and refine their ethical frameworks in a sequence of multiple simulations. The iterative approach models actual professional learning, in that ethical competency is developed progressively over time using experience, reflection, and mentoring.

Assessing Ethical Development and Learning Outcomes

To ensure the effectiveness of the simulation-based learning module, a comprehensive assessment framework is necessary. The evaluation process includes quantitative and qualitative measures that assess students' ethical growth and decision-making proficiency over time. Performance metrics embedded in the simulation track students' ethical decision accuracy, stakeholder trust ratings, and financial performance outcomes. These indicators provide empirical data on how students balance ethical considerations with business objectives. Pre- and post-simulation surveys measure changes in students' ethical awareness, confidence in decision-making, and attitudes toward ethical leadership. By analyzing responses before and after participation, educators can assess the simulation's impact on students' moral reasoning development (Dimitriou, 2022). Reflective journals and debriefing discussions provide qualitative insights into students' thought processes, ethical challenges encountered, and key takeaways from the simulation experience. These reflections encourage self-assessment and help students articulate lessons learned. Longitudinal studies can further enhance evaluation efforts by tracking students' ethical behavior after they enter professional roles. By examining how former participants apply ethical decision-making skills in their entrepreneurial ventures, educators can assess the long-term influence of simulation-based ethics training.

The simulation-based learning module represents a transformative approach to ethical education in entrepreneurship. By immersing students in realistic ethical dilemmas, it enhances ethical awareness, fosters adaptive leadership, and strengthens decision-making abilities. Through interactive and iterative learning, students develop practical skills that extend beyond theoretical knowledge, preparing them for real-world entrepreneurial challenges. As business ethics continues to evolve, simulation-based education will play a crucial role in shaping the next generation of ethical entrepreneurs.

DISCUSSION

The integration of simulation-based learning in entrepreneurship education is a pedagogical innovation that seeks to close the gap between theory and application. Conventional ethics education is created to expose learners to basic concepts of morality; yet it often fails to provide experiential knowledge required to help prospective entrepreneurs navigate real-life challenges in professional contexts. The use of simulations allows learners to gain a dynamic and riskless learning platform that is applicable to improving their decision-making, receiving instant feedback, and improving their reasoning via iterative learning processes. This section delves into the wide-reaching implications of using simulations in ethics education, evaluating its impact on creating responsible entrepreneurs, its impact on entrepreneurship education in general, and its potential to open up new areas of inquiry for future studies and curricula improvement.

The Role of Ethics in Entrepreneurship Education

Ethical decision-making is a key aspect of entrepreneurship education in response to growing pressures on business companies from consumers, investors, and regulatory agencies. Entrepreneurs need to navigate complex ethical contexts that involve corporate social responsibility, sustainability, data protection, fair labor practices, and diverse stakeholder engagement. Compared to their counterparts in established companies, entrepreneurs often face intense pressures typified by quick decisions, scarcity of resources, and unexpected ethical challenges (George & Dane, 2016; Le Breton-Miller and Miller, 2020). Such unique challenges require a forward-thinking approach to ethical reasoning that allows entrepreneurs to embed ethical aspects in strategic decisions at the initial stages.

Simulation learning is found to be highly effective in closing wide gaps in conventional entrepreneurship education, given that it allows learners to gain a realistic, immersive exposure to ethical decision processes. The interactive nature of simulations allows learners to interact with realistic ethical challenges in a practical way in contrast to passive analysis of case studies of business failure. Such experiential learning is highly useful in entrepreneurial education, given that it stimulates learners to develop the capacity to anticipate potential ethical challenges, assess potential consequences, and strike a balance between business expansion goals and ethical uprightness. The iterative nature of simulation activities also fosters a learning culture of constant ethical reflection, enabling learners to build their ethical frameworks in a practical manner without over-reliance on conceptual frameworks.

Enhancing Ethical Awareness and Leadership in Entrepreneurs

One of the key strengths of learning through simulation is its potential to enhance ethical sensitivity in prospective business owners. Most business failures in terms of ethics result not from ill intent but from a lack of sensitivity or failure to detect ethical issues when they arise (Sartzetaki et al., 2025; Palanski, & Vogelgesang, 2011). By engaging in realistic simulations, students gain a heightened ethical sensitivity, learning to detect and evaluate potential ethical risks before their escalation to crises. Such a preventive approach is crucial in entrepreneurship, in which decisions taken at initial stages of business formation can lead to long-term effects on ethics and reputation.

Simulation-based learning also fosters ethical leadership capabilities. Entrepreneurs not only carry a personal ethic of behavior but also a responsibility to set up a system of ethics in their companies (Zollo & Winter, 2002). The ethical leader is responsible for managing complex relationships between co-founders, employees, investors, and customers while ensuring business growth does not sacrifice ethical standards. Simulation that combines role-playing decision models, in which students become leaders in a start-up team, allows participants to apply practical leadership in a realistic context. Such exercises highlight the need to manage relationships with key stakeholders, negotiate ethically, and lead for values, hence providing students with practical competencies to build ethical cultures in their potential business entities.

Implications for Entrepreneurship Education and Institutional Adoption

The efficacy of simulation-based learning in entrepreneurship ethics has serious implications for entrepreneurship education in general. Business programs and business schools are increasingly recognizing the paramount importance of experiential learning approaches, moving beyond lecture-based instruction to interactive, practice-oriented pedagogics. Simulation-based ethics training is in line with new currents in entrepreneurial education that place a premium on experiential learning, cross-disciplinary cooperation, and problem-solving in response to actual business challenges.

For institutions looking to adopt simulation-based learning in their curricula, a number of key factors need to be given attention (Cappelli & Tavis, 2016). Most prominently, it is crucial to provide faculty with training to equip instructors with the pedagogical and technical skills to facilitate simulations effectively. Instructors need to be trained in experiential learning theory, in ethically informed reasoning assessment, and in simulation technologies to provide useful guidance and feedback to learners. Institutions also need to provide funding for infrastructure to support technologies, ensuring that platforms for simulations are accessible, scalable, and integrated in learning management systems (Treviño & Nelson, 2016). Such investment is crucial in particular when institutions move to blended and online learning models, in which digital tools for simulations can provide flexible and immersive learning opportunities. Another key concern is scalability and flexibility in simulation-based ethics training. Entrepreneurship's ethical challenges are highly contextual, varying in terms of industry, market, and cultural contexts. Institutions should consider developing modular frameworks for simulations that allow educators to tailor ethical situations in response to particular course learning objectives and regional business contexts. Such flexibility ensures that simulations are relevant and provocative for learners, hence reinforcing ethical knowledge in unique business contexts that learners are likely to encounter.

Challenges and Considerations in Simulation-Based Ethics Training

Notwithstanding its plethora of advantages, simulation-based learning presents multiple challenges that institutions of learning must face to maximize its overall effectiveness. One key challenge is to elicit student engagement and accountability in the simulated environment. Compared to traditional examinations, in which explicit grading standards are presented, simulation-based learning requires qualitative assessment strategies that capture accurately the subtlety of students' ethical reasoning and decision-making processes (Sartzetaki et al., 2023; Sims & Felton, 2006). Institutions need to design tight evaluation frameworks that combine both performance metrics and reflection-based measurement to comprehensively determine students' ethical capabilities.

The other key challenge is related to the ethical complexity of simulated scenarios. While simulations carry the potential to recreate realistic ethical dilemmas, they need to be carefully developed to avert over-simplification or over-abstraction of issues. Entrepreneurship's nature of ethical decision-making is highly complex, often compelling leaders to navigate between competing moral, financial, and strategic demands. If simulations portray ethical dilemmas in a binary nature, they undermine the sophistication of ethical reasoning and fail to equip students to handle ambiguities of actual business situations. In order to address this challenge, designers of simulations need to use multidimensional ethical scenarios that dynamically adjust to accommodate student decisions, hence mirroring the iterative nature of entrepreneurship's ethical problem-solving. Educational institutions also need to consider financial and resource implications of introducing simulation-based ethics education. Developing high-quality interactive simulations requires a heavy upfront investment in software design, instructor training, and technical support. Some institutions may choose to license existing simulation platforms, while others choose to undertake the design of tailor-made simulations specifically for their entrepreneurship programs. In either case, institutions need to dedicate sufficient resources to ensure sustainability and long-term effects of simulation-based ethics education.

CONCLUSION

Integrating simulation-based learning in entrepreneurship ethics education addresses theory-practice gaps. Classical ethics education is deprived of practical exposure to moral principles. Interactive simulations enhance interest in making decisions ethically and enhances moral reasoning via feedback. The chapter highlights experiential ethics education's significance in forming ethically sensitive and leadership-oriented businesspeople capable of managing stakeholders. Simulation-based learning enhances ethical sensitivity, enabling students to detect and resolve dilemmas in a timely manner. Simulation-based learning also links business needs to ethical principles, indicating that ethical decision making enhances trust and sustainability. Simulation-based ethics education, via live decisions and stakeholder bargaining, presents a dynamic learning approach to ethics.

This chapter delves into the principles, strategies, results, and implications of simulation-based ethics education in entrepreneurship education. Decision-making in a moral or ethical manner is conceptualized as a competency that is shaped by cognitive processes, situational pressures, and learning experiences. Conventional case-based ethics instruction is found to be lacking in engagement and problem-solving for developing ethics skills in entrepreneurship. Simulation-based learning requires instructor training, technology, logistics, and methods of measurement. Instructors facilitate discussions, moral reasoning, and interpreting feedback. Institutions need to invest in digital infrastructure and support services to deliver effective learning experiences. The course needs to incorporate multi-session simulations, role-playing, and debriefing to produce better ethical results.

Measurement of simulation-based training is a combination of quantitative indicators, qualitative reflection, peer review, and longitudinal studies. In contrast to static measurement, these models monitor students' reasoning, leadership, and decision-making capabilities. Reflective journals and debriefs enable instructors to track ethical development and provide targeted feedback for improvement. This study's findings are relevant to educators, entrepreneurship programs, and business professionals. Entrepreneurship ethics training needs to be interactive rather than passive learning. Institutions need to place a focus on faculty development to prepare instructors for simulations and reflection on the part of students. Programs need to work in conjunction with providers of technologies to design relevant ethical situations that simulate actual challenges.

For entrepreneurs, this work highlights the need to take ethics seriously in initial business planning. Failure in ethics results from inadequate foresight, mismanagement, and decisions resulting from pressures rather than actual malfeasance. The simulation approach allows for improving ethical decision making, strategies to cope with ethical risk, and trust-building. Generally, today's entrepreneurs need to navigate new learning processes to equip students to handle business in a realistic manner. Simulation learning increases ethical sensitivity and decision making in conjunction with leadership and strategic thinking. The inclusion of ethical challenges in learning provides students with practical knowledge to approach challenges in a confident manner and ethically.

Entrepreneurship education should be experiential in nature, incorporating interactive technologies and live decision-making to build responsible leaders. Simulation programs equip graduates to work in careers that involve ethics and corporate social responsibility. Changing partnership models and studies can revolutionize business education to build character and creativity in leaders of tomorrow.

REFERENCES

Alessi, S. M., & Trollope-Kumar, K. (2018). Experiential learning and simulation in business ethics education. Academic Press.

Ardichvili, A., Mitchell, J. A., & Jondle, D. (2009). Characteristics of ethical business cultures. *Journal of Business Ethics*, *85*(4), 445–451. DOI: 10.1007/s10551-008-9782-4

Briseño-García, A. & Husted, B. (2015). The Diffusion of CSR Practices: Past Research and Future Directions. Academic Press.

Buckingham, M., & Goodall, A. (2015). Reinventing performance management. *Harvard Business Review*, *93*(4), 40–50. https://hbr.org/2015/04/reinventing-performance-management

Buxton, M., Phillippi, J., & Collins, M. (2014). Simulation: A New Approach to Teaching Ethics. *Journal of Midwifery & Women's Health*, *60*(1), 70–74. Advance online publication. DOI: 10.1111/jmwh.12185 PMID: 25141791

Cappelli, P., & Tavis, A. (2016). The performance management revolution. *Harvard Business Review*, *94*(10), 58–67.

Carroll, A. B., & Buchholtz, A. K. (2003). *Business and society: Ethics and stakeholder management* (5th ed.). Cengage Learning.

Chakrabarty, S., & Bass, A. E. (2015). Comparing virtue, consequentialist, and deontological ethics-based corporate social responsibility: Mitigating microfinance risk in institutional voids. *Journal of Business Ethics*, *126*(3), 487–512. DOI: 10.1007/s10551-013-1963-0

Christensen, C. M. (1997). *The Innovator's Dilemma: When New Technologies Cause Great Firms to Fail*. Harvard Business School Press.

Culnan, M. J., & Williams, C. C. (2009). How ethics can enhance organizational privacy: Lessons from the Choice Point and TJX data breaches. *Management Information Systems Quarterly*, *33*(4), 673–687. DOI: 10.2307/20650322

Daymond, J., & Knight, E. (2023). *Design Thinking in Business and Management: Research History*. Themes, and Opportunities., DOI: 10.1093/acrefore/9780190224851.013.386

Dimitriou, D. (2022). Corporate ethics: Philosophical concepts guiding business practices. *Conatus*, *7*(1), 33–60. DOI: 10.12681/cjp.29864

Dimitriou, D., Sartzetaki, M., & Karagkouni, A. (2024). *Managing Airport Corporate Performance: Leveraging Business Intelligence and Sustainable Transition*. Elsevier., DOI: 10.1016/C2023-0-51427-2

Elms, H., Brammer, S., Harris, J., & Phillips, R. (2010). New Directions in Strategic Management and Business Ethics. *Business Ethics Quarterly*, *20*(3), 401–425. Advance online publication. DOI: 10.5840/beq201020328

Ferrell, O. C., Fraedrich, J., & Ferrell, L. (2018). *Business ethics: Ethical decision making and cases* (12th ed.). Cengage Learning.

George, J., & Dane, E. (2016). Affect, emotion, and decision making. *Organizational Behavior and Human Decision Processes, 136*, 47–55. DOI: 10.1016/j.obhdp.2016.06.004

Kirkman, B., Lowe, K., & Gibson, C. (2006). A Quarter Century of Culture's Consequences: A Review of Empirical Research Incorporating Hofstede's Cultural Values Framework. *Journal of International Business Studies, 37*(3), 285–320. DOI: 10.1057/palgrave.jibs.8400202

Kolb, D. A. (1984). *Experiential learning: Experience as the source of learning and development.* Prentice Hall.

Lawton, A., & Gabriunas, I. (2014). Developing a framework for ethical leadership. *Journal of Business Ethics, 130*(3), 639–651. DOI: 10.1007/s10551-014-2244-2

Le Breton-Miller, I., & Miller, D. (2020). Ideals-Based Accountability and Reputation in Select Family Firms. Journal of Business Ethics, 163(2), 183-196. DOI: 10.1007/s10551-019-04225-5

Palanski, M. & Vogelgesang, G. (2011). Virtuous Creativity: The Effects of Leader Behavioural Integrity on Follower Creative Thinking and Risk Taking. Canadian Journal of Administrative Sciences / Revue Canadienne des Sciences de l'Administration, 28. .DOI: 10.1002/cjas.219

Rest, J. R. (1986). *Moral development: Advances in research and theory*. Praeger.

Salas, E., Wildman, J. L., & Piccolo, R. F. (2009). Using simulation-based training to enhance management education. *Academy of Management Learning & Education, 8*(4), 559–573. DOI: 10.5465/AMLE.2009.47785474

Sartzetaki, M., Dimitriou, D., & Karagkouni, A. (2025). Assortment of the Regional Business Ecosystem Effects Driven by New Motorway Projects, Transportation Research. Procedia, 82, 515-529. DOI: 10.1016/j.trpro.2024.12.111

Sartzetaki, M., Karagkouni, A., & Dimitriou, D. (2023). A Conceptual Framework for Developing Intelligent Services (a Platform) for Transport Enterprises: The Designation of Key Drivers for Action. *Electronics (Basel), 12*(22), 4690. DOI: 10.3390/electronics12224690

Sims, R. R., & Felton, E. L.Jr. (2006). Designing and Delivering Business Ethics Teaching and Learning. *Journal of Business Ethics, 63*(3), 297–312. DOI: 10.1007/s10551-005-3562-1

Treviño, L. K., & Nelson, K. A. (2016). *Managing business ethics: Straight talk about how to do it right* (6th ed.). Wiley.

Werhane, P. H., & Freeman, R. E. (1999). Business ethics: The state of the art. *International Journal of Management Reviews, 1*(1), 1–16. DOI: 10.1111/1468-2370.00002

Zollo, M., & Winter, S. G. (2002). Deliberate learning and the evolution of dynamic capabilities. *Organization Science, 13*(3), 339–351. DOI: 10.1287/orsc.13.3.339.2780

Chapter 23
Integrating Simulation Tools Effect on Entrepreneurship Education by Mediation of Real-World Entrepreneurial Practices in the Horn of Africa

Shashi Kant
https://orcid.org/0000-0003-4722-5736
Bule Hora University, Ethiopia

Tafese Niguse
https://orcid.org/0009-0008-6536-6392
Bule Hora University, Ethiopia

Metasebia Adula
https://orcid.org/0000-0001-5732-2850
Bule Hora University, Ethiopia

Aynetu Terefe
https://orcid.org/0009-0003-3814-9548
Bule Hora University, Ethiopia

ABSTRACT

This chapter investigates the purpose that practical practices related with entrepreneurship manifest as a mediator and looks at the inclusion of tools employed for simulation in education related with entrepreneurship. The authors determine the direct and indirect impacts of tools employed for simulation on learning outcomes through quantitative analysis. The findings show a direct influence of 0.42, proving that the use of tools employed for simulation make betters education related with entrepreneurship considerably. Also, the computed indirect influence of 0.45 emphasizes how crucial practical experiences are in moderating this association. The results, which have an overall influence of 0.87, imply that effective learning requires a thorough approach that includes both theoretical and practical components.

DOI: 10.4018/979-8-3693-9040-5.ch023

The investigation has imperative managerial consequences and supports the inclusion of experiential learning and simulation-based learning in curriculum.

1. INTRODUCTION

Internationally, education related with entrepreneurship is becoming increasingly imperative for augmenting monetary progression, especially in marginalized areas like the Eastern Africa (Dereso et al., 2023). With countries depending more and more on invention and trade initiatives, including simulation into educational frameworks presents prospects for learners to incubate their entrepreneurial knowledge set. This assimilation is more than just a leading-edge training approach; it nurtures a association among theoretical inclusion and practical application by letting learners test out practical situations in a safe setting (Onjewu et al., 2021). The generation of works, monetary diversification, and communal mobility are three factors that highlight the worldwide significance of education related with entrepreneurship and make it essential to justifiable incubation (Hassan et al., 2021). The notion of using simulation into education related with entrepreneurship emerged from the necessity of incubating immersive learning ecosystem that replicate practical difficulties. Numerous advantages of simulations have been noted in empirical investigation, such as better decision-making abilities, increased capacity for problem-solving and heightened self-assurance in prospective trade owners (Adula et al., 2023).

Investigation has demonstrated that trade environment complexity may be accurately simulated by simulations, providing learners with the opportunity to apply abstract notions to practical situations (Jabo et al., 2024). Even so, the Eastern Africa continues to encounter particular difficulties in the field of education related with entrepreneurship, such as poor infrastructure, restricted access to resources, and socio-monetary constraints that impede the successful acquisition and use of entrepreneurial knowledge (Adeniyi, 2023). The region's practical issues make assimilating simulation into entrepreneurship instruction even more difficult. A lot of schools don't have the IT infrastructure or expertise needed to use them efficiently. Also, curricula frequently fail to effectively educate learners for the difficulties they will encounter as entrepreneurs due to a gap among academic programs and the realities of the local trade environment (Onjewu et al., 2021). This discrepancy draws attention to a major knowledge vacuum regarding the successful assimilation of simulation into regional entrepreneurial activities to make better learning outcomes (Rungsrisawat & Sutduean, 2019).

The incorporation of real-world practice into entrepreneurship education is critical in determining the link between simulation tool absorption and educational result effectiveness. As global economies adapt and the demand for innovative entrepreneurs grows, understanding how practical experiences affect learning becomes increasingly vital. The notion of incorporating real-world practice into education is rooted in experiential learning theories, which highlight the importance of hands-on experiences in improving information retention and skill acquisition (Panigarhi et al., 2023). The empirical research has consistently shown that experiential learning, particularly using simulation technology, increases student engagement and prepares students for real-world issues. Studies have indicated that when students participate in simulations that match genuine business settings, they are more likely to develop critical thinking skills. Despite this amount of information, many practical obstacles persist. Many educational institutions fail to effectively integrate simulation technology into their courses owing to limited resources, inadequate faculty training, and insufficient engagement with industry partners (Onjewu et al., 2021). Furthermore, there are study gaps in understanding the exact processes that real-world practice uses to moderate the link between simulation tool absorption and educational results. While previous research emphasizes the advantages of simulations, it frequently ignores the contextual aspects that impact these correlations, such as cultural variations and various educational settings. Addressing these shortcomings is critical to developing a complete framework for successful entrepreneurship education (Rungsrisawat & Sutduean, 2019).

This chapter aims to close these gaps by looking at how real-world experience may modify the relationship across simulation tool absorption and entrepreneurship education. This study will provide valuable insights for educators, legislators, and scholars by examining how these factors interact. It will highlight best practices for bringing simulations into curricula and propose strategies to improve cooperation among educational institutions and businesses (Guye et al., 2024). The study's fundamental question is: ***"How does the mediation of practical applications influence the relationship between simulation tool assimilation and entrepreneurship education effectiveness?"*** Answering this question will not only contribute to the scholarly discourse on entrepreneurial education, but will also provide practical ideas for improving educational frameworks, eventually equipping students to flourish in an increasingly complex business landscape.

1.1 Background of Study

In the past, education related with entrepreneurship has frequently overlooked the practical knowledge's required for navigating practical trade contexts in favor of theoretical frameworks. Consequently, a large number of graduates leave with insufficient knowledge to start or run their trades (Hassan et al., 2021). The lack of infrastructure and resources required to integrate contemporary educational technology, especially simulation technologies, is one major obstacle. For example, in Ethiopia, many educational institutions continue to receive inadequate funding and lack access to cutting-edge technology resources, despite a growing interest in entrepreneurship among young people (Adula et al., 2023). This problem is demonstrated by a practical case investigation from Addis Ababa University. Although the school's entrepreneurship program has received recognition for its creative curriculum, it finds it difficult to offer hands-on training because of limited access to hardware and simulation software. Because of this, learners frequently pass on practical learning prospects that could make better their comprehension of practical entrepreneurial difficulties (Hassan et al., 2022).

Also, the Eastern Africa's socio-monetary situation makes it more difficult to conduct successful entrepreneurship instruction. For instance, it is challenging for educational institutions to run regularly in Somalia due to the ongoing instability and insecurity. The University of Hargeisa has a strong entrepreneurship program, but there are few prospects for learners to participate in practical trade operations because of the continuous conflict, according to a case investigation of the institution. There is often a disconnect among what is learned in the classroom and what they can really do because many learners struggle to access the markets or resources needed for experiential learning (Shabbir et al., 2018). Also, there's sometimes a mismatch among the real needs of the local trade environment and the educational programs that are given. Even if universities like Strathmore University in Kenya have made progress in incorporating entrepreneurial education, there is still a big disconnecting among curricula and the needs of the regional economy (Guye et al., 2024).

An in-depth case investigation of Strathmore's entrepreneurship program demonstrates that although learners get imperative knowledge, the value of their education is diminished by the absence of practical application and mentorship from local trade owners. Many graduates have a degree in theory but lack the practical experience and connections necessary to thrive in a cutthroat industry (Adeniyi, 2023). In the Eastern Africa, cultural perspectives on entrepreneurship might also provide difficulties. Traditional notions about work and job stability may deter young people in some regions from exploring entrepreneurial endeavors. Despite receiving training in entrepreneurship, a case investigation conducted in rural Ethiopia reveals that young people frequently choose secure employment over launching their own enterprises because of communal constraints and the perceived risks involved in entrepreneurship (Rungsrisawat & Sutduean, 2019).

1.2 Statement of Problem

There is a great chance to make better learners' and future leaders' entrepreneurial knowledge through the use of simulation in education related with entrepreneurship in the Eastern Africa. In a notion world, this combination would result in a strong educational framework that fosters a generation of entrepreneurs who can successfully navigate the intricacies of the contemporary trade environment while also imparting theoretical knowledge and practical knowledge to learners. But this is not at all how education related with entrepreneurship is currently provided in the area (Onjewu et al., 2021). There is contradictory information about the efficacy of conventional entrepreneurship training methods. Some studies support the use of simulation to close the knowledge gap among theory and practice, while others draw attention to the ongoing difficulties that prevent its successful application. For example, studies indicate that learning through simulations can greatly make better one's ability to make decisions and solve problems (Panigarhi et al., 2023).

However, empirical information from the Eastern Africa demonstrates that many institutions lack the infrastructure and resources needed to successfully integrate such. This disparity indicates a imperative knowledge vacuum on how to apply and modify simulation in a way that is responsive to the particular difficulties faced by the area (Wata et al., 2020). Also, the findings of the investigation that has already been done on education related with entrepreneurship in the Eastern Africa are still unclear. Although there is evidence that practical training and simulation lead to better entrepreneurial success, there are no defined metrics to assess these results reliably. This discrepancy leaves theoretical gaps about optimal procedures and the particular circumstances in which simulation can be employed successfully. Also, little is known about how theoretical learning and practical entrepreneurial activities interact, especially in terms of how these components might be combined to make better the efficacy of education (Anosike, 2019).

Contextual gaps further complicate the situation. The diverse socio-monetary and cultural landscapes across the Eastern Africa mean that a one-size-fits-all approach to education related with entrepreneurship is ineffective. Practical challenges, such as infrastructural deficiencies, limited access to technology, and socio-political instability, exacerbate these context-specific issues, leading to disconnect among educational objectives and local entrepreneurial realities (Guye et al., 2024). By investigating the mediating purpose of actual trade activity in the successful assimilation of simulation into education related with entrepreneurship in the Eastern Africa, this investigation seeks to close these gaps. Through investigating the ways in which hands-on experiences might enhance theoretical education, the investigation will offer a sophisticated comprehension of the prerequisites for effective execution. In addition, the investigation looks for notions and best practices for getting over the obstacles that the region's educational institutions are currently facing (Rungsrisawat & Sutduean, 2019).

2. LITERATURE REVIEW

2.1 THEORETICAL FOUNDATION

2.1.1 Experiential Learning Theory (ELT)

is one pertinent theory. According to this notion, experience is transformed into knowledge during the learning process. Concrete experience, reflecting observation, abstract conceptualization, and active experimentation are Kolb's four stages of the learning cycle. This theory is especially relevant to the training of entrepreneurship because it highlights the value of practical experience in the incubation of entrepreneurial abilities. Through the inclusion of simulation, instructors can enable experiential learning, providing learners with prospects to participate in authentic trade scenarios, contemplate on their experiences, and utilize acquired concepts in their future undertakings (Hassan et al., 2021).

2.1.2 Communal Learning Theory

It is another imperative framework. This approach emphasizes how imperative tools and observation are to the learning process. Learners can gain from interacting with practical practices and seeing successful entrepreneurs in the context of education related with entrepreneurship. Learners can tool their behaviors after those they observe by using simulation as a medium for this observational learning. The assumption that collaborative simulations might make better the educational experience is reinforced by Bandura's theory, which emphasizes the significance of communal environment and peer interactions in teach (Shabbir et al., 2018).

2.1.3 Theory of Planned Behavior

Rendering to TPB, approaches, apparent behavioral regulator, and individual customs inspiration an entity's conduct. This hypothesis can assist in explaining how learners' views toward entrepreneurship, shaped by their experiences in simulations, can influence intends to pursue entrepreneurial endeavors in the context of education related with entrepreneurship. Teachers can help kids incubate better attitudes and more confidence in their entrepreneurial abilities by giving them positive simulations that represent practical difficulties (Cui et al., 2021).

2.1.4 Entrepreneurial Intention Theory (EIM)

focuses on the specific variables that drive people to become entrepreneurs. This tool is helpful for inclusion how educational experiences, especially those incorporating simulations, can affect learners' desires to become entrepreneurs since it integrates numerous psychological, communal, and contextual aspects that influence entrepreneurial inclinations (Tchokoté et al., 2024).

Finally, the combination of experience learning, community learning, the theory of planned behavior, and entrepreneurial intention theory provides a holistic framework for improving entrepreneurship education. These ideas emphasize the value of practical experience, observation, and collaborating interactions, highlighting the necessity for immersive learning settings that mirror real-world business issues. Such environments not only instill critical skills and attitudes in students, but also boost their confidence in their entrepreneurial ability. Using simulations and practical exercises, educators may effectively bridge the gap across theory and practice, eventually cultivating an entire new class of entrepreneurs capable of navigating the complexity of the commercial world.

2.2 DEFINITION AND ORIGIN OF TERMS

2.2.1 Entrepreneurship Education

the term "education related with entrepreneurship" refers to the educational approach that aims to provide people the abilities, information, and mindset needed to recognize prospects, launch and run new trades, and promote invention. It covers a broad range of subjects, such as leadership, marketing, financial management, and trade planning. In the latter half of the 20th century, the notion of education related with entrepreneurship began to take shape as more people realized how imperative entrepreneurship is to job generation and monetary progression. At first, trade schools were the main places where entrepreneurship was taught, with a concentration on conventional trade management (Adeniyi, 2023).

2.2.2 Simulation

With the use of instructional technology called simulation, learners can practice and apply their knowledge in risk-free, realistic scenarios. These can include case studies, role-manifesting games, and computer-based simulations. Because they are made to resemble realistic situations, users can manifest around with decision-making methods and see how their choices turn out without having to take on the real risks of becoming an entrepreneur. Simulation has been employed in education since the middle of the 20th century, when troops were being trained for complicated works in military and aviation training programs (Rungsrisawat & Sutduean, 2019).

2.2.3 Real World Entrepreneurship Practices

refers to the real experiences and actions that trade owners take when launching and running their ventures. This involves determining market prospects, creating trade notions, obtaining funding, and managing the difficulties involved in operating a firm. Unlike theoretical learning, these actions offer insightful perspectives into the day-to-day reality of entrepreneurship. The experiential learning movement, which emphasizes the value of firsthand experience in the learning process, is where the notion of practical entrepreneurship practice originated. Investigations and educators started arguing for a more practical approach to training entrepreneurship as it became apparent that it was a key factor in monetary progression (Hassan et al., 2022).

2.2.4 Competency

refers to a collection of abilities, know-how, and conduct that allow a person to carry out activities efficiently. Competencies related to education related with entrepreneurship may include communication, critical thinking, problem-solving, and financial literacy, all of which are necessary for profitable ventures. In corporate and educational settings, the word "competency" became more popular in the

1970s and 1980s, especially when talking about workforce incubation and human resource management (Cui et al., 2021).

3. EMPIRICAL LITERATURE REVIEW

3.1 Simulation Tools and Entrepreneurship Education

The inclusion of simulation technologies into education related with entrepreneurship yields substantial benefits by offering learners opportunity to apply theoretical concepts in practical scenarios in an immersive context. With the use of tools employed for simulation, educators may set up authentic trade settings in which learners can make decisions that closely resemble the challenges of actual entrepreneurship (Asefa et al., 2023). As a result of navigating obstacles and making strategic decisions in response to shifting market conditions, learners using this experiential learning method incubate critical thinking and problem-solving abilities. Learners learn about the complexities of running a trade, such as financial management, marketing tactics, and operational issues, through the simulation of the entrepreneurial process. These concepts are frequently challenging to explain using conventional lecture-based methods (Shabbir et al., 2018).

Additionally, learners are encouraged to actively participate and collaborate through simulation a technology, which fosters the cooperation and communication knowledge necessary for successful entrepreneurship. Similar to collaborative practical entrepreneurial endeavours, learners can work together in this virtual ecosystem to establish trade concepts, examine market information, and handle competitive scenarios (Kant & Adula, 2024). In addition to improving individual learning outcomes, this collaborative method gets learners ready for the interpersonal complexities they will face when they embark on their entrepreneurial adventures. Moreover, the instantaneous feedback provided by the simulation enables learners to contemplate their choices, absorb lessons from their errors, and modify their approaches correspondingly, so strengthening the iterative character of entrepreneurship (Adeniyi, 2023).

Additionally, learners are encouraged to actively participate and collaborate through simulation technologies, which foster the cooperation and communication knowledge necessary for successful entrepreneurship. Similar to collaborative practical entrepreneurial endeavours, learners can work together in this virtual ecosystem to establish trade concepts, examine market information, and handle competitive scenarios. In addition to improving individual learning outcomes, this collaborative method gets learners ready for the interpersonal complexities they will face when they embark on their entrepreneurial adventures. Moreover, the instantaneous feedback provided by the simulation enables learners to contemplate their choices, absorb lessons from their errors, and modify their approaches correspondingly, so strengthening the iterative character of entrepreneurship (Onjewu et al., 2021).

H1: Simulation tool has imperative impact on Education related with entrepreneurship

3.2 Simulation Tools and on Real-World Related Entrepreneurship

By giving aspiring entrepreneurs a secure space to test out their concepts and tactics, the inclusion of tools employed for simulation in entrepreneurial education has a imperative impact on the practice of entrepreneurship in the real world. With the use of these tools, which mimic the intricacies of practical trade situations, learners can participate in decision-making processes that are similar to those confronted by trade owners in the real world (Durga et al., 2024). Learners can explore different trade strategies, evaluate risks, and feel the consequences of their decisions without the financial costs of practical ventures by practicing in this simulated environment. Through fostering a deeper grasp of customer behaviour, market dynamics, and operational issues, experiential learning helps prepare learners for practical entrepreneurship (Cui et al., 2021).

Additionally, tools employed for simulation encourage the progression of vital abilities necessary for negotiating the terrain of entrepreneurship. Learners can incubate knowledge like flexibility, problem-solving, and strategic thinking through these simulations. For example, in a simulation, learners learn to pivot and alter their approach in real-time when faced with unanticipated problems or changing market conditions, matching the agility necessary in practical trade situations. Through practical experience, they gain confidence in their capacity to respond to unanticipated events, a critical knowledge for prosperous trade owners (Hassan et al., 2022). Also, incorporating tools employed for simulation promotes cooperation and teamwork, two essential elements of entrepreneurship. In order to accomplish shared objectives, a lot of entrepreneurial endeavours need people to collaborate, combining their varied perspectives and knowledge sets. Group activities are a common feature of simulations, where learners must work together to create trade notions, evaluate market information, and reach judgments. In addition to improving communication knowledge, this collaborative environment teaches learners the value of using group talents to solve complicated problems, mirroring the collaborative nature of practical entrepreneurial operations (Weber et al., 2023).

H2: Tools employed for simulation has imperative impact on the real world practice related with entrepreneurship

3.3 Real-World Entrepreneurship and Entrepreneurship Education

Through experiential learning, learners can better traverse obstacles and make well-informed decisions by applying theoretical concepts taught in the classroom to practical scenarios. It is possible for learners to contextualize their learning and increase its relevance and significance by having them watch and take part in practical trade activity (Abbink et al., 2022). Also, exposure to actual entrepreneurial activity fosters critical abilities that are necessary for success in the commercial world. Learners acquire knowledge like critical thinking, problem-solving, and flexibility through practical experiences (Shkabatur et al., 2022). Also, practicing entrepreneurship in the real world nurtures relationships and networking possibilities that are essential for budding trade owners. Learners can obtain essential information, mentorship, and potential partnerships by interacting with seasoned entrepreneurs, industry professionals, and peers. These relationships can result in partnerships, financing prospects, and industry trends insights, all of which greatly make better learners' chances of success. By including these practical encounters in education related with entrepreneurship, organizations can give their learners access to a stronger network of support (Cui et al., 2021).

Moreover, one of the most imperative aspects of the learning process is the feedback that comes from practical experiences. Learners get fast feedback from classmates, mentors, and consumers when they test their trade concepts in practical scenarios. They are able to make better their concepts, comprehend the demands of the market, and modify their strategies as a result of this feedback loop. The incubatement of a progression mind set in which pupils see difficulties as chances for progression require this kind of iterative learning (Adeniyi, 2023). Finally, assimilating practical entrepreneurial activities into the classroom fosters a creative and innovative atmosphere. Learners are motivated to think creatively and explore their own trade dreams when they witness directly how entrepreneurs overcome challenges and embrace prospects. Incorporating practical experience into the curriculum not only make betters the learning environment but also helps learners incubate a more entrepreneurial min dset, which will ultimately position them to become proactive and creative leaders in the trade sector (Dabić et al., 2022).

H3: Real World Practice related with entrepreneurship has a imperative impact on education related with entrepreneurship

3.4 Real-World Entrepreneurship Mediation

world can gain a better inclusion of the mechanisms that lead to successful learning by looking at how practical entrepreneurial experiences mediate the interaction among tools employed for simulation and education related with entrepreneurship (Anosike, 2019). By placing the theoretical frameworks given in tools employed for simulation in context, practical practice related with entrepreneurship enhances the educational experience. Learners can put the notions they have acquired through simulations into practice in practical situations when they participate in practical entrepreneurial activities, such as internships, start-up projects, or joint ventures. This association among theory and practice strengthens their comprehension and raises the educational value of their training. Learners receive insights that enhance their inclusion of entrepreneurial principles as they solve practical problems, which amplify the learning process (Hassan et al., 2022). Also, practical experience offers crucial input that increases the efficiency of simulation programs. Learners practice making decisions and incubateing strategies in a simulated setting, but also learn about the difficulties and uncertainties of entrepreneurship through practical experiences. Through this exposure, learners are able to hone their abilities and modify their tactics in response to first hand input from the industry. As a result, practical experience acts as a crucial prism through which learners can assess and refine their simulated learning, resulting in a deeper comprehension of the dynamics of entrepreneurship (Cui et al., 2021).

Also, practical practice related with entrepreneurship's collaborative character incubates vital interpersonal knowledge, which enhance the individual learning that takes place in simulation ecosystem. Working on real projects with peers or seasoned trade owners helps learners acquire the teamwork, communication, and negotiation knowledge that are necessary for success in the trade world. Through this collaboration, learners can exchange strategies and insights that further enrich their educational journey, which make betters the learning acquired from simulation technologies. Practical experience mediates the association in this way by encouraging a collaborative learning environment where concepts may be discussed and make better (Shabbir et al., 2018). Additionally, learners who engage in practical entrepreneurial activity incubate a progression mentality, which encourages them to rise to difficulties and see failures as training prospects. In contrast to the risk-free environment that simulations offer, practical encounters frequently entail real dangers and repercussions. Learners benefit from this exposure by incubating their resilience and adaptability, which are essential knowledge for negotiating the uncertainties of entrepreneurship. The ability of pupils to overcome challenges in practical situations boosts their self-confidence, which in turn make betters the overall efficacy of their education (Adeniyi, 2023).

H4: *Mediation of real world practice related with entrepreneurship influence the relationship among assimilation of tools employed for simulation and Education related with entrepreneurship*

4. CONCEPTUAL FRAMEWORK

A conceptual framework is a theoretical structure and visual aid that depicts how imperative variables in a investigation relate to one another. Within the framework of this investigation, the emphasis is on how simulation technologies may be included into education related with entrepreneurship and how practical entrepreneurial experience can operate as a mediating factor. The main elements of the conceptual framework are described below:

Figure 1. Conceptual framework (Authors)

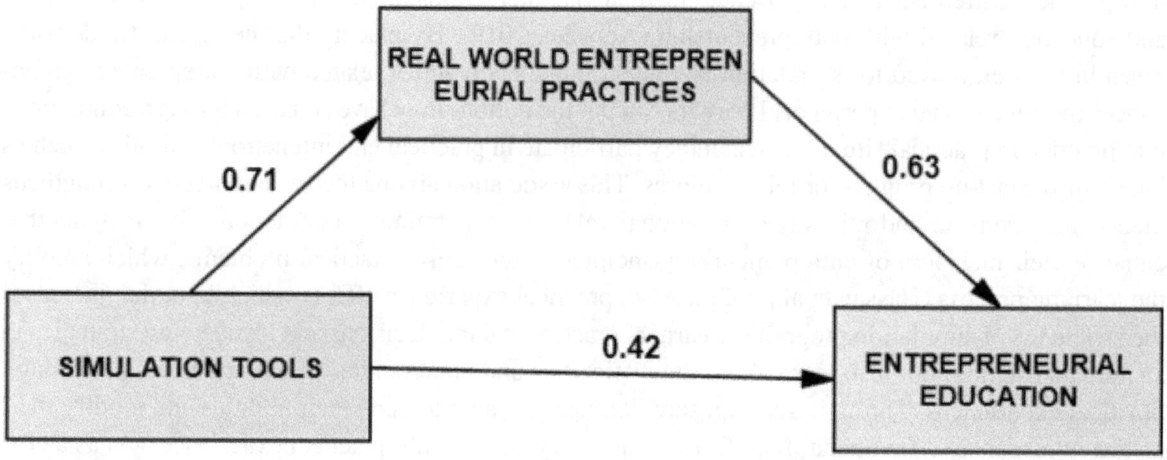

5. INVESTIGATION METHODOLOGY

A structured questionnaire was utilized in the investigation to collect information from a sample of 394 participants, utilizing a quantitative method. The purpose of this approach was to measure the connections among the inclusion of simulation technologies, actual entrepreneurial activity, and education related with entrepreneurship. In order to ensure a wide sample of learners enrolled in entrepreneurship programs, the respondents were chosen from a variety of educational institutions throughout the Eastern Africa. This approach made it possible to analyse the information in a methodical manner, which made it easier to thoroughly investigate the associations that were theorized. The investigation made use of Bartlett's Test of Sphericity and the Kaiser-Meyer-Olkin (KMO) measure of sample adequacy to evaluate the information's validity and eligibility for additional analysis. To evaluate if the sample size was sufficient for factor analysis, the KMO value was computed; values greater than 0.6 were deemed appropriate. Subsequently, the information underwent Exploratory Factor Analysis (EFA) in order to detect underlying factor structures and verify that the questionnaire items corresponded to the targeted constructs.

The suggested relationships inside the conceptual framework were then tested using AMOS software and structural equation model, or SEM. Through the simultaneous examination of various interactions made possible by SEM, education related with entrepreneurship was able to gain a thorough grasp of the impact of assimilating tools employed for simulation with practical entrepreneurial experience. A number of indices, such as the Chi-square statistic, RMSEA, CFI, and TLI, were employed to evaluate the tool fit and make sure the proposed tool appropriately captured the relationships in the information.

6. INFORMATION ANALYSIS

Table 1. KMO and Bartlett's test

Kaiser-Meyer-Olkin Measure of Sampling Adequacy.		**.857**
Bartlett's Test of Sphericity	Approx. Chi-Square	1419.735
	Df	90
	Sig.	.002

Source: Authors

The results of Bartlett's Test of Sphericity and the Kaiser-Meyer-Olkin (KMO) Measure of Sampling Adequacy, two crucial preliminary tests for evaluating the suitability of factor analysis, are shown in Table 1. The sample of 394 individuals appears to be well-suited for factor analysis, as indicated by the KMO value of 0.857, which depicts a high degree of sampling adequacy. KMO ratings vary from 0 to 1, where values nearer 1 suggest that the information is suitable for determining underlying causes. A KMO score of more than 0.8 is regarded as exceptional, supporting the notion that the information is sufficiently connected to produce imperative findings in further examinations. Bartlett's Test of Sphericity complements the KMO measure by assessing whether the correlation matrix is imperatively different from an identity matrix. The test produced an approximate Chi-Square value of 1419.735 with 90 degrees of freedom and a significance level (Sig.) of 0.002. This significance level indicates that the null hypothesis, which posits that the correlation matrix is an identity matrix (i.e., no correlations among the variables), can be rejected. Consequently, this result confirms that there are imperative relationships among the variables, further validating the appropriateness of conducting factor analysis.

All of these findings demonstrate how reliable the information set is for exploratory factor analysis (EFA). Sufficient inter-item correlations among the variables are revealed by the imperative Bartlett's Test result, and the strong KMO score indicates that the sample size is sufficient. These results offer a strong basis for further EFA since they suggest that the information set has imperative latent structures that warrant additional investigation. Consequently, deeper inclusion of the connections among the inclusion of tools employed for simulation, actual entrepreneurial activities, and education related with entrepreneurship is provided by the combined results of the KMO and Bartlett's Test.

Table 2. Total variance explained

Component	Initial Eigenvalues			Extraction Sums of Squared Loadings			Rotation Sums of Squared Loadings		
	Total	% of Variance	Cumulative %	Total	% of Variance	Cumulative %	Total	% of Variance	Cumulative %
1	4.51	32.229	32.229	4.51	32.229	32.229	3.01	21.451	21.451
2	1.43	9.792	42.027	1.43	9.792	42.027	2.17	15.486	36.941
3	1.37	9.083	51.128	1.46	9.083	51.128	1.95	14.168	51.128
4	.947	6.785	57.893						
5	.872	6.217	64.114						
6	.769	5.522	69.633						

Abstraction Routine: PCA
Source: Authors

Table 2 manifests the findings of the Total Variance Explained Exploratory Factor Analysis (EFA), which sheds light on the information set's factor structure. The initial eigenvalues show how much variance is explained by each component prior to rotation or extraction. With an eigenvalue of 4.51, the first component explains 32.229% of the variation in the whole. This large proportion implies that this component is imperative to the overall factor structure and captures a considerable amount of the variability in the information. With an eigenvalue of 1.43, the second component accounts for 9.792% of the variance, making the sum variance explained 42.027%. The eigenvalues of the following components decrease: the fourth component, at 0.947, explains 6.785% of the variance; the fifth and sixth components, at 0.872 and 0.769, respectively, show declining eigenvalues. Even if these factors still influence the total variance, their eigenvalues are less than 1, which means that they can only explain a decreasing amount of the information set's variability.

Table 3. Covariance

Covariance			Estimate	S.E.	C.R.	P	Hy.
Real-world entrepreneurship Practices	<-->	Simulation Tools	.244	.022	8.230	.00	H2
Real-world entrepreneurship Practices	<-->	Entrepreneurship Education	.303	.0322	7.693	.00	**H3**
Simulation Tools	<-->	Entrepreneurship Education	.248	.23	7.833	.00	**H1**

Source: Authors

The correlation among the three main studies constructs—Practical Practice related with entrepreneurship, Simulation Tool, and Education related with entrepreneurship—is shown in Table 3. With a standard error (S.E.) of 0.022, the correlation among the simulation tool and practical practice related with entrepreneurship is given as 0.241. This association has a critical ratio (C.R.) of 8.230 and a p-value of .00 (statistically imperative). The robust positive covariance indicates a favourable correlation among increased participation in authentic entrepreneurial activities and enhanced efficacy of simulation technologies in education related with entrepreneurship. Hypothesis 2 (H2), which proposes a positive association among these two conceptions, is supported by the large C.R. value, which further depicts that this relationship is robust. Next, there is a 0.303 correlation with a 0.0322 standard error among Practical Practice related with entrepreneurship and Education related with entrepreneurship. This association has a statistically imperative C.R. of 7.693. This result emphasizes the favourable correlation among increased participation in practical entrepreneurial activities and the general efficacy of education related with entrepreneurship. It backs up Hypothesis 3 (H3), which contends that practical experiences make better learning outcomes and that this association is an essential part of the framework for education. Finally, a covariance of 0.248, with a S.E. of 0.23 and a C.R. of 7.833, is reported among the simulation tool and education related with entrepreneurship. The observed positive covariance suggests a noteworthy correlation among the use of tools employed for simulation and their influence on the training of entrepreneurship. The relationship's statistical significance supports Hypothesis 1 (H1), which holds that tools employed for simulation are essential for improving education related with entrepreneurship.

Table 4. Validity concern

	CR	AVE	MSV	MaxR(H)	ST	RWEP	EE
ST	0.735	0.640	0.216	0.853	**0.652**		
RWEP	0.757	0.659	0.133	0.761	0.169	**0.670**	
EE	0.792	0.601	0.272	0.796	0.385	0.192	**0.681**

Note: ST= Tools employed for simulation; RWEP= Real world Practice related with entrepreneurship; EE=Education related with entrepreneurship
Source: Authors

Key metrics pertaining to the dimensions being studied—the Simulation tool (SM), Practical Practice related with entrepreneurship (RWEP), and Education related with entrepreneurship (EE)—are provided in Table 4, which addresses validity problems. To prove the validity and reliability of the measurements employed in the investigation, the table comprises Composite Reliability (CR), Average Variance Extracted (AVE), Maximum Shared Variance (MSV), and other pertinent indices. Each construct's Composite Reliability (CR) ratings show a reasonable degree of internal consistency. The simulation tool's CR of 0.735 is higher than the generally acknowledged cut-off of 0.7, indicating that the items employed to measure this construct are likely to accurately capture the intended notion. In a similar vein, the CRs for Education related with entrepreneurship and Practical Practice related with entrepreneurship are 0.792 and 0.757, respectively. These results, which show good internal consistency across all constructs, provide additional evidence for the validity of the scales that were utilized.

Another imperative metric for assessing validity is Average Variance Extracted (AVE), which depicts how much variation a concept extracts from its indicators compared to how much variation results from measurement error. The Education related with entrepreneurship AVE is 0.601, the Simulation tool is 0.640, and Practical Practice related with entrepreneurship is 0.659. Each of these figures depicts that each construct accounts for a sizable percentage of the variance among its indicators, above the suggested cutoff point of 0.5. This proves that the scales accurately capture the underlying concepts that they are designed to measure. The constructs with the strongest association with each other among all the constructs in the tool are shown by the Maximum Shared Variance (MSV) values. The MSVs are 0.216, 0.133, and 0.272 for the simulation tool, practical practice related with entrepreneurship, and education related with entrepreneurship, respectively. Because the MSV values for each construct are smaller than the corresponding AVE values, these information imply that the constructions are different from one another. In order to maintain the discriminant validity of the measures and guarantee that each concept is different and not unduly associated with the others, this separation is essential. The constructs' dependability is further supported by the Maximum dependability (MaxR(H)) values, which show that the Simulation tool has a value of 0.853, Practical Practice related with entrepreneurship has a value of 0.761, and Education related with entrepreneurship has a value of 0.796. These high numbers provide additional evidence for the validity of the investigation's measures.

6.1 Mediating Examination

Figure 2. Structural equation model (Authors)

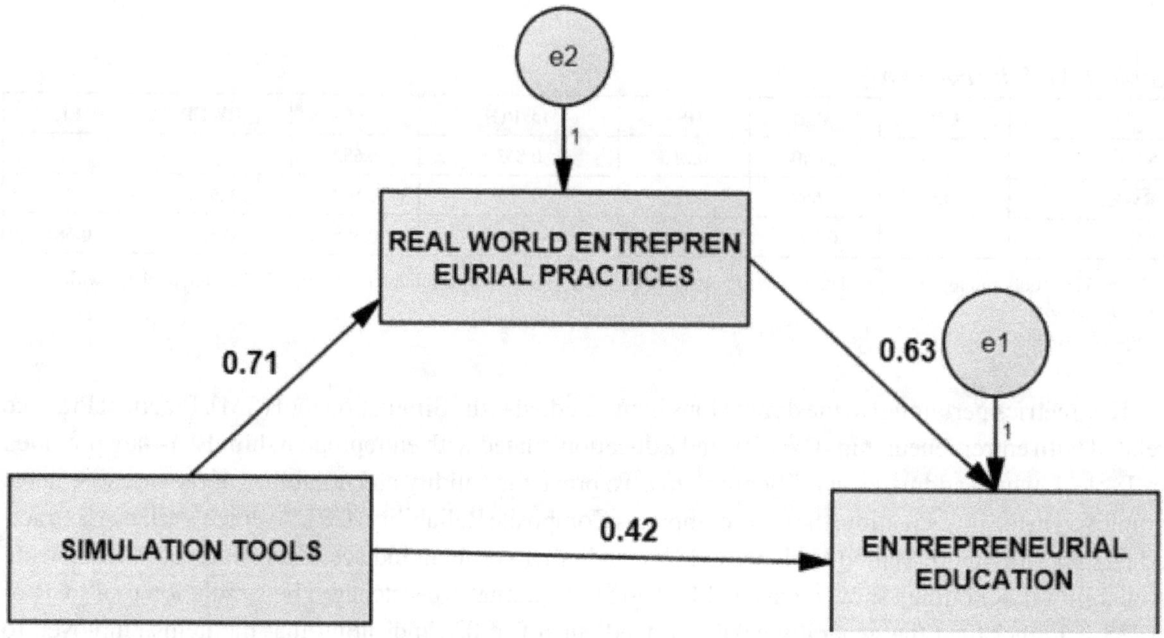

Table 5. Model fit

Sig.	Chi-Sq	RMR	Fitness Goodness	Fitness Confirmatory	TLI	RMSEA
0.004	1.951	.037	0.930	0.913	0.911	.02

Source: Authors

In order to investigate the mediating purpose of practical entrepreneurial activity among the assimilation of tools employed for simulation and education related with entrepreneurship, Table 5 presents the tool fit indices for the structural equation tool (SEM). Given that the tool's significance level (Sig.) is 0.004, it may be concluded that the associations it looks at are unlikely to have happened by accident. A low p-value indicates a meaningful relationship among the variables under investigation (tools employed for simulation, practical entrepreneurial activity, and education related with entrepreneurship), which in turn increases the tool's dependability. Positive tool fit is shown by the comparatively low Chi-Square value of 1.951. A smaller Chi-Square value in SEM indicates that the instrument closely resembles the observed information. The Chi-Square statistic is a crucial indicator for assessing the overall suitability of the instrument, even if it cannot offer a comprehensive evaluation on its own. The tool's fit is further supported by the Root Mean Square Residual (RMR) result of 0.037. When the RMR number is close to zero, it indicates that there are little differences among the observed and predicted values, indicating that the tool is capturing the connections among the components under investigation properly.

The stated values for the Fitness Confirmatory Index (CFI) and Fitness Goodness Index (GFI) are 0.913 and 0.930, respectively. These numbers show that the tool fits the user well, since they are higher than the suggested cutoff of 0.90. Both indices are critical for assessing the tool's fit since GFI depicts the percentage of variation explained by the instrument and CFI accounts for sample size. A good match is also shown by the Tucker-Lewis Index (TLI), which is at 0.911. Values above 0.90 indicate that the tool performs well in comparison to a baseline instrument. Lastly, as RMSEA values less than 0.05 denote a close match, the Root Mean Square Error of Approximation (RMSEA) value of 0.02 is especially imperative. The tool appears to offer a good estimate of the population covariance matrix, based on the low RMSEA.

Table 6. Regression examination

Relative			Estimate	S.E.	C.R.	P	Ass.
Real-world entrepreneurship Practices	<---	Simulation Tools	.860	.139	7.580	.00	H2
Entrepreneurship Education	<---	Real-world entrepreneurship Practices	.325	.130	2.849	.00	H3
Entrepreneurship Education	<---	Simulation Tools	.961	.188	7.960	.00	H1

Source: Authors

The findings of the regression analysis, are shown in Table 6. To shed light on the strength and importance of these associations, the regression coefficients, standard errors (S.E.), critical ratios (C.R.), p-values (P), and assumptions (Ass.) are presented. With a S.E. of 0.139, the regression coefficient for the route from the simulation tool to practical practice related with entrepreneurship is 0.860. This association has a C.R. of 7.580 and a .00 (statistically imperative) p-value. This strongly positive coefficient suggests that there is a substantial positive correlation among the effectiveness of tools employed for simulation and learners' participation with practical entrepreneurial activities. This result lends credence to Hypothesis 2 (H2), which holds that tools employed for simulation have a beneficial impact on actual entrepreneurial activities. The association among education related with entrepreneurship and practical practice related with entrepreneurship is examined in the following regression line, which produces a coefficient of 0.325 and a S.E. of 0.130. This association has a 2.849 coefficient of determination and a statistically imperative p-value.

This finding implies that more participation in practical entrepreneurial endeavors enhances the efficacy of education related with entrepreneurship. This investigation emphasizes the value of practical experiences in improving educational achievements for learners interested in entrepreneurship, hence supporting Hypothesis 3 (H3). Finally, a coefficient of 0.961 with a S.E. of 0.188 is shown by the regression line from the simulation tool to the entrepreneurial education. This association has a statistically imperative p-value of 7.960 and a C.R. of 7.960. The robust positive correlation suggests that tools employed for simulation imperatively influence the efficacy of entrepreneurship instruction. The inclusion of simulation technologies considerably make betters learners' educational experiences and prepares them for practical entrepreneurial difficulties, as suggested by the high coefficient supporting Hypothesis 1 (H1).

Table 7. Mediating role impact

	Influence	worth	Path Influence
Simulation Tools → Entrepreneurship Education	Direct Influence	.42	Direct influence stated
Simulation tool →Real-world entrepreneurship Practices → Entrepreneurship Education	Indirect Influence	.71*.63=.45	Indirect Influence Ensued
	Whole influence	.87	Partial mediation

Source: Authors

According to Table 7, there is a somewhat good correlation among tools employed for simulation and entrepreneurial education, as indicated by the direct impact value of 0.42. This depicts that using tools employed for simulation effectively can make better learning outcomes and experiences in education related with entrepreneurship. To enhance their training strategies, educators want to think about concentrating on this association. Also the association among tools employed for simulation and education related with entrepreneurship is mediated, as indicated by the indirect impact of 0.45, which points to practical entrepreneurial actions. Here, the impact of tools employed for simulation on practical behaviours is represented by 0.71, while the impact of such practices on educational results is represented by 0.63. This highlights the value of experiential learning by implying that putting notions acquired through simulations to use in actual situations make betters learning as a whole. As a result, the overall influence value of 0.87 depicts that both direct and indirect impacts have a imperative overall impact on education related with entrepreneurship. This high number supports the hypothesis that substantial gains in educational efficacy may be achieved by fusing simulation technologies with practical applications. It implies that education related with entrepreneurship benefits from a comprehensive approach.

Table 7 shows a significant link across the simulation tools used and entrepreneurial education, with a direct effect value of 0.42. This suggests that the proper use of simulation tools may considerably improve student results and educational experiences in entrepreneurship. Educators should thus highlight this relationship in order to strengthen their training tactics and increase student participation. Furthermore, the association between simulation tools and entrepreneurship education is mediated by real entrepreneurial behaviors, as indicated by an indirect impact value of 0.45. This shows that simulation technologies' effects are not entirely direct; rather, they alter practical actions, which in turn affect educational outcomes. More specifically, the influence of simulation tools on practical behaviors is measured at 0.71, whereas the effect of these activities on educational outcomes is 0.63. These principles emphasize the importance of experiential learning, demonstrating that applying concepts gained through simulations in real-world circumstances considerably improves the entire learning experience. As a result, the cumulative influence value of 0.87 demonstrates the significant impact that both direct and indirect factors have on entrepreneurship education. This high value backs up the premise that combining simulation technology with real-life applications leads to considerable increases in educational efficacy.

It highlights the need of a complete strategy that integrates academic knowledge with actual learning chances. In summary, the implications of mediation in this context demonstrate that the underlying worth of simulation tools is not just their immediate educational advantages, but also their capacity to bridge the gap among theory and practice. Educators may promote a more effective and comprehensive entrepreneurial education by creating an environment in which students can utilize simulation-acquired information in real-world circumstances. This comprehensive approach provides students with the required skills and confidence to handle the intricacies of the entrepreneurial world, eventually improving their preparedness for future difficulties.

7. DISCUSSION

The results shown in Table 7 highlight how imperative it is to incorporate tools employed for simulation into education related with entrepreneurship. It is evident from the direct impact of tools employed for simulation on student learning outcomes that theoretical information may be successfully imparted through engaging and interactive methods. Moreover, the significance of experience learning is underscored by the indirect impact transmitted by actual trade actions. This combined method not only make betters inclusion of entrepreneurial notions but also incubates the critical thinking and problem-solving abilities needed to succeed in the trade world. It is clear that a combination of theory and practice is necessary to prepare learners for the difficulties of entrepreneurship as educators use simulation-based learning more and more.

The outcomes of this study provide important insights into the mediating function of simulation tools in entrepreneurship education. The direct impact of simulation tools on entrepreneurship education, with a route influence of 0.42, demonstrates their usefulness in building a practical knowledge of entrepreneurial principles. This is consistent with prior studies emphasizing the relevance of experience learning in improving educational results (Kolb, 1984). Simulation technologies encourage greater involvement with entrepreneurial processes by giving learners hands-on experience (Adeniyi, 2023). Furthermore, the indirect impact of simulation tools on real-world entrepreneurial practices, with a total path influence of 0.45, indicates that these tools not only improve theoretical understanding but also bridge the gap between theory and practice. This conclusion is consistent with the community learning paradigm, which stresses learning via observation and engagement in real-world settings (Durga et al., 2024). The capacity of simulation tools to mimic actual entrepreneurial settings enables students to use theoretical information in a practical environment, strengthening their learning experience. The total effect of 0.87 demonstrates a substantial correlation between simulation tools and entrepreneurial education, which is supported by partial mediation. This shows that, while simulation technologies play an important role, other factors may also influence the success of entrepreneurship education. Future study should look at these other aspects, since knowing the full picture might give a more nuanced view on how to improve entrepreneurial training programs. In contrast to the current literature, our findings add to the expanding body of data supporting the incorporation of simulation-based learning into entrepreneurship education. While previous research has demonstrated the benefits of experiential learning, this study goes deeper by objectively establishing the mediating role of simulation tools. Thus, the study not only confirms previous hypotheses, but it also encourages future investigation into the particular processes by which simulation tools improve learning outcomes in entrepreneurship education.

8. CONCLUSION

In conclusion, using simulation technology into entrepreneurship education dramatically improves learning results, especially when combined with practical experiences. This study indicates that both direct and indirect factors have a significant impact on students' entrepreneurial skills, highlighting the varied character of the learning process. Understanding these dynamics is critical as educational institutions work to develop imaginative and skilled entrepreneurs who can succeed in an increasingly complicated commercial market. The findings demonstrate that simulation technologies are not only good teaching tools, but also catalysts for experiential learning. These tools help learners apply theoretical information in a practical situation, reinforcing essential ideas and abilities. This hybrid approach, which combines organized academic frameworks with hands-on experiences, results in a more diverse educational environment that develops critical thinking, problem-solving, and flexibility, all of which are necessary characteristics for aspiring entrepreneurs. Furthermore, the findings emphasize the value of a comprehensive educational plan that includes mentoring, peer cooperation, and real-world experience. This holistic approach guarantees that trainees are not only theoretically prepared but also have the actual skills required for commercial success. It is critical for educational institutions to identify the interaction of these many components and create curriculum that reflect this connectivity. Finally, the key to building effective entrepreneurial mindsets is to create an educational atmosphere that blends academic rigor with practical application. By adopting simulation technology and encouraging real-world involvement, educators may greatly improve their students' entrepreneurial talents, equipping them to face the difficulties of the corporate world with confidence and inventiveness. This study adds vital insights to the ongoing discussion about entrepreneurship education, calling for creative teaching techniques that will empower the future generation of entrepreneurs.

8.1 Managerial Implications

The findings of this analysis give significant recommendations for managers in developing effective curriculum and instructional methodologies for entrepreneurship programs. It is critical for both managers and educators to emphasize the use of simulation technology as a basic component of instructional design. By doing so, they may dramatically improve the learning experience and provide students with the skills required for business success. Creating an educational atmosphere that promotes experiential learning is critical. Managers should prioritize creating settings that promote active involvement, collaboration, and real-world applications. This may be accomplished by combining simulation technologies that simulate real-world entrepreneurial issues, allowing students to fully interact with the curriculum. This technique not only improves the overall quality of education, but it also boosts student involvement, making learning more dynamic and effective. Furthermore, investing in projects that encourage actual entrepreneurial activity is critical for closing the gap between theory and practice. Managers may help students apply their academic knowledge in real-world situations by supporting workshops, internships, and mentorship programs. This practical experience is vital, preparing graduates to confidently and competently negotiate the complexity of the corporate world. Finally, by embracing these management implications, educational institutions may foster a new generation of entrepreneurs who are not just informed but also skilled at putting theory into practice. This strategic emphasis on experiential learning and practical involvement will result in graduates who are more prepared to handle the demands of the entrepreneurial environment, increasing the overall efficacy of entrepreneurship education.

8.2 Practical Implications

This analysis has important practical consequences for entrepreneurship educators and practitioners. Using simulation technology, teachers may build immersive learning experiences that closely match real-world corporate contexts. This method not only improves students' memory of academic information, but also provides them with the real-world abilities required for success in today's competitive entrepreneurial world. Furthermore, educational institutions should aggressively pursue relationships with local companies to give students with hands-on learning opportunities that reinforce classroom topics. Collaborating with industry professionals enables students to participate in real-world initiatives, internships, and mentorship opportunities, closing the gap across academic learning and practical application. Such cooperation can improve the educational experience by making it more useful and efficient. Furthermore, educators may use these collaborations to invite guest speakers, provide seminars, and organize networking events, exposing students to the realities of business. By cultivating these linkages, institutions may improve the learning environment and enhance readiness students for the challenges that await them as future entrepreneurs. In conclusion, the practical implications of this study highlight the importance of a collaborative, experiential methodology for entrepreneurship education. Educators may create a more effective and interesting learning experience for students by embracing simulation technology and forming strong links with business.

8.3 Theoretical Implications

This study contributes greatly to our understanding of the potential advantages of simulation technology in entrepreneurship education. It adds to the current corpus of research on experiential learning by proving that including practical activities significantly enhances student learning outcomes. By providing actual proof of simulation tools' positive influence, the study emphasizes the relevance of hands-on experiences in building a better knowledge of entrepreneurial principles. Furthermore, the findings emphasize the need for more research into the particular processes by which practical experiences and simulation technology interact to impact learning outcomes. These offers up new areas for research into the intricacies of how these variables interact to improve educational efficacy. Understanding these relationships will be critical in enhancing pedagogical techniques in entrepreneurial education. Furthermore, this study provides useful information that might help to educate and improve existing theories about entrepreneurial teaching approaches. By clarifying the significance of experiential learning and simulation, the study invites educators and researchers to reconsider standard teaching methodologies, calling for a more integrated strategy that stresses active, experiencing participation. This theoretical progress not only enhances academic debate, but also lays the groundwork for establishing creative educational frameworks that can better prepare students for the difficulties of entrepreneurship. In conclusion, the study emphasizes the transformational potential of simulation technology in entrepreneurship education, urging more research and theoretical refinement to improve teaching practices and student results in this critical subject.

8.4 Recommendations

Based on the conclusions of this study, educational institutions should create a complete framework for incorporating simulation technologies into their entrepreneurship curricula. This framework should promote collaboration with industry practitioners in order to provide real learning experiences that bridge the gap among theory and practice. By involving experts with real-world experience, universities may improve the relevance of their courses while also providing students with insights into contemporary industry norms and issues. Furthermore, educators should be trained in successful simulation approaches. This course will educate teachers to provide interesting and meaningful learning experiences that use simulation technology. Continuous professional development opportunities should be made available, allowing educators to keep current on creative teaching approaches and advances in simulation technologies. Furthermore, to ensure that the educational experience remains relevant and successful, schools should adopt a frequent curriculum review process. This approach should include analyzing and revising course material to reflect current industry trends along with best practices. Institutions can better prepare students for the challenges of the business world by creating an adaptable learning environment that adapts to the changing landscape of entrepreneurship. To summarize, a systematic approach to incorporating tools for simulation, combined with robust educator training and ongoing curriculum review, will significantly improve the quality of entrepreneurship education. These suggestions aim to create a dynamic learning ecosystem that empowers learners to gain the skills and knowledge required to succeed as future entrepreneurs.

8.5 Future Directions

Future study should look at the long-term impact of simulation-based learning on graduates' performance as entrepreneurs. Understanding how these educational experiences lead to real-world business success is critical for assessing the efficacy of such pedagogical techniques. Furthermore, researchers should investigate the exact sorts of simulations and practical activities that have the most positive influence on student learning outcomes. Identifying the most successful approaches allows educators to customize their teaching tactics to increase student engagement and skill acquisition. Furthermore, broadening the research to encompass a variety of educational ecosystems and cultural contexts might give vital insights on how to tailor these techniques to different learning demands. Different cultural and institutional contexts may impact how simulation tools are perceived and used, and understanding these dynamics is critical for building inclusive and successful entrepreneurship education programs. Finally, more research into the relationship between practice and simulation is critical for improving our knowledge of effective entrepreneurship education. By diving further into how these aspects interact, researchers might discover techniques for optimizing learning experiences, eventually resulting to more successful entrepreneurial experiences for students. In a nutshell these future directions seek to expand our understanding of entrepreneurship education and inspire best practices that adapt to learners' changing requirements across varied contexts.

REFERENCES

Abbink, J., Ancel, S., Aziz, A. A. A., Fantini, E., Ferras, P., Mwakimako, H., & Záhořík, J. (2022). *Routledge handbook of the eastern Africa*. Routledge.

Adeniyi, A. O. (2023). The mediating impacts of entrepreneurial self-efficacy in the relationship among education related with entrepreneurship and start-up readiness. *Humanities and Communal Sciences Communications*, *10*(1), 1–14.

Adula, M., Birbirsa, Z. A., & Kant, S. (2023). The effect of interpersonal, problem solving and technical training skills on performance of Ethiopia textile industry: Continuance, normative and affective commitment as mediators. *Cogent Business & Management*, *10*(3), 2286672. Advance online publication. DOI: 10.1080/23311975.2023.2286672

Adula, M., & Kant, S. (2025). Impact of Smart Entrepreneurship and Territorial Marketing on Regional Branding: Case of Ethiopia. In *Sustainable and Intelligent Territorial Marketing and Entrepreneurship* (pp. 229–256). IGI Global. DOI: 10.4018/979-8-3693-9775-6.ch008

Anosike, P. (2019). Education related with entrepreneurship as human capital: Implications for youth self-employment and conflict mitigation in Sub-Saharan Africa. *Industry and Higher Education*, *33*(1), 42–54. DOI: 10.1177/0950422218812631

Anosike, P. (2019). Education related with entrepreneurship as human capital: Implications for youth self-employment and conflict mitigation in Sub-Saharan Africa. *Industry and Higher Education*, *33*(1), 42–54. DOI: 10.1177/0950422218812631

Asefa, K., & Debela, K. L. (2023). Effect of Transformational Leadership on Organizational Performance: The Mediating Role of Employee Commitment and Expert Systems (AI) Inclusion in Ethiopia. *2023 International Conference on Communication, Security and Artificial Intelligence (ICCSAI)*, 305-310. DOI: 10.1109/ICCSAI59793.2023.10421269

Birhane, M., Amentie, C., Borji, B., & Kant, S. (n.d.). Are Ethiopian Coffee Farmers Proficient to Predict Capital Structure with Mediation of AI Based Knowledge Systems and Asset Liquidity? In *AI in Agriculture for Sustainable and Economic Management* (pp. 199-215). CRC Press. DOI: 10.1201/9781003451648-15

Cui, J., Sun, J., & Bell, R. (2021). The impact of education related with entrepreneurship on the entrepreneurial mindset of college learners in China: The mediating role of inspiration and the role of educational attributes. *International Journal of Management Education*, *19*(1), 100296. DOI: 10.1016/j.ijme.2019.04.001

Dabić. (2022). *Women Entrepreneurs in Sub-Saharan Africa*. Springer Nature.

Dereso, C. W., Kant, S., Muthuraman, M., & Tufa, G. (2023). Effect of Point of Service on Health Department Student's Creativity in Comprehensive Universities of Ethiopia: Moderating Role of Public-Private Partnership and Mediating Role of Work Place Learning. In Proceedings of the International Health Informatics Conference. Lecture Notes in Electrical Engineering, vol 990. Springer. DOI: 10.1007/978-981-19-9090-8_13

Durga, P., Godavarthi, D., Kant, S., & Basa, S. S. (2024). Aspect-based drug review classification through a hybrid model with ant colony optimization using deep learning. *Discov Computing*, *27*(1), 19. DOI: 10.1007/s10791-024-09441-w

Guyo, D. M., Kero, C. A., & Kant, S. (2025). Is Marketing Intermediaries' Mediation Required for Livestock and Products Marketing to Improve the Economic Status of Pastoralist Communities in Ethiopia? In *AI in Agriculture for Sustainable and Economic Management* (pp. 216-234). CRC Press.

Guyo, K., & Kero, C. A. (2023). Mediation of Marketing Intermediaries and AI Adoption Between Livestock Products Marketing and Economic Status of Pastoralist in Ethiopia. *2023 International Conference on Communication, Security and Artificial Intelligence (ICCSAI)*, 311-316. DOI: 10.1109/ICCSAI59793.2023.10421261

Hassan, A., Anwar, I., Saleem, I., Islam, K. B., & Hussain, S. A. (2021). Individual entrepreneurial orientation, education related with entrepreneurship and entrepreneurial intention: The mediating role of entrepreneurial motivations. *Industry and Higher Education*, *35*(4), 403–418. DOI: 10.1177/0950422221 1007051

Hassan, H. K., Igel, B., & Shamsuddoha, M. (2022). Education related with entrepreneurship and communal entrepreneurial intentions: The mediating impacts of entrepreneurial communal network. *Frontiers in Psychology*, *13*, 860273. DOI: 10.3389/fpsyg.2022.860273 PMID: 35651573

Jabo, B., & Kant, S. (2024). Impact of Technical CRM on Ethiopia Bank Human-Computer Interface and Competitive Advantage as Mediators of Performance. *2024 IEEE International Conference on Computing, Power and Communication Technologies (IC2PCT)*, 679-682. DOI: 10.1109/IC2PCT60090.2024.10486237

Kant, S., & Adula, M. (2024). AI Learning and Work Attitude Mediation Between Reward and Organizational Support in Ethiopia. In Gomathi Sankar, J., & David, A. (Eds.), *Generative AI for Transformational Management* (pp. 109–136). IGI Global. DOI: 10.4018/979-8-3693-5578-7.ch005

Kant, S., & Adula, M. (2024). Mediated by AI-Based Generative Re-Enforcement Learning and Work Attitude: Are Intrinsic Rewards Transforming Employee Perceived Organizational Support? In Gomathi Sankar, J., & David, A. (Eds.), *Generative AI for Transformational Management* (pp. 83–108). IGI Global. DOI: 10.4018/979-8-3693-5578-7.ch004

Kant, S., & Adula, M. (2024). Human-Machine Interaction in the Metaverse in the Context of Ethiopia. In *Impact and Potential of Machine Learning in the Metaverse* (pp. 196–212). IGI Global. DOI: 10.4018/979-8-3693-5762-0.ch008

Kant, S., Adula, M., & Genale, M. (2025). Mediating of Smart Entrepreneurship Among Territorial Marketing on Place Branding in Ethiopia. In *Sustainable and Intelligent Territorial Marketing and Entrepreneurship* (pp. 257–284). IGI Global. DOI: 10.4018/979-8-3693-9775-6.ch009

Kant, S., Adula, M., Kumari, M., & Nimbrain, N. (2025). Role of SMEs in Greening the Economy by Mediation of Eco-Innovation in the Horn of Africa. In *Examining Green Human Resources Management and Nascent Entrepreneurship* (pp. 173–200). IGI Global. DOI: 10.4018/979-8-3693-7046-9.ch007

Niguse, T., Kant, S., & Adula, M. (2025). Mediation Effect of Customer Loyalty in Relationship Between Market Orientation, Entrepreneurial Orientation, and Firm Performance in Ethiopia. In *Leveraging AI for Effective Digital Relationship Marketing* (pp. 419–458). IGI Global. DOI: 10.4018/979-8-3693-5340-0.ch014

Nyoach, T. D., Lemi, K., Debela, T., & Kant, S. (2024). Does Organizational Commitment Mediate the Relationship between Employee Relationship Management and Bank Performance? The Case of Banks in Ethiopia. *International Journal of Organizational Leadership*, *13*(2), 355–376. DOI: 10.33844/ijol.2024.60419

Onjewu, A. K. E., Haddoud, M. Y., & Nowiński, W. (2021). The impact of education related with entrepreneurship on nascent entrepreneurship. *Industry and Higher Education*, *35*(4), 419–431. DOI: 10.1177/09504222211014038

Panigrahi, A., Pati, A., Sahu, B., Das, M. N., Nayak, D. S. K., Sahoo, G., & Kant, S. (2023). En-MinWhale: An ensemble approach based on MRMR and Whale optimization for Cancer diagnosis. *IEEE Access : Practical Innovations, Open Solutions*, *11*, 113526–113542. DOI: 10.1109/ACCESS.2023.3318261

Ratten, V., & Usmanij, P. (2021). Education related with entrepreneurship: Time for a change in investigation direction? *International Journal of Management Education*, *19*(1), 100367. DOI: 10.1016/j.ijme.2020.100367

Rungsrisawat, S., & Sutduean, C. (2019). Entrepreneurial education and entrepreneurial intention: The mediating role of creativity disposition among University Learners in Thailand. *Int J Innov Creat Change*, *6*(10), 213–232.

Shabbir, M., Shariff, M. N. M., Bin Bakar, M. S., & Yusof, M. S. (2018). The mediating role of trade simulations on the relationship among University role entrepreneurship curriculum and assessment of training approaches and entrepreneurial inclination. *International. The Journal of Supply Chain Management*, *7*(4), 223–233.

Shkabatur, J., Bar-El, R., & Schwartz, D. (2022). Invention and entrepreneurship for justifiable incubatement: Lessons from Ethiopia. *Progress in Planning*, *160*, 100599. DOI: 10.1016/j.progress.2021.100599

Tchokoté, I. D., & Bawack, R. E. (2024). Associationing Trade Games to Trade and Education related with entrepreneurship: Insights from a Bibliometric and Literature Review. *Theoretical Monetarys Letters*, *14*(02), 436–467. DOI: 10.4236/tel.2024.142024

Wata, C., Muthuraman, M., & Kant, S. (2020). Associations among Education related with entrepreneurship Outcomes and Entrepreneurship Behavior in Higher Education: A Review and Evaluation in Case of Ethiopia. *Journal of Indigenous Knowledge and Incubatement Studies*, *2*(2), 93–109.

Weber, C., Fasse, A., Haugh, H. M., & Grote, U. (2023). Varieties of necessity entrepreneurship–New insights from Sub Saharan Africa. *Entrepreneurship Theory and Practice*, *47*(5), 1843–1876. DOI: 10.1177/10422587221111737

KEY TERMS AND DEFINITIONS

Education: It is the systematic process of acquiring knowledge, skills, values, and attitudes through various forms of instruction and learning. It encompasses formal schooling, informal learning, and vocational training, aiming to foster personal and professional development.

Entrepreneurship: It is the process of designing, launching, and running a new business, typically a startup, in order to seek profit and address market needs. It involves identifying opportunities, mobilizing resources, and taking on financial risks to create innovative products or services.

Incubation: It refers to the supportive environment and resources provided to early-stage startups or entrepreneurs to help them develop their business ideas into viable enterprises. This process often includes mentorship, funding, office space, and access to networks, which facilitate growth and reduce the risks of failure.

Simulation Tools: These are software applications or platforms that allow users to create and analyze virtual models of real-world processes or systems. These tools are used to test hypotheses, predict outcomes, and make informed decisions by simulating various scenarios without the risks associated with real-world experimentation.

Compilation of References

. Jia, Q., Cui, J., Xiao, Y., Liu, C., Rashid, P., & Gehringer, E.F. (2021). ALL-IN-ONE: Multi-task learning BERT models for evaluating peer assessments. *arXiv*.

Abbas, M., & Bulut, M. (2024). Navigating the landscape of sustainable entrepreneurship research: A systematic literature review. *Discover Sustainability*, *5*(1), 171. Advance online publication. DOI: 10.1007/s43621-024-00293-4

Abbas, M., Jam, F. A., & Khan, T. I. (2024). Is it harmful or helpful? Examining the causes and consequences of generative AI usage among university students. *International Journal of Educational Technology in Higher Education*, *21*(1), 10. Advance online publication. DOI: 10.1186/s41239-024-00444-7

Abbink, J., Ancel, S., Aziz, A. A. A., Fantini, E., Ferras, P., Mwakimako, H., & Záhořík, J. (2022). *Routledge handbook of the eastern Africa*. Routledge.

Abdullah, N. L., Hanafiah, M. H., & Hashim, N. A. (2013). Developing creative teaching module: Business simulation in teaching strategic management. *International Education Studies*, *6*(6). Advance online publication. DOI: 10.5539/ies.v6n6p95

Abdullah, S. H., Rahim, M. S., & Zakaria, N. (2017). Riding the practice of technopreneur development: Innovative entrepreneurial teaching and learning in institutes of higher learning. *International Journal of Economic Research*, *14*(15), 213–219.

Abt, C. C. (1970). *Serious Games*. Viking Press.

Abu Hanieh, A., Abdelall, S., Krajnik, P., & Hasan, A. (2015). Industry-academia partnership for sustainable development in Palestine. *Procedia CIRP*, *26*, 109–114. DOI: 10.1016/j.procir.2014.07.184

Abwamiah, N., Maulani, G.A.F., Lindayani, & Hamdani, N.A. (2023). The effect of entrepreneurship education on student's entrepreneurship interest in entrepreneurship faculty of Universitas Garut. *Advances in Economics, Business and Management Research*, 1865-1876. .DOI: 10.2991/978-94-6463-234-7_197

Act, E. U. A. I. (n.d.). https://www.euaiact.com/#:~:text=The%20EU%20Artificial%20Intelligence%20Act,three%20years%20negotiations%20and%20entered

Adachi, P. J. C., & Willoughby, T. (2013). More than just fun and games: The longitudinal relationships between strategic video games, self-reported problem solving skills, and academic grades. *Journal of Youth and Adolescence*, *42*(7), 1041–1052. DOI: 10.1007/s10964-013-9913-9 PMID: 23344653

Adams, P. C. (1998). Teaching and learning with SimCity 2000. *The Journal of Geography*, *97*(2), 47–55. DOI: 10.1080/00221349808978827

Adedeji, S. B., & Rahman, M. M. (2018). Innovative Teaching Methods and Entrepreneurship Education: A Review of Literature. *Journal of Research in Business. Economics and Management, 10*(1), 1807–1813.

Adedeji, S. B., Rahman, M. M., Abdul, M. B., Ghani, M. F. B. A., Uddin, M. J., & Rahaman, M. S. (2020). Innovative teaching methods and entrepreneurship education: A synthesised literature review [Educational Administration Research and Review]. *EARR, 2*(1), 1–8. DOI: 10.17509/earr.v2i1.21713

Adeniyi, A. O. (2023). The mediating impacts of entrepreneurial self-efficacy in the relationship among education related with entrepreneurship and start-up readiness. *Humanities and Communal Sciences Communications, 10*(1), 1–14.

Adeyinka-Ojo, S., & Abdullah, S. K. (2021). Social media marketing in rural hospitality and tourism destination research. *University of South Florida (USF) M3 Publishing, 5*, 11.

Adula, M., Birbirsa, Z. A., & Kant, S. (2023). The effect of interpersonal, problem solving and technical training skills on performance of Ethiopia textile industry: Continuance, normative and affective commitment as mediators. *Cogent Business & Management, 10*(3), 2286672. Advance online publication. DOI: 10.1080/23311975.2023.2286672

Adula, M., & Kant, S. (2025). Impact of Smart Entrepreneurship and Territorial Marketing on Regional Branding: Case of Ethiopia. In *Sustainable and Intelligent Territorial Marketing and Entrepreneurship* (pp. 229–256). IGI Global. DOI: 10.4018/979-8-3693-9775-6.ch008

Aebersold, M., Tschannen, D., & Bathish, M. (2012). Innovative simulation strategies in education. *Nursing Research and Practice, 2012*(1), 765212. PMID: 22550573

Agoraki, K. K., Deirmentzoglou, G. A., Psychalis, M., & Apostolopoulos, S. (2024). Types of Innovation and Sustainable Development: Evidence from Medium-and Large-Sized Firms. *International Journal of Innovation and Technology Management, 21*(02), 1–18.

Agoraki, K. K., Deirmentzoglou, G. A., Psychalis, M., & Apostolopoulos, S. (2024a). Types of Innovation and Sustainable Development: Evidence from Medium-and Large-Sized Firms. *International Journal on Management of Innovation & Technology, 21*(02), 1–18. DOI: 10.1142/S0219877024500135

Agoraki, K. K., Deirmentzoglou, G. A., & Triantopoulos, C. (2024b). Cultural Values as Catalysts of Technological Innovation for a Sustainable Future. *Sustainability (Basel), 16*(5), 2064. DOI: 10.3390/su16052064

Ahmad, S. Z. (2013). The need for inclusion of entrepreneurship education in Malaysia lower and higher learning institutions. *Education + Training, 55*(2), 191–203. DOI: 10.1108/00400911311304823

Ahn, J. (2008). Application of the experiential learning cycle in learning from a business simulation game. *E-Learning and Digital Media, 5*(2), 146–156. DOI: 10.2304/elea.2008.5.2.146

Ahuja, V. (2024). Simulations in Business Education: Unlocking Experiential Learning. Practices and Implementation of Gamification in Higher Education, 1-21.

Ajzen, I. (1991). The Theory of planned behavior. *Organizational Behavior and Human Decision Processes, 50*(2), 179–211. DOI: 10.1016/0749-5978(91)90020-T

Akman, E., & Çakır, R. (2023). The effect of educational virtual reality game on primary school students' achievement and engagement in mathematics. *Interactive Learning Environments*, *31*(3), 1467–1484. DOI: 10.1080/10494820.2020.1841800

Alajmi, Q., Al-Sharafi, M. A., & Abuali, A. (2020). Smart learning gateways for Omani HEIs towards educational technology: Benefits, challenges and solutions. *International Journal of Information Technology and Language Studies*, *4*(1), 12–17. https://www.scirp.org/reference/referencespapers?referenceid=2989533

Al-Ansi, A. M., Jaboob, M., Garad, A., & Al-Ansi, A. (2023). Analyzing augmented reality (AR) and virtual reality (VR) recent development in education. *Social Sciences & Humanities Open*, *8*(1), 100532. DOI: 10.1016/j.ssaho.2023.100532

Aldosari, S. A. M. (2020). The Future of Higher Education in the Light of Artificial Intelligence Transformations. *International Journal of Higher Education*, *9*(3), 145. DOI: 10.5430/ijhe.v9n3p145

Aldrich, C. (2005). *Learning by doing: A Comprehensive Guide to Simulations, Computer Games, and Pedagogy in e-Learning and Other Educational Experiences*. Academic Press.

Aldrich, C. (2004). *Simulations and the Future of Learning: An Innovative (and Perhaps Revolutionary) Approach to e-Learning*. Pfeiffer.

Alessi, S. M., & Trollope-Kumar, K. (2018). Experiential learning and simulation in business ethics education. Academic Press.

Alessi, S. M., & Trollip, S. R. (2001). *Multimedia for Learning: Methods and Development*. Allyn & Bacon.

Alexiou, A., & Schippers, M. C. (2018). Digital game elements, user experience and learning: A conceptual framework. *Education and Information Technologies*, *23*(6), 2545–2567. DOI: 10.1007/s10639-018-9730-6

Alghamdi, E. (2023). Digital Games use in Entrepreneurhip Education at the Undergraduate Level: A Systematic Review. *Journal of Management and Business Education*, *6*(2), 172–198. DOI: 10.35564/jmbe.2023.0009

Al-Haimi, B., Hujainah, F., Nasir, D., & Alhroob, E. (2021). Higher Education Institutions with Artificial Intelligence: Roles, Promises, and Requirements. In *Studies in computational intelligence* (pp. 221–238). DOI: 10.1007/978-3-030-72080-3_13

Ali, O., Krsteska, K., Said, D., & Momin, M. (2023). Advanced technologies enabled human resources functions: Benefits, challenges, and functionalities: A systematic review. *Cogent Business & Management*, *10*(2), 2216430. Advance online publication. DOI: 10.1080/23311975.2023.2216430

Ali, O., Murray, P. A., Momin, M., Dwivedi, Y. K., & Malik, T. (2023). The effects of artificial intelligence applications in educational settings: Challenges and strategies. *Technological Forecasting and Social Change*, *199*, 123076. DOI: 10.1016/j.techfore.2023.123076

Aljohani, M. (2015). Innovation and entrepreneurship integration in education. Ohaio State Model. *International Journal of Teaching and Education*, *III*(3), 1–20. DOI: 10.20472/TE.2015.3.3.001

Allen, G. (2020). Concepturealize™: A new contribution to generate real-needs-focussed, user-centred, lean business models. *Journal of Innovation and Entrepreneurship*, *11*(1), 6. Advance online publication. DOI: 10.1186/s13731-022-00198-4 PMID: 35096505

Almaki, S. H., Gunda, M. A., Idris, K., Hashim, A. T. M., & Ali, S. R. (2023). A systematic review of the use of simulation games in K-12 education. *Interactive Learning Environments*, 1–25. DOI: 10.1080/10494820.2023.2205894

Alonso-Peña, M., & Álvarez Álvarez, C. (2023). Clinical simulation in health education: A systematic review. *Investigacion y Educacion en Enfermeria*, *41*(2), e08. DOI: 10.17533/udea.iee.v41n2e08 PMID: 38589326

Alper, A., Şengün Öztaş, E., Atun, H., Çınar, D., & Moyenga, M. (2021). A systematic literature review towards the research of game-based learning with Augmented Reality. *International Journal of Technology in Education and Science*, *5*(2), 224–244. DOI: 10.46328/ijtes.176

Al-Samarraie, H., & Hurmuzan, S. (2018). A review of brainstorming techniques in higher education. *Thinking Skills and Creativity*, *27*, 78–91.

Alshare, K., & Sewailem, M. F. (2018). A gap analysis of business students' skills in the 21st century: A case study of Qatar. *Academy of Educational Leadership Journal*, *22*(1), 1–22.

Alstete, J. W. (2023). Multiplying success: The power of multiple simulations with graduated weighting and coordinated sequencing for learner engagement. *Journal of International Education in Business*, *16*(3), 334–350. DOI: 10.1108/JIEB-04-2023-0018

Altinay, F., Tlili, A., Altinay, Z., Dagli, G., Adedoyin, O. B., Huang, R., Xu, L., Jemni, M., Mogavi, R. H., & Metwally, A. H. S. (2024). *Meta-In or Meta-Out of Students with Special Needs: A Systematic Review on the Use of Metaverse in Special Education*. DOI: 10.1007/978-981-97-1298-4_7

Amani, D., Ismail, I. J., Makona, A., Changalima, I. A., & Kazungu, I. (2024). Extending the mediation role of entrepreneurial self-efficacy on enhancing students' entrepreneurial intentions: A moderated mediation model. *International Journal of Management Education*, *22*(1), 100915. Advance online publication. DOI: 10.1016/j.ijme.2023.100915

Ambrosio Mawhirter, D., & Ford Garofalo, P. (2016). Expect the unexpected: Simulation games as a teaching strategy. *Clinical Simulation in Nursing*, *12*(4), 132–136. DOI: 10.1016/j.ecns.2015.12.009

Amoah, J., Egala, S. B., Keelson, S., Bruce, E., Dziwornu, R., & Duah, F. A. (2023). Driving factors to competitive sustainability of SMEs in the tourism sector: An introspective analysis. *Cogent Business & Management*, *10*(1), 2163796. Advance online publication. DOI: 10.1080/23311975.2022.2163796

Amon, T. (2004). Simulations and the Future of Learning: An Innovative (and Perhaps Revolutionary) Approach to e-Learning. *Journal of Educational Technology & Society*, *7*, 149–150.

Amri, F., Djatmika, E. T., Wahyono, H., & Widjaja, S. U. M. (2020). The Effect of Using Simulation on Developing Students' Character Education in Learning Economics. *International Journal of Instruction*, *13*(4), 375–392.

Amundam, D. N. (2019). Enhancing potential social innovative thinking, responsibility, social entrepreneurship education: A curriculum content and teaching method model. *Journal of Entrepreneurship Education, 22*(5).

Ananian, S., & Dellaferrera, G. (2024). *A study on the employment and wage outcomes of people with disabilities*. ILO Working Paper.

Ananya, S. A. (2021). Technology application in agri-tourism. In *Technology Application in the Tourism and Hospitality Industry of Bangladesh* (pp. 113-126). DOI: 10.1007/978-981-16-2434-6_7

Anastasiadis, T., Lampropoulos, G., & Siakas, K. (2018). Digital game-based learning and serious games in education. *International Journal of Advances in Scientific Research and Engineering, 4*(12), 139–144. DOI: 10.31695/IJASRE.2018.33016

Anastasiadou, S., Zirinoglou, P., Seremeti, L., Masouras, A., Komodromos, M., & Anastasiadis, L. (2025). Statistical implicative analysis: A distinguished statistical methodology in evaluating Greek students' attitudes toward the use of AI. In *Real-world tools and scenarios for entrepreneurship exploration* (pp. 133–168). IGI Global.

Anastasopoulos, I., Georgopoulos, N., Katsanakis, I., Klada, N., Konstantopoulou, C., Kopanaki, E., Stroumpoulis, A., Tsoupros, G., & Varelas, S. (2024). Management of sustainable tourism in tourist destination ports: The use of sustainable indicators in the case study of Piraeus port, Greece. *WIT Transactions on Ecology and the Environment, 263*, 23–35. DOI: 10.2495/ST240031

Anastasopoulos, I., & Varelas, S. 2023, September. A Literature Review and Emerging Trends on key Topics of Risks and Challenges Facing Tourism real Estate Investments. In *European Conference on Innovation and Entrepreneurship* (Vol. 18, No. 1, pp. 39-47). DOI: 10.34190/ecie.18.1.1738

Anderson, L. W., Krathwohl, D. R., & Bloom, B. S. (2001). *A taxonomy for learning, teaching, and assessing: A revision of Bloom's taxonomy of educational objectives*. Longman.

Anderson, T., & Rivera Vargas, P. (2020). A critical look at educational technology from a distance education perspective. *Digital Education Review, 2020*(37), 208–229. DOI: 10.1344/der.2020.37.208-229

Andrade-Valbuena, N., Baier-Fuentes, H., & Gaviria-Marin, M. (2022). An Overview of Sustainable Entrepreneurship in Tourism, Destination, and Hospitality Research Based on the Web of Science. *Sustainability (Basel), 14*(22), 14944. DOI: 10.3390/su142214944

Angolia, M., & Reed, A. H. (2019). A case for early semester utilization of business simulations. *Journal of Applied Research in Higher Education, 11*(1), 90–101. DOI: 10.1108/JARHE-07-2017-0082

Anosike, P. (2019). Education related with entrepreneurship as human capital: Implications for youth self-employment and conflict mitigation in Sub-Saharan Africa. *Industry and Higher Education, 33*(1), 42–54. DOI: 10.1177/0950422218812631

Antoncic, B., & Hisrich, R. (2001). Intrapreneurship: Construct refinement and cross-cultural validation. *Journal of Business Venturing, 16*(5), 495–527. DOI: 10.1016/S0883-9026(99)00054-3

Antonelli, G., Venesaar, U., Riviezzo, A., Kallaste, M., Dorożyński, T., & Kłysik-Uryszek, A. (2023). Find your limits and break them! Nurturing students' entrepreneurship competence through innovative teaching methods and self-assessment. Journal of Enterprising Communities: People and Places in the Global Economy. .DOI: 10.1108/JEC-10-2022-0148

An, Y.-J., Haynes, L., Alba, A., & Chumney, F. (2016). Using educational computer games in the classroom: Science teachers' experiences, attitudes, perceptions, concerns, and support needs. *Contemporary Issues in Technology & Teacher Education*, *16*(4), 415–433.

Aoki, N. (2020). An experimental study of public trust in AI chatbots in the public sector. *Government Information Quarterly*, *37*(4), 101490. DOI: 10.1016/j.giq.2020.101490

Apostolopoulos, N., Kakouris, A., Liargovas, P., Dermatis, Z., & Komninos, D. (2018). Evaluating the learning environment of a cross-institutional postgraduate programme in entrepreneurship. Entrepreneurship Education, 1, 105-123. https://doi.Org/10.1007/S41959-018-0007-6

Apostolopoulos, N., Makris, I., Apostolopoulos, S., & Anastasopoulou, E. E. 2023, September. Aligning Agri-food Business with Sustainable Development and Quality of Life in Rural Areas: Stakeholders' Perspectives from Greece. In *ECIE 2023 18th European Conference on Innovation and Entrepreneurship Vol 1*. Academic Conferences and Publishing Limited.

Apostolopoulos, N., Makris, I., Apostolopoulos, S., & Dimitrakopoulos, P. (2024). Resilience of rural micro-businesses in an adverse entrepreneurial environment: adapting to the energy crisis. Journal of Enterprising Communities: People and Places in the Global Economy.

Apostolopoulos, N., Makris, I., Apostolopoulos, S., & Dimitrakopoulos, P. (n.d.). Resilience of rural micro-businesses in an adverse entrepreneurial environment: adapting to the energy crisis. Journal of Enterprising Communities: People and Places in the Global Economy. DOI: 10.1108/JEC-08-2023-0144

Apostolopoulos, N., Petropoulos, D., Liargovas, P., & Anastasopoulou, E. 2024. Constraints to Green and Digital Transition in the Greek Agri-Food Sector. In *Proceedings of The 19th European Conference on Innovation and Entrepreneurship*. Academic Conferences International. DOI: 10.34190/ecie.19.1.2996

Apostolopoulos, S., Makris, I., & Stavroyiannis, S. (2022, September). Health digitalisation and innovative entrepreneurship status. A qualitative exploration of private sector in Greece and synthesis of main issues. In *ECIE 2022 17th European Conference on Innovation and Entrepreneurship*. Academic Conferences and Publishing Limited.

Apostolopoulos, N., Kakouris, A., Liargovas, P., Borisov, P., Radev, T., Apostolopoulos, S., & Anastasopoulou, E. E. (2023). Just transition policies, power plant workers and green entrepreneurs in Greece, Cyprus and Bulgaria: Can education and retraining meet the challenge? *Sustainability*, *15*(23), 16307.

Apostolopoulos, N., Kakouris, A., Liargovas, P., Dermatis, Z., & Komninos, D. (2018). Evaluating the learning environment of a cross-institutional postgraduate programme in entrepreneurship. *Entrepreneurship Education*, *1*(1), 105–123.

Apostolopoulos, N., Kakouris, A., Liargovas, P., Petropoulos, D., & Anastasopoulou, E. (2024). Agri-food enterprises and relationship marketing during COVID-19: A primary data research through commitment-trust theory. *Journal of International Food & Agribusiness Marketing*, *36*(1), 3–22. DOI: 10.1080/08974438.2023.2183300

Apostolopoulos, N., Kakouris, A., Liargovas, P., Petropoulos, D., & Anastasopoulou, E. E. (2024). Exploring the impact of crises on rural agri-food SMEs: The moderating role of support mechanisms, digitalisation, and networking. *International Journal of Entrepreneurship and Innovation*. DOI: 10.1177/14657503241270275

Apostolopoulos, N., Liargovas, P., Stavroyiannis, S., Makris, I., Apostolopoulos, S., Petropoulos, D., & Anastasopoulou, E. (2020). Sustaining Rural Areas, Rural Tourism Enterprises and EU Development Policies: A Multi-Layer Conceptualisation of the Obstacles in Greece. *Sustainability (Basel)*, *12*(18), 7687. DOI: 10.3390/su12187687

Apostolopoulos, N., Moon, C., & Walmsley, A. (2018b). The entrepreneurial university as an engine for sustainable development. *International Journal of Innovative Research and Development*, *8*(4), 358–372.

Apostolopoulos, N., Ratten, V., Petropoulos, D., Liargovas, P., & Anastasopoulou, E. (2021). Agri-food sector and entrepreneurship during the COVID-19 crisis: A systematic literature review and research agenda. *Strategic Change*, *30*(2), 159–167. DOI: 10.1002/jsc.2400

Apostolopoulos, S., Makris, I., & Stavroyiannis, S. (2022). Healthcare innovation in Greece: The views of private health entrepreneurs on implementing innovative plans. *Journal of Open Innovation*, *8*(2), 78.

Apostu, S., Mukli, L., Panait, M., Gigauri, I., & Hysa, E. (2022). Economic Growth through the Lenses of Education, Entrepreneurship, and Innovation. *Administrative Sciences*, *12*(3), 74. Advance online publication. DOI: 10.3390/admsci12030074

Ardichvili, A., Mitchell, J. A., & Jondle, D. (2009). Characteristics of ethical business cultures. *Journal of Business Ethics*, *85*(4), 445–451. DOI: 10.1007/s10551-008-9782-4

Arias-Aranda, D., & Bustinza-Sánchez, O. (2009). Entrepreneurial attitude and conflict management through business simulations. *Industrial Management & Data Systems*, *109*(8), 1101–1117. DOI: 10.1108/02635570910991328

Arroyo, C. G., Barbieri, C., & Rich, S. R. (2013). Defining agritourism: A comparative study of stakeholders' perceptions in Missouri and North Carolina. *Tourism Management*, *37*, 39–47. DOI: 10.1016/j.tourman.2012.12.007

Asefa, K., & Debela, K. L. (2023). Effect of Transformational Leadership on Organizational Performance: The Mediating Role of Employee Commitment and Expert Systems (AI) Inclusion in Ethiopia. *2023 International Conference on Communication, Security and Artificial Intelligence (ICCSAI)*, 305-310. DOI: 10.1109/ICCSAI59793.2023.10421269

Ashley, C., & Tuten, T. (2015). Creative strategies in social media marketing: An exploratory study of branded social content and consumer engagement. *Psychology and Marketing*, *32*(1), 15–27. DOI: 10.1002/mar.20761

Aswani, R., Kar, A. K., Ilavarasan, P. V., & Dwivedi, Y. K. (2018). Search engine marketing is not all gold: Insights from Twitter and SEOClerks. *International Journal of Information Management, 38*(1), 107–116. DOI: 10.1016/j.ijinfomgt.2017.07.005

Auchter, E., & Kriz, W. C. (2014). The impact of business simulations as a teaching method on entrepreneurial competencies and motivation—A review of 10 years of evaluation research in entrepreneurship education. *The shift from teaching to learning: Individual, collective and organizational learning through gaming & simulation*, 187-197.

Avramenko, A. (2012). Enhancing students' employability through business simulation. *Education + Training, 54*(5), 355–367. DOI: 10.1108/00400911211244669

AwangHarun, S., Md Hashim, N. H., & Kadiman, S. (2022). The Effectiveness of Simulation in Education 4.0: Application in a Transesophageal Echocardiography Training Program in Malaysia. *Frontiers in Surgery, 9*, 749092. Advance online publication. DOI: 10.3389/fsurg.2022.749092 PMID: 35445072

Ayad, A., Wilkinson, E., & Matthews, R. (2019). Systemic experiential learning model for the evaluation of technological learning: The case of small satellite capability-building in Algeria. *International Journal of Technology Management & Sustainable Development, 18*(1), 75–100. DOI: 10.1386/tmsd.18.1.75_1

Azmi, A. N., Kamin, Y., Noordin, M. K., &Nasir, A. N. M. (2018). Towards Industrial Revolution 4.0: Employers' expectations on fresh engineering graduates. International Journal of Engineering & Technology, 7(4.28), 267-272. https://doi.org/DOI: 10.14419/ijet.v7i4.28.23889

Azungah, T. (2018). Qualitative research: Deductive and inductive approaches to data analysis. *Qualitative Research Journal, 18*(4), 383–400.

Babin, M.-J., Rivière, E., & Chiniara, G. (2019). Theory for Practice: Learning Theories for Simulation. In *Clinical Simulation (Second Edition), Education, Operations, and Engineering* (pp. 97-114). Academic Press.

Bacca Acosta, J. L., Baldiris Navarro, S. M., Fabregat Gesa, R., & Graf, S. (2014). Augmented reality trends in education: A systematic review of research and applications. *Journal of Educational Technology and Society, 17*(4), 133–149.

Bacca, J., Baldiris, S., Fabregat, R., & Graf, S. (2014). Augmented Reality Trends in Education: A Systematic Review of Research and Applications. *Journal of Educational Technology & Society, 17*(4).

Bacigalupo, M., Kampylis, P., Punie, Y., & Van den Brande, G. (2016). *EntreComp: The Entrepreneurship Competence Framework.* European Commission.

Badawi, B. (2024). Entrepreneurial Character Education from an Early Age. Al-Hayat: Journal of Islamic Education. .DOI: 10.35723/ajie.v8i1.481

Baden, D., & Parkes, C. (2013). Experiential learning: Inspiring the business leaders of tomorrow. *Journal of Management Development, 32*(3), 295–308. DOI: 10.1108/02621711311318283

Badghish, S., & Soomro, Y. A. (2024). Artificial Intelligence Adoption by SMEs to Achieve Sustainable Business Performance: Application of Technology–Organization–Environment Framework. *Sustainability (Basel), 16*(5), 1864. DOI: 10.3390/su16051864

Badri, A., & Badri, P. (2020). Investigating The Impact Of Entrepreneurship And Education On Economic Growth. Open Journal of Management Science (ISSN: 2734-2107). DOI: 10.52417/ojms.v1i1.77

Bae, T. J., Qian, S., Miao, C., & Fiet, J. O. (2014). The relationship between entrepreneurship education and entrepreneurial intentions: A meta-analytic review. *Entrepreneurship Theory and Practice*, *38*(2), 217–254.

Bagheri, A., Lope Pihie, Z. A., & Krauss, S. E. (2017). Entrepreneurial leadership competencies among Malaysian university students: The pervasive effect of social support. *Asian Academy of Management Journal*, *22*(1), 79–101.

Bai, C., & Yang, J. (2023). Exploration on the Application of Virtual Simulation Platforms in the Practice Teaching of Financial Management Majors in Private Colleges and Universities. In *3rd International Conference on Education Studies: Experience and Innovation (ICESEI 2022)* (pp. 71-76). Athena Publishing. DOI: 10.55060/s.atssh.230306.013

Bailey, J. O., & Bailenson, J. N. (2017). Considering virtual reality in children's lives. *Journal of Children and Media*, *11*(1), 107–113. DOI: 10.1080/17482798.2016.1268779

Baiocco, S., Leoni, L., & Paniccia, P. M. A. (2023). Entrepreneurship for sustainable development: Co-evolutionary evidence from the tourism sector. *Journal of Small Business and Enterprise Development*, *30*(7), 1521–1546. DOI: 10.1108/JSBED-01-2023-0003

Baker, T., & Smith, L. (2019). *Educ-AI-tion Rebooted? Exploring the future of artificial intelligence in schools and colleges*. https://media.nesta.org.uk/documents/Future_of_AI_and_education_v5_WEB.pdf

Baker, S. D. (2020). The role of soft skills in employability: A systematic review. *Journal of Education and Work*, *33*(6), 617–634.

Bakoush, M. (2022). Evaluating the role of simulation-based experiential learning in improving satisfaction of finance students. *International Journal of Management Education*, *20*(3), 100690.

Ballard, J., & Butler, P. (2011). Personalised learning: Developing a Vygotskian framework for e-learning. *International Journal of Technology, Knowledge and Society*, *7*(2), 21–36. Advance online publication. DOI: 10.18848/1832-3669/CGP/v07i02/56198

Banks, G. C., McCauley, K. D., Gardner, W. L., & Guler, C. E. (2016). A meta-analytic review of authentic and transformational leadership: A test for redundancy. *The Leadership Quarterly*, *27*(4), 634–652. DOI: 10.1016/j.leaqua.2016.02.006

Bansal, P., & DesJardine, M. R. (2014). Business sustainability: It is about time. *Strategic Organization*, *12*(1), 70–78. DOI: 10.1177/1476127013520265

Bansal, P., & Knox-Hayes, J. (2013). The time and space of materiality in organizations and the environment. *Organization & Environment*, *26*(1), 61–82. DOI: 10.1177/1086026612475069

Barakat, B., & Shields, R. (2019). Just Another Level? Comparing Quantitative Patterns of Global Expansion of School and Higher Education Attainment. *Demography*, *56*(3), 917–934. DOI: 10.1007/s13524-019-00775-5 PMID: 31001732

Barbieri, C. (2013). Assessing the sustainability of agritourism in the US: A comparison between agritourism and other farm entrepreneurial ventures. *Journal of Sustainable Tourism, 21*(2), 252–270.

Barbieri, C. (2020). Agritourism research: A perspective article. *Tourism Review, 75*(1), 149–152. DOI: 10.1108/TR-05-2019-0152

Barbieri, C., & Mahoney, E. (2009). Why is diversification an attractive farm adjustment strategy? Insights from Texas farmers and ranchers. *Journal of Rural Studies, 25*(1), 58–66. DOI: 10.1016/j.jrurstud.2008.06.001

Barbieri, C., & Streifeneder, T. (2019). Agritourism advances around the globe: A commentary from the editors. *Open Agriculture, 4*(1), 712–714. DOI: 10.1515/opag-2019-0068

Barjis, J., Gupta, A., Sharda, R., Bouzdine-Chameeva, T., Lee, P. D., & Verbraeck, A. (2012). Innovative teaching using simulation and virtual environments. *Interdisciplinary Journal of Information, Knowledge, and Management, 7*, 237–255.

Barzilai, S. (2017). "Half-reliable": A qualitative analysis of epistemic thinking in and about a digital game. *Contemporary Educational Psychology, 51*, 51–66. DOI: 10.1016/j.cedpsych.2017.06.004

Bass, B. M., & Riggio, R. E. (2006). *Transformational leadership* (2nd ed.). Lawrence Erlbaum Associates Publishers., DOI: 10.4324/9781410617095

Batsaikhan, B., & Correia, A.-P. (2024). The effects of Generative Artificial Intelligence on Intelligent Tutoring Systems in higher education: A systematic review. *Studies in Technology Enhanced Learning, 4*(1). Advance online publication. DOI: 10.21428/8c225f6e.33570bb1

Bearman, M., Ryan, J., & Ajjawi, R. (2022). Discourses of artificial intelligence in higher education: A critical literature review. *Higher Education, 86*(2), 369–385. Advance online publication. DOI: 10.1007/s10734-022-00937-2

Beavis, C., Rowan, L., Dezuanni, M., McGillivray, C., O'Mara, J., Prestridge, S., Stieler-Hunt, C., Thompson, R., & Zagami, J. (2014). Teachers' beliefs about the possibilities and limitations of digital games in classrooms. *E-Learning and Digital Media, 11*(6), 569–581. DOI: 10.2304/elea.2014.11.6.569

Beckman, G. D. (2007). "Adventuring" Arts Entrepreneurship Curricula in Higher Education: An Examination of Present Efforts, Obstacles, and Best Practices. *The Journal of Arts Management, Law, and Society, 37*(2), 87–112. DOI: 10.3200/JAML.37.2.87-112

Beckman, S. L., & Barry, M. (2007). Innovation as a Learning Process: Embedding Design Thinking. *California Management Review, 50*(1), 25–56. DOI: 10.2307/41166415

Beckman, S. L., & Barry, M. (2020). Innovation and entrepreneurship education: A multidisciplinary approach. *Journal of Entrepreneurship Education, 23*(4), 1–12.

Bedwell, W. L., Salas, E. M., & Eduardo, J. (2014). Developing the future workforce: An approach for integrating interpersonal skills into the MBA classroom. *Academy of Management Learning & Education, 13*(2), 171–186. DOI: 10.5465/amle.2011.0138

Beghetto, R. A., & Kaufman, J. C. (2010). *Nurturing Creativity in the Classroom*. Cambridge University Press.

Bellas, F., Guerreiro-Santalla, S., Naya, M., & Duro, R. J. (2022). AI Curriculum for European High Schools: An Embedded Intelligence Approach. *International Journal of Artificial Intelligence in Education, 33*(2), 399–426. DOI: 10.1007/s40593-022-00315-0

Bell, B. S., & Federman, J. E. (2013). E-Learning and Development: The Use of Simulation Games in Workforce Training. *Human Resource Management Review, 23*(2), 239–251.

Bell, B. S., Kanar, A. M., & Kozlowski, S. W. J. (2008). Current issues and future directions in simulation-based training in North America. *International Journal of Human Resource Management, 19*(8), 1416–1434. DOI: 10.1080/09585190802200173

Bell, E., Bryman, A., & Harley, B. (2018). *Business Research Methods* (5th ed.). Oxford University Press.

Bell, J., & Waters, S. (2018). *Ebook: Doing Your Research Project: A Guide for First-Time Researchers*. McGraw-Hill Education.

Bellotti, F., Berta, R., De Gloria, A., & Primavera, L. (2013). Enhancing the educational value of business simulations through gaming. *Computers in Human Behavior, 31*, 135–146.

Bellotti, F., Kapralos, B., Lee, K., Moreno-Ger, P., & Berta, R. (2013). Assessment in and of serious games: An overview. *Advances in Human-Computer Interaction, 2013*, 1–11. DOI: 10.1155/2013/120791

Bell, R. (2021). Underpinning the entrepreneurship educator's toolkit: Conceptualising the influence of educational philosophies and theory. *Entrepreneurship Education, 4*(1), 1–18. DOI: 10.1007/s41959-020-00042-4

Bell, R., & Bell, H. (2020). Applying educational theory to develop a framework to support the delivery of experiential entrepreneurship education. *Journal of Small Business and Enterprise Development, 27*(6), 987–1004. DOI: 10.1108/JSBED-01-2020-0012

Bell, R., & Cui, J. (2023). Addressing progressive educational reforms: Fusing acquisition approaches and participation in Chinese entrepreneurship education. *International Journal of Management Education, 21*(1), 100748. DOI: 10.1016/j.ijme.2022.100748

Bell, R., & Liu, P. (2019). Educator challenges in the development and delivery of constructivist active and experiential entrepreneurship classrooms in Chinese vocational higher education. *Journal of Small Business and Enterprise Development, 26*(2), 209–227. DOI: 10.1108/JSBED-01-2018-0025

Bell, R., & Loon, M. (2015). The impact of critical thinking disposition on learning using business simulations. *International Journal of Management Education, 13*(2), 119–127. DOI: 10.1016/j.ijme.2015.01.002

Berson, I. R., & Berson, M. J. (2023). The Democratization of AI and its Transformative Potential in Social Studies Education. *Social Education, 87*(2). https://lists.aaai.org/ai4k12/cache/22236874/2.pdf

Berthon, P. R., Pitt, L. F., Plangger, K., & Shapiro, D. (2012). Marketing meets Web 2.0, social media, and creative consumers: Implications for international marketing strategy. *Business Horizons, 55*(3), 261–271. DOI: 10.1016/j.bushor.2012.01.007

Bessant, J., & Tidd, J. (2019). *Managing Innovation: Integrating Technological, Market and Organizational Change*. John Wiley & Sons.

Bhagat, S. V., & Kanyal, D. (2024). Navigating the Future: The Transformative Impact of Artificial Intelligence on Hospital Management- A Comprehensive Review. *Cureus*, *16*(2), e54518. [REMOVED HYPERLINK FIELD]DOI: 10.7759/cureus.54518 PMID: 38516434

Bharadiya, J. P. (2023). Machine learning and AI in business intelligence: Trends and opportunities. [IJC]. *International Journal of Computer*, *48*(1), 123–134.

Bharadwaj, A., El Sawy, O. A., Pavlou, P. A., & Venkatraman, N. V. (2013). Digital business strategy: Toward a next generation of insights. *Management Information Systems Quarterly*, *37*(2), 471–482. DOI: 10.25300/MISQ/2013/37:2.3

Bhardwaj, J. (2020). Working with others and enjoying it: CS1 students' experience of small-group collaboration on a business simulation. *Proceedings - Frontiers in Education Conference, FIE, 2020-Octob*. DOI: 10.1109/FIE44824.2020.9274161

Bhatia, N. L., Shukla, V. K., Punhani, R., & Dubey, S. K. 2021, June. Growing aspects of cyber security in e-commerce. In *2021 International Conference on Communication information and Computing Technology (ICCICT)* (pp. 1-6). IEEE. DOI: 10.1109/ICCICT50803.2021.9510152

Bhatti, M. A., Al Doghan, M. A., Saat, S. A. M., Juhari, A. S., & Alshagawi, M. (2021). Entrepreneurial intentions among women: Does entrepreneurial training and education matters? (Pre-and post-evaluation of psychological attributes and its effects on entrepreneurial intention). *Journal of Small Business and Enterprise Development*, *28*(2), 167–184. DOI: 10.1108/JSBED-09-2019-0305

Biggs, J. (1996). Enhancing teaching through constructive alignment. *Higher Education*, *32*(3), 347–364.

Bilad, M. R., Anwar, K., & Hayati, S. (2023). Nurturing Prospective STEM Teachers' Critical Thinking Skill through Virtual Simulation-Assisted Remote Inquiry in Fourier Transform Courses. *International Journal of Essential Competencies in Education*, *1*(1), 1–10. Advance online publication. DOI: 10.36312/ijece.v1i1.728

Bílek, M., Nodzyńska, M., Kopek-Putała, W., & Zimak-Piekarczyk, P. (2018). Balancing chemical equations using sandwich making computer simulation games as a supporting teaching method. *Problems of Education in the 21st Century, 76*(6), 779–799. DOI: 10.33225/pec/18.76.779

Billett, S., Choy, S., & Hodge, S. (2020). Enhancing the standing of vocational education and the occupations it serves: Australia. *Journal of Vocational Education and Training*, *72*(2), 270–296. DOI: 10.1080/13636820.2020.1751247

Binsztok, A., Butryn, B., Holowinska, K., Owoc, M. L., & Sobinska, M. (2023). Business Computer Simulations and its Role in Educational Processes from the Students' Perspective. *Procedia Computer Science*, *225*(7), 4006–4014. DOI: 10.1016/j.procs.2023.10.396

Birhane, M., Amentie, C., Borji, B., & Kant, S. (n.d.). Are Ethiopian Coffee Farmers Proficient to Predict Capital Structure with Mediation of AI Based Knowledge Systems and Asset Liquidity? In *AI in Agriculture for Sustainable and Economic Management* (pp. 199-215). CRC Press. DOI: 10.1201/9781003451648-15

Birley, S. (1985). Encouraging Entrepreneurship: Britain's New Enterprise Program. *Journal of Small Business Management, 23*, 6.

Birtill, M., King, J., Jones, D., Thyer, L., Pap, R., & Simpson, P. (2021). The use of immersive simulation in paramedicine education: A scoping review. *Interactive Learning Environments, 31*(4), 2428–2443. DOI: 10.1080/10494820.2021.1889607

Bisel, L. D. (2007). The role of SSL in cybersecutiry. *IT Professional, 9*(2), 22–25. DOI: 10.1109/MITP.2007.41

Blank, S. (2013). *The Four Steps to the Epiphany: Successful Strategies for Products that Win*. K&S Ranch.

Blauth, M., Sinha, D., & Schmidt, C. (2019). Socio-economic background and entrepreneurial intentions: Evidence from a developing country. *Journal of Business Research, 105*, 342–354.

Blažič, A. J., & Novak, F. (2015). *Challenges of business simulation games - a new approach of teaching business*. E-Learning - Instructional Design, Organizational Strategy and Management. DOI: 10.5772/61242

Bloom, N. (2019). The Use of Simulations in Entrepreneurship Education. *Journal of Business Education, 87*(2), 34–48. DOI: 10.1080/08832323.2018.1536028

Blouin, R. A., Riffee, W. H., Robinson, E. T., Beck, D. E., Green, C., Joyner, P. U., Persky, A. M., & Pollack, G. M. (2009). Roles of innovation in education delivery. *American Journal of Pharmaceutical Education, 73*(8), 154. DOI: 10.5688/aj7308154 PMID: 20221347

Bobek, E., & Tversky, B. (2016). Creating visual explanations improves learning. *Cognitive Research: Principles and Implications, 1*(1), 27. [REMOVED HYPERLINK FIELD]DOI: 10.1186/s41235-016-0031-6 PMID: 28180178

Bocken, N. M., Short, S. W., Rana, P., & Evans, S. (2014). A literature and practice review to develop sustainable business model archetypes. *Journal of Cleaner Production, 65*, 42–56. DOI: 10.1016/j.jclepro.2013.11.039

Boldureanu, G., Ionescu, A., Bercu, A., Bedrule-Grigoru ă, M., & Boldureanu, D. (2020). Entrepreneurship Education through Successful Entrepreneurial Models in Higher Education Institutions. *Sustainability (Basel), 12*(3), 1267. Advance online publication. DOI: 10.3390/su12031267

Bondarenko, Y. G., & Kozulin, A. V. (1991). The Democratization of education: basic principles. *Higher education in Europe, 16*(1), 74-78. https://unesdoc.unesco.org/ark:/48223/pf0000093679

Bongomin, O., Ocen, G. G., Nganyi, E., Musinguzi, A., & Omara, T. (2020). Exponential disruptive technologies and the required skills of Industry 4.0. *Journal of Engineering, 2020*, 1–17. DOI: 10.1155/2020/7074372

Bong, W. K., & Chen, W. (2024). Increasing faculty's competence in digital accessibility for inclusive education: A systematic literature review. *International Journal of Inclusive Education, 28*(2), 197–213. DOI: 10.1080/13603116.2021.1937344

Bonwell, C., & Eison, J. A. (1991). Active Learning: Creating Excitement in the Classroom. *ASHE-ERIC Higher Education Report*.

Bosman, L., Kotla, B., Madamanchi, A., Bartholomew, S., & Byrd, V. (2022). Preparing the future entrepreneurial engineering workforce using web-based AI-enabled tools. *European Journal of Engineering Education, 48*(5), 972–989. DOI: 10.1080/03043797.2022.2119122

Boston Consulting Group Report. (2015). Man and machine in Industry 4.0: How will technology transform the industrial workforce through 2025. Boston Consulting Group.

Botelho, F. H. F. (2021). Accessibility to digital technology: Virtual barriers, real opportunities. *Assistive Technology, 33*(sup1), 27–34.

Bouchard, S., Côté, S., St-Jacques, J., Robillard, G., & Renaud, P. (2006). Effectiveness of virtual reality exposure in the treatment of arachnophobia using 3D games. *Technology and Health Care, 14*(1), 19–27. DOI: 10.3233/THC-2006-14103 PMID: 16556961

Bouncken, R. B., & Kraus, S. (2022). Entrepreneurial ecosystems in an interconnected world: Emergence, governance and digitalization. *Review of Managerial Science, 16*(1), 1–14. DOI: 10.1007/s11846-021-00444-1

Boyle, E., MacArthur, E., Connolly, T. M., Hainey, T., Manea, M., Kärki, A., & van Rosmalen, P. (2014). A narrative literature review of games, animations and simulations to teach research methods and statistics. *Computers & Education, 74*, 1–14. DOI: 10.1016/j.compedu.2014.01.004

Brazhkin, V., & Zimmerman, H. (2019). Students' perceptions of learning in an online multiround business simulation game: What can we learn from them? *Decision Sciences Journal of Innovative Education, 17*(4), 363–386. DOI: 10.1111/dsji.12189

Briseño-García, A. & Husted, B. (2015). The Diffusion of CSR Practices: Past Research and Future Directions. Academic Press.

Brockbank, A., & McGill, I. (2007). Facilitating Reflective Learning in Higher Education. McGraw-Hill Education.

Brown, T. (2009). *Change by design: How design thinking creates new alternatives for business and society*. Collins Business.

Bruksle, I., Chwallek, C., & Krastina, A. (2023). Strengthening Sustainability in Entrepreneurship Education -Implications for Shifting Entrepreneurial Thinking Towards Sustainability at Universities. *ACTA PROSPERITATIS, 14*(1), 37–48. DOI: 10.37804/1691-6077-2023-14-37-48

Buckingham, M., & Goodall, A. (2015). Reinventing performance management. *Harvard Business Review, 93*(4), 40–50. https://hbr.org/2015/04/reinventing-performance-management

Buhalis, D., Leung, D., & Lin, M. (2023). Metaverse as a disruptive technology revolutionising tourism management and marketing. *Tourism Management, 97*, 104724. DOI: 10.1016/j.tourman.2023.104724

Buil, I., Catalán, S., & Martínez, E. P. (2018). Exploring students' flow experiences in business simulation games. *Journal of Computer Assisted Learning, 34*(2), 183–192. DOI: 10.1111/jcal.12237

Bulathwela, S., Pérez-Ortiz, M., Holloway, C., Cukurova, M., & Shawe-Taylor, J. (2024). Artificial Intelligence Alone Will Not Democratise Education: On Educational Inequality, Techno-Solutionism and Inclusive Tools. *Sustainability (Basel), 16*(2), 781. DOI: 10.3390/su16020781

Bulchand-Gidumal, J., Secin, E. W., O'Connor, P., & Buhalis, D. (2023). Artificial intelligence's impact on hospitality and tourism marketing: Exploring key themes and addressing challenges. *Current Issues in Tourism*, 1–18. DOI: 10.1080/13683500.2023.2229480

Burdon, W. M., & Munro, K. (2017). Simulation–is it all worth it? The impact of simulation from the perspective of accounting students. *International Journal of Management Education, 15*(3), 429–448. DOI: 10.1016/j.ijme.2017.07.001

Burgstahler, S., David, M. E., & Amey, M. J. (2020). Universal design for learning. In *The SAGE encyclopedia of higher education* (Vol. 4, pp. 1621–1622). SAGE Publications. DOI: 10.4135/9781529714395.n609

Burkhardt, J. M., & Lubart, T. I. (2010). *Creativity and Innovation in Education: Theory, Research, and Practice*. Routledge.

Buxton, M., Phillippi, J., & Collins, M. (2014). Simulation: A New Approach to Teaching Ethics. *Journal of Midwifery & Women's Health, 60*(1), 70–74. Advance online publication. DOI: 10.1111/jmwh.12185 PMID: 25141791

Cabrera, D., & Cabrera, L. (2023). What is systems thinking? In *Learning, design, and technology: An international compendium of theory, research, practice, and policy* (pp. 1495–1522). Springer International Publishing.

Cadenas, G., Cantú, E., Lynn, N., Spence, T., & Ruth, A. (2020). A programmatic intervention to promote entrepreneurial self-efficacy, critical behavior, and technology readiness among underrepresented college students. *Journal of Vocational Behavior, 116*, 103350. DOI: 10.1016/j.jvb.2019.103350

Cadotte, E. (2014). The use of simulations in entrepreneurship education: Opportunities, challenges and outcomes. *Business (Atlanta, Ga.), 2014*, 280–302. DOI: 10.4337/9781783471454.00021

Cadotte, E. R. (2016). Markstrat as a tool for teaching marketing strategy. *Marketing Education Review, 26*(1), 65–68.

Cadotte, E. R. (2022). How to use simulation games in the classroom? *The Journal of Entrepreneurship, 31*(2, suppl), S90–S134. DOI: 10.1177/09713557221107442

Çağataylı, M., & Çelebi, E. (2022). Estimating academic success in higher education using big five personality traits, a machine learning approach. *Arabian Journal for Science and Engineering, 47*(2), 1289–1298. DOI: 10.1007/s13369-021-05873-4

Cairns, P., Cox, A., & Nordin, A. I. (2014). Immersion in digital games: Review of gaming experience research. In *Handbook of Digital Games* (pp. 337–361). John Wiley & Sons, Inc. DOI: 10.1002/9781118796443.ch12

Calandra, D., Oppioli, M., Sadraei, R., Jafari-Sadeghi, V., & Biancone, P. Pietro. (2023). Metaverse meets digital entrepreneurship: a practitioner-based qualitative synthesis. *International Journal of Entrepreneurial Behavior & Research.*

Campos, N., Nogal, M., Caliz, C., & Juan, A. A. (2020). Simulation-based education involving online and on-campus models in different European universities. *International Journal of Educational Technology in Higher Education, 17*(1), 8. Advance online publication. DOI: 10.1186/s41239-020-0181-y

Cappelli, P., & Tavis, A. (2016). The performance management revolution. *Harvard Business Review, 94*(10), 58–67.

Carpenter, A., & Wilson, R. (2021). A systematic review looking at the effect of entrepreneurship education on higher education student. *International Journal of Management Education.* Advance online publication. DOI: 10.1016/j.ijme.2021.100541

Carpio, C. E., Wohlgenant, M. K., & Boonsaeng, T. (2008). The demand for agritourism in the United States. *Journal of Agricultural and Resource Economics*, 254–269.

Carroll, A. B., & Buchholtz, A. K. (2003). *Business and society: Ethics and stakeholder management* (5th ed.). Cengage Learning.

Carruth, D. W. (2017). Virtual reality for education and workforce training. *2017 15th International Conference on Emerging ELearning Technologies and Applications (ICETA)*, 1–6.

Casson, M. (1982). *The Entrepreneur: An Economic Theory.* Martin Robertson.

Castaldi, L., Sepe, E., Turi, C., & Iscaro, V. (2020). An experiential learning program for entrepreneurship education. *Global Business & Economics Review, 22*(1), 178–197. DOI: 10.1504/GBER.2020.105050

Centre for Applied Special Technology (CAST). (2024). *About universal design for learning.* Retrieved from https://www.cast.org/impact/universal-design-for-learning-udl

Černezel, A., & Heričko, M. 2013. A user-centric approach for developing mobile applications. In *7th International Conference on Knowledge Management in Organizations: Service and Cloud Computing* (pp. 455-465). Springer Berlin Heidelberg. DOI: 10.1007/978-3-642-30867-3_41

Chae, B., & Goh, G. (2020). Digital Entrepreneurs in Artificial Intelligence and Data Analytics: Who Are They? *Journal of Open Innovation, 6*(3), 56. Advance online publication. DOI: 10.3390/joitmc6030056

Chaffey, D., Edmundson-Bird, D., & Hemphill, T. (2019). *Digital business and e-commerce management.* Pearson Uk.

Chakrabarty, S., & Bass, A. E. (2015). Comparing virtue, consequentialist, and deontological ethics-based corporate social responsibility: Mitigating microfinance risk in institutional voids. *Journal of Business Ethics, 126*(3), 487–512. DOI: 10.1007/s10551-013-1963-0

Challa, A., & Anute, N. (2021). The effectiveness of Instagram content marketing on brand building of a company. *Journal of Sales. Service and Marketing Research, 2*(2), 1–7. DOI: 10.46610/JSSMR.2021.v02i02.001

Chandel, Tarana. (2022). Green Entrepreneurship and Sustainable Development. .DOI: 10.4018/978-1-6684-4666-9.ch009

Chandwaskar, P., & Jape, S. (2024). Case of learnbiz simulations: Challenges and opportunities ahead. *Emerging Economies Cases Journal*, *6*(2), 83–90. DOI: 10.1177/25166042241228367

Chang, Y., Kao, J.-Y., & Wang, Y.-Y. (2022). Influences of virtual reality on design creativity and design thinking. *Thinking Skills and Creativity*, *46*, 101127. DOI: 10.1016/j.tsc.2022.101127

Chan, V. (2011). Teaching oral communication in undergraduate science: Are we doing enough and doing it right? *Journal of Learning Design*, *4*(3), 71–79. DOI: 10.5204/jld.v4i3.123

Chaudhry, M. A., & Kazim, E. (2021). Artificial Intelligence in Education (AIEd): A high-level academic and industry note 2021. *AI and Ethics*, *2*(1), 157–165. DOI: 10.1007/s43681-021-00074-z PMID: 34790953

Chea, C. C., Tan, J., & Huan, J. (2019). Higher education 4.0: The possibilities and challenges. *Journal of Social Sciences and Humanities*, *5*(2), 81–85.

Chee, Y. S., Mehrotra, S., & Ong, J. C. (2015). Professional development for scaling pedagogical innovation in the context of game-based learning: Teacher identity as cornerstone in "shifting" practice. *Asia-Pacific Journal of Teacher Education*, *43*(5), 423–437. DOI: 10.1080/1359866X.2014.962484

Chege, S. M., Wang, D., & Suntu, S. L. (2020). Impact of information technology innovation on firm performance in Kenya. *Information Technology for Development*, *26*(2), 316–345.

Chen, L., Ifenthaler, D. & Yau, J.YK. (2021). Online and blended entrepreneurship education: a systematic review of applied educational technologies. *Entrep Educ*, 4(2), 191–232. DOI: 10.1007/s41959-021-00047-7

Chen, C. H., & Chang, C. L. (2024). Effectiveness of AI-assisted game-based learning on science learning outcomes, intrinsic motivation, cognitive load, and learning behavior. *Education and Information Technologies*, *29*(14), 18621–18642. Advance online publication. DOI: 10.1007/s10639-024-12553-x

Chen, I. J., & Popovich, K. (2003). Understanding customer relationship management (CRM): People, process and technology. *Business Process Management Journal*, *9*(5), 672–688. DOI: 10.1108/14637150310496758

Chen, J., Chen, Y., Ou, R., Wang, J., & Chen, Q. (2022). How to use artificial intelligence to improve entrepreneurial attitude in business simulation games: Implications from a quasi-experiment. *Frontiers in Psychology*, *13*, 856085. DOI: 10.3389/fpsyg.2022.856085 PMID: 36467165

Chen, L., Chen, P., & Lin, Z. (2020). Artificial Intelligence in Education: A Review. *IEEE Access : Practical Innovations, Open Solutions*, *8*, 75264–75278. DOI: 10.1109/ACCESS.2020.2988510

Chen, M.-H. M., Tsai, S.-T., & Chang, C.-C. (2019). Effects of game-based instruction on the results of primary school children taking a natural science course. *Education Sciences*, *9*(2), 79. DOI: 10.3390/educsci9020079

Chen, Z., Wu, J., Gan, W., & Qi, Z. (2022). Metaverse security and privacy: An overview. *2022 IEEE International Conference on Big Data (Big Data)*, 2950–2959. DOI: 10.1109/BigData55660.2022.10021112

Chernikova, O., Heitzmann, N., Stadler, M., Holzberger, D., Seidel, T., & Fischer, F. (2020). Simulation-Based Learning in Higher Education: A Meta-Analysis. *Review of Educational Research*, *90*(4), 499–541. DOI: 10.3102/0034654320933544

Chevalère, J., Yun, H. S., Henke, A., Pinkwart, N., Hafner, V. V., & Lazarides, R. (2023). A sequence of learning processes in an intelligent tutoring system from topic-related appraisals to learning gains. *Learning and Instruction*, *87*, 101799. DOI: 10.1016/j.learninstruc.2023.101799

Chigunta, F. (2017). Entrepreneurship as a possible solution to youth unemployment in Africa. Labour Market Institutions and Economic Outcomes in Africa, 433-451.

Choshin, M., & Ghaffari, A. (2017). An investigation of the impact of effective factors on the success of e-commerce in small- and medium-sized companies. *Computers in Human Behavior*, *66*, 67–74. DOI: 10.1016/j.chb.2016.09.026

Christensen, C. M. (1997). *The Innovator's Dilemma: When New Technologies Cause Great Firms to Fail*. Harvard Business School Press.

Chu, H., Tu, Y., & Yang, K. (2022). Roles and research trends of artificial intelligence in higher education: A systematic review of the top 50 most-cited articles. *Australasian Journal of Educational Technology*, *38*(3), 22–42. DOI: 10.14742/ajet.7526

Chulkov, D. & Wang, X. (2020). The Educational Value of Simulation as a Teaching Strategy in a Finance Course. e-Journal of Business Education & Scholarship of Teaching, 14(1), 40-56.

Chulkov, D., & Wang, X. (2020). The Educational Value of Simulation as a Teaching Strategy in a Finance Course. *E-Journal of Business Education & Scholarship of Teaching*, *14*(1), 40–56.

Činčera, J., Biberhofer, P., Binka, B., Boman, J., Mindt, L., & Rieckmann, M. (2018). Designing a sustainability-driven entrepreneurship curriculum as a social learning process: A case study from an international knowledge alliance project. *Journal of Cleaner Production*, *172*, 4357–4366. DOI: 10.1016/j.jclepro.2017.05.051

Clarke, V., Braun, V., Hayfield, N., & Smith, J. A. (2015). Qualitative psychology. A practical guide to research methods, 222, 248.

Clarke, E. (2009). Learning outcomes from business simulation exercises: Challenges for the implementation of learning technologies. *Education + Training*, *51*(5/6), 448–459.

Clark, G. L., Feiner, A., & Viehs, M. (2015). *From the stockholder to the stakeholder: How sustainability can drive financial outperformance*. Oxford University Press.

Clark, R. E., Yates, K., Early, S., & Moulton, K. (2010). An Analysis of the Use of Simulation Games in Education. *Educational Technology Research and Development*, *58*(5), 575–595.

Climate Interactive & MIT Sloan. (n.d.). En-ROADS Climate Policy Simulator. Retrieved from https://www.climateinteractive.org/tools/en-roads/

Collins, J. (2009). Lifelong learning in the 21st century and beyond. *Radiographics, 29*(2), 613–622. DOI: 10.1148/rg.292085179 PMID: 19325069

Colombelli, A., Loccisano, S., Panelli, A., Pennisi, O. A. M., & Serraino, F. (2022). Entrepreneurship education: The effects of challenge-based learning on the entrepreneurial mindset of university students. *Administrative Sciences, 12*(1), 10. DOI: 10.3390/admsci12010010

Colonna, L. (2023). *The AI Regulation and Higher Education: Preliminary Observations and Critical Perspectives*. De Lege., DOI: 10.33063/dl.vi.428

Connolly, T. M., & Stansfield, M. H. (2007). From eLearning to games-based eLearning: Using interactive technologies in teaching an IS course. *International Journal of Information Technology and Management, 26*(2), 188–208.

Cook, D. A., Brydges, R., Hamstra, S. J., Zendejas, B., Szostek, J. H., Wang, A. T., Erwin, P. J., & Hatala, R. (2012). Comparative effectiveness of technology-enhanced simulation versus other instructional methods: A systematic review and meta-analysis. *Simulation in Healthcare, 7*(5), 308–320. DOI: 10.1097/SIH.0b013e3182614f95 PMID: 23032751

Cook, D. A., Hatala, R., Brydges, R., Zendejas, B., Szostek, J. H., Wang, A. T., Erwin, P. J., & Hamstra, S. J. (2011). Technology-Enhanced Simulation for Health Professions Education. *Journal of the American Medical Association, 306*(9). Advance online publication. DOI: 10.1001/jama.2011.1234 PMID: 21900138

Costello, G. J. (2017). More than just a game: The role of simulation in the teaching of product design and entrepreneurship to mechanical engineering students. *European Journal of Engineering Education, 42*(6), 644–652. DOI: 10.1080/03043797.2016.1211992

Costin, Y., O'Brien, M. P., & Hynes, B. (2019). Developing cognitive and non-cognitive entrepreneurial competences through business simulation games. *Journal of Enterprising Culture, 27*(04), 471–498. DOI: 10.1142/S0218495819500171

Crampon, K., Giorkallos, A., Deldossi, M., Baud, S., & Steffenel, L. (2021). Machine-learning methods for ligand-protein molecular docking. *Drug Discovery Today*. Advance online publication. DOI: 10.1016/j.drudis.2021.09.007 PMID: 34560276

Crebert, G., Bates, M., Bell, B., Patrick, C., & Cragnolini, V. (2004). Developing generic skills during work placement and in employment: Graduate perceptions. *Higher Education Research & Development, 23*, 147–165. DOI: 10.1080/0729436042000206638

Creed, C., & Beale, R. (2005). Using emotion simulation to influence user attitudes and behavior. In *Proceedings of the 2005 Workshop on the role of emotion in HCI.*

Creswell, J. (2005). *Research Design: Qualitative, Quantitative, and Mixed Methods Approaches*. Sage Publications.

Creswell, J. W., & Poth, C. N. (2016). *Qualitative inquiry and research design: Choosing among five approaches*. Sage Publications.

Creswell, J. W., & Poth, C. N. (2018). *Qualitative Inquiry and Research Design: Choosing Among Five Approaches*. Sage Publications.

Crompton, H., & Burke, D. (2023). Artificial Intelligence in Higher education: The State of the Field. *International Journal of Educational Technology in Higher Education*, *20*(1), 1–22. DOI: 10.1186/s41239-023-00392-8

Crossan, M. M., & Apaydin, M. (2010). A Multi-Dimensional Framework of Organizational Innovation: A Systematic Review of the Literature. *Journal of Management Studies*, *47*(6), 1154–1191.

Csikszentmihalyi, M. (1975). *Beyond Boredom and Anxiety*. Jossey-Bass Publishers.

Csikszentmihalyi, M. (2014). Flow and the foundations of positive psychology: The collected works of Mihaly Csikszentmihalyi. In *Flow and the Foundations of Positive Psychology*. The Collected Works of Mihaly Csikszentmihalyi., DOI: 10.1007/978-94-017-9088-8

Cui, J., Sun, J., & Bell, R. (2021). The impact of education related with entrepreneurship on the entrepreneurial mindset of college learners in China: The mediating role of inspiration and the role of educational attributes. *International Journal of Management Education*, *19*(1), 100296. DOI: 10.1016/j.ijme.2019.04.001

Culnan, M. J., & Williams, C. C. (2009). How ethics can enhance organizational privacy: Lessons from the Choice Point and TJX data breaches. *Management Information Systems Quarterly*, *33*(4), 673–687. DOI: 10.2307/20650322

Cupać, J., Schopmans, H., & Tuncer-Ebetürk, İ. (2024). Democratization in the age of artificial intelligence: Introduction to the special issue. *Democratization*, *31*(5), 899–921. DOI: 10.1080/13510347.2024.2338852

Curta, N. C., Petrusel, R., & Iftinca, C. A. (2015). Business simulation of tourism companies using the level I exercise firm model. *Quaestus*, *7*, 65.

Curtis, V., Moon, R., & Penaluna, A. (2020). Active entrepreneurship education and the impact on approaches to learning: Mixed methods evidence from a six-year study into one entrepreneurship educator's classroom. *Industry and Higher Education*, *35*(4), 443–453. DOI: 10.1177/0950422220975319

D'Angelo, S., Ghezzi, A., Cavallo, A., Rangone, A., & Annunziata, S. (2023). Corporate experimentation: Antitode or oxymoron? *European Conference on Innovation and Entrepreneurship*, 18(1), 234-241. DOI: 10.34190/ecie.18.1.1771

Dabić. (2022). *Women Entrepreneurs in Sub-Saharan Africa*. Springer Nature.

Dai, C., & Ke, F. (2022). Educational applications of artificial intelligence in simulation-based learning: A systematic mapping review. *Computers and Education Artificial Intelligence*, *3*, 100087. DOI: 10.1016/j.caeai.2022.100087

Dakung, R. J., Orobia, L., Munene, J. C., & Balunywa, W. (2017). The role of entrepreneurship education in shaping entrepreneurial action of disabled students in Nigeria. *Journal of Small Business and Entrepreneurship*, *29*(4), 293–311. DOI: 10.1080/08276331.2017.1312217

Dal, M., Elo, J., Leffler, E., Svedberg, G., & Westerberg, M. (2016). Research on pedagogical entrepreneurship-a literature review based on studies from Finland, Iceland and Sweden. *Education Inquiry*, *7*(2), 159–182. DOI: 10.3402/edui.v7.30036

Dana, L. P. (2020). *Entrepreneurship in developing countries*. Routledge.

Dana, L. P., Salamzadeh, A., Mortazavi, S., & Hadizadeh, M. (2022). Investigating the impact of international markets and new digital technologies on business innovation in emerging markets. *Sustainability (Basel)*, *14*(2), 983. DOI: 10.3390/su14020983

Dangwal, A., Kukreti, M., Angurala, M., Sarangal, R., Mehta, M., & Chauhan, P. (2023). A Review on the Role of Artificial Intelligence in Tourism. 2023 10th International Conference on Computing for Sustainable Global Development (INDIACom), New Delhi, India, 2023, pp. 164-168. https://shorturl .at/G2NgW

Darling-Hammond, L., Hyler, M. E., & Gardner, M. (2017). *Effective teacher professional development*. Learning Policy Institute.

Dasgupta, A. (2015). Finding the right fit in academia and industry collaboration. Retrieved March 15, 2020, from https://www.geospatialworld.net/article/expectations-in-academia-and-industry-collaboration/amp/

Daskou, S., Masouras, A., & Reppa, A. (2022). Servicc-Dominant Logic: The Road Map to Valuc Co-Creation in Place Marketing. In *Business Development and Economic Governance in Southeastern Europe: 13th International Conference on the Economies of the Balkan and Eastern European Countries (EBEEC), Pafos, Cyprus, 2021* (pp. 369-382). Cham: Springer International Publishing, 2022.

Davenport, T., & Kalakota, R. (2019). The potential for artificial intelligence in healthcare. *Future Healthcare Journal*, *6*(2), 94–98. [REMOVED HYPERLINK FIELD]DOI: 10.7861/futurehosp.6-2-94 PMID: 31363513

David, L. (2014). *Social Development Theory (Vygotsky) - Learning Theories*. Learning Theories.

Davidson, E., & Vaast, E. 2010, January. Digital entrepreneurship and its sociomaterial enactment. In *2010 43rd Hawaii International Conference on System Sciences* (pp. 1-10). IEEE. DOI: 10.1109/HICSS.2010.150

Davidsson, P. (2004). *Researching Entrepreneurship*. Springer.

Davitadze, M., Ooi, E., Ng, C. Y., Zhou, D., Thomas, L., Hanania, T., Blaggan, P., Evans, N., Chen, W., Melson, E., Arlt, W., & Kempegowda, P. (2021). Simba: Using Kolb's learning theory in simulation-based learning to improve participants' confidence. *BMC Medical Education*, *22*(1), 116. [REMOVED HYPERLINK FIELD]DOI: 10.1186/s12909-022-03176-2 PMID: 35193557

Davoine, R., & Deitmer, L. (2020). German Dual Training through Apprenticeships: An Exportable Model? 133–141. DOI: 10.1002/9781119694793.ch16

Day, J., Chin, N., Sydnor, S., Widhalm, M., Shah, K. U., & Dorworth, L. (2021). Implications of climate change for tourism and outdoor recreation: An Indiana, USA, case study. *Climatic Change*, *169*(3-4), 29. DOI: 10.1007/s10584-021-03284-w PMID: 34924649

Daymond, J., & Knight, E. (2023). *Design Thinking in Business and Management: Research History*. Themes, and Opportunities., DOI: 10.1093/acrefore/9780190224851.013.386

De Carvalho, C. V. (2013). Improving experiential learning with haptic experimentation. *International Journal of Online Engineering, 9*(S8), 7–9. DOI: 10.3991/ijoe.v9iS8.3309

de Freitas, S., & Oliver, M. (2006). How can exploratory learning with games and simulations within the curriculum be most effectively evaluated? *Computers & Education, 46*(3), 249–264.

de Jong, T., & van Joolingen, W. R. (2018). Scientific discovery learning with computer simulations of conceptual domains. *Review of Educational Research, 68*(2), 179–201. DOI: 10.3102/00346543068002179

de la Fuente, J., Franco, C., Gabarda, V., & Zapata, L. (2021). The role of entrepreneurship education in the development of organizational resilience and value creation in new entrepreneurs. *Journal of Innovation & Knowledge, 6*(1), 27–34. DOI: 10.1016/j.jik.2020.06.001

De la Torre, R., Onggo, B. S., Corlu, C. G., Nogal, M., & Juan, A. A. (2021). The role of simulation and serious games in teaching concepts on circular economy and sustainable energy. *Energies, 14*(4), 1138. DOI: 10.3390/en14041138

De Villiers Scheepers, M. (2015). Creative problem-solving in management education. *Management in Education, 15*(2), 101–115.

Deci, E. L., & Ryan, R. M. (1985). *Intrinsic motivation and self-determination in human behavior*. Springer. DOI: 10.1007/978-1-4899-2271-7

Dede, C. (2010). *Comparing frameworks for 21st century skills. In 21st Century Skills*. Rethinking How Students Learn.

Deininger, M., Daly, S. R., Sienko, K. H., & Lee, J. C. (2017). Novice designers' use of prototypes in engineering design. *Design Studies, 51*, 25–65. DOI: 10.1016/j.destud.2017.04.002 PMID: 29398740

Deirmentzoglou, G. A., & Deirmentzoglou, E. A. 2022, September. Pest analysis of the e-commerce industry: The case of Greece. In *Business Development and Economic Governance in Southeastern Europe: 13th International Conference on the Economies of the Balkan and Eastern European Countries (EBEEC), Pafos, Cyprus, 2021* (pp. 315-323). Cham: Springer International Publishing.

Deirmentzoglou, G. A., Vlassi, E., & Agoraki, K. K. 2022, May. The Effect of the Hotel Attributes on Guest Satisfaction Due to the Covid-19 Pandemic Crisis: The Case of the Greek Tourism and Hospitality Sector. In *International Conference Economies of The Balkan And Eastern European Countries* (pp. 283-297). Cham: Springer Nature Switzerland.

Deirmentzoglou, E., Papakyriakopoulos, G., & Patsakis, C. (2019). A survey on long-range attacks for proof of stake protocols. *IEEE Access: Practical Innovations, Open Solutions, 7*, 28712–28725. DOI: 10.1109/ACCESS.2019.2901858

Deirmentzoglou, G. A., Agoraki, K. K., & Fousteris, A. E. (2020). Organizational culture and corporate sustainable development: Evidence from Greece. *International Journal of Business and Social Science, 11*(5), 92–98. DOI: 10.30845/ijbss.v11n5a9

Deirmentzoglou, G. A., Agoraki, K. K., & Patsoulis, P. (2024c). The nexus between cultural values and perceptions of corporate sustainable development. *Social Responsibility Journal*, *20*(2), 224–242. DOI: 10.1108/SRJ-09-2022-0373

Deirmentzoglou, G. A., Anastasopoulou, E. E., & Sklias, P. (2024a). International economic relations and energy security in the European Union: A systematic literature review. *International Journal of Sustainable Energy*, *43*(1), 2385682. DOI: 10.1080/14786451.2024.2385682

Deirmentzoglou, G. A., Vlassi, E., & Anastasopoulou, E. E. (2024b). DDMMO Website Quality, Destination Image and Intention to Use Metaverse Platforms. *Platforms*, *2*(4), 180–192. DOI: 10.3390/platforms2040012

Deitrick, E., Shapiro, R. B., Ahrens, M. P., Fiebrink, R., Lehrman, P. D., & Farooq, S. (2015). Using distributed cognition theory to analyze collaborative computer science learning. *Proceedings of the Eleventh Annual International Conference on International Computing Education Research*, 51–60. DOI: 10.1145/2787622.2787715

Del Vecchio, P., Secundo, G., Mele, G., & Passiante, G. (2021). Sustainable entrepreneurship education for circular economy: Emerging perspectives in Europe. *International Journal of Entrepreneurial Behaviour & Research*, *27*(8), 2096–2124. DOI: 10.1108/IJEBR-03-2021-0210

Demirkan, I., Srinivasan, R., & Nand, A. (2021). Innovation in SMEs: The role of employee training in German SMEs. *Journal of Small Business and Enterprise Development*, *29*(3), 421–440. DOI: 10.1108/JSBED-07-2020-0246

Denzin, N., & Lincoln, Y. (Eds.). (1994). *Handbook of Qualitative Research*. SAGE Publications Ltd.

Dereso, C. W., Kant, S., Muthuraman, M., & Tufa, G. (2023). Effect of Point of Service on Health Department Student's Creativity in Comprehensive Universities of Ethiopia: Moderating Role of Public-Private Partnership and Mediating Role of Work Place Learning. In Proceedings of the International Health Informatics Conference. Lecture Notes in Electrical Engineering, vol 990. Springer. DOI: 10.1007/978-981-19-9090-8_13

Desmarais, M. C., & Baker, R. S. D. (2012). A review of recent advances in learner and skill modeling in intelligent learning environments. *User Modeling and User-Adapted Interaction*, *22*(1-2), 9–38. DOI: 10.1007/s11257-011-9106-8

Dever, D. A., Azevedo, R., Cloude, E. B., & Wiedbusch, M. (2020). The impact of autonomy and types of informational text presentations in game-based environments on learning: Converging multi-channel processes data and learning outcomes. *International Journal of Artificial Intelligence in Education*, *30*(4), 581–615. DOI: 10.1007/s40593-020-00215-1

Devlin-Scherer, R., & Sardone, N. B. (2010). Digital simulation games for social studies classrooms. The Clearing House: A. *The Clearing House: A Journal of Educational Strategies, Issues and Ideas*, *83*(4), 138–144.

Dewettinck, K., Van De Walle, J., & Galle, D. (2021). Active learning in higher education: Exploring the role of instructor and student engagement. *Teaching in Higher Education*, *26*(3), 291–308.

Dewey, J. (1933). *How we think: a restatement of the relation of reflective thinking to the educative process*. D.C. Heath & Co Publishers.

Dewey, J. (1938). *Experience and Education*. Kappa Delta Pi.

Dhanesh, G., Duthler, G., & Li, K. (2022). Social media engagement with organization-generated content: Role of visuals in enhancing public engagement with organizations on Facebook and Instagram. *Public Relations Review, 48*(2), 102174. DOI: 10.1016/j.pubrev.2022.102174

Dharmastuti, C. F., Darmoyo, S., Gunawan, R. A., & Duka, M. N. (2021). Business simulation, student competency, and learning outcomes. *Jurnal Manajemen, 25*(1), 160. DOI: 10.24912/jm.v25i1.709

Dhliwayo, S. (2008). Experiential learning in entrepreneurship education. *Education + Training, 50*(4), 329–340. DOI: 10.1108/00400910810880560

Diepolder, C. S., Weitzel, H., & Huwer, J. (2021). Competence Frameworks of Sustainable Entrepreneurship: A Systematic Review. *Sustainability (Basel), 13*(24), 13734. DOI: 10.3390/su132413734

Dillenbourg, P., & Jermann, P. (2007). Designing Integrative Scripts. In *Springer eBooks* (pp. 275–301). DOI: 10.1007/978-0-387-36949-5_16

Dimitriou D. and Karagkouni A., (2022). Du-diligence of transport infrastructure operators sustainability: a circular economy driven approach, Frondiers in Sustainability: Circular Economy, DOI: https://doi.org/DOI: 10.3389/frsus.2022.916038

Dimitriou, D. J. (2016). Climate change implications in aviation and tourism market equilibrium. Climate Change Adaptation, Resilience and Hazards, 409-424.

Dimitriou, D. (2022). *Corporate Ethics: an arbitration of philosophical concepts and market practices*. CONATUS, International Journal of Philosophy, Scopus Indexed., DOI: 10.12681/cjp.29864

Dimitriou, D., & Karagkouni, A. (2022). 'Airports' Sustainability Strategy: Evaluation framework upon environmental awareness'. *Frontiers in Sustainability., 3*, 880718. Advance online publication. DOI: 10.3389/frsus.2022.880718

Dimitriou, D., & Karagkouni, A. (2022). Assortment of Airports' Sustainability Strategy: A Comprehensiveness Analysis Framework. *Sustainability (Basel), 14*(7), 4217. DOI: 10.3390/su14074217

Dimitriou, D., & Karagkouni, A. (2023). Appraisal of Critical Infrastructure Corporate Performance Upon Sustainability: An Analysis of Impact in National Branding and Welfare. In Masouras, A., Daskou, S., Pistikou, V., Dimitriou, D., & Friesner, T. (Eds.), *Global Developments in Nation Branding and Promotion: Theoretical and Practical Approaches* (pp. 1–24). IGI Global., DOI: 10.4018/978-1-6684-5902-7.ch001

Dimitriou, D., Sartzetaki, M., & Karagkouni, A. (2024). *Managing Airport Corporate Performance: Leveraging Business Intelligence and Sustainable Transition*. Elsevier., DOI: 10.1016/C2023-0-51427-2

Dinmore, S., & Stokes, J. (2015). Creating inclusive university curriculum: Implementing universal design for learning in an enabling program. *Widening Participation and Lifelong Learning : the Journal of the Institute for Access Studies and the European Access Network, 17*(4), 4–19. DOI: 10.5456/WPLL.17.4.4

Dionne, S. D., Gupta, A., Sotak, K. L., Shirreffs, K. A., Serban, A., Hao, C., & Yammarino, F. J. (2014). A 25-year perspective on levels of analysis in leadership research. *The Leadership Quarterly*, *25*(1), 6–35. DOI: 10.1016/j.leaqua.2013.11.002

Donnelly, M., & Evans, C. (2019). A 'home-international' comparative analysis of widening participation in UK higher education. *Higher Education*, *77*(1), 97–114. DOI: 10.1007/s10734-018-0260-3

Dreyfus, S. E. (1980). *A Five-stage model of the mental activities involved in directed skill acquisition.* Storming Media. DOI: 10.21236/ADA084551

Drieschner, C., Xiong, F., Bajraktari, F., Utesch, M., Weking, J., & Krcmar, H. (2024). Measuring the Effectiveness of Learning Economic Principles in a Sustainable Entrepreneurship Game-Based Setting: A Bootstrapping Approach. *IEEE Transactions on Learning Technologies*, 1–12. DOI: 10.1109/TLT.2024.3492073

Drury-Grogan, M. L., & Russ, T. L. (2013). A contemporary simulation infused in the business communication curriculum. *Business Communication Quarterly*, *76*(3), 304–321. DOI: 10.1177/1080569913493923

Du Toit, A. (2023). Entrepreneurial Learning: Creating Value towards Social Justice. *Research in Educational Policy and Management*, *5*(3), 1–19. DOI: 10.46303/repam.2023.18

Duchatelet, D., & Donche, V. (2022). Assessing student learning during simulations in education: Methodological opportunities and challenges when applying a longitudinal case study design. *Studies in Educational Evaluation*, *72*, 101129. DOI: 10.1016/j.stueduc.2022.101129

Dudley, J., Yin, L., Garaj, V., & Kristensson, P. O. (2023). Inclusive Immersion: A review of efforts to improve accessibility in virtual reality, augmented reality and the metaverse. *Virtual Reality (Waltham Cross)*, *27*(4), 2989–3020. DOI: 10.1007/s10055-023-00850-8

Duncan, I., Miller, A., & Jiang, S. (2012). A taxonomy of virtual worlds usage in education. *British Journal of Educational Technology*, *43*(6), 949–964. DOI: 10.1111/j.1467-8535.2011.01263.x

Duong, C. D., Wach, K., Vu, N. X., Ha, S. T., & Nguyen, B. N. (2022). Entrepreneurial education, government policies and programmes, and entrepreneurial behaviour: A serial moderated mediation model. *Entrepreneurial Business and Economics Review*, *10*(4), 37–54.

Durga, P., Godavarthi, D., Kant, S., & Basa, S. S. (2024). Aspect-based drug review classification through a hybrid model with ant colony optimization using deep learning. *Discov Computing*, *27*(1), 19. DOI: 10.1007/s10791-024-09441-w

Duval-Couetil, N. (2013). Assessing the impact of entrepreneurship education programs: Challenges and approaches. *Journal of Small Business Management*, *51*(3), 394–409. DOI: 10.1111/jsbm.12024

Du, X., Liechty, T., Santos, C. A., & Park, J. (2022). 'I want to record and share my wonderful journey': Chinese Millennials' production and sharing of short-form travel videos on TikTok or Douyin. *Current Issues in Tourism*, *25*(21), 3412–3424. DOI: 10.1080/13683500.2020.1810212

Dwiniasih, D., & Khumaeroh, I. (2021). How do pre-service teachers deliver their instruction during teaching practicum?: Voice from EFL classrooms. *Research and Innovation in Language Learning*, *4*(1), 1. DOI: 10.33603/rill.v4i1.3958

Dwivedi, Y. K., Hughes, L., Baabdullah, A. M., Ribeiro-Navarrete, S., Giannakis, M., Al-Debei, M. M., Dennehy, D., Metri, B., Buhalis, D., Cheung, C. M. K., Conboy, K., Doyle, R., Dubey, R., Dutot, V., Felix, R., Goyal, D. P., Gustafsson, A., Hinsch, C., Jebabli, I., & Wamba, S. F. (2022). Metaverse beyond the hype: Multidisciplinary perspectives on emerging challenges, opportunities, and agenda for research, practice and policy. *International Journal of Information Management*, *66*, 102542. DOI: 10.1016/j.ijinfomgt.2022.102542

Earl Rinehart, K. (2021). Abductive analysis in qualitative inquiry. *Qualitative Inquiry*, *27*(2), 303–311. DOI: 10.1177/1077800420935912

Edoho, F. M. (2015). Entrepreneurship paradigm in the new millennium: A critique of public policy on entrepreneurship. *Journal of Educational Leadership*, *15*(3), 27–39.

Egenfeldt-Nielsen, S. (2011). *Beyond edutainment: Exploring the educational potential of computer games*. Lulu. Com.

Egieya, Z. E., Ewuga, S. K., Omotosho, A., Adegbite, A. O., & Oriekhoe, O. I. (2023). A review of sustainable entrepreneurship practices and their impact on long-term business viability. *World Journal of Advanced Research and Reviews*, *20*(3), 1283–1292. DOI: 10.30574/wjarr.2023.20.3.2588

Elenurm, T. (2022). Choosing Collaborative Learning Options for Preparing Innovative Entrepreneurs. *European Conference on Innovation and Entrepreneurship*. DOI: 10.34190/ecie.17.1.379

Elia, G., Margherita, A., & Passiante, G. (2020). Digital entrepreneurship ecosystem: How digital technologies and collective intelligence are reshaping the entrepreneurial process. *Technological Forecasting and Social Change*, *150*, 119791. DOI: 10.1016/j.techfore.2019.119791

Elkington, J. (1997). *Cannibals with Forks: The Triple Bottom Line of 21st Century Business*. Capstone.

Ellinger, A. D., Trent, R., Wang, Y., Wofford, G., Howard, Y., Cho, I., & Wooten, B. (2007). Experiencing scholarly writing through a collaborative course project. In Reynolds, M., & Vince, R. (Eds.), *The Handbook of Experiential Learning and Management Education* (pp. 309–326)., DOI: 10.1093/oso/9780199217632.003.0019

Elms, H., Brammer, S., Harris, J., & Phillips, R. (2010). New Directions in Strategic Management and Business Ethics. *Business Ethics Quarterly*, *20*(3), 401–425. Advance online publication. DOI: 10.5840/beq201020328

Embarak, O. H. (2022). Internet of Behaviour (IoB)-based AI models for personalized smart education systems. *Procedia Computer Science*, *203*, 103–110. DOI: 10.1016/j.procs.2022.07.015

Englis, B. G., & Frederiks, A. (2023). Using experimental designs to study entrepreneurship education: A historical overview, critical evaluation of current practices in the field, and directions for future research. *Entrepreneurship Education and Pedagogy*, *7*(1), 93–149. DOI: 10.1177/25151274231161102

Ergazakis, K., & Metaxiotis, K. (2011). The knowledge-based development agenda:a perspective for 2010-2020. *Vine*, *41*(3), 358–377. DOI: 10.1108/03055721111171582

Esfahlani, S. S., Izsof, V., Minter, S., Kordzadeh, A., Shirvani, H., & Esfahlani, K. S. (2019). Development of an Interactive Virtual Reality for Medical Skills Training Supervised by Artificial Neural Network. In *Advances in intelligent systems and computing* (pp. 473–482). DOI: 10.1007/978-3-030-29513-4_34

European Commission. (2019). *European Accessibility Act.* Retrieved from https://eur-lex.europa.eu/legal-content/EN/TXT/?uri=CELEX%3A32019L0882

European Commission. (2020). *Artificial intelligence: A European perspective.* European Union Publications.

European Commission. (2022). *The Commission publishes guidelines to help teachers address misconceptions about Artificial Intelligence and promote its ethical use.*https://ec.europa.eu/commission/presscorner/detail/en/ip_22_6338

European eCompetence Framework. (n.d.). Retrieved from https://www.ecompetences.eu/

Facer, K. (2003). Computer games and learning. Futurelab discussion paper. Available at: www.futurelab.org.uk/resources/publications-reports-articles/discussion-papers/Discussion-Paper261

Fairlie, R. W., & Holleran, W. (2012). Entrepreneurship training, risk aversion and other personality traits: Evidence from a random experiment. *Journal of Economic Psychology*, *33*(2), 366–378. DOI: 10.1016/j.joep.2011.02.001

Faisal, N., Chadhar, M., Goriss-Hunter, A., & Stranieri, A. (2022). Business Simulation Games in Higher Education: A Systematic Review of Empirical Research. *Human Behavior and Emerging Technologies*, *2022*, 1–28. Advance online publication. DOI: 10.1155/2022/1578791

Fajar, A., & Sarno, R. (2019). Asynchronous agent-based simulation and optimization of parallel business. *Telkomnika*, *17*(4), 1731. DOI: 10.12928/telkomnika.v17i4.10846

Fanelli, R. M. (2022). Agritourism farms: A great way to promote local products. *Tourism Analysis*, *27*(3), 331–342. DOI: 10.3727/108354222X16449628077748

Fang, F., & Luo, X. (2018). Entrepreneurship Teaching Design Based On Case Study. .DOI: 10.2991/icesem-18.2018.299

Farhangmehr, M., Gonçalves, P., & Sarmento, M. (2016). Predicting entrepreneurial motivation among university students: The role of entrepreneurship education. *Education + Training*, *58*(7/8), 861–881. DOI: 10.1108/ET-01-2016-0019

Faria, A. J. (2001). The changing nature of business simulation/ gaming research: A brief history. *Simulation & Gaming*, *32*(1), 97–110. DOI: 10.1177/104687810103200108

Faria, A. J., & Dickinson, J. R. (1994). Simulation gaming for sales management training. *Journal of Management Development*, *13*(1), 47–59.

Faria, A. J., Hutchinson, D., & Wellington, W. J. (2009). The role of business simulations in international business education. *Journal of Teaching in International Business*, *20*(3), 207–223.

Faria, A. J., Hutchinson, D., Wellington, W. J., & Gold, S. (2009). Developments in business gaming: A review of the past 40 years. *Simulation & Gaming*, *40*(4), 464–487. DOI: 10.1177/1046878108327585

Farkas, A., & Nagy, V. (2008). Student assessment of desirable technical skills: A correspondence analysis approach. *Acta Polytechnica Hungarica*, *5*(2), 43–57.

Farooq, M. S., Salam, M., Rehman, S. U., Fayolle, A., Jaafar, N., & Ayupp, K. (2018). Impact of support from social network on entrepreneurial intention of fresh business graduates. *Education + Training*, *60*(4), 335–353. DOI: 10.1108/ET-06-2017-0092

Farshid, M., Paschen, J., Eriksson, T., & Kietzmann, J. (2018). Go boldly!: Explore augmented reality (AR), virtual reality (VR), and mixed reality (MR) for business. *Business Horizons*, *61*(5), 657–663. DOI: 10.1016/j.bushor.2018.05.009

Faulds, D. J., Mangold, W. G., Raju, P. S., & Valsalan, S. (2018). The mobile shopping revolution: Redefining the consumer decision process. *Business Horizons*, *61*(2), 323–338. DOI: 10.1016/j.bushor.2017.11.012

Fauske, I. M., Verhulst, E., Wigger, K. A., Solvoll, S., & Jakobsen, S. (2024). Teaching Entrepreneurship for Sustainability - a Review of Educational Tools. *Management Review*, *35*(1), 113–146.

Fauzan, A. C., Sarno, R., & Yaqin, M. A. (2017). Performance measurement based on coloured petri net simulation of scalable business processes. *Proceeding of the Electrical Engineering Computer Science and Informatics*, 4(1). DOI: 10.1109/EECSI.2017.8239121

Fayolle, A., & Gailly, B. (2008). From craft to science: Teaching models and learning processes in entrepreneurship education. *Journal of European Industrial Training*, *32*(7), 569–593. DOI: 10.1108/03090590810899838

Fayolle, A., & Gailly, B. (2015). The impact of entrepreneurship education on entrepreneurial attitudes and intention: Hysteresis and persistence. *Journal of Small Business Management*, *53*(1), 16–30.

Fayolle, A., & Liñán, F. (2014). The Future of Research on Entrepreneurial Intentions. *Journal of Business Research*, *67*(5), 663–666. DOI: 10.1016/j.jbusres.2013.11.024

Febrianti, B., Kussudyarsana, K., Setyawan, A., Sholahuddin, M., & Maimun, M. (2023). *The Role of Internship Program and Entrepreneurship Training to Hole Entrepreneur Capability and Startup Performance*. Jurnal Manajemen Bisnis. DOI: 10.18196/mb.v14i2.19251

Felin, T., Gambardella, A., Stern, S., & Zenger, T. (2020). Lean startup and the business model: Experimentation revisited. *Long Range Planning*, *53*(4), 101889. Advance online publication. DOI: 10.1016/j.lrp.2019.06.002

Felix, R., Rauschnabel, P. A., & Hinsch, C. (2017). Elements of strategic social media marketing: A holistic framework. *Journal of Business Research*, *70*, 118–126. DOI: 10.1016/j.jbusres.2016.05.001

Feng, Y., Lin, F., & Huang, M. (2024). Application of seminar teaching method combined with case-based learning and problem-based learning teaching models in oral clinical nursing teaching. *Journal of Contemporary Educational Research*, *8*(4), 176–181. DOI: 10.26689/jcer.v8i4.6521

Ferrell, O. C., Fraedrich, J., & Ferrell, L. (2018). *Business ethics: Ethical decision making and cases* (12th ed.). Cengage Learning.

Fiet, J. O. (2001). The Theoretical Side of Teaching Entrepreneurship. *Journal of Business Venturing, 16*(1), 1–24. DOI: 10.1016/S0883-9026(99)00041-5

Filteau, M. (2012). La créativité: Un processus complexe. *Review of Psychology, 42*(2), 73–85.

Fiore, E., Sansone, G., & Paolucci, E. (2019). Entrepreneurship Education in a Multidisciplinary Environment: Evidence from an Entrepreneurship Programme Held in Turin. *Administrative Sciences, 9*(1), 28. DOI: 10.3390/admsci9010028

Fitriany, F. (2024). The implementation of Project Based Learning method in building creativity, encouraging learning motivation and improving language skills. *BRIGHT VISION Journal of Language and Education, 4*(2), 108. DOI: 10.30821/brightvision.v4i2.3862

Flanigan, S., Blackstock, K., & Hunter, C. (2014). Agritourism from the perspective of providers and visitors: A typology-based study. *Tourism Management, 40*, 394–405. DOI: 10.1016/j.tourman.2013.07.004

Fleischer, A., Tchetchik, A., Bar-Nahum, Z., & Talev, E. (2018). Is agriculture important to agritourism? The agritourism attraction market in Israel. *European Review of Agriculture Economics, 45*(2), 273–296. DOI: 10.1093/erae/jbx039

Flick, U. (2018). *An Introduction to Qualitative Research.* Sage Publications.

Flora, H. K., Wang, X., & Chande, S. V. (2014). An investigation on the characteristics of mobile applications: A survey study. *IJ Information Technology and Computer Science, 11*(11), 21–27. DOI: 10.5815/ijitcs.2014.11.03

Foo, M., Vissa, B., & Wu, B. (2020). Entrepreneurship in Emerging Economies. PSN: Other Comparative Capitalism (Topic). DOI: 10.2139/ssrn.3666851

Forman, J., Creswell, J. W., Damschroder, L., Kowalski, C. P., & Krein, S. L. (2008). Qualitative research methods: Key features and insights gained from use in infection prevention research. *American Journal of Infection Control, 36*(10), 764–771. DOI: 10.1016/j.ajic.2008.03.010 PMID: 18834752

Fox, J., Pittaway, L., & Uzuegbunam, I. (2018). Simulations in Entrepreneurship Education: Serious Games and Learning Through Play. *Entrepreneurship Education and Pedagogy, 1*(1), 61–69.

Fox, J., Pittaway, L., & Uzuegbunam, I. (2018). Simulations in entrepreneurship education: Serious games and learning through play. *Entrepreneurship Education and Pedagogy, 1*(1), 61–89. DOI: 10.1177/2515127417737285

Frasson, C., & Blanchard, E. G. (2012). Simulation-Based Learning. In Seel, N. M. (Ed.), *Encyclopedia of the Sciences of Learning*. Springer., DOI: 10.1007/978-1-4419-1428-6_129

Freberg, K. (2012). Intention to comply with crisis messages communicated via social media. *Public Relations Review, 38*(3), 416–421. DOI: 10.1016/j.pubrev.2012.01.008

Freeman, R. E., Harrison, J. S., & Wicks, A. C. (2007). *Managing for Stakeholders: Survival, Reputation, and Success.* Yale University Press.

Fu, H., Su, L., & Yu, X. (2019). Enhancing student engagement and learning outcomes through business simulations in entrepreneurship education. *Journal of Entrepreneurship Education, 22*(1), 1–10.

Fullan, M. (2023). *The Principal 2.0: Three Keys to Maximizing Impact*. John Wiley & Sons.

Fullan, M. (2010). *The Moral Imperative of School Leadership*. SAGE Publications.

Gadanakis, Y. (2024). Advancing farm entrepreneurship and agribusiness management for sustainable agriculture. *Agriculture, 14*(8), 1288. DOI: 10.3390/agriculture14081288

Gajda, A., Karwowski, M., & Beghetto, R. A. (2017). Creativity and academic achievement: A meta-analysis. *Journal of Educational Psychology, 109*(2), 269.

Galloway, L., Sanders, J., & Deakins, D. (2011). Rural small firms' use of the internet: From global to local. *Journal of Rural Studies, 27*(3), 254–262. DOI: 10.1016/j.jrurstud.2011.05.005

Gandasegui, V. D. (2013). Entornos virtuales para el desarrollo de la educación inclusiva: Una mirada hacia el futuro desde el pasado de Second Life. *RELATEC: Revista Latinoamericana de Tecnología Educativa, 12*(2), 67–77.

Gao, C. A., Howard, F. M., Markov, N. S., Dyer, E. C., Ramesh, S., Luo, Y., & Pearson, A. T. (2022). Comparing scientific abstracts generated by ChatGPT to original abstracts using an artificial intelligence output detector, plagiarism detector, and blinded human reviewers. *bioRxiv*. 2022.12.23.521610

Gao, H. (2020). Research on the Construction of Virtual Simulation Experiment Teaching Courses of Economics and Management Majors. *Advances in Social Science, Education and Humanities Research, 416*.

Gao, H. (2020). Research on the construction of virtual simulation experiment teaching courses of economics and management majors. In *4th International Conference on Culture, Education and Economic Development of Modern Society (ICCESE 2020)* (pp. 973-978). Atlantis Press.

García, P. O., & Capitán, Á. O. (2019). The uniqueness of entrepreneurship of persons with disabilities in Spain. *Suma de Negocios, 10*(SPE22), 1–8.

Garcia, S., Kauer, R., Laesker, D., Nguyen, J., & Andujar, M. (2019). A virtual reality experience for learning languages. *Extended Abstracts of the 2019 CHI Conference on Human Factors in Computing Systems*, 1–4.

García, J. Y. S., Ríos, J. E. N., & Hernández, C. L. (2020). Systemic complementarity, an integrative model of cooperation among small and medium-sized tourism enterprises in Mexico. *International Journal of Business Innovation and Research, 23*(3), 354. DOI: 10.1504/IJBIR.2020.110968

Garcia, M. E., Guerrero, C. A., & Pérez, S. (2020). Enhancing innovative capacities in higher education: The importance of collaboration. *Innovation (Abingdon), 33*(3), 301–314.

García-Madurga, M., & Grilló-Méndez, A. (2023). Artificial intelligence in the tourism industry: An overview of reviews. *Administrative Sciences, 13*(8), 172. DOI: 10.3390/admsci13080172

García, P. O., & Capitán, Á. J. O. (2021). Entrepreneurship for people with disabilities: From skills to social value. *Frontiers in Psychology, 12*, 699833. DOI: 10.3389/fpsyg.2021.699833 PMID: 34305761

Gardner, J., O'Leary, M., & Yuan, L. (2021). Artificial intelligence in educational assessment:'Breakthrough? Or buncombe and ballyhoo? *Journal of Computer Assisted Learning*, *37*(5), 1207–1216. DOI: 10.1111/jcal.12577

Garnett, F., & O'Beirne, R. (2019). Digital Skills for Educators: Enhancing Technology Use in Teaching. *Educational Technology Research and Development*, *67*(2), 207–221.

Garris, R., Ahlers, R., & Driskell, J. E. (2002). Games, motivation, and learning: A research and practice model. *Simulation & Gaming*, *33*(4), 441–467.

Gartner, W. B. (1988). Who Is an Entrepreneur? Is the Wrong Question. *American Journal of Small Business*, *12*(4), 11–32. DOI: 10.1177/104225878801200401

Gbadegeshin, S. A. (2017). Commercialization process of high technology: A study of Finnish University Spin-off. *Academy of Entrepreneurship Journal*, *23*(2), 1–22.

Gefen, D., Karahanna, E., & Straub, D. W. (2003). Trust and tam in online shopping: An integrated model1. *Management Information Systems Quarterly*, *27*(1), 51–90. DOI: 10.2307/30036519

Gentry, J. W. (1990). *What is Experiential Learning? Guide to Business Gaming and Experiential Learning*. Nichols/GP Publishing.

Gentry, J. W. (1990). What is Experiential Learning? In *Guide to Business Gaming and Experiential Learning*. Nichols Publishing.

Gentry, J. W., Commuri, S., & Sulek, J. (2010). How experiential learning can be used in entrepreneurship education. *Simulation & Gaming*, *41*(1), 114–123.

Gentry, T., Wallace, J., Kvarfordt, C., & Lynch, K. (2010). Personal digital assistants as cognitive aids for high school students with autism: Results of a community-based trial. *Journal of Vocational Rehabilitation*, *32*(2), 101–107. DOI: 10.3233/JVR-2010-0499

George, B., & Wooden, O. (2023). Managing the Strategic Transformation of Higher Education through Artificial Intelligence. *Administrative Sciences*, *13*(9), 196. DOI: 10.3390/admsci13090196

George, J., & Dane, E. (2016). Affect, emotion, and decision making. *Organizational Behavior and Human Decision Processes*, *136*, 47–55. DOI: 10.1016/j.obhdp.2016.06.004

Georgiou, Y., Tsivitanidou, O., & Ioannou, A. (2021). Learning experience design with immersive virtual reality in physics education. *Educational Technology Research and Development*, *69*(6), 3051–3080. DOI: 10.1007/s11423-021-10055-y

Ghezzi, A., & Cavallo, A. (2020). Agile Business Model Innovation in Digital Entrepreneurship: Lean Startup Approaches. *Journal of Business Research*, *110*, 519–537. Advance online publication. DOI: 10.1016/j.jbusres.2018.06.013

Ghisu, T., Arca, B., Pellizzaro, G., & Duce, P. (2015). An improved cellular automata for wildfire spread. *Procedia Computer Science*, *51*, 2287–2296.

Gibb, A. (1996). Entrepreneurship and Small Business Management: Can We Afford to Neglect Them in the Twenty-first Century Business School? *British Journal of Management*, *7*(4), 309–321. DOI: 10.1111/j.1467-8551.1996.tb00121.x

Gibb, A. (2002). In Pursuit of a New 'Enterprise' and 'Entrepreneurship' Paradigm for Learning: Creative Destruction, New Values, New Ways of Doing Things and New Combinations of Knowledge. *International Journal of Management Reviews*, *4*(3), 233–269. DOI: 10.1111/1468-2370.00086

Gibbons, B., Fernando, M., & Spedding, T. (2022). Innovation Through Developing a Total Enterprise Computer Simulation: Teaching Responsible Decision Making. *Journal of Management Education*, *46*(1), 16–42. DOI: 10.1177/1052562920987591

Gillespie, G. L., Farra, S., Regan, S. L., & Brammer, S. V. (2021). Impact of immersive virtual reality simulations for changing knowledge, attitudes, and behaviors. *Nurse Education Today*, *105*, 105025. DOI: 10.1016/j.nedt.2021.105025 PMID: 34175566

Gilligan, J. (2020). Competencies for educators in delivering digital accessibility in higher education. *Universal Access in Human-Computer Interaction. Applications and Practice: 14th International Conference, UAHCI 2020, Held as Part of the 22nd HCI International Conference, HCII 2020, Copenhagen, Denmark, July 19–24, 2020Proceedings*, *22*(Part II), 184–199.

Gimmon, E., Farja, Y., & Greenberg, Z. (2020). Vocational education of owners and SME employment growth: Evidence from Israel. *International Journal of Training Research*, *19*(1), 21–46. DOI: 10.1080/14480220.2020.1864440

Gittins, P., Apostolopoulos, S., Anastasopoulou, E. E., & Apostolopoulos, N. (2025). Responding to Greece's constrained agricultural context: Farm diversification strategies used by family farmers. *Journal of Rural Studies*, *113*, 103522.

Gleason, N. W. (2018). Singapore's higher education systems in the era of the fourth industrial revolution: Preparing lifelong learners. In Higher education in the era of the fourth industrial revolution (pp. 145-169). Palgrave Macmillan, Singapore. DOI: 10.1007/978-981-13-0811-8_8

Global Entrepreneurship Monitor. (2024). *GEM 2023/2024 Global Report 25 Years and Growing*. Author.

Goch, M. (2023). Interdisciplinary students' reflections on the development of their epistemic fluency. *Frontiers in Education*, *8*, 1145227. Advance online publication. DOI: 10.3389/feduc.2023.1145227

Goh, Y. M., Lim, Y. T., & Ooi, K. B. (2021). Exploring the entrepreneurial intentions of university students: A comparative study between two Asian countries. *Asian Journal of Technology Innovation*, *29*(1), 1–16.

Goldin-Meadow, S. (2005). *Hearing gesture: How our hands help us think*. Harvard University Press. DOI: 10.2307/j.ctv1w9m9ds

Goldschmidt, G. (2014). Modeling the role of sketching in design idea generation. In *An anthology of theories and models of design: philosophy, approaches and empirical explorations* (pp. 433–450). Springer London. DOI: 10.1007/978-1-4471-6338-1_21

Gonçalves, M., Cardoso, C., & Badke-Schaub, P. (2014). What inspires designers? Preferences on inspirational approaches during idea generation. *Design Studies*, *35*(1), 29–53. DOI: 10.1016/j.destud.2013.09.001

González-Calatayud, V., Prendes-Espinosa, P., & Roig-Vila, R. (2021). Artificial Intelligence for Student Assessment: A Systematic Review. *Applied Sciences (Basel, Switzerland)*, *11*(12), 5467. DOI: 10.3390/app11125467

Gonzalez, E., Rodriguez, M., & Martinez, A. (2020). The impact of entrepreneurial education on students' innovation skills: An analysis of the Spanish case. *Journal of Business Research*, *118*, 63–71.

Gopalan, M., Rosinger, K. O., & Ahn, J. B. (2020). Use of quasi-experimental research designs in education research: Growth, promise, and challenges. *Review of Research in Education*, *44*(1), 218–243. DOI: 10.3102/0091732X20903302

Gopinath, C., & Sawyer, J. E. (1999). Exploring the learning from an enterprise simulation. *Journal of Management Development*, *18*(5), 477–489.

Gough, S., Hellaby, M., Jones, N., & MacKinnon, R. (2012). A review of undergraduate interprofessional simulation-based education (IPSE). *Collegian (Royal College of Nursing, Australia)*, *19*(3), 153–170. DOI: 10.1016/j.colegn.2012.04.004 PMID: 23101350

Gouskova, E. (2020). Why self-employment rates are higher among people with work limitations. *Journal of Disability Policy Studies*, *31*(1), 15–25. DOI: 10.1177/1044207319851244

Gove, S., & Marquez, J. (2012). The Business Strategy Game: Learning management principles. *Management Decision*, *50*(8), 1356–1372.

Goyal, D P & Sharma, Sarika & Singh, Archana. (2021). Systematic review on sustainable entrepreneurship education (SME): A framework and analysis" World Journal of Entrepreneurship, Management and Sustainable Development. *World Review of Entrepreneurship, Management and Sustainable Development*, *17*, 372–395.

Greco, M., Baldissin, N., & Nonino, F. (2013). An exploratory taxonomy of business games. *Simulation & Gaming*, *44*(5), 645–682. DOI: 10.1177/1046878113501464

Gredler, M. E. (2004). Games and simulations and their relationships to learning. Handbook of Research on Educational Communications and Technology, 571-581.

Gredler, M. E. (1996). Educational games and simulations: A technology in search of a (research) paradigm. In Jonassen, D. H. (Ed.), *Handbook of research on educational communications and technology* (pp. 521–539). Macmillan.

Greenhow, C., & Lewin, C. (2019). Social media and education: Reconceptualizing the boundaries of formal and informal learning. In *Social Media and Education* (pp. 6–30). Routledge. DOI: 10.4324/9781315121697-2

Gregory, P. A., & Austin, Z. (2020). COVID-19: How did community pharmacies get through the first wave? *Canadian Pharmacists Journal/Revue des Pharmaciens du Canada, 153*(5), 243-251.

Grierson, L., Norman, G., Monteiro, S., & Sibbald, M. (2019). Simulation-Based Education and the Challenge of Transfer. In *Clinical Simulation (Second Edition), Education, Operations, and Engineering* (pp. 115-127). Academic Press.

Grobbelaar, W., & Verma, A. (2020). Vocational training and industry IR 4.0 in a smart city. SSRN Electronic Journal. DOI: 10.2139/ssrn.3713780

Groß, E., Siegert, J., & Bauernhansl, T. (2017). Changing requirements of competence building due to an increase of personalized products. *Procedia Manufacturing*, *9*, 291–298. DOI: 10.1016/j.promfg.2017.04.045

Guerrero, M., Heaton, S., & Urbano, D. (2021). Building universities' intrapreneurial capabilities in the digital era: The role and impacts of Massive Open Online Courses (MOOCs). *Technovation*, *99*, 102139. Advance online publication. DOI: 10.1016/j.technovation.2020.102139

Guerrero, M., Urbano, D., Fayolle, A., Klofsten, M., & Mian, S. (2016). Entrepreneurial universities: Emerging models in the new social and economic landscape. *Small Business Economics*, *47*(3), 551–563.

Guilford, J. P. (1950). Creativity. *The American Psychologist*, *5*(9), 444–454. PMID: 14771441

Guillén-Yparrea, N., & Hernández-Rodríguez, F. (2024). Unveiling Generative AI in Higher Education: Insights from Engineering Students and Professors. *2022 IEEE Global Engineering Education Conference (EDUCON)*, 1–5. https://doi.org/DOI: 10.1109/EDUCON60312.2024.10578876

Gül, H.. (2023). The impact of project-based learning on creative thinking skills: A meta-analysis. *Educational Research Review*, *34*, 100405.

Gürpınar, E., Batı, H., & Tetik, C. (2011). Learning styles of medical students change in relation to time. *Advances in Physiology Education*, *35*(3), 307–311. [REMOVED HYPERLINK FIELD]DOI: 10.1152/advan.00047.2011 PMID: 21908841

Gustavsson, S. (2021). Simulation in vocational education. Skandinavisk Tidsskrift for Yrker Og Profesjoner I Utvikling, 6(1). DOI: 10.7577/sjvd.4076

Guyo, D. M., Kero, C. A., & Kant, S. (2025). Is Marketing Intermediaries' Mediation Required for Livestock and Products Marketing to Improve the Economic Status of Pastoralist Communities in Ethiopia? In *AI in Agriculture for Sustainable and Economic Management* (pp. 216-234). CRC Press.

Guyo, K., & Kero, C. A. (2023). Mediation of Marketing Intermediaries and AI Adoption Between Livestock Products Marketing and Economic Status of Pastoralist in Ethiopia. *2023 International Conference on Communication, Security and Artificial Intelligence (ICCSAI)*, 311-316. DOI: 10.1109/ICCSAI59793.2023.10421261

Haddad, G., Haddad, G., & Nagpal, G. (2021). Can students' perception of the diverse learning environment affect their intentions toward entrepreneurship? *Journal of Innovation & Knowledge*, *6*(3), 167–176. DOI: 10.1016/j.jik.2021.04.002

Haderer, B., & Ciolacu, M. (2022). Education 4.0: Artificial intelligence assisted task- and time planning System. *Procedia Computer Science*, *200*, 1328–1337. DOI: 10.1016/j.procs.2022.01.334

Hagebakken, G., Reimers, C. S., & Solstad, E. (2021). Entrepreneurship education as a strategy to build regional sustainability. *Sustainability (Basel), 13*(5), 2529. DOI: 10.3390/su13052529

Hägg, G., & Gabrielsson, J. (2019). Entrepreneurial learning in practice: The role of narrative in the development of entrepreneurial competencies. *International Journal of Entrepreneurial Behaviour & Research, 25*(3), 478–498.

Hägg, G., & Gabrielsson, J. (2020). A systematic literature review of the evolution of pedagogy in entrepreneurial education research. *International Journal of Entrepreneurial Behaviour & Research, 26*(5), 829–861. DOI: 10.1108/IJEBR-04-2018-0272

Hägg, G., & Kurczewska, A. (2019). Who is the student entrepreneur? Understanding the emergent adult through the pedagogy and andragogy of entrepreneurial learning. *Education + Training, 61*(9), 1071–1084.

Hair, J. F., Sarstedt, M., Ringle, C.M. and Gudergan, S.P. (2017), Advanced Issues in Partial Least Squares Structural Equation Modeling, Sage Publications, Thousand Oaks, CA.

Hallinger, P., & Wang, R. (2020). Analyzing the intellectual structure of research on simulation-based learning in management education, 1960–2019: A bibliometric review. *International Journal of Management Education, 18*(3), 100418. DOI: 10.1016/j.ijme.2020.100418

Hall, J. K., Matos, S., Sheehan, L., & Silvestre, B. S. (2013). Entrepreneurship and Innovation at the Base of the Pyramid: A Recipe for Inclusive Growth or Social Exclusion? *Journal of Management Studies, 49*(4), 785–812.

Hamari, J., Koivisto, J., & Sarsa, H. (2014). Does Gamification Work? — A Literature Review of Empirical Studies on Gamification. *Proceedings of the ... Annual Hawaii International Conference on System Sciences. Annual Hawaii International Conference on System Sciences, 10*, 1109. DOI: 10.1109/HICSS.2014.377

Hamari, J., Koivisto, J., & Sarsa, H. (2016). Does gamification work?—A literature review of empirical studies on gamification. *System Sciences, 2016*, 3025–3034.

Hamilton, L., Tee, S., & Considine, J. (2019). The impact of immersive simulation experiences on nurse educators' confidence, knowledge and skills. *Nurse Education Today, 78*, 37–42.

Hammoda, B. (2024). The impact of educational technologies on entrepreneurial competencies: A systematic review of empirical evidence. *Knowledge Management & E-Learning, 16*(2), 309–333. DOI: 10.34105/j.kmel.2024.16.015

Hamzeh, F., Theokaris, C., Rouhana, C., & Abbas, Y. (2017). Application of hands-on simulation games to improve classroom experience. *European Journal of Engineering Education, 42*(5), 471–481. DOI: 10.1080/03043797.2016.1190688

Han, E., & Bailenson, J. N. (2024). Lessons for/in virtual classrooms: designing a model for classrooms inside virtual reality. In *Communication Education* (Vol. 73, Issue 2, pp. 234–243). Routledge. DOI: 10.1080/03634523.2024.2312879

Hanandeh, R., Alharafsheh, M., Albloush, A., Lehyeh, S., & Kilani, Q. (2024). The impact of entrepreneurship self-concept, work motivation, and risk-taking on human resource department performance and business overall performance at Jordan private universities. *Uncertain Supply Chain Management*, *12*(1), 143–150. Advance online publication. DOI: 10.5267/j.uscm.2023.10.010

Hanney, R., & Savin-Baden, M. (2013). The problem of projects: Understanding the theoretical underpinnings of project-led PBL. *London Review of Education*, *11*(1), 7–19. DOI: 10.1080/14748460.2012.761816

Hannig, A., Kuth, N., Özman, M., Jonas, S., & Spreckelsen, C. (2012). Emedoffice: A web-based collaborative serious game for teaching optimal design of a medical practice. *BMC Medical Education*, *12*(1), 104. Advance online publication. DOI: 10.1186/1472-6920-12-104 PMID: 23110606

Harder, N. (2023). Advancing healthcare simulation through artificial intelligence and Machine Learning: Exploring Innovations. *Clinical Simulation in Nursing*, *83*, 101456. DOI: 10.1016/j.ecns.2023.101456

Hardesty, S. (2011). Agritourism operators embrace social media for marketing. *California Agriculture*, *65*(02), 56–57. DOI: 10.3733/ca.v065n02p56a

Hariyono, H. (2024). Building a future generation of entrepreneurs: An experimental study of the integration of PBL and AI in entrepreneurial. *EDUTEC: Journal of Education and Technology*, *7*(4), 444–453. DOI: 10.29062/edu.v7i4.921

Harris, R., & Clayton, B. (2020). The value of vocational education and training. *International Journal of Training Research*, *18*(3), 185–190. DOI: 10.1080/14480220.2020.1860309

Hart, H., & Smith-Glick, J. (1994). Training in technical communication: Ideas for a partnership between the academy and the workplace. *Technical Communication (Washington)*, *41*(3), 399–405.

Harvey, L., & Green, D. (1994). *Employer satisfaction*. Quality in Higher Education Project.

Hashim, Osman, & Elbadri. (2024). Pedagogical Approaches to Teaching Entrepreneurship to Higher Education Students: A Literature Review. DOI: 10.69481/PED06172024

Hassan, A., Anwar, I., Saleem, I., Islam, K. B., & Hussain, S. A. (2021). Individual entrepreneurial orientation, education related with entrepreneurship and entrepreneurial intention: The mediating role of entrepreneurial motivations. *Industry and Higher Education*, *35*(4), 403–418. DOI: 10.1177/0950422221 1007051

Hassan, H. K., Igel, B., & Shamsuddoha, M. (2022). Education related with entrepreneurship and communal entrepreneurial intentions: The mediating impacts of entrepreneurial communal network. *Frontiers in Psychology*, *13*, 860273. DOI: 10.3389/fpsyg.2022.860273 PMID: 35651573

Hassan, S., Mahsud, R., Yukl, G., & Prussia, G. E. (2013). Ethical and empowering leadership and leader effectiveness. *Journal of Managerial Psychology*, *28*(2), 133–146. DOI: 10.1108/02683941311300252

Hattie, J., & Timperley, H. (2007). The power of feedback. *Review of Educational Research*, *77*(1), 81–112. DOI: 10.3102/003465430298487

Hayes, A. F., & Krippendorff, K. (2007). Answering the call for a standard reliability measure for coding data. *Communication Methods and Measures*, *1*(1), 77–89. DOI: 10.1080/19312450709336664

Hays, S., Page, S. J., & Buhalis, D. (2013). Social media as a destination marketing tool: Its use by national tourism organisations. *Current Issues in Tourism*, *16*(3), 211–239. DOI: 10.1080/13683500.2012.662215

He, F. (2022). Application Research on Intelligent Design System of Indoor Public Space Based on Computer AI Technology, 2022 IEEE 2nd International Conference on Data Science and Computer Application (ICDSCA), Dalian, China, 2022, pp. 864-868, DOI: 10.1109/ICDSCA56264.2022.9988571

Heater, C. (1992). Being there: The subjective experience of presence. *Presence (Cambridge, Mass.)*, *1*(2), 262–271. DOI: 10.1162/pres.1992.1.2.262

Hecklau, F., Galeitzke, M., Flachs, S., & Kohl, H. (2016). Holistic approach for human resource management in Industry 4.0. *Procedia CIRP*, *54*(1), 1–6. DOI: 10.1016/j.procir.2016.05.102

Henczi, L., & Zöllei, K. (2007). *Kompetenciamenedzsment (Competence management)*. PerfektKiadó.

Hennessey, B. A., & Amabile, T. M. (2010). Creativity. *Annual Review of Psychology*, *61*, 569–598. PMID: 19575609

Hermann, R., & Bossle, M. (2020). Bringing an entrepreneurial focus to sustainability education: A teaching framework based on content analysis. *Journal of Cleaner Production*, *246*, 119038. DOI: 10.1016/j.jclepro.2019.119038

Heuer, A., Serratos-Sotelo, L., & Motel-Klingebiel, A. (2024). How perception affects participation: The case of adult learning and continued vocational education and training in Europe. *International Journal of Lifelong Education*, 1–21. DOI: 10.1080/02601370.2024.2398516

Hidalgo-Peñate, A., Nieves, J., & Padrón-Robaina, V. (2020). The influence of employees' knowledge, organisational commitment, and culture on the innovativeness of vocational educational. *Knowledge Management Research and Practice*, *20*(5), 755–766. DOI: 10.1080/14778238.2020.1774431

Hindle, K. (2002). A Grounded Theory for Teaching Entrepreneurship Using Simulation Games. *Simulation & Gaming*, *33*(2), 236–241. DOI: 10.1177/1046878102332012

Hindle, K. (2004). Choosing Qualitative Methods for Entrepreneurial Cognition Research: A Canonical Development Approach. *Entrepreneurship Theory and Practice*, *28*(6), 575–607.

Hirschi, A. (2018). The fourth industrial revolution: Issues and implications for career research and practice. *The Career Development Quarterly*, *66*(3), 192–204. DOI: 10.1002/cdq.12135

Hjalager, A. M. (2010). A review of innovation research in tourism. *Tourism Management*, *31*(1), 1–12. DOI: 10.1016/j.tourman.2009.08.012

Hlasny, V. (2023). Vocational training support and innovation at SMEs. *Asia Pacific Journal of Innovation and Entrepreneurship*, *17*(2), 99–120. DOI: 10.1108/APJIE-09-2022-0096

Hoang, G., Le, T. T. T., Tran, A. K. T., & Du, T. (2020). Entrepreneurship education and entrepreneurial intentions of university students in Vietnam: The mediating roles of self-efficacy and learning orientation. *Education + Training*, *63*(1), 115–133. DOI: 10.1108/ET-05-2020-0142

Hobson, C. J., Strupeck, D., Griffin, A., Szostek, J., & Rominger, A. S. (2014). Teaching MBA students teamwork and team leadership skills: An empirical evaluation of a classroom educational program. *American Journal of Business Education*, *7*(3), 191–212. DOI: 10.19030/ajbe.v7i3.8801

Hockerts, K. (2018). The Effect of Experiential Social Entrepreneurship Education on Intention Formation in Students. *Journal of Social Entrepreneurship*, *9*(3), 234–256. DOI: 10.1080/19420676.2018.1498377

Hogue, A., Kapralos, B., & Desjardins, F. (2011). The role of project-based learning in IT: A case study in a game development and entrepreneurship program. *Interactive Technology and Smart Education*, *8*(2), 120–134. DOI: 10.1108/17415651111141830

Hoidn, S., & Kärkkäinen, K. (2014). Promoting skills for innovation in higher education: A literature review on the effectiveness of problem-based learning and of teaching behaviours. Academic Press.

Hollan, J., Hutchins, E., & Kirsh, D. (2009). Distributed Cognition: Toward a New Foundation for Human-Computer Interaction Research, 2000. *ACM Transactions on Computer-Human Interaction*, *7*(2), 175.

Holmes, W., Bialik, M., & Fadel, C. (2019). *Artificial Intelligence in Education: Promises and Implications for Teaching and Learning*. Center for Curriculum Redesign.

Holuša, V., Vaněk, M., Beneš, F., Švub, J., & Staša, P. (2023). Virtual reality as a tool for sustainable training and education of employees in industrial enterprises. *Sustainability (Basel)*, *15*(17), 12886. DOI: 10.3390/su151712886

Ho, M. H. R., Uy, M. A., Kang, B. N., & Chan, K. Y. (2018). Impact of entrepreneurship training on entrepreneurial efficacy and alertness among adolescent youth. *Frontiers in Education*, *3*(13), 1–10. DOI: 10.3389/feduc.2018.00013

Hong, J.-C., Cheng, C.-L., Hwang, M.-Y., Lee, C.-K., & Chang, H.-Y. (2009). Assessing the educational values of digital games: Assessing the educational values. *Journal of Computer Assisted Learning*, *25*(5), 423–437. DOI: 10.1111/j.1365-2729.2009.00319.x

Hongyan, X. (2018). Construction and Practice of Virtual Simulation Experimental Teaching Platform for Economic Management. *Advances in Social Science, Education and Humanities Research, 264*.

Hooda, M., Rana, C., Dahiya, O., Rizwan, A., & Hossain, M. S. (2022). Artificial Intelligence for Assessment and Feedback to Enhance Student Success in Higher Education. *Mathematical Problems in Engineering*, *2022*, 1–19. DOI: 10.1155/2022/5215722

Horton, J., Macve, R., & Struyven, G. (2004). Qualitative research: experiences in using semi-structured interviews. In *The real life guide to accounting research* (pp. 339–357). Elsevier. DOI: 10.1016/B978-008043972-3/50022-0

Hsieh, H., & Maritz, A. (2023). A Study of the Impact of the Application of Digital Technology-Integrated Entrepreneurship Education on Entrepreneurship and Entrepreneurial Performance. *International Journal of Emerging Technologies in Learning*, *18*(20), 126–136. Advance online publication. DOI: 10.3991/ijet.v18i20.43907

Hsieh, Y.-J., & Wu, Y. J. (2019). Entrepreneurship through the platform strategy in the digital era: Insights and research opportunities. *Computers in Human Behavior*, *95*, 315–323. DOI: 10.1016/j.chb.2018.03.033

Hsu, C.-Y., & Wu, T.-T. (2023). Application of Business Simulation Games in Flipped Classrooms to Facilitate Student Engagement and Higher-Order Thinking Skills for Sustainable Learning Practices. *Sustainability (Basel), 15*(24), 16867. DOI: 10.3390/su152416867

Huang, C. (2021). The effects of experiential learning on creativity: A study of higher education. *Journal of Education and Training Studies*, *9*(1), 43–52.

Huang-Saad, A., Fay, J., & Sheridan, L. (2017). Closing the divide: Accelerating technology commercialization by catalyzing the university entrepreneurial ecosystem with I-Corps™. *The Journal of Technology Transfer*, *42*(6), 1466–1486.

Huang, Y.-M., Silitonga, L. M., & Wu, T.-T. (2022). Applying a business simulation game in a flipped classroom to enhance engagement, learning achievement, and higher-order thinking skills. *Computers & Education*, *183*(104494), 104494. DOI: 10.1016/j.compedu.2022.104494

Huang, Z., & Benyoucef, M. (2013). From e-commerce to social commerce: A close look at design features. *Electronic Commerce Research and Applications*, *12*(4), 246–259. DOI: 10.1016/j.elerap.2012.12.003

Huebscher, J., & Lendner, C. (2010). Effects of entrepreneurship simulation game seminars on entrepreneurs' and students' learning. *Journal of Small Business and Entrepreneurship*, *23*(4), 543–554. DOI: 10.1080/08276331.2010.10593500

Hühn, C., & Rausch, A. (2022). Collaboration and emotions during simulation-based learning in general management courses. *Studies in Educational Evaluation*, *73*, 101130. DOI: 10.1016/j.stueduc.2022.101130

Hui, A. N. N., Eason, M. S., Cheung, R. C. C., Lai, L. C. H., Lau, D., & Lam, T. (2021) The Relationships Among Simulation-Based Learning Creativity and the Learning Approach in Higher Education. In A. Hui & C. Wagner (Eds.), *Creative and Collaborative Learning through Immersion*. Creativity in the Twenty First Century. Springer. DOI: 10.1007/978-3-030-72216-6_6

Hunter, P. (2013). Research funding is not enough. Universities need more support for teaching and facility maintenance to stay fit for the future. *EMBO Reports*, *14*(2), 140–142. DOI: 10.1038/embor.2012.226 PMID: 23318630

Hurrell, S. A. (2016). Rethinking the soft skills deficit blame game: Employers, skills withdrawal and the reporting of soft skills gaps. *Human Relations*, *69*(3), 605–628. DOI: 10.1177/0018726715608001

Hutchins, E. (1995). How a cockpit remembers its speeds. *Cognitive Science*, *19*(3), 265–288. DOI: 10.1207/s15516709cog1903_1

Hutchins, E. (2020). The distributed cognition perspective on human interaction. In *Roots of human sociality* (pp. 375–398). Routledge. DOI: 10.4324/9781003135517-19

Hyams-Ssekasi, D., & Caldwell, E. F. (2018). An exploration of experiential education as a catalyst for future entrepreneurs. In Hyams-Ssekasi, D., & Caldwell, E. F. (Eds.), *Experiential learning for entrepreneurship: theoretical and practical perspectives on enterprise education* (pp. 71–83). Springer International Publishing. DOI: 10.1007/978-3-319-90005-6_4

Iakovleva, T., Kolvereid, L., & Stephan, U. (2020). Entrepreneurship and education in emerging economies. *Journal of Developmental Entrepreneurship*, *25*(4), 2050027.

Iandoli, L. (2023). Annual review article: The dual mindset of design-driven entrepreneurship: The case for a pedagogy of making and artefact-centred entrepreneurship education. *International Small Business Journal, 41*(4), 349–370. DOI: 10.1177/02662426231160525

Ibáñez, M.-B., & Delgado-Kloos, C. (2018). Augmented reality for STEM learning: A systematic review. *Computers & Education, 123*, 109–123. DOI: 10.1016/j.compedu.2018.05.002

Iborra, A., Álvarez, B., Sánchez, P., Pastor, J. A., & Suárez, T. (2016). ICT entrepreneurial ecosystem for engineering education. *International Journal of Engineering Education, 32*(5), 2033–2047.

Imran, M., Almusharraf, N., Abdellatif, M. S., & Abbasova, M. Y. (2024). Artificial Intelligence in Higher Education: Enhancing Learning Systems and Transforming Educational Paradigms. *International Journal of Interactive Mobile Technologies, 18*(18), 34–48. DOI: 10.3991/ijim.v18i18.49143

Ingram, K.W., & Jackson, M.K. (2004). Simulations as authentic learning strategies: Bridging the gap between theory and practice in performance technology. Academic Press.

Innerhofer, J., Nasta, L., & Zehrer, A. (2022). Antecedents of labor shortage in the rural hospitality industry: A comparative study of employees and employers. *Journal of Hospitality and Tourism Insights, 7*(1), 28–55. DOI: 10.1108/JHTI-04-2022-0125

Insight, E. (2023). *Business Simulation Games and Entrepreneurial Education*. Retrieved from Emerald Insight.

Ireland, R., & Webb, J. (2007). A Cross-Disciplinary Exploration of Entrepreneurship Research. *Journal of Management, 33*(6), 891–927. DOI: 10.1177/0149206307307643

Isaksen, S. G., & Ekvall, G. (2010). Managing for innovation: The importance of culture. *International Journal of Technology Management, 51*(1/2), 112–130.

Islam, M. A., Barna, S. D., Raihan, H., Khan, M. N. A., & Hossain, M. T. (2020). Depression and anxiety among university students during the COVID-19 pandemic in Bangladesh: A web-based crosssectional survey. *PLoS One, 15*(8), e0238162. DOI: 10.1371/journal.pone.0238162 PMID: 32845928

Ismail, I. J. (2022). My intentions, my choice! How does lecturers' competency influence entrepreneurial intention among undergraduate university students in Tanzania? *Cogent Education, 9*(1), 2151237. DOI: 10.1080/2331186X.2022.2151237

Issenberg, S. B. (2005). Features and uses of high-fidelity medical simulations that lead to effective learning: A BEME systematic review. *Medical Teacher, 27*(1), 1028. DOI: 10.1080/01421590500046924 PMID: 16147767

Ivcevic, Z., & Grandinetti, M. (2024). Artificial intelligence as a tool for creativity. *Journal of Creativity, 34*(2), 100079. DOI: 10.1016/j.yjoc.2024.100079

Jabo, B., & Kant, S. (2024). Impact of Technical CRM on Ethiopia Bank Human-Computer Interface and Competitive Advantage as Mediators of Performance. *2024 IEEE International Conference on Computing, Power and Communication Technologies (IC2PCT)*, 679-682. DOI: 10.1109/IC2PCT60090.2024.10486237

Janiesch, C., Zschech, P., & Heinrich, K. (2021). Machine learning and deep learning. *Electronic Markets, 31*(3), 685–695. DOI: 10.1007/s12525-021-00475-2

Jayawarna, D., Jones, O., & Macpherson, A. (2014). Entrepreneurial potential: The role of human and cultural capitals. *International Small Business Journal, 32*(8), 918–943. DOI: 10.1177/0266242614525795

Jehn, K. A. (1995). A multimethod examination of the benefits and detriments of intragroup conflict. *Administrative Science Quarterly, 40*(2), 256–282. DOI: 10.2307/2393638

Jena, R. K. (2020). Measuring the impact of business management Student's attitude towards entrepreneurship education on entrepreneurial intention: A case study. *Computers in Human Behavior, 107*, 106275. DOI: 10.1016/j.chb.2020.106275

Jeong, H. (2019). Rethinking Open Universities: What makes them unique? *International Review of Research in Open and Distance Learning, 20*(4), 152–166. DOI: 10.19173/irrodl.v20i4.4163

Jiwa, S., Lavelle, D., & Rose, A. (2005). E-entrepreneurship: Learning in a simulated environment. *Journal of Electronic Commerce in Organizations, 3*(3), 42–56. DOI: 10.4018/jeco.2005070103

Johnston, E., Olivas, G., Steele, P., Smith, C., & Bailey, L. (2018). Exploring pedagogical foundations of existing virtual reality educational applications: A content analysis study. *Journal of Educational Technology Systems, 46*(4), 414–439. DOI: 10.1177/0047239517745560

Jones, C. (2019). A signature pedagogy for entrepreneurship education. *Journal of Small Business and Enterprise Development, 26*(2), 243–254. Advance online publication. DOI: 10.1108/JSBED-03-2018-0080

Jones, P. (2024). Engaging With Lived Experience: Towards a Sociological Biography of a Sociological Category. *Sociological Research Online, 0*(0).

Jones, P., Apostolopoulos, N., Kakouris, A., Moon, C., Ratten, V., & Walmsley, A. (Eds.). (2021). *Universities and entrepreneurship: meeting the educational and social challenges*. Emerald Publishing Limited.

Jones, P., Jones, A., Williams-Burnett, N., & Ratten, V. (2017). Let's get physical: Stories of entrepreneurial activity from sports coaches/instructors. *International Journal of Entrepreneurship and Innovation, 18*(4), 219–230. DOI: 10.1177/1465750317741878

Jordan, K. (2014). Initial trends in enrolment and completion of massive open online courses. *International Review of Research in Open and Distance Learning, 15*(1), 133–160. DOI: 10.19173/irrodl.v15i1.1651

Jordan, T. (2020). *The Digital Economy*. Polity Press.

Jose, S. (2018). Strategic use of digital promotion strategies among female emigrant entrepreneurs in UAE. *International Journal of Emerging Markets, 13*(6), 1699–1718. DOI: 10.1108/IJoEM-10-2016-0268

Jossberger, H., Brand-Gruwel, S., van de Wiel, M. W. J., & Boshuizen, H. P. A. (2015). Teachers' Perceptions of Teaching in Workplace Simulations in Vocational Education. *Vocations and Learning, 8*(3), 287–318. DOI: 10.1007/s12186-015-9137-0

Justice, J., & Ritzhaupt, L. (2015). Identifying the barriers to games and simulations in education. *Journal of Educational Technology Systems, 44*(1), 86–125.

Kakouris, A., & Morselli, D. (2020). Addressing the pre/post-university pedagogy of entrepreneurship coherent with learning theories. Entrepreneurship education: A lifelong learning approach, 35-58.

Kakouris, A. (2017). *Constructivist entrepreneurial teaching: The telecc online approach in Greece.* Contemporary Issues in Entrepreneurship Research. DOI: 10.1108/S2040-724620170000007015

Kakouris, A., & Liargovas, P. (2021). On the about/for/through framework of entrepreneurship education: A critical analysis. *Entrepreneurship Education and Pedagogy*, *4*(3), 396–421.

Kakouris, A., Morselli, D., & Pittaway, L. (2023). Educational theory driven teaching in entrepreneurship. *International Journal of Management Education*, *21*(2), 100814.

Kalantari, S., Rounds, J. D., Kan, J., Tripathi, V., & Cruz-Garza, J. G. (2021). Comparing physiological responses during cognitive tests in virtual environments vs. in identical real-world environments. *Scientific Reports*, *11*(1), 10227. DOI: 10.1038/s41598-021-89297-y PMID: 33986337

Kallio, H., Pietilä, A. M., Johnson, M., & Kangasniemi, M. (2016). Systematic methodological review: Developing a framework for a qualitative semi-structured interview guide. *Journal of Advanced Nursing*, *72*(12), 2954–2965. PMID: 27221824

Kanematsu, H., Fukumura, Y., Barry, D. M., Sohn, S. Y., & Taguchi, R. (2010). Multilingual discussion in metaverse among students from the USA, Korea and Japan. *Knowledge-Based and Intelligent Information and Engineering Systems: 14th International Conference, KES 2010, Cardiff, UK, September 8-10, 2010Proceedings*, *14*(Part IV), 200–209.

Kant, S., & Adula, M. (2024). AI Learning and Work Attitude Mediation Between Reward and Organizational Support in Ethiopia. In Gomathi Sankar, J., & David, A. (Eds.), *Generative AI for Transformational Management* (pp. 109–136). IGI Global. DOI: 10.4018/979-8-3693-5578-7.ch005

Kant, S., & Adula, M. (2024). Human-Machine Interaction in the Metaverse in the Context of Ethiopia. In *Impact and Potential of Machine Learning in the Metaverse* (pp. 196–212). IGI Global. DOI: 10.4018/979-8-3693-5762-0.ch008

Kant, S., Adula, M., Kumari, M., & Nimbrain, N. (2025). Role of SMEs in Greening the Economy by Mediation of Eco-Innovation in the Horn of Africa. In *Examining Green Human Resources Management and Nascent Entrepreneurship* (pp. 173–200). IGI Global. DOI: 10.4018/979-8-3693-7046-9.ch007

Kaplan, A. M., & Haenlein, M. (2010). Users of the world, unite! The challenges and opportunities of Social Media. *Business Horizons*, *53*(1), 59–68. DOI: 10.1016/j.bushor.2009.09.003

Karagkouni, A., & Dimitriou, D. (2022). 'Sustainability Performance Appraisal for Airports Serving Tourist Islands'. *Sustainability (Basel)*, *14*(20), 13363. DOI: 10.3390/su142013363

Karakaş, Ö. (2024). The Persistence of Gender Inequality in e-Science: The Case of eSec. *Minerva*, *62*(4), 611–634. Advance online publication. DOI: 10.1007/s11024-024-09530-6

Karanassios, N., Pazarskis, M., Mitsopoulos, K., & Christodoulou, P. (2006). EU strategies to encourage youth entrepreneurship: Evidence from higher education in Greece. *Industry and Higher Education*, *20*(1), 43–50. DOI: 10.5367/000000006776150747

Karatas-Ozkan, M., Anderson, A., Fayolle, A., Howells, J., & Condor, R. (2014). Understanding entrepreneurship: Challenging dominant perspectives and theorising entrepreneurship through new post-positivist epistemologies. *Journal of Small Business Management*, *52*(4), 589–593.

Kassean, H., Vanevenhoven, J., Liguori, E. W., & Winkel, D. (2015). Entrepreneurship education: A need for reflection, real-world experience and action. *International Journal of Entrepreneurial Behaviour & Research*, *21*(5), 690–708. DOI: 10.1108/IJEBR-07-2014-0123

Katsande, C., Chigora, F., Mutipforo, G., & Marime, S. 2024. Redefining Social Media through Agritourism Business Marketing. In *Agritourism for Sustainable Development: Reflections from Emerging African Economies* (pp. 47-61). CABI. DOI: 10.1079/9781800623705.0004

Kaufman, J. C., Beghetto, R. A., & Roberts, A. M. (2022). Creativity in the schools: Creativity models and new directions. In *Handbook of positive psychology in schools* (pp. 335–345). Routledge.

Kaya, T., Erkut, B., & Thierbach, N. (2019). Entrepreneurial intentions of business and economics students in Germany and Cyprus: A cross-cultural comparison. *Sustainability (Basel)*, *11*(5), 1437. DOI: 10.3390/su11051437

Ke, F. (2019). Mathematical problem solving and learning in an architecture-themed epistemic game. *Educational Technology Research and Development. Educational Technology Research and Development*, *67*(5), 1085–1104. DOI: 10.1007/s11423-018-09643-2

Ke, F., & Xu, X. (2020). Virtual reality simulation-based learning of teaching with alternative perspectives taking. *British Journal of Educational Technology*, *51*(6), 2544–2557. DOI: 10.1111/bjet.12936

Kelley, D. J., & Thomas, B. (2011). *Entrepreneurship education: Learning by doing*. Edward Elgar Publishing.

Khalfallah, J., & Slama, J. B. H. (2018). The effect of emotional analysis on the improvement of experimental e-learning systems. *Computer Applications in Engineering Education*, *27*(2), 303–318. DOI: 10.1002/cae.22075

Khalifa, M., & Albadawy, M. (2024). Using Artificial Intelligence in Academic Writing and Research: An Essential Productivity Tool. *Computer Methods and Programs in Biomedicine Update*, *5*, 100145. DOI: 10.1016/j.cmpbup.2024.100145

Khanduri, V., & Teotia, D. A. (2023). Revolutionizing learning: An exploratory study on the impact of technology-enhanced learning using digital learning platforms and AI tools on the study habits of university students through focus group discussions. *International Journal of Research Publication and Reviews*, *4*(6), 663–672. DOI: 10.55248/gengpi.4.623.44407

Khoshtaria, T., Matin, A., Komodromos, M., & Kikutadze, V. (2024). The Impact of Word- of-Mouth Communication on Consumer Choices and Satisfaction: An Empirical Study of Students' Perspective. International Journal of Marketing. *Communication and New Media*, *12*(22), 6–33. DOI: 10.54663/2182-9306.2024

Kiat, T. Y., Jumintono, J., Kriswanto, E. S., Sugiri, S., Handayani, E., Anggarini, Y., & Rofik, M. (2020). The effectiveness of multimedia learning on academic achievement in reproduction topic science subject. *Universal Journal of Educational Research*, *8*(8), 3625–3629. DOI: 10.13189/ujer.2020.080839

Kickul, J., Gundry, L., Mitra, P., & Berçot, L. (2018). Designing With Purpose: Advocating Innovation, Impact, Sustainability, and Scale in Social Entrepreneurship Education. *Entrepreneurship Education and Pedagogy*, *1*(2), 205–221. DOI: 10.1177/2515127418772177

Kijkasiwat, P., Cave, J., Wellalage, N. H., & Locke, S. (2024). Forecasting symbiosis in tourism enterprise networks: Monte Carlo simulation of risk and return. *International Journal of Services Economics and Management*, *15*(1), 63–83. DOI: 10.1504/IJSEM.2024.136056

Kim, B., Suh, H., Heo, J., & Choi, Y. (2020). AI-Driven Interface Design for Intelligent Tutoring System Improves Student Engagement. *arXiv (Cornell University)*. /arxiv.2009.08976DOI: 10.48550

Kim, J., Park, M., & Shin, D. (2006). Case-based reasoning and simulation for decision support. *Expert Systems with Applications*, *30*(3), 484–492.

Kim, N., Belland, B., & Walker, A. (2018). Effectiveness of Computer-Based Scaffolding in the Context of Problem-Based Learning for Stem Education: Bayesian Meta-analysis. *Educational Psychology Review*, *30*(2), 397–429. DOI: 10.1007/s10648-017-9419-1

Kim, T., Planey, J., & Lindgren, R. (2023). Theory-Driven Design in Metaverse Virtual Reality Learning Environments: Two Illustrative Cases. *IEEE Transactions on Learning Technologies*, *16*(6), 1141–1153. DOI: 10.1109/TLT.2023.3307211

Kinkel, S., Schemmann, B., & Lichtner, R. (2017). Critical competencies for the innovativeness of value creation champions: Identifying challenges and work-integrated solutions. *Procedia Manufacturing*, *9*, 323–330. DOI: 10.1016/j.promfg.2017.04.005

Kirkman, B., Lowe, K., & Gibson, C. (2006). A Quarter Century of Culture's Consequences: A Review of Empirical Research Incorporating Hofstede's Cultural Values Framework. *Journal of International Business Studies*, *37*(3), 285–320. DOI: 10.1057/palgrave.jibs.8400202

Kirriemuir, J., & McFarlane, A. (2004). Games and learning. Futurelab Literature Review. Available at: www.futurelab.org.uk/resources/publications-reports-articles/literature reviews/Literature-Review378

Kirsh, D. (2013). Embodied cognition and the magical future of interaction design. *ACM Transactions on Computer-Human Interaction*, *20*(1), 1–30. DOI: 10.1145/2442106.2442109

Kirzner, I. M. (1973). *Competition and Entrepreneurship*. University of Chicago Press.

Kiyomi, A., Bayoumi, K. A., Din, N. S. E., Abuhassna, H., & Ali, E. A. (2022). Bibliometric analysis of entrepreneurship education research from 2012 to 2022. *International Journal of Academic Research in Business & Social Sciences*, *12*(11). Advance online publication. DOI: 10.6007/IJARBSS/v12-i11/15646

Klapper, R. G., & Fayolle, A. (2023). *A transformational learning framework for sustainable entrepreneurship education: The power of Paulo Freire's educational model. International Journal of Management Education (Elsevier Science), 21(1).*

Kleckner, M. J., & Marshall, C. R. (2014). Critical communication skills: Developing course competencies to meet workforce needs. *Journal for Research in Business Education, 56*(2), 59–81.

Kleibeuker, S. W., De Dreu, C. K. W., & Crone, E. A. (2016). The role of cognitive flexibility in creative thinking: Evidence from a multi-method approach. *Psychological Science, 27*(3), 366–373.

Kleij, F., Feskens, R., & Eggen, T. (2013). Effects of Feedback in a Computer-Based Learning Environment on Students' Learning Outcomes. *Review of Educational Research, 85*(4), 475–511. DOI: 10.3102/0034654314564881

Kloch, C., Petersen, E. B., & Madsen, O. B. (2011). Cloud based infrastructure, the new business possibilities and barriers. *Wireless Personal Communications, 58*, 17–30.

Klofsten, M., Jones-Evans, D., & Pereira, L. (2020). Teaching science and technology PhD students in entrepreneurship-Potential learning opportunities and outcomes. *The Journal of Technology Transfer, 46*(2), 319–334. DOI: 10.1007/s10961-020-09784-8

Klofsten, M., Urbano, D., & Heaton, S. (2019). Developing entrepreneurial competencies through education. *Journal of Small Business Management, 57*(S2), 500–513.

Kolb, D. A. (1984). Experiential learning: Experience as the source of learning and development, David A. Kolb, Prentice-Hall International, Hemel Hempstead, Herts., 1984. No. of pages: xiii + 256. *Journal of Organizational Behavior.*

Kolb, D. A. (2014). *Experiential learning: Experience as the source of learning and development.* FT Press.

Kolb, D. A., & Fry, R. E. (1974). Toward an Applied Theory of Experiential Learning. *Theories of Group Process.*

Kolb, A., & Kolb, D. (2009). Experiential learning theory: a dynamic, holistic approach to management learning, education and development. In Armstrong, S. J., & Fukami, C. V. (Eds.), *The SAGE Handbook of Management Learning, Education and Development* (pp. 42–68). SAGE., DOI: 10.4135/9780857021038.n3

Kolb, D. A. (1984). *Experiential learning: experience as the source of learning and development / David A. Kolb.* Prentice-Hall.

Kolb, D. A. (1984). *Experiential Learning: Experience as the Source of Learning and Development. Englewood Cliffs.* Prentice-Hall.

Kolb, D. A. (1984). *Experiential learning: Experience as the source of learning and development.* Prentice Hall.

Kolb, D. A. (1984). *Experiential Learning: Experience as the Source of Learning and Development.* Prentice Hall.

Kollmann, T. (2006). What is e-entrepreneurship? Fundamentals of company founding in the net economy. *International Journal of Technology Management, 33*(4), 322–340. DOI: 10.1504/IJTM.2006.009247

Komodromos, M. (2021). *Innovative Learning and Education Practices in European Universities: A Pathway to Modern Pedagogy*. Ktoridou (Ed.), *Cases on Engineering Management Education in Practice* (63-90). IGI Global.

Komodromos, M., Harkiolakis, T., Khoshtaria, T., & Vassiliou, M. (2024). Adoption of digital technology and investigation of the impact in the marketing industry for marketing communication professionals: The case study of Cyprus and Greece. *International Journal of Technology Enhanced Learning*, *16*(2), 173–191. DOI: 10.1504/IJTEL.2024.137650

Kondaveeti, H. K., Kumaravelu, N. K., Vanambathina, S. D., Mathe, S. E., & Vappangi, S. (2021). A systematic literature review on prototyping with Arduino: Applications, challenges, advantages, and limitations. *Computer Science Review*, *40*, 100364. DOI: 10.1016/j.cosrev.2021.100364

Kostenetskiy, P. S., Chulkevich, R. A., & Kozyrev, V. I. (2021). HPC resources of the higher school of economics. *Journal of Physics: Conference Series*, *1740*(1), 012050. DOI: 10.1088/1742-6596/1740/1/012050

Kotler, P., & Keller, K. L. (2007). *A Framework for Marketing Management* (3rd ed.). Prentice Hall.

Kountouridou, M., & Dino Domic, . (2022a). Reconditioning the Freshman Gene: Can a 'Positive Visualisation Course' Successfully modify Freshmen Students' Perceptions of a University's Brand Image? *Transnational Marketing Journal*, *10*(2), 203–214. DOI: 10.33182/tmj.v10i2.1988

Kountouridou, M., & Domic, D. (2022b). 'The Impact of a Positive Visualisation Course in Brand Identity on Freshmen Students' Perceptions of University Brand Image'. *Interdisciplinary Journal of Management Studies*, *15*(4), 945–962. DOI: 10.22059/ijms.2022.326021.674612

Kourkoumelis, A., Anastasopoulou, E., Deirmentzoglou, G., Masouras, A., & Anastasiadou, S. (2024). Artificial Intelligence and Managerial Decision-Making in International Business. In *Proceedings of The 19th European Conference on Innovation and Entrepreneurship*. Academic Conferences International. DOI: 10.34190/ecie.19.1.2573

Kovid, R. K., Rana, S., & Omrane, A. (2022). The promise of entrepreneurship and innovation as a strategic response to global turmoils. *FIIB Business Review*, *11*(1), 7–10.

Kozlowski, S. W. J., & Bell, B. S. (2007). A theory-based approach for designing distributed learning systems. In Fiore, S. M., & Salas, E. (Eds.), *Toward a science of distributed learning* (pp. 15–39). APA. DOI: 10.1037/11582-002

Krakauer, P. V. C., Serra, F. A. R., & de Almeida, M. I. R. (2017). Using experiential learning to teach entrepreneurship: A study with Brazilian undergraduate students. *International Journal of Educational Management*, *31*(7), 986–999. DOI: 10.1108/IJEM-09-2016-0189

Kratochvil, T., Vaculik, M., & Macak, M. (2023). Gamification tailored for novelty effect in distance learning during COVID-19. *Frontiers in Education*, *8*, 1051227. Advance online publication. DOI: 10.3389/feduc.2023.1051227

Kraus, M., Feuerriegel, S., & Oztekin, A. (2020). Deep learning in business analytics and operations research: Models, applications and managerial implications. *European Journal of Operational Research*, *281*(3), 628–641. DOI: 10.1016/j.ejor.2019.09.018

Kraus, S., Bouncken, R. B., & Aránega, A. Y. (2024). The burgeoning role of literature review articles in management research: An introduction and outlook. *Review of Managerial Science, 18*(2), 299–314. DOI: 10.1007/s11846-024-00729-1

Kraus, S., Burtscher, J., Vallaster, C., & Angerer, M. (2019). Sustainable Entrepreneurship Orientation: A Reflection on Status-Quo Research and Future Research Directions. *Journal of Cleaner Production, 235*, 1336–1350.

Kraus, S., Kanbach, D. K., Krysta, P. M., Steinhoff, M. M., & Tomini, N. (2022). Facebook and the creation of the metaverse: Radical business model innovation or incremental transformation? *International Journal of Entrepreneurial Behaviour & Research, 28*(9), 52–77. DOI: 10.1108/IJEBR-12-2021-0984

Kraus, S., Palmer, C., Kailer, N., Kallinger, F. L., & Spitzer, J. (2019). Digital entrepreneurship: A research agenda on new business models for the twenty-first century. *International Journal of Entrepreneurial Behaviour & Research, 25*(2), 353–375.

Krauss, J., Reschke, C., & Hartmann, C. (2020). The role of self-efficacy in entrepreneurship education: Evidence from Germany. *Education + Training, 62*(4), 455–473.

Kremel, A., & Edman, K.W. (2019). Implementing design thinking as didactic method in entrepreneurship education. The importance of through. *The Design Journal*, 22(sup1), 163-175. .DOI: 10.1080/14606925.2019.1595855

Krippendorff, K. (2018). *Content Analysis: An Introduction to its Methodology*. Sage Publications.

Krippendorff, K. (2018). *Content Analysis: An Introduction to Its Methodology*. Sage Publications.

Kritzinger, W. T., & Weideman, M. (2013). Search engine optimization and pay-per-click marketing strategies. *Journal of Organizational Computing and Electronic Commerce, 23*(3), 273–286. DOI: 10.1080/10919392.2013.808124

Kriz, W. C., & Auchter, E. (2016). 10 Years of Evaluation Research Into Gaming Simulation for German Entrepreneurship and a New Study on Its Long-Term Effects. *Simulation & Gaming, 47*(2), 179–205. DOI: 10.1177/1046878116633972

Król, K. (2019). Forgotten agritourism: Abandoned websites in the promotion of rural tourism in Poland. *Journal of Hospitality and Tourism Technology, 10*(3), 431–442. DOI: 10.1108/JHTT-09-2018-0092

Kuckertz, A., & Wagner, M. (2010). The influence of sustainability orientation on entrepreneurial intentions: Investigating the role of business experience. *Journal of Business Venturing, 25*(5), 524–539. DOI: 10.1016/j.jbusvent.2009.09.001

Kudła, J., Stachowiak-Kudła, M., & Figurski, A. (2014). The impact of funding on the quality of public higher education in Poland. SSRN *Electronic Journal*. DOI: 10.2139/ssrn.2537075

Ku, E. C., & Chen, C. (2024). Artificial intelligence innovation of tourism businesses: From satisfied tourists to continued service usage intention. *International Journal of Information Management, 76*, 102757. DOI: 10.1016/j.ijinfomgt.2024.102757

Kulik, J. A., & Fletcher, J. D. (2016). Effectiveness of Intelligent Tutoring Systems: A Meta-Analytic Review. *Review of Educational Research*, *86*(1), 42–78. DOI: 10.3102/0034654315581420

Kumar, N., & Benbasat, I. (2006). Research note: The influence of recommendations and consumer reviews on evaluations of websites. *Information Systems Research*, *17*(4), 425–439. DOI: 10.1287/isre.1060.0107

Kumar, S., & Gupta, S. (2021). The impact of digital skills on innovation: A study of small and medium-sized enterprises. *Journal of Small Business Management*, *59*(1), 142–165.

Kuratko, D. (2005). The Emergence of Entrepreneurship Education: Development, Trends, and Challenges. *Entrepreneurship Theory and Practice*, *29*(5), 577–597. DOI: 10.1111/j.1540-6520.2005.00099.x

Kuratko, D. F. (2020). *Entrepreneurship: Theory, Process, and Practice*. Cengage Learning.

Kuratko, D. F., & Morris, M. H. (2018). Examining the future trajectory of entrepreneurship education. *Journal of Small Business Management*, *56*(1), 11–23. DOI: 10.1111/jsbm.12364

Kurbjuhn, B., Kramer, F., & Turowski, K. (2014). Challenges for cloud-based simulation games. *Proceeding of the 47th Hawaii International Conference on System Sciences*. DOI: 10.1109/HICSS.2014.162

Kurotimi, M., Franklin, A., Aladei, G., & Helen, O. (2017). Entrepreneurship Education as a 21st Century Strategy for Economic Growth and Sustainable Development. World Academy of Science, Engineering and Technology, International Journal of Social, Behavioral, Educational, Economic. *Business and Industrial Engineering*, *11*, 2242–2253.

Kuruczleki, E., Pelle, A., Laczi, R., & Fekete, B. (2012). The readiness of the European Union to embrace the fourth industrial revolution. *Journal Title*, *11*, 327–347.

Kutz, J. N., Brunton, S. L., Brunton, B. W., & Proctor, J. L. (2016). *Dynamic mode decomposition: data-driven modeling of complex systems*. Society for Industrial and Applied Mathematics., DOI: 10.1137/1.9781611974508

Kwon, C. (2019). Verification of the possibility and effectiveness of experiential learning using HMD-based immersive VR technologies. *Virtual Reality (Waltham Cross)*, *23*(1), 101–118. DOI: 10.1007/s10055-018-0364-1

Lacatus, M., & Stăiculescu, C. (2016). Entrepreneurship in Education. International conference Knowledge-Based Organization, 22, 438 - 443. DOI: 10.1515/kbo-2016-0075

Lackéus, M. (2020). Comparing the impact of three different experiential approaches to entrepreneurship in education. *International Journal of Entrepreneurial Behaviour & Research*, *26*(5), 937–971. DOI: 10.1108/IJEBR-04-2018-0236

Lai, F.-Y., Tang, H.-C., Lu, S.-C., Lee, Y.-C., & Lin, C.-C. (2020). Transformational leadership and job performance: The mediating role of work engagement. *SAGE Open*, *10*(1), 1–12. DOI: 10.1177/2158244019899085

Laine, K. (2010). Fostering Innovation in Collaboration between Higher Education and Industry. A Systemic Model Based on Case Study. Academic Press.

Lalisan, A. K., Fresnido, M. B. R., Ramli, H. R., Aung, A., Utama, A. A. G. S., & Ating, R. (2024, July). Empowering the ASEAN Community through Digitalization of Agriculture for Rural Tourism Development: An NVIVO Analysis. *IOP Conference Series. Earth and Environmental Science*, *1366*(1), 012018. DOI: 10.1088/1755-1315/1366/1/012018

Lamie, R. D., Chase, L., Chiodo, E., Dickes, L., Flanigan, S., Schmidt, C., & Streifeneder, T. (2021). Agritourism around the globe: Definitions, authenticity, and potential controversy. *Journal of Agriculture, Food Systems, and Community Development*, *10*(2), 573–577. DOI: 10.5304/jafscd.2021.102.002

Land, S., & Jonassen, D. (2012). *Theoretical foundations of learning environments*. Routledge. DOI: 10.4324/9780203813799

Lane, B. (2009). Rural tourism: An overview. Academic Press.

Lans, T., Blok, V., & Wesselink, R. (2014). Learning apart and together: Towards an integrated competence framework for sustainable entrepreneurship in higher education. *Journal of Cleaner Production*, *62*, 37–47. DOI: 10.1016/j.jclepro.2013.03.036

Larios-Hernandez, G., Walmsley, A., & Lopez-Castro, I. (Eds.). (2022). *Theorising Undergraduate Entrepreneurship Education. Reflections on the Development of the Entrepreneurial Mindset*. Palgrave MacMillan. DOI: 10.1007/978-3-030-87865-8

Larkin, M. (2014). Building successful partnerships between academia and industry. Elsevier Connect. Retrieved from https://www.elsevier.com/connect

Larreche, J.-C. (2001). *Markstrat: A Marketing Strategy Simulation*. StratX International.

Lattacher, W., & Wdowiak, M. A. (2020). Entrepreneurial learning from failure. A systematic review. *International Journal of Entrepreneurial Behaviour & Research*, *26*(5), 1093–1131. DOI: 10.1108/IJEBR-02-2019-0085

Lave, J., & Wenger, E. (1991). *Situated learning: Legitimate peripheral participation*. Cambridge University Press. DOI: 10.1017/CBO9780511815355

Lavía, C., Otero, B., Albizu, E., & Olazaran, M. (2021). Exploring the Intensity of Relationships with Vocational Education Centres: A Typology of Spanish SMEs. *Sustainability (Basel)*, *13*(16), 9287. DOI: 10.3390/su13169287

Lawton, A., & Gabriunas, I. (2014). Developing a framework for ethical leadership. *Journal of Business Ethics*, *130*(3), 639–651. DOI: 10.1007/s10551-014-2244-2

Le Breton-Miller, I., & Miller, D. (2020). Ideals-Based Accountability and Reputation in Select Family Firms. Journal of Business Ethics, 163(2), 183-196. DOI: 10.1007/s10551-019-04225-5

Leal, L., Ribeiro, A., Romão, V., Amaral, G., Altmann, R., Kahn, R., Pacci, B., Avó, M., Salerno, M., Plonski, G., & Zancul, E. (2021). R&D approach based on multiple partners and Design Thinking, Lean Startup, and Agile concepts: case study in the electricity sector. .DOI: 10.14488/BJOPM.2021.003

Lean, J., Moizer, J., Towler, M., & Abbey, C. (2006). Simulation and games: Use and barriers in higher education. *Active Learning in Higher Education*, *7*(3), 227–242. DOI: 10.1177/1469787406069056

Lean, J., Moizer, J., Towler, M., & Abbey, C. (2006). Simulations and games: Use and barriers in higher education. *Active Learning in Higher Education, 7*(3), 227–242.

Lee, K., Nguyen, A. T., Nguyen, N. P., Nguyen, T. H., Tran, N., Nguyen, T. L., & Vu, T. T. (2024). Determinants of agritourism development in green tea farms of the northern mountains of Vietnam. *Multidisciplinary Science Journal, 6*(4).

Lee, A., Willis, S., & Tian, A. W. (2018). Empowering leadership: A meta-analytic examination of incremental contribution, mediation, and moderation. *Journal of Organizational Behavior, 39*(3), 306–325. DOI: 10.1002/job.2205

Lee, D., Arnold, M., Srivastava, A., Plastow, K., Strelan, P., Ploeckl, F., Lekkas, D., & Palmer, E. (2024). The impact of generative AI on higher education learning and teaching: A study of educators' perspectives. *Computers and Education Artificial Intelligence, 6*, 100221. DOI: 10.1016/j.caeai.2024.100221

Lee, I. (2016). *Encyclopedia of E-Commerce Development, Implementation, and Management*. IGI Global. DOI: 10.4018/978-1-4666-9787-4

Lee, J., Kao, H. A., & Yang, S. (2014). Service innovation and smart analytics for Industry 4.0 and big data environment. *Procedia CIRP, 16*(1), 3–8. DOI: 10.1016/j.procir.2014.02.001

Lee, M., Liang, P., & Yang, Q. (2022). CoAuthor: Designing a Human-AI Collaborative Writing Dataset for Exploring Language Model Capabilities. *CHI Conference on Human Factors in Computing Systems*. DOI: 10.1145/3491102.3502030

Lee, Y. E., & Benbasat, I. (2004). A framework for the study of customer interface design for mobile commerce. *International Journal of Electronic Commerce, 8*(3), 79–102. DOI: 10.1080/10864415.2004.11044299

Lee, Y. J., Davis, R. O., & Ryu, J. (2024). Korean in-Service Teachers' Perceptions of Implementing Artificial Intelligence (AI) Education for Teaching in Schools and Their AI Teacher Training Programs. *International Journal of Information and Education Technology (IJIET), 14*(2), 214–219. DOI: 10.18178/ijiet.2024.14.2.2042

Lee, Y. L., & Tee, M. Y. (2021). Facilitator's Scaffolding Strategies in a Design-based Learning Context. *Journal of Social Sciences and Humanities, 5*(2), 15–33.

Lefrid, M., Cavusoglu, M., Richardson, S., & Donnelly, C. (2023). Simulation-Based Learning Acceptance Model (SBL-AM): Expanding the Technology Acceptance Model (TAM) into Hospitality Education. *Journal of Hospitality & Tourism Education*, 1–15. DOI: 10.1080/10963758.2023.2188217

LeGary, R. A.Jr, & LaRocco, D. J. (2022). Job-embedded professional learning: Facilitating faculty implementation of UDL. *New Directions for Teaching and Learning, 2022*(172), 93–103. DOI: 10.1002/tl.20521

Lehikko, A. (2021). Measuring self-efficacy in immersive virtual learning environments: A systematic literature review. *Journal of Interactive Learning Research, 32*(2), 125–146.

Lehner, O. M., Grabmann, E., & Ennsgraber, C. (2015). Entrepreneurial implications of crowdfunding as alternative funding source for innovations. *Venture Capital, 17*(1-2), 171–189. DOI: 10.1080/13691066.2015.1037132

Lei, J., Hock, O., & Karim, A. (2021). Exploration of Entrepreneurship Education and Innovative Talent Training Model: New Economic Perspective. *International Journal of Academic Research in Business & Social Sciences*, *11*(11). Advance online publication. DOI: 10.6007/IJARBSS/v11-i11/11319

Lemos, S. I. C., Ferreira, F. F., Zopounidis, C., Galariotis, E., & Ferreira, N. C. M. Q. F. (2022). Artificial intelligence and change management in small and medium-sized enterprises: An analysis of dynamics within adaptation initiatives. *Annals of Operations Research*. Advance online publication. DOI: 10.1007/s10479-022-05159-4 PMID: 36597501

Leung, D., Law, R., Van Hoof, H., & Buhalis, D. (2013). Social media in tourism and hospitality: A literature review. *Journal of Travel & Tourism Marketing*, *30*(1-2), 3–22. DOI: 10.1080/10548408.2013.750919

Lévesque, M., Obschonka, M., & Nambisan, S. (2020). Pursuing Impactful Entrepreneurship Research Using Artificial Intelligence. *Entrepreneurship Theory and Practice*, *46*(4), 803–832. DOI: 10.1177/1042258720927369

Levie, J. (2014). Entrepreneurial innovation: The importance of narratives in the commercialization of technology. *Journal of Business Research*, *67*(8), 1644–1650.

Lewandowski, W. E. (2019). *Assessing and Planning for Simulation Implementation: An Approach to Instructional Design to Meet Organizational Needs*. Academic Press.

Liang, P., Bommasani, R., Lee, T., Tsipras, D., Soylu, D., Yasunaga, M., Zhang, Y., & Narayanan, D.. (2022). *Holistic evaluation of language models*. Arxiv.

Lichtenstein, B. M., & Brush, C. (2019). How entrepreneurship education shapes students' attitudes towards risk and uncertainty. *Entrepreneurship Theory and Practice*, *43*(3), 511–534.

Licorish, S. A., Owen, H. E., Daniel, B., & George, J. L. (2018). Students' perception of Kahoot!'s influence on teaching and learning. *Research and Practice in Technology Enhanced Learning*, *13*(1), 9. Advance online publication. DOI: 10.1186/s41039-018-0078-8

Liguori, E., & Winkler, C. (2020). From offline to online: Challenges and opportunities for entrepreneurship education following the COVID-19 pandemic. *Entrepreneurship Education and Pedagogy*, *3*(4), 346–351. DOI: 10.1177/2515127420916738

Liguori, E., Winkler, C., Neck, H., & Terjesen, S. (2019). Editorial: Special Issue on Entrepreneurship Education. *Journal of Small Business Management*, *57*(sup1, S1), 4–5. DOI: 10.1111/jsbm.12542

Li, J., & Pilz, M. (2021). International transfer of vocational education and training: A literature review. *Journal of Vocational Education and Training*, *75*(2), 185–218. DOI: 10.1080/13636820.2020.1847566

Li, J., Xue, E., Wei, Y., & He, Y. (2024). How popularising higher education affects economic growth and poverty alleviation: Empirical evidence from 38 countries. *Humanities & Social Sciences Communications*, *11*(1), 520. DOI: 10.1057/s41599-024-03013-5

Lim, D., Oh, C., & Clercq, D. (2016). Engagement in entrepreneurship in emerging economies: Interactive effects of individual-level factors and institutional conditions. *International Business Review*, *25*(4), 933–945. DOI: 10.1016/j.ibusrev.2015.12.001

Limone, P., Ragni, B., & Toto, G. A. (2023). The epidemiology and effects of video game addiction: A systematic review and meta-analysis. *Acta Psychologica*, *241*(104047), 104047. DOI: 10.1016/j.actpsy.2023.104047 PMID: 37897856

Lin, C., Huang, A. Y. Q., & Lu, O. H. T. (2023). Artificial intelligence in intelligent tutoring systems toward sustainable education: A systematic review. *Smart Learning Environments*, *10*(1), 41. Advance online publication. DOI: 10.1186/s40561-023-00260-y

Lin, H., Wan, S., Gan, W., Chen, J., & Chao, H.-C. (2022). *Metaverse in Education: Vision, Opportunities, and Challenges*. DOI: 10.1109/BigData55660.2022.10021004

Lin, Y., Chen, S., Tsai, C., & Lai, Y. (2021). Exploring Computational Thinking Skills Training Through Augmented Reality and AIoT Learning. *Frontiers in Psychology*, *12*, 640115. Advance online publication. DOI: 10.3389/fpsyg.2021.640115 PMID: 33708166

Lin, Y.-L., Lin, H.-W., & Yang, Y.-T. (2017). Players' value structure in digital games. *Games and Culture*, *12*(1), 72–99. DOI: 10.1177/1555412015581710

Liu, H., Ma, H., Meng, Q.-C., Fan, S.-S., & Dang, Z.-H. (2018). Reform and practice of electronic system design course based on CDIO educational philosophy. *DEStech Transactions on Social Science Education and Human Science, icss*. DOI: 10.12783/dtssehs/icss2017/19446

Liu, B., Zhu, W., Cao, Y., Liu, Y., & Sun, Y. (2018). Application of Virtual Reality Teaching Method in Combination with Practical Teaching Method in the Undergraduate Teaching of Colleges-Taking the Course of Rolling Technology as an Example. In *2018 International Conference on Social Science and Education Reform (ICSSER 2018)* (pp. 280-284). Atlantis Press.

Liu, F., Ma, J., & Li, R. (2019). Which role model is more effective in entrepreneurship education? An investigation of storytelling on Individual's entrepreneurial intention. *Frontiers in Psychology*, *10*, 837. [REMOVED HYPERLINK FIELD]DOI: 10.3389/fpsyg.2019.00837 PMID: 31068853

Liu, P., & Bell, R. (2019). Exploration of the initiation and process of business model innovation of successful Chinese ICT enterprises. *Journal of Entrepreneurship in Emerging Economies*, *11*(4), 515–536. DOI: 10.1108/JEEE-09-2018-0094

Liu, X., Sha, Y., & Yu, X. (2022). The Impact of Developmental HR Practices on Career Self-Management and Organizational Citizenship Behavior: A Moderated Mediation Model. *Psychology Research and Behavior Management*, *15*, 1193–1208. DOI: 10.2147/PRBM.S355376 PMID: 35586698

Liu, Y., Keller, R. T., & Shih, H.-A. (2011). The impact of team-member exchange, differentiation, team commitment, and knowledge sharing on R&D project team performance. *R & D Management*, *41*(3), 274–287.

Li, Y. M., & Yeh, Y. S. (2010). Increasing trust in mobile commerce through design aesthetics. *Computers in Human Behavior*, *26*(4), 673–684. DOI: 10.1016/j.chb.2010.01.004

Li, Y., Shen, W., & Lv, Y. (2020). Quality evaluation of entrepreneurship education in Chinese medical colleges–From the perspective of student cognition. *Frontiers in Psychology*, *11*, 1093. Advance online publication. [REMOVED HYPERLINK FIELD]DOI: 10.3389/fpsyg.2020.01093 PMID: 32625132

Lloyd, R., Martin, M. J., Hyatt, J., & Tritt, A. (2019). A cold call on work-based learning: A "live" group project for the strategic selling classroom. *Higher Education. Skills & Work-Based Learning*, *9*(3), 329–346. DOI: 10.1108/HESWBL-12-2017-0098

Lo Iacono, V., Symonds, P., & Brown, D. H. (2016). Skype as a tool for qualitative research interviews. *Sociological Research Online*, *21*(2), 103–117. DOI: 10.5153/sro.3952

Lobinger, K., & Mele, E. (2021). Visual Methods and Visual Analysis in Tourism Research. In Springer eBooks (pp. 1–28). DOI: 10.1007/978-3-030-05324-6_54-1

Longenecker, J. G., Petty, J. W., Palich, L. E., & Hoy, F. (2019). *Small Business Management: Launching and Growing Entrepreneurial Ventures* (19th ed.). Cengage.

Longva, K. K., & Foss, L. (2018). Measuring impact through experimental design in entrepreneurship education: A literature review and research agenda. *Industry and Higher Education*, *32*(6), 358–374. DOI: 10.1177/0950422218804912

Loon, M., Evans, J., & Kerridge, C. (2015). Learning with a strategic management simulation game: A case study. *International Journal of Management Education*, *13*(3), 227–236. DOI: 10.1016/j.ijme.2015.06.002

López, M. M. L. (2020). Project-based learning strategy: An innovative proposal for local education system. *International Journal of Psychosocial Rehabilitation*, *24*(1), 1666–1681. DOI: 10.37200/IJPR/V24I1/PR200267

Lourenço, F., Jones, O., & Jayawarna, D. (2012). Promoting sustainable development: The role of entrepreneurship education. *International Small Business Journal*, *31*(8), 841–865. DOI: 10.1177/0266242611435825

Lowden, K., Hall, S., Elliot, D., &Lewin, J. (2011). A report on employers' perceptions of the employability skills of new graduates. SCRE Centre at the University of Glasgow. SCRE Centre Report.

Low, M., Venkataraman, S., & Srivatsan, V. (1994). Developing an Entrepreneurship Game for Teaching and Research. *Simulation & Gaming*, *25*(3), 383–401. DOI: 10.1177/1046878194253006

Lubart, T. I., Zenasni, F., Barbot, B., & Botella, M. (2015). *The Creativity Maze: Implications for Teaching and Learning*. Creativity and Learning: A Theoretical Perspective, 17(4), 307-320.

Luckin, R., & Cukurova, M. (2019). Designing educational technologies in the age of AI: A learning sciences-driven approach. *British Journal of Educational Technology*, *50*(6), 2824–2838. DOI: 10.1111/bjet.12861

Lu, H., Xu, J., Wang, L., & He, W. (2021, December). The Basic Problems of Virtual Simulation Experimental Teaching in Higher Education. In *2021 Tenth International Conference of Educational Innovation through Technology (EITT)* (pp. 69-74). IEEE.

Lünich, M., Keller, B., & Marcinkowski, F. (2024). Diverging Perceptions of Artificial Intelligence in Higher Education: A Comparison of Student and Public Assessments on Risks and Damages of Academic Performance Prediction in Germany. *Computers and Education Artificial Intelligence*, *100305*, 100305. Advance online publication. DOI: 10.1016/j.caeai.2024.100305

Lu, O. H. T., Huang, A. Y. Q., Tsai, D. C. L., & Yang, S. J. H. (2021). Expert-authored and machine-generated short-answer questions for assessing students learning performance. *Journal of Educational Technology & Society*, *24*(3), 159–173. https://www.jstor.org/stable/27032863

Luo, Y. (2021). New OLI advantages in digital globalization. *International Business Review*, *30*(2), 101797. DOI: 10.1016/j.ibusrev.2021.101797

Lynch, M., Kamovich, U., Longva, K., & Steinert, M. (2019). Combining technology and entrepreneurial education through design thinking: Students' reflections on the learning process. *Technological Forecasting and Social Change*, *119689*. Advance online publication. DOI: 10.1016/j.techfore.2019.06.015

Maas, G., & Jones, P. (2015). An Overview of Entrepreneurship Education., 22-95. .DOI: 10.1057/9781137509802_2

Macayan, V. D., Baguistan, D. C., & Golias, J. B. (2022). *Game-based activities and gamification in the mastery of science process skills: a systematic literature review. EPRA International Journal of Multidisciplinary Research.* IJMR. DOI: 10.36713/epra10950

MacDermott, C., & Ortiz, L. (2017). Beyond the business communication course: A historical perspective of the where, why, and how of soft skills development and job readiness for business graduates. *The IUP Journal of Soft Skills*, *11*(2), 7–24.

Macht, S. A., & Ball, S. (2016). "Authentic Alignment"–a new framework of entrepreneurship education. *Education + Training*, *58*(9), 926–944. DOI: 10.1108/ET-07-2015-0063

Mack, E. A., Marie-Pierre, L., & Redican, K. (2017). Entrepreneurs' use of internet and social media applications. *Telecommunications Policy*, *41*(2), 120–139. DOI: 10.1016/j.telpol.2016.12.001

Maellaro, R. (2013). The learning journal bridge: From classroom concepts to leadership practices. *Journal of Leadership Education*, *12*(1), 234–244. DOI: 10.12806/V12/I1/234

Maheshwari, G., & Kha, K. L. (2022). Investigating the relationship between educational support and entrepreneurial intention in Vietnam: The mediating role of entrepreneurial self-efficacy in the theory of planned behavior. *International Journal of Management Education*, *20*(2), 100553. DOI: 10.1016/j.ijme.2021.100553

Makris, I., & Apostolopoulos, S. (2021). Investing in healthcare enterprises in the non-metropolitan areas: Incentives, reflections, and innovative ideas. In *European Conference on Innovation and Entrepreneurship* (pp. 1160-R17). Academic Conferences International Limited.

Makris, I., & Apostolopoulos, S. (2021, September). Investing in healthcare enterprises in the non-metropolitan areas: Incentives, reflections, and innovative ideas. In European Conference on Innovation and Entrepreneurship (pp. 1160-R17). Academic Conferences International Limited.

Makris, I., Apostolopoulos, S., & Anastasopoulou, E. E. (2024). An Entrepreneurial Perspective on the Transition of Lignite Rural Areas to a New Regime within a Suffocating Timeframe. *Administrative Sciences*, *14*(4), 64.

Makris, I., Apostolopoulos, S., & Dimitrakopoulos, P. (2024). Analysing supporting mechanisms, cultural shaping and incentives for circular economy: The case of local governments. *Interdisciplinary Environmental Review*, *23*(3), 218–235. DOI: 10.1504/IER.2024.139254

Malik, G., & Venkatraman, A. (2017). The great divide: Skill gap between the employer's expectations and skills possessed by employees. *Industrial and Commercial Training*, *49*(4), 175–182. DOI: 10.1108/ICT-11-2016-0071

Mallari, A. (2024). Arcie Mallari. In *Advances in Educational Technologies and Instructional Design* (pp. 479–484). IGI Global.

Malthouse, E. C., Calder, B. J., Kim, S. J., & Vandenbosch, M. (2016). Evidence that user-generated content that produces engagement increases purchase behaviours. *Journal of Marketing Management*, *32*(5-6), 427–444. DOI: 10.1080/0267257X.2016.1148066

Mandalia, S. (2023, November). Tourism Education in the Digital Era: Navigating Innovation and Transformation. In *International Conference on Social Science and Education (ICoeSSE 2023)* (pp. 509-530). Atlantis Press. DOI: 10.2991/978-2-38476-142-5_48

Mankiw, N. G. (2024). *Principles of Economics* (10th ed.). South-Western Cengage Learning.

Mansoori, Y., & Lackéus, M. (2020). Comparing effectuation to discovery-driven planning, prescriptive entrepreneurship, business planning, lean startup, and design thinking. *Small Business Economics*, *54*(3), 791–818. Advance online publication. DOI: 10.1007/s11187-019-00153-w

Mansour, S., Mkhize, N., & Alam, S. (2021). Innovative pedagogies: The role of active learning in higher education. *International Journal of Educational Management*, *35*(3), 569–586.

Maraza-Quispe, B., Traverso-Condori, L. C., Torres-Gonzales, S. B., Reyes-Arco, R. E., Tinco-Túpac, S. T., Reyes-Villalba, E., & Carpio-Ventura, J. D. R. (2024). Impact of the Use of Gamified Online Tools: A Study with Kahoot and Quizizz in the Educational Context. *International Journal of Information and Education Technology (IJIET)*, *14*(1), 132–140. Advance online publication. DOI: 10.18178/ijiet.2024.14.1.2033

Maresch, D., Harms, R., Kailer, N., & Wimmer-Wurm, B. (2016). The impact of entrepreneurship education on the entrepreneurial intention of students in science and engineering versus business studies university programs. *Technological Forecasting and Social Change*, *104*, 172–179. DOI: 10.1016/j.techfore.2015.11.006

Mariani, M. M., & Nambisan, S. (2021). Innovation analytics and digital innovation experimentation: The rise of research-driven online review platforms. *Technological Forecasting and Social Change*, *172*, 121009. DOI: 10.1016/j.techfore.2021.121009

Mariappan, L. (2024). Mindful teaching, diverse learning: Harnessing multiple intelligences for students success. *Journal of Electrical Systems*, *20*(7s), 1720–1725. DOI: 10.52783/jes.3768

Maritz, A., & Brown, C. (2013). Enhancing Entrepreneurial Self-Efficacy and Learning Orientation: A Regional Australian Perspective. *Education + Training*, *55*(6), 552–574.

Markham, T., Larmer, J., & Ravitz, J. (2003). *Project Based Learning Handbook: A Guide to Standards-Focused Project Based Learning for Middle and High School Students*. Academic Press.

Markowitz, D. M., Laha, R., Perone, B. P., Pea, R. D., & Bailenson, J. N. (2018). Immersive virtual reality field trips facilitate learning about climate change. *Frontiers in Psychology*, *9*, 2364. DOI: 10.3389/fpsyg.2018.02364 PMID: 30555387

Marriott, P., Tan, S. M., & Marriott, N. (2015). Experiential learning–A case study of the use of computerised stock market trading simulation in finance education. *Accounting Education*, *24*(6), 480–497.

Martínez-Carmona, M. J., Gil Del Pino, C., & Álvarez-Castillo, J. L. (2022). The Basic Cycles of Vocational Training: Student Satisfaction and Perceived Benefit. *European Journal of Investigation in Health, Psychology and Education*, *12*(4), 417–430. DOI: 10.3390/ejihpe12040030 PMID: 35447748

Martínez, J. G., Martí, M. C., & Cervera, M. G. (2019). Inside a 3D simulation: Realism, dramatism and challenge in the development of students' teacher digital competence. *Australasian Journal of Educational Technology*, *35*(5), 1–14.

Martínez, J. M. G., Martín, J. M. M., & Del Sol Ostos Rey, M. (2020). An analysis of the changes in the seasonal patterns of tourist behavior during a process of economic recovery. *Technological Forecasting and Social Change*, *161*, 120280. DOI: 10.1016/j.techfore.2020.120280

Martínez-Martí, M. L., & Ruch, W. (2017). Character strengths predict resilience over and above positive affect, self-efficacy, optimism, social support, self-esteem, and life satisfaction. *The Journal of Positive Psychology*, *12*(2), 110–119. DOI: 10.1080/17439760.2016.1163403

Martín-Gutiérrez, J., Fabiani, P., Benesova, W., Meneses, M. D., & Mora, C. E. (2015). Augmented reality to promote collaborative and autonomous learning in higher education. *Computers in Human Behavior*, *51*, 752–761. DOI: 10.1016/j.chb.2014.11.093

Masouras, A., Daskou, S., Pistikou, V., Dimitriou, D., & Friesner, T. (2024). Global Developments in Nation Branding and Promotion. (2023). In Advances in marketing, customer relationship management, and e-services book series. DOI: 10.4018/978-1-6684-5902-7

Masouras, A., Pistikou, V., & Komodromos, M. (2021). Innovation analysis in Cypriot small and medium-sized enterprises and the role of the European Union. In *Entrepreneurship, Institutional Framework and Support Mechanisms in the EU* (pp. 115-131). Emerald Publishing Limited. DOI: 10.1108/978-1-83909-982-320211011

Masouras, A., & Papademetriou, C. (2018). Digital Consumer Behaviour in Cyprus: From Uses and Gratifications Theory to 4C's Online Shopping Approach. *Journal of Advertising and Public Relations*, *1*(1), 1–11. DOI: 10.22259/2639-1953.0101006

Matera, M., Rizzo, F., & Carughi, G. T. (2006). Web usability: Principles and evaluation methods. *Web engineering*, 143-180.

Matute, J., & Melero, I. (2016). *Game-based learning: using business simulators in the university classroom* [Aprender jugando: la utilización de simuladores empresariales en el aula universitaria]. No. ART.

Maunze, O. R., Abratt, R., & Mingione, M. (2020). Impact of internal branding on student engagement: Insights from a South African University. *Services Marketing Quarterly*, *41*(2), 124–144. DOI: 10.1080/15332969.2020.1742979

Maxwell, J. A. (2021). Why qualitative methods are necessary for generalization. *Qualitative Psychology*, *8*(1), 111.

Mayer, R. E. (2019). Computer games in education. *Annual Review of Psychology*, *70*(1), 531–549. DOI: 10.1146/annurev-psych-010418-102744 PMID: 30231003

McCarthy, M. C. (2016). Experiential learning theory: From theory to practice. *Journal of Business & Economics Research*, *14*(3), 91–100. DOI: 10.19030/jber.v14i3.9749

McFarland, K. (2017). Entrepreneurship Education and Experiential E-Learning: A Literature Review. *Developments in Business Simulation and Experiential Learning*, 44.

McGrath, S., & Yamada, S. (2023). Skills for development and vocational education and training: Current and emergent trends. *International Journal of Educational Development*, *102*, 102853. DOI: 10.1016/j.ijedudev.2023.102853

McGuinness, S., & Ortiz, L. (2016). Skill gaps in the workplace: Measurement, determinants and impacts. *Industrial Relations Journal*, *47*(3), 253–278. DOI: 10.1111/irj.12136

McHaney, R., Reiter, L., & Reychav, I. (2018). Immersive simulation in constructivist-based classroom e-learning. *International Journal on E-Learning*, *17*(1), 39–64.

McKenna, L., Innes, K., French, J., Streitberg, S., & Gilmour, C. (2010). Is history taking a dying skill? An exploration using a simulated learning environment. *Nurse Education in Practice*, *11*(4), 234–238. [REMOVED HYPERLINK FIELD]DOI: 10.1016/j.nepr.2010.11.009 PMID: 21195667

McKeown, J. M. (2012). *Real Options in Practice*. Wiley.

McVeigh-Schultz, J., & Isbister, K. (2022). A "beyond being there" for VR meetings: Envisioning the future of remote work. *Human-Computer Interaction*, *37*(5), 433–453. DOI: 10.1080/07370024.2021.1994860

Mehta, M. G. D. K. (2023, March 30). *China's Next-Gen Artificial Intelligence Development Plan (Part 1)*. IMR. https://imrmedia.in/chinas-next-gen-artificial-intelligence-development-plan-part-

Melo, A., Melo, C., & Vasconcelos, S. (2023). 'Rota Dos Sabores' – Simulation-Based Learning in Tourism, Hospitality and Catering Education and Training. *INTED Proceedings*, 3384–3390. Advance online publication. DOI: 10.21125/inted.2023.0920

Memar, N., Sundström, A., & Larsson, T. (2020). Teaching causation and effectuation in the large classroom: A production–trade game. *Journal of Management Education*, *45*(3), 438–478. DOI: 10.1177/1052562920951971

Merchant, Z., Goetz, E. T., Cifuentes, L., Keeney-Kennicutt, W., & Davis, T. J. (2013). Effectiveness of virtual reality-based instruction on students' learning outcomes in K-12 and higher education: A meta-analysis. *Computers & Education*, *70*, 29–40. DOI: 10.1016/j.compedu.2013.07.033

Merry, K. L. (2024). *Delivering inclusive and impactful instruction: Universal design for learning in higher education* (1st ed.). CAST Professional Publishing.

Michael, D. R., & Chen, S. L. (2016). *Serious Games: Games That Educate, Train, and Inform*. Thomson Course Technology.

Middleton, K. W., & Donnellon, A. (2019). Personalizing entrepreneurial learning: A pedagogy for facilitating the know why. *Entrepreneurship Research Journal*, *4*(2), 167–204. DOI: 10.1515/erj-2013-0040

Mikić, M., Sopta, M., & Horvatinović, T. (2019). The Role Of Entrepreneurial Education In The Development Of Entrepreneurship. EMC Review - Časopis za ekonomiju - APEIRON. .DOI: 10.7251/EMC1802385M

Milgram, P., & Kishino, F. (1994). A taxonomy of mixed reality visual displays. *IEICE Transactions on Information and Systems*, *77*(12), 1321–1329.

Milgram, P., Takemura, H., Utsumi, A., & Kishino, F. (1995). Augmented reality: A class of displays on the reality-virtuality continuum. *Telemanipulator and Telepresence Technologies*, *2351*, 282–292. DOI: 10.1117/12.197321

Milmeister, P., Rastoder, M., & Houssemand, C. (2022). Mechanisms of Participation in Vocational Education and Training in Europe. *Frontiers in Psychology*, *13*, 842307. Advance online publication. [REMOVED HYPERLINK FIELD]DOI: 10.3389/fpsyg.2022.842307 PMID: 35707674

Milosz, E., & Milosz, M. (2012). Business simulation games during the summer schools–the case study. In *INTED2012 Proceedings* (pp. 1577-1583). IATED.

Ming, F. (2017). *Construction of experiment teaching center of virtual simulation of economic management in application-oriented Colleges Study on Shaan Xi Institute of International Trade & Commerce. In Advances in Engineering Research* (Vol. 123). Atlantis Press.

Miotto, G., Del-Castillo-Feito, C., & Blanco-González, A. (2020). Reputation and legitimacy: Key factors for Higher Education Institutions' sustained competitive advantage. *Journal of Business Research*, *112*, 342–353. DOI: 10.1016/j.jbusres.2019.11.076

Mir, A.A., Hassan, S. and Khan, S.J. (2022), "Understanding digital entrepreneurial intentions: a capital theory perspective", International Journal of Emerging Markets, Vol. ahead-of-print No. ahead-of-print, pp. 1-27.

Mirchi, N., Bissonnette, V., Yilmaz, R., Ledwos, N., Winkler-Schwartz, A., & Maestro, R. (2020). The Virtual Operative Assistant: An explainable artificial intelligence tool for simulation-based training in surgery and medicine. *PLoS One*, *15*(2), e0229596. Advance online publication. DOI: 10.1371/journal.pone.0229596 PMID: 32106247

Misfeldt, M. (2015). Scenario Based Education as a Framework for Understanding Students Engagement and Learning in a Project Management Simulation Game. *Electronic Journal of e-Learning*, *13*(3), 181–191.

Mishra, C., & Zachary, R. K. (2015). *The theory of entrepreneurship: Creating and sustaining entrepreneurial value*. Palgrave Macmillan.

Mishra, S. (2017). Open educational resources: Removing barriers from within. *Distance Education, 38*(3), 369–380. DOI: 10.1080/01587919.2017.1369350

Mitchell, R. K., Busenitz, L., Lant, T., McDougall, P. P., Morse, E. A., & Smith, J. B. (2002). Toward a Theory of Entrepreneurial Cognition: Rethinking the People Side of Entrepreneurship Research. *Entrepreneurship Theory and Practice, 27*(2), 93–104. DOI: 10.1111/1540-8520.00001

Mitchell, T. R. (2021). Expectancy-value models in organizational psychology. In *Expectations and actions* (pp. 293–312). Routledge.

Mittal, P., & Raghuvaran, S. (2021). Entrepreneurship education and employability skills: The mediating role of e-learning courses. *Entrepreneurship Education, 4*(2), 153–167. DOI: 10.1007/s41959-021-00048-6

Mohan, V. (2019). On the use of blockchain-based mechanisms to tackle academic misconduct. *Research Policy, 48*(9), 103805. DOI: 10.1016/j.respol.2019.103805

Monk, E., & Lycett, M. (2014). Measuring business process learning with enterprise resource planning systems to improve the value of education. *Education and Information Technologies, 21*(4), 747–768. DOI: 10.1007/s10639-014-9352-6

Monllor, J., Michels, N., & Adderley, S. (2023). Pivoting an entrepreneurship experiential learning module online: Applying a concrete experience framework. *Entrepreneurship Education and Pedagogy, 7*(4), 416–438. DOI: 10.1177/25151274231217953

Moon, C., Walmsley, A., & Apostolopoulos, N. (2018). Sustainability and entrepreneurship education. A survey of 307 UN HESI signatories. Academic Press.

Morales, B. (2020). Salvador & Martinez-Roig, Rosabel & Hernández-Amorós, Maria J. (2020). Sustainability and Educational Technology- A Description of the Teaching Self-Concept. *Sustainability (Basel), 12*(24), 10309. Advance online publication. DOI: 10.3390/su122410309

Moratis, L., Hoff, J., & Reul, B. (2006). A dual challenge facing management education: Simulation-based learning and learning about CSR. *Journal of Management Development, 25*(3), 213–231. DOI: 10.1108/02621710610648150

Morfaki, C. (2025). From Passion to Success: A Journey Through the Emotional Landscape of Entrepreneurial (He) arts. In *Real-World Tools and Scenarios for Entrepreneurship Exploration* (pp. 169–202). IGI Global.

Morris, M. H., Kuratko, D. F., & Cornwall, J. R. (2019). Entrepreneurship Programs and the Development of Entrepreneurial Skills: An Exploration of the Student Experience. *The International Entrepreneurship and Management Journal, 15*(4), 1193–1216.

Morris, T. H. (2019). Experiential learning - A systematic review and revision of Kolb's model. *Interactive Learning Environments, 28*(8), 1064–1077. DOI: 10.1080/10494820.2019.1570279

Morse, J. M. (1994). 'Emerging from the data': the cognitive processes of analysis in qualitative inquiry. In Morse, J. M. (Ed.), *Critical Issues in Qualitative Research Methods* (pp. 23–43). Sage.

Morselli, D., & Gorenc, J. (2022). Using the EntreComp framework to evaluate two entrepreneurship education courses based on the Korda Method. *International Journal of Management Education*, *20*(1), 100591. DOI: 10.1016/j.ijme.2021.100591

Morse, M. J., & Field, A. P. (1996). *Nursing Research: The Application of Qualitative Approach*. Chapman & Hall.

Moser, A., & Korstjens, I. (2018). Series: Practical guidance to qualitative research. Part 3: Sampling, data collection and analysis. *The European Journal of General Practice*, *24*(1), 9–18. PMID: 29199486

Mosyjowski, E. A., & Seifert, C. M. (2014). Integrating problem-solving methods in project-based learning. *International Journal of Educational Research*, *64*, 53–61.

Mousavinasab, E., Zarifsanaiey, N., Kalhori, S. R. N., Rakhshan, M., Keikha, L., & Saeedi, M. G. (2018). Intelligent tutoring systems: A systematic review of characteristics, applications, and evaluation methods. *Interactive Learning Environments*, *29*(1), 142–163. DOI: 10.1080/10494820.2018.1558257

Mousavi, S. M., & Beroza, G. C. (2020). A Machine-Learning Approach for Earthquake Magnitude Estimation. *Geophysical Research Letters*, *47*(1). Advance online publication. DOI: 10.1029/2019GL085976

Mubaraz, S., & Heikkilä, J. (2022). Business simulations as effective virtual and experiential learning environment. INTED2022 Proceedings, 6743-6749. DOI: 10.21125/inted.2022.1705

Mueller, S., & Anderson, A. R. (2014). Understanding the entrepreneurial learning process and its impact on students' personal development: A European perspective. *International Journal of Management Education*, *12*(3), 500–511. DOI: 10.1016/j.ijme.2014.05.003

Muldoon, J., Liguori, E. W., Solomon, S., & Bendickson, J. (2023). Technological Innovation and the expansion of Entrepreneurship Ecosystems. *Review of Managerial Science*, *17*(5), 1789–1808. DOI: 10.1007/s11846-022-00573-1

Murphy, J., Raffa, L., & Mizerski, R. (2003). The Use of Domain Names in e-branding by the World's Top Brands. *Electronic Markets*, *13*(3), 222–232. DOI: 10.1080/1019678032000108310

Musso, M., Hernández, C., & Cascallar, E. (2020). Predicting key educational outcomes in academic trajectories: A machine-learning approach. *Higher Education*, *80*(5), 1–20. DOI: 10.1007/s10734-020-00520-7

Mutanga, M. B. (2024). Students' perspectives and experiences in project-based learning: A qualitative study. *Trends in Higher Education*, *3*(4), 903–911. DOI: 10.3390/higheredu3040052

Muthukannan, P., Tan, B., Gozman, D., & Johnson, L. (2020). The emergence of a fintech ecosystem: A case study of the Vizag Fintech Valley in India. *Information & Management*, *57*(8), 1–18. DOI: 10.1016/j.im.2020.103385

Mutipforo, G., Muwani, T. S., Katsande, C., Marime, S., & Ranganai, N. (2024). ICTs and Their Influence on Agritourism. In *Agritourism for Sustainable Development: Reflections from Emerging African Economies* (pp. 174-188). CABI. DOI: 10.1079/9781800623705.0013

Muwani, T. S., Marime, S., Ranganai, N., & Mutipforo, G. (2024). Digital technologies for sustainable agritourism and human development. In *Agritourism for Sustainable Development* (pp. 189-206). CABI. DOI: 10.1079/9781800623705.0014

Mwasalwiba, E. S. (2010). Entrepreneurship education: A review of its objectives, teaching methods, and impact indicators. *Education + Training*, *52*(1), 20–47.

Mystakidis, S. (2022). Metaverse. *Encyclopedia*, *2*(1), 486–497. DOI: 10.3390/encyclopedia2010031

Mystakidis, S., Papantzikos, G., & Stylios, C. (2021). Virtual reality escape rooms for STEM education in industry 4.0: Greek teachers perspectives. *2021 6th South-East Europe Design Automation, Computer Engineering,Computer Networks and Social Media Conference (SEEDA-CECNSM)*, 1–5.

Nabi, G., Holden, R., & Walmsley, A. (2019). The role of entrepreneurial education in fostering innovation. *International Journal of Entrepreneurial Behaviour & Research*, *25*(2), 251–270.

Nabi, G., Liñán, F., Fayolle, A., Krueger, N., & Walmsley, A. (2017). The Impact of Entrepreneurship Education in Higher Education: A Systematic Review and Research Agenda. *Academy of Management Learning & Education*, *16*(2), 277–299. DOI: 10.5465/amle.2015.0026

Nagy, M., Lăzăroiu, G., & Valaskova, K. (2023). Machine Intelligence and Autonomous Robotic Technologies in the Corporate Context of SMEs: Deep Learning and Virtual Simulation Algorithms, Cyber-Physical Production Networks, and Industry 4.0-Based Manufacturing Systems. *Applied Sciences (Basel, Switzerland)*, *13*(3), 1681. DOI: 10.3390/app13031681

Naidoo, R. (2016). The competition fetish in higher education: Varieties, animators and consequences. *British Journal of Sociology of Education*, *37*(1), 1–10. DOI: 10.1080/01425692.2015.1116209

Nambisan, S., Wright, M., & Feldman, M. (2019). The digital transformation of innovation and entrepreneurship: Progress, challenges and key themes. *Research Policy*, *48*(8), 103773. DOI: 10.1016/j.respol.2019.03.018

Nambisan, S., Zahra, S. A., & Luo, Y. (2019). Global platforms and ecosystems: Implications for international business theories. *Journal of International Business Studies*, *50*(9), 1464–1486. DOI: 10.1057/s41267-019-00262-4

Nandi, V. T. N., Khan, S., Qureshi, M. A., & Ghias, S. (2020). Training & Development, Organizational Commitment and Turnover Intentions in SMEs. *Market Forces*, *15*(2), 24. DOI: 10.51153/mf.v15i2.457

Nasir, J., Ibrahim, R. M., Sarwar, M. A., Sarwar, B., Al-Rahmi, W. M., Alturise, F., Al-Adwan, A. S., & Uddin, M. (2022). The Effects of Transformational Leadership, Organizational Innovation, Work Stressors, and Creativity on Employee Performance in SMEs. *Frontiers in Psychology*, *13*, 772104. Advance online publication. [REMOVED HYPERLINK FIELD]DOI: 10.3389/fpsyg.2022.772104 PMID: 35529553

Nathan, M. J., & Martinez, C. V. J. (2015). Gesture as model enactment: The role of gesture in mental model construction and inference making when learning from text. *Learning: Research and Practice*, *1*(1), 4–37. DOI: 10.1080/23735082.2015.1006758

Naudin, A., & Agusita, E. (2021). Rethinking Cultural and Creative Entrepreneurship Education. *European Conference on Innovation and Entrepreneurship.*

Navarro-Parra, S. L., & Chiappe, A. (2024). Simulated Learning Environments as an Interdisciplinary Option for Vocational Training: A Systematic Review. *Simulation & Gaming*, *55*(2), 135–158. DOI: 10.1177/10468781231221904

Navío-Marco, J., Ruiz-Gómez, L. M., & Sevilla-Sevilla, C. (2018). Progress in information technology and tourism management: 30 years on and 20 years after the internet-Revisiting Buhalis & Law's landmark study about eTourism. *Tourism Management*, *69*, 460–470. DOI: 10.1016/j.tourman.2018.06.002

Nawir, F., & Hendrawan, S. A. (2024). The Impact of Website Usability and Mobile Optimization on Customer Satisfaction and Sales Conversion Rates in E-commerce Businesses in Indonesia. *The Eastasouth Journal of Information System and Computer Science*, *2*(01), 15–30. DOI: 10.58812/esiscs.v2i01.324

Ndou, V., Mele, G., & Del Vecchio, P. (2018). Entrepreneurship education and entrepreneurial intention: The role of information exposure and knowledge acquisition. *Journal of Business Research*, *94*, 209–221.

Ndou, V., Secundo, G., Schiuma, G., & Passiante, G. (2018). Insights for shaping entrepreneurship education: Evidence from the European entrepreneurship centers. *Sustainability (Basel)*, *10*(11), 4323. DOI: 10.3390/su10114323

Neck, H. M., & Greene, P. G. (2011). Entrepreneurship education: Known worlds and new frontiers. *Journal of Small Business Management*, *49*(1), 55–70. DOI: 10.1111/j.1540-627X.2010.00314.x

Neck, H. M., Greene, P. G., & Brush, C. G. (2014). *Teaching entrepreneurship: A practice-based approach*. Edward Elgar Publishing. DOI: 10.4337/9781782540564

Neck, H., & Corbett, A. (2018). The Scholarship of Teaching and Learning Entrepreneurship. *Entrepreneurship Education and Pedagogy*, *1*(1), 8–41. DOI: 10.1177/2515127417737286

Neergaard, H., & Ulhøi, J. P. (Eds.). (2007). Handbook of Qualitative Research Methods in Entrepreneurship. Edward Elgar Publishing.

Nelson, R. R., & Monsen, E. (2014). The role of research in the commercialization of technology. *Research Policy*, *43*(7), 1132–1143.

Neneh, B. N. (2022). Entrepreneurial passion and entrepreneurial intention: The role of social support and entrepreneurial self-efficacy. *Studies in Higher Education*, *47*(3), 587–603. DOI: 10.1080/03075079.2020.1770716

Neriz, L., Núñez, A., Fuentes-Caceres, V., Ramis, F., & Jerez, O. (2020). Simulation-based training as a teaching and learning tool for management education. *Innovations in Education and Teaching International*, *57*(6), 701–713. DOI: 10.1080/14703297.2019.1631874

Newbery, R., Lean, J., & Moizer, J. (2016). Evaluating the impact of serious games: The effect of gaming on entrepreneurial intent. *Information Technology & People*, *29*(4), 733–749. DOI: 10.1108/ITP-05-2015-0111

Newbery, R., Lean, J., Moizer, J., & Haddoud, M. (2018). Entrepreneurial identity formation during the initial entrepreneurial experience: The influence of simulation feedback and existing identity. *Journal of Business Research*, *85*, 51–59. DOI: 10.1016/j.jbusres.2017.12.013

Ngozwana, N. (2022). Experiential learning through simulations in business management education. *Journal of Business Education & Learning*, *18*(2), 147–161.

Nguy n, T. T., Nguyen, L. T. P., Phan, H. T. T., & Vu, A. T. (2021). Impact of entrepreneurship extra-curricular activities and inspiration on entrepreneurial intention: Mediator and moderator effect. *SAGE Open*, *11*(3), 21582440211032174. Advance online publication. DOI: 10.1177/21582440211032174

Nickerson, N. P., Black, R. J., & McCool, S. F. (2001). Agritourism: Motivations behind farm/ranch business diversification. *Journal of Travel Research*, *40*(1), 19–26. DOI: 10.1177/004728750104000104

Nidumolu, R., Prahalad, C. K., & Rangaswami, M. R. (2009). Why sustainability is now the key driver of innovation. *Harvard Business Review*, *87*(9), 57–64.

Nielsen. (2015). The sustainability imperative: New insights on consumer expectations. Nielsen Global Consumer Survey.

Niguse, T., Kant, S., & Adula, M. (2025). Mediation Effect of Customer Loyalty in Relationship Between Market Orientation, Entrepreneurial Orientation, and Firm Performance in Ethiopia. In *Leveraging AI for Effective Digital Relationship Marketing* (pp. 419–458). IGI Global. DOI: 10.4018/979-8-3693-5340-0.ch014

Nishikawa, K. (2021). The role of soft skills in enhancing team performance: A case study of Japanese companies. *Journal of Business Research*, *124*, 233–243.

Norlyk, A., & Harder, I. (2010). What makes a phenomenological study phenomenological? An analysis of peer-reviewed empirical nursing studies. *Qualitative Health Research*, *20*(3), 420–431. PMID: 20068190

Norman, D. A. (2013). *The Design of Everyday Things* (Revised and Expanded Edition). Basic Books.

Norwich, B. (2014). Recognising value tensions that underlie problems in inclusive education. *Cambridge Journal of Education*, *44*(4), 495–510. DOI: 10.1080/0305764X.2014.963027

Noyes, E. (2018). Teaching entrepreneurial action through prototyping: The prototype-it challenge. *Entrepreneurship Education and Pedagogy*, *1*(1), 118–134. DOI: 10.1177/2515127417737289

Nyoach, T. D., Lemi, K., Debela, T., & Kant, S. (2024). Does Organizational Commitment Mediate the Relationship between Employee Relationship Management and Bank Performance? The Case of Banks in Ethiopia. *International Journal of Organizational Leadership*, *13*(2), 355–376. DOI: 10.33844/ijol.2024.60419

Nyström, S., & Ahn, S. E. (2024). Teaching with simulators in vocational education and training – From a storing place to a new colleague. *Teaching and Teacher Education*, *138*, 104409. DOI: 10.1016/j.tate.2023.104409

Nzilano, K. L., Tundui, H. P., & Ndyetabula, D. W. (2022). Perceived university support and technical graduates' intentions to venture into business start-ups in Tanzania: Does institutional support matter? *Journal of Global Entrepreneurship Research*, *12*(1), 465–477. DOI: 10.1007/s40497-022-00334-0

Oberle, M., & Leunig, J. (2016). Simulation games on the European Union in civics: Effects on secondary school pupils' political competence. *Citizenship Social and Economics Education, 15*(3), 227–243. DOI: 10.1177/2047173416689794

Obschonka, M., & Audretsch, D. (2019). Artificial intelligence and big data in entrepreneurship: A new era has begun. *Small Business Economics, 55*(3), 529–539. DOI: 10.1007/s11187-019-00202-4

Ocares-Cunyarachi, L., & Andrade-Arenas, L. (2022). Mobile Application Prototype: Learning in the Programming Course in Computer Engineering Students. *International Journal of Advanced Computer Science and Applications, 13*(7). Advance online publication. DOI: 10.14569/IJACSA.2022.0130791

OECD. (2021). *The state of AI adoption in higher education in developing countries.* OECD Publishing. https://www.oecd.org/en/topics/sub-issues/higher-education.html

OECD. (2023). *Managing Shocks and Transitions. Future-Proofing SME and Entrepreneurship Policies.* https://www.oecd.org/cfe/smes/key-issues-paper-oecd-sme-and-entrepreneurship-ministerial-meeting-2023.pdf

Okoli, C. (2023). Inductive, abductive and deductive theorising. *International Journal of Management Concepts and Philosophy, 16*(3), 302–316. DOI: 10.1504/IJMCP.2023.131769

Okonkwo, C. W., & Ade-Ibijola, A. (2021). Chatbots applications in education: A systematic review. *Computers and Education: Artificial Intelligence, 2*, 100033. DOI: 10.1016/j.caeai.2021.100033

Oldemeyer, L., Jede, A., & Teuteberg, F. (2024). *Investigation of artificial intelligence in SMEs: a systematic review of the state of the art and the main implementation challenges.* Management Review Quarterly., DOI: 10.1007/s11301-024-00405-4

Olumekor, M., Mohiuddin, M., & Su, Z. (2023). Effective altruism and the dark side of entrepreneurship. *Frontiers in Psychology, 14*, 1247331. Advance online publication. DOI: 10.3389/fpsyg.2023.1247331 PMID: 37908811

Onjewu, A. K. E., Haddoud, M. Y., & Nowiński, W. (2021). The impact of education related with entrepreneurship on nascent entrepreneurship. *Industry and Higher Education, 35*(4), 419–431. DOI: 10.1177/09504222211014038

Ordonez-Ponce, E., Clarke, A., & Colbert, B. (2020). Collaborative Sustainable Business Models: Understanding Organizations Partnering for Community Sustainability. *Business & Society*, 1–42. DOI: 10.1177/0007650320940241

Oreg, S., & Berson, Y. (2019). Leaders' impact on organizational change: Bridging theoretical and methodological chasms. *The Academy of Management Annals, 13*(1), 272–307. DOI: 10.5465/annals.2016.0138

Oren, T., Mittal, S., & Durak, U. (2017). *Guide to Simulation-Based Disciplines. Simulation Foundations, Methods and Applications.* Springer. DOI: 10.1007/978-3-319-61264-5

Organ, J., O'Neill, S., & Shanahan, B. W. (2022). Development of Social Technology Entrepreneurial Ventures: A challenge project-based learning approach. *IFAC-PapersOnLine, 55*(39), 181–186. DOI: 10.1016/j.ifacol.2022.12.050

Othman, A., Chemnad, K., Hassanien, A. E., Tlili, A., Zhang, C. Y., Al-Thani, D., Altınay, F., Chalghoumi, H. S., Al-Khalifa, H., & Obeid, M. (2024). Accessible Metaverse: A Theoretical Framework for Accessibility and Inclusion in the Metaverse. *Multimodal Technologies and Interaction, 8*(3), 21. DOI: 10.3390/mti8030021

Ouahi, M. B., Hou, M. A., & Hassoun, I. T. (2021). Opinions of Moroccan teachers towards the use of PhET simulations in teaching and learning physics–chemistry. In *2020 6th IEEE Congress on Information Science and Technology (CiSt)* (pp. 274-278). IEEE.

Ouatik, F., Raoufi, M., Ouatik, F., & Skouri, M. (2021). E-Learning & decision making system for automate students assessment using remote laboratory and machine learning. *DOAJ (DOAJ: Directory of Open Access Journals)*. DOI: 10.20368/1971-8829/1135285

Palanski, M. & Vogelgesang, G. (2011). Virtuous Creativity: The Effects of Leader Behavioural Integrity on Follower Creative Thinking and Risk Taking. Canadian Journal of Administrative Sciences / Revue Canadienne des Sciences de l'Administration, 28. .DOI: 10.1002/cjas.219

Paliszkiewicz, J., Chen, K., & Mendel, M. (2024). *Trust in Social and Business Relations*. Trust in Social and Business Relations., DOI: 10.4324/9781032633749

Pan, J. (2017). *An empirical study of the impact of project-based learning on English major students' critical thinking skills*. Academic Press.

Panadero, E., Jonsson, A., & Botella, J. (2019). Effects of Self-Assessment on Self-Regulated Learning and Self-Efficacy: Four Meta-Analyses. *Educational Research Review, 28*, 100284.

Pane, J. F., Steiner, E. D., Baird, M. D., & Hamilton, L. S. (2017). *Informing Progress: Insights on Personalized Learning Implementation and Effects*. RAND Corporation. DOI: 10.7249/RR2042

Panigrahi, A., Pati, A., Sahu, B., Das, M. N., Nayak, D. S. K., Sahoo, G., & Kant, S. (2023). En-MinWhale: An ensemble approach based on MRMR and Whale optimization for Cancer diagnosis. *IEEE Access : Practical Innovations, Open Solutions, 11*, 113526–113542. DOI: 10.1109/ACCESS.2023.3318261

Papadakis, S. (2018). The use of computer games in classroom environment. *International Journal of Teaching and Case Studies, 9*(1), 1. DOI: 10.1504/IJTCS.2018.090191

Papademetriou, C. (2012). Leadership Impact on Elementary School's Effectiveness and Improvement. Paper presented at the 8th European Conference on Management, Leadership and Governance, Pafos, Cyprus.

Papademetriou, C., & Charalampous, C. (2018). Entrepreneurship and Innovation in Education: The model of the Inclusive Leader. *1st International Conference on Marketing and Entrepreneurship (ICME 2018)*. Neapolis University.

Papademetriou, C., Ragazou, K., Belias, D., Anastasiadou, S., Garefalakis, A., & Prodromou, A. (2024). The Importance of Green Human Resources: Green Ambidexterity and Environmental Performance. In *Sustainability Through Green HRM and Performance Integration*. IGI Global., DOI: 10.4018/979-8-3693-5981-5.ch004

Pardo-Garcia, C., & Barac, M. (2020). Promoting Employability in Higher Education: A Case Study on Boosting Entrepreneurship Skills. *Sustainability (Basel)*, *12*(10), 4004. Advance online publication. DOI: 10.3390/su12104004

Park, J. J., Tiefenbach, J., & Demetriades, A. K. (2022). The role of artificial intelligence in surgical simulation. *Frontiers in Medical Technology*, *4*, 1076755. DOI: 10.3389/fmedt.2022.1076755 PMID: 36590155

Park, S., & Kim, S. (2023). The Avaritia: Entrepreneurship practice to understand the problem of information control through gamification. *Sustainability (Basel)*, *15*(8), 6738. DOI: 10.3390/su15086738

Parong, J., & Mayer, R. E. (2021). Cognitive and affective processes for learning science in immersive virtual reality. *Journal of Computer Assisted Learning*, *37*(1), 226–241. DOI: 10.1111/jcal.12482

Passaro, R., Quinto, I., & Thomas, A. (2018). The impact of higher education on entrepreneurial intention and human capital. *Journal of Intellectual Capital*, *19*(1), 135–156. DOI: 10.1108/JIC-04-2017-0056

Patacsil, F., & Tablatin, L. (2017). Exploring the importance of soft and hard skills as perceived by IT internship students and industry: A gap analysis. *Journal of Technology and Science Education*, *7*(3), 347–368. DOI: 10.3926/jotse.271

Patil, M., Meena, M., Maste, D., Deshpande, R., & Kallurkar, S. P. (2018). Building effective association amongst the academia world and industry world. *IOSR Journal of Engineering*, *5*, 16–20. DOI: 10.9790/3021-0502061620

Patrício, L. D., & Ferreira, J. J. (2024). Unlocking the connection between education, entrepreneurial mindset, and social values in entrepreneurial activity development. *Review of Managerial Science*, *18*(4), 991–1013. DOI: 10.1007/s11846-023-00629-w

Patsoulis, P., & Deirmentzoglou, G. A. (2024). Entrepreneurship in the World of ESG Awareness: Tales from a Global Panel. *Available atSSRN* 4870078. DOI: 10.2139/ssrn.4870078

Patton, M. Q. (1990). *Qualitative evaluation and research methods*. SAGE Publications, inc.

Patton, M. Q. (2002). *Qualitative Research and Evaluation Methods* (3rd ed.). Sage.

Paunović, I., Apostolopoulos, S., Miljković, I. B., & Stojanović, M. (2024). Sustainable Rural Healthcare Entrepreneurship: A Case Study of Serbia. *Sustainability (Basel)*, *16*(3), 1143. DOI: 10.3390/su16031143

Paunović, I., Apostolopoulos, S., Miljković, I. B., & Stojanović, M. (2024). Sustainable Rural Healthcare Entrepreneurship: A Case Study of Serbia. *Sustainability*, *16*(3), 1143.

Paust, S., Korsgaard, S., & Thrane, C. (2024). Entrepreneurial prototyping: The role of purpose, prototype recycling, and skills bricolage. *Small Business Economics*, 1–25.

Pellas, N., Dengel, A., & Christopoulos, A. (2020). A Scoping Review of Immersive Virtual Reality in STEM Education. *IEEE Transactions on Learning Technologies*, *13*(4), 748–761. DOI: 10.1109/TLT.2020.3019405

Pellas, N., Mystakidis, S., & Kazanidis, I. (2021). Immersive Virtual Reality in K-12 and Higher Education: A systematic review of the last decade scientific literature. *Virtual Reality (Waltham Cross)*, *25*(3), 835–861. DOI: 10.1007/s10055-020-00489-9

Peng, J., & Abdullah, I. (2018). Building a market simulation to teach business process analysis: Effects of realism on engaged learning. *Accounting Education*, *27*(2), 208–222.

Perkins, G., Lean, J., & Newbery, R. (2017). The role of organizational vision in guiding idea generation within SME contexts. *Creativity and Innovation Management*, *26*(1), 75–90. DOI: 10.1111/caim.12206

Persico, L., & Lalor, J. D. (2019). A Review: Using Simulation-Based Education to Substitute Traditional Clinical Rotations. *Teaching and Learning in Nursing*, *14*(4), 274–278. DOI: 10.1016/j.teln.2019.03.006

Petchamé, J., Iriondo, I., Torné, O., & Solanellas, F. (2024). Student perceptions of project-Based Learning when studying 'Information Systems' in an ICT engineering program: Taking advantage of active learning. *Education Sciences*, *14*(11), 1148. DOI: 10.3390/educsci14111148

Peterková, J., Repaská, Z., & Prachařová, L. (2022). Best practice of using digital business simulation games in business education. *Sustainability (Basel)*, *14*(15), 8987. DOI: 10.3390/su14158987

Peterk, S., Koprivnjak, T., & Mezulić, P. (2015). Challenges Of Evaluation Of The Influence Of Entrepreneurship Education. *Econometric Reviews*, *13*, 74–86.

Peterman, N., & Kennedy, J. (2003). Enterprise Education: Influencing Students' Perceptions of Entrepreneurship. *Entrepreneurship Theory and Practice*, *28*(2), 129–144. DOI: 10.1046/j.1540-6520.2003.00035.x

Petersen, F. (2023). Business Simulation Games and Entrepreneurial Education. In Iwu, C. G., & Shambare, R. (Eds.), *Delivering Entrepreneurship Education in Africa*. Emerald Publishing Limited.

Peters, M. A. (2017). Technological unemployment: Educating for the fourth industrial revolution. *Educational Philosophy and Theory*, *49*(1), 1–6. DOI: 10.1080/00131857.2016.1177412

Peterson, J. S. (2019). Presenting a Qualitative Study: A Reviewer's Perspective. *Gifted Child Quarterly*, *63*(3), 147–158. DOI: 10.1177/0016986219844789

Petrakis, K., Wodehouse, A., & Hird, A. (2021). Prototyping-driven entrepreneurship: Towards a prototyping support tool based on design thinking principles. *The Design Journal*, *24*(5), 761–781. DOI: 10.1080/14606925.2021.1957531

Petridou, E., & Sarri, K. (2011). Developing "Potential Entrepreneurs" in Higher Education Institutes. *Journal of Enterprising Culture*, *19*(1), 79–99. DOI: 10.1142/S0218495811000647

Pham, M., Nguyen, A. T. T., Tran, D. T., Mai, T. T., & Nguyen, V. T. (2023). The impact of entrepreneurship knowledge on students' e-entrepreneurial intention formation and the moderating role of technological innovativeness. *Journal of Innovation and Entrepreneurship*, *12*(1), 80. Advance online publication. DOI: 10.1186/s13731-023-00351-7

Phan, P. H. (2014). The commercialization of technology: A review and future directions. *Research Policy*, *43*(6), 1138–1149.

Phelan, C., & Sharpley, R. (2011). Exploring agritourism entrepreneurship in the UK. *Tourism Planning & Development*, *8*(2), 121–136. DOI: 10.1080/21568316.2011.573912

Phillip, S., Hunter, C., & Blackstock, K. (2010). A typology for defining agritourism. *Tourism Management*, *31*(6), 754–758. DOI: 10.1016/j.tourman.2009.08.001

Piaget, J. (1971). The Theory of Stages in Cognitive Development. McGraw-Hill Education.

Piaget, J. (1952). *The origins of intelligence in children*. International University. DOI: 10.1037/11494-000

Piercy, N. (2013). Evaluating experiential learning in the business context: Contributions to group-based and cross-functional working. *Innovations in Education and Teaching International*, *50*(2), 202–213. DOI: 10.1080/14703297.2012.760870

Pietsch, M., Cramer, C., Brown, C., Aydin, B., & Witthöft, J. (2023). Open Innovation in Schools: A New Imperative for Organising Innovation in Education? *Technology Knowledge and Learning.*, *29*(2), 1051–1077. DOI: 10.1007/s10758-023-09705-2

Piperopoulos, P. (2012). Could higher education programmes, culture and structure stifle the entrepreneurial intentions of students? Journal of Small Business and Enterprise Rahman, H., & Day, J. (2015). Involving the entrepreneurial role model: A possible development for entrepreneurship education. *Journal of Entrepreneurship Education*, *18*(1), 86–95.

Pistikou, V., Flouros, F., Deirmentzoglou, G. A., & Agoraki, K. K. (2023). Sustainability Reporting: Examining the Community Impact of the S&P500 Companies. *Sustainability (Basel)*, *15*(18), 13681. DOI: 10.3390/su151813681

Pittaway, L., & Cope, J. (2007). Simulating Entrepreneurial Learning. *Management Learning*, *38*(2), 211–233. DOI: 10.1177/1350507607075776

Pittaway, L., Rodriguez-Falcon, E., Aiyegbayo, O., & King, A. S. (2011). The role of entrepreneurship clubs and societies in entrepreneurial learning. *International Small Business Journal*, *29*(1), 37–57. DOI: 10.1177/0266242610369876

Piu, A., Fregola, C., & Santoro, A. (2016). Using a simulation game to make learning about angles meaningful. an exploratory study in primary school. *European Journal of Science and Mathematics Education*, *4*(4), 490–500. DOI: 10.30935/scimath/9488

Platania, M. (2014). Agritourism farms and the web. An exploratory evaluation of their websites. *AGRIS On-Line Papers in Economics and Informatics*, *6*(3), 51–58.

Polas, M. R. H., Jahanshahi, A. A., Ahamed, B., & Molla, M. O. F. (2023). The Future of Artificial Intelligence in Education 4.0. In *Advances in educational technologies and instructional design book series* (pp. 1–20). DOI: 10.4018/978-1-6684-9103-4.ch001

Polikarpus, S., Luik, P., Poom-Valickis, K., & Ley, T. (2023). The Role of Trainers in Implementing Virtual Simulation-based Training: Effects on Attitude and TPACK Knowledge. *Vocations and Learning*, *16*(3), 459–486. DOI: 10.1007/s12186-023-09322-1

Polit, F. D., & Hungler, P. B. (1999). *Nursing Research: Principles and Methods*. Lippincott.

Politis, D. (2005). The process of entrepreneurial learning: A conceptual framework. *Entrepreneurship Theory and Practice*, *29*(4), 399–424. DOI: 10.1111/j.1540-6520.2005.00091.x

Porter, M. E. (1985). Competitive advantage: creating and sustaining superior performance: with a new introduction. Free Press, New York https://www.hbs.edu/faculty/Pages/item.aspx?num=193

Porter, M. E. (1980). *Competitive Strategy: Techniques for Analyzing Industries and Competitors*. Free Press.

Porter, M. E., & Kramer, M. R. (2011). Creating shared value. *Harvard Business Review*, *89*(1/2), 62–77.

Prenger, R., Tappel, A. P. M., Poortman, C. L., & Schildkamp, K. (2022). How can educational innovations become sustainable? A review of the empirical literature. *Frontiers in Education*, *7*, 970715. Advance online publication. DOI: 10.3389/feduc.2022.970715

Prensky, M. (2006). *Don't bother me mom — I'm learning!* Paragon House.

Price, S., Yiannoutsou, N., & Vezzoli, Y. (2020). Making the body tangible: Elementary geometry learning through VR. *Digital Experiences in Mathematics Education*, *6*(2), 213–232. DOI: 10.1007/s40751-020-00071-7

Prince, M. (2004). Does active learning work? A review of the research. *Journal of Engineering Education*, *93*(3), 223–231. DOI: 10.1002/j.2168-9830.2004.tb00809.x

Prinsloo, P., & Khalil, M. (2024). The Democratisation of AI in, for and through Education: A Position Paper. *Ubiquity Proceedings*, *8*, 8. Advance online publication. DOI: 10.5334/uproc.130

Prodromou, A., Efthimiou, I., & Apostolopoulos, S. (2024). Covid-19 and the Impact on Cyprus' SMEs Tourism - Enterprises: Lessons to be Learned. Conference Proceedings of the 19th European Conference on Innovation and Entrepreneurship ECIE 19(1), 2024 26-27 September 2024 CESI, Paris-Nanterre, France. DOI: 10.34190/ecie.19.1.2470

Prodromou, A. (2021). The Impact of Covid-19 on the Global Automotive Industry - Future Challenges. *American International Journal of Social Science*, *10*(1), 1–11. DOI: 10.30845/aijss.v10n1p1

Prodromou, A., & Kountouridou, M. (2024). Local Entrepreneurial Ecosystems for Global Market Diversification. In *Security and Strategy Models for Key-Solving Institutional Frameworks*. IGI Global., DOI: 10.4018/979-8-3693-5583-1

Purchase, H. C. (2000). Learning about interface design through peer assessment. *Assessment & Evaluation in Higher Education*, *25*(4), 341–352. DOI: 10.1080/026029300449245

Qin, X., Huang, Y.-N., Hu, Z., Chen, K., & Lin, L. (2023). Human resource management research in healthcare: a big data bibliometric study. *Human Resources for Health, 21*(1). https://www.ncbi.nlm.nih.gov/pmc/articles/PMC10696747/

Qiu, Y., Isusi-Fagoaga, R., & García-Aracil, A. (2023). Perceptions and use of metaverse in higher education: A descriptive study in China and Spain. *Computers and Education: Artificial Intelligence*, *5*, 100185. Advance online publication. DOI: 10.1016/j.caeai.2023.100185

Quality Assurance Agency for Higher Education. (2018). *Enterprise and entrepreneurship education: Guidance for UK higher education providers.* Retrieved from https://www.qaa.ac.uk/the-quality-code/enterprise-and-entrepreneurship-education

Radford, S. K., Hunt, D. M., & Andrus, D. (2015). Experiential learning projects. *Journal of Macromarketing*, *35*(4), 466–472. DOI: 10.1177/0276146715573834

Rae, D. (2018). Entrepreneurial learning: A conceptual framework for the development of graduate entrepreneurship. *International Journal of Entrepreneurial Behaviour & Research*, *24*(3), 724–744.

Raja, F. U., & Najmonnisa, K. (2018). Comparing Traditional Teaching Method and Experiential Teaching Method using Experimental Research. *Journal of Education and Educational Development*, *5*(2), 276. DOI: 10.22555/joeed.v5i2.1816

Rajapathirana, R. J., & Hui, Y. (2018). Relationship between innovation capability, innovation type, and firm performance. *Journal of Innovation & Knowledge*, *3*(1), 44–55.

Rajeswarie, S., Praveen, K., Sangam, M. R., Vinay, G., Bokan, R. R., Deka, R., & Kaur, A. (2022). Comparison of team-based learning over conventional didactic lecture among second-year MBBS students. *Cureus*. Advance online publication. [REMOVED HYPERLINK FIELD]DOI: 10.7759/cureus.21792 PMID: 35251859

Rajnai, Z., & Kocsis, I. (2018). Assessing industry 4.0 readiness of enterprises. IEEE 16th World Symposium on Applied Machine Intelligence and Informatics (SAMI), 225-230.

Rampersad, H., Ho, J., & Van der Meer, H. (2010). The role of pre-tests in qualitative research. *International Journal of Business Research*, *10*(3), 130–138.

Ramsgaard, M. B., & Blenker, P. (2022). Reinterpreting a signature pedagogy for entrepreneurship education. *Journal of Small Business and Enterprise Development*, *29*(2), 182–202. Advance online publication. DOI: 10.1108/JSBED-03-2021-0115

Rao, M. (2014). Enhancing employability in engineering and management students through soft skills. *Industrial and Commercial Training*, *46*(1), 42–48. DOI: 10.1108/ICT-04-2013-0023

Rashid, L. (2019). Entrepreneurship Education and Sustainable Development Goals: A literature Review and a Closer Look at Fragile States and Technology-Enabled Approaches. *Sustainability (Basel)*, *11*(19), 5343. Advance online publication. DOI: 10.3390/su11195343

Rastegar, R., Seyfi, S., & Shahi, T. (2023). Tourism SMEs' resilience strategies amidst the COVID-19 crisis: The story of survival. *Tourism Recreation Research*, 1–7. DOI: 10.1080/02508281.2023.2233073

Ratten, V. (2020). Entrepreneurial Leadership and VUCA Management: Competencies for Creativity and Innovation. *Creativity and Innovation Management*, *29*(2), 184–194.

Ratten, V., & Jones, P. (2021). Transformational entrepreneurship education through gamification. *International Journal of Entrepreneurial Behaviour & Research*, *27*(5), 1241–1257.

Ratten, V., & Usmanij, P. (2020). Entrepreneurship education: Time for a change in research direction? *International Journal of Management Education*. Advance online publication. DOI: 10.1016/j.ijme.2020.100367

Redondo, A., Castillo, S., Carro, L., & Martín, P. (2021). The Effects of European Recommendations on the Validation of Lifelong Learning: A Quality Assurance Model for VET in Spain. *Sustainability (Basel)*, *13*(13), 7283. DOI: 10.3390/su13137283

Reinhardt, K. (2023). Business Research Methods. SSRN Electronic Journal. DOI: 10.2139/ssrn.4488860

Research Anthology on Cross-Industry Challenges of Industry 4.0. (2021). In IGI Global eBooks. DOI: 10.4018/978-1-7998-8548-1

Rest, J. R. (1986). *Moral development: Advances in research and theory*. Praeger.

Reuben, B., Samuel, O., & Lawal, A. (2024). *A Review of Artificial Intelligence (AI) Readiness in Higher Education Institutions: A Case Study of Northern States of Nigeria BY.*https://shorturl.at/XQ4zz

Rezghi, S., Moghaddam, A., & Modarresi, M. (2022). The effect of digital games on entrepreneurial self-efficacy and occupational preferences of adolescents. Technology of Education Journal (TEJ), 339-350.

Ribeiro, G., & Leitão, J. C. (2024). Sustainable leadership and sustainable entrepreneurship: A systematic literature review. *Discover Sustainability*, *5*(1), 188. Advance online publication. DOI: 10.1007/s43621-024-00383-3

Richmond, A. S., & Cummings, R. (2005). Implementing Kolb's learning styles into online distance education. *International Journal of Technology in Teaching and Learning*, *1*(1), 45–54.

Rideout, E. C., & Gray, D. O. (2013). Does entrepreneurship education really work? A review and methodological critique of the empirical literature on the effects of university-based entrepreneurship education. *Journal of Small Business Management*, *51*(3), 329–351.

Ries, E. (2011). *The Lean Startup: How Today's Entrepreneurs Use Continuous Innovation to Create Radically Successful Businesses*. Crown Business.

Riivari, E., Kivijärvi, M., & Lämsä, A. M. (2021). Learning teamwork through a computer game: For the sake of performance or collaborative learning? *Educational Technology Research and Development*, *69*(3), 1753–1771. DOI: 10.1007/s11423-021-10009-4

Rios-Campos, C., Zambrano, E. O. G., Cantos, M. F. M., Anchundia-Gómez, O., León, M. E. C., Moya, G. E. M., García, E. M., Batalla, E. P., De La Oliva, N. R., & Zelada, O. S. (2024). Universities and artificial intelligence. *South Florida Journal of Development*, *5*(6), e4016. DOI: 10.46932/sfjdv5n6-010

Rippa, P., Landi, G. C., Cosimato, S., Turriziani, L., & Gheith, M. H. (2020). Embedding entrepreneurship in doctoral students: The impact of a t-shaped educational approach. *European Journal of Innovation Management*, *25*(1), 249–270. DOI: 10.1108/EJIM-07-2020-0289

Robinson, O. C. (2014). Sampling in interview-based qualitative research: A theoretical and practical guide. *Qualitative Research in Psychology*, *11*(1), 25–41. DOI: 10.1080/14780887.2013.801543

Robinson, S., Neergaard, H., Pedersen, L. T., & Krueger, N. (2016). New horizons in entrepreneurship education: From teacher-led to student-centered learning. *Education + Training*, *58*(7/8), 661–683. DOI: 10.1108/ET-03-2016-0048

Rodríguez, A. J. G., Barón, N. J., & Martínez, J. M. G. (2020). Validity of dynamic capabilities in the operation based on new sustainability narratives on nature tourism SMEs and clusters. *Sustainability (Basel)*, *12*(3), 1004. DOI: 10.3390/su12031004

Roepen, D. (2017). Australian business graduates' perceptions of non-technical skills within the workplace. *Education + Training*, *59*(5), 571–582. DOI: 10.1108/ET-01-2017-0016

Rogmans, T., & Abaza, W. (2019). The impact of international business strategy simulation games on student engagement. *Simulation & Gaming*, *50*(3), 393–407. DOI: 10.1177/1046878119848138

Ronstadt, R., Shuman, J., & Vesper, K. (2020). The early story: A brief history of the creation of entrepreneurship at Babson College and the discovery of innovation's missing imperative. *Industry and Higher Education*, *35*(2), 75–82. DOI: 10.1177/0950422220978563

Rosário, A. T., & Raimundo, R. (2024). Enhancing Business Higher Education Through Simulation-Based Learning, Problem-Based Learning, and Challenge-Based Learning. DOI: 10.20944/preprints202407.0747.v1

Rosário, A. T., & Raimundo, R. (2024). Sustainable Entrepreneurship Education: A Systematic Bibliometric Literature Review. *Sustainability (Basel)*, *16*(2), 784. DOI: 10.3390/su16020784

Rosário, A. T., Raimundo, R. J., & Cruz, S. P. (2022). Sustainable Entrepreneurship: A Literature Review. *Sustainability (Basel)*, *14*(9), 5556. DOI: 10.3390/su14095556

Rosenberg, S., Heimler, R., & Morote, E. S. (2012). Basic employability skills: A triangular design approach. *Education + Training*, *54*(1), 7–20. DOI: 10.1108/00400911211198869

Rosenthal, K., Ternes, B., & Strecker, S. (2021). Business process simulation on procedural graphical process models. *Business & Information Systems Engineering*, *63*(5), 569–602. DOI: 10.1007/s12599-021-00690-3

Ross, S. (2021). Simulation-based learning: From learning theory to pedagogical application. *The Internet Journal of Allied Health Sciences and Practice*, *19*(4), 15. DOI: 10.46743/1540-580X/2021.2056

Roth, W.-M. (2001). Gestures: Their role in teaching and learning. *Review of Educational Research*, *71*(3), 365–392. DOI: 10.3102/00346543071003365

Ruben, B. D. (1999). Simulations, Games and Experience Based Learning: The Quest for a New Paradigm for Teaching and Learning. *Simulation & Gaming*, *30*(4), 498–505.

Rubenstein, L. D., Callan, G. L., Neumeister, K. S., & Ridgley, L. M. (2020). Finding the problem: How students approach problem identification. *Thinking Skills and Creativity*, *35*, 100635. DOI: 10.1016/j.tsc.2020.100635

Rubia-Avi, B. (2022). The Research of Educational Innovation: Perspective and Strategies. *Education Sciences*, *13*(1), 26. DOI: 10.3390/educsci13010026

Rubmann, M., Lorenz, M., Gerbert, P., Waldner, M., Justus, J., Engel, P., & Harnisch, M. (2015). Industry 4.0: The future of productivity and the growth in manufacturing industries. BCG Report. Retrieved from https://www.zvw.de/media/media.72e472fb-1698-4a15-8858-344351c8902f.original.pdf

Rungsrisawat, S., & Sutduean, C. (2019). Entrepreneurial education and entrepreneurial intention: The mediating role of creativity disposition among University Learners in Thailand. *Int J Innov Creat Change*, *6*(10), 213–232.

Russell, R., Atchison, M., & Brooks, R. (2008). Business plan competitions in tertiary institutions: Encouraging entrepreneurship education. *Journal of Higher Education Policy and Management*, *30*(2), 123–138. DOI: 10.1080/13600800801938739

Russel, S., & Norvig, P. (2010). *Artificial intelligence - a modern approach.* Pearson Education.

Russo, M. V. (2003). The emergence of sustainable industries: Building on natural capital. *Strategic Management Journal*, *24*(4), 317–331. DOI: 10.1002/smj.298

Russo, S. G., Eich, C., Barwing, J., Nickel, E. A., Braun, U., Graf, B. M., & Timmermann, A. (2007). Self-reported changes in attitude and behavior after attending a simulation-aided airway management course. *Journal of Clinical Anesthesia*, *19*(7), 517–522. DOI: 10.1016/j.jclinane.2007.04.007 PMID: 18063206

Rutner, S., & Scott, R. (2022, September 1). *Use of Artificial Intelligence to Grade Student Discussion Boards: An Exploratory Study.* https://isedj.org/2022-20/n4/ISEDJv20n4p4.html

Saenz, M. J., & Cano, J. L. (2009). Experiential learning through simulation games: An empirical study. *International Journal of Engineering Education*, *25*(2), 296–307.

Sagar, H. (2015). *Entrepreneurial Schools. Part 2 - Entrepreneurial learning environments and a changed role for teachers., Entrepreneurship 360.* OECD and European Commission.

Salamzadeh, A., Tajpour, M., & Hosseini, E. (2022). Measuring the impact of simulation-based teaching on entrepreneurial skills of the MBA/DBA students. In *Technology and entrepreneurship Education: Adopting creative digital approaches to learning and teaching* (pp. 77–104). Springer International Publishing. DOI: 10.1007/978-3-030-84292-5_4

Salas, E. (2018). The power of teamwork: Building effective teams in organizations. *Organizational Psychology Review*, *8*(2), 78–102.

Salas, E., Wildman, J. L., & Piccolo, R. F. (2009). Using Simulation-Based Training to Enhance Management Education. *Academy of Management Learning & Education*, *8*(4), 559–573. DOI: 10.5465/AMLE.2009.47785474

Salavou, H., Chalkos, G., & Lioukas, S. (2021). Linkages between entrepreneurial intentions and entrepreneurship education: New evidence on the gender imbalance. *Education + Training*, *63*(6), 906–919. DOI: 10.1108/ET-10-2020-0301

Salehi, H., & Burgueño, R. (2018). Emerging artificial intelligence methods in structural engineering. *Engineering Structures*, *171*, 170–189. Advance online publication. DOI: 10.1016/j.engstruct.2018.05.084

Samašonok, K., Išoraitė, M., & Žirnelė, L. (2020). Education of entrepreneurship by participation in a business simulation enterprise activities: Conditions of effectiveness and opportunities for improvement. *Entrepreneurship and Sustainability Issues*, *7*(4), 3122–3144. DOI: 10.9770/jesi.2020.7.4(36)

Samrgandi, N. (2021). User interface design & evaluation of mobile applications. *International Journal of Computer Science & Network Security*, *21*(1), 55–63.

Sandirasegarane, S., Sutermaster, S., Gill, A., Volz, J., & Mehta, K. (2016). Context-driven entrepreneurial education in vocational schools. *International Journal for Research in Vocational Education and Training*, *3*(2), 106–126. DOI: 10.13152/IJRVET.3.2.3

Santeramo, F. G., & Barbieri, C. (2017). On the demand for agritourism: A cursory review of methodologies and practice. *Tourism Planning & Development*, *14*(1), 139–148. DOI: 10.1080/21568316.2015.1137968

Sarasvathy, S. D. (2001). Causation and Effectuation: Toward a Theoretical Shift from Economic Inevitability to Entrepreneurial Contingency. *Academy of Management Review*, *26*(2), 243–263. DOI: 10.2307/259121

Sarkar, P., Kadam, K., & Pillai, J. S. (2020). Learners' approaches, motivation and patterns of problem-solving on lines and angles in geometry using augmented reality. *Smart Learning Environments*, *7*(1), 1–23. DOI: 10.1186/s40561-020-00124-9

Sarker, I. H., Hoque, M. M., Uddin, M. K., & Alsanoosy, T. (2021). Mobile data science and intelligent apps: Concepts, AI-based modeling and research directions. *Mobile Networks and Applications*, *26*(1), 285–303. DOI: 10.1007/s11036-020-01650-z

Sarooghi, H., Sunny, S., Hornsby, J., & Fernhaber, S. (2019). Design Thinking and Entrepreneurship Education: Where Are We, and What Are the Possibilities? *Journal of Small Business Management*, *57*, 78–93. DOI: 10.1111/jsbm.12541

Sartzetaki, M., Dimitriou, D., & Karagkouni, A. (2025). Assortment of the Regional Business Ecosystem Effects Driven by New Motorway Projects, Transportation Research. *Procedia, 82*, 515-529. DOI: 10.1016/j.trpro.2024.12.111

Sartzetaki, M., Karagkouni, A., & Dimitriou, D. (2023). A Conceptual Framework for Developing Intelligent Services (a Platform) for Transport Enterprises: The Designation of Key Drivers for Action. *Electronics (Basel)*, *12*(22), 4690. DOI: 10.3390/electronics12224690

Saunders, B., Sim, J., & Kingstone, T. (2018). Saturation in qualitative research: Exploring its conceptualization and operationalization. *Quality & Quantity*, *52*, 1893–1907. PMID: 29937585

Scheepers, M. J. V., Barnes, R., Clements, M., & Stubbs, A. J. (2018). Preparing future-ready graduates through experiential entrepreneurship. *Education + Training*, *60*(4), 303–317. DOI: 10.1108/ET-11-2017-0167

Scherer, R., & Teo, T. (2019). Unpacking teachers' intentions to integrate technology: A meta-analysis. *Educational Research Review*, *27*, 90–109. DOI: 10.1016/j.edurev.2019.03.001

Schilling, B. J., Attavanich, W., & Jin, Y. (2014). Does agritourism enhance farm profitability? *Journal of Agricultural and Resource Economics*, 69–87.

Schmitt, A., Den Hartog, D. N., & Belschak, F. D. (2016). Transformational leadership and proactive work behaviour: A moderated mediation model including work engagement and job strain. *Journal of Occupational and Organizational Psychology*, *89*(3), 588–610. DOI: 10.1111/joop.12143

Schmitz, A., Urbano, D., Dandolini, G., Souza, J., & Guerrero, M. (2017). Innovation and entrepreneurship in the academic setting: A systematic literature review. *The International Entrepreneurship and Management Journal*, *13*(2), 369–395. DOI: 10.1007/s11365-016-0401-z

Schofield, T. (2012). Critical success factors for knowledge transfer collaborations between university and industry. *The Journal of Research Administration*, *44*, 38–56.

Schroder, C. (2016). The challenges for Industry 4.0 for small and medium sized enterprises. Friedrich-Ebert-Stiftung. Retrieved from https://www.fes.de/aktuell/publikationen

Schumpeter, J. A. (1942). *Capitalism, Socialism, and Democracy*. Harper & Brothers.

Schwab, K. (2016). The Fourth Industrial Revolution: What it means, how to respond. World Economic Forum. Retrieved from https://www.weforum.org/agenda/2016/01/the-fourth-industrial-revolution-what-it-means-and-how-to-respond

Schwaiger, M., Krajnčan, M., Vukovič, M., Jenko, M., & Doz, D. (2024). Educators' opinions about VR/AR/XR: An exploratory study. *Education and Information Technologies*, *29*(18), 24861–24880. Advance online publication. DOI: 10.1007/s10639-024-12808-7

Schwartz, R. A., & Weber, B. W. (2015). Simulation as a Research Tool for Market Architects. In Lee, C. F., & Lee, J. (Eds.), *Handbook of Financial Econometrics and Statistics*. Springer. DOI: 10.1007/978-1-4614-7750-1_4

Scott, J. M., & Hall, M. (2016). SimVenture: Embedding business simulation games in entrepreneurship education. *Education + Training*, *58*(1), 47–67.

Scott, J. M., Pavlovich, K., Thompson, J. L., & Penaluna, A. (2020). Constructive (mis)alignment in team-based experiential entrepreneurship education. *Education + Training*. Advance online publication. DOI: 10.1108/ET-06-2019-0113

Scuotto, V., & Morellato, M. (2013). Entrepreneurial knowledge and digital competence: Keys for a success of student entrepreneurship. *Journal of the Knowledge Economy*, *4*(3), 293–303. DOI: 10.1007/s13132-013-0155-6

Seaman, J. (2008). Experience, reflect, critique: The end of the "learning cycles" era. *Journal of Experiential Education*, *31*(1), 3–18. DOI: 10.1177/105382590803100103

Seidel, V., & Fixson, S. K. (2013). Adopting Design Thinking in Novice Multidisciplinary Teams: The Application and Limits of Design Methods and Reflexive Practices. *Journal of Product Innovation Management*, *30*(1), 19–33. DOI: 10.1111/jpim.12061

Seikkula-Leino, J., Ruskovaara, E., Pihkala, T., Rodríguez, I. D., & Delfino, J. (2019). Developing entrepreneurship education in Europe: Teachers' commitment to entrepreneurship education in the UK, Finland and Spain. In Fayolle, A., Kariv, D., & Matlay, H. (Eds.), *The Role and Impact of Entrepreneurship Education* (pp. 130–145)., DOI: 10.4337/9781786438232.00014

Selznick, P., & Mayhew, L. (2018). Innovation in Higher Education: A Critical Perspective. *Journal of Higher Education Policy and Management, 40*(1), 1–15.

Senyao, S., & Ha, S. (2022). How social media influences resident participation in rural tourism development: A case study of Tunda in Tibet. *Journal of Tourism and Cultural Change, 20*(3), 386–405. DOI: 10.1080/14766825.2020.1849244

Serdyukov, P. (2017). Innovation in education: What works, what doesn't, and what to do about it? *Journal of Research in Innovative Teaching & Learning, 10*(1), 4–33. DOI: 10.1108/JRIT-10-2016-0007

Setiawan, J. L. (2014). Examining entrepreneurial self-efficacy among students. *Procedia: Social and Behavioral Sciences, 115*, 235–242. DOI: 10.1016/j.sbspro.2014.02.431

Shabbir, M. S., & Pallares-Venegas, E. (2024). Influences of entrepreneurship skills and universities on the promotion of entrepreneurial intentions of students; mediating role of business simulation games. *On the Horizon, 32*(1), 1–14. DOI: 10.1108/OTH-10-2022-0062

Shabbir, M., Shariff, M. N. M., Bin Bakar, M. S., & Yusof, M. S. (2018). The mediating role of trade simulations on the relationship among University role entrepreneurship curriculum and assessment of training approaches and entrepreneurial inclination. *International. The Journal of Supply Chain Management, 7*(4), 223–233.

Shalwa. (2024, November 16). AI in Education: 2025 Statistics & the Future of Learning. *ARTSMART AI*. https://artsmart.ai/blog/ai-in-education-statistics-2024/

Shane, S. (2003). *A General Theory of Entrepreneurship: The Individual-Opportunity Nexus*. Edward Elgar Publishing. DOI: 10.4337/9781781007990

Shankar, D., Tewari, D., Rahman, M., Mishra, D., & Bajaj, M. (2023). *Impact of Virtual Reality (Vr) and Augmented Reality (Ar) in Education*. Tuijin Jishu/Journal of Propulsion Technology., DOI: 10.52783/tjjpt.v44.i4.1014

Sharma, A., Ahn, M., Levine, S., Kumar, V., Hausman, K., & Gu, S. (2020). Emergent Real-World Robotic Skills via Unsupervised Off-Policy Reinforcement Learning. *ArXiv*, abs/2004.12974. DOI: 10.15607/RSS.2020.XVI.053

Sharma, P. N., & Kirkman, B. L. (2015). Leveraging leaders: A literature review and future lines of inquiry for empowering leadership research. *Group & Organization Management, 40*(2), 193–237. DOI: 10.1177/1059601115574906

Sharma, S., Goyal, D. P., & Singh, A. (2021). Systematic review on sustainable entrepreneurship education (SEE): A framework and analysis. *World Journal of Entrepreneurship, Management and Sustainable Development, 17*(3), 372–395.

Sheikh, R. A., Abdalkrim, G. M., & Shehawy, Y. M. (2023). Assessing the impact of business simulation as a teaching method for developing 21st century future skills. *Journal of International Education in Business, 16*(3), 351–370.

Shepherd, D. A., & Patzelt, H. (2011). The New Field of Sustainable Entrepreneurship: Studying Entrepreneurial Action Linking "What is to be Sustained" with "What is to be Developed". *Entrepreneurship Theory and Practice*, *35*(1), 137–163. DOI: 10.1111/j.1540-6520.2010.00426.x

Shepherd, D., & Gruber, M. (2020). The Lean Startup Framework: Closing the Academic–Practitioner Divide. *Entrepreneurship Theory and Practice*, *45*(5), 967–998. DOI: 10.1177/1042258719899415

Shields, M. (2002). Learning and teaching through simulation. *Simulation & Gaming*, *33*(1), 111–126. DOI: 10.1177/1046878102033001010

Shkabatur, J., Bar-El, R., & Schwartz, D. (2022). Invention and entrepreneurship for justifiable incubatement: Lessons from Ethiopia. *Progress in Planning*, *160*, 100599. DOI: 10.1016/j.progress.2021.100599

Shrivastava, A. (2018). How to bridge the gap between academia and industry? Retrieved March 15, 2020, from https://www.peoplematters.in/article/campus-recruitment/how-to-bridge-the-gap-between-academia-and-industry-15203

Shrivastava, P. (1995). The role of corporations in achieving ecological sustainability. *Academy of Management Review*, *20*(4), 936–960. DOI: 10.2307/258961

Shrivastava, P., & Hart, S. (1995). Creating sustainable value through environmental strategy. *The Academy of Management Perspectives*, *9*(4), 101–119.

Silitonga, L. M., Dharmawan, B., Murti, A. T., & Wu, T. T. (2024). Promoting Entrepreneurial Intentions and Competencies Through Business Simulation Games. *Journal of Educational Computing Research*, *62*(3), 725–755. DOI: 10.1177/07356331231209772

Simonton, D. K. (2018). Creative Genius: A Trait Theoretical and Multivariate Perspective. *Personality and Social Psychology Review*, *22*(3), 218–240.

Simpson, M., Tuck, N., & Bellamy, S. (2004). Small business success factors: The role of education and training. *Education + Training*, *46*(8/9), 481–491. DOI: 10.1108/00400910410569605

Sims, R. R., & Felton, E. L.Jr. (2006). Designing and Delivering Business Ethics Teaching and Learning. *Journal of Business Ethics*, *63*(3), 297–312. DOI: 10.1007/s10551-005-3562-1

Sin, Z. P. T., Zhao, I. D., Wu, A. C. H., Li, R. C., Ng, P. H. F., Huang, X., Baciu, G., Cao, J., & Li, Q. (2023). Towards a Metaverse of Knowledge: A Constructivist Proposition on Immersive Learning and Visual Literacy. *Lecture Notes in Computer Science (Including Subseries Lecture Notes in Artificial Intelligence and Lecture Notes in Bioinformatics), 13869 LNCS*, 214–225. DOI: 10.1007/978-3-031-33023-0_19

Siregar, O. M., Ginting, B., Jali, M. F. M., & Nasution, M. D. T. P. (2024). Challenges in Integrating Agritourism with Sustainable Farming Practices: How Do the Willingness, Attitudes, and Entrepreneurial Competencies of Rural Youth Influence This Integration? In Harnessing, A. I. (Ed.), *Machine Learning, and IoT for Intelligent Business* (Vol. 1, pp. 439–450). Springer Nature Switzerland.

Sklias, G., Gkelios, S., Dimitriou, D., Sartzetaki, M., & Chatzichristofis, S. A. (2024). Synergizing global and local strategies for dynamic project management: An advanced machine learning-enhanced framework. *IEEE Access : Practical Innovations, Open Solutions, 12*, 85955–85968. DOI: 10.1109/ACCESS.2024.3413890

Slater, M., & Wilbur, S. (1997). A framework for immersive virtual environments (FIVE): Speculations on the role of presence in virtual environments. *Presence (Cambridge, Mass.), 6*(6), 603–616. DOI: 10.1162/pres.1997.6.6.603

Smirnov, I., Tsvetkova, N., & Borisova, L. (2023). Innovation-driven entrepreneurship education: New strategies for success. *International Journal of Educational Research, 113*, 101965.

Snyder, C. (2003). *Paper prototyping: The fast and easy way to design and refine user interfaces*. Morgan Kaufmann.

Song, R., Cao, Y., Xu, Z., Li, Y., & Liang, B. (2018). Exploring the Laboratory Construction in Finance and Economics Colleges and Universities by Adopting Virtual Simulation Technology. In *2018 2nd International Conference on Management, Education and Social Science (ICMESS 2018)* (pp. 491-494). Atlantis Press.

Song, R., Cao, Y., Xu, Z., Li, Y., & Liang, B. (2018, June). Exploring the Laboratory Construction in Finance and Economics Colleges and Universities by Adopting Virtual Simulation Technology. In *2018 2nd International Conference on Management, Education and Social Science (ICMESS 2018)* (pp. 491-494). Atlantis Press. DOI: 10.2991/icmess-18.2018.108

Sonnino, R. (2004). For a 'piece of bread'? Interpreting sustainable development through agritourism in Southern Tuscany. *Sociologia Ruralis, 44*(3), 285–300. DOI: 10.1111/j.1467-9523.2004.00276.x

Sophocleous, H. P. H. (2023). Nation Branding as a Strategic Asset for Local SMEs. In Advances in marketing, customer relationship management, and e-services book series (pp. 124–155). DOI: 10.4018/978-1-6684-5902-7.ch006

Sophocleous, H., & Prodromou, A. (2024). A Marketing - Business Plan and competition analysis for the Cyprus specialized /wellness tourism services / market. In *Real-World Tools and Scenarios for Entrepreneurship Exploration*. IGI Global. DOI: 10.4018/979-8-3693-3100-2.ch014

Sousa, A. E., Cardoso, P., & Dias, F. (2024). The Use of Artificial Intelligence Systems in Tourism and Hospitality: The Tourists' Perspective. *Administrative Sciences, 14*(8), 165. DOI: 10.3390/admsci14080165

Speicher, M., Hall, B. D., & Nebeling, M. (2019, May 2). What is mixed reality? *Conference on Human Factors in Computing Systems - Proceedings*. DOI: 10.1145/3290605.3300767

Sreenivasan, A., & Suresh, M. (2023). Twenty years of entrepreneurship education: A bibliometric analysis. *Entrepreneurship Education, 6*(1), 45–68. DOI: 10.1007/s41959-023-00089-z

Staiano, F. (2022). *Designing and Prototyping Interfaces with Figma: Learn essential UX/UI design principles by creating interactive prototypes for mobile, tablet, and desktop*. Packt Publishing Ltd.

Stainton, A. J., Johnson, J. E., & Borodzicz, E. P. (2010). Educational Validity of Business Gaming Simulation: A Research Methodology Framework. *Simulation & Gaming*, *41*(5), 705–723. DOI: 10.1177/1046878109353467

Stam, E. (2015). Entrepreneurial ecosystems and regional policy: A sympathetic critique. *European Planning Studies*, *23*(9), 1759–1769. DOI: 10.1080/09654313.2015.1061484

Stander, J., Grimmer, K., & Brink, Y. (2019). Learning styles of physiotherapists: A systematic scoping review. *BMC Medical Education*, *19*(1), 2. Advance online publication. [REMOVED HYPERLINK FIELD]DOI: 10.1186/s12909-018-1434-5 PMID: 30606180

Staroverov, A., Muravyev, K., Yakovlev, K., & Panov, A. (2023). Skill Fusion in Hybrid Robotic Framework for Visual Object Goal Navigation. *Robotics (Basel, Switzerland)*, *12*(4), 104. Advance online publication. DOI: 10.3390/robotics12040104

Statista (2023). Global total corporate artificial intelligence (AI) investment from 2015 to 2022 (in billion U.S. dollars). https://shorturl.at/v35mo

Statista (2024). Number of travel and tourism jobs worldwide from 2019 to 2023, with a forecast for 2024 and 2034 (in millions). https://shorturl.at/KZIhr

Stefanic, I., Campbell, R. K., Russ, J. S., & Stefanic, E. (2020). Evaluation of a blended learning approach for cross-cultural entrepreneurial education. *Innovations in Education and Teaching International*, *57*(2), 242–254. DOI: 10.1080/14703297.2019.1568901

Steiner, A., & Markantoni, M. (2014). Unpacking community resilience through capacity for change. *Community Development Journal: An International Forum*, *49*(3), 407–425. DOI: 10.1093/cdj/bst042

Steiner, A., & Steinerowska-Streb, I. (2013). *Why Use Franchising?: The Perception of Scottish Entrepreneurs*. LAP LAMBERT Academic Publishing.

Sternberg, R. J., & Lubart, T. I. (2019). Developing a model for creativity. *The Cambridge Handbook of Creativity*, 2, 3-15.

Stieff, M., Lira, M. E., & Scopelitis, S. A. (2016). Gesture supports spatial thinking in STEM. *Cognition and Instruction*, *34*(2), 80–99. DOI: 10.1080/07370008.2016.1145122

Stieler-Hunt, C. J., & Jones, C. M. (2017). Feeling alienated – teachers using immersive digital games in classrooms. *Technology, Pedagogy and Education*, *26*(4), 457–470. DOI: 10.1080/1475939X.2017.1334227

Stirling, A., Kerr, G., MacPherson, E., Banwell, J., Bandealy, A., & Battaglia, A. (2017). Do postsecondary internships address the four learning modes of experiential learning theory? An exploration through document analysis. *Canadian Journal of Higher Education*, *47*(1), 27–48. DOI: 10.47678/cjhe.v47i1.186196

Stirman, S. W., Kimberly, J., Cook, N., Calloway, A., Castro, F., & Charns, M. (2012). The sustainability of new programs and innovations: A review of the empirical literature and recommendations for future research. *Implementation Science : IS*, *7*(1), 17. Advance online publication. [REMOVED HYPERLINK FIELD]DOI: 10.1186/1748-5908-7-17 PMID: 22417162

Stöhr, C., Demazière, C., & Adawi, T. (2020). The polarizing effect of the online flipped classroom. *Computers & Education, 147*, 103789. DOI: 10.1016/j.compedu.2019.103789

Stoiber, K., Matzler, K., & Hautz, J. (2023). Ambidextrous structures paving the way for disruptive business models: A conceptual framework. *Review of Managerial Science, 17*(4), 1439–1485. DOI: 10.1007/s11846-022-00589-7

Strand, T., & Papastephanou, M. (2023). Education and democratization. An introduction. *Ethics and Education, 18*(3–4), 231–241. DOI: 10.1080/17449642.2023.2281856

Strickland, P. (2023). Business-Simulation Pedagogy, Assessments, and Barriers to Entry in an Australian Educational Environment. International Journal of Smart Business and Technology, 11(2), 1-14. DOI: 10.21742/IJSBT.2023.11.2.01

Stroumpoulis, A., Kopanaki, E., & Varelas, S. (2022). Role of artificial intelligence and big data analytics in smart tourism: A resource-based view approach. *WIT Transactions on Ecology and the Environment, 256*, 99–108. DOI: 10.2495/ST220091

Stubbs, W., & Cocklin, C. (2008). Conceptualizing a "sustainability business model". *Organization & Environment, 21*(2), 103–127. DOI: 10.1177/1086026608318042

Succi, C., & Canovi, M. (2020). Soft skills to enhance graduate employability: Comparing students and employers' perceptions. *Studies in Higher Education, 45*(9), 1834–1847.

Summers, G. J. (2004). Today's business simulation industry. *Simulation & Gaming, 35*(2), 208–241.

Sun, J., Gan, W., Chen, Z., Li, J., & Yu, P. S. (2022). Big data meets metaverse: A survey. *ArXiv Preprint ArXiv:2210.16282.*

Sung, C. S., & Park, J. Y. (2018). Sustainability orientation and entrepreneurship orientation: Is there a tradeoff relationship between them? *Sustainability (Basel), 10*(2), 379. DOI: 10.3390/su10020379

Sung, S. Y., & Choi, J. N. (2014). Do organizations spend wisely on employees? Effects of training and development investments on learning and innovation in organizations. *Journal of Organizational Behavior, 35*(3), 393–412. DOI: 10.1002/job.1897 PMID: 25598576

Sungur, S., Tekkaya, C., & Geban, Ö. (2006). Improving achievement through problem-based learning. *Journal of Biological Education, 40*(4), 155–160. DOI: 10.1080/00219266.2006.9656037

Sunny Yang, S., & Chandra, Y. (2013). Growing artificial entrepreneurs: Advancing entrepreneurship research using agent-based simulation approach. *International Journal of Entrepreneurial Behaviour & Research, 19*(2), 210–237. DOI: 10.1108/13552551311310383

Suseno, Y., & Abbott, L. (2021). Women entrepreneurs' digital social innovation: Linking gender, entrepreneurship, social innovation and information systems. *Information Systems Journal, 31*(5), 717–744. DOI: 10.1111/isj.12327

Sussan, F., & Acs, Z. J. (2017). The digital entrepreneurial ecosystem. *Small Business Economics, 49*(1), 55–73. DOI: 10.1007/s11187-017-9867-5

Su, Y., Zhu, Z., Chen, J., Jin, Y., Wang, T., Lin, C., & Xu, D. (2021). Factors influencing entrepreneurial intention of university students in China: Integrating the perceived university support and theory of planned behavior. *Sustainability (Basel)*, *13*(8), 4519. DOI: 10.3390/su13084519

Sweet, K. S., LeBlanc, J. K., Stough, L. M., & Sweany, N. W. (2020). Community building and knowledge sharing by individuals with disabilities using social media. *Journal of Computer Assisted Learning*, *36*(1), 1–11. DOI: 10.1111/jcal.12377

Tabrizi, B., Lam, E., Girard, K., & Vernon, I. (2019). Change management: Digital transformation is not about technology. Harvard Business Review. Retrieved from https://hbr.org/2019/03/digital-transformation-is-not-about-technology

Talukder, S. C., Lakner, Z., & Temesi, Á. (2024). Development and State of the Art of Entrepreneurship Education: A Bibliometric Review. *Education Sciences*, *14*(3), 295. DOI: 10.3390/educsci14030295

Tanina, A., Konyshev, E., & Tsahaeva, K. (2020). Agritourism development model in digital economy. In *Innovations in Digital Economy* (pp. 1-6). DOI: 10.1145/3444465.3444518

Tapalova, O., & Zhiyenbayeva, N. (2022). Artificial Intelligence in Education: AIEd for Personalised Learning Pathways. *Electronic Journal of e-Learning*, *20*(5), 639–653. https://files.eric.ed.gov/fulltext/EJ1373006.pdf. DOI: 10.34190/ejel.20.5.2597

Tardif, M. (2019). L'innovation pédagogique: Un levier pour la réussite des étudiants. *Revue internationale d'éducation*, 50(1), 55-73.

Taylor, D. L., Yeung, M., & Bashet, A. Z. (2021). Personalized and Adaptive Learning. In *SpringerBriefs in statistics* (pp. 17–34). DOI: 10.1007/978-3-030-58948-6_2

Tchokote, I., & Bawack, R. (2024). Linking Business Games to Business and Entrepreneurship Education: Insights from a Bibliometric and Literature Review. *Theoretical Economics Letters*, *14*(2), 436–467. DOI: 10.4236/tel.2024.142024

Teece, D. J. (2010). Business Models, Business Strategy and Innovation. *Long Range Planning*, *43*(2-3), 172–194. DOI: 10.1016/j.lrp.2009.07.003

Tena-Chollet, F., Tixier, J., Dandrieux, A., & Slangen, P. (2017). Training decision-makers: Existing strategies for natural and technological crisis management and specifications of an improved simulation-based tool. *Safety Science*, *97*, 144–153. DOI: 10.1016/j.ssci.2016.03.025

Tew, C., & Barbieri, C. (2012). The perceived benefits of agritourism: The provider's perspective. *Tourism Management*, *33*(1), 215–224. DOI: 10.1016/j.tourman.2011.02.005

Thavikulwat, P. (1995). Computer-assisted gaming for entrepreneurship education. *Simulation & Gaming*, *26*(3), 328–345. DOI: 10.1177/1046878195263005

Thimmanna, A. V. N. S., Sharma, M. S. N., & Radhakrishnan, A. S. (2024). Personalized Learning Paths: Adapting Education with AI-Driven Curriculum. *European Economic Letters*, *14*(1), 31–40. DOI: 10.52783/eel.v14i1.993

Thomke, S. (1998). Managing Experimentation in the Design of New Products. *Management Science*, *44*(6), 743–762. DOI: 10.1287/mnsc.44.6.743

Thompson, P. (2018). Developing entrepreneurial attitudes in the classroom: The role of entrepreneurship education. *Journal of Education and Work*, *31*(1), 27–40.

Thomsen, B., Muurlink, O., & Best, T. (2019). Backpack Bootstrapping: Social Entrepreneurship Education Through Experiential Learning. *Journal of Social Entrepreneurship*, *12*(2), 238–264. DOI: 10.1080/19420676.2019.1689155

Thurzo, A., Strunga, M., Urban, R., Surovková, J., & Afrashtehfar, K.I. (2023). Impact of Artificial Intelligence on Dental Education: A Review and Guide for Curriculum Update. *Education Sciences*, *13*(2), 150. DOI: 10.3390/educsci13020150

Tican, C. (2019). Pre-service primary school and pre-school teachers' perception of individual entrepreneurship and opinions about their creative thinking tendency. *International Journal of Educational Methodology*, *5*(4), 591–606. DOI: 10.12973/ijem.5.4.591

Tiggemann, M., Anderberg, I., & Brown, Z. (2020). # Loveyourbody: The effect of body positive Instagram captions on women's body image. *Body Image*, *33*, 129–136. DOI: 10.1016/j.bodyim.2020.02.015 PMID: 32151992

Timu , N., Bartlett, M. E., Bartlett, J. E., Ehrlich, S., & Babutsidze, Z. (2024). Fostering inclusive higher education through universal design for learning and inclusive pedagogy–EU and US faculty perceptions. *Higher Education Research & Development*, *43*(2), 473–487. DOI: 10.1080/07294360.2023.2234314

Tokarieva, A. V., Volkova, N. P., Harkusha, I. V., & Soloviev, V. N. (2019). Educational digital games: Models and implementation. *Educational Dimension*, *1*, 5–26. DOI: 10.31812/educdim.v53i1.3872

Toledano, N., & Urbano, D. (2008). Promoting entrepreneurial mindsets at universities: A case study in the south of Spain. *European Journal of International Management*, *2*(4), 382–399. DOI: 10.1504/EJIM.2008.021244

Tol, R. S. J. (2018). The Economic Impacts of Climate Change. *Review of Environmental Economics and Policy*, *12*(1), 4–25. DOI: 10.1093/reep/rex027

Tondeur, J., Howard, S., Van Zanten, M., Gorissen, P., Van der Neut, I., Uerz, D., & Kral, M. (2023). The HeDiCom framework: Higher Education teachers' digital competencies for the future. *Educational Technology Research and Development*, *71*(1), 33–53. DOI: 10.1007/s11423-023-10193-5 PMID: 37016717

Tong, L., Yan, W., & Manta, O. (2022). Artificial Intelligence Influences Intelligent Automation in Tourism: A Mediating Role of Internet of Things and Environmental, Social, and Governance Investment. *Frontiers in Environmental Science*, *10*, 853302. Advance online publication. DOI: 10.3389/fenvs.2022.853302

Torres, A., Domańska-Glonek, E., Dzikowski, W., Korulczyk, J., & Torres, K. (2020). Transition to online is possible: Solution for simulation-based teaching during the COVID-19 pandemic. *Medical Education*, *54*(9), 858–859. DOI: 10.1111/medu.14245 PMID: 32418247

Torres-Coronas, T., & Vidal-Blasco, M. (2021). *Predicting global entrepreneurship: An exploratory study*. Educar., DOI: 10.5565/rev/educar.1279

Tosto, S. A., Alyahya, J., Espinoza, V., McCarthy, K., & Tcherni-Buzzeo, M. (2023). Online learning in the wake of the COVID-19 pandemic: Mixed methods analysis of student views by demographic group. *Social Sciences & Humanities Open*, *8*(1), 100598. [REMOVED HYPERLINK FIELD]DOI: 10.1016/j.ssaho.2023.100598 PMID: 37366390

Tragazikis, P., Kirginas, S., & Gouscos, D. (2012). Digital games for entrepreneurial learning, innovation and creativity: Examples and evaluation criteria. *International Journal of Innovative Research and Development*, *4*(3/4), 314. DOI: 10.1504/IJIRD.2012.047564

Tran, T. T. (2016). Enhancing graduate employability and the need for university-enterprise collaboration. *Journal of Teaching and Learning for Graduate Employability*, *7*(1), 58–71. DOI: 10.21153/jtlge2016vol7no1art598

Trauth, E. M., Farwsell, D. W., & Lee, D. (1993). The IS expectation gap: Industry expectations versus academic preparation. *Management Information Systems Quarterly*, *17*(3), 293–307. DOI: 10.2307/249773

Treviño, L. K., & Nelson, K. A. (2016). *Managing business ethics: Straight talk about how to do it right* (6th ed.). Wiley.

Tsaknis, P. A., Sahinidis, A. G., & Vassiliou, E. E. (2022). Entrepreneurship education effectiveness: Does personality matter? *Development and Learning in Organizations*, *36*(6), 8–11. DOI: 10.1108/DLO-12-2021-0230

Tshuma, S., Dube, M., & Dangaiso, P. (2024). Agritourism Digital and Social Media Marketing in Africa: The Case Study of Zimbabwe. In *Agritourism in Africa* (pp. 191-211). Routledge.

Tsironis, G., Karagkouni, A., Dimitriou, D., & Tsagarakis, K. P. (2023). Mapping sustainable practices and concepts in the transportation ecosystem for the EU-27 countries, based on LinkedIn company profiles. *Frontiers in Sustainability*, *4*, 1268575. Advance online publication. DOI: 10.3389/frsus.2023.1268575

Tsitskaria, E., Goudas, M., Tsalouchou, E., & Michalopoulou, M. (2016). Employers' expectations of the employability skills needed in the sport and recreation environment. *Journal of Hospitality, Leisure, Sport and Tourism Education*, *20*, 1–9. DOI: 10.1016/j.jhlste.2016.11.002

Tuli, F. (2010). The basis of distinction between quantitative and qualitative in social science: Reflection on ontological, epistemological and methodological perspectives. *Ethiopian Journal of Education and Sciences*, *6*(1), 97–108.

Turban, E., Pollard, C., & Wood, G. (2018). *Information technology for management: On-demand strategies for performance, growth and sustainability*. John Wiley & Sons.

Uddin, M., Chowdhury, R. A., Hoque, N., Ahmad, A., Mamun, A., & Uddin, M. N. (2022). Developing entrepreneurial intentions among business graduates of higher educational institutions through entrepreneurship education and entrepreneurial passion: A moderated mediation model. *International Journal of Management Education*, *20*(2), 100647. DOI: 10.1016/j.ijme.2022.100647

UNESCO. (2018). *ICT competency framework for teachers (version 3).* Retrieved from https://unesdoc.unesco.org/ark:/48223/pf0000213475

United Nations Department of Economic and Social Affairs. (n.d.). *Disability factsheet on persons with disabilities.* Retrieved from https://www.un.org/development/desa/disabilities/resources/factsheet-on-persons-with-disabilities.html#:~:text=Disability%20rates%20are%20significantly%20higher,cent%20among%20the%20better%20educated

United Nations Educational, Scientific, and Cultural Organization (UNESCO). (2021). Education for sustainable development: A roadmap. Retrieved from https://www.unesco.org

United Nations. (2006). *Convention on the rights of persons with disabilities.* General Assembly of the United Nations. Retrieved from https://www.un.org/development/desa/disabilities/convention-on-the-rights-of-persons-with-disabilities.html#Fulltext

United Nations. (2015). Transforming our world: The 2030 Agenda for Sustainable Development. United Nations General Assembly. https://www.un.org/sustainabledevelopment

Urban, B., & Silva, M. (2019). The Influence of Creativity and Innovation on Entrepreneurial Intention. *International Journal of Entrepreneurial Behaviour & Research, 25*(4), 724–746.

Urbano, D., Aparicio, S., & Audretsch, D. B. (2019). Twenty-five years of research on institutions, entrepreneurship, and economic growth: What has been learned? *Small Business Economics, 53*(1), 21–49.

Usart, M., & Romero, M. (2014). Entrepreneurship competence assessment through a game based learning MOOC. In De Gloria, A. (Ed.), Lecture Notes in Computer Science: Vol. 8605. *Games and Learning Alliance. GALA 2013* (pp. 252–264). DOI: 10.1007/978-3-319-12157-4_20

Van Dijk, J., Van Der Lugt, R., & Hummels, C. (2014). Beyond distributed representation: embodied cognition design supporting socio-sensorimotor couplings. *Proceedings of the 8th International Conference on Tangible, Embedded and Embodied Interaction*, 181–188. DOI: 10.1145/2540930.2540934

Van Kolfschooten, H., & Van Oirschot, J. (2024). The EU Artificial Intelligence Act (2024): Implications for healthcare. *Health Policy (Amsterdam), 149*, 105152. DOI: 10.1016/j.healthpol.2024.105152 PMID: 39244818

van Krevelen, R., Warnier, M., Brazier, F. M. T., Verbraeck, A., & Corsi, T. M. (2011). Transparency, consistency and modularity of strategic reasoning: an agent architecture for interactive business simulations. *Proceedings of the 2011 Winter Simulation Conference (WSC)*, 1612-1623, DOI: 10.1109/WSC.2011.6147878

Van Zanten, A., & Rayou, P. (2017). *Dictionnaire de l'éducation.* Presses universitaires de France.

Vanevenhoven, J. (2013). Advances and Challenges in Entrepreneurship Education. *Journal of Small Business Management, 51*(3), 466–470. DOI: 10.1111/jsbm.12043

Varelas, S. (2022). Virtual immersive platforms as a strategic innovative destination marketing tool in the COVID-19 era. *Sustainability (Basel), 14*(19), 12867. DOI: 10.3390/su141912867

Vargas-Murillo, A. R., de la Asuncion Pari-Bedoya, I. N. M., & de Jesús Guevara-Soto, F. (2023). Challenges and Opportunities of AI-Assisted Learning: A Systematic Literature Review on the Impact of ChatGPT Usage in Higher Education. *International Journal of Learning, Teaching and Educational Research*. DOI: 10.26803/ijlter.22.7.7

Venkataraman, S., Sarasvathy, S. D., Dew, N., & Forster, W. R. (2012). Reflections on the 2010 AMR decade award: Whither the promise? Moving forward with entrepreneurship as a science of the artificial. *Academy of Management Review*, *37*(1), 21–33. DOI: 10.5465/armr.2011.0079

Verdú, E., Regueras, L. M., Gal, E., De Castro, J. P., Verdú, M. J., & Kohen-Vacs, D. (2016). Integration of an intelligent tutoring system in a course of computer network design. *Educational Technology Research and Development*, *65*(3), 653–677. DOI: 10.1007/s11423-016-9503-0

Vesci, M., Botti, A., & D'Auria, A. (2021). Simulation-based learning in higher education: Enhancing students' entrepreneurial skills through realistic virtual environments. *Computers & Education*, *170*, 104214. DOI: 10.1016/j.compedu.2021.104214

Viswanathan, V., Atilola, O., Goodman, J., & Linsey, J. (2014, October). Prototyping: a key skill for innovation and life-long learning. In 2014 IEEE Frontiers in Education Conference (FIE) Proceedings (pp. 1-8). IEEE. DOI: 10.1109/FIE.2014.7044423

Vivek, A. (2024). Simulations in Business Education. Advances in educational technologies and instructional design book series, 1-21. DOI: 10.4018/979-8-3693-0716-8.ch001

Vlachopoulos, D., & Makri, A. (2017). The effect of games and simulations on higher education: A systematic literature review. *International Journal of Educational Technology in Higher Education*, *14*(1), 2. DOI: 10.1186/s41239-017-0062-1

Vlassi, E., Deirmentzoglou, G. A., & Irakleidi, E. (2023b, September). Capturing Destination's Cognitive and Affective Image on Social Media. The Case of Pafos, Cyprus. In *The International Conference on Strategic Innovative Marketing and Tourism* (pp. 19-28). Cham: Springer Nature Switzerland.

Vlassi, E., Deirmentzoglou, G. A., & Irakleidi, E. 2023, September. Capturing Destination's Cognitive and Affective Image on Social Media. The Case of Pafos, Cyprus. In *The International Conference on Strategic Innovative Marketing and Tourism* (pp. 19-28). Cham: Springer Nature Switzerland.

Vlassi, E., Deirmentzoglou, G. A., Agoraki, K. K., & Papatheodorou, A. (2023a). When Tourism and Fashion Cocreate: Narratives From Greece. In *Fashion and Tourism: Parallel Stories* (pp. 93-106). Emerald Publishing Limited.

Vojtko, V., & Hesková, M. (2010). Constructivist use of business simulators in education. *Communications of the IBIMA*, 1–11. DOI: 10.5171/2010.366397

Von Mises, L. (1949). *Human Action: A Treatise on Economics*. Yale University Press.

Vorbach, S., Poandl, E., & Korajman, I. (2019). Digital Entrepreneurship Education - The Role of MOOCs. *Int. J. Eng. Pedagog.*, *9*(3), 99–111. DOI: 10.3991/ijep.v9i3.10149

Vos, L. (2015). Simulation games in business and marketing education: How educators assess student learning from simulations. *International Journal of Management Education, 13*(1), 57–74. DOI: 10.1016/j.ijme.2015.01.001

Vroom, V. H. (1964). *Work and motivation*. Wiley.

Vygotsky, L. S. (1978). *Mind in society: The development of higher psychological processes*. Harvard University Press.

Vygotsky, L. S. (1978). *Mind in Society: The Development of Higher Psychological Processes*. Harvard University Press.

Wagner, M., Schaltegger, S., Hansen, E. G., & Fichter, K. (2021). University-linked programmes for sustainable entrepreneurship and regional development: How and with what impact? *Small Business Economics, 56*(3), 1141–1158. DOI: 10.1007/s11187-019-00280-4

Walker, P. A., Greiner, R., McDonald, D. A., & Lyne, V. (1998). The Tourism Futures Simulator: A systems thinking approach. *Environmental Modelling & Software, 14*(1), 59–67. DOI: 10.1016/S1364-8152(98)00033-4

Walmsley, A., & Wraae, B. (2022). Entrepreneurship Education but not as we know it: Reflections on the relationship between Critical Pedagogy and Entrepreneurship Education. *International Journal of Management Education, 20*(3), 1–11. DOI: 10.1016/j.ijme.2022.100726

Walter, S. G., Parboteeah, K. P., & Walter, A. (2019). The role of culture and context in the relationship between entrepreneurship education and entrepreneurial intention. *Journal of Small Business Management, 57*(S1), 126–144.

Wang, R., & Yang, R. (2024). Research and Exploration on Virtual Simulation Teaching in Universities of Finance and Economics. International Journal of New Developments in Education, 6(4), 182-187. DOI: 10.25236/IJNDE.2024.060431

Wang, C. L., Chugh, H., & Malik, M. (2020). Entrepreneurship education and intention: A systematic review of the literature. *Journal of Small Business Management, 58*(2), 343–367.

Wang, H. W., Liu, G., & Yang, Z. D. (2013). Business-task coupled process management for complex product simulation. *Applied Mechanics and Materials, 394*, 531–535. . DOI: 10.4028/www.scientific.net/AMM.394.531

Wang, J., Guo, Y., Zhang, M., Li, N., Li, K., Li, P., Huang, L., & Huang, Y. (2022). The impact of entrepreneurship competitions on entrepreneurial competence of Chinese college students. *Frontiers in Psychology, 13*, 784225. Advance online publication. [REMOVED HYPERLINK FIELD]DOI: 10.3389/fpsyg.2022.784225 PMID: 35295399

Wang, K. (2024). Analysis of Image Interaction and Social Motivation in Virtual Communities:—Take the Example of Tiktok, Instagram Virtual Communities. *Transactions on Social Science. Education and Humanities Research, 7*, 194–200.

Wang, L., & Zhang, H. (2021). Leveraging experiential learning in higher education: The role of technology in shaping student outcomes. *International Journal of Educational Management, 35*(2), 285–299.

Wang, Q., & Huang, Q. (2024). Engaging Online Learners in Blended Synchronous Learning: A Systematic Literature Review. *IEEE Transactions on Learning Technologies*, *17*, 594–607. DOI: 10.1109/TLT.2023.3282278

Wang, R., & Yang, R. (2024). Research and Exploration on Virtual Simulation Teaching in Universities of Finance and Economics. *International Journal of New Developments in Education*, *6*(4).

Wang, S., Wang, F., Zhu, Z., Wang, J., Tran, T., & Du, Z. (2024). Artificial intelligence in education: A systematic literature review. *Expert Systems with Applications*, *252*, 124167. DOI: 10.1016/j.eswa.2024.124167

Wang, Z. (2023). Online language education recommendation based on personalized learning and edge computing. *Internet Technology Letters*, *2*, e408.

Wang, Z., & Le, T. T. (2022). The COVID-19 pandemic's effects on SMEs and travel agencies: The critical role of corporate social responsibility. *Economic Analysis and Policy*, *76*, 46–58. [REMOVED HYPERLINK FIELD]DOI: 10.1016/j.eap.2022.07.008 PMID: 35919271

Wardana, L. W., Narmaditya, B. S., Wibowo, A., Mahendra, A. M., Wibowo, N. A., Harwida, G., & Rohman, A. N. (2020). The impact of entrepreneurship education and students' entrepreneurial mindset: The mediating role of attitude and self-efficacy. *Heliyon*, *6*(9), e04922. DOI: 10.1016/j.heliyon.2020.e04922 PMID: 32995616

Ward, T. B. (2021). Creative cognition in entrepreneurship: An overview and some new research directions. *Journal of Business Venturing*, *36*(3), 106102.

Warhuus, J. P., Blenker, P., & Elmholdt, S. T. (2018). Feedback and assessment in higher-education, practice-based entrepreneurship courses: How can we build legitimacy? *Industry and Higher Education*, *32*(1), 1–10. DOI: 10.1177/0950422217750795

Wata, C., Muthuraman, M., & Kant, S. (2020). Associations among Education related with entrepreneurship Outcomes and Entrepreneurship Behavior in Higher Education: A Review and Evaluation in Case of Ethiopia. *Journal of Indigenous Knowledge and Incubatement Studies*, *2*(2), 93–109.

Watson, K., McGowan, P., & Cunningham, J. A. (2018). An exploration of the Business Plan Competition as a methodology for effective nascent entrepreneurial learning. *International Journal of Entrepreneurial Behaviour & Research*, *24*(1), 121–146. DOI: 10.1108/IJEBR-05-2017-0158

Web Accessibility Initiative (WAI). (n.d.). *Curricula*. Retrieved from https://www.w3.org/WAI/curricula/

Weber, C., Fasse, A., Haugh, H. M., & Grote, U. (2023). Varieties of necessity entrepreneurship–New insights from Sub Saharan Africa. *Entrepreneurship Theory and Practice*, *47*(5), 1843–1876. DOI: 10.1177/10422587221111737

Wei, X., Liu, X., & Sha, J. (2019). How does the entrepreneurship education influence the students' innovation? Testing on the multiple mediation model. *Frontiers in Psychology*, *10*, 1557. [REMOVED HYPERLINK FIELD]DOI: 10.3389/fpsyg.2019.01557 PMID: 31354574

Wellington, W. J., Hutchinson, D., & Faria, A. J. (2016). Measuring the impact of a marketing simulation game. *Simulation & Gaming*, *48*(1), 56–80. DOI: 10.1177/1046878116675103

Wenger, E., McDermott, R., & Snyder, W. M. (2002). Seven principles for cultivating communities of practice. *Cultivating Communities of Practice: A Guide to Managing Knowledge, 4*, 1–19.

Wenngren, J., & Rizk, A. (2024). Prototyping for Digital Innovation: Investigating the Impact of Digital Technology on Prototyping Elements. *Administrative Sciences, 14*(7), 142. DOI: 10.3390/admsci14070142

Werhane, P. H., & Freeman, R. E. (1999). Business ethics: The state of the art. *International Journal of Management Reviews, 1*(1), 1–16. DOI: 10.1111/1468-2370.00002

Wheadon, J. D., & Duval-Couetil, N. (2014). Business plan development activities as a pedagogical tool in entrepreneurship education. *The Journal of Engineering Entrepreneurship, 5*(1), 31–48. DOI: 10.7814/jeen5v5p3wd

Wikle, T., & Fagin, T. (2014). Hard and soft skills in preparing GIS professionals: Comparing perceptions of employers and educators. *Transactions in GIS, 19*(5), 641–799. DOI: 10.1111/tgis.12126

Wiklund, J., Patzelt, H., & Shepherd, D. A. (2009). Building an Integrative Model of Small Business Growth. *Small Business Economics, 32*(4), 351–374. DOI: 10.1007/s11187-007-9084-8

Wilkens, L., Haage, A., Lüttmann, F., & Bühler, C. R. (2021). Digital teaching, inclusion and students' needs: Student perspectives on participation and access in higher education. *Social Inclusion (Lisboa), 9*(3), 117–129. DOI: 10.17645/si.v9i3.4125

Williams, D. (2015a). Impact of Business Simulation Games in Enterprise Education University of Huddersfield Repository. *2010 University of Huddersfield Annual Learning and Teaching Conference, February 2011.*

Williams, A. J., & Williams, R. H. (2011). Multiple Identification Theory: Attitude and Behavior Change in a Simulated International Conflict. *Simulation & Gaming, 42*(6), 733–747. DOI: 10.1177/1046878111429228

Williams, D. (2015b). The Impact of SimVenture on the Development of Entrepreneurial Skills in Management Students. *Industry and Higher Education, 29*(5), 379–395. DOI: 10.5367/ihe.2015.0270

Williamson, B., Macgilchrist, F., & Potter, J. (2023). Re-examining AI, automation and datafication in education. *Learning, Media and Technology, 48*(1), 1–5. DOI: 10.1080/17439884.2023.2167830

Wilson, F., Kickul, J., & Marlino, D. (2007). Gender, Entrepreneurial Self-Efficacy, and Entrepreneurial Career Intentions: Implications for Entrepreneurship Education. *Entrepreneurship Theory and Practice, 31*(3), 387–406. DOI: 10.1111/j.1540-6520.2007.00179.x

Wilson, R. A., & Keil, F. C. (Eds.). (1999). *The MIT Encyclopedia of the Cognitive Sciences*. MIT Press. DOI: 10.7551/mitpress/4660.001.0001

Wilson, S. G., & Abel, I. (2002). So you want to get involved in e-commerce. *Industrial Marketing Management, 31*(2), 85–94. DOI: 10.1016/S0019-8501(01)00188-2

Wirts, J., & Lovelock, C. (2021). *Services Marketing: People, Technology, Strategy* (9th ed.). World Scientific Publishing Company. DOI: 10.1142/y0024

Wolfe, J., & Crookall, D. (1998). Developing a Scientific Knowledge of Simulation/Gaming. *Simulation & Gaming, 29*(1), 7–19. DOI: 10.1177/1046878198291002

Wolmarans, H. P. (2005). Business simulations in financial management courses: Are they valuable to learners? *Meditari. Research Journal of the School of Accounting, 13*(1), 121–133.

Wood, J., Oh, J., Park, J., & Kim, W. (2020). The relationship between work engagement and work–life balance in organizations: A review of the empirical research. *Human Resource Development Review, 19*(3), 240–262. DOI: 10.1177/1534484320917560

Woolf, B. P. (2010). *Building intelligent interactive tutors: Student-centered strategies for revolutionizing e-learning*. Morgan Kaufmann.

Woraphiphat, I., & Roopsuwankun, P. (2021). The impact of online design thinking-based learning on entrepreneurial intention: The case of vocational college. *Journal of Innovation and Entrepreneurship, 12*(1), 10. Advance online publication. DOI: 10.1186/s13731-023-00278-z PMID: 36911755

World Wide Web Consortium. (2024). *Web Content Accessibility Guidelines (WCAG) 2.1.* Retrieved from https://www.w3.org/TR/WCAG21/

Wright, A. M., Munz, S. M., & McKenna-Buchanan, T. (2023). Triage Teaching: Exploring Teacher. Self-Efficacy during COVID-19. In *Pandemic Pedagogies* (pp. 96-111). Routledge.

Wu, Y. J., Yuan, C.-H., & Pan, C.-I. (2018). Entrepreneurship Education: An Experimental Study with Information and Communication Technology. *Sustainability (Basel), 10*(3), 691. DOI: 10.3390/su10030691

Xiang, Z., & Gretzel, U. (2010). Role of social media in online travel information search. *Tourism Management, 31*(2), 179–188. DOI: 10.1016/j.tourman.2009.02.016

Xie, H. (2018). Construction and Practice of Virtual Simulation Experimental Teaching Platform for Economic Management. In *2018 5th International Conference on Education, Management, Arts, Economics and Social Science (ICEMAESS 2018)* (pp. 398-402). Atlantis Press.

Xie, H. (2018). Construction and Practice of Virtual Simulation Experimental Teaching Platform for Economic Management. In *2018 5th International Conference on Education, Management, Arts, Economics and Social Science (ICEMAESS 2018)* (pp. 398-402). Atlantis Press. DOI: 10.2991/icemaess-18.2018.83

Xie, H., Qin, Z., & Li, J. (2024). Entrepreneurship and Corporate ESG Performance—A Case Study of China's A-Share Listed Companies. *Sustainability (Basel), 16*(18), 7964. DOI: 10.3390/su16187964

Xie, Q. (2022). Using task-based approach in business English courses for English-majors at a Chinese university. *International Journal of Chinese Education, 11*(2), 2212585X221099104. Advance online publication. DOI: 10.1177/2212585X221099104

Xinaris, C., Kourtellis, A., Kakouris, A., & Georgiadis, P. (2011). Game based learning in entrepreneurship: The academic business planner. *Proceedings of the European Conference on Games-Based Learning.*

Xu, R., Yu, H., Li, B., & Miao, D. (2023). Research on the development path of e-commerce for rural tourism. *Applied Mathematics and Nonlinear Sciences, 9*(1).

Yan, P., & Guo, J. (2010, February). The research of web usability design. In *2010 The 2nd International Conference on Computer and Automation Engineering (ICCAE)* (Vol. 4, pp. 480-483). IEEE.

Yang, A. C. M., Chen, I. Y. L., Flanagan, B., & Ogata, H. (2021). Automatic generation of cloze items for repeated testing to improve reading comprehension. *Journal of Educational Technology & Society*, *24*(3), 147–158. https://www.jstor.org/stable/27032862

Yan, Y. (2020). Exploration and practice of maker education mode in innovation and entrepreneurship education. *Frontiers in Psychology*, *11*, 1626. Advance online publication. DOI: 10.3389/fpsyg.2020.01626 PMID: 33013496

Yasin, N., & Hafeez, K. (2018). Enterprise Simulation Gaming: Effective Practices for Assessing Student Learning with SimVenture Classic and VentureBlocks. In *Experiential Learning for Entrepreneurship* (pp. 51–69). Springer International Publishing. DOI: 10.1007/978-3-319-90005-6_3

Yasin, N., Gilani, S. A. M., Contu, D., & Fayaz, M. J. (2022). Simulation-based learning in business and entrepreneurship in higher education: A review of the games available. *Technology and Entrepreneurship Education: Adopting Creative Digital Approaches to Learning and Teaching*, 25-51.

Yasin, N., Gilani, S. A. M., Contu, D., & Fayaz, M. J. (2022). Simulation-based learning in business and entrepreneurship in higher education: A review of the games available. In *Technology and Entrepreneurship Education* (pp. 25–51). Springer International Publishing. DOI: 10.1007/978-3-030-84292-5_2

Yenduri, G., Kaluri, R., Rajput, D. S., Lakshmanna, K., Gadekallu, T. R., Mahmud, M., & Brown, D. J. (2023). From Assistive Technologies to Metaverse - Technologies in Inclusive Higher Education for Students with Specific Learning Difficulties: A Review. *IEEE Access : Practical Innovations, Open Solutions*, *11*, 64907–64927. DOI: 10.1109/ACCESS.2023.3289496

Yen, W. C., & Lin, H.-H. (2022). Investigating the effect of flow experience on learning performance and entrepreneurial self-efficacy in a business simulation systems context. *Interactive Learning Environments*, *30*(9), 1593–1608. DOI: 10.1080/10494820.2020.1734624

Yilmaz, R., Bakhaidar, M., Alsayegh, A., Hamdan, N., Fazlollahi, A., & Maestro, R. (2023). 828 Real-Time Artificial Intelligence Instruction in Comparison to Human Expert Instruction in Surgical Technical Skills Teaching a Randomized Controlled Trial. *British Journal of Surgery*, *110*(Supplement_7), znad258.077. Advance online publication. DOI: 10.1093/bjs/znad258.077

Yin, R. (2007). *Qualitative research from start to finish* (2nd ed.). Guilford.

Yin, R. K. (1994). Discovering the future of the case study. Method in evaluation research. *Evaluation Practice*, *15*(3), 283–290.

Yin, R. K. (2018). *Case Study Research and Applications: Design and Methods*. Sage Publications.

Yoehono, T., & Liliani, L. (2018). Innovativeness differences of studentpreneurs based on entrepreneurship experiential learning. *International Journal of Academic Research in Business & Social Sciences*, *8*(3). Advance online publication. DOI: 10.6007/IJARBSS/v8-i3/3932

Yuan, Y., Tseng, Y. H., & Li, C. (2022). e-Tourism research: A review. *Handbook of e-Tourism*, 75-93.

Yusof, R., Yin, K. Y., Norwani, N. M., Ismail, Z., Ahmad, A. S., & Salleh, S. M. (2020). Teaching through experiential learning cycle to enhance student engagement in principles of accounting. *International Journal of Learning. Teaching and Educational Research, 19*(10), 323–337. DOI: 10.26803/ijlter.19.10.18

Zainal, N. T. A., & Yong, K. (2020). Examining the digital entrepreneurship education effectiveness on soft skills among undergraduates [PPIB]. *MANU Jurnal Pusat Penataran Ilmu Dan Bahasa, 31*, 139–151. DOI: 10.51200/manu.vi.2112

Žalėnienė, I., & Pereira, P. (2021). *Higher Education For Sustainability: A Global Perspective*. Geography and Sustainability., DOI: 10.1016/j.geosus.2021.05.001

Zallio, M., & Clarkson, P. J. (2022). Designing the metaverse: A study on inclusion, diversity, equity, accessibility and safety for digital immersive environments. *Telematics and Informatics, 75*, 101909. DOI: 10.1016/j.tele.2022.101909

Zapalska, A. M. (2021). Designing an experiential learning with simulations and games to improve education in an undergraduate engineering major. *Asean Journal of Engineering Education, 5*(1), 32–43. DOI: 10.11113/ajee2021.5n1.59

Zapalska, A., Brozik, D., & Rudd, D. (2012). *Development of active learning with simulations and games*. Online Submission.

Zawacki-Richter, O., Marín, V. I., Bond, M., & Gouverneur, F. (2019). Systematic review of research on artificial intelligence applications in higher education – where are the educators? *International Journal of Educational Technology in Higher Education, 16*(1), 39. Advance online publication. DOI: 10.1186/s41239-019-0171-0

Zeithaml, C., & Rice, G. (1987). Entrepreneurship-Small Business Education in American Universities. *Journal of Small Business Management, 25*, 44.

Zeng, B., & Gerritsen, R. (2014). What do we know about social media in tourism? A review. *Tourism Management Perspectives, 10*, 27–36. DOI: 10.1016/j.tmp.2014.01.001

Zhang, J., Wang, C., & Zhao, H. (2021). Fostering entrepreneurial mindsets in higher education: A systematic review. *Journal of Entrepreneurship Education, 24*(1), 1–15.

Zhang, Z., Chen, Z., & Xu, L. (2022). Artificial intelligence and moral dilemmas: Perception of ethical decision-making in AI. *Journal of Experimental Social Psychology, 101*, 1–8. DOI: 10.1016/j.jesp.2022.104327

Zhao, H. (2021, October). The Application of Virtual Simulation Technology in Experimental Practice Course Teaching. In *Proceedings of the 2021 5th International Conference on Electronic Information Technology and Computer Engineering* (pp. 1526-1530).

Zhao, M., Yang, X., & Sheng, S. (2024). Transferring Political Capabilities Into Formal Entrepreneurship: The Moderating Role of Market Development in Emerging Markets. *IEEE Transactions on Engineering Management, 71*, 1504–1518. DOI: 10.1109/TEM.2023.3335161

Zheng, B., Zhang, Q., Geng, G., Chen, C., Shi, Q., Cui, M., Lei, Y., & He, K. (2021). Changes in China's anthropogenic emissions and air quality during the COVID-19 pandemic in 2020. *Earth System Science Data*, *13*(6), 2895–2907. DOI: 10.5194/essd-13-2895-2021

Zhou, Y., Li, H., & Shahzad, F. (2021). Does college education promote entrepreneurship education in China? *SAGE Open*, *11*(3), 21582440211031616. Advance online publication. DOI: 10.1177/21582440211031616

Zhurakovskaya, V., Sichinava, A., Simakova, T., Olicheva, O., Rykov, S., Valeeva, J., Kulachinskaya, A., & Ilyashenko, S. (2020). Innovations in Education—The Development of a New Pedagogical Technology of a Combinational Type, Focused on the Development of Personality of Students. *Journal of Open Innovation*, *6*(4), 123. DOI: 10.3390/joitmc6040123

Ziegler, R. (2022). Integrating technology and entrepreneurship: The role of higher education institutions. *Journal of Entrepreneurship Education*, *25*(1), 1–20.

Zimmerman, M. A., & Zeitz, G. J. (2002). Beyond Survival: Achieving New Venture Growth by Building Legitimacy. *Academy of Management Review*, *27*(3), 414–431. DOI: 10.2307/4134387

Zollo, M., & Winter, S. G. (2002). Deliberate learning and the evolution of dynamic capabilities. *Organization Science*, *13*(3), 339–351. DOI: 10.1287/orsc.13.3.339.2780

Zorn, M. L., Sexton, J. C., Bhussar, M. S., & Lamont, B. T. (2019). Unfinished business: Nested acquisitions, managerial capacity, and firm performance. *Journal of Management*, *45*(5), 1488–1516. DOI: 10.1177/0149206317737351

Zulfiqar, S., Al-reshidi, H. A., Al Moteri, M. A., Feroz, H. M. B., Yahya, N., & Al-Rahmi, W. M. (2021). Understanding and predicting students' entrepreneurial intention through business simulation games: A perspective of COVID-19. *Sustainability (Basel)*, *13*(4), 1838. DOI: 10.3390/su13041838

About the Contributors

Andreas Masouras is an Associate Professor of Communication and Marketing in the Department of Economics & Business at Neapolis University. He holds a PhD with distinction from the Department of Political Science and International Relations at the University of the Peloponnese. The title of his doctoral dissertation is "Entrepreneurship and Competitiveness through the Lens of Institutional Analysis: The Case of Cyprus," which is available in the National Archive of Doctoral Dissertations. He coordinates the following programs: the conventional MBA, the distance MBA (English-speaking), and the MBA in Tourism (distance learning). He is actively writing scientific articles and participates in international conferences. His book, "Entrepreneurship in Small and Medium-Sized Enterprises", published by the American publishing house Nova, has been indexed in the Scopus book list.

Sofia Anastasiadou is a Professor of Statistics and Research Methodology at the University of Western Macedonia (UOWM). Her teaching focuses in the field of cognitive Research Methodology (Quantitative and Qualitative), Educational Research and Statistical Data Analysis, Big Data. She has written three books on Statistics and Research Methodology and has published over 280 articles in International and Greek Journals as well as in International and Greek Conferences. She has participated in scientific dialogues/round tables in more than 200 lectures at International and Greek Conferences. She has organized and co-organized Greek and International Scientific Conferences. She is also a Member of a number of Scientific Committees of International Conferences and is an Associate Editor in a number of International Journals.

Georgios A. Deirmentzoglou is an Assistant Professor in International Entrepreneurship, Technology, and Sustainable Development at Neapolis University Pafos (Cyprus). He holds a PhD in Business Administration from the University of Piraeus, where he also earned an MBA with a specialization in Total Quality Management (MBA-TQM) and a Bachelor's degree in Industrial Management and Technology. His research interests focus on entrepreneurship, technological innovation, human-computer interaction, sustainable development, and tourism. Georgios has extensive experience as a Principal Investigator and Researcher in EU-funded projects, primarily focusing on digital transformation and sustainable development. Beyond academia, he has practical expertise in e-commerce, including the creation and management of online stores, and is the co-founder of a consulting firm specializing in information systems and software.

Harry Sophocleous is a researcher and visiting Lecturer at the University of Naples. He deals with Corporate Communication (Marketing), Political Communication and Electoral Behavior. and Nations' Branding He completed his studies in the UK with a BA (Hons) in Business Administration from the University of East Anglia, an MSc in Marketing and an Mphil in Social Sciences from the University of

Leicester. While, at this stage he is completing his PhD Thesis in Political Communication and Electoral Behavior, under the supervision of the Universities of Naples and Peloponnese.

Eleni E. Anastasopoulou is a Lecturer in Sustainable Entrepreneurship at the Neapolis University Pafos. She holds a Ph.D. in Sustainable Agri-food Entrepreneurship from the University of the Peloponnese, an M.Sc. in Pharmacognosy and Chemistry of Natural Products from the Faculty of Pharmacy at the National and Kapodistrian University of Athens, and a Bachelor's degree in Agriculture with a specialization in Food Science and Technology from the Aristotle University of Thessaloniki. During her studies, she received a scholarship from the Department of Economics, Faculty of Economic and Political Sciences of the University of Athens for the "Entrepreneurship in Practice" programme. Her research interest focuses on sustainable agri-food entrepreneurship, rural national and European policies, socio-economic crises as well as technological innovation. Her research has been published in high-impact international peer-reviewed journals, such as 'Strategic Change' (ABS:2), 'The International Journal of Entrepreneurship and Innovation' (ABS:2) and contributed as a co-author to a book chapter in an edited volume. She has presented at 19 international peer-reviewed conferences and has also extensive experience as a Researcher in the implementation of EU-funded research projects. Eleni served as a Teaching Assistant in Entrepreneurial Innovation at the Department of Management Science and Technology, University of the Peloponnese. She is currently working in the Rector's office for the academic development of the Neapolis University Pafos. Her previous work experience includes a variety of roles in both the public and private sectors, focusing on the management and monitoring of funded projects in the agricultural sector, as well as product management.

***

Konstantina K. Agoraki is an Assistant Professor in the Department of Business Administration, University of Piraeus. She holds a PhD from the Department of Business Administration, University of Piraeus and a Master's degree (MSc) in International Economics and Finance, Athens University of Economics and Business. Dr. Agoraki has taught in the Department of Tourism Studies, University of Piraeus, as well as at the University of Peloponnese, at both undergraduate and postgraduate levels. Additionally, she has taught at the postgraduate level at the Athens University of Economics and Business and the Open University of Cyprus. Her research interests include, among others, Knowledge Management, Innovation and Technology Management, Strategic Environmental Management and Sustainable Development, Entrepreneurship, and ESG (Environmental, Social, and Governance). She has published in high-quality international scientific journals such as the Journal of International Money and Finance (AJG/ABS 2024 List 3), International Journal of Innovation and Technology Management (AJG/ABS 2024 List 1), Social Responsibility Journal (AJG/ABS 2024 List 1), and Sustainability, and has participated in international scientific conferences. She is also a reviewer in international scientific journals.

Athanasios Anastasiou is an Associate Professor in the Department of Management Science and Technology at the University of the Peloponnese. He holds a Ph.D. in Economics and has 20 years of teaching experience in higher education in Greece and Cyprus. His research interests include Macroeconomics, Public Administration and Economics, Economic Development, International Economics, and European Integration. He has served as a member of the editorial board of the

International Journal of Behavioural and Healthcare Research and has published extensively in scientific journals and conferences on topics such as Macroeconomics, International Economics, Public Finance, and the Macroeconomy of the European Union. His research also focuses on applied econometrics, with an emphasis on Bayesian estimation methods. Dr. Anastasiou's earlier work has concentrated on the European Union and the policy independence of Central Banks. Additionally, he has conducted research using Data Envelopment Analysis (DEA) to measure efficiency in sectors such as industry, banking, and education, with several published works in these areas.

Ioannis Anastasopoulos is a Civil Engineer and PhD candidate in strategies and policies for tourism real estate investments and mixed-use developments, at the Department of Tourism Studies, at the University of Piraeus. He holds a Master's degree in Governance and Public Policies at the University of Peloponnese.

Sotiris Apostolopoulos is a Lecturer in Entrepreneurship and Development at the University of Neapolis (Paphos, Cyprus). He also acts as Coordinator of the Undergraduate Programs in Business Administration & Digital Business of the Department of Economics and Business for the same University. He holds a PhD degree from the School of Management of University of the Peloponnese and two Master's degrees (MSc) in Healthcare Administration and in Finance as well. He specialises in rural entrepreneurship, European policies and the socio-economic development of the rural areas with emphasis on private and social health enterprises. His research interests focus on local development, European policies, private and social enterprises as well as on innovation. In the past, he served as Chief Operating Officer (COO) for the largest regional private hospital of the Peloponnese Region. His research articles have been published in major scientific journals by publishers such as Elsevier, Wiley, Emerald,Springer, MDPI, while he has participated in studies that were included and published as book chapters in edited volumes (IGI Global, UCL Press Eburon, etc.). In parallel, he has taken part through research work in international and European conferences on Economics, Entrepreneurship and Innovation held in Greece, Cyprus, UK, Switzerland, Italy, Spain, Portugal and Montenegro. Recently, the World Health Organization included in its official database two research papers of Sotiris (co-author), concerning the rural health enterprises during the Covid-19 pandemic.

Christos N. Christodoulou-Volos is an accomplished Associate Professor of Economics and Finance at Neapolis University Pafos. He earned his PhD in Economics from the Graduate School of CUNY in 1997. He specializes in Macroeconometrics. Over his career, he has lectured at numerous universities across the globe, sharing his expertise with diverse academic audiences. His research contributions are extensive, with numerous publications in leading academic journals. His current research interests focus on empirical macroeconomics and financial economics. Beyond academia, Dr. Christodoulou-Volos has significant professional experience in the corporate world. He has held senior positions in prominent U.S. companies, including roles as a Senior Economist for a trade association and an Economist specializing in litigation economics for a financial firm. His blend of academic rigor and practical experience makes him a distinguished expert in his field.

Zacharias Dermatis is an Assistant Professor in the Department of Management Science and Technology at the University of the Peloponnese, specializing in "Innovative and Digital Technologies for Quality of Life." Since 2015, he has served at the University of the Peloponnese, initially in the

Department of Economics, and since 2020 in the Department of Management Science and Technology. He has taught a variety of courses, including Management Information Systems, E-Government, Health Informatics Applications, Strategic Management, and Geographic Information Systems (GIS). He holds a Ph.D. titled "Design and Development of an Information System Using GIS to Investigate Socioeconomic Indicators Affecting the Health Level of the Elderly" and a Master's degree in "Computer Science and Technology." His undergraduate degree is in Electrical Engineering from the University of West Attica. He is an active member of three laboratories within the Department of Management Science and Technology and the iLEADS Research and Training Center at the University of Piraeus. His expertise spans Quality of Life, Health Informatics Applications, GIS, Databases, Data Digitization, and programming and analytical tools such as Visual Basic, Python, SPSS, Jamovi, RapidMiner by Altair, and the Promethee multi-criteria decision analysis method. Dr. Dermatis has published numerous scientific articles and presented papers at international and national conferences. He has also contributed to books and book chapters, advancing knowledge and innovation in his areas of expertise.

Panos Dimitrakopoulos is an Adjunct Lecturer at the Department of Accounting and Finance, University of the Peloponnese, focusing on Energy Transition, Energy Efficiency, Sustainable Development, and Green Entrepreneurship. Their doctoral dissertation, titled "The Impact of Key Energy Indicators on the Economic Growth of EU Countries Based on the Industry Contribution to GDP Index and the Search for Optimal Energy Policies," explores the dynamic relationship between energy performance and economic growth, offering insights into the development of optimal energy policies tailored to diverse economic environments within the EU. Dimitrakopoulos has authored several publications in peer-reviewed journals and actively participates in international academic conferences, contributing to the fields of energy economics, green policies, and sustainable business practices. Their research highlights the importance of differentiated policy frameworks for enhancing energy efficiency and fostering sustainable growth across EU member states.

Dimitrios Dimitriou's educational background includes Doctorate in econometric modelling for quantitative demand forecasting, MSc in Airport Planning and Management, MSc in Infrastructures Environmental Management, and Diploma (equivalent to 4 years BA and 1-year MSc) in Civil Engineering (transportation sector). His specialization deals with the subjects of large investment appraisal, project financing, business planning, project management, transport and supply chain economics, corporate management performance, decision making for organizations/enterprises, investment economic impact assessment and Sustainable planning, management and economics for large projects. His direction focused on sector of energy, transport, logistics and supply chain.

Stavros G. Efthimiou is a Postdoctoral Researcher (Postdoc) and Academic Fellow at University of Piraeus. He holds a Ph.D. from the Department of International and European Studies– University of Piraeus at the field of International Economics.

Alexandros Kakouris, PhD, is an Assistant Professor in entrepreneurial learning and education at the Department of Management Science and Technology of the University of Peloponnese and at the Hellenic Open University. He holds PhD in Physics, PhD in Entrepreneurship and a MSc in Adult Education. His special interests concern: fostering entrepreneurship and innovation to science graduates, context-aware entrepreneurship, support of youth entrepreneurship through teaching and counselling as well as nascent entrepreneurship, transformative and experiential learning.

Aristi Karagkouni's educational background includes Doctorate (PhD) in Sustainable Development and Management of Infrastructure from Democritus University of Thrace (Department of Economics), MSc in Environmental Management for Business from Cranfield University (UK) and Diploma (equivalent to 4 years BA and 1-year MSc) in Civil Engineering (Transportation planning). She is currently an adjusted Lecturer in the Department of Economics (DUTh) as well as a Post Doctoral Researcher in the research field of Sustainable Development and Management of Infrastructure. She has participated in 60 publications in scientific missions, journals, international conferences, and workshops and she has contributed to 4 research projects.

Dimitrios Komninos holds a degree in Business Administration from the University of Cyprus and a degree in Automation from the University of West Attica (formerly TEI of Piraeus). He has earned two Master's degrees (Education Studies and Organization and Management of Public Services, Public Organizations, & Enterprises) and a Ph.D. from the University of the Peloponnese on "E-Government in Tax Organization and Administration." He works at the Tax Office of Tripoli and has significant teaching experience in adult education, providing training for public sector employees, teaching at the University of the Peloponnese, and collaborating with universities abroad. He is a member of the Sustainable Development and Entrepreneurship Laboratory in the Department of Economics at the University of the Peloponnese and the Hellenic Adult Education Association. Dr. Komninos has presented papers at international and national scientific conferences and published articles in international scientific journals related to his field of expertise.

Marcos Komodromos is an Associate Professor at the University of Nicosia's Department of Communications and holds accreditation as a Charter Instructor of Public Relations and Marketing Communications. With extensive experience over two years, he has made significant contributions to digital media, internal communication, corporate communication, and crisis management across Cyprus, Greece, and the UK. Beyond academia, Marcos serves as a trusted business consultant to numerous organizations both locally and internationally. His expertise extends to various facets of the media industry, notably radio and television, where he has spearheaded numerous successful projects. Marcos is a prolific author with a diverse range of publications covering topics such as public relations and marketing communications, digital media, strategic management, organizational trust, change management, internal communication, and corporate social responsibility.

Marilia Kountouridou holds a Ph.D. in Marketing from the European University Cyprus and an M.A. in Advertising and Marketing from the University of Leeds in the UK. Her research interests lie within the field of Marketing, specifically focusing on branding and consumer behaviour. Dr. Kountouridou is a scientific collaborator at the European University Cyprus and has considerable work experience in marketing communication, demonstrating strong communication skills.

Ilias Makris is a professor in Financial Analysis. He received his PhD on Business Administration at University of Patras. He currently serves as a Professor at the Department of Accounting and Finance, of the University of the Peloponnese, Teaching Economics and Finance, in undergraduate and postgraduate level. He has served as Scientific Director of Innovation and Entrepreneurship Unit of Technological Educational Institute of Peloponnese (2009-2015), Head of the Dept of Accounting and Finance and Director of postgraduate program in Finance, dept. of Accounting & Finance. He has authored many refereed publications in international journals, book chapters, collective volumes and international conferences. His scientific interests focus on sustainable economics, energy economics, innovation, entrepreneurship, and performance measures in Micro and macro level. His recent work has been published at J. Open Innov. Technol. Mark. Complex., Energy Sources, Part B: Economics, Planning, and Policy, Sustainability, and Energies.

Alexandra Morfaki works as a senior lecturer in Early Years at Norland College. She initially trained as a reception class teacher and worked in a range of early years settings in the capacity of teacher and manager prior to completing her Doctorate. Alexandra's research interests lie in inclusion in the early years for children with Special Educational Needs and Disabilities. Her doctoral thesis focused on early years educators' interpretation of inclusion in practice and explored interprofessional partnerships for inclusion and their influence on the formation of the role and identities of early years educators.

Christina Morfaki is an accomplished professional with a strong academic background, holding an MBA and a PhD specializing in Human Resources Management—Organizational Behavior. With over twenty years of experience in both the financial sector and multidisciplinary scientific research projects, she seamlessly integrates theoretical knowledge with practical application. Currently, Christina serves as an adjunct lecturer at Neapolis University and the University of West Attica Athens, while also holding a pivotal role as the head of human resources in a public organization. Her instructional repertoire spans a wide array of topics including human resources management, leadership, organizational behavior, entrepreneurship, technology and innovation, and financial engineering. She has authored numerous scientific articles and book chapters, in Greek and international journals. Her research interests revolve around organizational behavior, personality, business strategy, leadership, and education, underscoring her dedication to advancing both knowledge and practice within her field.

VidhyaPriya P. is a dedicated academician with a strong foundation in both computer science and business management. She holds an MBA from Avinashilingam Deemed University, Coimbatore, and earned her Ph.D. from Bharathiar University, Coimbatore, in 2010. Before transitioning to academia, she gained valuable industry experience working with a textile firm for over three years. In 2000, she joined Kongu Engineering College, where she has since built an illustrious career in research and teaching. With over 24 years of academic experience, Dr. VidhyaPriya's research interests lie in corporate finance, corporate governance, and behavioral finance. She has published 57 research papers in reputed national and international journals, including Scopus-indexed publications. Throughout her career, she has actively engaged with the academic community by attending numerous Faculty Development Programs (FDPs) at leading B-Schools, including IIM Bangalore, IIT Madras, Pondicherry University, and Mangalore University. Dr.VidhyaPriya has also presented papers at 30 national and international conferences and has organized multiple conferences, seminars, FDPs, workshops, and training programs. She has successfully completed two ICSSR-sponsored projects focused on start-up entrepreneurship and the Stand-Up India Scheme for entrepreneurs.

Christos Papademetriou teaches at the University of Neapolis in Pafos since 2010. He is an Assistant Professor in Management – Human Resources Management at the School of Economics, Administration and Computer Science. He is a Coordinator of the Distance Master in Business Administration (DMBA). He was teaching in the Department of Business Administration at the Open University of Cyprus (2017-2020). He obtained a BA (Hons) in Accounting and Business (2001) and MA in International Management (2002) from the University of Sunderland. He was awarded also a BSc (Hons) in Computing and the Postgraduate Certificate in Information Systems from the University of Portsmouth. He holds a doctorate (PhD) in Social Science from the University of Leicester, UK. The title of his thesis is "Investigating the Impact of Sequential Cross-Cultural Training on the Level of Sociocultural and Psychological Adjustment of Expatriate Mangers".

Amvrosios Prodromou holds a Doctorate of Business Administration (DBA) with specialization in SMEs, MBA in Marketing, MBA in Project Management, and Bachelor's (Hons) in Business Administration. He is a qualified Vocational Trainer by the Cyprus Human Resource Development Authority and qualified Sustainability expert by the Cyprus Chamber of Commerce and Industry. He runs his own business consulting firm. During his professional career in the private sector, he has managed to win the Cyprus Innovation Award in 2009 and the 2012 European Business Awards. He is an active academic with several publications. He has published several articles and co-authored numerous scholar/ academic books. He has participated in over twenty European Projects.

Vetrivel S. C. is a faculty member in the Department of Management Studies, Kongu Engineering College (Autonomous), Perundurai, Erode Dt. Having experience in Industry 20 years and Teaching 16 years. Awarded with Doctoral Degree in Management Sciences in Anna University, Chennai. He has organized various workshops and Faculty Development Programs. He is actively involved in research and consultancy works. He acted as a resource person to FDPs & MDPs to various industries like, SPB ltd, Tamil Nadu Police, DIET, Rotary school and many. His areas of interest include Entrepreneurship, Business Law, Marketing and Case writing. Articles published more than 100 International and National Journals. Presented papers in more than 30 National and International conferences including IIM Bangalore, IIM Kozhikode, IIM Kashipur and IIM Indore. He was a Chief Coordinator of Entrepreneurship and Management Development Centre (EMDC) of Kongu Engineering College, he was instrumental in organizing various Awareness Camps, FDP, and TEDPs to aspiring entrepreneurs which was funded by NSTEDB – DST/GoI.

Ioannis Sitaridis is a Research Associate in University of Macedonia, Thessaloniki Greece, Dept. of Applied Informatics. Ioannis research interests are in the field of Digital Entrepreneurship and Entrepreneurship Education.

Harry Sophocleous is an experienced corporate communications consultant, researcher, and visiting lecturer at Neapolis University, with a focus on Political Marketing, Consumer Behavior, and Cultural Branding. He has a robust academic foundation and practical expertise, having conducted extensive research and held various industry roles.

Arun V. P. is a driven and accomplished professional with a diverse educational background and extensive hands-on experience across various industries. Graduating with honors, Arun earned his Master of Business

Administration (M.B.A) with a specialization in Human Resources and Marketing from the renowned Sona School of Management in Salem in 2018, where he excelled academically with an impressive 8.3 Cumulative Grade Point Average (CGPA).Throughout his academic journey, Arun displayed an unwavering commitment to learning and personal growth, actively seeking opportunities to expand his knowledge and skills beyond the confines of traditional education. He sought practical experiences to complement his theoretical understanding, such as a 45-day summer internship focused on conducting a feasibility study for R-Doc Sustainability in the market. Additionally, Arun broadened his horizons through a 7-day industrial visit to Malaysia and Singapore, immersing himself in diverse cultural and professional environments. Arun's academic pursuits were further enriched by his involvement in hands-on projects, including a comprehensive study on Employee Job Satisfaction at Roots Cast Private Limited. His professional trajectory includes serving as a Growth Officer at Parle Agro Private Limited, where he played a crucial role in driving sales growth and market expansion. Arun is a dedicated professional, currently employed at JKKN Engineering College in the Management Studies Department. He holds expertise in his field and has contributed significantly to academia through the publication of two journal articles. Arun's work focuses on advancing knowledge and understanding in management studies, making valuable contributions to the academic community.

Sotirios Varelas is Assistant Professor at Tourism Studies Department - University of Piraeus with the academic field «Strategy of Hospitality Business and Tourism Organizations». Holds a Ph.D. degree in Business Administration from the Department of Business Administration – University of Piraeus at the field of Hospitality Strategic Management.

Eirini Vlassi is Assistant Professor in Brand Development of Tourism Businesses and Destinations in the University of the Aegean. She holds a PhD in Collaborative Destination Marketing and Branding (University of the Aegean), an MSc in Business Administration- Tourism Management (University of Piraeus) and a B.Sc. in Economics (University of Crete). She served as a lecturer in Neapolis University Pafos in the field of management and marketing of tourism business and tourism destinations and a coordinator of the MBA in Tourism in the same University. Since 2018, she has been an adjunct lecturer teaching Strategic Destination Management and Marketing in the MBA Programme in Aviation and Tourism Management that Frankfurt University of Applied Sciences, Germany offered in collaboration with the University of the Aegean, Chios (Greece). She had also served as an adjunct lecturer in the MSc in Digital and Social Media Marketing of the University of East London. Her research focuses on destination marketing and branding, digital marketing and co-creation in the tourism sector.

Andreas Walmsley is one of the core teaching team at Marjon Business and is highly experienced in the design and delivery of teaching business at both undergraduate and postgraduate levels having worked at five different UK higher education institutions, and been involved in external examining/ programme validations internationally (Ireland, Switzerland, Spain, Germany, Singapore, Vietnam and Nepal). Teaching and academic administration/management aside, Andreas is an active researcher, recognised nationally and internationally for his contributions in the areas of entrepreneurship education and responsible/sustainable employment, especially in the service sector. He is Editor (Research) for the United States Association for Business and Entrepreneurship's journal Entrepreneurship Education and Pedagogy, is a Research Fellow at Neapolis University Cyprus and Convenor of the SCION Research Group. Andreas is an experienced PhD supervisor and welcomes expressions of interest in topics around entrepreneurship, particularly entrepreneurship education, and also if there are links to sustainability/ responsible business practices.

Index

A

B

C

D

E

F

G

H

I

L

M

O

P

S

T

U

www.ingramcontent.com/pod-product-compliance
Lightning Source LLC
LaVergne TN
LVHW080357011026
849161LV00009B/2330